WEBSTER'S NEW WORLD™

EASY CROSSWORD KEY

WEBSTER'S NEW WORLD™

EASY CROSSWORD KEY

James H. Capps

Macmillan • USA

Webster's New World™
Easy Crossword Key

Macmillan General Reference
A Simon & Schuster Macmillan Company
1633 Broadway
New York, NY 10019-6785

A Webster's New World™ Book

Dictionary Editorial Offices:
New World Dictionaries
850 Euclid Avenue
Cleveland, OH 44114-3354

Library of Congress Cataloging-in-Publication Data

Capps, James H.
Webster's New World easy crossword key / James H. Capps.
p. cm.
"A Webster's New World book"—T.p. verso.
ISBN 0-02-861837-8 (pbk.)
1. Crossword puzzles—Glossaries, vocabularies, etc. I. Title.
GV1507.C7C27 1997
793.73'2'03—dc21 97–774
CIP

Manufactured in the United States of America

1 2 3 4 5 6 7 97 98 99 00 01 02

Contents

Webster's New World Staff

Editorial Director

Michael Agnes

Managing Editor

James J. Heaney

Editor and Database Administrator

Donald Stewart

Editorial Staff

Jonathan L. Goldman
James E. Naso
Katherine Soltis
Andrew N. Sparks
Stephen P. Teresi
Laura Borovac Walker

Administrative, Data Processing, and Clerical Staff

Alisa Murray Davis
Cynthia M. Sadonick
Betty Dziedzic Thompson

Citation Readers

Batya Jundef
Joan Komic

Foreword

This book is a compilation of crossword-puzzle clues and answers taken from a wide range of puzzles over a span of many years. While it is true that crossword puzzles, especially those designed to challenge the most experienced and skilled solvers, contain clues requiring a knowledge of all sorts of arcane and obscure information, it is equally true that there is a great deal of recurrence, a recycling of certain clues which, taken as a whole, form something of a core of crossword-puzzle knowledge. Scarcely a day passes without publication somewhere, for instance, of a crossword puzzle that asks for one of the following:

—the creator of Perry Mason (Erle Stanley Gardner)
—the famed Finnish architect (Eero Saarinen)
—one or another extinct bird (the dodo or the moa).

This is not to suggest that crossword-puzzle compilers rely solely upon recycling a limited inventory of stock clues. The core of crossword-puzzle knowledge is actually quite vast. In the aforementioned example, knowing that Gardner is "Erle" and not "Earl" is the first step. Solvers will need to know about Raymond Burr, Della Street, Paul Drake, and the fact that Perry Mason titles begin with "The Case of . . . " just to take on an easy puzzle. Experienced solvers who have acquired more esoteric knowledge would be likely to know the names, among others, of A. A. Fair, Barbara Hale, Bertha Cool, Doug Selby, Arthur Tragg, Warren William, and Donald Woods.

The number of possible clues used in crossword puzzles is as vast as the knowledge and ingenuity of those who compose them. No single reference could even begin to comprehend it all; at a minimum, one would need to be armed with a shelf of books including a dictionary, thesaurus, encyclopedia, almanac, and atlas and, to be really prepared, The Bible, Bartlett's *Quotations*, Bullfinch's *Mythology*, and others as well. This book does an exceedingly fine job of covering what was referred to above as the core of crossword-puzzle knowledge—that is, those names, places, dates, events, titles, aphorisms, foreign words, etc. which solvers are most likely to encounter over a wide range of puzzles, from the moderately easy to the highly difficult. This information, presented in puzzle clues under a variety of guises, is exhaustively reported here by James H. Capps. Using the same techniques employed by professional dictionary editors, Mr. Capps has amassed a treasure-trove of accurate and reliable data drawn from tireless field research. It is the soundness of his scholarship, together with the size and breadth of the entry list, that enables us to offer the reader this work with pride and the confidence that it stands among the very finest of such compilations.

Michael Agnes
Editorial Director
Webster's New World Dictionaries

GUIDE TO THE USE OF THIS BOOK

The simplest, most straightforward way to use this book is to match your unanswered clue with an identical or nearly identical entry. This method works especially well for certain clues, typically those which are seeking an invariable one-word answer. Examples include all clues whose answer forms the missing part of:

— a person's name (first, middle, last, nickname, etc.)
— a place name
— the name of an historical event
— the title of a book, film, play, song, poem, etc.
— an idiomatic phrase, aphorism, epigram, quotation, etc.

Because the same essential information is provided here in a variety of ways, the simple process of matching your clue to one in the book will prove successful in many instances. However, if you do not find an identical or nearly identical match, you should identify the key word or words in the clue and look for entries which begin with those words. For example, if you failed to find a match for the clue "Mother of Hamlet," you should look for entries at "Hamlet," where you will indeed find the clue "Hamlet's mother."

Since this book provides so many different variations, circuitous searches using several different key words should be unnecessary in most instances. Still, if you are especially desperate to find that elusive answer, you will discover a little bit of persistence in searching will often pay off.

In this regard, it helps to be a bit creative. If the key word or words in the clue have not taken you to the correct answer, you may wish to look under a closely related word. Thus, if the clue says "Dramatist," you may also wish to check under "Playwright" or "Author" or "Writer," just to name a few. While it would be impossible to provide a comprehensive list of related words and categories, the following examples should be suggestive of the type of creative association which could prove useful in conducting more involved searches:

— American / U.S.
— British / English / Scottish / Welsh
— Ireland / Eire / Erin / Hibernia
— ancient / classical
— fabled / legendary / mythological
— devout / holy / pious / religious / spiritual
— Hebrew / Jewish
— famed / famous / noteworthy / well-known
— deity / god
— Scandinavian / Northern European / Norwegian / Swedish

Some general comments on crossword-puzzle clues.

Crossword puzzle clues usually contain language, often coded language, that provides hints to correct answers. The form of the clue will often indicate in some manner the answer's part of speech (noun, verb, etc.), number (singular or plural), case (subjective, objective, possessive), or tense (present, past, etc.). It may indicate whether the answer word is colloquial or slang, whether it is in a particular variant form of English (archaic, British, dialectal, poetic, Scottish, etc.), or whether it is in a foreign language. It may also indicate whether the answer is to be spelled out in full or abbreviated.

Compilers of crossword puzzles do not always provide this information in clear and explicit terms. Often, they are deliberately vague. Proficiency in deciphering clues is obtained chiefly through the experience of working puzzles. Solvers who have had only limited experience will find browsing through this book instructive, as there are numerous examples where the same clue is presented in both an easy, straightforward form and a coded, elliptical form. Understanding the latter is necessary if one hopes to master more sophisticated—and difficult—puzzles.

Here are a few examples:

Answer singular or plural:

Florida locale — KEY
Florida locales — KEYS
Aaron or Raymond — BURR
Aaron and Raymond — BURRS
Ellington — DUKE
Ellington, et al. — DUKES
Ellington and others — DUKES

Answer in present, past, etc. Answer in first person, third person, etc.:

Made happy — ELATED
Make happy — ELATE
Makes happy — ELATES

Answer in abbreviated or shortened form:

Golf organization: Abbrev. — PGA
Golf org. — PGA
Golf instructor, for short — PRO

Answer in foreign language:

No, in Moscow — NYET
No, to a tsar — NYET
No, to Ivan — NYET
No, to Tolstoy — NYET

(Names of actual people are often used in clues. Expect to see Robert Burns for Scottish words and names like Cato, Julius Caesar, and Marc Antony where the answer is in Latin. Stereotypical names such as Ivan, Pierre, and Pedro are often used to indicate a particular country, language, or dialect.)

Answer in an old or archaic form:

No, in Shakespeare — NAY
No, once — NAY
No, formerly — NAY
No, at one time — NAY

Answer in a poetic form:

Over, in poesy — OER
Over, poetically — OER
Over, to Emily Dickinson — OER

A clue which ends in a question mark indicates some sort of play on words is involved. It will often take the form of an allusive reference to an aphorism, an idiomatic phrase, a well-known line in a poem or song lyric, etc. Expect to find nonsensical questions which require even more nonsensical answers:

A crowd? — THREE
Charge at the butcher shop? — JOINT ACCOUNT
Rural apothecary? — FARMACIST

In conclusion, readers are especially urged to consult the table of contents at the beginning of this book for information on the supplemental sections that follow the A-Z listing of clues and answers. In those sections the reader will find clues in unique formats that require precisely such special treatment in order to guarantee that they are always easy to find. These include clues that begin with numerals, clues that begin with answer blanks, and clues that are made up of or based upon quotations.

WEBSTER'S NEW WORLD™

EASY CROSSWORD KEY

A

A — HIGHEST MARK
A "9 to 5" actress — TOMLIN
A "Godfather" star — CAAN
A "good queen" — BESS
A "Landing" on TV — KNOTS
A "Moby Dick" harpoonist — TASHTEGO
A "mom and pop," e.g. — STORE
A "Pretty Woman" star — GERE
A "Quincy" star — ITO
A "stooge" of note — MOE
A "Treasure Island" sea dog — BONES
A "Wizard of Oz" star — LAHR
A _____ (dessert style) — LA MODE
A _____ (from boyhood, to Pliny) — PUERO
A _____ Able — AS IN
A _____ Apple — AS IN
A _____ in the bucket — DROP
A _____ minute — MILE A
A _____ throw — STONES
A 1914 Oriole who took wing — BABE RUTH
A 1918 hit song — BEAUTIFUL OHIO
A 1924 hit tune — CALIFORNIA HERE I COME
A 1932 hit song — LA HAY RIDE
A 1933 U.S. agency — NRA
A 1963 Oscar winner — NEAL
A 1965 U.S. Open winner — PLAYER
A 1977 movie — ORCA
A 1982 Oscar winner — GOSSETT
A 1984 running mate — FERRARO
A 1986 suspense film — BLACK WIDOW
A and B, e.g. — TYPES
A as in _____ — ALFA
A Baba — ALI
A bag at Fenway — BASE
A Barrymore — DREW, ETHEL, LIONEL
A Barrymore in "E.T." — DREW
A base of bone turquoise — IVORY
A basic Buddhist doctrine — ANATTA
A basic compound — AMINE
A beat in a musical direction? — ATEMPO
A Belafonte — SHARI
A bend — ESS
A Bennett of films — CONSTANCE
A bib catches this — DROOL
A big hand — PAW
A biographer of Henry James — EDEL
A Birgua inlaw — ESTE
A bit at a time — PIECEMEAL
A bit dishonest — SHADY
A bit nippy — CHILLY
A bit off-key — SHARP
A bit thick — DENSE
A bit too ripe? — GAMY
A Bobbsey and others — NANS
A Bobbsey twin — NAN
A body of matter collected into a lump — MASS
A boldface type — DORIC
A Bolger co-star in 1939 — LAHR
A bon marche — CHEAP
A Bond portrayer — DALTON
A book of maps — ATLAS
A Boone — PAT
A boy scout assembly — JAMBOREE
A Bradley — OMAR
A Broadway Role for Angela — MAME
A Bronte — EMILY
A brother of Hebe — ARES
A Brown of renown — LES
A brown pigment — OCHRE
A bugle call — TAPS
A buzzer — BEE
A Cabinet dept. — AGR
A Caesar — SID
A Canadian transient — GOOSE
A canonical hour — TERCE
A Cantor — UDA
A Capulet's question — WHATS IN A NAME
A card game for three — SKAT
A carny — GEEK
A Carson — KIT
A Carter, et al. — AMYS
A Castle — IRENE
A Caucasian — OSSET
A cause of corruption — GREED
A cause of mental and physical disturbances — ANOXIA
A caustic party for a popular star — ROAST
A Central or Southern African people — TWA
A cereal grass — OAT
A certain fisherman — EELER
A certain fool — APRIL
A certain J.F.K. departure — JATO
A cetacean — ORC
A Chaplin — OONA, SYD
A charge at the butcher's? — JOINT ACCOUNT
A chip off Woody's block — ARLO
A chosen one — SELECTED
A church tax — TITHE
A Churchill — SARAH
A circus has three — RINGS
A co-inventor of cordite — ABEL
A coach's fantasy — DREAM TEAM
A Cole — NAT
A colleague of Danton — MARAT
A companion of Falstaff — PETO
A computer language — ALGOL
A conception — IDEA
A concern of ecologists — SOOT
A contemproary of Loti — ANET
A continent — ASIA
A contraction for will not — WONT
A Cotton Belt grape — EDEN
A cotton fabric — CHINTZ
A Count — BASIE
A courtroom procedure — CROSS EXAMINATION
A cove for Cole? — PORTERS PORT
A cowfish — TORO
A crab on the roof — FIDDLER
A Crosby — BOB, BING, NORM
A Crosby-Hope destination — BALI
A crowd, in a saying — THREE
A crowd? — THREE
A cure-all, a panacea — ELIXIR
A Curie — MARIE
A Dadist — ARP
A dance — SAMBA
A Darling child — WENDY
A Darling dog — NANA

A daughter of Agamemnon — ELECTRA
A daughter of Cronus — HERA
A daughter of Hyperion — EOS
A daughter of Oedipus and Jocasta — ISMENE
A daughter of Phoebe — LETO
A daughter of Picasso — PALOMA
A daughter of Themis — IRENE
A Davis — BETTE
A Day — DORIS
A day in June? — RARE
A day's march — ETAPE
A de Mille — AGNES
A deadly sin — ANGER, ENVY
A degree — NTH
A delicate lace — MECHLIN
A democrat is one — WAGON
A descendant of Aaron — ELI
A Diamond — NEIL
A Dickinson — ANGIE
A dining-room surface — TABLE TOP
A dogma — TENET
A double reed — OBOE
A double star in the constellation Gemini — CASTOR
A dozen, to Juan — DOCE
A Dressler — MARIE
A dry red wine — CHIANTI
A Dumas — PERE
A Dumas character — ATHOS
A face that would _____ clock — STOP A
A faja is one — SASH
A feast _____ famine — OR A
A feather for your cap? — EGRET
A feeling of discomfort — MALAISE
A fertilizer — POTASH
A few — SOME
A few things for Franz to do? — LISZT LIST
A fight — SCRAP
A final word — AMEN
A First Lady of the 50's — BESS
A First Lady's monogram — AER
A first name in architect — EERO
A first name in fragrance — ESTEE
A Fisher — EDDIE
A Fitzgerald — ELLA
A flammable gas — PROPANE
A Flintstone — FRED
A flycatcher — PEWEE
A Flynn — ERROL
A foe of Pan — SMEE
A foe of Sparta — ARGOS
A Fonda — JANE, HENRY
A football play: Abbr. — SAF
A Ford — EDSEL, ERNIE
A Ford aide — NESSEN
A Ford, for short — GERRY
A Forsyte — IRENE
A founder of Dadaism — ARP
A framer of Roger Rabbit — TOON
A fray or fruit — RHUBARB
A fruit for a spirit — PEACH
A full house, in poker — A BOAT
A Gabor — EVA, MAGDA
A gal. has eight — PTS
A Gardener — AVA, ERLE
A garment — ROBE
A Gemini city — ST PAUL MINNESOTA
A gemstone — SPINEL
A gender — MALE
A genus — CLASS
A Gershwin — IRA
A Giant at 16 — OTT
A giant void — AIR
A goddess of the arts — ERATO
A golden vision — WISH
A good look — EYEFUL
A good place for dashes? — MEET
A grand — THOU
A Grant — CARY, LEE
A great distance — AFAR
A great number — MANY
A Greek goddess of vengance — ARA
A Greg Louganis dive — GAINER
A ground for running — TURF
A group of moths — DRAB
A growler for Giacomo? — PUCCINIS POOCH
A Guthrie — ARLO
A guy for ewe — RAM
A Gypsy language — CALO
A hardwood — TEAK
A Harrison — REX
A Hart — MOSS
A Hawaiian — KANAKA
A Heep of literature — URIAH
A hit song of 1922 — OHIO
A hit tune of 1967 — UP UP AND AWAY
A hole in one — ACE
A homemade Chinese soup? — BIRDS NEST
A Hope-Crosby location — RIO
A Houston athlete — ASTRO
A human score — NAILS
A hydrocarbon — TOLAN
A James Bond — ROGER MOORE, SEAN CONNERY
A Jane Addams org. — ACLU
A Japanese — AINU
A John — ELTON
A Johnson — ARTE
A Jones — INDIANA
A journey — TRIP
A k a lamb — ELIA
A Kansas Fort — RILEY
A Keaton — DIANE
A Kelly — GENE
A Kennedy — ROSE
A Kennedy, et al. — TEDS
A Khan and others — ALYS
A King — ALAN
A king and a poet — LEARS
A king of Egypt — TUT
A king of Israel — OMRI
A King of Judah — ASA
A King of Judea — ASA, HEROD
A King of Judea, et al. — ASAS
A king, in Asia — KHAN
A kingdom — ANIMAL
A knight of the round table — GALAHAD
A Knight to remember — TED
A Koblenz river — MOSEL
A Koestler title — DARKNESS AT NOON
A la follower — MODE
A la trailer — CARTE
A labor organization — CIO
A laboratory assistant — DIENER
A lack of red blood cells: Var. — ANAEMIA
A Ladd from Huron — CHERYL
A lagomorp — HARE
A Laker, e.g. — CAGER
A land in S.A. — URU
A land of plenty — GOSHEN
A land was named for him — DISNEY
A language of Pakistan — URDU
A Lauder — ESTEE
A leg of lamb — GIGOT
A Lewis — JERRY
A licensed victualler — VINTNER
A literary Bell — ELLIS
A little bit — SLIGHTLY
A little while, to Burns — A WEE
A living Dahl — ARLENE
A long rolling wave — BREAKER
A long time — AGES, EON
A long way off — AFAR
A loser in 1992 — PEROT
A lot — TONS
A Louisianan — CAJUN
A lover of Elizabeth I — ESSEX
A lug lead-in — CHUG
A lump on a battery part? — ANODE
A luncheon in Brighton — TIFFIN
A lure by Ludwig? — BEETHOVENS BAIT
A machine load floating — AWASH
A major anniversary — SILVER

A major leage: Abbr. — NATL
A major party — DEMOCRATIC
A man of morals — AESOP
A man's enunciation? — MALE DICTION
A manager of the Cards in 1990 — TORRE
A Manitoban — CREE
A many-splendoured thing? — LOVE
A Margaret Mead subject — SAMOA
A martial art — KARATE
A Marx — HARPO
A marzo date — IDI
A Massey — ILONA
A Maverick of TV — BRET
A May birthstone — AGATE
A mean or vile women — JADE
A memorable Bobby — DARIN
A memorable Erwin — STU
A memorable Mostel — ZERO
A Met score — ARIA
A mi. = 1,760 _____ — YDS
A mild cheese — EDAM
A Miller — ANN
A milquetoast — NOBODY
A mineral trona — URAO
A mite suspicious — LEERY
A Mo. patron? — LOUIS
A moment ago — JUST
A monetary claim — LIEN
A Montague — ROMEO
A month, in Madrid — ENERO
A moon of Jupiter — ELARA
A moon of Uranus — ARIEL
A Morrow medium — RADIO
A most devoted man — SIR GALAHAD
A Mother Goose pet — LAMB
A mule is its mascot — ARMY
A musical B — BACH
A musical Brown — LES
A musical Horne — LENA
A musketeer — ATHOS
A natural at Reno — SEVEN
A neighbor of Ky. — TENN
A neighbor of Norma — ARA
A Nero — PETER
A no-no — TABU
A Nobel Institute site — OSLO
A nucleic acid: Abbr. — RNA
A nut for pie — PECAN
A nymph pursued by Pan — ECHO
A Pa. airport code — PHL
A parent of a dzo — YAK
A parent: Lat. — PATER
A Paris airport — ORLY
A past tense: Abbr. — PRET
A Pequod owner in "Moby Dick" — PELEG
A Pharaoh — SETI
A pharoh, for short — TUT
A Phillies' manager: 1987 — ELIA
A piece of cake — EASY
A pig — FAT AS
A Pilgrim father — ALDEN
A place to remember — ALAMO
A Plato dialogue — ION
A Plummer from N.Y.C. — AMANDA
A political position — RIGHT
A poplar — ABELE
A Porter — COLE
A portmanteau word — SMOG
A poultry sum? — CHICKEN FEED
A Pound — EZRA
A practice of David — PSALMODY
A Preminger — OTTO
A president of Chile — ALLENDE
A Prot. — LUTH
A publication of seeds — CATALOG
A putting into circulation — EMISSION
A Queen of mystery — ELLERY
A queen of Thebes — NIOBE
A railroad car — SMOKER
A ratite — EMU
A real original — ONER
A real pal — FRIEND
A reciter of love poems, in Egypt — ENO
A Redgrave — LYNN
A Reese — DELLA
A Reiner — CARL, ROB
A report not to be sneezed at — POLLEN COUNT
A republic of Central America — PANAMA
A resin — ALK
A Rhine feeder — AARE
A rival of Agatha — ERLE
A rival of Hera — LEDA
A river at Rennes — ILLE
A Romance language — ITALIAN
A Roosevelt — SARA
A Roosevelt relative — DELANO
A Roosevelt successor — TAFT
A Rose — PETE
A Rose by any other name? — PETE
A Ross — DIANA
A Russian chess master — TAL
A science — OPTICS
A Scott — DRED
A seaman — TAR
A seasoning, in Savoie — SEL
A sect of Mennonites — AMISH
A Sedgwick — EDIE
A semisolid — GEL
A Seoul GI — ROK
A server — TRAY
A shaded area — UMBRA
A Shaw — ARTIE
A sheepdog — COLLIE
A sherry — FINO
A shield worn above the eyes — VISOR
A ship to remember — MAINE
A Shore — DINAH
A short solo in jazz — BREAK
A short, thickset haddock? — STOCKY FISH
A Shriver — EUNICE, MARIA
A sign of summer — LEO
A Sikh, in India — UDASI
A silk hat — SHINER
A silly trick — APERY
A Simon — NEIL
A Simpson — BART, HOMER
A Sinatra — NANCY, TINA
A single time — ONCE
A Siouan — OTOE
A sister of Calliope — ERATO
A sister of Eunomia — IRENE
A sister of Europa — ASIA
A sister of Goneril — REGAN
A sister of John Boy — ERIN
A sixth-day creation — BEAST
A size of paper — POTT
A skein of yarn containing 120 yards — RAP
A ski turn — CHRISTY
A Skinner — OTIS
A slight admixture — TINGE
A sloop has one — MAST
A slope — TALUS
A small bit — SMIDGEN
A smile with the teeth showing — GRIN
A Smith — KATE
A smooth, easy pace — CANTER
A Smothers brother — DICK
A snooze, in Oviedo — SIESTA
A soap — DALLAS
A social grace — TACT
A sodium carbonate — NATRON
A son of Bela: I Chr. 7:7 — IRI
A son of Bilhah — DAN
A son of Gad — ERI
A son of Jacob — ASHER, LEVI
A son of Jacob and Leah — SIMEON
A son of Jacob: Var. — ASER
A son of Midian: I Chr. 1:33 — HENOCH
A son of Priam — PARIS
A son of Seth — ENOS
A source of iron — SPINACH
A source of mother-of-pearl — ABALONE
A soviet adm. division — ASSR
A spar — FOREMAST
A spar extending sail — SPRIT
A spelling insect? — BEE

A spirit raiser? — SEANCE
A spouse, in Savoie — MARI
A Sprat preference — LEAN
A sq. is one — RECT
A Square one is desireable — MEAL
A squirrel at times — STORER
A standee lacks this — LAP
A star in Anaheim — MINNIE
A star of "Dr. Strangelove" — SELLERS
A star of "Naughty Marietta" — EDDY
A star of "Rashomon" and "Ugetsu" — MORI
A star of "The Collector" — EGGAR
A Starr — BELLE, RINGO
A step up — RISER
A stock exchange, for short — AMEX
A stooge — MOE
A Strasberg — SUSAN
A stringed instrument: It., — ARPA
A strong red shade — MADDER
A study — ETUDE
A sturdy chiffon — NINON
A subcontinent: Comb. form — INDO
A suburb of Pittsburgh — ETNA
A sucker holds it — BAG
A sugar — GLUCOSE
A sun screen — OZONE
A Superman — REEVE
A surface around the earth — GEOID
A Swell — NOB
A Tai language — SHAN
A taker of "notes" — STENO
A taste for life — ZEST
A teammate of Hodges — REESE
A teammate of Roe — REESE
A tear, perhaps — DROP
A tense — PAST
A tenth part — TITHE
A thick woolen cloth — LODEN
A thirst — EAGER
A Thomas — MARLO, SETH
A thousand kilograms — TONNE
A three-time A.L.M.V.P. — MANTLE
A tickbird — ANI
A tide — NEAP
A tippy canoe — KYAK
A to Z, for one — RANGE
A toast — TO LIFE
A top Japanese golfer — ONO
A toxic condition — SEPSIS
A Trask in "East of Eden" — ADAM
A tribe of Israel — LEVI
A trio of baseball teams? — THREE NINES
A triplet — TRIN
A tropical ray — MANTA
A troupial — ORIOLE
A Truman — BESS
A Tuesday not in the week — WELD
A Turner — IKE, LANA, NAT, TINA
A TV Ricky — DESI
A U.S. Chief Justice — TAFT
A unit of weight — CARAT
A USA or USN — SVCE
A valuable — ASSET
A verb for you — ARE
A very long time — EON
A very small person — MIDGE
A virus, for short — PHAGE
A voice vote — NAY
A vote for — AYE
A votre sante? — THE TOAST OF PARIS
A VP under FDR — HARRY TRUMAN
A VP under U.S. Grant — HENRY WILSON
A warm feeling — GLOW
A Wash. airport — NATL
A Washington — MARTHA
A watercolor by Wolfgang — MOZARTS ART
A Waugh — ALEC
A wave — BILLOW
A way in or out — DOOR
A way out — DOOR
A way to go: Abbr. — RTE
A way to learn with "by" — ROTE
A way to take the stairs — TWO AT A TIME
A way up — LADDER, STAIR, STEP
A way up in mil. service — OCS
A weedy grass — DARNEL
A West — MAE
A West African language — TSHI
A Western USA and Canadian mountain range — CASCADE
A white lie — FIB
A Whitney — ELI
A wife of Esau: Gen. 36:2 — ADAH
A Williams — VANESSA
A winner in the long run? — MARATHONER
A woodwind — OBOE
A year _____ day (legal period) — AND A
A Yokum — ABNER, PAPPY
A York river — OUSE
A Yugoslav — SERB
A Yugoslav: Abbr. — SLO
A&M subj. — GEOL
A&P rival — IGA
A+ is one — MARK
A, B, C and D, e.g. — MARKS
A, B, C, D, F — GRADE
A,K,Q,J,10 of spades? — ROYAL FLUSH
A-bomb plane — ENOLA GAY
A-F links — BCDE
A-frame — HOUSE
A-one — TOPS
A-Q combo, in bridge — TEN ACE
A-U connection — EIO
A. Miller play — AFTER THE MAN
A. Rand's "_____ Shrugged" — ATLAS
A.A. Milne's toy bear — POOH
A.B.A. member — ATTY
A.D.A. member — DDS
A.E.C. successor — NRC
A.E.S. defeater — DDE
A.F. unit — TAC
A.F.B. in Colorado — ENT
A.F.B. in Tex. — REESE
A.F.L. affiliate — CIO
A.F.L.'s partner — CIO
A.F.L.-C.I.O. court case? — UNION SUIT
A.F.T. rival — NEA
A.G. Eiffel's pride — TOWER
A.J. Cronin novel — THE GREEN YEARS
A.J. Cronin's "The _____" — CITADEL
A.k.a. — ALIAS
A.k.a. C. Lamb — ELIA
A.k.a., The Cowardly Lion — LAHR
A.L. batting champ of 1971 — OLIVA
A.L. member — VET
A.M.A members — MDS
A.M.s — MORNS
A.T.&T. or I.B.M.? — FAMILIAR STOCK
A/K/A — ALIAS
AAA way — RTE
AAA's concern — RTES
Aachen article — EIN
Aardvark's diet — ANTS
Aardvark's home — AFRICA
Aaron Burr's ego? — DUAL PERSONALITY
Aaron Burr, e.g. — DUELIST
Aaron of baseball — HANK
Aaron or Greenberg of baseball — HANK
Aaron or Raymond — BURR
Aaron specialty — HOMER
Aaron wallop — HOMER
Aaron's brother — MOSES
Aaron's son — ABIHU
AAU member — ATH

Ab _____ (from the start) — OVO
ABA member — ATT, LLD
Abaca — MANILA HEMP
Aback — AFT
Abacus — COUNTER
Abacus user, sometimes — ADDER
Abacus, at times — ADDER
Abadan currency — RIAL
Abadan native — IRANI
Abaft — ASTERN
Abalone — ORMER
Abalone lover — OTTER
Abandon — DESERT
Abandon restraint — CUT LOOSE
Abandoned — DERELICT, LOOSE
Abase — DEGRADE, DEMEAN, MEEK, MEAN, MILD
Abash — AMAZE
Abate — DECLINE, DECREASE, DWINDLE, SUBSIDE
Abate, as rain — LET UP
Abated — EASED, EBBED
Abatement — LET UP
Abates — DIES DOWN
Abating — LESSENING
Abba from Israel — EBAN
Abbess's assistant — PRIORESS
Abbess's counterpart — PRIORESS
Abbey or cathedral in some cities — MINSTER
Abbie's companion in comics — SLATS
Abbot's right-hand man — PRIOR
Abbr. for "The Bard" — SHAK, WILL
Abbr. for a potpourri — MISC
Abbr. for Signoras — SRAS
Abbr. in a to-let ad — RMS
Abbr. in apt. ads — RMS
Abbr. in grammar — MASC
Abbr. in physics — HTA
Abbr. in place names — HTS
Abbr. in Webster's — OBS
Abbr. on a bill of sale — RECD
Abbr. on a city map — AVE
Abbr. on a Roman standard — SPQR
Abbr. on a street map — AVE
Abbr. on a wanted poster — AKA
Abbr. on an overdrawn account — NSF
Abbr. on documents — ETAL
Abbr. on invoices — EOM
Abbr. on the NYSE — ATT
Abbr. used in geometry — QED
Abbreviate — CUT, SHORTEN
Abbreviated — SHORT
Abbreviated attribute — QUAL
Abbreviated garment — SHORTY
Abbreviation — SKETCH
Abbreviation on a race card — SCR
Abbreviations of street maps — AVES
ABC's Arledge — ROONE
Abcess — ULCER
Abdicate — DEMIT
Abdomen — BELLY, MIDRIFF
Abdominal pain — COLIC
Abdominal: Anat. — CELIAC
Abductors of the 70's: Abbr. — SLA
Abdul-Jabbar — KAREEM
Abe's adjective — HONEST
Abe's epithet — HONEST
Abecedarian — AMATEUR, TYRO
Abel's assailant — CAIN
Abel's land — EDEN
Abel's love — RIMA
Abel's parent — ADAM
Aberdeen _____ — ANGUS
Aberdeen river — DEE
Abet — AID, SECOND
Abet's complement — AID
Abet's partner — AID
Abets, with "on" — EGGS
Abeyant — LATENT
Abhor — HATE, DETEST, LOATHE
Abhorrence — ODIUM
Abide — ENDURE
Abigail _____ — ADAMS
Ability — ACUMEN, TALENT
Abject — SERVILE
Abjure — RETRACT
Ablaze — LIT
Able and Baker's relative — NAN
Able to cut smoothly with a knife — SECTILE
Able to pay one's debts — SOLVENT
Abnegate — DENY
Abner modifier — LIL
Abner's companion — LUM
Abner's radio pal — LUM
Abnormal occurence — ANOMALY
Abnormal Prefix — DYS
Abnormal: Comb. form — DYS, PARA
Aboard ship — ASEA
Abode of bliss — EDEN
Abode: Abbr. — HSE
Abolish — DESTROY, RID
Abolitionist author — STOWE
Abominable — HORRID
Abominates — HATES
Aboriginal Australian word — DINGO
Aborigine in Japan — AINU
Abort — END
Abounded — TEEMED
Abounding — RIPE
Abounding in fronds — FERNY
Abounding in monticles — HILLY
Abounding in stalks — STEMMY
Abounding with snow — NIVAL
Abounds in: Suffix — ULENT
About — ANENT, AS TO, CIRCA, INRE, OR SO
About 2 1/2 acres — HECTARE
About face — SHIFT
About two feet, in Denmark — ALEN
About-turn — REVERSAL
Above — ATOP, OVER, SUPRA, UPPER
Above or upon — ATOP
Above the Mason-Dixon line — NORTH
Above, in Augsburg — UBER
Above, in Berlin — UBER
Above, in poetry — OER
Above, to a poet — OER
Above: Lat. — SUPRA
Aboveboard — HONEST, NO STRINGS ATTACHED
Aboveboard — OPEN, OVERT
Abracadabra — SPELL
Abrade — CHAFE, RASP
Abraham's father — TERAH
Abraham's wife — SARAH
Abrasive — EMERY
Abrasive rock — PUMICE
Abridge — CONDENSE, ELIDE
Abroad — OVERSEAS
Abrogate — RESCIND
Abrogated — REPEALED
Abrupt — BRIEF, CURT
Abruzzi commune, central Italy — ATRI
Absalom to David — SON
Abscence of the skull — ACRANIA
Abscind brassica — CUT THE MUSTARD
Absconded — FLED
Absence of necessities — WANT
Absence of pain — ANALGESIA
Absent — AWAY
Absent-minded — DREAMY
Absentees at airports — NO SHOWS
Absolute — POSITIVE, SHEER
Absolute authority — TSAR
Absolute negative — NEVER
Absolute ruler — TSAR
Absolutely — TOTALLY
Absolutely first rate — A ONE
Absolutely intolerable — BEYOND ENDURANCE
Absolve — CLEAR
Absorb — BLOT, HOLD
Absorbed — RAPT
Absorbent — SPONGY

Absorbs water: Abbr. — ANH
Absorption in thought — BROWN STUDY
Absquatulate — FLEE
Absquatulated — FLED
Abstain — AVOID, DECLINE, FOREGO
Abstain from — SHUN
Abstain from food — FAST
Abstainer — HINDU, TEETO-TALER
Abstaining — ON THE WAGON
Abstinent — TEMPERATE
Abstract — COMPLEX
Abstract being — ESSE
Abstract entity — THING
Abstractions — IDEALS
Absurd — CRAZY, FOOLISH, SILLY
Absurdly eccentric — WACKY
Abtruse — DEEP, ESOTERIC, SUBTLE
Abundance — PLENTY, SCADS
Abundant — AMPLE, GALORE, RIFE
Abundantly filled — REPLETE
Abuse — DAMN, CURSE, FAULT, ILLTREAT
Abusive speech — DIATRIBE
Abutment — PROP, WALL
Abutting — ADJACENT, BESIDE, TANGENT
Abyss — CAVITY, CHASM, GAP, GULF, VOID
Abysses — CLEFTS, PITS
Abyssinian grains — TEFTS
Abyssinian prince — RAS
Abzug trademark — HAT
Academia — SCHOOL
Academic — CLASSIC
Academic achievement — DEGREE
Academic degree — DOCTOR-ATE
Academy _____ — AWARD
Academy award — OSCAR
Academy Award winner Hackman — GENE
Academy Award winner Thompson — EMMA
Academy founded in 1845 — NAVAL
Acapulco assent — SI SI
Acapulco aunt — TIA
Acapulco parrot — ALO
Acapulco wealth — ORO
Accelerate — REV
Accelerate a walk — TROT
Accent — STRESS
Accent mark like a wavy line — TILDE
Accept — RATIFY
Accept an IOU — LEND
Accept as true — BUY, CONCEDE
Accept formally — RATIFY
Accept philosophically — GRIN AND BEAR IT
Acceptable — WORTHY
Accepted — TAKEN
Accepted dlvy. — RCD
Accepted practice — USAGE
Accepts — TAKES
Accepts orders — OBEYS
Access — DOOR, ENTREE, ENTRY, GET AT
Access route — ENTRY
Access spaces — AREA WAYS
Accessible — OPEN
Accessories in Osaka — OBIS
Accident — MISHAP
Acclaim — ECLAT, LAUD
Acclimate — INURE
Acclivity — ASCENT
Accommodate — ASSIST, FAVOR, HUMOR, OBLIGE, PUT UP
Accommodates — SEATS
Accommodation — ROOM
Accompanied by — WITH
Accompanies — ESCORTS
Accompanies to the airport — SEES OFF
Accompany — ESCORT
Accomplice — COHORT
Accomplices of a kind — ABETTORS
Accomplished — DID, DONE
Accomplishes — DOES
Accomplishing — DOING
Accomplishments — DEEDS, FEATS
Accord — AMITY, RAPPORT
According to — A LA, PER
According to Hoyle — BY THE BOOK, RULES
According to the bill — A LA CARTE
According to the stars — ASTRALLY
Accost — GREET
Account — INVOICE, REPORT, SALE, SKETCH
Account statement — AUDIT
Accountant's entry — DEBIT
Accountant's listing — NET LOSS
Accounts officer on a ship — PURSER
Accouter — EQUIP
Accouterments — GEAR
Accra's land — GHANA
Accredited acct. — CPA
Accrete — GROW
Accrue — ENURE
Accrue wages — EARN
Acct. — CPA
Acct. bk. examiners — CPAS
Accumulate — AMASS
Accumulate money — BANK
Accumulated — GREW, RAN UP
Accumulated knowledge — LORE
Accumulated learning — LORE
Accumulated, with "up" — PLIED
Accumulation — GAIN
Accursed — DOOMED
Accusation — CHARGE
Accuse — BLAME
Accuse in court — ARRAIGN
Accused's answer — PLEA
Accuser — NAMER
Accuses — BLOWS THE WHISTLE
Accustom — ADAPT, INURE, ENNURE
Ace — ONE SPOT, ONER
Ace and 10 — BLACKJACK
Acedia — ENNUI
Acerb — ACRID, HARSH
Aces — PROS
Acetous — SOUR
Acetylene — GAS
Acey-deucy — AOK
Achaean League member — SPARTA
Ache — PINE
Ached — PINED
Aches — PAINS, YEARNS
Acheson — DEAN
Achier — SORER
Achieve — WIN
Achieve a balance — BREAKS EVEN
Achieve success — ARRIVE
Achievement — FEAT
Achieves — REALIZES
Achilles heel — DEFECT, WEAKNESS
Achilles killer — PARIS
Achilles' tissues — TENDONS
Achilles's tale — ILIAD
Aching — SORE
Achy — PAINING
Acicular — POINTED
Acid — LSD
Acid group — AMINO
Acid in apples — MALIC
Acid in soap — OLEIC
Acid neutralizer — ALKALI
Acid salt — OLEATE
Acidic salt — OLEATE
Acidity — ACOR
Acidulous — ACERBIC
Acier ingredient — EER
Acknowledge — AVOW, OWN, THANK
Acknowledge applause — BOW
Acknowledged a message — REPLIED
Acknowledgement — NOD
Acme — TOP
Acminate — TAPER
Acolyte — AIDE, NOVICE

Aconcagua's land — ARGENTINA
Aconcagua's location — ANDES
Acorn — NUT
Acorn producers — OAKS
Acquiesce — BOW, YIELD
Acquiescences — ASSENTS
Acquire — GET, OBTAIN
Acquired — GAINED
Acquires — GARNERS
Acquires quickly — SNAPS UP
Acquittal — EXONERATION
Acreage — AREA, LOTS
Acrobat — GYMNAST, TUMBLER
Acrobat suit — LEOTARD
Acrobatic feat — BACKBEND, HEADSTAND, STUNT
Acronym for "Relief to Everywhere" — CARE
Acronym for a Laker's player — NBA
Acronym for a quick-rising plane — STOL
Acronym for a sunscreen ingredient — PABA
Acronym for an aircraft's ascent — JATO
Acronym for an ex-treaty — SEATO
Acronym for Greek resistance: WWII — EDES
Acronym for sea-going reserve personnel — USNR
Acronym for some off-base GIs — AWOL
Acronym pt. — INIT
Across poetically — OER
Acrylic fiber — ORLON
Acrylic plastic — LUCITE
Act — APPEAR, BEHAVE, DEED, FAKE, IMITATE
Act — LAW, SEEM
Act affectedly — POSTURE
Act against — OPPOSE
Act aggressively against — ASSAIL
Act as chairperson — PRESIDE
Act as lookout — ABET
Act crabby — GRUMBLE
Act excessively expressively — EMOTE
Act independently — BE ONES OWN MAN
Act indicating disbelief — HEAD SHAKING
Act like lovebirds — BILL AND COO
Act like Mrs. Mitty — NAG
Act morosely — BROOD
Act of rising — ASCENT
Act opener — SCENE
Act parsimoniously — STINGE
Act playfully — DALLY
Act pts. — SCS
Act rashly — SHOOT FROM THE HIP, TAKE RISKS
Act servilely — FAWN
Act smugly — GLOAT
Act sullenly — MOPE
Act the ham — EMOTE
Act theatrically — EMOTE
Act up — EMOTE
Act uppity — SNOOT
Act, in a way — EMOTE
Acted — DID
Acted a little like Little — APED
Acted coquettishly — FLIRTED
Acting award — OBIE, OSCAR
Acting peer without peer — OLIVIER
Acting trophy — EMMY
Acting unselfishly — SHARING
Action is one — AGENCY, MEANS
Action often taken on campus — OPTING
Action or skill suffix — IER
Action re Napoleon: 1814 — ISLING
Action rec. — RPT
Action suffix — ANCE
Action words — VERBS
Actionable situations — TORTS
Actions banned on many campuses — HAZINGS
Activate — AROUSE
Active — AGILE, ASTIR, ALERT, BUSY, DOING
Active element — RADON
Active one — DOER
Active person — DOER
Active preceder — RETRO
Active starter — RETRO
Activists — DOERS
Activities — DOINGS
Activity — WORK
Activity at a joyful reunion — EMBRACING
Activity for the light-fingered — SWIPING
Actor-director Alan — ALDA, ARKIN
Actor "Mr. Average" Erwin — STU
Actor _____ Keith — BRIAN
Actor Adler — LUTHER
Actor Alain and family — DELONS
Actor Alan — ALDA, ARKIN, BATES
Actor Alan from Allestree — BATES
Actor Alastair — SIM
Actor Albert — EDDIE
Actor Auberjonois — RENE
Actor Ayres — LEW
Actor Baldwin — ALEC
Actor Barry — GENE
Actor Bates — ALAN
Actor Beatty — NED
Actor Beery's namesakes — NOAHS
Actor Ben — KINGSLEY
Actor Bert — LAHR
Actor Bert's family — LAHRS
Actor Billy _____ Williams — DEE
Actor Blore — ERIC
Actor Bogarde — DIRK
Actor Borgnine — ERNEST
Actor Bruce — DERN
Actor Bruce or Havers — NIGEL
Actor Brynner — YUL
Actor Buddy — EBSEN
Actor Burt — LAHR
Actor Byrnes — EDD
Actor Calhoun — RORY
Actor Cariou — LEN
Actor Ceasar's family — ROMEROS
Actor Chaney — LON
Actor Charlie's father — MARTIN SHEEN
Actor Charmichael — IAN
Actor Connery — SEAN
Actor Cross or Kingsley — BEN
Actor Darren — MCGAVIN
Actor David — NIVEN
Actor David Ogden — STIERS
Actor Davis — OSSIE
Actor Delon — ALAIN
Actor Denholm — ELLIOTT
Actor Dillon — MATT
Actor Dixon — IVAN
Actor Dobson — KEVIN
Actor Donny — MOST
Actor Dotrice — ROY
Actor Eastwood — CLINT
Actor Ed — ASNER
Actor Ed and family — ASNERS
Actor Eddie — ALBERT
Actor Eisenberg — NED
Actor Erwin — STU
Actor Estrada — ERIK
Actor Ewell — TOM
Actor Farrell — SHEA
Actor Fernando or Lorenzo — LAMAS
Actor Flynn — ERROL
Actor Foxx: 1922-91 — REDD
Actor Frobe — GERT
Actor from County Kerry — OTOOLE
Actor from Dublin — BRENT
Actor from Prague — LOM
Actor Gavin of "The Love Boat" — MACLEOD
Actor Gazarra — BEN
Actor George — RAFT
Actor George — SEGAL
Actor George C. _____ — SCOTT
Actor Griffith — ANDY
Actor Guinness — ALEC

Actor Gulager — CLU
Actor Gunn — MOSES
Actor Hackman — GENE
Actor Hardwicke — CEDRIC
Actor Harrison — REX
Actor Hayakawa — SESSUE
Actor Herbert from Prague — LOM
Actor Holbrook — HAL
Actor Holliman — EARL
Actor Horsely, et al. — LEES
Actor Howard — KEN
Actor Howard, from Trent — TREVOR
Actor in "A Summer Place" — EGAN
Actor in "American in Paris" — BOGART
Actor in "Family Plot" — DERI
Actor in "Fanny": 1961 — BOYER
Actor in "Four Daughters" — RAINS
Actor in "Grand Hotel" — MARCH
Actor in "Hold Back the Dawn" — WALTER ABEL
Actor in "Odd man out" — MASON
Actor in "Pretty Woman" — GERE
Actor in "The Addams Family" — ASTIN
Actor in "The Deep" — NOLTE
Actor in "The Ghost Goes West" — DONAT
Actor in "The Good Earth" — MUNI
Actor in "The Guardsman" — LUNT
Actor in "The Rain People" — CAAN
Actor in TV's "Hearts Afire" — ASNER
Actor in TV's "Reasonable Doubts" — HARMON
Actor Irons — JEREMY
Actor Jack — ELAM
Actor Jack of yesteryear — OAKIE
Actor Jacoby — DEREK
Actor Jacques — TATI
Actor James — CAAN, DEAN
Actor James _____ — WHITMORE
Actor James _____ Jones — EARL
Actor Jamie — FARR
Actor Jannings — EMIL
Actor Jeff or Wendell — COREY
Actor Jeremy — IRONS
Actor Jim — DALE
Actor John — AMOS
Actor John and family — ASTINS
Actor Johnson — VAN
Actor Jose — FERRER
Actor Joseph of "Citizen Kane" — COTTEN
Actor Julia and a Castro — RAULS
Actor Julia from San Juan — RAUL
Actor Kaplan — GABE
Actor Karl — MALDEN
Actor Karloff — BORIS
Actor Keach — STACY
Actor Keaton — BUSTER
Actor Keir _____ — DULLEA
Actor Kevin of "Sophie's Choice" — KLINE
Actor Ladd — ALAN
Actor Laurel — STAN
Actor Lee — MARVIN
Actor Leon _____: 1881-1951 — ERROL
Actor Linden — HAL
Actor Lionel — BARRYMORE, STANDER
Actor Little — CLEAVON
Actor Lloyd — NOLAN
Actor Lorenzo — LAMAS
Actor Lowe — ROB
Actor Lugosi — BELA
Actor MacDonald _____ — CAREY
Actor Majors — LEE
Actor Martin — BALSAM, STEVE
Actor Marvin — LEE
Actor Maurice — EVANS
Actor McDowall — RODDY
Actor McGavin — DARREN
Actor McKellan — IAN
Actor Michael — NOURI, TOLAN
Actor Michael of "Alfie" — CAINE
Actor Michael of "Broken Arrow" — ANSARA
Actor Mineo — SAL
Actor Montand — YVES
Actor Moses _____ — GUNN
Actor Moses _____ of "Roots" — GUNN
Actor Newman and namesakes — PAULS
Actor Nick — NOLTE
Actor Noah — BEERY
Actor Nolte — NICK
Actor O'Brien: 1915-85 — EDMOND
Actor O'Neal — RYAN
Actor O'Shea — MILO
Actor Ogilvy — IAN
Actor or actress — THESPIAN
Actor or mason — RENDERER
Actor Patrick of "Dallas" — DUFFY
Actor Paul _____ — MUNI
Actor Pendleton — NAT
Actor Penn — SEAN
Actor Peter — LORRE
Actor Philip et al. — DORNS
Actor Pickens — SLIM
Actor plays Fischer — DON AMECHESSMASTER
Actor plays Gaugin — RICHARD BASEHARTIST
Actor Poitier, et al. — SIDNEYS
Actor Porter — ERIC
Actor Porter of "The Forsyte Saga" — ERIC
Actor Portman — ERIC
Actor Power — TYRONE
Actor Ray — ALDO
Actor Reid — TIM
Actor Reynolds — BURT
Actor Rhodes of "Daktari" — HARI
Actor Richard — EGAN, GERE
Actor Richard and family — EGANS
Actor Richard from Philadelphia — GERE
Actor Richardson — IAN
Actor Rip — TORN
Actor Rob — LOWE
Actor Robert _____ — ITO
Actor Robert _____ — LOGGIA
Actor Robert De _____ — NIRO
Actor Robert or Alan — ALDA
Actor Roger — REES
Actor Ron — ELY
Actor Ronald — REAGAN
Actor Roscoe _____ — ATES
Actor Sam: 1891-1984 — JAFFE
Actor Santoni — RENI
Actor Savalas — TELLY
Actor Scott — BAIO
Actor Sean — PENN
Actor Shackleford — TED
Actor Sharif — OMAR
Actor Skinner — OTIS
Actor Tamblyn — RUSS
Actor Tamiroff — AKIM
Actor Taylor — ROD
Actor Tim — REID
Actor Tone — FRANCHOT
Actor Toomey — REGIS
Actor Torn — RIP
Actor Victor of "The Strangler" — BUONO
Actor Victor, 1902-82 — JORY
Actor Vidal — HENRI
Actor Vigoda — ABE
Actor Voight — JON
Actor Wallach — ELI
Actor Walter _____ — ABEL
Actor Walter and family — ABELS
Actor Waterston — SAM
Actor Wayne — JOHN
Actor Weathers — CARL
Actor Welles — ORSON

Actor who overacts — HAM
Actor who played Zola — MUNI
Actor who produced a director — WALTER HUSTON
Actor who sang "The Impossible Dream" — KILEY
Actor Will of "The Waltons" — GEER
Actor Williams — TREAT
Actor Williams of "A Different World" — AMIR
Actor Wynn — KEENAN
Actor's ambition — ROLE
Actor's award — TONY
Actor's goal — ROLE
Actor's last line — TAG
Actor's line — ASIDE
Actor's org. — SAG
Actor's ploy — UPSTAGE
Actor's plum — ROLE
Actor's quest — PART, ROLE
Actor's reps — AGTS
Actor's whispers — ASIDES
Actor-author Bogarde — DIRK
Actor-banjoist George — SEGAL
Actor-dancer Hal _____ — LEROY
Actor-director Elliott _____ — NUGENT
Actor-director Mel — BROOKS
Actor-folk singer from Vienna — BIKEL
Actor-singer Burl — IVES
Actor-singer David — BOWIE
Actor-singer Frankie and kin — AVALONS
Actor-singer from France — YVES MONTAND
Actors — TALENT
Actors Charlie and Martin — SHEENS
Actors Costner and Kline — KEVINS
Actors of yore — STAGERS
Actors' footwear of long ago — BUSKINS
Actors' plums — ROLES
Actress-author Chase — ILKA
Actress-writer Chase — ILKA
Actress _____ Dawn Chong — RAE
Actress _____ Margret — ANN
Actress Adams — EDIE, MAUDE
Actress Adorée — RENEE
Actress Alicia — ANA
Actress Anderson — LONI, BIBI
Actress Ann — SOTHERN
Actress Anna May _____ — WONG
Actress Anne — MEARA
Actress Arden — EVE
Actress Arlene — DAHL
Actress Arthur — BEA
Actress Balin — INA
Actress Balin's namesakes — INAS
Actress Bancroft — ANNE
Actress Bara, et al. — THEDAS
Actress Barbara — EDEN
Actress Bartok — EVA
Actress Belafonte — SHARI
Actress Berger — SENTA
Actress Bergman — INGRID
Actress Bernardt — SARAH
Actress Best — EDNA
Actress Black — KAREN
Actress Blyth and others — ANNS
Actress Blythe — ANN
Actress Bonet, et al. — LISAS
Actress Bow — CLARA
Actress Brennan — EILEEN
Actress Burke and others — DELTAS
Actress Burstyn — ELLEN
Actress Buzzi — RUTH
Actress Caron — LESLIE
Actress Carter — NELL
Actress Charlotte — RAE
Actress Chase — ILKA
Actress Christie — JULIE
Actress Christine _____ — LAHTI
Actress Cicely — TYSON
Actress Claire — INA
Actress Claire's namesakes — INAS
Actress Clarke of old films — MAE
Actress Claudette — COLBERT
Actress Collins and namesakes — JOANS
Actress Copley — TERI
Actress Crabtree: 1847-1924 — LOTTA
Actress Daly — TYNE
Actress Davis — BETTE
Actress Dawber — PAM
Actress Deborah — KERR
Actress Del Rio — DOLORES
Actress Dern — LAURA
Actress Dey — SUSAN
Actress Diana — DORS
Actress Dickinson — ANGIE
Actress Dorothy et al. — LAMOURS
Actress Dunne — IRENE
Actress Dunne and namesakes — IRENE
Actress Dyan — CANNON
Actress Edie — ADAMS
Actress Elaine — STRITCH
Actress Eleonora — DUSE
Actress Elisa — LANDI
Actress Elizabeth — TAYLOR
Actress Ella — RAINES
Actress Erin — MORAN
Actress Evans — MADGE
Actress Evans or Lavin — LINDA
Actress Eve — ARDEN
Actress Farrow — MIA
Actress Fawcett — FARRAH
Actress Fay: 1892-1968 — BAINTER
Actress Faye — WRAY
Actress Feldshuh — TOVAH
Actress Fleming — RHONDA
Actress Flora _____ — ROBSON
Actress Foch — NINA
Actress Freeman — MONA
Actress from Greece — PAPAS
Actress from N.Y.C. — MEARA
Actress from Washington D.C. — GOLDIE HAWN
Actress Garr — TERI
Actress Garson — GREER
Actress Gertrude — BERG
Actress Ghostley — ALICE
Actress Gilbert — SARA
Actress Gillette — ANITA
Actress Gish — LILLIAN
Actress Grant — LEE
Actress Gray — ERIN
Actress Hagen — UTA
Actress Hagen, et al. — UTAS
Actress Harding — ANN
Actress Harper, to friends — VAL
Actress Hartman — LISA
Actress Hasso — SIGNE
Actress Hayworth — RITA
Actress Hiller — WENDY
Actress Holm — CELESTE
Actress Hope — LANGE
Actress Hope or Jessica — LANGE
Actress Hughes — TRESA
Actress Hussey — OLIVIA
Actress in "Beserk" — DORS
Actress in "Brewster's Millions" — HAVOC
Actress in "Chitty Chitty Bang Bang" — HOWES
Actress in "Coal Miner's Daughter" — SPACEK
Actress in "Forever Amber" — DARNELL
Actress in "Good & Evil" — GARR
Actress in "Knots Landing" — NOONE
Actress in "Picnic": 1955 — KIM NOVAK
Actress in "Signore e Signori" — LISI
Actress in "Tea and Sympathy" — KERR
Actress in "The Flim Flam Man" — LYON
Actress in "The Wedding Night" — STEN

Actress in "Theatre Goes Wild" — DUNNE
Actress Ina — BALIN
Actress Irene — DUNNE
Actress Irene from Greece — PAPAS
Actress Irving — AMY
Actress Irving, et al. — AMYS
Actress Jackson — GLENDA
Actress Jacqueline — BISSET
Actress Jeanmaire of Paree — RENEE
Actress Jeanne — CRAIN
Actress Jergens — ADELE
Actress Joanne — DRU
Actress Jones (Mrs. Addams on TV) — CAROLYN
Actress Jones of "L.A. Law" — RENEE
Actress Julian — ANN
Actress Julie — CHRISTIE, HARRIS
Actress June from New York City — ALLYSON
Actress Keaton — DIANE
Actress Kedrova — LILA
Actress Kedrova and others — LILA
Actress Kerr — DEBORAH
Actress Kurtz — SWOOSIE
Actress Ladd — DIANE
Actress Lamarr — HEDY
Actress Lanchester — ELSA
Actress Lanchester and namesakes — ELSAS
Actress Lansbury — ANGELA
Actress Lee — LILA, RUTA
Actress LeGallienne — EVA
Actress Lenska — RULA
Actress Lenya — LOTTE
Actress Lilli or Betsy — PALMER
Actress Linda — LAVIN
Actress Lisi — VIRNA
Actress Lollobrigida — GINA
Actress Lombard — CAROLE
Actress Loretta — YOUNG
Actress Louise — TINA
Actress Louise from N.Y. — TINA
Actress Lupino and namesakes — IDAS
Actress MacGraw — ALI
Actress Madeline — KAHN
Actress Magnani — ANNA
Actress Marie Saint — EVA
Actress Marilu — HENNER
Actress Markey — ENID
Actress Martha — RAYE
Actress Mary — ASTOR
Actress Massey — ILONA
Actress May — ELAINE
Actress McClanahan — RUE
Actress McClurg — EDIE
Actress Meara — ANNE
Actress Meg of "Psycho II" — TILLY
Actress Merkel — UNA
Actress Merkel and namesakes — UNAS
Actress Merle — OBERON
Actress Merrill — DINA
Actress Meyer of "Kate and Allie" — ARI
Actress Miles — VERA
Actress Miller — ANN
Actress Mimieux — YVETTE
Actress Molly from N.Y.C. — PICON
Actress Montez — LOLA
Actress Moore — DEMI
Actress Moorehead — AGNES
Actress Moran — ERIN, NINA
Actress Munson — ONA
Actress Myrna of old — LOY
Actress Myrna, et al. — LOYS
Actress Naldi — NITA
Actress Nancy — OLSON
Actress Nazimova — ALLA
Actress Neagle — ANNA
Actress Negri of the silent days — POLA
Actress North — SHEREE
Actress O'Connor: 1880-1959 — UNA
Actress Oberon — MERLE
Actress of "Red River" — DRU
Actress Olin — LENA
Actress on "Murphy's Law — HAN
Actress Osa — MASSEN
Actress Paget — DEBRA
Actress Pagett — NICOLA
Actress Palmer — LILLI
Actress Palmer of "De Sade" — LILLI
Actress Papas — IRENE
Actress Parsons — ESTELLE
Actress Patricia — NEAL
Actress Patterson — LORNA
Actress Perlman — RHEA
Actress Petrova — OLGA
Actress Phillips — SIAN
Actress Piper — LAURIE
Actress Pitts — ZASU
Actress Polo or Copley — TERI
Actress Potts — ANNIE
Actress Prentiss — PAULA
Actress Purviance — EDNA
Actress Rainer — LOUISE
Actress Raines — ELLA
Actress Rehan — ADA
Actress Remick — LEE
Actress Renee and namesakes — ADOREES
Actress Rigg — DIANA
Actress Rita — GAM, MORENO
Actress Rowlands — GENA
Actress Ruby — DEE
Actress Rule — JANICE
Actress Russell, to friends — ROZ
Actress Ryan — MEG
Actress Samantha — EGGAR
Actress Samms — EMMA
Actress Sandra — DEE
Actress Sanford — ISABEL
Actress Scala — GIA
Actress Shaw — RETA
Actress Shearer — NORMA
Actress Shire — TALIA
Actress Singer — LORI
Actress Skye — IONE
Actress Slezak — ERIKA
Actress Smith — ALEXIS
Actress Sommer — ELKE
Actress Sophia — LOREN
Actress Spacek — SISSY
Actress Sten — ANNA
Actress Stevens — INGER, STELLA
Actress Streep — MERYL
Actress Stritch — ELAINE
Actress Susan — ANTON
Actress Suzanne — PLESHETTE
Actress Suzanne _____ — SOMMERS
Actress Swenson — INGA
Actress Sylvia — SIMS, SIDNEY
Actress Taina — ELG
Actress Talia _____ — SHIRE
Actress Talmadge — NORMA
Actress Tammy — GRIMES
Actress Tanguay — EVA
Actress Taylor — RENEE
Actress Teri — GARR
Actress Terry — ELLEN
Actress Thomas — MARLO
Actress Thompson — SADA
Actress Thorndike's namesakes — SYBILS
Actress Trevor — CLAIRE
Actress Turner — LANA
Actress Tyne — DALY
Actress Ullmann — LIV
Actress Ulric — LENORE
Actress Vaccaro — BRENDA
Actress Van Devere — TRISH
Actress Van Doren — MAMIE
Actress Velez — LUPE
Actress Verdon — GWEN
Actress Verdugo — ELENA
Actress Vivian and others — LEIGHS
Actress Wallace — DEE
Actress Waters — ETHEL
Actress Weld — TUESDAY
Actress Williams — CARA
Actress Winwood — ESTELLE
Actress Witherspoon — CORA
Actress Worth — IRENE
Actress Young — SEAN
Actress-dancer Champion — MARGE
Actress-singer Lenya — LOTTE

Actresses Bonet and Eilbacher — LISAS
Actresses Clair and Balin — INAS
Actresses Merkel and O'Connor — UNAS
Actresses Moran and Gray — ERINS
Actresses Olin and Nyman — LENAS
Actresses Parsons and Getty — ESTELLES
Acts — FEATS
Acts dreamily — MOONS
Acts for — REPRESENTS
Acts glum — MOONS
Actual — REAL
Actual being — ESSE
Actual double — CARBON COPY
Actual occurrence — FACT
Actually existing — IN ESSE
Actuary's concern — AGE
Actuate — AROUSE
Acuff and Rogers — ROYS
Acumen — WIT
Acuminate — TAPER
Acute — INTENSE, SHARP
Acute and obtuse — ANGLES
Acute myocardial infraction — HEART ATTACK
Acute or obtuse — ANGLE
Acute or rt. — ANG
Acute shortage — FAMINE
Ad _____ — HOC
Ad _____ — LIB
Ad _____ — REM
Ad _____ (committee) — HOC
Ad _____ (pertinent) — REM
Ad _____ (to a sickening degree) — NAUSEAM
Ad _____: to the point — REM
Ad award — CLIO
Ad hoc coalition — BLOC
Ad infinitum — EVER
Ad lib — FAKE, IMPROMPTU
Adage — MAXIM, SAW, SAYING
Adak man — ALEUT
Adak's neighbor — ATTU
Adam _____ — AND EVE
Adam's _____: water — ALE
Adam's address — EDEN
Adam's ale — WATER
Adam's grandson — ENOS
Adam's son — SETH
Adam's third son — SETH
Adamant — RIGID
Adamson's pet — ELSA
Adapt music for different voices — TRANSCRIBE
Adapted to rigors — INURED
Adapted to the desert — XERIC
Adapts for publication — REDACTS
ADC, for one — ASST
Add-on — WING
Add — ANNEX, COUNTS, TOTS UP, TOTAL
Add and delete — EDIT
Add flour — THICKEN
Add fuel to the flames — AGITATE
Add inches — GROW
Add lustre — BRIGHTEN
Add more bullets to a rifle — RELOAD
Add on — APPEND
Add spice — SEASON
Add spice to — SEASON
Add sugar — SWEETEN
Add to — APPEND, GAIN
Add up — TOT
Add value to — ENRICH
Add vitamins — ENRICH
Add whiskey — LACE
Add-on components — MODULES
Addage — MOTTO
Addams of Hull House — JANE
Addax's relative — ORIBI
Added coloring — TINTED
Added flavors — SPICED
Added in — INCLUDED
Added on — ATTACHED
Added spirits — LACED
Added to — WITH
Added unnecessary words — PLEONASM
Addendum — SUFFIX
Adder — SNAKE
Addict — FIEND, USER
Addiction — DEPENDENCE
Adding music to a sound track — DUB
Adding weight — GAINING
Addis _____, Ethiopia — ABABA
Addison's partner — STEELE
Addison's writing partner — STEELE
Addition — ADDING, COUNTING, ELL, EXTRA, SUMMATION
Additional — MORE, OTHER, PLUS
Additional amount — MORE
Additional clause — RIDER
Additional ones — OTHERS
Additionally — ALSO
Additions: Abbr. — SUPPS
Addle — CONFUSE, MIRE
Address — SPEECH
Address abbreviations — STS
Address for a king — SIRE
Address for a PFC — APO
Address for Raleigh — SIR
Addressee, often — RESIDENT
Addresses — GREETS
Adds coloring — TINTS
Adds more seed — RESOWS
Adduced — CITED
Ade medium — SLANG
Ade's "_____ Horne" — DOC
Ade's "Fables in _____" — SLANG
Adept — EXPERT
Adequate — AMPLE, DECENT, ENOUGH, PASSABLE
Adhere — FUSE, STICK
Adhered — STUCK
Adhered to duty — TOED THE MARK
Adherents: Suff. — ISTS, ITES
Adhesive — GLUE, PASTE
Adhesive ingredient — EPOXY
Adieu, in Avila — ADIOS
Adieux, in Bath — TATAS
Adipose — FAT
Adj. for some stock — PFD
Adj. for some verbs — IRR
Adjacent — NEAR
Adjacent to — NEARBY
Adjectival ending — ICAL
Adjectival suffix — INE, ITIC
Adjective aptly applied to Apley — LATE
Adjective for a bolt — NUTED
Adjective for a cadet — YOUNGEST
Adjective for a cherub — ADORABLE
Adjective for a judge — SOBER
Adjective for a ranger — LONE
Adjective for Abe — HONEST
Adjective for Abner — LIL
Adjective for certain sergeants — HARD BOILED
Adjective for champagne — BRUT
Adjective for diamond — HARDEST
Adjective for Galahad — NOBLE
Adjective for Loren — BELLA
Adjective for marine plants — ALGAL
Adjective for milk — SPILT
Adjective for Paris — GAI
Adjective for Pollyanna — GLAD
Adjective for Sarah Bernhardt — DIVINE
Adjective for shoppe — OLDE
Adjective for Susan — BLACK EYED
Adjective for Yorick — POOR
Adjective suffix — IAL, ILE, ULAR
Adjectives for Sea lions — EARED
Adjoin — ABUT
Adjudge — DEEM
Adjudged — RULED
Adjunct — TRIVIA
Adjunct to a parka — HOOD

Adjust — ADAPT, ALINE, RESET, SET
Adjust a clock — RESET
Adjust a spinet — RETUNE
Adjust a watch — RESET
Adjust accounts — SETTLE UP
Adjust again — RESET
Adjust anew — RESET
Adjust earlier — PRESET
Adjust exactly — TRUE
Adjust parts of a machine — ALIGN
Adjust precisely — ALIGN
Adjust the clock — RESET
Adjust the piano — TUNE
Adjust the sails — TRIM
Adjust unsatisfactorily — MISADAPT
Adjust: adapt — ORIENT
Adjustable piece in a machine — GIB
Adjusted — ALINED, TUNED
Adjusted a camera — FOCUSED
Adjusted a motor — TUNED
Adjusted the piano — TUNED
Adjusts anew — RESETS
Adjusts machinery — TRAMS
Adjusts oneself — ADAPTS
Adjusts, as a motor — TUNES UP
Adjutant — AIDE
Adlai _____ Stevenson — EWING
Adlai's opponent — IKE
Adlai's running mate — ESTES
Adm. Condor's group — NURSES
Adm. Kelso, e.g. — CNO
Adman — HUCKSTER
Adman's come-on — TEASE
Adman's product — SLOGAN
Admin. div. — DIST
Administer — EXECUTE
Administrative division of Greece — DEME
Administrative divisions of ancient Africa — DEMES
Administrator — LEADER
Admiral's aide: Abbr. — NSO
Admiral/historian — MAHAN
Admiralty abbr. — HMS
Admire greatly — REVERE
Admired complexion — PEACHES AND CREAM
Admired persons — IDOLS
Admirer — FAN
Admires — ESTEEMS
Admission — ENTRY
Admission fee — ANTE
Admit — LET IN, LET ON, OWN
Admit frankly — AVOW
Admit to, with "up" — FESS, OWN
Admits — LETS IN, OWNS
Admits defeat — CEDES
Admittance — ACCESS
Admitted — LET IN
Admittedly — INDEED
Admonish — REMONSTRATE
Admonition to Nanette — NO NO
Ado — CLAMOR, FUSS, TROUBLE
Adobe — COVER
Adolescence — YOUTH
Adolescent — TEEN
Adolescent years — TEENS
Adolf's bunkermate? — EVA
Adolphe of old movies — MENJOU
Adopt — ESPOUSE
Adopt as a law — ENACT
Adorable — CUTE
Adore — HONOR
Adore, with "on" — DOTE
Adored — LOVED
Adored one of groupies — IDOL
Adores — LOVES
Adorn — DECORATE, GARNISH, TRIM
Adorn, in a way — INSTAR
Adorned — GRACED
Adornment — FRILL, TRIM
Adornment for an angel — HALO
Adorns — ARRAYS
Adorns gaudily — TINSELS
Adrenal, for one — GLAND
Adriatic gulf — TRIESTE
Adriatic port — BARI, TRIESTE
Adriatic resort — LIDO
Adriatic winds — BORAS
Adrift — AT SEA
Adroit — CLEVER, DEFT
Ads required by law — LEGALS
Adult acorn — OAK
Adult doodlebugs — ANTLIONS
Adult insect — IMAGO
Adulterated — DOCTORED
Advance — FURTHER, MOVE, PROCEED
Advance exam — PRETEST
Advance scout — OUTRIDER
Advanced — LATE
Advanced course of study — SEMINAR
Advanced degree adjective — DOCTORAL
Advanced in rank — PROMOTED
Advanced student — INTERN
Advances — LOANS
Advantage — ASSET, AVAIL, EDGE, ODDS, PLUS
Advents — ARRIVALS
Adventure — GEST
Adventure tales — SAGAS
Adventurous — BOLD, RASH
Adventurous presidential aviator? — BUSH PILOT
Adventurous tale — CONTE
Adversary — FOE
Adverse — UNTOWARD
Advert — LEAFLET, REFER
Advertise — PARADE
Advertise a product — ENDORSE
Advertising medium? — BILL-BOARD
Advertising sign — NEON
Advice — COUNSEL
Advice to Clouseau — CHERCHEZ LA FEMME
Advice to eager beavers? — TAKE IT EASY
Advice to insomniacs — COUNT SHEEP
Advice to Nanette — NO NO
Advice to the overzealous? — EASY DOES IT
Advise — ALERT, DIRECT, URGE
Adviser to Odysseus — MEN-TOR
Advisory group — PANEL
Advocate — APOSTLE, BACK, PLEAD, URGE
Advocate of the most recent — NEO
Advocate or power symbol — EXPONENT
Advocate: Suffix — ARIAN
Advocated, as an idea — ESPOUSED
Advocates of a firm policy — HARDLINERS
Advocating détente, e.g. — DOVISH
Adz and awl — TOOLS
Adze — TOOL
Aegean gulf — SAROS
Aegean island — ICARIA, IOS, KOS, SAMOS
Aegean Island — TENOS, THA-SOS
Aegean isle — SAMOS
Aegean Sea island — RHODES
Aerial — WIRE
Aerial bomb — ROC
Aerial manuevers — BARREL ROLL, LOOP
Aerialist's foothold — WIRE
Aerials — ANTENNAS
Aerie — NEST
Aerie location, perhaps — TOR
Aerie newcomer — EYAS
Aerie resident — EAGLET
Aero ender — DROME
Aeronautics gp. — CAA
Aeschylus domestic trilogy — THE HOUSE OF ATREUS
Aeschylus's "_____ Against Thebes" — SEVEN
Aesir chief — ODIN

Aesir, e.g. — GODS
Aesop story — FABLE
Aesop's lessons — MORALS
Aesop's loser — HARE
Aesop's point — MORAL
Aesop's tales — FABLES
Aesopian loser — HARE
AF officer — TSGT
AFB in Fla. — EGLIN
Affable — GENIAL
Affair — INCIDENT
Affair of honor — DUEL
Affaire d'honneur — DUEL
Affaire de coeur — AMOUR
Affect — GET TO
Affectation — ACT, POSE, SHOW
Affectations — AIRS, FRILLS
Affected — MANNERED
Affected manner — AIR
Affected smile — SIMPER
Affected, suffering: Comb. form — OTIC
Affection — FONDNESS, LOVE, WARMTH
Affection, in Italia — AMORE
Affectionate — LOVEY DOVEY
Affectionately — DEARLY
Affiances — BETROTHS
Affiliate — ALLY
Affinity — KINSHIP
Affirm — ALLEGE, AVER, PREDICATE
Affirmation — AVERMENT, YES
Affirmative — APPROVING, AYE, YES, POSITIVE
Affirmative answers — YESES
Affirmative vote — YEA
Affirmative words — YESES
Affirmatives — YEAS, YESSES
Affix — ADD
Affixes — ATTACHES
Afflicted — AILING, SMITTEN
Afflicted by fatigue — LANGUID
Afflicted with ennui — BORED
Affliction on skid row — DTS
Afflictions — SORES
Affluence — EASE
Affluent ex-Veep in Virginia? — RICH MONDALE
Affluent ones — HAVES
Afford temporarily — LEND
Affray — MELEE
Affront — OFFEND, SLUR, SNUB
Affronts — INSULTS
Afghan city — HERAT
Afghan coin — PUL
Afghan native: var. — EIMAK
Afghan prince — AMIR
Aficionado — DEVOTEE, FAN
Afire with ire — ANGRY
Aflame — EXCITED
Afloat — NATANT
Afokre's poetic cousin — ERE
Afoot, in Quebec — A PIED
Afore — ERE
Aforementioned — SAME
Afr. antelope — ORIBI, TOPI
Afr. plant — ALOE
Afr. ruler — DEY
Afr. tree — SANDARAC
Africa's _____ Coast — IVORY
Africa's largest city — CAIRO
African antelope — BONGO, ELAND, GNU, IMPALA
African antelope — KOODOO, ORIBI, TORA
African antelope: Var. — PALA
African ape, for short — CHIMP
African boss — BWANA
African cape — RAS
African capital — CAIRO, RABAT, TRIPOLI
African cat — CIVET
African charm — JUJU
African cobra — ASP
African desert — SAHARA
African dog — BASENJI
African dominoes — DICE
African draught region — SAHEL
African expanse — SAHARA
African expedition — SAFARI
African falls — VICTORIA
African fish — ANABAS
African fly — TSETSE
African fox — ASSE
African gazelle — ADMI
African grassland — VELDT
African island — CANARY
African Jackal — DIEB
African kokoon — GNU
African Lake discoverd by Livingstone — NGAMI
African language — BANTU
African Lily plant — ALOE
African nation — ALGERIA, CHAD, MALI
African native — BANTU
African nuisance grass — DRINN
African outing — SAFARI
African people — BANTU
African plant — ALOE
African primates — BABOONS
African region — AFAR
African republic — CHAD, TOGA, ZAIRE
African republic or lake — CHAD
African river — ATHI, CONGO, NILE, UELE
African rodent — TREE RAT
African ruler — EMIR
African rulers — DEYS
African seaport — ORAN
African settlers — BOERS
African snake — PYTHON
African spear — ASAGAI
African succulent — ALOE
African tea plant — KHAT
African thongs — RIEMS
African title — RAS
African tree — COLA
African tribe — BANTU
African village — KRAAL, STAD
African villages — DORPS
African whip — JAMBOR
African wildcat — SERVAL
African's rawhide thong — RIEM
Afrikaan — BOER
Afrikaans — TAALS
Afrikaner — BOER
Afrit — DEMON
Afro-cuban dance — CONGA
Aft — ABAFT, REAR
Aft area — STERN
Aft deck — POOP
After-dinner treats — MINTS
After-ski warmer — COCOA
After — BEHIND
After 12:59 — ONE
After A — BCD
After a bit — LATER
After a while — ANON, LATER
After Aug. — SEPT
After bee — CEE
After danger or hazard — OUS
After docking down _____ — THE RIVER ROUND MIDNIGHT
After due — TRE
After Eleanor, before Mamie — BESS
After epsilon — ZETA
After eta — THETA
After FDR — HST
After follower — MATH
After Ford — CARTER
After HST — DDE
After job or mob — STER
After luncheon — ETTE
After nay or yea — SAYER
After Parr — CARSON
After pipe or day — DREAM
After printemps — ETE
After sigma — TAU
After taxes — NET
After twelve fifty-nine — ONE
After uno — DUE
After wye — ZEE
After yoo or boo — HOO
After young or old — STER
After, in Avignon — APRES
After, to Marcel — APRES
After-bath garment — ROBE
After-bath powder — TALC
After-dinner beverage — ESPRESSO
After-dinner drinks — CORDIALS, DEMITASSE
After-dinner serving — DEMITASSE
After-dinner wine — PORT
After-hours school gp. — PTA

After-shave — TALC
Afterdeck — POOP
Aftermath — RESULT, WAKE
Afternoon — SIESTA
Afternoon affairs — TEAS
Afternoon breaks — NAP, SIESTAS
Afternoon event — TEA DANCE
Afternoon hour — ONE
Afternoon hours — PMS
Afternoon in Australia — ARVO
Afternoon nap — SIESTA
Afternoon or high — TEA
Afternoon party — TEA
Afternoon ritual in London — TEA
Afternoon serial melodrama — SOAP
Afternoon siesta — NAP
Afternoon TV diversion — SOAPER
Afternoon TV fare — SOAPS
Aftersong — EPODE
Afterthoughts on a ltr. — PSS
Afton, e.g. — STREAM
Again — ANEW, OVER
Again, then again — THRICE
Against — ANTI, CONTRA, VERSUS
Against a thing: Law — IN REM
Against one's interests — ADVERSE
Against: Prefix — ANTI
Agape — GOGGLING
Agassi of tennis — ANDRE
Agate — MIG
Agate or taw — MARBLE
Agatha Christie hint — CLUE
Agave — SISAL, YUCCA
Agave fiber — SISAL
Agave product — SISAL
Agcy. concerned with pollution — EPA
Agcy. products — ADS
Agcy. with an eagle — NRA
Age — RIPEN, YEARS
Age from 1558 to 1603 — ELIZABETHAN
Age of old — AERA
Age preceder — TEEN
Age, as cheese — RIPEN
Age, time: It. — EVO
Age: Lat. abbr — AET
Aged — MATURED
Aged: L. Abbr. — AET
Ageless dwarf — GNOME
Agency — OFFICE
Agenda — LIST, PLAN, ROTA
Agenda part — ITEM
Agenda units — ITEMS
Agent — ASSIGNEE, FACTOR, PROXY
Agent in business matters — SYNDIC
Agent in place — MOLE
Agent of a kind — PROXY
Agent on a special mission — ENVOY
Agent, of a kind: Abbr. — ATTY
Agents — OPERANTS
Agents, for short — REPS
Agents: suffix — STERS
Ager of parents? — TEEN
Ageratum — PLANT
Ages — RIPENS
Ages and ages — EONS
Aggalach — ALOES
Agglomerate — AMASS
Agglomeration — PILE
Aggrandize — EXTEND
Aggravate — ANNOY, PROVOKE, RILE
Aggravates — MADDENS
Aggregate — ALL, AMOUNT, ENTIRE, SUM, TOTAL
Aggregate of good qualities — ARETE
Aggregate: Abbr. — AMT
Aggregation — NEST
Aggregation of animals — HERD
Aggregation of people — CROWD
Aggressive — MILITANT
Aggressive one — SHOVER
Aggressive person — TIGER
Aggressive pitch — HARD SELL
Aggressive salesmanship — HARD SELL
Aggressive, energetic person — GO GETTER
Aggressiveness — DRIVE
Aggressor — ASSAILER
Agha _____ — KHAN
Aghast — AFRAID
Agile — ACTIVE, QUICK, SPRY
Agile burglar — CATMAN
Aging vessel — VAT
Agitate — RILE, ROIL, ROUSE, SHAKE, STIR
Agitate violently — CHURN
Agitated — SHOOK
Agitated fits — SNITS
Agitated state — SNIT
Agitation — UNREST
Agitation of the mind — TUMULT
Agnes and Jeanne: Abbr. — STES
Agnes de Mille ballet — RODEO
Agnes, in Acapulco — INES
Agnes, in Avila — INES
Agnew — SPIRO
Agnew namesakes — SPIROS
Agnus _____ — DEI
Ago — PAST, SINCE
Agog — EAGER, IN A DITHER
Agons — CHOICES
Agora coin — STATER
Agouti's cousin — PACA
Agoutis — RODENTS
Agra address — SAHIB
Agra airs — RAGAS
Agra garb — SAREES
Agra site — TAJ MAHAL
Agrarian edifice — SILO
Agree — ASSENT, COME TO TERMS, SEE EYE TO EYE
Agree to a request — ACCEDE
Agree with — SIDE
Agreeable — AMIABLE, EXACT, NICE, PRECISE
Agreeable answer — YES
Agreeable in Scotland — COUTHIE
Agreeable signal — NOD
Agreeable words — YESES
Agreeable, old style — AMENE
Agreed — ATONE, GOT TOGETHER
Agreement — DEAL, PACT
Agreement between nations — ENTENTE, PACTS
Agrestral — WILD
Agri Dagi, to Turks — ARARAT
Agriclutural college student — AGGIE
Agriculture agcy.: 1937-42 — FSA
Agriculture: Comb. form — AGRO
Agriculturist — GRANGER
Agriculturist Jethro _____ — TULL
Agrippa's apparel — TOGA
Agronomy — FARMING
Agronomy unit — ACRE
Agt., of a sort — NARC
Agts. — REPS
Ah, me! — ALAS
Ahab's father — OMRI
Ahead — ONWARD
Ahead of — BEFORE
Ahead of, of yore — AFORE
Ahead of, to Ahab — AFORE
Ahoy! — YOO HOO
Ahs' partners — OHS
Ahura _____: Persian god — MAZDA
Ai-ling and Mei-ling — SOONGS
Aid — ABET, ASSIST
Aid an Italian town — ASSIST ASSISI
Aid in wrongdoing — ABET
Aid's companion — ABET
Aida or Radames — ROLE
Aida's locale — EGYPT
Aida's proposition to Burstyn — SAME TIME NEXT YEAR
Aide — ADVISER
Aide to a V.P. — ASST
Aider and abettor — ACCOMPLICE IN CRIME
Aider and abettor — FELLOW CONSPIRATOR

Aiders and abettors — COLLABORATIONISTS
Aides: Abbr. — ASSTS
Aids — ASSISTS
Aids and _____ — ABETS
Ail, in a way — ACHE
Ailerons — FLAPS
Ailing — ILL, UNDER THE WEATHER
Ailing while sailing — SEASICK
Ailurophile's rewards — PURRS
Ailurophobe's word — SCAT
Aim — DIRECT, GOAL, INTENT, POINT
Aim high — ASPIRE
Aimed a snide attack — SNIPED
Aimed at — ASPIRED
Aimless — IDLE
Aimless person — BUTTERFLY
Aims — DRAWS A BEAD
Ainu or Tamil — ASIAN
Air-show feature — STUNT
Air-strike warnings — RED ALERTS
Air — SONG, TUNE, VENTILATE
Air a view — OPINE
Air battles — DOGFIGHTS
Air bubble — BLEB
Air current — DRAFT
Air defense center — NORAD
Air deflector on a race car — SPOILER
Air Force Academy location — COLORADO SPRINGS
Air Force Chief of Staff: 1961-65 — LEMAY
Air force missile — THOR
Air group: Abbr. — WAFS
Air Hazards — SMOGS
Air hole — SPIRACLE
Air layer — OZONE
Air liner — JET
Air Medal — DECORATION
Air pirates — SKYJACKERS
Air pollutant — SMOKE
Air raid — BLITZ
Air show manuever — LOOP
Air term. data — ARRS
Air tube — TRACHIA
Air watching agency, for short — EPA
Air waves — RADIO
Air-borne — ALOFT
Air-condition — COOL
Air-press. unit — ATM
Air-quality watchdog agcy. — EPA
Air: Comb. form — AER, AERI, AERO, ATMO, PNEUMO
Air: Prefix — AERI
Airborn RN's — FNS
Airborne — ALOFT
Aircraft carrier — FLATTOP
Aircraft designation, for short — STOL
Aircraft enclosure — NACELLE
Aircraft gear — RADAR
Aircraft launching device — CATAPULT
Aircraft manuever — IMMELMAN
Aircraft manufacturer — PIPER
Aircraft operated by remote control — DRONE
Aircraft part — TAIL
Aircraft speed measure — MACH
Aired again — RERAN
Airedale — TERRIER
Airfield or kitchen item — APRON
Airfoil — FIN, RUDDER
Airgun ammo — BBS
Airheads — DOLTS
Airizona resort city — SCOTTSDALE
Airline abbr. — ARR, ETA
Airline employee — PILOT
Airman — ACE, PILOT
Airman's assent — ROGER
Airman: Abbr. — AMN
Airplane dimension — WINGSPAN
Airplane manuever — IMMELMAN, LOOP
Airplane's runner — SKID
Airplanes course — VECTOR
Airport — DROME
Airport abbr. — ARR, ETA, DEST, SST
Airport abbreviations — ETAS
Airport aid — RADAR
Airport area — APRON, TARMAC
Airport code for Copenhagen — CPH
Airport control device — RADAR
Airport device — RADAR
Airport info — ETD
Airport initials — ETA
Airport near Paris — ORLY
Airport optimist — STANDBY
Airport sched. heading — ARR
Airport towers — PYLONS
Airs — BROADCAST, MIENS, TUNES
Airships — AEROS
Airships of a sort — BLIMPS
Airwaves watchdog org — FCC
Airy — BREEZY
Airy hotel lobbies — ATRIA
Aisle seat finder — USHER
Ait — ISLET
Aix-les-Bains attraction — EAUX
Aix-la-Chapelle — ACHER
Aix-les-Bains, e.g. — SPA
Ajar — OPEN
Aka — ALIAS
Aka "City of Light" — PAREE
Aka Clem Kadiddlehopper — RED SKELTON
AKA Louise de la Ramee: Eng. novelist — OUIDA
Akihito — EMPEROR
Akihito's father — HIROHITO
Akihito's second son — AYA
Akin — ALIKE, KINDRED, LIKE, RELATED
Al _____ (to the tooth) — DENTE
Al _____, Algerian earthquake scene: 1980 — ASNAM
Al _____: cooking style — DENTE
Al Capp's "lil" hero — ABNER
Al-_____ Iraq port city — BASRAH
Alabama Indian — CREEK
Alabama State team player — HORNET
Alabama's Cole — NAT
Alabama's Crimson _____ — TIDE
Alabaster — GYPSUM
Alack's partner — ALAS
Aladdin's benefactor — GENIE
Aladdin's super servant — GENIE
Alain of France — DELON
Alain of the screen — DELON
Alamo — SHRINE
Alamogordo's county — OTERO
Alan _____ — ADALE
Alan Alda series — MASH
Alan and Cheryl — LADDS
Alan Bates movie: 1966 — KING OF HEARTS
Alan Ladd movie — SHANE
Alan Ladd role — SHANE
Alan or Cheryl — LADD
Alan, Frances or Robert — ALDA
Alarm — ALERT, FEAR, SCARE, SIREN, TOCSIN
Alarm bell — TOCSIN
Alarm turn-on — TIMER
Alarming letters — SOS
Alarming person — STARTLER
Alas — AH ME, OTOTOI
Alas's partner — ALACK
Alas, in Augsburg — ACH
Alas, in Berlin — ACH
Alas, in Munich — ACH
Alas, to Hans — ACH
Alaska bay — PRUDHOE
Alaska blizzard — PURGA
Alaska city — NOME
Alaska gold-rush center — NOME
Alaska purchaser — SEWARD
Alaska river — YUKON
Alaska sable — SKUNK

Alaska state tree — SPRUCE
Alaska, formerly: Abbr. — TER
Alaskan bear — KODIAK
Alaskan city — NOME
Alaskan highway, formerly — ALCAN
Alaskan island — ADAK, ATTU, PRIBILOFF
Alaskan islander — ALEUT
Alaskan metropolis — NOME
Alaskan native — ALEUT, AUK, ESKIMO
Alaskan river — TANANA, YUKON
Alaskan school ad? — GET YOUR BERING STRAIT
Alaskan seaport — NOME
Alaskan strait — BERING
Alastair or Kate — REID
Albacore — MACKEREL, TUNA
Alban and Gertrude — BERGS
Albania's Ramiz _____ — ALIA
Albanian capital — TIRANA
Albanian coin — FRANC, LEK
Albany or Austin, e.g. — STATE CAPITAL
Albatross — GOONIE, GOONEY BIRD
Albatross' cousin — GULL
Albee accountant's problem? — A DELICATE BALANCE
Albee specialty — DRAMA
Albee's "_____ and Yam" — FAM
Albee's Virginia — WOOLF
Albeit — BECAUSE, NOT WITHSTANDING, SINCE
Alberta lake — LOUISE
Alberta park — BANFF
Album — BOOK, FILE
Alcohol — BOOZE, LIQUOR
Alcohol heaters — ETNAS
Alcohol lamp — ETNA
Alcohol standard — PROOF
Alcoholic like compound — THIOL
Alcoholic liquor — TIPPLE
Alcoholic on a budget — WINO
Alcott girl — BETH, MEG
Alcott heroine — MEG
Alcott narative — LITTLE WOMEN
Alcott's "Little _____" — MEN
Alda and Arkin — ALANS
Alda and namesakes — ALANS
Alda or King — ALAN
Alda series — MASH
Alder tree — ARN
Alder: Scot — ARN
Alderman, for short — POL
Aldo and Milland — RAYS
Aldous Huxley novel — APE AND ESSENCE
Ale units — PINTS
Ale vessel — FLAGON, TANKARD
Ale, in Aachen — BIER
Alec Guiness film: 1960 — OUR MAN IN HAVANA
Alehouse — PUB
Aleichem's language — YIDDISH
Alencon — LACE
Alencon and Brussels — LACES
Alencon capital — ORNE
Alencon product — LACE
Alencon's department — ORNE
Aleppo native — SYRIAN
Alert — OPEN EYED, WARN
Alert watchman — ARGUS
Alert, asea — SOS
Alerted — WARNED
Aleut's dog — MALAMUTE
Aleutian Indian — ATTU
Aleutian island — ATTU, ADAK, ATKA
Aleutian islands — NEAR
Aleutian Isle — ATKA
Aleutian straight — BERING
Alewife — HERRING
Alewife's kin — SHAD
Alex Haley opus — ROOTS
Alexander Godunov, to friends — SASHA
Alexander of early "60 Minutes" — SHANA
Alexander the Great's birthplace — PELLA
Alexander's band plays this — RAGTIME
Alexandra's Nicholas — TSAR
Alexandrian V.I.P. — CLEO
Alf or E.T. — ALIEN
Alfalfa — HAY
Alfonse's polite ami — GASTON
Alfonso's queen — ENA
Alfred Noyes poem — THE HIGHWAYMAN
Alfred or Luther — ADLER
Alfred's taro treats — HOYESPOIS
Alfred, Larry, Luther and Polly — ADLERS
Alfresco meals — PICNICS
Algae causing fishy taste in water — ANABAENA
Algae extracts — AGARS
Alger hero's trait — PLUCK
Alger or Humphrey — HORATIO
Algerian city — ORAN
Algerian desert — SAHARA
Algerian governor, before 1830 — REY
Algerian island — IOS
Algerian money — DINARO
Algerian seaport — ORAN
Algiers quarter — CASBAH
Algonquian-speaker — CREE
Algonquian — CREE, OTTAWA
Algonquian Indian — CREE, WEA
Algonquian Indian spirit — MANITO
Algonquian language — CREE
Algonquin Indians — SACS
Algonquin's literary luncheon club — ROUND TABLE
Ali _____ — BABA
Ali once — CLAY
Alias — AKA
Alias acronym — AKA
Alias Ensign Pulver — LEMMON
Alias initials — AKA
Alias, for short — AKA
Aliases: Abbr. — AKAS
Alibi — PLEA
Alibi of a sort — EXCUSE
Alice _____, noted portraitist — NEEL
Alice and Julia — FAYES
Alice Cooper number — SCHOOLS OUT
Alice or Gary — COOPER
Alice's TV friend — FLO
Alicia of "Falcon Crest" — ANA
Alien — FOREIGN, OUTSIDER, STRANGE
Alien chaser — ATION
Alien Frisbee? — UFO
Alien in Iowa — AFIELD
Alien on TV — ALF
Alien transport? — UFO
Alienate — DIVIDE
Aliens — STRANGERS
Aliens' transport — SAUCER
Alighieri — DANTE
Alight — LAND
Align — EVEN
Aligned — TRUE
Aligned as a margin — FLUSH
Alike — SAME
Alike, in Arles — EGAL
Alive — ANIMATED
All-out efforts — ENERGIES
All — THE WHOLE BALL OF WAX
All _____ (attentive) — EARS
All _____ up — HET
All _____ work — IN A DAYS
All _____: everything considered — IN ALL
All a-tremble — SHAKEN
All a twitter — GAGA
All better? — OVER THE HILL
All done — OVER
All ears — ATTENTIVE
All ears — NOSY, RAPT
All fives — MUGGINS
All hot and bothered — UPSET
All in — SPENT, TIRED
All in _____ work — A DAYS
All in all — WHOLLY
All in order — NEAT
All inclusive — ETC, ET AL
All kidding _____ — ASIDE

All messed up — TOPSY TURVY
All of _____ (abruptly) — A HEAP
All out — DO OR DIE, TOTAL
All right — GOOD, OKAY
All right: Fr. — BIEN
All set — PREPARED, READY
All set and ready, to a astronaut — AOK
All the "worlds" — UNIVERSE
All the gossip — DIRT
All the players — CAST
All the rage — STYLISH
All the time — ALWAYS
All the world, to Shakespeare — STAGE
All thumbs — INEPT
All together — ENMASSE
All together, in music — TUTTI
All work and no play — DULL BOY MAKER
All- _____ — AMERICAN
All-purpose abbr. — ETC
All-purpose truck — UTE
All: Comb. form — OMNI
All: L. — OMME
Alla _____ — BREVE
Alladin's servant — GENIE
Allahabad's waterfront — GANGES RIVER
Allay — APPEASE, EASE
Allay inflammation — SUBDUE
Allegation — CHARGE
Allegation, in law — PLEA
Allege — AVER, AVOW, CLAIM
Alleged arson accompanist — NERO
Alleged cause of Cranmer's execution — HERESY
Alleged force — ODYL
Allegedly payless misdeed — CRIME
Allegory — PARABLE
Allegro _____ — ASSAI
Allen _____ — ADALE
Allen and _____ — ROSSI
Allen and Astaire — FRED
Allen and Guttenberg — STEVE
Allen and Martin — STEVES
Allen or Frome — ETHAN
Allen or Lawrence — STEVE
Allen or Martin — STEVE
Allen or Nathan — HALE
Allen or Young — STEVE
Allen's "_____ Hall" — ANNIE
Allergy sympton — RASH
Alleviate — EASE
Alleviated — EASED
Alleviates — EASES
Alley buttons — RESETS
Alley of the comics — OOP
Alley Oop's abode — CAVE
Alley or Oola — OOP
Alley target — TENPIN
Alleys — LANES
Allgood or Teasdale — SARAS
Alliance — ENTENTE
Alliance acronym — NATO, OAS, SEATO
Alliance of World War II — AXIS
Allie's TV friend — KATE
Allied group — BLOC
Alligator pear — AVOCADO
Alligator, e.g. — PEAR
Allman Brother's Band number — RAMBLIN MAN
Allmost unheard-of — SCARCE
Allocate — METE
Allot — METE, METE OUT
Allotment — SHARE
Allotments in Cluny — LACERATIONS
Allots, with "out" — METES
Allotted amount — QUOTA
Allow — ENTITLE, LET
Allow access — LET IN
Allow entry — LET IN
Allowance — RATION
Allowance for damage — BREAKAGE
Allowance for waste — TARE, TRET
Allowed — LICIT
Allows — LETS
Alloy-coated steel — TERNE
Alloy — METAL, MONEL
Alloy used to make tankards — PEWTER
Alloy used to reduce friction in bearings — BABBITT
Alloyed plating — TERNE
Allude (to) — REFER
Alluded — REFERRED
Alludes — REFERS
Allure — ATTRACT, TEASE
Allurement — APPEAL
Alluring creatures — SIRENS
Ally — HELPER
Alma _____ — MATER
Alma mater — COLLEGE
Alma mater of the 39th Pres. — USNA
Alma-_____ U.S.S.R. city — ATA
Alma-_____, capital of Kazakhstan — ATA
Almanac data — MOONSET
Almanack man — POOR RICHARD
Almeria aunts — TIAS
Almond — NUT
Almond colored — TANNED
Almond confection — NOUGAT
Almond-flavored liqueur: Var — RATAFFE
Almond-flavored syrup — ORGEAT
Almondy confection — MARZIPAN
Almondy drink — ORGEAT
Almost — ABOUT, NEARLY, NIGH, NINETYNINE PERCENT
Almost — NOT YET
Almost a direct hit — NEAR MISS
Almost aubergine — PUCE
Almost cylindrical — TERETE
Almost no time at all — SPLIT SECOND
Almost perfect — NINE
Almost unique — RARE
Almost, to the Bard — ANEAR
Alms box — ARCA, ARCAE
Alms seeker — BEGGAR
Aloe derivative — ALOIN
Aloha "boa" — LEI
Aloha wreath — LEI
Aloha's cousin — SHALOM
Aloha, in Israel — SHALOM
Alone — SOLO
Alone, in France — SEUL
Alone, in stage directions — SOLA, SOLUS
Alone, on the boards — SOLUS
Along the way — ENROUTE
Along with — ALSO
Alongside — ADJACENT
Aloof — REMOTE
Aloof one — SNOB
Aloud — ORAL
Alouette's neck — COU
Alp's high — MONT BLANC
Alp's togs — DIRNDLE
Alpaca — COAT
Alpaca's habitat — ANDES, PERU
Alpaca's relative — LLAMA
Alpert of Tijuana Brass — HERB
Alpert's "Spanish _____" — FLEA
Alpert's group — BRASS BAND
Alpha follower — BETA
Alpha's complement — OMEGA
Alpha's opposite — OMEGA
Alpha, beta and gamma — RAYS
Alphabet — ABCS
Alphabet run — ABC, BCDE, MNOP, RSTU
Alphabet used in Russia — CYRILLIC
Alphabet: abbr. — LTRS
Alphabetic quartet — BCDE
Alphabetic quintet — ABCDE
Alphonso's queen — ENA
Alpine abode — CHALET
Alpine city — BERN
Alpine communication — YODEL
Alpine country — ITALY
Alpine crest — ARETE
Alpine feature — ARETE
Alpine house — CHALET
Alpine pasture land — ALM
Alpine range — JUREA
Alpine river — AARE

Alpine slope receiving much sun warmth — ADRET
Alpine sound — YODEL
Alpine stream — AARE
Alpine wind — BISE
Already, in Anhalt — SCHON
Alsace also — AUSSI
Also — AND, TOO
Also extract — ORCIN
Also known as — ALIAS
Also not — NEITHER
Also-_____ (losers) — RANS
Also-ran — LOSER
Also-ran of fable — HARE
Alt. — ELEV, HGT
Alt. flyers — SSTS
Alt. names — AKAS
Alt. to int. — EXT
Alta. or Ont. — PROV
Altar-lights sight — RETABLE
Altar agreement — I DO
Altar area — APSE
Altar boy — ACOLYTE
Altar boy's garb — COTTA
Altar cloth — PALL
Altar in the sky — ARA
Altar on high — ARA
Altar pledge — I DO
Altar promises — VOWS
Altar screen — REREDOS
Altar stone — MENSA
Altar words — I DO
Altar's hanging tapestry — DOSSAL
Alter — REDO
Alter _____ — EGO
Alter a text — EMEND
Alter district lines — REZONE
Alter drastically — REDO
Alter plate — PATEN
Alteration — REDOING
Altercation — SET TO
Altercations, of sorts — SPATS
Alternate — STAGGER
Alternative choice — OTHER
Alternative to Fido — ROVER
Alters — CHANGES
Alters a line — REHEMS
Alters the text — REWRITES
Although — WHILE
Although: Lat. — ETSI
Altitude — HEIGHT
Alto lead-in — PALO
Altogether — IN TOTO
Altogether: mus. — TUTTI
Altos or Angeles — LOS
Alts. — HTS
Alum — GRAD
Aluminum Israeli coin: Var. — AGURA
Aluminum source — BAUXITE
Alumnus, for short — GRAD
Alveoli — AIR SACS
Alvin Childress's TV role — AMOS
Always — EVER, REGULARLY
Always, in Aachen — IMMER
Always, in music — SEMPRE
Always, in poesy — EER
Always, poetically — ETERNE
Always, to Keats — EER
Alyssums — MADWORTS
AM eye-openers? — ALARMS
AM time — MORN
Am. diplomat Silas — DEANE
Am. equivalent of a concierge — SUPER
AMA members — DRS, DOCTORS, MDS
Amalgamate — BLEND, FUSE, MERGE, MIX
Amalgamates — BLENDS
Amalgamation — MERGER
Amas follower — AMAT
Amas successor — AMAT
Amass — HEAP UP
Amassed — PILED UP, RAN UP
Amassment — HOARD
Amateur baseball league — BUSH
Amateur presidential baseball teams? — BUSH LEAGUE
Amateur-sports gp. — AAU
Amateurish painter — DAUBER
Amative — EROTIC
Amatory — EROTIC
Amaze — STUN
Amazon estuary — PARA
Amazon feeder — PARA
Amazon forest feature — RUBBER TREE
Amazon Indian — TUPI
Amazon racoon relative — COATI MUNDI
Amazonia's big cat — JAGUAR
Amazonia's language — PORTUGUESE
Amazonian viper — BUSHMASTER
Amazonian's little cat — OCELOT
Ambassador — ENVOY
Ambassador from the Vatican — NUNCIO
Ambassador John _____ — GAVIN
Amber-colored wine — SHERRY
Ambience — AURA
Ambiguous — OBSCURE
Ambit — CIRCUIT, SCOPE
Ambition — DRIVE
Amble — SAUNTER, WALK
Ambler of fiction — ERIC
Ambler or Blore — ERICS
Ambles — SAUNTERS
Ambling horse — PADNAG
Ambracia today — ARTA
Ambrosia — DESSERT, NECTAR
Ambrosial — TASTY
Ambry — PANTRY
Ambulance-chaser, e.g. — SHYSTER
Ambush — TRAP
Ameliorate — BETTER
Amelita _____ Curci of opera fame — GALLI
Amen — SO BE IT
Amend — ALTER
Amendment — RIDER
Amenhotep IV's god — ATEN
Amenity — COMFORT
Ament — FOOL
Amer. commercial vessels — USMM
Amer. Samoa and Guam — TERRS
Amerces — FINES
America's Cup entry — YACHT
America's Cup sport — SAILING
America's first child — VIRGINIA DARE
America's first printer, 1640 — DAYE
American — MAJOR LEAGUE, YANK
American anthropologist — MEAD
American artist George _____ — CATLIN
American artist Neiman — LEROY
American author — POE, OLIVER WENDELL HOLMES
American author Bret — HARTE
American author Stephen — CRANE
American beauty — ROSE
American capitalist — ASTOR
American cat — OCELOT
American century plant — ALOE
American Civil Rights leader — INNIS
American composer Charles — IVES
American dessert — APPLE PIE
American dogwoods — OSIERS
American etcher Adolf _____ — DEHN
American finch — JUNCO
American flag — RED WHITE AND BLUE
American flycatcher — KINGBIRD
American fur merchant — ASTOR
American fur trader and financier — ASTOR
American humorist — NYE
American Indian — ERIE, UTE
American Indian crest pole — TOTEM

American Indian people — PAWNEE
American Indian tribe — CREE
American Indian weapon of old — TOMAHAWK
American inventor Elmer Ambrose — SPERRY
American inventor Howe — ELIAS
American inventor Pliny _____ — EARLE
American Japanese — NISEI
American Judas tree — REDBUD
American League MVP 1953 — ROSEN
American milkwort — SENEGA
American national military park — SHILOH
American naturalist — MUIR
American nature writer — BEEBE
American naval initials — USS
American Nobel laureate — ERNEST HEMINGWAY
American novelist — JAMES FENIMORE COOPER
American novelist Chaim — POTOK
American novelist Howard — FAST
American or Foreign — LEGION
American painter: 1882-1967 — EDWARD HOPPER
American painting name — PEALE
American patriot of 1776 — HALE
American philosopher: 1855-1916 — ROYCE
American playwright — INGE, WILLIAMS
American plover — KILLDEER
American poet — WILLIAM CULLEN BRYANT
American poet Doolittle — HILDA
American poet Elinor — WYLIE
American poet Paul — DUNBAR
American Revolutionary general — PUTNAM
American Revolutionary hero — NATHAN HALE
American school of art — ASHCAN
American social worker, Jacob — RIIS
American socialist Eugene V. — DEBS
American Socialist: 1855-1926 — DEBS
American suffragette — CATT
American symbol — EAGLE
American trapper and capitalist — ASTOR
American uncle — SAM
American writer Hawthorne — NATHANIEL
American writer James — AGEE
American-born Japanese — NISEI
American-Revolutionary hero Ethan — ALLEN
Amerind — CREE
Amerind leader — CHIEF
Amerinds of N.M. — TEWAS
Ames and Asner — EDS
AMEX neighbor — NYSE
AMEX overseer — SEC
Amiable — NICE
Amicable revision — ADJUSTMENT
Amiens Cathedral feature — GARGOYLE
Amiens river — SOMME
Amin Dada — IDI
Amin, et al. — IDIS
Amino _____ — ACID
Amino acids — LEUCINES
Amino and boric — ACIDS
Amish pronoun — THEE
Amish, for one — SECT
Amiss — AWRY
Amity — COMITY, FRIENDSHIP
Amman is its capital — JORDAN
Ammo unit — SHELL
Ammonia compounds — AMIDES, AMINES
Ammonia derivatives — AMIDES
Ammunition — SHOT
Ammunition dump — DEPOT
Amneris' slave — AIDA
Amneris's rival — AIDA
Amnesty — PARDON
Amo, _____, amat — AMAS
Amo, amas, _____ — AMAT
Amonasro's daughter — AIDA
Among — AMID
Among other things — INTER ALIA
Among the quick — ALIVE
Among us — ALIVE
Amongst — AMID
Amor — EROS
Amor's counterpart — EROS
Amor's wings — ALAE, ALAR
Amorino — CUPID
Amorous grand jete? — LOVERS LEAP
Amorous stare — OGLE
Amos Alonzo _____ — STAGG
Amount — QUANTITY
Amount needed to fill a cask — ULLAGE
Amount of medicine — DOSE
Amounting to nothing — NULL
Amour — LOVE
Amour-propre — SELF RESPECT
Ampersand — ALSO
Ampersands — ANDS
Amphibian — FROG, NEWT, SEAPLANE, TOAD
Amphibious attacks — LANDINGS
Amphitheater — ARENA
Amphora — VASE
Amphora adjunct — ANSA
Amphoras — URNS
Ample room — LARGE
Ample shoe width — EEE
Ample supply — PLENTY
Ample, poetically — ENOW
Amplify — PAD
Ampulla's cousin — CRUET
Amritsar apparel — SARIS
Amsterdam-to-Utrecht dir. — SSE
Amtrack, et al. — RRS
Amtrak stop — STA
Amulet — CHARM
Amuse — CHEER, DELIGHT, DIVERT, TICKLE
Amused expression — HA HA, HEH
Amusement — DISTRACTION, DIVERSION
Amusement centers — ARCADES
Amusement park attractions — RIDES
Amusement rides — WHIPS
Amusements — PASTIMES
Amusing — COMICAL, PLEASANT
Amusing attendants? — FUNNY PAGES
Amusing bunch? — BARREL OF MONKEYS
Amusing fellow — COMIC
Amusing one — DIVERTER
An 1849 event — THE CALIFORNIA GOLD RUSH
An about face — REVERSAL
An ace is one — SERVE
An acid salt — BORATE
An acquired character — ECAD
An act of retribution — NEMESIS
An Adams — EDIE
An adjective for Sears Tower — TALLEST
An Aegean island — THERA
An affirmative — AYE
An Alaskan First Family — EGANS
An Alcott — AMOS
An Alda — ALAN
An Allen — ETHAN, STEVE
An Alou of baseball — MATTY
An altar promise — HONOR

An American's right — THE PURSUIT OF HAPPINESS
An Amerind — CREE
An amphibian — NEWT
An amusing production — JAPE
An anagram for nail — LAIN
An anagram for nails — SLAIN
An anagram for staple — PASTEL
An ancestor of Abraham — PELEG
An Anderson — LONI
An Anne from N.Y.C. — MEARA
An Annie Oakley — PASS
An answer to an RSVP — ACCEPT
An ant — EMMET
An antitoxin: Comb. form — SERO
An antonym for restores — ERASES
An appeal to reason — ARGUMENTUM
An apple inspired him — NEWTON
An Arab rep. — SYR
An archangel — URIEL
An arm of H.U.D. — FHA
An arm of the U.S. exec. branch — OMB
An Arthur — BEA
An assertion in church — AMEN
An Astaire — ADELE, FRED
An Attorney General under Regan — MEESE
An attorney's desk? — A LEGAL SECRETARY
An attractive quality — GRACE
An aunt of Princess Beatrice — DIANA
An eagle's defense — TALON
An easy gait — AMBLE
An easy plumbing assignment? — A LEAD PIPE CINCH
An echo's performance — REPEAT
An edible grain i.e. oats, corn or wheat — CEREAL
An elephant packs his — TRUNK
An end to motion — LESS
An entire range — GAMUT
An equal — MATCH
An equilateral parallelogram — RHOMBE
An evangelist's first name — AIMEE
An explosive — AMATOL
An explosive, for short — TNT
An eye opener — ALARM
An FDR VP — HST
An incarnation of Vishnu — RAMA
An incline — ATILT
An Indic language — PALI
An innermost layer of skin — ENDODERM
An instant — TRICE
An intentional misrepresentation — FRAUD
An interest of TAE — ELEC
An Iroquoian — SENECA
An Italian princely family — ESTE
An Italian sauce — PESTO
An L.B.J. beagle — HIM
An NCO — SARG, SFC
An O'Neal — TATUM
An O'Neill — OONA
An objective of NOW — ERA
An ointment — OLEATE
An old story from Paul? — HINDEMITHS MYTH
An old sweetie? — PENNY CANDY
An ore capital — COPENHAGEN
An Oscar winner in 1986 — CAINE
An Oscar winning screenwriter of "Casablanca" — KOCH
An S.S.R. — RUS
An uncle, to Robert Bruce — EME
An unsaturated hydorcarbon — TOLAN
An upward slope — ACCLIVITY
Ana or Barbara — SANTA
Anadama or panettone — BREAD
Anagram for Aden — DANE
Anagram for air — IRA
Anagram for ales — SALE
Anagram for alter — ALERT
Anagram for aunt — TUNA
Anagram for Australian — SATURNALIA
Anagram for chase — ACHES
Anagram for cots — SCOT
Anagram for door — ODOR
Anagram for Elba — ABEL
Anagram for Emile — ELEMI
Anagram for fade — DEAF
Anagram for FDR — RFD
Anagram for lamp — PALM
Anagram for leas — ALES
Anagram for Lees — ELSE
Anagram for nail — LAIN
Anagram for note — TONE
Anagram for oriental — RELATION
Anagram for pass — SPAS
Anagram for peculation — UNPOETICAL
Anagram for peon — OPEN
Anagram for reap — PARE
Anagram for rose — EROS
Anagram for sacred — SCARED
Anagram for seam — SAME
Anagram for sour — OURS
Anagram for tail — ALIT
Anagram for tales — STALE
Anagram for time — EMIT
Anagram of lane — ELAN
Anagram of master — TAMERS
Anagram of meal — MALE
Anagram of pear — REAP
Anagram of posh — SHOP
Anagram of stream — MASTER
Anagram of tag — GAT
Anagram of vile — EVIL
Anais, the author — NIN
Analgesic plant — ALOE
Analogous — AKIN, SAME
Analyze — DISSECT
Analyze a sentence — PARSE
Analyze grammatically — PARSE
Analyze ore — ASSAY
Analyze verse — SCAN
Analyzed a sentence — PARSED
Analyzed logically — EXPLICATED
Ananais, for one — LIAR
Anarchy — CHAOS
Anarctic ice shelf — AMERY
Anastasia's husband — TSAR
Anat. or chem. — SCI
Anatomic organism — SOMA
Anatomical cavity — SINUS
Anatomical duct — VAS
Anatomical fringe — FIMBRIA
Anatomical hollow — AEROLA
Anatomical loops — ANSAE
Anatomical network — RETE
Anatomical partition — SEPTUM
Anatomical passage — ITER
Anatomical sac — BURSA
Anatomical wrinkle — RUGA
Anatomy, mod style — BOD
Anc. Babylonian — CHAL
Anc. language — LAT
Ancestor — ELDER
Ancestor of David — PELEG
Ancestor of the modern horse — EOHIPPUS
Ancestoral — AVITAL
Ancestoral line — PEDIGREE
Ancestry — DESCENT
Ancestry — LINEAGE, STRAIN
Anchia — HERB
Anchor — MOOR
Anchor cable — HAWSER
Anchor hoist — CAPSTAN
Anchor hoister — CAPSTAN
Anchor position — ATRIP
Anchor with several flutes — GRAPNEL
Anchor's position — ATRIP
Anchorage — HAVEN
Anchored — MOORED
Anchoring place — MOORAGE
Anchorman Dan — RATHER
Anchovy — SPRAT
Anchovy sauce — ALEC

Ancient — OLD, OLDEN
Ancient Adriatic area — ILLYRIA
Ancient Aegean region — IONIA
Ancient and respected — VENERABLE
Ancient Armenia — ARAM
Ancient ascetics — ESSENES
Ancient Asia Minor region — IONIA
Ancient Asian — MEDE
Ancient Assyrian King — SARGON
Ancient Athenian freeman — THETE
Ancient Athenian judge — DICAST
Ancient Briton — CELT, PICT
Ancient bucket-shaped vessel — SITULA
Ancient capital of the Tartars — SARAI
Ancient celibates — ESSENES
Ancient Celtic priest — DRUID
Ancient chariot — ESSED
Ancient chest — ARCA
Ancient China — CATHAY
Ancient Chinese capital — SIAN
Ancient chipped stones — EOLITHS
Ancient chronicler — BELL
Ancient city — TANIS
Ancient city in Syria — EMESA
Ancient city near Argolis — ALEA
Ancient city of Egypt — TANIS
Ancient city of Italy — OSTIA
Ancient counsel — REDE
Ancient country — ELAM
Ancient country of SE Europe — DACIA
Ancient country south of the Dead Sea — EDOM
Ancient courtyards — ATRIA
Ancient dagger — SNEE
Ancient Dead Sea kingdom — EDOM
Ancient district of Asia Minor — IONIA
Ancient Ecuadoran Indians — CARAS
Ancient Egyptian capital — SAIS
Ancient Egyptian percussion instrument — SISTRUM
Ancient Egyptian, perhaps — HAMITE
Ancient Egyptians — SAITES
Ancient Ethiopian capital — MEROE
Ancient France — GAUL
Ancient French tribe — PARASII
Ancient galley — BIREME
Ancient Germanic people — FRANKS
Ancient gold — ASEM
Ancient Greek — SPARTAN
Ancient Greek capital — PELLA
Ancient Greek city-state — POLIS
Ancient Greek city — SPARTA
Ancient Greek coin — OBOL
Ancient Greek coin, Latin style — OBOLUS
Ancient Greek coins — OBOLI
Ancient Greek colony — IONIA
Ancient Greek contest — AGON
Ancient Greek dialect — IONIC
Ancient Greek flask — OLPE
Ancient Greek market place — AGORA
Ancient Greek physician — GALEN
Ancient Greek porticos — STOAS
Ancient Greek sanctuary — SECOS
Ancient Hebrew ascetic — ESSENE
Ancient Hebrew coin — GERAH
Ancient Hebrew linen apron — EPHOD
Ancient Hispania — IBERIA
Ancient ideogram — RUNE
Ancient instrument — LYRE, REBEC
Ancient instruments — ASORS, LUTES
Ancient Istanbul — BYZANTIUM
Ancient Italian — SABINE
Ancient Jewish monastics — ESSENES
Ancient king of Tyre — HIRAM
Ancient kingdom — ELAM, EDOM
Ancient kingdom in SW Asia — ELAM
Ancient kingdom near the Dead Sea — MOAB
Ancient Kingdom of the Persian Gulf — ELAM
Ancient land — ARABY
Ancient land near the Jordan — AMMON
Ancient Latium city — OSTIA
Ancient London prison — BRIDGEWELL
Ancient lyre — ASOR
Ancient lyric poems — EPODES
Ancient magistrates — EDILE
Ancient markers — STELES
Ancient marketplaces — AGORAE
Ancient measure — OMER
Ancient Mexican — OLMEC
Ancient money chest — ARCA
Ancient name for a N European area — SCANDIA
Ancient name for China — CATHAY
Ancient native of S. Mexico — OLMEC
Ancient Nile city — THEBES
Ancient Norse narrative — SAGA
Ancient Olympic Games site — ELIS
Ancient Persian — MEDE
Ancient Persian coin — DARIC
Ancient Persian kingdom — ELAM
Ancient Peruvian — INCA, INCAN
Ancient Phoenician city — BEIRUT
Ancient recluses — EREMITES
Ancient regime queen — REIN
Ancient region of Asia Minor — IONIA
Ancient region of Troy — TROAS
Ancient Roman magistrates — AEDILES
Ancient Roman official — EDILE
Ancient Roman port — OSTIA
Ancient Roman roads — ITERS
Ancient seat of Irish kings — TARA
Ancient site of Susa — ELAM
Ancient stone ax — CELT
Ancient stone implement — AMGARN
Ancient stringed instrument — ASOR, REBEC
Ancient strongbox — ARCA
Ancient Sumerian drum — ALA
Ancient Susa's country — ODIN
Ancient Syria — ARAM
Ancient temple — NAOS
Ancient temple site — KARNAK
Ancient theaters — ODEA
Ancient times — YORE
Ancient toiler ESNE
Ancient tower city — BABEL
Ancient town of Lucania, Italy — ELEA
Ancient tribe of Briton — ICENI
Ancient truth, in China — TAO
Ancient two-wheeled chariots — ESSEDAS
Ancient wall word — MENE
Ancient weapon — SPEAR
Ancient weight unit — MINA
Ancient zither — ASOR
Ancient zitherlike instruments — ASORS

Ancient: Comb.form — PALEO
Ancient: L Comb. form — ARCHEO
And elsewhere: Abbr. — ET AL
And no other — ONLY
And now, a word from Morris — MEOW
And others, for short — ET AL
And so forth: Abbr. — ETC
And the rest — ETC
And were witnesses as _____ — THE TOUCHABLES
And, to Hans — UND
Andalusian aunt — TIA
Andalusian dance — FLAMENCO
Andalusian song — SAETA
Andaman, for one — SEA
Andean — INCA
Andean animal — ALPACA, LLAMA
Andean beast — LLAMA
Andean capital — LIMA
Andean Indian — INCA
Andean land — PERU
Andean native — INCA
Andean republic — PERU
Andersen's birthplace — ODENSE
Anderson of TV — LONI
Anderson or Fonteyn — DAMES
Andersson of the stage — BIBI
Andes country — PERU
Andes dweller — INCA
Andes Indian — INCA
Andes indigenes — INCAS
Andes ruminant — LLAMA
Andes site — PERU
Andiron, in Roma — ALARE
Andover's rival — EXETER
Andre' or Dory — PREVIN
Andrea _____ — DORIA
Andrea del _____ — SARTO
Andress film: 1965 — SHE
Andretti and Unser — RACERS
Andretti or Puzo — MARIO
Andrew Jackson — OLD HICKORY
Andrew's sister — ANNE
Andrews and Carvey — DANAS
Andrews Sisters, e.g. — TRIO
Ands, in Nice — ETS
Andy Gump's wife — MIN
Andy Moog specialties — SAVES
Andy Taylor's boy — OPIE
Andy Warhol subject — SOUP CAN
Andy's crony — AMOS
Andy's radio mate — AMOS
Andy's sidekick — AMOS
Anecdotal collection — ANA
Anecdote — STORY
Anemic — PALE
Anemic color — PALLOR
Anent — AS TO, IN RE
Anesthesia — BLOCK, DULL
Anesthetic — ETHER
Aneurin Bevan familiarly — NYE
Angel Clare's bride — TESS
Angel topper — HALO
Angel's accessory — HALO
Angel's aura — HALO
Angel's delight — SRO
Angel's dream — BOX OFFICE HIT
Angel's favorite letters — SRO
Angel's favorite sign — SRO
Angel's instrument — HARP
Angel, in Avignon — ANGE
Angel? — PATRON
Angela Lansbury role — MAME
Angeles lead-in — LOS
Angelic — HOLY
Angelic headware — HALO
Angelic homeland — HEAVEN
Angelico's title — FRA
Angelico, for one — FRA
Angels, or Astros — TEAM
Anger — ENRAGE, FURY, IRE, OUTRAGE, WRATH
Anger to the point of bitterness — EXACERBATE
Anger, to Cato — IRA
Angered — IRED
Angers — IRES
Angina pectoris — PAIN
Angle — FISH, SLANT, TRICK
Angle for bass — CAST
Angle iron — L BAR
Angle or color preceder — TRI
Angle or plane lead-in — TRI
Angle ratio — SINE
Angled — ATILT
Angleo _____, memorable educator — PATRI
Angler of a kind — EELER
Angler on the move — TROLLER
Angler's aid — LURE
Angler's barb — HERL
Angler's basket — CREEL
Angler's casting plug — CHUGGER
Angler's catch — BASS, CARP, EEL, PERCH, PIKE, TROUT
Angler's item — REEL
Angler's line — SNELL
Angler's lure — SPINNER, WORM
Angler's need — BAIT, LINE, ROD
Angler's purchase — REEL
Angler's Schubert work? — TROUT QUINTETTE
Angler's shortened note — GONE FISHIN
Angler's supply — LURES
Anglers' gear — RODS
Angling need — ROD
Anglo-Saxon riddle — RUNE
Anglo-Saxon slave — ESNE
Anglo-Irish author Elizabeth — BOWEN
Anglo-Saxon coin — ORA
Anglo-Saxon hero — BEOWULF
Anglo-Saxon king: 46-55 — EDRED
Anglo-Saxon laborer — ESNE
Anglo-Saxon letter — EDH
Anglo-Saxon poet — SCOP
Anglo-Saxon village — HAM
Angora — GOAT
Angora goat fabric — MOHAIR
Angora goats home base — TIBET
Angry — IRATE, IRED, IREFUL, VEXED
Angry canine, e.g. — SNARLER
Angry dog reaction — SNARL
Angry dog sound — GRR
Angry dogs — GROWLERS
Angry looks — GLARES
Angry state — SNIT
Angry states for Bumstead's boss? — DITHERS
Angry Valletta native? — MALTESE CROSS
Angry with — MAD AT
Angry, with "off" — TEED
Angry; peeved — SORE
Angst — FEAR, WORRY
Anguine fish — EELS
Anguish — PAIN, WOE
Angular — ABRUPT
Angular border design — FRET
Anil and woad — DYES
Anil, e.g. — DYE
Anility — AGE
Anima — SPIRIT
Animal — BRUTE
Animal and plant life of a region — BIOTA
Animal bereft of its horns — POLLARD
Animal bred from two different species — HYBRID
Animal color — BRINDLE
Animal fat — SUET
Animal handler — TAMER, TRAINER
Animal life — FAUNA
Animal lover — ZOOFILE
Animal lovers' org. — SPCA
Animal MD — VET
Animal of the Andes — LLAMA
Animal pelts — HIDES
Animal shelter — COTE
Animal skin — PELT
Animal track — SPOOR
Animal trail — SPOOR
Animal wandering about homeless — WAIF
Animal's hideaway — LAIR

Animal's pouchlike part — SAC
Animals existing in a given area — FAUNA
Animals lacking pigmentation — ALBINOS
Animals of a given region — FAUNA
Animals that sound tasty — MOOSE
Animate — INSPIRE, LIVEN, SPARK
Animated — ALIVE
Animated sailor — POPEYE
Animation — LIFE
Animation frame — CEL
Animation, usually — CARTOON
Animations were his creations — DISNEY
Animosity — HATRED
Anita or Alan of songdom — O DAY
Anita or Clara — SANTA
Anjou — PEAR
Anjou or Comice — PEAR
Anjou season — ETE
Anjou's cousin — BOSC
Anka from Ottawa — PAUL
Ankara natives — TURKS
Ankara's country — TURKEY
Ankle bone — TALUS
Ankle bones — TALI
Ankle: Comb. form — TARSO
Ankles — ASTRAGALI, TARSI
Anklet — SOCK
Ann _____, Michigan — ARBOR
Ann Landers, for one — TWIN
Ann or Andy — RAG DOLL, RAGGEDY
Ann or Fear — CAPE
Ann or Mike — TODD
Ann Sothern role — MAISIE
Anna — COIN
Anna _____, memorabler singer-actress — HELD
Anna Mary Robertson — GRANDMA MOSES
Anna May of films — WONG
Anna of "Nana" — STEN
Anna Sten role — NANA
Annals — HISTORY
Annapolis freshmen — PLEBES
Annapolis grad — ENS
Annapolis graduates — ENSIGNS
Annapolis inst. — USNA
Annapolis monogram — USN
Annapolis river — SEVERN
Annapolis school, for short — USNA
Anne Boleyn's daughter — QUEEN ELIZABETH I
Anne Brontë's "The _____ of Wildfell Hall" — TENANT
Anne Nichols' hero — ABIE
Anne Sedgewick novel: 1911 — TANTE
Anne Sullivan's pupil — HELEN KELLER
Anne's 1,000 — DAYS
Anne, to Margaret — NIECE
Anneal — TEMPER
Annealing oven — LEHR
Annelid — WORM
Annette's co-star — FRANKIE
Annex — ADD, APPEND, ATTACH, JOIN, PROCURE, WING
Annexed — ADDED, OBTAINED
Annie _____ — OAKLEY
Annie Oakley — PASS
Annie's dog — SANDY
Annie's song — TOMORROW
Annie, for one — ORPHAN
Annie, of the West — OAKLEY
Anniversary of a royal accession — JUBILEE
Anno _____ — DOMINI
Annoited, old style — ANELED
Announce — SAY
Announcer for Jack Benny — WILSON
Announcer of hit songs — DEEJAY
Announcer Schenkel — CHRIS
Annoy — HARASS, IRK, MOLEST, NETTLE, PEEVE
Annoy — PESTER, RANKLE, RIDE, ROIL, VEX
Annoy no end — BADGER
Annoy with taunts — HECKLE
Annoy: Slang — BUG
Annoyance — BOTHER, GNAT, NUISANCE, PAIN, PEST
Annoyed — BADGERED, PESTERED, SORE
Annoying — PESKY
Annoying one — PEST
Annoying situations — HEADACHES
Annoys — CHAFES, GALLS, IRKS, RILES
Annual "first" — NEW YEARS DAY
Annual award — OSCAR
Annual event at Henley — REGATTA
Annual H.S. event — PROM
Annual in the garden — CHINA ASTER
Annual incomes, in Aries — RENTES
Annual presentation of honor — NOBEL PEACE PRIZE
Annual toast — HAPPY NEW YEAR
Annual TV award — EMMY
Annual visitor — SANTA
Annually — YEARLY
Annul — CANCEL, VOID
Annuls — ERASES
Anodyne — OPIUM
Anodyne's target — PAIN
Anoint — ANELE, OIL
Anoint, old style — ANELE
Anoint: archaic — ANELE
Anomaly — ODDITY
Anon — LATER
Anonym — ALIAS
Anonymous Jane — DOE
Anonymous John — DOE
Anonymous Richard — ROE
Anorak — PARKA
Anos openers — ENEROS
Another name for Hosea — OSEE
Another of the same — DITTO
Another time — ANON
Another, in Acapulco — OTRA
Another, in Madrid — OTRO
Answer — REPLY, RESPONSE, RIPOSTE
Answer for — REDEEM
Answer impudently — SASS
Answer in kind — REJOIN
Answer to a knock — COME IN
Answering machine playback — MESSAGES
Ant — EMMET, PISMIRE
Ant. for ant. — SYN
Ant. opposite — SYN
ANTA and UNESCO, e.g. — ACRONYMS
Antagonism — ENMITY
Antagonist — ENEMY
Antagonist of torrero — EL TORO
Antagonists — FOES
Antarctic arm of the Pacific — ROSS SEA
Antarctic bird — PENGUIN
Antarctic cape — ADARE
Antarctic coastal area — ADELIE
Antarctic covering — ICECAP
Antarctic explorer — ROSS
Antarctic penguin — ADELIE
Antarctic precipitation — SNOW
Antarctic Sea — ROSS
Antarctica null point — SOUTH POLE
Antares or Vega — STAR
Ante — STAKE
Antebellum — PREWAR
Antecedence — PRIORITY
Anted up, in a way — LOOED
Antediluvian — OLD
Antediluvian time — ANCIENT
Antelope — ELAND
Antelope — ORYX
Antelope of Africa — GNU
Antelope of E Africa — NYALA
Antelope of puzzledom — ELAND, GNU

Antelope or drum — BONGO
Antelopes of SE Africa — STEENBOKS
Antenna — LONG WIRE, PALP
Antenna connection — LEAD IN
Antenna for singer Eddie? — RABBITT EARS
Antenna housings on aircraft — RADOMES
Antennas — AERIALS
Anterior — FRONTAL
Anterior limb in a bird — WING
Anthologies — ANAS
Anthology — ALBUM, COLLECTION, DIGEST
Anthology of an author's works — OMNIBUS
Anthony _____, Earl of Avon — EDEN
Anthony and Barbara — EDENS
Anthony of the alleys — EARL
Anthony or Elmo — SAINT
Anthony Quinn role — ZORBA
Anthozoans — CORALS
Anthracite — COAL
Anthropod lips — LABRA
Anthropoid — APE
Anthropologist Claude _____ Strauss — LEVI
Anthropologist Fossey — DIAN
Anthropologist Franz — BOAS
Anthropologist Margaret — MEAD
Anthropologist Turnbull — COLIN
Anti-saccharin agcy. — FDA
Anti-Tweed cartoonist — NAST
Anti vote — NAY, NO
Anti-child abuse org. — SPCC
Anti-detonation stencil — TNT
Anti-mine device — PARAVANE
Anti-social one — LONER
Antic — CAPER
Anticipate — AWAIT
Anticipate with alarm — DRED
Anticipating — AGOG
Anticyclones — HIGHS
Antigone's uncle — CREON
Antilles Indian — CARIB
Antilles isle near Venezuela — ARUBA
Antipathetic — AVERSE
Antipathy — HATE, RANCOR
Antipodean soldier — ANZAC
Antipolio pioneer — SABIN
Antipollution devices — SCRUBBERS
Antiquate — DATE
Antiquated — DATED, OLD
Antique — CURIO
Antique auto — REO
Antique automobiles — REOS
Antique finish — PATINA
Antique pot? — CROCK OF AGES
Antique red — CANNA
Antique store caveat — AS IS
Antiquity — OLD, PAST
Antiseptic — IODINE, STERILE
Antislavery network — UNDERGROUND RAIL-ROAD
Antitoxic agents — SERUMS
Antitoxin — SERUM
Antitoxins — SERA
Antler subdivisions — TINES
Antler tip — PRONG
Antler's flat section — PALM
Antlered animal — STAG
Antlers — HORNS
Anton or Dey — SUSAN
Anton or Hayward — SUSAN
Antonio or Francisco — SAN
Antony — MARC
Antony or Connelly — MARC
Antonym for adore — ABHOR
Antonym of aloft — ALOW
Antonym of aweather — ALEE
Antonym of narrow — WIDE
Ants and mosquitoes — PESTS
Anvil location — EAR
Anvils — STITHIES
Anwar of Egypt — SADAT
Anxiety — ANGST
Anxiety relieving alkaloid — RESERPINE
Anxious — EAGER
Anxiously expecting — ATIP
Any — SOME
Any AL team — NINE
Any delicious drink — NECTAR
Any dog — CANID
Any dough — PASTE
Any human — MORTAL
Any NBA team — FIVE
Any NFL team — ELEVEN
Any of the 12 parts of the Zodiac — HOUSE
Any old time — WHENEVER
Any person that — WHO SO
Any planet — ORB
Any poet — BARD
Any rich man — DIVES
Any temporal ruler — CAESAR
Any time at all — EVER
Any Venetian canal — RIO
Any way at all — AD LIB
Any: Dial. — ONI
Anything of worth and stability — BLUE CHIP
Anything that is braided — PLAITING
Anything whatever — AUGHT
Anything's belief? — IMPOSSI-BLE
Año nuevo time — ENERO
Aorta — ARTERY
Apace — FAST
Apache masked dancers — GAHE
Apart — SEPARATE
Apart from anything else — MERE
Apart: Prefix — DIS
Apartment — FLAT, UNIT
Apartment adjuncts — TERRACES
Apartment dweller — TENANT
Apartment house sign — TO LET
Apartment no-no sometimes — PETS
Apartment on the roof — PENTHOUSE
Apartment, along the Thames — FLAT
Apartment, in London — FLAT
Apartments to Becky's kin — SHARPS FLATS
Apartments, in a way — UNITS
Apartments, in Mayfair — FLATS
Apathetic — BLASE, BORED, STOLID, TORPID
Apathy — DISINTEREST
Ape — ECHO
Ape of Sumatra — ORANG
Ape's foot — HAND
Apennines river — ARNO
Apennines stream — ARNO
Aper anagram — PEAR
Aperitif of white wine — KIR
Aperture: Abbr. — OPG
Apertures — SLOTS
Apes — SIMIANS
Apex — CUSP, TOP
Aphids — PESTS
Aphorism — ADAGE, GNOME, PROVERB
Aphrodisiac — EROTIC POTION
Aphrodite's husband — ARES
Aphrodite's love(r) — ADONIS
Aphrodite's son — CUPID, EROS
Apia is its capital — SAMOA
Apiarist — BEEKEEPER
Apiarist's assets — BEES
Apiary — HIVE
Apiculturist's concern — BEE
Apiece — EACH, PER
Aplenty, old style — ENOW
Apocalyptic — ARCANE
Apocopates — ELIDES
Apocryphal bk. — ESD
Apoidea member — BEE
Apollo 7 astronaut — EISLE
Apollo agcy. — NASA
Apollo festival — DELIA
Apollo's birthplace — DELOS
Apollo's mother — LETO
Apologetic — CONTRITE
Apologizer's ailment — CROW

Apologue — FABLE
Apostate — FALSE
Apostle of the Franks — REMI
Apostolic letter — EPISTLE
Apothegm — ADAGE
Apothegms — SAWS
Apothesize — CROWN
Appalachia product — COAL
Appalachian baseball organization? — MINER LEAGUE
Appalachian, for one — TRAIL
Appalling — GRIM
Apparatus — GEAR
Apparatus to induce change — REACTOR
Apparel at an "Animal House" orgy — TOGAS
Apparent self-contradiction — PARADOX
Apparition — SPECTER, WRAITH
Appeal — PLEA, PLEAD
Appealed for help — PRAYED
Appeals — REFERS
Appeals judge in Parliment — LAWLORD
Appear — LOOM, SEEM, TURN UP
Appear to be — SEEM
Appearance — MIEN, VISAGE
Appeared in a show — WAS ON
Appeared unexpectedly — CROPPED UP
Appearing as if gnawed — EROSE
Appears — SEEMS, SURFACES
Appears deadly pale — LOOKS LIKE A GHOST
Appears somber — GLOOMS
Appears to be — SEEMS
Appease — PLACATE, PROPITIATE
Appease or appoint follower — MENT
Appease with liquid — SLAKE
Appeased — PLACATED
Appeased thirst — SLAKED
Appeases hunger — SATES
Appelation — LABEL, NAME, NOMEN, TITLE
Append — ADD, AFFIX, ATTACH, JOIN, TIE TO
Appendage — LIMB
Appended — ADDED ON
Appends — ADDS
Appertain — BELONG
Appetence — NEED, WANT
Appetite appeaser — SNACK
Appetite rouser — AROMA
Appetizer for a gourmet — PATE
Appetizing — TOOTHSOME
Appia or Dolorosa — VIA
Appian Way, e.g. — ITER
Appian Way, once — ROAD TO ROME
Applaud — CLAP
Applauded — CHEERED
Applause — ECLAT
Applause for George? HANDELS HAND
Apple — GREEN, POME
Apple beverage — CIDER
Apple butter — SPREAD
Apple centers — CORES
Apple drink — CIDER
Apple juice acid — MALIC
Apple of one's eye — IDOL, PET
Apple or Cranberry follower — SAUCE
Apple or pear — POME
Apple parts — CORES
Apple polisher — BACK SLAPPER
Apple pudding — BROWN BETTY
Apple seed — PIP
Apple type — ROME
Apple variety — WINESAP
Apple-filled pastry — STRUDEL
Apples or pears — POMES
Appliances — IRONS
Application — USE
Applied calcium oxide — LIMED
Applied henna — DYED
Applied oneself to — GOT AT
Applies — USES
Applies heat to damp clothes — DRIES
Applies henna — DYES
Apply — PUT
Apply a new metallic coat — REPLATE
Apply chrism — ANOINT
Apply chrism, old style — ANELE
Apply cosmetics — MAKE UP
Apply elbow grease — SCOUR
Apply henna — DYE
Apply new pipe covering — RELAG
Apply pressure — TURN ON THE HEAT
Apply rouge — PAINT
Apply sequins to — SEW ON
Apply wrongly — MISUSE
Applying gold paint — GILDING
Appoint — NAME
Appointed — NAMED
Appointer — NAMER
Appointment — DATE, TRYST
Appomattox figure — LEE
Apportion — ALLOT, DEAL, METE, SHARE
Apportioned — DEALT
Apportioned potions — DOSED
Apportions (with "out") — METES
Appraisal — ASSESSMENT
Appraise — ASSESS, ESTIMATE, GAUGE, RATE, SIZE UP
Appraised — RATED, VALUED
Appraiser — EVALUATOR, RATER
Appraises — RATES
Appreciate — CHERISH, ESTEEM, PRIZE, VALUE
Apprehend — ARREST, CAPTURE, GRASP, NAB
Apprehend clearly — KNOW
Apprehender — CAPTOR
Apprehends — NABS
Apprehension — DREAD, MISGIVING
Apprentice — LEARNER, TRAINEE
Apprentice's state — CLERKSHIP
Apprise — INFORM
Apprize — VALUE
Apprizes — WARNS
Approach — ACOST, AVENUE, BUNT, COME, NEAR
Approach obliquely — SIDLE
Approach shot — CHIP
Approach stealthily — STALK
Approached — NEARED
Approached directly — ACCOSTED
Approaches — NEARS
Approbation — PRAISE
Appropriate — COMANDEER, COOPT, MEET, TAKE
Appropriate April wear? — DRENCH COATS
Appropriate as one's own — POCKET
Appropriated — TOOK
Appropriately — APTLY
Approval — ASSENT, KUDOS, YES
Approval word — AMEN
Approvals — SAMPLES
Approvals, for short — OKS
Approve — ADOPT, ENDORSE, OKAY, RATIFY
Approved — OKED
Approving gesture — NOD
Approving, in a way — OKING
Approx. — CIRCA
Approximate — NEAR
Approximately — ABOUT, OR SO
Appurtenance — ANNEX
Apr. "revenue enhancers" — IRS
Apres _____ — VOUS
Après six — SEPT
Après-ski drink — COCOA
April 1 baby, e.g. — ARIES
April 13, to Caesar — IDES
April 5, in old Rome — NONAE

April initials — IRS
April item — RAINDROP
Apron — STAGE
Apropos of — IN RE
Apse — ALCOVE
Apt anagram for notes — STENO
Apt anagram for vile — EVIL
Apt anagram of aye — YEA
Apt name for a mariner — SALTY
Apt pupils response — I SEE
Apt rhyme for confuse — BEMUSE
Apt rhyme for gain — ATTAIN
Apt. ad abbr. — RMS
Apt. house, e.g. — CONDO
Aptitude — FLAIR
Aptly matched — WELL SUITED
Aptly named Tommy of musicals — TUNE
Aqua _____ — PURA
Aqua _____ (nitric acid) — REGIA
Aqua vitae — ALCOHOL
Aqua vitae — BRANDY, WHISKY
Aquarelle — WATERCOLOR
Aquarium — TANK
Aquarium accesories — AERATORS
Aquarium favorite — TETRA
Aquarium fish — TETRA
Aquarium inhabitant — TETRA
Aquarium prop — EWER
Aquarius follower — PISCES
Aquarius' mo. — JAN
Aquatic — MARINE
Aquatic animal — OTTER
Aquatic animalcule — ROTIFER
Aquatic bird — TERN
Aquatic footwear? — WATER PUMPS
Aquatic mammals — MANATEE, OTTERS, SEALS
Aquatic performers — SEALS
Aquatic plant — ALGA
Aquatic rodents — MUSKRATS
Aquatic skill — BUTTERFLY STROKE
Aquatic viewing vessel — GLASS BOTTOM BOAT
Aqueduct — CANAL, RACETRACK
Aqueous — WATERY
Aquila — EAGLE
Aquiline — ROMAN
Aquiline abode — AERIE
Aquinas — ST THOMAS
Arab — SEMITE
Arab bigwig — EMEER
Arab caliph — ALI
Arab chieftan — SHEIK
Arab cloak — ABA
Arab garment — ABA
Arab or Roman add-on — ESQUE
Arab org.: 1958-61 — UAR
Arab port — ADEN
Arab prince — EMEER
Arab republic — YEMEN
Arab's garb — ABA
Arab, for one — SEMITE
Arabesque — BRAID
Arabian arroyo — WADIS
Arabian bigwig — AMEER, EMEER, EMIR
Arabian chiefs — EMIRS
Arabian chieftain — EMIR
Arabian coffee — MOCHA
Arabian garment — ABA
Arabian gazelle — ARIEL
Arabian gulf — OMAN
Arabian nation — YEMEN
Arabian nobleman — EMEER
Arabian pasta ad? — MECCA RONI
Arabian peninsula — SINAI
Arabian port — ADEN
Arabian prince — AMEER, EMIR
Arabian prince: Var. — AMIR
Arabian robes — ABAS
Arabian ruler — AMIR, EMIR
Arabian sailboat — DHOW
Arabian Sea gulf — ADEN, OMAN
Arabian Sea sultanate — OMAN
Arabian title — EMIR
Arabic A — ALIF
Arabic name meaning "dark as night" — LEILA
Arabic word for hill — TIL
Araceous — AROID
Arachnid — SPIDER
Arachnid's traps — WEBS
Arachnid's work — WEB
Arafat of the PLO — YASIR, YASSER
Arafat's gp. — PLO
Arafat's org. — PLO
Aramis sidekick — ATHOS
Aramis, to Athos — AMI
Ararat docker — ARK
Ararat landfall figure — NOAH
Arbitrary orders — FIATS
Arboreal frog — TREE TOAD
Arboreal marsupial — KOALA
Arboreal primate — LEMUR
Arboreal protection — BARK
Arboreal rodent — TREE RAT
Arboreal snake — MAMBA
Arboretum specimens — TREES
Arborvitae — CEDAR
Arc — SPARK
Arc. dweller — ESK
Arcade — MALL
Arcade in ancient Athens — LESCHE
Arcadian — PASTORAL
Arcane — ABSTRUSE, ESOTERIC, HIDDEN, SECRET
Arcane knowledge — LORE
Arcane symbol — RUNE
Arcaro or Shoemaker — JOCKEY
Arcaro, the jockey — EDDIE
Arcas — CHESTS
Arch — BOW, OGEE
Arch Bolshevik — LENIN
Arch de Triomphe locale — ETO ILE
Arch in a vault — RIB
Arch in St. Louis — GATEWAY
Arch types — OGEES
Archaeological areas — DIGS
Archaic — OLDEN
Archaic adverb — ERST
Archbishop Tutu — DESMOND
Archduchess — LADY
Archduke, e.g. — TITLE
Arched upper side of the human foot — INSTEP
Archeological find — TOMB
Archeological sites — DIGS
Archeologist's fragments — SHERDS
Archeologist's haunts — DIGS
Archeologist's milieu — DIGS, RUINS
Archer of myth — EROS
Archer or Baxter — ANNE
Archer William — TELL
Archer's forte — AIMING
Archers — BOWMEN
Archery target — BULLSEYE
Arches — OGIVES
Archfiend — SATAN
Archibald of the N.B.A. — NATE
Archie Bunker, for example — BIGOT
Archie or Roger — MOORE
Archie's spouse — EDITH
Archipelago unit — ISLE
Architect — ARTIST
Architect _____ van der Rohe — MIES
Architect Gottlieb _____ Saarinen — ELIEL
Architect I.M. — PEI
Architect Saarinen — EERO
Architect van der Rohe — MIES
Architect with a high IQ? — FRANK LLOYD BRIGHT
Architect's addition — ELL
Architect's annex — ELL
Architect's fillet — ORLE
Architect's wing — ELL
Architectural feature — NAVE
Architectural fillet — ORLE
Architectural item — STOA
Architectural order — DORIC, IONIC
Architectural piers — ANTAE

Architectural rib — LIERNE
Architecture style — DORIC, IONIC
Archway element — LINTEL
Arctic — GLACIAL, RAW
Arctic athlete? — NORTH POLE VAULTER
Arctic bird — AUK
Arctic craft — UMIAK
Arctic dwelling — IGLOO
Arctic explorer — PEARY
Arctic explorer and family — PEARYS, RAES
Arctic floater — BERG
Arctic hunters — ESKIMOS
Arctic pack — FLOE
Arctic seals — HARPS
Arctic sight — FLOE, ICECAP
Arctic surname — CLAUS
Arctic transport — DOG SLED, SLED
Arden and namesakes — EVES
Arden and Queler — EVES
Ardent — BURNING, EAGER, FIERY, INTENSE
Ardent enthusiasms — LUSTS
Ardent follower — DEVOTEE
Ardor — ELAN, WARMTH
Arduous journey — TREK
Area — BELT, DOMAIN, EXPANSE, REGION, TRACT
Area between the fetlock and the hoof — PASTERN
Area east of New York City — LONG ISLAND
Area east of the Blue Ridge — PIEDMONT PLATEAU
Area enframed by an arch — LUNETTE
Area equaling 1,000 square meters — DECARE
Area in Manhattan — SOHO
Area near a ship's keel — DEADRISE
Area of a cathedral — NAVE
Area of France — MIDI
Area of NW Greece — EPIRUS
Area of South Dakota — BADLANDS
Area of swift current — RAPIDS
Area on the moon — MARE
Area or zip — CODE
Areas in St. Peter's — APSES
Areas off fairways — ROUGHS
Areca nut — BETEL
Arena — HIPPODROME
Arena arbitrator — REFEREE
Arena area — TIER
Arena cries — OLES
Arena for the Hawks — OMNI
Arena parts — TIERS
Arena receipts — GATE
Arena sound — OLE
Arena structure — TIER
Arena surprise — UPSET
Arenaceous plant — SANDWORT
Arenas — STADIA
Areola — CELL, SPACE
Ares or Mars — GOD
Arête — CREST
Argentina's neighbor — CHILE
Argentine cowboy — GAUCHO
Argentine leader — PERON
Argentine weapon — BOLO
Argentinian plain — PAMPAS
Argentinian timber trees — TALAS
Argonaut skipper — JASON
Argosy — FLEET
Argot — CANT, JARGON, PATOIS, SLANG
Argument — SPAT, WORDS
Argument in favor of — PRO
Argus's specialty — EYES
Argyles — SOCKS
Argyles, e.g. — HOSE
Arhat — MONK
Aria — AIR, SOLO
Aria da _____ — CAPO
Aria for two — DUETTO
Aria, plus — SCENA
Ariabian sea gulf — OMAN
Arias — SOLI, SOLOS
Arias, for example — SOLI
Arid — DRY, SERE
Arid wastes — SAHARAS
Ariel's compeers — SPRITES
Ariel, for one — SPRITE
Aries — RAM
Arikaras — REES
Ariosto's patron — ESTE
Arising unexpectedly — EMERGENT, EMERGENCY
Arista — ANTENNA
Aristae — AWNS
Aristocles — PLATO
Aristocratic — NOBLE
Aristophanes was one — ATHENIAN
Aristophanes' "The _____" — WASPS
Aristotle irked? — GREEK CROSS
Arith. action — ADDN
Arith. solution — ANS
Arithmetical sign — PLUS
Ariz. Senator Dennis De _____ — CONCINI
Ariz. zone — MST
Arizona aristocrats? — TUCSON COUNTS
Arizona city — MESA, YUMA
Arizona Indian — PIMA, YUMA
Arizona Indians — NAVAHO, TEWAS
Arizona native — NAVAJO
Arizona State University city — TEMPE
Arizona's _____ Grande — CASA
Ark — VESSEL
Ark builder: Var. — NOE
Ark constructor — NOAH
Ark man — NOAH
Ark passenger — SHEM
Ark skipper — NOAH
Ark unit — PAIR
Ark. county — DESHA
Arkansas Indian — WICHITA
Arkansas river — RED
Arlene and Roald — DAHL
Arles' waterfront — RHONE
Arlette's school — ECOLE
Arlington, Va., structure — PENTAGON
Arlo, to Woody — SON
Arm — FORTIFY, LIMB
Arm bone — ULNA
Arm bones — ULNAS
Arm muscle — BICEP
Arm of HUD — FHA
Arm of the Amazon — PARA
Arm of the Med. — AEG
Arm of the sea — INLET
Arm of the South Pacific — CORAL SEA
Arm part — WRIST
Arm: Prefix — BRACHI
Armada — FLEET
Armadas — NAVIES
Armadillo — APAR, TATOU
Armed Egyptian goddess — ANTA
Armed force — MILITIA
Armed forces careerist — LIFER
Armed horseman — LANCER
Armed services br. — USMC
Armed vessel, British style — E BOAT
Armenia's capital — ERIVAN
Armies — HOSTS
Armistice — TRUCE
Armor — MAIL
Armor part — TASSE
Armored tank — PANZER
Armored vehicles — TANKS
Arms of a barnacle — CIRRI
Arms storehouse — ARSENAL
Armstrong and Sedaka — NEILS
Armstrong on trumpet — LOUIS
Army and Navy — SERVICES
Army bigwigs — BRASS
Army bugle call — TAPS
Army careerist — LIFER
Army chaplain, to some — PADRE
Army division — UNIT
Army eating place — MESS TABLE
Army group — UNIT
Army helicopters — APACHES
Army man: Abbr. — CPL
Army mascot — MULE

Army meal — MESS
Army officer — MAJOR
Army offs. — COLS
Army outfit — UNIT
Army partner to Hickam Field — SCHOFIELD BARRACKS
Army post exchange — CANTEEN
Army quarters — BILLET
Army rank: Abbr. — GEN, PFC
Army school — WEST POINT
Army school, for short — OCS
Army storehouse — ETAPE
Army unit — TROOP
Army unit: Abbr. — BDE
Army V.I.P.'s — CPOS
Arnaz — DESI
Arnie's fans — ARMY
Arnie's helper — CADDIE
Arnie's writing style? — PALMER METHOD
Arno river city — PISA
Arnold _____, memorable actor-puzzler — MOSS
Arnold of comedy — STANG
Arnold of golf — PALMER
Arnold or Tony — BENNETT
Arnt able? — CANST
Aroma — ODOR, SCENT, SMELL
Aromatic gum resin — AMMONIA
Aromatic herb — ANISE, DILL, MINT
Aromatic ointment — BALM
Aromatic resin — ELEMI, MASTIC
Aromatic resins — BALMS
Aromatic root — ORRIS
Aromatic seed — ANISE
Aromatic spice — MACE
Aromatic tea — TISANE
Aromatic tree — ALLSPICE
Aromatic wood — ALOES
Arose — STOOD
Around: Comb. form — AMBI, CIRCUM, PERI
Arouse — ALERT, STIR
Aroused — AWAKE
Aroused from sleep — WOKE
Arouses anger — INCENSES
Arow — IN A LINE
Arp follower — DADAIST
Arp's art — DADA
Arraign — ACCUSE
Arrange — SORT
Arrange in folds — DRAPE
Arrange in order — SORT
Arranged — SORTED
Arranged in piles — STACKED
Arranged in rows — SERIATE
Arranged in threes — TERNATE
Arrangement — DEAL, ORDER, SETUP
Arrangements — PLANS
Arranges beforehand — PRESETS
Arranges in rows — ALINES
Arrant — UTTER
Arrears — DEBT
Arrest — CAPTURE, CATCH, DELAY, GRAB, HALT
Arrest — MAKE A COLLAR, NAB, RUN IN
Arrested — RAN IN
Arris — RIDGE
Arrival at Heathrow? — ENGLANDING
Arrive — GET IN
Arrive as expected — SHOW
Arrive at — REACH
Arrive at Grand Central — DETRAIN
Arrived — CAME, GOT IN
Arrivederci — BYE
Arrives — COMES, VISITS
Arriving a la Currier & Ives — COMING IN SLEIGHS
Arrogance — DISDAIN, HUBRIS, PRIDE
Arrogant — HAUGHTY, UPPISH
Arrogate — PREMPT, USURP
Arrow-poison tree — UPAS
Arrow — SHAFT, WEAPON
Arrow case — QUIVER
Arrow feature — NOTCH
Arrow launcher — BOW
Arrow maker or aerospace scientist — JAMES FLETCHER
Arrow part — SHAFT
Arrow point — NEB
Arrow poison — INEE, UPAS, URARI
Arrow string — NOCK
Arrow's mate — BOW
Arrow-root — STARCH
Arrowed traffic sign — ONE WAY
Arrowhead, e.g. — NEOLITH
Arrows — SHAFTS
Arrowsmith's wife — LEORA
Arroyo — GORGE
Arroyo's relative — WADI
Ars' followers — ESSES
Arsenal — DEPOT, DUMP
Arsenal items — GUNS
Arson is one — CRIME
Art — CRAFT, DECO, HUMANITIES, KNACK, SKILL
Art — TALENT, TRADE
Art _____ — DECO
Art _____: 20's style — DECO
Art appreciator — AESTHETE
Art categories — GENRES
Art category — GENRE
Art colony near Santa Fe — TAOS
Art cult founded in 1916 — DADA
Art dealer? — BEARER OF GOOD NUDES
Art Deco artist — ERTE
Art Deco designer — ERTE
Art for art's _____ — SAKE
Art gallery — TATE
Art genre of 20th cen. — ASHCAN
Art material — CHALK
Art medium — OIL
Art movement — DADA
Art object — CURIO, VASE
Art rack — EASEL
Art sch. course — ANAT
Art show — OPENING
Art students' river — SEINE
Art supporter — EASEL
Art teacher's degree — MAE
Art work — OIL, SKETCH
Artemis gave him stardom — ORION
Artery — AORTA, ROAD
Artful — SKILLED
Artful move — END RUN
Arthur and Lillie — BEAS
Arthur of tennis — ASHE
Arthur of tennis fame — ASHE
Arthur of the courts — ASHE
Arthur of TV — BEA
Arthur of Wimbledon — ASHE
Arthur or Lillie — BEA
Arthur who was Maude — BEA
Arthur's dad — UTHER
Arthurian lady — ELAINE, ENID
Arthurian locale — ASTOLAT
Arthurian maid — ELAINE
Arthurian twin — BALIN
Arthurian wear — ARMOR
Article — ITEM, THE
Article printed daily — THE
Article worn to cover the body — DRESS
Articles of food — VIANDS
Articulate — FLUENT, SPEAK
Articulates — SAYS
Artifact — RELIC
Artifice — RUSE WILE
Artificial — ERSATZ, MANNERED
Artificial channel — CAT
Artificial gem — PASTE
Artificially high voice — FALSETTO
Artillery — CANNON
Artillery need — AMMO
Artisan of a kind — WOODWORKER
Artist — CREATOR
Artist _____ del Sarto — ANDREA
Artist Calder, to friends — ALEX
Artist Chagall — MARC
Artist Frankenthaler — HELEN
Artist grandma — MOSES

Artist Henri, et al. — MATISSES
Artist Hieronymus — BOSCH
Artist in the Louvre — DEGAS
Artist is short of a spring — NORMAN ROCK
Artist Joan — MIRO
Artist Max — ERNST
Artist Mondrian — PIET
Artist or wheel, e.g. — ESCAPE
Artist Shahn — BEN
Artist subject — NUDE
Artist's case — PORTFOLIO
Artist's choice — BLUE
Artist's colors — PALETTE
Artist's mate — GRANDPA MOSES
Artist's milieu — ATELIER
Artist's need — EASEL
Artist's pigment — OCHRE, SIENNA
Artist's stand — EASEL
Artist's studio — ATELIER
Artist's surface — GESSO
Artist, marmot and actor — GRANT WOODCHUCK CONNORS
Artistic — ESTHETIC
Artistic Grandma — MOSES
Artistic style — GENRE
Artists' wear — BERETS
Artless — NAIVE
Arty Paris "Quarter" — LATIN
Arum genus — ARALES
Arum lily — CALLA
Aryan of Central Caucasus — OSSET
As _____ (from this time on) — OF NOW
As _____ (normally) — A RULE
As _____ (often) — A RULE
As _____ (usually) — A RULE
As _____ a beet — RED AS
As _____ kite — HIGH AS A
As a result of this — HEREBY
As a substitute — INSTEAD
As an example — THUS
As an extreme limit — AT MOST
As bright _____ — AS DAY
As busy as _____ — A BEE
As close as possible — CHOCK
As free as _____ — A BIRD
As good as — NEARLY
As in former days — OLDEN
As it were — SO TO SPEAK
As long as — WHILE
As meek as _____ — A LAMB
As one — UNITED
As plain _____ — AS DAY
As soon as — ONCE
As such — PER SE
As to — IN RE
As usual — NORMAL
As well — ALSO, TOO
As well as — AND
As written: Mus. — STA
As yet — SO FAR
ASAP — PDQ
ASCAP's alley — TIN PAN
Ascend — CLIMB, LIFT, RISE, SCALE, SOAR
Ascended — AROSE, RISEN
Ascends, as Halfdome — CLIMBS
Ascent — CLIMB, GO UP
Ascertain — GET AT, LEARN, DETERMINE
Ascetic — LONER
Ascetic of yore — ESSENE
Asch's "The _____" — APOSTLE
Ascot — TIE
Ascribe — IMPUTE, REFER
Ascribed — CREDITED
Asgard chief — ODIN
Asgard resident — THOR
Ash — LUMBER, TREE
Ash holders — URNS
Ash or aspen — TREE
Ash receptacle of yore — SILENT BUTLER
Ashamed — CONTRITE, GUILTY, RED FACED
Ashcan target — SUB
Ashen — PALE
Ashley or Hobson — LAURA
Ashtabula's lake — ERIE
Ashton ballet — FACADE
Asia desert — GOBI
Asia Minor region — IONIA, TROAS
Asia or Ursa — MINOR
Asian antelope — SEROW
Asian border river — YALU
Asian calculator — ABACUS
Asian capital — SEOUL
Asian cattle — ZEBU
Asian cuisine — CHINESE
Asian desert — GOBI
Asian domestic — AMAH
Asian evergreen — ATLE
Asian export — TEA
Asian festival — TET
Asian fiber — RAMIE
Asian form of address — SAHIB
Asian gazelle — GOA
Asian goat antelope — SEROW
Asian holiday — TET
Asian land — IRAN, KOREA, LAOS
Asian monkey — LANGUR
Asian mountains — ALTAI
Asian nanny — AYAH
Asian nation — LAOS
Asian nation: Abbr. — KOR
Asian native — MEO
Asian nurse — AMAH
Asian occasions — TETS
Asian oxen — YAKS
Asian partridge — SEESEE
Asian peninsula — MALAY, MALAYA
Asian plant — RAMIE
Asian prince — RAJAH
Asian range — ALAI, URALS
Asian ruler — EMIR
Asian sailor — LASCAR
Asian sea — ARAL
Asian servant — AMAH
Asian staple — SOY
Asian transport — RICKSHA
Asian unit of weight — TAEL
Asian wild goat — TAHR
Asian wild ox — ANOA
Asian wild sheep — ARGALI
Asian, for one — FLU
Asiatic goat antelopes — SEROWS
Asiatic gulf — ADEN
Asiatic lemur — LORIS
Asiatic peninsula — MALAYA
Asiatic woody vine — ODAL
Aside — APART
Aside from — SAVE
Ask — QUERY
Ask for alms — BEG
Ask Rona — WHOM DID CHEVY CHASE
Ask with authority — DEMAND
Asked for boldly — DEMAND
Askew — ALOP, AWRY
Asleep at the switch — UNWARY
Asner and McMahon — EDS
Asner, Murrow and Mr. — EDS
Asparagus shoot — SPEAR
Asparagus stalk — SPEAR
Aspect — ANGLE, FACET, LOOK, PHASE
Aspect, manner — MIEN
Aspect: side — PHASE
Aspens — ALAMOS
Aspersion — SLUR
Asphalt, e.g. — BLACKTOP
Aspic — JELLY
Aspirant — HOPEFUL, WOULD BE
Aspirant's goal — MECCA
Aspirations — DREAMS
Aspire — HOPE
Aspires — AIMS
Aspirin — DRUG ON THE MARKET
Asprin compound — APC
Assail — BESET
Assail verbally — LASH
Assails — SETS AT
Assam product — TEA
Assam silkworm — ERI, ERIA
Assamese native — AOR
Assault — RUSH
Assault vessel — LST
Assay — TEST
Assay again — RETRY
Asse — FOX

Assemblage — TROOP
Assemblage of witches — COVEN
Assemble — AMASS, COLLECT, CONVENE, RALLY
Assemble — MEET
Assembled mechanism? — MANTLED MACHINE
Assembles — GATHERS
Assembles a collage again — REPASTES
Assembly — GATHERING, MEETING
Assembly hall — AULA
Assembly of churchmen — SYNOD
Assembly of ecclesiastics — SYNOD
Assembly of witches — COVEN
Assent — AGREE
Assent asea — AYE
Assent in Acapulco — SI SI
Assented — ACCEDED
Assenting phrase — I DO
Assenting sounds — UH HUHS
Assert — AFFIRM, AVER
Assert positively — AVOUCH
Asserts — HAS IT
Asserts without proof — ALLEGES
Assess — APPRAISE, ESTIMATE, RATE, VALUE
Assess property — TAX
Assess proportionately — PRORATE
Assessed — RATED
Assessed valuation — RATAL
Assessment basis — RATAL
Asset — ADVANTAGE, CAPITAL, CASH, WEALTH
Asset for a musician — EAR
Asset for an actress :Var. — GLAMOR
Asseverate — AVER, DECLARE, STATE
Assign — ALLOT
Assign a role in a play — CAST
Assign by contract — LET
Assign to new categories — REGRADE
Assigned areas: abbr. — TERS
Assigned tasks — DUTIES
Assignment — CHORE, LESSON, TASK
Assigns — ALLOCATES
Assigns to an evil fate — CURSES
Assimilate — ABSORB
Assimilated — ABSORBED
Assiniboin Indians — HOHE
Assinine — BANAL
Assist — ABET, AID, HELP, UPHOLD
Assist in wrongdoing — ABET
Assistant — AIDE
Assistants — HELPERS
Assn. — ORG
Asso. — ORG, SYND
Assoc. of a barrister — SOLR
Associate — ALLY, COHORT, PARTNER, RELATE
Associate Justice of the Supreme Court (1902-32) — HOLMES
Associate of Peter and Mary — PAUL
Associates — PARTNERS
Assortment — ARRAY
Asst. — DEP
Assuage — ALLAY, EASE, SALVE, SOOTHE
Assuage completely — SATE
Assuaged, as one's conscience — SALVED
Assuagement — MITIGATION
Assume — PUT ON, STRIKE, THROW
Assume a particular position — POSE
Assume a prayerful position — KNEEL
Assume another's job — FILL ONES SHOES
Assume as a fact — POSIT
Assumed authority — DISGUISE
Assumed haughtiness — AIRS
Assumed name — ALIAS, ANONYM
Assumes — TAKES ON
Assumptions — PREMISES
Assured air — ELAN
Assured, in a way — ON ICE
Assyrian chief deity — ASHUR
Assyrian god — ASUR
Assyrian god of war — ASHUR
Assyrian monarch — SARGON
Assyrian war god — ASUR
Asta's mister — NICK
Asta's mistress — NORA
Astaire — FRED
Astaire and namesakes — FREDS
Astaire and Rogers e.g. — TEAM
Astaire dancing partner — ROGERS
Astaire sister — ADELE
Astaire-Caron film: 1955 — DADDY LONG LEGS
Astaire-Rogers arena — DANCE FLOOR
Astaire-Rogers film: 1935 — TOP HAT
Aster for one — FALL BLOOM
Asterisk — STAR
Astern — AFT, IN THE REAR
Astonish — AMAZE, AWE
Astonished — AGOG
Astound — AMAZE, STUN
Astral — GRAND, STARRY, STELLAR
Astral body — COMET
Astral phenomena — NOVAE
Astrally bright — STARRY
Astride — ATOP
Astringent — ACERB, ALUM, BITTER, HARSH, STYPTIC
Astringent fruit — SLOE
Astro Ryan — NOLAN
Astrolabe plate — RETE
Astrologer's research source — ZODIAC
Astrological aspect — TRINE
Astrological lions — LEOS
Astrologist's tool — ZODIAC
Astromancers — SEERS
Astronaut Bean — ALAN
Astronaut Buzz — ALDRIN
Astronaut Evans — RON
Astronaut Gagarin — YURI
Astronaut Grissom — GUS
Astronaut Gus — GRISSOM
Astronaut John — GLENN
Astronaut Sally _____ — RIDE
Astronaut Senator John _____ — GLENN
Astronaut Shepard, et al. — ALANS
Astronaut Slayton — DEKE
Astronaut's "Perfect" — AOK
Astronaut's affimative — AOK
Astronaut's milieu — ETHER
Astronomer Knopf — OTTO
Astronomer Samuel _____ — LANGLEY
Astronomer's favorite song? — STARS FELL ON ALABAMA
Astronomer? — NIGHT WATCHMAN
Astronomical devices — TRANSITERS
Astronomical unit — PARSEC
Astute — KEEN
Asunder — APART
Aswan's river — NILE
Asyla — HAVENS
Asylum — HAVEN, REFUGE
At _____ (floundering) — A LOSS
At _____ (for words) — A LOSS
At _____ (free) — LARGE
At _____ (puzzled) — A LOSS
At _____ (relaxed) — EASE
At _____ and sevens — SIXES
At _____: disagreeing — ODDS
At _____: perplexed — A LOSS
At a _____ — LOSS
At a _____: perplexed — LOSS
At a distance — AFAR, ALOOF, AWAY
At a little distance — APART
At a loss — ASEA
At a low ebb — WEAK
At a previous time — EARLIER
At all — ANY, EVER
At an incline — ATILT

At anchor — BERTHED
At another time — ANON, LATER
At any time — EVER
At attention — ERECT
At close range — NEARBY
At ease — IDLE, RELAX
At full speed — PEDAL TO THE METAL
At great length — ON AND ON
At hand — IMMINENT, NEAR, ON TAP
At high speed — RAPID
At large — LOOSE, UNCAUGHT
At liberty — FREE, IDLE
At long last — FINALLY
At no time — NEVER
At no time, in poetry — NEER
At no time: Poet. — NEER
At once — NOW, PRONTO
At once, to an R.N. — STAT
At one's disposal — AVAILABLE, READY
At reduced prices — ON SALE
At right angles to a ship's length — ABEAM
At sea — BAFFLED, LOST
At some remote spot — AFAR
At that moment — THEN
At that place — THERE
At that time — THEN
At the age of: Lat. abbr. — AET
At the apex — ATOP
At the bar — IN COURT
At the bottom — LOWEST
At the center of — AMID
At the drop of _____ (instantly) — A HAT
At the helm — STEERING
At the peak — ATOP
At the ready — PREPARED
At the same age — COEVAL
At the same time — STILL
At the summit — ATOP
At the tail — AFT
At this place: Latin abbr. — AD LOC
At this time — NOW
At turbo-prop speed — SUB-SONIC
At what time? — WHEN
At-home garment — ROBE
Atahualpa's empire — INCA
Atahualpa, notably — INCA
Ate — DEVOUR, DINED, INGEST
Ate away — ERODED
Ate crow — RUED
Ate in courses — DINED
Ate well — DINED
Atelier — STUDIO, STUDY
Atelier furnishings — EASELS
Atelier headwear — BERET
Atelier item — EASEL
Atelier stand — EASEL
Atelier support — EASEL
Athanasian, for one — CREED
Atheism — DENIAL
Atheistic — GODLESS
Athena _____ — ALEA
Athena _____, war goddess — ALEA
Athena epithet — ALEA
Athena's challenger — ARACHNE
Athenian — ATTIC
Athenian citadel — ACROPOLIS
Athenian landmark — PARTHENON
Athenian lawgiver — SOLON
Athenian political subdivision — PHYLE
Athenian statesman — PERICLES
Athenian vow — ETA
Athenian's homeland — ELLAS
Athenians' domestic goddess — HESTIA
Athens and Sparta — TWO EYES OF GREECE
Athens' rival — SPARTA
Athlete — CONTENDER, JOCK, PLAYER, PRO, SPORT
Athlete Korbut — OLGA
Athlete/Actor — NAMATH
Athletes' features — PHYSIQUES
Athletic — ACTIVE, MUSCU-LAR, ROBUST, STRONG
Athletic group — TEAM
Athletic org. — NBA
Athletic shoe attachment — CLEAT
Athos friend — ARAMIS
Athos, Porthos and Aramis — MUSKETRY, TRIAD
Athrob — ACHY
Athwart — ACROSS
Atl. crossers — SSTS
Atl. flyers — SSTS
Atlanta arena — OMNI
Atlanta baseball player — BRAVE
Atlanta eleven — FALCONS
Atlanta time abbr. — EST
Atlanta University — EMORY
Atlanta's civic center — OMNI
Atlanta's Omni — ARENA
Atlantic City attractions — ONE ARM BANDITS
Atlantic City opening — SLOT
Atlantic crossers, for short — SSTS
Atlantic islands — AZORES, CUBA, ICELAND
Atlantic or Pacific — OCEAN
Atlantic sea — SARGASSO, WEDDELL
Atlantic treaty org. — NATO
Atlas abbr. — ISL, MTN, RTE
Atlas additions — INSERTS
Atlas aid — INSET
Atlas components — MAPS
Atlas contents — MAPS
Atlas feature — INSET
Atlas item — MAP
Atlas or Samson — HE MAN
Atlas was one — TITAN
Atmosphere — AIR, AURA, MILIEU, OZONE
Atmosphere: Comb. form — AER
Atmosphere: prefix — AER
Atmospheric — AIR, AURA, IONOSPHERE, OZONE
Atmospheric layer — STRATUM
Atmospheric phenomena — METEORS
Atmospheric pollution — SMOG
Atmospheric problem — SMOG
Atoll material — CORAL
Atom — BIT, IOTA, MONAD, SPECK
Atom nucleus — DEUTERON
Atomic _____ — PILE
Atomic particle — NEUTRON, PION
Atomic research center in Tennessee — OAK RIDGE
Atomizer — SPRAYER
Atomizer's spray — MIST
Atoms — PARTICLES
Atone for — EXPIATE
Atonement — AMEND, PENANCE
Atop — ABOVE, UPON
Atremble — ASPEN
Atrium — COURT
Atrocious actor — HAM
Att.'s degree — LLB
Atta _____! — GIRL
Attach — ADD, ANNEX, GRAFT, SEW ON
Attach in a way — NAIL
Attach to — TIE TO
Attached — ADDED, TIED TO
Attachment in law — LIEN
Attachments — TIES
Attack — ASSAIL, BESET, ONSET, STORM, SET ON
Attack verbally — TEAR INTO
Attack vigorously, with "in" — WADE
Attack with vigor — HAVE AT
Attack word — SIC
Attacked — CAME AT, HAD AT, RAN AT
Attacked by a bee — STUNG
Attacked vigorously, with "into" — WADED
Attacks — ASSAULTS, SETS UPON

Attacks flies — SWATS
Attacks with vigor — HAS AT
Attain — ACHIEVE, CATCH, EARN, HIT, REACH
Attain acclaim — ARRIVE
Attain stardom — ARRIVE
Attar and Neroli oil — ESSENCES
Attar sources — ROSES
Attempt — EFFORT, ENDEAVOR, ESSAY, STAB, TRY
Attempt to reach — AIM
Attempt, in Evian — ESSAI
Attempting — ESSAYING
Attempts — TRIES
Attempts something — BELLS THE CAT
Attend — APPEAR AT, MIND, VISIT
Attend a bee — SEW
Attend Choate — PREP
Attendance — GATE, PRESENCE
Attendance check — ROLL CALL
Attendant — PAGE
Attendant — SERVITOR
Attendant on Artemis — OREAD
Attendant to Bacchus — SATYR
Attendants at a spa — MASSEUSES
Attendants, in India — SYCES
Attended — CAME
Attender at the Gator Bowl — FLORIDIAN
Attending — PRESENT
Attends — IS AT
Attends Andover — PREPS
Attends Choate, e.g. — PREPS
Attention — EAR, CARE, HEED, NOTICE, REGARD
Attention getter — AHEM, PSST, YOOHOO
Attention getter, in court — GAVEL
Attention-getter — AHEM, HEY
Attention-getting sound — AHEM, HIST
Attention-getting word — HEIGH
Attentive one — HEEDER
Attentive, in Lanark — TENTIE
Attentive, of old — HEEDY
Attenuate — ABATE, DILUTE
Attenuated — SHRANK, THIN
Attest — CERTIFY, VOUCH
Attic market — AGORA
Attic natives — GREEKS
Attic promenade — STOA
Attic township — DEME
Attic, usually — STOREROOM
Attica theaters — ODEA
Attica township — DEME
Attican township — DEME
Attics — LOFTS
Attila's army — HORDE
Attila's followers — HUNS
Attila's men, e.g. — INVADERS
Attila, for one — HUN
Attire — DRESS, OUTFIT
Attire for neonates — BOOTEES
Attire for ranees — SARIS
Attire in Agra — SAREE
Attired — ENROBED
Attires — GARBS
Attitude — STANCE
Attitudinize — POSE
Attorney — AGENT, LAWYER
Attorney _____ — AT LAW
Attorney General Janet — RENO
Attorney's advice? — SUE
Attorney's jargon — LEGALESE
Attorneys' degs. _ — LLMS
Attract — DRAW, LURE
Attract attention — CUT A FIGURE
Attract love — ENDEAR
Attracted — DREW
Attraction — AFFINITY, APPEAL
Attractive — CUTE, MAGNETIC
Attractive face shape — OVAL
Attractive gift — PRETTY PRESENT
Attractive girl — BELLE
Attractive girl, informally — CUTIE
Attracts — DRAWS
Attribute — ALLOT, ASCRIBE, PLACE
Attribute a certain meaning to — READ
Attribute of good workers — THOROUGHNESS
Attributes — TRAITS
Attu canoe — OOMIAK
Attu islander — ALEUT
Attune — ADAPT
Attuned — IN HARMONY
Atty's org. — ABA
Attys.' group — ILA
Au _____ (with-it) — COURANT
Au contraire — AGAINST
Au fait — ABLE
Au naturel — NAKED
Auberges — INNS
Auberjonois — RENE
Auberjonois and Descartes — RENES
Auburn athlete — TIGER
Auch is its capital — GASCONY
Auckland's island — NORTH
Auction — SALE, SELL
Auction chaser — EER
Auction ending — EER
Auction hammer — GAVEL
Auction input — BID
Auction off — SELL
Auction unit — LOT
Auction warning — GOING
Auctioned off — SOLD
Auctioneer's call — GOING
Auctioneer's close — GONE
Auctioneer's condition — AS IS
Auctioneer's cry — GOING GOING GONE
Auctioneer's last word — GONE
Audacious — BRASH
Audacity — NERVE
Auden's "The _____ of Anxiety" — AGE
Auden, for example — POET
Audible — HEARD
Audibly — ALOUD
Audie Murphy was one — HERO
Audile — EAR MINDED
Audio distortion — STATIC
Audio systems — STEREOS
Audit a course — SIT IN
Audition — HEAR
Audition tape, briefly — DEMO
Auditioned — TRIED OUT
Auditions — READS FOR
Auditor, for short — CPA
Auditorium — HALL, ODEON
Auditors — CPAS
Auditory — OTIC
Audobon symbols — EGRETS
Audubon or Darwin, e.g. — NATURALIST
Auerbach — RED
Aug. 4, 1892, crime name — BORDEN
Aught — ZIP
Augment — ENHANCE
Augmentation: Abbr. — INCR
Augur — BODE, FOREBODE, FORSEE, ORACLE, SEER
Auguries — OMENS
Augury — OMEN
August — ROYAL
August babies — LEOS
August baby — LEO
August forecast in Miami — TROPICAL WEATHER
August person — LEO
August Zodiac sign — VIRGO
August, in Aries — AOUT
August, to friends — GUS
Augusta golf tournament — MASTERS
Augustine St. Clare's daughter — LITTLE EVA
Aujord' _____ (today, in Tours) — HUI
Auk — MURRE
Auk's relative — MURRE
Auld Lang _____ — SYNE
Aunt Betsy Trotwood's ward — DAVID COPPERFIELD

Aunt in "Oklahoma!" — ELLER
Aunt or Uncle: Abbr. — REL
Aunt Polly's ward — TOM SAWYER
Aunt's child — FIRST COUSIN
Aunt, for one — RELATION
Aunt, in Arles — TANTE
Aunt, in Avila — TIA
Aunt, in Dortmund — TANTE
Aunt, in Juarez — TIA
Aunt, in Normandy — TANTE
Aunt, in Tijuana — TIA
Aunt, to Pedro — TIA
Aunt: Abbr. — REL
Aunt: Sp. — TIA
Aunts, in Paris — TANTES
Aura — NIMBUS
Aural — OTIC
Aural insensitivity — TIN EAR
Auricles — PINNAE
Auricular — OTIC
Auriculate — EARED
Aurora — EOS
Aurora, in Greece — EOS
Auslander — ALIEN
Auspices — EGIS
Aussie — DIGGER
Aussie animal — ROO
Aussie birds — EMUS
Aussie gas pump — BOWSER
Aussie marsupial — ROO
Aussie natives — ABOS
Aussie rodent — RABBIT RAT
Aussie's air gp. — RAAF
Aussies' animals — ROOS
Austen character — DARCY
Austen heroine — EMMA
Austen or Eyre — JANE
Austen's Miss Wodehouse and namesakes — EMMAS
Austere — SPARTAN
Austin and Boston, e.g. — CAPITALS
Austin native — TEXAN
Australia's lowest point — LAKE EYRE
Australia's principal river — MURRAY
Australia's southern ocean — INDIAN
Australian bird — EMU
Australian bird or call — COOEE
Australian export — OPAL
Australian isl. — TAS
Australian lizard — MOLOCH
Australian marsupial — KOALA
Australian musical film: 1982 — STAR STRUCK
Australian non-flyer — EMU
Australian outback — BUSH
Australian peninsula — EYRE
Australian strait — TORRES
Australian teddy bear — KOALA
Australian tree — TUART
Australis or Borealis — AURORA
Austria's capital — VIENNA
Austrian composer Bruckner — ANTON
Austrian composer/conductor — MAHLER
Austrian contralto: 1803-77 — UNGER
Austrian essayist-editor — KRAUS
Austrian neighbor — ITALY
Austrian opera conductor : 1894-1981 — BOHM
Austrian river — DANUBE
Austrian river or town — ENNS
Austrian state — STYRIA
Austrian-born actor-singer — BIKEL
Austronesian language — MORO
Auth., "Kidnapped" — RLS
Authentic — REAL
Authentic, to Hitler — TREU
Authenticate — PROVE
Authenticator — NOTARY
Author-director Kazan — ELIA
Author — WRITE
Author _____ de Cervantes Saavedra — MIGUEL
Author _____ Passos — DOS
Author _____ Salinger — JEROME DAVID
Author _____ Vidal — GORE
Author _____ Yutang — LIN
Author A.A. — MILNE
Author A.A. Fair's real first name — ERLE
Author Alan — PATON
Author Alcott — LOUISA
Author Alex — HALEY
Author Alexander — SHANA
Author Alice _____ Miller — DUER
Author Ambler — ERIC
Author Anais — NIN
Author Andrew — LANG
Author Anita — LOOS
Author Asimov — ISAAC
Author Ayn — RAND
Author Bagnold — ENID
Author Balzac — HONORE
Author Bellow — SAUL
Author Benchley — ROBERT
Author Bombeck, et al. — ERMAS
Author Bontemps — ARNA
Author Bret — HARTE
Author Buck — PEARL
Author Calvino — ITALO
Author Carnegie — DALE
Author Cather — WILLA
Author Deighton — LEN
Author Delmar — VINA
Author Dinesen — ISAK
Author Earl _____ Biggers — DERR
Author Ephron — NORA
Author Eric — AMBLER
Author Ferber — EDNA
Author Fleming, et al. — IANS
Author Foley — RAE
Author Francis — BACON
Author Gallant — MAVIS
Author Gardner — ERLE
Author Gay — TALESE
Author George — SAND
Author Gertrude — STEIN
Author Godden — RUMER
Author Godwin — GAIL
Author Grey — ZANE
Author Haley — ALEX
Author Harte — BRET
Author Havelock — ELLIS
Author Hersey's "The _____" — WALL
Author Howard — FAST
Author Hunter — EVAN
Author Hyman — MAC
Author Ira — LEVIN
Author Irving — STONE
Author Jaffe — RONA
Author James — AGEE
Author James and family — AGEES
Author John Dos _____ — PASSOS
Author John Le _____ — CARRE
Author Jong — ERICA
Author Joyce Carol _____ — OATES
Author Kazan — ELIA
Author Kingsley — AMIS
Author Kundera — MILAN
Author Lafcadio _____ — HEARN
Author Laura's decision? — HOBSONS CHOICE
Author lecturer Mills — ENOS
Author Leon — URIS
Author Leverson — ADA
Author Levin — IRA
Author Lieblich — AMIA
Author Loos — ANITA
Author Ludwig — EMIL
Author Lurie — ALISON
Author Margaret — MEAD
Author Mary Ellen _____ — CHASE
Author Mazo _____ Roche — DE LA
Author McFadden — CYRA
Author Milne — ALAN
Author Nin — ANAIS
Author Norman — MAILER
Author O'Flaherty — LIAM
Author of "A Barn" — ANON
Author of "A Death in the Family" — AGEE

Author of "A Garden of Early Delights" — OATES
Author of "A Passage of Arms" — AMBLER
Author of "A Sentimental Journey" — STERNE
Author of "A Serendipiter's Journey" — TALESE
Author of "Advise and Consent" — DRURY
Author of "America the Beautiful" — BATES
Author of "Androcoles and the Lion" — SHAW
Author of "Atlas Shrugged" — RAND
Author of "Back Street" — HURST
Author of "Battle Cry" — URIS
Author of "Battle Hymn" — HOWE
Author of "Ben Hur" — WALLACE
Author of "Borstal Boy" — BEHAN
Author of "Brave New World" — HUXLEY
Author of "Bus Stop" — INGE
Author of "Butterfield 8" — OHARA
Author of "Cimarron" — EDNA FERBER
Author of "Common Sense" — PAINE
Author of "Cybele" — OATES
Author of "Das Capital" — MARX
Author of "Dead Souls" — GOGOL
Author of "Death on the Nile" — CHRISTIE
Author of "Delta of Venus" — NIN
Author of "Desire Under the Elms" — ONEILL
Author of "Divine Comedy" — DANTE
Author of "Dracula" _____ Stoker — BRAM
Author of "Duino Elegies" — RILKE
Author of "Eight Cousins" — ALCOTT
Author of "Exodus" — URIS
Author of "Fables in Slang" — ADE
Author of "Games People Play" — BERNE
Author of "Gentleman Prefer Blondes" — LOOS
Author of "Germinal" — ZOLA
Author of "Ghosts" — IBSEN
Author of "Giants in the Earth" — ROLVAG
Author of "Gods, Graves & Scholars — CERAM
Author of "Golden Boy" — ODETS
Author of "Goodbye, Columbus" — ROTH
Author of "Half Mile Down" — BEEBE
Author of "Hedda Gabler" — IBSEN
Author of "Heidi" — SPYRI
Author of "Honor Thy Father" — TALESE
Author of "Hop-Frog" — POE
Author of "Human Bondage" — MAUGHAM
Author of "Jakes Thing" — AMIS
Author of "Jo's Boys" — ALCOTT
Author of "Lady Windermere's Fan" — OSCAR WILDE
Author of "Les Miserables" — VICTOR HUGO
Author of "Les Plaisirs et les jours" — PROUST
Author of "Leviathan" — HOBBES
Author of "Little Minister — BARRIE
Author of "Little Women" — ALCOTT
Author of "Look Who's Talking!" — HAHN
Author of "Love Story" — SEGAL
Author of "Lucky Jim" — AMIS
Author of "Lummox" _____ Hurst — FANNIE
Author of "Marius the Epicurean" — PATER
Author of "Meeting at Potsdam" — MEE
Author of "Men of Iron" — PYLE
Author of "Mildred Pierce" — CAIN
Author of "Nat Turner" — STYRON
Author of "O Pioneers!" — CATHER
Author of "On the Beach" — SHUTE
Author of "One Human Minute" — LEM
Author of "Pal Joey" — OHARA
Author of "Pet Sematary" — KING
Author of "Riders to the Sea" — SYNGE
Author of "Romola" — ELIOT
Author of "Roots" — HALEY
Author of "Serpico" — MAAS
Author of "Silas Marner" — ELIOT
Author of "Spring Song" — REID
Author of "State Fair" — STONG
Author of "Steppenwolf" — HESSE
Author of "Tales of St. Austen" — WODEHOUSE
Author of "Taurus Bulba" — GOGOL
Author of "Ten Days That Shook The World" — REED
Author of "The Angry Hills" — URIS
Author of "The Citadel" — CRONIN
Author of "The Cloister and the Hearth" — READE
Author of "The Devil's Dictionary" — BIERCE
Author of "The Dinner Party" — FAST
Author of "The Dunciad" — POPE
Author of "The Dynasts" — HARDY
Author of "The Fountainhead" — RAND
Author of "The Gold Bug" — POE
Author of "The Golden Bowl" — JAMES
Author of "The Greening of America" — REICH
Author of "The Haj" — URIS
Author of "The High and the Mighty" — GANN
Author of "The Immoralist" — GIDE
Author of "The Lone Wolf" — VANCE
Author of "The Markropoulos Secret" — CAPEK
Author of "The Mill on the Floss" — ELIOT
Author of "The Moneychangers" — HAILEY
Author of "The Nose" — GOGOL
Author of "The Overcoat" — GOGOL
Author of "The Pisan Cantos" — POUND
Author of "The Pit" — NORRIS
Author of "The Power of Positive Thinking" — PEALE
Author of "The Prophet," Gibran — KAHLIL
Author of "The Raven" — POE
Author of "The Rebel" — CAMUS
Author of "The Stranger" — CAMUS
Author of "The Talisman" — SCOTT
Author of "The Telltale Heart" — POE

Author of "The Three Musketeers" — DUMAS
Author of "The Titans" — JAKES
Author of "The Valachi Papers" — MAAS
Author of "The White Company" — DOYLE
Author of "Thy Neighbor's Wife" — TALESE
Author of "To Kill a Mockingbird" — LEE
Author of "Toys in the Attic" — HELLMAN
Author of "Trinity" — URIS
Author of "Tristram Shandy" — STERNE
Author of "Tropic of Capricorn" — HENRY MILLER
Author of "Two Years Before the Mast" — DANA
Author of "Uhuru" — RUARK
Author of "Ulalume" — POE
Author of "What The Butler Saw" — ORTON
Author of "Why Not the Best?" — JAMES EARL CARTER
Author of "Wolsey": 1930 — BELLOC
Author of "Wonderland" — OATES
Author of "Wuthering Heights" — EMILY BRONTE
Author of western tales: first name — BRET
Author or poet follower — ESS
Author Paton — ALAN
Author Philip — ROTH
Author Potok — CHAIM
Author Prevost's title — ABBE
Author Rand and namesakes — AYNS
Author Roald — DAHL
Author Rölvaag — OLE
Author S.S. Van _____ — DINE
Author Santha Rama _____ — RAU
Author Segal — ERICH
Author Seton — ANYA, ERNEST
Author Sewell — ANNA
Author Shaw — IRWIN
Author Shere — HITE
Author Shusaku — ENDO
Author Sinclair — LEWIS
Author Sir James M. — BARRIE
Author Stephen Vincent _____ — BENET
Author Talese — GAY
Author Tarbell — IDA
Author Turin — ADELA
Author Umberto and others — ECOS
Author Uris — LEON
Author Vidal — GORE
Author Wiesel — ELIE
Author Wister — OWEN
Author Yutang — LIN
Author's "jackpot" — BEST SELLER
Author's concern — PLOT
Author's works: Abbr. — MSS
Author, runner Jim and kin — FIXXS
Author-actress Chase — ILKA
Author-scenarist James _____ — AGEE
Authority — SAY SO
Authority level — RANK
Authority on snakes? — HISTOLOGIST
Authorize — EMPOWER
Authorized — CERTIFICATED, OFFICIAL
Authorized reports — RELEASES
Authorizes — EMPOWERS
Authors? — BOOKMAKERS
Auto and pluto followers — CRATS
Auto attachment — CRAT
Auto court — MOTEL
Auto hood, in Soho — BONNET
Auto industry pioneer — OLDS
Auto key — IGNITION
Auto maker — OLDS
Auto of yore — REO, STANLEY STEAMER
Auto parts, for short — SHOCKS
Auto pioneer — OLDS
Auto race — RALLY
Auto racer Al — UNSER
Auto racing name of fame — UNSER
Auto's gauge illuminator — DASHLAMP
Autobiography item — MEMOIR
Autocrat — TSAR
Autocrats — DESPOTS, TSARS
Autograph — INK
Autograph book — ALBUM
Automaker — OLDS
Automatic hand weapon — STEN
Automatic pistol — LUGAR
Automaton — ROBOT
Automobile pioneer — OLDS
Automobile problem — STALLING
Automobile: Slang — BUS
Automotive flops — EDSELS
Automotive innovator — OLDS
Automotive passive restraint — AIRBAG
Automotive tryout — ROAD TEST
Autonomous oblast in the U.S.S.R. — OIROT
Autry's hat — STETSON
Autry's horse — CHAMPION
Autumn — FALL
Autumn beverage — CIDER
Autumn pear — BOSC
Autumnal hue — RUST
Autumnal quaff — CIDER
Auxiliary engine — STANDBY
Ava — GARDNER
Ava Gardner celestial movie? — ONE TOUCH OF VENUS
Ava's was barefoot — CONTESSA
Avail — USE
Available — HANDY, ON HAND, ON TAP, READY
Available buyer — TAKER
Avant-garde group — DADA
Avant- _____ — GARDE
Avant-garde — AHEAD
Avant-garde — MODERN
Avant-gardist — NEO
Avante-garde style — MOD
Avarice — GREED
Avaricious — GREEDY
Avatar of Vishnu — RAMA
Ave _____ vale — ATQUE
Ave Maria or Pater Noster — PRAYER
Ave! — HAIL
Avenue going east or west — TWO WAY STREET
Aver — AFFIRM, AVOUCH, DECLARE, CLAIM, STATE
Aver again — RESTATE
Average — MEAN, MILL RUN, SO SO
Average grades — CEES
Average Miss — JANE DOE
Average name — DOW
Avernus — HADES, HELL
Averred — STATED
Avers — ASSERTS
Averse — LOATH
Averse — OPPOSED
Averse to writing research papers? — ANTITHESES
Aversion — DISTASTE
Avert — BEND, PARRY
Aves. — STS
Aves. kin — STS
Avestan hero or demigod in Persian myth — YIMA
Avian — BIRD
Avian appendages — ALAE
Avian brood — COVEY
Avian chatterbox — MYNA
Avian diver — LOON
Avian food — BIRD SEED
Avian midwives? — STORKS
Aviary residence — NEST
Aviary sound — COO
Aviary utterance — WARBLE
Aviate — FLY
Aviated — FLEW
Aviation agency — FAA

Aviation: Prefix — AERO
Aviator — ACE, AIRMAN, LEADER, PILOT
Aviator Balboa — ITALO
Aviator's affirmative — ROGER
Aviator's chart — AIRMAP
Avid — EAGER
Avifauna — ORNIS
Avignon's river — RHONE
Avine abode — NEST
Avine activity — NESTING
Avocado center — PIT
Avocat's specialty — LOI
Avocation — HOBBY
Avocet — REE
Avocet's kin — STILT
Avoid — ESCHEW, IGNORE, SHIRK, SHUN, SKIRT
Avoid apprehension — ELUDE
Avoid arrests? — FLEE COLLARS
Avoid comment — EQUIVOCATE
Avoid commitment — HEDGE
Avoid looking at reality — UNSEE
Avoids — SKIRTS
Avoids work — LOAFS
Avouch — STATE
Avowed — SWORN
Avows — ADMITS
Avril's follower — MAI
Await — ABIDE
Await a decision — PEND
Await eagerly, in a way — DROOL
Awaiting the jeweler — UNSET
Awaiting, with "for" — IN STORE
Awaits — BIDES
Awake — ALERT, STIR
Awaken — ROUSE
Award — GRANT, TROPHY
Award for valor: Abbr. — DSO
Award recipient — HONOREE
Award-winning Broadway musical — CATS
Awards — PRIZES
Aware — ON TO
Aware of — IN THE KNOW, ON TO
Away — FRO, GONE, NOT IN
Away from — ALOOF
Away from land — ASEA
Away from the coast — INLAND
Away from the job — OFF
Away from the weather — ALEE
Away from the wind — ALEE
Away from the wind — ALEE
Away from: Prefix — APH
Awe — AMAZE, DREAD, REGARD
Aweather possible — ALEE
Aweather's opposite — ALEE
Awed by leading man's pickup? — STAR STRUCK
Aweigh — ATRIP
Awesome — EERIE, HOLY
Awful — DIRE, UGH
Awkward — BULKY, CLUMSY, CUMBERSOME, INEPT
Awkward crafts — ARKS
Awkward guys — GALOOTS
Awkward one — LOUT
Awkward position — SPRAWL
Awkward try — STAB
Awl, in Arles — ALENE
Awn — ARISTA, BARB
Awning — CANVAS
Awry — AMISS, ASKEW, UNEVEN, WRONG
Awry: Scot. var. — AGLEE
Axe — CHOP
Axelrod's "The Seven Year _____" — ITCH
Axila — ARMPIT
Axillary — ALAR
Axiom — ADAGE, LAW, PREMISE
Axis — BLOC, PIVOT, SHAFT
Axis power leader — TOJO
Axlike tool — ADZ
Ayatollah's predecessor — SHAH
Aye-aye on the Pinta — SI SI
Aye — YES
Aye neutralizer — NAY
Aye-aye and loris — LEMURS
Aye-aye's home — TREE
Ayers and Hoad — LEWS
Ayes' opposition — NOES
Ayesha — SHE
Ayn and Sally — RANDS
Ayn Rand novel — ANTHEM
Ayn Rand's shrugger — ATLAS
Ayres of films — LEW
Azimuth — ARC
Aztec or Toltec — NAHUA

B

B'klyn college — LIU
B'nai _____ — BRITH
B'way favorite sign — SRO
B, soundwise — HIVED DWELLER
B-flat — A SHARP
B-G connection — CDEF
B-H link — CDEFG
B.A. part — ARTS
B.L.T. option — MAYO
B.P.O.E. word — ORDER
B.S. part — SCI
B.S.A. outings — HIKES
B.S.A. unit — TRP
Baalim — IDOLS
Baba and MacGraw — ALIS
Baba and Pasha — ALIS
Baba au _____ — RHUM
Baba ingredient — RUM
Babbitt — ALLOY
Babbitt's creator — LEWIS
Babble — PRATE
Babe — BEAUTY
Babe _____ — RUTH
Babe in _____ — ARMS
Babe or Chatterton — RUTH
Babe Ruth's team, once — ORIOLES
Babe Ruth, The Sultan of _____ — SWAT
Babe's title — SULTAN
Babel — NARGON
Babel ambiance — DIN
Babiche — THONG
Babies' first words — DADAS
Babilonia namesakes — TAIS
Baboon — MANDRILL
Baboon genus — PAPIO
Babushka — SCARF
Baby — INFANT
Baby _____: W.C. Fields nemisis — LEROY
Baby beds — CRIBS
Baby bird? — STORK
Baby blues, e.g. — EYES
Baby buggy, in Brighton — PRAM
Baby clothing and accessories — LAYETTE
Baby fare — PAP
Baby food — PAP
Baby moray — ELVER
Baby music — LULLABY
Baby powder — TALCUM

Baby rose — BUD
Baby seal — PUP
Baby Snooks comedienne — BRICE
Baby soother — TALC
Baby ware — BIBS
Baby's call — MAMA
Baby's complaint — COLIC
Baby's cry — MAMA
Baby's face sometimes — EGGY
Baby's first word — MAMA
Baby's ring — TEETHER
Baby's shoe — BOOTIE
Baby's transport — BUGGY
Baby's wheels — PRAM
Baby's word — MAMA
Baby-care item — TALC
Babylon's neighbor — ELAM
Babylonian deity — ANU
Babylonian sky god — ANU
Bacall — LAUREN
Bacchanalia — ORGIES
Bacchanalian "Whoopee!" — EVOE
Bacchanalian cry — EVOE
Bacchus' attendant — SATYR
Bach composistion — CANTATA
Bach opus — ITALIAN CONCERTO
Bach's "_____ of Fugue" — THE ART
Bach's output — MUSIC
Bachelor boast — CANT TIE ME DOWN
Bachelor girl — SPINSTER
Bachelor party — STAG
Bachelor's button — CORNFLOWER
Bachelor's last words — I DO
Back — AID, BACKBONE, HEEL, HELP, LATE, OLD, PAST
Back — REAR, REVERSE, SPINE
Back 40 unit — ACRE
Back and sides of a pig — BACON
Back areas — DORSA
Back away from — WASH ONES HANDS OF
Back country — BUSH
Back from fore — AFT
Back gate — POSTERN
Back gear — REVERSE
Back of $20 bill — THE WHITE HOUSE
Back of $5 bill — LINCOLN MEMORIAL
Back of leaf — VERSO
Back of the head — OCCIPUT
Back of the neck — NAPE, NUQUE
Back off — PULL IN ONES HORNS
Back or baked starter — HALF
Back out — THROW IN THE TOWEL
Back talk — LIP
Back talk — SASS
Back up — REVERSE
Back-fence yowlers — TOMCATS
Backbone — SPINE
Backbone mountain range — ANDES
Backbone of South America — ANDES
Backcomb — TEASE
Backdrop — CURTAIN
Backdrop fabric — SCRIM
Backed — ENDORSED
Backed by an oath — SWORN
Backer — PATRON
Background, as in lacework — POND
Backing — AIDE, HELP
Backland — WILD
Backless slipper — MULE
Backpacked — HIKED
Backpacker — HIKER
Backpacker's bedroom — TENT
Backs — SUPPORTS
Backs of necks — NAPES
Backs up (with "with") — SIDES
Backs up the lines — ROVES
Backsheesh — ALMS
Backslide — REGRESS, RELAPSE
Backtalk — LIP, SASS
Backus' Mr. _____ — MAGOO
Backward — ASTERN
Backward and forward — TO AND FRO
Backward nautically — ASTERN
Backward: Prefix — RETRO
Backwash — WAKE
Backwoods corn converter — STILL
Backyard refresher — POOL
Bacon bringers — EARNERS
Bacon portion — RASHER
Bacon products — ESSAYS
Bacon slice — RASHER
Bacon units — RASHERS
Bacon's Rx for becoming "a full man" — READING
Bacon, "the Admirable Doctor" — ROGER
Bacteria — GERMS
Bacteria colony for medical research — CULTURE
Bacteria: abbr. — BACT
Bacterium that need air to live — AEROBE
Bad-luck glance — EVIL EYE
Bad-news ball — EIGHT
Bad _____ (German Spa) — EMS
Bad actor — HAM
Bad apple, in a way — LEMON
Bad beginning? — MAL
Bad blood — HATE
Bad boy — BRAT
Bad dog — BITER
Bad Ems, for one — SPA
Bad grades — DEES
Bad impression? — DENT
Bad luck — SETBACK
Bad moods — SNITS
Bad news from the scale — GAIN
Bad off — POOR
Bad place to lie — WITNESS STAND
Bad reviews — PANS
Bad scene — TRAUMA
Bad Soden is one — SPA
Bad tempered goddess — ERIS
Bad tempered one — TARTAR
Bad things — BANES, ILLS
Bad time for Caesar — IDES
Bad: Comb. form — CACO, MAL
Bad: Prefix — MAL
Baddie in a fairy tale — OGRESS
Bade — ORDERED
Baden-Baden, e.g. — SPA
Baden or Aix — SPA
Baden-Baden and Bath — SPAS
Badger — BESEIGE, HARASS, NAG
Badger relative — RATEL
Badger's African cousin — RATEL
Badger-like canivore — RATEL
Badgers — NAGS
Badinage — JESTS
Badinage and persifiage — RAILLERIES
Badly — ILLY
Baer or Beerbohn — MAX
Baffin or Biscayne — BAY
Baffle — ELUDE, STYMIE
Baffling — EERIE
Baffling question — POSER
Baffs a golf ball — LOFTS
Bag — GRAB
Bag and baggage — FULLY
Bag man — SANTA
Bag of bones — SKELETON
Bag of tools — KIT
Bag or board — TOTE
Bagatelle — GAME
Bagdad ruler more cantankerous — CALIPHORNERIER
Bagel emporium, for short — DELI
Bagel's partner — LOX
Bagellike roll — BIALY
Bagged — SNARED
Baggins of Tolkien's "The Hobbit" — BILBO
Baghdad native — IRAQI
Bagnio — BROTHEL
Bagnold — ENID
Bagnold and Markey — ENIDS

Bagpipe part — DRONE
Bagpipe's base drone — BURDEN
Bagpipe's shrill piercing sound — SKIRL
Bagpiper frequently — HIGHLANDER
Bah! — TOSH
Bah's buddy — POH
Bahamian baths? — NASSAU SAUNAS
Bahamian island — ABACO, BIMINI
Bahamian resort — NASSAU
Bahr _____, Egyptian name for the Nile — ENNIL
Bahrain, for example: Var. — AMIRATE
Baikal or Peipus — LAKE
Bail — BOND
Bail out — EJECT
Bailey of comics — BEETLE
Bailey or Minnie — PEARL
Bailiff's area of jurisdiction — BAILIWICK
Bain — DIRECT
Bait — DECOY, TEMPT
Bait fish — CHUB
Bake eggs — SHIRR
Bake in a casserole — SCALLOP
Baked Alaska topping — MERINGUE
Baked and smoked _____ — HAMS
Baked apple dessert — BROWN BETTY
Baked goods — PIES
Baker of music — ANITA
Baker's _____ — DOZEN
Baker's assistant — ICER
Baker's companion — ABEL
Baker's dozen plus five — EIGHTEEN
Baker's dozen, Roman style — XIII
Baker's hapless G.I. — SAD SACK
Baker's long handled shovel — PEEL
Baker's meas. — TSP
Baker's need — OVEN, PIE TIN, YEAST
Baker's plan? — KNEAD A LOT OF DOUGH
Baker's suit — LOAF
Baker's sweet concoction — HONEYBUN
Bakery buy — RYE
Bakery employee — ICER
Bakery item — CAKE, PIE, TART
Bakery order — RYE
Bakery products — ROLLS, POUND CAKES, TARTS
Bakery purchase — RYE, TART
Bakery specialty — CAKE
Bakery treats — ECLAIRS
Bakery worker — ICER
Bakes eggs — SHIRRS
Baking aid — YEASTCAKE
Baking chamber — OAST, OVEN
Baking soda — SALERATUS
Baklava — DESSERT
Balaam's "vehicle" — ASS
Balaam's mount — ASS
Balance — EQUATE, REST
Balance also called lever scales — STEEL YARD
Balance consisting of a pivoted bar — STEELYARD
Balance sheet entry — ASSET
Balance sheet for Amos? — PROPHET AND LOSS
Balance sheet item — ASSET
Balance weight — BALLAST
Balanced — SANE
Balances — POISES
Balanchine ballet — ROMA
Balanchine's forte — BALLET
Balata or banyan — TREE
Balcony — PORCH
Balcony offering a wide view — MIRADOR
Bald and smooth — GLABROUS
Bald one's bailiwick — AERY
Balderdash — BUNK, ROT
Baldwin and Guinness — ALECS
Baldwin-Wallace college site — BEREA
Baleful — SINISTER
Bali, e.g. — ISL
Balin or Claire — INA
Balk — FLINCH, REFUSE, SHUN
Balkan — SERB
Balkan brandy — RAKI
Balkan capital — SOFIA, TIRANA
Balkan citizen — SLAV
Balkan native — SERB
Balkan river — DANUBE
Balkan sea — BLACK
Ball — Dance
Ball c. 7,926 mi. in diameter — EARTH
Ball flower? — BELLE
Ball game — CATCH
Ball hit outside the base lines — FOUL
Ball holder — TEE
Ball of fire — SOL
Ball of yarn — CLEW, SKEIN
Ball park action — SWAT
Ball prop — TEE
Ball star — BELLE
Ball team — NINE
Ball up — BOTCH
Ball-gown fabric — TULLE
Ball-park offering — WIENER
Ballad — LAY, SONG
Ballad singer Ed — AMES
Ballerina Alessandra — FERRI
Ballerina Alicia from Cuba — ALONSO
Ballerina Alonso — ALICIA
Ballerina Evdokimova, et al. — EVAS
Ballerina Fracci — CLARA
Ballerina McKerrow — AMANDA
Ballerina Park — MERLE
Ballerina Plisetskaya — MAYA
Ballerina Shearer — MOIRA
Ballerina Spessivtseva — OLGA
Ballerina Susan — JAFFE
Ballerina's _____ seul — PAS
Ballerina's balancing aide — BARRE
Ballerina's knee bend — PLIE
Ballerina's leap — JETE
Ballerina's movement — PLIE, RELEVE
Ballerina's perch — TOE
Ballerina's poses — ATTITUDES
Ballerina's quality — GRACE
Ballet bend — PLIE
Ballet bird — SWAN
Ballet director Balanchine — GEORGE
Ballet duet — ADAGIO
Ballet element — CHASSE
Ballet jump — ROYALE
Ballet kneebend — FLY
Ballet leaps — JETES
Ballet maneuvers — LEAPS
Ballet movement — ENTRECHAT, PLIE
Ballet or charlotte follower — RUSSE
Ballet painter — DEGAS
Ballet point — TOE
Ballet step — PAS
Ballet studio warm-up rail — BARRE
Ballet term — ARABESQUE, PLIE
Ballet term: var. — ECART
Ballet's "Le _____ des Cygnes" — LAC
Ballet's George de _____ — LAPENA
Ballet's Peter Martin, for one — DANE
Ballet's Plisetskaya — MAYA
Balletomane, at times — STANDEE
Balletomane, for one — FAN
Balloon cabin — GONDOLA
Balloon gas — HELIUM
Balloon on a bike — TIRE
Balloon part — BASKET
Ballot — VOTE
Ballot marks — XES
Ballot winners — INS
Ballpark feature — BASE
Ballpark thrills — HOMERS

Ballpoint — PEN
Ballroom dance — ONE STEP, FOX TROT, TANGO
Ballroom dances — RYE WALTZES
Ballroom dances that end a ball — COTILLIONS
Ballroom oldie — ONE STEP
Balm — ODOR
Balm of Gilead — BALSAM
Balm or spice — ODOR
Balm-of-_____: perfumery resin — GILEAD
Balmoral Castle's river — DEE
Balmy — CALM
Balsam — TOLU
Balt — ESTH
Balt. and N.Y.C. — SPTS
Baltic feeder — ODER
Baltic gulf — RIGA
Baltic Island — AERO, ALAND, ALSEN, OLAND
Baltic native — ESTH, LETT
Baltic port — RIGA
Baltic region once — PRUSSIA
Baltic Sea feeder — ODER, PEENE
Baltic seaport — KIEL
Baltic, e.g. — SEA
Baltic-North Sea canal — KIEL
Baltimore birds — ORIOLES
Baltimore player — ORIOLE
Baltimore's boys of summer — ORIOLES
Baluchistan tribe — REKI
Balzac — HONORE
Balzac's "La Cousine _____" — BETTE
Balzac's "Le _____ Goriot" — PERE
Balzac's "Une Ténébreuse _____" — AFFAIRE
Balzac's birthplace — TOURS
Bamako is its capital — MALI
Bamako's country — MALI
Bambi of theater fame — LINN
Bambi's aunts — ENAS, ROES
Bambi's ilk — DEER
Bambi's mom — DOE
Bambi, for one — DEER
Bambino's parent — MADRE
Bamboo curtain — BORDER
Bamboo lover of China — PANDA
Bamboolike grasses — REEDS
Bamboozle — BLUFF
Ban — INTERDICT, PROHIBIT
Ban man — CENSOR
Ban the bottle — TEETOTAL
Banal — FATUOUS, STALE, TRITE
Banana bunch — STEM
Banana feature — PEEL
Banana kin — PLANTAIN
Banana leaf — FROND
Banana leaf fiber — ABACA
Bananas — BATTY
Bancroft and Boleyn — ANNES
Bancroft and Jackson — ANNES
Band — COMBO, TROOP
Band brass — CORNET
Band instruments — DRUMS, SAXOPHONES
Band member — SIDEMAN
Band of color on an insect — FASCIA
Band of lawmen — POSSE
Band of musicians — COMBO
Band of tissue — LIGAMENT
Band or dog — ONE MAN
Band section — REEDS
Band under a dog's tongue — LYTTA
Band's place — STAND
Bandage — DRESS
Bandar Seri Begawan — BRUNEI
Bandbox — NEAT
Bandeau — BRA
Bandicoot — RAT
Bandit — CROOK
Bandleader-songwriter Jones — ISHAM
Bandleader Alpert — HERB
Bandleader Bill and author Alex — HALEYS
Bandleader Brown — LES
Bandleader Fields — SHEP
Bandleader Kenton — STAN
Bandleader Lawrence — WELK
Bandleader Martin — FREDDY
Bandleader of "Heartache" fame — WEEMS
Bandleader Shaw — ARTIE
Bandleader Weems — TED
Bandleader, drummer — KRUPA
Bandman Lanin — LESTER
Bando and Maglie of baseball — SALS
Bando and Mineo — SALS
Bando of baseball — SAL
Bandsman Brown — LES
Bandsman Brown — LES
Bandsman Goodman — BENNY
Bandsman Hines — EARL
Bandsman Miller — GLENN
Bandsman Shaw — ARTIE
Bandy — GOSSIP
Bane — CURSE, WOE
Bane of grain — ERGOT
Bane of librarians? — BOOK-KEEPERS
Bane of some canines — MANGE
Bane of the farmer's wife — MICE
Baneful — EVIL
Banes — NEMESES
Bang — SHOT
Bangkok citizen — SIAMESE
Bangkok coins — BAHTS
Bangkok man — THAI
Bangkok monkey — ATT
Bangkok native — THAI
Bangkok-to-Hanoi dir. — NNE
Bangladesh capital's former spelling — DACCA
Bangor neighbor — ORONO
Bani- _____ of Iran — SADR
Banish — DEPORT, EXILE, EXPEL, OUST, RELEGATE
Banished — DEPORTED
Banished Olympian — ATE
Banishment — EXILE
Banister — RAIL
Banister terminus — NEWELL
Banjo _____ (Cantor sobriquet) — EYES
Banjo parts — FRETS
Banjos' kin — UKES
Bank — RELY, RIDGE
Bank abbr. — INT
Bank account, e.g. — ASSET
Bank annuities — CONSOLS
Bank business — LOAN
Bank clients — SAVERS
Bank deals — LOANS
Bank deposits — SILTS
Bank employee — CASHIER, TELLER
Bank instrument — NIGHT DRAFT
Bank jobs — HEISTS
Bank offering — MORTGAGE
Bank on — RELY
Bank patron — SAVER
Bank problems — OVER-DRAFTS
Bank robber's bonanza — PAYROLL
Bank specialties — LOANS
Bank transaction — LOAN
Bank workers — CASHIERS
Bankbook fig. — INT
Banker's decision — LOAN
Banker, at times — LENDER
Bankers at times — LENDERS
Banking abbr. — INT, NSF, SAV
Banking activity — LOANING
Banking fee — AGIO
Banking game — FARO
Banknote — BILL
Bankroll items — ONES
Bankrolls — WADS
Bankrupt — BUST, DEBTOR
Banks or Ford — ERNIE
Banks or Pyle — ERNIE
Banks' business — LOANS
Banky of silents — VILMA
Banned — TABOO
Banner — ENSIGN, FLAG
Bannockburn babe — BAIRN
Banquet — DINE, DINNER, FEAST
Banquet platform — DAIS

Banshee sounds — WAILS
Banshee's activity — WAILING
Banshee's outcry — WAIL
Banter — JOSH
Bantering criticisms — ROASTS
Bantu language — DUALA
Banyon — VINA
Baobab fruit — MONKEY BREAD
Baptism — BATH, RITE
Baptism by pouring water on the head — AFFUSION
Baptism, e.g. — RITE
Baptism, et al. — RITES
Baptismal basins — FONTS
Bar — ESTOP, HINDER, INGOT, INN, PUB, POLE
Bar — PROHIBIT, RAIL, ROD
Bar accommodation — STOOL
Bar bill — CHIT, TAB
Bar concoction — TODDY
Bar connecting wheels — AXLE
Bar drink — RYE
Bar grouping — GINS
Bar in a tavern — TAPROOM
Bar mat — COASTER
Bar measure — SHOT
Bar on a loom — EASER
Bar or therm — ISO
Bar order — ALE, BOURBON, CHASER, RYE
Bar seat — STOOL
Bar seating — STOOL
Bar serving food as well as drink — BRASSERIE
Bar setup — CHASER
Bar slug — SHORT ONE
Bar where Hemingway hung out — HARRYS
Bar, at the bar — ESTOP
Bar, legally — ESTOP
Bara of the silents — THEDA
Barabaras — HUTS
Barb — BRISTLE, SPIKE
Barbados capital — BRIDGETOWN
Barbara _____ Geddes — BEL
Barbara and Conrad — BAINS
Barbara Bush, _____ Pierce — NEE
Barbara Cartland's forte — ROMANCE
Barbara of TV — EDEN
Barbara or Anita — SANTA
Barbara or George — BUSH
Barbara Stanwyck role: 1941 — BALL OF FIRE
Barbara, for one — MAJOR
Barbara, of "Mission Impossible" — BAIN
Barbarians — GOTHS
Barbary apes — MAGOTS
Barbasco — TAM
Barbecue — ROAST
Barbecue area — PATIO
Barbecue buttinskis — ANTS
Barbecue equipment — SPIT
Barbecue favorite — T BONE
Barbecue gadget — SPIT
Barbecue host? — CHUCK WAGON
Barbecue item — SPARERIB
Barbecue locale — YARD
Barbecue necessities — SPITS
Barbecue skewer — SPIT
Barbecue treats — RIBS
Barbecue-pit fixture — SPIT
Barbecued treats — SPARE RIBS
Barbed head on a harpoon — FLUKE
Barber-ous? — TONSORIAL
Barber — HAIR
Barber of Seville — FIGARO
Barber's "_____ for Strings" — ADAGIO
Barber's call — NEXT
Barber's favorite — SWEET ADELINE
Barber's garb? — HAIRSHIRT
Barber's need — RAZOR, STROP
Barber's request — NEXT
Barber's service — SHAVE
Barbers' tool — STROP
Barbers? — HAIR AID WARDENS
Barbican _____, London — CENTRE
Barbie's beau — KEN
Barbie, for one — DOLL
Barbituate — DOWNER
Barbizon school painter — COROT
Barcelona baby boys — NINOS
Barcelona beast — TORO
Barcelona bigwig — DON
Barcelona bravos — OLES
Barcelona buddy — AMIGO
Barcelona-born tenor — JOSE CARRERAS
Bard — POET
Bard in ancient Scandinavia — SKALD
Bard of _____ — AVON
Bard's before — ERE
Bard's narrative — EPOS
Bard's river — AVON
Bard's specialty — LAY
Bard's stream — AVON
Bard's title starter — ALLS
Bard, in old England — SCOP
Bare — EMPTY, STRIPPED
Bare spot on a mountain — SCAR
Barefaced — BOLD
Barely — JUST
Barely beat with "out" — EDGED
Barely makes do, with "out" — EKES
Bares — EXPOSES
Barest trace — MODICUM
Barflies — SOUSES, SOTS
Barflies, generally — SOTS
Barfly — TOPER
Barfly's perch — STOOL
Bargain — AGREEMENT, BUY, CONTRACT, DEAL
Bargain — DICKER, DISCOUNT, PACT, STEAL
Bargain at court — PLEA
Bargain for — CONSIDER
Bargain hunter's event — GARAGE SALE
Bargain-basement — CHEAP
Bargains — BUYS, HAGGLES, STEALS
Barge's relative — SCOW
Barges — SCOWS
Baritone Gorin — IGOR
Baritone Opie — ALAN
Bark cloth — TAPA
Bark up the wrong tree — ERR
Barked, in a way — YIPPED
Barker — SPIELER, TOUT
Barker of film fame — LEX
Barker of the movies — LEX
Barker's babble — SPIEL
Barker's barkings — SPIELS
Barker's pitch — SPIEL
Barkin of films — ELLEN
Barking circus performers — SEALS
Barkley's sobriquet — VEEP
Barks — YAPS
Barley beard — ARISTA, AWN
Barley, in Bordeaux — ORGE
Barn — STABLE, STALL
Barn adjunct — SILO
Barn conversations — MOOS
Barn dances — REELS
Barn door — SHATE
Barn owl — LULU
Barn's neighbor — SILO
Barnaby Jones — EBSEN
Barney Google's horse — SPARK PLUG
Barney of NFL fame — LEM
Barney of the comics — GOOGLE
Barnstorm — TROUPE
Barnum fare — THREE RING CIRCUS
Barnum player — DALE
Barnum's prize attraction — GENERAL TOM THUMB
Barnum's Tom _____ — THUMB
Barnyard creature — GOOSE
Barnyard crone? — OLD SOW AND SOW
Barnyard denizens — PIGS, FOWL
Barnyard enclosure — STY
Barnyard sound — BAA, MOO
Barnyard strutter — ROOSTER
Baron Munchausen, e.g. — LIAR
Baronet's title — SIR

Baronet's wife — LADY
Baroque — ELABORATE, FLAMBOYANT, ORNATE
Baroque composer — BACH
Baroque or rococo — STYLE
Barracks bed — COT
Barracks berths — COTS
Barracks bunks — COTS
Barracks wall decor — PIN UP
Barracks' boss, familiarly — SARGE
Barracuda — SENNET
Barre exercises — PLIES
Barred partitions — GRATES
Barrel — CASK, KEG, TUB, VAT
Barrel _____ (hurdy gurdy) — ORGAN
Barrel along — RACE
Barrel band — HOOP
Barrel holding about 100 gallons — HOGSHEAD
Barrel of a gun — MUZZLE
Barrel part — STAVE
Barrel stave — LAG
Barrel stopper — BUNG
Barrel-shaped tunicate — SALPA
Barren — ARID, STERILE
Barren: Sp. — ARIDA
Barrett and Jaffe — RONAS
Barrie title from "Julius Caesar" — DEAR BRUTUS
Barrie's Peter — PAN
Barrier — DAM, FENCE, WALL
Barrier ditches — MOATS
Barrier for Becker — NET
Barrier of a sort — RAIL
Barrister — LAWYER
Barrow — CART
Barrymore and Merman — ETHELS
Barrymore film role — AHAB
Barrymore girl — ETHEL
Bars — TAVERNS
Bars, at the bar — ESTOPS
Bars, in law — ESTOPS
Bars, in music — MEASURES
Bars, legally — ESTOPS
Bartender's measure — SHOT
Bartender's need — ICE
Barter — SWAP
Barter item for G.I. Joe — HOSE
Bartlett — PEAR
Bartlett relative — BOSC
Bartok or Lugosi — BELA
Barton or Bow — CLARA
Barton, e.g. — NURSE
Baruch's "My _____ Story" — OWN
Baryshnikov never executes only one — ENTRECHAT
Baryshnikov, to friends — MISHA
Bas-relief material — GESSO
Basalt ingredient — LAVA
Base — GROUNDS, IGNOBLE
Base for Boggs — THIRD
Base for plaster — LATH
Base Gehrig covered — FIRST
Base of chewing gum — CHI-CLE
Base on balls — PASS, WALK
Base or hospital areas — DAYROOMS
Base runner's ploy — SLIDE
Base security — SAFENESS
Base, in baseball — HOME
Baseball "brotherhood" — ALOU
Baseball "trophy" — PENNANT
Baseball abbr. — ERA
Baseball bat — CLUB
Baseball bird — ORIOLE
Baseball bobble — ERROR
Baseball brothers' name — ALOU
Baseball call — SAFE
Baseball category — RBI
Baseball deal — TRADE
Baseball family name — ALOU
Baseball great — OTT
Baseball great Aaron — HANK
Baseball great Willie — MAYS
Baseball group — OWNERS
Baseball Hall of Fame member Walt — ALSTON
Baseball Hall of Fame's Ralph — KINER
Baseball Hall-of-Famer — REESE
Baseball Hall-of-Famer Tim _____ — KEEFE
Baseball Hall-of-Famer, Waite _____ — HOYT
Baseball hit of a sort — FOUL
Baseball league — AMERICAN
Baseball legend — RUTH
Baseball Mel and others — OTTS
Baseball name of fame — OTT
Baseball number — NINE
Baseball park in California — CANDLESTICK
Baseball pitcher's delight — SHUTOUT
Baseball play — HIT AND RUN
Baseball player — FIELDER
Baseball player from Iowa — FELLER
Baseball player from Texas — ASTRO
Baseball player, sometimes — HITTER
Baseball plays — ASSISTS
Baseball ploy — BUNT
Baseball putout — TAG
Baseball stat. — ERA, RBI
Baseball statistic — ERROR
Baseball tactic — BUNT
Baseball team — NINE
Baseball term — HOMER, NINE, PLATE
Baseball units — INNINGS
Baseball wear — CAP
Baseball's "Casey" — STENGEL
Baseball's Berra — YOGI
Baseball's Blue — VIDA
Baseball's Crab or Hoot — EVERS
Baseball's Felipe, Jesus and Matty — ALOUS
Baseball's Fordham flash — FRISCH
Baseball's Larry and family — DOBYS
Baseball's Matty — ALOU
Baseball's Mel — OTT
Baseball's Mike or Tom — TRESH
Baseball's Paul or Lloyd — WANER
Baseball's Pee Wee, et al. — REESES
Baseball's Penguin — CEY
Baseball's Phil or Joe — NIEKRO
Baseball's Pitcher Duren — RYNE
Baseball's Rod — CAREW
Baseball's Rookie of the Year: 1957 — KUBEK
Baseball's showcase game — ALL STAR
Baseball's Slaughter — ENOS
Baseball's Willie — MAYS
Baseball's Yogi — BERRA
Baseballer Guidry — RON
Baseballer Otis — AMOS
Based — SEWED
Based on mistaken ideas — FALSE
Baseman — SACKER
Basement — CELLAR
Basement feature — AREAWAY
Bases for poi — TAROS
Bases for predictability — TRAITS
Bashful — COY, SHY
Bashful's brother — DOC
Basic — ELEMENTAL, ROOT
Basic commodity — STAPLE
Basic component — UNIT
Basic facts — ABCS
Basic igneous rock — SIMA
Basic Latin verb — ESSE
Basic neccesity — ROOF OVER THE HEAD
Basic necessity — BREAD ON THE TABLE
Basic necessity — GOOD AIR AND WATER
Basic organisms — AMEBAE
Basic part — CORE
Basic school text — PRIMER
Basic start — ABC
Basic unit — MONAD

Basic unit of matter — ATOM
Basic: Abbr. — ELEM
Basics — ABCS
Basie of Jazz — COUNT
Basil — HERB
Basilica central area — NAVE
Basilica feature — APSE
Basilica part — APSE
Basin — TUB
Basin in W. China — TARIM
Basinger of "Batman" — KIM
Basinger of films — KIM
Basis for a suit — TORT
Basis of milady's coiffure — PINCURL
Basket fiber — RAFFIA
Basket for bass — CREEL
Basket for farm work — SKEP
Basket grass — OTATE
Basket material — RAFFIA
Basket of a kind — CREEL
Basket under a balloon — GONDOLA
Basket used for catching fish — COOP
Basketball coach Chuck — DALY
Basketball defense — PRESS
Basketball Hall-of-Famer — NAT
Basketball inventor — NAI-SMITH
Basketball org. — NBA
Basketball player — CAGER
Basketball ploy — FAST BREAK
Basketball star Larry — BIRD
Basketball tourn. — NIT
Basketry fiber — ISTLE
Basketry material — RAFFIA
Basketry palm — NIPA
Basketry twigs — OSIERS
Basketry willow — OSIER
Baskets — SKEPS
Basks — SUNS
Basks in the sun — TANS
Basque caps — BERETS
Basra native — IRAQI
Basra's land: var. — IRAK
Bass and Spade — SAMS
Bass baritone Simon — ESTES
Bass-baritone Scaria — EMIL
Basse-_____, city in Guadeloupe — TERRE
Basso Cesare — SIEPI
Basso Pinza — EZIO
Basso Ruggero _____ — RAI-MONDI
Basso Simon — ESTES
Bassoon — OBOE
Bassoon's little cousin — OBOE
Basswoods — LINDENS
Bast — BARK
Bast fiber — RAMEE
Baste — SEW
Basted — SEWN
Bastille: Brit — GAOL
Bastion — CITADEL
Basutoland, formerly — LESOTHO
Bat — IRON GRAY
Bat Masterson's weapon — CANE
Bat material — ASH
Bat of an eye — INSTANT
Bat the breeze — RAP
Bat the eyes — BLINK
Bat wood — ASH
Bataan group — AETA
Bataan native — AETA
Bates _____ ("Psycho locale) — MOTEL
Bates and Badel — ALANS
Bates or Alda — ALAN
Bates or Sillitoe — ALAN
Bates's "amber waves" — GRAIN
Bates's wayside stopover — MOTEL
Bath — SAUNA
Bath accessory — TOWEL
Bath byproducts — SUDS
Bath is one — SPA
Bath powder — TALC
Bath repast — TEA
Bath residue — RING
Bath's river — AVON
Bath, e.g. — SPA
Bath: comb. form — BALNEO
Bathe — LAVE, WASH
Bathed — LAVED
Bathhouse — CABANA
Bathhouse of a sort — SAUNA
Bathing suit style — ONE PIECE
Bathos — NADIR
Bathroom — CAN, JOHN, LOUNGE, PRIVY, LAVATORY
Bathroom feature — TUB
Bathroom hangup — TOWEL
Bathroom, in London — LOO
Bathsheba's son — SOLOMON
Bathysphere man — BEEBE
Batlike — ALIPED
Batman's friend — ROBIN
Batman? — COUNT DRACULA
Baton — ROD
Baton Rouge coll. — LSU
Baton, of a kind — WAND
Bats' hangout — CAVE
Batten — FEED
Batter — BEAT, BREAK, PELT, RAM
Batter holders — PANS
Batter's bane — SLUMP
Batter's destination — BASE
Batter's ploy — BUNT
Batter, in Born — TEIG
Battering _____ — RAM
Battering device — RAM
Batters — RAMS
Battery — ARRAY, ASSAULT, GROUP
Battery cell — ANODE
Battery or cell — SOLAR
Battery part — MINUS, ANODE
Battery terminal: Abbr. — NEG
Battery terminals — ANODES
Battle — CLASH
Battle of _____ July 3, 1940 — ORAN
Battle of Brit. heros — RAF
Battle of the _____ — BULGE
Battle of the _____ — SEXES
Battle scene: 1914, 1918 — MARNE
Battle site in Wars of the Roses — BARNET
Battle site: 1836 — ALAMO
Battle solo — ARIA
Battle style? — HAND TO HAND COMBAT
Battlement space — CRENEL
Battlers, at times — SEXES
Battleship part — GUNWALE
Battling — AT WAR
Battologize — ITERATE
Bauble — TRIFLE
Baudelaire's "Les Fleurs du _____" — MAL
Baum barker — TOTO
Bauxite and hematite — ORES
Bauxite, e.g. — ORE
Bavaria freeway — AUTOBAHN
Bavarian city — MUNICH
Bavarian river — ROTT
Bawl out — SCOLD
Baxter or Boleyn — ANNE
Baxter role in 1950 — EVE
Bay — COVE
Bay in SW Maine — CASCO
Bay of Biscay feeder — LOIRE
Bay of Funday attractions — TIDES
Bay of Funday phenomenon — TIDE
Bay or Acre port — HAIFA
Bay State cape — ANN
Bay State cape — COD
Bay window — ALCOVE, ORIEL
Bayh — BIRCH
Baylor University site — WACO
Bayonet — KNIFE
Bayreuth attraction — OPERA
Bazaar performer — COBRA
Bazzini's eerie "The Round of _____" — THE GOBLINS
BBC realm — ETHER
Bbls, etc. — STATS
Be _____ (play the powerhouse) — A LIVE WIRE
Be _____: act normally — ONE-SELF
Be a _____ in the neck — PAIN
Be a bear on Wall Street — SELL

Be a fan — ROOT
Be a flop — BOMB
Be a good enviornmentalist — REUSE
Be a majority — OUTNUMBER
Be a nosey-parker — PRY
Be a pal — HANG AROUND WITH
Be a party to — ABET
Be a somebody — RATE
Be a witness — ATTEST
Be against — OPPOSE
Be ahead — LEAD
Be all _____ (attentive) — EARS
Be all smiles — BEAM
Be ambitious — ASPIRE
Be appropriate — BEFIT, PERTAIN
Be as full as possible — BURST
Be at odds with — OBJECT
Be at the helm — STEER
Be at variance — DIFFER
Be aware of — NOTE
Be beholden — OWE
Be bested — LOSE
Be biddable — OBEY
Be bombastic — RANT
Be brazen — FLAUNT
Be buoyant — FLOAT
Be compassionate — HAVE A HEART
Be completely ineffective — CUT NO ICE
Be concerned — CARE
Be consistent — COHERE
Be contrite — RUE
Be curious — GAPE, STARE
Be deficient in — WANT
Be dishonest — FUDGE
Be displeased — RESENT
Be distressed — ACHE
Be finicky in selecting — PICK AND CHOOSE
Be follower — HEST
Be fretful — STEW
Be frugal — STINT
Be furious — FUME, RAGE
Be generous — GIVE
Be gloomy — MOPE
Be half-awake — DROWSE
Be happy — SMILE
Be human — ERR
Be idle — LAZE
Be important — RATE
Be in a turmoil — WELTER
Be in cahoots with — ABET
Be in charge of — HEAD
Be in debt — OWE
Be in session — SIT
Be inclined — TEND, TEND TO
Be infatuated — CARRY A TORCH
Be informed of — HEAR
Be intestate — LACK A WILL
Be kind — OBLIGE
Be masterful — RULE THE ROOST
Be meddlesome — PRY
Be merciful — PITY
Be morose — SULK
Be next to — ABET
Be obligated — OWE
Be obtrusively conspicuous — STARE
Be of _____ (avail oneself) — USE TO
Be of help — AVAIL
Be of use to — AVAIL
Be off guard — NAP
Be on the alert — WATCH
Be overly fond — DOTE
Be patient — WAIT
Be pregnant — GESTATE
Be present at — ATTEND
Be rude in a crowd — ELBOW
Be second in a match race — LOSE
Be servile — KOWTOW
Be silent — HSST
Be silent, in music — TACET
Be situated — LIE
Be still — HUSH
Be stimulated — REACT
Be stingy — PENNY PINCH
Be suitable — BELONG
Be sure of — RELY
Be together with — ESCORT
Be tremulous — QUAVER
Be uncertain — PEND
Be undecided — PEND
Be under the weather — AIL
Be unfair, in a way — PRE-JUDGE
Be unguarded — NAP
Be united — COHERE
Be unresolved — PEND
Be unsettled — PEND
Be unwilling, old style — NILL
Be valetudinarian — AIL
Be wary — HAVE A CARE
Be wicked — SIN
Be zetetic — SEEK
Be, in Aix — ETRE
Bea and Jean — ARTHUR
Bea Arthur TV role — MAUDE
Beach — BANK, COAST, STRAND, WATERFRONT
Beach acquistions — TANS
Beach bird — ERNE
Beach denizen — LIFEGUARD
Beach feature — DUNE
Beach find — DRIFTWOOD
Beach in Florida — VERO
Beach reading — THRILLER
Beach resort — LIDO
Beach sight — DUNE
Beach sight, in Britain — DENE
Beach stuff — SAND
Beachcomber — LOAFER, WAVE
Beachcomber's concern — TIDES
Beachcomber's tool — SIEVE
Beached — STRANDED
Beacon — FLARE, LIGHT, SIGNAL
Beacon or Nob — HILL
Bead — DROP
Beaded lizard — GILA
Beadle's bailiwick — PARISH
Beak — BILL, NEB, NOSE
Beak, in Bologna — BECCO
Beaked — ROSTRATE
Beaker — MUG
Beam — GIRDER, RAY, RAFTER, SHAFT, SMILE
Beam giving support to a roof — RAFTER
Beam upon — SMILE AT
Beame or Fortas — ABE
Beamed — RAYED
Beaming — BRIGHT, RADIANT
Beams — GRINS, SMILES
Bean — ORSON
Bean capital? — LIMA
Bean curd — TOFU
Bean or fleet — NAVY
Bean or horse — PINTO
Bean or quartet — STRING
Bean or Welles — ORSON
Bean town? — LIMA
Bean variety — LIMA
Beanery sign — EATS
Beanie — CAP
Beans — LIMA, NOBS
Beans' companion — PORK
Beantown event of 1773 — BOSTON TEA PARTY
Beantown team — SOX
Bear — ABIDE, CARRY, PRO-DUCE, STAND, SUFFER
Bear — SUPPORT, TOLERATE
Bear a lamb — YEAN
Bear down — PUSH
Bear false witness — LIE
Bear in the air — URSA
Bear in the sky — URSA
Bear malice — HATE
Bear of Alaska — KODIAK
Bear of mountains — SMOKY
Bear with — ENDURE
Bear witness — ATTEST
Bear's lair — DEN
Bear, Cat and mouse — BRYANT BALLOU AND A DANCE
Bear, in Barcelona — OSO
Bear, in Brest — OURS
Bear, to Pablo — OSO
Beard — AWN
Beard erasers — RAZORS
Beard of grain — ARISTA, AWN
Beard the lion in his den — CONFRONT
Beard, of a sort — ARISTA
Bearded bloomer — IRIS

Bearded sheep — URIALS
Bearded wild goat — TAHR
Beards group — BSA
Beards of a sort — AWNS
Bearer of enormous burden — ATLAS
Bearer of good tidings — MESSENGER
Bearing — MIEN
Bearing a burden — LADEN
Bearish times — DIPS, DROPS
Bearnaise, for one — SAUCE
Bears — SUPPORTS
Bears from Waco — BAYLOR
Bears or Lions — TEAM
Bears or Penguins — TEAM
Bears witness — ATTESTS
Beast — ANIMAL, BRUTE, FIEND
Beast of burden — BURRO
Beast of the plains — BISON
Beastly types — OGRES
Beasts of burden — ASSES, OXEN
Beat — BLEND, CLUB, DEFEAT, HIT, MIX, PULSE
Beat — THRASH, WHIP
Beat around the bush — MINCE WORDS
Beat into shape — FORGE
Beat it! — SCRAM
Beat it, old style — BEGONE
Beat one's gums — YAK, JAW
Beat the competition — WIN ONE
Beat the goalie — SCORE
Beat the odds — SCORE
Beat, in a way — CANE
Beat, in Melbourne — DING
Beatified — BLEST
Beatify — BLESS
Beatle name — LENNON
Beatles film: 1965 — HELP
Beatles movie — YELLOW SUBMARINE
Beatles' "_____ Fine" — I FEEL
Beatles' "_____ Pepper" — SERGEANT
Beatrice's admirer — DANTE
Beatrice, to Leonato — NIECE
Beats place or show — WIN
Beats, to Puccini — TEMPI
Beatty and Rorem — NEDS
Beatty and Sparks — NEDS
Beatty film: 1981 — REDS
Beatty movie — SHAMPOO
Beatty or Rorem — NED
Beau and Jeff, to Lloyd — SONS
Beau Brummell — DUDE, FOP
Beaut — LALLAPALOOZA, LULU, PIP
Beautician or couturier — STYLER
Beautician Westmore — ERN
Beautician's appliance — STYLER
Beautician's kooky plan? — HAIR BRAINED SCHEME
Beautician's offering — HENNA
Beautician's specialties — RINSES
Beautician, at times — DYER
Beautiful — FAIR, GRACEFUL, LOVELY, PRETTY
Beautiful and graceful beings — PERIS
Beautiful bird — ORIOLE
Beautiful girl — PERI
Beautiful girls — BELLES
Beautiful maiden — HOURI
Beautiful red-leaved poisonous plant — SUMAC
Beautiful woman — HOURI, PERI
Beautiful young man — ADONIS
Beautiful youth — ADONIS
Beautiful, in Berlin — SCHON
Beautiful: Comb. form — BEL, CALLI
Beautify — ADORN
Beautious — FAIR
Beauty — CHARM, GOOD LOOKS
Beauty culturist Adrien — ARPEL
Beauty in a bed — ROSE
Beauty parlor — SALON
Beauty parlor production — SET
Beauty salon extra — RINSE
Beauty salon? — PEACH PRESERVE
Beauty spot — SALON
Beauty treatment — FACIAL
Beauty's lover — BEAST
Beauty's suitor — BEAST
Beauty's swain — BEAST
Beauty-shop comparative — BLONDER
Beauvais's department — OISE
Beaux — ADMIRERS
Beaver — BEARD, RODENT
Beaver project — DAM
Beaver St. — ORE
Beaver State — OREGON
Beaver State capital — SALEM
Beaver State citizens — OREGONIANS
Beaver's den — LODGE
Beaver's structure — DAM
Becalm — SOOTHE
Became distant — COOLED
Became friendly, with "to" — WARMED
Because — SINCE
Because of — DUE TO
Béchemel or Bérnaise — SAUCE
Beck and Kite's org. — PGA
Becker forte — ACING
Becker hit — SMASH
Beckett's "_____ Dies" — MALONE
Becky of "Vanity Fair" — SHARP
Becloud — BLUR, DIM
Become — WAX
Become adult — MATURE
Become angry — SEETHE
Become boring — PALL
Become confused — ADDLE
Become corroded — RUST
Become disillusioned — SOUR
Become enraged — SEETHE
Become firm — GEL
Become friendly — THAW
Become harsh, as a voice — HOARSEN
Become hazy — BLUR
Become indistinct — BLUR
Become informed — LEARN
Become insipid — PALL
Become less desirable — WORSEN
Become less green — AGE
Become less severe — RELENT
Become lessor while lessee — SUBLET
Become lightheaded — FEEL FAINT
Become more solid — GEL
Become oxidized — RUST
Become publicly known — GET OUT
Become ragged — FRAY
Become raspy — HOARSEN
Become rigid — OSSIFY
Become scorched — PARCH
Become smitten — FALL IN LOVE
Become soft — MELT
Become stony — PETRIFY
Become tense — TAUTEN
Become weary — JADE, TIRE
Become well informed — READ UP
Become whole again — HEAL
Becomes a member — ENROLS
Becomes a participant — ENTERS
Becomes a partisan — SIDES
Becomes a partner — PAIRS UP
Becomes adjusted — ADAPTS
Becomes apparent — UNFOLDS
Becomes bushed — TIRES
Becomes innervated — REACTS
Becomes known — ARISES
Becomes less interesting — PALLS
Becomes liquefied — MELTS
Becomes more flexible — UNBENDS
Becomes semisolid — GELS
Becomes sunny — CLEARS
Becomes wan — PALES

Becoming — FITTING, SEEMLY
Becoming less green — AGING
Becoming proficient — MASTERING
Becoming raveled — FRAYING
Bed — BERTH, COT, SACK
Bed and breakfast spot — INN
Bed canopies — TESTERS
Bed cover — SHEET
Bed for baby — CRIB
Bed item — SPREAD
Bed linen — SHEET
Bed linen item — PILLOW CASE
Bed of coal — SEAM
Bed of roses — EASE
Bed or home follower — STEAD
Bed or home trailer — STEAD
Bed parts — SLATS
Bed sheets — LINEN
Bedazzle — AWE
Bedbug — CIMEX
Bedding item — SHEET
Bede of fiction — ADAM
Bede's first name — ADAM
Bedeck — ADORN
Bedecked — ADORNED, ARRAYED
Bedevil — HARASS, TAUNT, TEASE
Bedew — WET
Bedfellow — ALLY
Bedlam — ASYLUM, CHAOS, UPROAR
Bedloe's neighbor — ELLIS
Bedouin — ARAB, NOMAD
Bedouin chief — EMIR
Bedouin dwelling — TENT
Bedouin headband cord — AGAL
Bedouin's workout? — ARABIC EXERCISES
Bedouin, for one — ARAB
Bedraggled — GRIMY
Bedrock — HARDPAN
Bedroom _____ — FARCE
Bedroom furniture — DRESSER
Bedside item — ALARM
Bedspring support — SLAT
Bedstaff — SLAT
Bedtime treat for children — STORY
Bee — DRONE
Bee chaser — CEE
Bee colony — APIARY
Bee follower — CEE
Bee or horse lead-in — SEA
Bee participant — SPELLER
Bee proboscis part — LORA
Bee's quest — NECTAR
Bee's sometime abode? — BONNET
Bee, Cee follower — DEE
Bee, for one — STINGER
Beech or birch — TREE
Beecher's rewarder — HEN
Beef-to-be — STEER
Beef and Buffalo — MEATS
Beef fat — SUET
Beef Wellington, e.g. — ENTREE
Beefeater — GUARD
Beefeater's choice? — T BONE
Beefs — GRIPES
Beefy — FLESHY, STRONG
Beehive denizen — DRONE
Beehive state — UTAH
Beehive State dweller — UTE
Beekeeping unit — HIVE
Beelzebub — SATAN
Beelzebub's area — EVIL
Been fed — EATEN
Beeped — PAGED
Beer — BREW, LAGER
Beer _____: bar sign — ON TAP
Beer alternative — ALE
Beer barrel — TUN
Beer cousin — ALE
Beer garden quaff — LAGER
Beer glass — SCHOONER
Beer head — FROTH
Beer holder — KEG
Beer ingredient — HOPS
Beer mug — STEIN
Beer picturing a billy goat — BOCK
Beer, informally — SUDS
Beer-party cask — KEG
Beersheba's locale — NEGEV
Beersheba's region — NEGEV
Bees' bounty — HONEY
Beet product — SUGAR
Beethoven concerto — THE EMPEROR
Beethoven output — SONATAS
Beethoven trio, Op. 121a — KAKADU
Beethoven's "_____ Solemnis" — MISSA
Beethoven's "Archduke _____" — TRIO
Beethoven's "Choral" symphony — NINTH
Beethoven's "Fur _____" — ELISE
Beethoven's "Minuet _____" — IN G
Beethoven's "Moonlight _____" — SONATA
Beethoven's birthplace — BONN
Beethoven's opera — FIDELIO
Beethoven's Sixth — PASTORAL
Beethoven's Third — EROICA
Beetle — DOR, SCARAB
Beetle Bailey character — SARGE
Beetle Bailey's boss — SARGE
Beetle Bailey's general — HALFTRACK
Beetle Bailey's nemesis — SARGE
Beetle larva — GRUB
Beetle type — ELATER
Befitting a monarch — REGAL
Befitting holiness — SAINTLY
Before — AGO, ERE
Before angle or corn — TRI
Before angle or cycle — TRI
Before bat or phobia — ACRO
Before Beth or Heath — MAC
Before birth — PRENATAL
Before bow, road or word — CROSS
Before bus or mobile — AUTO
Before cake or meal — OAT
Before carp or dermis — ENDO
Before cast or conduct — MIS
Before center or cure — EPI
Before center or cycle — EPI
Before chi — PHI
Before chute or trooper — PARA
Before classic or circle — SEMI
Before clear and out — ALL
Before corn and form — UNI
Before corn or color — TRI
Before corn or cycle — UNI
Before cotta or firma — TERRA
Before cycle or sect — TRI
Before DDE — HST
Before dee — CEE
Before deux — UNE
Before Diego or Jose — SAN
Before Downs or salts — EPSOM
Before drome or dyne — AERO
Before eater or steak — BEEF
Before fact or fice — ARTI
Before freeze — ANTI
Before game or race — PRE
Before gamma — BETA
Before grapes or orange — SOUR
Before hostilities — PREWAR
Before JFK — DDE
Before king or mode — A LA
Before la-la — TRA
Before land or world — NETHER
Before legal or medic — PARA
Before long — ERE, SOON
Before lunch or dinner — PRE
Before Major or Minor — CANIS, URSA
Before meter or tude — ALTI
Before mi — DO RE
Before mode — A LA
Before pay or runner — BASE
Before phase or physics — META
Before plan or program — PRE
Before plane or drome — AERO
Before play or pleasure — DIS

Before Ranger or Eagle — LONE
Before room or date — ANTE
Before shirt or pony — POLO
Before shooter or pack — SIX
Before sigma — RHO
Before space or sphere — AERO
Before state or collegiate — INTER
Before such time — UP TILL
Before Sun. — SAT
Before surgeon — NEURO
Before taxes — GROSS
Before tee — ESS
Before the ans. — QUES
Before the crowing starts — PREDAWN
Before the steam era — SAILAGE
Before toad or scotch — HOP
Before way or where — ANY
Before weed or motor — LOCO
Before word or port — PASS
Before, either way — ERE
Before, in Berlin — VOR
Before, in poetry — ERE
Before, once — ERE
Before, poetically — ERE
Before, to a bard — ERE
Before, to Byron — ERE
Before, to Keats — ERE
Before-mentioned — SAME
Before: pref. — ANTE, PRE
Before: prefix — PRE
Befpre drink or pedal — SOFT
Befuddle the brain — ADDLE
Befuddled — ASEA, AT SEA
Beg — ASK, BUM, COAX, ENTREAT, PLEAD
Beg off — DROP, DECLINE, REFUSE
Beg. course on human behavior — PSYCHI
Began — FOUND, INITIATE, STARTED
Began to appear — DAWNED
Began to use — TAPPED
Begat — SIRED
Beget — GENERATE, SIRE, YEAN
Beggar, for example — NEEDER
Beggarly — SCANT
Begged — ENTREATED, PLED
Begin — COMMENCE, GET TO, SET ABOUT, START
Begin a journey — EMBARK
Begin again — ANEW, RESTART
Begin anew — REOPEN, RESTART
Begin to function — SET IN
Begin too soon — JUMP THE GUN
Begin, as winter — SET IN
Begin, in poesy — OPE
Beginner — NEOPHYTE, TIRO
Beginner's book — PRIMER
Beginners of a type — TRAINEES
Beginners, of sorts — TYROS
Beginning — ALPHA, ONSET, ORIGIN, OUTSET, SEED
Beginning of a career — DEBUT
Beginning of a certain tale — TELL
Beginning of a jazz piece — INTRO
Beginning of a new day — DAWN
Beginning of a river — HEAD
Beginning of adolescence — PUBERTY
Beginning of something — GENESIS
Beginning, in Ayr — ONCOME
Begins — SETS IN, SETS OUT
Begins the hand — DEALS
Begins to appear — DAWNS
Begins to grow — BUDS
Begley and Asner — EDS
Begley and Lopat — EDS
Begley and Wynn — EDS
Begone! — SCAT
Begot — SIRED
Begrimed — SOOTED
Begrudges — RESENTS
Begs — CADGES, ENTREATS
Beguile — AMUSE, LEAD ON
Beguiles — DELIGHTS, DELUDES
Begum — SOIL
Begum's spouse — AGA
Behave — ACT, HEED, MIND, OBEY
Behave badly — ACT UP
Behave rudely — ACT UP
Behaved — ACTED
Behaved abstractedly — MOONED
Behaved shrewishly — NAGGED
Behaves — DEPORTS
Behavior: Fr. — TENUE
Behest — DICTATE
Behind schedule — LATE
Behind the eight-ball — SUNK
Behind time — LATE
Behind which Polonius hid — ARRAS
Behold — ESPY, LOOK, NOTE, VOILA
Behold, to Brutus — ECCE
Beholden — INDEBTED
Beiderbecke's forte — JAZZ
Beiderbecke's instrument — CORNET
Beige — ECRU
Beige hue — ECRU
Beijing baby sitters — AMAHS
Being — ESSE
Being mulled over — ON ONES MIND
Being three in one — TRIUNE
Being, in Brest — ETRE
Being, in France — ETRE
Being, in Grenada — ENTE
Being, to Caesar — ESSE
Being, to Cato — ESSE
Being, to Cicero — ESSE
Being, to Sartre — ETRE
Being: Lat. — ESSE
Beknighted women — DAMES
Bel _____: formal singing style — CANTO
Bel _____: Italian cheese — PAESE
Bel Kaufman's "Love, _____": 1979 — ETC
Bel-esprit — WIT
Bela _____: Hungarian revolutionary — KUN
Belabor the point — ARGUE
Belafonte favorite of 1956 — DAYO
Belafonte forte — CALYPSO
Belafonte hit — MATILDA
Belasco portrayer: 1940 — RAINS
Belay that! — STOP IT
Beldam — CRONE, HAG
Belém, Brazil — PARA
Belfast barker? — IRISH SETTER
Belfry — SPIRE
Belfry denizen? — BAT
Belfry inhabitants — BATS
Belg. city — ALOST
Belg. river — YSER
Belgian _____ — HARE
Belgian coin — FRANC
Belgian Congo, today — ZAIRE
Belgian export — LACE
Belgian king: 1909-34 — ALBERT
Belgian marbles — RANCES
Belgian moppets? — BRUSSELS SPROUTS
Belgian pilgrimage town, to a Parisian — HAL
Belgian port — GHENT, OSTEND
Belgian resort town — SPA
Belgian river — YSER
Belgian river to North Sea — YSER
Belgian seaport — OSTEND
Belgian steel center — LIEGE
Belgian town — YPRES
Belgian waterway — YSER
Belgium city on the Meuse — LIEGE
Belgradian — SERB
Belie — DISTORT

Belief — CREDENCE, ISM, TENET
Belief differing from an orthodox view — HERESY
Belief in God — DEISM
Belief that things have souls — ANIMISM
Belief, acceptance as true — CREDENCE
Beliefs — CREDOS, ISMS
Believable — CREDIBLE
Believe _____ Not — IT OR
Believe in — ACCEPT
Believe, old style — TROW
Believe; trust — CREDIT
Believed — TRUSTED
Believer in — IST
Believer in a Hindu religion — SIKH
Believer in a personal God — DEIST
Believer in God — DEIST
Believer: Suffix — ARIAN, IST
Believers — ITES
Believes, of yore — TROWS
Belittle — ABASE, DECRY, DETRACT
Belittling word — MERE
Bell and sweet — PEPPERS
Bell boy — PORTER
Bell part — CLAPPER
Bell ringer, for short — PHONE
Bell ringers' science — CAMPANOLOGY
Bell song — BONG
Bell sound — DING, DONG, PEAL, TINKLE
Bell sounds — PEALS
Bell the cat — DARE
Bell tongue — CLAPPER
Bell used for sending alarm signals — TOCSIN
Bell's code — AREA
Belle or Bart — STARR
Belle or Ringo — STARR
Belle's millieu — BALL
Bellerophon's transportation — WINGED HORSE
Belles- _____ (certain literature) — LETTRES
Bellhop — PAGE
Bellicose Olympian — ARES
Belligerent — HOSTILE
Belligerent god — ARES
Belligerent goddess — ERIS
Belligerent sea groups — ARMADAS
Bellini opera — NORMA
Bellow — BLARE, ROAR
Bellow work — NOVEL
Bellow's "_____ the Day" — SEIZE
Bellowed — CRIED
Bellowing loudly — AROAR
Bellringers at Christmas — SANTAS
Bells of a kind — ALARMS
Belly laugh, a' la Variety — BOFF
Belmont feature — RIDE
Belmont or Churchill Downs — TRACK
Belmont racers — EQUINES
Belong — INHERE, PERTAIN
Belong intrinsically — INHERE
Belonging of value — ASSET
Belonging to "that talking horse" — MR EDS
Belonging to architect Saarinen — EEROS
Belonging to Harry's successor — IKES
Belonging to the past — HISTORICAL
Belonging to us — OURS
Belongings — GEAR
Belorussian town — PINSK
Beloved — DEAR
Beloved Blanc — MEL
Beloved of Radames — AIDA
Beloved of Rose — ABIE
Beloved: Fr. — AIME
Below an aud. — ACCT
Below the earth's surface — NETHER
Below, in Berlin — UNTER
Below, in Bonn — UNTER
Below, in poetry — NEATH
Below, to Whittier — NEATH
Below: Prefix — INFERO
Belt — STRAP
Belt area — WAIST
Belt's locale — WAIST
Belt-mounted beeper — PAGER
Belts — STRAPS
Beltway signs — EXITS
Bemoan — DEPLORE, RUE
Bemused — AT SEA
Ben _____ — HUR
Ben Bradlee, e.g. — EDITOR
Ben Canaan and Onassis — ARIS
Ben Ezra — RABBI
Ben Hur was one — CHARIOTEER
Ben's 1961 island — BLUE HAWAII
Ben-Hur's drag strip — ITER
Ben-Hur's racer — CHARIOT
Benatar of song — PAT
Bench-made — CUSTOM
Bench and Carter — CATCHERS
Bench warmer? — JUDGE
Bench wear — ROBES
Bench, in Bologna — BANCO
Bend — FLEX
Bend an ear — TALK
Bend for a ballerina — PLIE
Bend in a ship's timber — SNY
Bend over — STOOP
Bend, at the bar — PLIE
Bender — SPREE, TEAR, TOOT
Beneath — BELOW, UNDER
Beneath the earth's surface — NETHER
Beneath the Laptev's surface — SUBSEA
Benedict Arnold — TRAITOR
Benedict Arnold's crime — TREASON
Benedict was this, once — BACHELOR
Benefactor — DONOR, PATRON
Beneficiary: Law — USEE
Benefit — AID, AVAIL, BOON
Benefited — AVAILED
Benefits — BOONS
Benevolent org. — SPCA
Benign swellings — OSTEOMATA
Benin native — FON
Benin's neighbor — TOGO
Benison — BOON
Benito's daughter — EDDA
Benjamin Britten opera — PETER GRIMES
Benjamin or Rebecca — WEST
Bennett of publishing fame — CERF
Bennington homecomers — ALUMNAE
Benny Goodman forte — SWING
Benny Goodman's kingdom — SWING
Benny retort — CUT THAT OUT
Benny, to Burns — FRIEND
Bensten's st. — TEX
Bensten, for one — TEXAN
Bent — FLEXED, LEANED
Bent backward — RETROFLEX
Bent, as a bow — DREW
Bequeath — ENDOW
Bequeathed — LEFT
Bequests — LEGACIES
Berate — CHIDE, CENSURE, REBUKE, SCOLD
Bereave — DEPRIVE, ROB
Bereavement — GRIEF
Bereft — LORN
Beret — CAP, TAM
Beret wearer — CHE GUEVARA
Beret's cousin — TAM
Beret, e.g. — CAP
Berg detachment — FLOE
Berg opera — LULU
Bergen — EDGAR
Bergen dummy — SNERD
Bergen's Mortimer — SNERD
Bergen's Snerd — MORTIMER
Bergère, e.g. — CHAIR, SEAT
Bergman role in "Casablanca" — ILSA

Bergman's "_____ From a Marriage" — SCENES
Bergman-Bogart classic — CASABLANCA
Beria's boss — STALIN
Bering Sea island — ATTU
Bering Straight peninsula — SEWARD
Berkshire racecourse — ASCOT
Berlin airport — TEMPELHOF
Berlin exclamation — ACH, HOCH
Berlin freeways familiarly — BAHNS
Berlin highway — BAHN
Berlin hit: 1925 — ALWAYS
Berlin lady — FRAU
Berlin mister — HERR
Berlin musical: 1940 — LOUISIANA PURCHASE
Berlin output — SONG
Berlin public square — PLATZ
Berlin song — LIED
Berlin street — ALLEE
Berlin sweetheart — LIEBCHEN
Berlin's "He's _____ Picker" — A RAG
Berlin's "Say It _____ So" — ISNT
Berlin's "When _____ You" — I LOST
Berlin, once — DIVIDED CITY
Berlin-to-Dresden dir. — SSE
Berliner's "I" — ICH
Berliner's alas — ACH
Berliner's pronoun — ICH
Berlioz' "Harold in _____" — ITALY
Berm — BRIM, EDGE, SHOULDER
Bermuda _____ — TRIANGLE
Bermuda bike — MOPED
Bermuda or red — ONION
Bermuda transport — MOPED
Bern's waterway — AAR
Bernard who played "M" — LEE
Berne's river — AARE
Berne's river — AARE
Bernhardt — SARAH
Bernie _____, former Red Sox slugger — CARBO
Bernstein opera — TROUBLE IN TAHITI
Bernstein score — MASS
Bernstein, for short — LEN
Berra and Bear — YOGIS
Berry and Howard — KENS
Berserk — AMOK
Bert _____, silent film star — LYTELL
Bert Bobbsey's twin — NAN
Bert of stage and screen — LAHR
Bert's "Sesame Street" friend — ERNIE
Berth — BED, BUNK, COT, PALLET, SLIP
Berth choice — UPPER, LOWER
Berths — UPPERS
Bertolucci film: 1979 — LUNA
Beseech — BEG, PRAY
Beseeched — PLED
Beset — AFFLICT, ASSAIL
Beset with trouble — IN HOT WATER
Beset with trouble — UP THE CREEK
Beside — ALONG
Beside (with "of") — ABREAST
Beside oneself — FRANTIC, IRATE
Besides — ELSE
Besides, to Burns — FOR BY
Besiege — BESET
Besmear — SOIL
Besmeared — GRIMED
Besmirch — ASPERSE, SMEAR, SOIL
Besmirches — TAINTS
Bess Truman, _____ Wallace — NEE
Bess' man — HARRY
Best — EDNA, FINEST, FOREMOST, OUTDO, TOP
Best Actress: 1961 — LOREN
Best and Ferber — EDNAS
Best mark — 100
Best men, e.g. — AIDES
Best of films — EDNA
Best of Hollywood — EDNA
Best or Millay — EDNA
Best part of Ivan Isevic's game — SERVE
Best Picture Oscar winner: 1969 — MIDNIGHT COWBOY
Best seller — HIT
Best seller by Barbara Taylor — HOLD THE DREAM
Best seller by Larry McMurtry — LONESOME DOVE
Best seller by Sidney Sheldon — IF TOMORROW COMES
Best seller in 1885 — RAMONA
Best seller in 1924 — SO BIG
Best source of news — HORSES MOUTH
Best suit — SPADES
Best way to be endowed — HEAVILY
Bested — OUTDONE
Bested or worsted — OUTDONE
Bestow a right upon — ENTITLE
Bestow knighthood upon — DUB
Bestow without a return — GIVE
Bestowed — GAVE AWAY, GRANTED
Bestowed abundantly — RAINED
Bestowed upon — AWARDED
Bestowing profusely — LAVISH
Bestseller by Bill Cosby — LOVE AND MARRIAGE
Bestseller by Dale Brown — DAY OF THE CHEETAH
Bestseller by Truddi Chase — WHEN RABBIT HOWLS
Bet — CHANCE, GAMBLE, PLOT, RISK, STAKE, WAGER
Bet acceptors — TAKERS
Bet modifier — HEDGE
Beta and gamma — RAYS
Betakes oneself — REPAIRS
Bete _____ (bugbear) — NOIRE
Betel palm — ARECA
Betelgeuse or Deneb — STAR
Betelgeuse's constellation — ORION
Beth preceder — ALEF
Beth's Greek cousin — BETA
Bethel — CHAPEL
Bethlehem sight — STEEL MILL
Betoken — SHOW
Betray — SELL
Betray: sl. — RAT ON
Betrayer; traitor — ISCARIOT
Betrayers — RATS, TRAITORS
Betroth — PROMISE
Betrothed — VOWED
Betsey _____ (Dickens character) — PRIG
Betsy and Diana — ROSSES
Betsy whose work was saluted — ROSS
Betsy, the flagmaker — ROSS
Better — AMEND, FINER
Better _____ (spouse) — HALF
Better aligned — TRUER
Better prepared — READIER
Better than better — BEST
Better than never — LATE
Better than sorry — SAFE
Better times, we hope — NEW ERA
Betters — WORSTS
Betting considerations — ODDS
Betting group — POOL
Bettor's choices — EVENS
Bettor's concern — ODDS
Bettor's plan? — PLAY THE FIELD
Betty Boop quality — PERKINESS
Betty of song and friends — COED
Betty or Gerry — FORD
Betty's 1985 evenings? — WHITE NIGHTS
Betulaceous tree — ALDER

Between — AMID, AMONG
Between 12 and 20 — TEENS
Between A and U — EIO
Between AM and PM — NOON
Between dix and douze — ONZE
Between friends and countrymen — ROMANS
Between hic and hoc — HAEC
Between high and low tide — SEA LEVEL
Between Hubert and Gerald — SPIRO
Between larva and imago — PUPA
Between Man. and Que. — ONT
Between Michigan and Ontario — ERIE
Between ourselves — ENTRE NOUS
Between pi and sigma — RHO
Between Q and U — RST
Between quod and faciendum — ERAT
Between rho and tau — SIGMA
Between stem and stern — AMID
Between the sheets — ABED
Between Thomas and Edison — ALVA
Between Tinker and Chance — EVERS
Between, in Bologna — TRA
Between-the-acts entertainment — ENTRACTE
Between: Comb. form — INTER, META
Between: Prefix — INTER
Betwixt's associate — BETWEEN
Bevel — CHAMFER
Bevels — CANT
Beverage — ALE, BEER, COLA, SODA, TEA
Beverage for a cold day — COCOA
Beverage for fall — CIDER
Beverage holder — MUG
Beverage nut — KOLA
Beverage server — CARAFE
Beverage unit — QUART
Beverage, in Wiesbaden — BIER
Beverly _____ — HILLS
Beverly of opera fame — SILLS
Bevy — BUNCH
Bewail — MOURN
Bewail, Irish style — KEEN
Bewails — WEEPS
Bewhiskered Union General — AMBROSE BURNSIDE
Bewildered — AT SEA
Bewildered state — PUZZLEMENT
Bewildered statement — ITS ALL GREEK TO ME
Bewitch — ENCHANT
Bewitched — RAPT
Beyond — AFAR
Beyond a doubt — CERTAIN
Beyond calculation — COUNTLESS
Beyond doubt — ASSURED
Beyond help — SUNK
Beyond measure — IMMENSE
Beyond the _____ — PALE
Beyond the megalopolis — EXURBAN
Beyond X-rated — PORNO
Beyond, to Burns — AYONT
Bhuddist sect — ZEN
Bhuddist shrine — STUPA
Bhuddist temple — WAT
Bhutan's location — ASIA
Bialy or bagel — ROLL
Bianchi opponents — NERI
Bianco or Carlo — MONTE
Bias — ANGLE, BENT, LEANING, SLANT, WARP
Biased — SKEWED, SLANTED
Biased man, to NOW ladies — MCP
Biased one — BIGOT
Biases — BENTS
Bib — APRON, DICKEY
Bibl. book — OBAD
Bible — BOOK
Bible book — AMOS, ACTS, EXODUS
Bible city — SODOM
Bible segments: Abbr. — VSS
Bible version: Abbr. — VULG
Biblical allegory — PARABLE
Biblical angel — GABRIEL
Biblical animal — UNICORN
Biblical ascetic — ESSENE
Biblical battle — JERICHO
Biblical boat — ARK
Biblical brother — ABEL, ESAU
Biblical city — BABYLON, SIDON
Biblical comforter — STAFF
Biblical country — EDOM, SHEBA
Biblical craft — ARK
Biblical dancer — SALOME
Biblical dill — ANET
Biblical event — FLOOD
Biblical food — MANNA
Biblical garden — EDEN
Biblical Hebrew measure — EPNA
Biblical herbs — ANETS
Biblical hunter — NIMROD
Biblical judge — ELI
Biblical king — ELAH
Biblical kingdom — EDOM, JUDAH, MOAB
Biblical land — ELAM, NOD
Biblical land I Kings 9:28 — OPHIR
Biblical land of plenty — GOSHEN
Biblical land, rich in gold — OPHIR
Biblical landfall — ARARAT
Biblical lion — ARI
Biblical lovers — SOLOMON AND SHEBA
Biblical Mary — MAGDALEN
Biblical measure — CUBIT
Biblical mother-in-law — NAOMI
Biblical mount — NEBO
Biblical mountain — ARARAT, HOREB, SINAI
Biblical oldster — ENOS
Biblical opponents — DAVID AND GOLIATH
Biblical parents — SOLOMON AND SHEBA
Biblical patriarch — ENOS
Biblical peak — SINAI
Biblical poems: Abbr. — PSA
Biblical pottage buyer — ESAU
Biblical preposition — UNTO
Biblical pronoun — THOU
Biblical prophet — AMOS, ELIHU
Biblical queen — ESTHER
Biblical river — JORDAN
Biblical sailor — NOAH
Biblical scribe — EZRA
Biblical seamstress — DORCAS
Biblical society — GIDEON
Biblical song — PSALM
Biblical spy — CALEB
Biblical stargazers — MAGI
Biblical Syria — ARAM
Biblical temptress — EVE
Biblical tower — BABEL
Biblical tower town — BABEL
Biblical town — ENDOR
Biblical twin — ESAU
Biblical verb — CANST, GIVETH, HATH, SHALT
Biblical verb suffix — ETH
Biblical villain — CAIN, HEROD
Biblical wall words — MENES
Biblical warrior — CALEB
Biblical weed — ANTES, TARE
Biblical well — AIN, ESEK
Biblical wise men — MAGI
Biblical witch's home — ENDOR
Biblical witching site — ENDOR
Biblical word — UNTO
Biblike shirt front — DICKEY
Bibliophile — COLLECTOR
Bibliotheca — LIBRARY
Bibulous — TIPSY
Biceps locale — ARM
Bicker — SPAT
Bicuspid's neighbor — MOLAR
Bicycle — RACER
Bicycle built for two — TANDEM

Bicycled — RODE
Bid — CALL, OFFER
Biddies — HENS
Biddy — HEN
Bide one's time — WAIT
Bide time — AWAIT
Bided one's time — WAITED
Bids — OFFERS
Bier — PYRE
Biergarten item — STEIN
Bifocal — LENS
Big-time spender — SPORT
Big — AWSOME, GREAT, HUGE, LARGE, VAST
Big "D" — DALLAS
Big _____ — AS LIFE
Big _____ — BEN
Big _____ theory — BANG
Big _____, Calif. — SUR
Big A offshoot — OTB
Big and clumsy — HULKING
Big band leader Jones — ISHAM
Big bargain — STEAL
Big bash — WING DING
Big bashes — FETES
Big bear — GRIZZLY
Big beetle — CHAFER
Big bell sound — BONG
Big Ben — CLOCK
Big Ben locale — LONDON
Big Bertha's birthplace — ESSEN
Big bird — EMU, OSTRICH
Big blazes — THREE ALARM FIRES
Big blow — GALE
Big Board initials — ITT
Big board initials — NYSE
Big Board's big brother — SEC
Big buck — ELK
Big business assumption — TAKEOVER
Big casino's spot — TEN
Big cat — TIGER
Big cats — PUMAS
Big containers — VATS
Big Daddy portrayer — IVES
Big dipper — LADLE
Big do's — FETES
Big eater — HOG
Big events at school — FINALS
Big game — ELK, MOOSE
Big gato — TIGRE
Big hit — SMASH
Big house — PRISON
Big job for L.I. Water Dept.? — FLUSHING NY
Big leagues — MAJORS
Big lunk — BOZO
Big mess — HODGEPODGE
Big moment at the opera — ARIA
Big mouth? — MAW
Big name in Argentina — PERON
Big name in farm machinery — DEERE
Big name in Monte Carlo — RAINIER
Big name in New Haven — ELI
Big name in Ohio — TAFT
Big name in publishing — HEARST, LUCE
Big name in publishing — OCHS
Big name in The Hague — BEATRIX
Big oaf — BOZO
Big one — LIE
Big pots — VATS
Big ref. work — OED
Big rigs, for short — SEMIS
Big shallow lake in Novgorod Oblast — ILMEN
Big shot — MOGUL, NABOB
Big sip — SWIG
Big Sky team — UTES
Big sleeper — RIP
Big spender — HIGH ROLLER
Big swallow — GULP
Big swig — BELT
Big Ten inst. — OSU
Big Ten team — GOPHERS
Big Three meeting place: WW II — YALTA
Big Top — TENT
Big top leader — RINGMASTER
Big top principal — CLOWN
Big Top star — TAMER
Big Top's top — TARP
Big truck, for short — SEMI
Big wins — GRAND SLAMS
Big Woman on Campus? — CATHERINE WHEEL
Big, in Bayonne — GROS
Big-A action — BET
Big-A laggard — ALSO RAN
Big-bang maker — TNT
Big-top employee — CARNY
Bigfoot of Asia — YETI
Bigger than life — HEROIC
Bigger than med. — LGE
Biggers sleuth — CHARLIE CHAN
Biggers' detective — CHAN
Biggest part for Sue? — LYONS SHARE
Biggies at the zoo — HIPPOS
Biggin — CAP
Bight of Benin port — LAGOS
Bight or fjord — ARM
Bigot — RACIST
Bigoted — NARROW
Bigotry — RACISM
Bihar and Kerala — STATES
Bijou — GEM
Bike — CYCLE, PEDAL
Bike feature — PEDAL
Biked — CYCLED
Bikini _____ — ATOLL
Bikini and Kwajalein — ATOLLS
Bikini feature — BRA
Bikini part — BRA
Bikini time — SUMMER
Bikini top — BRA
Bikini, e.g. — TWO PIECE SUIT
Bikini, et al. — ATOLLS
Bikini, for one — ATOLL
Bilbao boy — NINO
Bilbo — SWORD
Bilge — PUMP
Bilge covering — FLOOR-BOARD
Bill-topper — STAR
Bill — NEB, ONE, TEN, TAB
Bill _____: Dickens villain — SYKES
Bill of _____ — FARE
Bill of fare — MENU
Bill of Rights guarantee — FREEDOM
Bill's companion — COO
Bill's partner — COO
Bill, in Nice — BEC
Billboard? — HIGH SIGN
Billed cap — ETON
Billfold — PURSE, WALLET
Billhooks — SNAGGERS
Billiard opening action — LAG
Billiard stroke — MASSE
Billiards establishment — POOLROOM
Billiards items — CUEBALLS
Billiards shot — CAROM
Billion pursuer — AIRE
Billion years — EON
Billow — RISE, WAVE
Billowy — RISING, SURGING, WAVING
Bills — NEBS, ONES, TENS
Billy _____ Williams — DEE
Billy _____, pop singer — OCEAN
Billy Budd's captain — VERE
Billy of rock — IDOL
Billy Ray Cyrus's "_____ Breaky Heart" — ACHY
Bin — CRIB
Binary — DUAL
Binaural — STEREO
Binaural system — STEREO
Bind — ENLACE, LASH, STRAP, TIE
Bind again — RETIE
Bind by affection — ENDEAR
Bind firmly — CEMENT
Bind matrimonially — WED
Bind tightly — TRUSS
Binders — TIES
Binding words — I DO
Binds — LIGATES
Bing Crosby's birthplace — TACOMA
Bing in the Holy City? — JERUSALEM CHERRY
Binge — BENDER, SPREE, TEAR
Bingo's brother — BEANO
Biochemist's abbr. — RNA

Biographer _____ Ludwig — EMIL
Biographer Leon — EDEL
Biographer of "What Maisie Knew" — EDEL
Biographer of Henry James — EDEL
Biographer Winslow — OLA
Biography — MEMOIR, VITA
Biography beginner — AUTO
Biol. or social — SCI
Biol. topic — RNA
Biol., for one — SCI
Biological classes — GENERA
Biological groups — GENERA
Biologically connected — ADNATE
Biologists Jacques — LOEB
Biology and physics — SCIENCES
Bionomics — ECOLOGY
Biota — LIFE
Biped, e.g. — MAN
Birch — ALDER
Birch family member — ALDER
Birch trees — ALDERS
Birchbark — CANOE
Bird — ERNE, JAY, MOA, OWLET, SERIN
Bird beak — NEB
Bird bill — BEAK
Bird crop — CRAW
Bird dog — SETTER
Bird encountered by Sinbad — ROC
Bird food — SEED
Bird from Down Under — EMU
Bird life — ORNIS
Bird noises — CHIRPS
Bird of Australia — KIWI
Bird of Hawaii — NENE
Bird of legend — ROC
Bird of peace — DOVE
Bird of prey — ERNE
Bird of the Florida Keys — GREAT WHITE HERON
Bird of the night — OWLET
Bird of white plumage — EGRET
Bird or Birdsong — CAGER
Bird or fruit — KIWI
Bird or player — ORIOLE
Bird pads — NESTS
Bird rests — ROOSTS
Bird sanctuary — PRESERVE
Bird shot — LAYUP
Bird snarer — LIMER
Bird sound — CAW, TWEET
Bird talk? — CHAT
Bird with remarkably long legs — FLAMINGO
Bird's beak — NEB
Bird's crop — CRAW
Bird, to Brutus — AVIS
Birdbrain — FOOL
Birdfood — SEEDS
Birdhouse — COTE
Birdie beater — EAGLE
Birdie topper — EAGLE
Birdie's better — EAGLE
Birdlife of a region — ORNIS
Birdman — AVIATOR
Birds and Holmes — LARRYS
Birds beak — ROSTRUM
Birds do it — ROOST
Birds in the walls? — HEATING DUCKS
Birds of a region — ORNIS
Birds of passage — TRAMPS
Birds of prey — RAPTORS
Birds that utter booming notes — EMUS
Birds' "thumbs" — ALULAE
Birds' beaks — NEBS
Birds' resting place — ROOST
Birds, to Brutus — AVES
Bireme gear — OARS
Birl — ROTATE
Birler's footing — LOG
Birnam, in "Macbeth" — WOOD
Birth — NASCENCE
Birth "veil" — CAUL
Birth related — NATAL
Birthmarks — NEVI
Birthplace of Ceres — ENNA
Birthplace of Columbus — GENOA
Birthplace of Constantine the Great — NIS
Birthplace of Hippocrates — KOS
Birthplace of Honore' de Balzac — TOURS
Birthplace of HST — LAMAR
Birthplace of St. Francis — ASSISI
Birthplace of Toulouse-Lautrec — ALBI
Birthright — HERITAGE, LEGACY
Birthright seller — ESAU
Birthstone for October — OPAL
Bis — ENCORE, TWICE
Biscay roller — ONDE
Biscuit color — DOE
Biscuit Tortoni — DESSERT
Biscuit's cousin — ROLL
Bisect — CUT, HALVE
Bishop — ABBA, PRELATE
Bishop and Sexton — POETS
Bishop of Canterbury's headdress — MITRE
Bishop or ballet skirt — TUTU
Bishop who won a Nobel prize — TUTU
Bishop's headdress — MITRE
Bishop's representative — VICAR
Bishop, e.g. — PRELATE
Bishopric — MITER, SEE
Bishops — ECCLESIASTICAL OFFICIALS
Bismarck — OTTO
Bismarck is its cap. — N DAK
Bismarck's first name — OTTO
Bismarck, the "_____ Chancellor" — IRON
Bismuth or bullion — METAL
Bismuth, e.g. — ORE
Bison — AUROCHS
Bisque or Borscht — SOUP
Bistro — CAFE, NIGHT SPOT, PUB
Bit — ATOM, TAD
Bit by bit — SLOWLY
Bit of a job — STINT
Bit of bric-a-bac — CURIO
Bit of butter — PAT
Bit of canvas — STUNSAIL
Bit of change — CENT
Bit of fiction — FABLE
Bit of food — DOLLOP, NIBBLE
Bit of gossip — ITEM
Bit of hardware — T NUT, U BOLT
Bit of information — FACT, ITEM
Bit of smoke — WISP
Bit of work — CHORE
Bit part — MAID, SPOT
Bit parts — CAMEOS
Bit role — CAMEO
Bite — MORSEL, NIP
Biting — ACID, ACRID, MORDANT
Biting bugs — MOSQUITOES
Bits — SHREDS
Bits for Benji — ORTS
Bits of butter — PATS
Bits of food — SOPS
Bits of gossip — ITEMS
Bits of marginalia — STETS
Bits of wit — EPIGRAMS
Bits or hints — SOUPCONS
Bitsy's partner — ITSY
Bitter — ACERB, ACID, ACRID, HARSH, SOUR, TART
Bitter disagreement — IMBROGLIO
Bitter feud — VENDETTA
Bitter herb — TANSY
Bitter medicine — ALOIN
Bitter regret — REMORSE
Bitter resinous juice — ALOE
Bitter vetch — ERS
Bitter: Comb. form — PICRO
Bitterness — BILE
Bittersweet, e.g. — VINE
Bivalve — CLAM, MUSSEL
Bivalve mollusk — SCALLOP
Bivalvular shellfish — CLAM
Bivouacked — TENTED
Bivouacs — CAMPS, ETAPE
Bizarre — ODD, OUTRE, OUTLANDISH, WEIRD
Bizet opera — CARMEN

Bjorn of tennis — BORG
Bjorn of the courts — BORG
Bk. notation — PTO
Bk. of Revelations — APOC
Bk. of the Apoc. — MAC
Bk. of the Bible — MIC
Bks. before publication — MSS
Blab — SPILL THE BEANS
Blabbed — SPILLED THE BEANS
Black — CROW, DARK, DISMAL, EBON, EBONY, INKY
Black — RAVEN, SOIL, SOOT
Black _____ cattle — ANGUS
Black _____ HOLE
Black and _____ — BLUE
Black and blue — LIVID
Black and tan — ALE AND STOUT
Black Bears' home — ORONO
Black bird — ANI, DAW
Black cat's favorite day? — FRIDAY THE THIRTEENTH
Black cat, e.g. — OMEN
Black cat, to some — OMEN
Black cuckoo — ANI
Black enamel-like alloy — NIELLO
Black entry — ASSET
Black eye — MOUSE, SHINER
Black Forest locale — GERMANY
Black gem — ONYX
Black gold — OIL
Black gum trees — TUPELOS
Black gums — TUPELOS
Black hardwood — EBONY
Black Hawk was one — SAC
Black Hawk's followers — SACS
Black Jack's outfit — AEF
Black Kettle was one — CHEYENNE
Black Maria — PADDY WAGON
Black or baked starter — HALF
Black or blue ending — BERRY
Black or Red — SEA
Black or Red follower — EYE
Black or silver — SMITH
Black or White — SEA
Black piano key — D FLAT
Black pigment — INDIA INK
Black Sea arm — AZOV
Black Sea feeder — RION
Black Sea peninsula — CRIMEA
Black Sea port — ODESSA
Black sheep — OUTCAST, RENEGADE
Black stone — ONYX
Black tea — BOHEA
Black tea: var. — PECO
Black tie get-up — TUX
Black wood — EBON, EBONY
Black, in Blois — NOIR
Black, in Bordeaux — NOIR
Black, in Brest — NOIR
Black, in verse — EBON
Black, to a poet — EBON
Black, to Byron — EBON
Black-and-tan terrier — MANCHESTER
Black-eyed _____ — PEAS
Black-eyed Susan — DAISY
Black-footed albatross — GOONEY BIRD
Black-ink item — ASSET
Black: Prefix — MELA
Blackball — REJECT
Blackberry drupelets — ACINI
Blackbird — ANI, DAW, MERL
Blackbirds — OUZELS
Blackboard — SLATE
Blackboard crayon — CHALK
Blackboard item — ERASER
Blacked — TARRED
Blacken — CHAR
Blackfoot homes — TEPEES
Blackguard — CAD
Blackguards — KNAVES
Blackhawks' arena — RINK
Blackjack player's request — HIT ME
Blackjack's big brother — BILLY CLUB
Blackjack's relative — COSH
Blackleg — SCAB
Blacklist — LABEL
Blackmail — BRIBE, RANSOM
Blackmailer's words — OR ELSE
Blackmore heroine — DOONE
Blackmore outlaw — DOONE
Blackmore's Doone — LORNA
Blacksmith — FARRIER, SHOER
Blacksmith's adjunct — ANVIL
Blacksmith's device — ANVIL
Blacksmith, at times — SHOER
Blackthorn — SLOE
Blackthorn fruits — SLOES
Blade for Gaston — EPEE
Blake of "Gunsmoke" — AMANDA
Blake subject — TIGER
Blake's "The Book of _____" — LOS
Blake's model of symmetry — TIGER
Blame — ACCUSE, ONUS
Blame bearer — GOAT
Blame bearer in a song — MAME
Blanc and Brooks — MELS
Blanc and Torme — MELS
Blanc or Cenis — MONT
Blanch — FADE, WHITEN
Blanche DuBois's sister — STELLA
Blanched — ASHEN, PALED
Blanches — PALES
Blandly urbane — SUAVE
Blank intervals between words — SPACES
Blanket — COVER
Blarney — FLATTERY
Blaspheme — CURSE, PROFANE
Blasphemous — IMPIOUS
Blasphmemer — CURSER
Blast or carp precursor — ENDO
Blast or plasm lead-in — ECTO
Blast-furnace steel — COKE
Blaster's letters — TNT
Blaster's need — TNT
Blasting stuff — TNT
Blather — DROOL, GAB, YAK
Blaze — BURN, FIRE, FLAME, FLARE, GLOW
Blazing — AFIRE, ON FIRE
Blazing bijou — OPAL
Blazon — COAT OF ARMS
Bldg. material — CEM
Bleach — ETIOLATE
Bleacher creature — FAN
Bleaching vat — KIER
Bleak — STARK
Bleat — BAA, MAA
Blemish — MAR, SOIL, STAIN, TAINT
Blemish of a sort — SCAR
Blemishes — STAINS, WARTS
Blend — AGREE, FUSE
Blend of smoke and fog — SMOG
Blend thoroughly — GETS AT
Blende and turgite — ORES
Blended — MIXED
Blender button — PUREE
Blender yield — PUREE
Blends together — FUSES
Blenheim blue — BLAU
Bless, in a way — ANOINT
Blessed _____ — EVENT
Blessed woman — BEATA
Blessed woman, in the Vatican — BEATA
Blessing — BOON, GRACE, PRAYER
Blest — SACRED
Blew one's stack — RAVED
Blew the whistle — SPILLED THE BEANS
Blight — SMUT
Blighted area — SLUM
Blighted expanse — SAHARA
Blind — AMBUSH, COVER, CURTAIN, SCREEN
Blind a falcon — SEEL
Blind as _____ — A BAT
Blind feature — SLAT
Blind mice, e.g. — TRIO
Blind part — SLAT
Blind unit — SLAT
Blindfolded, in falconry — SEELED
Bliss — RAPTURE
Blissful — BLEST
Blissful abodes — EDENS
Blissful place — EDEN

Blissful, in Berlin — SELIG
Blister — BLAIN
Blisters — SORES
Blitz, in football — RED DOG
Blitzen — FLASH IN GERMAN
Blizzard configuration — SWIRL
Blob or lump — DOLLOP
Block — BRICK, CHUNK, DAM, STEM, STOP
Block fragment — CHIP
Block grant — FUNDS
Blockade — CLOSURE
Blocked up — CLOGGED
Blockhead — DOLT, DUNCE, OAF
Blockheads, in Brest — ANES
Blocks access — SHUTS
Blocks or crushes — SCOTCHES
Blocks, as at the pass — HEADS OFF
Bloke — BOD, CHAP, EGG, GENT
Blokes from Stoke-on-Trent — BRITISH
Blond — FAIR
Blonde shade — ASH
Blondie, to Dagwood — SPOUSE
Blood — ANCESTRY, FLUID, LINEAGE
Blood carrier — AORTA
Blood color — SANGUINE
Blood components — PLATELETS, PLASMA
Blood condition: Comb. form — HEMIA
Blood element — PLASMA
Blood line — AORTA
Blood state: Comb. form — EMIA
Blood sugar — GLUCOSE
Blood vessel — AORTA, ARTERY
Blood vessel: Comb. form — ANGI
Blood-related — HEMAL, HEMIC
Blood: Comb. form — HEMA, HEMAT
Blood: Prefix — HEMO
Bloodhound's clue — SCENT
Bloodhound, e.g. — TRACER
Bloodhounds, e.g. — SCENTERS
Bloodless — ASHEN, PALE, WAN
Bloodshed — CARNAGE, VIOLENCE
Bloodshoot — RED
Bloody — BRUTAL, GORY
Bloody Mary's daughter — LIAT
Bloom — BLOSSOM, FLOWER
Bloom from Holland — TULIP
Bloomer girl? — VIOLET
Blossom — BLOOM, FLOWER
Blossom for Batista — FLOR
Blossom of silents — SEELY
Blossom part — PETAL
Blot — STAIN
Blot out — ERASE
Blotch — BLUR, GLOB, PATCH
Blots out — ANNULS, ERASES
Blotter — LIST, RECORD
Blotter item — ARREST
Blotto — TIPSY
Blouse — SHIRT
Blow — JOLT, PUFF
Blow down — FELL
Blow hot and cold — WAVER
Blow in — ARRIVE
Blow off steam — RANT
Blow one's horn — BRAG
Blow one's stack — SHOUT, YELL
Blow out — FEED, QUASH
Blow over — CEASE, END, PASS
Blow the whistle on — SING
Blow up — SOLI
Blowgun ammunition — DART
Blowhard — BRAGGART
Blown-up photo: Abbr. — ENL
Blown — RUINED
Blown over — PAST
Blowout — BASH
Blows a horn — TOOTS
Blows away — ZAPS
BLT spread — MAYO
Blubber — SOB
Bludgeon — CLUB
Blue-chip edging — GILT
Blue-pencil wielder — EDITOR
Blue — GLOOMY, SAD
Blue and White glazed pottery — DELFT
Blue bird — JAY
Blue blood — ARISTO
Blue chip — STOCK
Blue corundum — SAPPHIRE
Blue denim — DUNGAREE
Blue dye — ANIL, WOAD
Blue Eagle agcy. — NRA
Blue Eagle org. — NRA
Blue flag — IRIS
Blue flowered plants — AGERATUMS
Blue Frost subject? — SAPPHIRED MAN
Blue grass — GRAMA, POA
Blue Grotto island — CAPRI
Blue hue — NAVY
Blue Jay's rival — ORIOLE
Blue Jays or Cardinals — TEAM
Blue jeans — DENIMS
Blue Nile source — TSANA
Blue of baseball — VIDA
Blue or green — BICE
Blue or White river — NILE
Blue ribbon — IST, AWARD
Blue Ridge and Smokies: Abbr. — MTNS
Blue shade — ALICE
Blue suit, sometimes — SERGE
Blue-footed petrel — TITI
Blue-green — CYAN
Blue-green shade — AQUA
Blue-greens — AQUAS
Blue-pencil — EDIT
Blue-pencil wielders — REDACTORS
Blue-pencillers — REDACTORS
Blue-plate special, e.g. — MEAL
Bluebeard's last wife — FATIMA
Bluebell's bloom in these — BEDS
Blueblood — BARON
Bluefin — TUNA
Bluegrass State — KENTUCKY
Bluejackets — TARS
Bluenose — PRIG, PRUDE
Blueprint — MODEL, PLAN
Blueprint datum — SPEC
Blues — AGUES
Blues singer _____ Smith — BESSIE
Blues singer Bessie — SMITH
Bluff — DECEIVE, FOOL, TRICK
Bluff — FAKE
Bluish-green — AQUA, EMAIL
Bluish-gray — SLATE
Blunder — ERROR, FLUFF
Blunderbore — GIANT
Blundered — ERRED
Blunders — ERRS
Blunt — DEADEN
Blunt sword — EPEE
Blunted — DULLED
Blunted blade — EPEE
Bluntly — POINT BLANK
Blunts — DULLS
Blur — SMEAR
Blurbs — RAVES
Blurred — MISTY
Blurts out — BLATS
Blush — REDDEN
Blushed — ROSED
Blusters — RAVES
Blustery — LIVELY, RAW
Blyth and Jillian — ANNS
Blyth of film — ANN
BMT's kin — IRT
Bo Derek's 1977 "Whale of a Film" — ORCA
Bo Derek's number — TEN
Boa — NECKLET
Boa constrictor's cousin — ANACONDA
Boa family member — ANACONDA
Boadicea's tribe — ICENI
Boar: Ger. — EBER
Board — PLANK, TABLE
Board and missle game — DARTS
Board at Belmont — TOTE
Board game — CHECKERS, CHESS, KENO, LOTTO

Board game piece — TILE
Board members: Abbr. — TRS
Board mems. — TRS
Board of _____ — TRADE
Board the Metroliner — ENTRAIN
Board up — CLOSE
Board's partner — BED
Boarded up — SHUT DOWN
Boarder — ROOMER
Boardinghouse occupant — ROOMER
Boas for milady — SCARVES
Boast — BRAG, CROW
Boaster — WINDBAG
Boasts — BRAGS
Boat-bottom timber — KEEL
Boat basin — MARINA
Boat bows, on the Seine — AVANTS
Boat covers? — SHYAWLS
Boat house item — OAR
Boat or bike starter — MOTOR
Boat or blow — SMACK
Boat pin — THOLE
Boat rest — MARINA
Boat spar — SPRIT
Boat's berth — SLIP
Boat's rope "ladders" — RATLINES
Boater adornment — HATBAND
Boater or porkpie — HAT
Boater's haven — BASIN
Boater, e.g. — HAT
Boaters and bowlers — HATS
Boaters and sailors — HATS
Boatman — OAR
Boatman's waterway? — VOLGA
Boats of a sort — PROAS
Bob-o-link — ORTOLAN
Bob _____, pop singer — SEGER
Bob Burns — ARKANSAS TRAVELER
Bob follower — SLED
Bob Hope film of 1951 — THE LEMON DROP KID
Bob Hope's "Have _____, Will Travel" — TUX
Bob of "Full House" — SAGET
Bob of folk / rock music — DYLAN
Bob or Thomas — DYLAN
Bob starts them — SLEDS
Bob, for one — HAIRDO
Bobbin — REEL, SPOOL
Bobbins — SPOOLS
Bobble the ball — ERR
Bobby of Hockey — ORR
Bobby of rink fame — ORR
Bobby Orr was one — BRUIN
Bobby's traffic stint — POINT DUTY
Bobbysoxer's sock — ANKLET
Bobcats' kin — LYNXES
Bobolink's relative — ORIOLE
Bobwhite — COLIN
Boca _____, Fla. — RATON
Boccaccio's "The _____ Heart" — EATEN
Bode — AUGUR
Bodega quaff — SANGRIA
Bodice — WAIST
Bodies of water: Abbr. — SDS
Bodkin — AWL
Bodkins and dibbles — TOOLS
Body-shop problem — DENT
Body — CARCASS
Body art — TATTOOS
Body building — EXERCISE
Body covering 71 percent of the earth — OCEAN
Body meeting in Paris — SENAT
Body membrane — TELA
Body of an organism — SOMA
Body of brave African warriors — IMPI
Body of facts or information — SCIENCE
Body of jurors — PANEL
Body of knowledge — LORE
Body of law — CODE
Body of learning — LORE
Body of water — COVE, POND, RIVER
Body of water at International Falls — RAINY LAKE
Body of water surrounded by land — LAKE
Body part — ABDOMEN, HIP
Body powder — TALC
Body trunks — TORSI
Body-shop item — PAINT
Body: Comb. form — SOMAT
Bodyguard — ESCORT
Boer burg — STAD
Boer legislature — RAAD
Boer statesman — SMUTS
Boer town — STAD
Boesky and Tors — IVANS
Boesky of finance — IVAN
Boffin — BRAIN
Bog — MIRE
Bog down — MIRE
Bog fuel — PEAT
Bog product — PEAT
Bogart classic — THE MALTESE FALCON
Bogart fans, e.g. — CULT
Bogart film, 1943 — SAHARA
Bogart role, 1941 — SPADE
Bogart's Betty — LAUREN
Bogart's Lauren — BABY
Bogart-Hepburn film — THE AFRICAN QUEEN
Bogey — SPOOK
Bogey beater — PAR
Bogey minus one — PAR
Bogey's better — PAR
Bogged down — MIRED
Boggle — FALTER, HESITATE
Boggs of baseball — WADE
Boggy wasteland — MOOR
Bogie classic — THE AFRICAN QUEEN
Bogota awakener? — COLOMBIAN COFFEE
Bogs — MIRES, QUAGS
Bogus — FAKE, FALSE, SHAM
Bohea, e.g. — TEA
Bohemia's neighbor — MORAVIA
Bohemian — ARTY
Bohemian headgear — BERET
Bohemian religious leader Jan — HUS
Bohr and Borge — DANES
Boil — SCALD, SEETHE
Boil down — DECOCT, DIGEST
Boiled _____ — IN OIL
Boiled shirt adornment — STUD
Boiler-room workers — PHONERS
Bois de Boulogne, e.g. — PARC
Boisterous — LOUD
Boisterous frolics — ROMPS
Boite de _____ (nightclub) — NUIT
Boito works — OPERAS
Bokhara or Tuzla — RUG
Bold — BRAZEN
Bold and free — MOD
Bold one — DARER
Bold, merry women — PEATS
Boleyn or Hathaway — ANNE
Bolger or Charles — RAY
Bolger sang about her — AMY
Bolivian export — TIN
Bolivian tanager — YENI
Bollix — ERR
Bologna bye-bye — CIAO
Bolognese boniface — OSTE
Bolognese painter: 1665-1747 — CRESPI
Bolshevik victim — TSAR
Bolster — PILLOW
Bolster, in a way — PROP UP
Bolt — ABSCOND
Bolt holder — T NUT
Bolt together — ELOPE
Bolt's partner — NUT
Bolt-head sides — PANES
Bolted — ATE, RAN
Bolted grain — MEAL
Bolus — PILL
Bomb — ATTACK
Bombard — BLITZ, PELT
Bombarded — SHELLED
Bombardment by actor Jimmy? — SMITS BLITZ
Bombast: rant — RODOMONTADE
Bombastic talk — RANT

Bombastic talker or writer — WORDSTER
Bombay baby sitter — AMAH
Bombay bigwig — RANA
Bombay royalty members — RANEES
Bombay wraps — SARIS
Bombeck and namesakes — ERMAS
Bombeck, the columnist — ERMA
Bomber force, for short — SAC
Bomber's door — BOMB BAY
Bombinate — DRONE
Bombs, etc — AMMO
Bombs: sl. — LAYS AN EGG
Bomito genus — SARDA
Bon-voyage party — SEND OFF
Bon _____ (cheap) — MARCHE
Bon ton — ELITE, TASTE
Bon vivant — GOOD TIME CHARLIE, EPICURE, SPORT
Bon-voyage bashes — SEND OFFS
Bona _____ — FIDE
Bonbon — SWEET
Bonbons — CHOCOLATES
Bond — BAIL, JOIN, TIE, UNION
Bond foe — AURUM FINGER
Bond or Smiley, e.g. — MASTER SPY
Bond providers — BAILSMEN
Bond rating — AAA
Bond ratings — AAS
Bond's alma mater — ETON
Bond-servant — SLAVE
Bonds — TIES
Bondsman of old — ESNE
Bondsman's client — BAILEE
Bondsmen — SERFS
Bone — ULNA
Bone below a humerus — ULNA
Bone breakers, in a way — STICKS AND STONES
Bone cavities — ANTRA
Bone cavity — ANTRUM
Bone dividing the nostrils — VOHEE
Bone docs — OSTEOS
Bone juncture — JOINT
Bone marrow: Prefix — MYEL
Bone or fish — CUTTLE
Bone up — STUDY
Bone: Comb. form — OSSI, OSTE, OSTEOS
Bone: Prefix — OSSI, OSTE
Bonebreaker's cousin — ERNE
Boner — FOUL UP
Bones — OSSAS
Bones of the forearm — RADII
Bones up on — CRAMS
Bones, in Vegas — DICE
Bonet of "A Different World" — LISA
Bonheur and Ponselle — ROSAS
Boniface's bonhomie — HEARTINESS
Boniface's domain — INN
Bonito sharks — MAKOS
Bonkers — LOCO
Bonkers, in Britain — SCATTY
Bonn article — EINNE
Bonn expletives — ACHS
Bonn wife — FRAU
Bonnet buzzer — BEE
Bonnet's cousin — TAM
Bonneville and Hoover — DAMS
Bonnie babies — BAIRNS
Bonnie bairn — LASS
Bonnie or Clyde — OUTLAW
Bono and Liston — SONNYS
Bonsai tree — MING
Bony — OSSEOUS, OSTEAL
Bony fish — TELEOST
Boo-boo — ERROR
Boo-boos — SLIPS
Boob-tube precursor — RADIO
Booboos — SLIPUPS
Booby _____ — TRAP
Boodle — HAUL
Boogie-man chaser — NIGHT LIGHT
Boojum — SNARK
Book — OPUS, TOME
Book after Joel — AMOS
Book appendixes — ADDENDA
Book back — SPINE
Book by Admiral Byrd — ALONE
Book by Bryn: 1976 — EST
Book by Byrd — ALONE
Book by Ciardi — AS IF
Book by D.S. Freeman — R E LEE
Book by Gore Vidal — BURR
Book by Haggard — SHE
Book by Julian Huxley — ANTS
Book by Oates — THEM
Book by Peter Evans — ARI
Book club offering — NOVEL
Book cover — JACKET
Book holder — RAMP, SHELF
Book jacket plug — BLURB
Book leaf — FOLIO
Book of hours — HORA
Book of maps — ATLAS
Book of prayers — MISSAL
Book of religious chants — GRADUAL
Book of the Apoc. — MACC
Book of the bible — ACTS, HOSEA, MICAH
Book of the Bible: Abbr. — HOS
Book of the N.T. — APOC
Book page — LEAF
Book page size — OCTAVO
Book part — CHAPTER, SPINE
Book parts — SPINES
Book people: Abbr. — EDS
Book repository — STUDY
Book review? — AUDIT
Book that's full of meaning? — DICTIONARY
Book-cover displays — TITLINGS
Book-jacket item — BLURB
Book: Abbr. — VOL
Bookbinding leather — ROAN
Booked — ENGAGED
Booked the boondocks — BARNSTORMED
Booker T.'s group — MGS
Bookie's concern — ODDS
Bookie's quote — ODDS
Bookies give these — ODDS
Bookish person — PEDANT
Bookkeeping abbr. — ACCT
Bookkeeping entry — DEBIT
Books of records — LIBRI
Bookworm — BIBLIOPHAGE, PORER, READER
Bookworm's challenge — TOME
Boom — HUM, ROAR, SPAR
Boom type — SONIC
Boom variety — SONIC
Boon — GIFT
Boone or O'Brien — PAT
Boons — GODSENDS
Boor — LOUT
Boor's problem — GROSSNESS
Boorish — RUDE
Boorish one — LOUT
Boost in price — HIKE
Booster — FAN
Booster rocket — AGENA
Boot — TRAINEE
Boot bottom — SOLE
Boot camp's cousin — DEPOT
Boot country — ITALY
Boot extension — SPUR
Boot loop — STRAP
Boot material — COWHIDE
Boot nation — ITALY
Boot tie — LACET
Boot-camp housing — BAR-RACKS
Boot-camp pastimes — DRILLS
Booted — SHOD
Booted feline — PUSS
Booth — STAND
Booth at a state fair — CONCESSION
Booth's target — LINCOLN
Boothbay Harbor locale — MAINE
Booths — LOGES
Bootless — NOUSE
Booty — LOOT, PELF, SPOILS
Booze — DRINK, HOOCH
Boozers — SOTS
Borax carriers — MULE TRAINS

Borax once imported from Tibet — TINCAL
Border on — ABUT
Bordered — EDGED
Borders — EDGES
Boredom — ACEDIA
Borg, e.g. — SWEDE
Borgia in-law — ESTE
Boring tool — AUGER, BIT
Boris Karloff, aka William Henry _____ — PRATT
Born — NEE
Borne by the wind — EOLIAN
Borne by the wind — EOLIC
Borneo ape, for short — ORANG
Borodin hero — IGOR
Borodin's prince — IGOR
Borodin's unfinished opera "_____ Igor" — PRINCE
Borscht ingredient — BEET
Bosh! — ROT
Bosox's park — FENWAY
Boss — UMBO
Boss Tweed's nemesis — NAST
Bossa _____ — NOVA
Bosses, in Roma — CAPOS
Boston Bobby — ORR
Boston or ground follower — IVY
Boston Red _____ — SOX
Boston's airport — LOGAN
Boswell was one — SCOT
Botanical interstices — AREOLAS
Botanist Gray — ASA
Botanist Gray and namesakes — ASAS
Botch — SPOIL
Bother — AFFLICT, PESTER, TEASE
Bothered — IRKED
Bothers — ANNOYS, IRKS
Bothersome — IN ONES HAIR
Botswanna boss — BWANA
Bottle stopper — CORK
Bottom line — SUM
Bottom line figures — NETS
Bottomless hole — ABYSS
Bottomless pit — ABYSS
Bottoms — BASES
Boudoir attire — NEGLIGEE
Bounce — BOUND, RECOIL, SKIP, VIGOR
Bouncy dance — SHAG
Bound together — JOINED
Bound with leather — STRAPPED
Boundary — LIMIT, METE
Bounders — CADS
Boundless — VAST
Bouquet — AROMA
Bouquet sans color — AROMAS
Bourse — SALE
Bout of indulgence — SPREE
Boutique — SHOP
Boutique worker — SALESWOMAN
Bovary namesakes — EMMAS
Bovine bellow — MOO
Bow or Barton — CLARA
Bow-tie style — CLIP ON
Bowie's last stand — ALAMO
Bowler or boater — HAT
Bowler's problem — SPLIT
Bowler's woe — SPLIT
Bowlers — HATS
Bowline or sheepshank — KNOT
Bowling alley — LANE
Bowling division — FRAME
Bowling is his game — KEGLER
Bowling score — SPARE
Bows out — EXITS
Bowsprit — SPAR
Box — ENCASE, SPAR
Box a bit — SPAR
Box camera man — EASTMAN
Box for oolong — CADDY
Box in — ENCASE
Box office signs — SROS
Box-elder genus — ACER
Boxeo or béisbol — DEPORTE
Boxer Griffith — EMILE
Boxer Spinks — LEON
Boxer's poke — JAB
Boxers' aides — HANDLERS
Boxing finish — TKO
Boxing great — ALI
Boxing ploys — FEINTS
Boxing practice — SPARRING
Boy detective of fiction — EMIL
Boy Scout beginner — TENDERFOOT
Boy Scout group — PATROL
Boy Scout of ranking — EAGLE
Boy sponsored at a baptism — GODSON
Boyer-Bergman thriller — GASLIGHT
Boys from Syracuse — ORANGEMEN
Boys of Aberdeen — LADS
Boys' org. — BSA
Boys, in Baza — NINOS
BPOE member — ELK
BPOE word — ELKS
Br. composer — ERNE
Br. fliers — RAF
Br. gun — STEN
Br. money — LSD
Br. naval letters — HMS
Brace — BEND, STAY, TWO
Bracelet, e.g. — BANGLE
Bracing — COLD, TONIC
Bracing drink — TODDY
Bracket — CONCH, SCONCE
Bracket-supported window — ORIEL
Brackish — BRINY, SALINE
Brackish lake in the USSR — ARAL
Brad and spad — NAILS
Brad's cousin — NAIL
Bradbury's field — SCI FI
Bradley and Sharif — OMARS
Bradley campus site — PEORIA
Bradley from NJ — SEN
Bradley or Bentsen — SENATOR
Bradley or Nunn — SENATOR
Brads and spads — NAILS
Braes — HILLSIDES
Brag — BOAST
Brag musically, in a way — BLOW ONES HORN
Braga of films — SONIA
Braggart — CROWER
Braggarts — BOASTERS
Brahma — HINDU
Brahman, e.g. — CASTE
Brahmin — SNOB
Brahms or Mendelssohn composition: Abbr. — CTO
Braid — COIL, PLAIT
Braided — WOVE
Braided hair — PIGTAIL
Braids — ENLACES
Brain — MIND
Brain canal — ITER
Brain covering — DURA
Brain passage — ITER
Brain scan, for short — EEG
Brain specialist's rec. — EEG
Brain wave — EEG
Braincases — CRANIA
Brainchild — IDEA
Brains or beauty — ASSET
Brainstorm — IDEA
Brainstorming product — IDEA
Brake part — SHOE
Bram Stoker subject — VAMPIRE
Bramble — BRIER
Bran source — CEREAL
Branagh of "Dead Again" — KENNETH
Branch — ARM, RAMUS, SPUR, TWIG
Branch angle — AXIL
Branch of dentistry — ODONTOLOGY
Branch of knowledge — OLOGY
Branch of learning — OLOGY
Branch of math. — GEOM
Branch of mathematics — ALGEBRA
Branch of peace — OLIVE
Branch of physics: Abbr. — DYN
Branch, to a Botanist — RAMUS
Branched — RAMOSE
Branches — ARMS, RAMI
Branches off — DIVERGES
Branching — RAMOSE
Brand — BURN
Brand new — UNUSED

Brand of fiber — ARNEL
Brand of oat — WILD
Brand or Chamberlain — NEVILLE
Brandish — WAVE, WIELD
Brando role in "I Remember Mama" — NELS
Brando's last dance in Paris — TANGO
Brandy cocktail — ALEXANDER, SIDECAR
Brandy glasses — SNIFTERS
Brandy vessel — SNIFTER
Brandy-based cocktail — STINGER
Brants — GEESE
Brash — SAUCY
Brass alloy — LATTEN
Brass or pewter — ALLOY
Brass player — HORNIST
Brass silencer — MUTE
Brass wheels — LIMO
Brass wind instrument — HORN
Brassica oleracea acephala — KALE
Brassica oleracea caulorapa — KOHLRABI
Brassica rapa — TURNIP
Brat — IMP
Brat Pack's Rob — LOWE
Brat's blowipe — PEA SHOOTER
Brat's rebuttal — SASS
Brats — HELLIONS
Brats are often holy ones — TERRORS
Bratty, friend of Hobbes — CALVIN
Braun or Le Gallienne — EVA
Braun or Marie Saint — EVA
Brava or Rica preceder — COSTA
Brave bull — TORO
Brave lass — HEROINE
Brave Nixon — OTIS
Brave who could really hammer — HENRY AARON
Bravery — VALOR
Bravo or Branco — RIO
Bravo, in Barcelona — OLE
Bravos, in Bilbao — OLES
Bravura — DASH
Brawl — RIOT
Brawl aftermaths — SHINERS
Brawl, in Bologna — RISSA
Brawl? — DONNYBROOK
Brawled — RIOTED
Brawls — AFFRAYS
Brawny — MUSCULAR
Braxton and Thomas of the C.S.A. — BRAGGS
Bray — HEEHAW
Brazen — INSOLENT
Brazier — HIBACHI
Brazil city on the Para — BELEM
Brazil's _____ Branco — RIO
Brazilian airline — VARIG
Brazilian bean — COFFEE
Brazilian bird — MACAW
Brazilian city — RECIFE
Brazilian coffee — RIO
Brazilian dance — SAMBA
Brazilian Indian — CARIB
Brazilian macaw — ARARA
Brazilian mammal — TAPIR
Brazilian money of old — REIS
Brazilian novelist Jorge — AMADO
Brazilian parrots — ARAS
Brazilian plantations — FAZENDAS
Brazilian seaport — BELEM, NATAL
Brazilian soccer star — PELE
Brazilian state — ACRE, CEARA, NATAL
Brazilian title — DOM
Brazos — RIVER
Brea pit product — TAR
Breach — GAP, RIFT
Bread — MOOLAH
Bread and butter — LETTER
Bread choice — WHITE
Bread in Beauvais — PAIN
Bread part — CRUST
Bread spread — OLEO
Bread spread for short — MAYO
Bread unit — LOAF
Bread, in Brest — PAIN
Bread: Comb. form — ARTO
Breadbasket — TUMMY
Breadth — WIDTH
Breadth; scope — GAMUT
Breadwinner — WAGE EARNER
Break — BUST, REST, SMASH, SNAP
Break a commandment — SIN
Break a fast — EAT
Break bread — EAT, DINE
Break down — COLLAPSE
Break down one's spirit — UNMAN
Break ground — DIG
Break in — INTERRUPT
Break into smithereens — SHATTER
Break loose — FLY THE COOP
Break of day — DAWN
Break one's word — RENEGE
Break open — TAP
Break out — ITEMIZE
Break suddenly — SNAP
Break the ice — BEGIN
Break the tape — WIN
Break with — DITCH, LEAVE
Breakable — FRAIL
Breaker of a camel's back — LAST STRAW
Breakers — SURF
Breakfast cereal — BRAN, FARINA
Breakfast choice — BACON, BRAN, CEREAL
Breakfast comestible — BACON
Breakfast dish — OMELET
Breakfast fare — EGGS BENEDICT, OATMEAL, OMELET
Breakfast food — CEREAL
Breakfast item — OATMEAL
Breakfast items — EGGS
Breakfast option — CEREAL
Breakfast room — DINETTE
Breakfast starter — GRAPEFRUIT
Breakfast table item — CREAMER
Breakfast treat — BACON, RASHERS, WAFFLE
Breakfast treat from Philly — SCRAPPLE
Breakfast-food magnate — POST
Breakout at high school? — ACNE
Breaks a confidence — LEAKS
Breaks a habit — WEANS
Breaks a law — VIOLATES
Breaks apart — SHATTERS
Breaks to harness — TAMES
Breaks up — PARTS
Breaks, as broncos — TAMES
Breakwater — MOLE, PIER, WHARF
Breastbone — STERNUM
Breastplate — PECTORAL
Breath of life — SOUL
Breathe — INHALE, RESPIRE
Breathe hard — HEAVE, PANT
Breathed — RESPIRED
Breather — LUNG
Breather's needs — NARES
Breathes — LIVES
Breathes audibly — PANTS
Breathes heavily — PANTS
Breathing — ALIVE
Breathing apparatus — LUNGS
Breathing disorder — ASTHMA
Breathing noise — RALE
Breathing sound — RALE
Brecht-Weill opus — THREEPENNY OPERA
Bred — RAISED
Breeches — PANTS
Breed — BEGET
Breed of dairy cattle — HOLSTEIN
Breed of duck — PEKIN
Breed of hog — DUROC
Breed of horse — ARAB, MORGAN
Breed of sheep — MERINO

Breeding ground — HOTBED
Breezes: Lat. — AURAE
Breezy — AIRY, BLOWY
Breezy greeting — HI YA
Breezy OK's — YEPS
Breezy turn-down — NOPE
Brenda of comics — STARR
Brenda or Bart — STARR
Brenda or Kay — STARR
Breslau's river — ODER
Brest beast — ANE
Breton kin — CELT
Bretons or Britains — CELTS
Bretons, e.g. — CELTS
Brevity — SHORTNESS
Brew — ALE, BOIL, MIX
Brewer of note — TERESA
Brewer or Wright — TERESA
Brewer's buy — MALT
Brewer's grain — MALT
Brewer's need — HOPS, MALT
Brewers' city in France? — ALES
Brewery unit — OAST
Brezhnev — LEONID
Brian _____, early Irish king — BORU
Brian De _____ — PALMA
Brian Piccolo player — CAAN
Bribe of a sort — KICKBACK
Bribes — SOPS
Bric-a- _____ — BRAC
Bric-a-brac — CURIO
Brice's Snooks — BABY
Brick-baker — OVEN
Brick Brewer's staple — MALT
Brick for a mesa home — ADOBE
Brick layers — MASONS
Bridal accessory — GARTER
Bridal car sign — JUST MARRIED
Bridal party — SHOWER
Bridal path — AISLE
Bridal shower gift — CHINA
Bride of Angel Clare — TESS
Bride of Lohengrin — ELSA
Bride or groom — VOWER
Bridge — BOND, GAME, OVERPASS, SPAN, VIADUCT
Bridge action — REBID
Bridge assets — HONORS
Bridge authority — GOREN
Bridge beam — I BAR
Bridge between electrodes — ARC
Bridge bid — DOUBLE, PASS, SLAM
Bridge call — REBID
Bridge coup — SLAM
Bridge declarations — BIDS
Bridge designer — EADS
Bridge expert — GOREN
Bridge expert Jacoby — OSWALD
Bridge feats — SLAMS
Bridge fees — TOLLS
Bridge forerunner — WHIST
Bridge frameworks — TRESTLES
Bridge gaffe — RENEGE
Bridge holding — HONORS, TEN ACE
Bridge in St. Louis — EADS
Bridge maven Charles — GOREN
Bridge no-no, for short — NIG
Bridge opener — I CLUB, NORTH
Bridge option — PASS
Bridge over the East River — TRIBORO
Bridge part — DECK
Bridge participants — PLAYERS
Bridge passes — BYS
Bridge play — TRUMP
Bridge players — EASTS
Bridge plays — RUFFS
Bridge position — EAST, SOUTH
Bridge requirement — CARDS
Bridge reversal — SET
Bridge savant — GOREN
Bridge seat — WEST, EAST
Bridge section — SPAN
Bridge stratagem — SIGNAL
Bridge suit — HEARTS
Bridge support — ABUTMENT, PIER, TRESTLE
Bridge supports — PIERS
Bridge term — PASS
Bridge thrill — SLAM
Bridge to paradise, in Islam — SIRAT
Bridge toppers — TRUMPS
Bridges — SPANS
Bridle — REIN IN
Bridle flaps — BLINDERS
Bridle hand — LEFT
Bridle part — BIT
Brie portion — WEDGE
Brief — CONCISE
Brief appearance in a movie — CAMEO
Brief cheer — RAH
Brief contests — SET TOS
Brief effort — STAB
Brief follower — CASE
Brief gander — GLIM
Brief joy rides — SPINS
Brief look — GLIM
Brief missive — NOTE
Brief nap — WINK
Brief news release — BLURB
Brief news report — FLASH
Brief news story — ITEM
Brief piece of writing — SCRIP
Brief quarrel — SPAT
Brief respites — PAUSES
Brief sheepish comment — BLEAT
Brief try — STAB
Brief vacation — WEEKENDER
Brief, violent argument — SET TO
Briefly brilliant stars — NOVAE
Brier — ERICA
Brigade — FORCE
Brigadier's neighbor — COLONEL
Brigand — BANDIT
Brigette _____ — BARDOT
Bright — APT, RIANT, SMART, SUNNY
Bright and amusing — WITTY
Bright beam — LASER
Bright Bear — URSA
Bright color — STRAWBERRY
Bright decorations — SPANGLES
Bright idea? — BULB
Bright light — NEON
Bright reds — SCARLETS
Bright sign component — NEON
Bright star — NOVA
Bright thought, to Pierre — IDEE
Bright-green municipal officials? — EMERALDERMEN
Brighten up — ILLUME
Brightest star in a constellation — COR
Brightly colored fish — OPAH, TETRA
Brightly-colored sea anemone — OPELET
Brightness — GLARE, SHEEN
Brighton's neighbor — HOVE
Brilliance — ECLAT, EFFULGENCE, SPLENDOR
Brilliant — RADIANT
Brilliant displays — POMPS
Brilliant fish — OPAH
Brilliant ploy — COUP
Brilliant star — NOVA
Brilliant stroke — COUP
Brilliant success — ECLAT
Brilliant unit — CARAT
Brilliant, as a color — NEON
Brilliantly colored fish — BETTA
Brim — EDGE, LIP, RUT
Brimless hat — TOQUE
Brine — PICKLE
Brine treatment specialists — PICKLERS
Bring — DELIVER
Bring _____ (animate) — TO LIFE
Bring about — ENGENDER, INDUCE
Bring back — RENEW, RESTORE, REVIVE
Bring down — RAZE
Bring down the house — WIN
Bring forth a lamb — YEAN
Bring home the bacon — EARN
Bring into agreement — ALIGN

Bring into court — CITE
Bring into existence — GENERATE
Bring into harmony — ATTUNE
Bring into memory — ADAPT
Bring joy — ELATE
Bring off — ATTAIN
Bring on — INCUR
Bring out — AIR, EDUCE, EVOKE
Bring to an end — FOLD
Bring to bear — EXERT
Bring to earth — LAND
Bring to life — CREATE
Bring to light — EXPOSE
Bring to mind — RECALL
Bring to ruin — UNDO
Bring to terms — RECONCILE
Bring together — AMASS, MARRY
Bring together at a focal point — CONCENTER
Bring up — RAISE, REAR
Bring up the rear — LAG, LAST, TRAIL
Bring up to date — REVISE
Bringing up — REARING
Bringing up the rear — BEHIND
Brings bad luck to — JINXES
Brings forth — SPAWNS
Brings forth young — YEANS
Brings home the bacon — EARNS
Brings into accord — ATTUNES
Brings into being — CREATES
Brings on — CAUSES
Brings out — EDUCES
Brings to court — SUES
Brings up — REARS
Brings up baby — REARS
Brink — BRIM, VERGE
Brink or border — RIM
Brinker — HANS
Brinker or Henie — SKATER
Brinker's bravery? — DUTCH COURAGE
Brinker's land — HOLLAND
Brinker, the skater — HANS
Briny — SALINE
Brisk — AGILE
Brisk and cheerful — PERKY
Briskly — APACE
Bristish molasses — TREACLE
Bristle — RESENT, SETA
Bristle: Comb. form — SETI
Bristlelike appendages — ARISTAS
Bristlelike structure — ARISTA
Bristles — SETA, SETAE, ARISTAE
Bristling — ERECT
Bristly — SETAL, SETOSE
Bristly appendages — ARISTAE
Bristly part — SETA
Bristly plant — TEASEL
Brit's vacation — HOL
Brit. — ENG
Brit. army institute — RMA
Brit. award — DSO
Brit. business abbr. — LTD
Brit. capital — LON
Brit. carbines — STENS
Brit. coins, of old — SHS
Brit. colony in SE Spain — GIB
Brit. commoner — BARONET
Brit. county — SHIRE
Brit. courtesy titles — ESQS
Brit. dance org. — RAD
Brit. decoration — OBE
Brit. dictionary — OED
Brit. gumshoe — TEC
Brit. gun — STEN
Brit. lexicon — OED
Brit. medieval pennies — STERS
Brit. mil. gp. — RAF
Brit. monetary base — STG
Brit. money — STER
Brit. money, formerly — LSD
Brit. navigation aid — DECCA
Brit. office holder — MP
Brit. prince — EDW
Brit. raincoat — MAC
Brit. standby unit — RNR
Brit. weapon — STEN
British _____ — ISLES
British abbreviation "p" — PENCE
British actor Jeremy — IRONS
British actress Johnson — CELIA
British actress Mary — URE
British actress Wendy — HILLER
British alphabet end — ZED
British ballerina — TAIT
British biscuit — COOKIE
British bishop's headdress — MITRE
British boob tube — TELLY
British bread — QUID
British bye-bye — TA TA
British carbine — STEN
British center — CENTRE
British chariot — ESSED
British chinaware — SPODE
British Christmas entertainment — PANTOMINE
British cleaning lady — CHAR
British coins — PENCE
British coins, for short — SOVS
British collation — TEA
British Columbia sound — NOOTKA
British comic Idle — ERIC
British composer Frederick — DELIUS
British conservative — TORY
British container of a kind — DUSTBIN
British court for probate, divorce, admiralty — PDA
British customs documents — TRANSIRES
British dance org. — RAD
British emblem — LION
British exclamation — BLOODY
British fabric — TWEED
British farewells — TATAS
British folklorist Peter Mason — OPIE
British football — RUGBY
British gun — STEN
British handcuffs — DARBIES
British Honduras today — BELIZE
British hoods — YOBS
British hooligans — YOBS
British import from Chile — NITRE
British island — LUNDY
British jails — GAOLS
British Keno or Lotto game — HOUSEY HOUSEY
British marquee — TENT
British measure — METRE
British measure of volume — LITRE
British medical org. — NHS
British miler — COE
British mothers — MUMS
British musician Brian — ENO
British neighbors — WALES AND ENGLAND
British nobleman — EARL
British North America — CANADA
British Nova Scotia — BNS
British novelist Geoffrey — HOUSEHOLD
British painter John _____: 1761-1807 — OPIE
British painter-designer Roger _____ — FURSE
British passenger vehicles — TRAMS
British PM during the U.S. Civil War — PALMERSTON
British policeman — BOBBY
British politicians — TORIES
British prime minister: 1970-74 — HEATH
British prince — EDWARD, WILLIAM
British princess — ANNE
British pub order — PINT
British public school — ETON
British race-track tout — SPIV
British refresher — TEA
British refresher, informally — CUPPA
British river city — LONDON
British sailor — MATELOT
British sailor, of old — LIMEY
British sausages — BANGERS

British scientist John Scott _____ — HALDANE
British sneaker — SAND SHOE
British symbol — LION
British taps signal — LAST STOP
British title — BARONET
British title holders — LORDS
British title of honor — BARONET
British traffic cops — POINTS-MEN
British TV — TELLY
British unit of length — ROOD
British V.I.P.'s — PMS
British vehicles — TRAMS
British version of a biblical name — BEULA
British W.W.II heroes — RAF
British weapon — STEN
British writer known for his romantic novels — HAWKINS
Brittany seaport — BREST
Britten opus — OPERA
Bro. and dau. — RELS
Bro. or sis. — REL, SIB
Broach — AIR, CUT, OPEN
Broad-topped hill — LOMA
Broad — VAST, WIDE
Broad _____, in a church — AISLE
Broad expanse — ACRES
Broad shoulders — WIDE
Broad-beamed — STOUT
Broad-brimmed hat — SHOVEL
Broad-minded — OPEN
Broad: Comb. form — LATI
Broadcast — AIR, AIRED, SEND
Broadcast — SHOW, STREW, TELEVISE
Broadcast agcy. — FCC
Broadcast medium — RADIO
Broadcast network — ABC
Broadcast to Europe — TRANS-MIT
Broadcaster's need — AIR
Broadcaster's problem? — MIKE FRIGHT
Broadcasting — AIRING, ON AIR
Broadcasts seed again — RESOWS
Broadhorns — ARKS
Broadloom — RUG
Broadside — SALVO
Broadside's opposite — END ON
Broadway acronym — ANTA
Broadway area — RIALTO
Broadway backer — ANGEL
Broadway beginning — ACT I
Broadway benefactor — ANGEL
Broadway blockbuster — CATS
Broadway dazzle — NEONS
Broadway gas — NEON
Broadway gp. — ANTA
Broadway group — CAST
Broadway hit — CATS
Broadway hit of 1977 — EVITA
Broadway hit of 1982 — NINE
Broadway Joe — NAMATH
Broadway lights — NEONS
Broadway luminary — STAR
Broadway musical — ANNIE
Broadway musical since 1982 — CATS
Broadway musical: 1982 — NINE
Broadway offering — DRAMA, PLAY
Broadway org. — ANTA
Broadway play: 1985 — AS IS
Broadway show — MAME
Broadway sign — SRO
Broadway smash — HIT
Broadway Tevye — ZERO
Broadway tune? — LULLABUY
Broadway VIP — DIR
Broadway's Bailey — PEARL
Broadway's Cariou — LEN
Broadway's Jane — COWL
Broadway's Logan — JOSH
Broadway's long-running smash, with "A" — CHORUS LINE
Broadway's singing orphan — ANNIE
Broadway's Tune — TOMMY
Brobdingnagian — HUGE, LARGE, MIGHTY
Brocaded fabric — LAME
Brochette — SPIT
Brochure of advertising — LEAFLET
Brock or Gehrig — LOU
Brogan — SHOE
Brogue — SHOE
Brogue for one — ACCENT
Brogue or buck — SHOE
Broil a steak rare — CHAR
Brokaw specialties — NEWSCASTS
Brokaw's beat — NEWS
Brokaw, for one — BROAD-CASTER
Broke bread — ATE
Broke the law — VIOLATED
Broke up a shutout — SCORED
Broke up or in — STAVED
Broken out — ACNED
Broken pottery — SHARD
Broken-down — KAPUT
Broker — REALTOR
Broker's Swiss shares selection? — ALPEN STOCK
Broker's tip — BUY
Broker, often — SELLER
Brokerage fee — ROYALTY
Brom Bones's creator — IRVING
Bronco's home st. — COLO
Bronco-busting event — RODEO
Bronowski's "The _____ of Man" — ASCENT
Bronte heroine — EYRE
Bronte or Dickinson — EMILY
Bronte settings — MOORS
Bronte's Jane — EYRE
Brönte's trap? (White) — CHARLOTTES WEB
Bronx attraction — ZOO
Bronze — TAN
Bronze and iron — AGES
Bronze Star — DECORATION
Bronze, for one — AGE
Brooch — CAMEO, CLASP
Brooch part — PIN
Brooches — PINS
Brood — MOPE
Brood of pheasants — NIDE
Brook — RILL
Brook or Mary — ASTOR
Brooke and Hughes — RUPERT
Brooklet — RILL
Brooklyn follower — ITE
Brooklyn music cntr. — BAM
Brooklyn or Manhattan follower — ITE
Brooklyn's "field of dreams" — EBBETS
Brooklyn's _____ Institute — PRATT
Brooks and Blanc — MELS
Brooks or Allen — MEL
Brooks or Ferrer — MEL
Brooks or Ott — MEL
Broom _____: comic witch — HILDA
Bros. — RELS
Brosnan TV role — STEELE
Brothel — BATH
Brother — FRA
Brother of Electra — ORESTES
Brother of Eris — ARES
Brother of Jacob — ESAU
Brother of JFK and Robt. — EDW
Brother of Moses — AARON
Brother of Romulus — REMUS
Brother of Seth — ABEL
Brother's daughter — NIECE
Brother's son — NEPHEW
Brother's wife — SISTER IN LAW
Brothers in an abbey — FRAS
Brought about deviously — WORMED
Brought back into use — RESTORED
Brought down — FELLED
Brought down the house — RAZED
Brought forth — ISSUED
Brought forth a lamb — YEANED

Brought in from the driveway — GARAGED
Brought into being — BORN
Brought into harmony — TUNED
Brought into memory — ATTUNED
Brought legal action — SUED
Brought to a halt — ARRESTED
Brought to court — SUED
Brought under control — REINED
Brought up — REARED
Brouhaha — ADO, MELEE, ROW, SET TO, TO DO
Brown bear found in Alaska — KODIAK
Brown color — TAWNY
Brown earth pigment — UMBER
Brown feline from Africa — ABYSSINIAN
Brown horse — BAY
Brown October quaff of song — ALE
Brown of renown — LES
Brown pigments — SEPIA
Brown study — REVERIE
Brown, in Brittany — BRUN
Browne's comic Viking — HAGAR
Browned — TOASTED
Browned by the sun — TANNED
Browned-off — BORED
Brownies' org. — GSA
Browning's "_____ Lippo Lippi" — FRA
Browning's "_____ Vogler" — ABT
Browning's Ben Ezra — RABBI
Brownish gray — TAUPE
Brownish orange — TAWNY
Brownish photo — SEPIA
Brownish pigment — SEPIA, SIENNA
Brownish purple — PUCE
Brownish yellow — TAWNY
Brownish-crimson — MAROON
Brownish-yellow — TAWNY
Browns — TANS
Brows — FOREHEADS
Browses — LEAFS
Brubeck of music — DAVE
Bruce and Sebastian — CABOTS
Bruce of films — NIGEL
Bruce of the flicks — DERN
Bruce or Laura — DERN
Bruckner namesakes — ANTONS
Bruhn of the ballet — ERIK
Bruin — BEAR
Bruin Bobby, and family — ORRS
Bruins coll. — UCLA
Bruins' campus — UCLA
Brumal blanket — SNOW
Brume — MIST
Brummell — BEAU
Brunch — MEAL
Brunch choice, perhaps — LOX OR BAGEL
Brunch dish from Wales — RAREBIT
Brunch or lunch — MEAL
Brunch, for instance — MEAL
Brunched — ATE
Brunei V.I.P. — SULTAN
Brunei's location — BORNEO
Brunt — IMPACT
Brunt of the hurricane — FORCE
Brush off — SNUB
Brush partner — COMB
Brush, in Brest — BROSSE
Brusque — BLUNT, SHORT
Brusque person's command — CUT IT SHORT
Brussels-based command — NATO
Brussels-based org. — NATO
Brutal — BESTIAL
Brute — YAHOO
Brutus was one — ROMAN
Brutus' book — LIBER
Bryant and Baker — ANITAS
Bryant or Loos — ANITA
Bryant, but not Gumbel — ANITA
Bryce and Grand — CANYONS
Bryce Canyon locale — UTAH
Bryce Canyon state — UTAH
Brynner's namesakes — YULS
Bryophyte — ELI
Bu. or Pk. — AMT
Bubble — BLEB, BOIL
Bubble up — SEETHE
Bubbled — BOILED
Bubbling — PERKING
Bubbly drink — COLA
Buccal — ORAL
Buccaneer — PIRATE
Buccaneer's base — TAMPA
Buccaneers of _____ Bay — TAMPA
Bucephalus, e.g. — STEED
Bucharest capital — ROMANIA
Bucharest native — ROUMANIAN
Buck — DOLLAR, ONE, SINGLE, SMACKER, STAG
Buck character — OLAN
Buck chaser — AROO
Buck farmer's planting — DRAGON SEED
Buck heroine — OLAN
Buck or bull — MALE
Buck or byte preceder — MEGA
Buck or doe — HARE
Buck or ram — MALE
Buck private — ROOKIE
Buck's appendages — ANTLERS
Buck's mate — DOE
Buckaroo — COWBOY
Bucket — PAIL
Bucket handle — BAIL
Bucket wood — OAK
Buckeye or piroque — CANOE
Buckeye state — OHIO
Buckeye's coll — OSU
Buckingham or Kensington — PALACE
Buckingham's river — OUSE
Buckle, old style — TARGE
Buckler leader — SWASH
Buckles — TACHES
Bucknell mascot — BISON
Bucks — CASH, MALE RABBITS, ONES
Bucks and stags — MALES
Bucks' beginning — MEGA
Bucks' consorts — DOES
Buckshot — AMMO
Buckwheat — KASHA
Buckwheat cereal — KASHA
Buckwheat tree — TITI
Bucolic — RURAL
Bucolic events — FAIRS
Bucs or Cubs — NINE
Bud-producing branch — STOLON
Bud — GEMMA
Bud and George — ABBOTS
Bud of a sort — GEMMA
Bud or Arnie — PALMER
Bud's comic buddy — LOU
Buddhist concept — TAO
Buddhist discipline — ZEN
Buddhist monk — BONZE, LAMA
Buddhist monk, free from karma — LOHAN
Buddhist monument — STUPA
Buddhist mound — STUPA
Buddhist priests — LAMAS
Buddhist sacred mountain — OMEI
Buddhist sect — ZEN
Buddhist shrine — STUPA
Buddies — CHUMS, PALS, MATES
Buddy — CHUM, MATE, PAL
Buddy of "haw" — HEM
Buddy of Hollywood — EBSEN
Buddy or Max of boxing — BAER
Buddy or Rock fame — HOLLY
Buddy, the drummer — RICH
Budget feature: Abbr. — EST
Budget item — RENT
Buenos _____ — AIRES
Buenos _____ — DIAS
Buff — POLISH
Buffalo — BISON

Buffalo athlete — SABRE
Buffalo Bill — CODY
Buffalo Bill and others — CODYS
Buffalo bird — STARLING
Buffalo Bob Smith's co-star — HOWDY DOODY
Buffalo celebration? — BISON-TENNIAL
Buffalo from the Bronx — UPSTATE
Buffalo hide — BUFF
Buffalo hockey team — SABRES
Buffalo player — BISON
Buffalo roaming grounds — GREAT PLAINS
Buffalo skater — SABRE
Buffalo's lake — ERIE
Buffalo's river — NIAGARA
Buffalo's waterfront — ERIE
Buffalo, for one — CITY
Buffer — PAD
Buffet — SMITE, TABLE, TOSS
Buffet about — TOSS
Buffet features — SALADS
Buffoon — FOOL, PIERROT, ZANY
Bufonidae — TOADS
Bug — BEETLE, GERM, NETTLE, RILE
Bug killer — DDT
Bug of a sort — VIRUS
Bug of sort — FLU
Bug the landlord — HARASS OWNER
Bug's palp — FEELER
Bug's relative — TAP
Bugaboo — OGRE
Bugbear — OGRE
Buggies — PRAMS
Buggy or umbrella — BEACH
Bugle call — TAPS
Bugle call at sunset — TAPS
Bugs Bunny's voice — BLANC
Build — ERECT
Build again — RESTRUCTURE
Builder — ERECTOR, MAKER
Builder of wooden horse — EPEUS
Builder's finishing touches — COPE STONES
Builder's plot — SITE
Builder's rod — REBAR
Builder's unit — LOT
Builders — ERECTORS
Building — ERECTING
Building add-on — ELL
Building addition — ELL, WING
Building annex — ELL
Building beam — I BAR
Building block — BRICK
Building burned by British: 1814 — CAPITOL
Building custodian — JANITOR
Building extension — ELL
Building girder — H BEAM
Building greeters — DOOR-MEN
Building in Bologna — CASA
Building locale — SITE
Building lot — SITE
Building material — ADOBE, CEMENT, GLASS, MORTAR
Building material — STEEL, STONE, TILE, WOOD
Building on Fifth Avenue — EMPIRE STATE
Building part — EAVE, ELL
Building section — ELL
Building sites — LOTS
Building steel — I BARS
Building stone — ASHLAR
Building wing — ALETTE
Building wings — ELLS
Building yard — AREA
Buildings in capital cities — SENATES
Builds — ERECTS
Builds a lawn — SODS
Builds up again — REDEVELOPS
Built — ERECTED
Bulb from Holland — TULIP
Bulb holder — SOCKET
Bulbous plant — TULIP
Bulbous stem base — CROM
Bulgaria's capital — SOFIA
Bulgarian — SLAV
Bulgarian coin — LEV
Bulgarian gold coins — LEVA
Bulgarian salad green? — SOFIARUGULA
Bulgarian weight — TOVAR
Bulge of a barrel — BILGE
Bulging — PROTRUDING
Bulging part of a sail — BAG
Bulks large — LOOMS
Bulky boat — TUB
Bulky package — BALE
Bull — COP, ERROR
Bull — TAURUS
Bull _____ party — MOOSE
Bull chaser — PEN
Bull fiddle — BASS
Bull or jam — SESSION
Bull or Miss — OLE
Bull run site — MANASSAS
Bull Run, to Confederates — MANASSAS
Bull thrower — LASSO
Bull's eye — CENTER
Bull's order — BUY
Bull-session event? — RODEO
Bull: Comb. form — TAURO
Bull: Sp. — TORO
Bulldogs — ELIS
Bulldogs' cousins — BOSTON TERRIERS
Bulldogs, for example — PIPES
Bulldoze, in Soho — RASE
Bullet, in Bilboa — BALA
Bulletin — REPORT
Bullets — AMMO, PELLETS
Bullets, e.g. — TEAM
Bullets, in poker — ACES
Bullfight cheer — OLE
Bullfighter — MATADOR
Bullish indicator — UPTREND
Bullish investor's song — IM A DREAMER
Bullish time — RISE
Bullring — ARENA
Bullring bravos — OLES
Bullring cheers — OLES
Bullring cries — OLES
Bullring hooray — OLE
Bullwinkle, for one — MOOSE
Bully — PICK ON
Bulrush — TULE
Bulwark — TOWER OF STRENGTH
Bulwer-Lytton heroine — IONE
Bulwer-Lytton novel — LEILA
Bum around — DRIFT
Bump — NODE, THUD
Bump into — MEET
Bump mark — DENT
Bump off — DO IN
Bump on the head — SMACK
Bump, in poker — RAISE
Bumper coating — CHROME
Bumpkin — BOOR, CLOD, HICK, OAF, YOKEL
Bumpkin's cousin — NERD
Bumps a Durant — DENTS
Bumps on the skin — MILIA
Bumps or lumps — KNOBS
Bumpy — UNEVEN
Bunch — CLUMP, CLUSTER, CROWD, GANG, GROUP
Bunch — HOST, HUDDLE, PACK
Bunch of cub scouts — PACK
Bundle — BALE, PARCEL, SHEAF, WAD, WRAP
Bundle of "dough" — WAD
Bundle of cotton — BALE
Bundle of stalks — SHEAF
Bundle of twigs — FAGOT
Bundled, as grain — SHEAVED
Bundlers — BALERS
Bundles — BALES
Bundles of energy — DYNAMOS
Bungle — ERR, MUFF, SLIP
Bungled, with "up" — MESSED
Bungling — INEPT, RUIN, SPOIL
Bungo or buckeye — CANOE
Bungo, e.g. — CANOE
Bunk — HOKUM, HOOEY
Bunk! — APPLESAUCE
Bunk's cousin — COT
Bunker — ARCHIE, TRAP
Bunker or Lavender — HILL
Bunker, for one — HILL
Bunkhouse — CABIN
Bunny tails — SCUTS
Bunny's mother — DOE

Bunyan's blue ox — BABE
Bunyan's companion — BABE
Bunyan's ox — BABE
Buonarroti creation — PIETA
Buonarroti masterpiece — PIETA
Buoy — MARKER
Buoy follower — ANCY
Buoyant — LITHE
Burbank specialty — POTATO
Burble — BOIL
Burbot — LING
Burden — CARGO, CHORE, LOAD, ONUS
Burden for Cliff, in "Cheers" — MAIL BAG
Burden, to the Bard — FARDEL
Burdened — LADEN, LADED, TAXED
Burdens — LOADS
Burdensome — ONEROUS
Burdensome obsession — A MONKEY ON ONES BACK
Bureau — CHEST
Bureau attachment — CRAT
Bureau, in Brest — AGENCE
Bureaucracy, with "red" — TAPE
Bureaucratic wrapping — RED TAPE
Burgees — FLAGS
Burgeon — GROW, SWELL, SPROUT
Burger adjunct — FRIES
Burger stop — EATERY
Burger toppings — ONIONS
Burgher — CITIZEN
Burghoff on M*A*S*H — RADAR
Burghoff role — RADAR
Burglar's booty — LOOT
Burglary, mod style — HEIST
Burgoo — STEW
Burgoo and matelote — STEWS
Burgs — TOWNS
Burgundy and Bordeaux, sometimes — REDS
Burgundy buddy — CAMA-RADE
Buries — ENTOMBS
Burin — CHISEL
Burlap — GUNNYSACK
Burlesque — FARCE, PARODY, SPOOF
Burlesque act? — COMIC STRIP, SKIT
Burlesque piece — SKIT
Burlesque queens, often — FAN DANCERS
Burlington's Bean — ORSON
Burls on trunks — KNARS
Burly antecedent — HURLY
Burma's locale — ASIA
Burma's U _____ — THANT
Burmese capital — RANGOON
Burmese gravure ad? — ROTO MANDALAY
Burmese or Chinese — ASIAN
Burmese statesman — UNU
Burmese statesman U _____ — THANT
Burmese, e.g. — ASIAN
Burn — GO UP IN SMOKE
Burn _____ in one's pocket — A HOLE
Burn brightly — FLARE
Burn out — OVERDO
Burn slightly — CHAR
Burn superficially — SINGE
Burn the surface — CHAR
Burn treatment — ALOE
Burn with steam — SCALD
Burned — FLAMED
Burned completely — ASHED
Burning — AFIRE
Burning bush — WAHOO
Burning zeal — ARDOR
Burnish — BUFF, POLISH
Burnoose wearers — ARABS
Burns brightly — BLAZES
Burns setup — GRACIE HOWS YOUR BROTHER
Burns' countrymen — SCOTS
Burns' denial — NAE
Burns' prop — CIGAR
Burns' word for tiny — SMA
Burns's "Scots _____ Hae" — WHA
Burns / Matthau film: 1975 — THE SUNSHINE BOYS
Burr role — IRONSIDE
Burr-Hamilton combat — DUEL
Burrow — HOLE
Burrow's kin — DENS
Burrowed — TUNNELED
Burrowers — MOLES
Burrowing animal — GOPHER
Burrowing animals — MOLES
Burrowing clam — GAPER
Burrowing rodent — GERBIL, RABBIT
Burrows of B'way — ABE
Burrows or Vigoda — ABE
Burst — EXPLODE
Burst of activity — RUSH
Burst of approval — ECLAT
Burst out — ERUPTED
Burstyn — ELLEN
Burstyn or Barkin — ELLEN
Burstyn or Terry — ELLEN
Burt Lancaster role: 1960 — ELMER GANTRY
Burt Reynolds film: 1978 — HOOPER
Burt Reynolds movie of 1973 — WHITE LIGHTNING
Bury — INHUME, INTER
Bus station — STOP
Bus stop — DEPOT
Bus stop structure — SHELTER
Bus. abbr. — ASSN, CPA
Bus. addr. — INC
Bus. degree — MBA
Bus. group — ORG
Bus. leader — EXEC
Bus. letter plus — ENC
Busboy's prop — TRAY
Bush-whackers, of a sort — SNIPERS
Bush and Clinton, for example — ELIS
Bush or Bentsen, e.g. — TEXAN
Bush or Taft — ELI
Bush role in 1988 — DOLE
Bush was one in '48 — ELI
Bush's alma mater — YALE
Bush's Amsterdam statement? — READ MY TULIPS
Bush's chief of staff — SUNUNU
Bushed — TIRED
Bushel's partner, in song — PECK
Bushes' Millie, e.g. — PET
Bushy-tailed hoarder — WOOD RAT
Business abbr. — INC
Business affairs — MERGERS
Business association — FIRM
Business center in New York — WALL STREET
Business combo — POOL
Business deal — MERGER
Business deg. — MBA
Business degree — DBA
Business establishment — SHOP
Business giant — CAPTAIN OF INDUSTRY
Business letter abbr. — ENC, INST
Business man in April? — WET COLLAR WORKER
Business transaction — DEAL
Business tycoon — MAGNATE
Business watchdog agcy. — FTC
Business watchdog: Abbr. — FTC
Business-like — FORMAL
Businessman's alias: Abbr. — DBA
Bustle — ADO, DASH, FLUT-TER, FLY, HURRY, STIR
Bustle at bargain basement sale — COUNTER ACTION
Bustling excitements — ADOS
Busy — IN USE, TIED UP
Busy airport — OHARE
Busy as _____ — A BEE
Busy Athenian's breakfast? — A KAPPA COFFEE
Busy bug — ANT
Busy flautists — PIPERS PIPING
Busy insect — ANT, BEE

Busy place — HIVE
Busy place, 4:00 P.M., London — TEA SHOP
Busy places in June — ALTARS
Busy spot — HIVE
Busy times at the I.R.S. — APRS
Busy unionizer? — JACK OF ALL TRADES
Busy with — INTO
Busybodies — SNOOPS
Busybody of a sort — YENTA
But — UNLESS, YET
But for — SAVE
But not if — UNLESS
But of course! — NATCH
But, in Berlin — ABER
But, in Bonn — ABER
But, to Brutus — SED
But, to Caesar — SED
But, to Cato — SED
But: Fr. — MAIS
But: Lat. — SED
Butcher shop purchase — CAPON
Butcher shop: Fr. — ETAL
Butcher's cut — LOIN
Butcher's garb? — LOIN CLOTH
Butcher's ware — MEAT
Butcher, baker, etc — JOBS
Butchers? — MERCHANTS OF VENISON
Butler — STEWARD
Butler of fiction — RHETT
Buts and maybes pal — IFS
Butt of jokes — STOOGE
Butte — HILL
Butte native — MONTANAN
Butte's brother — MESA
Butter at Fordham — RAM
Butter bean — LIMA, WAX
Butter in the sky — ARIES
Butter makers — CHURNERS
Butter or skim — MILK
Butter portion — PAT
Butter sub — OLEO
Butter trees — SHEAS
Butter units — PATS
Butter-and- _____ — EGG MAN
Buttercup relative — ANEMONE
Buttercup's craft — HMS PINAFORE
Butterfinger's word — SLIP
Butterfingers' remark — OOPS
Butterflies, sometimes — SATYRS
Butterfly — SATYR
Butterfly's relative — MOTH
Butterfly's sashes — OBIS
Butterine — OLEO
Butterlike oil — OLEO
Butters up — YESES
Buttinski — MEDDLER
Buttinsky — PEST, YENTA
Buttocks — HEINIE
Button for a bowler — RESET
Button of a type — SNAP
Button or bolt — TOGGLE
Button, cubby or key — HOLES
Buttons or Barber — RED
Buttons up — FASTENS
Buttons' replacer — ZIPPER
Buttons, for one — RED
Buttonwood — SYCAMORE
Buttress — PROP, SHORE
Butts — RAMS
Buy now, pay later — CHARGE
Buyer's concern — COST
Buys the sponsor's wares — CONSUMES
Buzz — HUM
Buzz or see — SAW
Buzz-y place — HIVE
Buzzed — RANG
Buzzer — BEE
Buzzing beetle — DOR
Buzzing insects — DORS
Buzzing sound — SKIRR, WHIRR
Bway sign — SRO
By _____ (mechanically) — ROTE
By _____ and bounds — LEAPS
By _____ of (effort) — DINT
By _____! — JOVE
By a fraction — IN HALF
By airmail from France — PAR AVION
By all means — CATCH AS CATCH CAN
By all means! — YES
By all means: Slang — INDEEDY
By and by — ANON, SOON
By any chance — EVER
By any means — AT ALL
By birth — NEE
By favor: Law — DE GRATIA
By fits and starts — BROKENLY
By its very nature — PER SE
By itself — PER SE
By jove! — EGAD
By myself — ALONE
By oneself — ALONE, SOLO
By the sea — COASTAL
By the year: Abbr. — PER AN
By way of — VIA
By, in Salamanca — POR
Bye, in Britain — TATA
Bye-bye — TATA
Byelorussia capital — MINSK
Byelorussian city — MINSK
Byelorussian hub — MINSK
Bygone — AGO, PAST
Bygone Bara — THEDA
Bygone bird — DODO
Bylaws — RULES
Bypass — EVADE, SKIP
Bypasses — IGNORES
Bypath — LANE
Byrd book — ALONE
Byrd, Hart, or Hatch — SENATOR
Byre Livery, Mass — BARNSTABLE
Byrnie, e.g. — ARMOR
Byron — POET
Byron and Keats — POETS
Byron or Betty — WHITE
Byron poem — LARA
Byron's "_____ Harold's Pilgrimage" — CHILDE
Byron's "The Lament of _____" — TASSO
Byron's first published work — HOURS OF IDLENESS
Byron's Rx — SODA WATER THE DAY AFTER
Byron, for one — POET
Byronic hero — LARA
Bystander — ONLOOKER
Byte or hertz preceder — MEGA
Bytom natives — POLES
Byway — LANE
Byways — ROADS
Byword — ADAGE
Byzantium, today — ISTANBUL

C

C & W singer Travis — RANDY
C to C, e.g. — OCTAVE
C&W singer McEntire — REBA
C'est _____ — A LUI
C'est _____ — LA VIE
C'est _____ (it is mine) — A MOI
C'est _____ (it's his) — A LUI

C'est la _____ — VIE
C, soundwise — ONE OF SEVEN
C-notes — IOOS
C. _____ Smith of old films — AUBREY
C. Moore beast of burden — DASHER
C. Porter's "_____ Sensational" — YOURE
C.B. activity — RADIOING
C.B. deMille's genre — EPICS
C.E.O.'s aide — TREAS
C.E.O.'s degree — MBA
C.G. Norris novel — BREAD
C.I.A. predecessor — OSS
C.I.O. partner — AFL
C.P. and Phoebe — SNOWS
C.P. Snow's title — LORD
C.P.A. — ACCT
C.P.A.'s record — ACC
C.S.A. general — FORREST
C.S.A. man — REB
C.S.A. state — ALA
C3PO in "Star Wars" — ROBOT
CA-NV lake — TAHOE
CA resort — PALM SPRINGS
Caama — ASSE
Cab — HACK, TAXI
Cab Calloway specialty — JIVE
Caba da _____, Portugal — ROCA
Cabal — CLIQUE, JUNTA, PLOT
Caballero — HORSEMAN
Caballero, e.g. — SENOR
Cabana — HUT
Cabaret — TAVERN
Cabaret dance — APACHE
Cabaret employee — TAXI DANCER
Cabaret fare — REVUE
Cabaret offering — REVUE
Cabarets — NIGHTCLUBS
Cabbage — KALE, MOOLA
Cabbage concoction — SLAW
Cabbage dish — SLAW
Cabbage in brine — KRAUT
Cabbage or Kale — DOREMI, DOUGH
Cabbage Patch dolls, e.g. — FAD
Cabbage salad — SLAW
Cabbage unit — HEAD
Cabbage variety — HEAD
Cabbage's kin — KALES
Cabbage, in Cannes — CHOU
Cabbage, in Koln — KRAUT
Cabbage; clams — BREAD
Cabby's customers — FARES
Cabby's passenger — FARE
Cabell of baseball — ENOS
Cabernet — WINE
Cabin — CAMP, HUT
Cabin builders' tools — ADZES
Cabinet appliance in 1867 — SEWARDS ICE BOX
Cabinet joint — MITRE
Cabinet Nobelist? — MADAME CURIO
Cabinet of a type — CURIO
Cabinet on short legs and ornamented — COMMODE
Cabinet post: Abbr. — EDUC
Cabineted — SHUT UP
Cable — CHAIN, ROPE, WIRE
Cable car — TELPHER
Cable channel, for short — HBO
Cable conduit — DUCT
Cable for towing — HAWSER
Cable railway — TRAMWAY
Cable-car V.I.P. — MOTORMAN
Cable: Abbr. — CATV
Cablegram — MESSAGE
Caboodle — LOT
Caboodle's complement — KIT
Caboose — GALLEY
Caboose neighbor, perhaps — BOXCAR
Caboose position — REAR
Cabot Cove's Jessica — ANGELA
Cabriolet — CARRIAGE
Cachalot — WHALE
Cache — HIDE, STORE
Cache box? — TILL
Cache, as cash — STASH
Cachet — PRESTIGE, SEAL, STAMP
Cacholong — OPAL
Cackle — CHATTER, GIGGLE
Cacomistle — CIVET
Cacophonous — NOISY
Cacophony — DIN, DISCORD, NOISE
Cad — HEEL, ROTTER
Cad in charge? — STEERING HEEL
Cadaver — CORPSE
Caddis — BRAID, LINT
Caddo Indians — IONIS, REES
Caddoan — ARIKARA
Caddy's contents — TEA
Cadence — BEAT, COUNT, RHYTHM
Cadet — RECRUIT
Cadets' inst. — USMA
Cadge — BEG
Cadmium and tungsten — METALS
Cadre — GROUP
Caducity — OLD AGE
Caen clergyman — ABBE
Caen crumb — MIE
Caen's neighbor — ST LO
Caen's river — ORNE
Caesar — SID
Caesar _____ — SALAD
Caesar conquest — GAUL
Caesar namesakes — SIDS
Caesar or Luckman — SID
Caesar was here — GAUL
Caesar was one — EDILE
Caesar's "I rate" — AESTIMO
Caesar's "I seize" — CAPIO
Caesar's "myself" — IPSE
Caesar's 506 — DVI
Caesar's 700 — DCC
Caesar's base — ROMA
Caesar's brother-in-law — ANTONY
Caesar's brother — FRATER
Caesar's co-star — COCA
Caesar's eulogist — ANTONY
Caesar's farewell — VALE
Caesar's friend — COCO
Caesar's hand — MANU
Caesar's one-time partner — COCA
Caesar's path — ITER
Caesar's road — ITER
Caesar's robe — TOGA
Caesar's route — ITER
Caesar's sister — SOROR
Caesar's tongue — LATIN
Caesar's unlucky date — IDES
Caesar's wife — UXOR
Caesar's wings — ALAE
Caesar's words — ET TU
Caesar, for one — SALAD
Caesar, when a lad — PUER
Caesura — PAUSE, REST
Caesurae — RESTS
Cafe — BISTRO, DINER
Café au _____ — LAIT
Café cup — TASSE
Cafe guests — DINERS
Cafe patron — EATER
Cafeteria help — CASHIER
Cafeteria item — TRAY
Caffard — BIGOT
Caffeine source — KOLA
Caffeine-containing seed — KOLA NUT
Caftan — ROBE
Cage — BOX, CRIB, COOP
Cage for hawks — MEW
Cager Archibald — NATE
Cager Frazier's nickname — CLYDE
Cager from NJ — NET
Cager Karl or Moses — MALONE
Cagers' org. — NBA
Cagier — SLYER
Cagney and Lacey's Daly namesakes — TYNES
Cagney film — TORRID ZONE
Cahn-Styne product — AIR
Cahn or Davis Jr. — SAMMY
Cahn product — SONG
Cain's "_____ Pierce" — MILDRED
Cain's nephew — ENOS
Cain's postman — TWICE RINGER
Cairo cobra — ASP
Cajole — COAX, WHEEDLE

Cajoled — URGED
Cake — CRUST, HARDEN, PASTRY, TORTE
Cake _____ — MIX
Cake cover — ICING
Cake decorators — ICERS
Cake enhancer — ICER
Cake finisher — ICER
Cake flavoring — MOCHA
Cake mixture — BATTER
Cake topper — ICER
Cake topping — CRUMBS, ICING
Cake, in Capri — TORTA
Caked — HARD
Cakewalked — STRUTTED
Cal. _____ — TECH
Cal. campus — UCLA
Cal. entry — APR
Cal.-Wash. separator — ORE
Calaboose — HOOSEGOW
Calabria cash — LIRA
Calabria's country — ITALIA
Calais entree — ROTI
Calais-to-Paris dir. — SSE
Calais-to-Rouen dir. — SSW
Calamities — EVILS
Calamity — HARM, MISERY, WOE
Calaveras County jumpers — FROGS
Calcar — OVEN
Calcars — OVENS
Calchas or Mopsus — SEER
Calcium oxide — LIME
Calculate — TALLY
Calculated — TALLIED
Calculates — ADDS
Calculating — SHARP
Calculator key — PLUS
Calculus calculation — AREA
Calculus, for short — MATH
Calcutta cigarette — BIRI
Calder creation — MOBILE
Caldwell or Bernhardt — SARAH
Calembour — PUN
Calendar abbr. — AUG, FRI, OCT, SAT, SUN
Calendar abbr. — THURS, WED, TUES
Calendar heading — YEAR
Calendar in use before Gregorian — JULIAN
Calendar noting religious events — MENOLOGY
Calendar period — YEAR
Calendar word — MAY
Calf covers — HOSIERY
Calf gone astray — DOGY
Calf location — LEG
Calf meat — VEAL
Calf's cry — BLAT
Calf-skin — HIDE
Calgary hockey team — FLAMES
Calgary roundup — STAMPEDE
Calgary's prov. — ALTA
Calhoun — RORY
Calhoun of Hollywood — RORY
Calhoun of the movies, et al. — RORYS
Caliber — BORE, CLASS, MERIT
Calico — PIEBALD
Calico bass — FISH
Calico creature — CAT
Calico horse — PINTO
Calico pony — PINTO
Calif. beach — REDONDO
Calif. campus — UCLA
Calif. observatory — PALOMAR
Calif. pearl-fishing center — LA PAZ
Calif. pitching arms, slangily — ANGEL WINGS
Calif. resort — TAHOE
Calif. spot for Mr. America — MUSCLE BEACH
Calif. university — UCLA
Calif. wine valley — NAPA
Calif.'s Big _____ — SUR
California city east of L.A. — ONTARIO
California college — POMONA
California concern — SAN ANDREAS FAULT
California flag animal — GRIZZLY BEAR
California Fort — ORD
California hot dry wind — SANTA ANA
California Indian — MAIDU
California landmark — GOLDEN GATE
California parade — ROSE
California red wine — ZINFANDEL
California rockfishes — RENAS
California seafood? — SALMONTEREY
California team, once — RAMS
California town poll — BIG SURVEY
California university town — BERKELEY
California wine-growing valley — NAPA
California's Big _____ — SUR
California's first capital — SAN JOSE
Caligula's nephew — NERO
Call — PHONE
Call _____ day (quit) — IT A
Call a president to account — IMPEACH
Call at a barn dance — PROMENADE
Call at a deli counter — NEXT
Call at sea — AHOY
Call at Wimbledon — LET
Call back — CANCEL
Call backs — ENCORES
Call balls and strikes — UMPIRE
Call by the ump — OUT
Call down — CHIDE
Call for silence — HIST
Call forth — ELICIT, EVOKE
Call in coin tossing — TAILS
Call into question — CHALLENGE
Call it a day — RETIRE
Call it quits — RESIGN
Call off — DROP
Call off a launch — SCRUB
Call on — VISIT
Call out — EVOKE
Call repeatedly by name — PAGE
Call to a bellhop — FRONT
Call to order — OPEN
Call up — ASSEMBLE, DRAFT
Call upon for help — EVOKE
Call, in poker — SEE
Calla and sego — LILIES
Calla lillies — ARUMS
Calla lily, e.g. — ARUM
Calla, e.g. — ARUM
Callahan-Roberts song — SMILES
Callas — LILIES
Callas or Tallchief — MARIA
Called — PHONED
Called loudly — CRIED
Called on — VISITED
Called out — CRIED
Calligrapher — LETTERER
Calligraphers' needs — INKS
Calling — CAREER, TRADE
Callisto and Ganymede — MOONS
Callous — HARD
Callowness — INEXPERIENCE
Calls — DIALS
Calls a halt — STOPS
Calls at Fenway Park — OUTS
Calls at Wimbledon — LETS
Calls it a day — RETIRES
Calls up — RINGS
Calls, at poker — SEES
Calls, in cards — SEES
Calm — COOL, QUIET, SERENE
Calm and collected — SEDATE
Calm before the storm — LULL
Calm down — SUBSIDE
Calm spot amid turbulence — EYE OF THE HURRICANE
Calm state of restfulness — REPOSE
Calm, in a way — DEFUSE
Calm, in Calabria — CHETO
Calmed — ALLAYED, SEDATED
Calming process — SEDATION
Calms — SEDATES
Caloric meas. — BMR
Caloric rating: Abbr. — BTU

Calorie counter — DIETER
Calumet — PIPE
Calumniate — ASPERSE
Calumnies — SLURS
Calvados capital — CAEN
Calvary initials — INRI
Calves on the loose — DOGIES
Calvin of the P.G.A. — PEETE
Calvin's Hobbes — TIGER
Calvin's home city — GENEVA
Calyx leaf — SEPAL
Calyx part — SEPAL
Calyx segment — SEPAL
Cam-wheel projections — LOBES
Camaguey's locale — CUBA
Camaraderie — ESPRIT DE CORPS
Camber — BOW
Cambers — BOWS
Cambio in Calabria — LIRE
Cambodia's monetary unit — RIEL
Cambodia's neighbor — LAOS
Cambodian coin — RIEL, SEN
Cambodian neighbor — LAOS
Cambodian people — KHMER
Cambodian's 100 sen — RIEL
Cambria — WALES
Cambria, today — WALES
Cambridge inst. for would-be attorneys — HLS
Cambridge school letters — MIT
Cambridgeshire "isle" and town — ELYS
Came across — MET
Came back — RECURRED
Came close — NEARED
Came down — ALIT, LANDED
Came down in buckets — TEEMED
Came down to earth — ALIT
Came first — ANTECEDES
Came home — SCORED
Came in — ENTERED
Came into being — AROSE
Came off the track — DERAILED
Came prior to — FORERAN
Came to — WOKE
Came to a conclusion — ENDED
Came to a halt — STALLED
Came to rest — ALIT
Came to roost — ALIT
Came up — AROSE
Came up with — LIT ON
Came upon — MET
Camel habitat — DESERT
Camel hair robe — ABA
Camel in the Sahara — MEHARI
Camel kin — LLAMA
Camel's backbreaker — STRAW
Camel's chew — CUD
Camel's hair fabric — ABA
Cameleopard of Africa — GIRAFFE
Camelot combat — JOUST
Camelot king — ARTHUR
Camelot lady — ENID
Camembert — CHEESE
Camembert's cousin — BRIE
Cameo carver's agate — ONYX
Cameo stone — ONYX
Cameo's opposite — INTAGLIO
Cameo, for one — ROLE
Camera _____, sketching aid — OBSCURA
Camera adjustments — FOCI
Camera feature — LENS
Camera genius Edwin — LAND
Camera openings — STOPS
Camera part — LENS
Camera stand — TRIPOD
Cameroons tribe — ABO
Camilla of films — SPARV
Camilli of the B'klyn Dodgers — DOLF
Camise — SHIRT
Camote — YAM
Camouflage — BLIND, HIDE, MASK
Camp — BIVOUAC, CROWD
Camp beds — COTS
Camp covers — TENTS
Camp David — RETREAT
Camp David locale — MARY-LAND
Camp feature — TENT
Camp follower — FIRE
Camp rouser — BUGLE
Camp sight — TENT
Campaign — BATTLE, RUN FOR OFFICE
Campaign confrontations — DEBATES
Campaign flier? — AIR FORCE ONE
Campaign issue — CRIME
Campaign issue in '92 — ECON
Campaign topic — ISSUE
Campaign-fund source: Abbr. — PAC
Campaigned — RAN
Campaigned for office — RAN
Campaigner Clinton, tunefully? — ARKANSAS TRAVELER
Campaigner, for short — POL
Campaniles — BELL TOWERS
Campbell of song — GLEN
Camped under canvas — TENTED
Camper abodes — WALL TENTS
Camper's accessory — BED ROLL
Camper's cover — TENT
Camper's curfew — TAPS
Camper's home — TENT
Camper's light — LANTERN
Camper's route — TRAIL
Camper's shelter — LEANTO
Camping equipment — TENT
Camping need, for short — TARP
Campus areas, for short — QUADS
Campus Betty — COED
Campus climber — IVY
Campus climbers — IVIES
Campus costumes — GOWNS
Campus do — PROM
Campus event — SENIOR PROM
Campus figure — DEAN
Campus figures — COEDS
Campus finals — EXAMS
Campus military org. — ROTC
Campus notable — DEAN
Campus org. — NSA, ROTC
Campus org. in the 60's — SDS
Campus residences, for short — DORMS
Campus segments — TERMS
Campus social gp. — FRAT
Campus V.I.P. — DEAN, PROF
Can — TIN
Can a S. American city be cool? — IS SANTIAGO CHILE
Can be augmented — ADDABLE
Can be endured — BEARABLE
Can't or won't, e.g. — CON-TRACTION
Can't stand — HATE
Can. peninsula — GASPE
Can. province — ALTA, ONT
Canaanite — SINITE
Canaanite army commander: Judges 4:2 — SISERA
Canaanite god — BAAL
Canada's capital — OTTAWA
Canada's financial center — BAY STREET
Canada, once — DOMINION
Canadian bay — FUNDY
Canadian city — TORONTO
Canadian court decree — ARRET
Canadian Indian — CREE
Canadian lake — CREE
Canadian mystery writer Howard _____ — ENGEL
Canadian physician Sir William _____ — OSLER
Canadian prov. — NFLD, ONT, PEI
Canadian provinces, with "The" — MARITIMES
Canadian summer treat? — OTTAWATERMELON
Canadian territory — YUKON
Canadian wild goose — BRANT
Canal — ERIE, SOO, SUEZ
Canal of song — ERIE

Canal started in 1817 — ERIE
Canal Zone town — ANCON
Canals in Michigan and Canada — SOO
Canals, for short — SOO
Canapé — HORS DOEUVRE
Canapé spreads — PATES
Canapé supplier — CATERER
Canapés — DIPS
Canaries — YELLOW BIRDS
Canary Island port — LOS PALMOS
Canary Island's sea — ATLANTIC
Canary Isls. location — ATL
Canary kin — SERIN
Canary's cousin — SERIN
Canary's relative — SERIN
Canary's sound — CHIRP
Canasta card — TREY
Canasta item — TREY
Canasta play — MELD
Cancel — ABORT, ANNUL, DISANNUL, ERASE, RESCIND
Cancel — SCRUB, UNDO, VOID
Cancel a bombing mission — ABORT
Cancel a command — COUNTERMAND
Cancel a debt — REPAY
Cancel a punishment — REMIT
Cancels — NEGATES, VOIDS
Cancels editorial changes — STETS
Cancer — CURSE, TUMOR
Cancun gelt — PESOS
Candelabrum with seven branches — MENORAH
Candid — FRANK, ON THE LEVEL
Candid camera shot? — X RAY
Candidate — NOMINEE
Candidate for a kind of salad — EGG
Candidate Harold from Minnesota — STASSEN
Candidate Jack from Buffalo — KEMP
Candied — SUGARY
Candied fruit, e.g. — SWEETMEAT
Candle — TAPER, TORCH, WAX
Candle eggs — INSPECT
Candle or holiday — ROMAN
Candle or nose — ROMAN
Candlelighting affairs — BIRTHDAYS
Candlemaker — CHANDLER
Candlemas — FEAST
Candlepin sport — BOWLING
Candles — TAPERS
Candlestick — STANDARD
Candlestick Park info — STATS
Candor — OPENNESS
Candy — BONBON, NOUGAT, SWEET
Candy _____ — CANES
Candystriper, e.g. — AIDE
Canea is the capital — CRETE
Canea' isle — CRETE
Caner's material — RATTAN
Canine — SETTER
Canine breed — BOXER
Canine chatter — ARF, YAPPING
Canine comment — ARF, BARK, YELP, YIP
Canine crossbreeds — CURS
Canine of film fame — RIN TIN TIN
Canine of flicks — ASTA
Canine remark — YIP
Canine sound — YELP
Canine threat — SNARL
Canine tooth — CUSPID
Canine TV star — LASSIE
Canine warning — GNARL, GRR
Canine's neighbor — BICUSPID, INCISOR
Canine, e.g. — TOOTH
Canines — TEETH
Canines on the Concorde? — JET SETTERS
Cannabis — HASHISH
Cannabis plant — MARIJUANA
Canned beef — BULLY
Canned brew — ALE
Canned fish — SARDINE
Canned from the job — FIRED
Cannel — COAL
Canner's kin — BOTTLER
Cannery worker — STONER
Cannes cap — BERET
Canning container — TIN
Canning equipment — JARS
Cannon Ball's engineer — CASEY JONES
Cannon has three — ENS
Cannon of pictures — DYAN
Cannon shot — GRAPE
Cannonballed — TORE
Canny — ASTUTE
Canoe — DUGOUT
Canoe bark — BIRCH
Canoeist's concern — RAPID
Canola and cottonseed — OILS
Canon — DECREE, EDICT
Canonical hour — MATIN, NONES, SEXT
Canonized one: Abbr. — STE
Canoodle — PET
Canopy — TESTER
Canopy over altar — TESTER
Cans, in Canterbury — TINS
Cant — LINGO
Cant and patois — ARGOTS
Cantankerous — CROSS
Canted — LEANED
Canteens — FLASKS
Canter — GAIT, LOPE
Canter or gallop — GAIT
Canter or shamble — GAIT
Canter or trot — GAIT
Canter's cousin — LOPE
Canterbury bell variety — CUP AND SAUCER
Canterbury stories — TALES
Canterbury's saint — ANSELM
Canticle — ODE
Cantilever — TRUSS
Cantina offering — CHILI
Cantina snack — TAMALE
Canting — ATILT
Canto — SONG
Canton dwellers — SWISS
Canton follower — ESE
Canton's state — OHIO
Cantonese chicken dish — MOO GOO GAI PAN
Cantor and Lupino — IDAS
Cantrell or Turner — LANA
Cants — LEANS, TIPS
Canvas covering, for short — TARP
Canvas holder — EASEL
Canvas shelter — TENT
Canvas shoe — SNEAKER
Canvas support — EASEL
Canvass — POLL
Canvassed — POLLED
Canvasser's concern — VOTE
Canyon — ARROYO, GORGE, GULCH, RAVINE
Canyon feature — GORGE
Canyon mouth — ABRA
Canyon phenomenon — ECHO
Canzone — ODE
Caoutchouc — RUBBER
Cap — BEANIE, TAM
Cap addendum — EARFLAP
Cap attachment — EARMUFF
Cap brim — VISOR
Cap for a highlander — TAM
Cap for Malcolm — TAM
Cap for Monsieur — BERET
Cap or coat — RED
Cap or collar — ETON
Cap's partner — GOWN
Cap, collar or jacket — ETON
Cap, in Madrid — TAPA
Cap- _____ — A PIE
Cap-and-gown occasions — GRADUATIONS
Capable — ABLE, APT, SMART
Capable of — UP TO
Capable of being appeased — SATIABLE
Capable of being felt — TACTILE
Capable of being heard — AUDIBLE
Capable of being molded — PLASTIC
Capacitance unit — FARAD

Capacity — POWER
Cape — CLOAK, POINT, RAS
Cape _____ — COD
Cape buffalo — BISON
Cape Cod abodes — COTTAGES
Cape Cod town — TRURO
Cape fox — ASSE
Cape hartebeest — CAAMA
Cape in Massachusetts — ANN
Cape of Good Hope discoverer — DIAS
Cape on Honshu — OMA
Cape Town gun — BOER
Cape Town's county: Abbr. — RSA
Cape Town's famous son — SMUTS
Cape, in Arabic — RAS
Capek play — RUR
Capek play about "Star Wars" — RUR
Capek's robot play — RUR
Capella, for one — STAR
Caper — ANTIC, DIDO, PRANK
Caper — GAMBOL
Caper for a yegg — HEIST
Caper of a sort — NIPUP
Capgun — TOY
Capita preceder — PER
Capital 100 — SENS, SENATE
Capital of Albania — TIRANA
Capital of Ancient Assyria — NINEVEH
Capital of ancient Laconia — SPARTA
Capital of ancient Macedonia — EDESSA
Capital of Armenia — EREVAN
Capital of Azerbaijan — BAKU
Capital of Baleares province, Spain — PALMA
Capital of Bangledesh, old style — DACCA
Capital of Belorussia — MINSK
Capital of Calvados — CAEN
Capital of Campania — NAPLES
Capital of Canada — OTTAWA
Capital of Cape Verde — PRAIA
Capital of Carthage — CARALIS
Capital of County Clare — ENNIS
Capital of Elam — SUSA
Capital of Eritrea — ASMARA
Capital of Fiji — SUVA
Capital of Guam — AGANA
Capital of Italia — ROMA
Capital of Jordan — AMMAN
Capital of Jorge Amado's homeland — BRASILIA
Capital of Laconia — SPARTA
Capital of Lombardy — MILAN
Capital of Macapa, Brazil — AMAPA
Capital of Maine — AUGUSTA
Capital of Manche — ST LO
Capital of Nigeria, once — LAGOS
Capital of Okinawa — NAHA
Capital of old Macedonia — PELLA
Capital of Oman — MUSCAT
Capital of Oregon — SALEM
Capital of Orne Department — ALENCON
Capital of Perak State, Malaysia — IPOH
Capital of Rhone Department — LYONS
Capital of Russian America — SITKA
Capital of Sicily — PALERMO
Capital of the Bahamas — NASSAU
Capital of the Beaver State — SALEM
Capital of the First State — DOVER
Capital of the Maldives — MALE
Capital of the Treasure State — HELENA
Capital of the Ukraine — KIEV
Capital of Tibet — LHASA
Capital of Turkey — ANKARA
Capital of Valais, Switzerland — SION
Capital of Venezuela — CARACAS
Capital of Vietnam — HANOI
Capital of Western Australia — PERTH
Capital of Yemen — ADEN, SANA
Capital on a fjord — OSLO
Capital on the South Platte — DENVER
Capital site — HILL
Capitalize — USE
Capitol — STATE HOUSE
Capitol _____ — HILL
Capitol _____, Utah — REEF
Capitol body — SENATE
Capitol feature — DOME
Capitol figure — SENATOR
Capitol Hill list — CALENDAR
Capitol Hill name — DOLE
Capitol Hill person: Abbr. — SEN
Capitol Hill turndown — NAY
Capitol Hill worker — PAGE
Capitol topping — DOME
Capitulate — YIELD
Capone nemesis — NESS
Capone's successor — NITTI
Capote's Golightly — HOLLY
Capout or Scott — HUGH
Capp and Capone — ALS
Capp and Hirt — ALS
Capp creature — SHMOO
Capp hero — ABNER
Capp's "Lil _____" — ABNER
Capp's _____ the Hyena — LENA
Capp's Fearless fellow — FOSDICK
Capp's Leapin _____ — LENA
Capri — ISLE
Capri or Sicily — ISOLA
Capri or Wight — ISLE
Capri, to Capriotes — ISOLA
Caprice — FAD, WHIM
Capricious — ERRATIC
Capricious escapade — CAPER
Capricious indulgences — FLINGS
Capricorn — GOAT
Capriole — LEAP
Caps or cans — SEALS IN
Capsize — UPSET
Capsizes — KEELS
Capsule's relative: Var. — AMPULE
Capt. Andy in 1936 "Show Boat" — WINNINGER
Capt. Hook's aide — SMEE
Capt. Louis Renault — CLAUDE RAINS
Captain _____, the pirate — KIDD
Captain Hook Portrayer Cyril — RITCHARD
Captain Hook's henchman — SMEE
Captain Hook's look — LEER
Captain Hook's sidekick — SMEE
Captain Nemo's creator — VERNE
Captain of the "Caine" — QUEEG
Captain of the Nautilus — NEMO
Captain of the Pequod — AHAB
Captain Shotover's domicile — HEARTBREAK HOUSE
Captain's boat — GIG
Captain's chronicle — LOG
Captains' bosses — COLONELS
Captains' diaries — LOGS
Caption — TITLE
Captivate — ENAMOR
Captivates — INTERESTS
Captive G.I. — POW
Captor or Jerusalem — OMAR
Capture — BAG, NAB, NAIL, POT, SEIZE, SNARE
Capture, in a heartfelt way — ENAMOR
Captured — GOT, NABBED, TAKEN, TOOK
Captured again — RETOOK
Captured long ago — TAEN
Captured, in poesy — TAEN
Captures — NABS, TAKES

Capuchin monkey — SAI
Capulet query — WHERE FOR ART THOU ROMEO
Capulet, to Montague — FOE
Car-door feature — ARMREST
Car adjuncts — RADIOS
Car appurtenances — RADIOS
Car bar — AXLE
Car barn — STATION
Car coverups — LAP ROBES
Car dealer's lure — REBATE
Car driven by prospective buyer — DEMO
Car feature — BRAKE
Car for hire — TAXI
Car makers' gp. — UAW
Car mishap — DENT
Car of 1957 — EDSEL
Car of yesteryear — REO
Car on wheels — TROLLEY
Car or television — CABLE
Car part — AXLE, PISTON, WHEEL
Car pool participant — RIDER
Car style — SEDAN
Car support — AXLE
Car type — SEDAN
Car with a rumble seat — ROADSTER
Car with folding roof over rear seat — LANDAU
Car-wash step — RINSE
Car: Comb. form — AUTO
Cara or Papas — IRENE
Caramel — CANDY
Caravan — CONVOY, TRAIN
Caravan beast — CAMEL
Caravan stopover — SERAI
Caravansaries — INNS
Caravansary — SERAI
Caravel of 1492 — NINA
Caravel or coaster — SHIP
Carbamide — UREA
Carbohydrate suffix — OSE
Carbolic acid — PHENOL
Carbon Chief, Hawaii — DIAMOND HEAD
Carbon compound — ENOL
Carbon compounds: suffix — INES
Carbonize — CHAR
Carbonized organic matter — COAL
Carboy holder — CRATE
Carburetor part — FLOAT
Carcassonne's river — AUDE
Card-sharp — CHEAT
Card — JOKER, TREY
Card display — MELD
Card game — CANASTA, FARO, GIN, LOO, MONTE
Card game — PINOCHLE, POKER, SEVEN UP, SKAT
Card game — STOPS
Card game for three — SKAT
Card game for two — ECARTE, HONEYMOON BRIDGE
Card game starters — DEALS
Card holding — TENACE
Card player on dealer's right — PONE
Card position — FACE UP
Card sequence — TIERCE
Card term — PASS
Cardigan Welsh _____ — CORGI
Cardin creations — DRESSES
Cardinal — CHIEF
Cardinal and scarlet tanager — RED BIRDS
Cardinal assembly — COLLEGE
Cardinal Newman hymn — LEAD KINDLY LIGHT
Cardinal number — THREE
Cardinal point — EAST
Cardinal's nest — ST LOUIS MISSOURI
Cardinal's quarters — NEST
Cardplaying move — ANTE
Cards left over after a deal — TALON
Cards of a kind — JOKERS
Care — TRUST, WORRY
Care for — MINISTER, TEND
Care of horsehair? — MANE-TENANCE
Cared for — LIKED
Career military person — LIFER
Careerist with a mentor — PROTEGE
Carefree rover's activity — GADDING
Careful — CIRCUMSPECT
Carefully selected — HAND-PICKED
Careless — REMISS
Careless seamstress's situation? — ON PINS AND NEE-DLES
Cares for — NURSES
Caresses — DANDLES
Caretaker — JANITOR
Caretaker for baby — SITTER
Carews beloved — CELIA
Carfares — TOKENS
Cargo — LOAD
Cargo carrier — OILER
Cargo lifter — DAVIT
Cargo ship: Abbr. — STR
Cargo space — HOLD
Cargo spot — HOLD
Cargo weight — TON
Caribbean cruise ship's destination — NASSAU
Caribbean dance — LIMBO
Caribbean isle — CUBA
Caribbean resort island — ARUBA
Caribbean's Gulf-of _____ — PARIA
Caribou herdsmen — LAPP
Caricaturist Berger — OSCAR
Carillon players? — RINGMASTERS
Carioca — RUMBA
Cariou or Deighton — LEN
Carl Lewis or Flo Jo with a baton — RELAY
Carl, Fritz or Rob — REINER
Carlo Bergonzi e.g. — TENOR
Carlos S. _____, 1936 Nobelist for peace — LAMAS
Carlsbad attraction — CAVERN
Carmer or Sandburg — CARL
Carmichael or Fleming — IAN
Carmichael song — GEORGIA ON MY MIND
Carmine — RED
Carmine and cerise — REDS
Carnation variety — PICOTED
Carnegie Hall performer — TENOR
Carnegie or Jackson — ANDREW
Carnelian — SARD
Carnera's sport — BOXING
Carney — ART
Carney and Buchwald — ARTS
Carney and Garfunkel — ARTS
Carney and Linkletter — ARTS
Carney and Tatum — ARTS
Carney or Buchwald — ART
Carney or Linkletter — ART
Carney or Tatum — ART
Carnival — GALA
Carnival attraction — FERRIS WHEEL, RIDE
Carnival feature — COTTON CANDY, RIDE
Carnival wheel — FERRIS
Carol Burnett specialty — SKIT
Carol opener — ADESTE
Carol or Citizen — KANE
Carol starter — ADESTE
Carolina rail — SORA
Carolina river — PEEDEE, SANTEE
Carolina's river, _____ Dee — PEE
Caroline's daughter — ROSE
Caroline's Island — TRUK
Caron film of 1953 — LILI
Caron film of 1963 — THE L SHAPED ROOM
Caron role — LILI
Carotid — ARTERY
Carousals — HIGH TIMES, SPREES
Carouse — LIVE IT UP, MAKE THE ROUNDS
Carouse — PAINT THE TOWN RED, REVEL
Carousing — ON A TEAR
Carp — CAVIL
Carpal — WRIST
Carpathian mountain group — TATRA

Carpathian range — TATRA
Carpe _____ — DIEM
Carpenter with six legs — ANT
Carpenter's device — SCREW
Carpenter's heavy beam — GIRT
Carpenter's necessity — LATHE
Carpenter's pin — DOWEL
Carpenter's power machine — PLANER
Carpenter's shaping tool — NOOG
Carpenter's squares — MITERS
Carpenter's tool — ADZ, HAMMER, LEVEL
Carpenter's tool — PLANE, ROUTER, SANDER, SAW
Carpenters' affliction? — ACHING JOINTS
Carpentry — TRADE
Carpentry and pottery, e.g. — CRAFTS
Carpentry file — RASP
Carpentry groove — DADO
Carpentry items — SAWS
Carpentry joint — MITRE
Carpentry tool — LATHE
Carpentry tools — PLANES
Carpet — RUG
Carpet cleaner — SWEEPER, VAC
Carpet feature — NAP, PILE
Carpet fiber — ISTLE
Carpet's nap — PILE
Carpeted again — RELAID
Carpi — WRISTS
Carping remarks — BARBS
Carps — NAGS
Carriage — CHAISE, MIEN
Carriage type — CALASH
Carriages — VICTORIAS
Carrie or Louis — NYE
Carried — BORNE, TOTED
Carried along — SWEPT UP
Carried away — RAPT
Carried away, as property — ELOINED
Carried on — MAINTAINED, RAGED, RANTED
Carried on the wind — BLOWN
Carried out — TRANSACTED
Carried the ball — RAN
Carried the day — WON
Carrier for leftovers — DOGGY BAG
Carries — CARTS, LUGS, TOTES
Carries away — ABLATES
Carries on — RANTS, RAVES, WAGES
Carries the day — WINS
Carroll character — ALICE
Carroll or Josephine — BAKER
Carroll's heroine — ALICE
Carrot family member — PARSLEY
Carrot family plant — ANISE
Carrot hydrocarbons — CAROTENES
Carrot tops — REDHEADS
Carrot, briefly — VEG
Carrots companions — PEAS
Carrots partners often — PEAS
Carry — CONVEY, TOTE
Carry away — SEDUCE
Carry debts — OWE
Carry more import or pounds — OVERWEIGH
Carry Nation's targets — SALOONS
Carry off — KIDNAP, TAKE
Carry off forcibly, old style — REAVE
Carry on — RAGE, RANT, RAVE, WAGE
Carry on vocally — RANT
Carry out — FULFIL
Carry through — COMPLETE
Carry, to a nudnick — SHLEP
Carryalls — BASKETS, TOTES
Carrying — TOTING
Carrying a burden — LADEN
Carrying cargo — LADEN
Carrying case — ETUI
Carryon — BAG
Carson City state — NEVADA
Carson City's neighbor — RENO
Carson predecessor — PARR
Carson successor — LENO
Carson's "_____ Around Us" — THE SEA
Carte — MENU
Carte preceder — A LA
Cartel — POOL
Carter-cliff-hanger phrase — IN THE NICK OF TIME
Carter and Gwyn — NELLS
Carter country — PLAINS
Carter daughter — AMY
Carter of "Ain't Misbehavin'" — NELL
Carter of stage and TV — NELL
Carthage loc. — AFR
Cartilages — GRISTLES
Cartographer's output — MAPS
Cartographer's product — MAP
Cartographic creation — MAP
Cartographic product — MAP
Cartography compendium — ATLAS
Carton — BOX, CONTAINER
Carton's "_____ better thing" — FAR FAR
Cartons — CASES
Cartoon — DRAWING, SATIRE, SKETCH
Cartoon by Hoest, with "The" — LOCKHORNS
Cartoon by the Sansoms, with "The" — BORN LOSER
Cartoon caption, as a rule — ONE LINE
Cartoon duck — DAFFY
Cartoon ghost — CASPER
Cartoon kid — DONDI
Cartoon miser — MAGOO
Cartoon portrait — CARICATURE
Cartoon screech — EEK
Cartoon section — COMICS
Cartoonist Addams — CHAS
Cartoonist Chast — ROZ
Cartoonist Dean — ABNER
Cartoonist Fisher — HAM
Cartoonist Gardner — REA
Cartoonist Goldberg — RUBE
Cartoonist of "Happy Hooligan" — OPPER
Cartoonist of "Iodine" — HATLO
Cartoonist Peter — ARNO
Cartoonist Soglow — OTTO
Cartoonist Thomas — NAST
Cartoonist's light bulb — IDEA
Cartoonist's org. — NCS
Cartoonist's scream — EEK
Cartoonist / author |Silverstein — SHEL
Cartoons by, "The New Yorker" stalwart — THURBERS
Cartouche — MESA
Cartridge holder — CHAMBER
Carve — INCISE
Carve a roasting turkey — SLICE
Carved gemstones — CAMEOS
Carved ornament on a gable — CROCKET
Carved pillar — STELE
Carwash step — RINSE
Cary or Lee — GRANT
Cary or Ulysses — GRANT
Casa _____: Toronto tourist attraction — LOMA
Casa component — SALA
Casa room — SALA
Casa's rooms — SALAS
Casaba — MELON
Casaba or crenshaw — MELON
Casablanca heroine — ILSA
Casals — PABLO
Casanova — LADY KILLER
Casanova's list — LOVES
Casanovanic spiel — HOTLINE
Casca thrust — STAB
Cascades — WATERFALLS
Cascades peak — SHASTA
Case for trivia — ETUI
Case or knot — SLIP
Case presentation — HEARING
Case: Abbr. — CTN
Casement — SASH
Casey Jones — ENGINEER
Casey's place — AT BAT

Cash — COIN, LUCRE
Cash attachment — IER
Cash container — MONEY BAG
Cash for Czechs — KORUNAS
Cash holders — TILLS
Cash in — REDEEM
Cash of baseball — NORM
Cash or charm — ASSET
Cash register figure — TOTAL
Cash register key — NO SALE
Cash stash — SAFE, TILL
Cash substitute — SCRIP
Cash surpluses — BALANCES
Cash to run a business — LIQUIDITY
Cash, for one — ASSET
Cashews — NUTS
Cashier — PURSER
Cashier in a cage — TELLER
Cashier's stamp — PAID
Casino action — BET
Casino cash-collector — SLOT
Casino choice — KENO
Casino cube — DIE
Casino cubes — DICE
Casino customers — BETTORS
Casino employee's — DEALERS
Casino game — MONTE
Casino option — ODDS OR EVEN
Casino principals — DEALERS
Cask — TUN
Cask and tub makers — COOPERS
Cask plug — SPILE
Casket platform — BIER
Casks: Abbr. — BBLS
Casper — Pierre direction — ENE
Caspian feeder — ARAS, URAL
Caspian Sea country — IRAN
Caspian Sea feeder — URAL
Cassandra's country — TROY
Cassandra's gloomy prediction — DOOM
Cassandra, for one — SEER
Cassava grains — TAPIOCA
Casserole — DISH
Cassette — TAPE
Cassette input — TAPE
Cassin and Clair — RENES
Cassini — OLEG
Cassini of fashion — OLEG
Cassius and Antony, e.g. — ENEMIES
Cassowaries — RATITES
Cassowary's cousin — EMEUR, EMU, EMEU
Cast — HEAVE, MOLT, SLING
Cast a ballot — VOTE, VOTED
Cast a glance — PEER
Cast a spell — HEXED
Cast a spell over — BEWITCH
Cast about — SEARCH
Cast aside — REJECT
Cast by John Wellington Wells — SPELL
Cast down — CRUSH
Cast in a play — TROUPE
Cast in one's lot — CHOOSE
Cast in the same mold — ALIKE
Cast off — SHED
Cast or gram lead-in — TELE
Cast, in London — CHUCK
Cast-off — REJECT
Castanet dances — FANDANGOS
Caste — RANK
Castigated — PUNISHED
Castigates — ASSAILS, CHASTEN
Castile — SOAP
Casting — BLOCK
Castle adjunct — MOAT
Castle and Dunne — IRENES
Castle defense — MOAT
Castle ditch — MOAT
Castle in France — CHATEAU
Castle manager — CHATELAIN
Castle of note — IRENE
Castle part — DRAWBRIDGE
Castle protection — MOAT
Castle trench — MOAT
Castle's protector — MOAT
Castor and Pollux — STARS
Castor bean product — RICIN
Castor follower — AND POLLUX
Castor or corn product — OIL
Castor Oyl's daughter — OLIVE
Castor's slayer — IDAS
Castor, e.g. — TWIN
Castor, to Pollux — TWIN
Castrate — NEUTER
Castro's home ground — ORIENTE
Castro's predecessor — BATISTA
Castro, e.g. — CUBAN
Casts — TONES
Casts about — SEEKS
Casts doubt on — DISCREDITS
Casual — INFORMAL
Casual conversations — CHATS
Casual greetings — HIS
Casual hats — CAPS
Casual shirt — POLO
Casual shoes — PENNY LOAFERS
Casual wear — DUDS
Casualty, military: Abbr. — MIA
Cat- ______ -tails — O NINE
Cat-quick — AGILE
Cat (catamaran) — HOBIE
Cat breed — ANGORA, MANX
Cat call — MEW
Cat cry — MEOW
Cat family member — FELID
Cat nation — ERIE
Cat's-paw — TOOL
Cat's cry — MEW
Cat, in Cadiz — GATO
Cat, in Catania — GATTO
Cat, in Cordova — GATO
Cat, to Cato — FELIS
Cat-swinger's need — ROOM
Cat-walk — PLANK
Cat: Comb. form — FELIN
Cat: Fr. — CHAT
Cataclysm — DISASTER, SPASM
Catacomb — TOMB
Catafalque — BIER
Catalina Island town — AVALON
Catalina: Abbr. — ISL
Catalog — FILE
Catalog enclosure — ORDER BLANK
Catalogue — ASSORT
Catalogue company's activity — MAILING
Catalogued — INDEXED
Catalpa or ceiba — TREE
Catalyst — YEAST
Catamarans — RAFTS
Catamount — PUMA
Catania citizens: Abbr. — ITALS
Catapult — LAUNCH, ONAGER
Catarrh — RHEUM
Catbird seat? — ROOST
Catcall — RASPBERRY
Catch-22, perhaps — RUB
Catch — BAG, GET, ENMESH, ENTRAP, NAB, SNAG, SNARE
Catch a glimpse of — PEEK
Catch cod — NET
Catch in the act — NAB, NAIL
Catch one's breath — REST
Catch oysters — TONG
Catch sight of — ESPY, SPOT
Catch something — AIL
Catch unaware — STARTLE
Catch up with — OVERTAKE
Catch-22 — BIND, PLIGHT
Catchall abbr. — ET AL, ETC
Catcher in the Rhine — SEINE
Catcher's base — HOME
Catchers' gloves — MITTS
Catches — ENTRAPS, LANDS
Catches flies — SHAGS
Catches napping — STARTLES
Catches on — UNDERSTANDS
Catches on guns — SEARS
Catches red-handed — NAILS
Catchword — EPITHET
Catchwords — PHRASES
Catchy phrase — MOTTO
Categorize — LABEL
Category in "Twenty Questions" — ANIMAL
Cater basely — PANDER
Catercousin — PAL
Caterpillar home — TENT
Caterpillars' hair — SETAE
Catfights — SPATS

Catfish or Cannery — ROW
Catfish Row dealer — BESS
Catfish's lookalike — LOACH
Cathedral — TEMPLE
Cathedral area — APSE
Cathedral church of Rome — LATERAN
Cathedral city in Devon — EXETER
Cathedral city of Germany — ULM
Cathedral city of SE France — ARLES
Cathedral city, Italy — MILAN
Cathedral feature — APSE, ALTAR
Cathedral on Fifth Avenue — ST PATRICKS
Cathedral part — NAVE
Cathedral projection — APSE
Cathedral section — APSE
Cathedral segments — APSES
Cathedral toppers — SPIRES
Cather biographer — EDEL
Cather's "Death _____ for the Archbishop" — COMES
Cather's "One of _____" — OURS
Catherine de Médicis was one — REINE
Catherine de Médicis, e.g. — REINE
Catherine of _____ — ARAGON
Catheter — TUBE
Cathode heater — A BATTERY
Catholic devotions — NOVENA
Catholic tribunal — ROTA
Catkin bearer — ALDER
Catkins — AMENTS
Catnapped — SLEPT
Cato the _____ — ELDER
Cato the Elder was one — EDILE
Cato's 104 — CIV
Cato's 161 — CLXI
Cato's 2550 — MMDL
Cato's 649 — DCIL
Cato's ampersands — ETS
Cato's country — NATIC
Cato's road — ITER
Cato's tomorrow — CRAS
Cato's tongue — LATIN
Cats and dogs — PETS
Cats' prey — MICE
Cats, goats or rabbits — ANGORAS
Catskills place — RESORT
Cattail — REED, RUSH
Cattail or clarinet — REED
Cattiness — SPITE
Cattle — ANGUS, LIVESTOCK
Cattle breed — ANGUS
Cattle drivers — PRODS
Cattle feature — RUMEN
Cattle group — HERD
Cattle pen — CORRAL
Cattle roundups — DRIVES
Cattle stall — CRIB
Cattle, in poesy — KINE
Cattle, old style — KINE
Cattle, to a poet — SWINE
Cattle-raising island — ALDERNEY
Catty sound — MEW
Caucasian — OSSET
Caucasian goat — TEHR
Caucasian language — AVAR
Caucasian native — OSSET
Caucasian tongue — UDIC
Caucasian, in Hawaii — HAOLE
Caucasians — OSSETES
Caucasus native — OSSET
Caucho tree — ULE
Caucho yielder — ULE
Caudal parts — TAILS
Caudle — DRINK
Caught — OVERTAKEN, SNARED, TAKEN
Caught by oarsmen — CRAB
Caught congers — EELED
Caught forty winks — DOZED
Caught in a lasso — NOOSED
Caught in the act — NAILED
Caught lepidopterans — NETTED
Caught sight of — ESPIED, SPIED
Caught, in a way — ROPED
Cauldron — TUB
Cauldron of a sort — ALFET
Cause — BASIS, CREATOR, ORIGIN, ROOT
Cause — INDUCE
Cause — PRIME MOVER, RESULT IN, SOURCE
Cause — THE REASON WHY
Cause — THE WHY AND WHEREFORE
Cause bad luck at the dinner table — SPILL THE SALT
Cause bad luck by walking here — UNDER A LADDER
Cause bad luck while walking — STEP ON A CRACK
Cause concern — ALARM
Cause consternation — ALARM, APPAL
Cause discontent — RUB
Cause distaste — REPEL
Cause euphoria — ELATE
Cause for a suit — TORT
Cause for divorce — GROUNDS
Cause for pride — BOAST
Cause loss — ENDAMAGE
Cause much distress — TORMENT
Cause of a bong or dong — STROKE
Cause of a suit — LIBEL
Cause of Archimedes' cry, "Eureka" — IDEA
Cause of ennui — TEDIUM
Cause of eruptions — ACNE
Cause of irritation — THORN
Cause of sepsis — GERMS
Cause pain — HURT
Cause resentment — IRK
Cause seven years bad luck — BREAK A MIRROR
Cause to fit — TAILOR
Cause to go — SEND
Cause to lose courage — UNMAN
Cause to make a mistake — TRIP UP
Cause to turn turtle — UPEND
Cause want — WASTE
Cause: Comb. form — ETIO
Cause: Fr. — RAISON
Caused — EFFECTED
Caused a rubber check — OVERDREW
Caused annoyance — NETTLED
Caused by — DUE TO
Caused by touch — TACTUAL
Caused distaste — REPELLED
Caused turbulence — MADE WAVES
Causes — REASONS
Causes anger — ENRAGES
Causes bitterness — RANKLES
Causes detritus — ERODES
Causes of nagging pains? — CHARLEY HORSES
Causes to think of — REMINDS
Causing a disturbance — ACTING UP
Causing fear and anxiety — OMINOUS
Caustic — ACRID, BITING, LYE
Caustic substance — LYE
Caustic wit — SARCASM
Caustics — ACIDS
Cauterize — SEAR
Cautionary imperative — DONT
Cautions — WARNS
Cautious — CHARY, WARY
Cav. units — TRPS
Cavalcade — COLUMN
Cavalier — LANCER
Cavalier poet — CAREW
Cavalry horse — CHARGER
Cavalry men — HUSSARS
Cavalry soldier — DRAGOON
Cavalry sword — SABER
Cavalry weapon — SABER
Cavaradossi, Tosca's lover — MARIO
Cavatina — AIR
Cave _____: Beware the dog — CANEM
Cave denizen — BAT
Cave in a cliffside — COVE

Cave, to Coleridge — GROT
Caveat — ALARM
Caveat _____ — EMPTOR
Caveat emptor phrase — AS IS
Cavelike structure — GROTTO
Caves — GROTTOS
Caviar — ROE
Caviar base — ROE
Caviar source — ROE
Cavil — CARP, DISSENT
Cavities of a sort — ENTRA
Cavort — FRISK, FROLIC
Cavorted — ROMPED
Cavy's cousin — MARA
Caxton or Zenger — PRINTER
Cay and Holm — ISLES
Cays — ISLES, ISLETS
Cayuga's neighbor — SENECA
CBer's licensed cousin — HAM
CBS logo — EYE
CD predecessors — LPS
Cease-fire — TRUCE
Cease — DESIST, STOP
Cease to be — END
Cease, on the Bounty — AVAST
Cease: Naut. — AVAST
Ceases — STOPS
Cecil _____, famed photographer — BEATON
Cecil's niece — AGNES DEMILLE
Cecile and Jeanne — STES
Cede — LEAVE
Cedric _____ (Little Lord Fauntleroy) — ERROL
Cee follower — DEE
Ceiba or ipil — TREE
Ceiling decorated with paintings — PLAFOND
Celebes dwarf buffalo — ANOA
Celebes island — MUNA
Celebes ox — ANOA
Celebes, e.g. — SEA
Celebrate — FETE
Celebrated archer — TELL
Celebrated caravel — NINA
Celebrated essayist — ELIA
Celebrated etcher — DURER
Celebrated fabler — AESOP
Celebrated Giant — OTT
Celebrated log — YULE
Celebrated odist — KEATS
Celebrated sign — VEE
Celebrated vow — I DO
Celebration — FEST, FETE, GALA, PARTY, RITE
Celebration at Yuletide — WASSAIL
Celebration conflagration — BONFIRE
Celebration, Spanish style — FIESTA
Celebrations — FETES, GALAS
Celebrity — ECLAT, HONOR, LION
Celebrity's attainment — FAME
Celebrity's following — ENTOURAGE
Celebrity-roast host — DEAN MARTIN
Celebrity: Colloq. — BIG NAME
Celerity — ALACRITY, HASTE, SPEED
Celeste from N.Y.C. — HOLM
Celestial — ASTRAL
Celestial Altar — ARA
Celestial being — SERAPH
Celestial beings, in Brest — ANGES
Celestial bodies — SPHERES
Celestial body — COMET
Celestial canapes? — MANNA
Celestial Eagle — AQUILA
Celestial hunter — ORION
Celestial matter — NEBULA
Celestial phenomenon — ECLIPSE
Celestial Ram — ARIES
Celestial sci. — ASTR
Celestial sign-oriented — ZODIACAL
Celestial sphere — ORB
Celestial streaker — COMET
Celestial terrier? — SKYE
Cell acids, for short — RNAS
Cell body — SOMA
Cell division in genetics — MITOSIS
Cell feature — BAR
Cell finish — ULAR
Cell material: Comb. form — PLASM
Cella — NAOS
Cellar entrance — AREAWAY
Cellar player in 78 — MET
Cellars and attics, usually — STOREROOMS
Cellini's skill — ARTE
Cellist Ma and namesakes — YO YOS
Cellular instrument — PHONE
Cellulose fabric — RAYON
Celt language — IRISH
Celtic — ERSE
Celtic deity — DANU
Celtic group — CLAN
Celtic language — ERSE
Celtic Neptune — LER
Celtic republic, once — EIRE
Celtic sea god — LER
Celtic tribe — ICENI
Celtic word for river — AVON
Celtics' "33" — BIRD
Celtics, for one — TEAM
Cement component — SILICATE
Cemented — GLUED, LUTED
Cen. Florida city — OCALA
Cen. Italian river — LIRI
Cenotaph — TOMB
Censor — BAN
Censor's objective? — PRIM TIME TV
Censure — BLAME, CORRECT, REPROOF
Censure cruelly — SCORCH
Censure severely — SCOLD
Census — BLAME, LIST
Census figs. — STATS
Census taker's dearth — FEW OF YOU
Cent. Amer. peninsula — YUC
Centenial choice for U.S. President — HAYES
Centenial state — COLORADO
Centenial State projection? — TECHNICOLORADO
Center — CORE, HIVE
Center of a famed palindrome — ERE
Center of a simple game — TAC
Center of attraction — ARENA
Center of Fifth Avenue — ROCKEFELLER
Center of operations — BASE
Center the ball — SNAP
Center the cross hairs — AIM
Center: Comb. form — MESO
Centerfold subject — BEEFCAKE
Centers of activity — FOCI
Centers of attention — FOCI
Centers; hubs — FOCI
Centipede — INSECT
CENTO member — IRAN
Central — POLAR
Central America country — PANAMA
Central American — LATINO
Central American monkey — MARMOSET
Central American rodents — PACAS
Central Asian range — ALTAI
Central Caucasian — OSSET
Central Europeans — SLAVS
Central fingerprint ridge — WHORL
Central Florida city — OCALA
Central Italian tourist stop — ASSISI
Central marketplace of Rome — FORUM
Central New York body of water — ONEIDA LAKE
Central or Hyde — PARK
Central part — MIDST
Central point — NODE
Central points — FOCI
Central positions — CORES
Central Tex. town — LLANO
Central U.S.S.R. city — OSH
Central veins of leaves — MIDRIBS
Centuries — EONS
Century letter — CEE

Century plant — AGAVE, ALOE
Century unit — YEAR
Cephalopod's "cover" — INK
Cephalopods — OCTOPI
Cephalopods defenses — INKS
Ceraceous — WAXY
Ceramic material — CLAY
Ceramic paving pieces — TILES
Ceramic piece — TILE
Ceramic ware — PORCELAIN
Ceramics from Holland — DELFTWARE
Ceramist's need — KILN, OVEN
Ceramist's requisite — OVEN
Cerated — WAXY
Cereal blight — ERGOT
Cereal bristles — AWNS
Cereal grain — OAT
Cereal grass — BARLEY, MILLET, RYE, SORGO
Cereal product — MEAL
Cereal spike — AWN
Cereal spikes — EARS
Ceremonial — RITUAL
Ceremonial acts — RITES
Ceremonial prayer — LITANY
Ceremonial Roman chariot — TENSA
Ceremonial staff — MACE
Ceremonial wrestling — SUMO
Ceremonials — RITES
Ceremonies — RITES
Ceremonious — FORMAL
Ceremony — LITURGY, RITE, RITUAL, SERVICE
Ceres, to Socrates — DEMETER
Cerise — RED
Cerise and scarlet — REDS, STELAR
Cerris or roble — OAK
Certain — ASSURED, POSITIVE, SURE
Certain A.L. batters — DHS
Certain acids — AMINOS
Certain actors — HAMS
Certain admiral — REAR
Certain adult — MAN
Certain airline initials — SAS
Certain Alaskan — ALEUT
Certain algae — DIATOMS
Certain alphabet or number — ARABIC
Certain amateurs — HAMS
Certain amplifier — MASER
Certain ants — SLAVES
Certain Arab — OMANI
Certain artwork — OILS
Certain astringent — WITCH HAZEL
Certain athletes — PROS
Certain Australians — MAORIS
Certain barren area — BADLANDS
Certain barriers — CORDONS
Certain bass — STRIPER
Certain bear's song? — AMAPOLA
Certain beards — GOATEES
Certain beverages — SOURS
Certain bills — ONES
Certain birds of a feather — BLOC
Certain black-nosed rabbits — HIMALAYANS
Certain board members — PEGS
Certain books — FICTION
Certain bottom lines — HEMS
Certain brick — ADOBE
Certain broadleaf — MAPLE
Certain buoys — NUNS
Certain businessmen — MANAGERS
Certain button — PANIC
Certain cabbages — KALES
Certain canines — SETTERS, TEETH
Certain cap wearers — DUNCES
Certain carbonated drinks — COLAS
Certain cards, for short — IDS
Certain cars — SEDANS
Certain case — TEST
Certain cats and goats — ANGORRAS
Certain cattle or canines — PUREBREDS
Certain check signers — ENDORSERS
Certain chess pcs. — KTS
Certain China — TEA CUPS
Certain chord — TRIAD
Certain church corner — AMEN
Certain circuit courts — EYRES
Certain clarinets — ALTOS
Certain climbers — IVIES
Certain coals — COKES
Certain cocktails — SOURS
Certain code — AREA, MORSE
Certain coils and currents — TESLA
Certain collars — ETONS
Certain combat zone — BOXING RING
Certain consonants — LEENS
Certain copies — CARBONS
Certain couturier's creations — DIORS
Certain cross — TAU
Certain current, for short — ELEC
Certain daises — OXEYES
Certain dances — HOPS
Certain decks — ORLOPS
Certain degree — NTH
Certain deliveries — CODS
Certain detectives — TRACERS
Certain discs, for short — LPS
Certain disks: Abbr. — EPS
Certain dive — JACKKNIFE
Certain docs — VETS
Certain donations — SLMS
Certain driver's warning — FORE
Certain ed. of the Bible — RSV
Certain empress — TSARINA
Certain engines — DIESELS
Certain English schoolboy — ETONIAN
Certain entrance fees — ANTES
Certain enzymes — MALTASES
Certain European — SERB, CROAT
Certain exam — ORAL
Certain fabric — LINEN
Certain fabrics — WEFTS
Certain farms — DAIRIES
Certain favorite — PIE A LA MODE
Certain feasts — BAKES
Certain fertilizer — NITRATE
Certain fight fans — RINGSIDERS
Certain fighter — PLANE
Certain fisherman — CODDER, EELER, TROLLER
Certain flyers — PILOTS
Certain folding money — TENNERS
Certain folks — ELDERS
Certain football players: Abbr. — LGS
Certain fracture — HAIRLINE
Certain French paintings — MONETS
Certain gaits — LOPES
Certain game pursuit — TRIVIA
Certain GI's — PFCS
Certain glance — CAROM
Certain golf stroke — BAFF
Certain graduates — BAS
Certain grains — WHEAT
Certain greenbacks — ONES
Certain grime — SOOT
Certain ground cover — CORD MOSS
Certain group — TRIO
Certain heights — TREETOPS
Certain herbs — WORTS
Certain highway — BLACKTOP ROAD
Certain hormone — ANDROGEN
Certain horses — BAYS, PACERS
Certain horseshoe throw — LEANER
Certain hose — SHEERS
Certain howlers — WOLVES
Certain illegal voter — REPEATER
Certain Indian soldier — SEPOY

Certain Indonesians — JAVANESE
Certain inlets — COVES
Certain inspectors — ROUNDSMEN
Certain ironworker — GATER
Certain Iroquoians — ERIES
Certain items of tangible property — CHATTELS
Certain jugs — TOBIES
Certain Khans — AGAS
Certain Latvians — LETTS
Certain leaf tip — MUCRO
Certain left wingers — SOUTHPAWS
Certain legumes — LENTILS
Certain lodge members — ELKS, MASONS
Certain logs — YULES
Certain long bones — ULNAE
Certain luminary — C STAR
Certain macaws — ARAS
Certain madrilena — SENORA
Certain Manhattanite — EAST SIDER
Certain marketeers — ADMEN
Certain materials — ORLONS
Certain means of escape — LOOPHOLE
Certain membranes — SEPTA
Certain Mennonites — AMISH
Certain metals — ALLOYS
Certain millworkers — SAWYERS
Certain mining sites — PLACERS
Certain minstrel — END MAN
Certain molding — YMAS, OVOLO
Certain mortals — MEN
Certain movie — REMAKE
Certain music — BLUEGRASS
Certain musician — TONALIST
Certain Muslim — SUNNI
Certain nail — SPAD
Certain naval ordnance — MINES
Certain NCO — SGT
Certain Nebraskan — OTO
Certain necktie — FOUR IN HAND
Certain nests — NIDI
Certain news items, for short — OBITS
Certain newspaper page — OP ED
Certain Nigerians — EDOS
Certain nightclubs, for short — DISCOS
Certain North African — BERBER
Certain notebooks — LLS
Certain nuclide — ISOMER
Certain numbers — EVENS
Certain orange or duck — MANDARIN
Certain oranges — NAVELS
Certain ovens — OASTS
Certain paintings — OILS
Certain paints — LATEXES
Certain papers — EXTRAS
Certain parallelograms — RHOMBI
Certain peers — BARONS
Certain peppers — CHILIS
Certain performer — COMIC
Certain phantom's haunt — OPERA
Certain physicist — ATOMIST
Certain pickles — DILLS
Certain piece of sculpture — MOBILE
Certain pipe — BRIAR
Certain pitch — BREAKING BALL, SLIDERS
Certain Plains precipitation — RAIN
Certain plant workers — WELDERS
Certain plastic tubes — PARISONS
Certain players' assn. — SAG
Certain policemem: Abbr. — SGTS
Certain powder — TALC
Certain priestly figures — LAMAS
Certain primates — APES
Certain properties — RENTAL
Certain quaffs — ALES
Certain racer — MILER
Certain radius — SPOKE
Certain railroaders — TRAINMEN
Certain railroads — ELS
Certain railways — ELS
Certain rays — GAMMAS
Certain reds — MAROONS
Certain refreshments — BEERS
Certain retail outlet — CHAIN STORE
Certain rivers — MUDDY
Certain runners — MILERS
Certain sale gds. — IRRS
Certain saucers — UFOS
Certain savings accts. — IRAS
Certain Scandinavians — SWEDES
Certain school, for short — ELEM, PREP
Certain sculptures — TORSI
Certain sea gull — TERN
Certain ship — OILER
Certain shoe size TRIPLE ETAS
Certain shrub — SUMAC
Certain singer — ALTO
Certain singers — BASSI
Certain sizes — TALLS
Certain skirt — MIDI
Certain Slav — CROAT
Certain slippers — MULES
Certain small countries — BANANA REPUBLICS
Certain socials — TEAS
Certain South African — BOER
Certain Spaniards — IBERI
Certain statesman: Abbr. — PMS
Certain steeplejack — RIVETER
Certain stitch — PURL
Certain stocks — BLUE CHIPS
Certain street sign — ONE WAY
Certain sub — U BOAT
Certain summaries — SYLLABI
Certain surfer — WAHINE
Certain surveyors — MONARCHS
Certain sweaters — SLIP ONS
Certain teen — SUBDEB
Certain teenage Ninja turtles — MUTANTS
Certain telegs, once — NLS
Certain television — COLOR
Certain territorial units — ENCLAVES
Certain tests — ORALS, SCANS, WRITTEN
Certain theater-goers — APPLAUDERS
Certain theatre locale — FAMILY CIRCLE
Certain tide — EBB, NEAP
Certain time measurement — EPACT
Certain tires — RADIALS, RETREADS
Certain tollgate employees — PIKEMEN
Certain tournaments — OPENS
Certain track measurement — OO GAUGE
Certain trailers, for short — SEMIS
Certain tree pests — BORERS
Certain trucks — SEMIS
Certain trumpeter — SWAN
Certain trunks — TORSOS
Certain turkeys — BOURBON REDS
Certain TV offerings — REPEATS
Certain types — PICAS
Certain undesirable passengers? — BACK SEAT DRIVERS
Certain utility conduits? — GAS MAINS
Certain verb: Abbr. — IRR
Certain vote — AYE, NAY, YEA
Certain voter — WOMAN
Certain wader — STORK
Certain waters — SHOALS
Certain wax — SEALANT
Certain weasel — OILER
Certain Wednesday — ASH
Certain whip — CAT O NINE TAILS
Certain wines — REDS

Certain wood — EBONY
Certain word puzzle — ACROSTIC
Certain worker, for short — TEMP
Certain wrench — ALLEN
Certain Yugoslavian — SERB
Certainly, to Jacques — SANS DOUTE
Certainties — LEAD PIPE CINCHES
Certainty — FACT
Certificate — BOND
Certificates, in Durango — ACTAS
Certifies — ATTESTS
Certify — ATTEST, AUDIT
Certify (to) — ATTEST
Cerumen — EARWAX
Cervantes hero — QUIXOTE
Cerveza ingredient — AGUA
Cervine animal — DEER
César Franck's birthplace — LIEGE
Cetus — WHALE
Ceylonese langur — MAHA
Cezanne's "Boy With _____ Vest" — A RED
Cezanne's contemporary — MONET
CGS units — ERGS
Cha-cha — DANCE
Chabas painting — SEPTEMBER MORN
Chabrier favorite — ESPANA
Chad or Onega — LAKE
Chadian town — LERE
Chafe — RUB
Chaff — BANTER
Chagall — MARC
Chagall, e.g. — ARTIST
Chagrin — DISMAY
Chain components — LINK
Chain of hills — RIDGE
Chain sound — CLANK
Chains heard from coast to coast — NETWORKS
Chains, in Paris — FERS
Chair — PRESIDE, SEAT
Chair crosspiece — STAVE
Chair designer Charles — EAMES
Chair makers — CANERS
Chair material — CANE
Chair name — EAMES
Chair of state — THRONE
Chair or auto — SEDAN
Chair part — RUNG
Chair seat repairman — CANER
Chaired a meeting — PRESIDED
Chairman's request — VOTE
Chairman: abbr — CHM, CHMN
Chairperson's accessory — GAVEL
Chairs — SEATS
Chairwomen — MADAMS
Chalcedony — AGATE, ONYX, SARD
Chalcedony gem — SARD
Chalet and chateau — HOMES
Chalet features — EAVES
Chaliapin, e.g. — BASSO
Chalice — CUP
Chalice veil — AER
Chalk — DRAW
Chalk talks — LESSONS
Chalk up to — CHARGE
Chalked up _____ (triumphed) — A WIN
Chalky — WAN
Challenge — CONFRONT, DARE, DEMAND, TEST, TRIAL
Challenge the house — BET
Challenge to a surfer — BREAKER
Challenged — DARED
Challenger — DARER
Challengers, in a way — ANTIS
Challenges — DARES
Chamber — OVEN, ROOM
Chamber for Child — OVEN
Chamber group — TRIO
Chamber music ensemble — TRIO
Chamber or gazer — STAR
Chamber-music composition — TRIO
Chamber-music piece — TRIO
Chamberlain — SERVANT
Chameleon — ANOLE
Chamfer — BEVEL
Chamois — ANTELOPE
Champ — BIT, CHEW
Champ at the bit — FUSS
Champ at Wimbledon: 1975 — ASHE
Champagne buckets — ICERS
Champagne feature — BUBBLE
Champagne term — BRUT
Champagne-orange juice cocktails — MIMOSAS
Champion — ACE, HERO, VICTOR
Champion of a doctrine — ADVOCATE
Champion of a medieval prince — PALADIN
Champion of peace — GANDHI
Championship — TITLE
Champlevé — ENAMEL, INLAID
Chan portrayer — OLAND, TOLER
Chan's exclamation — AH SO
Chance — HAP, ODD, LOT
Chance upon — MEET
Chancel seat — SEDILE
Chancy — RISKY
Chancy social engagement — BLIND DATE
Chandelier — LUSTER, SCONCE
Chanel — COCO
Chanel port — DIEPPE
Chanel recess — APSE
Chanel, to friends — COCO
Chaney — LON
Chaney classic, "The_____" — PHANTOM OF THE OPERA
Chang's counterpart — ENG
Chang's Siamese twin — ENG
Change — ALTER, CASH, TRANSIT
Change a hem — RESEW
Change a shade — RECOLOR
Change addresses — MOVE
Change an appellation — RENAME
Change back — REVERT
Change color — DYE
Change costume — REROBE
Change course — TURN, VEER
Change direction — VEER
Change for a five — ONES
Change for a rupee — ANNAS
Change for the better — ENHANCE
Change in Como — LIRE
Change of five — ONES
Change of mind on an impulse — WHIM
Change slowly by degrees — GRADUATE
Change the angle of a propellor blade — FEATHER
Change the clock — RESET
Change the color — DYE
Change the decor — REDO
Change the flower bed — REPLANT
Change the wallpaper — REDECORATE
Change the wording — REDRAFT
Change, as text — AMEND
Change, to Solti — MUTA
Change: Comb. form — TROPO
Change: Mus. dir. — MUTA
Changeable — FICKLE
Changed — ALTERED
Changed color — DYED
Changed colors again — REDYED
Changed, as leaves — TURNED
Changes — ALTERS
Changes course — VEERS
Changes direction — VEERS
Changes the circuit — REWIRES
Changes the clock — RESETS
Changes the color — DYES

Changes the wall coloring — REPAINTS
Changing stars — NOVAE
Changing the packaging — REBOX
Channel — ARTERY, CANAL, ROUTE
Channel changer — SELECTOR
Channel for molten metal — GATE
Channel markers — BUOYS, CATS
Channel off Greenland — SMITH SOUND
Channels — COURSES
Chanson de _____ — GESTE
Chanson follower — ETTE
Chanson topic — AMOUR
Chant — INTONE, SING
Chanted — INTONED
Chanteur Jacques _____ — BREL
Chanteuse — THRUSH
Chanteuse Edith — PIAF
Chanteuse Horne — LENA
Chanteuse Page — PATTI
Chanticleer — ROOSTER
Chanticleer's realm — ROOST
Chantilly — LACE
Chantilly product — LACE
Chantilly's department — OISE
Chantlike — SING SONG
Chaos — FUROR, RUIN
Chap — BLOKE
Chap trap — VAMP
Chap, in Cordoba — ENTE
Chapeau — TOQUE
Chapeau rest — TETE
Chapeau's place — TETE
Chapeaux — HATS, TOQUES
Chaperon — ESCORT, TUTOR
Chaperone — DUENNA
Chaplain — PADRE
Chaplain, to some — PADRE
Chaplet for Galahad — ORLE
Chaplin and Coward — SIRS
Chaplin character — TRAMP
Chaplin's "_____ My Song" — THIS IS
Chaplin's "_____ Times" — MODERN
Chaplin's prop — CANE
Chaplin's widow — OONA
Chapparal chapeau — TEN GALLON HAT
Chaps — MEN
Chapter — PART, SECTION
Char — BURN, SINGE
Char a steak — SEAR
Char force — MAIDS
Char slightly — SEAR
Character — ROLE
Character actor Leon — AMES
Character actor Tamiroff — AKIM
Character actress Shaw — RETA
Character created by Oscar Wilde — DORIAN GRAY
Character in "B.C." — GROG
Character in "Barbe Bleu" — BLUEBEARD
Character in "G.W.T.W." — ASHLEY
Character in "Henry IV, Pt. 2" — PETO
Character in "Oliver Twist" — MR BUMBLE
Character in "Peter Pan" — SMEE
Character in "Silas Marner" — EPPIE
Character in "Tarzan" — BOY
Character in "The Canterbury Tales" — ALISON
Character in "The Marble Faun" — HILDA
Character in "The Rivals" — ACRES
Character in "The Tempest" — PROSPERO
Character in "The Wind in the Willows" — MR RAT
Character in a beaver lawsuit? — BADGER THE WITNESS
Character in Faulkner's "The Town" — EULA
Character in the "Iliad" — AJAX
Character in Trollope's "Phineas Finn" — ERLE
Character, to a computer — BYTE
Characteristic — TRAIT
Characteristic of wine — AROMA
Characterized by melody — ARIOSE
Characterized by: Suffix — ULOSE
Characters in "Emma" (with "the") — ELTONS
Characters in "Star Wars" — ROBOTS
Characters in "The Sound of Music" — NUNS
Charactor actor Benny — RUBIN
Charade — RIDDLE
Chard — BEET
Charge — ADJURE, ASSESS, COST, FEE, LUNGE
Charge it — OWE
Charge on property — LIEN
Charge opener — SUR
Charge per unit — RATE
Charge with a crime — INDICT
Charge with gas — AERATE
Charge: sl. — RAP
Charged — RAN AT
Charged atoms — IONS
Charged electrons — IONS
Charged particles — IONS
Charged with gas — AERATED
Charger — STEED
Charger in Mexico City — TORO
Chargers or coursers — HORSES
Charges — FEES, RATES, TOLLS
Charges with gas — AERATES
Chariot — WAGON
Chariot in ancient Britain — ESSED
Chariot of yore — ESSED
Chariot's path — ITER
Chariot's way — ITER
Charioteer Ben — HUR
Charitable — LIBERAL
Charitable gifts — ALMS
Charitable items — ALMS
Charitable ones — DONORS
Charity — ALMS, MERCY, AT HOME BEGINNER
Charlatans — QUACKS
Charlemagne and Napoleon: Abbr. — EMPS
Charlemagne and others — EMPERORS
Charlemagne's domain: Abbr. — HRE
Charlemagne's doughty dozen — PALADINS
Charlemange's realm: _____ Abbr. — HRE
Charles _____, Coolidge's VP — DAWES
Charles _____, grandfather of Charlemagne — MARTEL
Charles _____, silents actor — OGLE
Charles and Mary — LAMBS
Charles Dickens — BOZ
Charles Dickens' pen name — BOZ
Charles Evans Hughes was one — BAPTIST
Charles Laughton role — QUASIMODO
Charles Laughton's wife — ELSA
Charles Lutwidge Dodgson character — ALICE
Charles' dog — ASTA
Charles' wife — DIANA
Charleses' dog — ASTA
Charley horse, e.g. — ACHE, CRAMP
Charley's aunt — MEG
Charley's Donna Lucia — AUNT
Charley's relative — AUNT
Charlie and clan — CHANS
Charlie Brown exclamation — RATS
Charlie Brown's cussword — RATS
Charlie Brown's plaint — RATS

Charlie Chan creator — BIGGERS
Charlie McCarthy's nemesis — SNERD
Charlie Parker nickname — BIRD
Charlie's comic brother — SYD
Charlie's wife — OONA
Charlie, the detective — CHAN
Charlie, the fictional sleuth — CHAN
Charlotte _____ — RAE, RUSSE
Charlotte _____, Virgin Islands — AMALIE
Charlotte and Norma — RAES
Charlotte Bronte heroine — JANE
Charlotte Corday's victim — MARAT
Charlotte of "Facts of Life" — RAE
Charlotte of TV — RAE
Charlotte or Norma — RAE
Charm — ENAMOR
Charm — ENDEAR
Charmed creature — ELF
Charming New York City square — GRAMERCY PARK
Charms — DRAWS, ENTHRALS
Charon's river — STYX
Charon, for one — FERRYMAN
Charpentier heroine — LOUISE
Charpoy — COT
Charred — SEARED
Chart — PLAT
Chart a course — PILOT
Chart again — REMAP
Charter — HIRE, LEASE
Charter car — RENTAL
Chartered — LEASED, LET, RENTED
Charteris hero, with "The" — SAINT
Charters — RENTS
Chartres cherub — ANGE
Charwoman's tool — MOP
Chas. Wick's bailiwick — USIA
Chase of "Fletch" — CHEVY
Chase or jack — STEEPLE
Chase, the author — ILKA
Chaser — SODA
Chasm — GORGE
Chassé, e.g. — STEP
Chassepot — RIFLE
Chaste — CLEAN, DECENT, VESTAL
Chasten — SCOLD
Chastise — PUNISH, REPROVE, SCOLD
Chastise, in a way — SPANK
Chastity — VIRTUE
Chastity or Sonny — BONO
Chastity's mother — CHER
Chat — TETE A TETE
Chateau — CASTLE
Chateaubriand, e.g. — STEAK
Chattanooga's State: Abbr. — TENN
Chattel — ESTATE
Chatter — GAB, GABBLE, PRATE, YAP
Chatter idly — JABBER
Chatter in bed? — PILLOW TALK
Chatters — YAKS
Chatty — WORDY
Chauvinism in the fold? — NO EWE TURNS
Chauvinist — JINGO
Chaw — QUID
Cheap-skate — MISER
Cheap — CUT RATE, TIGHT
Cheap cigar — EL ROPO
Cheap hotels — FLOP HOUSES
Cheap newspaper — RAG
Cheap smoke — STOGY
Cheap thin cigar — STOGY
Cheap: Slang — TWOBIT
Cheaper — TINNIER
Cheat — BILK, FLEECE
Cheat the bookie — WELSH
Check — ARREST, DETER, REIN, STEM
Check (money) — TAB
Check a flow of blood — STANCH
Check booster — KITER
Check by pulling — REIN
Check copy — EDIT
Check for Checkers — LEASH
Check for content — TEST
Check for speed — TIME
Check for time — CLOCK
Check or play follower — MATE
Check out — ASSESS
Check over — STUDY
Check part — STUB
Check recipient — ENDORSEE
Check recipients — PAYEES
Checked the joint — CASED
Checkered — PLAID
Checking the physical boundaries of land — SURVEY
Checkmate — BLOCK, HALT
Checkout counter items — BAGS
Checkout machines — SCANNERS
Checkpoint Charlie, was one — BARRIER
Checks — LOWERS THE BOOM, STOPS
Checks for errors — PROOFS
Checks for prints — DUSTS
Checks text — PROOFREADS
Checks the experiment — RETESTS
Checks, a la Cordero — REINS
Cheddar or cottage — CHEESE
Cheek — JOWL
Cheek to cheek — BESIDE
Cheekbone — MALAR
Cheeks like roses, e.g. — SIMILE
Cheeky — BOLD
Cheep — CHIRP
Cheer — GLADDEN, RAH, ROOT
Cheer (Japanese style) — BANZAI
Cheer (up) — CHIRK
Cheer for a matador — OLE
Cheer for El Cid — OLE
Cheer for El Cordobes — OLE
Cheer for Pavarotti — BRAVO
Cheer for the home team — ROOT, YELL
Cheer up — ELATE
Cheer's cousin — PROSIT
Cheer, at a flamenco dance — OLE
Cheer, in Oviedo — OLE
Cheer, of a sort — RASPBERRY
Cheered the home team — ROOTED
Cheerful — CHIRPY, GAY, PERT, RIANT
Cheerful conclusion? — UP END
Cheerful little earful — DITTY
Cheerful sound — HA HA
Cheerful sprite — PIXY
Cheerful tune — LILT
Cheering section — ROOTERS
Cheering words — RAHS
Cheerio — TATA
Cheerleading staple — LOCOMOTIVE
Cheerless — GRAY
Cheers — BOTTOMS UP, RAHS, SHOUTS
Cheers for the matador — OLES
Cheers for the torero — OLES
Cheers or chin-chion — TOASTS
Cheers, e.g. — TOAST
Cheers, in Cadiz — OLES
Cheery final story on newscast — KICKER
Cheese a la Athens — FETA
Cheese choice — SWISS
Cheese city — EDAM
Cheese dish — RAREBIT, WELSH RABBIT
Cheese for a baguette — BRIE
Cheese for quiche — SWISS
Cheese from France — BRIE
Cheese from Meaux — BRIE
Cheese lover — MOUSE
Cheese that's not bad? — GOUDA
Cheese town of Holland — EDAM
Cheese tray item — BRIE, EDAM

Cheese, in Oslo — OST
Cheesecake viewer — OGLER
Cheesecloth — NET
Cheeselike — CASEOUS
Cheeseparer — MISER
Cheesy — PALTRY
Chef — COOK
Chef of a very high rank — CORDON BLEU
Chef's art — COOKERY
Chef's attire — APRON
Chef's concoction — SAUCE
Chef's need — POTS
Chef's references — COOK-BOOKS
Chef's specialty — ROAST
Chekhov and Bruckner — ANTONS
Chelsea beltways — RING ROADS
Chelsea domain — MANOR
Chelsea Hotel resident: 1962-68 — ARTHUR MILLER
Chem. classroom — LAB
Chem. compound — AZIDE, DDT, OXIDE
Chem. ending — ENE
Chem. milieus — LABS
Chem. or biol. — SCI
Chem. or bot. — SCI
Chem. pollutants — PCBS
Chem. suffix — ANE
Chem. unit — ATM
Chemical — ELEMENT
Chemical analysis — ASSAY
Chemical antiseptic: Comb. form — IOD
Chemical bases — ALKALIS
Chemical compound — AMIDE, ENOL, IMIDE
Chemical compound — ESTER, ISOMER, IODIDE, PURIN
Chemical compound: Suff. — IDE
Chemical compounds — AMYLS
Chemical container — BEAKER
Chemical element — BORON
Chemical ending — ANE, ENE, ENOL, INE, OLS
Chemical flower? — OXIDE DAISY
Chemical haze — SMOG
Chemical instrument — ETNA, STILL
Chemical measure — GRAM
Chemical oxide — ALUMINA
Chemical prefix — ACI, AMIDO, OXO, THIO
Chemical preparation — ROSI-NATE
Chemical salts — MALATES, SAL
Chemical solvent — ACETAL
Chemical substances — AMIDES
Chemical suffix — ANE, ASE, IDE, ITOL, ENE, YNE
Chemical suffix: sugars — OSE
Chemical test — ASSAY
Chemical used in film devel oping — AMIDOL
Chemical vessel — ALUDEL
Chemically treated — BORATED
Chemin de _____ — FER
Chemise — SMOCK, TEDDY
Chemist Harold — UREY
Chemist Pauling — LINUS
Chemist prefix — THIO
Chemist's workplace, for short — LAB
Chemistry Nobelist in 1934 — UREY
Chemistry or physics: Abbr. — SCI
Chemistry suffix — ANE
Chemists' hangouts — LABS
Chenille — YARN
Cheongsam features — SLITS
Cher's Academy Award winner: 1987 — MOONSTRUCK
Cher's ex — BONO
Cher's former partner — BONO, SONNY
Cherish — ADORE, ENSHRINE, TREASURE
Cherished — DEAR
Cherished ones — DEARS
Cherokee's booster — HURON
Cheroot or corona — CIGAR
Cherries — BINGS
Cherries Jubilee, for one — DESERT
Cherry — BING, GLAD
Cherry brandy — KIRSCH
Cherry color — CERISE
Cherry or tomato — RED
Cherry picker, e.g. — TOWER WAGON
Cherry stone — CLAM
Cherry stone clam — QUAHOG
Cherry-red — CERISE
Cherub — AMORETTO, BABE
Cherub, in Chamonix — ANGE
Cherub, in Chartres — ANGE
Cheryl — — — of "Charlie's Angels" — LADD
Chesapeake Bay is one — RETRIEVER
Chesapeake Bay island — KENT
Chesapeake Bay island and sound — TANGIERS
Cheshire borough — CREWE
Cheshire-Cat's leftover — GRIN
Chess castle — ROOK
Chess game ender — MATE
Chess manuever — MOVE
Chess move — CASTLE
Chess or Scrabble — BOARD GAME
Chess pc. — KNT
Chess piece — MAN
Chess pieces — KNIGHTS, MEN, PAWNS, ROOKS
Chess pieces to Alan and Larry? — KINGS QUEENS
Chess strategy — MOCWA
Chess term — MATE
Chess, for instance — BOARD GAME
Chessman — KING, PAWN
Chest — THORAX
Chest bones — RIBS
Chest fastener — HASP
Chest for valuables, of old — ARCA
Chest lining — CEDAR
Chest material — CEDAR
Chest of drawers — COM-MODE, HIGHBOY
Chest rattle — RALE
Chest sound — RALE
Chest wood — CEDAR
Chest: Comb. form — STETH
Chesterfield — COAT
Chesterfield, e.g. — SOFA
Chesterfieldian — ELEGANT
Chesterfields — SOFAS
Chesterton's Father — BROWN
Chestnut case — BUR
Chestnut-colored horse — SORREL
Chevalier film — GIGI
Chevalier hit song — MIMI
Chevet — APSE
Cheville — PEG
Chevrotains' genus — TRAGU-LUS
Chevy — HUNT
Chevy's "Foul Play" co-star — GOLDIE
Chew — CHOMP, MASTICATE
Chew at — GNAW
Chew noisily — CHAMP
Chew the _____ (ponder) — CUD
Chew the fat — GAB, JAW, RAP
Chew the rag — GOSSIP
Chew the scenery — EMOTE
Chewed the fat — RAPPED
Chewed the rag — GABBED
Chews like a beaver — GNAWS
Chews the rag — GABS
Chews the scenery — EMOTES
Chewy candy — CARAMEL, TAFFY
Chewy chocolate — NOUGA-TINE
Cheyenne's home — TEPEE
Chez Scarlett — TARA
Chg. for a loan — INT
Chi-chi — TONY
Chi. airport code — ORD
Chi. suburb — NILES
Chi. trains — ELS

Chi. transportation — ELS
Chi.-Ft. Wayne vector — ESE
Chiang-_____-shek — KAI
Chiang _____, Mao's widow — CHING
Chic — ELEGANT, SMART
Chicago-born actress — RAQUEL WELCH
Chicago — WINDY CITY
Chicago airport — OHARE
Chicago area, with "The" — LOOP
Chicago basketball team — BULLS
Chicago Bears' coach — DITKA
Chicago club — CUBS
Chicago district, with "The" — LOOP
Chicago fire cow owner? — OLEARY
Chicago footballer — BEAR
Chicago hoopster — BULL
Chicago landmark — SEARS TOWER
Chicago recruiter — CUB SCOUT
Chicago stopover — OHARE
Chicago team — BEARS
Chicago to Columbus vector — ESE
Chicago university — DE PAUL
Chicago-to-Detroit dir. — ENE
Chicago / Bangor vector — ENE
Chicanery — BLARNEY, FRAUD
Chick sound — PEEP
Chick Webb, for one — DRUMMER
Chickaree's morsel — ACORN
Chicken-_____, like a certain "Little" — HEARTED
Chicken _____ — LITTLE
Chicken _____ King — A LA
Chicken choice — BREAST
Chicken coop — ROOST
Chicken farm structure — HEN HOUSE
Chicken Little's cry — DEAR ME
Chicken Little, for one — ALARMIST
Chicken of the future — EGG
Chicken or turkey — FOWL
Chicken parts — NECKS
Chicken pox — VIRUS
Chicken, in Calabria — POLLO
Chicken-eaters choice — LEG
Chicle gum — BALATA
Chico or Gummo — MARX
Chide — BERATE
Chider — SCONDER
Chief — HEAD, PRIMAL
Chief artery — AORTA
Chief city in Avon County — BRISTOL
Chief city in Morocco — RABAT
Chief city of New Britain — RABAUL
Chief city of old Cyprus — SALAMIS
Chief city of the Ukraine — KIEV
Chief comics — TOP BANANAS
Chief commodity — STAPLE
Chief ductwork — MAINS
Chief Egyptian divinity — PTAH
Chief engineer on the Enterprise — SCOTTY
Chief Etruscan god — TINIA
Chief god of Thebes — AMON
Chief honcho of the Aesir — ODIN
Chief island of Tanzania — ZANZIBAR
Chief island of the Seychelles — MAHE
Chief Japanese island — HONSHU
Chief Justice Warren — EARL
Chief Justice: 1941-46 — STONE
Chief Justice: 1953-69 — WARREN
Chief magistrate of a Scottish burgh — PROVOST
Chief magistrate of Venice, once — DOGE
Chief Norse deity — ODIN
Chief of naval operations (1942-1945) — KING
Chief of the Paris police — PREFECT
Chief officer: Abbr. — PRES
Chief ore of aluminum — BAUXITE
Chief ore of lead — GALENA
Chief Ouray's people — UTES
Chief part of honey — NECTAR
Chief river of Pakistan — INDUS
Chief White Cloud's people — IOWAS
Chiffon and voile — SHEERS
Chigger — MITE
Chihuahua cheer — OLE
Chihuahua's language? — ESPANIEL
Chilcan coins — PESOS
Child and Howe, grab, L.B.J. pet — JULIASSEIZEHER
Child star Jackie — COOGAN
Child's "piggies" — TOES
Child's collection: Abbr. — RPS
Child's companion — PLAYMATE
Child's coverup — APRON
Child's game — TAG
Child's marble — AGATE
Child's need — OVEN
Child's pet — HAMSTER
Child's play — MARBLES, SNAP
Child's spinner — TOP
Child's toy — TOP
Child, for one — CHEF
Child, in Scotland — BAIRN
Child: Comb. form — PED, PEDO
Child: Sp. — NINO
Childhood — YOUTH
Childish, in Chartres — PUERIL
Childlike — OPEN
Children — TADS
Children's aid org. — SPCC
Children's classic — THE TALE OF PETER RABBIT
Children's game — TAG
Children's garments — SMALLS
Children's Halloween game? — HIDE AND GO SHRIEK
Children's television — KIDVID
Children's-song character — THE FARMER IN THE DELL
Chile export — NITER
Chile saltpetre — NITRO
Chilean bird — TURCO
Chilean capital — SANTIAGO
Chilean export — NITRO
Chilean grouse? — PHEASANTIAGO
Chilean south winds — SURES
Chilean stream — LOA
Chilean timber tree — RAULI
Chili con _____ — CARNE
Chill — ICE
Chilled — ICED
Chilled dessert — GELATIN
Chilled, old style — ACOLD
Chilling — EERY, ON ICE
Chills — COOLS, ICES
Chills and fever — AGUE
Chilly — ALGID
Chilly apple seed — COLD PIT
Chilly time in Spain — ENERO
Chime — PEAL
Chimes from "Hades" — HELLS BELLS
Chimney accumulation — SOOT
Chimney particles — SOOT
Chimney problem — SOOT
Chimney residue — SOOT
Chimp's cousin — ORANG
Chimp, e.g. — APE
Chimps — APES
Chin or Malt finish — ESE
Chin. dynasty — HAN
Chin. name — MAO
China — TEA SET
China follower — WARE
China item — PLATE
China lead-in — INDO
China piece — PLATE

China prefix — INDO
China's _____ En-lai — CHOU
China's Chou En- _____ — LAI
China's Great _____ — WALL
China's neighbor — KOREA
China, Japan, etc. — ASIA
China, Korea, etc. — ASIA
China-Russia divider — AMUR
Chinatown's famed street — MOTT
Chinese-Russian river — ILI
Chinese betting game — FAN-TAN
Chinese black tea — BOHEA
Chinese border river — YALU
Chinese character — IDEOGRAM
Chinese civet — RASSE
Chinese concubine — TSIP
Chinese councils — YUANS
Chinese dialect — CAN-TONESE
Chinese dish — EGG FOO YOUNG
Chinese dumplings — DIM SUM
Chinese dynasty — HAN CHIN, MING, TANG, TSIN
Chinese dynasty: 1368-1644 — MING
Chinese dynasty: 960-1279 — SUNG
Chinese green tea with twisted leaves — HYSON
Chinese hair style — PIGTAIL
Chinese horns — OBOES
Chinese idol — JOSS
Chinese idol or stick — JOSS
Chinese legendary dynasty — HSIA
Chinese martial art — KUNG FU
Chinese mystical word — TAO
Chinese nursemaid — AMAH
Chinese or Indian coin — CASH
Chinese or Japanese — ASIAN
Chinese organization — TONG
Chinese ornamental tree — SANDPEAR
Chinese pagoda — TAA
Chinese peak — OMI
Chinese pleasure craft? — SUN YACHT SEN
Chinese poet: 701-62 — LI PO
Chinese pref. — SINO
Chinese province — HONAN, SHENSI
Chinese seaport — AMOY
Chinese singing ads? — BEIJINGLES
Chinese skiff — SAMPAN
Chinese society — TONG
Chinese territory — MANCHURIA
Chinese truth — TAO
Chinese warehouse — HONG
Chinese weight — LIANG, TAEL
Chinese: Comb. form — SINO
Chink — CRANNY
Chinook or sirocco — WIND
Chinquapin or ginkgo — TREE
Chins — GABS
Chintzy ones — MISERS
Chip a glass — DAMAGE
Chip in — ANTE
Chip in chips — ANTES
Chip off the old block — SON
Chip on chip on chip — STACK
Chipmunk's kin — GOPHER
Chipped — FLAKED
Chips in a chip — ANTES
Chips' companion — FISH
Chiquita _____ — BANANA
Chiropteran — BAT
Chiropterous — BATTY
Chirp — TWEET
Chirping sound — TWEET
Chisel — CARVE
Chisholm Trail town — ENID
Chisholm, for example — TRAIL
Chit — IOU
Chitchats — SHOOTS THE BREEZE
Chiton's cousin — STOLA
Chivalry — VALOR
Chivy — TEASE
Chivy or chevy — TEASE
Chloroform's cousin — ETHER
Cho-choo sounds — CHUGS
Chock — WEDGE
Chockful — ABRIM
Chocolate — CACAO
Chocolate flavor — BITTER-SWEET
Chocolate source — CACAO
Chocolate substitute — CAROB
Chocolate tree — COLA
Choctaw — INDIAN
Choice — ELITE, OPTION, RARE, SELECT
Choice assignment — PLUM
Choice cut — FILET
Choice item — PLUM
Choice meat — T BONE STEAK
Choice part — LEADING LADY, PLUM
Choice part for a Shakespearean — LEAR
Choice seating — RINGSIDE
Choice steak — T BONE
Choice word — EITHER
Choice words — OR ELSE, ORS
Choices: Abbr. — SELS
Choir gallery — LOFT
Choir gown — ROBE
Choir group — ALTOS
Choir leader — CANTOR
Choir member — ALTO, TENOR
Choir member's dream — SOLO
Choir persons — ALTOS
Choir recess — APSE
Choir response — AMEN
Choir voice — ALTO, TENOR
Choir wear — ROBE
Choir-related — CHORAL
Choke — THROTTLE
Chokes; stifles — DAMPS
Choler — ANGER, BILE, IRE
Choleric — — ANGRY, IRATE
Cholesterol source — LARD
Cholla and opuntia — CACTI
Chomp — EAT
Choo Choo Coleman was one — MET
Choose — CULL, ELECT, OPT, PICK, SELECT
Choose and follow — ADOPT
Choose for membership — TAP
Choose from a menu — ORDER
Choose partners — PAIR OFF
Chooses — APPOINTS, OPTS, SELECTS
Chop — HACK, HEW
Chop choice — LOIN
Chop chops — CLEAVE
Chop off — LOP
Chop up — HASH
Chop wood — HEW
Chopin — PIANIST
Chopin composition — ETUDE
Chopin crowd pleaser — MINUTE WALTZ
Chopin opus — ETUDE
Chopin piece — ETUDE
Chopped — AXED, HEWED
Chopped cabbage — SLAW
Chopped fish — CHUM
Chopped food, of a kind — MINCED MEAT
Chopped up — DICED
Chopper — AXE
Chopper part — ROTOR
Chopper, of a sort — APE
Choppers — AXMEN
Choppy sea — RACE
Chops — AXES
Chops to pieces — HASHES
Choral composition — CAN-TATA, MOTET
Choral syllables — LALAS
Choral voice — ALTO
Choral work — GLEE, MOTET
Chordal — HOMOPHONIC
Chore — TASK
Choreographer-director from Chicago — FOSSE
Choreographer Alvin — AILEY
Choreographer and director Bob — FOSSE
Choreographer Cunningham — MERCE

Choreographer de Mille — AGNES
Choreographer Kurt — JOOSS
Choreographer Twyla — THARP
Choreographer White — ONNA
Choreographer's concern — STEP
Chores — TASKS
Chorister — ALTO
Chorister's big moment — SOLO
Chorister's garb — ROBE
Chortle — LAUGH
Chorus — REFRAIN
Chorus of a song — REFRAIN
Chorus rejects — MONOTONES
Chose — OPTED, VOTED
Chose chow — ORDERED
Chose for jury duty — IMPANELED
Chosen — ELECTED
Chosen (country) — KOREA
Chosen few — ELITE
Chosen, in Caen — ELU
Chosen, in Chartres — ELU
Chou En _____ — LAI
Chow _____ — MEIN
Chowder base — CLAM
Chowed down — ATE
Chris of tennis fame — EVERT
Chris of the courts — EVERT
Christ fest. abbr. — XMAS
Christen — NAME, BAPTIZE
Christened — NAMED
Christener — NAMER
Christian and Mayan — ERAS
Christian creations — DIORS
Christian equivalent of Ramadan — LENT
Christian love — AGAPE
Christian of fashion — DIOR
Christian of the East — LUNIAT
Christian symbol of the cross — IHS
Christian's creations — DIORS
Christiana, today — OSLO
Christiania today — OSLO
Christie and namesakes — AGATHAS
Christie character — ESA
Christie of mystery — AGATHA
Christie or Karenina — ANNA
Christie sleuth — MISS MARPLE
Christie title from "Twelth Night" — SAD CYPRESS
Christie's "_____ at End House" — PERIL
Christie's "There _____ Tide" — IS A
Christina Crawford book — MOMMIE DEAREST
Christine of Hollywood — LAHTI
Christmas — NOEL, YULE
Christmas and eared — SEALS
Christmas candy — CANES
Christmas cookie flavoring — ANISE
Christmas decoration — HOLLY, MISTLETOE
Christmas dinner entree — GOOSE
Christmas displays — CRECHES
Christmas Eve item — YULE LOG
Christmas feature — NOEL
Christmas figure — MAGI, SANTA
Christmas gift for Donald Trump — A SQUARE DEAL
Christmas gift for Mike Tyson — BOXER SHORTS
Christmas gift for Miss Muffet — INSECT REPELLENT
Christmas gift for Superman — PIE IN THE SKY
Christmas poem starter — TWAS
Christmas presents for dad — TIES
Christmas singer — CAROLLER
Christmas song — CAROL, NOEL
Christmas stollen gredient — YEAST
Christmas travellers — MAGI
Christmas tree star, for example — ORNAMENT
Christmas visitor — SANTA CLAUS
Christmas visitors — MAGI
Christophe's homeland — HAITI
Christopher _____ of rhyme — ROBIN
Christopher Carson "alias" — KIT
Christopher Columbus, for one — GENOESE
Christopher Robin's creator — MILNE
Chromolithograph on cloth — OLEO
Chromosome component — GENE
Chromosome constituents — GENES
Chronicle — NOVEL
Chronicle item — EVENT
Chronological period — EPACT
Chronologist's concern — TIME
Chronometric letters — GMT
Chrysler cars of 1928-61 — DE SOTO
Chub — DACE
Chubby — PLUMP
Chubby Checker's forte — TWIST
Chubby one — ROLY POLY
Chuckle — TITTER
Chuckling carnivore — LAUGHING HYENA
Chuckling sound — HEH
Chug-a-lug — SWIG
Chum — PAL, PARD
Chummy — PALSY WALSY
Chump's cousin — NERD
Chums — PALS
Chunk — SLAB
Chunk of turf — SOD
Chunk, in Chelsea — WODGE
Church — CHAPEL, ECCLESIA, MOSQUE, SHRINE
Church advisory council — SYNOD
Church area — AISLE, ALTAR, APSE, NAVE
Church area — AMEN CORNER
Church assembly — SYNOD
Church assistant — ELDER
Church bench — PEW
Church books — HYMNALS
Church calendar — ORDO, ROTA
Church caretaker — SEXTON
Church closing — AMEN
Church contribution — TITHE
Church council — SYNOD
Church council site — TRENT
Church crucifix — ROOD
Church desk — AMBO
Church dignitary — PRELATE
Church elder — DEACON
Church feature — ALTAR, APSE
Church features — STEEPLES
Church gp. — CONG
Church group leader — CHOIR MASTER
Church headwear — MITER
Church instruments — ORGANS
Church law — CANON
Church leaders — PONTIFFS, POPES
Church members — — BRETHREN
Church musician — ORGANIST
Church officer — DEACON, ELDER
Church officers: Abbr. — DEAS
Church official — ELDER
Church part — APSE, NAVE
Church pledge — TITHE
Church projections — APSES
Church recess — APSE
Church rite — MASS
Church seats — PEWS

Church section — APSE, TRANSEPT
Church Society since 1714 — AMANA
Church tax — TITHE
Church teaching — CREED
Church title — FRA
Church topper — SPIRE, STEEPLE
Church tribunal — ROTA
Church vessel — AMAS
Church vestment — ALB
Church vestment — ALB, AMICE, ORGAN
Church vocal composition — MOTET
Church vocalists — CHOIR
Church words — AMENS
Church-goer — REGULAR
Church-going sailor? — PIOUS GOB
Church-supper dish — CASSEROLE
Churchill _____ — DOWNS
Churchill family home — BLENHEIM
Churchill's "_____ Country" — A FAR
Churchill's "enigma" — RUSSIA
Churchill's daughter — SARAH
Churchill's few — RAF
Churchill's gesture — VEE
Churchill's Labor Minister — BEVIN
Churchillian sign — VEE
Churchillian word — TOIL
Churchman — CLERIC, DEACON
Churchmen: Abbr. — BPS
Churchwarden — PIPE
Churl — CAD
Churlish child — BRAT
Churn — WHIP
Chute — SLIDE
Chute material — NYLON
Chute opener? — PARA
Chutney, e.g. — RELISH
CIA predecessor — OSS
Ciao — TATA
Ciao, on Oahu — ALOHA
Cicatrix — SCAR
Cicero was one — ORATOR
Cicero's "I maintain" — ALO
Cicero's 503 — DIII
Cicero's bread — PANIS
Cicero's famous scribe — TIRO
Cicero's heat — CALOR
Cicero, e.g. — ORATOR, RHETOR
Cicerone — GUIDE
Cigar — PANATELA
Cigar end? — ETTE
Cigar litter — ASH
Cigar or crown — CORONA
Cigar remains — ASHES
Cigar tree, e.g. — CATALPA
Cigar-shaped — PROLATE
Cigarette — CIGGY, SMOKE, WEED
Cigarette end — ASH
Cigarette user — SMOKER
Cilium — LASH
Cinch — SHOO IN, SNAP
Cinch belt's cousin — SASH
Cinci players — NINE, REDS
Cincinnati — QUEEN CITY
Cincinnati nine — REDS
Cincinnati players — REDS
Cincinnati Rose — PETE
Cincinnati team — REDS
Cincinnati's team — REDLEGS
Cincinnati-N.Y. vector — ENE
Cincture — BELT
Cinder — SLAG
Cinder follower — ELLA
Cinderella' stepsisters, e.g. — MEANIES
Cinders — ASHES
Cinema — FLICKS
Cinema's M. Hulot — TATI
Cinema's Orson — WELLES
Cinema-TV detective Helm — MATT
Cinematographer Nykvist — SVEN
Cinnabar — ORE
Cinnabar and bauxite — ORES
Cinnabar or galena — ORE
Cinnamon — SPICE
Cinnamon bark — CASSIA
Cinque follower — SEI
Cio-Cio San: — MADAME BUTTERFLY
Cio-Cio-San's sash — OBI
Cioppino leavings — SHELLS
Cipher system — CODE
Ciphers — ZEROS
Circa — ABOUT
Circle — TURN
Circle dance — HORA
Circle meas. — DIAM
Circle of color — AREOLA
Circle of light — HALO, CORONA
Circle or sanctum — INNER
Circle parts — ARCS, DEGREES, RADII
Circle sections — ARCS
Circle segments — ARCS, RADII
Circle the earth — ORBIT
Circle, NASA style — ORBIT
Circled — ORBED
Circles — ORBS
Circuit — AMBIT
Circuit breaker — SWITCH
Circuitous — ROUND ABOUT
Circuits of a utility system — MAINS
Circular — CURVED, FLIER, ROTARY, ROUND
Circular diamond — RONDELLE
Circular painting — TONDO
Circular, towerlike fort — MARTELLO
Circular: Abbr. — RND
Circumferences — GIRTHS
Circumnavigate — SKIRT
Circumscribe — LIMIT
Circumspect — CHARY
Circumvent — EVADE
Circus cover — TENT
Circus employee — TAMER
Circus equipment — TRAPEZES
Circus figure — TAMER
Circus group — BARE BACK RIDERS
Circus Maximus official — EDILE
Circus partner of P.T. Barnum — RINGLING
Circus people — TRAINERS
Circus performer — CLOWN, SEAL
Circus performers to Billy? — WILDERS TAMERS
Circus performers: Abbr. — ACROS
Circus star — TAMER
Circus swing — TRAPEZE
Circus worker — TAMER
Circus workers' brawls — CLEMS
Cistern — VAT
Cistern's catch — RAINWATER
Citadel in ancient Greece — ACROPOLIS
Citizen — FREE MAN
Citizen Kane's "Rosebud" — SLED
Citizens of a Japanese port — OSAKANS
Citole — LUTE
Citric quenchers — ADES
Citrine — FALSE TOPAZ
Citronlike — LEMONISH
Citrus belt — FLORIDA
Citrus center — OCALA
Citrus fruit source — LEMON TREE
Citrus fruits — LIMES, ORANGES, TANGELOS
Citrus hybrid — TANGELO
Citrus trees — LIMES
City-state — POLIS
City-state of old Greece — SPARTA
City — BURG
City and river in central Europe — EGERS
City area — SLUM
City at the foot of Mt. Etna — CATANIA
City blight — SLUM
City brighteners — NEONS

City building — TENEMENT
City captured by the French in 1859 — SAIGON
City celebrated by Cole Porter — PAREE
City cruisers — TAXIS
City district — UPTOWN
City E. of Phoenix — MESA
City east of Erie — OLEAN
City ENE of Wichita — IOLA
City ESE of Dayton, O. — XENIA
City eyesore — SLUM
City facing Lake Huron — ALPENA
City for split decisions? — RENO
City in Alabama, W of Montgomery — SELMA
City in Argentina — MORON
City in Bangladesh — DACCA
City in Bolivia — SUCRE
City in California — MADERA
City in Camus' "The Plague" — ORAN
City in Canada — SOREL
City in central Florida — SEBRING
City in central Neb. — ORD
City in China's Kansu province — WUWEI
City in County Kerry — KILLARNEY
City in East Germany — GOTHA
City in Egypt — ASWAN
City in France — BREST
City in Georgia — MACON
City in Germany — LAHR
City in Greece — ARGOS
City in Hungary — EGER
City in Ill. — KANKAKEE
City in Illinois or Mississippi — MOLINE
City in Italy — GEMPA, PADUA, ROMA
City in Libya — TRIPOLI
City in Mo. — AVA
City in Montana — BUTTE
City in N. France — LAON
City in N. Italy — CESENA
City in N. Oklahoma — ENID
City in NE France — NANCY
City in NE Nevada — ELKO
City in NE Romania — JASSY
City in NE Texas — WACO
City in New Hampshire — KEENE
City in Nigeria — EDE
City in Normandy — CAEN
City in NW Algeria — ORAN
City in NW France — DINAH, RENNES
City in NW Germany — EMDEN
City in NW Illinois — GALENA
City in Ohio — NILES
City in Oklahoma — ENID
City in Peru — ICA
City in Provence — ARLES
City in Puerto Rico — CATANO, PONCE
City in Quebec — SOREL
City in Roumania — ARAD
City in S France — ALES
City in S Netherlands — BREDA
City in S. Turkey — ADANA
City in SE Alaska, U.S. naval air base — SITKA
City in SE Florida — TAMARAC
City in SE France — LYON
City in SE Kansas — IOLA
City in SE New Hampshire — PORTSMOUTH
City in SE Siberia — IMAN
City in SE Turkey — URFA
City in SE Wyoming — LARAMIE
City in Serbia — NISH
City in Sicily — ENNA
City in southern China — KWEILIN
City in Spain — CIUDAD
City in SW Connecticut — ANSONIA
City in SW Ga. — PELHAM
City in SW Idaho — NAMPA
City in SW New York — OLEAN
City in the Nile Delta — TANTA
City in the Ruhr region — HERNE
City in the Ruhr valley — ESSEN
City in Thessaly — LARISSA
City in Tuscany — SIENA
City in Uruguay — SALTO
City in Utah — OGDEN, OREM, SALT LAKE
City in Vermont — BARRE
City in Vermont — MONTPELIER
City in Virginia — ROANOKE
City in W Alaska — NOME
City in W Algeria — BECHAR
City in W. Romania — ARAD
City in western North Carolina — LENOIR
City in Yemen — ADEN
City known for damascene ware — TOLEDO
City map — PLAT
City N of Bombay — SURAT
City N of Des Moines — AMES
City N of Detroit — UTICA
City NE of Boston — SALEM
City NE of Paris — LAON
City NE OF Syracuse — ONEIDA
City NE of Venice — UDINE
City near Amhem — EDE
City near Assisi — SIENA
City near Babylon's site — CAIRO
City near Barcelona — LERIDA
City near Boston — SALEM
City near Boys Town — OMAHA
City near Chicago — ELGIN
City near Dayton — XENIA
City near Daytona Beach — DELAND
City near Köln — BONN
City near Lake Tahoe — RENO
City near Leipzig — ERFURT, HALLE
City near Lille — ARRAS
City near Los Angeles — ELMONTE, POMONA
City near Milwaukee — RACINE
City near Montpelier — BARRE
City near Moray Firth — INVERNESS
City near Oakland — ALAMEDA
City near Osaka, Japan — NARA
City near Padua — ESTE
City near San Francisco — ALAMEDA
City near Tahoe — RENO
City near Turin — ASTI
City near Vesuvius — NAPLES
City night sights — NEONS
City NNE of Lake Tahoe — RENO
City NNE of Paris — LILLE
City NNW of Gdansk — SOPOT
City NNW of Oklahoma City — ENID
City north of Des Moines — AMES
City not built in a day — ROME
City NW of Bologna — MODENA
City NW of Buenos Aires — TIGRE
City NW of Grenoble — LYONS
City NW of Leipzig — HALLE
City NW of Madrid — AVILA
City NW of Napoli — ROMA
City NW of Nimes — ALES
City NW of Orlando — OCALA
City NW of Trieste — UDINE
City NW of Venice — TRENT
City NW of Waco — HICO
City of central Florida — OCALA
City of famous aqueduct, Pont du Gard — NIMES
City of Gaul — ALESIA
City of Germany — ESSEN

City of India — DELHI
City of lace — ALENCON
City of light — PARIS
City of Light native — PARISIENNE
City of lights — PERTH
City of masts — LONDON
City of N central Hungary — EGER
City of N. central N. Dak — MINOT
City of N. France — LILLE
City of N. India — DELHI
City of N. Italy — MILAN
City of NW Louisiana — SHREVEPORT
City of NW Spain — LEON
City of NW Turkey — BURSA
City of Old Castile — AVILA
City of palaces — CALCUTTA
City of S. Italy — OTRANTO
City of the Nobel Peace Prize — OSLO
City of the Oka — OREL
City of the Peloponnesus — ARGOS
City of the Sacher torte — VIENNA
City of W Colombia — CALI
City of W. India — SURAT
City official — ALDERMAN, MAYOR
City official: Abbr. — ALD
City on Casco Bay — BANGOR
City on Hawaii — HILO
City on Honshu — NARA
City on Lake Erie — HURON
City on Lake Michigan — RACINE
City on Lake Ontario — TORONTO
City on Lake Superior — DULUTH
City on Long Island Sound — BRIDGEPORT
City on Long Island Sound, N.Y. — RYE
City on Puget Sound — TACOMA
City on Sabine Lake, Tex — PORT ARTHUR
City on Seward peninsula — NOME
City on the Aar — BERN
City on the Aare — BERNE
City on the Adige — VERONA
City on the Aire — LEEDS
City on the Allegheny — OLEAN
City on the Arkansas — TULSA
City on the Arno — PISA
City on the Avon — BATH
City on the Bay of Acre — HAIFA
City on the Brazos — WACO
City on the Clyde — GLASGOW
City on the Colorado — YUMA
City on the Columbia — PORTLAND
City on the Danube — BRAILA
City on the Danube — VIENNA
City on the Don — ROSTOV
City on the Donau — WIEN
City on the Douro — OPORTO
City on the Elbe — PIRNA
City on the Garonne — AGEN
City on the Hari Rud — HERAT
City on the Hudson — ALBANY, NYACK, TROY
City on the Irtysh — OMSK
City on the Jumma — DELHI
City on the Katun River — ULALA
City on the Loire — BLOIS, NANTES
City on the Missouri — OMAHA
City on the Mohawk — UTICA
City on the Mosel — TRIER
City on the Moselle — METZ
City on the Niagara — BUFFALO
City on the Nile — ASWAN, CAIRO
City on the Nile, N of Lake Nasser — ASWAN
City on the Ocmulgee River — MACON
City on the Oka — OREL
City on the Orne — CAEN
City on the Orontes — HAMA
City on the Ouche — DIJON
City on the Ouse — YORK
City on the Po — TURIN
City on the Rhine — BONN
City on the Rhine, old style — BASLE
City on the Rhone — ARLES, BASEL, LYON
City on the Rio Grande — LAREDO
City on the Ruhr — ESSEN
City on the Saone — MACON
City on the Seine — PARIS
City on the Seyhan — ADANA
City on the Shannon — LIMERICK
City on the Skunk — AMES
City on the Somme — AMIENS
City on the St. Lawrence — SOREL
City on the Tagus — TOLEDO
City on the Tay — PERTH
City on the Tevere — ROMA
City on the Tiber — ROME
City on the Truckee — RENO
City on the Ural — ORSK
City on the Vistula — CRACOW, KRAKOW
City on the Volga — SARATOV
City on the Wabash — PERU, VINCENNES
City on the Wesser — BREMEN
City on the Yamuna — AGRA
City on the Yonne — SENS
City once Japanese — TAKAO
City or country features — PARKS
City or prefecture, Honshu — NARA
City pests — ROACHES
City prominent in civil rights — SELMA
City R R's — ELS
City residence — TENEMENT
City S of Albany — TROY
City SE of Cleveland — AKRON
City SE of Hue, Vietnam — DANANG
City SE of Sacremento — LODI
City SE of San Francisco — FRESNO
City sight — CAB
City slicker — DUDE
City south of Florence — SIENA
City south of Moscow — OREL
City SSE of Dallas — ENNIS
City SSW of Moscow — OREL
City SW of Algiers — BLIDA
City SW of Buenos Aires — MORON
City SW of Jacksonville — OCALA
City SW of Tokyo — ATAMI
City that may make you tired? — AKRON
City trains, for short — ELS
City transits — ELS
City transports — LIMOS
City visited by Tarzan — OPAR
City W of Cleveland — ELYRIA, LORAIN
City W of Erfurt — GOTHA
City W of Houston — KATY
City W of Warsaw — POSEN
City WNW of Enid — ALVA
City WNW of Madrid — AVILA
City WSW of Colorado Springs — SALIDA
City, lake or Indian — ERIE
Civet — RASSE
Civet's cousin — GENET
Civet's kin — GENETS
Civetlike animal — GENET
Civil — CORDIAL, POLITE
Civil court case — LAWSUIT
Civil disobedience — RIOT
Civil disobedience activist — GANDHI
Civil eng. — BLDR

Civil melee — RIOT
Civil rights activist Medgar _____ — EVERS
Civil war battle site — MANASSA
Civil war battle site: 1862 — SHILO
Civil war general — MEADE, SHERMAN
Civil War issue — SLAVERY
Civil War monogram — CSA
Civil War org. — GAR
Civil War photographer — BRADY
Civil War warship — MONITOR
Civil wrong — TORT
Civil-rights org. — ACLU
Civilian garb — MUFTI
Civvies — MUFTI
Clad — ATTIRED, ROBED
Clad, to the Bard — DREST
Claim — ALLEGE, AVER, LIEN, PLEA
Claim on a property — LIEN
Claimed a tort — SUED
Claims — AVERS
Clair de _____ (porcelain) — LUNE
Clair of films — RENE
Clair or Coty — RENE
Claire and Balin — INAS
Claire or Lacoste — RENE
Clairvoyance — PSI
Clairvoyant's forte — ESP
Clairvoyant's talent — ESP
Clairvoyants — SEERS
Clambake item — STEAMER
Clammy — DAMP, SLIMY
Clamor — DIN, HUE, NOISE, UPROAR
Clamorous — LOUD
Clamorous state capital — NOISY BOISE
Clamp — VISE
Clamping device — VISE
Clan — GENS, TRIBE
Clan branch — SEPT
Clan cloth — TARTAN
Clan emblem — TOTEM
Clan leader — CHIEFTAIN
Clan member — SCOT
Clan subdivisions — SEPTS
Clan symbol — TOTEM
Clan units — SEPTS
Clandestine — COVERT, SECRET
Clandestine meeting — TRYST
Clanging — PEALING
Clangor — PEAL
Clapboards or shingles — SIDING
Clapton of rock — ERIC
Clapton or Sevareid — ERIC
Clapton, et al. — ERICS
Clara or Maria — SANTA
Clare Boothe — LUCE
Clarence of the courts — DARROW
Clarence or Doris — DAY
Claret or port — WINE
Clarified butter — GHEE
Clarify — DEFINE
Clarinet's cousin — OBOE
Clarinet's large cousin — BASS SAX
Clarinet, e.g. — REED
Clarinetist Goodman — BENNY
Clarinetist Jimmie _____ — NOONE
Clarinetist Shaw — ARTIE
Clark _____ — KENT
Clark Kent's girl — LOIS
Clark of Butler role — GABLE
Clark or Spitz — MARK
Clark's co-explorer — LEWIS
Clark's companion — LEWIS
Clark's girl — LOIS
Clark's girlfriend — LOIS
Clark's Lane — LOIS
Clark's show — AMERICAN BANDSTAND
Claro or corona — CIGAR
Claro or stogy — CIGAR
Clasps or clamps — BRACES
Class — BREED, ILK
Class between tourist and first — CABIN
Class cap — ETON
Class Clown — CUTUP, TOM FOOLERY
Class comprising ants, flies, etc — INSECTA
Class distinction — CASTE
Class of plants — TRIBE
Class of sort — ILK
Class or aid — FIRST
Class or birth — UPPER
Class subj. — SCI
Class with common attributes: Comb. form — SPECI
Class, in Bombay — CASTE
Classes — GENERA
Classic — EPIC
Classic auto — REO
Classic beginning — NEO
Classic binge of fiction — LOST WEEKEND
Classic by Capek — RUR
Classic car — REO
Classic greek beauty — LAIS
Classic introduced by Whiteman: 1924 — RHAPSODY IN BLUE
Classic Japanese drama — NOH
Classic oater — SHANE
Classic prefix — NEO
Classic role for Ladd — SHANE
Classic villain — IAGO
Classic Von Stroheim film — GREED
Classical apple-picker — ATLANTA
Classical Chinese poet — LI PO
Classical geometer — EUCLID
Classical prefix — NEO
Classified — SORTED, SUBSUMED, TYPED
Classified book — YELLOW PAGES
Classified items — ADS
Classified words — FOR SALE
Classifieds, for short — ADS
Classifies — ASSORTS, SORTS
Classify — ASSORT, GRADE, RATE, SORT
Classrm. aides — TAS
Classroom equipment — ERASER
Classy — SMART
Claude Atkins TV role — LOBO
Claude's friend — AMI
Claudia _____ Johnson — ALTA
Claus and Callas's caravel? — SANTA MARIA
Clause connectors — ANDS
Claw — TALON, UNGUIS
Claw: Comb. form — CHELI, UNCI
Clay or Webster — WHIG
Clay used as a pigment — BOLE
Clay, today — ALI
Clayey earth — MARL
Clayey rock — SHALE
Clayey soil — MARL
Claymore — SWORD
Clayton Moore's Ranger — LONE
Clayware — POTTERY
Clean-up place — SHOWER-BATH
Clean — MOP UP
Clean a pipe — REAM
Clean air org. — EPA
Clean as a whistle — SPOTLESS
Clean energetically — SCOUR
Clean the board — ERASE
Clean the orlop — SWAB
Clean the slate — ERASE
Cleaned a pipe — REAMED OUT
Cleaned the yard — RAKED
Cleaner's associate — DYER
Cleaning agent — AMMONIA
Cleaning aid — SCRUB BRUSH, LIQUID SOAP
Cleaning aids — DETERGENTS, MOP AND PAIL
Cleaning implement — MOP
Cleaning lady in Soho — CHAR
Cleaning tools — MOPS
Cleaning woman, old style — CHARER
Cleaning women, British style — CHARS

Cleans the slate — ERASES
Cleanse — BATHE, DETERGE, SCOUR
Cleanse by rubbing — SCRUB
Cleanses — DETERGES
Cleansing agent — BORAX
Clear — ALERT, BRIGHT, FAIR, FREE, LUCID, NET
Clear — PLAIN, SUNNY
Clear a tape — ERASE
Clear air — OZONE
Clear as mud — ABSTRUSE, ILLEGIBLE
Clear of blame — REDEEM
Clear sky — ETHER
Clear soup, Scotch style — BROO
Clear the slate — ERASE
Clear up — SOLVE
Clear's partner — LOUD
Cleared — NETTED
Clearing in a forest — GLADE
Clearing the garden — WEEDING
Cleavage — GAP
Cleave — ADHERE, SEVER, SPLIT
Cleaves — RIVES
Cleaving tool — FROE
Cleavon's 1979 indulgence — A LITTLE ROMANCE
Cleft — FISSURE, PARTED, SPLIT, TORN
Clefts — SLITS
Clematis, for one — VINE
Clemency — MERCY
Clemens — TWAIN
Clement — MILD
Clement Moore opening word — TWAS
Clement one — SPARER
Clementine's father — MINER
Clemson or Princeton player — TIGER
Clenched hand — FIST
Cleo of songdom — LAINE
Cleo's handmaid — IRAS
Cleo's killer — ASP
Cleo's river — NILE
Cleo's suitor — MARC
Cleo's way out — ASP
Cleopatra's attendant — IRAS
Cleopatra's maid — IRAS
Cleopatra's Needle, e.g. — OBELISK
Cleopatra's nemesis — ASP
Clergyman — CANNON, PRELATE, PRIEST, RABBI, RECTOR
Clergyman — REVEREND, VICAR
Clergyman's residence — MANSE
Cleric-poet — DONNE
Cleric — ABBE, DEACON, PADRE
Cleric's home — MANSE
Cleric's vestments — ALBS
Clerical breast piece — RABAT
Clerical garb — ALBS
Clerical residence — MANSE
Clerical vestment — AMICE
Clerical wear — ORALE, ORB
Clerk — SCRIBE
Clerk Cratchit — BOB
Clerk Heep — URIAH
Clerk, in India — BABU
Cleveland Brown QB — KOSAR
Cleveland landmark "The _____" — ARCADE
Cleveland player — INDIAN
Cleveland team — CRUNCH
Clever — DEFT
Clever comeback — RIPOSTE
Clever manipulator — FOX
Clever saying — MOT
Cleverly sly — ARCH
Clew makeup — YARN
Cliburn and Heflin — VANS
Cliburn's forte — PIANO
Cliburn's instrument — PIANO
Click beetle — DORS, ELATOR
Client — USER
Client cost — FEE
Clientele — TRADE
Cliff dwelling — AERIE, AERY
Cliff dwellings: Var. — EYRIES
Cliff line — SCARP
Climax — CRISIS, TOP OFF
Climax for "The 1812 Oveture" — PEALS
Climb — SHIN
Climb a slope on skis — HERRINGBONE
Climb aboard — GET ON
Climb up — SCALE
Climb, in a way — SHIN, SHINNY
Climbed — SCALED
Climbed again — RESCALE
Climber's goal — ARETE
Climbing ferns — NITOS
Climbing palm — RATTAN
Climbing pepper — BETEL
Climbing perch — ANABAS
Climbing spot — TRELLIS
Climbing vine — LIANA, LIANE
Climbs a pole — SHINS
Climbs, in a way — SHINS
Clinch breaker — REFEREE
Clinch first place — WIN
Clinched — ON ICE
Cline of music — PATSY
Cling — ADHERE
Clinger — VINE
Clinging — ADHESIVE
Clings to — ADHERES
Clink aboard ship — BRIG
Clinquant — TINSEL
Clinton's canal — ERIE
Clinton's hometown — HOPE
Clintonian section of London or Manhattan? — CHELSEA
Clio and Edgar — AWARDS
Clio's sister — ERATO
Clio, et al. — MUSES
Clip a Merino — SHEAR
Clip joint? — BARBER SHOP
Clipped — SHORN
Clippers — PRUNERS
Clipping or tripping — FOUL
Clips — TRIMS
Clique — CIRCLE, CLAN, SET
Cliques — COTERIES
Clit — CLOSE
Cloaca — SEWER
Cloak — CAPE, GUISE, WRAP
Cloak, in Malaga — CAPA
Cloaked — SECRET
Clobber — BELT, SHELLAC, SWAT
Clobbers — BEATS, SMITES
Cloche, for one — HAT
Clock — TIME
Clock face — DIAL
Clock feature — MAINSPRING
Clock features — DIALS
Clock numeral — III
Clock sound — TICK, TOCK
Clock symbol — XII
Clock watcher — EYER
Clock, in Koln — UHR
Clock, to some — WAKER
Clocked a race — TIMED
Clockmaker Thomas — SETH
Clockwork — MOVEMENT
Clockwork part — DETENT
Clodhopper — OAF
Clods — OAFS
Clogs or pumps — SHOES
Cloisonné artisan — ENAMELER
Cloisonné feature — ENAMEL
Cloister — ARCADE
Cloistered women — NUNS
Clone — ROBOT
Close-fitting — SNUG
Close-fitting cap — CALOT, COIF
Close — CONNECT, END, FASTEN, FINISH, FINALE, NEAR
Close — SEAL, SHUT
Close again — RESEAL
Close an envelope — SEAL
Close at hand — NEARBY
Close by — NEAR, NIGH
Close by, old style — ANEAR
Close companion — CRONY
Close connection — KINSHIP
Close friend — PAL
Close in — NEAR
Close kinsman — SIB
Close of the day, to Byron — EVENTIDE
Close scrutiny — TABS

Close the eyes, in falconry — SEEL
Close tight — SEAL
Close tightly — CLAM, CLENCH, SEAL
Close to — NEAR
Close to being top dog — SECOND BEST
Close to, in poetry — ANEAR
Close up shop — CALL IT A DAY
Close, in Kohn — BEI
Close, poetically — ANEAR
Close, to Frost — ANEAR
Close-fitting jackets — COATEES
Close-knit groups — CLANS
Close-lipped — TACITURN
Close-mouthed one — CLAM
Closed-shop sign in May — GONE FISHIN
Closed — ENDED
Closed car — SEDAN
Closed or open position, in golf — STANCE
Closed shop — UNION
Closely associated — ALLIED
Closely pressed package — BALE
Closes a falcon's eyes — SEELS
Closes after opening — RESEALS
Closes off the flow, again — REDAMS
Closet accessories — HANGERS
Closet contents — FINERY
Closet item — BROOM
Closing letters — ETC
Closing passage in music — CODA
Closing words — AMENS
Cloth — TEXTILE
Cloth covering for a cap — HAVELOCK
Cloth for a kilt — TARTAN
Cloth for Dior — TISSU
Cloth of gold — LAME
Cloth or cash endings — IERS
Clothe — ARRAY, ENDUE, ENROBE
Clothes — TOGS
Clothes for sentries — HALTERS
Clothes to be washed — LAUNDRY
Clothing — APPAREL, ATTIRE, RAIMENTS, LINEN
Clothing category — KNITS
Clothing designer — STYLIST
Clothing in Moscow? — RUSSIAN DRESSING
Clotho, for one — FATE
Cloud — HAZE
Cloud of ice crystals: Comb. form — CIRR
Cloud, to Baudelaire — NUE
Cloud: Comb. form — CIRRI
Cloudburst — RAIN
Cloudland — SKY
Cloudy — OVERCAST
Clouseau's servant — CATO
Clouseau, for one: Abbr. — INSP
Clout — PULL, SWAT
Clove hitch, e.g. — KNOT
Clown in "Pagliacci" — TONIO
Clown Kelly — EMMET
Clown's repertory — PRATFALLS
Clownish — ZANY
Clowns' specialties — ANTICS
Cloy — SATE
Cloy with overabundance — SATE
Cloyed — SATED
Cloying — SYRUPY
Cloying or sticking — TREACLY
Cloying sentimentality — GOO
Cloys — GLUTS
Club assessments — DUES
Club for Kite — IRON
Club for Ray Floyd — IRON
Club for Snead — IRON
Club moss — LYCOPOD
Club receipts — DUES
Club tab — CHIT
Club type — GLEE
Clublike weapon of New Zealand — PATU
Clubs, e.g. — SUIT
Clue — TRACE
Clump — TUFT
Clump of grass — TUFT
Clump of Ivy — TOD
Clumsy — AWKWARD, BULKY, CLUMSY, INEPT, OAFISH
Clumsy craft — ARK, SCOW, TUB
Clumsy one's cry — OOPS
Clumsy ones — CLODS, OAFS
Clumsy, in Callao — TORPE
Clunk — THUD
Clunker — HEAP
Cluny product — LACE
Cluny's pride — LACE
Cluny, for one — LACE
Clupeid fishes — SHADS
Clusium's Porsena — LARS
Cluster of fruit or nut trees — GROVE
Clustered — TUFTED
Clusters of fiber — NEPS
Clutch — GRIP
Clutched — HELD
Clutter — MUSS
Clyde and Forth — FIRTHS
Clytemnestra's mother — LEDA
CN _____: Toronto — TOWER
Cnemis or zygoma — BONE
Co-author of "Animal Crackers" — KAUFMAN
Co-signer with Hancock — RUSH
Co-star in "The Seven Year Itch" — EWELL
Co-worker — TEAM MATE
Co-writer of the other woman — MEARA
CO resort — ASPEN
Co-author of a 1930 tariff act — SMOOT
Co-conspire — ABET
Co-inventor of cordite — AABEL
Co-Nobelist for Peace: 1907 — RENAULT
Co-Nobelist for Peace: 1978 — SADAT
Co-Nobelist in Medicine: 1977 — YALOW
Co-star of "Hellzapoppin" — OLSEN
Co. in Cannes — CIE
Co., in France — CIE
Coach — TRAINER
Coach Alonzo Stagg — AMOS
Coach Lombardi — VINCE
Coach Parseghian — ARA
Coach's area in Kansas City — ROYAL BOX
Coach's request — TIME
Coaches — TUTORS
Coachman (fishing) — FLY
Coachman's command — WHOA
Coagulate — CLOT, CURD
Coagulate, as cream — CLOT
Coagulated part of milk — CURD
Coagulates — CURDS
Coagulating enzyme — RENNIN
Coal — EMBER
Coal _____ — TAR
Coal barge — KEEL
Coal bed — SEAM
Coal car, e.g. — HOPPER
Coal carrier — HOD, SCOW, TRAM
Coal case — BIN
Coal front — CHAR
Coal measure — TON
Coal mine tunnel — SHAFT
Coal miner — PITMAN
Coal or gas — FUEL
Coal or oil, for example — FUEL
Coal region of central Europe — SILESIA
Coal residue — COKE
Coal scuttle — HOD
Coal source — MINE
Coal tar product — CRESOL
Coal, e.g. — FUEL
Coalesce — UNITE

Coalition in 1941 — AXIS
Coalitions — BLOCS
Coals — EMBERS
Coarse — RIBALD
Coarse corundum — EMERY
Coarse fabric — CADDIS
Coarse file — RASP
Coarse hominy — SAMP
Coarse quality — GROSSNESS
Coarse sugars, in East India — RAABS
Coarse wool — ABB
Coarse woolen fabrics — STAMINS
Coarse, island cloth — TAPA
Coast — SEABOARD
Coast or Rush preceder — GOLD
Coastal avian — ERN
Coastal birds — ERNES
Coastal coasters — ERNES
Coastal flyer — ERNE, TERN
Coastal region — SEABOARD
Coaster — SLED
Coat — TOG
Coat fold — LAPEL
Coat food with flour — DREDGE
Coat of arms — CREST
Coat or shirt — POLO
Coat part — LAPEL
Coat rack — VALET
Coat type — CHAR
Coat with an alloy of tin and lead — TERNE
Coat with plaster — PARGE
Coated with crumbs — BREADED
Coated with pitch — PAYED
Coated with tin-lead alloy — TERNED
Coati's coat — HIDE
Coats applied before paint — SEALER
Coats with plaster — PARGES
Coax — TEASE
Coaxed — WANGLED
Coaxes — URGES
Cob and Pen — SWANS
Cobb and namesakes — TYS
Cobbler's academy? — SCHOOL FOR SANDAL
Cobbler's concern — LASTS
Cobbler's mend these — SOLES
Cobbler's model — LAST
Cobbler's save these — SOLES
Cobbler's sparable — NAIL
Cobbler's tool — AWL
Cobblers' block — LAST
Cobbling tool — AWL
Coblenz cry — ACH
Cobra or cottonmouth — SNAKE
Cobra's cousin — MAMBA
Cobra's relative — MAMBA
Cobras' cousins — KRAITS
Cobs and pens, e.g. — MATES
Cobs' companions — PENS
Coca of television — IMOGENE
Coca's partner — CAESAR
Cochise was one — APACHE
Cochlea location — EAR
Cock's territory — ROOST
Cockatoo or lory — PARROT
Cockatoo palms — ARAS
Cockcrow — DAWN
Cockeyed — ASLANT
Cockfight locale — PIT
Cockle — OAST
Cockloft — ATTIC
Cockney crony — MATEY
Cockney dwellings — OMES
Cockney family in comics — CAPPS
Cockney's problem — AITCH
Cockpit — NACELLE
Cockpit — NACELLE
Cocktail _____ — PARTY
Cocktail accompaniment — CANAPE
Cocktail party treat — DIP
Cocktail shaker? — BAR MEN
Cocktail with gin or vodka and lime juice — GIMLET
Cocky — PERT
Coconino County cutie — KRAZY KAT
Coconut and pineapple — TROPICAL TREES
Coconut fiber — COIR
Coconut meat — COPRA
Coconut or banana — OIL
Coconut, e.g. — SEED
Cocoon dwellers — PUPAE
Cocteau's "L' _____ Heurtebise" — ANGE
Cod cousin — HAKE
Cod or Hatteras — CAPE
Cod's kin — HAKE
Coda — FINALE
Coda, for one — FINALE
Coddle — BABY
Code inventor — MORSE
Code man — MORSE
Code name for a Virgin Islands airport — STT
Code of beliefs — CREED
Code of laws — CANON
Code of morals — ETHICS
Code of silence — OMERTA
Code or rug — AREA
Code signal — DIT
Code type — AREA
Code units — DOTS
Code word — ALFA, DIT
Code word for "A" — ALFA
Code word for "B" — BETA
Code word for "Z" — ZULU
Codified — DIGESTED
Coe or Cram — MILER
Coe's distance — MILE
Coed's habitat — DORM
Coerce — BULLY, COMPEL
Coerced — PRESSURED
Coercion — DURESS, FORCE
Coeur d' _____, Idaho — ALENE
Coeur d' _____, Indian tribe — ALENE
Coexistent — CURRENT
Coffee — BREW, DRIP, JAVA, MOCHA
Coffee accompaniment — TOAST
Coffee and tea services — SETS
Coffee and vanilla — BEANS
Coffee breaks, Brit. style — TEATIMES
Coffee containers — URNS
Coffee flavor — MOCHA
Coffee maker — SILEX, URN
Coffee or cocktail item — TABLE
Coffee pot — URN
Coffee server — CARAFE, URNS
Coffee service item — CREAMER
Coffee variety — MOCHA
Coffee, Italian style — ESPRESSO
Coffee, tea and china — SETS
Coffeebush — PEABERRY
Coffer — CHEST
Cogent — STRONG
Cognate — ALIKE
Cognizant — AWARE
Cognomen — NAME
Cohan song, 1907 — HARRIG-AN
Cohan's "_____ Popular Man" — IM A
Cohan's "_____ There" — OVER
Cohesive group — UNIT
Cohort of Larry and Curly — MOE
Coif cover — HAIRNET
Coif items — BOBBY PINS
Coiffeur's accessory — RAT
Coiffeur's creation — UPDO
Coiffeuse's appliance — DRYER
Coiffure — AFRO, BANG, WAVE
Coiffure feature — BANGS
Coiffure style — PART
Coil — CURVE, KINK
Coil about — ENWIND
Coil or curl — SPIRE
Coil, in Calabria — SPIRA
Coil: Comb. form — SPIRO
Coiled: Comb. form — SPIRO
Coin-toss result — HEADS, TAILS
Coin — CENT, DIME, SILVER
Coin aperture — SLOT
Coin collector — SLOT
Coin depository — SLOT

Coin for a taco — PESO
Coin for Antonio — DUCAT
Coin for Cato — TRIENS
Coin for Malaga — PESETA
Coin for Pedro — PESO
Coin for Père Noël — FRANC
Coin in Stockholm — KRONA
Coin machine feature — SLOT
Coin marking — DATE
Coin of Abyssinia — GIRSH
Coin of ancient Greece — OBOL
Coin of Cuba — PESO
Coin of Ecuador — SUCRE
Coin of India — PICE
Coin of Iran — RIAL
Coin of Italy — LIRA
Coin of little worth — SOU
Coin of old England — GROAT
Coin of Yugoslavia — DINAR
Coin receiver — SLOT
Coin receptacle — SLOT
Coin taker — SLOT
Coin, to a bloke — SOU
Coinage — CURRENCY
Coined money — SPECIE
Coins for Caesar — AUREI
Coins in Como — LIRE
Coins in Tirana — LEKS
Coins of Belgrade — PARAS
Coins of Kerman — RIALS
Coir, ramie, etc — FIBERS
Col. pts. — CRS
Col. subj. — ECOL
Col.'s junior — MAJ
Colander — SIEVE
Colanders — STRAINERS
Colanders cousin — SIEVE
Colberteen, e.g. — LACE
Colby or Gillette — ANITA
Cold-water seaweed — KELP
Cold _____ — CASH, CREAM, COMFORT, CUTS, DUCK
Cold _____ — FISH, FEET, FRONT, FRAME, SNAP, SHOULDER
Cold _____ — TURKEY, WAR
Cold confections — ICES
Cold country — NORTH
Cold country vehicle — SLED
Cold cream — COSMETIC, EMULSION
Cold cut center — DELI
Cold cut shop — DELI
Cold desserts — ICES
Cold north wind of the alps — BISE
Cold sensation — ACHE
Cold snap comment — BRR
Cold symptom — COUGH
Cold weather garb — OVERCOAT
Cold wind — BISE, WESTER
Cold wind from the Andes — PAMPERO
Cold, dry wind — MISTRAL
Cold, in Cadiz — FRIO
Cold, in Colima — FRIO
Cold-climate craft — KAYAK
Cold-cuts counter — DELI
Cold-cuts shop — DELI
Cold-weather card game — DRESS POKER
Cold: Prefix — FRIGO
Coldcut counter — DELI
Colds cure — HOT SOUP
Cole of song — NAT
Cole or Turner — NAT
Cole Porter heroine — KATE
Cole Porter song: 1929 — PAREE
Cole Porter song: Nelson Eddy film, 1937 — ROSALIE
Cole Porter's "_____ Clown" — BE A
Cole Porter's _____ Sweeney — RENO
Cole's fiddlers — THREE
Cole's musicians — FIDDLERS
Cole, et al. — NATS
Colema cover-up — SERAPE
Coleridge contribution — POETRY
Colesium — ARENA
Colette novel — CHERI
Colette's "The _____ One" — OTHER
Coleus — HERB
Coliseum — ARENA, STADIUM, THEATER
Coliseum area — TIER
Coll. award — DEG
Coll. basketball tourney — NIT
Coll. course — BIOL, ECOL
Coll. degree — ABS, MED
Coll. degs. — BAS
Coll. in Cambridge — MIT
Coll. reunion prospect — ALUM
Coll. sports org. — NCAA
Coll.'s big sister — UNIV
Collage — GEL
Collage-maker's need — SCISSORS
Collapse — BUST, FOLD UP, RUIN
Collapsed, with "in" — CAVED
Collar — ARREST, BAND, CHOKER, NAB
Collar and cap — ETONS
Collar attachment — LEASH
Collar fastener — STUD
Collar for a scholar — ETON
Collar insert — STAY
Collar maker — COP
Collar or jacket — ETON
Collar part — TAB
Collars — ARRESTS, NABS
Collates — SORTS
Colleague — CRONY
Colleague of a DDS — DMD
Colleague of an alim — IMAM
Colleague of Dashiell — ERLE
Colleague of Paul, John and George — RINGO
Colleague of Rep. — SEN
Colleague of Rita and Hedy — LANA
Collect — AMASS, GATHER, RAISE
Collect bit by bit — GLEAN
Collect by legal authority — LEVY
Collect one's pension — RETIRE
Collected — AMASSED, GARNERED, PILED
Collected items of information: Suffix — ANA
Collected writings — ANA
Collected, as votes — GARNERED
Collection — ANA, GROUP, SERIES, SET
Collection of anecdotes — ANAS
Collection of books — LIBRARY
Collection of Icelandic heroic poems — EDDA
Collection of literary passages: Abbr. — ANTH
Collection of memorable sayings — ANA
Collection of religious sayings — LOGIA
Collection of reminiscences — ANA
Collection of sayings — ANAS
Collection of stamps — ALBUM
Collection of stories — ANA
Collection of studies by Oscar Wilde — INTENTIONS
Collection of writings — DIGEST
Collections — ANAS
Collections of memorabilia — ANAS
Collective farm of the Soviet — ARTEL
Collector from John Q. — IRS
Collector of useless items — PACK RAT
Collector's car — PACKARD
Collector's item — STAMP, SEASHELL
Collector's milieux — FLEA MARKET
Collector, of a kind — PACK RAT
Collector, of a sort — AMASSER
Collectors' cars — EDSELS
Colleen — LASS
Colleen's country — EIRE
Colleen's land — ERIN
College accom. — DORM

College area, for short — QUAD
College at Saratoga, N.Y. — SKIDMORE
College athelete, usually — AMATEUR
College boards, briefly — PSAT
College credit unit — HOUR
College degrees: Abbr. — ABS, BAS, BSCS
College employee — ELECTOR
College entrance exam — SATS
College figure — DEAN
College football conference — BIG TEN
College in Lewiston, Me. — BATES
College in Michigan — ALMA
College in North Carolina — ELON
College in Northfield, Minn. — SAINT OLAF
College in Portland, Ore. — REED
College in Washington, D.C. — TRINITY
College lang. org. — CLA
College mil. group — ROTC
College milieu — CAMPUS
College near Phila. — BRYN MAWR
College of Cedar Rapids — COE
College of Doakes — JOE
College of N.C. — ELON
College officials — DEANS
College on the Thames — ETON
College sports gp. — NCAA
College student — COED
College studies — ARTS
College subj. — GEOL
College teacher: Abbr. — PROF
College town in Iowa — AMES
College town on the Thames — ETON
College town SE of Cleveland — HIRAM
College VIP — PROF
Collegian — STUDENT
Collegian's goal — DEGREE
Collegian's monetary aid Abbr. — GSL
Collegian's prerogative — CUT
Collegian's quest — DEGREE
Collegians — STUDENTS
Collegians pad — DORM
Collegiate Betty of song — COED
Collegiate team — VARSITY
Collegio's offerings — ARTI
Collier's cooler — ALE
Colliers' entry — ADIT
Colliery — MINE
Colliery access — ADIT
Colliery entrances — ADITS
Collins and Mix — TOMS
Collinsworth of N.F.L. fame — CRIS
Collision — IMPACT
Colloquial dissimilarity — DIF
Colloquial failures — NOGOODS
Colloquial realm — TURF
Colloquial speech — SLANG
Colloquial thousand — GRAND
Colloquialism — SLANG
Collusive behavior — PRICE FIXING
Colo. resort — ASPEN
Colo. Shoshones — UTES
Colo. time — MST
Cologne constituent — NEROLI
Colombian city — CALI
Colombian export — COCAINE
Colombian gem — EMERALD
Colombian gem — EMERALD
Colombian Indian — ICA
Colombian poncho — RUANA
Colombian seaport — TUMACO
Colonel in "Hogan's Heroes" — KLINK
Colonial — COMMUNITY, GROUP, VILLAGE
Colonial freethinkers — DEISTS
Colonial patriot — OTIS
Colonial philosopher — PAINE
Colonist — SETTLER
Colonist greeting to Indian — NETOP
Colonize — SETTLE
Colonizer — SETTLER
Colonizer of New Mexico — ONATE
Colony denizen — ANT
Colony group — ANTS
Colony member — ANT, NUDIST
Color — DYE, HUE, ECRU, NILE, SAPPHIRE BLUE
Color — STAIN, TINGE, TINT
Color again — RETINT
Color also called meadowlark — ACORN
Color change on old silver — PATINA
Color changers — DYES
Color for a British scholar — OXFORD GREY
Color for a Canton bride — CHINESE RED
Color of a certain badge — RED
Color of a different horse — ROAN
Color of a whole decade — MAUVE
Color of Androcles' friend — TAWNY
Color of raw silk — ECRU
Color or angle leader — TRI
Color or city — HUE
Color or cycle starter — TRI
Color, in a way — TINT
Colorado flag eye-catcher — GOLD CIRCLE
Colorado Indian — UTE
Colorado resort — ASPEN, VAIL
Colorado resort city — ASPEN
Colorado river — GILA
Colorado ski resort — ASPEN
Coloratura Jenny — LIND
Coloratura Mills — ERIE
Colored — DYED, HUED
Colored flare: Var. — FUZEE
Colored or layered start — MULTI
Colorful — VIVID
Colorful bird — PARROT, TANANGER
Colorful bloomer — CANNA
Colorful carp — KOI
Colorful cheese tray item — EDAM
Colorful duck — TEAL
Colorful fish — OPAH
Colorful flower — ANEMONE
Colorful flyer — ORIOLE
Colorful gem — OPAL
Colorful jewel — RED CORAL
Colorful marble — TAW
Colorful marine fish — OPAH
Colorful marine sights — CORALS
Colorful pennant — STREAMER
Colorful plant with showy flowers — PORTULACA
Colorful rural sight — RED BARN
Colorful tree — RED MAPLE
Coloring — PIGMENT, SHADE, TINCT
Coloring agent — STAIN, DYE
Coloring agents — TONERS
Coloring matter — EOSIN, PAINT
Coloring workers — DYERS
Colorist — DYER
Colorless — WAN
Colorless character — NERD
Colorless gas: Comb. form — OXO
Colorless personality — DULL
Colorless poison gas — ARSINE
Colorless, odorless gas — ETHANE
Colorless, odorless, tasteless, gaseous mixture — AIR
Colors — DYES, FLAG, STAINS, TINTS
Colors slightly — TINTS
Colossal — ENORMOUS, GIGANTIC, HUGE, LARGE
Colossal — HOMERIC

Colossal collisions — SMASH UPS
Colosseum combatants — LIONS
Colossus of _____ — RHODES
Colossus of Rhodes — STATUE
Colour — GREY
Colour of the cloudless skies — BLUE
Colt on the loose? — FILLYANDERER
Colt's Hall of Famer — UNITAS
Colts — FORTY FIVES
Colts or fillies — FOALS
Colts or Rams — ELEVEN
Columbia mascot — LION
Columbia, in a song — GEM
Columbo portrayer — FALK
Columbus caravel — NINA, PINTA
Columbus Day, e.g. — FETE
Columbus departure port — PALOS
Columbus ed. inst. — OSU
Columbus' birthplace — GENOA
Columbus' quest — NEW ROUTE TO INDIA
Column — PILLAR
Column base — PLINTH
Column moldings — TORES
Column style — DORIC, IONIC
Column tops — ABACUSES
Column type — DORIC, IONIC
Columnist _____ Chase — ILKA
Columnist Alexander — SHANA
Columnist Barrett — RONA
Columnist Bombeck — ERMA
Columnist Buchwald — ART
Columnist John — HESS
Columnist Landers — ANN
Columnist Le Shan — EDA
Columnist of "Conning Tower" — FPA
Columnist Royko — MIKE
Columnist Stewart — ALSOP
Columnist's specialty — RUMORS
Columnist's tidbit — ITEM
Colzie of the N.F.L. — NEAL
Com preceder — NON
Com. market area — EUR
Comaneci — NADIA
Comb components — TEETH
Comb or eyeglass frame material — TORTOISE SHELL
Comb projections — TEETH
Comb. form for 12 — DODECA
Comb. form for a ridge of the eye — CANTH
Comb. form of skin — DERM
Comb: Comb. form — CTEN, CTENO
Combat milieu — ARENA
Combat mission — SORTIE
Combat site — ARENA
Combat zones — ARENAS, LISTS
Combatants — SOLDIERS
Combatants of a kind — MIDGET WRESTLERS
Combative person — TIGER
Combats to settle a point of honor — DUELS
Comber's comb — CREST
Combers — SURF
Combination for Serkin — CHORD
Combination of musical notes — CHORD
Combine — UNITE
Combine, e.g. — REAPER
Combined — POOLED
Combiner with dyne or doxy — HETERO
Combo — BAND
Combo on the keys — CHORD
Combos — TRIOS
Combustible heap — PYRE
Combustion residue — ASH
Combustion's companion — SMOKE
Come-on for sales — ADS
Come a cropper — FAIL
Come about — SLUE
Come across — FIND
Come again — RETURN
Come apart — BREAK
Come apart, with "off" — PEEL
Come ashore — LAND
Come back — RECUR
Come before — PRECEDE
Come by — PROCURE
Come clean — ADMIT
Come clean (with up) — FESS
Come down in buckets — RAIN CATS AND DOGS
Come down with — CATCH
Come forth — EMANATE, EMERGE
Come forth from — GUSH, SPEW
Come from — DERIVE
Come in — ENTER
Come in last — LOSE
Come in second — LOSE
Come in third, in a horserace — SHOW
Come into focus — APPEAR
Come into view — EMERGE
Come of _____ (mature) — AGE
Come off — OCCUR
Come on — PROPOSAL
Come out — DEBUT, EMERGE
Come out on top — WIN
Come out right — ADD UP
Come to — AWAKEN
Come to _____ (fail) — GRIEF
Come to _____ (suffer a mishap) — GRIEF
Come to a conclusion — CEASE
Come to a standstill — STOP
Come to fruition — RIPEN
Come to know — REALIZE
Come to light — DEVELOP, EMERGE
Come to pass — BETIDE
Come to pass — OCCUR
Come to terms — SETTLE
Come to understand — REALIZE
Come together — MEET, UNITE
Come up — ARISE
Come up against — ABUT, OPPOSE
Come up short — FAIL
Come up to expectations — CUT THE MUSTARD
Come up with, as an idea — HIT ON
Come upon — FIND, MEET
Come-on — TEASER
Comeback — ANSWER, REPLY
Comedian — WAG
Comedian _____ Fields — WILLIAM CLAUDE
Comedian Arnold — STANG
Comedian Bert — LAHR
Comedian Carney — ART
Comedian Costello — LOU
Comedian Dan — ROWAN
Comedian Edward _____ Horton — EVERETT
Comedian Foxx — REDD
Comedian from Montreal — SAHL
Comedian Jay — LENO
Comedian Jay and family — LENOS
Comedian Joey — PENNER
Comedian Johnson — ARTE
Comedian Lee — PINKY
Comedian Lew — LEHR
Comedian Lewis — SHARI
Comedian Louis — NYE
Comedian meets an actor — DICK GREGORY PECK
Comedian Mickey's dupes? — KATZ PAWS
Comedian Mort — SAHL
Comedian Olsen — OLE
Comedian Phillips — EMO
Comedian Richard — PRYOR
Comedian Rudner — RITA
Comedian Sahl — MORT
Comedian Skelton — RED
Comedian Sparks — NED
Comedian Stang — ARNOLD

Comedian turned traveler — TIM CONWAYFARER
Comedian's foil — STOOGE
Comedian's start remark — DID YOU HEAR THE ONE ABOUT
Comedian-actor Arnold _____ — STANG
Comedians Allen and _____ — ROSSI
Comedians stock in trade — HUMOR
Comedienne Anne and kin — MEARAS
Comedienne Denise — LOR
Comedienne Imogene — COCA
Comedienne Martha — RAYE
Comedienne Pearl — MINNIE
Comedienne Perlman — RHEA
Comedienne Pitts — ZASU
Comedienne-actress from Brooklyn — MEARA
Comedies — FARCES
Comedy team — LAUREL AND HARDY
Comedy team — MARTIN AND LEWIS
Comedy team of vaudville and movies — RITZ BROTHERS
Comely — HANDSOME
Comer — ARRIVER
Comes across — MEETS
Comes apart at the edges — FRAYS
Comes ashore — LANDS
Comes before — PREDATES
Comes close — NEARS
Comes closer to — NEARS
Comes down hard — RAINS
Comes earlier than — PRE-DATES
Comes first — PRECEDES
Comes forth — EMANATES
Comes in — ARRIVES, ENTERS
Comes in again — REENTERS
Comes in second — LOSES
Comes into view — EMERGES, LOOMS
Comes off second best — LOSES
Comes onstage — ENTERS
Comes out — EMERGES
Comes to an end — CLOSES
Comes to mind — RECALLS
Comes to nothing — FIZZLES
Comes up — ARISES
Comes up on suddenly — STARTLES
Comet discoverer — HALLEY
Comet that returns every 76 years — HALLEYS
Cometic path — ARC
Comeuppance — JUST DESERTS
Comeuppance place — WOODSHED
Comeuppance, in a way — DESERTS
Comfort — CHEER, EASE, SOLACE, SOOTHE
Comfort — CONSOLE, SOLACE
Comfortable in Paris — AISE
Comforted — EASED
Comforter — EASER
Comforting word — THERE
Comforts — EASES
Comforts — EASES, SOLACES
Comfy — SNUG
Comic — ABSURD, FUNNY, MAG
Comic actor Bill — COSBY
Comic actor Conway — TIM
Comic actor Jack — OAKIE
Comic actress Anne — MEARA
Comic Arnold — STANG
Comic bit — STRIP
Comic Caesar — SID
Comic Chevy — CHASE
Comic Costello and others — LOUS
Comic cries — YIPES
Comic Dom De _____ — LUISE
Comic Foxx / Chief Justice Chase — REDD SALMON
Comic Fred — ALLEN
Comic Gilliam — STU
Comic Harold — TEEN
Comic Imogene — COCA
Comic Jay — LENO
Comic Jay's folks — LENOS
Comic John — BYNER
Comic Johnson — ARTE
Comic Johnson's namesakes — ARTES
Comic King — ALAN
Comic Kovacs — ERNIE
Comic Leon — EARL
Comic Louis — NYE
Comic Martha and others — RAYES
Comic Morris — HOWIE
Comic Mort, et al. — SAHLS
Comic operatives? — NEWHART TO HART
Comic preceder — SERIO
Comic reporter — BRENDA STARR
Comic Sahl — MORT
Comic Skelton — RED
Comic sketches — SKITS
Comic Soupy — SALES
Comic strip box — FRAME
Comic strip cry — YIPE
Comic strip hero Harold — TEEN
Comic strip Viking — HAGAR
Comic turn — BIT
Comic Wil _____ — SHRINER
Comic with a hearty line? — SOUPY SALES
Comic's offering — JOKE
Comic's relief? — HAHA
Comic's squeal — EEK
Comic's stock in trade — GAGS
Comic-strip word — EEK
Comical — DROLL, MERRY
Comical Richard — LITTLE
Comical sketch — SKIT
Comice — PEAR
Comics' Kett — ETTA
Comics' Miss Kett — ETTA
Coming to rest — SETTLING
Comm. mode — TEL
Comm. network — NPR
Command — BEHEST, CON-TROL, EDICT, ORDER
Command from the helm — ALEE
Command in a library — SHH
Command to a canine — HEEL
Command to a cat — SCAT
Command to a dog — SPEAK, STAY
Command to a guard dog — SIC
Command to a horse — GEE, WHOA
Command to a husky — MUSH
Command to Dobbin — GEE
Command to Fido — SIT, SPEAK
Command to Gabriel — BLOW
Command to Lassie — STAY
Command to Mr. Ed — WHOA
Command to Rover — HEEL
Command: Abbr. — ORD
Commanded — BADE
Commandeer — CONFISCATE
Commander at Bunker Hill — GAGE
Commander of David's army — JOAB
Commander of forces in Korea — CLARK
Commander's order — HOLD FIRE
Commanding — ORDERING
Commandment breaker — SINNER
Commandment word — THOU
Commando specialties — RAIDS
Commands — MANDATES
Comme il faut — PROPER
Commedia dell' _____ — ARTE
Commemorative — STAMP
Commemorative pillar — MONUMENT
Commemorative slab — STELA
Commemorative stone — STELA
Commemorative stones — STE-LAE

Commemorative tablets — STELAE
Commence — BEGIN
Commencement wear — CAP
Commend a G.I. — CITE
Commended for gallantry — CITED
Comment — CLARIFY, DISCUSS, REMARK, REVIEW
Comment _____ vous? (How are you?) — ALLEZ
Comment follower — ATOR
Comment from Leo — ROAR
Commentator Sevareid — ERIC
Commented — SAID
Commerce — TRADE
Commercial abbr. — MDSE
Commercial boat — TUG
Commercial prefix — TOL
Commercial premium — AGIO
Commercial signs — NEONS
Commercial traveler — SALESMAN
Commercial vessel — OILER
Commercials — ADS
Commercials, for short — ADS
Commercials, in a way — SPOTS
Commingle — CONFUSE
Commiserates with — PITIES
Commiseration — PITY
Commissioned rank in the U.S.N. — CDR
Commit — PERPETUATE
Commit a gaffe at bridge — RENEGE
Commits a bull — ERRS
Committee employees — STAFFERS
Committee head — CHAIR
Commodity org. — CEA
Common — AVERAGE, BANAL, MERE, PUBLIC
Common — SIMPLE, TRITE, UNNOBLE
Common abbr. — ET AL
Common adder — SNAKE
Common ancestry — KINSHIP
Common beetle — DOR
Common boundary — INTERFACE
Common complaint — COLD
Common conjunction — NOR
Common conjunctions — ANDS
Common connective — AND
Common contraction — ARENT, DIDNT, HADNT
Common contraction — ISNT, ITLL, IVE, WEVE
Common follower — SENSE
Common French verb — ETRE
Common Great Lakes cargo — ORE
Common Latin abbr. — ET AL
Common Latin phrase — ID EST
Common law — CUSTOM
Common link — AND
Common Market abbr. — EEC
Common Market country — ITALY
Common Market initials — EEC
Common Market milieu — EUROPE
Common Muslim name — ALI
Common noun ending — ENCE
Common noun endings — TIONS
Common or non — SENSE
Common or proper word — NOUN
Common papal name — PIUS
Common people — PLEBS
Common remedy — ANTACID
Common roadside site — SUMAC
Common scene in westerns — ROUNDUP
Common solecisms — AINTS
Common soup base — LENTILS
Common street name — ELM
Common suffix — ANCE
Common sympton — ACHE
Common talk — RUMOR
Common title starter — THE
Common verb — ARE
Common word — THE
Common, Hawaiian style — NOA
Common, in Hawaii — NOA
Common-sense — SOUND
Commoner — PROLE
Commonly — OFTEN
Commonly, to Cato — VULGO
Commonplace — HUMDRUM, PROSAIC, PROSY
Commonplace — TRITE, TRIVIAL, USUAL
Commonwealth — NATION
Commotion — ADO, BUSTLE, FLAP, POTHER
Commotion — TEMPEST, TO DO
Commune in Greece — DEME
Commune in Iowa — AMANA
Commune in Sicily — ENNA
Commune in the Netherlands — EDE
Commune near Caen — ST LO
Commune near Padua — ESTE
Commune on the Arno — PISA
Communication — MESSAGE
Communication service — TELEX
Communications boat — AVISO
Communications check — RADIO TEST
Communications code word — ALFA
Communications devices — TELEPHONES
Communications, collectively — MEDIA
Communion is one — RITE
Communion plate — PATEN
Communists in Providence? — RHODE ISLAND REDS
Community character — ETHOS, MORES
Community head — ELDER
Community pursuer of pooches — DOG CATCHER
Community standard — ETHOS
Commuter area — RESIDENTIAL
Commuter car — SMOKER
Commuter carrier — SHUTTLE
Commuter group — CARPOOL
Commuter train time — SEVEN TEN
Commuter transportation — DIESEL TRAIN
Commuter's hangout — RAILROAD STATION
Commuter's shelter: Abbr. — STA
Commuters' arrangement — CARPOOL
Como _____ usted? — ESTA
Como is one — LAGO
Como or Garda — LAGO
Como or Maggiore — LAGO
Como the barber — PERRY
Como's forte — WONG
Compact — DENSE
Compact mass — CLUMP
Compacts — TREATIES
Compacts, for example — CARS
Compadre of Fidel — CHE
Companies — FIRMS
Companion — BUDDY, MATE
Companion for a lass — LAD
Companion of "humbug" — BAH
Companion of a bottle — BIRD
Companion of Aeneas — ABAS
Companion of Artemis — THEA
Companion of bitsy — ITSY
Companion of Blitzen — DONNER
Companion of end-all — BE ALL
Companion of hither — YON
Companion of mighty — HIGH
Companion of pains — ACHES
Companion of Paul — TITUS
Companion of spick — SPAN
Companion of Thummim — URIM
Companion of to — FRO

Companion of Wynken and Blynken — NOD
Companions of "O" and "U" — AEI
Companions of chips — DIPS
Companions of crafts — ARTS
Companionway — STAIR
Company — FIRM
Company for Carson — GUEST
Company lover — MISERY
Company's man — REP
Comparative ending — ERS, IER, IOR
Compare — CONTRAST, LIKEN
Compare to — LIKEN
Compare, with "to: — LIKEN
Compared — LIKENED
Compares prices — SHOPS
Comparison conjunction — THAN
Compartmentalize — PIGEON-HOLE
Compass — BEARING
Compass direction — NNE
Compass heading — ENE
Compass letters — SSE
Compass point — SSW, ENE, SSE, ESE, NNE
Compass pt. — ENE, ESE, NNE
Compassion — MERCY, MILK OF HUMAN KINDNESS
Compassionate — KIND
Compatibility — ACCORD
Compatriot — ALLY
Compatriots — PAISANOS
Compeer — EQUAL
Compel — COERCE, DRIVE
Compel by force — COERCE
Compel obedience to — ENFORCE
Compendious — TERSE
Compendious plus mellifluous — SHORT AND SWEET
Compensate — REQUITE, REWARD
Compensated — PAID
Compensation — GAIN, PAY, STIPEND
Compere — HOST
Compete — VIE
Competed for the Little Brown Jug — PACED
Competed with — RIVALLED
Competent — ABLE, ADEPT, EXPERT
Competently — ABLY, SKILL-FULLY
Competes at Henley — ROWS
Competing — VYING
Competition — MATCH
Competition prize winner — PLACER
Competitions — CONTESTS
Competitor — ENTRANT, RIVAL
Compiegne's river — OISE
Compile — AMASS
Complacency — EASE
Complain — CARP, GRIPE, PROTEST
Complain about the entree? — ROAST BEEF
Complain persistently — YAM-MER
Complainer — BEWAILER, GROUSER
Complains — MOANS
Complains violently — RAILS
Complaints — ILLS
Complaisant — GENIAL
Complete — DONE, END, ENTIRE, EVERY, FINISH
Complete — INTACT, PLE-NARY, UTTER
Complete confusion — CHAOS
Complete control — MASTERY
Complete copy — CLONE
Complete failure — BANK-RUPTCY, FIASCO
Complete musical scale — GAMUT
Complete surprise — BOLT FROM THE BLUE
Complete undivided unit — WHOLE IN ONE
Complete: Comb. form — TELEO
Completed — DONE, ENDED, OVER
Completed hang gliding — ALIT
Completed, in Caen — FINI
Completely — ALL, HEAD OVER HEELS
Completely absorbed — RAPT
Completely covered — ENCASED
Completely sealed — HERMETIC
Completes — ENDS
Completion — END
Complexion — HUE
Compliance — ASSENT
Complication — SNAG
Complied with commands — OBEYED
Compliment — FAVOR, PRAISE
Compline or sext — HOUR
Comply — ACCEDE
Comply with — OBEY
Comply with policy — FALL IN LINE
Component — ITEM, UNIT
Components of psyches — EGOS
Compos mentis — SANE
Compose — WRITE
Composed — CALM, SEDATE, SERENE, WROTE
Composed of two parts — BINARY
Composer-musicologist Taylor — DEEMS
Composer _____ Carlo Menotti — GIAN
Composer _____ Hoffman: Inits. — ETA
Composer Adolphe — ADAM
Composer Alban — BERG
Composer Barraine — ELSA
Composer Bartok — BELA
Composer Berg — ALBAN
Composer Bloch — ERNEST
Composer Bruckner — ANTON
Composer César's folks — CUIS
Composer Chasins — ABRAM
Composer Copland — AARON
Composer Debussy — CLAUDE
Composer Delibes — LEO
Composer Dvorak — ANTON
Composer Erik — SATIE
Composer Francesco Antonio _____ — ROSETTI
Composer Franck — CESAR
Composer Franz — LISZT, LEHAR
Composer from Hungary — LEHAR
Composer Grofé — FERDE
Composer Gustav — MAHLER
Composer Harold — ARLEN
Composer Jacques — IBERT
Composer Janacek — LEOS
Composer Janácek — LEOS
Composer Jerome — KERN
Composer Jones — ISHAM
Composer Joplin — SCOTT
Composer Khachaturian — ARAM
Composer Leopold _____: 1899-1964 — MANNES
Composer Luigi _____ — NONO
Composer Montemezzi — ITALO
Composer Musgrave — THEA
Composer Ned — ROREM
Composer of "Alceste" — GLUCK
Composer of "Angelique": 1927 — IBERT
Composer of "Carmen" — BIZET
Composer of "Daphnis et Chloé" — RAVEL
Composer of "El Amor Brujo" — DE FALLA
Composer of "Eliza" — ARNE
Composer of "Enigma Variations" — ELGAR
Composer of "Firefly" — FRIML
Composer of "Funny Girl" — STYNE

Composer of "Giselle" — ADAM
Composer of "Grand Canyon Suite" — FERDE GROFE
Composer of "Happy Days Are Here Again" — AGER
Composer of "Judith" — ARNE
Composer of "King Olaf" — ELGAR
Composer of "La Cenerentola" — ROSSINI
Composer of "La Valse" — RAVEL
Composer of "Le Roi D'ys" — LALO
Composer of "Liebestraum" — LISZT
Composer of "Lohengrin" — WAGNER
Composer of "Merry Widow" — LEHAR
Composer of "Namouna" — LALO
Composer of "Rigoletto" — VERDI
Composer of "Roberta — KERN
Composer of "Rule Britannia" — ARNE
Composer of "Show Boat" — KERN
Composer of "Socrates" — SATIE
Composer of "Statements" — COPLAND
Composer of "Stormy Weather" — ARLEN
Composer of "Sylvia" — DELIBES
Composer of "Symphonie Espagnole" — LALO
Composer of "Tannhauser" — WAGNER
Composer of "The Barber of Seville" — ROSSINI
Composer of "The Planets" — HOLST
Composer of "The Princess on the Pea" — ENNA
Composer of "The Rosary" — NEVIN
Composer of "The Three Penny Opera" — WEILL
Composer of "The Wiz" — SMALLS
Composer of "Villa" — LEHAR
Composer of nine symphonies — MAHLER
Composer Philip — GLASS
Composer Porter — COLE
Composer Rorem — NED
Composer Satie — ERIK
Composer Schifrin — LALO
Composer Shostakovich — DMITRI
Composer Siegmeister — ELIE
Composer Stravinsky — IGOR
Composer Wilder — ALEC
Composers Corp. — BMI
Composition — OPUS, THEME
Composition for eight — OCTET
Composition for sitar — RAGA
Composition for two — DUET
Composition in verse — POEM
Composition theme — LEMMA
Composure — CALM
Compound — COMPLEX, ISOMERE, VARIED
Compound used as a disinfectant — CRESOL
Compound used as a photographic developer — AMIDOL
Compound whence caffeine is derived — PURINE
Compound with rust — OXIDE
Comprehend — GET, SEE
Comprehended — GOT
Comprehending — SEEING
Comprehension — GRASP
Comprehensive — LARGE
Comprehensiveness — WIDTH
Compress — CROWD
Comprise — INCLUDE
Compromise — SETTLE, SETTLEMENT
Compromises — STEERS A MIDDLE COURSE
Compromises — STRIKES A HAPPY MEDIUM
Compunction — REMORSE
Compute — ADD
Computer-display pointers — CURSORS
Computer acronym — DOS
Computer adjunct — PRINTER
Computer card readers — SORTERS
Computer channels — BANDS
Computer data unit — BYTE
Computer device — MOUSE
Computer facts — DATA
Computer grist — DATA
Computer in "2001" — HAL
Computer input — DATA
Computer key — ENTER
Computer language — PASCAL
Computer list — MENU
Computer memory — RAM
Computer method — OFFLINE
Computer monitor — SCREEN
Computer part — CHIP
Computer picture — GRAPHIC
Computer plate — DISC
Computer pointer — CURSOR
Computer product — READOUT
Computer programming language — ADA
Computer screen offering — MENU
Computer software items — PROGRAMS
Computer unit — BYTE
Computer's sustenance — DATA
Computers of a kind — PROCESSORS
Comrade-in-arms — ALLY
Comstock lode — MINE
Comte de la Fere — ATHOS
Con — AGAINST, ANTI, SCAM
Con _____ (tenderly) — AMORE
Con _____ (with vigor) — BRIO
Con artfully — STING
Con artist — FAST TALKER
Con artist's residence — DUPLEX
Con con — PRO
Con game — BUNCO, FRAUD, SCAM
Con man — ANTI
Con man's game — SCAM
Concave — DISHED, HOLLOW
Concave moldings — SCOTIAS
Conceal — CACHE, HIDE, MASK, SECRETE, SCREEN
Conceal, in a way — ENSHROUD
Conceal, of old: Var. — ELOIN
Concealed — HID, PERDU
Concealed again — REHID
Concealed complication — CATCH
Concealed fence — HAHA
Concealed obstacles — SNAGS
Concealed zapper — SNIPER
Concealed, as motives — ULTERIOR
Conceals — HIDES
Conceals cleverly — PALMS
Concede — AGREE, GRANT
Conceded — AGREED, ALLOWED
Conceit — EGO, EGOTISM, IDEA
Conceited — VAIN
Conceited character — EGOIST
Conceited ones — EGOS
Conceits — EGOS
Conceive — IDEATE
Concentrate — CENTER, FOCUS
Concentration — TRAIN OF THOUGHT
Concept — EGO, IDEA, IMAGE, PLAN
Concept: Comb. form — IDEO
Conception — IDEA
Conception of perfection — IDEAL

Concern — AFFAIR, CARE, WORRY
Concern of Chanoyu — TEA
Concern of some sportsmen — THE SNOW AT STOWE
Concern of the cobbler — LAST
Concern on Wall St. — ECON
Concerned — CARING, INTERESTED, UNEASY
Concerned parents' gps — PTAS
Concerned with — ABOUT
Concerning — ABOUT, ANENT, AS TO, IN RE, IN TERMS OF
Concerning word parts — SYLLABIC
Concerning, to a lawyer — IN RE
Concerning: Lat — IN RE
Concert-hall — ODEON
Concert — CHORUS
Concert follower — INA
Concert halls — ODEA
Concert highlights — ENCORES
Concert number — TRIO
Concession chaser — AIRE
Concierge — JANITOR
Concious — SENTIENT
Concise — BRIEF, COMPACT, TERSE
Concisely — IN SUM
Conclamation — SHOUT
Conclude — CLOSE, END, FINISH, INFER, RESOLVE
Conclude prematurely a la NASA — ABORT
Concluded — DEDUCED, OVER
Concluding musical passage — CODA
Concluding stanza — ENVOI
Conclusion — END, FINIS
Concoct — BREW, DEVISE, HATCH
Concocted — MADE
Concoction — MIXTURE
Concord — FRATERNITY
Concord, Ma. neighbor — LEX
Concorde — ENIENTE
Concorde, e.g. — SST
Concordes, for short — SSTS
Concrete leveler — SCREED
Concupiscence — LUST
Concur — AGREE
Concurrence — YES
Concurring — ATONE
Conde, the publisher — NAST
Condemn — DECRY, DOOM
Condemnation — BLAME
Condemns — DAMNS
Condensed — THICK
Condensed vapor — RAIN
Condescends — DEIGNS, STOOPS
Condign — JUST
Condiment — FENNEL
Condiment bottle — CRUET
Condiment containers — CRUETS
Condition — AILMENT, CASE, MUST, REPAIR, STATE
Condition — STATUS, TERM
Condition of sale — AS IS
Condition of servitude — PEONAGE
Condition situation — UNITED STATES
Conditional — IFFY
Conditional release — PAROLE
Conditionally released prisoner — PAROLEE
Conditions — IFS
Condo offering — DUPLEX
Condo or coop — ABODE
Condor — FALCON
Condor habitat — AERIE
Condor or eagle — RAPTOR
Condor's castle: Var. — EYRIE
Condor's claw — TALON
Condor's home: Var. — AERI
Condor's roost — AERIE
Conduce — TEND
Conduct — CHAPERONE, DEMEANOR, DIRECT, GUIDE, LEAD
Conducted — CONVOYED, ESCORTED, HELD, LED
Conductive substance — METAL
Conductor _____ -Pekka Salonen — ESA
Conductor Akira _____ — ENDO
Conductor Ansermet — ERNEST
Conductor Caldwell — SARAH
Conductor De Waart — EDO
Conductor Dorati — ANTAL
Conductor Fritz — REINER
Conductor Klemperer — OTTO
Conductor Koussevitzky — SERGE
Conductor Masur — KURT
Conductor Mehta — ZUBIN
Conductor Paul _____ — WHITEMAN
Conductor Previn — ANDRE
Conductor Rapee — ERNO
Conductor Santi — NELLO
Conductor Walter — BRUNO
Conductor Zubin — MEHTA
Conductor's aide — TRAINMAN
Conductor's concerns — TEMPI
Conductor's need — BATON
Conductor / composer — PREVIN
Conductors — MAESTROS
Conducts — DIRECTS
Conduit — MAIN
Conduits — WATER MAINS
Cone-shaped — PINEAL
Cone-shaped tent — TEEPEE
Conestoga wagon setting — PRAIRIE
Conf. — SESS
Conf. component — SESS
Confabulations — CHATS
Confection — JELLY, NOUGAT
Confection fruits — KUMQUATS
Confederate — ALLY
Confederate gen. — R E LEE
Confederate in the audience — PLANT
Confederate Johnny _____ — REB
Confederate leader — R E LEE
Confederate soldier — REB
Confederate soldiers, for short — REBS
Confederates — ALLIES
Confederation — UNION
Confer — BESTOW
Confer ender — ENCE
Confer knighthood — DUB
Confer priesthood — ORDAIN
Conference before a hearing — PRETRIAL
Conference city — GENEVA
Conference grp. — DEL
Conference or ritual ceremony — POWWOW
Conference seg. — SESS
Conference sight, 1943 — TEHERAN
Conference site: 1945 — YALTA
Confers holy orders — ORDAINS
Confess — ADMIT, AVOW, LET ON
Confess to stealing the stole? — TAKE THE WRAP
Confessor's earful — SINS
Confide — RELY
Confidence game — SCAM, STING
Confident — ASSURED, SECURE
Confidential — UNDER ONES HAT
Confidential matters — SECRETS
Confidential; recondite — ESOTERIC
Configured in folds — PLEATED
Confine — KEEP TO, LIMIT, PEN
Confine, with "in" — HEM
Confined — CAGED, PENT
Confines, in a way — PENS
Confining — NARROW
Confirm — ATTEST, VALIDATE
Confirmation — ASSENT
Confirmation slap — ALAPA

Confirmation, e.g. — RITE
Confiscated — SEIZED
Conflict — STRUGGLE
Conflicts — WARS
Conform — ADAPT, FIT, KEEP STEP
Conforming — IN STEP
Confound! — DRAT
Confounded — HAZY
Confounds — ADDLES
Confront — FACE
Confront boldly — ACCOST
Confronted — ACCOSTED, MET
Confronts — FACES, STANDS UP TO
Confronts head on — FACES
Confucian truth — HSIN
Confucianist principles — TAO
Confuse — ADDLE, BEFOG, CLOUD, JUMBLE, POSE
Confused — ADDLEHEADED
Confused — ASEA, AT SEA, MUDDLED
Confused cluster — SPLATTER
Confused struggle — MELEE
Confusion — ADO
Confusion that is noisy — BEDLAM
Confute — REBUT
Cong. period — SESS
Congeal — GEL
Conger — EEL
Conger catcher — EELER
Conger chasers — EELERS
Conger or moray — EEL
Conger seeker — EELER
Congo feeder — UELE
Congo native — PYGMY
Congo, today — ZAIRE
Congou, for one — TEA
Congregation — ECCLESIA
Congress financial watchdog — GAO
Congress: Abbr. — LEGIS
Congressional barrel — PORK
Congressional title — REP
Congressional vote — NAY
Congressman in last term — LAME DUCK
Congressman's concern: Abbr. — DIST
Congressman: Abbr — SEN
Congruous — FIT
Conical skin tent: Var. — TIPI
Conical tent: var. — TEEPEE
Conical tents: Var. — TIPIS
Conifer — FIR, PINE
Coniferous tree — LARCH
Conjecture — GUESS, OPINE
Conjunction — ACCORD, UNION
Conjunctions — ORS
Conk out — FAIL
Conked — BEANED
Conks — BOPS
Conn — CONTROL
Conn. town — AVON
Connect — ATTACH, JOIN, LINK, RELATE
Connect with — TIE TO
Connect, in a way — RELATE
Connected — LINKED
Connected series — CATENA
Connected series of rooms — SUITE
Connecticut bulldogs — YALE
Connecticut flag greenery — GRAPEVINES
Connecticut senator — DODD
Connecticut state bird — ROBIN
Connecticut tourist town — MYSTIC
Connecting devices — ADAPTERS
Connecting word — AND, NOR
Connection — LINK, TIE
Connectives — ANDS
Connell's "_____ Bridge" — MRS
Connery and Penn — SEANS
Connery from Edinburgh — SEAN
Connery or O'Casey — SEAN
Connery role — BOND
Connery's namesakes — SEANS
Connie of baseball — MACK
Connived in a crime — ABETTED
Connives — ABETS
Connors coup — ACE
Connors or Wallace — MIKE
Conquer — MASTER
Conquered — WON
Conquerer — VICTOR
Conquistador's booty — ORO
Conquistador's dream — ELDORADO
Conquistador's goal — ORO
Conquistadors' quest — ORO
Conrad opus — HEART OF DARKNESS
Conrad or Cotten — JOSEPH
Conrad's "Lord _____" — JIM
Cons — ANTIS
Conscious — AWAKE
Conscript — DRAFT
Conscription agcy. — SSS
Consecrate — ANOINT, BLESS, DEVOTE
Consecrated oil — CHRISM
Consecrated, in Cannes — SACRE
Consecreated — BLESSED
Consent — ACCEDE
Consents — AGREES
Consents concerning — AGREES TO
Consequence — RESULT
Consequential clause — APODOSIS
Consequently — ERGO
Conservative — DISCREET, MODERATE, REASONABLE
Conservative fasteners — WILLIAM F BUCKLES
Conservatives — TORIES
Conserve of fruits boiled with sugar and water — JAM
Consider — DEEM
Consideration — CHARITY
Considered — HEARD
Consign — SEND
Consisting of two chambers — BICAMERAL
Console — COMFORT
Consolidate — UNITE
Consolidates — MERGES
Consonants' connection — AEIOU
Consort of Zeus — HERA
Conspicuous — SALIENT
Conspicuousness — SALIENCE
Conspiracy — CABAL
Conspirator — CATILINARIAN
Conspirator agiangst Peter III — ORLOV
Constable and Turner paintings — LANDSCAPES
Constables — OFFICERS
Constant — TRUE
Constant factor: Abbr. — COEF
Constanta coin — LEU
Constantine's vision — CROSS
Constantly — EVER
Constellation — ARA, CETUS, CLUSTER
Constellation Grus — CRANE
Constellation Lepus — HARE
Consternation — ALARM
Constitution — IRONSIDES
Constrain — RESTRICT
Constraint — DURESS
Constrict — CLOG, CRAMP
Constricting scarf? — BOA
Construct — ASSEMBLE, ERECT, FORGE, REAR
Constructed anew — REMADE
Construction beam — I BAR
Construction contractor — ERECTOR
Construction girder — H BEAM
Construction material — PLYWOOD
Construction member — CROSSBEAM, I BAR
Construction piece — I BAR
Construction toy — ERECTOR
Construction worker — HARD HAT
Constructional item — T BEAM
Constructive — HANDY
Constructor — ERECTOR
Constructors in a fairy tale — THREE LITTLE PIGS

Constructs — ERECTS
Constructs again — REMAKES
Construe — INFER
Consumed — ATE, EATEN
Consumer — USER
Consumer activist — NADER
Consumer advocate — NADER
Consumer's choice — BRAND
Cont. — AFRICA
Contact with the spirits — SEANCE
Contained — CALM
Container — CAN, CARTON, CASE, JAR, PAIL
Container — TIN, TUB, VAT, VESSEL
Container business? — PAN BROKERAGE
Container for a hiker — PACK
Container for café — TASSE
Container for callas — VASE
Container for film — CAN
Container for flour — BIN
Container for Hancock — INKPOT
Container for needles — ETUI
Container for water — EWER
Container of cigarettes — PACK
Container of cigars — HUMI-DOR
Container of coal — HOPPER
Container of oranges — CRATE
Container of toothpaste — TUBE
Container weight — TARE
Containers — BINS
Containers larger than six-packs — CASES
Containing carbamide — UREAL
Containing gold — AURIC
Containing iron — FERRIC
Containing oil — OLEIC
Containing silver — ARGENTIC
Containing sulfur: Prefix — THIO
Containing the most open work — LACIEST
Containing Tl — THALLIC
Contaminate — INFECT, TAINT
Contaminate again — REIN-FECT
Contaminated — TAINTED
Contemn — DERIDE
Contemning — SCORNING
Contemplation of the past — RETROSPECTION
Contemporaries of Hudsons — NASHES
Contemporary — COEVAL
Contemporary artist and set designer — ERTE
Contemporary French author — AYME
Contemporary of Edison — TESLA
Contemporary of H. Wells — G SHAW
Contemporary of Henry Wadsworth — EDGAR ALLAN
Contemporary of Magritte — DALI
Contemporary of Shelley — KEATS
Contemporary of T.S.E. — WHA
Contempt — BAH, SCORN
Contempt breeder — FAMILIARITY
Contemptibility — VILENESS
Contemptible — GRUBBY, MEAN
Contemptible one — INSECT, LICE, TOAD
Contemptible person — SNIPE
Contemptible person — TOAD
Contemptuous look — SNEER
Contend — ARGUE, BATTLE, CLASH, STRIVE, VIE
Contend in a game — PLAY
Contended — VIED
Contends — COPES, DEALS WITH
Contented-baby sound effects — GURGLES
Contented baby's sound — COO
Contented employee? — GRUNTLED WORKER
Contented sound — AAH, PURR
Contentious item? — BONE
Contents of heisters' holsters — GATS
Contest — BATTLE, DUEL, FRAY, GAME, MATCH
Contest — RACE, SPORT, STRUGGLE, VIE
Contest for Atlanta — RACE
Contests — BOUTS, EVENTS, GAMES, RACES, TILTS
Contests for spellers — BEES
Contiguous — ABUTTING, ADJACENT, ADJOIN, BOUND, NEAR
Continence — PURITY
Continent bordering Urals — EUROPE
Continent connectors — AIR-LINERS
Continent: Abbr. — S AMER
Continental capital — ROMA
Continental divide — URALS
Continental divider — OCEAN
Continental is one — SHELF
Continental prefix — EURO
Continental range — URALS
Continental subdivision — EAST ASIA
Continual — NONSTOP
Continuation of a subscription — RENEWAL
Continue — ADD, BIDE, GO ON, PERSIST
Continue — PROTRACT, RESUME
Continue a subscription — RENEW
Continue to hold — KEEP
Continue to survive — SUBSIST
Continue with to the end — SEE OUT
Continue working — RESUME
Continued along — STOOD ON
Continued without pause — RAN ON
Continuous — DAY AFTER DAY, NONSTOP
Continuous — PERPETUAL
Continuous coming — INFLUX
Continuously — YEAR IN YEAR OUT
Contort — BEND, TWIST, WARP
Contorted — BENT, WRESTED
Contract — DEFLATE
Contract of a sort — LEASE
Contraction for Keats — EER
Contraction of the pupil — MIOSIS
Contractions — SPASMS
Contracts — SHRINKS
Contracts, of a sort — LEASES
Contradict — BELIE, DENY, REBUT
Contradiction, British style — MY EYE
Contralto Nikolaidi — ELENA
Contrary — BALKY
Contrary adage first part — WHEN THE CATS AWAY
Contrary adage second part — THE MICE WILL PLAY
Contrary Mary's milieu — GARDEN
Contrary newscaster — DAN RATHERNOT
Contrary words — BUTS
Contravene — DENY
Contribute — CHIP IN
Contribute in a way — ANTE
Contributes — ADDS TO
Contribution — INPUT
Contribution commitment — TITHE
Contribution to support a church — TITHE
Contributor — FACTOR
Contrite — HUMBLE, SORRY
Contrite one — RUER
Contrition — REMORSE
Contrivance for emptying — TILTER
Contrived sentimentally — TREACLE

Contriver of Balder's death — LOKI
Contrives — INVENTS
Control — DIAL, REIN, RESTRAIN, SWAY
Control buttons — ONS
Control spot — HELM
Controlled — RAN
Controlling influence — SWAY
Controls — CURBS, RESTRAINS
Controversial — POLEMICAL
Controversial amendment — ERA
Controversial compounds — STEROIDS
Controversial implant — SILICONE
Controversial pesticide — ALAR
Controversial pesticide for short — DDT
Controversial Supreme Court case — ROE VERSUS WADE
Controversial wraps — FURS
Controversy — RHUBARB
Conundrum — POSER
Conv. attendees — DELS
Convalesces — HEALS
Convene — CONGREGATE, RALLY, SIT
Convened — MET, SAT
Convened anew — REMET
Convenient — USEABLE
Convent — FRIARY, NUNNERY
Convent dwellers — NUNS
Convent head — ABBESS
Convent rooms — CELLS
Conventicle group — SECT
Convention figures — DELEGATES, NOMINATOR
Convention showstopper — KEYNOTE ADDRESS
Convention site for blacksmiths? — HORSE SHOE BEND ID
Convention site for distillers? — WHISKEY BOTTOM MD
Convention site for gamblers? — BLACK JACK MO
Convention site for orthopedists? — WOUNDED KNEE SD
Convention site for phrenologists? — SKULL VALLEY AZ
Conventional, Downeast? — MAINE STREAM
Conventioneer — DELEGATE
Convents — PRIORIES
Conventual superior — ABBESS
Converge — CENTER, FOCUS, MEET, MERGE
Converging — FOCAL
Conversation á deux — TETE A TETE
Conversation piece — CURIO
Converse — CHAT, TALK
Converses, informally — CHATS
Convert — ALTER, CHANGE
Convert into cash — REDEEM
Convert into cipher — ENCODE
Converted the chips — CASHED
Convertible — RAGTOP
Convertible piece of furniture — ATO
Convertibles — AUTOS
Converts messages — ENCODES
Convex molding — OGEE, OVOLO, TORI, TORUS
Convex moldings — OVOLI
Convey — IMPART, TRANSFER
Convey feeling — INFECT
Convey in a way — TELEPORT
Conveyed in shifts — RELAYED
Conveyed through conduits — PIPED
Conveys the written word — READS TO
Convict falsely and quickly — RAILROAD
Convince — ASSURE
Convinced — CERTAIN, SOLD
Convoy constituent — SEMI
Convoys — ESCORTS
Convy of TV — BERT
Conway — TIM
Cooch _____, West Bengalese city — BEHAR
Cook book — COMA
Cook eggs — SHIRR
Cook too long — OVERDO
Cook up — BREW
Cook who has a lot of crust — PASTRY CHEF
Cook's abbr. — TBSP
Cook's amts. — TSPS
Cook's cover — APRON
Cook's herb — OREGANO
Cook's meadow, Calif. — BAKERSFIELD
Cook's measure — DASH
Cook's needs — PANS
Cook, in a way — BAKE
Cook? — PANHANDLER
Cookbook abbr. — TBSP
Cookbook amt. — TSP
Cookbook direction — DICE, STIR
Cookbook instruction — SERE, STIR
Cooked — DONE
Cooked again — REHEATED
Cooked cereal — GRUEL, MUSH
Cooked in a French oven — ROTI
Cookery direction — STIR
Cookery method — WATERLESS
Cookie — OATMEAL, SNAP, WAFER
Cookie king "Famous _____" — AMOS
Cooking abbr. — TBSP, TSP
Cooking amts. — TSPS
Cooking direction — HEAT, SAUTE, SCALD, STIR
Cooking fat — LARD
Cooking herb — BASIL, SAGE
Cooking measurement: Abbr. — TSPS
Cooking utensils — POTS AND PANS
Cookout item — SPARE RIB
Cookout specialty — CORN ON THE COB
Cooks — CHEFS
Cooks necessity: abbr. — REC
Cooks needs — RECIPES
Cooks with hot air — BAKES
Cookware — PANS, POTS
Cool — CRISP, DISTANT, HIP
Cool and reserved state — STANDOFFISHNESS
Cool desserts — ICES
Cool guys — DUDES
Cool horsewoman — GODIVA
Cool Italian desert — SPUMONE
Cool one, in presidential lore — CAL
Cooled ember — ASH
Cooled the champagne — ICED
Cooler — ICIER
Coolest wear — FIG LEAF
Coolidge and Peete — CALS
Coolidge from Nashville — RITA
Coolidge's running mate — DAWES
Coolidge's V.P. — DAWES
Coolidge, et al. — CALS
Coolidge, to family — CAL
Cooling drink — MALT
Cooling-off period — TRUCE
Cools in a way — ICES
Coop dwellers — HENS
Coop group — CAGE, BROOD, HEN AND CHICKENS, HENS
Coop resident — HEN
Coop roost — PERCH
Coop sounds — PEEPS
Coop up — CAGE
Cooper or Coleman — GARYS
Cooper role, with "Mr." — DEEDS
Cooper title role — DEEDS
Cooper's tool — CROZE
Cooperate — COME TO AN AGREEMENT
Cooperates, informally — PLAYS BALL

Cooperative type of man — YES
Cooperatives in the USSR — ARTELS
Cooperstown name — COBB, OTT, TRIS
Coordinated clothing item? — WEAR WITH ALL
Coordinated effort — TEAMWORK
Coordinated procedure — SYSTEM
Coordinates — TIES IN
Coot — FOOL
Cooter — TURTLE
Cop — LIFT, NAB
Cop _____ — A PLEA
Cop making a collar — ARRESTER
Cop org., in Moose Jaw — RCMP
Copenhagen amusement garden — TIVOLI
Copenhagen attraction — TIVOLI
Copenhagen change — ORE
Copenhagen citizen — DANE
Copenhagen coin — KRONE, ORE
Copenhagen money — KRONE
Copenhagen natives — DANES
Copenhagen park — TIVOLI
Copenhagen's Swedish neighbor — MALMO
Copernicus predecessor — PTOLEMY
Copied — APED
Copier — APER
Copier solution — TONER
Copies — APES
Copies, for short — REPROS
Copland ballet score — RODEO
Copland's "El _____ Mexico" — SALON
Copland's "The Tender Land": e.g. — OPERA
Copper — CENT, POLICEMAN
Copper alloy — BRASS
Copper center of Venezuela — AROA
Copper or Bronze: Lat. — AES
Copper: Comb. form — CUPRO
Copperfield — DAVID
Copperfield's first wife — DORA
Copperfield's second wife — AGNES
Copperfield, to friends? — DAVIE
Coppers — CENTS
Copse — THICKET
Copter — WHIRLYBIRD
Copter blade — ROTOR
Copter feature — VTO
Copter part — ROTOR
Copter propulsion — ROTORS
Copter's cousin — GIRO
Coptic church title — ABBA
Copy — CLONE, CARBON, DITTO, REPLICA
Copy — REPRINT, TRANSCRIPTION
Copy editor's word — STET
Copy of a kind — XEROX
Copy, in a way — XEROX
Copycat — MIME
Copycats — APERS
Copying machine necessity — TONER
Copyread — EDIT
Copyreader's word — STET
Copyright — PATENT
Copyright violator — PIRATE
Coq au _____ — VIN
Coquettes — FLIRTS
Coquettishly — COYLY
Cor or core — HEART
Coral — ROSE
Coral and cerise — REDS
Coral form — SEAFAN
Coral island — ATOLL, REEF
Coral or Black — SEA
Coral or Red — SEA
Coral reef — ATOLL
Coral ridge — REEF
Coral structure — ATOLL
Corbeled widow — ORIEL
Corbie — CROW
Corbin's "L.A. Law" role — ARNIE
Cord — TWINE
Cord holding down Arab's headdress — AGAL
Cord of goat's hair — AGAL
Cord or Opel — AUTO
Cord or pod lead-in — TRI
Cord tip — AGLET
Cordage fiber — BAST, ISTLE
Cordage plant — RAMIE
Corday's victim — MARAT
Corded fabric — REP
Corded silk — REP
Cordelia's father — LEAR
Cordell and Henry — HULLS
Cordial — WARM
Cordial flavoring — ANISE
Cordial welcome — GLAD HAND
Cordoba coin — PESETA
Cordoba friends — AMIGOS
Cordoban curse — ANATEMA
Cordon _____ (chef) — BLEU
Cordon bleu — COOK
Cordon bleu entree — ROTI
Corduroy rib — WALE
Corduroy ridge — WALE
Cordwood measure — STERE
Core — CENTER, ESSENCE
Core of solipsism — SELF
Cores — PITHS
Corium — DERM
Cork Harbour port — COBH
Cork-oak bark — SUBER
Cork-to-Kilkenny dir. — ENE
Corked — SEALED
Corker — LULU
Corkscrewed — SPIRALED
Corkscrews, e.g. — OPENERS
Corkwood — BALSA
Corm — BULB
Corn and palm products — OILS
Corn Belt institution — FAMILY FARM
Corn bread — PONE
Corn cake — PONE
Corn centers — COBS
Corn cores — COBS
Corn field items — EARS
Corn goddess — CERES
Corn holder — COB, CRIB
Corn lead-in — TRI
Corn lily — IXIA
Corn meal-meat mixture — SCRAPPLE
Corn oil product — OLEO
Corn on _____ — THE COB
Corn or form beginning — UNI
Corn or form starter — UNI
Corn or oat follower — MEAL
Corn or sect starter — TRI
Corn or verse predecer — UNI
Corn pest — BORER
Corn porridges — SAMPS
Corn serving — EAR
Corn stick — PONE
Corn unit — EAR
Corn's may be smoked — SILK
Corneille tragedy — ARIANE
Cornelia _____ Skinner — OTIS
Cornell's locale — ITHACA
Corner — TREE
Corner of a sail — CLEW
Corner sign — STOP
Cornered — CAUGHT, TREED
Corners — NOOKS
Cornerstone — BASIS
Cornfield state, in the vernacular — IOWAY
Cornflower — BLUEBOTTLE, IXIA
Cornhusker city — OMAHA
Cornhusker state — NEBRASKA
Cornhusker's capital: abbr. — LIN
Cornhuskers — NEBRASKANS
Cornice molding — CYMA
Cornmeal cakes — PONES
Cornmeal goodies — HOECAKES
Cornstarch syrup — GLUCOSE
Cornucopia — HORN
Cornwall coins — PENCE
Cornwell's pen name — LE CARRE
Corny actors — HAMS

Corny or square — MICKEY MOUSE
Corolla part — GALEA, PETAL
Corolla petal — ALA
Corona's density — ASH
Corona, e.g. — CIGAR
Coronach — DIRGE
Coronado's quest — ORO
Coronation gown — KIRTLE
Coronation jewel — TIARA
Coronet — TIARA
Coronet's cousin — TIARA
Corot, for example — LANDSCAPE ARTIST
Corp. abbreviations — INCS
Corp. board — TRS
Corp. brass — EXEC
Corp. giant — ITT
Corp. officer — TREAS
Corp. or sgt. — NCO
Corporate "marriage" — MERGER
Corporate monogram — RCA
Corporate symbol — LOGO
Corporate titles — INCS
Corporate VIPs — CEOS, EXECS, TREAS
Corporeal vessel — AORTA
Corps de ballet — CHORUS
Corpsman — MEDIC
Corpulent — OBESE, PORTLY
Corral — POUND
Corral sound — SNORT
Corrals — PENS
Correct — AMEND, EMEND, RIGHT
Correct a seam again — RERIP
Correct copy — EMEND
Correct texts — EMEND
Correct the wheels — ALIGN
Correct: Abbr. — RGT
Corrected — AMENDED
Corrected a text — EMENDATED
Corrected copy — EDITED
Corrected the text — EMENDED
Corrections — ERASURES
Correctly reasoned — LOGICAL
Corrects — AMENDS, CHECKS
Corrects copy — EDITS
Corrects texts — EMENDS
Correspond — AGREE, TALLY, WRITE
Correspond exactly — COINCIDE
Correspondence — EPISTLE
Correspondence abbr. — MRS
Correspondent of a sort — PENPAL
Corrida beast — TORO
Corrida bravo — OLE
Corrida celebration — FIESTA
Corrida cheer — OLE
Corrida combatants — TOROS
Corrida cries — OLES
Corrida figure — MATADOR, TORERO, TORO
Corrida hero — MATADOR
Corrida participant — TORO
Corrida principal — TORRERO
Corrida shouts — OLES
Corrida star — BULL, TORO
Corridors — PASSAGES
Corrigenda — ERRATA
Corrigendum — ERROR
Corrode — EAT, RUST
Corroded — EATEN
Corrosion — RUST
Corrosive — ERODENT
Corrosives — ACIDS
Corrugated — FLUTED
Corrupt — EVIL, ROTTEN, TAINT, VENAL
Corrupts — SEDUCES
Corsage — BOUQUET, FLOWER
Corsage favorite — ORCHID
Corsair — PIRATE
Corsair's quest — LOOT
Corset bone — STAY
Corset feature — STAY
Corsica is one: abbr. — ISL
Corsica, for one — ILE
Corsican's neighbor — SARD
Corso money — LIRE
Corteges — TRAINS
Cortes victim — AZTEC
Cortex — RIND
Cortices — RINDS
Corundum — EMERY
Corvette or packet — SHIP
Corvette, for one — SHIP
Corvettes, to the USN — DDCS
Corvine bird — MAGPIE
Corvine comments — CAWS
Corvis — BIRDS
Coryphaeus — LEADER
Cosby — BILL
Cosby show character — THEO
Cosby's "_____ Albert" — FAT
Cosmetic — ROUGE
Cosmetic ingredient — ALOE
Cosmetic item — ROUGE
Cosmetic liquid — LOTION
Cosmetic plant — ALOE
Cosmetic used by Cleopatra — KOHL
Cosmetician Lauder — ESTEE
Cosmetician Madeleine _____ — MONO
Cosmetics ingredient — ALOE
Cosmic principle — KARMA
Cosmic times — EONS
Cosmonaut Gagarin — YURI
Cosmos — EARTH, UNIVERSE
Cossack Bulba — TARAS
Cossack chief — ATAMAN
Cosset — CARESS, PAMPER, PET
Cost a loser — ADAM
Cost of living — COLA
Cost of maintenance — UPKEEP
Cost, courtwise — DAMAGES
Costa _____, Spain — BRAVA
Costa _____: , home of Arias — RICA
Costae — RIBS
Costello — LOU
Costello and Ferrigno — LOUS
Costello namesakes — LOUS
Costello or Gossett — LOU
Costello or Groza — LOU
Costello's query — WHOS ON FIRST
Costlier — STEEPER
Costly — DEAR, STEEP
Costly vase — MING
Costner role: 1987 — NESS
Costume — ATTIRE, CLOTHE, DRESS, GETUP
Costume for Coppelia — TUTU
Cosy — SNUG
Cote cries — BAAS
Cote d' _____ — AZUR
Cote d'Or capital — DIJON
Cote dweller — DOVE, EWE
Cote female — EWE
Cote occupant — EWE
Cote residents — EWES, RAMS
Cote sound — BAA, BLEAT, COO
Coterie — CENACLE, SET
Cotillion event — ROUND DANCE
Cotswold — SHEEP
Cotta lead-in — TERRA
Cotta or firma — TERRA
Cottage cheese ingredient — CURD
Cottage style — A FRAME
Cotter — PIN
Cotterways — SLOTS
Cotton bundle — BALE
Cotton by-product — OILSEED
Cotton castoff — LINT
Cotton cloth — DRILL, SILESIA
Cotton fabric — LISLE, LENO
Cotton fiber knot — NEP
Cotton filament — THREAD
Cotton flowers — BOLLS
Cotton gin inventor Whitney — ELI
Cotton machine — GIN
Cotton packer — BALER
Cotton separators — GINS
Cotton textile remnant — RAG
Cotton thread — LISLE
Cotton to — LIKE
Cotton unit — BALE
Cotton worker — BALER
Cotton's castoff — LINT
Cottontail — DOE

Cottontail's sibling — MOPSY
Cottonwoods — ALAMOS
Coty of France — RENE
Coty or Cassin — RENES
Coty or Clair — RENE
Coty or Descartes — RENE
Couch — SETTEE
Couch potato's favorite show? — MASH
Couch potato's meals, often — SNACKS
Cougar — PUMA
Cougar or Jaguar — CAT
Cougar's color — TAWNY
Cough — RALE
Cough-drop — LOZENGE
Could and would — VERBS
Couloir — GORGE, GULLY
Coulter — BLADE
Council city of Italy — TRENT
Council site: 1545-63 — TRENT
Counsel — LAWYER, REDE
Counsel of law — BARRISTER
Counsel, of old — REDE
Counseled — ADVISED
Counselers for Joan of Arc — VOICES
Counsellor-at-Law in Ireland — ADVOCATE
Count — NUMBER, TOTAL
Count _____: take attendance — NOSES
Count calories — DIET
Count follower — ESS
Count of Jazz — BASIE
Count of music — BASIE
Count on — RELY
Count points — TALLY
Count up — TALLY
Countenance — AIR, FEATURE, LOOK
Counter — CALCULATOR, REBUT
Counter covers — TILES
Counteract — INTERFERE
Counterbalance — OFFSET
Counterclockwise: Abbr. — CCW
Counterfeit — SHAM
Counterfeit, in Paris — FAUX
Counterfeited — FAKED
Countermarch — ABOUT FACE, RECOIL
Counterpart — PARALLEL
Counterpart of Mars — ARES
Counterstroke — RIPOSTE
Countertenor — ALTO
Counterweight — TARE
Countess, for example — NOBLEWOMAN
Counties in Fla. and Ga. — DADES
Counties, in Germany — KREISE
Counting frame — ABACUS
Counting sheep — SLEEPLESS
Counting-out rhyme word — EENE
Countless years — EONS
Countrified character — RURALITY
Countrified name? — ZEKE
Country — LAND, NATION
Country bordering on the Mekong — LAOS
Country byway — LANE
Country club fees — DUES
Country club? — UNITED NATIONS
Country dance — BARN, REEL
Country estate — VILLA
Country home near Moskova — DACHA
Country house — VILLA
Country in NW Africa — ALGERIA
Country in West Africa — TOGO
Country lass — WENCH
Country of Juan Carlos — SPAIN
Country residences — ESTATES
Country road — LANE
Country singer Bandy — MOE
Country singer Johnny — CASH
Country singer McEntire — REBA
Country singer Mel — TILLIS
Country singer Murray — ANNE
Country singer turned Yeti? — HANK SNOWMAN
Country Slaughter — ENOS
Country stopover — INN
Country store? — SILO
Country without women? — STAGNATION
Country, to Caesar — PATRIA
Country-rock group — ALABAMA
Country: Comb. form — ITALO
Country: Lat. — RUS
Countrymen of Goya and Dali — SERT
Counts calories — DIETS
Counts on — DEPENDS
County center — SEAT
County in Ireland — CLARE
County in Kentucky or Texas — OLDHAM
County in Munster — CLARE
County in N cen. England — NOTTS
County in New York — TIOGA
County in NW Ireland — MAYO
County in Western Michigan — OCEANA
County Kerry seaport — TRALEE
County Kerry town — TRALEE
County of N Ireland — ARMAGH
County stopover — INN
County-fair racer — NAG
Coup d' _____ — ETAT
Coup de grace — END
Coup plot — CABAL
Couperin's "Tic-_____-choc" — TOC
Couple — BRACE, DUO, DYAD, MATCH, PAIR
Coupled — PAIRED
Couples — DUOS
Couples' game — GOLF
Couples's org. — PGA
Couples, but not Fred — DYADS
Coupon — CHIT, STUB
Courage — GRIT, HEART, NERVE, VALOR
Courage; spirit — METTLE
Courageous act — DEED
Courier — PORTER
Courier's concern — MAIL
Course — GUIDE
Course for a horse — OVAL
Course for TV's Quincy: Abbr. — ANAT
Course necessity — TEE
Course participant — LEARNER
Course peg — TEE
Courser — STEED
Courses for horses — OVALS
Court — WOO, BENCH
Court action — PLEA, TRIAL
Court attire — ROBE, SNEAKERS
Court business — CASE
Court call — LET
Court champ: 1963 — OSUNA
Court champion — EVERT
Court decision — ARRET
Court decisions — VERDICTS
Court decree — ARRET
Court defense — PRESS
Court divider — NET
Court event — TRIAL
Court feature — LINES
Court fig. — ATTY, REF
Court figure — ASHE, LITIGANT, SUER
Court follower — IER
Court great Arthur — ASHE
Court high shot — LOB
Court hits — LOBS
Court immortal — BORG
Court minutes — ACTA
Court name — ASHE
Court officers: Abbr. — DAS
Court order — WRIT
Court painter for Charles III and IV — GOYA
Court personality — ASHE
Court plea — NOLO
Court proceeding — TRIAL

Court proceedings — ACTA
Court sport — HANDBALL, TENNIS
Court team — NETS
Court units — SETS
Court VIPs — ATTYS
Court vow — I DO
Court wear — SNEAKERS
Court winners — ACES
Court's Jimmy — CONNORS
Court's John — MCENROE
Courted — WOOED
Courted danger — RISKED
Courteous — CIVIL, POLITE
Courtesan — HARLOT, WHORE
Courtesy — FAVOR
Courtfoom figure — FELON
Courtier in "Hamlet" — OSRIC
Courtman — ASHE
Courtroom routines — PLEAS
Courtroom shrewdies — PHILADELPHIA LAWYERS
Courtyards — ATRIA
Cousin of "Belay!" — AVAST
Cousin of a baluga — ORCA
Cousin of a Civet — GENET
Cousin of a hootmaganzy — SMEW
Cousin of a smash — ADE
Cousin of a twp. — VIL
Cousin of a union — GUILD
Cousin of a walk-on — CAMEO
Cousin of acad. — INST
Cousin of an ophidid — EEL
Cousin of bingo — BEANO
Cousin of bonkers — FANTEE
Cousin of Chris — TINA
Cousin of etc. — ET AL
Cousin of Mae — MAY
Cousin of teehee — HAHA
Cousin of the heron — IBIS
Cousin of vague or flot — ONDE
Cousins of hammerheads — HERONS
Cousins of Okies — ARKIES
Cousins of satyrs — SILENI
Cousins, e.g. — KINSMEN, RELATIVES
Cousteau apparatus — SCUBA
Cousteau's fld. — OCEANOG
Cousteau's milieu — SEA
Cousy's team — CELTICS
Couth — REFINED
Couturier — SEAMSTRESS
Couturier's annual surprise — NEW LINE
Couturier's concern — HEM, SEAM
Cove — BAY, INLET, LAGOON, NOOK
Covenant — PACT
Covenant chest — ARK
Covent Garden — MARKET
Cover — AWNING, BLANKET, CANOPY, GUARD, LID
Cover — SHEATH, TOP
Cover a bet — RISK
Cover coat — PAINT
Cover for a con — ALIAS
Cover for a Ninja turtle — SHELL
Cover for the iris — CORNEA
Cover girl — MODEL
Cover girl Carol _____ — ALT
Cover of a sort — LID
Cover story — ALIBI
Cover up for — TAKE THE RAP
Cover up of a sort — MASK
Cover with a hard surface — PAVE
Cover with asphalt — PAVE
Cover with feathers — FLEDGE
Cover with metal again — REPLATE
Cover with soot — BLACKEN
Cover, as with onions — SMOTHER
Covered — CLAD
Covered cart — CARIOLE
Covered containers — URNS
Covered on the inside — LINED
Covered passageways — ARCADES
Covered with asphalt — PAVED
Covered with evergreens — PINEY
Covered with frost — RIMED, RIMY
Covered with green — MOSSY
Covered with hoarfrost — RIMED
Covered with morning moisture — DEWED
Covered with sticky stuff — GOOEY
Covered with terra cotta — TILED
Covering — ROOF
Covering more area — WIDER
Covering of a sort — PEEL
Coverings at marinas — TARPS
Coverlet — BEDSPREAD
Covers — LIDS, SHROUDS
Covers a chimney sweep — SOOT
Covers of a type — LIDS
Covers with coal dust — SOOTS
Covert — LAIR
Covert news release — LEAK
Coverts cousin — LAIR
Coves — INLETS
Covet — ENVY
Coveted (with "for") — HUNGERED
Coveted award — OSCAR
Coveted statuette — OSCAR
Coveting — DESIROUS
Covetous ones — ENVIERS
Covets — DESIRES
Covey — BROOD
Cow — BOVINE
Cow _____ — BELL, BOY
Cow and slow follower — POKES
Cow barn, in Devon — BYRE
Cow sounds — MOOS
Cow that has lost its horns — POLLARD
Cow's milieu — LEA
Cow-headed goddess — ISIS
Coward of note — NOEL
Coward's "To Step _____" — ASIDE
Coward's problem — FEAR
Coward's reaction — PANIC
Coward, et al. — NOELS
Cowardly — YELLOW
Cowardly Lion actor — LAHR
Cowardly ones — CAITIFFS
Cowardly vine — YELLOW JESSAMINE
Cowardly, lyin', fictional fatso — FALSTAFF
Cowboy at times — ROPER
Cowboy competition — RODEO
Cowboy contest — ROPING
Cowboy flick — OATER
Cowboy gear — ROPES
Cowboy Gene — AUTRY
Cowboy or combat wear — BOOTS
Cowboy or disputant — WRANGLER
Cowboy star Tom — MIX
Cowboy wear — CHAPS
Cowboy's blade — BOWIE KNIFE
Cowboy's grub — CHOW
Cowboy's loop — NOOSE
Cowboy's milieu — CORRAL
Cowboy's need — LARIAT
Cowboy's need — ROPE
Cowboy's protective wear — CHAPS
Cowboy's rope — RIATA
Cowboy's sidekick — PARD
Cowboy, Spanish style — VAQUERO
Cowboys and Indians — TEAMS
Cowboys' home — RANCH
Cowcatcher — LASSO, REATA
Cowpoke's milieu — RANGE
Cowpoke's mount — PINTO
Cowpoke's pal — PARD
Cowpoke's poker — SPUR
Cowpuncher's need — LASSO
Cowpuncher's pal — PARD
Cows, the old way — KINE
Cows, to Cowper — KINE
Cowshed — BYRE

Cowslip — MARIGOLD
Coxa — HIP
Coy — ARCH
Coyly decorous — DEMURE
Coyote St. — S DAK
Cozened — DUPED
Cozy — SNUG
Cozy corner — NOOK
Cozy homes — NESTS
Cozy living room areas — FIRE-SIDES
Cozy place — NEST
Cozy retreat — DEN, NOOK
Cozy room — DEN
Cozy treetop home — NEST
Cozy, protected place — COCOON
Cozy: Var. — HOMY
CPA's concern — NOS
CPA's reading matter — LEDGERS
Cpl. or Sgt. — NCO
Cpls.' bosses — SGTS
Crab and grouse — NEEDLE
Crab apple — SCRAB
Crab constellation — CANCER
Crab's claw — NIPPER
Crabbed — SOUR
Crack — CHAP
Cracked — RIMOSE
Cracker — WAFER
Cracker jack — ACE, DANDY
Cracker state — GEORGIA
Crackerjack — WHIZ
Crackers — SALTINES
Crackle — SNAP
Cracklings — SCRAPS
Cradle — ROCKER
Cradle of Texas liberty — ALAMO
Cradle rocker — MAMA
Cradle setting — TREETOP
Cradle tenders — MAMMAS
Cradle's cousin — BASSINET
Craft — ART, SHIP, SKILL
Craft for Hiawatha — CANOE
Craft, in Cadiz — ARTE
Craftier — SLYER
Craftiness — WILINESS
Craftman's collection — TOOLS
Crafts partner — ARTS
Crafts' companion — ARTS
Crafts' mate — ARTS
Crafts, in the barrio — ARTES
Craftsman / river sign? — CAR-PENTER
Craftsmen — ARTISIANS
Crafty — ARCH, SLY, WILY
Crafty plan — SCHEME
Crafty plotting — INTRIGUE
Crafty villains — SCHEMERS
Crag — TOR
Craggy abode — AERIE
Craggy crests — TORS
Craggy hill — TOR
Craggy nest — EYRIE
Cram for an exam — PREP
Cramps a cowboy's style — FENCE IN
Crams — STUFFS
Crandall and Webb — DELS
Crane fly's kin — TSETSE
Crane of fiction — ICHABOD
Crane's cousin — IBIS
Crane's kin — EGRET
Cranial feature — BASION
Cranial membranes — TELAE
Crash — RAM INTO
Crash a party — INTRUDE
Crash diets — FASTS
Crash-helmet wearer — EVEL KNIEVEL
Crass — RUDE
Crater contents — LAVA
Cravat — TIE
Cravat adornments — TIE PINS
Crave — WANT, YEARN
Craved — WANTED
Craving — ITCH, YEN
Cravings — YENS
Craw — MAW
Crawled, Australian style — SWAM
Crawly creature — ASP, SER-PENT
Craze — FAD, MANIA
Crazed — MANIC
Crazy — DAFT, LOCO
Crazy as _____ — A LOON
Crazy Legs Hirsch — ELROY
Crazy talk — MAD CHATTER
Crazy TV columnist? — ANDY LOONEY
Creaky joint — KNEE
Cream — ELITE, LATHER
Cream of the crop — BEST
Cream of the crop — ELITE, FIRST RATE, TOP DRAWER
Cream or dough lead-in — SOUR
Cream puff — ECLAIR
Cream queen Lauder — ESTEE
Creamy cheese — NEUFCHA-TEL
Crease — LINE
Creased — FOLDED
Create — MAKE
Create a cardigan — KNIT
Create joy — ELATE
Created — MADE
Created a rowdydow — RIOTED
Creates with wool — KNITS
Creation named for a Roosevelt — TEDDY BEAR
Creative ability — TALENT
Creative graduate course — SEMINAL SEMINAR
Creator — MAKER
Creator of "Come Back Little Sheba" — INGE
Creator of "Lil Abner" — CAPP
Creator of "Little Eyolf" — IBSEN
Creator of "Shropshire Lad" — A E HOUSMAN
Creator of "Sister Carrie" — THEODORE DREISER
Creator of "Tears" — REESE
Creator of "The Medium" — GIANCARLO MENOTTI
Creator of "Winnie the Pooh" — MILNE
Creator of Ah Sin — HARTE
Creator of Arthur Gordon Pym — POE
Creator of Christopher Robin — MILNE
Creator of Dr. Fu Manchu — ROHMER
Creator of Euphues — LYLY
Creator of Lady Windermere — OSCAR WILDE
Creator of Mrs. Tanqueray — PINERO
Creator of Pooh — MILNE
Creator of some Easter bon-nets? — THE MAD HAT-TER
Creator of the March family — LOUISA MAY ALCOTT
Creator of the Moffats — ESTES
Creator of the New Look — DIOR
Creator or "Shropshire Lad" — A E HOUSMAN
Creature — ANIMAL
Creature in German folklore — NIX
Creature that lives a "sheltered" life — BOX TURTLE
Creature with 14 legs — ISO-POD
Creatures of Greek myth — CENTAURS
Creatures: Fr. — ETRES
Creche figures — MAGI
Credence — TRUST
Credit — ACCLAIM, ASSET, CHARGE, HONOR, TIME
Credit card alternative — CASH
Credo — TENET
Credos — BELIEFS
Creek — RIA
Creel contents — BAIT
Creep — HEEL
Creep like a crab — SIDLE
Creeper — VINE
Creepers — IVIES
Creepy — WEIRD
Creepy plant — IVY
Creil's river — OISE
Crème _____ crème — DE LA
Creme de _____ — CACAO
Crème de la crème — ELITE
Cremerie, for one — SHOP

Cremona creations, for short — STRADS
Cremona family name — AMATI
Cremona instr. — STRAD
Cremona name — AMATI
Cremona product, for short — STRAD
Cremona violin-maker — AMATI
Creole — FRENCH
Creole shellfish dish — LANGOSTINO
Crepe de _____ — CHINE
Crepitate — GRATE
Crescendo — SURGE
Crescent — LUNAR
Crescent-shaped — LUNATE
Crescent-shaped body — MENISCUS
Crescent-shaped item — LUNE
Crest — ACME
Crest of a small hill, in Britain — KNAP
Crested bird — TITMOUSE
Crested duck — SMEW
Crested European birds — HOOPOES
Crested parrot — COCKATOO
Crests — ARETES
Cretan peak — IDA
Cretan-born Spanish painter El _____ — GRECO
Crete's capital — CANEA
Crete's sea — AEGEAN
Crevice — CHINK
Crew — BAND, FORCE, HANDS, MEN, STAFF, TEAM
Crew cut's antithesis — AFRO
Crew member — OAR
Crew member of a locomotive — FIREMAN
Crews — TEAMS
Crib of a sort — BIN
Cribbage markers — PEGS
Cribbage pieces — PEGS
Crick — ACHE
Cricket need — BAT
Cricket position — MIDON
Cricket sides — ONS
Cricket sound — CHIRP
Cricket team — ELEVEN
Cricket term — TICE
Cricket variation — SINGLE WICKET
Cried — SOBBED, WEPT
Cried loudly — BAWLED
Cried out sharply — YIPED
Cries — SOBS
Cries at Greek orgies — EVOES
Cries of delight — AHS
Cries of disgust — FIES
Cries of glee — WHOOPS
Cries of repugnance — UGHS
Cries of surprise — HAHS, OHS, AHS
Cries of triumph — AHAS
Cries out sharply — YIPES
Crime investigator Kefauver — ESTES
Crime punishable by death — FELONY
Crime punishable by imprisonment — FELONY
Crime-solving "insect" — THE GREEN HORNET
Crimean resort — YALTA
Crimean river — ALMA
Criminal charge — IMPEACH
Crimps again — RECURLS
Crimson rambler — ROSE
Crimson Tide — ALABAMA
Crimson Tide fan — ALABAMIAN
Crimson Tide's archrival — AUBURN
Cringe — COWER, GROVEL
Cringed — COWERED
Cringes and flatters — FAWNS ON
Crinkle the brow — FROWN
Crinkled — CREPED
Crinkled fabric — CREPE
Crinky fabric — PLISSE
Crisp — BRISK
Crisp bread — RUSK
Crisp cake — WAFER
Crisp confection — PRALINE
Crisp cookie — SNAP
Crisp cracker — SALTINE
Crispin's product — SHOE
Cristu concoctions — PIES
Criterion — TEST
Criterion: Abbr. — STD
Critic and poet Charles _____ — OLSON
Critic Barnes — CLIVE
Critic Faure and namesakes — ELIES
Critic Reed — REX
Critic Siskel — GENE
Critic's praise — RAVE
Critic's seat — TWO ON THE AISLE
Critic, at times — RAVER
Critic-writer James _____ — AGEE
Critical approval — RAVE
Critical examiner — ANALYZER
Critical remark — STRICTURE
Critical studies — EXAMS
Criticize severely — FLAY, LASH, ROAST
Criticize slyly — SNIPE
Criticized harshly — SCATHED
Criticized sharply — RAPPED
Criticizes — RAPS
Critique — COMMENTARY
Critter for Tex to tame — BRONC
Critter's cry — BAA
Croak — CAW
Croaked — CAWED
Croaky — HOARSE
Croat or Bulgar — SLAV
Croat or Czech — SLAV
Croat, for one — SLAV
Croats and Serbs — SLAVS
Croc's cousin — GATER, GATOR
Croce's "_____ Got a Name" — IVE
Crochet — TAT
Crock or trick ending — ERY
Crocked — TIPSY
Crockett or Jones — DAVY
Crocodile Dundee, for one — AUSSIE
Crocus — IRID
Croissants — ROLLS
Crone — HAG, BELDAME
Crone-like — ANILE
Cronies — PALS
Cronus or Rhea — TITAN
Crony — PAL
Cronyn and Tandy, often — COSTARS
Cronyn's mate — TANDY
Crook — STAFF
Crook in a branch — KNEE
Crook's cover-up — ALIAS
Crooked — AGEE, ALOP, AWRY, BENT, WRY
Crooked letter — ESS
Crooked or ironic — WRY
Crooned — SANG
Crooner Crosby — BING
Crooner Vallee — RUDY
Crop — CRAW, CUT, MAW
Crop duster — PILOT
Cropped up — AROSE
Crops up — ARISES
Crosby — BING
Crosby, et al. — CROONERS
Crosby, Stills and Nash, e.g. — TRIO
Cross — FRETFUL, ROOD
Cross one's mind — OCCUR
Cross out — DELETE, OMIT
Cross paths — MEET
Cross swords — DISAGREE
Cross the plate — SCORE
Cross words — SPAT
Crossbeam — TRAVE
Crossbill's genus — LOXIA
Crossbreeds — MONGRELS
Crossed out — XED
Crosses — ROODS
Crosses out — EXES
Crossing on a letter — SERIF
Crossing the plate — SCORING
Crosspatch — CRAB
Crosswd. clue — DEF
Crosswise of a ship — ABEAM
Crossword clues: Abbr. — DEFS
Crossword diagram — GRID

Crossworder's Latin verb — AMAT
Crotchety — CROSS
Crotophaga member — ANI
Croupier, e.g. — RAKER
Crow — BOAST, BRAG, GLOAT
Crow cries — CAWS
Crow's comment — CAW
Crow's cry — CAW
Crow's cry — CAW
Crow's home — TEPEE
Crow's nest site — MAST
Crow, e.g. — TRIBE
Crowbar — LEVER
Crowd — HERD
Crowd — HERD, MOB
Crowd number — THREE
Crowd number — THREE
Crowd or squeeze — SCROUGE
Crowd shouts — RAHS
Crowd-scene actor — EXTRA
Crowded — DENSE
Crowded — DENSE
Crowds — MOBS
Crowds — MOBS
Crown — CORONET
Crown of a hill — KNOLL
Crown of laurel — HONOR
Crown protector — ENAMEL
Crowned head — EMPEROR
Crowning glory — HAIR
Crowns of furnaces — DOMES
Crows' cousins — DAWS
CRT unit — PIXEL
Crucial point, with "The" — BOTTOM LINE
Crucible — TRIAL
Crucifix — ROOD
Crucifix inscription — INRI
Crucifix letters — INRI
Crude — COARSE, RUSTIC
Crude abode — HUT
Crude metals — ORES
Crude person — BOOR
Crude shelters — HUTS
Crude vessels? — OILERS
Cruel — BRUTAL, MEAN, PITILESS
Cruel creditors — SHYLOCKS
Cruel one — SADIST
Cruel people — ABUSERS
Cruel person — ABUSER, BEAST, SADIST
Cruise — SAIL, TOM
Cruise hand — STEWARD
Cruise port, for short — RIO
Cruise ship — LINER
Cruise ship employee — STEW-ARD
Cruise ship pastime — SKEET
Cruises for Soupy? — SALES SAILS
Cruising — ASEA
Crumb toter — ANT
Crumble — BREAK UP
Crumble into bits — MOLDER
Crumbly soil — MARL
Crumbs: Sp. — MIGAS
Crummy — LOUSY
Crumple — CREASE
Crusader's foe — SARACEN
Crusader's weapon — POLEAX
Crush — MASH
Crusoe's creator — DEFOE
Crusoe, for one — CASTAWAY
Crust of bread — RIND
Crustacean — CRAB
Crustaceans' projections — EGG SACS
Crusting over — CAKING
Crux — MEAT
Cruxes — CORES
Cry — WEEP
Cry from Richard III — A HORSE
Cry from the bridge — AVAST
Cry from the captain — AVAST
Cry like a banshee — WAIL
Cry of amused surprise — OHO
Cry of contempt — POH
Cry of despair — AIE
Cry of discovery — HAH
Cry of disgust — BAH
Cry of lament — ALAS
Cry of pleasure — OOH
Cry of relief — PHEW
Cry of surprise — AHA, OHO
Cry of triumph — AHA, HAH
Cry of woe — ALAS
Cry on a roller coaster — WHEE
Cry out — HOWL
Cry over — MOURN
Cry's partner — HUE
Cryptic — ENCODED
Cryptogram — CODE
Crystal clear — DISTINCT
Crystal-ball gazer — SEER
Crystal-lined stone — GEODE
Crystalline medicine — ALOIN
Crystalline mineral — FELDSPAR, SPAR
CSA fighter — REB
CSA general — REL, R E LEE
CSA soldier — REB
Cub group — DEN
Cub or Eagle — SCOUT
Cub Scout groups — DENS
Cub Scout pack leader — AKELA
Cub Scout units — DENS
Cub unit — PACK
Cub's output — REPORTAGE
Cuba or Bali: Abbr. — ISL
Cuba, e.g. — ISLE
Cuba, for one — ISLA
Cuban bay — PIGS
Cuban blade — MACHETE
Cuban castle — MORRO
Cuban coins — PESOS
Cuban dances — CONGAS
Cuban export — CIGARS
Cuban exports — PANATEL-LAS
Cuban pennies — CENTAVOS
Cuban revolutionary — MARTI
Cubbyhole — BIN, NOOK
Cube and sphere — SOLIDS
Cube inventor Rubik — ERNO
Cube root of 27 — THREE
Cube root of eight — TWO
Cube, as carrots — DICE
Cube, for coffee — SUGAR
Cubes and pyramids — SOLIDS
Cubes up — DICES
Cubic — SOLID
Cubic meter — STERE
Cubicle — CELL
Cubist designer? — RUBIK
Cubist Max _____ — WEBER
Cubits — ELLS
Cubs or Mets — NINE
Cuchulain's wife — EMER
Cuckoo — ANI, LOCO
Cuckoo pint — ARUM
Cuckoo's announcement — HOUR
Cuckoopint, e.g. — AROID
Cuckoopints — ARUMS
Cucumbers — PEPOS
Cud — RUMEN
Cudgel — BATON, STAVE
Cue — SIGNAL
Cue on a musical score — PRESA
Cuisine master — CHEF
Culbertson, et al. — ELYS
Culinary ads — SANDWICH BOARDS
Culinary appliance — BLENDER
Culinary Julia — CHILD
Culinary preparation — DISH
Cull — WEED
Culled out — SELECTED
Culminating point — APEX, HIGH TIDE
Culmination — APEX, APOGEE
Culp-Cosby series — I SPY
Culpabilities — GUILTS
Culpability — GUILT
Culprit, in Roman law — RIAE
Cult — ISM, SORT
Cult member — IST
Cultivable — ARABLE
Cultivate — RAISE, TILL
Cultivate again — REWEED
Cultivate the land — FARM
Cultivated — GREW
Cultivates — TENDS
Cultivation of land — TILLAGE
Cultural characteristics — ETHOS
Cultural city of India — POONA
Cultural degree — LHD

Cultural entertainment — OPERA
Culture — ART, MUSIC
Culture lead-in — AGRI
Culture medium — AGAR
Culture of ancient Crete — MINOAN
Cultured-milk product — YOGURT
Cumberland — GAP
Cumberland river — TEES
Cumberland, e.g. — GAP
Cumin, e.g. — SPICE
Cumulus — HEAP
Cunctatious — LATE
Cunegonde's creator — VOLTAIRE
Cunning — ARCH, FOXY, WILY
Cunning trick — DODGE
Cuomo or Lanza — MARIO
Cuomo's title, briefly — GOV
Cup-holder of the Orient — ZARF
Cup — CHALICE, GOBLET, MUG
Cup for cafe — TASSE
Cup one's ear — LISTEN
Cup or pay finish — OLA
Cup to International Lawn Tennis Champion — DAVIS
Cup, in Caen — TASSE
Cup, in Cannes — TASSE
Cup, in Paris — TASSE
Cup-shaped — HOLLOW
Cupbearer of the gods — HEBE
Cupid — AMOR, DAN, EROS
Cupid — SAM COOKE SONG
Cupid on canvas — AMOR
Cupid's bow items — LIPS
Cupid's collections — OBJECTS D HEART
Cupid's counterpart — EROS
Cupid's Greek counterpart — EROS
Cupid's mother — VENUS
Cupid's weapon — DART
Cupid, in Art — AMOR
Cupidinous — AVID
Cupidity — GREED
Cupids — AMORINI
Cupola — DOME
Cuprite and limonite — ORES
Cur — MUTT
Cur. unit — DOL
Curator — CARETAKER
Curator's deg. — BFA
Curb — BRIDLE
Curd — CLOT
Curdle — TURN
Curdled masses — COAGULA
Curdles — CONGEALS
Cure-all — PANACEA
Cure — AGE, TAN
Cure lead-in — EPI
Cure or center — EPI
Cure, as leather — TAN
Curfew — LIMIT
Curia garment — TOGA
Curie's discovery — RADIUM
Curios — VIRTU
Curiosity victim — CAT
Curious — NOSY
Curl — RINGLET
Curl the lip — SNEER
Curled as a Torah — SCROLLED
Curlicue, in writing — TAG
Curlicues — COILS
Curling one's lip — SNEERING
Curling or hurling — SPORT
Curls — SPIRALS
Curls the lip — SNEERS
Curly coiffure — AFRO
Curly variety of lettuce — COS
Curly's friend — MOE
Curmudgeon's word — BAH
Currant — GOOSEBERRY
Currants, e.g. — ACINI
Currency agcy. of the UN — IMF
Currency in Como — LIRA
Currency units on Capri — LIRE
Current — FLOW, NEW, TIDE, VOGUE
Current abbr. — AMPS, ELEC
Current alternatives — ACDC
Current and blessed — EVENTS
Current event coverage — NEWS
Current event film — NEWS-REEL
Current fashion — MODE
Current measuring device — AMMETER
Current unit — AMPERE
Current version: Comb. form — NEO
Current: Comb. form — RHEO
Current: Prefix — RHEO
Currently topical — NEWSY
Currents caused by cars — AIRFLOWS
Curriculum item — ARTS
Currier's partner — IVES
Curse — BANE, OATH
Cursed — REVILED
Curses — DAMNS, IMPRE-CATES
Curt — TERSE
Curtail — CLIP, DRAPE, ELIDE, LIMIT
Curtain band — TIEBACK
Curtain closers — BOWS
Curtain color — ECRU
Curtain fabric — NINON, SCRIM
Curtain feature — TIEBACK
Curtain fixture — ROD
Curtain holder — ROD
Curtain material — LENO, MADRAS, NINON
Curtain material — ORGANDY
Curtain pull tufts — TASSELS
Curtain raiser — PRELIMINARY
Curtain requests — ENCORES
Curtain staff — VOILE
Curtain supports — RODS
Curule-chair occupants — EDILES
Curvaceous letter — ESS
Curve — ARC, ESS
Curve around — CIRCLE
Curve in a ship's plank — SNY
Curve into an arch — EMBOW
Curve of a ship's plank — SNY
Curve the lip — SNEER
Curve type — ESS
Curved — BENT
Curved arch — OGEE, OGIVE
Curved inward — INVOLUTE
Curved letter — ESS
Curved line — ARC
Curved moldings — OGEES
Curved outward — CONVEX
Curved surface of a vault — GROIN
Curved swords — SABERS
Curves — ESSES
Curving inward as a beak — ADUNC
Curving out — CONVEX
Curvy letter — ESS
Cushion — PAD
Cushions — PILLOWS
Cushy — EASY
Cuss — CURSE
Cussed — SWORE
Cusswords — OATHS
Custard dessert — FLAN
Custard pie — FLAN
Custard-apple tree — PAPAW
Custardy desserts — FLANS
Custer's finale — STAND
Custer's last major — RENO
Custer's righthand man — RENO
Custodian — KEEPER
Custom — NORM, WONT, USAGE
Customary — USUAL
Customary charge — FEE
Customary itinerary — ROUTINE ROUTING
Customer — CLIENT
Customs — MORES, USAGES
Cut-rate vaccinations? — CHEAP SHOTS
Cut-up — CARD
Cut — AXE, CARVE, DICE, GASH, HEW, NOTCH
Cut — SAW, SEVER, SHEAR, SLASH

Cut — SLICE, SLIT, SNIP
Cut _____ (make no difference) — NO ICE
Cut _____ (transact) — A DEAL
Cut a groove — DADO
Cut a turkey — CARVE
Cut across — SLICE
Cut and dried — FIXED, RIGID
Cut another cassette — RETAPED
Cut away — LOP, PARED
Cut back — PARED, TRIM
Cut back underbrush again — RECLEARED
Cut down — HEWN
Cut down on — DECREASE
Cut from a film — EDIT
Cut in — INTERRUPT
Cut in squares — DICE
Cut in two — BISECT, HALVE
Cut into cubes — DICE
Cut into three — TRISECT
Cut molars — TEETHE
Cut of beef — SHANK
Cut of meat — LOIN, RUMP, SIDE, STEAK
Cut off — CLIP, LOP, SEVER, SNIP
Cut off the rind — PARE
Cut one's eyeteeth — MATURE
Cut or slant — BEVEL
Cut out — EXCISE
Cut short — ABORT, BOBTAIL, CROP, NIP, TRIM
Cut short, as a lamb — SHORN
Cut short, at NASA — ABORT
Cut the grass — MOW
Cut the hair — BARBER
Cut the turkey — CARVE
Cut with a toothed blade — SAWN
Cut with cleats — SPIKE
Cut with scissors — SNIP
Cut wood — SAWED
Cut's partner — DRIED
Cut, as prices — SLASH
Cut-price — CHEAP
Cut: Scot. — SNEG
Cutaway — COAT
Cutback weapon? — AXE
Cute creatures from down under — KOALAS
Cutesy — COY
Cuticle — DERM, SKIN
Cutie Knievel guided — DISHEVELLED
Cutlet meat — VEAL
Cuts — AXES, SEVERS, SNIPS
Cuts back — PARES
Cuts down — FELLS, REDUCES
Cuts for agts. — PCTS
Cuts into cubes — DICES
Cuts longitudinally — TRANSECTS
Cuts of beef — BARONS
Cuts of meat — CHOPS
Cuts off — AXES, LOPS
Cuts short — CROPS
Cuts up — SHREDS
Cuts wood — SAWS
Cutter — SLED
Cutter or pung — SLED
Cutting — CAUSTIC
Cutting along a line — SLITTING
Cutting device — DIE
Cutting edge — BEZEL
Cutting remark — BARB
Cutting tool — ADZE, DIE, SHEAR
Cuttings — SECTIONS
Cuttlefish — SQUID, OCTOPUS
Cuzco cookpot — OLLA
Cuzco country — PERU
Cuzco native — INCA
Cuzco was their capital — INCAS
Cyberneticist's hot dog — NORBERTS WEINER
Cycle — PEDAL
Cycle front — TRI
Cyclist — PEDALER
Cyclist LeMond — GREG
Cyclones play here — AMES
Cyclops feature — ONE EYE
Cygnet's mother — SWAN
Cygnet's parent — COB
Cygnet's sire — COB
Cygnets when mature — SWANS
Cygnus twinkler — DENEB
Cylinder — PISTON, ROLL
Cylindrical — TERETE, TUBULAR
Cylindrical and tapered — TERETE
Cylindrical seat — TABORET
Cyma — OGEE
Cyma _____ (molding) — RECTA
Cyma reversa — OGEE
Cymbal noise — CLASH
Cymbals worked with a foot pedal — HIGHHAT
Cymric — WELSH
Cynic — SNEERER
Cynic's look — SNEER
Cynical — SNEERY
Cypher — CODE
Cypress _____, swamp wood in room decor — KNEES
Cypress family shrubs — THUJAS
Cypress feature — KNEE
Cypress or larch — TREE
Cyprinoid fish — DACE
Cyprus port — LIMASSOL
Cyrano's creator — ROSTAND
Cyrano's problem — NOSE
Cyrus or Philo — VANCE
Cyst — BLISTER, WEN
Cytologist's interest — CELL
Cytoplasm substance, for short — RNA
Czar called "the Great" — PETER I
Czar's edict — UKASE
Czar's name: Abbr. — NICH
Czars' jeweler — FABERGE
Czech capital, to Czechs — PRAHA
Czech coin — HALER
Czech industrialist — SKODA
Czech or Bulgar — SLAV
Czech politician-playwright — HAVEL
Czech region — MORAVIA
Czech religious reformer — HUS
Czech river to the Elbe — EGER
Czech statesman — BENES
Czech-German river — ELBE
Czech. neighbor — AUS, POL
Czechoslovakian river — ITER

D

D-day beach — OMAHA
D-day craft — LST
D'Anjou, for one — PEAR
D'Artagnan's friend — ATHOS
D'Artagnan's sidekick — ARAMIS
D'Urberville girl — TESS
D, soundwise — ACTRESS RUBY
D-day craft — LST
D-H connection — EFG

D. Arnaz's costar — L BALL
D.A.'s helper — ASST
D.A.'s need — EVIDENCE
D.A.'s obstacle — FERRUM CLAD ALIBI
D.A.'s staff — ASSTS
D.C. agcy. — FDA
D.C. body — CONG
D.C. denizen — SEN
D.C. ecology group — EPA
D.C. group protecting minorities — CRC
D.C. House — BLAIR
D.C. mortgage insurer — FHA
D.C. movers and shakers — SENS
D.C. orchestra — NSO
D.C. regulatory body — FAA
D.C. VIP — SEN
D.C.-based org. — DAR
D.D.E. — IKE
D.D.E.'s W.W II post — ETO
D.O.D. div. — USAR
D.S. Freeman subject — R E LEE
D.W. Griffith product — EPIC
DA's aide — ASST
Dabbed — PATTED
Dabbling ducks — TEALS
Dabchicks or didapers — GREEBS
Dabs — PATS
Dacha, e.g. — VILLA
Dad — PAPA
Dad's bro — UNC
Dad's Dad — GRAMP
Dad's daughter — SIS
Dad's second wife — STEPMOTHER
Dad, in Damascus — ABOU
Dad, in London — PATER
Dada artist — ARP
Dadaism and Cubism — GENRES
Dadaist Hans — ARP
Dadas — PAPAS
Daddy-o — PAW
Daddy — POPS
Daddy-long-legs — SPIDER
Dads — PAPAS
Daedalian — CLEVER
Daffy — LOCO
Daft — LOONEY, MAD
Dag Hammarskjold's successor — U THANT
Dagger — SKEEN, SNEE, STILETTO
Dagger handle — HAFT
Dagger of yore — SKEEN, SNEE
Dagger's confrere — CLOAK
Dagger's partner — CLOAK
Dahl from Minnesota — ARLENE
Dahl or Francis — ARLENE
Dahlia's kin — ASTERS
Dahomey — BENIN
Daily — DIURNAL
Daily beginnings — DAWNS
Daily bread — SUPPORT
Daily doings, for short — SKEDS
Daily dozen — PUSHUPS
Daily fare — DIET
Daily grind — RATRACE, ROUTINE
Daily in recurrence — DIURNAL
Daily newspapers — EDITIONS
Daily TV fare — SOAPS
Daimler invention — ENGINE
Daimler or Rolls — AUTO
Daimler's partner — BENZ
Dainty — PETITE
Dainty drinks — SIPS
Daiquiri base — RUM
Daiquiri ingredient — RUM
Dairy — FARM
Dairy bar items — CONES
Dairy sound — MOO
Dairyman's anathema — OLEO
Dairyman's garden items? — SWISS CHEESE PLANTS
Dais — BENCH, PULPIT, SEAT
Dais V.I.P. — EMCEE
Daisy — ASTER
Daisy _____ Scraggs — MAE
Daisy feature — PETAL
Daisy Mae's son — ABE
Daisy type — OXEYE, SHASTA
Daisylike flower — ASTER
Dakar is its capital — SENEGAL
Dakar's location — SENEGAL
Dakota Indians — REES
Dalai _____ — LAMA
Dalai Lama's city — LHASA
Dale or Linda — EVANS
Dale or Maurice — EVANS
Dali work, e.g. — OBRA
Dali's "Nostalgic _____" — ECHO
Dallas "Southfork", e.g. — RANCH
Dallas airport — LOVE
Dallas campus: Abbr. — SMU
Dallas-Chicago vector — NNE
Dallas-to-San Antonio dir. — SSW
Dallas-to-Tulsa dir. — NNE
Dallied — TOYED
Dallies — FLIRTS
Dally — LINGER
Dalmatia — SERBIA
Dalmatian — COACH DOG
Dalmatians are spotted in these — FIRE HOUSES
Daly of TV — TYNE
Daly who plays Lacey — TYNE
Daly's co-star — GLESS
Dam — WALL, WEIR
Dam device — GATE
Dam for diverting water — WEIR
Dam in a rill — WEIR
Dam of Arizona — HOOVER
Dam on the Missouri — OAHE
Dam on the Nile — ASWAN
Dam org. — RVA, TVA
Dam wall across a waterway — BARRAGE
Dam's mate — SIRE
Dama's drawing room — SALA
Damage — HARM, INJURE, MAR, SPOIL
Damage beyond repair — RUIN
Damage through neglect — BLIGHT
Damaged-goods rendition — FIRE SALE
Damages — INJURES, MARS
Damages awarded in excess of actual loss — EXEMPLARY
Daman — CONY
Damascene's land — SYRIA
Damascus native — SYRIAN
Damascus' country — SYRIA
Damask — CLOTH, LINEN
Dame Edith _____, English poet — SITWELL
Dame Ellen and family — TERRYS
Dame Myra _____ — HESS
Dame on the Seine — NOTRE
Dame's opposite — SIR
Damine — DEER
Dammam denizens — SAUDIS
Damnation curse — ANATHEMA
Damned — CURST
Damon and Pythias — FRIENDS
Damp — CLAMMY, MOIST, SOGGY, WET
Dampens — BEDEWS
Damper — MOISTER
Dams — STOPS
Damsel — GIRL, MAIDEN
Damsel's lament — ALAS
Dana and Greeley — EDITORS
Dana of films — LEORA
Dana tames Broadway — THE LION IN WYNTER
Dance — HOP, PROM
Dance and music — ARTS
Dance band — COMBO
Dance critic Arlene — CROCE
Dance exhibition — TAP
Dance for a flapper — BUNNY HOP
Dance for a jitterbug — SHAG
Dance for a nude — BUBBLE
Dance for Gene Kelly — TAP
Dance for Hines — TAP
Dance for Miranda — SAMBA
Dance for seniors — PROM
Dance for the piper — HIGHLAND FLING
Dance from France — GAVOTTE
Dance hall — BALLROOM

Dance in a single file — CONGA
Dance in Lahaina — HULA
Dance lightly — TRIP
Dance movements — STEPS
Dance named after famed flyer — LINDY HOP
Dance of the 20's — CHARLESTON
Dance of the early 1900's — TURKEY TROT
Dance of the late '30's — SUSY Q
Dance or song — FOLK
Dance or state capital — CHARLESTON
Dance org. headed by Margot Fonteyn — RAD
Dance shoes — PUMPS
Dance step — PAS
Dance with joy — KICK UP YOUR HEELS
Dance, e.g. — ART
Dance, in the Southwest — BAILLE
Dance-drama of Japan — NOH
Dance: Comb. form — CHOREO
Dancer — TARANTIST
Dancer Bambi — LINN
Dancer Charisse — CYD
Dancer Coles — HONI
Dancer Dolin — ANTON
Dancer Driver — SEMTA
Dancer Duncan — ISADORA
Dancer Eddie _____ Jr. — FOY
Dancer George de la _____ — PENA
Dancer Jeanmaire — RENEE
Dancer Jose — LIMON
Dancer Kelly, et al. — GENES
Dancer McKenzie — KEVIN
Dancer Miller and namesakes — ANNS
Dancer of a sort — CHORUS GIRL
Dancer Tamblyn — RUSS
Dancer Ted, et al. — SHAWNS
Dancer Verdon — GWEN
Dancer's concern — SLIPPERS
Dancer's costumer — PAULS DRAPER
Dancer's garb — TIGHTS
Dancer's garment — LEOTARD
Dancers of first rank — PRIMA BALLERINAS
Dancing Castle — IRENE
Dandelion drink — WINE
Dandelions — WEEDS
Dander — IRE
Dandies — FOPS, PEACOCKS
Dandle — CARESS
Dandy — FOP
Dandy's partner — FINE
Dandyism — FOPPERY
Dane's monetary unit — KRONE
Danger — MENACE, PERIL
Dangerous curves — ESSES
Dangerous game — RUSSIAN ROULETTE
Dangerous Hawaiian shark — MANOS
Dangerous heading — COLLISION COURSE
Dangerous kind of wave — TIDAL
Dangerous place for a tympanist? — BERMUDA TRIANGLE
Dangerous shark — MAKO
Dangled — HUNG
Dangles a fish hook — DAPS
Daniel arap Moi's land — KENYA
Daniel or Pat — BOONE
Danielle Steele's "Message From _____" — NAM
Danielle's dream — REVE
Danish actress Nielsen — ASTA
Danish atomic physicist — BOHR
Danish author — ANDERSEN
Danish coin — ORE
Danish dwarf — TROLL
Danish first name — SVEN
Danish gnome — TROLL
Danish Island — FYN
Danish Islands — FAROE
Danish king of England — CANUTE
Danish king of England: 1017-35 — CNUT
Danish king of England: Var. — CNUT
Danish measure — ALEN
Danish money — ORE
Danish Possession — ICELAND
Danish seaport — ODENSE
Danish toast — SKOAL
Danish weights — ESER
Danish, perhaps — CAKES
Danish-American journalist-reformer — RIIS
Danish-born American writer: 1849-1914 — RIIS
Danny DeVito role — LOUIE
Danny Kaye role — MITTY
Danny's daughter — MARLO
Danson and Knight — TEDS
Danson and Koppel — TEDS
Danson and Williams — TEDS
Danson role in "Cheers" — SAM
Dante work — INFERNO
Dante's beloved — BEATRICE
Dante's homeland: Abbr. — ITAL
Dante's trade — POET
Danube city — ULM
Danube delta — BLACK SEA
Danube feeder — ENNS, ILLER
Danube gorge — IRON GATES
Danube tributary — ISAR, SIRET
Danzig — GDANSK
Daphne turned into this tree — LAUREL
Daphnis' love — CHLOE
Dapper — NATTY, TRIM
Dapper Dan's footwear — SPATS
Dapper David of films — NIVEN
Dapper one — DAN
Dapple-gray, e.g. — PONY
Darbies — MANACLES
Dardan — TROJAN
Dare — VENTURE
Daredevil Knievel — EVEL
Daredevil Robbie's daredevil Dad — EVEL
Daredevil's delight — RISK
Daredevil's trait — FEARLESSNESS
Dares to, in ye olde days — DAST
Daring — BOLD, RASH
Daring person — RISKER
Darius's subjects — PERSIANS
Darius, to his spouse? — PERSIAN LAMB
Dark — MURKY, UNLIT
Dark ale — STOUT
Dark and obscure — MURKY
Dark beer — BOCK
Dark blue fruit — DAMSON
Dark bodied terns — NODDIES
Dark continent — AFRICA
Dark grayish blue — PERSE
Dark horse — SLEEPER
Dark look: Var. — LOUR
Dark Martian spot — OASIS
Dark of night — GLOOM
Dark olive brown — SEPIA
Dark purple — PUCE
Dark red — RUBY
Dark reddish-brown — SEPIA
Dark time: Abbr. — NGT
Dark, brownish gray — TAUPE
Dark, in poesy — EBON
Dark-eyed beauty — HOURI
Dark-haired man — BRUNET
Dark-red pigment — LAKE
Dark: comb. form — MELANO, NYCTO
Darken — BEDIM
Darkens — DIMS
Darkness — GLOOM
Darkroom activity — DEVELOPING
Darling dog — NANA
Darling of baseball — RON
Darling of the Mets et al. — RONS
Darling or Ely — RON
Darling or Hiller — WENDY

Darlings — PETS
Darlings team — METS
Darlings' dog — NANA
Darn good worker? — SEWER
Darn it! — DRAT
Darn kin — HECK
Darn! — RATS
Darn's relative — DRAT
Darnel — TARE
Darners' target — HOLES
Dart — ARROW, FLIT, SCOOT
Dart off — SCOOT
Dart throwing line — OCHE
Darth — VADER
Darwin's ship — BEAGLE
Darwin's theory — EVOLUTION
Dash — ELAN, SCOOT, SCURRY, STREAK
Dash designators — DAHS
Dash man — SPRINTER
Dash off — SCOOT
Dash preceder — SLAP
Dash unit — METER
Dash water about — SPLATTER
Dashboard calcs. — RPMS
Dashboard info — MPH
Dashboard instrument — ODOMETER
Dashboard reading's: Abbr. — RPMS
Dashed — TORE
Dasher — PART OF A CHURCH
Dashes' companion — DOTS
Dashiell's contemporary — ERLE
Dashing display — BRAVURA
Dashing fellow — BLADE
Dasht-i- _____ (Iranian desert) — LUT
Dastard — CAD
Data — FACTS
Data digester — ANALYST
Data entry — INPUT
Data fed to a computer — INPUT
Data gatherers for short — STATISTS
Data repository — FILE
Data transmission device — TELEMETER
Data, briefly — INFO
Date — TRYST
Date line on coin — EXERGUE
Date preceder — ANTE
Date, for one — PALM
Date-setting phrase — AS OF
Dated — PASSE
Dated student org. — SDS
Dates frequently -SEES
Dating from — AS OF, SINCE
Dating from birth — NATAL
Dative or ablative — CASE
Datum — FACT
Dau, e.g. — REL
Daub — SMEAR
Daube — LARD
Daughter of Atlas — PLEIAD
Daughter of Cadmus — INO, SEMELE
Daughter of Clytemnestra and Agamemnon — ELECTRA
Daughter of David — TAMAR
Daughter of Elon the Hittite — ADAH
Daughter of Juan Carlos — ENENA
Daughter of Loki — HEL
Daughter of Minos, et al. — ARIADNES
Daughter of Mnemosyne — ERATO
Daughter of Theodore Roosevelt — ALICE
Daughters — GIRLS
Daughters of Zeus and Themis — HORAE
Daunt — AWE, COW, FAZE
Dauntless — BOLD, BRAVE
Dauphin's dad — ROI
Davenport — SOFA
Davenport's locale — IOWA
Davenport's place — IOWA
David and others — CAMPS
David Copperfield's first wife — DORA
David Copperfield's forte — MAGIC
David Hare play — PLENTY
David Lean's milieu — CINEMA
David of films and kin — NIVENS
David or James — BOWIE
David Rabe play — STREAMERS
David's weapon — SLING
David, for one — CAMP
David, the film director — LEAN
DaVinci painting — MONA LISA
Davis and Midler — BETTES
Davis Cup divisions — SETS
Davis Cup Winner Arthur — ASHE
Davis from Ga. — OSSIE
Davis in "The Hill" — OSSIE
Davis of "Dark Victory" — BETTE
Davis or Midler — BETTE
Davis's "Yes _____" — I CAN
Davis's gold at its best — LOVE IN BLOOM
Davits — CRANES
Davy or hurricane — LAMP
Dawber or Shriver — PAM
Dawdle — LAG, WASTE TIME
Dawdle in the park — LOITER
Dawdled — IDLED
Dawn — EOS, SUNUP, SUNRISE
Dawn goddess — AURORA, EOS
Dawn to dusk — ALL DAY
Dawns, poetically — MORNS
Dawson of football fame — LEN
Dawson or Deighton — LEN
Dawson's river — YUKON
Day _____ — LILY
Day after Day — OFTEN
Day bed — SOFA
Day before — EVE
Day by day — DAILY
Day dream — FANCY
Day for the blues — MONDAY
Day in Quito — DIA
Day in September — LABOR
Day nursery — CRECHE
Day of musicals — DORIS
Day of note — DORIS
Day of rest — SABBATH
Day of the wk — TUES, WED
Day or Duke — DORIS
Day or Holiday — SINGER
Day or night lead-in — MID
Day star — SUN
Day time — NOON
Day to honor M.L. King — JANUARY FIFTEENTH
Day to save for — RAINY
Day, Duke and Hart — DORISES
Day, in Durango — DIA
Day, in Madrid — DIA
Day-Cagney movie — LOVE ME OR LEAVE ME
Day-dreamed — MOONED
Dayan — MOSHE
Dayan's land: Abbr. — ISR
Daybooks: Abbr. — JLS
Daybreak — DAWN, PRIME
Daydream — REVERIE, STARGAZE
Daydreaming — REVERIE
Daylight-saving time — SUMMER
Days march — ETAPE
Days of _____ — YORE
Days of yore, to Burns — LANG SYNE
Days' start — DAWN
Daytime tube fare — SOAP OPERAS
Daze — STUN
Dazzle — DAZE, ECLAT
Dazzler — ONER
Dazzles a disciple — AWES
Dazzling display — ECLAT
DC agent — G MAN
DC eleven — WA REDSKINS
DC personage — REP, SEN
DC times — DSTS
DC VIPs — SENS
DC-based org. — DAR
DCCLII x II — MDIV
DCL doubled — MCCC

DDE — IKE
DDE was one — GEN
DDE's command — ETO
DDE's domain — ETO
DDE's lady — MAMIE
DDE's opponent — AES
DDT targets — PESTS
De _____ ("Green Pastures" role) — LAWD
De _____ (anew) — NOVO
De _____ (sumptuous) — LUXE
De _____ (too much) — TROP
De _____ of Shamrock land — VALERA
De bon _____ (genuine): Fr. — ALOI
De facto — ACTUAL
De jure — BY RIGHT
De la Mare poem — NOD
De Larrocha and Markova — ALICIAS
De Laurentiis — DINO
De Mille epic, with "The": 1927 — KING OF KINGS
De Mille of dance — AGNES
De Mille specialties — EPICS
De Mille's Delilah — HEDY
De natura _____ (of the nature of things) — RERUM
De Palma's field — CINEMA
De Valera of Ireland — EAMON
De Valera's land — EIRE
De-creased? — IRONED
DEA agent — NARC
Deacon — LAYMAN
Dead duck — GONER
Dead ember — ASH
Dead end — CUL DE SAC
Dead end for some — RAT TRAP
Dead heat — DRAE, TIE
Dead Sea product — POTASH
Dead to the world — ASLEEP
Dead weight — BALLAST
Dead, in Glasgow — DREE
Deaden — DAMP
Deadeye and Rackstraw — TARS
Deadhead — EMPTY
Deadlocked — HUNG, TIED
Deadly — FATAL, LETHAL
Deadly fly — TSETSE
Deadly snakes — ASPS
Deafening — AROAR, LOUD
Deal in money — LEND
Deal or deed prefix — MIS
Deal out — DISBURSE
Deal-consummating word — SOLD
Dealer's car, for short — DEMO
Dealer's demand — ANTE
Dealers in Au — GOLDSMITHS
Deals straight — LAYS IT ON THE LINE
Deals straight — TELLS IT LIKE IT IS
Dealt — TRADED
Dealt in stocks — BROKERED
Dealt with problems — COPED
Dealt with successfully — COPED
Dean and Downey — MORTONS
Dean of baseball — DIZZY
Deans — DOYENS
Dear — CLOSE, COSTLY, EXPENSIVE, PET, PRECIOUS
Dear — PRIZED, RICH
Dear followers, sometimes — SIRS
Dear John, for one — LETTER
Dear ones — PETS
Dear Sir — SALUTATION
Dear, in Italy — CARO
Dear, in Paris — CHERIE
Dear, in Venice — CARA
Dear, on the Via Condotti — CARA
Dear, to Francoise — CHERE
Dear: Fr. — CHERE
Dearie — HON
Dearth — PENURY
Death blow — COUP DE GRACE
Death Valley adjective — DRIEST
Death-defying — BOLD
Debase oneself — GROVEL
Debate — ARGUE, CONTEST, DISCUSS, MATCH, PARLEY
Debate-limiting method — CLOTURE
Debates — MOOTS
Debauch — CORRUPT, RUIN
Debauchee — RAKE, ROUE
Debby or Daniel — BOONE
Debilitate — SAP
Debilitated — ENERVATED
Debit — ARREARS, DETRIMENT, LIABILITY, OBLIGATION
Debits — LOSSES
Debonair — JAUNTY, NATTY, SUAVE
Deborah Kerr movie of 1946 — BLACK NARCISSUS
Deborah, Walter or Jean — KERR
Debris — RUBBLE
Debt — ARREAR
Debtor's role — IOU
Debunk — EXPOSE
Debussed — ALIT
Debussy heroine — LIA
Debussy opus — LA MER
Debussy work — IBERIA
Debussy's "_____ of a Faun" — AFTERNOON
Debussy's "La _____" — MER
Debussy's "Prodigal Son" heroine — LIA
Debussy's sea — MER
Dec. 24 and 31 — EVES
Dec. holiday — XMAS
Dec. visitor — KRINGLE
Decade — TEN
Decadent — EFFETE
Decaf — COFFEE
Decalogue adverb — NOT
Decalogue figure — TEN
Decamped — FLED
Decamps — ELOPES
Decant — POUR
Decanters — CARAFES
Decarlo of Hollywood — YVONNE
Decathlon numbers — TENS
Decay — FESTER, ROT
Deceit — SHAM
Deceitful — FALSE, TRICKY
Deceitful sculptor? — CHISELER
Deceitfully affable — OILY
Deceive — DUPE, LEAD DOWN THE GARDEN PATH, SPOOF
Deceive — TRICK
Deceivers — DELUDERS, LIARS
Decelerate — SLOW
December 24 or 31 — EVE
December 31st happening — REVEL
December flower — HOLLY
December platitude — CHRISTMAS COMES ONCE A YEAR
December song — NOEL
December star — ST NICK
December VIP's — SANTAS
Deceptions — FRAUDS, LIES
Deceptive act — CHARADE
Deceptively difficult — EASIER SAID THAN DONE
Decide — ELECT, RESOLVE
Decide against the diner — EAT IN
Decided — OPTED
Decides upon — OPTS
Deciduous horn — ANTLER
Deciduous tree — MAPLE
Decimal base — TEN
Decimal point — DOT
Decimal-system base — TEN
Decimals — TENTHS
Decipher — READ, SOLVE
Decision for Sugar Ray — TKO
Decision in stormy weather — ANY PORT
Decisions for Tyson — TKOS
Decisive defeat — WATERLOO
Decisive experiment — ACID TEST
Decisive factor — CLINCHER
Deck — FLOOR, ORLOP, TIER
Deck opening — SCUPPER

Deck post — BITT
Deck units — CARDS
Deck VIP — BOSN
Deck wood — TEAK
Decked with leis — GARLANDED
Declaim — ATTACK, ORATE, SPEAK
Declaim noisily — RANT
Declaim violently — RANT
Declaim, in a way — SPOUT OFF
Declaims — RANTS
Declaration — EDICT
Declaration of Independence signer — JAMES SMITH
Declare — ALLEGE, ANNOUNCE, AVER, AVOW, CLAIM
Declare — NOTIFY, STATE
Declare a pinochle hand — MELD
Declare an oath? — AVOW
Declare frankly — AVOW
Declare null and void — CANCEL
Declare without proof — ALLEGE
Declarer's choice — SUIT
Déclassé — OUT
Declination — NO SIR
Decline — DROP, EBB, WANE
Decline in power — WANE
Declined — SLID
Declines — WANES
Declining stock market — BEAR
Decorate — ADORN, REDO
Decorate a lily — GILD
Decorate anew — REDO
Decorate food — GARNISH
Decorate lavishly with jewels — ENCRUST
Decorate with raised patterns — EMBOSS
Decorated all over — REDID
Decorated anew — REDID
Decorated fabric — BATIK
Decorated metal — TOLE
Decorated one — HERO
Decorates anew — REDO
Decoration — INLAY
Decoration of a page — ILLUMINATION
Decorations akin to D.S.O.'s — VCS
Decorative — FANCY
Decorative accents — KNICK KNACKS
Decorative altar structure — RETABLE
Decorative design — PATTERN
Decorative garden structure — TRELLIS
Decorative moulding — EGG AND DART
Decorative trim — RICKRACK
Decorator of a kind — LANDSCAPE GARDENER
Decorator's advice — REDO
Decorator's asset — TASTE
Decorator's color — BEIGE, ECRU
Decorator's garb? — COAT OF PAINT
Decorators — PAINTERS
Decorous — FORMAL, PRIM, SEDATE
Decorticate — PEEL
Decoy — BAIT, LURE
Decrease — LESSEN, LOSS
Decrease gradually — TAPER
Decrease in mental activity — STUPOR
Decreased in size — SCALED DOWN, SHRUNK
Decreases — WANES
Decreases the bankroll — SPENDS
Decree — ARRET, EDICT, FIAT
Decree _____ — NISI
Decree by Hussein, e.g. — IRADE
Decreed judiciously — DECERNED
Decrees — EDICTS, FIATS
Decrepit — LAME
Decrepit, in Dijon — CADUC
Decrypt — SOLVE
Dedicate — DEVOTE
Dedicated — VOTIVE
Deduce from a remark — INFER
Deduces — INFERS
Deduct — ABATE
Deduction of a sort — REBATE
Deductive reasoning anal. — SYL
Deed — ACT, GEST
Deed placed in custody — ESCROW
Deed-holder — LANDLORD, OWNER
Deeds — ASSETS
Deeds of paladins — FEATS
Deems — OPINES
Deep affection — LOVE
Deep black — EBON
Deep blue — ANIL
Deep breath — SIGH
Deep cut — GASH
Deep drawers — BINS
Deep gap in earth's surface — GULF
Deep green — EMERALD
Deep guttural sound — GRUNT
Deep holes — PITS
Deep in the earth's crust — MARIANA TRENCH
Deep mud — MIRE
Deep orange-red quartz — SARD
Deep ravine — GORGE
Deep red — GARNET
Deep respect — VENERATION
Deep sleep — SOPOR
Deep tone — BASS
Deep, dark, and empty — CAVERNOUS
Deep, hearty guffaw — BELLY LAUGH
Deep-dish pie — PANDOWDY
Deep-red gadfly? — GARNETTLER
Deep-seated — INNATE
Deep: Comb. form — BATH
Deepen a river bed — DREDGE
Deepest within — INMOST
Deer — ROES
Deer family member — MOOSE
Deer hunter, e.g. — STALKER
Deer meat — JERKY
Deer young — SPAY
Deer's trail — SLOT
Deface — MAR
Defamation — SMEAR
Defamatory statement — LIBEL
Defame — TRADUCE
Defeat — BEST, BLOW, LOSS, OVERPOWER, REVERSE
Defeat — SETBACK, VANQUISH, WORST
Defeat at bridge — SET
Defeat decisively — ROUT, THUMP, TROMP
Defeat overwhelmingly — ROUT
Defeated at chess — MATED
Defeated politicians — OUTS
Defeats — BESTS, UPENDS
Defective automobile — LEMON
Defective vision — ANOPIA
Defects — FLAWS
Defendant at law — REI
Defendant in a divorce action — RESPONDENT
Defendants: Lat. — REI
Defended a client — REPRESENTED
Defender of Scopes — DARROW
Defense against oppression — BASTION
Defense arm — NAVY
Defense made of trees — ABATIS
Defense on a court — PRESS
Defense weapon: Abbr. — ABM
Defenses — RAMPARTS
Defensible — TENABLE
Defensive alliance — SEATO
Defensive linemen: Abbr. — NTS
Defer — STAY

Deferred — ON THE BACK BURNER
Deficiency of vigor — ANERGY
Deficiency: Comb. form — OLIG
Deficient in energy — ANEMIC
Defies — DARES
Defile — PASSAGE
Defoe — DANIEL
Defraud — BILK, COZEN, CHEAT
Defrauds — CONS
Defrost — THAW
Deft — ADROIT
Deftness — AGILITY
Defunct cage gp. — ABA
Defunct gold coin of England — GUINEA
Defunct motor vehicles — EDSELS
Defy danger — DARE
Deg. — LLB
Deg. for a cellist, e.g. — BMUS
Deg. for a museum worker — AFA
Deg. for a thespian — BDA
Deg. for a yuppie — MBA
Deg. in education — BSED
Deg. in religion — THM
Deg. of urgency — PRI
DeGaulle's birthplace — LILLE
Degenerates — GOES TO THE DOGS, ROTS
Degrade — ABASE, LOWER
Degree for a future C.E.O — BBA
Degree for a hosp. worker — BSN
Degree of grade — HEIGHT
Degree of shine of a gemstone — LUSTER
Degree paper — THESIS
Degree type — NTH
Degrees — AMS
Degs. for industrialists — MBAS
Dehumidifies — DRIES
Dehydrated — DRY
Dei _____: by the grace of God — GRATIA
Deighton or Cariou — LEN
Deighton's "_____ in Berlin" — FUNERAL
Deity — ALLAH, GOD, LORD
Deity akin to Cronus — SAT-URN
Deity heathen — IDOL
Deja vu for Michael J. Fox — BACK TO THE FUTURE
Dejected, old style — AMORT
Dejection — GLOOM
Del _____, Colorado city on the Rio Grande — NORTE
Del of baseball fame — ENNIS
Delaware capital — DOVER
Delaware Indian — LENAPE
Delaware seaport — LEWES
Delaware Water _____ — GAP
Delayer at Wimbledon — RAIN
Delbert Mann's 1955 Oscar winner — MARTY
Dele's opposite — STET
Dele, in printing — ELIDE
Delectate — PLEASE
Delegate — LEGATE
Delete — ERASE
Deleted — TOOK OUT
Deletes — EXES
Deletion — ERASURE
Delhi dress — SARI
Delhi garb — SAREE, SARI
Delhi garment — SARI
Deli — MARKET
Deli buys — SALAMIS
Deli choice — RYE
Deli delight — SALAMI
Deli favorites — BAGELS AND LOX
Deli item — MAYO
Deli machine — SLICER
Deli offering — SALAMI
Deli order — TO GO
Deli specialty — HERO, KNISH
Deli treat — HERO
Deli treats — SALAMIS
Deliberate indifference — THE COLD SHOULDER
Delibes and Durocher — LEOS
Delibes opus — LAKME
Delicacy — ROE, TASTE, TREAT
Delicate — FINE
Delicate — LACY
Delicate; graceful — FLOWER-LIKE
Delicately ornamented — FILIGREED
Delicatessen item — BAGEL
Delicious — LUSH
Delicious center — CORE
Delicious food? — APPLE
Delight — ELATE
Delighted — TICKLED PINK
Delightful — NICE
Delights in — GLOATS
Delights or thrills — SENDS
Delineate — TRACE
Delineates — DRAWS
Delinquency — FAULT
Delinquency pickups — REPOS
Delinquent — REMISS
Deliquesce — MELT
Delirium — FEVER
Deliver — GIVE, PITCH, SAVE
Deliver a deed in advance — PREMEDITATE
Deliver a sermon — PREACH
Deliver one to the jaw — BELT
Deliver or perform follower — ANCE
Deliverance — RESCUE
Delivered — SENT
Delivered a knockout punch — DECKED
Delivered an oration — SPOKE
Deliverer — SAVIOR
Deliverer of a perfect pitch — TUNING FORK
Delivery — RENDITION, SPEECH
Delivery ramp — CHUTE
Delivery service — UPS
Delivery to a pub — KEGS
Dell dweller — FARMER
Della and Pee Wee — REESES
Della from Detroit — REESE
Della of song — REESE
Della or Pee Wee — REESE
Della who played a Della — REESE
Delon namesakes — ALAINS
Delores _____ Rio — DEL
Deloul, for one — CAMEL
Delphic datum — OMEN
Delta — MOUTH OF THE RIVER, RIVER MOUTH
Delta material — SILT
Deluded — MISLED
Delusion's companion — SNARE
Delusion's partner — SNARE
Delve — PROBE, SEARCH
Dem bums — DODGERS
Demagogue — AGITATOR
Demand — CLAIM
Demand as one's due — CLAIM
Demander — CLAIMER
Demands — EXACTS
Demands payment — DUNS
Demean — ABASE, REDUCE
Demeanor — AIR, MIEN
Demesne house — MANOR
Demeter, to the Romans — CERES
Demi _____ — TASSE
Demi or Dudley — MOORE
Demi or Roger — MOORE
Demigod — IDOL
Demitasse beverage — COFFEE
Demo — MODEL
Demo ending — CRAT
Democrat's adjective for Grant — USELESS
Democritus or Dalton — ATOMIST
Demolish — LEVEL, RAZE, TOTAL, WRECK
Demolish, British style — RASE
Demolish, in Chelsea — RASE
Demolished, in London — RASED
Demolishes — RASES
Demon — FIEND
Demon in a bottle — GENIE
Demonic — EVIL
Demonstrate — EVINCE
Demonstrated — SHOWED
Demonstrative — EVINCIVE
Demonstrative pronoun — WHOM

Demosthenes for one — ORATOR
Demote — BUST
Demotic — POPULAR
Demotion — COME DOWN
Dempsey challenger: 1923 — FIRPO
Dems. opposition — GOP
Demure — COY, PRIM
Den — LAIR
Den alert — ROAR
Den denizen — BEAR, LION
Den of iniquity — SNAKEPIT
Dendrites' counterparts — AXONS
Deneb or Mizar — STAR
Denial — DOUBT, REFUSAL, VETO
Denial of an allegation in a lawsuit — TRAVERSE
Denial, in Dusseldorf — NEIN
Denials — NOES
Denials, in Dogpatch — NAWS
Denied — REFUSED
Denier — COIN
Denies the truth of — NEGATES
Denigrate — BELITTLE
Denise of "The Garry Moore Show" — LOR
Denizen of an aerie — EAGLE
Denizen of the Andes — LLAMA
Denizens of the deep — FISH
Denmark's _____ Islands — FAEROE
Dennis and Doris — DAYS
Dennis or Calvin — BRAT
Dennis or Duncan — SANDY
Dennis's Mame — AUNTIE
Dennis, the Menace, e.g. — BRAT
Denomination — SECT
Denotes — MEANS
Denounce — DAMN
Denpasar's island — BALI
Dens — NESTS
Dense groves — THICKETS
Dent or vent ending — URE
Dent. degrees — DOSS
Dental _____ — FLOSS
Dental deg. — DDS, LDS
Dental degree — LDS
Dental standby of old — ETHER
Dental work — INLAY
Dentifrice — WASH
Dentist's advice — BRUSH
Dentist's dearth? — LOSS OF FLOSS
Dentist's degree — DMD
Dentist's plan? — GET DOWN IN THE MOUTH
Dentist's request — OPEN
Dentists' offices? — FILLING STATIONS
Dentists' org. — ADA
Denture — PLATE
Denude — STRIP
Denuded — BARE
Denunciate bitterly, with "at" — RAIL
Denver institution — MINT
Denver is one mile above it — SEA LEVEL
Deny — ABJURE, BELIE, GAINSAY, IMPUGN, NEGATE
Deny responsibility — DISAVOW
Deo _____ (thanks to God) — GRATIAS
Deodar — CEDAR
Dep. — STA
Dep. complement — ARR
Dep.'s counterpart — ARR
Depart — LEAVE
Departed — DECEASED, GONE, LEFT, WENT
Department of France — OISE
Department of NW France — ORNE
Department-store plan — LAY AWAY
Departure — LEAVE
Depend — RELY
Depend (on) — RELY
Dependable — TRUSTY
Depended (upon) — LEANT
Depends — HINGES
Depict sharply — ETCH
Deplaned — ALIT
Deplete — DRAIN
Depletion — DRAIN
Deplore — BEMOAN
Deport — BANISH
Deportee — EXILE
Deposit — BANK, DROP, SAVE, SEDIMENT, SILT
Deposit of dust layed down by the winds — LOESS
Deposited in pledge — PAWNED
Depositories, of a sort — SLOTS
Deposits — LODES, MOUNDS
Depot — RAILROAD STATION
Depots: Abbr. — STAS
Depreciate — CHEAPEN
Depreciated — ABASED
Depress — SADDEN
Depressed — SAD
Depressed areas of earth's crust — GRABENS
Depressed areas? — SINK HOLES
Depressed state — FUNK, LOW WATER
Depression — DENT
Depression agcy. — WPA
Depression in bottle bottom — KICK
Depression letters — NRA
Depression program — NRA
Deprivation — HARDSHIP, LOSS
Deprive — DENY, REFUSE
Deprive fraudulently — CHEAT
Deprive of — DIVEST
Deprive of attractive properties — DEMAGNETIZE
Deprive of self-confidence — UNMAN
Deprive of strength — UNMAN
Deprive of weapons — UNARM
Deprive of wind — BECALM
Dept. head — MGR
Depth — STEEPNESS
Depth charge — ASHCAN
Depth of water — DRAFT
Deputy — AGENT, AIDE
Der _____: Adenauer — ALTE
Der of Asia — SAMBUR
Deranged — MAD
Derby entrant — HORSE
Derby, e.g. — RACE
Derby-winner Earle — SANDE
Derby-winning filly: 1915 — REGRET
Deride — FLEER, SCOFF
Deride; mock — JAPE
Derides — GIBES, JEERS
Deriding — RAZZING
Derision — CONTEMPT, RIDICULE, SCORN
Derisive calls — HOOTS, YAHS
Derisive sound — HOOT
Derivation — ROOT
Derivative of morphine — HEROIN
Derive — GAIN
Derived from oil — OLEIC
Dermal blemish — COMENDO
Dermatologist concern — ACNE
Dermatologist, sometimes — ITCH DOCTOR
Dermatologists plan? — GET UNDER YOUR SKIN
Dernier — FINAL
Dernier _____ — CRI
Dernier _____ (latest fashion) — CRI
Derogatory — SNIDE
Derogatory name — SISSY
Derogatory remark — SLUR
Derogatory term for a German — BOSCH
Derrick — CRANE
Derrick booms — JIBS
Dervish — FAKIR
Dervish movement — WHIRL
Dervish's cap — TAJ
Des _____ — MOINES
Descartes and Coty — RENES
Descartes or Lacoste — RENE
Descartes, e.g. — RENE

Descend — SINK
Descend a mountain by rope — ABSEIL
Descend the gangplank — GO ASHORE
Descendant — HEIR, SCION
Descendant of Esau — EDOMITE
Descendant of Noah's son — SHEMITE
Descendants of an Eden dweller — SERPENTS
Descended — ALIT, SANK
Descent — LINEAGE
Describe — DEPICT, LIMN
Describe grammatically — PARSE
Described a half-circle — ARCED
Described a parabola — ARCED
Described in brief — OUT-LINED
Describes honestly — PAINT IN ITS TRUE COLOR
Describing a 9 to 5 job — FULL TIME
Describing a better comeback — SNAPPIER
Describing a certain Andy — RAGGEDY
Describing a certain hatter — MAD
Describing a common cold — VIRAL
Describing a desert — ARID
Describing a doting husband — UXORIOUS
Describing Ann or Andy — RAGGEDY
Describing food for fast days — MAIGRE
Describing Lady Macbeth — EVIL
Describing neon — INERT
Describing Norse poetry — RUNIC
Describing some beavers — EAGER
Describing some courts — MOOT
Describing some faces — HEARTSHAPED
Describing some interest rates — USURIOUS
Describing some numerals — ARABIC
Describing some walls — IVIED
Describing some wines — DRY
Describing Superman's vision — X RAY
Describing winds from the Orient — EASTERLY
Descries — SPOTS
Descriptive title for a Gandhi — MAHATMA
Descriptive wd. — ADJ
Descry — DETECT, ESPY, SPY
Desdemona's handkerchief , e.g. — PROP
Desdemona's nemesis — IAGO
Desert — ABANDON, SAHARA
Desert "sights" — MIRAGES
Desert blooms — CACTI
Desert coat — ABA
Desert depression — WADI
Desert dry — ARID
Desert dweller — NOMAD
Desert fruits — DATES
Desert green spot — OASIS
Desert in S. Israel — NEGEV
Desert incline — DUNE
Desert islands? — OASES
Desert juniper — RETEM
Desert lizard of the US — UMA
Desert menace — SCORPION
Desert one's party — BOLT
Desert plants — CACTI
Desert rat — MINER
Desert region — ERG
Desert region of N Africa — SAHARA
Desert scenery — DUNES
Desert shelter — TENT
Desert shrub — RETEM
Desert stops — OASES
Desert transport — CAMEL
Desert transportation — CAMEL
Desert travelers — CARAVANS
Desert vision — MIRAGE
Desert wanderer — NOMAD
Desert, in Deamante — YERMO
Desert-like — ARID
Desert-like region of the Arabian Peninsula — DAHNA
Deserters — RATS
Deserts — REWARD
Deserve — BE WORTHY OF, EARN, MERIT, RATE
Deserved — EARNED, MERIT-ED
Desi Arnaz's autobiography — A BOOK
Desi's daughter — LUCIE
Desiccate — PARCH
Desiccated — SERE
Desideratum — HOPE, NEED
Design — INTEND, MOTIF, PLAN
Design glass — ETCH
Designate — DENOTE, DENOMINATE, NAME, TAP
Designate falsely — MISLABEL
Designated — ENTITLED, TABBED, TERMED
Designated for use in flying — AERO
Designates — NAMES
Designation — TITLE
Designed for singing — CHORAL
Designed to fly — AERO
Designer Ashley — LAURA
Designer Cassini — OLEG
Designer de la _____ — RENTA
Designer of chocolates? — COCOA CHANEL
Designer of the new look — DIOR
Designer Oscar de la _____ — RENTA
Designer Rykiel — SONIA
Designer Simpson — ADELE
Designer's device — DRAPE
Designer's forte — STYLE
Designers' logos — LABELS
Designing name — DIOR
Designs — INTENTS, PLANS
Desinence — END
Desirable theater seat location — AISLE
Desirable thing — ASSET
Desire — COVET, NEED, WANT, WILL, YEN
Desire fiercely — CRAVE
Desire greatly — CRAVE
Desire to eat chalk, clay, etc. — PICA
Desires — WANTS
Desirous — AVID
Desist — CEASE, STOP
Desist from — HALT
Desisted — CEASED
Desk compartment for bureau-crats — PIGEONHOLE
Desk feature — KNEEHOLE
Desk item — CALENDAR, CLIP, ERASER
Desk style — ROLLTOP
Desolate — LONESOME, LORN
Desolate regions — WILDS
DeSoto, e.g. — CAR
Desperate — DIRE
Despicable — VILE
Despina, in "Cosi fan tutte" — MAID
Despise — DETEST, HATE, LOATHE
Despised — DETESTED
Despises — HATES
Despoilers — ROTTERS
Despondent — LOW
Despot — TSAR, TYRANT
Dessert — BLANC MANGE, CHEESE CAKE, MOUSSE
Dessert — KEY LIME PIE, RUM CAKE, ZABAGLIONE
Dessert choice — APPLE PIE, TORTE
Dessert choice — CHERRIES JUBILEE, TART
Dessert choice — CHOCO-LATE MOUSSE

Dessert item — CUSTARD
Dessert named for an opera star — PEACH MELBA
Dessert offering — PIE
Dessert specialty — BAKED ALASKA
Dessert treat — BANANA SHORTCAKE
Dessert wine — TOKAY
Dessert with oranges and flaked coconut — AMBROSIA
Desserts — ICES
Destination — FINISH
Destine — FATE, PREORDAIN
Destined — FATED
Destines — ORDAINS
Destinies — ENDS
Destiny — DOOM, KARMA, LOT
Destiny in Buddhism — KARMA
Destiny, to Domenico — FATO
Destitution — NEED
Destroy — RUIN, SHRED, TOTAL
Destroy, in a way — GUT
Destroyed — UNDONE
Destroyed, as by fire — GUTTED
Destroyer — TINCAN
Destroyer function — ESCORT
Destroyer's gun platform — SPONSON
Destroyers to Dinah and Eddie — SHORES SHIPS
Destroys documents — SHREDS
Destructive one — VANDAL
Destructive whelk — WINKLE
Detach a brooch — UNPIN
Detached — ALOOF, IMPERSONAL
Detail — FACT, ITEM, POINT
Detailed info — CHAPTER AND VERSE
Details — NICETIES, NITTY GRITTY, SETUP
Detect — ESPY, FIND, UNEARTH
Detected — SEEN
Detection device — RADAR, SONAR, SENSOR
Detective Charlie — CHAN
Detective Charlie's creator — EARL DERR BIGGERS
Detective Sam — SPADE
Detective Spade and others — SAMS
Detective story writer Michael _____ — INNES
Detective Tibbs — VIRGIL
Detective Wolfe — NERO
Detective's find — CLUE
Detective, at times — TRACER
Detectives Nick and _____ Charles — NORA
Deter — STEM
Detergent — CLEANER
Deteriorate — DROOP, ROT, WORSEN
Deteriorated — DEGENERATED
Determinant — CAUSE
Determination: Abbr. — ANAL
Determine — ASCERTAIN, GET AT, INTEND, RESOLVE, RULE
Determined — RASH
Detest — ABHOR, HATE
Detestable / tenants' motto? — ABHORRENT
Detonations — BLASTS
Detriment — DAMAGE, HARM
Detritus — DEBRIS, FLOTSAM AND JETSAM
Detroit action — RECALL
Detroit athlete — TIGER
Detroit centerfielders? — LAIR OF TIGERS
Detroit eleven — LIONS
Detroit export — AUTOS
Detroit from Chicago, dir. — ENE
Detroit headache — RECALL
Detroit model — SEDAN
Detroit offering — AUTO
Detroit pioneer — OLDS
Detroit's Della — REESE
Detroit's icemen — RED WINGS
Detroit / Rochester vector — ENE
Deuce beater — TREY
Deuce follower — TREY
Deuce topper — TREY
Deuces — TWOS
Deutsch one — EIN
Deux follower — TROIS
Devastate — RUIN
Devastating calamity — CRUSHING BLOW
Devastation — HAVOC
Develop — GROW, ENLARGE, MATURE, SWELL
Developed gradually — EVOLVED
Developed into — BECAME
Developer's charts — PLATS
Developer's concern — SITE
Developer's interest — SITE
Developer's map — PLAT
Developers' interests — SITES
Deviating from course — YAWING
Deviating from proper course — ERRANT
Deviating, as a storm-swept ship — YAWING
Device for lettering — STENCIL
Device for spraying pesticide — DUSTGUN
Device on a loom — REED
Device used in tape recording — DOLBY
Devil — TEASE
Devil's bones — DICE, YAM
Devil's walking stick, e.g. — TREE
Devil-may-care — CASUAL, RASH
Devilfish — MANTA, OCTOPUS
Devilish — DEUCED
Devilish Broadway chronicler? — DEMON RUNYON
Devilish features — HORNS
Devilishly bad exposures? — PRINTS OF DARKNESS
Devilkin — IMP
Devious — EVASIVE, SLY, SHREWD
Devise — COIN
Devise a scheme — PLAN
Devoid — EMPTY
Devoid of excitement — DEAD
Devoid of interest — ARID
Devoid of native minerals — ORELESS
Devoid of superfluity — TERSE
Devon river — EXE
Devonshire cathedral — EXETER
Devonshire river — TAMAR
Devoted — LOVING
Devotee — FAN, LOVER
Devotion — PIETY
Devotional prayer — ANGELUS
Devour — CONSUME, EAT
Devoured — EATEN
Devout — PIOUS, SAINTLY
Devout insect? — MANTIS
Devout Turk — MUSLIM
Devoutness — PIETY
Dew-covered — WET
Dewey or Nimitz — ADMIRAL
Dewey, in poetry — RORAL
DeWitt Clinton's ditch — ERIE
DeWitt of Erie Canal fame — CLINTON
Dexterous — AGILE, DEFT
Dey or Brownell Anthony — SUSAN
DH for one — BATTER
Dhurrie — RUG
Di-dah's preceder — LAH
Diable and d'Yeu — ILES
Diabolical — DEMONIC, SATANIC
Diacritical mark — TILDE
Diacritics, e.g. — MODIFIERS
Diadem adornment — GEM
Diadem for Diana — TIARA
Diagonal — BIAS, SLANT
Diagonal line — BIAS
Dial backward — LAID
Dialect — IDIOM

Dialect of ancient Greece — ATTIC
Dialectic — LOGIC
Dialogue — TALK
Diamond — GEM
Diamond _____ — LIL
Diamond and Armstrong — NEILS
Diamond arbiter — UMPIRE
Diamond arbiter, for short — UMP
Diamond award — GOLDEN GLOVE
Diamond bags — BASES
Diamond call — SAFE
Diamond champs: 1976 — REDS
Diamond clubs — BATS
Diamond corner — BASE
Diamond covering — TARP
Diamond covers — TARPS
Diamond cutter's device — DOP
Diamond decision — SAFE
Diamond feat — HOMER
Diamond figs. — UMPS
Diamond figure — UMPIRE
Diamond glove — MITT
Diamond Hall of Famer Lloyd or Paul — WANER
Diamond Head site — OAHU
Diamond imitation — PASTE
Diamond judges — UMPS
Diamond lady, et al. — LILS
Diamond location — BATTERS BOX, THIRD
Diamond man — JIM
Diamond name — LIL
Diamond numbers — NINES
Diamond of song — NEIL
Diamond point — BASE, HOME
Diamond shape — PEAR
Diamond source — MINE
Diamond stat. — ERA
Diamond State poetry? — RONDELAWARE
Diamond unit — CARAT
Diamond unit of weight — CARAT
Diamond units — INNINGS
Diamond wear — MITTS
Diamond weights — CARATS
Diamond's "_____ Believer" — IM A
Diamond, actually — CARBON
Diamondback or hawkbill — TURTLE
Diamonds in Don Juan's deck — OROS
Diamonds, to a yegg — ICE
Diamonds, to Legs Diamond — ICE
Diana _____: 1934-73 — SANDS
Diana is its princess — WALES
Diana of song — ROSS
Diana or Katherine — ROSS
Diana Ross was one — SUPREME
Diana's beloved — ORION
Diana's realm — MOON
Diane or Buster — KEATON
Diapers, in Dover — NAPKINS, NAPPIES
Diaphoretic — CLOSE
Diarist Frank — ANNE
Diarist of the 17th century — PEPYS
Diarize — ENTER
Diarized — ENTERED
Diary — JOURNAL
Diary abbr. — APR
Diaskeuast — EDITOR
Diatom or nostoc — ALGA
Diatoms — ALGAE
Diatribe — TIRADE
Dic. entry — SYN
Dice naturals — SEVENS
Dice throw — ACES, SEVEN
Dice, to some — BONES
Dicer or skimmer — HAT
Dicer's lucky throw — NATURAL
Diciembre follower — ENERO
Dick and Jane's pet dog — SPOT
Dick and Schick — TESTS
Dick Bogarde film: 1955 — SIMBA
Dick or Ramsey — CLARK
Dickens character Edwin — DROOD
Dickens clerk — HEEP
Dickens Edwin _____ — DROOD
Dickens girl — NELL
Dickens hardware merchant — GRADGRIND
Dickens hero — DROOD, TWIST
Dickens Mr. Heep — URIAH
Dickens novel of 1852 — BLEAK HOUSE
Dickens offering — TALE
Dickens pen name — BOZ
Dickens Uriah — HEEP
Dickens villain — FAGIN, SYKES
Dickens' "Barnaby _____" — RUDGE
Dickens' "Little _____" — DORRIT
Dickens' foundling — TWIST
Dickens' Heep — URIAH
Dickens' lad — PIP
Dickens' Little _____ — NELL
Dickens' Miss Dartle — ROSA
Dickens' Miss Manette — LUCIE
Dickens' Rosa _____ — DARTLE
Dickens' Tim — TINY
Dickens' Uriah — HEEP
Dickens's forte — FICTION
Dickens, sometimes — BOZ
Dicker — BARTER
Dickinson of Amherst — EMILY
Dickinson of Hollywood — ANGIE
Dickinson of poetry — EMILY
Dickinson or Whitman — POET
Dict. entry — DEF
Dict. published in England — OED
Dicta — FIATS
Dicta from the Court — OPINIONS
Dictate — ORDER
Dictated — ORAL
Dictatee — STENO
Dictator's phrase — IN RE
Dictators — DUCES
Diction — EXPRESSION, RHETORIC, STYLE
Dictionary compilation — LEXICOGRAPHY
Dictionary info — DEF
Dictum — MAXIM
Did a cobbler's job — SOLED
Did a cotton-pickin' job — BALED
Did a fall job — RAKED
Did a garden chore — RAKED
Did a gardening job — SPADED
Did a grand jete — LEAPED
Did a kitchen chore — PARED
Did a lawn job — RAKED
Did a pre-laundry job — SORTED
Did a publishing job — EDITED
Did a Tuesday chore — IRONED
Did an inside job — LINED
Did an usher's job — SEATED
Did business — DEALT
Did business, in a way — BARTERED
Did field work — HOED, PLANTED, WEEDED
Did garden work — HOED
Did in — SLEW
Did in, gangster style — ICED
Did lawn work — MOWED
Did penance — ATONED
Did ranch work — RODE
Did road work — PAVED
Did some home work — SIDED
Did some nitpicking — CARPED
Did some ranch work — ROPED
Did some sewing — PLANTED
Did sums — TOTALED
Did the cancan — KICKED
Did the human thing — ERRED
Did undercover work — SPIED
Did wickerwork — CANED
Didactic — MORAL

Diddle — CHEAT, JOG, SWINDLE
Didn't lose at musical chairs — SAT
Didn't sink — SWAM
Dido — ANTIC, CAPER, NIPUP
Dido died on one — PYRE
Dido's deserter — AENEAS
Die down — SUBSIDE
Die out — STOP
Die spots — PIPS
Die-cast — FORCE
Died without issue: Lat. abbr. — DSP
Diego or Mateo lead-in — SAN
Diemaker's tool — BURR
Dieppe donkey — ANE
Dies _____ — IRAE
Dies non — SUNDAY
Diet — BANT, FARE, FAST, REGIMEN
Diet follower — ICIAN
Diet periods — LENTS
Diet reneger — FATSO
Diet, in a way — BANT
Dietary staple — RICE
Dieter's bane — SCALE
Dieter's concern — FLAB
Dieter's concern — OVERWEIGHT
Dieter's dish — FRUIT SALAD
Dieter's enemy — SWEET TOOTH
Dieter's fare — MELBA TOAST, SALAD
Dieter's need — SCALE
Dieter's nemesis — SCALE
Dieter's no-no — SNACK
Dieter's place? — ON A SCALE
Dieter's problem — WEIGHT
Dieter's turndown — ECLAIR
Dieting goal — WASTE NOT WANT NOT
Dieting no-nos — SWEETS
Diets successfully — SLIMS
Diets, British style — SLIMS
Differ ending — ENCE
Differ or prefer finisher — ENCE
Difference in pressure — DRAFT
Different — UNLIKE
Different: Comb. form — ALLO
Different: Prefix — HETERO
Difficult — UNEASY
Difficult age, often — TEENS
Difficult feat — STUNT
Diffident — SHY, TIMID
Diffuse — STREWN
Diffusion of liquid: Prefix — OSMO
Dig for coal — MINE
Dig for data — DELVE
Dig further — DEEPEN
Dig into — EXPLORE
Dig out — EXTRACT
Dig up — UNEARTH
Digest — GRASP
Digestive enzyme — LIPASE
Digests, for short — ABRS
Digger — SPADE
Digger of TV's "The Life of Riley" — ODELL
Diggers' need — SHOVELS
Digging tools — SPUDS
Digit — TOE
Digital watch display — LCD
Digitate — TOED
Dignified — LORDLY, SOBER, STATELY
Dignified woman of a "certain age" — DOWAGER
Dignitary — VIP
Dignity — FACE
Digress — STRAY, VARY
Digression — ASIDE
Digs up — SEEKS
DII doubled — MIV
Dijon darlings — CHERIES
Dijon donkey — ANE
Dijon dream — REVE
Dik-dik's big cousin — ELAND
Dik-dik's cousin — ORIBI
Dike, Eunomia and Irene — HORAE
Dilapidated — SHAKY
Dilapidated structure — RAT TRAP
Dilate — SWELL
Dilemma — KNOT, TEASER
Dilemma appendages — HORNS
Dilemma items — HORNS
Dilettante — AESTHETE, AMATEUR, NOVICE
Diligence — ZEAL
Diligent — ACTIVE
Dill, in olden days — ANET
Dill, of the bible — ANET
Dill, of yore — ANET
Dillon of the movies — MATT
Dillon or Houston — MATT
Dilly-dally — LOAF
Dillydally — TOY
Dilo and dita — TREES
Dilute — THIN, WATER
Diluted — WATERY
Dilutes — THINS
Dim — BLEAR, BLUR, FAINT
DiMaggio — JOE
DiMaggio brother — DOM
Dime a dozen — CHEAP
Dimension — RANGE, SIZE, WIDTH
Diminish — ABATE, DETRACT, FADE, LESSEN, SIZE, WANE
Diminish gradually, with "out" — PETER
Diminish in a way — PARE
Diminish in intensity — WANE
Diminish speed — SLOW
Diminishes quickly — EVAPORATES
Diminution — CUT
Diminutive — BANTAM, PETITE, PUNY, TEENSY, TINY
Diminutive coloratura — PONS
Diminutive ending — ETTE, ULA
Diminutive of a girl's name — ETTA
Diminutive suffix — CLE, ULA, ULE
Diminutive suffix, Irish style — EEN
Diminutive suffixes — ETTES, ULAS, ULES, ETS
Dimitri's dangerous game? — RUSSIAN ROULETTE
Dimmed again — REDARKENED
Dimmer — RHEOSTAT
Dims — PALES
Din — BLARE, CLAMOR, NOISE
Dinah from Tennessee — SHORE
Dinar fraction — PARA
Dinars are spent here — ORAN
Dine (with) — EAT
Dine at home — EAT IN
Dine in a meadow — GRAZE
Dined at home — ATE IN
Dined sparingly — DIETED
Dined to well — OVERATE
Diner order — TO GO
Diner sign — EATS, NEON
Diner's protectors — BIBS
Dines at a restaurant — EATS OUT
Dines informally — SUPS
Dines late — SUPS
Ding-a-ling things — BELLS
Ding companion — DONG
Ding-a-ling — CRACKPOT
Dinge — GLOOM
Dinghy — SKIFF
Dinghy adjunct — OAR
Dingle — DALE, DELL, GLEN, VALE
Dingy — SHABBY
Dingy place — DIVE
Dingy, in Dijon — TERNE
Dining halls on liners — SALOONS
Dining room, to some — MESS
Dinky — TRIM
Dinner bell, of a sort — GONG
Dinner check — TAB
Dinner course — ENTREE
Dinner course, dressed up? — SMOCK TURTLE SOUP
Dinner fare — ROAST
Dinner for "Spend a Buck" — OATS

Dinner hour, e.g. — MEALTIME
Dinner item: Abbr. — VEG
Dinner menu item — FILETS
Dinner starter — SOUP
Dinner wear for young ones — BIBS
Dinosaur, e.g. — REPTILE
Dinsmore of fiction — ELSIE
Diocese — SEE
Dionysian reveler — SATYR
Dionysus specialty — ORGY
Dior creation — GOWN
Dior ending — AMA
Dip — BATHE, LADE
Dip flax — RET
Dip into — TRY
Dip out — SAIL
Dip site — POND
Diplomacy — CRAFT, TACT
Diplomas — SHEEPSKINS
Diplomat Abba — EBAN
Diplomat Eban — ABBA
Diplomat Root — ELIHU
Diplomat Silas — DEANE
Diplomat's desire — RAPPORT
Diplomat's forte — TACT
Diplomatic skill — TACT
Diplomatic VIP — AMB
Dipper — LADLE
Dippy or dotty — GAGA
Dips — DUNKS, LADES
Dipteran — FLY
Dir. from Bath to London — ENE
Dir. from NYC to Boston — NNE
Dir. of Dallas from Austin — NNE
Dir. of L.A. from Reno — SSE
Dir. of San Diego from L.A. — SSE
Dir. to Rochester from Buffalo — ENE
Dire — TERRIBLE
Direct — MANAGE, STEER
Direct a jet — NAVIGATE
Direct a team — MANAGE
Direct a weapon — AIM, POINT
Direct an activity — CONTROL
Direct insult — SLAP
Direct phone link for Bush — HOT LINE
Direct the affairs of others — ADMINISTER
Direct, as a road — THRU
Directed — LED
Directed a course, with "at" — AIMED
Directed toward — AIMED
Direction finder — MAP
Direction of sunrise — EAST
Direction on a destroyer — PORT
Direction to a violinist — ARCO
Direction to play loudly — FORTE
Direction, asea — PORT
Direction, in music — ATEMPO
Directional controls — REINS
Directional ending — ERN
Directionally straight — LINEARLY
Directive to a sinner — REPENT
Directly — SOON
Director-author Kazan — ELIA
Director Buñuel's billow — OLA
Director Clair — RENE
Director Delbert or Daniel — MANN
Director Flaherty's "Man of _____" — ARAN
Director Fritz — LANG
Director Fritz and family — LANGS
Director Gene — SAKS
Director Jean-_____ Godard — LUC
Director Kazan — ELIA
Director Kenton — ERLE
Director Logan from Tex. — JOSHUA
Director Lubitsch, 1892-1947 — ERNST
Director Lumet — SIDNEY
Director May — ELAINE
Director Norman — LEAR
Director of "Breaking Away" — YATES
Director of "It Happened One Night" — CAPRA
Director of "Network" — LUMET
Director of "Psycho" — HITCHCOCK
Director of "The Big Sleep" — HOWARD HAWKS
Director of "The Birds" — HITCHCOCK
Director of "Two Hundred Motels" — ZAPPA
Director Preminger — OTTO
Director Russell — KEN
Director Spielberg — STEVEN
Director Stanley — DONEN
Director Stone — OLIVER
Director Vittorio De _____ — SICA
Director Wertmüller — LINA
Director William _____ — WYLER
Director's request — ACTION
Director-writer Kazan — ELIA
Directs — SENDS
Directs a ship's navigation — CONNS
Dirge — ELEGY
Dirigible description: Abbr. — LTA
Dirk — SKEAN
Dirk of yore — SNEE
Dirndl — SKIRT
Dirt — DINGE
Dirt dauber — WASP
Dirty — SOIL, UNCLEAN
Dirty group out of Hollywood — DOZEN
Dis pater — HADES
Disabled — LAMED
Disaccustoms — WEANS
Disaffect — ESTRANGE
Disagree sharply — CLASH
Disagreeable — NASTY, UGLY
Disagreeable one — PILL
Disagreeably — NASTILY
Disagreeably moist and cold — CLAMMY
Disagreement — SPAT
Disallow — BAN, NIX
Disappeared — GONE
Disappoint — LET DOWN
Disapprover's sounds — TSKS
Disapproving look — FROWN
Disarrangement — MESS
Disarray — MESS
Disassemble — DEMOUNT, UNDO
Disassociate — SEVER
Disasters — CATASTROPHES
Disastrous — DIRE
Disavow — DENY
Disavowals — RETRACTIONS
Disbelief — DOUBT
Disburden — FREE
Disburdens — EASES
Disburse — METE, SPEND
Disburser — PAYER
Disc brakes adjunct — CALIPERS
Discard — SCRAP
Discard a card — SLUFF
Discard unnecessarily — WASTE
Discard, in a way — MOLT
Discarding — RIDDING
Discards — THROWS TO THE DOGS
Discern — ESPY
Discernment — INSIGHT, TASTE
Discerns — ESPIES
Discharge — EGEST, EMIT, FIRE, RELEASE
Discharge from milit. service — DEMOB
Discharge of artillery — SALVO
Discharge slowly — EXUDE
Discharge violently — EXPLODE
Discharge, as lava — OUT-POUR
Discharged light — ARCED
Discharges — EGESTS, FIRES

Disciple — ADHERENT, IST, PETER
Disciple of Ananias — TWO FACED LIAR
Disciple of: Suffix — ITE
Disciple's emotion — AWE, REVERENCE
Disciplinary measure — PENALTY
Discipline — CHASTEN, PUNISH
Disciplines — SPANKS
Discloses — REVEALS
Discomfit — ABASH, FOIL
Discomfiture — UNEASE
Discomfort — PAIN
Disconcert — ABASH
Disconcert — ABASH, FAZE
Disconcerted — ABASHED, FAZED, IN A SPOT
Disconnected, as notes — STACCATO
Discontinuance — HALT, LAPSE
Discontinue — CEASE, DROP, QUIT, STOP
Discontinues — HALTS
Discontinuing — CEASING
Discontinuity — GAP
Discord — CONFLICT, DIN, STRIFE
Discord deity — ERIS
Discordant — AJAR, HARSH
Discordia — ERIS
Discordia, to Demosthenes — ERIS
Discotheque dancing style — GOGO
Discotheque term — A GOGO
Discount — LOWER, REBATE, REJECT
Discount allowances — REBATES
Discourage — DEMORALIZE, DEPRESS, DETER
Discourse — TALK
Discourteous — RUDE
Discover — PUT ONES FINGER ON
Discovered — ESPIED, LEARNT
Discoverer Abel — TASMAN
Discoverer of Greenland — ERIC
Discoverer of radium — CURIE
Discovers — FINDS
Discovery shouts — AHAS
Discredit — SHAME
Discreet — WARY
Discretion — PRUDENCE
Discriminate — PREJUDGE, SEPARATE
Discriminating — SELECT
Discrimination — TASTE
Discriminator against older people — AGEIST
Discuss — TALK OVER
Discuss the real business — TALK TURKEY
Discusses at length — DWELLS ON
Discusses Thanksgiving dinner? — TALKS TURKEY
Discussion group — PANEL
Disdain — SCORN
Disdainful of — LOOKING DOWN ONES NOSE AT
Disease — VIRUS
Disease of cereals — ERGOT
Disease producers — BACILLI
Diseases of rye — ERGOTS
Disembark — LAND
Disembarked — ALIT
Disencumber — RID
Disencumbers, with "of" — RIDS
Disengage — DETACH, UNDO
Disentangle, in football — UNPILE
Disentangles — FREES
Disfigure — MAR
Disfigured — SCARRED
Disgrace — SHAME
Disgraceful — SHAMELESS
Disgraces — SMEARS
Disgruntled — PEEVED
Disguise — CAMOUFLAGE, MASK
Disgust — LOATHING, REPEL
Disgusted — REPELLED
Disgusting — NASTY, YUCKY
Disgusts — REVOLTS
Dish apples, celery and lettuce — WALDORF SALAD
Dish for a King? — COLE SLAW
Dish list — MENU
Dish of the South — MUSH
Dish similar to grits — GROATS
Dish the _____ (gossip) — DIRT
Disharmony — DIN
Disharmony, per Tennyson — RIFT WITHIN THE LUTE
Dishearten — DETER
Dishes out — METES
Disheveled — MUSSED
Dishonest gain — GRAFT
Dishonor — ABASE, SHAME
Disinclined — AVERSE
Disinclined to action — LAZY
Disinformation — LIES
Disintegrate — DECAY, ERODE
Disintegrate slowly — ERODE
Disintegrated — SHATTERED
Disintegrates — ERODES
Disintegrating roost? — CRUMBLE SEAT
Disk for sealing letters — WAFER
Disk jockey — RECORD HOLDER
Disk jockey's disc — RECORD
Disk's list for a dee-jay — LPS
Dislike intensely — HATE
Dislikes — AVERSIONS
Dislodge from office — UNSEAT
Dismal cry — YOWL
Dismiss — DROP, FIRE, OUST
Dismounted — ALIT
Dismounts — ALIGHTS
Disney — WALT
Disney creation — MICKEY MOUSE
Disney creatures — MICE
Disney deer — BAMBI
Disney dog — LADY, PLUTO
Disney mermaid — ARIEL
Disney or Whitman — WALT
Disney products — CARTOONS
Disney sci-fi film: 1982 — TRON
Disney World locale — ORLANDO
Disney's "World's Greatest Athlete" — NANU
Disney's middle name — ELIAS
Disorder — AILMENT, DERANGE, RIOT
Disorder in the streets — RIOT
Disordered — DERANGED
Disorderly — MESSY
Disorderly crowd — RABBLE
Disparage — DECRY, SLUR
Disparagement — DETRACTION
Disparaging remark — SLUR
Dispassionate — COLD BLOODED
Dispatch — FORWARD, HASTE, ISSUE, ROUTE, SEND
Dispatch — SEND OFF, SPEED
Dispatch across the sea — SEND OVER
Dispatch vessel — AVISO
Dispatched — SENT
Dispatcher — STARTER
Dispense with — ABANDON, DROP
Dispensed equably, with "out" — METED
Disperse — ROUT, SCATTER, SPREAD
Dispirited — CRESTFALLEN, LOW
Dispirits — PALLS
Displace — MOVE, UPROOT
Display — EXHIBIT, EXPOSE, LAYOUT, SET OUT
Display boredom — YAWN
Display cases — ETAGERES
Display concern — FROWN
Display in a toy shop — DOLLS
Display instability — TOTTER
Display otiosity — LAZE
Display patience — AWAIT

Display pretentiously — FLAUNT
Displayed — SHOWN, WORE
Displayed displeasure — HOOTED
Displays boredom — NODS
Displays contempt — SNEERS
Displease — ANGER, MIFF, ROIL
Dispose — RID
Dispose of — RID
Disposed — APT
Disposition — MOOD, SPIRIT
Dispossession — EVICTION, OUSTER
Disprove — REFUTE
Dispur is its capital — ASSAM
Dispute — CONTEST, DEBATE, REFUTE
Dispute strongly — CONTEND
Disputes — ARGUES, ROWS
Disquiet — ALARM, UNEASE
Disregard — OMIT
Disregards — NEGLECTS
Disreputable — SHADY
Disrobed — BARE
Disrupt — REND
Dissect a sentence — PARSE
Dissected a sentence — PARSED
Disseminate — STREW
Dissent — DENIAL, DIFFER
Dissertation — TRACTATE
Dissertation — TREATISE
Disserve — HARM
Dissident — ANTI
Dissimilar — UNLIKE
Dissimulation — PRETENSE
Dissipate — BURN, WASTE
Dissolute man — RAKE
Dissolute one — ROUE
Dissolve — MELT
Dissonant — ATONAL
Dissuade — DAMPEN, HINDER
Dissuades — DETERS
Dist. _____ — ATTY
Dist. or pros. — ATTY
Distaff title — MAAM
Distance between railroad tracks — GAUGE
Distance between rails — GAUGE
Distance between ship and shore — BERTH
Distance equaling 1,482 meters — MILE
Distance from shore — OFFING
Distance measures — MILES
Distant — AFAR, ALOOF, REMOTE
Distant actor? — TELE SAVALAS
Distant ancestor — APEMAN
Distant view — PERSPECTIVE
Distant witness — ESPIER
Distant: Comb. form — TELE
Distant: Prefix — TELE
Distantly related — SHIRT TAIL
Distasteful — UNSAVORY —
Distillation leftovers — RESIDUA
Distilled grape juice: Var. — RAKEE
Distiller's grain — MALT
Distillery residue — POT ALE
Distinct parts — UNITS
Distinct: Abbr. — DIF
Distinction — EMINENCE, GLORY
Distinctive — RARE
Distinctive air — AURA
Distinctive atmosphere — AURA
Distinctive doctrine — ISM
Distinctive flavor — TANG
Distinctive period — ERA
Distinctive time period — ERA
Distinguished 1776 group — FOUNDING FATHERS
Distort — ANGLE, GARBLE, SKEW
Distorted — BENT, WRY
Distress — AIL, GRIEVE, PAIN
Distress deeply — AFFLICT
Distress letters — SOS
Distress signal — SOS, TEARS
Distressed — SORE
Distressful matter — BANE
Distribute — ALLOT, DIVIDE, METE, PARCEL
Distribute cards — DEAL
Distribute cards anew — REDEAL
Distribute, with "out" — DOLE
Distributed — DEALT
Distributed by measure — METED
Distributed cards — DEALT
Distributed the cards — DEALT
Distributed to jobbers — FARMED OUT
Distributes — ALLOTS, DEALS, ISSUES, METES OUT
Distributes impartially — EVENS
Distributes sparingly — DOLES
Distributor — AGENT
District — AREA
District in Greenland — THULE
District in SW Saudi Arabia — ASIR
District of Columbia river — POTOMAC
District of Paris — MONT-MARTE
District of W. India — GOA
Distrustful — LEERY, WARY
Disturb — ALARM, JAR, RILE
Disturb the nocturnal peace — SNORE
Disturbances — RIOTS
Disturbed ghost, in Hindu myths — PRETA
Ditch — TRENCH
Ditch, of a sort — MOAT
Dithers — FURORS
Ditsy seniors — GEEZERS
Ditto — DUPE, SAME
Ditty — AIR, LAY, SONG
Ditty from Down Under — WALTZING MATILDA
Ditty syllable — TRA
Diurnal — BOOK
Div. or sect. — SEG
Diva _____ Te Kanawa — KIRI
Diva Amara — LUCINE
Diva Dame Nellie — MELBA
Diva deliveries — ARIAS
Diva Geraldine — FARRAR
Diva Gilla-Cucie — AMELITA
Diva Jenny — LIND
Diva Lehmann — LOTTE
Diva Lily — PONS
Diva Lucine — AMARA
Diva Maria — CALLAS
Diva Melba — NELLIE
Diva Mitchell — LEONA
Diva Moffo — ANNA
Diva Pons who sang "Lucia" — LILY
Diva Renata — SCOTTO
Diva Stevens — RISE
Diva Tibaldi — RENATA
Diva's number — ARIA
Diva's solo — ARIA
Divagate — STRAY
Divan — SOFA
Dive — DIP, JOINT
Diver Louganis — GREG
Diver's device — SCUBA
Diver's perch — SPRING BOARD
Diver's position — PIKE
Diverge — OPEN, SPREAD
Diverges from the straight and narrow — STRAYS
Diverse — SUNDRY
Diversion — GAME
Diversion, of a sort — RED HERRING
Diversionary tactic — RED HERRING
Diversions — PASTIMES
Divert — AMUSE
Divide — FORK, SEVER, SHARE
Divide into two equal parts — HALVE
Divide the profits — CUT A MELON
Divided — SLICED
Divided Asian land — KOREA
Divided by — INTO
Divided into vertical stripes in heraldry — PALY
Divided land — KOREA
Divided, as highways — LANED
Divided, in heraldry — PALY

Dividend — BONUS
Divider, in biology — SEPTUM
Divides — SEPARATES
Dividing walls — SEPTA
Dividing word — INTO
Divine — GODLY, HOLY
Divine gift — GRACE
Divine nourishment — MANNA
Diviner — SEER
Diving bell inventor — EADS
Diving bird — AUK, GREBE, LOON, OSPREY
Diving duck — SCAUP
Divining rod — WAND
Divinity — DEITY
Divinity deg. — STD
Divinity sch. degree — STM
Division — CHAPTER, DISTRICT
Division of a book — CHAPTER
Division of a city — WARD
Division of a newspaper — DESK
Division of society — CASTE
Division word — INTO
Divisions of a boxing match — ROUNDS
Divisions of basketball games — QUARTERS
Divisions of hockey games — PERIODS
Divisions: Abbr. — DEPTS
Divorce — SPLIT
Divorce lawyer's suit? — PILLOW CASE
Divorce payment — ALIMONY
Divorcee's concern — ALIMONY
Divorcees — EXES
Divulge — REVEAL, TELL
Divulged — IMPARTED
Divulgement — EXPOSURE
Divulges — IMPARTS
Dix and Lee — FORTS
Dix and Sumter, e.g. — FORTS
Dixie alliance — CSA
Dixie joints — JOOKS
Dixie tree — LIVER OAK
Dixie, with "The" — SOUTH
Dixieland — JAZZ, SOUTH
Dixmude's river — YSER
Dizzied — AREEL
Dizzy and son, Steve, of baseball — TROUTS
Dizzy one — REELER
Djakarta's land: abbr. — INDON
Djibouti's sea — RED
Do-gooder's concerns — REFORMS
Do-it-yourself book — HOW TO
Do-it-yourselfers' purchases — KITS
Do _____ (all out) — OR DIE
Do a 180 degree — CHANGE
Do a baker's job — KNEAD
Do a cobbler's job — RESOLE
Do a conn job — STEER
Do a cotton-picking job — BALE
Do a detective's job — TRAIL
Do a disappearing act — VANISH
Do a do — COMB
Do a double take — REACT
Do a fall job — RAKE
Do a farm job — MOW
Do a farmer's job — SOW, REAP
Do a farrier's job — SHOE
Do a gardener's job — RAKE, REPOT
Do a good turn — HELP
Do a grammar chore — PARSE
Do a hair-dresser's job — TEASE
Do a hawker's job — VEND
Do a journalist's job — EDIT
Do a laundry chore — SOAK
Do a mending job — RESEW
Do a party job — CATER
Do a photographer's job — ENLARGE
Do a plasterer's job — CEIL
Do a pressing chore — IRON
Do a publishing job — EDIT
Do a razing job — BLAST
Do a road job — PAVE, WIDEN
Do a roundup job — ROPE
Do a sailor's job — SWAB
Do a schuss — SKI
Do a selling job — FLOG
Do a slow burn — FUME, SMOULDER
Do a stevedore's work — LADE
Do a tailor's job — REFIT, RESEW
Do a tailoring job — ALTER
Do a Tuesday job — IRON
Do again — REPEAT
Do an about-face — FLIP
Do an auditing chore — RE ADD
Do an usher's job — SEAT
Do aquatints — ETCH
Do archeology work — DIG
Do arithmetic — ADD
Do art work — PAINT
Do as told — OBEY
Do away with — CANCEL, DISCARD, DROP, VOID
Do away with completely — ABOLISH
Do better — TOP
Do business — TRADE
Do business on Wall Street — INVEST
Do come in — ENTER
Do cryptography — DECIPHER
Do damage — MAR
Do detective work — SOLVE
Do farm work — PLOW
Do handiwork — TAT
Do handwork — KNIT
Do housework — CLEAN, MOP
Do in — BEAT, DEFEAT
Do in, comic style — ZAP
Do Latin homework — PARSE
Do like — MIMIC
Do needlework — KNIT
Do not rush in dressing — PREEN
Do nothing — REST, SLEEP
Do oneself proud — PREVAIL
Do or go — VERB
Do over — REVAMP
Do over the bathroom — RETILE
Do over the lawn — RESOD
Do over the walls — REPAPER
Do penance — ATONE
Do pull-ups — CHIN
Do regular exercise — KEEP FIT
Do road work — PAVE
Do roadwork — REPAVE
Do sums — ADD
Do tailoring — ALTER
Do the backstroke — SWIM
Do the crawl — SWIM
Do the sights — TOUR
Do time — SERVE
Do up — ADORN, WASH, WRAP
Do up brown — CHEAT
Do up gifts — WRAP
Do ushering — SEAT
Do well — PROSPER
Do winter road job — PLOW
Do without — FORGO
Do wrong — SIN
Do's and dont's — CUSTOMS, RULES
Do, re and mi — NOTES
Do-gooder — LIBERAL
Do-it-yourself bar — SALAD
Dobbin — MARE
Dobbin gait — TROT
Dobbin's domicile — STABLE
Dobbin's fare — OATS
Dobbin's guide — REIN
Dobbin's morsel — OAT
Dobos or Sacher — TORTE
Doc — MEDIC
Docile — TAME
Dock — BASIN, BOB, PIER
Dock area — SHIPSIDE
Dock landing — PIER
Dock support — PILE
Dockers' org. — ILA
Docket — AGENDA
Docket items — CASES
Dockmackie — SHRUB
Docks — MOORS
Dockworkers' org. — ILA

Doctor — HEALER, MEDICATE, PHD, TREAT
Doctor Bubbles? — FIZZICIAN
Doctor Mirabilis — ROGER BACON
Doctor or shaman — HEALER
Doctor with bedside manner? — GENTLE BEN CASEY
Doctor's bills — FEES
Doctor's favorite Bach works? — ORGAN SONATAS
Doctor's org. — AMA
Doctor's prescription — DOSAGE
Doctor's residence? — BEDSIDE MANOR
Doctor-author — SPOCK
Doctoral degree hurdles — ORALS
Doctoral exams — ORALS
Doctorow novel — LOON LAKE
Doctrinal divisions — SECTS
Doctrinal groups — SECTS
Doctrine — DOGMA, ISM, RULE, TENET
Document: Abbr. — CERT
Documentary film hero — NANOOK
Dodder — SHAKE, TOTTER
Doddering — ANILE, FEEBLE, INFIRM
Dodecanese dazzler? — GREEK GODDESS
Dodecanese Island — LEROS, RHODES
Dodecanese Island: It. sp. — LERO
Dodge — ELUDE, EVADE, PARRY
Dodge City lawman — EARP
Dodge City location — KANSAS
Dodge, as taxes — EVADE
Dodger "preacher" — ROE
Dodger great — REESE
Dodger Hall of Famer — REESE
Dodger mound man — PENA
Dodger's action — EVADING
Dodgers' forte — BASEBALL
Dodgers' home turf — LOS ANGELES
Dodgers' old field — EBBETS
Dodges — AVOIDS
Dodo — NINNY
Doe or ewe — FEMALE
Doe or Roe — DEER, NAME
Doer — WORKER
Doer's suffix — ATOR, ISTS
Does a baker's job — KNEADS
Does a farm job — SOWS
Does a good turn — HELPS
Does a journalist's job — REPORTS
Does a narrator's job — RETELLS
Does a roofing job — TARS
Does a supermarket chore — BAGS
Does an editor's job — REVISES
Does an office job — FILES
Does exceptionally well — STARS
Does farming — PLOWS
Does handiwork — TATS
Does household chores — CLEANS
Does lawn work — SODS
Does simple math — ADDS
Does some landscaping — SODS
Does some whittling — PARES
Does some woolgathering — DAYDREAMS
Does the correct thing — FLIES RIGHT
Does the floor — MOPS
Does the unexpected — SURPRISES
Does' spouses — HARTS
Does, e.g. — DEER
Doesn't heed — IGNORES
Doff — REMOVE, SHED
Doffs the lid — UNHATS
Dog — AIREDALE
Dog _____ — TAG
Dog buried in Hyde Park — FALA
Dog disease — MANGE
Dog doc — VET
Dog follower — SLED
Dog in "Annie" — SANDY
Dog in "Punch and Judy" — TOBY
Dog in a Barrie play — NANA
Dog in Garfield's life — ODIE
Dog lovers' org. — AKC
Dog of 104A — ASTA
Dog of primer fame — SPOT
Dog of whodunits — ASTA
Dog or flop attachment — EARED
Dog or schooner — PRAIRIE
Dog owner's need — LEASH
Dog show entry — POODLE
Dog star — SIRIUS
Dog tag — IDENT
Dog tags, for short — IDS
Dog that went to Oz — TOTO
Dog used for hunting badgers? — DACHSHUND
Dog with two Tins on his tail — RIN
Dog's bane — FLEA
Dog's doc — VET
Dog's foot — PAW
Dog's home away from home — KENNEL
Dog, for one — STAR
Doge's domain, once — VENICE
Dogear — FOLD
Dogface — SOLDIER
Dogfall — KEELS
Dogfall, in wrestling — TIE
Dogged pursuers? — BLOODHOUNDS
Doggie-bag cadidate — ORT
Doggie-bag items — ORTS
Doggle lead-in — BOON
Doggone it — RATS
Doghouse — KENNEL
Dogie — CALF
Dogie catcher — LASSO
Dogie's domain — RANGE
Dogie's kin — STEER
Dogie, e.g. — STRAY
Dogma — CREDO, CREED, DOCTRINE, ISM, TENET
Dogmatic — FORMAL
Dogpatch family — YOKUM
Dogpatch hero — ABNER
Dogpatch sobriquet — LIL
Dogpatcher — ABNER
Dogs and cats — PETS
Dogs give them — PAWS
Dogwood pests — BORERS
Doha's emirate — QATAR
Doily's cousin — COASTER
Doing — ACTING
Doing a circus job — TAMING
Doing business — OPEN
Doing road shows — ON TOUR
Doit — SOU
Dolce _____ niente — FAR
Dolce far _____ (pleasant idleness) — NIENTE
Dolce vita — GOOD LIFE
Doldrums — BLUES
Dole out — ALLOT, METE, RATION
Doled out — METED
Doleful — LOW, SAD
Doles — METES
Dolittle and Kildare — DRS
Dolittle, e.g. — DOCTOR
Doll baby — TOY
Doll talk — MAMA
Doll up — DRESS, PREEN
Doll's utterance — MAMA
Dollar bills — ONES, SINGLES
Dollar fig. — AMT
Dollars for quarters — RENT
Dolley or James — MADISON
Dollops — LUMPS
Dolly Varden, e.g. — DRESS
Dolly's welcome — HELLO
Dolmans — SLEEVES
Dolores _____ Rio — DEL
Dolorous — SAD, SORROWFUL
Dolphin — FISH
Dolphin's blind cousin — SUSU
Dolphins' coach — SHULA
Dolphins' home — MIAMI
Dolt — DULLARD, OAF
Dolts — ASSES
Dom. Health aide — HHA

Domain — AREA, REALM, RULE, SPHERE
Dombey's kin — SON
Dome in Rome — DUOMO
Domelike structure — CUPOLA
Domesday book money — ORA
Domestic — MAID, SERVANT
Domestic chirper — HOUSE SPARROW
Domestic fowl — DORKING
Domestic pest — ROACH
Domestic prelate — PRIEST
Domestic travel slogan — SEE AMERICA FIRST
Domesticate — TAME
Domesticated bird — FOWL
Domicile — HOME
Domicile in London — DIGS
Domicile in Paris — MAISON
Domicile: Abbr. — RES
Dominant themes — MOTIFS
Dominate — RULE
Domineer — BULLY
Domineering — LORDLY
Domingo — PLACIDO
Domingo specialty — ARIA
Domingo's domain — OPERA
Domingo, for one — TENOR
Domini lead-in — ANNO
Dominion — EMPIRE, RULE
Dominion _____ (Canada) — DAY
Dominique's donation — EGG
Domino — MASK
Domino or Waller — FATS
Don — WEAR
Don _____ — JUAN
Don _____ de la Vega (Zorro) — DIEGO
Don Giovanni, as a seaman? — LATEEN LOVER
Don Ho prop — LEI
Don Jose's love — CARMEN
Don Juan type — TRIFLER
Don Juan's kiss — BESO
Don Juan's mother — INEZ
Don Juan, for one — ROUE
Don Marquis's cockroach — ARCHY
Don or San — JUAN
Don Pasquale's nephew — ERNESTO
Don who played Barney — KNOTTS
Don's January — ENERO
Don's PGA warm-up? — JANUARY THAW
Don't dele — STET
Don't look _____! — AT ME
Don't, in Dundee — DINNA
Dona's domain — CASA
Donahue — PHIL
Donahue and Silvers — PHILS
Donald's ex — IVANA
Donate — BESTOW
Donate, in Dundee — GIE
Donated — GAVE, GIVEN
Donates — GIVES
Donations — ALMS
Done — COMPLETE
Done for — KAPUT
Done in — SLAIN
Done with — OVER
Donees — TAKERS
Donets Basin area — UKRAINE
Donizetti opera — LUCIA
Donizetti's _____ Bolena — ANNA
Donkey — ASS
Donkey sounds — BRAYS
Donkey's alternative — CARROT
Donkey's cousin — ASS
Donkey's Mexican cousin — BURRO
Donkey, e.g. — ENGINE
Donkey, in Bavaria — ESEL
Donkey, in Frankfurt — ESEL
Donkeys — ASSES
Donkeys, to Brits — MOKES
Donkeys: Fr. — ANES
Donned — WORE
Donner or Khyber — PASS
Donnybrook — BRAWL, MELEE
Donovan or Shaw — ARTIE
Donovan's agcy. — OSS
Dons — WEARS
Donut — SINKER
Doodle — JOT
Doohickey fancier — GADGETEER
Dooley's first name — SAM
Doolittle and namesakes — ELIZAS
Doom — FATE
Doomed area in Chekhov play — ORCHARD
Doomsday Book money — ORA
Doone — LORNA
Doone and Luft — LORNA
Doone of fiction — LORNA
Door clasp — HASP
Door description — AJAR
Door fasteners — HINGES
Door fastening — HASP
Door feature — HINGE, SILL
Door hinge — HASP
Door in a floor — TRAP
Door part — HINGE, JAMB, KNOB
Door section — PANEL
Door sign — ENTER
Door support — HINGE
Door-frame part — LINTEL
Doorkeeper becomes Broadway composer — COLE PORTER
Doorway — PORTAL
Doorway curtain — PORTIERE
Doorway sign — EXIT
Doozy — LULU
Dope — INFO
Dopey, Doc, Sneezy et al. — DWARFS
Doppelgänger's kin — CLONE
Dorcas was one — SEWER
Doris Duke and Barbara Hutton — HEIRESSES
Doris or Clarence — DAY
Doris or Dennis — DAY
Doris's 1937 diversion — A DAY AT THE RACES
Dorm mate — ROOMIE
Dorm resident — COED
Dormant — ASLEEP, LATENT
Dormant Calif. volcano — SHASTA
Dormant state — LATENCY
Dormer units — PANES
Dormouse — LEROT
Dorothea _____ Dix — LYNDE
Dorothy _____ of "See No Evil" — ALISON
Dorothy Lamour's trademark — SARONG
Dorothy's destination — KANSAS
Dorothy's pet — TOTO
Dorset town — BEAMINS
Dory accessory — OAR
Dos Passos trilogy — USA
Dos preceder — UNO
Dossier — FILE
Dostoyevsky novel — CRIME AND PUNISHMENT, IDIOT
Dostoyevsky's Prince Myshkin — IDIOT
Dot — DAB, FLECK, MARK, PERIOD, POINT
Dot in a radio code — DIT
Dote — ADMIRE, BABY, CODDLE, FAVOR, HUMOR
Dote on — ADORE, LOVE
Doted on — ADULATED
Doting — FOND
Dotted, in heraldry — SEME
Dotters of i's, crossers of t's — PEDANTS
Douar denizens — ARABS
Douay Bible book — OSEE
Double — DUAL, PAIR, STAND IN
Double agent — MOLE, SPY
Double apartment — DUPLEX
Double back — RETURN
Double barrelled _____ — SHOTGUN
Double boiler — SAUCEPAN
Double curve — ESS, OGEE
Double edge or seam — WELT
Double feature — MOVIES
Double or triple follower — DECKER
Double quartet — OCTET

Double road curve — ESS
Double shuffle, to Hines — STEP
Double this for a Chilean river — BIO
Double this for a perfume — YLANG
Double wing — FORMATION
Double-chambered — BICAMERAL
Double-cross — BETRAY, CHEAT
Double-eagle — GOLD COIN
Double-edged sword — EPEE
Double-hung — SASHES
Double-reed instrument — OBOE
Double-reed player — OBOIST
Double-runner — SLED
Double-talk — GIBBERISH
Doubleday — ABNER
Doubleday and Yokum — ABNERS
Doubles — PAIRS, TWO BASE HITS, TWOS
Doublet — COUPLE
Doubly strange — ODDER
Doubly stylish — DRESSIER
Doubly tender — SORER
Doubly: Prefix — TWI
Doubt — MISGIVE, UNCERTAINTY
Doubter — SKEPTIC
Doubtful — MOOT
Doubting Thomas — SKEPTIC
Doubtless — CERTAIN, SURE
Douce — SOBER, SWEET
Douceur — BRIBE, TIP
Dough — MONEY, MOOLA
Dough leavening — YEAST
Dough raiser — YEAST
Doughboy's alley — POILU
Doughboy? — BAKER
Doughboys — DOG SOLDIERS
Doughnut feature — HOLE
Doughnut shaped — TORIC
Doughnut shop? — A HOLE IN ONE
Doughnut: Slang — SINKER
Douglas _____ — FIRS
Douglas Fairbanks Sr. role — ZORRO
Douglas fir — CONIFER
Douglas Hyde's republic — EIRE
Douglas, for one — FIR
Dour — GLUM
Douse — IMMERSE
Douse in clean water — RINSE
Dove sound — COO
Dove's quest — PEACE
Dove, in Barcelona — PALOMA
Dover or lemon — SOLE
Dover's fish — SOLE
Dover's st. — DEL
Doves sounds — COOS
Dovetail part — TENON
Dow-Jones average — INDEX
Dowdy old gossip — FRUMP
Dowel — PEG, PIN, ROD
Down and out — DESTITUTE
Down at the heels — SEEDY, TACKY
Down dweller — DOE
Down in the dumps — BLUE
Down in the mouth — DISCOURAGED
Down market players — WALL STREET BEARS
Down payment — DEPOSIT
Down provider — EIDER
Down source — EIDER
Down to earth — PRAGMATIC
Down under animals — DINGOS, KOALAS, ROOS
Down under bird — EMEU
Down under capital — CANBERRA
Down Under fellows — AUSSIES
Down under leaper — ROO
Down Under leaper, for short — ROO
Down under lumberman — PINER
Down under metropolis — ADELAIDE
Down Under sea mile — NAUT
Down under symbols — EMUS
Down wind — ALEE
Down with, in Paris — A BAS
Downcast — BLUE, SAD
Downed — ATE
Downfall — RAIN, RUIN
Downgraded — ABASED, DEMOTED
Downhill — DECLINING
Downhill surface — SLOPE
Downhill track — DESCENT
Downing Street lady — THATCHER
Downing Street number — TEN
Downright — ABSOLUTE, ARRANT, OPEN, PLAIN
Downright — TOTAL, UTTER
Downright plain — STARK
Downright stupid — IDIOTIC
Downs of TV — HUGH
Downs or salts — EPSOM
Downslide — FALL
Downswing — TREND
Downtown sign — EATS
Downward slides — SLUMPS
Downwind — ALEE
Downy — FLOSSY, SOFT
Downy duck — EIDER
Downy or hairy tree climber — WOODPECKER
Dowry — DOT, GIFT
Dowse — DRENCH, SOAK
Dowser — WAND, WATERWITCH
Dowser's needs — RODS
Doxology — HYMN
Doxy — TRULL
Doyen — DEAN, ELDER
Doyle novel "Micah _____" — CLARKE
Doyle opus of 1887 — A STUDY IN SCARLET
Doyle opus of 1891 — RED HEADED LEAGUE
Doyle's "The _____ of the Four" — SIGN
Doyle's middle name — CONAN
Doze — CATNAP, NOD, SLEEP
Dozens of mos. — YRS
Dozes off — NAPS
Dozing one — NAPPER
DP gear — DTE
Dr. _____, "Buck Rogers" scientist — HUER
Dr. Dan, of "Doonesbury" — ASHER
Dr. Dolittle's Sophie, e.g. — SEAL
Dr. K's target — HOME PLATE
Dr. K's turf — SHEA
Dr. Kildare portrayer — AYRES
Dr. Rhine's field — ESP
Dr. Salk — JONAS
Dr. Seuss classic — HOW THE GRINCH STOLE CHRISTMAS
Dr. Seuss's Thidwick — MOOSE
Dr. Slops creator — STERNE
Dr. Spooner's "_____ wenches" — BEERY
Dr. Zhivago's love — LARA
Drab — DULL, MOUSEY
Drab condition — UNINTERESTING
Drab shade — OLIVE
Drab; not stylish — DOWDY
Drachm — DRAM
Dracula — VAMPIRE
Draft — OUTLINE, SKETCH
Draft again — REDO
Draft animal — MULE
Draft board letters — SSS
Draft classification — ONE A
Draft horses — PERCHERONS
Draft in London — CHEQUE
Draft inits. — SSS
Draft or train endings — EES
Drafting-yard occupants — CATTLE
Drag — LUG
Drag along — HAUL
Drag out — PROTRACT
Dragged — HAULED
Dragged, as to court — HALED
Draggletail — SLATTERN
Dragon — MONSTER
Dragon head, ginger tail — SNAP

Dragon killed by Hercules — LADON
Dragon of song — PUFF
Dragon of the skies — DRACO
Dragonfly — DARNING NEEDLE
Drags along — LUGS
Drain — EMPTY, SAP, TAP
Drainage aid — SWALE
Drainage ditches — SOUGHS
Drains — SUMPS
Drains the strength — SAPS
Drains, in a way — SAPS
Drake and Buck — MALES
Drake or gander — MALE
Drakes or harts — MALES
Dram — BIT, MITE
Dram or gram — UNIT
Drama award — OBIE
Drama by Goethe — FAUST
Drama critics baseball delights? — TRIPLE PLAYS
Drama lead-in — MELO
Drama suited for reading — CLOSET PLAY
Dramatic comment — ASIDE
Dramatic creations — SCENES
Dramatic devices — ASIDES
Dramatic element in "Key Largo" — GALE
Dramatic locale — THEATER
Dramatic spot for a cat — HOT TIN ROOF
Dramatic streetcar — DESIRE
Dramatics — ACTING
Dramatis personae — CAST
Dramatist — WRITER
Dramatist Ben — HECHT
Dramatist Chekhov — ANTON
Dramatist Clifford — ODETS
Dramatist David from Dubuque — RABE
Dramatist de Vega — LOPE
Dramatist Fugard — ATHOL
Dramatist Jones (Baraka) — LEROI
Dramatist O'Casey — SEAN
Dramatist turns apiarist — EDWARD ALBEEKEEPER
Dramatize — EMOTE
Drape — ADJUST, CLOTHE, COVER
Draped — HUNG
Drapery — SWAG
Drapery cord — TORSADE
Drat — BOTHER, CON-FOUND, DASH
Drat or shucks, e.g. — MINCED OATH
Draught — DRAFT, SKETCH
Draught beer container — CASK, KEG
Dravidian language — TAMIL
Draw — TIE
Draw _____ on (aim at) — A BEAD
Draw a _____: split hairs — FINE LINE
Draw a conclusion — INFER
Draw forth — EDUCE, EVOKE
Draw into — EMBROIL
Draw liquid — POUR, TAP
Draw off — SIPHON
Draw off through a bent tube — SIPHON
Draw out — EDUCE
Draw up plans — DESIGN
Draw wages — EARN
Draw, in a way — ETCH
Drawer pull — KNOB
Drawing for a winner — LOTTING
Drawing need — CRAYON
Drawing room — SALON
Drawl — TWANG
Drawn — LINED, TIED
Drawn out — LENGTHY
Drawn tight — TAUT
Draws a bead on — SIGHTS
Draws attention to oneself — UPSTAGES
Draws closer — NEARS
Draws out — ELICITS
Dray — CART
Dread — FEAR
Dreaded — FEARED
Dreaded Amazonian serpent — FERDELANCE
Dreaded fly — TSETSE
Dreaded one — OGRE
Dreadful — DIRE
Dreadful place to hole up — HIDEOUS HIDEOUT
Dream of every gold digger — BIG SPENDER
Dream, in Madrid — SUENO
Dream, in Paris — REVE
Dream: Comb. form — ONEIR, ONEIRO, ONIRO
Dream: Prefix — ONIRO
Dreamers — WISHERS
Dreamily romantic — MOON STRUCK, STARRY EYED
Dreaming — ASLEEP
Dreamland — SLEEP
Dreary, in Dundee — DREE
Dred Scott decision Justice — TANEY
Dredged the dough — FLOURED
Dregs — LEES, SEDIMENT
Dreiser novel, with "The" — TITAN
Drench — SOAK, SOUSE
Drenches — SOAKS, SOUSES
Dresden duck — ENTE
Dresden's river — ELBE
Dress — CLOTHE, GARB, GOWN, RIG
Dress a salad — TOSS
Dress accessories — BELTS
Dress accessory — PIN, SASH
Dress carefully — PREEN
Dress designer Simpson — ADELE
Dress fabrics — MOIRES
Dress feathers — PREEN
Dress for a rani — SARI
Dress for display — ARRAY
Dress fussily — PREEN
Dress gaudily — BEDIZEN
Dress in — DON
Dress in fine clothing, with "up" — TOG
Dress material — ORGANDY
Dress ornament — FALLAL
Dress style — A LINE
Dress trims — RICKRACKS
Dress with care — PREEN
Dress wood — PLANE
Dress, with "up" — TOG
Dressed — CLAD
Dressed for a ball — GOWNED
Dressed for the stage — COSTUMED
Dressed to the _____ — NINES
Dresser — BUREAU
Dresser part — DRAWER
Dresses — INVESTS
Dresses up — ADORNS
Dressing accompaniment — SALAD
Dressing holders — CRUETS
Dressing ingredient — VINEGAR
Dressing of gauze and plaster of Paris — CAST
Dressing rooms? — CLOTHES QUARTERS
Dressler and Osmond — MARIES
Dressler of old films — MARIE
Dressmaker's need — PATTERN
Dressmaker's tuck — DART
Dressmakers concerns — HEMS
Dressy gloves from Britain — DOESKINS
Dressy operetta? — HMS PINAFORE
Drew — ATTRACTED
Drew a bead on — AIMED
Drew back in fear before — SHIED AT
Drew out — EDUCED
Dreyfus defender — ZOLA
Dreyfus or Housman — ALFRED
Dribble — SEEP
Driblet — BITE, SCRAP
Dried — SERE
Dried and withered — SERE
Dried fish — HERRING
Dried flower head — TEASEL
Dried fruit — PRUNE

Dried grape — RAISIN
Dried orchid tubers — SALEP
Dried out — STALE
Dried up — ARID, SERE
Dries — SERES
Driest Spanish sherry — FINO
Drift — TENOR, TREND
Drifter — TRAMP
Drill — TRAIN
Drill command — AT EASE, HALT
Drill's partner — BIT
Drilled — BORED
Drink additive — ICE
Drink cooler — ICE
Drink for Ivan — VODKA
Drink made with eggs — NOG
Drink noisily — SLURP
Drink of the gods — NECTAR
Drink to excess — TOPE
Drink too much — BESOT, TOPE
Drink with gusto — QUAFF
Drink without moderation — TOPE
Drinker — SOT
Drinking bout — BENDER
Drinking spree — JAG
Drinks at the fountain — COLAS
Drinks for football fans — COCOAS
Drinks gingerly — SIPS
Drinks like a cat — LAPS
Drinks to — TOASTS
Drip stopper — WASHER
Dripping — ASOAK
Drippy sound — PLOP
Drive — MOTOR, PROPEL, PUSH, URGE
Drive a nail obliquely — TOE
Drive along leisurely — TOOTLE
Drive away — REPEL, ROUT, SHOO
Drive back — REPEL
Drive crazy — MADDEN
Drive forward — PROPEL
Drive in — TAMP
Drive of a kind — LIBIDO
Drive off — REPEL
Drive or officer — LINE
Drive out — EXPEL, ROUST
Drive out of bed — ROUST
Drive the car — MOTOR
Drive-in — MOVIE
Drive-in waitress or waiter — CARHOP
Driver for Nicklaus — WOOD
Driver's command — GEE
Driver's exam — ROAD TEST
Driver's lic., cr. card, etc. — IDS
Driver's main course? — CLUB STEAK
Driver's org. — AAA
Driver's turn — ESS
Driver's visual aid — WIND-SHIELD WIPER
Drives at high speed — BAR-RELS
Drives nails obliquely — TOES
Drives the getaway car — ABETS
Driveways, at times — OVALS
Driving force — ENGINE
Driving hazard — SLEET
Driving jacket — CARCOAT
Driving mishap — DENT
Driving need: Abbr. — LIC
Drizzle — RAIN, MIST
Drizzled — RAINED
Droll — FUNNY
Drome beginning — AERO
Drome lead-in — AERO
Drone — HUM
Drone of a bagpipe — BURDEN
Drone's home — HIVE
Drool — DRIBBLE, SLAVER
Droop — LOP, SAG, SLOUCH, SLUMP, TIRE, WILT
Droop sharply — PLUMMET
Droop to one side — SAG
Droop-nosed flyers, for short — SSTS
Drooping — ALOP, LANGUID, LIMP
Droops — SAGS
Droopy eared dog — SPRINGER SPANIEL
Drop — FALL
Drop _____(write) — A LINE
Drop a brick — GOOF
Drop a fly — ERR
Drop a line — WRITE
Drop a stitch — ERR
Drop anchor — MOOR
Drop behind — LAG
Drop by unexpectedly — POP IN
Drop heavily — PLOP
Drop in — VISIT
Drop in the Vegas bucket — CHIP
Drop off — NOD
Drop shots, in the ring — KOS
Drop-lid desks — STIPOS
Dropped — FELL
Dropped back — RECEDED
Drops a bundle — LOSES
Drops a fly — ERRS
Drops bait — DAPS
Drops in the morning — DEW
Drops off — SHEDS
Drops pounds — DIETS
Drops the ball — ERRS
Drops: Lat. abbr. — GTT
Dropsy — EDEMA
Droshky — CARRIAGE
Dross of metal — SLAG
Droughty — ARID
Drove — HERD, RODE
Drove (with "off") — TEED
Drove a nail on the slant — TOED
Drove away — SHOOED
Drove of cattle — HERD
Drover's concern — HERD
Drown out — DEAFEN
Drowse — NAP
Drowsy — LOGY
Drs. org. — AMA
Drub — CANE, FLOG
Drudge — GRIND, MOIL, PLOD
Drudgery — GRIND, MOIL
Drudges — PEONS
Drug — LSD
Drug addict — NARCOMANIAC
Drug buster — NARC
Drug cop — NARC
Drug dealers? — PHARMA-CISTS
Drug plant — ALOE
Drug-culture leader in the 60's — LEARY
Drugged drink — MICKEY
Druggist's measure — DRAM
Drugstore cowboys, usually — OGLERS
Drugstore purchase — ASPIRIN
Drum — SNARE
Drum beat — RATATAT
Drum call to arms — RAPPEL
Drum on — THRUM
Drum roll — TATTOO
Drum up — SOLICIT
Drum's companion — FIFE
Drumbeat — TATTOO
Drumbeat in a regular, even rhythm — TATTOO
Drummer's gear — TRAPS
Drummers' cousins — XYLO-PHONISTS
Drunk, in Dijon — IVRE
Drunkard — SOT, SOUSE
Drury Lane composer — ARNE
Drury or Tate — ALLEN
Dry — ARID, BLOT, DRAIN, DULL, DROLL, SAHARAN, SERE
Dry — THIRSTY, WIPE, WRY
Dry cleaner's focus — STAIN
Dry cleaners' problems — SPOTS
Dry comic? — XERO MOSTEL
Dry condition — ARIDNESS
Dry goods — LINENS
Dry goods dealer — MERCER
Dry gully — ARROYO
Dry Lakes — PLAYAS
Dry martini with a pickled onion — GIBSON
Dry measure — PECK
Dry off — WIPE
Dry out — PARCH
Dry red wine — CHIANTI

Dry riverbed — WADI
Dry run — TEST
Dry streambed — COULEE
Dry up — SHRIVEL
Dry watercourse of the Middle East — WADI
Dry, as an environment — XERIC
Dry, as bubbly — BRUT
Dry, as wine — SEC
Dry, in a way — BLOT
Dry, powdered starch — SAGO
Dry, to a vintner — SEC
Dry: Comb. form — XER, XERO
Dry: Prefix — XER
Dryad's home — TREE
Dryden's "The _____ Ladies" — RIVAL
Dryer trap item — LINT
Drying chambers — KILNS
Drying frame — AIRER
Drying ovens — OASTS
Drysdale or Mattingly — DON
Du Maurier's "Jamaica _____" — INN
Duad — TWO
Duant — DEE
Dub — ENTITLE
Dub — NAME
Dub over — RENAME
Dubai or Kuwait — EMIRATE
Dubai or Kuwait: Var — EMEERATE
Dubbed — NAMED
Dubbed one — SIR
Dubious — FISHY
Dublin natives — IRISH
DuBose Heyward hero — PORGY
Dubuque native — IOWAN
Ducat — SEQUIN
Duchamp subject — NUDE
Duchy of _____-Coburg — SAXE
Duck — AVOID, BEND, CROUCH, DODGE, EIDER, EVADE
Duck — STOOP, TEAL
Duck blind — SHELTER
Duck down — EIDER
Duck for apples — BOB
Duck genus — ANAS
Duck hunter's dog — GOLDEN RETRIEVER
Duck or under follower — LING
Duck, in Essen — ENTE
Ducks — AVOIDS
Ducks the issue — EVADES
Duct — VAS
Ducts — VASA
Dud — LEMON
Dude ranch events — HAYRIDES
Dudley Do-Right's love — NELL
Dudley or Garry — MOORE
Dudley or Roger — MOORE
Dudley, Melba or Roger — MOORE
Duds — LEMONS
Due — OWED
Due e cinque — SETTE
Due follower — TRE
Due preceder — UNE
Due-process process — TRIAL
Duel memento — SCAR
Duel preceders — SLAPS
Duel weapon — SABER
Dueler's weapon — EPEE
Dueling sword — EPEE, ESTOC, RAPIER
Dueling weapon — EPEE
Duelist Burr — AARON
Dues — FEE
Dues paying constituent — MEMBER
Duffer's curving drive — SLICE
Duffer's dream — PAR
Dug a stope — MINED
Dugout — ABRI, CANOE, DEN
Dukakis or Bentsen — DEMOCRAT
Dukas' "La _____" — PERI
Duke Ellington-Billy Strayhorn opus — PERFUME SUITE
Duke in Cannes — DUC
Duke of Cornwall's wife — REGAN
Duke of Edinburgh — PHILLIP
Duke of Elchingen — NEY
Duke of Milan in "The Tempest" — PROSPERO
Duke or Day — DORIS
Duke or earl — NOBLEMAN
Duke's ex — ASTIN
Duke's wife — PEERESS
Duke, for one — TITLE
Dulcet — MUSICAL, SWEET
Dulcimer's descendant — PIANO
Dull — ARID, BLAH, BLUNT, MATTE, OBTUSE
Dull boy maker — ALL WORK AND NO PLAY
Dull finish — ARD, MATTE
Dull hollow sounds — CLONKS
Dull pain — ACHE
Dull partygoer — DRAG
Dull person — BORE, DRIP
Dull sounds — THUDS
Dull surface — MATTE
Dull, annoyingly slow — POKY
Dull, explosive sound — CHUG
Dull, to Donne — DREAR
Dull-witted — OBTUSE
Dull: Slang — BLAH
Dullard — DODO
Dullards — BORES
Dulls — BLUNTS
Dumas character — ARAMIS, HOS
Dumas Dantes — EDMOND
Dumas Musketeer — ATHOS
Dumas' words of togetherness — ALL FOR ONE
DuMaurier's "Jamaica _____" — INN
Dumb — DENSE
Dumb bunny — STUPE
Dumbarton natives — SCOTS
Dumbarton Oaks, e.g. — ESTATE
Dumbbell — MORON
Dumbfounds — AMAZES, AWES
Dumbo or Jumbo — ELEPHANT
Dumbo's were jumbo — EARS
Dummy — SIMP
Dummy Charlie's voice — EDGAR BERGEN
Dump — UNLOAD
Dumpy — STOCKY
Duncan or Dennis — SANDY
Dunce — ASS
Dunces — DOPES, OAFS
Dundee dances — REELS
Dundee denial — NAE
Dundee denizens — SCOTS
Dundee dowry — TOCHER
Dundee inheritance — LAIRDSHIP
Dundee no — NAE
Dunderhead — ASS
Dungaree fabric — DENIM
Dungarees — LEVIS
Dunne or Cara — IRENE
Duo — PAIR
Duo after em — EN O
Duo quadrupled — OCTO
Duomo statue in Firenzo — PIETA
Duos: Abbr. — PRS
Dupe — HOCUS, STOOGE
Duped — GULLED
Duplicate — CLONE, COPY, SPARE, DITTO
Duplicate of a sort — CLONE
Duplicate, for short — FAX
Duplicate, in a way — CLONE
Duplicated genetically — CLONED
Durable columnist in California? — OAK LANDERS
Durable fiber — SISAL
Durable film star — CARY GRANT
Durable material — SERGE
Durable pop singer — TONY MARTIN
Durable wood — EBONY
Durango day — DIA
Durango demonstrative — ESA
Durango dog — MEXICAN HAIRLESS

Durante song word — INKA
Durante's heritage — ITALIAN
Duration — LIFE, TERM
Duration of life — AGE
Duration of position — TENURE
Durer's "Paumgärtner _____" — ALTAR
Duress — FORCE
Durham campus: Abbr. — UNH
During — AMID, AMIDST
Duroc — HOG, PIG
Duroc's home — STY
Durocher and Gorcey — LEOS
Durocher and namesakes — LEOS
Durocher of baseball — LEO
Durum — WHEAT
Dusk to dawn — NIGHT
Dusk to dusk — DAY
Dusk, to Donne — EEN
Dusseldorf donkey — ESEL
Dusters — RAGS
Dusters make up — FEATHERS
Dustin Hoffman role — RATSO
Dustin Hoffman role: 1974 — LENNY
Dustin in "Midnight Cowboy" — RATSO
Dusting powders — TALCS
Dustup — RHUBARB
Dutch _____ — TREAT
Dutch Antilles — ARUBA
Dutch artist Hals — FRANS
Dutch bulb — TULIP
Dutch cheese — EDAM
Dutch cheese town — EDAM
Dutch cheeses — GOUDAS
Dutch city — EDE
Dutch commune — EDE
Dutch commune and Nigerian city — EDES
Dutch explorer — TASMAN
Dutch export — EDAM, TULIP
Dutch genre display — STEENS
Dutch genre painter — STEEN
Dutch gentleman — HEER
Dutch head of state — QUEEN
Dutch humanist — ERASMUS
Dutch name of French river — MAAS
Dutch navigator Tasman — ABEL
Dutch or French follower — DOOR
Dutch painter — STEEN
Dutch painter Frans — HALS
Dutch painter Jan — STEEN
Dutch painter: 1638-1709 — HOBBEMA
Dutch philosopher: 1632-77 — SPINOZA
Dutch South African — BOER
Dutch town — STAD
Dutch treat — EDAM
Dutch uncle — EME, OOM
Dutra and Sarazen, to Ben? — HOGANS HEROES
Duty — TARIFF
Dwarf — STUNT
Dwarf _____ iris — CRESTED
Dwarf buffalo — ANOA
Dwarfed plant — BONSAI
Dweeb — NERD
Dwell — ABIDE, RESIDE
Dwelled — LIVED
Dweller in a Yemeni port — ADENI
Dweller in Hades — SHADE
Dweller in Salalah, e.g. — OMANI
Dwelling — ABODE
Dwellings, in Spain — CASAS
Dwelt — RESIDED
Dwight _____, U.S. high jumper — STONES
Dwight's opponent — ADLAI
Dwight's wife — MAMIE
Dwindle — EBB, WANE
Dwindling — WANING
Dyads — PAIRS
Dybbuks — DEMONS
Dye — CYANIN
Dye containers — VATS
Dye for the Picts — WOAD
Dye plant — ANIL
Dye vessel — VAT
Dyed rabbit fur — CONY
Dyed Stake, N.Y. — PAINTED POST
Dyeing method — BATIK
Dyeing specialist — TANNER
Dyes — ANILS
Dyestuff — ANIL
Dykstra of baseball — LEN
Dynamic beginning — AERO
Dynamic monogram? — TNT
Dynamiter's need — FUSE
Dynamites — BLASTS
Dynamo parts — STATORS

E

E African republic — KENYA
E Asian weight — TAEL
E followers — EFFS
E Indian cereal grass: var. — RAGI
E Indian herb — TIL
E Indian herb roots — CHOYS
E Indian instrument — VINA
E Indian sailor — LASCAR
E Indian tree with honey-filled flowers — MOWRA
E of Wyo — NEB
E St. Louis, e.g. — ILL CITY
E Texas river — SABINE
E to J connection — FGHI
E Wisconsin city — NEENAH
E-J links — FGHI
E. Power Bigg's instrument — ORGAN
E.B. White's Charlotte, for one — SOW
E.C. Bently's sleuth — TRENT
E.M. Forster's "A _____ to India" — PASSAGE
E.M.K. is one — SEN
E.O.M. item — BILL
E.R. personnel — RNS
E.R.A. or R.B.I. — STAT
E.T. — ALIEN
E.T. or Alf — ALIEN
E.T.'s transport? — UFO
E.T., e.g. — ALIEN
E.T.O. leader — DDE
E.T.O. town — ST LO
Each — APIECE, EVERY
Each and every — ALL
Eager — AGOG, AVID, EARNEST, EXCITED
Eager beaver — DOER, HUSTLER
Eager with curiosity — AGOG
Eagerly desires — ASPIRES
Eagerly expecting — A TIP
Eagerness — ALACRITY
Eagle — ERN
Eagle ex-coach "Greasy" — NEALE
Eagle on high — AQUILA
Eagle or Ranger — LONE
Eagle Scout — RANK
Eagle's claw — TALON
Eagle's nest — AERIE
Eagle, for one — SCOUT

Eagle: Comb. form — AETO
Eagled a par-three hole — ACED
Eagles and Oilers — FOOTBALL PLAYERS
Eaglet's birthplace — AERIE
Eagre — BORE
Eaker and Wolfert — IRAS
Eamon de _____ — VALERA
Ear ache — PAIN
Ear bone — STAPES
Ear covering — MUFF
Ear features — LOBES
Ear of grain — SPIKE
Ear part — DRUM, LOBE
Ear section — INNER
Ear trumpet — CORNET
Ear-grabber — HEY
Ear: Comb. form — AURI, OTO
Ear: Pref. — OTO
Eardrop — EARRING
Eared seal — OTARY
Eared vessel — EWER
Earhart — AMELIA
Earhart's copilot — NOONAN
Earl _____ Biggers — DERR
Earl _____ Hines, jazz pianist — FATHA
Earl Biggers' middle name — DERR
Earl Derr Biggers sleuth — CHAN
Earl Grey, for one — TEA
Earl Hines nickname — FATHA
Earl of Avon — EDEN
Earl of Baltimore — WEAVER
Earl of Chatham's surname — PITT
Earl or baron — PEER
Earl's equals — COUNTS
Earless or elephant — SEAL
Earlier — OLDER
Earlier bid — PREOFFER
Earliest — ORIGINAL
Earlobe adjuncts — TRAGI
Early — BEGINNING, FIRST, INITIAL, PRIOR
Early 1900's school of painters — ASHCAN
Early American "money" — BEADS
Early American dwelling — TEPEE
Early April game — OPENER
Early auto magnate — OLDS
Early autos — REOS
Early aviator? — ICARUS
Early bird's time — DAYBREAK
Early bloomer — ANEMONE, CANDY TUFT, IRIS
Early boat — ARL
Early boat-builder and Webster — NOAH
Early Breton — CELT
Early Briton — PICT
Early Britons — CELTS
Early calculator — ABACUS
Early car — REO
Early Castro ally — CHE
Early cenobite — ESSENE
Early Christian — ESSENE
Early Christian center — EDESSA
Early Christian church — BASILICA
Early cinema mogul — LOEW
Early color — OCHRE
Early days — ONSET
Early dwelling — CAVE
Early Egyptian — NILOT
Early English council — WITAN
Early fig-leaf wearer — EVE
Early fruit fancier — ADAM
Early furrier — ASTOR
Early garden — EDEN
Early German — TEUTON
Early Greek colony — IONIA
Early guitar — LUTE
Early harpsichord — SPINET
Early hours — AMS
Early in the 4th cen.: Rom. — CCCI
Early Iranian — MEDE
Early Japanese immigrant — ISSEI
Early late show host — PAAR
Early Latin version of Scriptures — ITALA
Early man — PEKING
Early monk — ESSENE
Early mystery writer — POE
Early N.A. money — WAMPUM
Early New England houses — SALTBOXES
Early New York railroad — ERIE
Early nuclear agcy. — AEC
Early O'Neill play — ILE
Early or late Crawford — PEACH
Early penman's chore — SCRIBING
Early people of Mexico — AZTECS
Early Persian — MEDE
Early Peruvian — INCAN
Early porch — STOA
Early post of J Caesar — EDILE
Early pre-college exam — PSAT
Early product of Morgantown, W.Va — GLASS
Early Quaker — PENN
Early residents — SETTLERS
Early safety lamp for miners — DAVY
Early Scandinavian — GEAT
Early seamstress — ROSS
Early settler — COLONIST
Early shelter — CAVE
Early show — MATINEE
Early space traveler — ENOS
Early superliner? — ARK
Early television picture — MONOCHROME
Early Turkish leader — OSMAN
Early TV couple — OZZIE AND HARRIET
Early TV sensation — BERLE
Early TV surname — DOODY
Early TV's March — HAL
Early Venetian trader — POLO
Early victim — ABEL
Early weight lifter — ATLAS
Early, to Pepys — BETIMES
Early-American fur merchant — ASTOR
Earmark — BAND, TAG
Earn — MERIT
Earn a living — BRING HOME THE BACON
Earned — GARNERED
Earned 10%, perhaps — REPRESENTED
Earned, before tax — GROSSED
Earnest — EAGER
Earnest money — DEPOSIT
Earnest reformer — DO GOODER
Earnest request — APPEAL
Earnings — GAIN, PAY, WAGES
Earns before deductions — GROSSES
Earring — BAUBLE, DROP, JEWEL
Earring locale — LOBE
Earring sites — LOBES
Ears catch note of derision? — SCORN ON THE COB
Earth-borer — AUGER
Earth — DIRT, SOD, SOIL
Earth circuit — GROUND
Earth color, for Turner — OCHRE
Earth goddess — GAEA, TERRA
Earth mover — BULLDOZER
Earth movers — HOES
Earth or baseball — SPHERE
Earth pigment — OCHRE
Earth sci. — GEOL
Earth used as a fertilizer — MARL
Earth's envelope: Abbr. — ATM
Earth's nearest neighbor — MARS
Earth, for one — ORB, PLANET
Earth: Comb. form — AGRO, GEO
Earth: Prefix — GEO
Eartha of song — KITT
Earthborn — HUMAN, MORTAL
Earthen jar — OLLA
Earthen pot — CRUSE
Earthen pot for stew — OLLA
Earthen pots — OLLAS
Earthenware — POTTERY
Earthenware jar — OLLA
Earthenware maker — POTTER

Earthenware pot — OLLA
Earthenware vessel — OLLA
Earthling — MORTAL
Earthly — WORLDLY
Earthnut — GOOBER
Earthquake — SEISM, TREMBLER
Earthquake feature — TREMOR
Earthquake geologists? — FAULT FINDERS
Earthquake measuring equipment — SEISMOGRAPH
Earthquake measuring scale — RICHTER
Earthquake shock — TREMOR
Earthquake site: June 21, 1990 — IRAN
Earthquake: Comb. form — SEISMO
Earthquakes — SEISMS
Earthwork — BULWARK
Earthy — FUNKY, SALTY, SEXY
Earthy color — OCHRE, SIENNA
Earthy deposit — MARL
Earthy pigment — OCHRE
Earthy yellow or red — OCHOR
Earwax — CERUMEN
Ease — ABATE
Ease of movement — FREEDOM
Ease off — WANE
Easel — FRAME
Easel adjunct — PALETTE
Eases — LETS UP
Easier to reach — CLOSER
Easier, as a job — SOFTER
Easiest — SOFTEST
Easily — HANDILY
Easily bent — LITHE
Easily carried — PORTABLE
Easily frightened — SKITTERY
Easily tempted — FRAIL
Easily understood — LUCID
Easing of tension between nations — DETENTE
Easing up — ABATING
East — ORIENT
East African native — SOMALI
East China Sea island — MATSU
East coast time — EST
East ending — ERN
East Flanders capital — GHENT
East Flanders city: Fr. — ALOST
East German city — HALLE
East in Essen — OST
East India Co. VIP — CLIVE
East Indian cedar — DEODAR
East Indian herb — TIL
East Indian pepper plants — BETELS
East Indian sailor — LASCAR
East Indian tree — ROHAN, TEAK, UPSO
East Indies water bird — KORA
East Netherlands commune — EDE
East of Ill. — IND
East of the Urals — ASIA
East of Zaire — UGANDA
East or West ender — ERN
East or West follower — ENDER
East Orange, N.J. college — UPSALA
East River span — HELLGATE BRIDGE
East wind personification — EARUS
East, in Berlin — OST
East-Northeast abbr. — ENE
East-West confrontation — COLD WAR
Easter _____ — BUNNY
Easter bloom — LILY
Easter celebrant — CHURCHGOER
Easter celebrants — GENTILES
Easter entree — HAM
Easter finery — HATS
Easter Island goes native — RAPA NUI
Easter Island statue — MOAI
Easter quarry fragment? — SHARD BOILED EGGS
Easter season: Abbr. — SPR
Easter stroller — PARADER
Eastern — ASIATIC
Eastern accessories — OBIS
Eastern Bishop's title — ABBA
Eastern Bloc country — USSR
Eastern chief — EMEER
Eastern Chinese province — HONAN
Eastern Church oraria — STOLES
Eastern coll. — NYU
Eastern country — JAPAN
Eastern deity — ALLAH
Eastern dinner treat — HAM
Eastern European — SERB, SLAV
Eastern garb — SARI
Eastern Hemisphere — ORIENT
Eastern Hemisphere continent — ASIA
Eastern inn — SERIA
Eastern land mass — ASIA
Eastern leader — EMEER
Eastern maid — AMAH
Eastern name — ALI
Eastern nanny — AMAH
Eastern newts — EFTS
Eastern noble — AMIR
Eastern obeisance — SALAAM
Eastern observance — TET
Eastern part of the Earth — ASIA
Eastern potentate — EMIR
Eastern redskin — ERIE
Eastern religion — BUDDHISM, ISLAM
Eastern ruler — AMEER, EMEER
Eastern salutations — SALAAMS
Eastern shrine — PAGODA
Eastern state — DELAWARE
Eastern temple — PAGODA
Eastern title — EMEER, IMAM
Eastern V.I.P. — AMIR, EMIR
Eastern weight — TAEL
Easy — A PIECE OF CAKE, EFFORTLESS, FACILE, NAIVE
Easy — LIGHT, RELAXED, SIMPLE
Easy as _____ — ABC, PIE
Easy as pie — PIECE OF CAKE
Easy existence — LIFE OF RILEY
Easy gait — CANTER, LOPE
Easy job — SNAP
Easy mark — SOFT TOUCH
Easy on the eyes — AS PRETTY AS A PICTURE, COMELY
Easy on the eyes — NOT HARD TO LOOK AT
Easy on the eyes — WELL FAVORED
Easy or grub — STREET
Easy pace — DOGTROT
Easy stride — LOPE
Easy target — SITTING DUCK
Easy thing in a saying — PIE
Easy to achieve — CINCH
Easy to handle, at sea — YARE
Easy to understand — LUCID
Easy touch — SOFTY
Easy's partner — FREE
Easy's symbol — PIE
Easy-going — CALM, LAX
Easy: Scot. — EITH
Eat — CONSUME, DEVOUR, INGEST
Eat (one's) words — RETRACT
Eat a calorie-free diet? — PUT WORDS IN ONES MOUTH
Eat away — ERODE
Eat elegantly — DINE
Eat late — SUP
Eat like a bird — PECK
Eat like a chicken — PECK
Eat like a horse — CHAMP
Eat like a mouse — GNAW
Eat or drink greedily — LAP UP
Eat sparingly — FAST
Eatable — GOOD
Eatable pine seeds — PINONS
Eaten away — CORRODED
Eater's alcove — DINETTE
Eatery — DINER
Eatery order — BLT
Eatery special — BLUEPLATE
Eating implement — FORK

Eating places — LUNCHROOMS
Eating plan — DIET
Eating regimen — DIET
Eats — DINES, FOOD
Eats well — DINES
Eats with "down" — CHOWS
Eau de vie — BRANDY
Eaves drop — ICICLE
Eaves spout — GUTTER
Eavesdropping aid — TAP
Eban of Israel — ABBA
Ebb — WANE
Ebb and neap — TIDES
Ebb's opposite — FLOW
Ebb, e.g. — TIDE
Ebbed — RECEDED
Ebbs — ABATES
Ebenezer — CHAPEL
Ebenezer's word — BAH
Eber's son — PELEG
Ebert and Siskel, e.g. — REVIEWERS
Ebony — BLACK, WOOD
Ebro and Segura — RIOS
Ebro for one — RIO
Ebroy Tajo — RIOS
Ecce — BEHOLD
Eccentric — ODD, POTTY, STRANGE
Eccentric orbit point — APSIS
Eccentric person — GINK
Eccentrically — ODDLY
Eccles. title — RT REV
Ecclesiastic — CLERIC
Ecclesiastic states ruler — POPE
Ecclesiastic vestment — ALB
Ecclesiastical cap — BIRETTA
Ecclesiastical cape — ORALE
Ecclesiastical courts — ROTAS
Ecclesiastical division — PARISH
Ecclesiastical tribunal — ROTA
Ecclesiastical vessel — AMPULLA
Ecclesiastical vestment — ALB, STOLE
Ecclesiastical wear — ALB, FANON, ORALE
Echelon — GRADE, LEVEL
Echelon formation — VEE
Echidna's diet — ANTS
Echidna's morsel — ANT
Echidna's snack — ANTS
Echinate — THORNY
Echo — PARROT, REPEAT, REPORT, RESOUND
Echoed — RESOUNDED
Eclat — FLAIR
Eclectic — BROAD
Eclipse — OBSCURE
Eclipse cycle — SAROS
Ecol. agcy. — EPA
Ecol. watchdog — EPA
Ecole event — LECON
Ecole inhabitant — ELEVE
Ecole people — ELEVES
Ecologist's concern — EROSION
Economic — FISCAL, MONEY
Economic measure: Abbr. — GNP
Economic or logical starter — SOCIO
Economically disadvantaged — POOR
Economist Adam — SMITH
Economist John Maynard — KEYNES
Economist Thorstein — VEBLEN
Economize — SAVE
Economize, in a way — RETRENCH
Economizes — SCRIMPS
Ecru — BEIGE
Ecstasy — BLISS, RAPTURE
Ecstasy's partner — AGONY
Ecuador island group — GALAPAGOS
Ecuador's capital — QUITO
Ecuador's tennis champ — SEGURA
Ecuadorean salad ingredient? — QUITOMATO
Ecumenical — UNITY
Ed Koch's former question — HOW AM I DOING
Ed Norton's milieu — SEWER
Ed or Leon — AMES
Ed or Nancy — AMES
Ed's notation — DELE
Ed, of Lou Grant — ASNER
Ed. degrees — MAS
Ed. partnership — PTA
Ed.'s reading matter — MSS
Edacious — GREEDY
Edam or Gouda — CHEESE
Eddie Cantor hit of 1926 — BYE BYE BLACKBIRD
Eddies — SWIRLS
Eddy — SWIRL
Eddy role — MOUNTIE
Eddy, in "Rose Marie" — MOUNTIE
Eddy-MacDonald number — DUET
Edema — SWELLING
Eden dweller — ABEL, ADAM
Eden exile — ABEL
Eden outcast — CAIN
Eden resident — EVE
Eden's earldom — AVON
Eden: anagram — NEED
Edenite — ABEL, CAIN
Edgar _____ Masters — LEE
Edgar _____ Poe — ALLAN
Edgar and Emmy — AWARDS
Edgar Rice Burroughs hero — TARZAN
Edge — BORDER, BRIM, FRINGE, LIP, MARGIN, RIM, TIP
Edge — SIDLE, VERGE
Edge along — INCH
Edge forward — SIDLE
Edge of a sort — ACE UP ONES SLEEVE
Edge: Abbr. — MARG
Edged — BORDERED
Edges a razor — STROPS
Edges furtively — SIDLES
Edging — PICOT
Edgy — TENSE
Edible bud — CAPER
Edible fruit — PAPAW
Edible fruit of black nightshade — SUNBERRY
Edible fungi — CEPES
Edible fungus — MOREL
Edible grain — OAT
Edible green fruit — APPLE, KIWI
Edible Japanese plant — UDO
Edible mollusk — ABALONE, CLAM
Edible mushroom — CEP, MOREL
Edible pods — OKRA
Edible ring — ONION
Edible root of the tropics — TARO
Edible seaweed — DULSE
Edible seeds — SESAMES
Edible starch — SAGO
Edible tuber — TARO
Edict — FIAT, UKASE
Edicts — FIATS
Edifice — HOUSE
Edifice extension — ELL
Edifice occupied by Congress — CAPITOL
Edinburgh and York — DUKES
Edison — INVENTOR
Edison contemporary — TESLA
Edison's birthplace in Ohio — MILAN
Edison's middle name, et al. — ALVAS
Edison's Ohio birthplace — MILAN
Edit — CENSOR, CORRECT, EMEND, REVISE
Edit a text for publication — REDACT
Edith or Maurice — EVANS
Edith or Maurice of theater fame — EVANS
Edith Wharton opus — THE HOUSE OF MIRTH
Editing action by editors — REJECTING
Edition — COPY
Editor — DIASKEUAST, REDACTOR

Editor of "The Masses" — EASTMAN
Editor's concern — MSS
Editor's count — LINEAGE
Editor's insertion mark (^) — CARET
Editor's mark — CARET, DELE
Editor's need — ERASERS
Editor's notations — STETS
Editor's note — DELE, STET
Editor's tool — ERASER
Editor's word — STET
Editor, at times — EMENDER
Editor, sometimes — FIDDLER ON THE PROOF
Editorial touches — STYLINGS
Editors' are blue — PENCILS
Edits — EMENDS, REDACTS
Edmond O'Brien film: 1949 — DOA
Edmonton athlete on ice — OILER
Edmonton hockey player — OILER
Edmonton's Prov. — ALTA
Edna Ferber book — SO BIG
Edna May Oliver role: 1933 — THE RED QUEEN
Edna of Broadway — BEST
Edna's edibles? — MILLAYS FILETS
Edomite's ancestor — ESAU
Edomites' capital — PETRA
Edson-Hasen comic strip — DONDI
Educ. degree — EDD, SBED
Educ. group — PTA
Educ. TV — NET
Educand — STUDENT
Educate — INSTRUCT, SCHOOL, TRAIN, TUTOR
Educated — LETTERED
Education — INSTRUCTION
Education deg. — BAE
Education org. — NEA
Education specialists — TEACHERS
Educator Horace — MANN
Educator Nicholas ____: 1862-1947 — MURRAY BUTLER
Educator Willard — EMMA
Educe — ELICIT
Edward Kennedy Ellington — DUKE
Edward Lear specialty — LIMERICK
Edward's sister — ANNE
EEC country — GER
Eek! — YIPE
Eels — MORAYS, CONGERS
Eerie door opener? — SKELETON KEY
Eerie scribe? — GHOST WRITER
Eerie solution? — WITCH HAZEL
Eero Saarinen's dad — ELIEL
Efface — NULLIFY
Effect — RESULT
Effect's companion — CAUSE
Effect's partner — CAUSE
Effective — OPERANT, POTENT
Effervesce — FOAM
Effervescing device — AERATOR
Effete — DECADENT, WEAK
Efficacy — VIRTUE
Effigy — DUMMY
Efflux — EMANATION
Effort — STAB, TRY
Effort to find a lost letter — TRACE
Effortless — EASY, FACILE, FLUENT, SIMPLE
Effortlessness — EASE
Effrontery — GALL
Effulge — RADIATE
Effulgence — SHINE
Effuse — POUR
Efrem Zimbalist's teacher — AUER
Eft — NEWT
Eg. and Syr. once — UAR
Egg-shaped — OVATE, OVOID
Egg — IMPEL
Egg ____ yong — FOO
Egg a la ____ — RUSSE
Egg beater — MIXER
Egg beverage — NOG
Egg box — CARTON
Egg case — SHELL
Egg cell — OVUM
Egg dishes — OMELETS
Egg drinks — NOGS
Egg on — COAX, GOAD, SPUR, URGE
Egg part — YOLK
Egg shelters — HATCHERIES
Egg specialties — OMELETS
Egg white — ALBUMEN
Egg white liquid — GLAIR
Egg, in Paris — OEUF
Egg, to Nero — OVUM
Egg-shaped fruit — LIME
Egg: Comb. form — OVI
Egged on — GOADED
Egghead — BRAIN, HUMPTY DUMPTY, SMART BELL
Eggnog additive — NUTMEG
Eggs — OVA, ROE
Eggs needing a wash? — DIRTY DOZEN
Eggs to Ovid — OVA
Eggs, for Caesar's salad — OVA
Eggs, in ancient Rome — OVA
Ego — CONCEIT, PRIDE, SELF, VANITY
Egotist of myth — NARCISSUS
Egotistic — SMUG, VAIN
Egregious — INANE
Egress — EXIT
Egret's territory — MARSH
Egrets — HERONS
Egyp.-Syr. alliance 1958-61 — UAR
Egypt's Anwar — SADAT
Egypt's capital — CAIRO
Egypt's dam — ASWAN
Egypt's first president — NASSER
Egypt's Sadat — ANWAR
Egypt's second president — SADAT
Egypt, formerly (1958-1961) abbr. — UAR
Egypt, queen for short — CLEO
Egypt, statesman — SADAT
Egyptian — NILOT
Egyptian amulet — MENAT, SCARAB
Egyptian beetle — SCARAB
Egyptian Christians — COPTS
Egyptian church language — COPTIC
Egyptian city on the Nile — ASYUT
Egyptian cobra — ASP
Egyptian cotton — SAK
Egyptian courage? — COPTIC NERVE
Egyptian cross — ANKH
Egyptian dam site — ASWAN
Egyptian dancing girl — ALME
Egyptian deity — ATON, ISIS
Egyptian dry measure — ARDEB
Egyptian geishas — ALMAS
Egyptian god — AMON, ATEN, OSIRIS
Egyptian god of artisans — PTAH
Egyptian god of pleasure — BES
Egyptian goddess — ISIS
Egyptian goddess of sky — NUT
Egyptian killer — ASP
Egyptian king — RAMESES, SETI
Egyptian king, familiarly — TUT
Egyptian king, for short — TUT
Egyptian lake — NASSER
Egyptian lettuce? — CAIRO-MAINE
Egyptian maid — IRAS
Egyptian manipulator? — CAIRO PRACTOR
Egyptian moon goddess — ISIS
Egyptian port — SUEZ
Egyptian queen of the gods — SATI
Egyptian river — NILE
Egyptian setting-sun god — TEM
Egyptian skink — ADDA
Egyptian solar diety — ATEN
Egyptian statesman — SADAT
Egyptian sun disk — ATEN
Egyptian sun god — AMON, TEM
Egyptian talisman — SCARAB

Egyptian tomb — PYRAMID
Egyptian units of capacity — ARDEBS
Egyptian-born film actor — OMAR SHARIF
Eh _____! — BIEN
Eh, to Pierre: Fr. — HEIN
Eheu! — ALAS
Eider — DUCK
Eidolon — GHOST, IDEAL
Eiffel or ivory — TOWER
Eiger, for one — ALP
Eight bits — BYTE
Eight follower — TEEN
Eight furlongs — MILE
Eight maids a-singing — OCTET
Eight tones above a given one — OCTAVE
Eight, in Ancona — OCHO
Eight, in Essen — ACHT
Eight, in Oaxaca — OCHO
Eight, in Oviedo — OCHO
Eight- _____ shell — OARED
Eight: Comb. form — OCTA, OCTO
Eighteenth letter — SIGMA
Eighth-century Chinese poet — LI PO
Eighth greek letter — THETA
Eighth part of a circle — OCTANT
Eights, in Spain — OCHOS
Eighty-six — EJECT
Eins plus zwei — DREI
Einstein — ALBERT
Einstein's birthplace — ULM
Einstein's fourth dimension — TIME
Einstein's Princeton hdqrs. — IAS
Einzellage: Ger. — VINEYARD
Eisenhower and Turner — IKES
Eisenhower waist-hugger — JACKET
Eisenhower's "Crusade in _____" — EUROPE
Eisenhower's Secretary of State — DULLES
Eisenhut, e.g. — ALP
Eisenhut, for one — ALP
Eiswein — WINE
Either — AND OR
Either or or: Lat. — AUT
Either team — SIDE
Eject — OUST
Eject from school — EXPEL
Eject, as lava — SPEW
Ejected — SPEWED
Ekberg or Bryant — ANITA
Ekberg or Loos — ANITA
Eke out — STRETCH
El _____, artist — GRECO
El _____, Heston role — CID
El _____, on the Rio Grande — PASO
El _____, Spanish hero — CID
El _____, Texas — PASO
El _____, Toledo painter — GRECO
El Bahr — NILE
El Greco's "View of _____" — TOLEDO
El Greco's homeland — CRETE
El Misti's locale — ANDES
El Prado favorite — GOYA
El-_____, WW II battle — ALAMEIN
Elaborate — ORNATE
Elaborate carving on molding — GARDON
Elaborate inlaid work — BUHL
Elaborate pretense — CHARADE
Elan — PANACHE
Elanet — KITE
Elapids — SERPENTS
Elapsed — PAST
Elastic — GARTER
Elastic substances — GUMS
Elastic undergarment — CORSET
Elastic wood — YEW
Elate — INSPIRE
Elated — COCK A HOOP, GLAD, HAPPY AS A LARK
Elated — IN SEVENTH HEAVEN, WALKING ON AIR
Elated — JUMPING FOR JOY, ON CLOUD NINE
Elated — ON TOP OF THE WORLD, IN HIGH SPIRITS
Elbe feeder — ISER, SAALE
Elbe tributary — EGER, OHLE, SAALE
Elbow — JOSTLE, POKE, PROD, SHOVE
Elbow bender — SOT
Elbow grease — EFFORT
Elbow one's way in a crowd — JOSTLE
Elbow room — LEEWAY, SPACE
Elbridge _____; VP under Madison — GERRY
Elder — SENIOR
Elder (girl): Gr. — AINEE
Elder Beery brother — NOAH
Elder or Trevino — LEE
Eldest member of a group — DOYEN
Eldest, in Essone — AINE
Eldritch — EERIE, EERY, WEIRD
Eleanor Roosevelt's column — MY DAY
Elec. abbr. — AMP, REL
Elec. measures — AMPS
Elect — OPT
Elect. meas. — AMP HR
Elected — CHOSE, OPTED
Elected the incumbent — RESEATED
Electees — INS
Electing — OPTING
Election district — PRECINCT
Election grouping — SLATE
Election winners — INS
Electioneer — STUMP
Elector — VOTER
Electra's brother — ORESTES
Electric — STATIC
Electric _____ — EEL
Electric catfish — RAAD
Electric light — ARC
Electric measures — OHMS
Electric power — WATT
Electric spark — ARC
Electric swimmers — EELS
Electrical actuator — SOLENOID
Electrical adjunct — ADAPTOR
Electrical device — LAMP
Electrical failure — BROWNOUT
Electrical force — ELOD
Electrical generator — DYNAMO
Electrical outputs — AMPERES
Electrical parts produced by friction — STATIC
Electrical resistance units — OHMS
Electrical safety device — FUSE
Electrical strength — AMPERAGE
Electrical unit of resistance — OHM
Electrical units — AMPS, FARADS, OHMS, RELS, VOLTS, WATTS
Electrically charged atom — ION
Electrically charged particles — IONS
Electrician's unit — VOLT
Electrician, at times — WIRER
Electrician-inventor — EDISON
Electrician-inventor Nikola — TESLA
Electricity abbr. — AMP
Electrified particle — ION
Electrify — SHOCK, STUN
Electrifying agcy. — REA
Electro-magnetic unit of magnetomotive force — GILBERT
Electro-magnetic wave amplifier — MASER
Electrocardiogram, for short — ECG
Electrode — ANODE
Electrode bridge — ARC
Electrode type — CATHODE
Electron tube — DIODE, TRIODE
Electron tube replacement — TRANSISTOR
Electron tube used to generate microwaves — KLYSTRON

Electronic device — DIODE
Electronic medical device — PACEMAKER
Elects — OPTS
Eleemosynar's largess — ALMS
Elegance — LUXE, STYLE
Elegant — CHIC, POSH, REFINED, RITZY, SWANKY
Elegant apartment — SALON
Elegant room — SALON
Elegiac forms — ODES
Elem. and gram. — SCHS
Element — FACTOR, IRON
Element #10 — NEON
Element of a moral code — ETHIC
Element resembling tin — CADMIUM
Elementary — BASIC
Elephant Boy of filmdom — SABU
Elephant driver and keeper, in India — MAHOUT
Elephant of children's books — BABAR
Elephant of yore — MASTODON
Elephant rider's seat — HOWDAH
Elephant's tooth — TUSK
Elephantine — GIANT
Elevate — LIFT, RAISE, UPRAISE
Elevate in rank — PROMOTE, RAISE
Elevated — LIFTED
Elevated habitation — AERIE
Elevated in pitch — STEEPED
Elevated railroads — ELS
Elevating posts — STILTS
Elevation — HEIGHT
Elevation: Abbr. — HGT
Elevations: Abbr. — HTS
Elevator button — DOWN
Elevator cages — CARS
Elevator carriage — CAR
Elevator inventor — OTIS
Elevator man — OTIS
Elevator route — DOWN
Eleve's school — ECOLE
Eleven's numerals — ONES
Eleven: Fr. — ONZE
Eleventh letter of the Greek alphabet — LAMBDA
Eleventh president — POLK
Elevs. — ALTS, MTS
Elf — FAY, OUPHE, PIXIE
Elf of Persian myth — PERI
Elf or imp — SPRITE
Elgar's "_____ and Circumstance" marches — POMP
Elgar's "_____ Variations" — ENIGMA
Eli's place — YALE
Elia — LAMB
Elia's specialty — ESSAY
Elia, to Lamb — ALIAS
Elias or Gordie — HOWE
Elicit — EDUCE
Elide — OMIT
Eliel's son — EERO
Eligible — FIT
Eliminate — ERASE, PURGE
Eliminate malfunctions — DEBUG
Elimination game — MUSICAL CHAIRS
Eliot bartender's gig? — THE COCKTAIL PARTY
Eliot's "_____ Bede" — ADAM
Eliot's "cruellest month" — APRIL
Eliot's "The _____ on the Floss" — MILL
Eliot's Adam — BEDE
Eliot's cruelest mo. — APR
Eliot's Marner — SILAS
Elis — YALIES
Elissa of old movies — LANDI
Elite — CREME
Elite group within an organization — CADRE
Elitist — SNOB
Elixir — CURE
Eliz II, for one — SOV
Elizabeth II's title — QUEEN
Elizabeth Mackintosh's pen name — TEY
Elizabeth or Arden — EVE
Elizabeth or Bob of Kansas — DOLE
Elizabeth's daughter and others — ANNES
Elizabeth's I and II, e.g. — RULERS
Elk — WAPITI
Elk or rank — EXALTED RULER
Elk's cousin — MOOSE
Elks' acronym — BPOE
Ell — ANNEX, ELBOW
Ella and Barry — FITZGERALDS
Ella of note — LOGAN
Ella's forte — SCAT
Ella's kind of singing — SCAT
Ellás — GREECE
Ellery Queen portrayer on TV: 1958-59 — NADER
Ellesmere Island explorer — BAFFIN
Ellington or Wellington — DUKE
Ellington's "_____ Doll" — SATIN
Ellington's "Take _____ Train" — THE A
Elliot Ness — G MAN
Ellipses — OVALS
Elliptical — OBLONG, OVAL
Ellis Island visitor — IMMIGRANT
Elm fruit — SAMARA
Elm or mackerel — WAHOO
Elm or maple seed — SAMARA
Elm's offering — SHADE
Elmer Gantry's wife — CLEO
Elongated fish — GAR
Elongated swimmer — EEL
Elongated, as a spheroid — PROLATE
Eloper's secret — NO ONE KNOWS
Elopes — BOLTS
Elopment need, maybe — LADDER
Eloquent speaker — ORATOR
Els, e.g. — RRS
Elsa or Sylvester — FELID
Elsa's champion — LOHENGRIN
Elsa's cousin — LEO
Else — OTHER
Eluate — WASH
Elucidate — CLARIFY
Elude — DODGE
Elusive — CAGEY, EELY
Elusive one — EEL
Elusory — EVASIVE
Elvers — EELS
Elves — SPRITES
Elvis — PRESLEY
Elvis Presley hit — DONT
Elvis Presley's middle name — ARON
Elysium — PARADISE
Em or Jay follower — CEE
Em, to Dorothy — AUNT
Emaciated — GAUNT
Emaciated hunting dog? — BONY SETTER
Emanate — ARISE, OOZE
Emanates — EMITS
Emanation — EFFLUX
Emanations — AURAS
Emancipate — FREE, LET GO, RELEASE
Emancipation Proclamation — DECREE
Emasculate — CASTRATE, UNMAN
Emb. bigwig — AMB
Embankment — LEVEE
Embankment surrounding a fort — RAMPART
Embarrassed — RED, RED FACED, SHEEPISH
Embarrassing moments — SCENES
Embarrassment symptom — REDNESS
Embassy spies — MOLES
Embattled personae — SEXES
Embdem and quink — GEESE
Embellish — ADORN, DECORATE
Embellished — ORNATE
Embellisher — EMBOSSER

Ember — ASH, COAL
Ember _____ — DAYS
Embezzle — FILCH
Emblem — BADGE
Emblem of a sort — LOGO
Emblem of Wales — LEEK
Emblem on British arms — UNICORN
Emblem tag-on — ATIC
Emblem: Abbr. — SYM
Embodiment — AVATAR, EPITOME
Embossed — RAISED
Embossed emblem — SEAL
Embouchure — LIP
Embrace — CLINCH, HOLD, HUG, SQUEEZE
Embrace closely — PRESS
Embraced — ADOPTED
Embraces — CLASPS
Embroided cloths — SAMPLERS
Embroidered with openwork — FAGOTED
Embroidery edging — PURL
Embroidery fabrics — SCRIMS
Embroidery frame — HOOP
Embroidery yarn — CREWEL
Embroil — ENTANGLE, INVOLVE
Embroiled — KNEE DEEP
Emcee Parks — BERT
Emcee's bit — INTRO
Emend — CORRECT, REVISE
Emerald Isle — EIRE, ERIN, IRELAND
Emerald Isle native — IRISHER
Emerge — APPEAR, ARISE, LOOM, SHOW
Emerged — ARISEN
Emergency — CRISIS
Emergency band — POSSE
Emergency guest room — DEN
Emergency resource — SHEET ANCHOR
Emergency troops — MILITIA
Emerges victorious — WINS
Emerson's forte — ESSAY
Emerson's middle name — WALDO
Emery — ABRASIVE
Emery and sandpaper — ABRASIVES
Emery board's cousin — RASP
Emigrate — LEAVE
Emigrations — HEGIRAS
Emily and Wiley — POSTS
Emily of etiquette, et al. — POSTS
Emily or Charlotte — BRONTE
Eminence — NOTE
Eminent — GRAND, NOTED
Eminent evangelist — BILLY GRAHAM
Emir's garment — ABA
Emirate's cargo carrier — OILER
Emissary — LEGATE
Emissions — VAPORS
Emit — EXUDE, SEND UP
Emit an intense beam — LASE
Emit fumes — REEK
Emit like Etna — SPEW
Emit rays — RADIATE
Emit smoke — REEK
Emit violently — ERUCT
Emits vapor — STEAMS
Emitted — EXHALED
Emitted a coherent light — LASED
EMK — TED
Emma Thompson's award — OSCAR
Emmenthaler, e.g. — CHEESE
Emmet — ANT
Emmy-winning series — MASH
Emmy — AWARD
Emmy recipient, e.g. — PRIZE WINNER
Emollient — LOTION
Emoters — HAMS
Emotion — ARDOR
Emotion center — HEART
Emotional — PATHETIC
Emotional disturbance — APATHY
Emotionless — CALLOUS
Emperor of Japan — AKIHITO
Emphasis — ACCENT, STRESS
Emphasis on yes or no — SIREE
Emphasize — STRESS
Emphasize unduly — OVERDO
Emphatic denial — UH UH
Emphatically — FLATLY
Emplace — SITE
Emplaces — SEATS
Employ — APPLY, ENGAGE, HIRE, USE
Employ again — REHIRE
Employ radar — SWEEP
Employed — USED
Employee's quest — RAISE
Employee's reward — RAISE
Employees — HELP, STAFF
Employer — BOSS, MANAGER, USER
Employment training act: Abbr. — CETA
Emporia — MARTS
Emporium — MART, SHOP
Emporium event — SALE
Empower — ENABLE, WARRANT
Emptied the hold — UNLOADED
Empties — DRAINS
Empty — IDLE, INANE, VOID
Empty talk — GAS
Empty words — CLAPTRAP
Empty-headed — DUMB, INANE
Ems and Evian — SPAS
Emu or ostrich — RATITE
Emulate — COPY, ECHO, FOLLOW, IMITATE
Emulate a certain Tom — PEEP
Emulate a farmer — PLOW
Emulate a fish — SWIM
Emulate a ham — EMOTE
Emulate a squirrel — STORE UP
Emulate Al Unser — RACE
Emulate an adder — SLITHER
Emulate Betsy Ross — SEW
Emulate Bing — CROON
Emulate Blossom Seeley — SING
Emulate Brian Boitano — SKATE
Emulate Buonarroti — CARVE
Emulate Casey Stengel — MANAGE
Emulate Charles Carroll — SIGN
Emulate Cicero — ORATE
Emulate closely — APE
Emulate Cohen at Los Angeles — SWIM
Emulate Crosby — CROON
Emulate Debi Thomas — SKATE
Emulate Demosthenes — ORATE
Emulate Dick Weber — BOWL A THREE HUNDRED GAME
Emulate Dürer — ETCH
Emulate Earhart — AVIATE
Emulate ecdysiasts — DISROBE
Emulate Ederlee — SWIM THE ENGLISH CHANNEL
Emulate Edward VIII — ABDICATE
Emulate Electra — MOURN
Emulate Emmett Kelly — CLOWN
Emulate Fawn and Ollie — SHRED
Emulate Fleming — SKATE
Emulate Gorgeous George — WRESTLE
Emulate Goya — ETCH, PAINT
Emulate Gulliver — TRAVEL
Emulate Heiden or Hamill — SKATE
Emulate Henry — ORATE
Emulate Hershiser — PITCH
Emulate Hillary — WORK ONES WAY UP
Emulate Hogarth — ETCH
Emulate Holmes — DEDUCE
Emulate Horner — EAT
Emulate Izaak Walton — FISH
Emulate Jack and Jill — FETCH
Emulate John Hancock — SIGN
Emulate Kanonen — SKI
Emulate Katrina Witt — SKATE
Emulate Lorelei — TEMP
Emulate Madonna — SING
Emulate Mata Hari — SPY

Emulate Mme. Defarge — KNIT
Emulate Niobe — WEEP
Emulate Odom — AVIATE
Emulate Penelope — WEAVE
Emulate Peter Funk — CON
Emulate Petruchio — TAME
Emulate Rembrandt — ETCH
Emulate Roger Bannister — RUN A FOUR MINUTE MILE
Emulate Roger Maris — HIT SIXTY ONE HOME RUNS
Emulate Romeo and Juliet — ELOPE
Emulate S.C. in 1860 — SECEDE
Emulate Scrooge — SNEER
Emulate Sergei Bubka — POLE VAULT NINETEEN FEET
Emulate Slaney — RUN
Emulate some collegians — REUNE
Emulate Tom? — PEEP
Emulate Tomba — SKI
Emulate Vale — CROON
Emulate W.W. II's Rosie — RIVET
Emulate Willem de Kooning — PAINT
Emulate Xanthippe — NAG
Emulate Zayak — SKATE
Emulated — IMITATED
Emulated a roo — LEAPT
Emulated an ecdysiast — STRIPPED
Emulated Bob Richards — VAULTED
Emulated Bonnie and Clyde — ROBBED
Emulated Chaplin — MIMED
Emulated Daedalus — FLEW
Emulated Dorcas — SEWED
Emulated Edwin Booth — ACTED
Emulated Epimenides — SLEPT
Emulated Harvey Birch — SPIED
Emulated Huck Finn — RAFTED
Emulated Irons — ACTED
Emulated Jean-Claude Killy — SKIED
Emulated Jessica — ELOPED
Emulated John Lithgow — ACTED
Emulated Maxwell Perkins — EDITED
Emulated Mehta — LED
Emulated Mr. Chips — TAUGHT
Emulated Mr. Lendl — ACED
Emulated Niobe — WEPT
Emulated Patti LaBelle — SANG
Emulated Pavarotti in concert — ENCORED
Emulated Pearl White — EMOTED
Emulated Red Jacket — ORATED
Emulated Yma Sumac — SANG
Emulated Yorick — JESTED
Emulates — VIES
Emulates a pack rat — SAVES
Emulates a shore bird — WADES
Emulates Baryshnikov — DANCES
Emulates Betsy Ross — SEWS
Emulates Dennis Conner — SAILS
Emulates Dorcas — SEWS
Emulates Gompers — UNIONIZES
Emulates Jehu — SPEEDS
Emulates Marky Mark — RAPS
Emulates Marple — SOLVES
Emulates Muffet — SITS
Emulates Olivier — ACTS
Emulates Petruchio — TAMES
Emulates Spike Lee — DIRECTS
Emulates W.J. Bryan — ORATES
Emulates Xanthippe — NAGS
Emyd — TURTLE
En _____ — GARDE
En _____: short-haired — BROSSE
En pointe — A TIP
En preceders — EMS
Enact — ORDAIN
Enamel — PAINT
Enamel work — CLOISONNE
Enamel-ornamented metalware — TOLE
Enameled metalware — TOLE
Enamelware — TOLE
Enamelware from France — CLOISONNE
Enamored — IN LOVE
Enamored of a knight — SMIT
Encamp — TENT
Encapsulate — ENCYST
Encase — WRAP
Encephalogram — X RAY
Enchant — CHARM, DISARM
Enchantress described in the "Odyssey" — CIRCE
Enchantress who changed men into swine — CIRCE
Encipher — CODE
Encircle — GIRD, RING, WREATHE
Encircle with a belt — GIRD
Encircled — GIRDED
Encircled the moon — ORBITED
Encircled, of old — ORBED
Encircles — BEGIRDS, GIRDS
Enclose — SHUT IN
Enclosed — PENT
Enclosed with a fence — PALED
Enclosed, as a gift — WRAPT
Enclosure — PALE, PEN
Enclosure with a ms. — SASE
Enclosure with a ticket order: Abbr. — SASE
Encolure — MANE
Encomium — ELOGE
Encompassing — AMBIENT
Encore plea — MORE
Encore! — AGAIN, BIS
Encounter — MEET
Encountered — MET
Encounters — MEETS
Encourage — ABET, CHEER ON, INSPIRE, PROD, PROMOTE
Encourage — SPUR, URGE
Encourage a felony — ABET
Encourage, in a way — STOKE
Encouraged — ABETTED, BOOSTED
Encouraged, with "on" — EGGED
Encourages — PRODS, PROMOTES, URGES
Encourages a felon — ABETS
Encouraging shout in Latin America — HOLA
Encroach — USURP
Encrypted — CODED
Encryption keys — CODES
Encumber — SADDLE
Encumber — SADDLE
Encumbrance — LIEN
Encumbrances — DRAGS
Encyclopedic — VAST
End — OMEGA, STOP
End decisively — PUT ONES FOOT DOWN
End in Lyon — COUP DE GRACE
End of a 7:58 AM alert 12 / 7 / 41 — THIS IS NO DRILL
End of a band — ANA
End of a Burns title — SYNE
End of a Doris Day hit — SERA
End of a fable — MORAL
End of a loaf — HEEL
End of a Pope title — THE LOCK
End of a Stein line — A ROSE
End of an O'Neill title — ELMS
End of mob or lob — STER
End of Montana's title — PLATA
End of Poe title — USHER
End of the line — GOAL
End of vigil — ANCE
End product — RESULT
End unexpectedly — ABORT
End with young and old — STER
End-alls' partners — BE ALLS
End-users — PEOPLE
End: Comb. form — TELO
Endanger — JEOPARDIZE
Endangered buffalo — ANOA
Endangered species of Celebes — ANOA
Endangered tree — ELM

Endeavor — AIM, TRY
Endeavored — TRIED
Ended — OVER
Endemic — LOCAL
Ender beginner — REAR
Ending — AIM, FINISH, GOAL, STOP, SWAN SONG
Ending for 76 — ERS
Ending for a niña's name — ITA
Ending for an adjective — IAL
Ending for an inchoative verb — ESCE
Ending for assist or appear — ANCE
Ending for buck or smack — EROO
Ending for cash or front — IERS
Ending for court — ESY
Ending for depend — ENT
Ending for differ or insist — ENT
Ending for labor — ITE
Ending for leg or man — ATEE
Ending for pant or scant — IES
Ending for scant or pant — IES
Ending for tele or talka — THON
Ending for Tyrol or Bengal — ESE
Ending for velvet — EEN
Ending for what or when — EVER
Ending for win or sin — NER
Ending with convey — ANCE
Ending with Dan or span — IEL
Ending with differ or depend — ENCE
Ending with hex or malt — OSE
Ending with Japan or Nepal — ESE
Ending with Japan or Siam — ESE
Ending with Max or Joseph — INE
Ending with myth or iron — ICAL
Ending with part or vint — NER
Ending with Paul or Bernard — INE
Ending with slug or song — FEST
Ending with walk or talk — ATHON
Endings for draft and employ — EES
Endings for lobby and palm — ISTS
Endings for opera and idea — TIONS
Endings for pant and scant — IES
Endings with auction and profit — EERS
Endings with bal and val — ANCES
Endings with farm and bed — STEADS
Endings with oct and eth — ANES
Endless time period — EON
Endlessly — DAY IN AND DAY OUT
Endorse — SEAL
Endorses, for short — OKS
Endow — INDUE, INVEST
Ends — PURPOSES, CEASES
Ends of flights — LANDINGS
Ends' friends — ODDS
Ends, often — LOOSE
Endurance — STAMINA
Endure — ABIDE, BEAR, CONTINUE, LAST, OUTLAST, STAND
Endure distress — SMART
Endure longer — OUTLAST
Endure: Scot. — DREE
Endured — BORNE
Endures — GOES ON, LASTS
Enduring — ENDLESS
ENE plus 90 degrees — SSE
Enemy — FOE
Enemy of the Axis — ALLIES
Enemy snaps? — FOETOGRAPHS
Energetic — EAGER, SPIRITED
Energetic doer — MAN OF ACTION
Energetic one — DYNAMIST
Energizes — LIVENS
Energizes, with "up" — PEPS
Energy — BIRR, LIFE, STEAM, VIM
Energy based on motion — KINETIC
Energy measure — ENTROPY
Energy of motion — KINETIC
Energy restorer — TONIC
Energy source — ATOM, FUEL
Energy units — ERGS, RADS
Enero or febrero — MES
Enervates — SAPS
Enesco's homeland — RUMANIA
Enfant terrible — BRAT
Enfold — EMBRACE
Enfolds — DRAPES
Enforce by threat — COERCE
Enforcement group — POSSE
Enforcement, figuratively — TEETH
Eng. _____ — LIT
Eng. money — STER
Eng. philosopher — LOCKE
Eng. poet — KEATS
Eng. title — OBE
Engage — HIRE, MESH
Engage in _____: (cross swords) — A DUEL
Engage in a physical struggle — WRESTLE
Engage in a skirmish — SPAR
Engage in swordplay — FENCE
Engage the gears — MESH
Engage uke strings — STRUM
Engaged in — WAGED
Engagement: Abbr. — APPT
Engages — HIRES
Engaging one — HIRER
Engagingly disreputable — RAFFISH
Engender — BREED, PROPAGATE
Engendered — BRED
Engine — MOTOR, TURBINE
Engine cooler — RADIATOR
Engine covers — HOODS
Engine fittings — MANIFOLDS
Engine for an aircraft — RADIAL
Engine inventor Rudolf — DIESEL
Engine part — LIFTER
Engine parts — CAMS
Engine sound — CHUG, PURR
Engine valve regulating flow — THROTTLE
Engineer — PLAN
Engineering deg. — BME
England's "Great Commoner" — PITT
England's stand, at one time — ALONE
English — SPIN
English airforce — RAF
English ale month: Abbr. — OCT
English and Irish canines — SETTERS
English apartment — FLAT
English architect Christopher — WREN
English art patron — TATE
English boy's best friend? — HIS MATER
English carbines — STENS
English carpet town — AXMINSTER
English cathedral city — ELY
English cathedral town — ELY
English Channel feeder — EXE, ORNE, TAMAR
English Channel island — SARK
English Channel port — DOVER, POOLE
English chemist: 1877-1945 — ASTON
English chinaware — SPODE
English city with a minster — YORK
English coin — POUND
English commando trained in U.S. — RANGER
English composer — WATTS
English composer and family — ARNES
English composer: 1710-1788 — ARNE
English country festivals — ALES

English county — DORSET, KENT, SHIRE
English county noted for cream — DEVON
English crime fiction writer John _____ — CREASY
English daisy — GOWAN
English derby town — EPSOM
English diplomat — EDEN
English dramatist — PINERO
English dry-goods dealers — DRAPERS
English emblem — ROSE
English essayist — PATER
English explorer — DRAKE, RALEIGH
English institution — TEA
English isle — JERSEY
English monk-historian — BEDE
English musician: 1835-1909 — PROUT
English novelist — READE
English novelist C.P. — SNOW
English novelist Charles — READE
English or French follower — HORN
English painter and art critic — EASTLAKE
English philosopher John — LOCKE
English physicist-inventor: 1802-1875 — WHEATSTONE
English physicist: 1877-1945 — ASTON
English playwright — NOEL COWARD
English playwright-poet — PEELE
English poet — KEATS
English poet Alexander — POPE
English poet John — DONNE
English poet laureate: 1715-18 — ROWE
English poet-diplomat: 1664-1721 — PRIOR
English poet-novelist: 1886-1967 — SASSOON
English princess — ANNE
English pub game — DARTS
English religious reformer: 1485-1555 — LATIMER
English royal family — STUARTS
English royal house — TUDOR
English school — ETON
English school symbol — TIE
English snack shop? — TEA AND SYMPATHY
English stage actor McCowen — ALEC
English star-gazer: 1868-1939 — DYSON
English statesman William — PITT
English subways — TUBES
English tear-jerker? — LONDONION
English title — EARL
English track — ASCOT
English TV inits. — BBC
English weight — STONE
English word for matrimony — WEDLOCK
English: Comb. form — ANGLO
Englishman colloquially — BRIT
Englishmen — BRITONS
Engrave — ETCH, INCISE
Engraved pillar — STELE
Engraver — CHASER
Engraver's pad — DABBER
Engraves — ETCHES
Engraving on a gem — CAMEO
Engraving on wood — WOOD-CUT
Engross — ABSORB, ENGAGE
Engrossed — IMMERSED, RAPT
Engrossed in emotion — RAPT
Engulf — FLOOD
Enhances — ADDS, DEEPENS
Enigmas in the Himalayas — YETIS
Enigmatic — PERPLEXING
Enigmatical — MYSTIFYING
Eniwetok — ATOLL
Enjoy — LIKE, SAVOR
Enjoy a dip — SWIM
Enjoy a lot — GO FOR
Enjoy a meal — DINE
Enjoy a repast — EAT
Enjoy a summer sport — WATER SKI
Enjoy a winter sport — SKI
Enjoy oneself — PARTY
Enjoy the cuisine — DINE
Enjoy the slopes — SKI
Enjoy, with "up" — EAT
Enjoyable — NICE
Enjoyed a julep — DRANK
Enjoyed a repast — ATE
Enjoyed the taste — SAVORED
Enjoyers of haute cuisine — EPICURES
Enjoying great popularity? — RIDING HIGH
Enjoying the QE2 — ASEA
Enjoys literature — READS
Enjoys special privilege — RATES
Enjoys the sun — BASKS
Enl. men — GIS
Enlarge — ADD ON
Enlarge, in a way — WIDEN
Enlarges — DILATES
Enlarging gradually — EVASE
Enlighten — EDIFY, INFORM
Enlist — JOIN, ENROL
Enlist again: G.I. slang — RE UP
Enmesh — TRAMMELL
Enmity — HATRED
Ennis and Crandall — DELS
Ennobled — EDIFIED
Ennui — TEDIUM
Enoch's cousin — ENOS
Enoch's father — CAIN
Enoch, to Seth — NEPHEW
Enos' grandfather — ADAM
Enough — ADEQUATE
Enough, Antonio! — BASTA
Enough, for Shakespeare — ENOW
Enough, musically — ASSA
Enough, old style — ENOW
Enplane — BOARD
Enrage — INCENSE, IRE
Enraged — IRATE, IRED
Enraged one — FUMER
Enrich oneself — FEATHER ONES NEST
Enriched — LARDED
Enriches with fat — LARDS
Enrico Caruso portrayer — MARIO LANZA
Enroll — ENTER
Ensemble — COSTUME, SUITE
Enshrine — ADORE, CHERISH
Enshrined objects — RELICS
Ensign — FLAG
Ensign, for one — RANK
Ensiles — ISOLATES
Ensnare — TRAP
Ensnare, old style — BETRAP
Enstate — INSTAL
Ensue — FOLLOW, SUPER-VENE
Entangle: Var. — IMMESH
Entangled — MIRED
Entanglement — HITCH
Entanglements — WEBS
Entangles — MIRES, SNAGS
Enter — GO IN
Enter a port — PUT IN
Enter a yacht race — SAIL
Enter one's mind — OCCUR
Enter ranks — FALL IN
Enter statistics into a computer — KEY, TYPE
Enter surreptitiously — SNEAK IN
Enter the picture — APPEAR
Entered a race — RAN
Enterprising lad's objective — BRING HOME THE BACON
Enterprising lad's objective — THE TOP OF THE LADDER
Enterprising seafarers of old — PRIVATEERS
Entertain — AMUSE, HOST, REGALE
Entertain queuers in the Strand — BUSK
Entertained, as an idea — HARBORED
Entertainer — ARTISTE
Entertainer Adams — EDIE
Entertainer Bob — HOPE
Entertainer D'Orsay — FIFI

Entertainer Della — REESE
Entertainer Ed — ASNER
Entertainer Gorme — EDIE
Entertainer Horne — LENA
Entertainer Jacques — BREL
Entertainer Johnny — CASH
Entertainer Kazan — LAINIE
Entertainer Little — RICH
Entertainer Lou — RAWLS
Entertainer Luft — LORNA
Entertainer Midler — BETTE
Entertainer Minnelli — LIZA
Entertainer Moore — GARRY, MELBA
Entertainer Rivera — CHITA
Entertainer Susan — ANTON
Entertainer Tennille — TONI
Entertainer Turner — TINA
Entertainer Vic — DAMONE
Entertainer Zadora — PIA
Entertainer's date — GIG
Entertainer's engagement — GIG
Entertainer, old style — ARTISTE
Entertainers — DIVERTERS
Entertainment — PASTIME
Entertainment centers of yore — PENNY ARCADES
Entertainment host, for short — EMCEE
Entertainment to Variety readers? — SHOW BIZNIZ
Entertains — AMUSES
Entertains sumptuously — REGALES
Enthrall — CHARM, ENSLAVE, GRIP, RAVISH
Enthralled — RAPT
Enthrone — SEAT
Enthuse — ELATE, GUSH, INSPIRE
Enthusiasm — ELAN, VIM, ZEAL
Enthusiast — ADDICT, BOOSTER, BUFF, CHAMPION
Enthusiast — EAGER BEAVER, FAN, ZEALOT
Enthusiastic — AVID, EAGER, KEEN
Enthusiastic applause — OVATION
Enthusiastic review — RAVE
Enthusiastically — EAGERLY
Entice — ALLURE, BAIT, LURE, TEMPT
Enticed — WILED
Enticed via deception — ROPED IN
Enticement — BAIT
Enticers — SIRENS
Entices — LEADS ON
Enticing — TEMPTING
Entire — ALL, GROSS, WHOLE
Entire number — ALL
Entire range — GAMUT
Entire; complete — TEETOTAL
Entirely — ALL
Entirety — TOTAL
Entities — UNITS
Entitled to — DUE
Entitlement — BENEFIT
Entitlement program — MEDICARE
Entomb — INTER, INURN
Entr' _____: interlude — ACTE
Entrains — DEPARTS
Entrance — PORTAL
Entrance court — ATRIUM
Entrance fees — ADMISSION
Entrance for a U.M.W. man — ADIT
Entrance for Clementine's dad — ADIT
Entrance of a fugue subject — ANSWER
Entrance to a mine — ADIT
Entrances — ADITS
Entrap — SNARE, TREE
Entre- _____ — NOUS
Entre-nous — HUSH HUSH
Entreat — ASK, BEG, PRAY, PLEAD
Entreated — PLED
Entreaties — PLEAS
Entreats — ASKS
Entreaty — PLEA
Entrechat — LEAP
Entree item — VEAL
Entree, often — ROAST
Entrench oneself — DIG IN
Entries — ITEMS
Entrust once more — RECOMMIT
Entrusted — RELIED
Entry — ITEM
Entry in a list — ITEM
Entry in many a crossword — QUOTE
Entry island — ELLIS
Entry on a French map — ASIE
Entwine — BRAID
Enumerate — COUNT
Enunciation — DICTION
Env. directive — ATTN
Env. enclosure — ENC, SASE
Env. word — ATTN
Envelop — SWATHE, WRAP
Envelope abbr. — ATT, ATTN
Envelope encl. — SASE
Envelope wd. — ATTN
Environmental sci. — ECOL
Environmental subj. — ECOL
Environmental subspecies — ECOTYPE
Environmental watchdog agcy. — EPA
Environs — AREA
Envisioned — DREAMED
Envoy — LEGATE
Enzyme — ASE
Enzymes — PROTEINS
Eosin or henna — DYE
EPA concerns — SMOGS
Ephah / 10 — OMER
Ephalite — HUN
Ephemeral — AERY, BRIEF, PASSING
Ephemeral heavenly blaze — NOVA
Ephriam — BEAR
Ephron of "Heartburn" — NORA
Ephron or Helmer — NORA
Ephus name — DIANA
Epic — HEROIC
Epic finishes? — ENES
Epic poems — EPOS
Epic poetry — EPOPE, EPOS
Epic poetry unit — CANTO
Epic tales — SAGAS
Epical — ILIADIC
Epicede — ODE
Epicurean — GOURMET
Epicurean activity — FEASTING
Epidermis — SKIN
Epigram — SAYING
Epigrams — MOTS
Epinicion — ODE
Epiphany trio — MAGI
Episode — EVENT
Episperm — TESTA
Epitaph for many a monarch — GREAT
Epitaph of Athena — ALEA
Epitaph starter — HERE
Epithelium — TISSUE
Epithet for Samuel Johnson — CHAM
Epithet of Athena — ALEA
Epithet of Gen. Henry Lee — LIGHT HORSE HARRY
Epitome — IDEAL
Epoch — ERA
Epochal — ERAL
Epochs — ERAS
Eponym of an Eastern state — PENN
Eponym's relative — NAMESAKE
Epsom _____ — DOWNS
Equable — EVEN, JUST
Equal — EVEN, MATCH, PEER, RIG, SAME, TIE
Equal quantity — ANA
Equal Rights Amendment acronym — ERA
Equal share for two — HALF
Equal, in Marseilles — EGAL
Equal, to Jacques — EGAL
Equal: Comb. form — ISO, EQUI
Equal: Fr. — EGAL
Equal: Prefix — ISO, PARI
Equaled — RIVALED, TIED
Equality — PAR
Equalize — EVEN
Equals — PEERS
Equatorial country — GABON

Equestrian — RIDER
Equestrian command — GEE
Equestrian events — MEETS
Equestrian reign? — HORSEPOWER
Equestrian school — MANEGE
Equestrian's order — GEE
Equestrian's shop — SADDLERY
Equestrian's way — BRIDLE PATH
Equilateral parallelograms — RHOMBI
Equind — BAY
Equine armor — BARD
Equine control — REIN
Equine extremeties — POINTS
Equine feature — MANE
Equine neckpieces — MANES
Equine pace — TROT
Equine sounds — CLOPS, SNORTS
Equine stride — GAIT
Equip — ARM, GIRD, RIG
Equip a stripped ship — REFIT
Equip for action — ARM
Equip with lance and shield — ENARM
Equip with weapons, formerly — ENARM
Equip with weapons, once — ENARM
Equipment — CAPITAL, GEAR, RIG
Equipment for Eisenstaedt — CAMERA
Equipped — GEARED
Equipped for rowing — OARED
Equipped with breast plate and lance — ENARMORED
Equipped with horns — ANTLERED
Equipped with rowing gear — OARED
Equipped with tires — SHOD
Equipped with towers — TURRETED
Equipped with weapons — ARMED
Equitable — FAIR, JUST
Equity stock — COMMON
Equivalent — ANALOG, SAME
Equivalent cans in London — IDENTICAL TINS
Equivalent of 1,000 rin — YEN
Equivocate — HEDGE, LIE, WAVER
Equivocated — QUIBBLED
Er _____: hilly region of N Morocco — RIF
Era — TIME
ERA concern — WOMEN
ERA or RBI — STAT
Erase — CANCEL, DELE, DELETE, ERADICATE, UNDO
Erases a chalkboard — WIPES
Erasmus was one — SCHOLAR
Erato, for one — MUSE
Ere — BEFORE
Erechtheum site — ATHENS
Erect — ON END, REAR
Erect levees — EMBANK
Erected — BUILT
Erects — REARS
Erelong — SOON
Eremite — LONER
Ergate or kelep — ANT
Ergate, for one — ANT
Ergs and phots — UNITS
Erhard's therapy — EST
Eric _____ Red — THE
Eric Berne's 1964 book — GAMES PEOPLE PLAY
Eric of "Monty Python" — IDLE
Eric of movies — BLORE
Eric's sister — JULIA ROBERTS
Erica — HEATH
Ericaceous shrub — AZALEA
Erich _____ Stroheim — VON
Erie — LAKE
Erie and Huron — TRIBES
Erie Canal — WATERWAY
Erie Canal city — UTICA
Erie or Huron — GREAT LAKE
Erie or Seneca — TRIBE
Erie's better? — LAKE SUPERIOR
Erie, for one — CANAL
Erik of "CHiPs" — ESTRADA
Erin — HIBERNIA
Erin of TV — MORAN
Erin's other name — EIRE
Erin, to a Gael — EIRE
Eritrea sea — RED
Eritrea's capital — ASMARA
Eritrea's urethane riches — BURIED TREASURE
Erivan's country — ARMENIA
Ermine — STOAT
Ermine, in summer — STOAT
Ern is one — EAGLE
Ernie — PYLE
Ernie, the Gi's friend — PYLE
Ernst's eight — ACHT
Erode — ABLATE, EAT, ROT, WEAR
Eroded — ATE
Eros — CUPID
Eros anagram — ORES
Erotic — SEXY
Erotic dancer? — SALLY RAND
Err — MISDO, SLIP
Err at bridge — RENEGE
Errand — CHORE, MISSION
Errand runners — GOFERS
Errant — STRAY
Errant golf shot — SLICE
Errata — MISTAKES
Erred — MISDID
Erroneous — FALSE
Error — MISSTEP
Error for Evert — DOUBLE FAULT
Errors at Wimbledon — FAULTS
Ersatz — BOGUS, FAKE, SHAM
Ersatz butter — OLEO
Ersatz gem — PERIDOT
Erse — GAELIC
Erstwhile — ONCE
Erstwhile campus cutup — STREAKER
Erstwhile Hellas — ELLAS
Erstwhile movie fare — NEWSREEL
Erstwhile Persia — IRAN
Erstwhile Pleasant Island — NAURU
Erstwhile Russian provs. — SSRS
Erstwhile Sov. Estonia — ESSR
Erstwhile srs. — GRADS
Erstwhile Ulyanov — LENIN
Erstwhile Washington hostess — MESTA
Erubescent — ROSY
Erudition — CULTURE, LORE, REFINEMENT
Erupt — SPEW
Eruption — OUTBURST
Eruption site: 1883 — KRAKATOA
Erwin from Squaw Valley — STU
Erwin of early TV — STU
Esau's country — EDOM
Esau's father-in-law — ELON
Esau's father — ISAAC
Esau's wife — ADAH
Escalator unit — STAIR
Escamillo, e.g. — TOREADOR
Escamillo, for one — TOREADOR
Escapade — LARK
Escape — ELUDE, FLEE
Escape from — ELUDE
Escape notice — ELUDE
Escape punishment — GO SCOT FREE
Escape to wed — ELOPE
Escaped — GOT AWAY, OUTRAN
Escapee — FLEER
Escapees from a mythical box — ILLS
Escapees from Pandora's box — ILLS
Escapes — BREAKS OUT, ELUDES, FLIES, GETS OUT
Escargot — SNAIL
Escarpments — STEEPS
Eschew — AVOID, SHUN
Eschew a big wedding — ELOPE
Eschew food — FAST
Escort — ATTEND, DATE, GUIDE, SQUIRE
Escort down the aisle — SEAT
Escort in a way — CHAPERONE

Escort of a sort — GIGOLO
Escort's offering — ARM
Escorted — SQUIRED
Escorted anew — RELED
Escorts — ATTENDS
Escritoire — DESK
Esculents — EDIBLES
Escutcheon — SHIELD
Escutcheon border — ORLE
Escutcheon stain — BLOT
Escutcheons — SHIELDS
Eshkol or Eban — ISRAELI
Eshkol's successor — MEIR
Eskers — OSAR
Eskimo boats — UMIAKS
Eskimo boot — MUKLUK
Eskimo craft — UMIAKS
Eskimo home — IGLOO
Eskimo knives — ULUS
Eskimo settlement — SEAH
Eskimo woman's knife — ULU
Eskimo's boat — UMIAK
Eskimo's vehicle — SLED
Eskimos — ALEUTS
Esme's creator — SALINGER
Esophagus — GULLET
Esoteric — ARCANE, DEEP, PROFOUND
ESP practioners — SEERS
Espionage agent — SPY
Esplanade — MALL, WALK
Esposa de su padre — MADRE
Esprit de corps — ELAN, MORALE
Espy — SEE, SPOT
Ess follower — TEE
Essay — ATTEMPT, TRY
Essay in perfection — UTOPIA
Essay style — PROSE
Essayist — ELIA
Essayist Lamb — ELIA
Essayist's irony — SATIRE
Essayist's pseudonym — ELIA
Essays — TRIES
Essen eight — ACHT
Essen exclamation — ACH
Essen expletive — ACH
Essence — ATTAR, CORE, GIST, NATURE
Essence of motherhood or womanhood — FEMALE-NESS
Essential — KEY
Essential item — NEED
Essential oil — ATTAR
Essential part — GIST
Essential parts — VITALS
Essential point — CRUX
Essential to completeness — INTEGRAL
Essex or Reo — AUTO
Essex' title — EARL
EST minus 1 — CST
Establish — SET UP
Establish as true — PROVE
Establish radio communication — RAISE
Establish validity — PROVE
Established order — FORMALITY
Established principles — CRITERIA
Established: British slang — TRAD
Establishes — SETS UP
Estaminets — CAFES
Estate — ACRES
Estate house — MANOR
Estate residence — MANOR
Estate unit — ACRE
Estate; property — REALTY
Estee _____ LAUDER
Estee or Harry — LAUDER
Esteem — ADMIRE, HONOR
Esteem highly — ADMIRE
Estelle Getty role — SOPHIA
Ester — OLEATE
Esters of lactic acid — LACTATE
Esther of "Good Times" — ROLLE
Esther of TV — ROLLE
Esther Williams celestial movie — JUPITERS DARLING
Esther Williams film "_____ Island With You" — ON AN
Esther's antagonist — HAMAN
Esther's enemy — HAMAN
Esthetic course for freshmen — ART I
Estimate — APPRAISE, ASSESS, EVALUATE, GAUGE
Estimate — JUDGE, RATE
Estimated — ASSESSED
Estimates officially — ASSESSES
Estimation — RATE
Estimator — RATER
Estonia, Latvia, etc. — SSRS
Estonian — BALT
Estonian capital — TALLINN
Estonian chess master — NEI
Estonian city — TARTU
Estonian river — EMA
Estonian's parents — MATERS
Estoy, _____, esta' — ESTAS
Estrada of "Chips" — ERIK
Estrange — ALIENATE, DIVIDE, SEVER
Estrangement — RIFT
Estuaries — INLETS, RIAS
Estuary — ARM, INLET
Estuary spate — EAGRE
Et _____: and others — ALII
Et cetera — ALSO
Eta follower — THETA
Etats _____: U.S., French style — UNIS
Etc. — ET AL
Etc.'s relative — ET AL
Etch — BURN, ENGRAVE
Etcher's need — ACID
Etchers' purchases — ACIDS
Etching method — AQUATINT
Etching supplies — ACIDS
Eternal — EVER
Eternal city — ROME
Eternal vigilance — THE PRICE OF LIBERTY
Eternally — EVER, EVERMORE
Eternally, in poesy — EER
Eternities — EONS
Eternity — EONS
Ethan Frome's "other woman" — MATTIE
Ethan or Steve — ALLEN
Ethel Merman role — ANNIE OAKLEY
Ethel Water's classic — AM I BLUE
Ethel's grandniece — DREW BARRYMORE
Ether — SPACE
Ethereal — AERY
Ethical — MORAL
Ethical customs — MORES
Ethically neutral — AMORAL
Ethics — MORALS
Ethiopia neighbor — SUDAN
Ethiopia's largest province — HARAR
Ethiopian lake — TSANA
Ethiopian prince — RAS
Ethiopian province — SHOA
Ethiopian title, once — RAS
Ethiopian VIP — HAILE
Ethmoid — BONE
Ethnarch — RULER
Ethnic — RACIAL
Ethnic ending — ISH
Ethnic group — RACE
Ethnic hairdo — AFRO
Ethyl acetate, e.g. — ESTER
Ethyl alcohol derivative — ETHYLATE
Ethyl chaser — ENE
Ethyl ender — ENE
Etna feature — CONE
Etna has one — CONE
Etna issue — LAVA
Etna's output — LAVA
ETO head — DDE
Eton alumni — OLD BOYS
Eton boy's father — PATER
Eton's river — THAMES
Etonian's father — PATER
Etonian's mother — MATERS
Etonian's straw hat — BOATER
Eubie's music — RAG
Eucalyptus — GUM
Eucalyptus eater — KOALA
Eucharist — MANNA
Eucharistic plate — PATEN
Eucharistic rite — MASS
Eucharistic vestment — ALB
Eugene O'Neill's daughter — OONA

Eulogize — EXTOL, LAUD, PRAISE
Eunomia and Dike — HORAE
Eunuch's milieu — HAREM
Euphemistic oath — EGAD
Euphonium — BRASS
Euphoria — ELATION
Eur. country. — BELG, GER, ITAL
Eur. financial pact — EMA
Eur.-Amer. link — ATL
Eurasian range — URAL
Eurasian region of Middle Ages — TATARY
Eureka! — AHA
Euripides protagonist — MEDEA
Euripides tragedy — MEDEA
Europ. defense org. — EDC
Europe's 2nd largest lake — ONEGA
Europe's longest river — VOLGA
Europe's neighbor — ASIA
European — FINN
European annual herbs — MODESTIES
European blackbird — MERL, OUSEL
European capital — BONN, OSLO, ROME, WARSAW
European Community — COMMON MARKET
European deer — ROE, STAG
European finch — SERIN
European industrial area — SAAR
European juniper — CADE
European kite — GLEDE
European lake — ENARE
European moth — SPRAWLER
European mountain goat — IBEX
European mountains — ALPS
European neighbors — ITALY AND AUSTRIA
European peninsula — IBERIA
European plover — DOTTEREL
European range — ALPS
European republic — EIRE
European river — EDER, ISER
European shad — ALOSE
European shrub — GORSE
European song thrush — MAVIS
European subways — METROS
European thrush — OUZEL
European treaty org. — NATO
European tree — ALDER
European valley — RUHR
European waterway — ELBE
European winter resort — PAU
Europium and samarium — RARE EARTH METALS
Eustace Tilley's creator — IRVIN
Euterpe's sphere — MUSIC
Eva _____ — GABOR
Evade — AVERT, GEE
Evade a commitment — WEASEL
Evade work — SHIRK
Evaded — SKIRTED
Evaded, as an issue — SKIRTED
Evaluate — ASSAY, ASSESS, GRADE, JUDGE, RATE
Evaluate again — BERATE
Evaluated — ASSESSED
Evangel — GOSPEL
Evangeline land — ACADIA
Evangeline's Grand — PRE
Evangeline's home — ACADIA
Evangelist McPherson — AIMEE
Evangelist's advice — REPENT
Evans or Carnegie — DALE
Evasions — ELUSIONS
Evasive — CAGEY
Evasive action — ZIGZAG
Evasive ones — ELUDERS
Evasive speech — WEASEL WORDS
Eve's beginning — RIB
Eve's grandson — ENOS
Eve's origin — RIB
Eve's poor job — RAISING CAIN
Evel Knievel upheaval — CRASH
Evelyn or Frances Parkinson — KEYES
Evelyn Waugh novel — A HANDFUL OF DUST
Even — STRAIGHT, TIED
Even choices — TOSS UPS
Even game — TIE
Even if, for short — THO
Even money — ODDS
Even one — ANY
Even so — STILL
Even steven — TIED
Even surface — LEVEL
Even the score — AVENGE
Even up — TIE
Even- _____: tied — STEVEN
Evening bell — CURFEW
Evening dress — TAILS
Evening event — SOIREE
Evening party — SOIREE
Evening star — VENUS
Evening, in Naples — SERA
Evening, in Paris — SOIR
Evening, in Roma — SERA
Evening, in Siena — SERA
Evening, to Keats — EEN
Evens out — SMOOTHES
Evensong — VESPERS
Event at Vicksburg in 1862-63 — SIEGE
Event for Retton — GYMNASTICS
Event in 1780 — BATTLE OF KINGS MOUNTAIN
Event of 1812 — WAR
Event of 476 A.D. — FALL OF ROME
Eventide — EVENING
Events at Belmont — RACES
Events at meets — HEATS
Events at ovals — MEETS
Eventually — IN TIME
Ever — ONCE
Ever and _____ — ANON
Ever's antithesis — NEVER
Ever-abiding — AGELESS
Everest stat. — ELEV
Everett of TV and films — CHAD
Everglade state abbr. — FLA
Everglades denizen — EGRET
Everglades lake — OKEECHOBEE
Everglades sight — HERON
Everglades wader — EGRET
Evergreen — BALSAM, FIR, ILEX, YEW
Evergreen herb — GALAX
Evergreen Park, Ill. — SUBURB
Evergreen trees — CEDAR, FIRS, PINE
Evergreen trees and shrubs — YEWS
Evergreens — OLEANDER, YEWS
Evergreens, in Spain — PINOS
Everlasting — AGE LONG
Everlasting, in poesy — ETERNE
Everlasting, poetically — ETERNE
Evert of tennis — CHRIS
Evert's ex — LLOYD
Every — ALL, ANY, EACH, ENTIRE
Every 30 days — MONTHLY
Every corner or con man has one — ANGLE
Every mall has one — PARKING LOT
Every man _____ — JACK
Every one — EACH
Every partner — EACH
Every story has one — PLOT
Every suit has one — TREY
Every's companion — EACH
Every's partner — EACH
Everybody — ALL
Everybody's concern — WEATHER
Everybody's problem — INCOME TAX
Everybody, in Essen — ALLE
Everyday — BANAL
Everyone included — IN ALL
Everything — ALL, THE WORKS
Everything counted — IN ALL
Everything, in Darmstadt — ALLES
Everything, in Emden — ALLES
Evian or Dax — SPA
Evian or Menton — SPA

Evict — OUST, UNHOUSE
Evidence — SIGNS
Evidence of property ownership — TITLE
Evidence to preserve in plaster — BOOTPRINT
Evident — OVERT
Evil — BAD
Evil — SIN
Evil jinni — APRIT
Evil spirit — SATAN
Evil spirits — DAIMONS, DEMONS
Evil spirits: Var. — DAEMONS
Evil Tolkien creature — ORC
Evils — ILLS
Evince affection — CARESS
Evinced malice — SPITED
Evinces ennui — SIGHS
Evita — PERON
Evita Peron, e.g.; Abbr. — SRA
Evoked by ques. — ANS
Evoked much wonderment — AWED
Evokes wonder — AWES
Evolution pioneer — CHARLES DARWIN
Ewe gamboled here — LEA
Ewe's comment — BLEAT
Ewe's love — RAM
Ewe's mate — RAM
Ewe's youngster — LAMB
Ewelike — OVINE
Ewer's edge — RIM
Ewers' features — EARS
Ex-constellation — ARGO
Ex-jockey of note — SANDE
Ex-Met director — BING
Ex _____ (book owner's ID) — LIBRIS
Ex _____ (one-sided) — PARTE
Ex-astronaut on the Hill — GLENN
Ex-baseballer Fain — FERRIS
Ex-coach Parseghian — ARA
Ex-Dodgers ace Clem — LABINE
Ex-employee — RETIREE
Ex-head of Japan — YOSHIDA
Ex-king? — HAS BEEN
Ex-member — ASH
Ex-Red's Rose — PETE
Ex-Senator Long of Hawaii — OREN
Exacerbate — SOUR
Exact — TRUE
Exact copy — CLONE, RINGER
Exact opposite — ANTIPODE
Exacta — BET
Exactly vertical — PLUMB
Exactly what golfers need? — A TEE
Exaggerate — INFLATE, OVERDO
Exalted — ENNOBLED, SUBLIME
Exalts — ELEVATES
Exam — ORAL
Exam choice — FALSE
Exam for law school: Abbr. — LSAT
Exam taker — TESTEE
Examination — TEST, TRIAL
Examination of a kind — MIDTERM
Examination of a sort — ORAL
Examine — INSPECT, PERUSE, PROBE, TEST
Examine anew — REPROBE
Examine carefully — CASE, SIFT, VET
Examine closely — SIFT
Examine syntax — PARSE
Examine the facts — LOOK INTO
Examined closely — EYED
Examinee's T or F — ANS
Examiner — PERUSER
Example — CASE
Example of resin — LAC
Exams — ORALS
Exams for would-be Ph.D.'s — ORALS
Exams for would-be attorneys — LSATS
Exams for would-be Ed.D.'s — ORALS
Exasperate — IRK
Excalibur — SWORD
Excavate — DIG, DELVE
Excavated — MINED
Excavator — MINER
Excavator's egress — ADIT
Excavator's find — RELIC
Exceeded limits — OVERRAN
Exceedingly — VERY
Exceeds — PASSES
Exceeds in personnel — OUTMANS
Excel — OUTSHINE, SHINE
Excel on the track — OUTRUN
Excellence — MERIT, QUALITY, VIRTUE
Excellence to the Greeks — ARETE
Excellent — DANDY, NEAT, RARE
Excellent poker hand — AAAAQ
Excellent! — CAPITAL
Exceller — ACE
Excelsior — SHAVINGS
Except — BAR, BUT, REJECT, SAVE, UNLESS
Except for — BAR, SAVE
Except that — BUT, SAVE
Exceptional — NOVEL, ODD, RARE, SCARCE
Exceptional Egyptian — SADAT
Excess — GLUT, OVERKILL, SURPLUS
Excessive — STEEP, TOO TOO, ULTRA, UNDUE
Excessive as to interest — USURIOUS
Excessive: Prefix — HYPER
Excessively — TOO, UNDULY
Excessively decorated — OVERELABORATE
Exchange — BARTER, ECHO, SWAP, TRADE
Exchange fee — AGIO
Exchange premium — AGIO
Exchange witty remarks — BANTER
Exchanged — TRADED
Exchanged for — REPLACED, SWAPPED
Exchanges — TRADES
Exchequer — FISC
Excise — ERASE, TAX
Excite — AGITATE, BESTIR, STIR
Excited — AFIRE, AGOG, AMOK, FLUSH, INFLAMED
Excited about — ENTHUSED
Excited by desire — EAGER
Excitedly — AGOG
Excitement — FUSS, HOOPLA, ROW
Excites — WHETS
Excites again — RESTIRS
Excites pity — MELTS
Exciting — FAR OUT
Exclaim — CRY OUT
Exclaimed — OOHED
Exclamation — GOSH, HAW
Exclamation of astonishment — WHAT
Exclamation of contempt — POH, ROT
Exclamation of disbelief — PSHAW
Exclamation of discovery — AHA, OHO
Exclamation of disgust — UGH, YUCK
Exclamation of dismay — OH NO
Exclamation of exultant discovery — EUREKA
Exclamation of impatience — OOF
Exclamation of regret — ALAS
Exclamation of surprise — YIPES
Exclamation on sight of a mouse — EEK
Exclamations from Scrooge — BAHS
Exclamations of disgust — BAHS
Exclamations of triumph — AHAS
Exclude — DEBAR, OMIT, SKIP
Excluded — OUT IN THE COLD

Excludes — BANS, BARS
Exclusive — SOLE
Exclusiveness — ISOLATION
Excoriate — SCORCH
Excrescence — WART
Exculpate — ABSOLVE, ACQUIT, EXONERATE, PARDON
Excursion — DRIVE
Excuse — ALIBI
Excuse for a filibuster? — HASTE MAKES WASTE
Excuse, please — OOPS
Excuses of a sort — ALIBIS
Exec's brain, on occasion — STENO
Exec's car — LIMO
Exec's note — MEMO
Exec's reminder — MEMO
Exec. — MNGR
Exec. aide — ASST
Exec. rule — REG
Exec. skill — MGT
Execrate — DETEST, HATE
Execrated — HATED
Executed by auth. — SGD
Executive — MANAGER
Exemplar — MODEL
Exemplify — ILLUSTRATE
Exempted — SPARED
Exercise — LESSON
Exercise around the track — JOG
Exercise feverishly? — RUN A TEMPERATURE
Exercise in a way — JOG
Exercise influence — EXERT
Exercise on Everest — ASCENT
Exercise one's franchise — VOTE
Exercise, as authority or power — WIELD
Exercised — VEXED
Exercises — DRILLS
Exercises constitutionally — RIDES SHANKS MARE
Exercises hazardously — SKATES ON THIN ICE
Exercises in frustration — DASHES ONES HOPES
Exercising cheaply — DRIVING A BARGAIN
Exertion — ELBOW GREASE
Exertion of energy — WORK
Exerts traction on — HAULS
Exeter's river, appropriately — EXE
Exfoliate — PEEL, SCALE
Exhalations — SIGHS
Exhale — EJECT
Exhaust — DRAIN, SAP, SPEND
Exhausted — ALL IN, BURNED OUT, SPENT, TIRED
Exhausted with toil — WORN
Exhausts — TIRES, VENTS
Exhausts energy — SAPS
Exhausts, as resources — DEPLETES
Exhibit — SHOW
Exhibited disinterest — YAWNED
Exhibiting a play of colors — OPALESCING
Exhibition — FAIR, SHOW
Exhilarate — ELATE
Exhilarated — EAGER, ON AIR
Exhort — URGE
Exhorted — URGED
Exigency — NEED
Exigent — ACUTE
Exiguous — SPARSE
Exile — BANISH, DEPORT
Exile Amin — IDI
Exile island — ELBA
Exile isle — ELBA
Exile isle of 1814 — ELBA
Exiles — REFUGEES
Exist — ARE, BREATHE, LIVE, OCCUR
Existed — WAS, WERE
Existence — ACTUALITY, ESSE
Existence: Lat. — ESSI
Existent — ACTUAL
Existing — ALIVE
Existing for many yrs. — ANC
Existing in fact — ACTUAL
Exists — LIVES
Exit — EGRESS, OUTLET
Exited — WENT
Exodus character — ARI
Exodus obstacle — RED SEA
Exonerate — CLEAR
Exonerates — VINDICATES
Exorcist's target — EVIL
Exordium — PREFACE
Exotic — RARE
Exotic dinner bell — GONG
Expand — DILATE, WIDEN
Expand, in a way — PAD
Expandable table supports — GATE LEGS
Expanse — AREA
Expanse fed by the Amu Darya — ARAL
Expansion — DILATION
Expatriate of a sort — EMIGRE
Expect — AWAIT, HOPE
Expect confidently — TRUST
Expectancy — HOPE
Expectant — AGOG
Expectant dad, perhaps — PACER
Expectant mother's method — LAMAZE
Expectations — HOPES
Expected — USUAL
Expectorate — EXPEL
Expects — HOPES, PLANS ON
Expedite — HASTEN, SPEED UP
Expedited — SPED
Expedition — HASTE, TRIP
Expeditions of a sort — RAID
Expeditious — DIRECT
Expel — EGEST, OUST
Expend — PAY, USE
Expended — USED
Expenditure — LOSS, OUTGO
Expenditures — COST
Expense item — RENT
Expenses — COST, OUTGO, OVERHEAD
Expensive — DEAR
Expensive sport — POLO
Experience again — RELIVE
Experience anew — RELIVE
Experienced — SEASONED, SKILLED
Experienced hands — PROS
Experiences again imaginatively — RELIVES
Experiencing togetherness — IN THE SAME BOAT
Experiment — TEST, TRY
Experimental — TRIAL
Expert — ACE, ADEPT, MAVEN, PRO
Expert athelete — PRO
Expert combat flier — ACE
Expert ending — ISE
Expert of a sort — MAVEN
Expert skill — MASTERY
Expert witness in a sanity trial — ALIENIST
Expert, briefly — PRO
Expert, for short — PRO, WIZ
Expertise — ART
Experts in Jewish law — DAYANS
Expiate — ATONE, REPENT
Expiator — ATONER
Expire — ELAPSE
Expire, a la Tennyson — CROSS THE BAR
Expiring — LAPSING
Explain — SOLVE
Explanation seeker's query — WHY
Explicate — BUILD
Explode — BURST, ERUPT
Exploded — WENT OFF
Exploding material, for short — TNT
Exploit — DEED, EMPLOY, MISUSE, UTILIZE
Exploited — USED
Exploiter — USER
Exploits — FEATS, USES
Explore beforehand — PRETEST
Explorer Amundsen — ROALD
Explorer Bartholomew — DIAS
Explorer Cook — JAMES
Explorer De _____ — SOTO
Explorer Ericsson — LIEF
Explorer Francisco _____ — CORONADO
Explorer Hedin — SVEN

Explorer in a bathysphere — BEEBE
Explorer Johnson — OSA
Explorer of N.M.: 16th century — ONATE
Explorer of the far West — FREMONT
Explorer Tasman — ABEL
Explorer Uemura — NAOMI
Explorer Vasco de _____ — GAMA
Explorer Vespucci — AMERIGO
Explorer who named Louisiana — LA SALLE
Explorer's chef? — CAPTAINS COOK
Exploring Admiral — BYRD
Explosion — BLOWUP
Explosive — NITRO, TNT, VOLATILE
Explosive force — KILOTON
Explosive French dessert? — BOMBE
Explosive headwear? — DYNAMITE CAPS
Explosive initials — TNT
Explosive letters — TNT
Explosive mixture — AMATOL
Explosive noises — REPORTS
Explosive sound — REPORT
Explosive trio — TNT
Explosive, for one — TNT
Explosive, for short — TNT
Explosive: Abbr. — TNT
Expo 74, was one — WORLDS FAIR
Export from France — BRIE
Export of Chile — NITRO
Expose — BARE
Expose phoniness — DEBUNK
Expose to air — AERATE
Expose to danger — HAZARD
Exposed — OPENED
Exposes — BARES
Exposes a laughing stock — MAKES A MONKEY OUT OF
Exposure outdoors — AIRING
Express — FAST, NONSTOP
Express a viewpoint — OPINE
Express and air — MAILS
Express appreciation — THANKS
Express approval — ENDORSE
Express boredom — YAWN
Express contempt — POOH POOH, SNEER, SNORT
Express derision — HOOT, SNEER
Express gratitude — THANK
Express happiness — SMILE
Express nausea — RETCH
Express views — OPINE
Expressed disdain — SNORTED
Expressed dislike — BOOED
Expressed gratitude — THANKED
Expresses joy — GRINS
Expressing in words — STATING
Expression — CAST, IDIOM, PHRASE, TERM
Expression of amused surprise — OHO
Expression of annoyance — GRIMACE
Expression of beauty — ART
Expression of censure — REPROOF
Expression of chagrin — OOPS
Expression of disapproval — PSHAW
Expression of discovery — AH SO
Expression of disgust — UGH
Expression of dismay — OH NO
Expression of eagerness — WHOOP
Expression of enthusiasm — GEE
Expression of hearty approval — AMENS
Expression of inquiry — EHS
Expression of joy — HUZZAH
Expression of mild disbelief — DO TELL
Expression of pleasure — GRIN
Expression of surprise — HEAVENS, HUH
Expression of understanding — I SEE
Expression on a face — VISAGE
Expressions of consent — AMENS
Expressions of inquiry — EHS
Expressive dance — HULA
Expressive understatement — MEIOSIS
Expressway in Germany — BAHN
Expressway in USA — INST
Expropriate — SEIZE
Expunge — DELETE, ERASE
Expunged by a redactor — DELED, ERASED
Expurgate — DELETE, PURGE
Exquisite — FINE, RARE
Ext. paved area — TCE
Extempore — OFFHAND
Extend — ELONGATE, LENGTHEN
Extend a subscription — RENEW
Extend credit to — TRUST
Extend one's subscription — RENEW
Extend oneself — REACH OUT
Extend over — SPAN
Extend to — REACH
Extended — LONG
Extended a contract — RENEWED
Extended a subscription — RENEWED
Extended ungracefully — SPRAWLED
Extended walrus teeth — TUSK
Extension — ARM
Extension of a sort — ARM
Extensive — BROAD, VAST, WIDE
Extensive period — EON
Extensive tract of land — RANGE
Extent — RANGE, SCOPE
Extents — GAMUTS
Exterior — FACADE, OUTER
Exterior boundary — SURFACE
Exterminate — RID
External — OUTER, OUTSIDE
External boundary — AMBIT
External ear — PINNA
External world — NON EGO
External: Comb. form — ECTO
Extinct bird — DODO, MOA
Extinct cousin of NATO — SEATO
Extinct New Zealand bird — MOA
Extinct ratite bird — MOA
Extinct wild ox — URUS
Extinct workers? — ICEMEN
Extinct: Comb. form — NECRO
Extol — LAUD
Extort — BLEED
Extorted — BLED
Extra — ODD
Extra benefits: Colloq. — PERKS
Extra dividend — BONUS, MELON
Extra jobs — SIDELINES
Extra large sizes — SUPERS
Extra pay — BONUS
Extra troughs? — SPARE CRIBS
Extra, in theater jargon — SUPE
Extra-base hit — TRIPLE
Extract — ELICIT
Extract from — REND
Extract juice from — REAM
Extract metal from ore — SMELT
Extraordinary — ODD, ONE OF A KIND, RARE
Extraordinary person — ONER
Extraordinary: Abbr. — SPEC
Extras — ADD ONS
Extraterrestial — UFO
Extravagance — WASTE
Extravagant — LAVISH
Extravagant praise — RAVE
Extreme — ARRANT, DIRE, NTH, ULTRA, UNDUE
Extreme cruelty — SADISM
Extreme degree — NTH

Extremely — RATHER, UNDULY, VERY
Extremely bad — DIRE
Extremely bitter — ACRID
Extremely black — INKY
Extremely confidential — TOP SECRET
Extremely dark — INKY
Extremely dry — ARID, SERE
Extremely embarrassed — BEET RED
Extremely silly — APEISH
Extremely small — MICRO
Extremely: Fr. — TRES
Extremeties — ENDS
Extremeties of cold, etc. — RIGORS
Extremists, for short — RADS
Extremity — LIMB
Extremity of a plate — EDGE
Extricate — UNTIE
Extroverted — OUTGOING
Exuberance — ELAN
Exuberance — GLEE
Exude — EMIT, OOZE, REEK
Exude slowly — OOZE
Exuded color — BLED
Exudes fumes — REEKS
Exudes smoke — REEKS
Exultant — ELATED
Exultation — GLEE
Exurban — RURAL
Exuviate — MOLT
Eydie's spouse — STEVE
Eye — OGLE, ORB
Eye _____: visor — SHADE
Eye affliction — STYE
Eye ailment — STYE
Eye appeal — CHARM
Eye area — UVEA
Eye at the end of a lariat — HONDA
Eye boldly — OGLE
Eye cheesecake — OGLE
Eye cover — PATCH
Eye feature — UVEA
Eye gland — TEAR SAC
Eye layer — UVEA
Eye liner — RETINA
Eye makeup — LINER
Eye of _____: Macbeth — NEWT
Eye of the wind — CENTER
Eye part — CORNEA, LENS, UVEA
Eye part: Comb. form — IRID
Eye portion — UVEA
Eye problem — STYE
Eye section — UVEA
Eye shade — VISOR
Eye socket — ORBIT
Eye sore — STYE
Eye splice — LOOP
Eye tooth — CANINE
Eye with a sigh — OGLE
Eye woe — STYE
Eye, in Oveido — OJO
Eye-related — OPTIC
Eye: Comb. form — OCULO
Eyeball — ORB, OGLE
Eyeball covering — SCLERA
Eyebrow or commotion: Scot — BREE
Eyed like a thug — CASED
Eyed wolfishly — LEERED
Eyeglass holders — EARS
Eyelashes — CILIA
Eyelet — GROMET
Eyelike: var. — OCELLATE
Eyeopener — ALARM
Eyepiece — LENS
Eyes — OGLES, ORBS
Eyes amorously — LEERS, OGLES
Eyes and ears — ORGANS
Eyes the guys — FLIRTS
Eyes, in a way — OGLES
Eyeshade — VISOR
Eyesore — DEBRIS
Eyewash aid — EYECUP
Eyot — AIT
Eyrie — NEST
Ezra or Irving — STONE
Ezra the poet — POUND

F

F's forerunners — ABCDE
F-J connection — GHI
F-J link — GHI
F.A.A. airport service — ATC
F.B.I. agents — G MEN
F.D.R. and D.D.E., e.g. — INITS
F.D.R. measure — NRA
F.D.R.'s Secretary of the Interior — ICKES
F.D.R.'s successor — HST
Fa's followers — SOLS
Fa-la connector — SOL
Fa-la go-between — SOL
Fabius's foot — PES
Fable ending — MORAL
Fable with a moral message — APOLOGUE
Fabled birds — ROCS
Fabled fox's subject — SOUR GRAPES
Fabled racer — HARE
Fabled sisters — FATES
Fabled sword — EXCALIBUR
Fabray namesakes — NANS
Fabray, to friends — NAN
Fabric-hungry bug — EGGER, MOTH
Fabric — CAMELS HAIR, CLOTH, DRY GOOD, REP
Fabric — SATEEN, TEXTILE
Fabric border — SELVAGE
Fabric ends? — ATORS
Fabric floor cover — CARPET
Fabric for a filly? — STABLE LINEN
Fabric for formal wear — LAME
Fabric joiners — SEAMS
Fabric maker — LOOM
Fabric merchant — DRAPER
Fabric texture — WALE
Fabricate — FORM, LIE, MAKE
Fabricated — MADE
Fabricates — CONCOCTS
Fabrication — FALSEHOOD
Fabricator — LIAR
Fabulist — AESOP
Fabulist: Var. — ESOP
Fabulous — GREAT
Fabulous birds — ROCS
Fabulous fabrics — SATINS
Fabulous fiddle — STRAD
Fabulous fur — CHINCHILLA, SABLE
Facade — FACE, FRONT, MASK, VENEER
Face-stubble time — FIVE
Face — ABOUT, EXPRESSION, FACADE, FRONT, IMAGE
Face — LOOK, MASK
Face a pitcher — BAT
Face card — KING
Face cream ingredient — ALOE
Face down — PRONE
Face of a building — FRONTAGE
Face on $1,000 bill — GROVER CLEVELAND
Face on $100 bill — BENJAMIN FRANKLIN

Face on a $50 bill — ULYSSES S GRANT
Face shape — OVAL
Face the day — ARISE
Face the footlights — ACT
Face the pitcher — BAT
Face to face — OPPOSITE, WITH
Face up to — ADMIT
Face with riprap — REVET
Face with stone — REVET
Face, as an embankment — REVET
Face-lift — OPERATION
Faced — SMOOTHED
Faced the New Year — ROSE
Faceguard of a helmet — BEAVER
Faces up to — CONFRONTS
Facet — ANGLE, PANE
Facetious — MERRY, JOCULAR, WAGGISH
Facial — TREATMENT
Facial area — BROW
Facial blowholes — NAIRS
Facial expression — FROWN
Facial features — CHINS, EYELIDS, LIPS, NOSES
Facial shape — OVAL
Facial trimmer — RAZOR
Facile — EASY
Facilitate — EASE, ENABLE
Facilitates — AIDS, PROMOTES
Facility — EASE, PLANT
Facing — FRONT
Facing a glacier — STOSS
Facing Orel — AT BAT
Facing the pitcher — AT BAT
Facsimile — COPY
Facsimile, briefly — REPRO
Fact — DATUM
Fact finish — ORY
Fact or fiction lead-in — NON
Fact-find — TAKE A TRIP
Faction — SECT, SIDE
Factor — ELEMENTS
Factor in football — WIND
Factories — PLANTS
Factors — AGENTS
Factory of a kind — MILL
Factory of money — MINT
Factory return — CALL BACK
Factotum — DO ALL, HANDYMAN, MAN OF ALL WORK
Facts — DATA
Facts and figures — DATA
Factual — REAL, TRUE
Faculty head — DEAN
Faculty member — DEAN
Faculty of seeing — VISION
Fad — CRAZE, HOBBY, RAGE, WHIM
Faddish fruit — KIWI
Fade — DIM, PALE
Fade gradually — EVANESCE
Fade out — DISAPPEAR
Faded — PALE, WANED
Fades — DIES
Fading stars — NOVAE
Faeces — DREGS, LEES
Fagin, for one — FENCE
Fahr. or C — TEMP
Fail — BLUNDER, BREAK, CRACK, SNAP
Fail in business — FOLD
Fail to hear the alarm — OVERSLEEP
Fail to impress — CUT NO ICE
Fail to mention — OMIT
Fail to notice — IGNORE, PASS OVER
Fail to place — LOSE
Fail to win — LOSE
Failed — STALLED
Failed in a way — LOST OUT
Failed NOW goal — ERA
Failed to keep appointment — STOOD UP
Failing grade — DEE, POOR
Fails to mention — OMITS
Failure — WASHOUT
Faineant — IDLER
Faint — SWOON
Faint dead away — SWOON
Faint sound — THUMP
Fainter — PALER
Fair — EXPO, JUST, PASSABLE, SO SO
Fair grades — CEES
Fair haired — SANDY
Fair Lady Eliza — DOOLITTLE
Fair likeness — FACSIMILE
Fair locale — COUNTY
Fair location — BOOTH
Fair play — CRICKET
Fair portions — SHARES
Fair to middling — SO SO
Fair-haired — BLOND
Fair-haired one — PET
Fairbanks familiarly — DOUG
Fairbanks people — ALASKANS
Fairgrounds offering — RIDE
Fairy-tale sign-off — AFTER
Fairy-tale title — THE THREE BEARS
Fairy godmother's male — SUGAR DADDY
Fairy godmother, e.g. — GIVER
Fairy king — OBERON
Fairy queen — MAB
Fairy tale — FABLE
Fairy tale beginning — ONCE
Fairy tale in Berlin — MARCHEN
Fairy tale monster — OGRE
Fairy tale opener — ONCE
Fairy tale's penultimate word — EVER
Fairy-tale character — OGRE
Fairy-tale heavy — OGRE
Fairy-tale intruder — GOLDILOCKS
Fairy-tale sibling — GRETEL
Fairy-tale siblings — HANSEL AND GRETEL
Fairy-tale starter — ONCE
Fairy-tale villain — OGRE
Fairy-tale villain — OGRE
Faith — TRUST
Faith follower — HOPE
Faithful — LIEGE, LOYAL, RESOLUTE
Faithful one — PENELOPE OR ACHATES
Faithfulness to the facts — FIDELITY
Faithless — DISLOYAL
Faithlessness — PERFIDY
Fake — BOGUS, SHAM
Fake coin — SLUG
Fake jewelry? — SHAM ROCKS
Fakir — YOGI
Fala and Asta — PETS
Fala and Checkers — PETS
Fala was one — SCOTTIE
Falana of song — LOLA
Falcon — SAKER
Falcon feature — CLAW
Falconer's strap — JESS
Falconry equipment — CADGE
Falconry verb — SEEL
Falcons or Cardinals — TEAM
Falderal — FINERY
Falk or Finch — PETER
Falk, Finch or Fonda — PETER
Falk-Arkin film, with "The" — INLAWS
Falkland Isl. penguins — GENTOOS
Fall — COLLAPSE, DROP, PLUNGE, SIN
Fall apart — SHATTER
Fall away — DWINDLE
Fall back — LAG
Fall behind — LAG, STRAGGLE
Fall birthstone — OPAL
Fall bloomer — ASTER
Fall blooms, for short — MUMS
Fall calls — RAHS
Fall Classic — WORLD SERIES
Fall dessert treat — PUMPKIN PIE
Fall down — FAIL
Fall drink — CIDER
Fall end over end — TUMBLE
Fall fabrics — TWEEDS
Fall flat — BOMB
Fall flower — ASTER
Fall flower, for short — MUM
Fall for a gag — BITE
Fall from grace — SIN
Fall from one level to the next — CASCADE
Fall frost — HOAR
Fall guy — GOAT, SAP, SCAPEGOAT

Fall heavily — CRASH
Fall in — SINK
Fall mo. — NOV, OCT, SEPT
Fall off — DECLINE
Fall on one's knees — FAWN
Fall over — TRIP
Fall preceder — PRIDE
Fall quaffs — CIDERS
Fall quencher — CIDER
Fall short — LAG, MISS
Fall sound — RAH
Fall sporting event — WORLD SERIES
Fall through — FAIL
Fall tumbler — LEAF
Fallacy — ERROR
Fallen-rock debris — SCREE
Faller on Bacharach's head — RAINDROP
Falling barometer, e.g. — OMEN
Falling into error — LAPSING
Falling out — RIFT
Falling prices on Wall Street — BEAR MARKET
Fallow — ARID
Falls — AUTUMNS, CATARACTS
Falls behind — LAGS
Falls for honeymooners — NIAGARA
Falls into a chair — PLOPS
Falls short — FAILS
Falls, north of Buffalo — AMERICAN
False — NOT SO, SHAM
False appearance — GUISE
False colors — DISGUISE
False front — FACADE
False gem material — PASTE
False god — BAAL
False gods — BAALIM
False hair — CHIGNON, RAT, WIG
False hint — MISCUE
False move — FEINT
False move verbally — SLIP OF THE TONGUE
False name — ANONYM
False or fire — ALARM
False rumor — CANARD
Falsehood — FABLE, LIE
Falsehoods — TALES
Falstaff's prince — HAL
Falstaff's princely pal — HAL
Falstaff's title — SIR
Falstaffian — FAT
Falter — FAIL, HESITATE
Fam. member — DAU, REL, SIS
Fame — ECLAT
Famed "Dragnet" role — FRIDAY
Famed African-American diva — MARIAN ANDERSON
Famed American photorealist — ESTES
Famed apple-splitter — TELL
Famed architect of Barcelona — GAUDI
Famed Austrian singers — TRAPPS
Famed basso Cesare — SIEPI
Famed Canadian physician — OSLER
Famed cartoon animator — DISNEY
Famed charioteer — HUR
Famed chef — CAESAR
Famed choreographer: 1880-1942 — FOKINE
Famed columnist — ALSOP, RESTON
Famed elegist — GRAY
Famed English author — ANTHONY TROLLOPE
Famed English engraver — PYE
Famed English potter — SPODE
Famed epicist — HOMER
Famed essayist — ELIA, LAMB
Famed fabulist — AESOP
Famed family of German organists — BACHS
Famed feline — ELSA
Famed fiddle — STRAD
Famed film official: 1879-1954 — HAYS
Famed Florentine — DANTE
Famed Florentine family — MEDICI
Famed flyers of the 1940's — RAF
Famed folk singer — ODETTA
Famed fountain — TREVI
Famed French author — JULES VERNE
Famed fur trader — ASTOR
Famed German author — THOMAS MANN
Famed Giant quarterback — TITTLE
Famed hill near Dublin — TARA
Famed horticulturist Luther — BURBANK
Famed inventor's monogram — TAE
Famed Irish author — OSCAR WILDE
Famed jurist — TANEY
Famed lioness — ELSA
Famed loch — NESS
Famed lyrist — CAHN
Famed midnight rider — REVERE
Famed muralist — SERT
Famed novelist-dramatist — DUMAS
Famed obelisk — CLEOPATRAS NEEDLE
Famed office — OVAL
Famed Oglala chief — NED CLOUD
Famed Ore. lake — CRATER
Famed penologist — LAWES
Famed Pharaoh — TUT
Famed physicist Bohr — NIELS
Famed puppeteer — SARG
Famed researcher Jonas — SALK
Famed Russian author — LEO TOLSTOY
Famed Seminole chief — OSCEOLA
Famed Seminole leader — OSCEOLA
Famed Sing Sing penologist — LAWES
Famed soprano — EAMES
Famed tenor José — CARRERAS
Famed toxophilite — TELL
Famed twin — ORVILLE
Famed U.S. painter — ANDREW WYETH
Famed violin — STRAD
Famed WWII riveter — ROSIE
Famed Yale football coach — DUCKY POND
Fameuse and pippin — APPLES
Familiar — INWARD, KNOWN
Familiar goodbyes — TATAS
Familiar reference book — ROGETS
Familiar titles — SRAS
Familiar with — PRIVY TO
Family-tree twigs: Abbr. — RELS
Family _____: pedigree — TREE
Family branch — SEPT
Family car — SEDAN
Family circle member — AUNT, NIECE
Family created by Poe — USHERS
Family diagram — TREE
Family drs. — GPS
Family favorite — PET
Family femme — AUNT
Family group — CLAN
Family history — TREE
Family in "Look Homeward, Angel" — GANTS
Family lineage — TREE
Family man — DAD
Family member — AUNT, IN LAW, MAMA, NIECE, PAPA
Family member — PARENT, POP, SON
Family member, briefly — BRO
Family member, for short — POP, SIS
Family member, in Madrid — TIA
Family members — FATHERS, INLAWS, UNCLE
Family members: Abbr. — BROS
Family mems. — BROS
Family name in "A Rage to Live" — TATE
Family name of Princess Diana — SPENCER

Family of "The Minister's Wooing" author — STOWES
Family of 1922 Nobelist for physics — BOHRS
Family of a 1944 Nobelist in Chemistry — HAHNS
Family of a Giant star — OTTS
Family of a memorable cartoonist — NASTS
Family of a music-hall star — OSHEAS
Family of an actor in the "Godfather" films — PACINOS
Family of French scientists — CURIES
Family of Israel's Abba — EBANS
Family of languages — SLAVIC
Family of lions — PRIDE
Family of Portnoy's creator — ROTHS
Family of Reagan's first Sec. of Treasury — REGANS
Family of the twenty-seventh president — TAFTS
Family of winged robbers — ASILIDAE
Family pet — FIDO
Family relative — NIECE
Family room, for short — REC
Family rooms — DENS
Family roots — TREE
Family tree — PEDIGREE
Family VIP's — DADS
Famine — HUNGER
Famines — DEARTHS
Famines antithesis — FEAST
Famished — STARVED
Famous — NOTED, REPUTED
Famous "stooge" — MOE
Famous archer — TELL
Famous Borgia — CESARE
Famous boy king — TUT
Famous Bruin and family — ORRS
Famous Cambridge institution — MIT
Famous caravel — PINTA
Famous charwoman of TV — BURNETT
Famous Chevy — CHASE
Famous code name — MORSE
Famous comic character — POGO
Famous cow's namesakes — ELSIES
Famous dean of St. Paul's — INGE
Famous diamond — HOPE
Famous Dolly — PARTON
Famous English potter — SPODE
Famous essayist's pen name — ELIA
Famous express — ORIENT
Famous fabulist — AESOP
Famous fictional Faulkner family — SNOPES
Famous first name in spydom — MATA
Famous Fleming — IAN
Famous former weakling — ATLAS
Famous fountain in Rome — TREVI
Famous frontiersman — KIT CARSON
Famous fur merchant — ASTOR
Famous golf cup — RYDER
Famous hostess of the past — MESTA
Famous Italian family — ESTE
Famous jockey — SANDE
Famous Lamb — ELIA
Famous last words — ET TU
Famous maitre d'hötel — OSCAR
Famous Marechal — FOCH
Famous Mariner — SILAS
Famous marshal of France — NEY
Famous Met basso — SCOTTI
Famous military headquarters — PENTAGON
Famous mountain — OSSA
Famous New England name — CABOT
Famous New England school — PHILLIPS ANDOVER
Famous nom de plume — ELIA, MARK TWAIN
Famous old frigate — IRONSIDES
Famous opera singer Nellie — MELBA
Famous Orkan — MORK
Famous painting, 1917 — SEPTEMBER MORN
Famous paintings — RENOIRS
Famous park in Vienna — PRATER
Famous pen name — ELIA
Famous person — STAR
Famous pharaoh — "King _____" — TUT
Famous pharaoh — TUT
Famous physicist — RABI
Famous poem of 1922 (with "The") — WASTE LAND
Famous quarter of Paris — LATIN
Famous racing site — LE MANS
Famous recorder — PEPYS
Famous Red — ERIC
Famous redhead — ERIC
Famous reporter — NELLIE BLY
Famous Roman — NERO
Famous Scott — DRED
Famous seamstress — ROSS
Famous sidekick — TONTO
Famous singing family — TRAPP
Famous tennis family — EVERTS
Famous tennis player — BILLIE JEAN KING
Famous US planes — DCS
Famous Virginia river — JAMES
Famous Virginians — LEES
Fan — ROOTER
Fan follower — ATIC
Fan in the 40's — BOBBY-SOXER
Fan sound — RAH
Fanatic — FIEND, ZEALOT
Fanatical — RABID
Fancies — DREAMS
Fanciful, as a yarn — TALL
Fancy — IDEA, IMAGE, RITZY
Fancy bloke — SWELL
Fancy case — ETUI
Fancy dive — GAINER
Fancy dive — JACKKNIFE
Fancy fabric — LAME
Fancy lace — FILET
Fancy one — DAN
Fandango — DANCE
Fane — FLAG
Fanfare — BLARE, CALL, ECLAT, TANTARA
Fanfare on a trumpet — TUCKET
Fanfaron — GASCON
Fang — TOOTH
Fang: Fr. — CROC
Fannie _____ (Government issue) — MAE
Fanny — SEAT, TUSHY
Fanon — ORALE
Fantails locations — STERNS
Fantasize — DREAM
Fantasized — DREAMT
Fantastic — GREAT
Fantastic ideas — MAGGOTS
Fantastic ornamentation — ROCAILLE
Fantasy — VISION
Far and wide — ABROAD, UNIVERSAL
Far East — ASIA
Far East capital — TAIPEI
Far eastern alcoholic beverage — ARAK
Far flung — VAST
Far from abundant — SCARCE
Far from altruistic — SELFISH
Far from bright — GRIM
Far from cordial — ICY
Far from daring — TIMID
Far from faithless — LOYAL
Far from fragrant — OLID
Far from fresh — TIRED
Far from optimistic — CYNICAL
Far from plentiful — SCARCE
Far from pushy — RETICENT

Far from torpid — ANIMATED
Far left and far right — EXTREMES
Far out — ULTRA
Far out person — MOD
Far superior to — HEAD AND SHOULDERS ABOVE
Far-fetched — REMOTE
Far-from-simple Simon — NEIL
Far-sighted — SHREWD
Far: Comb. form — TELE
Farce — SHAM
Fare — PASSENGER, RIDER
Fare for Fido — ORT
Fare from an olla — SOPA
Fared — GOT ON
Fares — DIETS
Farewell — ADIEU, BON VOYAGE, CONGE, GOODBYE, TATA
Farewell formerly — AVE
Farewell, Esteban — ADIOS
Farewell, in Burgos — ADIOS
Farewell, in Florence — CIAO
Farewell, to Caesar — VALE
Farewell, to Cato — VALE
Farinaceous — MEALY
Farinaceous meal — SALEP
Farm — PLANT
Farm animals — EWES, OXEN
Farm baby — CALF
Farm beast — OXEN
Farm building — BARN, GRANGE, SHED, SILO
Farm cat — MOUSER
Farm crossing — STILE
Farm dog — COLLIE
Farm enclosures — PENS
Farm equipment: Abbr. — TRAC
Farm females — EWES, HENS, MARES
Farm fixture — SILO
Farm horse — DOBBIN
Farm implement — PLOW, SEEDER
Farm in Spain — HACIENDA
Farm mach. — TRAC
Farm machine — BALER, REAPER, SEEDER
Farm measure — ACRE
Farm out — HIRE
Farm output — CROP
Farm plot — ACRE
Farm power bureau: Abbr. — REA
Farm sight — SILO
Farm sound — BAA, MOO
Farm structure — SILO
Farm team — OXEN, ROOKIES
Farm towers — SILOS
Farm unit — ACRE
Farm vehicle — TRACTOR
Farm wagons — WAINS
Farm yard — PEN
Farm yield — CROP
Farm youngster — KID
Farm-implement pioneer — DEERE
Farm-machine pioneer — DEERE
Farmable — FRIABLE
Farmer in the spring — SOWER
Farmer played by Lange — FRANCES
Farmer with a big spread — RANCHER
Farmer's address — RFD
Farmer's concern — CROPS
Farmer's field: Abbr. — AGRIC
Farmer's locale — DELL
Farmer's milieu — DELL
Farmer's need, pre-tractor — OXEN
Farmer, at times — SOWER
Farmer, in Spring — SOWER
Farming machines — REAPERS
Farmland — ACREAGE
Farmlike — RURAL
Farouk's father — FUAD
Farouk, Tut, Arthur and George? — FOUR KINGS
Farrago — JUMBLE
Farrell's "Bernard ____" — CLARE
Farrell's knee bend — PLIE
Farrier — SMITH
Farrier, at times — SHOER
Farrow — MIA
Farrow and Korf — MIAS
Farrow's second — PREVIN
Farthest from the outside — INMOST
Farthest point — APOGEE
Farthest: Abbr. — ULT
Farthing — COIN
Fasces items — RODS
Fascinate — CHARM, INTEREST
Fascinate at the gate? — ENTRANCE
Fascinated — CHARMED
Fascination — ALLUREMENT
Fascist alliance of 1941 — AXIS
Fashion — CREATE, CUSTOM, DESIGN, MAKE, MANNER, MODE
Fashion — STYLE, VOGUE
Fashion barometers — HEMS
Fashion color — ECRU
Fashion designer Geoffrey — BEENE
Fashion designer Simpson — ADELE
Fashion item — BEADS
Fashion magazine — ELLE
Fashion magazine from France — ELLE
Fashion on the farm — OVERALLS
Fashion passions — FADS
Fashion style — MOD
Fashion writer's concern — STYLE
Fashion's Geoffrey — BEENE
Fashion's Oleg — CASSINI
Fashion's Oscar de la ____ — RENTA
Fashionable — MODISH, SMART
Fashionable equestrian addiction? — RIDING HABIT
Fashionable London thoroughfare — BOND STREET
Fashionable resort — SPA
Fashionable shoulder enhancers — PADS
Fashionable skirt — MINI
Fashionable society — BON TON
Fashioned — CREATED, FORMED, MADE
Fashions — MODES, MOLDS, VOGUES
Fast — QUICK, RAPID, SPEEDY
Fast break — RUSH
Fast complex style of jazz — BEBOP
Fast curve — SLIDER
Fast driver — JEHU
Fast escort vessel — CORVETTE
Fast feline — CHEETAH
Fast flyer, for short — SST
Fast food — MINUTE STEAK
Fast food order — FRIES
Fast food restaurants — DINERS
Fast freight — HOT SHOT
Fast jet — SST
Fast season — LENT
Fast talking comedian — PATTERER
Fast time — LENT
Fast's companion — LOOSE
Fast-food magnate — KROC
Fast-food order — FRIES, TO GO
Fast-talking — GLIB
Fasten — BIND, FIX, PIN, RIVET
Fasten anew — RENAIL
Fasten firmly — RIVET
Fastened with certain ropes — MARLED
Fastener — HASP, NAIL, RIVET, SNAP
Fastener for Rosie — RIVET
Fastener of a type — HASP
Fasteners — PINS, SNAPS
Fastening — HASP
Fastening device — SCREWDRIVER
Fastens — NAILS
Fastens securely — MORTISES
Fastidious — NICE
Fasting season — LENT
Fat — FLAB, LARD, SUET
Fat belly — PAUNCH

Fat farm — SPA
Fat in living cells — LIPID
Fat occuring in butter — CAPRIN
Fat, in Paris — GRAS
Fat: Comb. form — STEAR, STEARO
Fat: Pref. — SEBO
Fata morgana — MIRAGE
Fatal — DEADLY, DIRE
Fatal follower — IST
Fate — DOOM, KARMA, LOT
Fated — MAJOR
Fateful assent — I DO
Fateful day for Caesar — IDES
Fateful time — IDES
Fates, Norse style — NORNS
Fathead — DOPE
Father — BEGET, DAD, PADRE, PATER, POP, SIRE
Father _____ — TIME
Father _____, in a Wolff opera — TYL
Father _____, in Wolff's "The Bluebird" — TYL
Father figure — SENIOR
Father of Abner — NER
Father of Canute — SVEN
Father of Geometry — EUCLID
Father of Horus — OSIRIS
Father of psychoanalysis — FREUD
Father of Queen Elizabeth — KING HENRY VIII
Father of Remus and Romulus — MARS
Father of Spanish drama — ENCINA
Father of the Holy Roman Empire — OTTO
Father of the sea nymphs — OCEANUS
Father of the Seven Little Foys — EDDIE
Father of the Sphinx — TYPHON
Father of Wm. — CHAS
Father of young Simpson — HOMER
Father, at Eton — PATER
Father, in Bhopal — BABI
Father, in Paris — PERE
Father, to René — PERE
Father-in-law of Moses — JETHRO
Father: Comb. form — PATRI
Fathered — SIRED
Fatherland — PATRIA
Fatherly — PATERNAL
Fathers — SIRES
Fathers brother — UNCLE
Fathers of dauphins — ROIS
Fathers: Fr. — PERES
Fathom — SIX FEET
Fathoms — GETS
Fatigue — TIRE, WEAR
Fatigued — SPENT, WEARY
Fatima slept here — ODA
Fatima's husband — BLUEBEARD
Fats — LARDS
Fats and family — DOMINOS
Fats of "Blueberry Hill" — DOMINO
Fats Waller hit of 1943 — EARLY TO BED
Fatso — BUTTERBALL, OBESE
Fatty — ADIPOSE
Fatty acid-related — OLEIC
Fatty ester — OLEATE
Fatuous — IDIOTIC, STUPID
Faucet — TAP
Faucet fault — DRIP
Faulkner character — ANSE, EULA
Faulkner female — EULA
Faulkner hero — ANSE
Faulkner protagonist — ANSE
Faulkner's "_____ in the Dust" — INTRUDER
Faulkner's "As _____ Dying" — I LAY
Faulkner's "Requiem for _____" — A NUN
Fault — DEMERIT, SIN
Fault at Shea — ERROR
Faultfinder — CRITIC, SCOLD
Faulty — AMISS
Faulty: Prefix — DYS
Faun's fellow traveler — SATYR
Fauna's companion — FLORA
Fauna's counterpart — FLORA
Faux pas — BONER, ERROR, GAFFE, MISSTEP
Favor — BOON
Favorable — ROSY
Favorable margin — EDGE
Favored — TALENTED
Favoring — PRO
Favorite — PET
Favorite breakfast treat — MARMALADE
Favorite by Ravel — BOLERO
Favorite place to visit — HAUNT
Favorite pop — COKE
Favorite potato — IDAHO
Favorite season — SUMMER
Favorite song — OLDIE
Favorites — PETS
Favoritism — BIAS
Favus — TILE
Fawn — DEER
Fawn's boss — OLLIE
Fawner — BOOT LICKER
Fawns parents — DOES
Fawns upon — ADULATES
Fax — REPRO
Fax predecessor — TELEX
Faxed — SENT
Fay — PIXIE
Fay of "King Kong" — WRAY
Fay of old flicks — WRAY
Faye Dunaway movie? — EYES OF LAURA MARS
FBI counterpart — CIA
FBI people — AGTS
FDR agency — NRA
FDR or HST — PRES
FDR Secretary of Labor — PERKINS
FDR's Blue Eagle org. — NRA
FDR's coin — DIME
FDR's dog — FALA
FDR's Fala, for one — SCOTTIE
FDR's mother — SARA
FDR's pooch — FALA
FDR's price agency — OPA
FDR, to Bellamy — ROLE
FDR-DDE separator — HST
Feague — WHIP
Fear — PANIC
Fear or hate, e.g. — EMOTION
Fear: Fr. — PEUR
Feared — SUSPECTED
Fearful — DIRE
Fearful in a way — AWED
Fearful of criticism — AFRAID
Fearing that — LEST
Fearless — INTREPID
Fears greatly — DREADS
Fearsome — SCARY
Fearsome threesome — FATES
Feast — DINE, EAT
Feast day — SEDER
Feast of lights — CHANUKAH
Feast of Lots — PURIM
Feast, Hawaiian style — LUAU
Feast, kind of — SPREAD
Feasted — ATE, DINED
Feasted one's eyes — GAZED
Feasts — DINES
Feat — STUNT
Feat at Fenway — HOMER
Feat follower — URE
Feat for Debi Thomas — AXEL
Feat for Secretariat — TRIPLE CROWN
Feather-shaped marine life — SEA PENS
Feather — PLUME
Feather an arrow — FLEDGE
Feather in one's cap — REWARD
Feather scarf — BOA
Feather stole — BOA
Feather: Comb. form — PTER
Feather: Lat. — PINNA
Featherbed homebuilder — NESTER
Feathered Arctic pirate — SKUA
Feathered neckpiece — BOA
Featherlike — PINDATE
Featherweight Attell — ABE
Featherweight boxer Attell — ABE

Featherweight champ: 1942-48 — PEP
Feathery scarves — BOAS
Feats of courage — DEEDS
Feats of Keats — VERSES
Feature of a capitalist society — COMPETITIVENESS
Feature of a frigate — MAST
Feature of a porcupine — SPINE
Feature of boat motors — SCREW PROPELLERS
Feature of Columbus: Abbr. — OSU
Feature of large cities — ZOOS
Feature of some .38's — SNUBNOSE
Feature of the opera — ARIA
Feature of the southwestern landscape — ARROYO
Feature on some campuses — IVY
Featured player — STAR
Features of tall ships — MASTS
Febrero preceder — ENERO
February card — VALENTINE
February figure — AMOR
February offering — VALEN-TINE
February, 1988 sports event — WINTER OLYMPICS
Fecund — POTENT
Fed "extraction" org. — IRS
Fed a meter — PARKED
Fed the kitty — ANTED
Fed the pot — ANTED
Fed up — BORED
Fed. agency — CIA
Fed. agency concerned with retirees — SSA
Fed. agent — T MAN
Fed. airport service — ATC
Fed. arts agcy. — NEA
Fed. collector — IRS
Fed. support program — SSI
Fedayeen grp. — PLO
Fedellini or fettucine — PASTA
Federal drug agent, for short — NARC
Federal irrigation-power bd. — TVA
Federal Reserve note — ONE DOLLAR BILL
Federal stamp — POSTAGE
Federate — JOIN
Federation — UNITED STATES
Fedora — HAT
Fedora and toque — HATS
Fedora feature — BRIM
Fedora part — BRIM
Feds — G MEN, T MEN
Fee-fi-fo-fum — OGRE
Fee — RATE
Fee receiver — PAYEE
Feeble — FRAIL
Feeble imitations — PARODY
Feeble person — DOTARD
Feebleminded — DIM
Feed-grain unit — EAR
Feed — EAT, OATS
Feed a fire — STOKE
Feed bin — SILO
Feed feasters — REGALE
Feed for a finch — SUET
Feed for Dobbin — OATS
Feed grain wheat — EMMER
Feed on — GRAZE
Feed the furnace — STOKE
Feed the hogs — SLOP
Feed the kitty — ANTE
Feedback system, for short — SERVO
Feedbag contents — OATS
Feedbag morsel — OAT
Feedbag tidbit — OAT
Feeder artery — SIDE ROAD
Feeder of Lake Erie — MAUMEE
Feeds the computer — INPUTS
Feeds the flame — FANS
Feedstuff — FODDER
Feel — GROPE, HANDLE, PROBE, SENSE, TOUCH
Feel blue — MOPE
Feel compassion (for) — YEARN
Feel compunction — REPENT
Feel guilt — RUE
Feel ill will — RESENT
Feel one's _____ — OATS
Feel one's way — GROPE
Feel poorly — ACHE, AIL
Feel remorse — REPENT
Feel sympathy — ACHE
Feel the absence of — MISS
Feel unwell — AIL
Feeler — ANTENNA, PALP, TENTACLE
Feeling — SENSE, SENTIMENT
Feeling acutely — SMARTING
Feeling blue — SAD
Feeling contrite — RUING
Feeling great — ON TOP OF THE WORLD
Feeling of regret — REMORSE
Feeling of remorse — PANG
Feeling one's oats — FULL OF BEANS
Feeling persecuted — PARA-NOID
Feeling regret — RUING
Feeling, in Ferrara — SENSO
Feelings of regret — PANGS
Feelings, mod style — VIBES
Feels bitterness — RANKLES
Feels blah — AILS
Feels comtempt for — DETESTS
Feels poorly — AILS
Feet of _____ — CLAY
Feign — ACT, PRETEND
Feigned — ACTED
Feigned manner — FRONT
Feigns — SHAMS
Feint — MOCK
Feint, in ice hockey — DEKE
Feisty baseball manager — BILLY MARTIN
Feisty ones — SCRAPPERS
Feldspar — ALBITE
Felicitous — APT
Feline — CAT, TIGER, CATLIKE
Feline musical — CATS
Feline sound — MEOW, MIAOU
Feline sports name — TIGER
Feline, in France — CHAT
Felis pardalis — OCELOT
Felix of "The Odd Couple" — UNGER
Felix or Larry — ADLER
Felix Unger's daughter — EDNA
Felix's roommate — OSCAR
Fell — DESCENDED
Fell like _____ of bricks — A TON
Fella — BUB
Feller and Garcia, for years — INDIAN PITCHERS
Fellies — RIMS
Fellow — CHAP, DUDE
Fellow members — PEERS
Fellow, in Madrid — ENTE
Fellow, to a Brit — BLOKE
Fellows — LADS
Fellowship — CAMARADERIE
Fells — HEWS
Felon — CON
Felony — ARSON
Felt — SENSATE, SENSED
Felt compelled — HAD TO
Felt ill — AILED
Felt one's _____ — OATS
Felt one's way around — GROPED
Felt remorse — RUED
Felt shoe — PAC
Felt silly? — LEFT
Felt the effects of a blow — SAW STARS
Felt under the weather — AILED
Fem's counterpart — MASC
Fem. holy person — STE
Fem. suffixes — ETTES
Fem. title — MRS
Female — MOM, SHE, WOMAN
Female advisor — EGERIA
Female assistant — GIRL FRIDAY
Female bear: Sp. — OSA
Female deer — DOE, HINS
Female demon — LAMIA
Female demon of folklore — LILITH
Female fowl — HEN
Female friend — AMIGA, GIRL
Female goat — DOE

Female hare — DOE
Female hormone — ESTROGEN
Female horse — MARE
Female insect — QUEEN
Female kangaroo — DOE
Female lobster — HEN
Female oracles — SIBYLS
Female prayer figure — ORANT
Female rabbit — DOE
Female ruff — REE
Female saint: Lat. — SANCTA
Female slave — BOND WOMAN
Female swan — PEN
Female vampire — LAMIA
Female water buffalo — ARNEE
Female water spirit — UNDINE
Female: Comb. form — ETTE, GYNE
Females of the forest — DOES
Feme sole — SPINSTER
Feminine — SOFT
Feminine endings — ETTES, INES
Feminine fabrics — SHEERS
Feminine nickname — NAN
Feminine suffix — ESS, ETTE
Feminist Bloomer — AMELIA
Feminist Carrie Chapman _____ — CATT
Feminist Friedan — BETTY
Feminist Germaine _____ — GREER
Feminist Kate — MILLETT
Feminist pitcher's concern? — ERA
Femme de chambre — CHAMBERMAID
Femme fatale — SIREN
Femme's mate — MARI
Femur — BONE
Fen — MARSH, MERE
Fen footing — MIRE
Fence — BARRIERS, PALE
Fence access — STILE
Fence appurtenance — GATE
Fence crossings — STILES
Fence entrance: Scot. — YETT
Fence features — POSTS
Fence in — ENCLOSE
Fence material — SPLIT RAIL
Fence of a sort — HEDGE
Fence of stakes — SLAT
Fence opening — GATE
Fence pickets — PALES
Fence repairer? — MENDER
Fence sitter — MUGWUMP
Fence steps — STILE
Fence straddler — STILE
Fence-crossing — STILE
Fenced — PALED
Fenced off area — ENCLOSURE
Fencer's "En _____" — GARDE
Fencer's blade — EPEE
Fencer's call — EN GARDE
Fencer's manuever — LUNGING
Fencer's sword — EPEE
Fencer's thrust — LUNGE
Fencers' weapons — EPEES
Fencing and curling — SPORTS
Fencing foils — EPEES
Fencing moves — APPELS
Fencing ploy — APPEL, LUNGE
Fencing position — TIERCE
Fencing term — SIXTE
Fend off — AVERT
Fended off — STAVED
Fender bender — DENT
Fender fault — SCRATCH
Fender flaw — DENT
Fender mishaps — DENTS
Fends off — REPELS
Fenestration accessory — WINDOW SASH
Fennel's relative — ANISE
Fenway Pk. figure — UMP
Feral — WILD
Feral feline — OCELOT
Ferber — EDNA
Ferber and Best — EDNAS
Ferber and Millay — EDNAS
Ferber book — SO BIG
Ferdinand was one — REY
Fergie's sister-in-law — ANNE
Ferlinghetti novel — HER
Fermata — HOLD, PAUSE
Ferment — YEAST
Fermented — SIMMERED
Fermented dairy food: Var. — YOGURT
Fermented Furmints — TOKAY
Fermented palm — SURAS
Fern — BRAKE, PLANT
Fern feature — SPORE
Fern grouping — BRACKEN BRACKET
Fern with feathery fronds — MAIDEN HAIR
Fernando or Lorenzo — LAMAS
Ferrara family — ESTE
Ferrara's famous family — ESTE
Ferrari, in "Casablanca" — GREENSTREET
Ferret — SEEK OUT
Ferret out — PRY, SEEK
Ferric — IRONY
Ferrigno and Rawls — LOUS
Ferrous metal — IRON
Fertile desert area — OASIS
Fertile loam — LOESS
Fertile plain in ancient Palestine — SHARON
Fertile planting medium — LOAM
Fertilized eggs — OSPORES
Fertilizer component — NITRATE
Fervent — ARDENT, EAGER
Fervent love — ADORATION
Fervid — HOT
Fervor — ARDOR, ELAN, HEAT, RAGE
Fescennine — OBSCENE
Fescue or rye — GRASS
Fester — RANKLE
Festival — REVELRY
Festive — GALA
Festive affairs — GALAS
Festive celebration — GALA
Festive color — RED
Festive decorations — RIB-BONS
Festive drinks — EGGNOGS
Festive fliers — STREAMERS
Festoon — SWAG
Festoons — DRAPES
Fetch — BRING, GET
Fetching — CHARMING
Feted — REGALED
Fetid — OLID
Fetor — ODOR
Fetter — CHAIN
Feud — VENDETTA
Feudal farm workers — SERFS
Feudal fee — FIEF
Feudal field hand — ESNE
Feudal folk — SERFS
Feudal laborer — SERF
Feudal lord — BARON, LIEGE
Feudal retainer — VASSAL
Feudal slaves — SERFS
Feudal state — FIEF
Feudal tenant — VASSAL
Feudal underlings — VASSALS
Feudal V.I.P. — THANE
Feudal vassal — LIEGE
Feudal worker — ESNE, SERF
Fever — AGUE
Few: Prefix — OLIGO
Fewer — LESS, LESS THAN
Fewest — LEAST
Feydeau works — FARCES
Feydeau's forte — FARCE
Fez or fedora — HAT
FFV family — LEES
Fiasco — BOMB
Fiascos — FLOPS, WASHOUTS
Fiat — ACT, EDICT
Fiat's cousin — UKASE
Fib — YARN
Fibbed — LIED
Fibber — LIAR
Fiber — HEMP, THREAD
Fiber food — BRAN
Fiber for cordage — SISAL
Fiber from a jute — TOSSA
Fiber shrub — RAMIE
Fiber source — RAMIE
Fibers for bags — ISTLES
Fibers for carpets — ISTLES
Fibrous — STRINGY
Fibrous material — BAST
Fibrous silicate: Abbr. — ASB

Fickle — GIDDY
Fickle lady — LUCK
Fiction — STORY, TALE
Fiction series by Paul Scott — JEWEL IN THE CROWN
Fiction series by Paul Scott — THE RAJ QUARTET
Fictional alter ego — HYDE
Fictional Bede — ADAM
Fictional Bell town — ATRI
Fictional captain — NEMO
Fictional castle — ZENDA
Fictional crossword-addicted detective — MORSE
Fictional elephant — BABAR
Fictional English sleuth — PETER WIMSEY
Fictional feline — CHESHIRE CAT
Fictional feline — PUSS IN BOOTS
Fictional form — NOVEL
Fictional girl detective — DREW
Fictional harbor heroine — TUGBOAT ANNIE
Fictional lady with a fan — WINDERMERE
Fictional man of crime — FU MAN CHU
Fictional mansion — TARA
Fictional marine — AHAB
Fictional plantation — TARA
Fictional sailor — SINBAD
Fictional sea captain — NEMO
Fictional sleuth — CHAN
Fictional sleuth Vance — PHILO
Fictional Thompson — SADIE
Fictional whaler — AHAB
Fictitious name — ALIAS
Fictitious names of court figures — ROES
Fiddle with a uke — STRUM
Fiddle-de-dee — BAH
Fiddle-faddle — DRIVEL
Fiddled — TINKERED
Fiddler of a summer's night — KATYDID
Fiddler, from the sea? — CRAB
Fide beginning — BONA
Fidel's compadre — CHE
Fidel's former aide — CHE
Fidelity — ATTACHMENT
Fidget — FRET
Fidgety — ANTSY, RESTLESS
Fido's best friend: Abbr. — ASPCA
Fido's favorite plant? — FLEA-BANE
Fido's feet — PAWS
Fido's foot — PAW
Fido's friend — ROVER
Fido's friendly assn. — ASPCA
Fido's front foot — FOREPAW
Fido's gesture of affection — SLURP
Fido's gruff remarks — WOOFS
Fido's pal — ROVER
Fido's problem — FLEAS
Fido's supper, perhaps — ORTS
Fiduciary — TRUSTEE
Field — AREA, LEA
Field biologist, e.g. — NATURALIST
Field cover, for short — TARP
Field event — DISCUS, JAVELIN THROW, MARATHON
Field event — POLE VAULT, SHOT PUT
Field game devised by Indians — LACROSSE
Field hockey number — ELEVEN
Field judge, for short — REF
Field measure — ACRE
Field mice — VOLES
Field mouse — VOLE
Field of floating ice — FLOE
Field of interest — AREA
Field of view — VISTA
Field rodents — VOLES
Field role — RAE
Field workers — GLEANERS
Field yield — CROP
Field, at Fenway — LEFT
Field, in old Roma — AGER
Field, to Caesar — AGER
Fielder's boot — ERROR
Fielding novel — AMELIA
Fieldpieces — CANNON, MORTAR
Fields — SPHERES
Fields comedy classic — THE BANK DICK
Fields, to Fabius — AGRI
Fiend — DEMON, DEVIL
Fiendish ones — DEMONS
Fierce — EAGER
Fierce anger — WRATH
Fierce attack — ONSLAUGHT
Fierce look — GLARE
Fierce ones — TARTARS
Fiercely — HOTLY
Fierceness — FEROCITY
Fiery bosses — HOT HEADS
Fiery felony — ARSON
Fifi's friend — AMIE
Fifteen percent item — TIP
Fifteenth letter — OMICRON
Fifteenth letter: Pl. — OES
Fifth canonical hour — NONE
Fifth century German migrant — SAXON
Fifth columnist, perhaps — SABOTEUR
Fifth day — THURSDAY
Fifth finger — PINKY
Fifth largest planet — EARTH
Fifth letter — EPSILON
Fifth-largest cont. — EUR
Fifth: Comb. form — QUINT
Fifties' milkshake — MALT
Fifty minutes past — TEN OF
Fifty percent — HALF
Fifty-fifty — EQUAL
Fig or fir — TREE
Fig tree — PIPA
Fig. expert — CPA
Figaro — BARBER OF SEVILLE
Figaro's betrothed — SUSANNA
Figaro's city — SEVILLE
Figaro's forte — SHAVE
Fight — SCRAP
Fight _____ (avoid) — SHY OF
Fight back — REPLY
Fight ending for short — TKO
Fight finisher — KAYO
Fight for breath — GASP
Fight formation: Abbr. — ECH
Fight seg. — RND
Fight site — ARENA
Fight-card entry — PRELIM
Fighter from Down Under, for short — ANZAC
Fighter Lee — OMA
Fighter plane: Abbr. — AWAC
Fighters — BOXERS
Fighters of 1776 — MILITIA
Fighting — AT WAR
Fighting groups — ARMIES
Fighting machine: 1917 — SPAD
Fighting mad — IRATE
Fighting time — AGAINST THE CLOCK
Fighting, of a kind — FISTICUFFS
Fights back — REVOLTS
Fights, quarrels, etc. — STRIFES
Figs. — NOS
Figuratively, ornate — FLOWERY
Figure — DIGIT
Figure in court — CITEE
Figure of speech — SIMILE, TROPE
Figure out — PLAN
Figure skater Midori — ITO
Figure skating jump — LUTZ
Figure to be totaled — ADDEND
Figured fabric — PRINT
Figured out — DOPED
Figures in the theater — DRAMATURGES
Figures the bill — ADDS
Figures' Abbr. — NOS
Figurine — STATUETTE
Figwort — HERB
Fiji Island group — TONGA
Fiji sarongs — SULUS
Filament — THREAD
Filbert — NUT
Filberts — HAZELS
Filch — LIFT, PILFER, STEAL
Filch, old style — NIM
Filched — STOLE, STOLEN
File — RASP

File folder projection — TAB
File or flail — TOOL
File's partner — RANK
Filed — ARRANGED, RASPED, REPLETE
Filet border — ORLE
Filet mignon source — STEER
Filing aid — TAB
Fill — SATE
Fill in — SUB
Fill the bill — SERVE
Fill the hold — LOAD
Fill the suitcase — PACK
Fill to repletion — SATE
Fill to the brim — TOP
Fill up tight — CRAM
Fill with dismay — APPAL
Fill with joy — ELATE
Fill with lethargy — TIRE
Fill with pride — ELATE
Fill-in — STANDBY
Filled the tummy — ATE
Filled to excess — OVER-LOADED, SATED
Filled to repletion — SATED
Filled with cargo — LADEN, LOADED
Filled with danger — PERILOUS
Filled with ennui — BORED
Filled with fear — AFRAID
Filled with wonder — AWED
Filled-in land around Boston — BACK BAY
Filler of the general coffers — TAXPAYERS
Fillet — BONE, STRIP
Filleted — BONELESS
Filling — INLAY
Filling for shells — TNT
Filling for sleeping bags — KAPOK
Fillings after drillings — AMAL-GAMS
Fillip — GOAD, INCITE, PROD
Fills the hold — LADES
Fills to repletion — SATES
Fills with dread — AWES
Fills with resolution — STEELS
Fills with reverential respect — AWES
Film — MOVIE
Film _____ — NOIR
Film about Salvadoran refugees — EL NORTE
Film actor Leon — ERROL
Film awards — OSCARS
Film based on biblical phrase — ARISE MY LOVE
Film canine — ASTA
Film critic and author James — AGEE
Film day-player — EXTRA
Film director Frank — CAPRA
Film director Fritz _____ — LANG
Film director Kenton — ERLE
Film director Kurosawa — AKIRA
Film director's order — ROLL
Film from a Burnsian phrase — OF MICE AND MEN
Film magazine — CASSETTE
Film maker Jacques — TATI
Film on bronze — PATINA
Film producer Wallis — HAL
Film site — SET
Film spool — REEL
Film starring Cary Grant — CHARADE
Film starring Debra Winger — BLACK WIDOW
Film starring John Travolta — GREASE
Film starring Julie Andrews — DUET FOR ONE
Film starring Paul Hogan — CROCODILE DUNDEE
Film starring Paul Newman — THE COLOR OF MONEY
Film studios — SETS
Film superstar — ELIZABETH TAYLOR
Film text — SCREEN SCRIPTS
Film theater magnate — LOEW
Film unit — REEL
Film var. — POS
Film with Roger Moore — THUNDERBALL
Film yeast — FLOR
Film's Flynn — ERROL
Film's Navarro — RAMON
Film's Toulouse-Lautrec — FERRER
Film-festival locale — CANNES
Film: 1953 — LILI
Filmdom's Farrow — MIA
Filmdom's Kazan — ELIA
Filmland's Cisco Kid — ROMERO
Filmmaker Louis — MALLE
Filmmaker of "The African Queen" — HUSTON
Filmmaker Spike — LEE
Filmmaker's second try — RETAKE
Films' Arthur Stanley Jefferson — LAUREL
Films' M. Hulot — TATI
Filmy — THIN
Filmy net material — NINON
Filter — STRAIN
Filter out — REMOVE
Filthy — DIRTY, FOUL
Filthy places — STIES
Fin — DORSAL
Fin. adviser — ACCT
Fin. return — INT
Fin. units — ONES
Finagle — CHEAT
Final — END, EXAM, LAST
Final authority — SAY SO
Final checks for Karpov — MATES
Final dignity — LAST STRAW
Final disposal — MOP UP
Final ending — IST
Final notice — OBIT
Final notice, of a sort — OBIT
Final outcome — FATE
Final part — TAG END
Final resting place for Wild Bill Hickok — DEADWOOD
Final sale — CLOSEOUT
Final sound in a word — AUSLAUT
Final stanza — ENVOI
Final sum — TOTAL
Final word — AMEN
Final, for one — EXAM
Finale — CLOSE, OMEGA
Finales — CODAS, ENDS
Finally — AT LAST
Finals, on campus — TESTS
Finan haddie — SMOKED HADDOCK
Financial — MONETARY
Financial certificate — SCRIP
Financial Fed — T MAN
Financial institution officer — BANKER
Financial obligation — LIABILITY
Financial plum — SINECURE
Financial plus — ASSET
Financial record: Abbr. — ACCT
Financial windfall — MELON
Financial-world elites — BLUE CHIPS
Financially discriminates against — REDLINES
Financier's Fannie _____ — MAE
Finch — SERIN
Finch, fish or crossing — ZEBRA
Find — LOCATE
Find a sudden solution — PULL A RABBIT OUT OF A HAT
Find another chair — RESEAT
Find fault — CARP, SNIPE
Find fault needlessly — CAVIL
Find fault with — BLAME
Find out — LEARN
Find the answer — SOLVE
Finder of the Holy Grail — GALAHAD
Finder start — PATH
Finding a function for — USING
Finds — RECOVERS
Finds a second renter — SUBLETS
Finds a solution for, with "out" — DOPES
Finds a way around — DETOURS
Finds colloquially — SCARES UP
Finds fault with — CENSURES

Fine-wooled sheep — MERINO
Fine — DELICATE, PENALIZE, PENALTY
Fine _____ — ARTS
Fine and liberal — ARTS
Fine cheese — EDAM
Fine china — BONE
Fine china from England — SPODE
Fine cigar — CORONA
Fine cloth fiber — RAMIE
Fine cotton — PIMA
Fine cotton fabric — BATISTE, PIMA
Fine cotton thread — LISLE
Fine equine — STEED
Fine fabric — LACE, TULLE
Fine fabrics — BATISTES
Fine fiber — SILK
Fine fiddle — AMATI
Fine French lace — ALENCON
Fine fur — SABLE
Fine horse — ARAB
Fine Japanese porcelain — IMARI
Fine lava — ASH
Fine line of a letter — SERIF
Fine linen — FAWN
Fine marks — AAAA
Fine porcelain — MING
Fine powder of antimony — KOHL
Fine rain — MIST
Fine shines — LUSTERS
Fine soap — CASTILE
Fine spray — MIST
Fine steed — ARAB
Fine violin — AMATI
Fine wool — MERINO
Fine-feathered bird — EGRET
Fine-grained chalcedony — AGATE
Fine-grained granite — APLITE
Fined — AMERCED
Finely tempered sword — TOLEDO
Finery — ARRAY
Fines — AMERCES
Finess — OUTWIT
Finest — BEST
Finger — DIGIT
Finger Lake — SENECA
Finger Lakes — NEW YORK
Finger tip — NAIL
Fingerling salmon — SAMLET
Fingerprint features — ARCHES
Finial — EPI, CREST, ORNAMENT
Finial of a weather vane — EPI
Finicky — NEAT
Finis — END
Finish — COME TO A CLOSE, COMPLETE, END UP
Finish — OMEGA, RESOLVE, SETTLE
Finish first — WIN
Finish line — TAPE
Finish out of the ribbons — LOSE
Finish, as with lace — EDGE
Finished — ALL OVER, DONE, ENDED, OVER
Finished — OUT OF THE RUNNING, PAST
Finished — OVER AND DONE WITH, THRU
Finished hang gliding — ALIT
Finished last — LOSES
Finished: Poet. — OER
Finisher in "Wayne's World" — NOT
Finishes — ENDS
Finishes last — LOSES
Finishes off — SLAYS
Finishing nail — BRAD
Finishing tool — REAMER
Fink — RAT
Finland to Sibelius — SUOMI
Finland, to a Finn — SUOMI
Finn — HUCK
Finn's chum — SAWYER
Finn's cousin — ESTH
Finn's friend — SAWYER
Finn's language group — URALIC
Finn's neighbor — LAPP
Finnbogadóttir — VIGDIS
Finnic language — LAPP
Finnish bath — SAUNA
Finnish canto — RUNE
Finnish fruit? — HELSINKIWI
Finnish islands — ALAND
Finnish lake, to Swedes — ENARE
Finnish poem — RUNE
Finnish: Abbr. — FIN
Finno-Ugric language group — URALIC
Fiord — BAY
Fiord on the coast of Denmark — ISE
Fiord or city — OSLO
Fipple flutes — FLAGEOLETS
Fir or pine board — DEAL
Fire — ARSON, CAN
Fire _____ (semiprecious stone) — OPAL
Fire call exercise — DRILL
Fire crime — ARSON
Fire inspector's concern — ARSON
Fire remains — ASHES
Fire residue — ASH, EMBER
Fire retardant material — ASBESTOS
Fire starter — FLINT
Fire starters — TINDERS
Fire up — ANGER
Fire up, in a way — FAN THE FLAME
Fire worshiper — PARSI
Fire! — SHOOT
Fire-resistant fibers: Abbr. — ASB
Fire: Comb. form — IGNI
Fire: Prefix — IGNI
Firearm part — TRIGGER
Fireball — METEOR
Firebird — ORIOLE
Firebomb material — NAPALM
Firebug — PYRO
Firecracker — PETARD
Fired — LIT
Fired up — EAGER
Firedogs — ANDIRONS
Firefighters' gear — HOSES
Firehouse dog? — SPOT
Firenza's river — ARNO
Firenze friend — AMICO
Fireplace — GRATE, HEARTH, INGLE
Fireplace accessory — ANDIRON
Fireplace adjunct — MANTEL
Fireplace item — ANDIRON
Fireplace ledges — HOBS
Fireplace part — GRATE
Fireplace residue — EMBERS
Fireplace shelf — MANTEL
Fires — PULLS THE TRIGGER, SACKS
Fires up the furnace: Abbr. — IGNS
Fireside area — HEARTH
Fireside receptacle — ASHCAN
Firewood measure — STERE
Fireworks — PINWHEELS, SPARKS
Firing pin — DOTTLE
Firm — HARD, RIGID, SOLID, STIFF
Firm abbr. — BROS
Firm attachment — ADHESION
Firm fiber — SISAL
Firm or quick — FAST
Firm, unbroken soil — HARDPAN
Firmament — ETHER, HEAVEN, SKY
Firmly fixed: Var. — STEDFAST
Firmly in place — ROOTED
Firms up — SETS
Firms up muscles — TONES
Firn — NEVE
First — BASIC, INITIAL, LEADING
First — PRIMARY, MAIN, WINNER
First "Today Show" host — GARROWAY
First _____ — AID
First _____ (super) — RATE
First _____: 264-41 B.C. — PUNIC WAR
First American female astronaut — RIDE
First American in Orbit — GLENN

First and third first ladies — MARTHAS
First appearance — DEBUT
First Arabian country to strike oil — BAHRAIN
First Arabic letter — ALIF
First asteroid discovered — CERES
First attempt — DEBUT
First baseball commissioner — LANDIS
First baseman Kluszewski, to fans — KLU
First baseman of comedy — WHO
First book of the Old Testament — GENESIS
First class — A ONE
First commissioner of baseball — LANDIS
First couple's home — EDEN
First Dracula of film — BELA LUGOSI
First Duke of Normandy — ROLLO
First dynasty in Chinese history — HSIA
First event of a series — OPENER
First Family at Albany — CUOMOS
First family member — ABEL, SETH
First family's home — EDEN
First father — ADAM
First five Old Testament books — TORAH
First flag component — STAR
First flier lost at sea — ICARUS
First four of 26 — ABCD
First game of the season — OPENER
First garden — EDEN
First German president — EBERT
First Hebrew letter — ALEF
First horse — EOHIPPUS
First in a trio — TOM
First Indian ruler to embrace Buddhism — ASOKA
First introduction? — CALL ME ADAM
First King of Egypt — MENES
First King of Israel — SAUL
First king of Saudi Arabia — IBN SAUD
First king of the English — EGBERT
First known — EARLIEST
First lady — EVE
First Lady of Scat — ELLA
First lady of Versailles: Fr. — REINE
First lady's man — ADAM
First letter, Greek style — ALPHA
First man — ADAM
First man on the moon — NEIL ARMSTRONG
First Marxist President of Chile — ALLENDE
First mate — ADAM, EVE
First minor prophet — HOSEA
First Monday in September — LABOR DAY
First month, in Madrid: Sp. — ENERO
First Mother's Day celebrants? — ADAM AND EVE
First name for Blackmore heroine — LORNA
First name in "sleuthery" — ERLE
First name in architecture — EERO
First name in flight — ORVILLE, WILBUR
First name in heliocopters — IGOR
First name in musicals — FLO
First name in mystery — ERLE
First name in scat — ELLA
First name in solidarity — LECH
First name in westerns — WYATT
First name in whodunits — ERLE
First name of a first lady — MAMIE
First name of a memorable loner — GRETA
First name of a star on the bars — OLGA
First name of British actor Sanders — GEORGE
First name of popular silent star — POLA
First name of Swedish actor Olin — LENA
First name of the 18th President — HIRAM
First nine in golf — FRONT
First of a Latin trio — AMO
First of the Cavalier poets — ELIOT
First Olympics site — ELIS
First opera's composer Jacopo _____ — PERI
First or foreign — AID
First parts, as in trios — PRIMOS
First performance — PREMIERE
First person — ADAM
First place — EDEN
First planet discovered — CERES
First planet outside Earth's orbit — MARS
First president of Mali — KEITA
First Prime Minister of India — NEHRU
First rate — A ONE
First recorded king of Egypt — MENES
First Republican presidential candidate: 1856 — FREMONT
First seen asteroid — CERES
First shepherd — ABEL
First State — DELAWARE
First strike — ONE
First stroke of Big Ben — HOUR
First telegrapher — MORSE
First to come — EARLIEST
First to stab Caesar — CASCA
First to strike Caesar — CASCA
First to wear bifocals — FRANKLIN
First transplant site? — EDEN
First U.S. astronaut to circle the earth — GLENN
First U.S. Postmaster General — OSGOOD
First Vicount Templewood — HOARE
First wife of Jacob — LEAH
First women's Wimbledon champ: 1946 — PAULINE BETZ
First word in Massachusetts motto — ENSE
First word of "Home, Sweet Home" — MID
First word of "Paul Revere's Ride" — LISTEN
First word of Poe's "The Raven" — ONCE
First word of the Declaration — WHEN
First year Latin word — AMO
First zoo? — ARK
First, in Berlin — ERSTE
First, once — ERST
First, second, third or home — BASE
First-act finale in "La Bohème" — DUET
First-aid contrivance — SLING
First-born — ELDEST
First-discovered asteroid — CERES
First-prize color — BLUE
First-rate — A ONE, KNOCKOUT, TIPTOP
First-string — REGULAR
First: Comb. form — ARCHI
Firsts, in Mexican olympics — OROS
Firth of Clyde island — BUTE
Fiscal — MONEY
Fischer-Dieskau's songs — LIEDER
Fish-eater — ERN, ERNE
Fish-eating bird — ERN, LOON

Fish-eating diving birds — LOONS
Fish-eating hawk — OSPREY
Fish — ANGLE, COD, SMELT, SOLE, TUNA
Fish _____, in "The Green Pastures" — FRY
Fish basket — CREEL
Fish catcher — SEINE
Fish choice — SOLE
Fish complement — LEMON
Fish covering — SCALE
Fish dam — WEIR
Fish delicacies — ROES
Fish dish — EELS, SCRODSOLE
Fish eggs — ROES
Fish feature — GILL
Fish food — SOLE
Fish from Dover — SOLE
Fish fry — PICNIC
Fish hook — GAFF
Fish hook accessory — SWIVEL
Fish line leader — SNELL
Fish migration — RUN
Fish of the herring family — SHAD
Fish of the perch family — DARTER
Fish on a French menu — POISSON
Fish or cook attachment — ERY
Fish or cut bait — STAND
Fish or pear — TUNA
Fish or voice — BASS
Fish organ — FIN, GILL
Fish preparation — SCALING
Fish sauce — ALEC, TARTARE
Fish sign — PISCES
Fish stories — LIES
Fish traps — FYKES
Fish with a net — TRAWL
Fish's respiratory organ — GILL
Fish, in a way — TROLL
Fish-eating birds — OSPREYS
Fish-eating seabird — GANNET
Fisher or Foy — EDDIE
Fisherman of a sort — EELER
Fisherman's bend — KNOT
Fisherman's leader — SNELL
Fisherman's need — BAIT
Fisherman's plan? — TACKLE THE JOB
Fisherman's rig — BANK LINE
Fisherman's view — HOOK LINE AND SINKER
Fisherman, perhaps — LURER
Fishermen's profit? — NET
Fishes of the future — ROES
Fishes with nets — TRAWLS
Fishhook food — BAIT
Fishhook replacement — SNELL
Fishing — EELING
Fishing aid — NET
Fishing basket — CREEL
Fishing boat — SMACK
Fishing device — REEL, SET NET
Fishing fleets, for example — ARMADAS
Fishing fly — CAHILL, HERL
Fishing gadget — FLY, LURE
Fishing gear — RODS, TACKLE
Fishing grounds of the Shetlands — HAAF
Fishing lure — SPINNER
Fishing need — BAIT, LINE
Fishing net — FLUE, SEINE
Fishing trawl — SET LINE
Fishing vessel — SMACK
Fishlike — SCALY
Fishmonger's dearth? — OUT OF TROUT
Fishpoles — RODS
Fishwife's cousin — NAG
Fishy — SHADY
Fishy date — IDES
Fishy feature — SCALES
Fissile rock — SHALE
Fissure — CHUNK, RIFT
Fist — MITT, PAW
Fist fights — SET TOS
Fist tag-on — IANA
Fisticuffs — BRAWL
Fit — ABLE, READY, SUITABLE
Fit as a fiddle — HEALTHY, SOUND
Fit for a king — REGAL
Fit for farming — ARABLE
Fit for sampling — TASTABLE
Fit for scrutiny — STUDIABLE
Fit for the job — ABLE
Fit of anger — SNIT, SPLEEN
Fit of gossip, French style — ONDIT
Fit of pique — SNIT
Fit the mizzen — RIG
Fit to _____ — A TEE
Fit to be _____ — TIED
Fit to be marketed — SALEABLE
Fitness — HEALTH, RELEVANCE
Fitness center — SPA
Fitness facility — SPA
Fitness spot — SPA
Fits of temper — SNITS, TANTRUMS
Fits partner — STARTS
Fitted outer garments — REDINGOTES
Fitted piece — TENON
Fitting — APT, DUE, MEET, RIGHT
Fitzgerald and Logan — ELLAS
Fitzgerald and Raines — ELLAS
Fitzgerald of Jazz — ELLA
Fitzgerald or Logan — ELLA
Fitzgerald or Raines — ELLA
Fitzgerald specialty — SCAT
Fitzgerald's rhyme for "thou" — ENOW
Fitzgerald's Zelda — SAYRE
Five-year period — PENTAD
Five and ten: Abbr. — NOS
Five by _____ — FIVE
Five cents — NICKEL
Five Goren points — KING AND QUEEN
Five Nations tribe — MOHAWK
Five o'clock shadow — STUBBLE
Five of trumps — PEDRO
Five or nine at times — TEAMS
Five-and-ten — DIME STORE
Five-angled figures — PENTAGONS
Five-buck bills — FINS
Five-dollar bill — FIN
Five-franc piece of yore — ECA
Five-hundredth anniversary — QUINCENTENARY
Five-liners named for an Irish port — LIMERICKS
Five-spot — FIN
Five: Comb. form — PENTA
Fiver — FIN
Fix — AMEND, MEND, REPAIR
Fix an argyle — DARN
Fix an electrical device — REWIRE
Fix copy — EDIT
Fix laces again — RETIE
Fix potatoes — MASH
Fix the boundaries of — DEFINE
Fix the clocks again — RESET
Fix the lawn — SOD
Fix the roof — RETAR
Fix up — SOLVE
Fix up copy — EDIT
Fix up the house with new things — REDO
Fixation — FETISH, HANG UP
Fixations — FETISHES, TICS
Fixed — FAST
Fixed a flat — SOLED
Fixed amount — UNIT
Fixed charge — FEE
Fixed charges — RATES
Fixed course or routine — ROTE
Fixed quantity — UNIT
Fixes beforehand — PRESETS
Fixes boundaries — DELIMITS
Fixes the squeaks — OILS
Fixture — TOOL
Fizzles — FAILS
Fizzwater — SODA
Fizzy drink — SODA
Fizzy drinks — SODAS
Fjord — INLET
Fjord city — OSLO
Fjord, for one — ARM
FL feature — KEYS
FL teams — DOLPHINS AND BUCCANEERS

FL trees — TALLOW BERRIES
Fla. Cape — SABLE
Fla. city — OCALA
Fla. coastal city — DANIA
Fla. county — DADE
Fla. neighbor — ALA
Flabbergast — AMAZE
Flabby — FAT
Flaccid — LAX, LIMP, FLABBY
Flag — IRIS, PENNON, TIRE
Flag feature — STRIPE
Flag maker's name — ROSS
Flag-lowering ceremony — RETREAT
Flagitious — VILE
Flagpole rope — HALYARD
Flagrant — EGREGIOUS, WANTON
Flags — IRISES, TIRES
Flaherty film — MAN OF ARAN
Flaherty's "_____ of the North" — NANOOK
Flaherty's "Man of _____" — ARAN
Flair — KNACK, SKILL, TALENT
Flaky — DRY
Flaky dessert — PIE
Flame feeder — FUEL
Flamed up — BLAZED
Flaming — ABLAZE, AFIRE
Flaminian Way — ROAD
Flanders river — YSER
Flâneur — IDLER
Flange — EDGE, RIM
Flank — LOIN
Flap — FUSS, TAB
Flapjack — PANCAKE
Flapper of long ago? — PTERADACTYL
Flare — OUTBURST
Flare, sometimes — DISTRESS SIGNAL
Flared up — ERUPTED
Flaring outward — EVASE
Flash — BOLT, GLINT, SEC
Flash fish — OPAH
Flash Gordon's foe — MING
Flash of light — GLEAM
Flashed the _____ — COLOR OF MONEY
Flashlight, British style — TORCH
Flashy — CHICHI, GARISH, LOUD, SPORTY
Flashy fellow — SPORT
Flask — BOTTLE
Flat-bottomed boat — PUNT, SCOW
Flat — EDICT, STALE, TAME
Flat boat — SCOW
Flat double fold in cloth — PLEAT
Flat elevations — MESAS
Flat finish — MATTE
Flat fish — DAB
Flat out — APACE
Flat plinth — ORLO
Flat replacement — SPARE
Flat sign — TO LET
Flat straw hat — BOATER
Flat-bottomed ship — JUNK
Flat-bottomed vessel — BARGE
Flat-topped hill — MESA
Flat-topped vehicle — SURREY
Flat: Comb. form — PLANO
Flat: Prefix — PLANO
Flatbush hero of yore — REESE
Flatfish — PLAICE, SOLE
Flatfish of northern seas — HALIBUT
Flatout — POST HASTE
Flats — BAD TIRES
Flats: Abbr. — APTS
Flatten — CRUSH, SQUASH
Flatten a flat — RAZE
Flattened at the poles — OBLATE
Flattens, in a way — KOS
Flatter — LAUD
Flatter, in a way — IMITATE
Flatterer — ADULATOR
Flattery for the boss — YOURE THE TOP
Flattop on land — MESA
Flatulent — WINDY
Flatwear item — SPOON
Flaubert's "_____ Bovary" — MADAME
Flaunt — DISPLAY
Flautist — TOOTER
Flavor — SAPOR, TANG
Flavor enhancer — SPICE
Flavorful — SAPID, SAPOROUS
Flavorful bean — VANILLA
Flavorful plant of the lily family — LEEK
Flavorful quality — SAPOR
Flavorful veggie — ONION
Flavoring agent — SESAME
Flavoring for a Caen cordial — ANIS
Flavoring for a Cannes cordial — ANIS
Flavoring for Christmas cookies — ANISE
Flavoring seed — ANISE
Flavoring substance, in cooking — RIND
Flavors — TASTES
Flavors with — ENDOWS
Flavorsome — SPICED
Flavorsome liqueur — ANISETTE
Flaw — DEFECT
Flawed entrances — MISCUES
Flawless — IDEAL
Flaws — MARS
Flax product — LINEN
Flaxen haired — BLOND
Flay — STRIP
Fld. goal — BSKT
Flèche — SPIRE
Fleck — DUST
Fled — RAN
Fledermaus — BAT
Fledgling — NESTLER, TENDERFOOT
Fledgling sounds — PEEPS
Fledgling's home — NEST
Flee — BOLT, DECAMP
Flee: Slang — LAM
Fleece — COAT
Fleeced — STRUNG
Fleecy females — EWES
Fleer — LAUGH
Flees — ESCAPES
Flees to a J.P. — ELOPES
Fleet — ARMADA, FAST
Fleet initials — USN
Fleet monogram — USN
Fleet St. product — TIMES
Fleet Street — PRISON
Fleet Street locale — LONDON
Fleet V.I.P.'s — REAR ADMIRALS
Fleet-footed — AGILE
Fleeting things — EPHEMERA
Fleetwood _____ — MAC
Fleming — IAN, RHONDA
Fleming and Hunter — IANS
Fleming and namesakes — IANS
Fleming of "Rawhide" — ERIC
Fleming or Richardson — IAN
Fleming or Smith — IAN
Flemish painter — RUBENS
Flesh — TISSUE
Flesh-colored — INCARNADINE
Flesh: Comb. form — SARC
Flesh: Prefix — SARC
Fleshy — PAUNCHY
Fleshy fruit — POME
Fleshy part — PULP
Fleshy plant — SEDUM
Fleshy root — TUBER
Fleur-de- _____ — LIS, LYS
Fleur-de-lis — IRIS
Fleuret's kin — EPEE
Fleuret's relative — EPEE
Fleurets — EPEES
Flew — RAN
Flew alone — SOLOED
Flew, in a way — JETTED
Flex — BEND
Flexibility — GIVE
Flexible — PLIANT
Flexible armor — MAIL
Flexible plastic resin — SARAN
Flick — PIC
Flick fortaste — PREVUE
Flickering — LAMBENT
Flier's emblem — WINGS
Flier's-helmet wearer — SNOOPY
Fliers plucky under fire? — GAMEBIRDS

Flies alone — SOLOS
Flies heavenward — SOARS
Flies high — SOARS
Flies in flight fashion — KITES
Flies like a butterfly — FLITS
Flight attendant — STEWARD
Flight delayer, perhaps — SMOG
Flight formation: Abbr. — ECH
Flight of steps — STAIR
Flight segment — STEP
Flight unit — STEP
Flight unit — STEP, STAIR
Flight: Slang — LAM
Flightless — EARTHBOUND
Flightless bird — EMU, MOA
Flightless birds — EMUS
Flighty — GIDDY
Flimflam — TRICK
Flimflammed — CONNED
Flimsy — JERRYBUILT
Flimsy garment — NEGLIGEE
Flinders — PIECES, WINCES
Fling — CAST, TOSS
Fling carelessly — TOSS
Flintstone principal — FRED
Flintstones' pet — DINO
Flip — TOSS
Flippant — GLIB, PERT
Flipped up — ONED
Flipper — FIN
Flipper of a whale — FIN
Flippers — PADDLES
Flirt — OGLE, OGLER
Flirt with — MASH
Flirtation — DALLIANCE
Flirtatious glances — GOO-GOO EYES
Flirtatious look — OGLE
Flirtatious man — MASHER
Flitting — FLYING
Flivver — AUTO, HEAP
Flivvers — CARS
Flo Jo or Rono — MEDALIST
Float — BOB, BUOY, PONTOON, RAFT
Float outward — STREAM
Float through the air — SOAR
Floating — AWASH, NATANT
Floating guardhouse — BRIG
Floating hotel — LINER
Floating ice mass — BERG
Floating matter of the upper White Nile — SUDD
Floating palace — OCEAN LINER
Floating platform — RAFT
Floating zoo — ARK
Flock — DROVE, HERD
Flock fellows — RAMS
Flock female — EWE
Flock of felines — PRIDE
Flock of finches — CHARM
Flock of geese — SKEIN
Flock of geese in flight — SKEIN
Flock of geese on land — GAGGLE
Flock of herons — SIEGE
Flock of Peacocks — MUSTER
Flock of sheep — FOLD
Flock's cousin — HERD
Flocks — HERDS
Flocks of turkeys — RAFTER
Floe — BERG, ICE
Flog — LASH
Flood — FRESHET, GLUT, INRUSH
Flood follower — GATE
Flood refuge — ARK
Flooded — AWASH
Floodgate — SLUICE
Floodgates — DAMS
Floor — DECK, STUN
Floor cleaner — MOP
Floor cover — LINOLEUM
Floor covering, for short — LINO
Floor coverings — MATS, RUG, TILES
Floor exit — TRAP DOOR
Floor material — TILE
Floor of a fireplace — HEARTH
Floor piece — TILE
Floor support — JOISTS
Flooring — TERRAZZO, TILE
Flooring experts — TILERS
Flop — BOMB, FIASCO
Flop down — COLLAPSE
Flop, as a show — DIE
Flora — FAUNA
Flora and fauna — BIOTA
Flora and fauna of a region — BIOTA
Flora of the moors — ERICA
Floral arrangements — WREATHS
Floral asset — AROMA
Floral neckware — LEIS
Floral organ — STAMEN
Floral perfume — ATTAR
Florence native — TUSCAN
Florence's river — ARNO
Florence's waterfront — ARNO
Florentine architectural order — TUSCAN
Florentine family — MEDICI
Florentine flower — FIORE
Florentine palace — PETTI
Florid — RED
Florid: Fr. — ORNEE
Florida _____ — KEYS
Florida citrus center — — OCALA
Florida city — OCALA
Florida county — DADE
Florida divers' quests — SUNKEN TREASURES
Florida game fish — TARPON
Florida locales — KEYS
Florida resort — PALM BEACH
Florida's discoverer — DE LEON
Florida's Saint _____ — AUGUSTINE
Florist — PETAL PUSHER
Florist's favorite song? — ORCHIDS IN THE MOONLIGHT
Flotation device — LIFEBELT
Flotsam — DEBRIS
Flounces on blouses — PEPLA
Flounder — DAB
Flour sprinklers — DREDGERS
Flourish — GROW, THRIVE
Flourisher — THRIVER
Flow — CURRENT
Flow freely — POUR
Flow from a volcano — LAVA
Flow's counterpart — EBB
Flow's partner — EBB
Flowed back — EBBED
Flowed out — EBBED
Flowed to and fro — TIDED
Flower — BLOOM, BLOSSOM
Flower arranging in Nagoya — IKEBANA
Flower box favorite — PETUNIA
Flower clusters — CYMES
Flower essence — ATTAR
Flower extract — ATTAR
Flower features — PETALS, STEMS
Flower for Wordsworth — DAFFODIL
Flower from the Vosges — SAAR
Flower holder — VASE
Flower O'Keeffe painted — POPPY
Flower of the south — COTTON BLOSSOM
Flower part — CALYX, PETAL, SEPAL
Flower petals — COROLLAS
Flower pot of a sort — TUB
Flower stalks — SCAPES
Flower State — FLORIDA
Flower support — STEM
Flower through Florence — ARNO
Flower's petals, collectively — COROLLA
Flower's Saturday night special? — PISTIL
Flower-to-be — BUD
Flowering shrub — AZALEA, LILAC
Flowering water plant — LOTUS
Flowers flower in these — BEDS
Flowers from the Vosges — SAAR
Flowers' forerunners — BUDS
Flowery — ORNATE

Flowery arbor — BOWER
Flows — RUNS
Flt. data — ETAS
Flt. info — ETA
Flu sign — AGUE
Flu symptom — AGUE
Flub — BLUNDER
Fluctuate — SWAY
Flue coating — SOOT
Fluent — GLIB
Fluff — LINT
Fluffy fur piece — BOA
Fluffy neckpiece — BOA
Fluffy scarf — BOA
Fluffy stuff — LINT
Fluffy wool — ANGORA
Fluid accumulation — EDEMA
Fluid conveyor — HOSE, PIPE
Fluid in Zeus's veins -ICHOR
Fluorescent lamp gas — ARGON
Flurries — ADOS
Flurry — STIR
Flush — EVEN
Flush out game, in a way — BATTUE
Flushed — ROSY
Flushed corvine — BLUSHING CROW
Flushed to the max — RUDDIEST
Flustered — HET UP
Flute family member — FIFE
Flute sound — TOOTLE
Flute's kin — PICCOLO
Flutter — PULSE, TREMOR, WAVER
Fly — FLIT
Fly about — FLIT
Fly aloft — SOAR
Fly apart — BUST
Fly catcher — HONEY
Fly high — SOAR
Fly hit by a coach — FUNGO
Fly in the ointment — SNAG
Fly off the _____ — HANDLE
Fly off the handle — RANT
Fly that falls safely — TEXAS LEAGUER
Fly the coop — ESCAPE, FLEE
Fly weight — BOXER
Fly without an instructor — SOLO
Fly-by-night — SHADY
Flyboy — PILOT
Flyboys — AIRMEN
Flycatcher — REESE
Flyer Earhart — AMELIA
Flyers' org. — RAF
Flying — AERI
Flying ace Balboa — ITALO
Flying ace Don of WW II — GENTILE
Flying boat — SEAPLANE
Flying elephant-eaters of folklore — ROCS
Flying insect — GNAT
Flying mammal — BAT
Flying manuever — LOOP
Flying Mary — MARTIN
Flying org. — FAA
Flying prefix — AERO, AERI
Flying saucers — UFOS
Flying spray — SCUD
Flynn of film fame — ERROL
Flynn of films — ERROL
Flynn of old flicks — ERROL
Flynn of the movies — ERROL
Flyway din — HONKS
Fo'c'sle pacer — BOSN
Foam; froth — YEAST
Foamy brew — BEER
Foamy wave — WHITECAP
Fob — PASS OFF
Focal point — CENTER, HUB, TARGET
Foci — CENTERS
Focus — CENTER
Focus of Buckeye fans — OHIO STATE
Focusing device — LENS
Fodder — ENSILAGE, HAY, WHEAT
Fodder for computer — SOFTWARE
Fodder of a type — SILAGE
Fodder or bedding — STRAW
Fodder pit — SILO
Fodder plant — VETCH
Fodder shrub — GORSE
Foe — ENEMY
Foe of S. Grant — E LEE
Fog — MIST, MURK
Fog and smoke — SMOG
Fog fallout — DEW
Fog tatters — WISPS
Foghorn, for one — ALARM
Fogies — DODOS
Fogs companion — MIST
Fogy — DUFFER
Foil — STUMP
Foil's cousin — EPEE
Foil's relative — EPEE
Foiled by a Fisk throw — CAUGHT
Foiled the posse — ESCAPED
Fokker foe — SPAD
Fold — CREASE, CRINKLE, GATHER, PEN
Fold and fade away — CLOSE
Fold females — EWES
Fold over — LAP
Fold sound — BAA
Foliage used for crowns — LAUREL
Folk-rock singer Jim — CROCE
Folk foreword — KIN
Folk music of a sort — BLUES
Folklore character — OGRE
Folklore figure — GNOME, OGRE
Folklore heavies — OGRES
Folklore queen — MAB
Folksinger Burl — IVES
Folksinger Joan — BAEZ
Folksinger Richard _____ - Bennet — DYER
Folksingers' fest — HOOTENANNY
Folksong of the West Indies — CALYPSO
Folkways — MORES
Follow — ENSUE, TAIL, TRAIL
Follow along — GET ON THE BAND WAGON
Follow doggedly — PURSUE
Follow orders — OBEY
Follow rain or snow — SHOWERS
Follow the hounds — HUNT
Follow too closely — TAILGATE
Follow, to Solti — SEGUE
Followed — ENSUED
Followed a marriage vow — HONORED
Followed slavishly — APED
Follower — TAILOR
Follower of the Way — TAOIST
Follower: Suffix — IST, ITE
Followers of a sort — GEESE
Followers of canon and musket — EERS
Followers of ens — OES
Followers of Zeno — STOICS
Followers of zetas — ETAS
Followers of: Suffix — ISTS
Followers: Suffix — ITES
Following — AFTER, AUDIENCE, NEXT, PUBLIC
Following a curving course — ARCING
Following the sun — WESTING
Following this — HERE AFTER
Following young or old — STERS
Follows bee — CEE
Follows Cancer — LEO
Follows epsilon — ZETA
Follows fict or nutr — ITIOUS
Follows ham or mob — STER
Foment — STIR
Fond _____, WI — DU LAC
Fond du _____ — LAC
Fonda / Sutherland movie — KLUTE
Fondle — CARESS
Fontaine Fox strip — THE TOONERVILLE TROLLEY
Fontainebleu woods — FORET
Fontanne's partner — LUNT
Fonteyn and Markova — DAMES
Fonteyn bend — PLIE
Fonteyn's title — DAME
Fonts — SOURCES
Foo yong — EGG
Food — EDIBLES

Food _____ thought — FOR
Food additive: Abbr. — MSG
Food and drink — CHEER
Food and lodging — BOARD
Food and sport fish — YELLOW PERCH
Food enhancer — HERB
Food fish — BASS, CARP, CODS, EEL, SHAD, SOLE
Food fish — SHAD, SNAPPER, SNOOK, SALMON
Food fish akin to the pompanos — SCAD
Food fit for a fitness fiend — YOGURT
Food for the birds — SUET
Food from orchids — SALEP
Food in Florence — PASTA
Food in red paraffin — EDAM
Food item — COMESTIBLE
Food list — MENU
Food mixture in a small bowl — TIMBALE
Food of the gods — AMBROSIA
Food portion — PLATE
Food previously cooked — HASH
Food producers — FARMS
Food regimen — DIET
Food scrap — ORT
Food stabilizing agent — AGAR
Food staple — RICE
Food store — DELI
Food thickening agent — AGAR
Food vouchers — CHITS
Food wrap — SARAN
Food, shelter, etc. — NEEDS
Food: Comb. form — SITO
Foods — EDIBLES
Foodstuff, Dublin style — IRISH SODA BREAD
Foofaraws — ADOS
Fool — ASS, IDIOT, NINNY, NODDY, SAY, SIMP
Fool away time — IDLE
Fool's day mo. — APR
Fool's play of yore — SOTIE
Fooled — DELUDED
Foolish — ASININE, DAFT, SAPPY, SILLY
Foolish fancies — CHIMERAS
Foolish fancy — CHIMERA
Foolish fellow — SIMPLE SIMON
Foolish guillemot — MURRE
Foolish mistakes — BLOOPERS
Foolish, tree climbing bird? — NUTTY HATCH
Foolishly affected — APISH
Foolishness — FOLLY
Fools — SAPS, SIMPS
Foolscap figure? — PAPER EIGHT
Foot — PES
Foot bones — TALI, TARSI
Foot for Frost — IAMB
Foot form — LAST
Foot movement — STEP
Foot part — INCH, INSTEP, SOLE
Foot parts — TARSI
Foot soldier in India — PEON
Foot soldiers ammo? — GROUND ROUND
Foot soldiers of medieval Ireland: var. — KERNES
Foot the bill — TREAT
Foot woes — CORNS
Foot, for one — UNIT
Foot: Comb. form — PED, PEDI
Foot: L. — PES
Foot: Prefix — PED
Foot: Suffix — PEDE
Football — STEP
Football coach Amos Alonzo — STAGG
Football coach Warner — POP
Football factory worker — LACER
Football figure — ELEVEN
Football first name — ARA
Football footage: Abbr. — YDS
Football formation — SINGLE WINGBACK
Football goal — FIELD
Football Hall-of-Famer Parker — ACE
Football infraction — CLIP
Football interception — SNAG
Football kick — PUNT
Football no-no's — CLIPS
Football pass — LATERAL
Football play — LATERAL, TRAP
Football player — HARRIS, ROCKNE, STARR
Football players — ENDS
Football ploy — PASS
Football position — END
Football Q. or C. — POS
Football strategy — ENDPLAY
Football term — THIRD DOWN
Football's _____ Simpson — ORENTHAL JAMES
Football's fleetest — RUNNING BACKS
Football's Panthers, for short — PITT
Football's Tarkenton — FRAN
Footboy — PAGE
Footed vases — URNS
Footfall — STEP
Foothold — ROOST
Foothold provider — CLEAT
Footing — BASIS
Footle — CAPER
Footless — APOD
Footless animals — APODS
Footless creature — APOD
Footlike parts — PES
Footlocker — TRUNK
Footloose — ITINERANT
Footmen of India — PEONS
Footnote abbr. — IBID
Footnote direction — VIDE
Footnote notation — IBID
Footnote word — IBIDEM, IBID
Footpace — DAIS
Footpath — TRAIL
Footprint — TRACE
Footprints — TRACKS
Footrest — STOOL
Foots it — HIKES
Footsteps — TREADS
Footstool — HASSOCK
Footware form — SHOE TREE
Footway — PATH
Footwear — BOOT, MULES, SHOE
Footwear for Franz Peter? — SCHUBERT SHOE
Footwear of a dandy — SPATS
Fop — BEAU, DANDY, DUDE
For _____ sake — PITYS
For a _____: cheaply — SONG
For a brief time — AWHILE
For a fact — TRUE
For all time, poetically — EER
For each — PER
For example — SUCH AS, TO WIT
For fear that — LEST
For good — FINALLY
For keeps — EVER
For love or money — EVER
For men only — STAG
For nothing — FREE
For or where follower — EVER
For Pete's _____! — SAKE
For rent — TO LET
For shame! — TSK
For the time being — PRO TEM
For this reason — HEREAT
For. diplomat — AMB
Forage — HAY, GRASS, OATS, PASTURE
Forage bean — URD
Forage crop — SORGO
Forage grass — REDTOP
Forage plant — ERS, ERVIL
Forage wheat — EMMER
Foray — INROAD, RAID
Forays — — RAIDS
Forbear — CEASE
Forbearer — STOIC
Forbears — OMITS
Forbid — BAN, DENY
Forbidden — TABOO, TABI
Forbidden things — NONOS
Forbidding — PRAWN, STERN
Forbidding look — SCOWL
Forbidding words — DONTS
Forbids — BANS
Force — COMPEL, DINT, DIS, POTENCE
Force afloat — NAVY
Force out — EJECT
Force upon — FOIST

Force: Lat — VIS
Forced to go — HALED
Forces to go to court — HALES
Ford — WADE
Ford and Guidry, e.g. — SOUTHPAWS
Ford flop — EDSEL
Ford follower — CARTER
Ford of "Can You Top This? — SENATOR
Ford or Pyle — ERNIE
Ford's friend from Kansas — DOLE
Ford, of Tennessee — ERNIE
Fordable — WADABLE
Fordham athletes — RAMS
Fore's partner — AFT
Forearm bone — ULNA
Forearm bones — ULNAE
Foreboding — DIRE, OMEN
Forecaster — SEER
Forecaster, in a sense — SEER
Forefront — VAN
Foreign — ALIEN
Foreign film ending — FINI
Foreign moviehouse — CINE
Foreign service man — ENVOY
Foreign: Prefix — XEN
Foreigner — ALIEN
Foreigner: Comb. form — XENO
Foremen — OVERSEERS
Foremost — CHIEF, MAIN, PREMIER, SUPREME
Foremost sail of a ship — JIB
Forenoon hours — AMS
Forensic competition — DEBATE
Forerunner of NRC — AEC
Forerunner of TV — RADIO
Forest clearing — GLADE
Forest creature — HART, DOES
Forest cut-up — LUMBERJACK
Forest denizen — DEER
Forest dwellers — STAGS
Forest features — TREES
Forest female — DOE
Forest gods — SATYRS
Forest Hills, N.Y. fame — TENNIS
Forest in "As You Like It" — ARDEN
Forest in France — BOIS
Forest near London — EPPING
Forest trembler — ASPEN
Forestage — APRON
Forestall — PREVENT
Foretell — BODE
Foretoken — OMEN
Forever _____ day — AND A
Forever and a day — AGES
Forever in poesy — ETERN
Forever: Archaic — ETERNE
Forewarning — ALERT, CAUTION, OMEN
Foreword — PROEM
Forfeiture — LOSS
Forfend — PROTECT
Forgave — ABSOLVED
Forge — FAKE
Forget-me- _____ — NOT
Forget — OMIT
Forget where one put — MISLAY
Forgets — OMITS
Forgive — PARDON, REMIT
Forgoes food — DIETS
Fork-tailed flyer — TERN
Fork — SPLIT
Fork ball — PITCH
Fork components — TINES
Fork features — PRONGS, TINES
Fork part — TINE
Fork point — TINE
Fork prong — TINE
Fork unit — TINE
Fork-lift — TRUCK
Forked-tailed hawk — KITE
Forktails — TERNS
Forlorn — DESOLATE
Form — CREATE, SHAPE
Form an aspic — GEL
Form ideas — IDEATE
Form into a ball — WIND
Form into one — UNIFY
Form of address — SIR
Form of address: Sp. — DONA
Form of currency — SCRIP
Form of energy — MASS
Form of fuel — COKE, PEAT
Form of poker — STUD
Form of trapshooting — SKEET
Form of verse — RONDEL
Formal — PROM
Formal dance — BALL, PROM
Formal dance in France — BAL
Formal headdress — TIARA
Formal statements — DICTA
Formal wear — TAILS, TUX
Formalwear fastener — STUD
Format — PLAN, SET UP
Formation of words like "buzz or "hiss" — ONOMATOPOEIA
Formed — MADE
Formed a joint, in carpentry — RABBETED
Formed a rainbow — ARCED
Formed a sphere — ORBED
Formed an electrical circle — ARCED
Formed by one eruption — MONOGENE
Former — ERST, ONE TIME, WHILOM
Former A.L. team — NATS
Former acorn — OAK
Former actor Ralph — MEEKER
Former actress Ritter — THELMA
Former Alaskan-capital — SITKA
Former Annamese capital — HUE
Former Arab org. — UAR
Former Asian kingdom — SIAM
Former Asian treaty org. — SEATO
Former Attorney General — MEESE
Former Austrian Chancellor — RAAB
Former ballerina _____ Grey — BERYL
Former Boston pitcher — SAIN
Former British protectorate — KUWAIT
Former Brooklyn pitcher — ERSKINE
Former capital of Japan — KYOTO
Former capital of Myanmar — AVA
Former champ, for short — INGO
Former chess champ — TAI
Former Chief Justice — TANEY, WAITE
Former Chinese leader — MAO
Former Chinese PM, _____ Kuo-feng — HUA
Former city now part of Tel-Aviv — JAFFA
Former Congolese prime minister — ILEO
Former county in NE Scotland — NAIRN
Former court figure — JESTER
Former D.C. agency — USIS
Former D.C. team — NATS
Former Dean of State — RUSK
Former despot — TSAR
Former diva Lucrezia — BORI
Former draft org. — SSS
Former dynast — TSAR
Former Eastern rulers — SHAHS
Former Egyptian leader — SADAT
Former Estonian coin — KROON
Former European gold coin — PISTOLE
Former Far East treaty org. — SEATO
Former fastballer Duren — RYNE
Former Fawcett role — ANGEL
Former filly — MARE
Former first lady — BESS
Former first lady in Moscow — RAISA
Former former — ERST
Former French coin — LIARD
Former German coin — TALER
Former Giant Rote — KYLE

Former Giant's family — OTTS
Former group of stars — ARGO
Former H. S. senior — GRAD
Former head of actors' org. — ASNER
Former hostage Terry _____ — WAITE
Former Hungarian premier and family — NAGYS
Former Indian P.M. Shastri — LAL
Former Indian potentate — RAJAH
Former Iranian ruler — SHAH
Former Israeli Prime Minister and family — MEIRS
Former Italian Prime Minister — MORO
Former Japanese premier — SATO
Former Korean president — RHEE
Former Lithuanian coins — LITAI
Former mates — EXES
Former mayor of New York City — BEAME
Former Met conductor Alberto — EREDE
Former Met diva — ALDA
Former Met soprano — MOFFO
Former Mideast org. — UAR
Former Mlle. — MME
Former money of Portugal — REIS
Former N.Y. senator — KEATING
Former N.Y.C. mayor — BEAME
Former N.Y.C. skyline letters — RCA
Former name of Antalya, Turkey — ADALIA
Former name of England — ANGLIA
Former name of Guyana: Abbr. — BGU
Former name of Lake Malawi — NYASSA
Former name of Mongolian capital — URGA
Former name of the Saone — ARAR
Former name of Tokyo — EDO
Former Neareast ruler — SHAH
Former New England players? — EXPATRIOTS
Former New Jersey governor — KEAN
Former New York City mayor — BEAME
Former New York governor — CAREY
Former occupant of Gracie Mansion — BEAME
Former org. for Dr. J. — NBA
Former Ph.D. tests — PASTORALS
Former Pleasant Island — NAURU
Former president of Costa Rica — ARIAS
Former President of Nicaragua — ORTEGA
Former price agcy. — OPA
Former Prime Minister of Ireland — DE VALERA
Former quarterback Y.A. _____ — TITTLE
Former queen of Italy — ELENA
Former queen of Jordan — ALIA
Former queen of Spain — ENA
Former Red head — MAO, LENIN, STALIN
Former Red Sox star — YAZ
Former Ringling star — UNUS
Former Romanian capital — IASI
Former ruler of Iran — SHAH
Former rulers of India — RAJAHS
Former rural-credit org. — FSA
Former Russian council — DUMA
Former Russian measure — VERST
Former S.F. mayor — ALIOTO
Former Scandinavian notables? — LAPPS OF MEMORY
Former Secretary of State — HAIG
Former shah — PAHLAVI
Former slugger Tony — OLIVA
Former South African prime minister — MALAN
Former Spanish coins — REALS
Former Spanish enclave in Morocco — IFNI
Former Spanish queen — ENA
Former spouses — EXES
Former srs. — GRADS
Former stage direction — SOLUS
Former Sultan of Turkey — AHMED
Former Surgeon General — KOOP
Former symbols for British money — LSD
Former talk show host — PAAR
Former Teheran title — SHAH
Former Thai coin — TICAL
Former theater org. — ANTA
Former treaty org. — SEATO
Former Turkish title — PASHA
Former TV host — PAAR
Former U.A.W. head — FRASER
Former U.K. judicial writ — ELEGIT
Former UAR head — NASSER
Former White House pet — FALA, HIM
Former Winter Palace residents — CZARS
Former Yankee pitcher — TOMMY JOHN
Former, in other days — ERST
Formerly — ERST, ONCE, PREVIOUS, PRIOR
Formerly called — NEE
Formerly called, French style — NEE
Formerly Castrogiovanni — ENNA
Formerly named — NEE
Formerly Peking — BEIJING
Formerly, formerly — ERST
Formerly, once — ERSE
Formicary dwellers — ANTS
Formicary occupants — ANTS
Formicary residents — ANTS
Formicary, at times — HILL
Formidable — GREAT
Formidable fellow — STRAPPER
Formosa Straight island — AMOY
Formosa Straight port — AMOY
Formosa's other name — TAIWAN
Formosan bar ad? — TAIWAN ON TODAY
Forms a connection with — ALLIES
Forms a new paragraph — INDENTS
Forms a new structure — REGROUP
Forms spirals — COILS
Forsake — SHUN
Forsake one's duty — DESERT
Forsakes — ABANDONS
Forsooth — VERILY
Forswear food — FAST
Forsyte — SOAMES
Forsyth's "The _____ File" — ODESSA
Forsyth's "The _____ of the Jackal" — DAY
Forsythia's color — YELLOW
Fort- _____, Chad city — LAMY
Fort — GARRISON
Fort _____, Calif. — ORD
Fort _____, near Monterey — ORD
Fort Knox item — INGOT
Fort Knox stash — GOLD
Fort Worth inst. — TCU
Forte — METIER
Forte of Boris Becker — SERVE
Forth — ALONG
Forthright — OPEN

Forthwith — SOON
Fortification — REDAN
Fortified — ARMED
Fortified station — PRESIDIO
Fortified town of old — BERG
Fortifies anew — REARMS
Fortify — ARM
Fortissimo — LOUD
Fortress in Israel: siege site 66-73 AD — MASADA
Fortunate — IN LUCK
Fortune — HAP, LOT
Fortune hunter — PIRATE
Fortune tellers — SEERS
Fortune's partner — FAME
Fortune-teller — MENTALIST
Fortune-teller's phrase — I SEE
Fortune-telling card — TAROT
Forty-_____ — NINERS
Forty-niner, e.g. — MINER
Forty — TWO SCORE
Forty follower — ISH
Forty per furlong — RODS
Forty weekdays — LENT
Forty winks — CATNAP, NAP
Forty-niners' race — GOLD RUSH
Forum — BODY
Forum garment — TOGA
Forum villain — CASCA
Forum wear — TOGA, TUNIC
Forward — AHEAD, ANTERIOR, SEND
Forward a package — REMAIL
Forward and Reverse — GEARS
Forward end — BOW
Forward letters — REMAIL
Forward movement — PROGRESS
Forward, leading — AHEAD
Forwarded — SENT
Fossil — BONE, NEOLITH, RELIC
Fossil: Comb. form — NECRO
Foster — NURSE, REAR, TEND
Foster Brooks "comment" — HIC
Foster classic — MY OLD KY HOME
Foster's "Old Uncle _____" — NED
Fostered — REARED
Fosters — REARS
Fought — WARRED
Fought city hall — BUCKED THE SYSTEM
Foul up — RUIN
Foul weather cover — TARP
Foul weather footwear — PACS
Foul weather gear — GALOSHES
Foulard fastener — CLASP
Fouled-up — SNARLED
Found a place for the Picasso — HUNG
Found before "MacDonald" — OLD
Found fault — SCOLDED
Found in bunkers — COAL
Found in museums — NUDES
Found in the lab — ETNA
Found's opposite — LOST
Foundation — BASIS
Foundation gift — GRANT
Foundation piece — SILL
Foundations — BASES, BASIS
Founded — BASED
Founded: Abbr. — EST, ESTAB
Founder of bacteriology — COHN
Founder of Dadaism — ARP
Founder of Embryology — BAER
Founder of famed Academy — PLATO
Founder of Methodism — WESLEY
Founder of Providence — WILLIAMS
Founder of the Carmelite reform — ST TERESA
Founder of the Ottoman empire — OSMAN
Founder of Troy — ILUS
Founding father of a Commonwealth — PENN
Fountain — SPRING
Fountain drinks — MALTS
Fountain fare — SODAS
Fountain favorites — BANANA SPLITS, SHAKES, SODAS
Fountain favorites — SUNDAES
Fountain gleaming with lire — TREVI
Fountain of Rome — TREVI
Fountainhead — ORIGIN
Four-fifths of the atmosphere — NITROGEN
Four-star off. — GEN
Four _____ kind — OF A
Four balls — WALK
Four balls to a Torontonian — JAYWALK
Four bells — TEN
Four for Goren — SUITS
Four gills — PINT
Four in refrigerators — ARS
Four inches — HAND
Four o'clock beverage — TEA
Four of _____ (high poker hand) — A KIND
Four quarters — ONE
Four roods — ACRE
Four seasons — YEAR
Four time Wimbledon winner — LAVER
Four, in Frankfurt — VIER
Four-bagger — HOME RUN
Four-in-hand — TIE
Four-poster — BED
Four-wheeled carts — WAGONS
Four: Comb. form — TETR
Fourgon — VAN
Foursquare — HONEST
Fourteenth president — PIERCE
Fourth estate — PRESS
Fourth King of Troy — ILUS
Fourth man — SETH
Fourth of a pint — GILL
Fourth-greatest Great Lake — ERIE
Fowl dish — CAPON
Fowl enclosure — COOP
Fowl parts — LEGS
Fowl pen — COOP
Fox-drawn vehicle — BACK TO THE FUTURE
Fox breed — SILVER
Fox follower — TROT
Fox hunter's goad — SPUR
Fox hunter's shout — HARK
Fox of southern Africa — ASSE
Fox or mink — FUR
Fox or rabbit — BRER
Fox shark — THRESHER
Fox shelter — TEPEE
Fox's friend — SAC
Fox's relative — SAC
Foxhole — PIT
Foxlike — SLY
Foxx — REDD
Foxy — SLY
Foxy lady — VIXEN
Foyle of fiction — KITTY
Fr. adj. pronoun — SES
Fr. airport — ORLY
Fr. artist — ARP
Fr. cap — BERET
Fr. coin — FRANC
Fr. companies — CIES
Fr. council — SENAT
Fr. engineer — ING
Fr. head — TETE
Fr. holy woman — STE
Fr. king — ROI
Fr. ladies — MMES
Fr. landlords due — RENTE
Fr. money — CENTIMES
Fr. political philosopher — MONTESQUIEU
Fr. religious title — STE
Fr. river — AISNE, LOIRE, MARNE, SAONE
Fr. ruler — ROI
Fr. titles — MMES
Fr. town — NESLE
Fra — MONK
Fra Lippo _____ — LIPPI
Fracas — MELEE
Fraction — PART
Fraction of a yen — SEN
Fragile — FLIMSY
Fragile footing — TOE HOLD
Fragile last resort? — STRAW

Fragment — END, PIECE, SCRAP, SHERD
Fragment: Var. — SHERD
Fragrance — AROMA, PERFUME, REDOLENCE
Fragrance from a rose — ATTAR
Fragrant — OLENT, REDOLENT
Fragrant blooms — SWEETPEAS
Fragrant compound — ESTER
Fragrant evergreen — CEDAR
Fragrant flower — LILAC, ROSE
Fragrant foot stock — ORRIS
Fragrant grass — BENA
Fragrant marsh shrubs — GALES
Fragrant oil — ATTAR
Fragrant oleoresin — ELEMI
Fragrant resin — ELEMI
Fragrant rootstock — ORRIS
Fragrant shrub — LILAC
Fragrant southern tree — MIMOSA
Fragrant with herbs — THYMEY
Fragrant wood — CEDAR
Fragrant woods — ALOES
Fraidy-cat — YELLOW BELLY
Frail — THIN
Frame — HULL, RAILROAD, SHELL
Frame braces — TIE RODS
Frame of a car — CHASSIS
Frame of mind — HUMOR
Framework — CADRE, CASING, RACK
Framework used by sculptors — ARMATURE
France of France — ANATOLE
France or Litvak — ANATOLE
France's longest river — LOIRE
France's neighbor — ANDORRA
France's West Point — ST CYR
Frances Gumm's little girl — LIZA
Francesca _____, British actress — ANNIS
Franchot of films — TONE
Francis and namesakes — ARLENES
Francis of "What's My Line?" — ARLENE
Francis or Dahl — ARLENE
Francis Scott ___ — KEY
Franciscan abbr. — OSF
Franciscan mission — ALAMO
Francoise or Carl — SAGAN
Frangipani, e.g. — SCENT
Frank — OPEN
Frank, with "dog" — HOT
Frankenstein's flunky — IGOR
Frankenstein's office — LAB
Frankfurt's river — MAIN, ODER
Frankie Laine hit — MULE TRAIN
Frankie of song — AVALON
Frankie or Cleo — LAINE
Frankie or Johnny — LOVER
Franklin — BEN
Franklin and namesakes — BENS
Franklin D Roosevelt Museum site — WARM MANS GEORGIA
Franklin flyer — KITE
Franklin invented one — STOVE
Franklin's mother — SARA
Franz of operetta — LEHAR
Fraser of tennis — NEALE
Fraternal baseball trio — ALOUS
Fraternal brother — MASON
Fraternal club — LODGE
Fraternal fellow — ELK
Fraternal member — MOOSE
Fraternal order — ELKS
Fraternal org. — LOM
Fraternal organization — ELKS
Fraternity — CIRCLE
Fraternity letter — CHI, BETA, ETA, PSI
Fraternity letters — PHIS, PSIS
Fraternity novice — PLEDGE
Fraternity off. V.I.P. — PRES
Frau's husband — HERR
Frau's spouse — HERR
Fraud — SHAM
Fraud attachment — ULENT
Fraud follow-up — ULENT
Fraulein — MISS
Fraulein's refusal — NEIN
Fraulein's song — LIED
Fray — MELEE
Fray Bayou, Mich. — BATTLE CREEK
Frazil — ICE
Freburg or Musial — STAN
Freckle — SPOT
Fred Allen's milieu — RADIO
Fred or Adele — ASTAIRE
Fred or Steve — ALLEN
Fred or Woody — ALLEN
Fred's sister — ADELE
Free-for-all — DONNYBROOK, MELEE, RIOT
Free — LET OUT, LOOSE, LOOSED, RELEASE, RID
Free (of) — RELEASE, RID
Free and clear — OUT OF THE RED
Free electron — ION
Free from — RID, WEAN
Free from blame — CLEAR
Free from care — AT EASE
Free from doubt — ASSURE
Free from error: Abbr. — COR
Free from pride — HUMBLE
Free throw's value — ONE
Free time — INDEPENDENCE DAY
Free world defense pact — NATO
Free's companion — EASY
Freebie — PASS
Freebooter — PIRATE
Freed — DISENGAGED, RELEASED
Freedom from constraint — EASE
Freedom from prejudice — TOLERANCE
Freedom from sin — PURITY
Freeload — SPONGE
Freeloader — GUEST, PARASITE
Freeman biography — R E LEE
Freeman Gosden role — AMOS
Frees — LETS LOOSE, RIDS
Frees from a predicament — RESCUES
Frees from dependence — WEANS
Frees from frost — DEICES
Freeway access — RAMP
Freeway sign — EXIT, NO HITCHING
Freeways: Abbr. — RTES
Freeze — ICE, ICE UP
Freeze starter — ANTI
Freight — CARGO, LOAD
Freight haulers — RIGS
Freight shipment — CAR LOT
Freight train units — HOPPER CARS
Freight weight — CARLOAD
Freighter's "ears" — SONAR
Fremont County, Wyo. town — LANDER
French _____ — HEEL
French airport — ORLY
French area, rich in coal — LOIRE
French article — UNE
French assembly — SENAT
French assent — OUI
French auto racing locale — LE MANS
French ball — BOLA
French book — LIVRE
French brandy — MARC
French business: Abbr. — CIE
French cap — BERET
French cathedral city — AMIENS
French cheese — BRIE
French chef's pie — TARTE
French cherub — ANGE
French circle — RONDE
French city — CAEN, CALAIS
French city on the Rhone — LYON
French city with Roman antiques — NIMES
French cleanser — EPONGE

French clergyman — ABBE
French cleric — ABBE, CURE
French co. — CIE
French coin — FRANC, SOU
French coins of old — ECUS
French coins: 1929-38 — ECUS
French comic Jacques — TATI
French commune noted for lace — CLUNY
French composer — LALO
French composer and kin — SATIES
French Composer Edouard: 1823-92 — LALO
French composer Erik — SATIE
French conjunctions — ETS
French connection — ETS
French coronations — SACRES
French council — SENAT
French department or river — DROME, OISE
French designer Alix — GRES
French director Clair — RENE
French director Jean — RENOIR
French disbeliever — ATHEE
French dramatist Jean _____ — GENET
French dramatist: 1639-99 — RACINE
French dramatist: 1791-1861 — SCRIBE
French dream — REVE
French dynast — CAPET
French ecclesiastical figure — ABBE
French existential philosopher — SARTRE
French explorer — ACO
French explorer in Colonial America — ACO
French fare — CROISSANTS
French farewell — ADIEU
French fashion designer — DIOR
French father — PERE
French females — ELLES
French fighter-planes — SPADS
French film director Marcel — CARNE
French film director-actor Jacques _____ — TATI
French flatfoot — FLIC
French flower — LIS
French fluid — ENCRE
French fried potatoes — CHIPS
French friend — AMI, AMIE
French from — DES
French general — FOCH
French general, in-law of Napoleon — LECLERC
French girl friend — AMIE
French God — DIOS
French governing body — SENAT
French government C.I.D. — SURETE
French Guiana capital — CAYENNE
French handle — ANSE
French head — TETE
French I verb — ETIE, ETRE
French impressionist — MONET
French income — RENTE
French king — ROI
French lace place — CLUNY
French lake — LAGO
French landscape painter — WATTEAU
French landscapist — COROT
French legislative body — SENATE
French lending institutions — BANCS
French machine — ENGIN
French magazine — ELLE
French marshall and family — NEYS
French marshall of 19th century — NIEL
French menu item — POIS
French menu word — ROTI
French military cap — KEPI
French mineral water — EVIAN
French modern artist Fernand _____ — LEGER
French money — FRANC
French moon — LUNE
French morning — MATIN
French mother — MERE
French Mrs.: Var. — MDME
French naval battle area: 1692 — LA HOGUE
French negative — NON
French noble — DUC
French nobleman — COMTE
French nobleman, to revolutionists — ARISTO
French noblemen? — PARISTOCRATS
French notions — IDEES
French novelist — GIDE
French novelist _____ Fournier — ALAIN
French number — CINQ
French oenophiles' delights — VINS
French one — UNA, UNE
French Open champ: 1989 — CHANG
French or Dutch item — DOOR
French ordnance — BALLES
French painter — DORE, MATISSE, MONET
French painter Fernand _____ — LEGER
French painter of theater scenes — DEGAS
French painter-lithographer — LAUTREC
French painter: 1881-1955 — LEGER
French pal — AMI
French pancake — CREPE
French passage — STILE
French pastry — TARTE
French philosopher Rene — DESCARTES
French philosopher-historian — TAINE
French physician-novelist: 1894-1961 — CELINE
French pioneer in treating the mentally ill — PINEL
French political writer 1800-36: init — NAC
French port — DIEPPE, TOULON
French possessive — SES
French preposition — AVEC
French President Coty — RENE
French president: 1954-59 — COTY
French pronoun — CES, ELLES, ILS, MES, SES, SOI
French Republic personification — MARIANNE
French revolutionary leader — DANTON
French river — AIN, OISE
French river or department — CHER
French room — SALLE
French ruling family of yore — CAPET
French saint — MARTIN
French saint: Dec. 1 — ELOI
French saying — MOT
French school — ECOLE, LYCEE
French sculptor — RODIN
French seaport — BREST
French seas — MERS
French season — ETE
French seasoning — SEL
French seat of learning — ECOLE
French secular clergyman — ABBE
French senior — AINEE
French shelter — ABRI
French ship's course — ERRE
French shoe — SABOT
French silk — SOIE
French silver — ARGENT
French Socialist leader of the 1930's — BLUM
French soldier — POILU
French soul — AME
French spa — DAX, EVIAN
French star — ETOILE
French state — ETAT
French statesman: 1872-1950 — BLUM

French students — ELEVES
French summers — ETES
French table delicacy — SNAIL
French toast — SANTE
French town — USSEL
French treat — BRIE
French trench — ABRI
French upper house — SENAT
French vegetables — POIS
French verb — ETRE
French victor at Fortenoy — SAXE
French vineyard — CLOS, CRUS
French violinist: 18th century — ANET
French W.W. I commander — FOCH
French W.W. I plane — SPAD
French wave — ONDE
French weather pattern — CLIMAT
French wines — VINS
French working girl — GRISETTE
French wrinkles — PLIS
French writer Andre — GIDE
French writer-director — VADIM
French-Algerian existentialist author — CAMUS
French-built rockets — ARIANES
French: very — TRES
Frenchman — GAUL
Frenchman's smoke or snuff — TABAC
Frenzied — AMOK, BERSERK, DEMONIC, MANIAC
Frenzy — AMOK, RAGE
Freq. of 3000 megacycles per second — UHF
Frequency — SPEED
Frequent — HAUNT, USUAL, VISIT
Frequent catchall abbr. — ET AL
Frequent driveway shape — OVAL
Frequent salad ingredient — CRESS
Frequent title starter — THE
Frequenter of Lincoln Center — BALLETOMANE
Frequently — OFTEN
Frequently, to poets — OFT
Frequents — HAUNTS
Fresco _____, musical term — SECCO
Fresh-water fishes — GAR
Fresh — ANEW, SASSY
Fresh _____ (alert) — AS A DAISY
Fresh air — OZONE
Fresh and unusual — ORIGINAL
Fresh answer — SASS
Fresh as _____ — A DAISY
Fresh crews — RELAYS
Fresh information — NEW
Fresh out of — SOLD
Fresh talk — LIP
Fresh water fish — DACE, IDE
Freshen — RENEW
Freshen again — RENEW
Freshen an aloe — REPOT
Freshen the atmosphere — AERATE
Freshen, as a room — AIR OUT
Freshens the room — AERATES
Fresher — SASSIER
Freshest — NEWEST
Freshet — SPATE
Freshly — ANEW
Freshman — NOVICE
Freshman cadet — PLEBE
Freshman of a sort — PLEB
Freshwater duck — TEAL
Freshwater fish — BREAM, CHUB, LOACH
Freshwater food fish — GRAYLING, SMELT
Freshwater mussel — UNIO
Freshwater worm — NAID
Fret — STEW
Fret on a guitar — STOP
Fretful discontent — PET
Fretful state — STEW
Fretting — IN A STEW
Freud contemporary — ADLER
Freud's "_____ und Tabu" — TOTEM
Freud's appointments — SESSIONS
Freudian concern — EGO
Freudian concerns — IDS
Fri. utterance — TGIF
Friable — CRISP
Friars' feisty fete — ROAST
Fribble — WASTE
Frick collection — ART
Friction matches — LOCO FOCOS
Friday's friend — CRUSOE
Friday, et al. — COPS
Friday, for one — GIRL
Friday, usually — PAYDAY
Fridge gas — FREON
Fridge unit — ICER
Friend — ALLY, BUDDY, COMRADE, PAL, PATRON
Friend from Mexico — AMIGO
Friend in a fray — ALLY
Friend indeed — ALLY, PAL
Friend of Aramis — ATHOS
Friend of Hercules — TELAMON
Friend of Kukla — OLLIE
Friend of Pythias — DAMON
Friend of Queen Elizabeth — DRAKE
Friend of Solomon — HIRAM
Friend of the Fox — SAC
Friend of the Lone Ranger — TONTO
Friend of Trajan and Tacitus — PLINY
Friend south of the border — AMIGO
Friend, in Angers — AMI
Friend, in France — AMIE
Friend, in Granada — AMIGO
Friend, in Nice — AMI
Friendless — ALONE
Friendliness — AMITY, WARMTH
Friendly — AMIABLE, WARM
Friendly associate — ALLY
Friendly chat — HOB NOB
Friendly frictions — RIFTS
Friendly fungus — YEAST
Friendly Islands — TONGA
Friendly talk — CHAT
Friends — CHUMS, SIDEKICKS
Friends adjective — THY
Friends in need — PALS
Friendship — AMITY, BROTHERHOOD, HARMONY, RAPPORT
Friendships — AMITIES
Fries lightly — SAUTES
Frigate — SHIP
Frigate feature — HULL, MAST
Frigga's husband — ODIN
Frighten — SCARE, STARTLE
Frightened out of one's wits — SCARED STIFF
Frightened reactions — STARTS
Frightening — SCARY
Frightening word — BOO
Frightens — ALARMS
Frightens away — SHOOS
Frightful — HORRID, ALARMING
Frigid — COLD, ICY
Frill for chops — PAPILLOTE
Frilled collar — RUFF
Friml specialty — OPERETTA
Fringe — BORDER
Fringe benefit of a sort — PERK
Frisbee, e.g. — DISC, TOY
Frisbee, for one — DISC
Frisco gridder — NINER
Frisco's skinny serenader? — BONY BENNETT
Frisk — SEARCH
Frisky — ROMP
Frittata — OMELET
Frittata, e.g. — OMELET
Fritter — WASTE
Fritter away — WASTE
Frivolous — PETTY
Frivolous folks — FEATHER HEADS
Frivolous offerings — CONFECTIONS
Frog — RANID
Frog's relative — TOAD
Frogman — DIVER

Frogner Park city — OSLO
Frogs-to-be — TADPOLES
Frogs — RANIDS
Frolic — KICK UP ONES HEELS
Frolic — LARK, ROMP, SPREE
Frolics — DISPORTS
From (a date) — AS OF
From _____ (afterwards) — THEN ON
From _____ (completely) — A TO Z
From a distance — AFAR
From Aries to Pisces — ZODIAC
From here — THENCE
From memory, with "by" — ROTE
From Miami to Malibu — SUN-BELT
From now on — HENCE
From one end to another — THRU
From Oslo — NORSE
From side to side — ACROSS
From the _____ (long time) — YEAR ONE
From the beginning — AB OVO
From the Greek: wood or matter — HYLE
From the largest continent — ASIATIC
From the sign; in music — DAL SEGNO
From the start — AB OVO
From these come frustrums — CONES
From this date — AS OF
From this time — HENCE
From whence Columbus sailed — PALOS
From: Fr. — DES
Frome or Allen — ETHAN
Frond — LEAF
Front cover of a book — RECTO
Front or cash follower — IER
Front-page boxes — EARS
Front-wheels alignment — TOE IN
Fronted on — FACED
Frontier — EDGE
Frontier lawman — EARP
Frontiersman — BOONE
Frontiersman Wyatt, et al. — EARPS
Fronton shouts — OLES
Fronton word — ALAI
Frontons — ARENAS
Frosh teasers — SOPHS
Frosh's superior — SOPH
Frost — HOAR, RIME
Frost and colleagues — POETS
Frost or Preston — ROBERT
Frost product — POEM
Frost work — POEM
Frost's "The Road Not _____" — TAKEN
Frost's "The Witch of _____" — COOS
Frosted — ICED
Frostier — ICIER
Frosting — ICING
Frosty coating — RIME
Frosty look — GLARE
Frosty, for one — SNOWMAN
Froth — FOAM, LATHER, SPUME
Frothed — SPUMED
Frothy — CREAMY
Frown — SCOWL
Froze up — JAMMED
Frozen — ON ICE
Frozen desert — BOMBE
Frozen drip — ICICLE
Frozen rains — SLEETS
Frozen treats — ICES
Frozen water crystal — SNOWFLAKE
Frugal one — SAVER
Frugality in expenditures — ECONOMY
Frugally coped — EKED
Fruit — DATES, ORANGE
Fruit basket item — PEAR
Fruit bowl items — BOSC PEARS
Fruit center — PIT
Fruit drink — CIDER
Fruit drinks — ADES
Fruit for Buster? — CRABBE APPLE
Fruit jar — MASON
Fruit of forgetfulness — LOTUS
Fruit of the apple family — ROME
Fruit of the oak — ACORNS
Fruit parts — PITS
Fruit pies — TARTS
Fruit salad components — PEARS
Fruit seed — PIT
Fruit skin — RIND
Fruit tree — PEAR
Fruit type — POME
Fruit-filled desserts — TARTS
Fruitless — BARREN, VAIN
Fruits of the Amazon — BRAZIL NUTS
Frustrate — FOIL
Frustrated golfers discard — IRON IN THE FIRE
Frutti start — TUTTI
Fry in butter — SAUTE
Fry lightly — SAUTE
Fryers need — OIL
Frying pan — SPIDER
Fudd or Gantry — ELMER
Fuddy follower — DUDDY
Fudge — FAKE
Fudge or taffy — CANDY
Fuel — COAL, FOOD, GAS, PEAT
Fuel for a lorry — PETROL
Fuel from a bog — PEAT
Fuel gas — ETHANE
Fuel source — OIL WELL
Fuel used in welding — ACETYLENE
Fueled — FED
Fugard's "A Lesson From _____" — ALOES
Fugard's forte — DRAMA
Fugitive — ESCAPEE
Fulcrum feature — THOLE
Fulda feeder — EDER
Fulfill a Hippocratic promise — HEAL
Fulfill an obligation — REPAY
Fulfillment — FRUITION
Fuliginous — SOOTY
Full — AMPLE, BURSTING, CROWDED, LADEN, PACKED
Full _____ — TILT
Full authority — CARTE BLANCHE
Full follower — HOUSE
Full of eggs — GRAVID
Full of energy — PEPPY, ZIPPY
Full of fear — PANICKY
Full of flavor — SAPID
Full of life — ZESTY
Full of specks — MOTEY
Full of verve — SPRY
Full of vim — PEPPY
Full of vim and vigor — ALIVE
Full of wheel tracks — RUTTY
Full of zeal — AFIRE
Full of: Suff. — OSE
Full stop or period: Sp. — PUNTO
Full-blooded — HEARTY
Full-blown — RIPE
Full-bodied — ROBUST
Full-flavored — MELLOW
Fully awake — ALERT
Fully developed insect — IMAGO
Fully grown — ADULT
Fully revenged — EVEN
Fully, to an attorney — PLENE
Fully-fledged — SENIOR
Fully: Poesy — ENOW
Fulminate — RAGE, RAIL, RANT
Fulsome — FOUL
Fulton's Clermont, et al. — STEAMSHIPS
Fumarole's cousin — VENT HOLE
Fumble — ERR
Fumbles — GROPES
Fumbles on the diamond — DROPS
Fume — REEK
Fuming — IRATE

Fun and games — PASTIME
Function — ACT, ROLE, SERVE, USE, WORK
Functioning continuously — IN GEAR
Functions — USES
Fund-raising org., in a way — IRS
Fund — POOL
Fund-raising venture — CAR-WASH
Fundamental — BASAL, BASIC
Fundamental values — ETHOS
Funds — FINANCES
Funeral — BURIAL
Funeral hymn — DIRGE
Funeral oration — ELOGE
Funeral piece — DIRGE
Funeral sight — HEARSE
Funest — FATAL
Fungi — OIDIA
Fungus — ERGOT
Fungus gnat — SCIARID
Fungus spores — AECIA
Funicello of TV fame — ANNETTE
Funky — FOUL
Funnel-shaped — CONIC
Funnel-shaped flower — HONEYSUCKLE
Funnies' Ms Kett — ETTA
Funny-bone locale — ELBOW
Funny — BIZARRE, COMIC, ODD
Funny Amalekite king? — AGAG
Funny and Jolly, e.g. — BOATS
Funny bone? — HUMERUS
Funny fellows — RIOTS
Funny folks — WITS
Funny King — ALAN
Funny Martha — RAYE
Funny Ole — OLSEN
Funny one — CARD
Funny Raye — MARTHA
Funny stories — JAPES
Funnyman Foxx — REDD
Funnyman Johnson — ARTE
Funnyman Wilson — FLIP
Fur-lined cloaks — PELISSES
Fur — OTTER
Fur coat component — PELT
Fur for Redd? — GRAY FOXX
Fur magnate — ASTOR
Fur merchant of old — ASTOR
Fur or stream follower — LINED
Fur pieces — STOLES
Fur seal — SEA CAT
Fur trader John — ASTOR
Fur wrap — STOLE
Furbelow — FRILL
Furbish — POLISH
Furious — BURNING UP, FIT TO BE TIED, IRATE
Furious — LIVID
Furl — COIL
Furl a sail — STOW
Furlong — STADE
Furloughed — ON LEAVE
Furnace — OVEN
Furnace in Berlin — OFEN
Furnish a bank service — LEND
Furnish with income — ENDOW
Furnish with new weapons — REARM
Furnished floor covering — TILE
Furnishing help — AIDANT
Furniture classic — DROP LEAF TABLES
Furniture fastener's — DOWELS
Furniture feature — GATE LEG
Furniture item — DAYBED
Furniture mover — DOLLY
Furniture on casters — TRUNDLE BEDS
Furniture set — SUITE
Furniture style — ADAM, SHERATON
Furniture wood — TEAK
Furniture worker — GLUER
Furore — FLAP
Furrier's raw material — PELTS
Furrier's stock — PELTS
Furrow — DITCH, RUT, SEAM, STRIA
Furrow maker — PLOW
Furrow the brows — KNIT
Furrowed — LINED, STRIATE
Furrows — SEAMS
Furrows in phonograph records — GROOVES
Furry beasts — OTTERS
Furry pet — CAT
Furry pets — HAMSTERS
Furry scarves — BOAS
Furry surface — PILE
Furry swimmer — MINK, OTTER
Furs — WRAPS
Further — ABET, AGAIN
Further than — BEYOND
Furtive — COVERT, SLY, UNDERHANDED
Furtive glance — PEEP
Furuncles — BOILS
Fury — RAGE
Furze — GORSE, ULEX
Fuse — COMBINE, SMELT, UNITE
Fused metal — WELDED
Fuses — UNITES
Fusible substance — METAL
Fusion — BLEND
Fuss — ADO, FRET, TO DO
Fussed — STEWED
Fusses — ADOS, TO DOS
Fusspot — CHOOSY
Fussy dressers — DUDES
Fussy one — PRIG
Fustian — RANT
Futhark letter — RUNE
Futile — IDLE, NOT POSSIBLE, NOUSE, OTIOSE, VAIN
Futility — WASTE OF TIME
Future — LATER
Future blooms — SEEDS
Future citizen's designation — ALIEN
Future doc.'s major — PREMED
Future explosive matters — TIME BOMBS
Future farmer — AGGIE
Future fireflies — GLOW-WORMS
Future flower — SEED
Future fowl — EGGS
Future frog — TADPOLE
Future oak — ACORN
Future of a sort — ROSEATE
Future rose — BUD
Future, e.g. — TENSE
Fuzz — LINT
Fuzzy surfaces — NAPS

G

G-K connection — HIJ
G-men — FEDS
G. & S. princess — IDA
G. and S. heroine — PATIENCE
G. Burgess creature — GOOP
G. Cohan's ancestors — IRISH
G. Cooper role — DEEDS
G. Herbert's comments — CLOTHES BUT MAN
G.E. subsidiary — NBC
G.I. address — APO

G.I. aides to cooks — KPS
G.I. concern — K RATIONS
G.I. fare — CHOW
G.I. Joe's entertainer — USO
G.I. meal — CHOW
G.I. refectory — MESS
G.I. who can't shoot straight — BOLO
G.I.'s at times — KPS
G.I.'s award — DSC
G.I.'s devil-dodger — PADRE
G.I.'s hangout — USO
G.I.'s overseas address — APO
G.I.'s supervisors — OGS
G.P.O. items — USM
G.R.F. was one — PRES
G.W.T.W. estate — TARA
Ga. capital — ATL
Ga. city — MACON
Ga. river — COOSA
Ga.'s neighbor — FLA
Gab — CHAT, YAK, YACKETY YACK
Gabber — CHATTERBOX, LOOSE TONGUE
Gabble — TALK
Gabby — BABBLATIVE, BLATHERING, GARRULOUS
Gabby — LONG WINDED, VERBOSE, TALKATIVE
Gabby person — CHATTERBOX
Gable and hip — ROOFS
Gable's Butler, e.g. — ROLE
Gable-top feature — FINIAL
Gabler or Hopper — HEDDA
Gabon Republic's ocean — ATLANTIC
Gabon's Prime Minister and family — MBAS
Gabor and Braun — EVAS
Gabor and Le Galliene — EVAS
Gabor and Peron — EVAS
Gabriel — DANTE ROSSETTI
Gad — ROAM
Gad about — TRAIPSE
Gadabout — ROVER
Gadabout's cousin — ROAMER
Gadding about — ROVING
Gadfly in Washington — NADER
Gadfly: Comb. form — OEST
Gadget — DOODAD
Gadget in sports — TEE
Gadget: Var. — HICKIE
Gadgets — GISMOS
Gads — REAMS
Gads about — ROAMS
Gadsden native — ALABAMAN
Gael — ERSE
Gael's land — EIRE
Gaelic — ERSE
Gaelic language — ERSE
Gaelic Neptune — LER
Gaelic poet — OSSIAN
Gaels' republic — EIRE
Gaff — SPEAR
Gaffe — BONER, BRICK, ERROR
Gag — JOKE, SILENCE
Gaga — INFATUATED
Gaggle members — GEESE
Gagne _____ (French breadwinner) — PAIN
Gaiety — ELAN
Gain — ACHIEVE
Gain by force — WREST
Gain control — CORNER
Gain ground — PROCEED
Gain knowledge — LEARN
Gain possession — GET
Gain with difficulty — WREST
Gainer, e.g. — DIVE
Gainsaid — DENIED
Gainsay — DENY
Gainsborough's river — TRENT
Gait — PACE, TROT
Gait between walk and canter — TROT
Gait like a canter — LOPE
Gait, in Grenada — PASO
Gaited horse — PACER
Gaiter — SPAT
Gal — LASS
Gal of song and others — IDAS, SALS
Gal of songdom — SAL
Gal of the twenties — FLAPPER
Gal pal of Pierre — AMIE
Gala affair — FETE
Gala blowout — BASH
Gala occasions — FETES
Galahad's garb — ARMOR
Galahad's mother — ELAINE
Galahad's quest — GRAIL
Galahad's strong suit — ARMOR
Galapagos denizen — IGUANA
Galas — FETES
Galatea's beloved — ACIS
Galatea's lover — ACIS
Galatea, originally — STATUE
Galaxy — NEBULA
Galba's 502 — DII
Galba's successor — OTHO
Galbraith's subject — ECON
Gale — GUST, STORM
Gale and Veronica's boating area? — STORM LAKE
Galena and siderite — ORES
Galena or bauxite — ORE
Gales — ERSES
Gales biting force — TEETH OF THE WIND
Galileo taught there — PADUA
Galileo was one — PISAN
Galileo's "crime" — HERESY
Galileo's birthplace — PISA
Galileo, et al. — PISANS
Gall — CHAFE, NERVE, OFFEND, SPITE
Gallant — BRAVE, COURTLY
Galled — IRATE
Galleon — BOAT
Gallery — ARCADE, SALON
Gallery displays — ART, OILS
Gallery near the Thames — TATE
Gallery offering — ART
Gallery offerings — PRINTS
Galley — CARVEL
Galley essential — OAR
Galley implements — OARS
Galley mark — DELE, STET
Galley tools — PANS, POTS
Galley word — STET
Galley's propulsion — OARS
Galley-proof symbol — CARE
Gallic girlfriend — AMIE
Gallic name — RENE
Gallic seraph — ANGE
Gallic: — FRENCH
Gallimaufry — OLIO
Gallinaceous entree — CAPON
Gallinaceous female — PEA HEN
Gallivant — GAD
Gallop, for example — GAIT
Gallow trapdoor — DRO
Gallup undertaking — POLL
Galosh — SHOE
Gals of a sort — MOLLS
Galsworthy play: 1909 — STRIFE
Galsworthy's "_____ of Devon" — A MAN
Galvanic: Comb. form — ELECTR
Galvanize — STIR
Galveston gent — TEXAN
Galway Bay Islands — ARAN
Galway county's neighbor — CLARE
Gam and Moreno — RITAS
Gam or Tushingham — RITA
Gambit — PLOY
Gamble — TAKE A CHANCE
Gambler — BETTOR
Gambler's act — BET
Gambler's choice — TAILS
Gambler's concern — ODDS
Gambler's cube — DIE
Gambler's decoy — STOOGE
Gambler's Mecca — VEGAS
Gambler's nickname — LUCKY
Gambling chance — EDGE
Gambling chip — JETON
Gambling cube — DIE
Gambling device — PINBALL
Gambling game — BEANO, BINGO, KENO, POKER
Gambling mecca — RENO
Gambling resort — RENO
Gambling spot for littlenecks — CLAMS CASINO
Gambling town — LAS VEGAS
Gambol — CAPER, ROMP

Game — TAG
Game akin to roulette — BOULE
Game bird — GROUSE, SNIPE
Game divided into chukkers — POLO
Game dog — SETTER
Game fish — BASS, MARLIN, TARPON
Game fish of the Caribbean — CERO, STRIPED BASS
Game for a Bird — BASKETBALL
Game for Karpov or Kasparov — CHESS
Game for ringers — HORSESHOES
Game for swingers — GOLF
Game in "The Color of Money" — POOL
Game in "The Sting" — POKER
Game like bingo — KENO
Game like chemin de fer — LET FALL
Game locale — ARENA
Game machine — PINBALL
Game of American Indian origin — LACROSSE
Game of chance — KENO, LOTTO
Game of kings — CHESS
Game official — JUDGE
Game on horseback — POLO
Game piece — DICE, MAN, ROOK
Game place — ARENA
Game played for money in a hat — SHUFFLECAP
Game played in a pool — WATER POLO
Game played in school yards — HOPSCOTCH
Game played on 64 alternate colored squares — CHESS
Game played with a cue — BILLIARDS, POOL
Game played with a shuttlecock — BADMINTON
Game played with burning brandy — SNAP DRAGON
Game ragout — SALMI
Game show host at times — ASKER
Game trail — SPOOR
Game with 32 cards — SKAT
Game with numbered squares — LOTTO
Game with wooden peg — CRIBBAGE, TIPCA
Game, _____, match — SET
Game-show group — PANEL
Gamecock spurs — GAFFS
Gamekeeper, in Glasgow — GAMIE
Games — CONTESTS
Games supervisor in ancient Rome — EDILES
Gamete — OVUM
Gamin — URCHIN
Gaming cube — DIE
Gamut — RANGE
Gamy — STRONG
Gander's call — HONK
Ganders — GEESE
Ganef's job — HEIST
Gang follower — STER
Gang in "West Side Story" — JETS
Gang of swans? — CYGNET RING
Gang or road ending — STER
Ganges river locale — INDIA
Gangland group — GOONS
Gangling New Englander? — LANKY YANKEE
Gangplanks — RAMPS
Gangster's gat — ROD
Gangster's gun — GAT
Gangsters — HOODS
Gangsters' gals — MOLLS
Gannet — SOLAN
Gannon University site — ERIE
Gantry and Fudd — ELMERS
Gantry and Rice — ELMERS
Gap — LAPSE
Gape — STARE
Gaper — STARER
Gaping — AJAR
Garage employee — GREASER
Garage event — SALE
Garage of yore — BLACKSMITH SHOP
Garage size — ONE CAR
Garage worker: Abbr. — MEC
Garand — RIFLE
Garb — APPAREL, ATTIRE, TOG
Garb for a kid brother — HAND ME DOWN
Garb for a posh party — TUX
Garb for a rani — SARI
Garb for a Stapleton? — JEANS
Garb for Giselle — TUTU
Garb for Lakma — SARI
Garb for Livy — TOGA
Garb for Patricia McBride — TUTU
Garb for shieks — ABAS
Garb for Wapner, Sirica, et al. — TOGAS
Garb formally — ENROBE
Garb in regal garments — ENROBE
Garb of young Sinatra's fans — BOBBY SOCKS
Garbed — CLAD
Garbed, to Donne — DREST
Garble — DISTORT
Garbo — GRETA
Garbo and namesakes — GRETAS
Garbo speaks — I WANT TO BE ALONE
Garbo, reportedly — LONER
Garcon — WAITER
Gard's capital — NIMES
Garden activity — PLANTING
Garden area — ARBOR
Garden areas — BEDS
Garden bean — LIMA
Garden beauties — PEONIES
Garden beauties, for short — GLADS
Garden beauty — TULIP
Garden bloomer — CANNA, PANSY, PEONY
Garden bowers — ARBORS
Garden center retailers — SEEDSMEN
Garden dweller — ADAM
Garden equipment — HOSE
Garden favorite — ROSE
Garden feature — PATH, MOSS
Garden flower — POPPY
Garden herbs — AROIDS
Garden implement — HOE
Garden insect — APHID
Garden lifelines — HOSES
Garden need — HOSE
Garden of Eden — IDYLL
Garden party — FETE
Garden pest — APHID
Garden plant — MUM
Garden plant of the voilet family — PANSY
Garden plots — BEDS
Garden raider, for short — COON
Garden scenters — TEA ROSES
Garden shelter — ARBOR
Garden sight — PETAL
Garden spot — EDEN
Garden tool — HOE, SNIPS
Garden tool used for planting bulbs — DIBBLE
Garden tools — RAKES
Garden walk in ancient Rome — XYST
Garden worker — HOER
Gardener — FARMER
Gardener's bailiwick — GREENHOUSE
Gardener's bane — APHID, WEED
Gardener's gift — GREEN THUMB
Gardener's gift to Mom? — GORGEOUS LADYS SLIPPERS
Gardener's need — HOSE, MOWER, SOIL, SOD
Gardener's problem — PESTS
Gardener's tool — EDGER, HOE, SHEARS, SPADE
Gardener, at times — HOER, PLANTER

Gardeners' assets — GREEN THUMBS
Gardening device — HOSE
Gardner namesakes — AVAS, ERLES
Gardner of mystery — ERLE
Gardner of the many cases — ERLE
Gardner sleuth — PERRY MASON
Gardner's "_____ Calls it Murder" — THE DA
Gare — DEPOT
Garfield lovers — AIL-UREOPHILIA
Garfield or Felix — CAT
Garfield's friend? — ODIE
Garfunkel or Carney — ART
Garfunkel's ex-partner — SIMON
Garganeys — TEALS
Gargantuan — LARGE
Garish — CRUDE, GAUDY, LOUD, TAWDRY
Garish light source — NEON
Garland — LEI, CHAPLET
Garland or M-1 — RIFLE
Garlic mayonnaise — AIOLI
Garlic root — BULB
Garlic-flavored mayonnaise — AIOLI
Garment — ROBE, TUNIC
Garment carriers — CLOTHES RACKS
Garment for a dancer — LEOTARD
Garment for Brutus — TOGA
Garment for Geraint — TABARD
Garment leather — DEERSKIN
Garment of yore — HOOP SKIRT
Garment style — A LINE
Garment with strings — APRON
Garment worker — TAILOR
Garments for Caesar — TOGAS
Garments for Judges — ROBES
Garments for sheiks — ABAS
Garner — AMASS, REAP
Garner birthplace — TEXAS
Garner standard — MISTY
Garner-McQueen film: 1963 — THE GREAT ESCAPE
Garners — HIVES
Garnet of greenish hue — DEMANTOID
Garnish — LARD
Garnish unit — SPRIG
Garr of "Mr Mom" — TERI
Garret — ATTIC
Garroway — DAVE
Garrulous — LOQUACIOUS
Garson of filmdom — GREER
Garth, in "Ivanhoe" — ESNE
Gary Cooper comment — YUP
Gary Cooper role — DEEDS
Gary Grimes in 1971 O'Neill film — COSTAR
Gary or Mary — HART
Gary or Moss — HART
Gary's locale — INDIANA
Gary, John or Moss — HARTS
Gas-electricity agcy. — FPC
Gas-pump word — OCTANE
Gas burner — CAR
Gas plant's family — RUE
Gas: Comb. form — AER, AERO, ATMO, PNEUMO
Gas: Prefix — AERI
Gasbag — BALLOON
Gaseous element — RADON, XENON
Gaseous element in the news — RADON
Gaseous hydrocarbon — ETHANE
Gash — NOTCH
Gasket — SEAL
Gasman's reading matter? — METERS
Gasoline and Shubert — ALLEYS
Gasoline containers — JERRY CANS
Gasp — PANT
Gasp for breath — PANT
Gasp of delight — OOH
Gasper at Bethlehem, e.g. — ADORER
Gaspump word — ANTI-KNOCK
Gasthaus — INN
Gaston's gals — AMIES
Gaston's picnic area — PARC
Gate City of the West — OMAHA
Gate guard — SENTRY
Gatekeepers — WARDENS
Gater's cousins — CROCS
Gateway — ENTRY
Gather — AMASS, FOLD, MEET, PLEAT, PUCKER
Gather — REAP, RUFFLE, UNITE
Gather and store — GARNER
Gather bit by bit — GLEAN
Gather flowers — CULL
Gather in — REAP
Gather large amounts — AMASS
Gather together — AMASS
Gather up — GARNER
Gather, as oysters or logs — TONG
Gather, at times — AMASS
Gathered — DEDUCED
Gatherers of honey for Georges? — BIZETS BEES
Gathering — MEET
Gathering clouds — OMEN
Gathering leaves — RAKING
Gathering places — AGORAS
Gatlin of song — LARRY
Gator's relative — CROC
Gatwick letters — ETA
Gauche — CRASS, OBTUSE
Gaucho gear — RIATAS
Gaucho trees — ULES
Gaucho's gold — ORO
Gaucho's lariat — REATA, RIATA
Gaucho's milieu — PAMPAS
Gaucho's weapon — BOLA
Gauchos' cow catchers — BOLAS
Gaudi country — SPAIN
Gaudy — GARISH
Gaudy psittacine bird — ARA
Gauges: Abbr. — STDS
Gauguin or Cezanne — PAUL
Gauguin's birthplace — PARIS
Gauguin's island paradise — TAHITI
Gaul — CELT
Gaul's chariot — ESSED
Gaulish garb — SAGUM
Gaunt — LANK, LEAN
Gauntlet — GLOVE
Gautama — BUDDHA
Gave _____ on the back — A PAT
Gave a discount to — REBATED
Gave a gold watch — RETIRED
Gave a hand — AIDED
Gave a hoot — CARED
Gave a knife new life — HONED
Gave a party — THREW
Gave a party for — FETED
Gave a roast for — HONORED
Gave a shove — PUSHED
Gave a smile of sorts — SIM-PERED
Gave alms — DOLED
Gave an unfavorable review — PANNED
Gave consent — ACCEDED
Gave for a time — LENT
Gave medicine to — DOSED
Gave off sleigh sounds — JINGLED
Gave orders — BOSSED
Gave out — DEALT
Gave permission — ALLOWED
Gave structure to — FORMED
Gave succor — AIDED
Gave the cold shoulder — REBUFFED
Gave the gate — AXED, SACKED
Gave the once over — EYED
Gave the raspberry to — BOOED
Gave the word — ORDERED
Gave zest to — LACED

Gavel — MALLET
Gawk — GAPE, STARE
Gawkers — GAPERS
Gawking — ASTARE
Gawks at — EYEBALLS
Gawp — STARE
Gay _____ — PAREE
Gay blade — ROUE
Gay deceiver — RAKE
Gay tunes — LILTS
Gayelord — HAUSER
Gaynor or Leigh — JANET
Gaze intently — STARE
Gaze with malicious pleasure — GLOAT
Gazebo — SUMMER HOUSE
Gazed idly — MOONED
Gazelle — ARIEL, GOA
Gazelle gait — STOT
Gazelle of Africa — ADMI
Gazette — PAPER
Gazetteer item — AREA
Gazetteer letters — ENE
Gazpacho ingredients — TOMATOES
Gazzara and Bernie — BENS
Gear — CAM, COG, OUTFIT, PINION, TACKLE
Gear containers — KITS
Gear on a bireme — OARS
Gear parts — COGS
Gear teeth — COGS
Gear tooth — COG
Gee whiz! — GOSH
Gee, to a horse — RIGHT TURN
Geezer — COOT
Gehrig — LOU
Geisha belts — OBIS
Gel-forming substance — PECTIN
Gel — CLOT
Gelada or pongo — APE
Gelatinous extract — AGAR
Gelatinous materials — AGARS
Geld — ALTER
Gelid, in Granada — FRIO
Gelled — SET
Gelling agent — AGAR
Gelling substance — AGAR
Gem for Libras — OPAL
Gem from S. Australia — OPAL
Gem of a movie star, et al. — GOLDIES
Gem of a singer-composer — NEIL DIAMOND
Gem of an entertainer — RUBY DEE
Gem of country music — MINNIE PEARL
Gem or Egyptian charm — SCARAB
Gem shaped — OVAL
Gem State — IDAHO
Gem state capital — BOISE
Gem state veggie — POTATO
Gem weight — CARAT
Gem, maybe — STONE
Gemayel of Lebanon — AMIN
Gemini, e.g. — PAIR, TWINS
Gems — JEWELS
Gems are his setting — LAPIDARIST
Gemstone — JADE, SARD
Gemstone engraved with a raised design — CAMEO
Gemstone set by itself — SOLITARY
Gen. _____ Arnold — HAP
Gen. _____ E. Lee — ROBERT
Gen. Alexander and family — HAIGS
Gen. Arnold, to friends — HAP
Gen. Bradley — OMAR
Gen. Custer was here — LITTLE BIG HORN
Gen. from Israeli — DAYAN
Gen. Grant's first name — HIRAM
Gen. Lee — ROBT
Gen. Schwarzkopf's new title — SIR
Gen. units — YRS
Gen. Wingate of W.W. II — ORDE
Gendarme's law — LOI
Gender — SEX
Gender abbr. — MASC
Gender altering suffix — ESS
Gender bias — SEXISM
Genders — SEXES
Gene component — RNA
Gene from Tioga, Tex. — AUTRY
Gene Kelly exuberance — SINGING IN THE RAIN
Gene Kelly film: 1951 — AN AMERICAN IN PARIS
Gene Kelly's "Brigadoon" side-kick — VAN JOHNSON
Gene letters — RNA
Gene or green — KELLY
Genealogy — HOUSE, LIN-EAGE, PEDIGREE, RACE
General — EXTENSIVE, PUBLIC, WIDESPREAD
General "Vinegar Joe" — STILWELL
General (Light Horse Harry) _____ — LEE
General Anthony or Fort — WAYNE
General arrangement of a TV program — FORMAT
General assemblies — PLENA
General at Gettysburg — MEADE
General Bradley — OMAR
General Chennault of the "Flying Tigers" — CLAIRE
General cost — OVERHEAD
General direction — TREND
General George — PATTON
General Hampton — WADE
General idea — HANG
General pardon — AMNESTY
General Powell — COLIN
General president — EISENHOWER
General Rommel — ERWIN
General tendency — TREND
General Tom — THUMB
General who became president — EISENHOWER
General Wingate of the Chindits — ORDE
General's _____-camp — AIDE DE
Generalized term of disapproval — TATTY
Generalized title of respect — SQUIRE
Generally — AS A RULE
Generals' secretaries — AIDES
Generate — BEGET, CREATE, FATHER, SIRE
Generation — AGE, CRE-ATION, START
Generation _____ — GAP
Generator of direct current — DYNAMO
Generator's power output — LOAD
Generic — COMMON, GEN-ERAL
Generous — FERTILE, FREE HANDED, LIBERAL
Generous and charitable — ALTRUISTIC
Generous gifts — LARGESSES
Generous one — DONOR
Genes can carry it — TRAIT
Genes carrier: Abbr. — DNA
Genesis — CREATION, RISE, SEED
Genesis figure — EVE, SEED
Genesis name — ADAM, ABRAHAM, EVE
Genesis site — EDEN
Genesis verb — BEGAT
Genetic acids: Abbr. — RNA
Genetic cell material — DNA
Genetic duplicate — CLONE
Genetic initials — DNA, RNA
Genetic inits. — RNA
Genetic letters — DNA
Genetic material — DNA
Genetic offshoot — CLONE
Genetic replica — CLONE
Genetic unit — RNA
Genetically abnormal one — ALBINO
Genetically depilated — BALD
Genetically deviant organism — MUTANT
Genghis or Kubla — KHAN
Genial — CHEERY
Genie's abode — LAMP
Genie's home — LAMP

Genista specimen — BROOM
Genoa coin — LIRA
Genoa gate — PORTA
Genoa greeting — CIAO
Genoese Admiral — ANDREA DORIA
Genovese magistrates — DOGES
Gentle — AMENE, KIND, MILD, SOFT SPOKEN
Gentle gait — LOPE
Gentle one — LAMB
Gentle people — DOVES
Gentle soul — LAMB
Gentle wind — BREEZE
Gentleman — SIR
Gentleman in New Delhi — SAHIB
Gentleman of Veronna — ROMEO, SIGNOR
Gentlemen's gentlemen — VALETS
Gentlemen, from Veronna — SRES
Gentlemen, in München — HERREN
Gentles — TAMES
Gentry — ELITE
Genu — KNEE
Genuflect — KNEEL
Genuflected — KNELT
Genuine — KOSHER, REAL, TRUE
Genuine one — REAL MCCOY
Genus — CLASS
Genus of bees — APIS
Genus of blue-footed boobies — SULA
Genus of evergreen shrubs — THEA
Genus of frogs — RANA
Genus of grape — VITIS
Genus of maples — ACER
Genus of marine worms — NEREIS
Genus of mosquitoes — AEDES
Genus of stoneworts — NITELLA
Genus of trees — ACER
Geodesic _____ — DOME
Geog. area — TERR
Geog. limit — BDY
Geographical abbr. — ELEV
Geographical features — CLIFFS
Geographical origin: Suffix — ESE
Geography — LAYOUT
Geologic ending — CENE
Geologic interludes — ERAS
Geologic periods — ERAS
Geologic-time division — NEOCENE
Geological division — EPOCH, ERA
Geological fracture — FAULT
Geological times — ERAS
Geom. e.g. — MATH
Geom. fig. — RECT
Geom. figure — CIRC
Geom. or Trig. — MATH
Geom. shape — CIR
Geometer's straight line — SECANT
Geometric curve — ELLIPSE
Geometric figure — ISOGON, RHOMB, SOLID
Geometric figures — CONES, CYLINDERS
Geometric measure — AREA
Geometric surface — PLANE
Geometry verb — BISECT
Geometry word — SINE
George _____ (1783-1820) — III
George _____ Welles — ORSON
George _____, French novelist — SANS
George _____: former Chicago Bears' owner — HALAS
George and T.S. — ELIOTS
George Barr McCutcheon hero — BREWSTER
George Brummel's nickname — BEAU
George Burns companion — CIGAR
George Burns film — OH GOD
George Burns prop — CIGAR
George Burns sequel: 1980 — OH GOD BOOK II
George C. Scott movie: 1981 — TAPS
George Eliot hero — BEDE
George Eliot's "Silas _____" — MARNER
George Eliot's real name — EVANS
George Hamilton acquirement — TAN
George Herman Ruth — BABE
George Lucas classic — AMERICAN GRAFFITI
George of "A Touch of Class" — SEGAL
George of "The Owl and the Pussycat" — SEGAL
George of the silver screen — BRENT
George or Gracie — ALLEN
George or T.S. — ELIOT
George Peppard's TV group — A TEAM
George Washington _____ — CARVER
George Westinghouse invention — AIR BRAKE
George's brother — IRA
George's collaborator — IRA
George's veep — DAN
George's were wooden — TEETH
George, in Spain — JORGE
Georgetown athlete — HOYA
Georgetown, capital of _____ — GUYANA
Georgia beauties — PEACHES
Georgia bird? — MACONDOR
Georgia city — ATHENS
Georgia O'Keeffe specialty — STILL LIFE
Georgia or Armenia: Abbr. — SSR
Georgia Tech player — YELLOW JACKET
Georgia's capital — ATLANTA
Georgia's nickname — PEACH STATE
Georgia, once: Abbr. — SSR
Georgia-Alabama border river — CHATTAHOOCHEE
Geraint's beloved — ENID
Geraint's lady — ENID
Gerald Ford, by birth — OMAHAN
Gerald Green novel — THE LAST ANGRY MAN
Geraldine Chaplin's grandfather — EUGENE ONEILL
Geraldine of opera fame — FARRAR
Gerard _____ Borch, Dutch painter — TER
Germ — BUD, SEED, VIRUS
Germ cell — GAMETE, SPORE
Germ-free — STERILE
Germ-free state — ASEPSIS
German-Polish border river — NEISSE
German admiral — SPEE
German article — DAS, DER, EIN
German artist — DURER
German astronomer Johannes _____: 1571-1630 — KEPLER
German author noted for anecdotes — SCHAFER
German brew — BIER
German canal — KIEL
German city — COLN, GOTHA, HALLE
German city or the Lippe — WERNE
German coal-mining region — RUHR
German conjunction — UND
German count — GRAF
German emperors — KAISERS
German engraver-painter — DURER
German engraver: 1471-1528 — DURER
German expletive — ACH
German firearm — MAUSER
German four — VIER

German gentleman — HERR
German grandson — ENKEL
German granny — OMA
German gun — LUGER
German heroine — HELDIN
German ice cream — EIS
German industrial area — RUHR
German industrial city — ESSEN
German island in the North Sea — SYLT
German mark — UMLAUT
German mathematician / astronomer — GAUSS
German mister — HERR
German money — MARK
German name for a Polish port — STETTIN
German name for a Polish river — ODER
German name for Poznan — POSEN
German negative — NEIN
German news agency — DPA
German oldster — ALTE
German painter Albrecht — DURER
German philosopher Georg — HEGEL
German philosopher, 1734-1804 — KANT
German poet — HEINE
German politidal leader 1863-1919 — HAASE
German port — EMDEN
German region — SAAR
German reservoir dam — EDER
German river — ALLER, EGER, ELBE, PEENE
German river or valley — RUHR
German river to the North Sea — WESER
German ruler — OTTO
German seaport on the Ems — EMDEN
German society — BUND
German soldier of World War I — HUN
German song — LIED
German sophisticate? — BONN VIVANT
German spa — EMS
German textile center — GERA
German title — HERR
German-born British artist Carl _____: — HAAG
German: Abbr. — TEUT
Germany's _____ -Coburg — SAXE
Germany's Count Von — SPEE
Germicide — ANTISEPTIC
Geronimo was one — APACHE
Geronimo, e.g. — INDIAN
Gershwin favorite, "An _____" AMERICAN IN PARIS
Gershwin musical — LADY BE GOOD
Gershwin tune — SOMEBODY LOVES ME
Gershwin's "Rhapsody in _____" — BLUE
Gershwin, et al. — IRAS
Gertrude Stein subject — ROSE
Gertrude's apertif — STEINS WINE
Gerund ending — ING
Gesture made by thumbing the nose — SNOOK
Gestures of agreement — NODS
Get — ATTAIN, FETCH, GAIN, PROCURE, REACH
Get _____ (succeed) — ALONG
Get _____ in one's throat — A LUMP
Get _____ of: eliminate — RID
Get _____ on (stir) — A MOVE
Get _____ out of: enjoy — A BOOT
Get a free ride in baseball — WALK
Get a move on — HIE
Get a new lease — RELET
Get a touchdown — SCORE
Get ahead — PROSPER, THRIVE
Get along — HURRY
Get an eyeful — STARE
Get around — AVOID, EVADE
Get away — ESCAPE
Get away from — ELUDE
Get back — REGAIN
Get better — MEND
Get by trickery — FINAGLE
Get cosy — NESTLE
Get even — AVENGE
Get even again — RETIE
Get going — BEGIN
Get in shape — TRAIN
Get more weapons — REARMS
Get new equipment — REFIT
Get off one's high horse? — ALIGHT
Get off the ground — FLY
Get off the Pullman — DETRAIN
Get off track — DERAIL
Get on a soapbox — ORATE
Get one's ankles wet — WADE
Get one's dander up — RILE
Get one's goat — IRK, RILE
Get one's hand on — OBTAIN
Get or comprehend — LATCH ON TO
Get out of — AVERT, EVADE
Get out of bed — ARISE
Get out of town — FLEE
Get out! — SCAT, SCRAM, SHOO
Get ready for the O.R. — PREP
Get ready to drive — TEE UP
Get ready to propose — KNEEL
Get rid of a law — REPEAL
Get rid of, Stalin style — PURGE
Get smashed in Formosa — TAI WAN ON
Get some shuteye — SLEEP
Get some z's — SLEEP
Get the better of — EXCEL
Get the edge on — NOSE OUT
Get the lead out? — ERASE
Get the news — HEAR
Get together — MEET
Get under way — SAIL
Get up — AWAKEN, RISE, STAND
Get up _____ — AND GO
Get well — HEAL, RECOVER
Get wrong — MISUNDER-STAND
Get-together time — THANKS-GIVING DAY
Get-up — RIG
Getaway — ELOPE
Gethsemane monks — TRAP-PISTS
Gethsemane's locale — OLIVET
Gets — SECURES
Gets a circuit ahead in a race — LAPS
Gets a hint of — SCENTS
Gets along — FARES
Gets an "F" — FAILS
Gets away — ESCAPES
Gets better — HEALS, MENDS
Gets by, with "out" — EKES
Gets close to — NEARS
Gets even — AVENGES
Gets it all together — COL-LECTS
Gets married — WEDS
Gets off the Yankee Clipper — DETRAINS
Gets on well with — LIKES
Gets one's goat — RILES, IRKS
Gets out more soap — RERINSES
Gets out of bed — RISES
Gets out, in poker — FOLDS
Gets rid of — SCRAPS
Gets smart — WISES UP
Gets some shuteye — NAPS
Gets spliced — WEDS
Gets the job done — SEES TO IT
Gets the motor boat — SHOVES OFF
Gets the point — SEES
Gets the sun — TANS
Gets the wet out — DRIES
Gets the wrinkles out — IRONS

Gets to the presents — UNWRAPS
Gets together — TEAMS UP
Gets up steam — PRIMES
Gets uptight — TENSES
Gets, by persuasion — WANGLES
Getting boring — PALLING
Getting burned, in a way — BATHING IN THE SUN
Getting cold feet — CHICKENING OUT
Getting older — AGING
Getting on — AGED
Getting ready for battle — ARMING
Gettysburg loser — LEE
Gettysburg, for one — ADDRESS
Getz and Laurel — STANS
Getz instrument — SAX
Getz of jazz — STAN
Getz or Kenton — STAN
Geum genus — AVENS
Gewgaws — BANGLES
Ghana seaport — ACCRA
Ghana's capital — ACCRA
Ghanian export — COCOA
Ghanian neighbor — TOGO
Ghastly — LURID
Ghengis Khan was one — TATAR
Gherig or Rawls — LOU
Ghillie or solleret — SHOE
Ghost — SHADE, SPOOK
Ghost stories, perhaps — THRILLERS
Ghost: Dialect — HANT
Ghostly event — SEANCE
Ghostly garb — SHEET
Ghostly hangout in "Hamlet" — BATTLEMENT
Ghostly sound — BOO
Ghosts of the dead in ancient Rome — MANES
Ghoulish — EERIE
GI address — APO
GI mail drops — APOS
GI meal — MESS
GI no-show — AWOL
GI of World War I — DOUGHBOY
GI pinups — CHEESECAKE
GI wear, in WW II — ODS
GI's address — APO, FPO
GI's favorite org. — USO
GI's haven — USO
Giant armadillo — TATU
Giant at 16 — OTT
Giant ending — ESS
Giant grass — OTATE
Giant Hall of Famer Melvin — OTT
Giant in "The Pilgrim's Progress" — DESPAIR
Giant jets — SSTS
Giant killer — JACK
Giant Mel's family — OTTS
Giant of British legend — MAGOG
Giant petrel — NELLY
Giant redwood — SEQUOIA, TREE
Giant slain by Apollo — OTUS
Giant step — STRIDE
Giant with 100 eyes — ARGUS
Giant, to a Hamburger — RIESE
Gibberish — JABBER WOCKY, GALIMATIAS
Gibbet — LYNCH
Gibbon — APE, LAR
Gibbon of Malay peninsula — LAR
Gibbs of "227" — MARLA
Gibe — TAUNT
Gibe at — TWIT
Gibraltor denizen — APE
Gibraltor tourist attractions — APES
Gibraltor, e.g.: Abbr. — STR
Gibson garnish — ONION
Gibson of tennis fame — ALTHEA
Gibus or kady — HAT
Giddiness — VERTIGO
Gide's "_____ Die" — IF IT
Gift — BESTOWAL, PRESENT
Gift for a moppet — SLED
Gift for an old woman in a shoe? — A BABY SITTER
Gift for contrary Mary? — A LANDSCAPE ARTIST
Gift for Dr. Foster? — A PAIR OF HIP BOOTS
Gift for Hugo's Bishop? — SOME SILVER POLISH
Gift for milady — SCENT
Gift for Mother Hubbard? — A BAG OF BONES
Gift for Mrs. Sprat? — POUND OF LARD
Gift for Old King Cole? — PIPE TOBACCO
Gift getter — DONEE
Gift of gab — LINE
Gift tag word — FROM
Gift to charity — DONATION
Gifted — TALENTED
Gifted people — TALENTS
Gifts — TALENTS
Gig — BOAT
Gig implement — OAR
Gigantic — HUGE, LARGE
Giggle — TEHEE
Gigolo's friend? — SUGAR MAMA
Gil _____: Lesage hero — BLAS
Gil or Roy — BLAS
Gilbert & Sullivan expert John _____ — REED
Gilbert & Sullivan opera — MIKADO
Gilbert & Sullivan producer — CARTE
Gilbert & Sullivan star John _____ — REED
Gilbert & Sullivan vessel — PINAFORE
Gilbert & Sullivan's "_____ by Jury" — TRIAL
Gilbert and Jeb — STUARTS
Gilbert or Manchester — MELISSA
Gilbertian peeress — IDA
Gilda's father — RIGOLETTO
Gilded silver — VERMEIL
Gimcrack gems — PASTE
Gimlet — COCKTAIL
Gimlet ingredient — LIME
Gimlet's larger cousin — AUGER
Gimmick — ANGLE, GADGET
Gin — SNARE
Gin mill — BAR
Ginger chasers — SNAPS
Ginger cookie — SNAP
Ginger-snap — COOKY
Gingery — REDDISH
Gingiva — GUM
Gins — TRAPS
Ginseng — HERB, ROOT
Ginseng plant — UDO
Giraffe's kin — OKAPI
Giraffe's little cousin — OKAPI
Giraffe's relative — OKAPI
Giraffes — CAMELOPARDS
Girasol — OPAL
Gird up — ARM
Girdle — TRUSS
Girdle or belt, Latin style — CESTUS
Girdle's cousin — CORSET
Girl — MISS
Girl Fri. — ASST
Girl from Guadalajara — NINA
Girl graduate in "Princess Ida" — ADA
Girl in "Great Expectations" — ESTELLA
Girl in "Le Nozze di Figaro" — SUSANNA
Girl in "The Devil's Disciple" — ESSIE
Girl in "Twelfth Night" — VIOLA
Girl in a calypso song — MATILDA
Girl in Maude Nugent's 1896 song — ROSIE
Girl of Glasgow — LASS
Girl of song — CHLOE, DAISY, SUSIE, SWEET SUE
Girl of song, 1936 — IRENE
Girl with great expectations — HEIRESS

Girlfriend of Clark Kent — LOIS
Girls and women — SHES
GIs' wake-up call — REVEILLE
Gist — ESSENCE, MEAT, MEET, NUB, SUM
Gitche Gumee craft — CANOE
Give — AND TAKE, AWARD, CONTRIBUTE, DONATE, GRANT
Give — PRESENT, PROVIDE, SUPPLY
Give (someone) _____ deal — A RAW
Give _____ (care) — A DARN
Give _____ (chew out) — IT TO
Give _____ (listen) — EAR TO
Give _____ (take a stab) — A TRY
Give _____ a little (roughly) — OR TAKE
Give _____ to: approve — A NOD
Give _____ whirl (try) — IT A
Give _____: care — A HOOT
Give 52 to four — DEAL OUT
Give a bad time — TEASE
Give a boost to — HYPE
Give a bum steer to — MISLEAD
Give a darn — CARE
Give a face-lift to — RENEW
Give a hand — AID, ASSIST, HELP
Give a hoot — CARED
Give a leg up — ABET, AID
Give a leg up to a yegg — ABET
Give a new title — RENAME
Give a rendition of a poem — RECITE
Give a second scanning — REREAD
Give a sermon — PREACH
Give a wide berth — AVOID
Give advice — ADVISE
Give aid — ABET
Give all the info — LET IT ALL HANG OUT
Give an _____ (look after) — EYE TO
Give an angry look — GLARE
Give another polishing — REWAX
Give assistance to — ABET
Give away — MELT
Give back — REBATE
Give birth to — BEAR
Give birth: Scots — EAN
Give comfort — EASE
Give confidence — REASSURE
Give confidence to — ASSURE
Give conspicuous newspaper display — SPLASH
Give courage — EMBOLDEN
Give for awhile — LEND
Give forth — EMIT, EXUDE
Give homework — ASSIGN
Give in — ACCEDE, CONCEDE, RELENT, YIELD
Give in exchange — SWAP
Give in to — DEFER
Give it _____ (attempt) — A TRY
Give it a whirl — TRY
Give joy — ELATE
Give new form to — RESHAPE
Give off — EMIT, EXUDE, POUR OUT
Give off fumes — REEK
Give one an answer — REPLY TO
Give one's hand to — WED
Give oppurtunity to — ENABLE
Give or yield formally — CEDE
Give orders — DICTATE
Give out — EMIT, METE
Give over — CEDE
Give power to — ENABLE
Give private instruction — TUTOR
Give rise to — SPAWN
Give sanction to — RATIFY
Give shape — MOLD
Give shape to — HEW
Give shelter to — HOUSE
Give short measure — STINT
Give short shrift — SCANT
Give sparingly — INCH
Give Strawberry the raspberry — DERIDE
Give support — SUSTAIN
Give support to — ASSIST
Give temporarily — LEND
Give temporary custody to — LEND
Give the _____ (fire) — GATE TO
Give the ball to the fullback — HANDOFF
Give the boot — OUST
Give the eye — OGLE
Give the eye to — OGLE
Give the gate — BOOT, DISMISS, DRUM OUT
Give the nod — AGREE
Give the onceover — INSPECT
Give the slip to — ELUDE, LOSE
Give the valedictory — ORATE
Give up — CEDE, RENOUNCE
Give up power — ABDICATE
Give up the ball — FUMBLE
Give up the pigskin — PUNT
Give up, at the casino — CASH IN ONES CHIPS
Give up, at the ringside — THROW IN THE TOWEL
Give vent to — EMIT
Give voice to severe criticism — ROAST
Give-and-take — BANTER, EXCHANGE
Give-away — CLUE, HINT, IDEA, SLIP
Given — STATED
Given a hint — CLUED
Given a new life — REBORN
Given name of 26th president: Abr. — THEO
Given to conversation — CHATTY
Given to coquetry — FLIRTY
Given to panting — GASPY
Given to reverie — DREAMY
Given to wearing wools — TWEEDY
Given to wild laughter — SHRIEKY
Giver of titles, in a way — NAMER
Givers of unsolicited advice — BACK SEAT DRIVERS
Gives a bad review — PANS
Gives a leg up — AIDS
Gives a once-over — EYES
Gives a rating — RANKS
Gives a sly look — LEERS
Gives approval — ACCEDES
Gives chapter and verse — CITES
Gives ear — HEEDS
Gives expression to — VENTS
Gives forth — EMITS
Gives in — ACCEDES
Gives joy — PLEASES
Gives off — EMITS
Gives out — EMITS
Gives power to — ENABLES
Gives support (to) — LENDS
Gives temporarily — LENDS
Gives the cold shoulder to — SNUBS
Gives the go-ahead — OKS
Gives the heave-ho — OUSTS
Gives the nod — OKS
Gives the nod to — OKAYS
Gives thumbs up — OKAYS
Gives up occupancy — VACATES
Giving aid to the enemy — TREASON
Giving an account of — RELATING
Giving permission — ALLOWING
Giving positive views — ASSERTIVE
Giving voice to — EXPRESSING
Giving witness — VOUCHING
Glace — ICED
Glacial — ICY
Glacial deposits — ESKARS, MORAINES
Glacial dune — OSAR
Glacial epoch — ICE AGE
Glacial ice — NEVE

Glacial ice block — SERAC
Glacial mass — ICECAP
Glacial peak — SERAC
Glacial phenomena — SERACS
Glacial ridge — ASAR, ESKER, OSAR
Glacial ridge: Var. — ESKAR
Glacial ridges — OSAR
Glacial slope — STOSS
Glacial snow — FIRN, NEVE
Glaciarium — RINK
Glacier pinnacles — SERACS
Glaciers — ICECAPS
Glad plantings — BULBS
Gladden — CHEER, ELATE
Gladdens — PLEASES
Gladiator's three prong spear — TRIDENT
Gladiator's turf — ARENA
Gladly — FAIN, LIEF
Gladly, old style — FAIN
Gladly: Ger. — GERN
Gladstone or Queen Elizabeth — BRITON
Gladstone's kin — VALISES
Gladys Knight and the _____ — PIPS
Glairs' lairs? — EGGSHELLS
Glamorous fabric — LAME
Glamorous Turner — LANA
Glance at quickly — SCAN
Glance over — SCAN
Glance over or read carefully — SCAN
Glanced — PEEKED
Glancing rebound — RICOCHET
Gland: Comb. form — ADENO
Glaringly vivid — LURID
Glasgow adhesive? — SCOTCH TAPE
Glasgow girl — LASS
Glasgow negatives — NAES
Glasgow or Goodman — ELLEN
Glasgow topper — TAM
Glaspell's "Norma _____" — ASHE
Glass — LENS, TUMBLER
Glass container once used in distilling — MATRASS
Glass dish with an overlapping cover — PETRI
Glass enclosed porch — SOLARIUM
Glass gardens — TERRARIA
Glass having a rounded bottom inside — TUMBLER
Glass in Colorado? — ASPEN PANES
Glass setters — GLAZIERS
Glass support — STEM
Glass window — PANE
Glasses with compound lenses — BIFOCALS
Glassmakers' material — FRIT
Glassmakers' ovens — LEHRS
Glassware — CRYSTAL
Glassy — VITRIC
Glassy mineral — SILICA
Glaswegian — SCOT
Glaswegian boy — LADDIE
Glaswegian's great grandchild — IEROE
Glaze — COAT, SLEET
Glaze component — FRIT
Glazed fabrics — CIRES
Gleam — SHINE
Gleamed — SHONE
Glean — COLLECT
Glee club — SINGERS
Glen — VALE
Glencannon — GILPATRIC
Glenn Miller hit, 1943 — CHATTANOOGA CHOO CHOO
Glenn Miller's forte — SWING
Glenn's state — OHIO
Glens — VALES
Gless of "Cagney and Lacey" — SHARON
Gless role — CAGNEY
Gli _____ Unit: U.S.A., to Mario — STATI
Glib — FACILE
Glib or graceful — FLUENT
Glide — SOAR
Glide along — SKATE
Glide along or strut — SASHAY
Glide nonchalantly — SASHAY
Glide on ice — SKATE
Glide on wheels — SKATE
Glide on wings — SOAR
Glide without power — VOLPLANE
Glided — SLID
Glimmered — SHONE
Glimmering — IDEA
Glimpse — SEE
Glissade — SLIDE
Glisten — SHINE
Glistened — GLEAMED, SHONE
Glitch — SNAG
Glitch maker — GREMLIN
Glitter — SHINE, TINSEL
Glitters — SPANGLES
Glittery — SHINY
Glittery cloth — LAME
Glittery fabric — LAME
Glitzy dos — GALAS
Glitzy fabric — LAME
Glitzy topper — TIARA
Gloaming — EEN
Gloat — CROW, PREEN
Global — ROUND
Globe-trotters' Holland site? — HAARLEM
Globe-trotters' reference — ATLAS
Globes — ORBS
Globular jar — OLLA
Globular tear-jerker — ONION
Globule — BEAD
Gloom — PALL
Gloom's partner — DOOM
Gloomy — DARK, DISMAL, DOUR, MOROSE, SOMBER
Gloomy and taciturn — SATURNINE
Gloomy fellow? — GUS
Gloomy on the Left Bank — NOIR
Gloomy, poetically — DREAR
Gloppy — ICKY
Glorifies — EXALTS
Glorify — ENTHRONE, EXALT
Gloriole — HALO
Glorioles — HALOES
Glorious — GRAND
Glory — ECLAT
Gloss — LUSTER, SHEEN, SHINE
Gloss over, in a way — WHITEWASH
Gloss paint — ENAIL
Glossary — LIST
Glossy — SLEEK
Glossy coat — VARNISH
Glossy coating — ENAMEL
Glossy cotton cloth — SATEEN
Glossy fabric — SATEEN, SATIN
Glossy finish — ENAMEL
Glossy paint — ENAMEL
Glove — MITT
Glove leather — NAPA
Glove material — SUEDE
Gloves for Gehrig and Berra — MITTS
Glow — FLAME, SHINE
Glower — GLARE
Glower at — LEER
Glowing — FERVENT, RADIANT
Glowing bit — SPARK
Glowing coal — EMBER
Glowing fragment — EMBER
Glowing review — RAVE
Glows — RADIATES
Gluck works — OPERAS
Gluck's "_____ ed Euridice" — ORFEO
Gluck's "Paride ed _____" — ELENA
Gluck's output — OPERAS
Glue — PASTE
Glues — CEMENTS
Glum — MOROSE, SAD
Glut — SATE
Glutted — SATED
Glutting — SATING
Glutton — PIG
Glycerides — ESTERS
Gnarl — KNUR
Gnash — BITE

Gnat or rat — PEST
Gnaw — CHEW
Gnaw on — CHEW
Gnawed away — EROSE
Gnome — DWARF
Go-aheads — OKS
Go _____ for — TO BAT
Go _____ kite — FLY A
Go _____ tear — ON A
Go _____: deteriorate — TO SEED
Go _____: travel — ABROAD
Go a round — SPAR
Go about again — RETACK
Go after — CHASE, SEEK
Go after game — HUNT
Go ahead — LEAD, PROCEED
Go all out — KNUCKLE DOWN
Go along with — SWIM WITH THE TIDE
Go around — DETOUR
Go around in the ring — SPAR
Go around the edge — SKIRT
Go astray — ERR, SIN
Go astray, in a way — DERAIL
Go at full speed — CAREER
Go at top speed — CAREEN
Go at with _____ — HAMMER AND TONGS
Go away — BEGONE, LEAVE
Go away! — SCAT, SCRAM
Go AWOL — TAKE FRENCH LEAVE
Go back — REVERT
Go back to a former state — REVERT
Go backward — RECEDE
Go bad — ROT
Go before — ANTECEDE, PRECEDE
Go berserk — SNAP
Go between — AGENT, MESSENGER
Go between for illicit affairs — PANDERER
Go by — ELAPSE
Go by boat — SAIL
Go by car — MOTOR
Go by shanks' mare — WALK
Go cruising, in a way — SAIL
Go down — LOSE
Go down again — RESINK
Go down easily — MELT IN ONES MOUTH
Go first — LEAD
Go fishing — ANGLE
Go for — LIKE
Go for a spin — RIDE
Go for broke — SHOOT THE WORKS
Go forward — PROCEED
Go full tilt — RUSH
Go gaga over — ADORE, ENTHUSE
Go getter — BALL OF FIRE
Go gliding — SOAR
Go headlong — CAREEN
Go hire _____ — A HALL
Go hungry — STARVE
Go in haste — HARE
Go inside — ENTER
Go into — ENTER
Go into service — ENLIST
Go it alone — SOLO
Go lickety split — TEAR
Go off course — VEER
Go on all fours — CREEP
Go on horseback — RIDE
Go on the road — TOUR
Go or lead follower — ETH
Go out with — DATE
Go over — STUDY
Go oystering — TONG
Go silently — STEAL
Go sky-high — SOAR
Go slack-jawed — GAPE
Go the route — LAST
Go through the door — ENTER
Go to a dinner — EAT OUT
Go to bed — HIT THE HAY, RETIRE
Go to court — APPEAL
Go to court again — RETRY
Go to Gretna Green — ELOPE
Go to sleep — RETIRE
Go to the mat with — WRESTLE
Go to the top — RISE
Go together — DATE
Go up — RISE
Go up against — DEFY
Go whole _____ — HOG
Go wild over — FLIP
Go with — DATE
Go with the gale — SCUD
Go with the tide — DRIFT
Go wrong — ERR
Go-cart — WAGON
Go-getter — DOER, POWER-HOUSE, RAMROD, TIGER
Go-off — START
Go-to-meeting — CLOTHES
Goad — NEEDLE, PERTURB, PROD, SPUR, URGE
Goads — PRODS
Goads, with "on" — EGGS
Goal — AIM
Goal of a sunbather — TAN
Goal of actors — ROLE
Goal of every hockey team — STANLEY CUP
Goal of thespians — ROLE
Goal post (bowling) — SPLIT
Goal, in Geesthacht — ZIEL
Goalie feat — SAVE
Goanna — LIZARD
Goat — RAM
Goat note — MAA
Goat on a bender? — TOOT-NENANNY
Goat's offspring — KIDS
Goatee — BEARD, TUFT
Goatee setting — CHIN
Goatlike figure — FAUN
Goats' hair fabrics — MOHAIRS
Gob — TAR
Gob's greeting — AHOY
Gobble up — CHOMP
Gobbled up — ATE
Gobbledy-gook — JARGON
Gobbler — TURKEY
Gobbles down compliments — EATS UP
Gobelin product — TAPESTRY
Gobi and Mojave — DESERTS
Gobi or Negev — DESERT
Gobi-like — SERE
Goblet — CHALICE
Goblet part — STEM
Goblet, filled to the brim — BUMPER
Goblin — BOGLE, SPRITE
God — DIETY
God of fire — AGNI
God of heaven — URANUS
God of love — AMOR, EROS
God of marriage — HYMEN
God of Mecca — ALLAH
God of mischief — LOKI
God of the North Wind — BOREAS
God of the underworld — DIS, ORCUS
God of the winds — AEOLUS
God of thunder — THOR
God of war — ARES, MARS
God worshipped by Ahab's wife — BAAL
God, in Genoa — DIO
God, in Paris — DIEU
God, in Spain — DIOS
God, to Caeser — DEUS
God, to Chinese Protestants — SHEN
God, to Luigi — DIO
God: Fr. — DIEU
God: Lat. — DEO
Goddess — DEA
Goddess in Grenoble — DEEDE
Goddess in old Rome — DEA
Goddess of abundance — OPS
Goddess of agriculture — CERES
Goddess of dawn — EOS
Goddess of discord — ERIS
Goddess of grain — CERES
Goddess of healing — EIR
Goddess of hope — SPES
Goddess of horses — EPONA
Goddess of knights — HECATE
Goddess of Law — MAAT
Goddess of love — VENUS
Goddess of mischief — ATE
Goddess of peace — IRENE

Goddess of plenty — OPS
Goddess of strife — ERIS
Goddess of the dawn — EOS
Goddess of the harvest — CERES
Goddess of the hearth — VESTA
Goddess of the moon — LUNA, SELENE
Goddess of the rosy hue — EOS
Goddess of the seasons — HORAE
Goddess of vengeance — ARA
Goddess of victory — NIKE
Goddess of volcanoes — PELE
Goddess of wisdom — ATHENA
Goddess of youth — HEBE
Goddess who knew her oats — CERES
Goddess, to Caesar — DEA
Goddesses of the seasons — HORAE
Godfather — SPONSOR
Godfrey's companion — UKELELE
Godfrey's Julius — LA ROSA
Godiva's garb situation — BARE
Godiva's lover — LEOFRIC
Godiva's title — LADY
Godless — WICKED
Godlike youths — APOLLOS
Godsend — BOON, BLESSING, GIFT
Godunov or Badenov — BORIS
Godunov, for one — TSAR
Goering or Goebbels — NAZI
Goes _____ (deteriorates) — TO POT
Goes after trout — CASTS
Goes ashen — PALES
Goes astray — ERRS
Goes back on his word — RENEGES
Goes bad — ROTS, SOURS
Goes before and leads — PACES
Goes before ine or age — ENG
Goes by dog cart — RIDES
Goes by jet — FLIES
Goes cycling — PEDALS
Goes down — SETS
Goes down swinging — STRIKES OUT
Goes for glory — ASPIRES
Goes for the gold — VIES
Goes from gate to runway — TAXIS
Goes in with — JOINS
Goes into debt — OWES
Goes like a house afire — RACES
Goes off course — VEERS
Goes out with again — REDATES
Goes over 65 — SPEEDS
Goes quickly — HIES
Goes rapidly — HIES
Goes to the plate — BATS
Goes to the polls — VOTES
Goes weeding — HOES
Goes without food — FASTS
Goes wrong — ERRS
Gofer's task — ERRAND
Gogol tale — NOSE
Gogol's "_____ Bulba" — TARAS
Gogol's "_____ Souls" — DEAD
Gogol's "Taras _____" — BULBA
Going strong — ON A ROLL
Going to be married — ENGAGED
Going up fast — ROCKETING
Going-to-Jerusalem prop — CHAIR
Goings' opposite — COMINGS
Golconda — MINE
Gold _____ — DIGGER
Gold _____ — LEAF
Gold and silver — METALS
Gold cloth — LAME
Gold coin in Edam — FLORIN
Gold coins for Caesar — AUREI
Gold cup, e.g. — PRIZE
Gold digger — A GIRL WHO LIKES TO GO BUY BUY
Gold embroidery — ORPHERY
Gold fabric — LAME
Gold holder — ORE
Gold lace for upholstery — ORRIS
Gold look-alike — OROIDE
Gold measure — KARAT
Gold measures: Abbr. — KTS
Gold medalist Biondi — MATT
Gold medalist Louganis — GREG
Gold mold — INGOT
Gold or Silver — METAL
Gold or silver in mass — BUL-LION
Gold Rush seaport — FRISCO
Gold rush site of 1897-98 — KLONDIKE
Gold thread — PURL
Gold, e.g. — METAL
Gold, in Genova — ORO
Gold, in Oviedo — ORO
Gold, in Toledo — ORO
Gold-medal winner Louganis — GREG
Gold-rush mill owner — SUTTER
Gold: Sp. — ORO
Golda of Israel — MEIR
Golda, et al. — MEIRS
Goldbrick — IDLER, LOAF, SLACKER
Golden-rule preposition — UNTO
Golden _____ — GATE
Golden braid — ORRIS
Golden calf — IDOL
Golden dogs — RETRIEVERS
Golden fleece carrier — ARGO
Golden Gate, for one — SPAN
Golden girl Getty — ESTELLE
Golden ide — ORFE
Golden oldie favorites? — CHANTS OF A LIFETIME
Golden or Walden — POND
Goldfinch — YELLOW BIRD
Goldfinger — MIDAS
Goldie Hawn role — PRIVATE BENJAMIN
Goldie of movies — HAWN
Goldings's island idyll? — THE LORD OF THE FLIES
Goldwyn product — MOVIE
Golf "Army" leader — ARNIE
Golf bag items — TEES
Golf club — IRON, MASHIE, SPOON, WOOD
Golf club bigwig — PRO
Golf course — LINKS
Golf course area — GREEN
Golf course dogleg — FAIRWAY
Golf course location — TEE, TRAP
Golf course norm — PAR
Golf course unit — HOLE
Golf event — OPEN
Golf gadget — TEE
Golf gaffes — SLICES
Golf gizmo — TEE
Golf goal — PAR
Golf great — SNEAD
Golf hazard — TRAP
Golf instructor — PRO
Golf irons — WEDGES
Golf name of fame — SNEAD
Golf org. — PGA
Golf shoe feature — CLEAT
Golf shot — LOFT
Golf situation — LIE
Golf standard — PAR
Golf stroke — BAFF, PUTT
Golf teacher — PRO
Golf tournament — OPEN
Golf's "Champagne Tony" — LEMA
Golf's Arnie — PALMER
Golf's Ballesteros — SEVE
Golf's Gary — PLAYER
Golfer Andy's garden aids? — BEAN POLES
Golfer Baker-Finch — IAN
Golfer Ballesteros — SEVE
Golfer Calvin — PEETE
Golfer Curtis — STRANGE
Golfer from Japan — ONO
Golfer gaffes — SLICES
Golfer Hal's Gotham pad? — SUTTON PLACE

Golfer Irwin — HALE
Golfer Jay — HAAS
Golfer Louise — SUGGS
Golfer Palmer — ARNIE
Golfer Sam — SNEAD
Golfer Stewart — PAYNE
Golfer Sutton — HAL
Golfer turns merchant — ARNOLD PALMERCHANT
Golfer with an army — ARNIE
Golfer Woosman — IAN
Golfer's _____ in one — HOLE
Golfer's bane — TRAP
Golfer's choice — IRON
Golfer's concern — LIE
Golfer's gadgets — TEES
Golfer's goal — HOLE, PAR
Golfer's grp. — PGA
Golfer's hat — CAP
Golfer's hole _____ — IN ONE
Golfer's need — IRON, TEE
Golfer's obstacle — TRAP
Golfer's situation — LIE
Golfer's stroke over par — BOGEY
Golfer's transport — CART
Golfer's warning cry — FORE
Golfer, at times — TEER
Golfing area — GREEN
Golfing events — OPENS
Golfing name of fame — SNEAD
Golfing pro — SIKES
Goliath — GIANT
Goliath's slayer — DAVID
Golly — GOSH
Golly's cousin — GOSH
Gomorrah's neighbor — SODOM
Gomper's org. — AFL
Gon lead-in — PENTA
Gondolier — BOATMAN
Gondolier's need — POLE
Gone — PAST
Gone by — AGO, PAST
Gone con? — ESCAPE
Gone up — RISEN
Goner's name — MUD
Goneril's father — LEAR
Gong — TAM TAM
Goo — GUNK
Goober — PEANUT
Good-bye, amigo — ADIOS
Good blade — TOLEDO
Good cheese or chocolate — SWISS
Good cigar — CLARO
Good earth — LOAM, MARL
Good for nothing — IDLER
Good fortune — LUCK
Good Friday song of Andalusia — SAETA
Good garden's need — LOAM
Good golf score — EAGLE
Good health or wealth, e.g. — ASSET
Good judgement — TASTE
Good looker — DISH
Good loser — SPORT
Good luck charm — MASCOT
Good moods — UPS
Good name for short — REP
Good natured — CORDIAL
Good neighbor of the United States — CANADA
Good or adequate reason — CAUSE
Good or bad practice — HABIT
Good or kind follower — NESS
Good periods — UPS
Good quality paper — BOND
Good reply to a dope pusher — NOPE
Good sense — REASON
Good sense: Sp. — TINO
Good service award — BONUS
Good sort — GEM
Good taste — ELEGANCE
Good times — UPS
Good turn — FAVOR
Good weather at Stowe — SNOW
Good weather words — FAIR AND PLEASANT
Good, French word — BON
Good, to Gina — BUONA
Good-bye, in St. Lo — ADIEU
Good-for-nothing — WASTREL
Good-humored and jolly — JOVIAL
Good-looking taxi? — HANDSOME CAB
Good-luck charm — RABBITS FOOT
Good-luck piece — AMULET
Good-old high notes — ELAS
Good-time Charlie — SPORT
Goodbye on the Ginza — SAYONARA
Goodbye, in Granada — ADIOS
Goodbye, in Oahu — ALOHA
Goodie — TREAT
Goodies for a spread — EATS
Goodies for elevenses — SCONES
Goodies from the past — OLDIES
Goodman's instr. — CLAR
Goodman's jazz — SWING
Goodnight girl of song — IRENE
Goods cast adrift — LAGAN
Gooey — ICKY
Goof — BOO BOO, BONER, ERR, FLUB
Goof off — GOLDBRICK, LOAF
Goofed — ERRED
Goofs — BONERS, SLIPUPS, MISSTEPS
Goon — GORILLA
Goons — THUGS
Goose — BRANT
Goose cry — HONK
Goose egg — WELT, ZERO
Goose eggs — OOOOO
Goose feature — NECK
Goose genus — ANSER
Goose of Hawaii — NENE
Goose to a gander — MATE
Goose, in Gironde — OIE
Goose, in Rome — OCA
Goose: L. — ANSER
Goosefoot herb — ORACH
Gooselike — ANSERINE
GOP birthplace — RIPON
GOP's opposition — DEMS
Gorbachev in A.M. action? — RUSSIAN DRESSING
Gorbachev's denials — NYETS
Gordie of hockey — HOWE
Gordon and Lerner — MAXES
Gordon or Irish — SETTER
Gordon Shumway — ALF
Gore — PIERCE
Gore and family — VIDALS
Gore and Pacino — ALS
Goren partner Helen _____ — SOBEL
Goren's game — BRIDGE
Gorge — ABYSS, CHASM, RAVINE
Gorge with a stream — FLUME
Gorgon's mother — CETO
Gorilla — APE
Gormandize — EAT, OVEREAT
Gorp — MIX
Gosh! — GEE
Goshen card entry — TROT
Gospel — EVANGEL
Gospel author — LUKE, MARK
Gossip — BABBLE, CHAT, DIRT, HEN, IDLE TALK
Gossip — RUMOR, TALK
Gossip of a sort — YENTA
Gossip tidbit — DIRT, ITEM
Gossip's delight — KAFFEEKLATCH
Gossips — TALKS, TATTLES
Gossipy — NEWSY
Gosson — LAD
Got — AQUIRED
Got a bill — OWED
Got a hole-in-one — ACED
Got a lift — RODE
Got along — FARED
Got an eyeful — OGLED
Got around — EVADED
Got boring — PALLED
Got comfy — NESTLED
Got going — MOVED
Got it — GRASPED
Got it! — I SEE
Got mad — SAW RED
Got off a 747 — DEPLANED
Got off a steed — ALIT
Got on the soapbox — ORATED

Got one's goat — RILED
Got rid of — UNLOADED
Got rid of the weeds — HOED
Got the decision — WON
Got the lead out — ERASED
Got the soap out — RINSED
Got top billing — STARRED
Got up — AROSE, WOKE
Got up a second time — REROSE
Got very cross — IRED
Got wind of — HEARD
Gotcha! — AHA, HAH
Gotha and Coburg — SAXE
Gotham, for short — NYC
Gothamite — NEW YORKER
Gothic novelist Victoria — HOLT
Gothic windows — ORIELS
Gotlander — SWEDE
Gouda — CHEESE
Gouda's competitor — EDAM
Goulash — STEW
Gould railroad — ERIE
Gourd — MELON, PEPO
Gourd fruit — PEPO
Gourmand — EATER
Gourmandized — OVERATE
Gourmands — EATERS
Gourmet Claiborne — CRAIG
Gourmet pancake — CREPE
Gourmet treat — PATE
Gourmet's delight — DISH FIT FOR A KING
Gov. agt. — T MAN
Gov. Cuomo's concern — NYS
Govern — RULE
Governed — RULED
Governed by bishops — EPISCOPAL
Governess — ABBESS
Governing bodies — SENATES
Government body — SENATE
Government fiscal problem — BUDGET
Government of a sort — REGENCY
Governor — REGENT, REGULATOR
Governor Cuomo — MARIO
Governor of Virginia: 1827-30 — GILES
Governor Winthrop, e.g. — DESK
Governor Winthrop, for instance — DESK
Governors — REGENTS
Govt. advisory board — REC
Govt. agcy. responsible for broadcasting — FCC
Govt. agency of the past — HEW
Govt. collection agency — IRS
Govt. communications org. — USIA
Govt. group — AGCY
Govt. info org. — USIA
Govt. investigator — T MAN
Govt. meat stamp — USDA
Govt. mediation group — FMCS
Govt. news dispenser — USIA
Govt. org. — ICC, USIA
Govt. sponsor of opera, etc. — NEA
Govt. watchdog — FDA
Gowdy and namesakes — CURTS
Gown for Calpurnia — STOLA
Gown for O'Connor — ROBE
Goya duo, for short — MAJAS
Goya subject — MAJA
Goya's "Duchess of _____" — ALBA
Goya's "The Naked _____" — MAJA
Goya's duchess — ALBA
Goya's land — ESPANA
Goya, for one — ARTIST
Gozo's neighbor — MALTA
Gr. Island — TENOS
Gr. letter — ETA, TAU, CHI
Gr. marketplace — AGORA
Gr. meeting place — AGORA
Gr. pastry — BAKLAVA
Gr. porch — STOA
Gr. theaters — ODEA
Grab a flying object — CATCH
Grab away — WREST
Grab some shut-eye — SNOOZE
Grabber's cry — MINE
Grabbiness — GREED
Grable, to many W.W. II G.I.'s — PINUP
Grabs — NABS
Grabs forcibly — SEIZES
Grace — FAVOR
Grace or Melba — MOORE
Graceful aquatic bird — TERN
Graceful bird — SWAN
Graceful garments — SARIS
Graceful girl — SYLPH
Graceful horse — ARABIAN
Graceful looking birds — SWANS
Graceful sprite — PERI
Graceful steed — ARAB
Graceful tree — ELMS
Graceland, to Elvis — HOME
Graceless — HAM HANDED
Gracie Allen's heritage — IRISH
Gracie or Steve — ALLEN
Gracious — POLITE
Grackle — BLACKBIRD, DAW
Grad of MIT — ENGR
Grad, at times — REUNER
Grad. class members — SRS
Grad. degree in sci. — SCD
Grad. degrees — AMS
Grad. degrees for teachers — EDDS
Grad. sch. entrance exam — LSAT
Gradation — NUANCE, SHADE
Grade — LEVEL
Grade for a beginner in Judo — KYU
Grade sch. — ELEM
Gradiate — SCALE
Gradient — RAMP, SLOPE
Grading — RANK
Grading system — CURVE
Grads-to-be — SRS
Grads — ALUMNI, ALUMS
Grads, ere long — SRS
Gradual disappearance — EVANESCENCE
Gradually diminishing: Mus. — RIT
Gradually paid off a debt — AMORTIZED
Gradually slower: Mus. dir. — RALL
Graduate — ALUMNA
Graduate degree — DSC
Graduate exam — ORAL
Graduate of Balliol, e.g. — OXONIAN
Graduate school hurdles — ORALS
Graduate's acquisition — DEGREE
Graduate-to-be — SENIOR
Graduates — AULUMI
Graduates exam — ORAL
Graduating class — SENIORS
Graduating group — SRS
Graduation prom — SENIOR DANCE
Graf _____ — SPEE
Graf shot — LOB
Graff of "Mr. Belvedere" — ILENE
Graft — SHOOT
Graft, as a plant — INARCH
Graft, as plants: Var. — ENARCH
Grafted, in hearldry — ENTE
Grafted: Her. — ENTE
Grafter's item — CION
Grafting twig — SCION
Graham et al. — REVS
Graham or Raye — MARTHA
Graham's group — DANCERS
Grail — CUP
Grain — OAT, SEED
Grain appendage — AWN
Grain awn — ARISTA
Grain beard — ARISTA, AWN
Grain for Vassar — MALT
Grain fungus — ERGOT
Grain germinator — SPROUTER
Grain grinding place — MILL
Grain husk — BRAN
Grain product — CEREAL

Grain sorghum — DURRA, MILO
Grain spikes — EARS
Grain unit — EAR
Gram and dram — UNITS
Gram and stat starter — HELIO
Gram or graph — TELE
Gram or graph lead-in — EPI
Gram or graph starter — EPI
Gram or logic preceder — IDEO
Gram. case — ACC, DAT
Grammatical no-no — SPLIT INFINITIVE
Grammatical trumpeter? — VERB ALPERT
Grammer of "Cheers" — KELSEY
Grampus — ORC, ORCA, WHALE
Grampuses — ORCS
Granada cheer — OLE
Granada gentlemen — SENOR
Granada gruels — ATOLES
Granary — SILO
Grand _____ — PRIX, SLAM
Grand _____ (Western range) — TETONS
Grand _____ Dam — COULEE
Grand _____ National Park — TETON
Grand _____ Opry — OLE
Grand _____ Ruler (B.P.O.E. big-wig) — EXALTED
Grand _____, Evangeline's home — PRE
Grand _____, Mich. — RAPIDS
Grand and Plaza — HOTELS
Grand Canal worker — POLER
Grand Central: Abbr. — STA
Grand Coulee, for one — DAM
Grand Exalted Ruler, e.g. — ELK
Grand follower — SLAM
Grand homes — MANORS
Grand item — SLAM
Grand National or Iditarod — RACE
Grand O-Lei Opry? — HEE HAWAII FIVE O
Grand or Cedar — RAPIDS
Grand or little — SLAM
Grand or South — TETON
Grand Pee Dee — RIVER
Grand places — STANDS
Grand slam — HOMER
Grand slam outfit? — BRIDGE SUIT
Grand slam, in cards — VOLE
Grand time — GALA
Grand Tour site — EUROPE
Grand-tour cont. — EUR
Grande and Branco — RIOS
Grande or Bravo — RIO
Grande, for one — RIO
Grandeur — NOBILITY
Grandfather-grandson U.S. Presidents — HARRISONS
Grandiflora — ROSE BUSH
Grandiloquent writings — BOMBASTS
Grandiose — COSMIC, PALATINE
Grandiose tale — SAGA
Grandiosity of a sort — MAGNILOQUENCE
Grandma — NANA
Grandma _____ — MOSES
Grandma Moses — ANNA
Grandma's daughter — MOM
Grandmother of Kaiser Wilhelm II — QUEEN VICTORIA
Grandmother of Timothy — LOIS
Grandpa on "The Waltons" — GEER
Grandpa's car? — REO
Grandparental — AVAL
Grands — PIANOS
Grandson in Granada — NIETO
Grandstand rows — TIERS
Grange — FARM
Grange and Buttons — REDS
Grange of football — RED
Grange or Buttons — RED
Grange's team — ILLINI
Granite State — NEW HAMPSHIRE
Granny Smith is one — APPLE
Granny Smiths — APPLES
Granny's other daughter — AUNT
Granny, e.g. — KNOT
Granny, for one — KNOT
Granolalike breakfast food — MUESLI
Grant-Hepburn film — CHARADE
Grant — BESTOW, CEDE, GIVE, PERMIT
Grant advance — SECURED LOANS
Grant and Majors — LEES
Grant Fuhr and Andy Moog — GOALIIES
Grant giving org. — NSF
Grant of "Being a Woman" — TONI
Grant opponent — LEE
Grant portrayer — ASNER
Grant's _____ — TOMB
Grant's discarded name — HIRAM
Grant-Bennett film classic — TOPPER
Granted, as territory — CEDED
Granular snow — FIRN, NEVE
Grape — UVA
Grape growing — VITICULTURE
Grape mashing time? — CRUSH HOURS
Grape used for raisins — MUSCAT
Grape variety — PINOT
Grape, in Concordia — UVA
Grape: Comb.form — RHAG
Grapefruit's relative — POMELO
Grapes — UVA
Grapevine — GOSSIP
Grapevine growth — RUMOR
Graph — CHART
Graph or biography — AUTO
Graphic beginning — GEO
Graphic lead-in — CALLI
Graphic or logic starter — ZOO
Graphite — LEAD
Graphologist's concern — HANDWRITING
Grappling surface — MAT
Grasp — GET, SEE
Grass — SOD, TURF
Grass court — LAWN, TENNIS
Grass cutter — SCYTHE
Grass moisture — DEW
Grass roots — STICKS
Grass trimmer — EDGER
Grass variety — REDTOP
Grasses — REDS
Grassland — LEA, PRAIRIE
Grassy area — LAWN, LEA, SWARD
Grassy expanse — LAWN
Grassy plains of Argentina — LLANOS
Grassy plains of S. America — LLANOS
Grassy plant — SEDGE
Grate — ABRADE
Grate — RASP
Grate glower — EMBER
Grate harshly — RASP
Grateau's wave — MARCEL
Grateful — AWARE
Gratified — GLAD
Gratified completely — SATED
Gratifies — SATES
Gratify — SATE
Gratify to overflowing — SATE
Gratify totally — SATE
Gratifying — PLEASANT
Grating — HARSH, RASPY, STRIDENT
Gratis — FREE, ON THE HOUSE
Gratuities — PERKS, TIPS
Gratuity — FEE, TIP
Gratutitous — PERKS
Grave — SEDATE, SERIOUS
Grave marker — STELE
Gravel _____ of "Dick Tracy" — GERTIE
Gravel ridge in a glacier — ESKER
Graven image — IDOL
Gravesend goodbye — TATA

Gravestone — STELA
Gravitates — LEANS
Gravure lead-in — ROTO
Gravy dish — BOAT
Gray and black plaid — MAUD
Gray and Candler — ASAS
Gray and Moran — ERINS
Gray general — LEE
Gray wolf — LOBO
Gray, in Grenoble — GRIS
Grayer — SLATIER
Grayish green — SAGE
Grayish green color — RESEDA
Grayish wildcat — JAGUARUNDI
Grayish yellow — ECRUS
Grayish-green shade — RESEDA
Grayish-white — ASHEN
Graylags, for example — GEESE
Grayness — PALLOR
Graze — EAT, SKIM
Grazed — NICKED
Grazers — CATTLE
Grazing fields — LEAS
Grazing land — PASTURE
Grazing spots — LEAS
Grease jobs — LUBES
Grease monkey's job — LUBE
Grease pencil — LINER
Grease the palm — BRIBE
Great — TERRIFIC
Great _____ (N.A. region) — PLAINS
Great _____ of China — WALL
Great _____, Mont. — FALLS
Great _____: Bahama Island — ABACO
Great abundance — SCAD
Great amounts — SEAS
Great Antilles Island — CUBA
Great bargains — STEALS
Great Barrier Island — OTEA
Great Barrier Reef sight — ATOLL
Great books — EPICS
Great care — PAINS
Great circle — EQUATOR
Great deed — FEAT
Great destruction — HAVOC
Great distance — AFAR
Great distress — WOE
Great ending — EST
Great enthusiasm — MANIA
Great Greek geometrician — EUCLID
Great Greek writer — ARISTOTLE
Great Lake — ERIE, HURON
Great Lake canals, for short — SOO
Great Lake port — ERIE
Great Lakes boat — ORE
Great Lakes canals — SOO
Great Lakes city — ERIE
Great love, to a Sloane ranger — PASH
Great number — ARMY, SLEW
Great offense — SIN
Great Plains denizen — HARE
Great Pyramid builder — CHEOPS
Great quantities — LOTS
Great quantity — OCEAN
Great respect — AWE
Great review — RAVE
Great Seal word — ORDO
Great source of supply — MINE
Great state cops? — SUPER DUPER TROOPERS
Great surprise — AMAZEMENT
Great White Way light — NEON
Great work — EPIC
Great: Comb. form — MEGA
Greater Antilles island natives — CUBANS
Greater London borough — BARNET
Greater part — MOST
Greatest number — MOST
Greatly surprised — ASTONISHED, BOWLED OVER
Greatly surprised — DUMFOUNDED, SPEECHLESS
Greco and Cid — ELS
Greece to Greeks — HELLAS
Greece's Gulf of _____ — ARTA
Greed — AVARICE
Greedy — AVID
Greedy king — MIDAS
Greedy one — PIG
Greedy ones — AMASSERS
Greek — ARGIVE, IONIAN
Greek "H" — ETA
Greek and Roman, e.g. — ERAS
Greek arcade — STOA
Greek beauty — HELEN, LAIS
Greek capital — ATHENS
Greek cheese — FETA
Greek citadel — ACROPOLIS
Greek city-state — POLIS
Greek coin — OBOL
Greek coins of old — STATEERS
Greek colonnade — STOA
Greek colony, of old — IONIA
Greek commune — DEME
Greek dawn-goddess — EOS
Greek earth goddess — GAEA
Greek epic poet — HOMER
Greek fabulist — AESOP
Greek flask — OLPE
Greek god — ARES, EROS
Greek god of mockery — MOMUS
Greek goddess — HERA
Greek goddess of infatuation — ATE
Greek goddess of strife and discord — ERIS
Greek goddess of victory — NIKE
Greek goddess of wisdom — ATHENE, ATHENA
Greek goddesses of the season — HORAE
Greek Greece — ELLAS
Greek hero of the Trojan war — AJAX
Greek island — SAMOS
Greek islander — CRETAN, DELIAN
Greek isle — DELOS, SAMOS
Greek isles — IONIAN
Greek Juno — HERA
Greek letter — ALPHA, BETA, CHI, ETA, GAMMA
Greek letter — KAPPA, LAMBDA, PHI, PSI, OMICRON
Greek letter — RHO, SIGMA, TAU, THETA, ZETA
Greek letter on a sweater — ETA
Greek liqueurs — RAKIS
Greek long e — ETA
Greek marketplace — AGORA
Greek mountain chain — OETA
Greek mountain of mythical renown — OSSA
Greek muse — ERATO
Greek music halls — ODEA
Greek neckwear ad? — RHODES COLLAR
Greek official — EPARCH
Greek peak — ETNA, IDA, OSSA
Greek philosopher with a lamp — DIOGENES
Greek phonetician — ETACIST
Greek physician — GALEN
Greek pitcher — OLPE
Greek poet — PINDAR
Greek poet who rode a dolphin — ARION
Greek port — SALONIKA
Greek portico — STOA
Greek promenade — STOA
Greek resistance force of W.W. II — ELAS
Greek sacred city — ARGOS
Greek sculptor-architect — SCOPAS
Greek sea: Var. — EGEAN
Greek shipping domain? — CHRISTINAS WORLD
Greek sorceress — MEDEA
Greek stoic, circa 250 B.C. — ZENO
Greek sun god — HELIOS
Greek theaters — ODEA
Greek theologian — ARIUS
Greek to a Trojan — ENEMY
Greek victory goddess — NIKE
Greek war goddess — ENYO

Greek weights — OBOLI
Greek wine pitcher — OLPE
Greek writer of long ago — AESOP
Greek's ligneous ruse — HORSE
Greeks' Greece — HELLAS
Greel island, aka Santorim — THIRA
Greeley's direction — WEST
Green — NEW AT THE JOB, VERDANT
Green and snap — BEANS
Green Bay athlete — PACKER
Green bean — SNAP
Green bird of New Zealand — KEA
Green chalcedony — PRASE
Green films — PATINAS
Green Gables girl — ANNE
Green grazing spots — VERDANT PASTURES
Green ice cream — PISTACHIO
Green land — EIRE, ERIN
Green light — SIGNAL
Green Mountain "boy" — ETHAN
Green Mountain state — VERMONT
Green or black beverage — TEA
Green or glade starter — EVER
Green or soft follower — SOAP
Green parrots — KEAS
Green position — AWAY
Green quartz — PLASMA
Green shade — NILE
Green side dish: Fr. — SALADE
Green spaghetti sauce — PESTO
Green spot in Paris — PARC
Green stone — JADE
Green tea — HYSON
Green vegetable — BEAN, KALE, PEA
Green's shot — PUTT
Green's target — HOLE
Green: Comb. form — VERDI
Greenback — DOLLAR, NOTE
Greenbacks — PAPER MONEY, TENS
Greene of "Bonanza" — LORNE
Greengage — PLUM
Greengrocer's item — PEAR
Greengrocers' garb? — PEA JACKETS
Greengrocery — STORE
Greenhorn — NOVICE
Greenhorns — TYROS
Greenhouse calamity? — SHRINKING VIOLETS
Greenhouse shrub — CAMELLIA
Greenish blue — AQUA, TEAL, TURQUOISE
Greenish yellow paper — BOSC
Greenish-blue pigment — BICE
Greenland air base — THULE
Greenland base — ETAH
Greenland Bay — BAFFIN
Greenland eskimo — ITA
Greens — SALADS
Greens dish — SALAD
Greens feature — HOLE
Greens for the general? — CAESAR SALAD
Greens stroke — PUTT
Greensward — SWARTH
Greenwich time — GMT
Greer of "Mrs. Miniver" — GARSON
Greet — HAIL, SALUTE
Greet the day — ARISE
Greet with open arms — RECEIVE
Greet wordlessly — NOD
Greeted — HAILED
Greeted the dawn — AROSE, AWOKE
Greetin' for TV's Child? — WHATS COOKIN
Greeting — HANDSHAKE, HELLO, SALUTE
Greeting from Clinton — HAIL
Greeting from Hilo — ALOHA
Greeting in Lod — SHALOM
Greetings — REGARDS
Greets — HAILS
Greets intrusively — ACCOSTS
Greets the dawn — WAKES
Greets the villain — HISSES
Greg Norman, for one — AUSTRALIAN
Gregg grad — STENO
Gregg's system, for short — STENO
Gregorian cycle — YEAR
Gregors _____ in "The Wild Duck" — WERLE
Gregory Hines needs these — TAPS
Grenada gala — BAL, FIESTA
Grenoble girlfriend — AMIE
Grenoble grain — BLE
Grenoble's Department — ISERE
Grenoble's river — ISERE
Greta _____ — GARBO
Gretna Green arrival — ELOPER
Gretzky's stats — GOALS
Gretzky's target — CAGE
Grew faint — WANED
Grew rapidly — SNOWBALLED
Grew serious with "up" — SOBERED
Grew tall and thin — SPINDLED
Grey of ballet fame — BERYL
Grid — GRATING
Grid action — PASS
Grid distances, for short — YDS
Grid gains — YDS
Grid linemen, for short — RGS
Grid measures — YDS
Grid passes — LATERALS
Grid turf — ASTRO
Gridiron grippers — CLEATS
Gridiron group — ELEVEN
Gridiron groups — TEAMS
Gridiron infractions — CLIPS
Gridiron inits. — NFL
Gridiron pass option — LATERAL
Gridiron period abbr. — QTR
Gridiron Zebra — REFEREE
Grief — DOLOR, WOES
Grief symbol — ASHES
Grieg dancer — ANITRA
Grieg's "_____'s Dance" — ANITRA
Grieg's people — NORSE
Grievance — PEEVE
Grieve — ACHE, MOURN REPENT
Grieved — HEARTSORE, PAINED
Grievously — SORELY
Griffin — MERV
Griffith and Downs — HUGHS
Griffith or Rooney — ANDY
Griffith or Williams — ANDY
Grifter's accomplice — SHILL
Grifter's game — STING
Grill — BROIL
Grill counterfeits? — SHAM BURGERS
Grill item — BRIQUET
Grill or grid — MESH
Grill's partner — BAR
Grills — BROILS
Grim — BLEAK, DARK, SOLEMN, SOMBER, STERN
Grimace, old style — MUMP
Grimalkins — CATS, HAG
Grime — SOOT
Grimes golden pippin — APPLE
Grimm character — OGRE
Grimy — DINGY
Grin — SMILE
Grin and _____ — BEAR IT
Grinch's creator — SEUSS
Grind — GNASH
Grind engine valves — RESEAT
Grind the teeth — GNASH
Grind, on campus — BOOKWORM
Grinder — MOLAR
Grinders, e.g. — TEETH
Grinding powder — EMERY
Grinding tooth — MOLAR
Grip — CLENCH
Grip for a Giant — CLEAT
Gripes — BEEFS

Gripper — VISE
Gripper for the Gipper — CLEAT
Gripping instrument — CLAMP, WRENCH
Gripping tool — PLIERS, VISE
Grips for swashbucklers — Hilts
Grips for trips — TRAVELING BAGS
Gris-gris — AMULET
Grist for ed.'s mill — MSS
Grist for U.S. Mail mill — CORR
Grist of the opera — RERI
Grit — SAND
Grizzilies — BEARS
Grizzled — HOARY
Grizzled civet — RASSE
Grizzly's Alaskan cousin — KODIAK BEAR
Grocery clerk? — APPLE POLISHER
Grocery item — OLEO
Grocery vehicle — CART
Grofe's "Grand Canyon _____" — SUITE
Groggy — TIRED
Gromyko — ANDREI
Groom — CURRY
Groom on the Ganges — SYCE
Groom's milieu — STABLES
Groom's view — HORSE OF ANOTHER COLOR
Groom, in a way — CLIP
Grooming — TOILET
Grooming process — TOILET
Grooms' ring holders — BEST MEN
Grooved — STRIATE
Grope — SEARCH
Grosgrains, e.g. — REPS
Gross — SORDID
Gross in Granada — CRASO
Gross injustice — RAW DEAL
Gross receipts — SALES
Grosse _____, Mich. — POINTE
Grossly stupid — CRASS
Grotto — CAVE
Grouch — CRAB, CRANK
Grouch's problem — MUTTER COMPLEX
Groucho wore one — BERET
Ground corn — SAMP
Ground covered with fine grass — LAWN
Ground hominy — GRITS
Grounded — ON LAND
Grounded Australian — EMU
Grounded bird — EMU
Groundless — IDLE
Grounds — CAUSE, PREMISES
Grounds beautifier? — LANDSCAPE GARDENER
Grounds for belief — EVIDENCE
Groundskeeper's implement — EDGER
Groundwork — BASIS
Group "Tennessee River" — ALABAMA
Group akin to the "Highbinders" — TONG
Group beliefs — ETHOS
Group character — ETHOS
Group for a DA — ABA
Group having same trait — CLASS
Group in an oater — POSSE
Group of African languages — BANTU
Group of badgers — CETE
Group of crows — MURDER
Group of dogs or wolves — PACK
Group of eight — OCTAD, OCTED, OCTET
Group of eight divine beings: Gnos — OGDOADS
Group of experts — PANEL
Group of five — PENTAD
Group of girls — BEVY
Group of gorillas — BAND
Group of jurors — PANEL
Group of lions — PRIDE
Group of Muslim scholars — ULAMA
Group of nine — ENNEAD, NENET
Group of office workers — POOL
Group of paid applauders — CLAQUE
Group of poems — EPOS
Group of quails — BEVY
Group of railroad workers — GANG
Group of saddle horses — REMUDA
Group of servants — RETINUE
Group of seven — HEPTAD, SEAS
Group of seven musicians: Brit. — SEPTETTE
Group of teal — DUCKS
Group of three — TRIAD, TRINE, TRIUNE
Group of trained leaders — CADRE
Group of turtles — BALE
Group of warriors — COHORTS
Group of witches — COVEN
Group of workers — GANG
Group on one side — TEAM
Group on The Hill — SENATE
Group once ruled by J.E.H. — FBI
Group under a col. — RGT
Group under a master — TROOP
Group's senior member — DOYEN
Groupies — FANS
Groupies, in a sense — IDOLATORS
Groups — SETS
Groups of devotees — CULTS
Groups of eight — OCTADS
Groups of nine — ENNEADS
Groups of sayings — ANAS
Groups of three — TRIADS, TRINES, TRIOS
Groups of warships — NAVIES
Groups' guiding beliefs — ETHOS
Grouse — GRUMBLE
Grouse house — NEST
Groused — BEEFED
Grouses — MOPES
Grout — MORTAR
Grovel — FAWN
Grow — RAISE
Grow canines — TEETHE
Grow fair — CLEAR UP
Grow furious — SEETHED
Grow larger — DILATE
Grow milder — SOFTEN
Grow molars — TEETHE
Grow tiresome — PALL
Grow together — ACCRETE, COALESCE, KNIT
Grow toward sunset — LATEN
Grow upon — TOUCH
Grow warmer — MELLOW
Grow wearisome — PALL
Grow weary — TIRE
Growing conspiracy? — GARDEN PLOT
Growing healthy — THRIVING
Growing out — ENATE
Growl — GNAR
Growl, snarl: Scot. — GURR
Growlers — BERGS
Grown — ADULT
Grown up — ADULT
Grown up pullet — HEN
Grown-up chigger — MITE
Grownup — ADULT
Grows bright — DAWNS
Grows pale — FADES
Grows tiresome — STALES
Grows weary — TIRES
Growth in all directions — ISOTROPY
Growth on a trunk — KNAR
Grub — EATS, HUNT, LARVA
Grub; chow — EATS
Grubby — DIRTY
Grudge — ANIMUS, PEEVE, RANCOR, SPITE
Gruff — SURLY
Grumble — MUTTER, REPINE
Grumbled: nagged — HARPED
Grump — CRAB
Grunter's home — STY

Guacamole base — AVOCADOS
Guadalajara gold — ORO
Guadeloupe or Martinique — ILE
Guam's capital — AGANA
Guanaco's descendant — LLAMA
Guanaco's kin — ALPACAS
Guarantee — ENSURE
Guard — SENTINEL, SENTRY
Guard follower — IAN
Guard of a sort — DOOR-KEEPER
Guarded sticker — EPEE
Guardhouse — BRIG
Guardian spirits — GENII
Guardian's concern — WARD
Guardsman's side arm — SABRE
Gucci of fashion — ALDO
Gudrun's King — ATLI
Gudrun's mate — ATLI
Gudrun's victim — ATLI
Guernsey lillies — NERINES
Guernsey or Jersey — ELM
Guesses: Abbr. — ESTS
Guest of verse — EDGAR
Guest or Gray — POET
Guest room, frequently — DEN
Guevara — CHE
Guffaw — HAHA, HORSE LAUGH, ROAR
Guffaw or whinny — HORSE LAUGH
Gugelhupf — CAKE
Guidance — COUNSEL
Guide — STEER
Guide dogs, usually — GERMAN SHEPHERDS
Guide for Holmes — CLUE
Guided — LED, STEERED
Guides — LEADS, STEERS
Guiding beliefs — ETHOS
Guido notes — ELAS
Guido of art — RENI
Guido's high note — ELA
Guido's lowest note — GAMUT
Guidonian note — ELA
Guidry and Howard — RONS
Guidry of baseball — RON
Guidry or Nessen — RON
Guillotine — BEHEAD
Guiltless — INNOCENT
Guilty one — CULPRIT
Guilty or not guilty — PLEA
Guilty persons, usually — PENITENTS
Guinea pig — CAVY
Guinea pig kin — AGOUTI
Guinness — ALEC
Guinness or Waugh — ALEC
Guinness-Davis film: 1959 — THE SCAPEGOAT
Guipure, e.g. — LACE
Guitar feature — FRET
Guitar kin — UKE
Guitar ridge — FRET
Guitar's cousin — BANJO
Guitar's relative — LUTE
Guitarfish — RAY
Guitarist arpeggios — RASGADOS
Guitarist Ed — BICKERT
Guitarist Flatt — LESTER
Guitarist Lofgren — NILS
Guitarist Montgomery — WES
Guitarist Paul — LES
Guitars' kin — LUTES
Gula and cyma — OGEES
Gulag — PRISON
Gulch — RAVINE
Gulf _____ system — STREAM
Gulf in the Indian Ocean — ADEN
Gulf N. of Gallipoli peninsula — SAROS
Gulf of _____ — ADEN
Gulf of _____ — OMAN
Gulf of Sidra locale — LIBYA
Gulf of Suez neighbor — RED SEA
Gulf of the Indian Ocean — ADEN
Gulf on the Aegean — SAROS
Gulf scene of WWII victory — LEYTE
Gulf State's marsh — BAYOU
Gulfs — CHASMS
Gull — TERN
Gull genus — LARUS
Gull relatives — TERNS
Gull's cousin — TERN
Gull-like predator — SKUA
Gullet — CRAW, MAW
Gullible — CREDULOUS, EASY, NAIVE, SIMPLE
Gulls — DUPES
Gulls, terns, etc. — LARI
Gully — CANYON, DITCH, GORGE, GULCH
Gully in a desert — WADI
Gulps — SWIGS
Gum resin — ELEMI
Gum shoe — GALOSH
Gumbo basic — OKRA
Gumbo ingredient — OKRA
Gumlike — CHEWY
Gummy — TACKY
Gump or Grundy — MRS
Gump's wife — MIN
Gumption — SENSE, SPUNK
Gums — RESINS
Gums: Comb. form — ULO
Gumshoe — TEC
Gun — REVOLVER
Gun a motor — REV
Gun aimed at a bomber — ACK ACK
Gun charge — LOAD
Gun for a gangster — GAT
Gun for Tommy — STEN
Gun grp. — NRA
Gun muzzle covers — TAMPIONS
Gun org. — NRA
Gun parts — BORES
Gun the motor — REV
Gun-crew member — AIMER
Gun-toters in oaters — POSSE
Gunfighter at the O.K. Corral — EARP
Gung-ho — AVID, EAGER, ZEALOUS
Gunk — GOO
Gunman — THUG
Gunned down — SHOT
Gunnery command — FIRE
Gunny — HEMP
Gunpowder component — NITER
Gunpowder plot conspirator — FAWKES
Gunpowder, for example — TEA
Guns a motor — REVS
Gunsel's job — HEIST
Gunther subject in 1947 — USA
Gunwhale pin — THOLE
Gurth, in "Ivanhoe" — SWINE-HERD
Guru — MENTOR
Gush — SPEW, SPURT
Gush forth — SPEW
Gushed — SPEWED
Gushes — POURS
Gussets — INSERTS
Gussy up — PREEN
Gustav _____ former Swedish king — ADOLF
Gusto — ARDOR, ELAN, ZEST
Gut fish — GIP
Guthrie — ARLO
Guthrie scion — ARLO
Gutta — DROP
Guy's companion — GAL
Guy's partner — GAL
Guys — GENTS, MEN, STUDS
Guys not confused or upset? — COMBOBULATED MEN
Guzzle — TOPE
Gweducs — CLAMS
GWTW word — GONE
Gym accouterments — MATS
Gym assistant? — BARTENDER
Gym twist — CONTORTION
Gymnasium item — HORSE
Gymnast — ACROBAT
Gymnast becomes singer — TINA TURNER
Gymnast Comaneci — NADIA
Gymnast Korbut — OLGA
Gymnast's goal — TEN
Gymnast's prop — BEAM
Gymnast's turn — KIP
Gymnastic feat — KIP

Gymnastics move — SPLIT
Gynt's mother — ASE
Gyps — CONS
Gypsies — ROMS
Gypsum — YESO
Gypsum, from the Spanish — YESO
Gypsy _____ Lee — ROSE
Gypsy card — TAROT
Gypsy gentlemen — ROM
Gypsy husband — ROM
Gypsy Rose _____ — LEE
Gyrate — SPIN
Gyrated — SPUN
Gyrations — ANTICS
Gyre — SPIN
Gyves — CHAINS

H

H. _____ Perot — ROSS
H. Broun's "Pieces of _____" — HATE
H. Hoover or H. Wallace — IOWAN
H. Rider Haggard novel — SHE
H.G. — WELLS
H.H. Munro — SAKI
H.S. Jrs. test — PSAT
H.S. subject — ALG, GEOM
H.S.T., _____, J.F.K. — DDE
H.W.L. subject — REVERE
Ha-ha — TEHEE
Habeas corpus for one — WRIT
Haberdasher — TAILOR
Haberdasher's wares — SUITS
Haberdashery — MENS STORE
Haberdashery item — ASCOT, SHIRT, TIE
Habiliments — DRESS, TOOLS
Habilitated — GARBED
Habilitates — ATTIRES
Habit — WONT
Habit: custom — PRAXIS
Habitat — ABODE, HOME
Habitat: Prefix — ECO
Habitual procedure — ROTE
Habituate — ACCUSTOM, ADAPT, ENURE, INURE
Habituated — INURED
Hacienda — FARM
Hacienda for one — CASA
Hacienda pots — OLLAS
Hack — CAB
Hack of baseball — STAN
Hack or Musial of baseball — STAN
Hack's vehicle — CAB
Hackberry — ELM
Hackensack neighbor — TEANECK
Hacker — GOLFER
Hackman — JEHUS
Hackman and Autry — GENES
Hackman and Kelly — GENES
Hackman film — MISSISSIPPI BURNING
Hackman of films — GENE
Hackman or Wilder — GENE
Hackmatack — LARCH
Hackney coach — FIACRE
Hackney's gait — TROT
Hackneyed — CORNY, STALE, TIRED, TRITE
Hackneyed expression — CLICHE
Hacks — CABMEN, CABS
Had — OWNED
Had a bite — ATE
Had a little lamb — ATE
Had a look — EYED
Had a meal — DINED
Had a peek — LOOKED
Had a steady — DATED
Had a yen for — ACHED, YEARNED
Had affection for — CARED
Had an advantage on: comp. wd. — ONE UPPED
Had an aversion — DISLIKED
Had an aversion to — DETESTED
Had an outstanding bill — OWED
Had been — WAS
Had bills — OWED
Had deep longing — PINED
Had doubts — QUESTIONED
Had expectations — HOPED
Had in mind — MEANT
Had intentions — AIMED
Had legal title to — OWNED
Had lunch — ATE
Had misgivings — FEARED
Had on — WORE
Had regrets — RUED
Had status — RATED
Had the lead — STARRED
Had the misery — AILED
Had the sniffles — AILED
Haddock — FISH
Hades — DIS, HELL, PURGATORY
Hafez al- _____ of Syria — ASSAD
Hag — BELDAME, CRONE, OGRESS
Hagar and Helga's dog — SNERT
Hagar's dog — SNERT
Hagar's spouse — HELGA
Hagen of the stage — UTA
Hagen won four of these — PGAS
Haggard — DRAWN, GAUNT, PALE, WORN
Haggard appearance — WEARY
Haggard novel — SHE
Haggard's Ayesha — SHE
Haggis ingredient — OATMEAL
Hagiologist's topic — SAINTS
Hah, hah, e.g. — MIRTH
Haha, e.g. — FENCE
Hail — GREET, HELLO, HONOR, SALUTE
Hail's kin — SLEET
Hail, to Caesar — AVE
Hailed — GREETED
Hailey best seller: 1965 — HOTEL
Hailing call — AHOY
Hails — AVES
Hair — CURLS, FILAMENT, LOCKS, MANE, MOP
Hair — THREAD, TRESSES
Hair clasp — BARRETTE, BOBBY PIN
Hair covering — PERUKE, RUG, WIG
Hair dressing — POMADE
Hair dye — HENNA
Hair dyes — RINSES, TINTS
Hair found in "name" — MANE
Hair holder — SNOOD
Hair line — PART
Hair ornament — BOW
Hair over the eyes — BROWS
Hair pad — RAT
Hair raising — EERIE, SCARY
Hair rinse — HENNA
Hair style — AFRO, BANGS, UPDO
Hair tint — RINSE
Hair treatment — TINT
Hair's breadth — WHISKER
Hair-raising — EERIE, SCARY

Hair: Comb. form — PILO
Haircut — BUTCH, TRIM
Haircut or warship — FLAT-TOP
Hairdo — AFRO, BUN, SET, SHAG, UPDO
Hairdo, for short — PERM
Hairdresser's union? — COMBING COMBINE
Hairdressers, at times — STYLERS, TEASERS
Hairdressers? — LOCKSMITHS
Hairnet — SNOOD
Hairpiece — FALL
Hairpiece for Sir Roger — PERIWIG
Hairpin curves — ESSES
Hairy — CRINOSE, PILAR, SHAGGY
Hairy covering — PELAGE
Hairy herb — BORAGE
Hairy or downy bird — WOODPECKER
Haitian religious rites — VOODOOS
Hajj goal — MECCA
Hakenk Reuzler — NAZI
Halberd part — AXEO
Halcyon — BIRD
Hale — HARDY, ROBUST
Hale, the 1776 hero — NATHAN
Haley novel — ROOTS
Haley of roots — ALEX
Haley tome — ROOTS
Half-done — RARE
Half-time fare — PARADES
Half _____ — A LOAF
Half a blunder — BOO
Half a bray — HEE
Half a Broadway title — I DO
Half a celebrated panda — LING
Half a comforting phrase — THERE
Half a dance name — CHA, HOKEY
Half a decade — PENTAD
Half a drum — TOM
Half a farthing — MITE
Half a fly — TSE
Half a fortnight — WEEK
Half a laugh — HEE
Half a locomotive — CHOO
Half a native drum — TOM
Half a Samoan capital — PAGO
Half a Samoan island's name: Var. — PANGO
Half a score — TEN
Half a small antelope — DIK
Half a ticket — STUB
Half an anti-aircraft burst — ACK
Half boot — PAC
Half breed — HYBRID
Half in Paree, Fr. — SALLE
Half note — MINIM
Half of 11? — ONE
Half of a Samoan port — PAGO
Half of a Thor Heyerdahl title — AKU
Half of a Washington city — WALLA
Half of a West Indian dance rattle — CHAC
Half of all newlyweds — BRIDES
Half of an old refrain — NONNY
Half of CCVI — CIII
Half of CCVII — CIV
Half of CDII — CCI
Half of CDXIV — CCVII
Half of CIV — LII
Half of CMII — CDLI
Half of CXXII — LXI
Half of DCC — CCCL
Half of DCII — CCCI
Half of Ethiopia's capital — ABABA
Half of MCCCII — DCLI
Half of MCCII — DCI
Half of MCII — DLI
Half of MCIV — DLII
Half of MCVIII — DLIV
Half of MIV — DII
Half pint of ale — NIP
Half pints — RUNTS
Half sister of Liza — LORNA
Half, in Hamburg — HALB
Half, in Messina — MEZZO
Half-baked — IGNORANT, SILLY
Half-breed — CROSS, MONGREL
Half-finished — HALFWAY
Half-hearted — COOL, CURSORY, NEUTRAL
Half-moon, old style — LUNET
Half-note — MINIM
Half: Comb. form — DEMI
Half: Prefix — HEMI
Halfhitch — KNOT
Halfwit — DOLT, DUNCE, IDIOT, MORON
Halifax, Nova _____ — SCOTIA
Halite producers — SALTERNS
Hall — FOYER, WAY
Hall çarpet — RUNNER
Hall of _____ — FAME
Hall of Fame basketball coach Hank — IBA
Hall of Fame catcher — BERRA
Hall of Fame Hank — AARON
Hall of Fame jockey Sande — EARLE
Hall of Fame outfielder — GOOSE GOSLIN
Hall of Fame pitcher Warren _____ — SPAHN
Hall of Fame shortstop — REESE
Hall of Fame surgeon — REED
Hall of Famer Hank — AARON
Hall of Famer Slaughter — ENOS
Hall of Famer Warren — SPAHN
Hall or Letterman, e.g. — HOST
Halley's _____ — COMET
Hallow — BLESS
Halloween alternative — TRICK, TREAT
Halloween costume — PIRATE
Halloween creatures — CATS
Halloween cries — BOOS
Halloween exclamation — BOO
Halloween headgear — HOODS
Halloween message from C. Moore? — TO ALL A GOOD FRIGHT
Halloween option — TREAT
Halloween transport — WITCHES BROOM
Hallstand — HAT TREE
Hallucinogenic monogram — LSD
Hallway — ENTRY, FOYER
Halo — AURA
Halt — ARREST, CEASE, STEM
Halt by legal means — ESTOP
Halt, to Ahab — AVAST
Halters — NOOSES
Halting device — BRAKE
Halyard — ROPE
Ham-handed — INEPT
Ham — EMOTER
Ham _____ (emote) — IT UP
Ham additive — STER
Ham Berger's creator — ERLE
Ham it up — EMOTE
Ham saver — ARK
Ham to Noah — SON
Ham's brother — SHEM
Ham's equipment — RADIO
Ham's hobby — RADIO
Ham's temporary home — ARK
Hamate — CURVED
Hambletonian pace — TROT
Hambletonian, e.g. — RACE
Hamburg hair — HAAR
Hamburg's river — ELBE
Hamburger turner — SPATULA
Hamburgers, for example — PATTIES
Hamelin figure — PIED PIPER
Hamelin spice? — PIED PEPPER
Hamelin's problem — RATS
Hamilton and Burr, e.g. — ENEMIES
Hamilton's bills — TENS
Hamlet — VILLAGE
Hamlet and Borge — DANES
Hamlet and others — DANES
Hamlet or Borge — DANE
Hamlet or Ophelia — ROLE
Hamlet was one — DANE

Hamlet's exclamation — FIE
Hamlet's friend — HORATIO
Hamlet's mother — GERTRUDE
Hamlet, to Olivier — ROLE
Hamlets — DORPS
Hammarskjold — DAG
Hammer — BEETLE, MAUL, SLEDGE
Hammer and tongs — IMPLEMENTS
Hammer associated with Russia — ARMAND
Hammer away — PERSIST, PLOD
Hammer end — PEEN
Hammer head — PEEN
Hammer into form — SHAPE
Hammer of fiction — MIKE
Hammer or tongs — TOOL
Hammer out — FORM, MOLD, SHAPE
Hammer part — PEEN
Hammer type — CLAW, PEEN
Hammer's target — NAIL
Hammerhead — SHARK
Hammering surface — ANVIL
Hammerlike weapon — MARTEL
Hammerlock or half nelson — HOLD
Hammerstein — OSCAR
Hammett canine — ASTA
Hammett dieter? — THIN MAN
Hammett sleuth — SPADE
Hammett's "Spade" — SAM
Hammett's "The _____ Curse" — DAIN
Hammy — THEATRIC
Hamper — CRAMP
Hampton _____, Va. — ROADS
Hampton of Jazz — LIONEL
Hams — EMOTERS
Hand-woven curtain — TAPIS
Hand — MITT
Hand feature — NAIL
Hand game? — PATTY CAKE
Hand holder — WRIST
Hand holding, in bridge — TENACE
Hand luggage — VALISES
Hand out — ALLOT, DISPENSE
Hand warmer — GLOVE, MITTEN, MUFF
Hand wave — PARTING
Hand-dried — TOWELLED
Hand-dyed fabric — BATIK
Hand-seeker — WOOER
Handbag material — SUEDE
Handbags — PURSES, WALLETS
Handel highlight — ARIA
Handel or Haydn works — OPERAS
Handel oratorio — SAUL
Handel specialty — ORATORIO
Handel's "_____ the Priest" — ZADOK
Handel's "Messiah," for one — MASTERWORK
Handel's "Messiah," for one — ORATORIO
Handel's birthplace — HALLE
Handful — FISTFUL, MODICUM, SOME
Handicap — CURB, RESTRICTION
Handicraft — ART, CRAFT, SKILL
Handle — ANSA, FEEL, HILT, HEFT, HOLD
Handle awkwardly — FUMBLE
Handle clumsily — PAW
Handle inappropriately — MISUSE
Handle roughly — MAUL
Handle used books — RESELL
Handle, to Hadrian — ANSA
Handle, to Henri — ANSE
Handle: Fr. — ANSE
Handled — ANSATE, DEALT
Handled the situation — COPED
Handled the tea — POURED
Handles clumsily — PAWS
Handout — ALMS, CHARITY, DONATION
Handout to the press — RELEASE
Handrails, for danseurs — BARRES
Handsome — GOOD LOOKING
Handsome man — ADONIS
Handsome youth — APOLLO
Handwork adjunct — EMBROIDERY NEEDLE
Handwriting on the wall — MENE
Handy — ADROIT, NEARBY
Handy _____ — ANDY
Handy abbr. — ET AL
Handy Andy, for example — DOER
Handy fastener — SAFETY PIN
Handy man — JACK OF ALL TRADES
Hang-up — HITCH
Hang _____ (loiter) — AROUND
Hang about — LOITER
Hang around — HAUNT, LOAF, LOLL, WAIT
Hang back — SHIRK
Hang behind — DRAG
Hang fire — PEND
Hang in there — LAST, PERSEVERE, STICK TO YOUR GUNS
Hang in there, in poker — STAY
Hang loose — RELAX
Hang loosely — DRAPE, LOP
Hang over — HOVER
Hang suspended in air — HOVER
Hang the laundry outside — AIR DRY
Hang-out — HAUNT
Hanger-on — LEECH
Hanger-on — PARASITE
Hanging — LOOSE
Hanging "icicle" in a cave — STALACTITE
Hanging ends — DAGS
Hanging fire — IN SUSPENSE
Hanging in the balance — IFFY
Hangman's loop — NOOSE
Hangs around — WAITS
Hangs fire — PENDS
Hangs loosely — DANGLES
Hank or Phoebe of songdom — SNOW
Hank, the hitter — AARON
Hanker for — CRAVE
Hankered — YEARNED
Hankering — ITCH, WISH, YEN
Hanks vehicle — BIG
Hanky-panky — TRICKS
Hannah, for one — PALINDROME
Hannibal's conqueror — SCIPIO
Hannibal's family name — BARCA
Hannibal's invasion obstacle — ALPS
Hanoi holiday — TET
Hanoi people — VIETS
Hanover, N.H. college — DARTMOUTH
Hans Brinker, e.g. — SKATER
Hans of "Die Meistersinger" — SACHS
Hans of Dada — ARP
Hans of the silver skates — BRINKER
Hans' word for himself — ICH
Hansen's disease — LEPROSY
Hansom — CAB
Hansom command — GEE
Haphazard — RANDOM
Haphazard courses: Abbr. — RDMS
Haphazardly — ANY WAY, WILLY NILLY
Haphazardly, with "miss" — HIT OR
Happen — BEFALL, OCCUR, PASS
Happen again — RECUR
Happen once more — RECUR
Happen repeatedly — RECUR
Happened as by fate — BEFALLEN
Happening — EVENT
Happenstances — FORTUITOUS EVENTS
Happenstances — PECULIAR CIRCUMSTANCES

Happenstances — UNFORSEEN OCCURENCES
Happenstances — VICISSITUDES OF FORTUNE
Happifies — ELATES
Happily — ELATE
Happiness — BLISS
Happy — GLAD
Happy _____ — NEW YEAR
Happy _____ lark — AS A
Happy as _____ — A LARK
Happy expression — GRIN
Happy face — SMILE
Happy reaction — GRIN
Happy recipient — DONEE
Happy response — GRIN
Happy sign for angels — SRO
Happy sound — TEHEE
Happy-go-lucky — BLASE, CAREFREE
Hara-kiri — SUICIDE
Harald's predecessor — OLAV
Harangue — BLAST, DECLAIM, RANT, TIRADE
Harangues — SPOUTS
Harass — BESET, HASSLE, TEASE, TRY
Harass freshmen — HAZE
Harasses a British actor? — BATES ALAN
Harassment — BOTHER, TORMENT
Harbinger — HERALD, OMEN
Harbor — HAVEN
Harbor birds — GULLS
Harbor boat — TOW
Harbor features — PIERS
Harbor in Guam — APRA
Harbor seal — SEACAT
Harbor sights — FERRIES, MASTS
Harbor site — BOAT, WHARF
Harbor sound — FOGHORN
Harbors — PORTS
Hard — ADAMANT, COMPLEX, FIRM, RIGID, STONY
Hard _____ — TIMES
Hard abrasive — EMERY
Hard and fast — FIXED, RIGID
Hard as nails — SIMILE
Hard at work — BUSY AS A BEE
Hard ball — BASEBALL
Hard cheeses — SWISSES
Hard cider — APPLEJACK
Hard coal — ANTHRACITE
Hard core crew — CADRE
Hard cotton thread — LISLE
Hard goods — HARDWARE
Hard hit ball — LINER
Hard knock — POLT
Hard liquor — BOOZE
Hard minerals — BERYLS
Hard or soft — SELL
Hard puzzle — POSER
Hard road to hoe — RISK
Hard surfaced — TILED
Hard to believe — TALL
Hard to find — RARE
Hard to penetrate — DENSE
Hard to read — ILLEGIBLE
Hard to understand — DEEP
Hard up — BROKE
Hard water — ICE
Hard wood — EBONY, TEAK
Hard worker — DEMON, PEON
Hard, black rubbers — EBONITES
Hard, glassy mineral — SILICA
Hard, tough wood — ELM
Hard-and-fast — SET
Hard-bitten — RIGID, STRONG, TOUGH
Hard-boiled — STRAIGHT, TOUGH
Hard-boiled item — EGG
Hard-core — EXTREME
Hard-handed — BRUTAL, CRUEL, HARSH
Hard-headed — COOL, PRACTICAL, SHREWD
Hard-hearted — COLD, STONY
Hard-hit ball — LINER
Hard-hitting — TOUGH
Hard-luck case — LOSER
Hard-surfaced — TILED
Hard: Comb. form — SCLERO
Hardanger or Sogne — FIORD
Hardback — BOOK
Harden — ENURE, GEL, INURE, OSSIFY, SET
Harden — STEEL, SETTLE
Harden off — ACCUSTOM
Harden up — TOUGHEN
Hardened — CAKED, GELLED
Hardened skin — CALLOUS
Hardened, as mud — CAKED
Hardens — CEMENTS
Hardest to come by — RAREST
Hardest to find — RAREST
Hardhearted one — MEANIE
Harding was one — OHIOAN
Harding's Secretary of Commerce — HOOVER
Hardly ever — ON RARE OCCASIONS
Hardscrabble — ARID
Hardship — RIGOR
Hardships — TRIALS
Hardtack — BREAD
Hardtop or fastback — CAR
Hardware — APPLIANCE, GEAR, TOOLS
Hardware dealer at Harwich — IRONMONGER
Hardwood — ELM
Hardwood trees — LOCUSTS
Hardy — FIT
Hardy cabbage — KALE
Hardy grasses — RYES
Hardy hero — JUDE
Hardy heroine — TESS
Hardy horse of the west — MUSTANG
Hardy lass — TESS
Hardy one — OLIVER
Hardy protagonist — TESS
Hardy red wheat — EMMER
Hardy unfortunate — TESS
Hardy villain — ALEC
Hardy's "Pure Woman" — TESS
Hardy's chum — LAUREL
Hardy's partner — LAUREL
Hare-_____, like Bugs Bunny — BRAINED
Hare, in a fable — LOSER
Harem — SERAI
Harem feature — ODA
Harem room — ODA
Hari of espionage — MATA
Hari or Hale — SPY
Hari, the spy — MATA
Haricot, for one — STEW
Hark — LISTEN
Harlan, Irving or Lucy — STONE
Harlequin — CLOWN
Harlot — HUSSY
Harm — ABUSE, ENDAMAGE, SCATHE
Harmful — NOCENT
Harmful insect — JIGGER, LOCUST
Harmless hawk — OSPREY
Harmless reptile — GARTER SNAKE
Harmless reptile of N.A. — PINE SNAKE
Harmonic group — OCTET
Harmonica — MOUTH ORGAN
Harmonious — IN TUNE
Harmonious set — CHOIR
Harmonium — ORGAN
Harmonize — AGREE, ATTUNE, TONE
Harmonizes — BLENDS
Harmony — ACCORD, UNISON
Harms — IMPAIRS
Harness — SADDLE, TACK, TAME
Harness equipment — TACK
Harness horse — PACER
Harness item — REIN, BIT
Harness part — HAME, REIN
Harness race gait — TROT
Harness racer — TROTTER
Harness racing gear — TRAP
Harness that hero — HITCH YOUR STAR TO A WAGON
Harness-race horses — PACERS
Harnesses together — YOKES
Harold _____, English political scientist — LASKI
Harold Arlen's "_____ Rainbow" — OVER THE
Harold from Minnesota — STASSEN

Harold Lipshitz today — HAL LINDEN
Harold of "Safety Last" — LLOYD
Harold of the comics — TEEN
Harold of Tin Pan Alley — ROME
Haroun-al-Raschid, e.g. — ARAB
Harp — STRINGS
Harp and violin followers — ISTS
Harp constellation — LYRA
Harp kin — LYRE
Harp on — NAG, RUB IN
Harp, in Roma — ARPA
Harp: It. — ARPA
Harper and Peggy — LEES
Harper from Suffern, N.Y. — VALERIE
Harper Valley gp. — PTA
Harpoon — SPEAR
Harpsichord — KEYBOARD
Harridan — HAG
Harried — BESET
Harrier — DOG
Harriet Beecher _____ — STOWE
Harriette Lake — ANN SOTHERN
Harrington's "The _____ America" — OTHER
Harris of "Camelot" — RICHARD
Harris of "Harper" — JULIE
Harris or Silvers — PHIL
Harrison-O'Hara film — THE FOXES OF HARROW
Harrison and Reed — REXES
Harrison Ford's role in "Star Wars" — SOLO
Harrison of "Cleopatra" — REX
Harrison with the Beatles — GEORGE
Harrison's running mate — TYLER
Harrovian rival — ETONIAN
Harrow — REND
Harrow's rival — ETON
Harrowed — TILLED
Harry Houdini, nee Ehrich _____ — WEISS
Harry's first lady — BESS
Harry's successor — IKE
Harry-to-Jack link — IKE
Harsh — ACERB, SEVERE, STARK
Harsh circumstances — RIGOR
Harsh or clanging — TIN PANNY
Harsh pulmonary sound — RALE
Harsh sounds — RASPS
Harsh, grating sound — CREAK
Harsh: bleak — GRIM
Hart — DEER, STAG
Hart's "_____ One" — ACT
Hart's cereal source? — CRANES GRAIN
Hart's playmate, to Shakespeare — HIND
Harte — BRET
Hartebeest — ANTELOPE, ASSE, TORA
Harts — STAGS
Harum _____ — SCARUM
Haruspices — SEER
Harvard classics motto — KNOW THYSELF
Harvard newspaper — CRIMSON
Harvard president: 1869-1909 — ELIOT
Harvard's neighbor: abbr. — MIT
Harvest — CROP, PICK, PRODUCE, REAP, YIELD
Harvest goddess — CERES
Harvest goddess — OPA
Harvest machine — COMBINE
Harvest time — FALL
Harvested alfalfa, e.g. — HAYED
Harvester — REAPER
Has — OWNS
Has a ball — SWINGS
Has a bite — EAT
Has a hangover — ACHES
Has a late meal — SUPS
Has a little lamb? — EATS
Has a meal — DINES
Has a real fit — RAGES
Has a right to — RATES
Has a siesta — NAPS
Has a tete-a-tete — CHATS
Has an aversion — DETESTS
Has an overabundance — TEEMS
Has brunch — EATS
Has charge of — RUNS
Has dinner — SUPS
Has ess trouble — LISPS
Has high regard for — ESTEEMS
Has markers out — OWES
Has one's say in the U.S.A. — VOTES
Has pain — ACHES
Has qualms — FEARS
Has restaurant food — EATS OUT
Has the chair — PRESIDES
Has the deed — OWNS
Has the power — RULES
Has the sulks — POUTS
Has to — MUST
Has trouble with esses — LISP
Has-beens place — SHELF
Hasenpfeffer — RABBIT STEW
Hash house — DINER
Hassle — SET TO
Haste — DISPATCH
Haste, in Hannover — EILE
Hasten — HIE, HURRY
Hastened — HIED, RACED, SPED
Hastens — RACES
Hasty — RAPID, RASH, SPEEDY
Hasty departure — FRENCH LEAVE
Hasty mark — SCRATCH
Hat adornment — MARABOU
Hat adornments — PLUMES
Hat feature — BRIM
Hat fiber — STRAW
Hat for a Buckingham Palace guard — SHAKO
Hat for Hassan — FEZ
Hat material — SENNIT, STRAW
Hat material: pl. — FELTS
Hat or ship — TALL
Hat part — BRIM
Hat with a slightly rolled brim — HOMBURG
Hatch covering — TARP
Hatchback — CAR
Hatchet's relative — ADZ
Hatching post — NEST
Hate — ABHOR, DETEST
Hateful one — TOAD
Hatfields and McCoys, e.g. — ENEMIES
Hatred — ODIUM
Hatred in Buddhism — DOSA
Hatred: It. — ODIO
Haughty — PROUD, SUPERCILIOUS
Haughty contempt — SNOOTINESS
Haul — LUG, TOTE, TOW
Haulage vehicle — DRAE
Hauled — TOWED
Haulers — SEMIS
Hauling chg. — CTGE
Hauls — TOWS
Hauls again — RECARTS
Haunt — DEN, FREQUENT, HANGOUT, LAIR, OBSESS
Haunted — SPOOKY
Hausfrau's cry — ACH
Haut monde — ELECT
Hautboy — OBOE
Haute couture name — DIOR
Haute-Savoie spa — EVIAN
Havana — CIGAR
Havana habitant — CUBAN
Havana houses — CASAS
Havana landmark — MORRO CASTLE
Have — CONTAIN, HOLD, OWN, POSSESS
Have 'em rolling in the aisles — SLAY
Have _____ (be bored) — TIME ON ONES HANDS
Have _____ (be merciful) — A HEART
Have _____ (be upset) — A FIT
Have _____ (beware) — A CARE

Have _____ (enjoy oneself) — A BALL
Have _____ (lock horns) — AT IT
Have _____ (take a shot) — A FLING
Have _____ (watch out) — A CARE
Have _____ in one's bonnet — A BEE
Have _____ on (claim) — DIBS
Have _____ to fill — A SLOT
Have _____ to pick — A BONE
Have _____ to the ground — AN EAR
Have a _____ — HEART
Have a _____ (act like an odd one) — SCREW LOOSE
Have a bawl — CRY
Have a bite — EAT
Have a change of heart — RELENT
Have a chinfest — SHOOT THE BREEZE
Have a cold — AIL
Have a craving for — WANT
Have a go — TRY
Have a go at — TRY
Have a good feeling for — LIKE
Have a hirsute chin — BEARDED
Have a late meal — SUP
Have a meal — DINE
Have a repast — DINE
Have a second try at the plate — REHIT
Have a snack — EAT
Have a talk — CHAT
Have a trick up one's _____ — SLEEVE
Have a type of traffic mishap — REAR END
Have a yen for — CRAVE
Have an _____ (intend) — EYE TO
Have an _____ (look after) — EYE TO
Have an _____ grind — AX TO
Have an _____ the ground — EAR TO
Have an aversion — HATE
Have charge of — HEAD
Have comestibles — EAT
Have coming — EARN
Have confidence in — TRUST
Have creditors — OWE
Have debts — OWE
Have dibs on — CLAIM
Have done with — HALT
Have ess trouble — LISP
Have faith — TRUST
Have faith in a former Tarzan — TRUST BUSTER
Have feelings for — CARE
Have fun in the snow — SKI
Have hopes — ASPIRE
Have in hand — CONTROL, POSSESS
Have in tow — DRAG
Have lunch together — BREAK BREAD
Have magnetic power — ATTRACT
Have markers on — OWE
Have no use for — DETEST
Have nothing to do with — ESCHEW
Have notions — IDEATE
Have on — WEAR
Have one's head in the sand — IGNORE
Have one's say, in a way — VOTE
Have pains — ACHE
Have second thoughts — RUE
Have status — RATE
Have strings attached — ENTAIL
Have sway — GOVERN
Have the flu — AIL
Have the lead — STAR
Have the wherewithal — AFFORD
Have title to — OWN
Have to — MUST
Have to have — NEED
Have trouble with esses — LISP
Have trust in , with "on" — RELY
Have words — SPAT
Have, in Scotland — HAE
Haven — HOME, PORT
Haven for Ham? — ARK
Havens for bactrians? — OASES
Haversack — BAG
Having _____ ; silent — NOT A WORD TO SAY
Having a curved doorway — ARCHED
Having a delicate open pattern — LACY
Having a dotted pattern — SEME
Having a feast — DINING
Having a flair for painting — ARTISTIC
Having a handle — ANSATE
Having a healthy color — RUDDY
Having a keener edge — SHARPER
Having a new decor — REDONE
Having a reddish color — RUDDY
Having a scent — ODORED
Having a shallow sound — TINNY
Having an S-shaped molding — OGEED
Having claws — TALONED
Having color — HUED
Having creases — LINED
Having documents of ownership — DEEDED
Having exornation — ADORNED
Having frills — LACY
Having hair like Elsa — MANED
Having I trouble — EGOTISTICAL
Having independence — UNREINED
Having inherited status — BORN TO THE PURPLE
Having inordinate self-esteem — PROUD
Having kinship — RELATED
Having layers — TIERED
Having leaflike structures — STIPULAR
Having leafy divisions — SEPALED
Having less free time — BUSIER
Having long, rounded grooves — FLUTED
Having many hairs: Comb. form — TRICHI
Having new life — REBORN
Having no backbone — TIMID
Having no chance to win — OUT OF IT
Having no key — ATONAL
Having no shoes — UNSHOD
Having nothing left out — ENTIRE
Having one element — UNARY
Having pillars: Comb. form — STYLAR
Having prickly flower heads — TEASELED
Having returned to starting point — FULL CIRCLE
Having roof extensions — EAVED
Having rounded projections — LOBED
Having seed coverings — ARILLIATE
Having set limits — FINITE
Having sound judgement — LEVEL HEADED
Having strata — LAYERED
Having teeth — DENTATE
Having the _____ (spiritless) — BLAHS
Having the know-how — ABLE
Having the potential — POSSIBLE
Having tiny openings, as leaves — STOMATE
Having two ground floors — BILEVEL
Having uneven edges — EROSE
Having winglike toes, as a bat — ALIPED
Having wings — ALAR, ALATE
Having wrinkles — CREASY

Havoc — CHAOS
Haw preceder — HEE
Haw's companion — GEE
Haw's opposite — GEE
Haw's partner — HEM
Haw. or Born. — ISL
Haw., once — TERR
Hawaii is one — STATE
Hawaii Island port — HILO
Hawaii state nickname — ALOHA
Hawaii's nickname — ALOHA STATE
Hawaii, Alaska, etc. — STATES
Hawaiian avian — IIWI, NENE
Hawaiian bird — NENE
Hawaiian city — HILO
Hawaiian cookout — LUAU
Hawaiian dance — HULA
Hawaiian exports — PINEAPPLES
Hawaiian feast — LUAU
Hawaiian fiber — SOLA
Hawaiian floral pieces — LEIS
Hawaiian food — POI
Hawaiian food fish — MOANA
Hawaiian geese — NENES
Hawaiian goose — NENE
Hawaiian greeting — ALOHA
Hawaiian harbor city — HILO
Hawaiian hawks — IOS
Hawaiian head — DIAMOND
Hawaiian hub — HILO
Hawaiian Island — MAUI, OAHU
Hawaiian island chain? — LEI
Hawaiian kava — AWA
Hawaiian landmark — DIAMOND HEAD
Hawaiian picnic — LUAU
Hawaiian porch — LANAI
Hawaiian port — HILO
Hawaiian seaport — HILO
Hawaiian sport — SURFING
Hawaiian state bird — NENE
Hawaiian symbols — LEIS
Hawaiian taro paste — POI
Hawaiian thrush — OMAO
Hawaiian timber trees — KOAS
Hawaiian veranda — LANAI
Hawaiian wreath — LEI
Hawk — MILITARIST, PEDDLE, SELL
Hawk aggressively — OVERSELL
Hawk habitat — AERIE
Hawk parrot — HIA
Hawk's antithesis — DOVE
Hawk's asset — TALON
Hawk's fly here — OMNI
Hawk's opposite — DOVE
Hawked — PEDDLED
Hawker — DUFFER, PEDLAR
Hawkeye — ALDA
Hawkeye — IOWAN
Hawkeye state — IOWA
Hawkeye state half diameters? — RADIIOWA
Hawkeye's unit — MASH
Hawkins or Thompson — SADIE
Hawkish — BELLIGERENT
Hawkish deity — MARS
Hawks and hooks — TOOLS
Hawks' home court — OMNI
Hawley-_____ Tarriff Act — SMOOT
Haws' accompanists — HEMS
Hawser — LINE, ROPE
Hawthorn — MAY
Hawthorne collection — TWICE TOLD TALES
Hawthorne's "The Marble _____" — FAUN
Hawthorne's birthplace — SALEM
Hawthorne's Prynne — HESTER
Hawthorne, to friends? — NATE
Hay bundle — BALE
Hay fever symptom — SNEEZE
Hay fever, for one — ALLERGY
Hay follower — LOFT
Hay machine — BALER
Hay or cotton unit — BALE
Hay spreaders — TEDDERS
Hay wain crossings — FORDS
Hay-fever cause — RAGWEED
Hay; stubble — STOVER
Hayden and Manchester — MELISSAS
Haydn or Hemingway — PAPA
Haydn sobriquet — PAPA
Haydn's "_____ Symphony" — SURPRISE
Haydn's homeland — AUSTRIA
Haydn, to friends — PAPA
Hayes or Hallas — COACH
Hayfork parts — PRONGS
Haying machine — BALER
Haymaker — ONER
Hayseeds — HICKS, RUBES, YOKELS
Haystack — PILE
Haywire — GAGA
Hayworth and Moreno — RITAS
Hayworth namesakes — RITAS
Hayworth role — GILDA
Hayworth, of films — RITA
Hazard — CHALLENGE, DANGER, MENACE, PERIL, RISK
Hazard — TAKE A CHANCE, WAGER
Hazard a guess — SAY
Hazard for the superstitious — SIDEWALK CRACKS
Hazard in navigation — SANDBAR
Hazard on Mont Blanc — CREVASSE
Hazard, to Trevino — TRAP
Hazardous trick — STUNT
Hazel or walnut — TREE
Hds. of state — LDRS
He — MAN
He "loves mambo" — PAPA
He "runs the show" — CEO
He authored "A Boys Will" — FROST
He backs the Beavers and Ducks — OREGONIAN
He bested Brutus — ANTONY
He built the Great Pyramid — CHEOPS
He burned up the courts in the 70's — ASHE
He cameth before the refrigerator — ICEMAN
He cashed forged checks — KITER
He caused earthquakes — POSEIDON
He claimed Louisiana for France — LA SALLE
He cleans his plate — DISHWASHER
He climbed Mt. Everest first — HILLARY
He comes in time — NICK
He commits grave crimes — GHOUL
He could build castle's in Spain — REY
He created Anna Karenina — LEO TOLSTOY
He created Sad Sack — BAKER
He created the Democratic donkey — NAST
He dealt in pelts — ASTOR
He debuted in "The Sundowners" — ELAM
He defeated T.E.D. — HST
He didn't finish his sentence — PAROLEE
He didn't give a damn — RHETT
He directed "Never on Sunday" — DASSIN
He does the write thing — PENNER
He fought Joe Gans — ERNE
He gets around — ROVER
He goes where congers congregate — EELER
He had a way with Proust — SWANN
He had the golden touch — MIDAS
He hangs around — LOITERS
He has estrange feelings? — ALIENEE
He has his pride — LION
He hit 61 home runs in '61 — MARIS
He introduced the sack — DIOR

He invented dynamite — NOBEL
He is held — DETAINEE
He laughs: Fr. — ONRIT
He leads a good life — RILEY
He led first settlers to Ohio — PUTNAM
He lived 905 years — ENOS
He lived 912 years — SETH
He lost his shadow — PAN
He lost to D.D.E. — AES
He loved Lucy — DESI
He loves, in old Roma — AMAT
He loves, to Cicero — AMAT
He Loves: Lat — AMAT
He made a beginning with Begin — SADAT
He made a pile for Nabors — GOMER
He makes a lot of dough — BAKER
He makes vein efforts — MINER
He married Pocahontas — ROLFE
He may be tight — END
He may come from Qum — IRANI
He may do some stripping — MINER
He may use faint praise — DAMNER
He minded the stoa — ZENO
He must have slipped _____! — A COG
He opposed Girondists — MARAT
He outranks the sarge — LOOIE
He overthrew Fulgencio — FIDEL
He painted "Old Battersea Bridge" — WHISTLER
He painted "Red and White Domes" — KLEE
He painted "Sens Cathedral" — COROT
He painted "The Last Supper — DALI
He painted Helena Rubinstein — DALI
He peregrinates — TRAVELER
He played Ahab — GREGORY PECK
He played Ashley — LESLIE
He played Captain Bly (1935) — LAUGHTON
He played Cochise on TV — ANSARA
He played Dr. Kildare — AYRES
He played Fred Sanford — REDD FOXX
He played Gershwin — ALDA
He played Goldfinger — FROBE
He played Henry Goldblume — SPANO
He played Hutch — SOUL
He played in "Waiting for Godot" — LAHR
He played in 2,130 consecutive games — GEHRIG
He played Joel Cairo — LORRE
He played Max Smart — ADAMS
He played O.K. Crackerby — IVES
He played Pasteur — MUNI
He played the Saint — ROGER MOORE
He plays Mr. Micelli on TV — DANZA
He plays to the gallery — HAM
He portrayed Chan after Oland — TOLER
He pours out whines — PULER
He practices i-dolatry! — EGOIST
He practices pettifoggery — SHYSTER
He prepares the way — PAVER
He ran and ran and ran — STASSEN
He really makes money — COINER
He recruited Lafayette — DEANE
He rode with Revere — DAWES
He sang "Mack the Knife" — DARIN
He sang "Start Movin'": 1957 — MINEO
He shared a pea green boat — OWL
He shared rooms at 221B Baker Street — WATSON
He smooths the way — PAVER
He struck out — CASEY
He summons: Lat. — CITAT
He thinks "Whatever will be, will be" — FATALIST
He took a ribbing — ADAM
He traded his birthright — ESAU
He was a "Yankee Doodle Dandy" — CAGNEY
He was a hairy man — ESAU
He was Devine? — ANDY
He was down and out in "Beverly Hills" — NOLTE
He was Hutch on TV — SOUL
He was once Bud's buddy — LOU
He was raised from the dead — LAZURUS
He was terrible — IVAN
He was TV sleuth Jones — EBSEN
He was: Lat. — ERAT
He wed an Irish Rose — ABIE
He went to town — DEEDS
He won an Oscar for Mitch — MALDEN
He wrote "A Delicate Balance" — ALBEE
He Wrote "A Serendipiter's Journey" — TALESE
He wrote "Airport" — HAILEY
He wrote "Bambi" — SALTEN
He wrote "Esther Waters" — MOORE
He wrote "Ghosts" — IBSEN
He wrote "Hard Cash" — READE
He wrote "Hedda Gabler" — IBSEN
He wrote "His Family" — POOLE
He wrote "I Like It Here" — AMIS
He wrote "I Marry You" — CIARDI
He wrote "If I Ran the Zoo" — SEUSS
He wrote "Les Miserables" — HUGO
He wrote "Marius the Epicurean" — PATER
He wrote "Night Music" — ODETS
He wrote "Now We Are Six" — A A MILNE
He wrote "Off the Court" — ASHE
He wrote "Retaliation — OLIVER GOLDSMITH
He wrote "The Autocrat of the Breakfast Table" — HOLMES
He wrote "The Brave Bulls" — LEA
He wrote "The Chosen" — POTOK
He wrote "The Dynasts" — HARDY
He wrote "The Gremlins" — DAHL
He wrote "The Hive" — CELA
He wrote "The Morning Watch": 1951 — AGEE
He wrote "The Name of the Rose" — ECO
He wrote "The Prisoner of Zenda" — HAWKINS
He wrote "The Purloined Letter" — POE
He wrote "The Scarlet Letter" — HAWTHORNE
He wrote "The Sultan of Sulu" — ADE
He wrote "Watership Down" — ADAMS
He wrote "What Maisie Knew" — JAMES
He wrote "You Know Me, Al" — LARDNER
He's a phony — FAKER

He's Columbo — PETER
He's got the goods — TRADER
He's Hunter on TV — DRYER
He's in "de cold, cold ground" — MASSA
He's often robbed — PETER
He's three sheets in the wind — INEBRIATE
He, in Aquila — ESSO
He, she or it — PRONOUN
He, to Henri — LUI
He, to Luigi — ESSO
He, to Pierre — LUI
He-man — BRUTE
He: L. — ILLE
Head-shaped, to botanists — CAPITATE
Head — PATE
Head bandage — GALEA
Head cavity — SINUS
Head complaint — ACHE
Head cook — CHEF
Head cover for Sandy — TAM
Head covering for a poilu — KEPI
Head covers — HOODS
Head for Gretna Green — ELOPE
Head for the door — LEAVE
Head garland — ANADEM
Head honcho — BOSS
Head line? — PART
Head lock? — TRESS
Head nun — ABBESS
Head of a comet — COMA
Head of a tale — ONCE
Head of armor — COIF
Head of the haus — FRAU
Head of the Sanhedrin — NASI
Head off — AVERT
Head or ear ending — ACHE
Head or herring — RED
Head or hot starter — RED
Head over heels? — CAPONE
Head part — EAR
Head swellers — EGOS
Head table site — DAIS
Head the bill — STAR
Head up the gangplank — BOARD
Head, in France — TETE
Headache remedy — BROMO
Headbands — SNOODS
Headcheese — SOUSE
Headcheese, e.g. — MEAT
Headdress — COIF
Headdress for a princess — TIARA
Headdress for the Archbishop of Canterbury — MITRE
Headed — LED
Headgear — HELMET, LID
Headgear & frock coat — DERBY AND PRINCE ALBERT
Headgear for a peer — CORONET
Heading on a roll book — ABSENT
Headland — NESS, RAS
Headlight device — DIMMER
Headlight setting — LOW BEAM
Headline — BANNER
Headliner — STAR, TOP BANANA
Headliner's status — STARDOM
Headlong — HASTY
Headquartered — BASED
Headquarters — BASE
Headquarters of the U.S. Atlantic Fleet — NORFOLK
Heads — POLLS
Heads in Calais — TETES
Heads in Rouen — TETES
Heads of certain colleges — RECTORS
Heads of comets — COMAS
Heads of hair — MOPS
Heads or tails — CHANCE
Heads, to Henri — TETES
Headstall's kin — NOOSE
Headstrong — INTEMPERATE, RASH
Headware — CAP
Headware fit for a princess — CORONET, TIARA
Headway — DENT
Headwear for royal personages — TIARAS
Headwork — IDEAS
Heal mark — SCAR
Healed — CURED
Healing agent — SALVE
Healing goddess — EIR
Healing salve — BALM
Healing sign — SCAB
Healing: Comb. form — IATRY
Health club — SPA
Health club feature — SAUNA
Health enhancer — TONIC
Health food — BRAN, FRUIT
Health food also called bean curd — TOFU
Health Genus — ERICA
Health haven — SPA
Health maintenance organization — HMO
Health place — SPA
Health resorts — BATHS, SANATORIA, SPAS
Health spa feature — SAUNA
Health-care personnel — AIDES
Health-club feature — SAUNA
Health-enhancing — SALUTARY
Healthier, in a way — SANER
Healthy — FIT, HALE
Healthy water — SPA
Healthy, in Madrid — SANO
Healthy: Sp — SANO
Heap — CLUSTER, GROUP, PILE, STACK
Heap of hay — MOW
Heap of stones — SCREE
Heap up — AMASS
Heap upon — LOAD
Heaped — PILED
Heaps — A LOT
Heaps of wood — PILES
Hear — LISTEN, PAY ATTENTION
Hear a case — TRY
Hear about — LEARN
Heard from the herd — LOW
Hearing — TRIAL
Hearing aid — EAR
Hearing device — EAR
Hearing distance — EARSHOT
Hearing-oriented — AURAL
Hearing: Comb. form — ACOUO
Hearken to — HEAR
Hears about gale warnings? — GETS WIND OF
Hears of — LEARNS
Heart — BREAST, CORE, SOUL, SPIRIT
Heart action reading, for short — EKG
Heart and soul — DEVOTEDLY, ENTIRELY
Heart chambers — ATRIA
Heart exam-chart — ANG
Heart of gold — KINDNESS
Heart of the matter — CORE
Heart part — AORTA
Heart parts — ATRIA
Heart test, for short — EKG
Heart track, initially — EKG
Heart-to-heart — CANDID, INTIMATE
Heartbeat — PULSE, EMOTION
Heartburn — INDIGESTION
Hearted or headed starter — HARD
Hearten — STEEL
Hearth — ASTRE, FOYER
Hearth item — ANDIRON
Hearth residue — ASH, CINDERS
Hearth shelves — MANTELS
Hearth tools — POKERS
Hearth, to Pierre — ATTE
Hearts or diamonds — SUIT
Heartthrob — FLAME
Heartwarming — INSPIRATIONAL
Hearty — SINCERE
Hearty dishes — STEWS
Hearty partner, Cockney style — ALE
Hearty soup — LENTE
Hearty's companion — HALE
Hearty's pal — HALE

Heat condition — ESTRUS
Heat meas. — BTU
Heat measures: Abbr. — BTUS
Heat source — COAL, STEAM
Heat unit — BTU, THERM
Heat units — LAPS
Heat up — WARM
Heat, at times — RACE
Heat, sweeten and spice — MULL
Heat: Comb. form — THERM
Heated — ANGRY
Heated argument — SET TO
Heated contests — SET TOS
Heater — ROD
Heaters and roscoes — GATS
Heath — ERICA
Heath for Heathcliff — MOOR
Heathcliff's creator — EMILY BRONTE
Heathen — PAGAN
Heather — LOCK
Heather genus — ERICA
Heatherton — JOEY
Heathrow arrivals — SSTS
Heathrow speed demons — SSTS
Heaths for Heathcliff — MOORS
Heating devices — ETNAS
Heating specs. — BTUS
Heating unit: Abbr — BTU
Heating vessels — ETNAS
Heats lightly — WARMS
Heave — PANT
Heaven — BLISS, PARADISE, VALHALLA
Heaven: Comb. form — URANO
Heavenly — BLEST, COSMIC, MASS, SPIRITUAL
Heavenly adman — SKY-WRITER
Heavenly altar — ARA
Heavenly bear — URSA
Heavenly being — SERAPH
Heavenly body — MOON
Heavenly butter — ARIES
Heavenly creature — ANGEL
Heavenly fare — MANNA
Heavenly food — MANNA
Heavenly hawk — ARES
Heavenly headdress — HALO
Heavenly headgear — HALO
Heavenly hunter — ORION
Heavenly instrument — HARP
Heavenly light — STAR
Heavenly peacock — PAVO
Heavenly political promise? — PIE
Heavenly rapture — BLISS
Heavenly scent — AROMA
Heavenly sight? — UFO
Heavenly sights — COMETS
Heavenly streaker — COMET
Heavenly strings — LYRES
Heavenly substance — MANNA
Heavenly topper — HALO
Heavens — ETHER, SKIES
Heavens-related — ASTRAL
Heavens: clear sky: Var. — AETHER
Heavens: Comb. form — URANO
Heavier — FATTER
Heavily favored — ODDS ON
Heavy-faced type — IONIC
Heavy — VILLAIN
Heavy actor loses his way — SYDNEY GREEN
Heavy barge — HOY
Heavy blow — ONER
Heavy British draft horses — SHIRE
Heavy cart: dial. — BOGIE
Heavy dark beer — BOCK
Heavy hammers — MAULS
Heavy handed — INEPT
Heavy headed hammer — PEEN
Heavy hearted — SAD
Heavy Irish tweed — DONE-GAL
Heavy metal's "_____ Sister" — TWISTED
Heavy military sword — SABER
Heavy plus — OBESE
Heavy rains — TORRENTS
Heavy reading — TOME
Heavy reading material — TOMES
Heavy satin — PANNE
Heavy shoes — BROGANS
Heavy shower — DOWN-POUR
Heavy silk fabric in the Middle-Ages — SAMITE
Heavy spar — BARITE
Heavy volume — TOME
Heavy weight — TON
Heavy weight I'm lifting in N.D.? — MINOT
Heavy weight: Fr. — TONNE
Heavy weights — TONS
Heavy wts. — TNS
Heavy's heater — GAT
Heavy, dark wood — EBONY
Heavy-bodied brews — STOUTS
Heavy-handed painting — IMPASTO
Heavyweight champ: 1934-35 — BAER
Heavyweight Max — BAER
Heb. letter — DALETH
Heb. month — ADAR
Hebdomadal — WEEKLY
Hebrew A — ALEPH
Hebrew Bible reading: Var. — KRI
Hebrew dry measure — EPHA, OMER
Hebrew hell — SHEOL
Hebrew instrument — ASOR
Hebrew judge — ELI
Hebrew letter — ALEF, ALEPH, AYIN, MEM, RESH
Hebrew letter — TAV, TETH, TSADE, ZAIN
Hebrew letter: Var. — TSADE
Hebrew letters — ALEFS, TAVE
Hebrew lyre — ASOR
Hebrew measure — KOR, OMER
Hebrew month — ADAR, ELUL, NISAN, SIVAN, TEBET
Hebrew month, of old — ABIB
Hebrew musical instruments — ASORS
Hebrew name meaning "exalted father" — ABRAM
Hebrew prophet — AMOS, EZRA
Hebrew prophet in Douay version — ELIAS
Hebrew school — HEDER
Hebrew scriptures — TORAHS
Hebrew T — TAV
Hebrew word in the Psalms — SELAH
Hebrides bird dog — SKELARK
Hebrides Island — IONA
Hebrides pet — SKYE TERRIER
Heckle — NEEDLE
Heckle noisily — RAZZ
Hecklephone, etc — OBOES
Heckles — GIVE SOMEONE THE NEEDLE
Hector — BULLY, HARASS, TEASE
Hector Hugh Muro — SAKI
Hector's hometown — TROY
Hector, Hercules et al. — HEROES
Hedda Gabler's creator — IBSEN
Hedda of fiction — GABLER
Heddles place — LOOM
Hedge — HEM
Hedge in — LIMIT
Hedge shrub — PRIVET
Hedge sparrow — PRUNELLA
Hedge-row — BUSHES
Hedren of "The Birds" — TIPPI
Hedy Lamarr film — ECTASY
Hee-bee-jee-bies — JITTERS
Heed — LISTEN
Heeded — OBEYED
Heehaw — BRAY
Heel-_____ — AND TOE
Heel — CUR
Heel _____; dance step — AND TOE
Heel and toe doctor — PODI-ATRIST
Heel end — CRUST
Heel over — CAREEN
Heel stepped on by women — SPIKE

Heelers' bailiwicks — WARDS
Heeling — ALIST
Heels — CADS
Heeltap — LIFT
Heeltaps — LEES
Heep — URIAH
Heep's adjective for himself — UMBLE
Heffalump's creator — MILNE
Heft — LIFT
Hefty weight — TON
Hegel's forte — LOGIC
Heiden's forte — SPEED SKATING
Heidi heights — ALPS
Heidi's creator — SPYRI
Heidi's home — ALPS
Heifers — COWS
Height for a little kite — AERIE
Height: Abbr. — ALT, ELEV
Height: Comb. form — ACRO
Height: Prefix — ACRO
Heighten — ENHANCE
Heighten the spirits — ELATE
Heine's sigh — ACH
Heinous — EVIL
Heir — SCION
Heir's interest — ESTATE
Heirless financier — MEYER-ROTHS
Hekzebiah Hawkin's daughter — SADIE
Held — KEPT
Held a get together — REUNED
Held a job in Las Vegas — DEALT
Held a spear in "Aida" — SUPERED
Held accountable — BLAMED
Held and Neagle — ANNAS
Held back — RETARDED
Held dear — VALUED
Held dear to one's heart — TREASURED
Held in bondage — ENSLAVED
Held in contempt — DESPISED
Held in veneration — ADORED
Held or Neagle — ANNA
Held together — COHERED
Helen Hayes lives here — NYACK
Helen Hunt Jackson novel — RAMONA
Helen Mirren film: 1984 — CAL
Helen of Troy's mother — LEDA
Helen or Roland — HAYES
Helen was here — TROY
Helen's abductor — PARIS
Helen's mother — LEDA
Helen's new home — TROY
Helga's portraitist — WYETH
Helical — COILED
Helices — SPIRALS
Helicons — TUBAS
Helicopter — EGGBEATER
Helicopter feature — ROTOR
Helicopter part — ROTOR
Helios — SUN
Helix — SPIRAL
Hell and low water — RIVER STYX
Hell kite — BEAST
Hell, to Sherman — WAR
Hell-bent — INTENT
Hellbound — FIEND
Hellenic — GREEK
Heller offering — NOVEL
Hellhound — DEMON
Hellman book: 1979 — THERE
Hellman's attic clutter? — TOYS
Hellman's attic treasures — TOYS
Hello, in Hilo — ALOHA
Helm dir. — ENE, NNE, SSE
Helm letters — SSE, NNE
Helm position — ALEE
Helmet border — ORLE
Helmet decorations — ORLES
Helmet part — VISOR
Helmet, to Hadrian — GALEA
Helmet: Lat. — GALEA
Helmsman's direction — ALEE
Helmsman's function — STEERAGE
Helmut's highway — BAHN
Helmut's ice — EIS
Heloise's beloved — ABELARD
Helot — ESNE, SERF
Helot for one — SLAVE
Help — ABET, AID, ASSIST, AVAIL
Help call — SOS
Help freshmen adjust — ORIENT
Help in a heist — ABET
Help in time of need — TIDE
Help on a "job" — ABET
Help the waiter — BUS
Help wanted — SOS
Help with the dishes — WIPE
Help! — SOS
Help!: Fr. — AMOI
Helper — AIDE, AIDER
Helper bringing a drink? — AIDE
Helper: Abbr. — ASST
Helpers — AIDES
Helpful one — AIDER
Helpful person — AIDER
Helping hand — BENEFACTOR
Helpings — PORTIONS
Helpless — UNABLE
Helpmate — WIFE
Helps — AIDS, ASSISTS
Helps the teacher — ERASES
Helps with the dishes — DRIES
Hem — EDGE
Hem and _____ — HAW
Hem anew — RESEW
Hem partner — HAW
Hematite and galena — ORES
Hemi's meaning — HALF
Hemidemisemiquaver — NOTE
Hemingway — ERNEST
Hemingway heroine — PILAR
Hemingway novel — A FAREWELL TO ARMS
Hemingway to friends — PAPA
Hemingway's "In _____ Time" — OUR
Hemingway's "The _____" — KILLERS
Hemingway's nickname — PAPA
Hemingway, to some — PAPA
Hemline region — KNEE
Hemlock, e.g. — TREE
Hemmed in by — AMID
Hemoglobin groups — HEMES
Hemp source — SISAL
Hems and haws — STUTTERS
Hemsley sitcom — AMEN
Hemsley TV vehicle — AMEN
Hen — LAYER
Hen house — COOP
Hen's home — ROOST
Hen, for one — LAYER
Hence — ERGO, THUS
Henchman — ALLY, SATRAP
Henfruit — EGGS
Henhouse infants — CHICKS
Henley action — OARING
Henley competitor — ROWER
Henley event — REGATTA
Henley on Thames event — REGATTAS
Henna — HAIR DYE
Henna user — DYER
Henna, e.g. — DYE
Henneries? — EGGPLANTS
Henning of magic — DOUG
Henny Youngman's forte — ONE LINER
Henpeck — NAG
Henpecker — NAG
Henri Christophe's land — HAITI
Henri ender — ETTA
Henri of art — MATISSE
Henri's donkey — ANE
Henri's head — TETE
Henri's lady friends — AMIES
Henry _____ Lodge — CABOT
Henry _____ Longfellow — WADSWORTH
Henry Aldrich portrayer Stone — EZRA
Henry Higgins' "Fair Lady" — ELIZA
Henry Higgins' pupil — ELIZA
Henry IV's birthplace — PAU
Henry IV's second wife — MARIE
Henry James biographer — EDEL
Henry James forte — PROSE
Henry Miller novel — SEXUS

Henry Morgan was one — PIRATE
Henry or Jane — FONDA
Henry or Marianne — MOORE
Henry the sculptor — MOORE
Henry VII's surname — TUDOR
Henry VIII was one — TUDOR
Henry VIII's second wife — ANNE
Henry VIII's sixth — PARR
Henry VIII's wife — ANNE
Henry Winkler — FONZ
Henry's Katharine of _____ — ARAGON
Henry's last Catherine — PARR
Hens' homes — COOPS
Hens' pens — COOPS
Hep — COOL, ON TO
Hepburn-O'Toole film: 1968 — THE LION IN WINTER
Hepburn — ACTRESS
Hepburn's "_____ Holiday" — ROMAN
Hepburn-Grant film: 1938 — HOLIDAY
Heptad — SEVEN
Her cupboard was bare — MOTHER HUBBARD
Her lover drowned — HERO
Her mate is ruff — REE
Her motto was "Semper Paratus" — SPAR
Her temple is at Philae — ISIS
Hera's husband — ZEUS
Hera's mate — ZEUS
Hera's son — ARES
Heraclitus was one — IONIAN
Heraldic band — ORLE
Heraldic bearings — ORLES
Heraldic border — ORLE
Heraldic design — ENTE, SEME
Heraldic fur — VAIR
Heraldic green — VERT
Heraldic insignia — ARMS, CREST
Heraldic pattern — ORLE
Herault hour — HEURE
Herb for flavoring — ANISE
Herb of goosefoot family — ORACH
Herb of lily family — SCILLA
Herb of medicinal value — ALOE
Herb of the Bible — ANET
Herb of the carrot family — ANISE, CORIANDER
Herb of the lily family — SCILLA
Herb of the nightshade family — MANDRAKE
Herb or blue dye — WOAD
Herb or spaghetti — OREGANO
Herb resembling spinach — ORACH
Herbaceous plants — ANISES
Herbal "Diff'rent Strokes" actress? — SHALLOT RAE
Herbal forecast? — PARSLEY SUNNY
Herbal infusions — TEAS
Herbert _____: "Panther" co-star — LOM
Herbert of films — HUGH, LOM
Herbert sci-fi novel — DUNE
Herbert's "_____ Toyland" — BABES IN
Herbs liked by felines — CATARIAS
Herbs of the mustard family — ALYSSUMS
Herbs resembling Indian pipes — PINESAPS
Herbs, in Yorkshire — YARBS
Herculean — TOUGH
Herculean serpent — HYDRA
Hercules' captive — IOLE
Hercules' victim — HYDRA
Herd animal — STEER
Herd of seals — PATCH
Herd sounds — LOWS
Here _____ again! — I GO
Here and there — AROUND, WILLY NILLY
Here's partner — THERE
Here's to you — TOAST
Here, along the Seine — ICI
Here, in Havana — AQUI
Here, in Paris — ICI
Here, to Henri — ICI
Here, to Pierre — ICI
Hereafter — LATER
Hereafter (Blake) — GATES OF PARADISE
Hereafter (F.D. Hemens) — THAT RADIANT SHORE
Hereafter (hymn) — THE PROMISED LAND
Hereafter (I. Watts) — MAN-SION IN THE SKY
Hereafter (legend) — THE BOWER OF BLISS
Hereafter (New Testament) — KINGDOM OF HEAVEN
Hereditary — INNATE
Hereditary factor — GENE
Hereditary initials — RNA
Heredity determiners — GENES
Heredity factors — TUNNEY, KRUPA, AUTRY
Heredity unit — GENE
Heresy — DISSENT
Heretofore — ERE, ERENOW
Heretofore named — NEE
Heritage — PAST
Hermetic — SEALED, SHUT
Hermit — EREMITE, LONER
Hermit or fiddler — CRAB
Hermit's dwelling — CELL
Hermitic device — INNER SEAL
Hermits — MONKS
Hernia — RUPTURE
Hero — ACE, IDLE, WHITE KNIGHT
Hero of "Exodus" — ARI
Hero of "Giants in the Earth" — PER
Hero of "Star Wars" — SOLO
Hero of a Gluck opera — ORFEO
Hero of a Sheed book — ALI
Hero of Hindi epics — RAMA
Hero of the 1936 Olympics — OWENS
Hero tag-on — INE
Hero worship — ADULATION
Hero's hero — LEANDER
Hero's medal — PURPLE HEART
Hero, for short — SUB
Hero-actor Murphy — AUDIE
Herodia's daughter — SALOME
Heroic — EPIC, EPICAL
Heroic act — DEED
Heroic Alaskan dog — BALTO
Heroic deed — GEST
Heroic narratives — SAGAS
Heroic people — VALIANTS
Heroic poem — EPIC, EPOPEE, EPOS
Heroic poetry — EPOS
Heroic stories — SAGAS
Heroic tales — SAGAS
Heroic verse — EPOS
Heroic works — EPICS
Heroine — IDOL, STAR
Heroine in "Ivanhoe" — ROWENA
Heroine of "The Flying Dutchman" — SENTA
Heroine of "The Old Curiosity Shop" — NELL
Heroine of "The Thorn Birds" — MEGAN
Heroine of 1880 novel — NANA
Heroine of a Broadway show — EVITA
Heroine of a Dickens novel — NELL
Heroine of Beethoven's "Fidelio" — LEONORE
Heroine of Conrad's "Victory" — LENA
Heron — EGRET
Heron's cousin — CRANE, EGRET, IBIS
Heron's kin — EGRET, IBIS
Heron, for one — WADER
Heros — SUBS
Herpetological fruit? — ASP BERRIES
Herpetologist's subject — REPTILES

Herr's "Alas!" — ACH
Herr's heir — SOHN
Herr, in Houston — MISTER
Herrick's choice in dress — SWEET DISORDER
Herring color? — RED
Herring measure in Hereford — CRAN
Herring or pepper — RED
Herringbone — CHEVRON
Herringlike fish — SMELT
Hersey novel — THE WALL
Hersey novel locale — ADANO
Hersey novel setting — ADANO
Hersey town — ADANO
Hersey's "_____ the Valley" — INTO
Hersey's bell town — ADANO
Hersey's fictional town — ADANO
Hershfield cartoon character — ABIE
Hershiser — OREL
Hershiser is one — ACE
Hes — MALES
Hesitant — STALLING
Hesitant one's sound — PEEP
Hesitant sounds — ERS
Hesitant syllables — ERS
Hesitate — FALTER
Hesitating sounds — ERS
Hesitation of a sort — STAMMER
Hesperia — SPAIN
Hesperous, for one — STAR
Hesse's river — EDER
Hessian river — EDER
Heterogeneous mix — HODGE PODGE
Hew — CHOP
Hew a yew — FELL
Hew out — CARVE
Hew, as a yew — CHOP
Hewer — — AXE
Hewer's tool — AXE
Hexagonal flagstones — FAVI
Hexahedra — CUBES
Heyday — PRIME
Heyerdahl — THOR
Heyerdahl craft — RAI
Heyerdahl's "Kon _____" — TIKI
Hgt. — ALT, ELEV
Hi-fi component, for short — PREAMP
Hi-fi feature — STEREO
Hi there! — HELLO
Hi-fi — STEREO
Hi-fi equipment — STEREO SET
Hi-fi part — SPEAKER
Hi-fi term — AUDIO
Hi-tech beam — LASER
Hialeah attractions — RACES
Hialeah hand — GROOM
Hiatus — LULL, SPACE
Hiawatha's craft — CANOE
Hibachi feature — GRATE
Hibachis — JAPANESE STOVES
Hibernate — SLEEP
Hibernating animal — BEAR
Hibernia — ERIN
Hibernia poetically — ERIN
Hibernian — CELT
Hibernian brouhaha? — IRISH STEW
Hic and hock separator — HAEC
Hic, _____, Hoc — HAEC
Hicksville? — ONE HORSE TOWN
Hidden — PERDU, VEILED
Hidden away — STASHED
Hidden evil — SNAKE IN THE GRASS
Hidden menace — SNAKE IN THE GRASS
Hidden spot — NOOK
Hidden stores — CACHES
Hide — CACHE, PELT, SECRETE
Hide _____ hair — NOR
Hide and go seek — GAME
Hide away — STASH
Hide in the hand — PALM
Hide the loot — STASH
Hide the swag — STASH
Hide's partner — SEEK
Hide, as a dog's bone — BURY
Hideaway — DEN
Hideaways — RETREATS
Hideous giant — OGRE
Hideouts — LAIRS
Hides — CACHES, PELTS
Hiding place — CACHE, LAIR
Hiding place of a sort — BUSHEL
Hiding spot for Polonius — ARRAS
Hie — RUSH
Hiemal sound in comics — BRR
Hierophant — PRIEST
High-rise structure — SKY-SCRAPER
High — AERIAL
High _____ — JINKS
High _____ — TEA
High _____ (avant garde) — TECH
High _____ kite — AS A
High aims — IDEALS
High alt. carriers — SSTS
High and dry — MAROONED
High and low phenomenena — TIDES
High ball at Wimbledon — LOB
High cards — ACES
High class — PLUSH
High craggy hill — TOR
High crest — ARETE
High dam — HOOVER
High degree — NTH
High dudgeon — IRE, SNIT, WRATH
High dwelling — AERI
High esteem — HONOR
High explosive — TNT
High fashion — TON
High fliers for the govt. — USAF
High flyer — KITE
High ground — UPLAND
High hat — SNUB
High hatter — SNOB
High hideout — AERIE
High hills — TORS
High home — AERIE
High house — AERIE
High kicking dance — CAN CAN
High mountain — ALP
High mountain pass — COL
High nest — AERIE
High note — ELA
High officials — TOP BRASS
High or low _____ — TIDE
High order of angels — SERAPHIM, THRONES
High peaks — ALPS
High pitch — BALL
High pitched — SHRILL
High point — ACME, PEAK
High praise — ACCOLADE, EULOGY
High ranking British officer — AIR MARSHALL
High regard — ESTEEM
High ridges — ARETES
High rises in a way: Abbr. — MTS
High rocky hill — EMBANK-MENT
High school dance — PROM
High school event — PROM
High school farming course: Abbr. — VOAG
High school years — TEENS
High schooler — TEEN
High schooler, e.g. — MINOR
High schoolers — TEENS
High sign — SIGNAL
High silk hat — TILE
High spirits — ELATION
High spot — PEAK
High tableland — MESA
High time — NOON
High time of day — NOON
High transit lines — ELS
High transits — ELS
High winds — GALE
High wire performer — ROPE DANCER
High, in music — ALT
High, in the French Alps — HAUT
High, low and flood — TIDES
High-_____ — RISE
High-five — HANDSLAP
High-flown — FANCY

High-handed — BOSSY
High-hat — SNOB, SNOOT, SNUB
High-level computer language — PASCAL
High-lives selection — AERY
High-melting element — BORON
High-minded — NOBLE
High-pitched sound — TING
High-pressure — URGE
High-priced — STEEP
High-ranking angels — SERAPHS
High-ranking Muslim woman — BEGUM
High-ranking person, for short — ARISTO
High-school subj. — ENG, MATH
High-schooler — TEEN
High-sticking penalty — HOCKEY
High-strung — TENSE
High: Comb. form — ALTI
High: Prefix — ALTI
Highball ingredient — MIXER
Higher — ABOVE
Higher part — UPSIDE
Higher salary — RAISE
Highest degree — NTH
Highest peak in Ethiopia, _____ Dashian — RAS
Highest point — ACME
Highest spot in Japan — MT FUJI
Highland between two geological faults — HORST
Highland dance — REEL
Highland games tree — CABER
Highland group — CLAN
Highland head cover — TAM
Highland headwear — TAM
Highland hillside — BRAE
Highland instruments — BAGPIPES
Highland lord — THANE
Highland miss — LASS
Highland pony — SHELTIE
Highland river — SPEY
Highland Scots, e.g. — CELTS
Highland turndown — NAE
Highlander — GAEL, SCOT
Highlander's denial — NAE
Highlander's garb — KILT
Highlander's log — CABER
Highlander's negatives — NAES
Highlander's tongue — GAELIC
Highlander's weapon — DIRK
Highlander's wrap — PLAID
Highlanders — SCOTS
Highlands Celt — GAEL
Highlands headwear — TAM
Highlands inhabitant — GAEL
Highlands loch — NESS
Highlands monster, familiarly — NESSIE
Highlands uncle — EME
Highlight — ACCENT
Highlight from Handel — ARIA
Highlight of some musicals — THE SONDHEIM RHYME
Highlights for some — TRILLS BY MISS SILLS
Highly amused — IN STITCHES
Highly amusing — RICH
Highly disciplined — SPARTAN
Highly excited — AGOG
Highly regarded — ESTEEMED
Highly volatile fuel: Abbr. — LNG
Highly-glazed fabric finish — CIRE
Highs — UPS
Highway — ROAD, ROUTE
Highway behemoths — SEMIS
Highway division — LANE
Highway features — LANES, RAMPS
Highway havens — MOTELS
Highway hazard — FALLEN ROCK
Highway man — JOHN MCADAM
Highway motors — SEMIS
Highway sights — VANS
Highway sign — SLO, YIELD
Highway to Alaska — ALCAN
Highway to Fairbanks — ALCAN
Highwayman — PAD, THIEF
Highways: Abbr. — RTES
Hijack — ROB
Hike — MARCH
Hiked — LEGGED
Hiked, in a way — RAISED
Hiker's vessels — CANTEENS
Hikers — BACK PACKERS
Hilaire Germain Edgar _____ — DEGAS
Hilarious — MERRY
Hilarity — GLEE, MIRTH
Hildegarde of films — NEFF
Hill — SLOPE
Hill dwellers — ANTS
Hill in D.C. — CAPITOL
Hill in San Francisco — NOB
Hill inhabitant — ANT
Hill maker — ANT
Hill region of India and Burma — NAGA
Hill workers — SENATORS
Hill's companion — DALE
Hill's partner — DALE
Hill, to an Arab -TEL
Hillary Clinton, _____ Rodham — NEE
Hillbilly negative — NAW
Hilloc's Matilda — LIAR
Hillock — KNOLL, RISE
Hillside — CLIFF, SLOPE
Hillside dugout — ABRI
Hillside near a loch — BRAE
Hillside shelter — ABRI
Hillside, in Dumfries — BRAE
Hillsides, to Burns — BRAES
Hilltop house — AERIE
Hilly — STEEP
Hilo dance — HULA
Hilo fare — POI
Hilo feast — LUAU
Hilo garlands — LEIS
Hilo geese — NENES
Hilo greeting — ALOHA
Hilo hello — ALOHA
Hilum — SCAR
Him: Fr. — LUI
Himalayan challenge — EVEREST
Himalayan enigma — YETI
Himalayan goat — TAHR
Himalayan kingdom — NEPAL
Himalayan monk's hood: Var. — ATEES
Himalayan mythical figure — YETI
Himalayan peak — EVEREST, KAMET
Himalayan racoon — PANDA
Himalayan resident — YETI
Himalayan sight — YETI
Himalayan snowman — YETI
Hind — ROE, STAG
Hind or hart — DEER
Hinder — DETER, IMPEDE
Hinder nice blokes? — DETERGENTS
Hindi master — SAHIB
Hindi titles — SRIS
Hindmost — AREAR, REAR
Hindrance — HITCH, SNAG
Hindu — NAWAB
Hindu "Sir" — BABU
Hindu "World Soul" — ATMAN
Hindu angel — DEVA
Hindu archaeological site — ELURA
Hindu ascetic — FAKIR
Hindu ascetic philosophy — YOGA
Hindu call to prayer — AZAN
Hindu caste — AHIR
Hindu coin — ANNA
Hindu cupid — KAMA
Hindu cymbal — TAL
Hindu deity — DEVA, KAMA, RAMA, SIVA
Hindu discipline — YOGA
Hindu dress — SARI
Hindu fire god: Var — AGNI, AGNIS, SIVA
Hindu foot sodiers — PEONS
Hindu garment — SAREE, SARI
Hindu god — DEV, DEVA, INDRA, SIVA, YAMA
Hindu god of love — KAMA

Hindu god of thunder — INDRA
Hindu goddess — DEVI
Hindu goddess of dawn — USHAS
Hindu good spirits — DEVAS
Hindu guitar — SITAR
Hindu hero — RAMA
Hindu honcho — NAWAB
Hindu honorifics — SRIS
Hindu incarnation — AVATAR
Hindu Kush people — KAFIR
Hindu Kush's locale — ASIA
Hindu land grant — ENAM
Hindu language — INDIC
Hindu legendary hero — NALA
Hindu merchant — BANIAN
Hindu monotheist — SIKH
Hindu noblewoman — RANEE
Hindu outergarment — SAREE0
Hindu prince — RAJA
Hindu princes — RANAS
Hindu princess — RANI
Hindu queen — RANEE
Hindu religious rite — PUJA
Hindu religious writing — TANTRA
Hindu scripture — TANTRA
Hindu sect — SIKH
Hindu sect members — JAINUS
Hindu title — NAWAB, SRI
Hindu wonder worker — FAKIR
Hindu's hello or goodbye — NAMASTE
Hindu's unsorted wheat flour — ATTA
Hindus' sacred book — VEDA
Hindustan — URDU
Hindustan kin — URDU
Hindustani — URDU
Hindustani emperor: 16th century — AKBAR
Hinge — JOINT, PIVOT
Hinged cover — LID
Hint — CUE, DASH, IDEA, MENTION, SUGGEST, TRACE
Hint at — INTIMATE
Hint: Abbr. — SUG
Hinterlands — WILDS
Hints — CLUES, INKLINGS, TRACES
Hip — ALERT, AWARE, ONTO
Hip bones — ILIA
Hipbone-related — ILIAC
Hipbones — ILIA
Hippie hangouts — PADS
Hippie's English counterpart — MOD
Hippies' homes — PADS
Hippo chaser — DROME
Hippo's cousin — TAPIR
Hippocampus of myth — SEA HORSE
Hippodromes — ARENAS
Hippolyte of France — TAINE
Hippolyte's sire — ARES
Hippopotamus — SEA COW
Hipsters — CATS
Hircine god — PAN
Hire — EMPLOY, GET, LEASE
Hire a fresh crew — REMAN
Hire Mutt to play Jeff? — MISCAST
Hired — LEASED, RENTED
Hired an atty. — RETD
Hirsch of football fame — ELROY
Hirsch sitcom — TAXI
Hirsute — HAIRY
Hirt and Haig — ALS
Hirt and Johnson — ALS
Hirt and Smith — ALS
His _____ (the boss) — NIBS
His business is looking up — ASTRONOMER
His law relates to thermodynamics — BOYLE
His message: "What hath God wrought!" — MORSE
His Monday is our Sunday — ASIAN
His or her: Fr. — SES
His or Hers — TOWEL
His peers think so — IS RAY NOBLE
His purchase was called "Folly" — SEWARD
His son wrote "Jaws" — BENCHLEY
His was the salty wife — LOT
His, in Hyeres — ALUI
His, in Paris — SES
His, their: Fr. — SES
His: Fr. — SES
Hispanic — LATINO
Hispanic homes — CASAS
Hispanic-American — LATINO
Hispaniola republic — HAITI
Hispaniola, e.g. — ISLA
Hiss — BOO
Hissed reproof — TST
Historian Nevins — ALLAN
Historian's concern — DATES, FACTS
Historian's study — ERA
Historians' interest — ERAS
Historic 1974 event — RESIGNATION OF NIXON
Historic Alabama city — SELMA
Historic April shower? — THE RAIN OF TERROR
Historic atoll — BIKINI
Historic beginning — PRE
Historic Belgian city — LIEGE
Historic Canton — URI
Historic city in Alabama — SELMA
Historic city of Greece — CORINTH
Historic city of NE Massachusetts — SALEM
Historic city on the Meuse — LIEGE
Historic city on the Nile — CAIRO
Historic explorer — CHRISTOPHER COLUMBUS
Historic home of golf — ST ANDREWS
Historic Hungarian city — EGER
Historic island — MALTA
Historic island in New York Bay — ELLIS
Historic landfall: Oct. 12, 1492 — WATLING ISLAND
Historic Massachusetts town — SALEM
Historic Normandy town — ST LO
Historic patron — KING FERDINAND
Historic patroness — QUEEN ISABELLA
Historic peak — ARARAT, IDA
Historic period — ERA, STONE AGE
Historic periods — ERAS, AGES
Historic port — PALOS SPAIN
Historic Portuguese City — EVORA
Historic region of Czechoslovakia — BOHEMIA
Historic river — RHINE
Historic river of Spain — EBRO
Historic Scott — DRED
Historic ship — NINA
Historic site near Salisbury — STONEHENGE
Historic site, at times — RUIN
Historic Spanish river — EBRO
Historic stage — ERA
Historic stretches — ERAS
Historic Swedish city — LUND
Historic Syrian city — ALEPPO
Historic time — ERA
Historic town near Lisbon — EVORA
Historic town near Padua — ESTE
Historic vessel — SANTA MARIA
Historical — CELEBRATED, NOTABLE, NOTED
Historical narrative — SAGA
Historical periods — AGES, ERAS
Historical records — ANNALS
Historically a fortified town — BURG

History — ANNALS, PAST, RECORD
Hit — SMITE, SOCK, SWAT
Hit _____ — AND RUN
Hit _____ (start traveling) — THE ROAD
Hit a pop fly — LOFTED
Hit from the tee — DRIVE
Hit gone but not forgotten — OLDIE
Hit hard — SLAM, SMITE
Hit hard: Slang — SOCK
Hit heavily — SMITE
Hit like _____ of bricks — A TON
Hit like Ruth — SWAT
Hit man or hero — TORPEDO
Hit movies' problems — LINES
Hit musical — ANNIE
Hit pay dirt — MINED
Hit show signs — SRO
Hit sign — SRO
Hit song of 1958 — VOLARE
Hit squad's ploy — RAID
Hit the bell — RANG
Hit the ceiling — FLY OFF THE HANDLE, RAGE
Hit the deck — ARISE
Hit the hay — CALLED IT A DAY
Hit the jackpot — WIN
Hit the road — PACE
Hit the sack — RETIRE
Hit the showers — BATHE
Hit the silk — PARACHUTE
Hit TV show — OPRAH
Hit upon — HAPPEN
Hit with a ray gun — ZAP
Hit, as in tennis — LOB
Hit, Biblical style — SMOTE
Hit, old style — SMIT
Hit-or-miss — CASUAL
Hitch — SNAG, TERM
Hitch up — HARNESS, HIKE, TETHER, YOKE
Hitch-hiker's query? — GOING MY WAY
Hitchcock film: 1964 — MARNIE
Hitchcock movie — STRANGERS ON A TRAIN
Hitchcock thriller — PSYCHO
Hite of "Hite Reports" — SHERE
Hither — HERE
Hits a fly — SWATS
Hits a high fly — LOFTS
Hits a homer — BELTS
Hits hard — SLUGS
Hits the books — PORES
Hits the slopes — SKIS
Hitter Hank — AARON
Hive dwellers — BEES
Hive part — CELL
Hive worker — DRONE
Hiver or printemps — SAISON
Hiver's opposite — ETE
Hives — UREDO
Hives: urticaria — UREDO
Ho and Marquis — DONS
Ho Chi _____ City — MINH
Ho Chi Minh City, formerly — SAIGON
Ho hello — ALOHA
Ho's partner — HEAVE
Ho-hum — SOSO
Hoagie — HERO, LUNCH
Hoar frosts — RIMES
Hoard — STORE
Hoarder — MIDAS
Hoarder's pronoun — MINE
Hoarfrost — RIME
Hoary — ANCIENT, AGED, GRAY
Hoax — PUT ON
Hoaxes — FRAUDS
Hobbies — PASTIMES
Hobbled — GIMPED
Hobbled horse — NAG
Hobby — AVOCATION
Hobby — HORSE
Hobby-horse — TOY
Hobgoblins — SPOOKS
Hobo — TRAMP, VAGABOND
Hobo's transport — BOXCAR, RAILS
Hobo-hat wearer — EMMETT KELLY
Hobos — TRAMPS
Hock — ANKLE
Hock and sack — WINES
Hockey check — BODY
Hockey disk — PUCK
Hockey great — ORR
Hockey manuevers — DEKES
Hockey position — GOALIE, WING
Hockey score — CAGE, GOAL
Hockey star Bobby and family — ORRS
Hockey star Tikkanen — ESA
Hockey statistics — ASSISTS
Hockey surface — ICE
Hockey's _____ Ross Trophy — ART
Hockey's Bobby — ORR
Hockey-stick wood — ASH
Hocus _____ — POCUS
Hodgepodge — FARRAGO, HASH, MISHMASH, OLIO, SALAD
Hodgepodges — MESSES
Hoffmann compositions — TALES
Hoffmann output — TALES
Hoffmann's initials — ETA
Hog — PIG
Hog feed — MASH
Hog food — SLOPS
Hog hair — SETA
Hog-tie — STRAP
Hogan of golf — BEN
Hogarth subject — RAKE
Hogback — RIDGE
Hogback's kin — ARETE
Hogfish — WRASSE
Hogged the conversation? — OINKED
Hogs hovel — STY
Hogs or shirt — SWEAT
Hogs's comment — GRUNT
Hogsheads — BARRELS
Hogwash — BUNK, ROT
Hoi Polloi — MOB
Hoist — ELEVATE, LIFT
Hoisting devices — CRANES
Hokaido aborigine — AINU
Hokaido city — OTARU
Hokaido port — OTARU
Hokkaido native — AINU
Hokum of old — BANANA OIL
Holbrook or Linden — HAL
Hold — CLUTCH, CONTAIN, DETAIN, GRASP, GRIP
Hold — IMPRISON, KEEP
Hold _____ (own) — TITLE TO
Hold _____: respect — IN AWE
Hold a position firmly — TAKE A STAND
Hold a watch on — TIME
Hold back — RESTRAIN
Hold dear — ADORE
Hold down — LIMIT
Hold fondly — CUDDLE
Hold forth — DEFER, ORATE
Hold high — ADORE
Hold in awe — REVERE
Hold in mind — HARBOR
Hold it sailor! — AVAST
Hold off — RESIST
Hold on — CLING, GRIP
Hold on for — AWAIT
Hold on to — KEEP
Hold on! — WAIT
Hold one's ground — STAND PAT
Hold onto — RETAIN
Hold out — LAST
Hold sway — RULE
Hold the deed on — OWN
Hold tight — CLASP, GRIP
Hold together — COHERE
Hold up — DELAY
Hold up under — BEAR
Hold your tongue — HUSH
Hold, in music — TENUTO
Hold, on 4th down — STOP
Holders for spinners — DISTAFFS
Holders of salt or wine — CELLARS
Holding back — STEMMING
Holding the bag at Shea — ON BASE
Holdings — ASSETS
Holds — GRASPS, HAS

Holds back — DETAINS, SAVES, STINTS, WAITS
Holds court — SITS
Holds for the future — SAVES
Holds in contempt — DISLIKES
Holds on to — SEIZES
Holds or holds back — CONTAINS
Holds up — ELEVATES, WAITS
Holdup — DELAY
Hole — CAVE
Hole _____ (ace) — IN ONE
Hole for an anchor cable — HAWSE
Hole in one — ACE
Hole makers — AWLS
Hole out — PUTT
Holey — RIDDLED
Holey roll — BAGEL
Holiday beverage — NOG
Holiday bread — STOLLEN
Holiday ending — MAS
Holiday event — SALE
Holiday for short — VAC
Holiday forerunners — EVES
Holiday happenings — SALES
Holiday highlight — SALE
Holiday inspiring Irish puns — SAINT PATRICKS DAY
Holiday music — CAROL
Holiday offering — NOG
Holiday pie — MINCE
Holiday season — YULE
Holiday song — NOEL
Holiday times — EVES
Holiday, in Madrid — FESTA
Holiday, in Scotland — VACANCE
Holier _____ thou — THAN
Holier-than-thou — HAUGHTY, SMUG
Holiness — PIETY
Holland or Lincoln — TUNNEL
Hollander life style? — HIGH ON THE HAGUE
Hollander's lottery goal? — WIND MILLIONS
Hollander's trouser plant? — DUTCHMANS BREECHES
Hollanders — DUTCHMEN
Holler — YELL
Hollered — BAWLED
Hollers — BAWLS
Hollow — CRATER, DELL, DENT
Hollow cell: Suffix — CYTE
Hollow out — CAVE
Hollow stem — REED
Hollow stone — GEODE
Hollows — DELLS
Holly — ILEX
Holly of Dixie — ASSI
Hollywood Academy people — AWARDERS
Hollywood back lots — SETS
Hollywood costume designer — ADRIAN
Hollywood figure — AGENT
Hollywood headliners — STARS
Hollywood hopeful — STARLET
Hollywood hopefuls — UNKNOWNS
Hollywood intersector — VINE
Hollywood name — AVA
Hollywood negator? — DANNY DEVETO
Hollywood P.S.? — SEQUEL
Hollywood Sommer — ELKE
Hollywood supernumerary — EXTRA
Hollywood supers — EXTRAS
Hollywood superstar, 1899-1957 — HUMPHREY BOGART
Hollywood's "cattle call" spot — CENTRAL CASTING
Hollywood's "Elephant Boy" — SABU
Hollywood's Bo or John — DEREK
Hollywood's Cruise — TOM
Hollywood's Day — DORIS
Hollywood's Hayworth — RITA
Hollywood's Kazan — ELIA
Hollywood's Keaton — BUSTER
Hollywood's Lubitsch — ERNST
Hollywood's May — ELAINE
Hollywood's Pat — MORITA
Hollywood's Preminger — OTTO
Hollywood's Sharif — OMAR
Hollywooders going steady — ITEMS
Holm oak — ILEX
Holm or Carmichael — IAN
Holm or key — ISLET
Holmes calabash — PIPE
Holmes called him "The Oldest" — ALI
Holmes creator — DOYLE
Holmes quarry — SLAYERS
Holmes' "one-hoss carriage" — SHAY
Holmes, Spade and Wolfe — SLEUTHS
Holt or Conway — TIM
Holy — SACRAL, SAINTLY
Holy _____ — SEE
Holy Ark's contents — TORAH
Holy book — BIBLE
Holy city of Spain? — TOLEDO
Holy cup — GRAIL
Holy Grail, e.g. — RELIC
Holy man's title — FRA
Holy river in India — GANGES
Holy rollers — HOOPS
Holy Roman emperor — OTTO
Holy state — SAINTDOM
Holy terror — BRAT
Holy: Comb. from — HAGI
Holyoke Center designer — CERT
Homage — FAVOR
Homburg — HAT
Home — ABODE, HOUSE, REFUGE
Home base — PLATE, RUBBER
Home buyers' org. — FHA
Home electrical piece — ADAPTOR
Home extensions — ELLS
Home for 25,000 Buckeyes — XENIA OHIO
Home for a Brahman — INDIA
Home for a Spitfire — HANGAR
Home for a Viking — NORWAY
Home for high flyers — EYRIE
Home for short — RES
Home for the "Enterprise" — EARTH
Home from Brooklyn — LENA
Home heater in Madrid — HORNO
Home in Paris — DEMEURE
Home in Rome — VILLA
Home loan, reduced — MTGE
Home of — CHEZ
Home of a biblical witch — ENDOR
Home of Abraham — HEBRON
Home of Aeneas — TROY
Home of Annapurna — NEPAL
Home of Ariz. Sun Devils — TEMPE
Home of Creighton University — OMAHA
Home of Helen Hayes — NYACK
Home of Henry VII's first wife — ARAGON
Home of Iowa State — AMES
Home of Irish kings — TARA
Home of Italian festival — SPOLETO
Home of Juarez — OAXACA
Home of Katharina and Bianca — PADUA
Home of leprechauns — ERIN
Home of many Tlingits — ALASKA
Home of N.Y.'s Blackbirds — LIU
Home of ouzo — GREECE
Home of over 25,000 Garden Staters — LODI NJ
Home of Phillips and Abbot Academies — ANDOVER
Home of Phillips U. — ENID
Home of primates — APERY
Home of six presidents — OHIO

Home of the Black Bears — MAINE, ORONO
Home of the Blue Jays — TORONTO
Home of the brave: Vari — TIPI
Home of the Braves — ATLANTA
Home of the Bruins: Abbr. — UCLA
Home of the Chargers — SAN DIEGO
Home of the Cyclones — AMES
Home of the Dolphins — MIAMI
Home of the first lady — EDEN
Home of the gods — OLYMPUS
Home of the Golden Hurricane — TULSA
Home of the helot — SPARTA
Home of the Incas — PERU
Home of the Jungfrau — ALPS
Home of the Kashmir goat — TIBET
Home of the llama — ANDES
Home of the Mets — SHEA
Home of the Padres — SAN DIEGO
Home of the slave — HOVEL
Home of the storied Mouse Tower — BINGEN
Home of the Tafts — OHIO
Home of the Yellow Jackets of Ga.: Abbr. — ATL
Home of Vance A.F.B. — ENID
Home of Zeno — ELEA
Home on high — AERIE
Home on the pampas — HACIENDA
Home on the range? — FARM, TEEPEE
Home or blue — PLATE
Home plate — DISH
Home Rehabilitation Agency — HRA
Home run — SWAT
Home run champ — AARON
Home run king — MARIS
Home safety device — SMOKE DETECTOR
Home site — LOT
Home site measure — ACRE
Home sites — LOTS
Home spun — PLAIN
Home to an Inuit — IGLOO
Home to the Olympics — ELIS
Home, for one — PLATE
Home, in Honduras — CASA
Home-based enterprise — COTTAGE INDUSTRY
Home-coming — GAME
Home-run — HIT
Homebase for the RAF — ENG
Homeland of Tom Jones — WALES
Homeless — OUTCAST
Homemade — NATIVE
Homeowner in Fall — RAKER
Homeowners' pride and bane — LAWN
Homer classic — ILIAD
Homer epic — ILIAD
Homer king — AARON
Homer's "homer"? — ILIAD
Homer's "Illiad" hero — ACHILLES
Homer's "Rosy-fingered _____" — DAWN
Homer's "scourge of mortals" — ARES
Homer's one horse town — TROY
Homer's opus — ILIAD
Homeric epic — ILIAD
Homeric warrior — AJAX
Homeric works — EPICS
Homes for hoods — HOOSGOWS
Homes for porkers — STIES
HOMES quintet — LAKES
HOMES, for example — LAKES
Homespun — PLAIN
Homestead — FARM, GRANGE, HOUSE, SETTLE
Homesteader on the range — NESTER
Homesteaders — SETTLERS
Homework — LESSONS
Homilies: Abbr. — SERS
Homily — LECTURE, SERMON
Homily: Abbr. — SER
Hominy — GRITS
Hominy — MAIZE
Homo sapiens, e.g. — BIPED, MAN
Homogenize — BLEND, COMBINE, FUSE, EMULSIFY
Homophone for air — ERE
Homophone for Astor — ASTER
Homophone for one — WON
Homophone for rights — RITES
Homophone for seize — SEES
Homophone for spade — SPAYED
Homophone for the verb use — YOUS
Homophone for use — EWES
Homophone for wood — WOULD
Homophone of raze — RAISE
Homophone of waste — WAIST
Homunculus — DWARF
Hon — DEARY
Honcho — BOSS
Honchos — CHIEFS
Hondo — ARROYO
Honduran island — ROATAN
Honduran seaport — TELA
Hone — WHET
Hone a fine edge — STROP
Hones — SHARPENS
Honest — OPEN, OPEN AND ABOVE BOARD
Honest — STRAIGHT UP AND DOWN
Honest _____ — ABE
Honest name — ABE
Honey — DEARY
Honey _____, Rose Kennedy's dad — FITZ
Honey badger — RATEL
Honey bee — APIS
Honey drinks — MEADS
Honey in prescriptions — MEL
Honey of a drink? — MEAD
Honey producer — BEE
Honey source — NECTAR
Honey-eating bird — IAO
Honeybunch — DEARIE
Honeycombed home — HIVE
Honeydews — MELONS
Honeyed word — SUGAR
Honeymakers' homes — HIVES
Honeymooners' haven — NIAGARA FALLS
Hong Kong's capital — VICTORIA
Hong Kong's neighbor — MACAO
Honi Coles' dance — TAP
Honing device — WHETSTONE
Honker's home — CANADA
Honkers — GEESE
Honks — TOOTS
Honky Tonk — DIVE
Honolulu greeting — ALOHA
Honolulu locale — OAHU
Honolulu's island — OAHU
Honor — ESTEEM, FETE
Honor card — TEN
Honor roll — LIST
Honor Societies' org. — ACHS
Honor the flag — SALUTE
Honor with ridicule — ROAST
Honor, in Halle — EHRE
Honora derivative — NORAH
Honorary degree — DLIT
Honorary law degree — LLD
Honored — FETED, SALUTED
Honored with a party — FETED
Honored with entertainment — FETED
Honorees' adjudicator — TOME
Honorific — SIR, TITLE
Honors — CITES, ESTEEMS
Honors a debt — REPAYS
Honshu bay — ISE
Honshu brew — SAKE
Honshu city — DEMO, DOMA, NARA, OSAKA, SETO
Honshu city N of Tokyo — SENDAI
Honshu port — ATAMI, KOBE, OSAKA, UBE
Honshu seaport — OSAKA, SAKAI

Honshu seaport city — TSU
Hooch or all-night flight — REDEYE
Hood — VEIL
Hood of armor — CLOAK
Hood or Olympus — MOUNT
Hood or Tell — ARCHER
Hood or Williams — ROBIN
Hood's decision re a payoff — WHERE OR WHEN
Hood's exit — LAM
Hood's gun — ROSCOE
Hood's weapon — GAT
Hooded cloak — COWL
Hooded cloaks — CAPOTES
Hooded garments — COWLS
Hooded jacket — ANPRAK
Hooded snake — COBRA
Hoodlum's knife — SHIV
Hoods' forest — SHERWOOD
Hoodwink — FOOL
Hoof sound — CLOP
Hoofbeat sound — CLOP
Hoofbeats — CLOPS
Hoofers — DANCERS
Hoohas — TODOS
Hook — BARB, SNARE
Hook or Bligh — CAPT
Hook's first mate — SMEE
Hook's henchman — SMEE
Hook's opposite — SLICE
Hook, line and sinker — WHOLLY
Hookah — PIPE
Hooked at the tip — HAMATE
Hooper or Nielsen: Abbr. — RTG
Hoopla — HYPE
Hoople or Barbara — MAJOR
Hoople whoops — EGADS
Hoople's expletive — EGAD
Hoopster — CAGER
Hoopster Abdul-Jabbar — KAREEM
Hoopster Bill — WALTON
Hoopster's shot — LAYUP
Hoopsters' org. — NBA
Hooray for the matador! — OLE
Hoosegow — CLINK, STIR
Hoosier humorist George and family — ADES
Hoosier State, for short — IND
Hoosier State: Abbr. — IND
Hooter — OWL
Hooters and screechers — OWLS
Hoover and Boulder — DAMS
Hoover and others — DAMS
Hoover Dam's lake — MEAD
Hop drying kiln — OAST
Hop's kiln — OAST
Hopalong Cassidy's portrayer — BOYD
Hope-Crosby title word, often — ROAD
Hope — GOAL
Hope and Carson — WITS
Hope chest item — LINEN
Hope components? — RAYS
Hope holder — CREST
Hope or cedar — CHEST
Hope or Jessica — LANGE
Hope sign-off — THANKS FOR THE MEMORY
Hope-Crosby course — ROAD
Hope-Crosby movie highway? — ROAD
Hope-Crosby movie: 1947 — ROAD TO RIO
Hopeful plunger's song? — IF I WERE A RICH MAN
Hopeless cases — GONERS
Hopeless one — GONER
Hopi or Zuni — PUEBLO
Hopi village — PUEBLO
Hoplite's weapon — SOEAR
Hopped-up drink — ALE
Hopper and Turner — PAINTERS
Hopper of Hollywood — HEDDA
Hopping dance step — SHAG
Hopping mad — IRATE
Hops brew — ALE
Hops dryer — OAST
Horace or Pindar — ODIST
Horace's "_____ Poetica" — ARS
Horaces's forte — ODES
Horatian creation — EPODE
Horatian gem — ODE
Horatio — ALGER
Horatio Alger book, e.g. — SUCCESS STORY
Horatio and Claudius, e.g. — DANES
Horatio, et al. — ALGERS
Horation creation — EPODE
Horatious helmet — GALEA
Hordeola — STYES
Hordeolum — STY
Horehound and mad-dog — MINTS
Horizon sights — STEEPLES
Horizontal timber — SILL
Horizontal: Abbr. — LIN
Hormone — ACTH
Horn — ANTLER, CORNU, CORONET
Horn emanations — TOOTS
Horn of a crescent moon — CUSP
Horn of plenty — CORNUCOPIA
Horn or clef — ALTO
Horn player's pet — BASSET HOUND
Horn sounds — BEEPS
Horn-nosed beast, briefly — RHINO
Horn: Comb. form — KERAT, URALITE
Horne — LENA
Horne and Nyman — LENAS
Horne from Brooklyn — LENA
Horne in the hurdles — LEAPING LENA
Horne of Broadway — LENA
Horne of music — LENA
Horne of note — LENA
Horne of plenty? — LENA
Horne of song — LENA
Horned animal — GOAT
Horned beast, for short — RHINO
Horned toad's relative — MOLOCH
Horned tropical fish — UNIE
Horned vipers — ASPS
Horner's capture — PLUM
Horner's prize — PLUM
Hornet — WASP
Hornet during WW II — CARRIER
Hornet's home — NEST
Hornplant — KELP
Horns 1 / 4 as loud as Preston's — NINETEEN TROMBONES
Hornswoggle — ROOK
Horologe — SUNDIAL
Horologe face — DIAL
Horologer Thomas — SETH
Horoscope — CHART
Horror film adjective — GORY
Horror film sounds — SCREAMS
Horror story — CHILLER
Horse-collar part — HAME
Horse — MARE
Horse _____ — HAIR PIN WHEEL CHAIR LIFT
Horse and buggy — RIG
Horse breed — MORGAN
Horse color — ROAN
Horse course — OVAL
Horse doctor, for short — VET
Horse exercise yard — PADDOCK
Horse feed — OATS
Horse follower — CART, SENSE
Horse for hire — HACK
Horse hair — MANE
Horse in the Racing Hall of Fame — KELSO, SEA BISCUIT
Horse of a certain color — ROAN
Horse of a certain style — PACER
Horse of different colors — ROAN
Horse opera — OATER
Horse or leather — BUCKSKIN
Horse race — DERBY, STEEPLE CHASE

Horse with a mixed coat — ROAN
Horse's ankle — HOCK
Horse's attribute — SENSE
Horse's checkrein — HALTER
Horse's gait — CANTER, TROT
Horse's home — STABLE
Horse's mouth — SOURCE
Horse's mouthpiece — BIT
Horse-drawn Indian vehicle — TONGA
Horse-drawn vehicle — CARRIAGE
Horse-opera command — REACH
Horse-racing event — PREAKNESS STAKES
Horse-racing prize — ROSES
Horsely and Meriwether — LEES
Horseplayers' concerns — SCRATCHES
Horses — ROANS
Horseshoe part — CALK
Horseshoe toss — NEARS
Horsey sound — SNORT
Hose blemish — SNAG
Hose down — WET
Hose fabric — NYLON
Hose fault — SNAG
Hose mishap — SNAG
Hose woe — RUN
Hosiery blemish in — SNAG
Hosiery hue — TAN
Hosiery material — LISLE
Hosiery shade — TAN
Hosiery thread — LISLE
Hosp. employees — RNS
Hosp. feeders — IVS
Hosp. people — RNS
Hosp. personnel — RNS
Hosp. tests — EEGS
Hospital "pronto" — STAT
Hospital areas — WARDS
Hospital camera art? — X RAY
Hospital ER word — STAT
Hospital talk for "now!" — STAT
Hospital trainee — INTERNE
Hospital worker — INTERN
Host — EMCEE
Host at Valhalla — ODIN
Host Donahue — PHIL
Host's pickup — TAB
Hostage — PAWN
Hosted on TV — EMCEED
Hostel — INN
Hostelries — INNS
Hostelry — INN
Hostess Maxwell — ELSA
Hostess Perle — MESTA
Hostility — ENMITY
Hot-plate holders — TRIVETS
Hot-tempered person — FIRE EATER
Hot — AIR, COMB, CORNER, HEAD, HOUSE
Hot — POTATO, ROD, SEAT, SHOT, SPRINGS
Hot — STUFF, TODDY, TUB, WIRE
Hot alcoholic drink — TODDY
Hot application — STUPE
Hot cakes — PANCAKES
Hot clothes towels — PACK
Hot compartment — OAST
Hot compress — STUPE
Hot diggetty — HURRAH
Hot dish — CHILI
Hot dog stop — DELI
Hot dog, in a way — WEENIE
Hot dogs — FRANKS
Hot drink — COCOA, TODDY
Hot drinks from sassafras — SALOOPS
Hot Lips' given name — MARGARET
Hot Lips' portrayer — SWIT
Hot off the presses — LATEST
Hot outpouring — LAVA
Hot sauce or dance — SALSA
Hot spot — INFERNO, KILN, OVEN
Hot springs — SPAS
Hot stuff — CHILI, FIRE
Hot time — JULY
Hot time, in Paris — ETE
Hot times — DOG DAYS OF SUMMER
Hot times in St. Tropez — ETES
Hot times in Tours — ETES
Hot times, in Metz — ETES
Hot tub — SPA
Hot under the collar — RILED
Hot water bottle, for some — FOOT WARMER
Hot water injury — SCALD
Hot wine drink — NEGUS
Hot, dry, Arabian wind — SIMOOM
Hot, old style — CALID
Hot-tempered — FIERY
Hotbed — NEST
Hotcake enhancer — MAPLE SYRUP
Hotel ______ Invalides, Paris — DES
Hotel accoms. — RMS
Hotel attendant — DOORMAN
Hotel for hounds — KENNEL
Hotel lobby transmitter — PAY PHONE
Hotel Lombardy resident 1930-35 — EDNA FERBER
Hotel Lombardy resident: 1939-40 — SINCLAIR LEWIS
Hotel or Forks — GRAND
Hotels — INNS
Hotels' country cousins — INNS
Hotfoot it — HURRY
Hotheaded — SHORT TEMPERED
Hothouse — BAGNIO
Hotplate — STOVE
Hotrod — CAR
Hotspur — PERCY
Houdini role — ESCAPER
Houlihan of M*A*S*H — SWIT
Hound — BASSET
Hound sound — YAP
Hound type — BASSET
Hound's clue — SCENT
Hound's companion — HARE
Hound's strong point — SCENT
Hour of sext — NOON
Hourglass contents — SAND
Hourglass filler — SAND
Hourglass holding — SAND
Hourglass material — SAND
Hourly — HORAL
House-lizard — GECKO
House — HOME, PROTECT, VILLA
House a GI — BARRACK
House addition — ELL
House and grounds — ESTATE
House bird — WREN
House design — SALTBOX
House divided? — SPLIT LEVEL
House extensions — ELLS
House front — PENT
House leaf collector — EAVE
House member, for short — REP
House of correction — WORKHOUSE
House of Windsor princess — ANNE
House on high — AERIE
House on The Hill group — REPRESENTATIVES
House or room lead-in — TOOL
House plant — BOSTON FERN, FERN
House style — TUDOR
House yard — AREA
House, in Seville — CASA
House, of fiction — BLEAK
Houseboats — ARKS
Housebreaks — TRAINS
Housedress — WRAP
Household — MENAGE
Household appliance — DRYER, IRON
Household concern — BUDGET
Household convenience — TRAY
Household god: Fr. — LARE
Household item — CLEANER
Household man — PAPA
Household member — PET
Household need — SPREAD
Household need, usually — ASHTRAY

Household pitcher — CREAMER
Housekeeper — MATRON
Houseplants used medicinally — ARALIAS
Houses of worship — TEMPLES
Housetop — ROOF
Housetop indicator — VANE
Housetop material — ROOFING
Housewife to Rene — MENAGERE
Housewife's problem — WASH
Housewife, in Hamburg — FRAU
Housman's "A Shropshire _____" — LAD
Houston and Coleridge — SAMLS
Houston and Dillon — MATTS
Houston and Donaldson — SAMS
Houston arena — ASTRODOME
Houston athlete — ASTRO
Houston baseballer — ASTRO
Houston eleven — OILERS
Houston gridder — OILER
Houston or Shepard — SAM
Houston org. — NASA
Houston player — ASTRO, OILER
Houston pro — ASTRO, OILER
Houston team — OILERS
Houston's The Summit, e.g. — ARENA
Houston: No hits, runs or errors — ASTRO-NOUGHTS
Hovel — HUT
Hover — FLOAT
How Godiva rode! — BARELY
How goose-steppers march — STIFFLY
How herds of cattle arrive — IN DROVES
How madcaps act — RASHLY
How one trio found Goldilocks? — UNBEARABLE
How sad! — ALAS
How sashimi is eaten — RAW
How tennis player's make noise? — RAISE A RACKET
How they lived — HAPPILY EVER AFTER
How to address the queen — MAAM
How to feed kitty? — ANTE
How we stand — UNITED
How's that again? — HUH
How, in Aachen — WIE
Howard _____ in "The Fountainhead" — ROARK
Howard and Ely — RONS
Howard and Liebman — RONS
Howard Fast novel — FREEDOM ROAD
Howard of musicals — KEEL
Howard or Ely — RON
Howard or Ernie — PYLE
Howard or Guidry — RON
Howard or Kesey — KEN
Howard or Murray — KEN
Howard's family — COSELLS
Howe won here: 9 / 11 / 77 — BRANDYWINE
However, briefly — THO
However, for short — THO
Howl — ULULATE
Howler — BONER
Howler monkey — ALOUATTA
Howls, in Le Harve — CRIS
Hoyden — TOMBOY
HRE name — OTTO
HRE ruler and namesakes — OTTOS
HST or LBJ — PRES
HST successor — DDE
HST's mate — BESS
Ht. — ALT, ELEV
Huarache, e.g. — SANDAL
Huaraches — MEXICAN SANDALS
Hub — NAVE
Hub of old Athens — AGORA
Hubbell of Cooperstown — CARL
Hubbub — ADO, NOISE, TUMULTS, UPROAR
Huck, to Tom — PAL
Huckle — HIP
Huckster — ADMAN, VENDOR
Huckster's helper — SHILL
HUD relative — FHA
Huddle — GATHER
Hudson Bay Indian — CREE
Hudson contemporary — NASH, REO
Hudson or Desoto — AUTO, CAR
Hudson or Essex — CAR
Hudson River span — TAPPANZEE BRIDGE
Hudson's "_____ Moon" — HALF
Hue — TINT
Hue and cry — NOISE
Hue's partner — CRY
Hues — COLORS, DYES, TINTS
Huesca houses — CASAS
Huey and Ted's sleepless time? — LONG KNIGHT
Huey or Shelly — LONG
Huff — SNIT
Huffy — CRANKY
Hug — CLASP, EMBRACE
Huge amount — OCEAN
Huge boat — ARK
Huge crowds — DROVES
Huge hideosity — OGRE
Huge number — GOOGOPLEX
Huge SE Asian fish — CATLA
Huge star in Cygnus — DENEB
Huge supply — TONS
Huge volume — TOME
Hugger-mugger — MESS
Hugh Capet was one — ROI
Hugh Johnson's legislation: Abbr. — NIRA
Hugh Johnson's org. — NRA
Hugh O'Brian role — EARP
Hughes' _____ Goose — SPRUCE
Hugo's "_____ Miserables" — LES
Hugo's "L'_____ terrible" — ANNEE
Hugo's "Toute la _____" — LYRE
Hugs and kisses symbols — OOXX
Huguenot center — NERAC
Hula follower — HOOPS
Hulk _____ — HOGAN, SHELL
Hulk Hogans milieu — MAT
Hull — RIND
Hullabaloo — ADO, FLAP, FUROR, NOISE, RUCKUS
Hulled grain — GROATS
Hum — DRONE
Hum bug — BEE
Human — MORTAL
Human ankle — TARSUS
Human being — EARTHLING, MORTAL
Human beings — PERSONS
Human incarnation of a deity — AVATAR
Human kindness juice? — MILK
Human rights org. — ACHR
Human trunk — TORSO
Human-rights president — CARTER
Humane — KIND, MILD
Humane org. — ASPCA, SPCA, SPCC
Humanity — MERCY
Humanoid — MANLIKE
Humber feeder — AIRE
Humble — ABASE, COMMON, DEMEAN, MEEK
Humble — MODEST, PLAIN, SERVILE, SIMPLE
Humble abode — CABIN, COTTAGE, HOVEL
Humble dwelling — HOVEL
Humble home — HOVEL
Humbled — ABASED
Humbles — ABASES, DEMEANS
Humbug — BUNCOMBE, FAKER, GAMMON, SHAM
Humbug's lead-in — BAH
Humbugs — CHEATS, FLAMS

Humdinger — ACE, LULU, ONER, PIP, RIP SNORTER, WINNER
Humdrum — DREARY, DULL, HO HUM, PROSEY, VAPID
Humerus neighbor — ULNA
Humerus, for one — BONE
Humid — CLAMMY, DAMP, DANK, MUGGY
Humiliate — ABASE, SNUB
Humiliated — SHAMED
Humiliation — ABASEMENT
Humiliator — ABASER
Humility — MODESTY
Hummable pieces — TUNES
Hummeling machines — AWNERS
Humor — WIT
Humor of a sort — IRONY
Humore — INDULGE
Humorist — CLOWN, COMIC, JOKER
Humorist Arthur (Bugs) _____ — BAER
Humorist Bill — NYE
Humorist Bombeck — ERMA
Humorist Edgar Wilson — NYE
Humorist Myron — COHEN
Humorist Ogden — NASH
Humorist Sahl — MORT
Humorous — COMIC, JOCOSE
Humpback or beluga, e.g. — WHALE
Humperdinck heroine — GRETEL
Humperdinck opera — HANSEL AND GRETEL
Humperdinck role — GRETEL
Humphrey in '68 — NOMINEE
Humphrey's widow — LAUREN
Humpty Dumpty — EGG
Humpty Dumpty, after his fall — SCRAMBLED EGG
Hums — CROONS
Hun King — ATLI
Hun leader — ATLI
Hun of Norse myth — ATLI
Hunch — BEND
Hundred percent — ENTIRELY
Hundred pounds, for short — CWT
Hundred-eyed monster — ARGUS
Hundred-weights: Abbr. — CWTS
Hundred: Comb. form — HECT, HECTO
Hundreth of a peso — CENTAVO
Hungarian city — PECS
Hungarian composer — LEHAR
Hungarian conductor Rapee — ERNO
Hungarian violinist Leopold — AUER
Hungarian wine — TOKAY
Hungarian-born conductor — DORATI
Hunger — LUST
Hunger, to Henri — FAIM
Hungered — YEARNED
Hungers — YENS
Hungry — UNFED
Hungry words — LETS EAT
Hunk — SLAB
Hunk of bread — SLAB
Hunk of cheese — BLOCK, SLAB, SLICE
Hunky-dory (copacetic) — FINE, JAKE
Hunky trailer — DORY
Hunt hero — ABOU
Hunt hinds — TRACK DEER
Hunt illegally — POACH
Hunted for food — STALKED GAME
Hunter — TAB
Hunter in the skies — ORION
Hunter of lampreys — EELERS
Hunter or angler, e.g. — SPORTSMAN
Hunter or Kelly — GREEN
Hunter's helpers — SETTERS
Hunter's prey — DEER
Hunter's quarry — PREY, STAG
Hunter's souvenir — PELT
Hunter's take — BAG
Hunters — YAGERS
Hunters' gear — SHOTGUNS
Hunting — CHASE
Hunting companion — POINTER
Hunting dog — GOLDEN RETRIEVER, SETTER
Hunting knife — BOWIE
Hunting trophy — DEER HEAD
Huntley or Atkins — CHET
Huntley, of TV fame — CHET
Hunts — CHASES
Hur's highway — ITER
Hurdle — LEAP OVER
Hurdles for would-be Ph.D.'s — ORALS
Hurdles in Hollywood — SCREEN TESTS
Hurdy-_____ — GURDY
Hurdy-gurdies — ROTAS
Hurl — HEAVE, THROW, TOSS
Hurled — SLUNG, THREW
Hurler's miscue — BALK
Hurls — SLINGS
Hurly-burly — ADO, UPROAR
Hurok, et al. — SOLS
Huron's cousin — ERIE
Huron's sister — ERIE
Hurrah — CHEER
Hurricane — CYCLONE
Hurricane center — EYE
Hurried — RAN, SPED, TORE
Hurried along — SPED
Hurries — HIES
Hurry-up letters — ASAP
Hurry — HASTEN, HIE
Hurt — AIL, PAINED, SCATHE
Hurt all over — ACHE
Hurt severely — MAIM
Hurt's victim in "Body Heat" — CRENNA
Hurtful spots — SORES
Hurting — ACHY
Hurting sensation — PAIN
Hurtle — SHOOT
Hurtled — SPED
Hurts a bit — SMARTS
Husband — MATE, SAVE
Husband and wife — PARTNERS
Husband of Faulkner's Addie Bundren — ANSE
Husband of Jezebel — AHAB
Husband of Judith — ESAU
Husband of Otrera — ARES
Husband of Pocohontas — ROLFE
Husband of Semiramis — NINUS
Husband, in Paris — MARI
Husbands — MEN
Hush-hush agency — CIA
Hush — CALM, QUIET, SHH, STILL
Hushed — CALM, STILLED
Hushes up — SILENCES
Husing and Weems — TEDS
Husk — PEEL, STRIP
Husk corn — SHUCK
Husk of grain — BRAN
Huskie's burden — SLED
Huskie's vehicle — SLED
Husky group — TEAM
Husky's home ground — SIBERIA
Hussar's weapon — SABER
Hussein's queen — NOOR
Hussein's queen and others — NOORS
Hussein, for one — IRAQI
Hustlers after rustlers — POSSE
Hut at the end of town — SHANTY
Hut, in old England — BYRE
Hutch display — CHINA
Hutch items — PLATES
Hutch occupants — DOES
Hutches — PENS
Huts — SHANTIES
Huxley's "_____ Hay" — ANTIC
Huxley's "Ape and _____" — ESSENCE
Huzzah — JOY, RAH
Huzzahs' cousins — RAHS
Hwy. — RTE
Hwy. and rd. — RTES
Hwy. hydrants — FPS
Hwy. sign — RTE
Hyalescent — CLEAR
Hybrid — CROSS

Hybrid animal — MULE
Hybrid floral beauties — TEA ROSES
Hybrid, of a sort — ALLOY, MESTEE
Hybridize a shrub — INGRAFT
Hyde or Central — PARK
Hyde Park baby carriages — PRAMS
Hyde Park vehicle — PRAM
Hyde, et al.: Abbr. — PKS
Hydriys — WATERY
Hydrocarbon — HEXANE, OLEFINE, TOLAN
Hydrocarbon found in natural gas — ETHANE
Hydrocarbon type: Suffix — YLENE
Hydrocarbon: Suffix — ENE
Hydrogen, for one — GAS
Hydroplane — SKIM
Hyla — TREE TOAD
Hyla genus frog — TREE TOAD
Hyman of the theater — EARLE
Hymn — CHORALE
Hymn — PSALM
Hymn by A.M. Toplady: 1775 — ROCK OF AGES
Hymn canary — STOOLIE
Hymn of praise — TE DEUM
Hymnals relative — PSALTER
Hymnist John Mason _____ — NEALE
Hype — PUFFERY
Hyperion, for one — TITAN
Hypocorism — PET NAME
Hypocrisy — SHAM
Hypothermal — TEPID
Hypothesis — THEORY
Hyson — TEA
Hyson and gunpowder — TEAS
Hyson and oolong — TEAS
Hyson, e.g. — TEA
Hysteresis — LAGGING

I

I _____ with my own eyes — SAW IT
I adornment — DOT
I am present: Lat — ADSUM
I believe: Lat. — CREDO
I came, to Caesar — VENI
I cannot tell _____ — A LIE
I love, to Antony — AMO
I love, to Livia — AMO
I love: Lat. — AMO
I smell _____ — A RAT
I toppers — DOTS
I trouble — EGOISM
I wander, to Ovid — ERRO
I, in Bonn — ICH
I, in Essen — ICH
I, to Claudius — EGO
I-95, 66, etc. — RTES
I.C.C. concerns — RATES
I.e. — ID EST
I.Q. tester — BINET
I.R.S. collection time — APR
I.R.S. employee — ACCT
I.R.S. employees — CPAS
I.R.S. inquiries — AUDITS
I.R.S. procedure — AUDIT
I.R.S. quarry — EVADER
I.R.S. targets — EVADERS
I.W. or Walter — ABEL
Iago's aria in Verdi's "Otello" — CREDO
Iago's forte — LIES
Iago, for example — ROLE
Iambi — FEET
Ian Fleming character — DR NO
Ian's cousin, in Cardiff — EVAN
Ian's Welsh cousin — EVAN
Iberian plain phenomenon — RAIN IN SPAIN
Ibis cousin — STORK
Ibsen character — ASE
Ibsen domestic opus — A DOLLS HOUSE
Ibsen heroine — NORA
Ibsen play — THE WILD DUCK
Ibsen role — NORA
Ibsen woman — ASE
Ibsen's "_____ Gabler" — HEDDA
Ibsen's "An _____ of the People" — ENEMY
Ibsen's "Lady from the _____" — SEA
Ibsen's first name — HENRIK
Ibsen's homeland — NORWAY
Ibsen's mountain king, for example — TROLL
ICBM housing — SILO
Ice — FREEZE, CHILL
Ice box — COOLER
Ice cold — FRIGID, GELID, SHARP
Ice cream _____ — CONE
Ice cream additive — AGAR
Ice cream container — CONE
Ice cream dish — BOMBE, SODA
Ice cream portions — DIPS
Ice cream treat — CONE
Ice crystals — FROST, SNOW
Ice Cube's music — RAP
Ice cubes — ROCKS
Ice fishing instrument — JIG
Ice formation — FLOE, SERAC
Ice house — IGLU
Ice mass — FLOE
Ice masses — BERGS
Ice pendant — ICICLE
Ice pinnacle — SERAC
Ice queen Katarina — WITT
Ice queen of yesteryear — HENIE
Ice seller? — YEGG
Ice skating leap — AXEL
Ice star Phil, to friends — ESPO
Ice, in Innsbruck — EIS
Ice-cold — FROSTY
Ice-cream in Rome — GELATO
Ice-cream treat — CONE
Ice-hockey team — SIX
Ice-shaped often — CUBIC
Iceberg feature — TIP
Iceblink — GLARE
Icebreaker, e.g. — SHIP
Iced — COOLED
Iced tea, in a way — SLAKER
Icel. or Ire. — ISL
Icel. poetry — EDDA
Iceland's language — NORSE
Icelandic coin — KRONA
Icelandic epic — EDDA
Icelandic hero — EILIF
Icelandic literary work — EDDA
Icelandic lore — EDDA
Icelandic monetary unit — KRONA
Icelandic poems — EDDAS
Icelandic saga — EDDA
Icelandic volcano — HEKLA
Icelandic work — EDDA
Icelandic writings — EDDAS
Ices — CHILLS
Ich dien — I SERVE
Ichabod's "headless horsemen" — BROM
Ichneumon — FLY
Ichorus — THIN

Ichthyic — FISHY
Ici on _____ francais — PARLE
Icing on an exec.'s cake — PERK
Icky — MUSHY, SYRUPY
Icky foods — GLOP
Icon — FIGURE, IMAGE, PICTURE
Icon site — NICHE
Iconoclast — REBEL, SCORNER
Iconoclast's target — IDOL
Iconoscopes, for short — IKES
Ictus — STRESS
Ictus syllable — ARSIS
Icy — FROZEN, GELID, RIMY
Icy coating — RIME
Icy dessert — SORBET
Icy or frosty — GELID
Icy rain — SLEET
Id _____ — EST
ID card — TAG
ID item — ALIAS, LAST NAME
ID mark — SCAR
Id relative — EGO
Idaho city — POCATELLO
Idaho resort — SUN VALLEY
Idaho river — SNAKE
Idaho state flower — SYRINGA
Idaho's capital — BOISE
Idaho's Coeur d' _____ — ALENE
Idea — CONCEPT, MODEL, NOTION, TYPE
Ideal — MODEL
Ideal example — EPITOME
Ideal place — EDEN
Ideal spot — EDEN
Ideal state — UTOPIA
Idealist — DREAMER
Idealistic — UTOPIAN
Ideality — ILLUSION, MYTH
Idealize — DEIFY
Ideas — CONCEPTS
Ideate — THINK
Idee _____ — FIXE
Idee-fixe — OBSESSION
Identical — DITTO, MATCHING, SAME
Identical copy — CLONE
Identification — BADGE, CACHET, DETECTION, DOG TAG
Identification — MARK, NAMING, SCAR
Identification aids — TABS
Identification tag — STICKER
Identifies — NAMES, PEGS
Identifying design — EMBLEM
Identifying label — MARKING
Identifying mark — SCAR
Identity — DETECT, KNOW, SEE
Ideologies — ISMS
Ideology — CREED, CREDO, GOSPEL, THESIS
Ides, for example — DATE
Idi — AMIN
Idiom — JARGON, LINGO, PARLANCE, PHRASE
Idiom finish — ATIC
Idiosyncrasy — QUIRK, TRAIT, TWIST
Idiot — CLOD, FOOL, JERK, MORON, OAF
Idiotic — ASININE, FATUOUS, INANE, STUPID
Idle — DALLY, LAZE, OTIOSE
Idle chatter — BABBLE
Idle hours — LEISURE
Idle state — INACTION
Idle talk — GAB, PALAVER, RUMOR
Idled — LOAFED
Idler — SLUG
Idol — HERO
Idol time — MATINEE
Idolize — ADORE, HONOR, REVERE
Idolizer — ADMIRERER
Idols — BAALIM
Ids — EGOS
Ids' kin — EGOS
Ids' relatives — EGOS
Idyll — BUCOLIC, PASTORAL
Idyllic — PASTORAL
Idyllic spots — EDENS
If ever — ONCE
If not — ELSE, UNLESS
If red, these may mislead — HERRINGS
If there should be — IN CASE OF
Iffy — UNSURE
Iffy sufix — ISH
Ifs, ands, or _____" — BUTS
Iglesias, e.g. — SENOR
Igloo — ICEHOUSE
Igloo footwear — MUKLUK
Igloo knife — ULU
Igloos, e.g. — ICE PRODUCTS
Ignatius of Loyola's order — JESUIT
Igneous rock — NORITE
Ignis fatuus — FLAME
Ignite — BURN, KINDLE, LIGHT
Ignited — LIT
Ignited again — RESPARKED
Ignited substance — SPARK
Ignites — SPARKS
Ignition component — SPARK
Ignoble — BASE, FOUL, LOW, MEAN, PETTY
Ignominious — WICKED
Ignominious Amin — IDI
Ignominy — SHAME, SPREE
Ignoramous — DUNCE, FOOL, SIMPLE SIMON
Ignorant — ILLITERATE, UNREAD
Ignore — DISREGARD, SHUN
Ignore haughtily — SNUB
Ignore, in a way — ELIDE
Ignored? — LEFT OUT
Iguana — LIZARD
Ike — DDE
Ike and Monty bailiwick — ETO
Ike's boyhood home — ABILENE
Ike's command — ETO
Ike's milieu — ETO
Ike's onetime command — ETO
Ike's opponent — ADLAI
Ike's rival — ADLAI
Ike's W.W. II command — ETO
Ike's WW II arena — ETO
Il _____ (he loves): Fr. — AIME
Ilex — HOLLY
Iliad — EPIC
Iliad character — PARIS
Iliad hero — AJAX
Ilk — SORT, TYPE
Ilka Chase's "_____ We Cry" — IN BED
Ill-bred ones — BOORS
Ill — ACHING, AILING, HURT, INJURY, INVALID
Ill — SICK, UNWELL
Ill at ease — ANXIOUS
Ill humor — ANGER, SPLEEN
Ill will — ANIMUS, HATE, PIQUE, SPITE
Ill- _____ (acquired improperly) — GOTTEN
Ill-advised — FOOLISH, HASTY
Ill-at-ease — EDGY, UNEASY
Ill-disposed — ANTI, AVERSE
Ill-fated — DOOMED
Ill-fated lover of yore — ABELARD
Ill-fated Montague — ROMEO
Ill-fated ship — TITANIC
Ill-favored — HOMELY, PLAIN, UGLY
Ill-humored — CURT, HUFFY, SHORT, TESTY
Ill-judged — UNWISE
Ill-kempt — TATTY
Ill-mannered — RUDE
Ill-natured — CROSS, HOSTILE
Ill-smelling — AREEK, STINKY
Ill-tempered — CRABBY, DOUR, MEAN, TART
Ill-treat — HARM
Ill-wisher — FOE
Ill. coal city — PANA
Ill.'s neighbor — IND
Illawarra Shorthorn — CATTLE
Illegal — CRIMINAL
Illegal acts — CRIMES
Illegal alcohol — HOOCH
Illegal baseball pitch — SPITTER
Illegal blow — RABBIT PUNCH
Illegal offer of money — BRIBE
Illegal stratum? — CRIMINAL LAYER
Illegal voter — FLOATER
Illegality — TORT
Illinois airport — OHARE

Illinois bird? — DECATURKEY
Illinois city — POSEN
Illinois city on the Mississippi — ALTON
Illinois native — SUCKER
Illinois refresher — LEMON-ADECATUR
Illinois river — CHICAGO
Illium — TROY
Illium, to Octavian — TROY
Ills — WOES
Illucidate — CLARIFY
Illuminated — AGLOW, LIT, LIT UP
Illuminated in a way — SUNLIT
Illumination unit — CANDELA, LUX
Illumined — LIT
Illustrate — DRAW
Illustrator of "Alice in Wonderland" — TENNIEL
Illustrious — NOBLE
Illustrious warriors — HEROES
Ilmenite and uraninite — ORES
Ilsa Lund — INGRID BERGMAN
Image-makers' avenue — MADISON
Image — ICON
Image: Comb. form — EIDO
Imaginary — UNREAL
Imaginary creature — ELF
Imaginary line through earth's center — AXIS
Imaginary monster — CHIMERA
Imagination — DREAM
Imaginative — CREATIVE
Imagine — ENVISION, IDEATE, PRETEND, SUPPOSE
Imagined — DREAMED UP
Imagines — ENVISAGES
Imagist Doolittle — HILDA
Imagoes — ADULTS
Imam's deity — ALLAH
Imam's text — KORAN
Imaret, e.g. — INN
Imbibe — TOPE
Imbibed — DRANK
Imbroglio — BRAWL, PROBLEM, STRIFE
Imbue — PERVADE
Imelda with the shoes — MARCOS
Imitate — APE, EMULATE
Imitated Judas — BETRAYED
Imitated Marceau — MIMED
Imitates Polonius — PRATES
Imitates Tinkerbell — FLITS
Imitating — APING
Imitation — APERY, FAKE, SHAM
Imitation autograph? — FORGERY
Imitation gold — ORMOLU
Imitation gold leaf — ORMULU
Imitation jewelry — PASTE
Imitation: Suffix — EEN
Imitative — ECHOIC
Imitator — APER
Immaculate — CLEAN, PRISTINE, SHINY
Immaterial — AIRY
Immature — GREEN, RAW, UNRIPE
Immature insect — LARVA
Immature newt — EFT
Immature, in a way — LARVAL
Immeasureable — UNTOLD
Immediately — AT ONCE, PRONTO
Immense — GREAT, LARGE, VAST
Immense quantity — OCEAN
Immersed — DIPPED, DUNKED, SOAKED
Immie's mate — AGGIE
Immigrate — ENTER
Immigration island — ELLIS
Imminent — IN STORE
Immobile — FIXED, INERT, STILL
Immodest glances — LEERS
Immoral — BAD
Immovability — INERTIA
Immovable — ADAMANT
Immune system factor — OPSONIN
Immured — PENT
Imogene _____ — COCA
Imp. mdse. label — IRR
Impact — SHOCK
Impaired gradually — WORE
Impairs — HURTS, MAIMS
Impart — LEND
Impart bit by bit — INSTILL
Impart color to wood — STAIN
Impart knowledge — TEACH
Imparted — LENT
Impartial — EVEN, FAIR
Impartiality or law — EQUITY
Imparts — LENDS
Imparts gradually — INSTILLS
Impasse — STANDSTILL
Impassive — STOIC, STOICAL, STOLID
Impatient — EDGY
Impede — HAMPER, LET
Impede, with "down" — BOG
Impedes — HINDERS
Impediments — SNAGS
Impel — CAST, MOVE, URGE
Impel to action — URGE
Impel to win — GOAD
Impend — LOOM
Imperfect — DAMAGED, DEFECTIVE, FAULTY, FLAWED
Imperfect: Comb form — ATELO, MAL
Imperfection — BLEMISH, FLAW
Imperfections — MARS
Imperfective, as a verb — ATELIC
Imperial Valley city — CALIPATRIA
Imperils — MENACES, RISKS
Impersonated — APED
Impertinence — LIP, SASS
Impertinent — SASSY
Impertinent lass — SNIP
Impertinent one — PRESUMER, SNIP
Impertinent youngster — SNIP
Imperturbable — STOICAL
Impetuosity — ARDOR, ELAN, HASTINESS
Impetuous — BRASH, RASH
Impetuous ardor — ELAN
Impetuous guest's question — WHEN DO WE EAT
Impetuous motorist's sound — HONK HONK HONK
Impetuous ones — HOT HEADS
Impetuous person's advice — GET A MOVE ON
Impetus — IMPULSE, MOMENTUM
Impiety — SIN
Impignorate — PAWN
Impignorated — PAWNED
Impinge, in a way — OVERLAP
Impious — UNHOLY
Impious person — ATHEIST
Impish — MISCHIEVOUS
Impish youngster — SCAMP
Implacable — ADAMANT
Implant — ENGRAFT
Implant deeply — ENROOT
Implants — IMBEDS
Implead — SUE
Implement for a shell — OAR
Implement for catching a crab? — OAR
Implement for Poseidon — TRIDENT
Implements — TOOLS
Implicit — TACIT
Implied — TACIT
Implore — PLEAD, PRAY
Implored — PLED
Implores — ENTREATS
Impolite — RUDE
Import — BARTER, CONVEY, MOMENT, SENSE
Import — TENOR, TRADE
Import chaser — ANCE
Import tax — DUTY
Importance — WORTH
Important — BIG, MAJOR, WEIGHTY
Important article — THE
Important beam — LASER

Important blood vessel — AORTA
Important city in Texas — SAN ANTONIO
Important cranial nerve — VAGUS
Important document — WILL
Important historical document — BILL OF RIGHTS
Important historical document — THE CONSTITUTION
Important hosp. group — RNS
Important intersection — CROSSROADS
Important legislation initials — NRA
Important name in Chicago — DALEY
Important ore of boron — KERNITE
Important paper: Abbr. — CERT
Important papers — DEEDS
Important period — ERA
Important person — BIG CHEESE
Important points — NUBS
Important role in a motion picture — LEAD
Important Theban god — AMON
Important times — ERAS
Importune — BEG, ENTREAT, PLEAD, URGE
Importunes — DUNS
Impose — ABUSE, SET
Impose upon — DUPE
Impossible — NO HOW, NO WAY
Impost — TOLL
Imposters — PHONIES
Imposts — TAXES
Impoverished — BEGGARED, NEEDY
Impractical — UNVIABLE
Imprecation — ANATHEMA, CURSE
Impress — STAMP
Impressario — DIRECTOR, MAESTRO
Impressario Hurok — SOL
Impressed — AWED
Impressed mightily — AWED
Impresses indelibly — ENGRAVES
Impression — CAST, DENT, MOLD
Impressionist painter — MANET
Impressions — IDEAS
Impressive entries — PORTALS
Imprest — LOAN
Imprint permanently — ETCH
Imprison — EMBAR
Improper contraction — AINT
Improve — AMEND, AMELIORATE, REVISE
Improve spiritually — ELEVATE
Improved the lawn — RESODDED
Improves by editing — EMENDING
Improves the soil — LOAMS
Improvisation of African rhythm — CALYPSO
Improvise — AD LIB, WING IT
Improvised — AD HOC, AD LIB
Improvised, with up — COOKED
Impudent — BOLD, FRESH, PERT, SASSY
Impudent ones — SNOTS
Impugn — DENY
Impulse — DESIRE, IMPETUS, MOTIVE, URGE
Impulse transmitters — SENSORS
Impulsive — RASH
Imputed — LAID
Imputes — ASCRIBES
In — AT HOME, TRENDY
In _____ (bogged down) — A RUT
In _____ (completely) — TOTO
In _____ (completely) — TOTO
In _____ (entirely) — TOTO
In _____ (going nowhere) — A RUT
In _____ (having problems) — A JAM
In _____ (having trouble) — A JAM, A SPOT
In _____ (instantly) — A SNAP
In _____ (mired in monotony) — A RUT
In _____ (peevish) — A PET
In _____ (piqued) — A PET
In _____ (position) — SITU
In _____ (prosperous) — CLOVER
In _____ (quickly) — A TRICK
In _____ (socially active) — THE SWIM
In _____ (stagnating) — A RUT
In _____ (stuck) — A RUT
In _____ (stunned) — A DAZE
In _____ (to a certain extent) — A SENSE
In _____ of (instead) — LIEU
In _____ parentis — LOCO
In _____ way (ailing) — A BAD
In _____?: poker dealer's query — OR OUT
In a _____ — SNIT
In a _____ (bewildered) — FOG
In a _____ (on the spot) — BIND
In a _____ (strapped) — BIND
In a bad way — ILLY
In a believable way — COGENTLY
In a bit — SOON
In a body — EN MASSE
In a box — STUCK
In a certain manner — SOMEWAYS
In a courageous manner — MAN TO MAN
In a dangerous spot — BETWEEN WIND AND WATER
In a different manner — ELSE
In a direct line — LINEAL
In a dither — AGOG
In a dudgeon — IRATE
In a fatal way — LETHALLY
In a fit way — APTLY
In a flagrant manner — EGREGIOUSLY
In a fog — AT SEA, LOST
In a foxy manner — SLYLY
In a frenzied manner — AMOK
In a frenzy — AMOK
In a fuzzy state — BEMUSED
In a gold mine, it can be a mile down — STOPE
In a good-natured way — GENIALLY
In a grandiose manner — EXTRAVAGANTLY
In a group — EN MASSE
In a heap — PILED
In a huff — CROSS, IRATE
In a hurry — HYING
In a jiffy — SOON
In a lather? — SOAPED
In a leisurely fashion — IDLY
In a mire — STUCK
In a moment — ANON
In a mournful way — SADLY
In a natty way — SNAPPILY
In a nutshell — BRIEFLY
In a pacific way — SERENELY
In a peculiar manner — ODDLY
In a perfect world — IDEALLY
In a pet — SORE
In a pile — HEEPED
In a pique — IRED
In a plausible way — CREDIBLY
In a pleasant manner — GENIALLY
In a private session — CLOSETED
In a proper way — MEETLY
In a prudent way — SANELY
In a quandary — AT SEA
In a rage — HOPPING MAD
In a rank — AROW
In a rational way — SENSIBLY
In a risky position — ON THIN ICE
In a risqué manner — RACILY
In a rococo fashion — ORNATELY
In a seemly way — PROPERLY
In a short time — ANON
In a short while — ANON

In a shrewd manner — CANNILY
In a silent way — MUTELY
In a sincere manner — TRULY
In a slower style — POKIER
In a sluggish way — LAZILY
In a smooth manner — SLEEKLY
In a sneaky way — COVERTLY
In a snit — IRED
In a sparse manner — THINLY
In a spin — AREEL
In a standing position — UPRIGHT
In a state of parvitude — SMALL
In a state of ruin — ON THE ROCKS
In a stubborn way — CONTRARILY
In a stupid way — DOLTISHLY
In a stupor — DAZED
In a superb manner — NOBLE
In a swivet — IRATE
In a tangle, with "of" — AFOUL
In a tick — SECOND
In a tie — EVEN
In a tizzy — HOT AND BOTHERED
In a trice, old style — ANON
In a vertical position: Naut. — APEAK
In a weird way — EERILY
In a while — SOON
In a whisper — SOTTO VOCE
In a wicked manner — EVILLY
In a wise manner — SAGELY
In a wretched manner — SORDIDLY
In action — ON THE FIRING LINE
In addition — ALSO, TOO
In adequate measure — AMPLY
In advance — AHEAD
In after-work-out condition — SWEATY
In agreement — UNITED
In an aloof way — ICILY
In an elegant manner — DAINTILY
In an icy manner — GELIDLY
In an impassive way — STOLIDLY
In an inexpensive way — CHEAPLY
In an untenable position — TREED
In any case — AT LEAST, LEAST
In any event — ANYHOW
In any way — AT ALL, EVER
In arrears — OWING, SHORT
In back — AREAR
In baroque style — ORNATELY
In better condition — HALER
In better health — HALER
In business — OPEN
In cars it's subject to change — OIL
In case — LEST
In Christ's name: L. abbr. — INC
In common — ALIKE
In concert — AS ONE
In conclusion — LASTLY
In conflict — AT ODDS, AT CROSS PURPOSES
In conformity with — ALONG
In control — ON TOP OF, VESTED
In current condition — AS IS
In debt — OWING
In debt to — OWING
In difficulty — ON THE ROCKS, OUT ON A LIMB
In disarray — MESSY
In dreamland — ABED
In due time — ANON
In error — WRONG
In every case — UNEXCEP-TIONALLY
In excess — SPARE
In excess of — ABOVE
In existence — ALIVE, REAL
In existence now — CURRENT, CONTEMPORARY, EXISTING
In existence now — PRESENT, PRESENT DAY
In fact — ACTUALLY
In favor — FOR
In favor of — FOR, PRO
In fine fashion — SPLENDIDLY
In fine fettle — HALE
In flames — AFIRE
In flight — AWING
In for _____ awakening — A RUDE
In for the night — ABED
In front — AHEAD
In front of — AHEAD
In full measure — AMPLY
In general — OVER ALL
In general circulation — ABROAD
In good health — FIT, HALE
In good shape — FIT, TRIM
In good spirits — JOLLY
In good supply — AMPLE
In good time — ANON
In great shape — HALE
In Greek odist's style — PINDARIC
In Hades — BELOW
In harmony — ATONE
In harness — AT WORK
In high dudgeon — ENRAGED, IRATE, MAD
In holiday spirits — GALA
In honor of — AFTER
In hot pursuit — CLOSE ON THE HEELS
In irons — BOUND
In its original condition — RAW
In its present condition — AS IS
In its present state — AS IS
In itself — PER SE
In lieu — INSTEAD
In lieu of — STEAD
In line — AROW
In Los Angeles, The Forum — ARENA
In love — HOOKED
In medias _____ — RES
In misty style — DREAMILY
In name only — TITULAR
In need of medication — ILL
In need of nursing — ILL
In no time — SOON
In Norway, 100 ore — KRONE
In olden days — OF YORE
In on — HIP
In one's right mind — SANE
In opposition to — ATHWART
In or out follower — SIDER
In order — TIDY
In pain — ACHING, HURT
In past times — AGO
In person — BODILY, LIVE
In place — SET
In place of — FOR
In plain view — OVERT
In play, as a ball — LIVE
In progress — AFOOT
In proper manner — MEETLY
In proportion — PRO RATA
In proximity — NEAR TO
In re — AS FOR, AS TO
In recent days — NEWLY
In reference — AS TO
In regard to — ANENT
In reserve — ASIDE, ON ICE, SAVED
In rhythm — METRICAL
In Roma, one — UNO
In round numbers — AVERAGE
In search of — AFTER
In shipshape fashion — TRIMLY
In short supply — RARE, SCARCE
In solitary — ALONE
In solitude — ALONE
In Spain its "mainly on the plain" — RAIN
In Spain, it's "Miercoles" — WEDNESDAY
In spite of — OVER
In stitches — CLAD
In style — CHIC, NEW
In style a la sweaters — TUR-TLE NECKED
In suitable fashion — APTLY
In that case — THEN
In that place — THEREIN
In the _____: healthy — PINK
In the act of — DOING
In the arms of Morpheus — A DREAM
In the attic, e.g. — STOWED

In the bag — CINCH, WON
In the beginning — AT FIRST
In the buff — BARE, NAKED
In the capacity of — QUA
In the cards — FATED
In the cellar — LAST
In the center — AMID
In the center of — AMID, AMIDST
In the chips — SOLVENT
In the company of — WITH
In the distance — AFAR, REMOTE
In the doldrums — MOPEY
In the dumps — MOROSE, SAD, SUNK
In the end — FINALLY
In the event — AS IF
In the flesh — LIVE
In the future — LATER
In the know — AWARE, HEP, UP ON
In the land of Nod — ASLEEP
In the last month — ULTIMO
In the lead — AHEAD
In the manner of — A LA
In the manner of a Dutch uncle — SEVERELY
In the middle — AMONG
In the midst — AMONG
In the midst of — AMONGST
In the money — FLUSH, LOADED
In the offing — NEAR
In the open — OVERT
In the past — AGO, ONCE
In the plus column — ASSET
In the same league as ERA — RBI
In the slightest degree — AT ALL
In the spotlight — ON STAGE
In the stars — FATED
In the style of — A LA
In the thick of — AMID
In the vicinity — CLOSE, NEARBY, NIGH
In the wild blue yonder — ALOFT
In the wink of an eye — INSTANTLY
In the works — AFOOT
In the wrong — ERRING
In the wrong role — MISCAST
In the year of: Lat. — ANNO
In the: It. — NEI
In things — TRENDY
In time — ANON
In top shape — FIT
In toto — ALL, UTTERLY
In two — APART
In two parts — DUAL
In uniform — SUITED
In unison — AS ONE
In want — NEEDY
In what place — WHERE
In what way — HOW
In which the scene is set — ACT I
In wonder — AWED
In-box item — MEMO
Inability to remember — AMNESIA
Inaccurate — FAULTY
Inactive — ASLEEP, IDLE, LEAN
Inadequately financed — UNDERFUNDED
Inadmissible evidence — HEARSAY
Inane — FOOLISH, SILLY
Inanimate — DEAD
Inanimate land tract? — LIFE-LESS BARREN
Inanimate objects — THINGS
Inappropriate — UNAPT
Inapt — ALIEN, DULL, OAFISH
Inasmuch as — SINCE
Inaudible — QUIET
Inaugural ball, e.g. — GALA
Inaugural promises — OATHS
Inaugurate — OPEN, START, BEGIN
Inauthentic — SPURIOUS
Inborn — NATIVE
Inc. — LTD
Inc. in London — LTD
Inc. in the U.K. — LTD
Inca country — PERU
Inca empire — PERU
Inca territory — PERU
Incandescence — GLOW
Incandescent — BULB
Incantation — SPELL
Incapacitates — LAMES
Incarcerate — IMPRISON, JAIL
Incarnadine — RED
Incarnate deity — AVATAR
Incarnation — AVATAR
Incarnation of Vishnu — AVATAR
Incautious — RASH
Incavate — HOLLOW
Incendiary jell — NAPALM
Incense — ANGER, ENRAGE, GALL, INFLAME, PROVOKE
Incense emanation — ODOR
Incense sources? — SANDAL-WOOD TREES
Incensed — IRATE
Incensement — IRE
Incenses — ODORS
Incentive for Seattle Slew? — FODDER IMAGE
Incentives of a sort — SPUR
Inception — START
Inch along — CRAWL
Inch or foot — UNIT
Inched along — CREPT
Incident — EVENT
Incidental — BYE
Incidental excursion — SIDE TRIP
Incipient grads — SRS
Incipient oak — ACORN
Incipient turmoil — UNREST
Incise — CUT, ENGRAVE
Incise for printing — ENGRAVE
Incision — SLIT
Incisor's neighbor — CANINE
Incite — ABET, EGG ON, GOAD, SPARK, ROUSE
Incite to action — SET ON
Incite to attack — SIC
Incite, with "on" — EGG
Incited a criminal — ABETTED
Incited to action — GOOSED
Incites — ABETS, AROUSES
Inclination — BENT, SLOPE, TREND
Incline — GRADE, RAMP, READY, SLOPE, TEND, TILT, TIP
Incline — TREND
Inclined — ATILT, SLANTED, SLOPED, LEANED, LEANT
Inclined passage — RAMP
Inclined plane — RAMP
Inclined to knock on wood — SUPERSTITIOUS
Inclined walk — RAMP
Inclined, as a ship — ALIST
Inclined, at sea — ALIST
Inclines — LEANS, TENDS
Inclining — ATILT
Inclose — ENCASE
Including — AND
Including everything — ENTIRE
Inclusive expression — ET AL
Inclusive list ending — ET AL
Income — PAY, SALARY, WAGE
Income extras — TIPS
Income for Julio — RENTA
Income for TV — ADS
Income property — RENTAL
Income source — JOB
Income's opposite — OUTGO
Income, in France — RENTE
Incommunicado — LONELY
Incomparable person — ONER
Incompetent — UNABLE
Incomplete — SKETCHY
Inconclusive: Abbr. — ET AL
Incongruity — ANOMALY, IRONY
Inconsistent — PATCHY
Inconspicuous — LOW PRO-FILE, MODEST
Inconspicuous position — BACKGROUND
Incontestable — POSITIVE
Incontrovertible — CERTAIN
Incorporated gradually — PHASED IN
Incorporated: Abbr. — INC
Increase — ADD, BOOM, GAIN, GROW, HIKE, INFLATE, RAISE
Increase — SPREAD, STEP UP

Increase in intensity — STEP UP
Increased — HIKED
Increased by 10 — TENFOLD
Increased faster — OUTGREW
Increased in size — DILATED
Increased the amount — ADDED
Increased threefold — TREBLED
Increases — ADDS TO
Increases — ADDS, RISES
Increases threefold — TREBLES
Increasingly brilliant, then fading, star — NOVA
Incriminating Eden garbage — CORE
Incrustations of bronze — PATINA
Incubator sounds — CHEEPS
Incursion — ASSAULT, RAID
Ind. bigwig — RAJAH
Ind. city — AGRA
Ind. hoopsters — PACERS
Ind. queens — RANIS
Indecent — RANK, SMUTTY
Indecent planter? — DIRTY FARMER
Indeed — TRULY, YEA
Indefinite amount — SOME
Indefinite place — ANYWHERE
Indefinite time — EONS
Indefinitely long period — AEON
Indefinitely: L. — SINE DIE
Indehiscent fruits — AKENES
Indemnify — REPAY
Indentation — DINT
Independence — AUTONOMY
Independence Day — FOURTH OF JULY
Independent — STANDING ON ONES OWN FEET
Independent org.: 1935-55 — CIO
Independently — APART
Indestructable unit — MONAD
Indeterminate — IFFY
Index — GUIDE
India _____ — INK
India dress fabric — MADRAS
India mail — DAK
India, for one — INK
Indian actor — SABU
Indian antelope — SASIN
Indian attendants — SYCES
Indian badge of victory — SCALP
Indian cattle — GIRS
Indian cedars — DEODARS
Indian chief — RAJAH
Indian cigar tree — CATALPA
Indian city — AGRA, CALCUTTA, RAMPUR
Indian coin — RUPEE
Indian comforter — NAVAJO BLANKET
Indian corn — MAIZE
Indian craft — CANOE
Indian deer — AXIS
Indian dress — SARI
Indian film: 1950 — BROKEN ARROW
Indian film: 1956 — THE SEARCHERS
Indian film: 1957 — NAKED IN THE SUN
Indian film: 1969 — TELL THEM WILLIE BOY IS HERE
Indian film: 1970 — SOLDIER BLUE
Indian film: 1975 — I WILL FIGHT NO MORE FO REVER
Indian foot soldier — PEON
Indian for whom a sea was named — CARIB
Indian from Illinois — FOX
Indian from tribe in Oklahoma — CHEROKEE
Indian fuel-company ad — BLACK COAL OF CALCUTTA
Indian islands in the Bay of Bengal — ANDAMAN
Indian language — FARSI, TAMIL
Indian lute — SITAR
Indian matting — TAT
Indian melodies — RAGAS
Indian military man — GURKHA
Indian moccasin — PAC
Indian money — RUPEE
Indian musical composition — RAGA
Indian name for Mount Rainier — TACOMA
Indian native — HINDU, TAMIL
Indian noble — SIRDAR
Indian Ocean gulf — ADEN
Indian Ocean island — NIAS
Indian Ocean vessel — DHOW
Indian of Colorado — LIOWA
Indian of N.M. — SIA
Indian of the N. Mississippi valley — DAKOTA
Indian official — DEWAN
Indian or Arctic — OCEAN
Indian or orange — OSAGE
Indian otter — NAIR
Indian peasant — RYOT
Indian plays? — MADRAS DRAMAS
Indian potentate — RAJA
Indian prince — RAJA, RAJAH, RANA
Indian princess — RANEE, RANI
Indian princess wear — SAREE
Indian queen — RANEE, RANI
Indian religious sect — PARSI, SIKH
Indian rice — BORO
Indian river landings — GHATS
Indian royal personage — RANI
Indian ruler — RAJAH
Indian shawl — PATTU
Indian sheep — SHA
Indian shoe, for short — MOC
Indian song from "Jam Session" — CHEROKEE
Indian state — ASSAM
Indian statesman — NEHRU
Indian symbol — TOTEM
Indian tent — TEPEE
Indian title — RANA, RANI
Indian title of respect: Var. — SHRI
Indian tobacco mixture — KINNIKINNICK
Indian token of victory — SCALP
Indian tourist stop — AGRA
Indian tribe — OTOES
Indian turban — PUGGAREE
Indian water vessels — LOTAS
Indian weight — SER, TOLA
Indian wild dog — DHOLE
Indian Zoroastrians — PARSEES
Indian's protector — TOTEM
Indian, e.g. — OCEAN
Indian, for one — OCEAN
Indian-born screen star — SABU
Indiana city — GARY
Indiana college — PURDUE
Indiana flag highlight — TORCH OF KNOWLEDGE
Indiana flower — PEONY
Indiana Indian — MIAMI
Indiana native — HOOSIER
Indiana port — GARY
Indiana river — WABASH
Indianapolis gridder — COLT
Indians — ERIES, UTES
Indians of Northern U.S. — OTTAWAS
Indians of the Dakotas — ARIKARA
Indians of the Southwest — HOPIS
Indic language — PALI, URDU
Indicate — DENOTE, EVINCE
Indicate faltering speech — ELLIPSIS
Indicates — DENOTES
Indications — SIGNS
Indicative and comparative — MOODS
Indicator — GAUGE, OMEN
Indicators — TRENDS
Indict — TAX
Indies export — RUM
Indifference — APATHY
Indifferent — SOSO
Indifferent about — COOL TO
Indigenous — ENDEMIC, NATIVE
Indigenous animals — FAUNA
Indigent — NEEDY, POOR

Indigestion — STOMACH ACHE
Indignation — ANGER
Indigo — ANIL
Indigo dye — ANIL
Indigo plant — ANIL
Indira Gandhi's father — NEHRU
Indira's father — JAWAHARLAL NEHRU
Indirect light — SKY SHINE
Indirectly — THIRD HAND
Indiscretion — LAPSE
Indisposition — AILMENT
Indistinct — FAINT, PALE
Individual — ENTITY, MAN, ONE, PERSON, SELF
Individual performers — SOLI
Individual substance — MONAD
Individual: Comb. form — IDIO
Individualist — ONER
Individualist of sorts — LONER
Individualize — CLASSIFY
Individuals — ONES, PERSONS, SOULS
Individuals: Abbr. — PERS
Indivisible units — MONADS
Indo-Aryan language — HINDI
Indo-Chinese — LAO, TAI
Indo-Chinese country — LAOS
Indo-Chinese group — SHAN
Indo-European — ARYAN
Indoctrinate — ORIENT, TEACH
Indolent — LAZY, OTIOSE
Indonesian beast — ANOA
Indonesian boat — PROA
Indonesian city — JAKARTA
Indonesian coin — RUPIAH
Indonesian craft — PROA
Indonesian fabric — BATIK
Indonesian island — ALOR, BALI, NIAS, TIMOR
Indonesian island group — ARU
Indonesian isle — BALI
Indonesian law — ABAT
Indoor — INSIDE
Indoor pest — ROACH
Induce — CAUSE
Induce by bribery — SUBORN
Induce yawns — BORE
Induces to perjury — SUBORNS
Induct — SWEAR IN
Inductance unit — HENRY
Indulge — HUMOR, SPOIL
Indulge in a sport — FENCE
Indulge in cabotinage — EMOTE
Indulged overmuch — DOTED
Indulgence in cabotinage — EMOTE
Indulgent — SOFT
Indulges in idol talk — VAPORS
Indurate — HARDEN, STARCH
Industrial activities, at times — ACCELERATION
Industrial city in Japan — NAGOYA
Industrial Cyrus — EATON
Industrial Revolution inventions — MACHINES
Industrialist Cyrus — EATON
Industrious — BUSY, OPEROSE
Industrious insects — ANTS
Industry — TRADE
Indy 500 — RACE
Indy 500 car — RACER
Indy 500 round — LAP
Indy 500 vehicle — RACER
Indy 500 winner: 1986 — RAHAL
Indy 500, e.g. — RACE
Indy cars lack these — FENDERS
Indy entrant — RACER
Indy event — RACE
Inebriated vege-taters? — SMASHED POTATOES
Inedible flower? — FORGET ME NOT
Ineffectual — USELESS
Ineffectual person — MILK-TOAST
Inept — UNGRACEFUL
Inept athletes — PALOOKAS
Inert — PASSIVE
Inert gas — NEON
Inert gaseous element — NEON
Inexorable — STERN
Inexpensive smoke — STOGIE
Inexperienced — GREEN, RAW
Infallible forecasters — ORACLES
Infamies — ODIUMS
Infamous alliance — AXIS
Infamous Amin — IDI
Infamous fiddler's namesakes — NEROS
Infamous Idi — AMIN
Infamous Marquis — SADE
Infamous wife of Ahab — JEZEBEL
Infant — BABY
Infant ferry? — STORK
Infant food — PAP
Infant's garment — BOOTEE
Infant's recreation area — PLAYPEN
Infant's slip buttoned at the shoulder — GERTRUDE
Infant's toe — PIGGY
Infant, terrible — BRAT
Infantry — SOLDIERS
Infantry gps. — BNS
Infatuate — BESOT
Infatuation — CRUSH
Infect — AFFECT
Infection — VIRUS
Infection type — VIRAL
Infecund — STERILE
Infer — EDUCE, GUESS
Inferential — EDUCTIVE, TACIT
Inferior — BAD, LESS, LESSER
Inferior imitator — EPIGONE
Inferior in quality — WORSE
Infernal — HELLISH
Infest — OVERRUN
Infidel — ATHEIST
Infield cover — GRASS
Infields — DIAMONDS
Infiltration — SEEPAGE
Infiltrator — SPY
Infinite time — EONS
Infinitesimal amount — IOTA
Infirm — WEAK
Infirm with age — DECREPIT
Inflammation of tonsils — QUINSY
Inflammation: Suffix — ITIS
Inflatable beach mattress — LILO
Inflatable life jacket — MAE WEST
Inflatable toy — BALLOON
Inflections — TONES
Inflexible — ADAMANT, FIRM, IRON, RIGID, TENSE
Inflict — WREAK
Inflicted, of yore — SMIT
Inflorescence — CYME, RACEME
Influence — BIAS, CLOUT, HEFT, HOLD, LEVERAGE
Influence — SWAY, WREAK
Influence deeply — IMPRESS
Influence illegally — BRIBE
Influence, in a way — MOLD
Influence, informally — PULL
Influenced — LED
Influenza's cousin — GRIPPE
Inform — ADVISE, EDUCATE, SNITCH, TELL
Inform — NOTIFY
Informal — CASUAL
Informal conversation — CHAT
Informal dance — HOP
Informal footwear — LOAFER
Informal garb — SLACKS
Informal gathering — FEST
Informal get-togethers — BULL SESSIONS
Informal invitation — COME AS YOU ARE
Informal talk — CHAT
Informality — EASE
Informant — REVEALER
Information — DATA
Information agency — USIA
Information of a kind — NEWSLETTERS
Information source — VOICE
Information, with "the" — DOPE
Informative — NEWSY

Informed — ABREAST, ADVISED, AWARE, UP ON
Informed about — UP ON
Informer — TELLTALE
Informer of a sort — TATTLE-TALE
Informer, informally — STOOLIE
Informs — TELLS
Infrequency — RARENESS
Infrequent — RARE
Infrequently — SELDOM
Infringement of rights — TORT
Infuriate — ENRAGE, INCENSE, MADDEN
Infuriated — ENRAGED, IRATE
Infuriates — ANGERS, IRES
Infuse — IMBUE, SOAK, STEEP
Infuse with an antiseptic — IODATE
Infuse with oxygen — AERATE
Inge play — PICNIC
Inge's "_____ Roses" — A LOSS OF
Ingenious — ARTLESS, CANNY, CLEVER, NAIVE
Ingenious Whitney — ELI
Ingenue — GIRL
Ingested — ATE
Ingot — BAR
Ingratiate — COAX, ENDEAR, FLATTER
Ingredient — FACTOR, PIECE
Ingredient in beer — MALT
Ingredient of a barman's cubes — WATER
Ingredient of a southern pie — SWEET POTATO
Ingredients for succotash — LIMAS
Ingredients of gimlets — LIMES
Ingress — ENTRANCE, ENTRY
Ingrid's daughter — PIA
Ingrid's role in "Casablanca" — ILSA
Inhabit — DWELL, LIVE, LODGE, PEOPLE
Inhabitant of Latvia — LETT
Inhabitant of: Suffix — ITE
Inhabitant: Suffix — OTE
Inhabitants: Suff. — ESE, ITES
Inhale sharply — GASP
Inheritance — LEGACY
Inheritance of the meek — EARTH
Inherited — GENETIC
Inheritor — HEIR
Inhibit — DETER, STUNT
Iniquities — EVILS
Iniquitous — EVIL
Iniquity units — DENS
Inisfail — EIRE
Inishmore's Island group — ARAN
Initial — ORIGINAL
Initial alphabet sequence — ABCD
Initial lap of an automobile race — PACE
Initial letters — ABCD
Initial quartet — ABCD
Initial scripts — DRAFTS
Initials — LETTERS
Initials advising a reader — PTO
Initials at Tempe — ASU
Initials for a monarch — HSM
Initials for the Intrepid — USS
Initials in the 30's — NRA
Initials of "Blue Eagle" — NRA
Initials of 1933 — NRA
Initials of a "Cats" collaborator — TSE
Initials of ancient Rome — SPQR
Initials of author of "Travels With a Donkey" — RLS
Initials of the 1960's — SDS
Initials of the 30's — CCC
Initials on a navy vessel — USS
Initials on a rap sheet — AKA
Initiate — TIRO
Initiated — BEGAN, BEGUN
Initiative — PEP
Inits. for Judith Anderson, e.g. — DBE
Inits. on an invitation — RSVP
Injection — SHOT
Injunction — ORDER
Injure — DAMAGE, JAR, HARM, HURT, WOUND
Injure severely — MAIM
Injured a joint — SPRAINED
Injures — HARMS, HURTS
Injury — DAMAGE, SPRAIN
Ink — FLUID, SIGN, WRITE
Ink soaked cushion for rubber stamp — PAD
Ink spots — BLOTS
Ink, in Berlin — TINTE
Ink, to Sartre — ENCRE
Inked — SIGNED
Inkling — IDEA
Inks — SIGNS
Inky — BLACK
Inky, poetically — EBON
Inlaid work — MOSAIC
Inland sea — ARAL
Inland sea of Asia — ARAL
Inlet — ARM OF THE SEA, BAY, BAYOU, COVE
Inlet — ESTUARY, RIA, STRAIT
Inlet, to Cortez — ESTERO
Inn's descendant — MOTEL
Inn, in Istanbul — SERAI
Innate — BORN, INHERENT
Inner circle — CLIQUE
Inner city sight — SLUM
Inner contentment — PEACE
Inner courtyards — ATRIA
Inner drive — URGE
Inner Hebrides island — IONA
Inner tubes — BRONCHI
Inner workings — DYNAMICS
Inner: Comb. form — ENT, ENTO
Innermost orbiter — PLANET HYDRARGYRUM
Inning ender — OUT
Inning sextet — OUTS
Innisfail — EIRE, ERIN
Innisfree, for one — ISLE
Innkeeper — HOSTELER
Innocent — NAIF
Innocent one — LAMB
Innocents — BABES
Innsbruck is here — TIROL
Innsbruck site — TIROL
Innsbruck's locale — TYROL
Innuendo — HINT
Inorganic — MINERAL
Inquire — ASK, SEEK
Inquired — ASKED
Inquires — SEARCHES
Inquiries — PROBES
Inquiring expressions — EHS
Inquisitive — ASKING
Inquisitive Carlin? (Rey) — CURIOUS GEORGE
Inquisitive interjections — EHS
Inquisitive lady of myth — PANDORA
Inquisitive one — ASKER
Inroads — RAIDS
Ins and outs of tennis — ADS
Insatiable — AVID
Inscribed pillars — STELAE
Inscribed stone pillar — STELA
Inscribed stone slab — STELA
Inscription in memoriam — EPITAPH
Inscriptions of a sort — EPITAPHS
Insect — ANT, ELATER, FLEA, LOUSE
Insect egg — NIT
Insect genus — CICADA, MANTIS
Insect larva — GRUB
Insect sci. — ENTOM
Insect stage — IMAGO, LARVA, PUPA
Insect stage — PUPA
Insect stages — PUPAE
Insect that bugged Alice — GNAT
Insect trap — WEB
Insect, such as the botfly — NITTER
Insect-eating bird — FLY-CATCHER
Insecticide — ALLETHRIN, DDT, PARIS GREEN
Insecticide for short — OMPA
Insecticide in disrepute — DDT
Insecticides — DDTS
Insectivore of Madagascar — TENREC

Insects' tongues — GLOSSAE
Insects' wings — ALAE
Insecure — RISKY
Insel, to a Frenchman — ILE
Insensible — BLIND, OBTUSE
Insensitive — BLUNT, COOL, OBTUSE
Insensitive one — BOOR
Insensitivity, of a kind — TIN EAR
Insert — ENTER, PLACE
Insert another round — RELOAD
Insert cartridges again — RELOAD
Insert for growth — GRAFT
Insert mark — CARET
Insert sign — CARET
Insert the plug — ACTIVATE
Insertion — INSET
Insertion in a mortise — TENON
Insertion mark — CARET
Inside — ENCLOSED
Inside dope — SCOOP
Inside: Comb. form — ENTO
Inside: Prefix — INTRA
Insider's song? — ONE ALONE
Insides of boundaries — AREAS
Insidious cunning — GUILE
Insignia of Rome — SPQR
Insignificant — PETTY, PUNY, TRIVIAL
Insignificant bit — SOU
Insincere — WILY
Insincere show of sorrow — CROCODILE EL ACRIMAE
Insincere talk — BUNK
Insinuating — SNIDE
Insinuation — HINT, OVER-TONE
Insipid — BLAND, INANE, BORING, FLAT, JEJUNE
Insipid — STALE, TAME
Insist upon — DEMAND
Insisted — PRESSED
Insolent — SASSY
Insouciant — CAREFREE
Inspiration — IDEA
Inspiration for "Cats" — ELIOT
Inspiration for Blake — TIGER
Inspiration for W.C. Bryant — GENTIAN
Inspire — ANIMATE
Inspire with passion — INFATUATE
Inspired — AWED, CREATIVE
Inspired affection — ENDEARED
Inspired reverence — AWE
Inspired with love — SMITTEN
Inspires — BREATHES
Inspires reverence in — AWES
Inspires wonder — AWES
Inspiring intense fear — GRISLY
Inspiring profound respect — AWING
Inspirit — ELATE, RAISE
Inst. at Annapolis — ACAD
Inst. at Dallas — SMU
Inst. at Lexington, Va. — VMI
Inst. at Nashville — TSU
Inst. attended by Abdul-Jabbar — UCLA
Inst. near Harvard — MIT
Inst. on the Hudson — USMA
Install — SEAT
Install again — RESEAT
Installed — INDUCTED
Installs a room top — CEILS
Instance — CASE
Instance of ostentatious display — SPLASH
Instances — TIMES
Instances of tautology — REDUNDANCIES
Instant — FLASH, JIFFY, SUDDEN, TRICE, WINK
Instantly — AT ONCE
Instants — MOMENTS
Instead — ELSE
Instigators — STARTERS, URGERS
Instiller of confidence — ASSURER
Institute in Brooklyn — PRATT
Institutionalized one — INMATE
Instruct — ADVISE, EDUCATE, TUTOR
Instruct again — RETEACH
Instruct differently — RETEACH
Instruct the waiter — ORDER
Instructed — TAUGHT
Instructions — LESSONS
Instructions component — STEP
Instructions to broker — SELL
Instructor — TUTOR
Instructs — TEACHES
Instrument category — REED
Instrument for Casals — CELLO
Instrument for Dame Hess — PIANO
Instrument for Erato — LYRE
Instrument of yore — LUTE
Instrument to blow — HORN
Instrument to measure current — AMMETER
Instrument to weigh gases — AEROMETER
Instrument used for drawing ellipses — TRAMMEL
Instrument: Comb. form — LABE
Instrumental composition — RONDO
Instrumental silencer — MUTE
Instrumentalist's concern — TONE
Instruments — TOOLS
Insulate — PROTECT
Insulates — DEADENS
Insult — AFFRONT
Insult — SLUR, SMEAR
Insulting blow — SLAP
Insulting remark — SLUR
Insults — SLAPS, SLURS
Insurance abbr. — ILO
Insurance transaction — CLAIM
Insurgent — REBEL
Insurrection — REVOLT, RISING
Int. acct — IRA
Intact — WHOLE
Integer — DIGIT, ENTITY
Integral — WHOLE
Integrate — MESH
Integument — ARIL, SKIN
Integuments — ARILS
Intellect — MIND, PSYCHE, WIT
Intellectual's retreat — IVORY TOWER
Intelligence — HORSE SENSE
Intelligent — SMART
Intelligentsia — BRAINS
Intemperance — EXCESS
Intend — GET AT, PLAN
Intended — AIMED, IMPLIED, MEANT
Intense — ACUTE, DEEP, POTENT
Intense beam — LASER
Intense desires — YENS
Intense dislike — ODIUM
Intense emotion — ECSTASY
Intense fears — TERRORS
Intense feeling — PASSION
Intense look — STARE
Intense yearnings — ACHES
Intensified exclamation — OOH
Intention — AIM, END, GOAL, MARK, OBJECTIVE
Intention — PLAN, PURPOSE
Intentional — DESIGNED
Intentionally apart — ALOOF
Intentions — MEANINGS
Inter — ENTOMB
Inter _____ — ALIA
Inter _____: among other things — ALIA
Inter follower — ALIA
Intercept — CATCH
Interchange — EXCHANGE
Interchanges of a kind — LOANS
Intercom — SQUAWKBOX
Interconnect — MESH
Interdict — BAN, DEBAR
Interest — USANCE
Interest groups — BLOCS
Interest on a mortgage — LIEN
Interface — TWINE
Interfere with — IMPEDE

Interfere, with "with" — TAMPER
Interfered — TAMPERED
Interior — CORE, INSIDE, MIDST, PITH
Interior designers' expertise — DECOR
Interior designers' forte — DECOR
Interior: Prefix — ENTO
Interjection — AHEM
Interjections — OHS
Interjections expressing delight — AHS
Interjections of disgust — FIES
Interlace — WEAVE
Interlaced — WOVEN
Interlaken's river — AARE
Interlock — MESH
Interlocks — KNITS
Intermediary — AGENT
Intermediate, in law — MESNE
Interminable — ENDLESS
Intermittent — STOP AND GO
Intermittently — OFF AND ON
Internal revenue agent — TAXMAN
Internal: Prefix — ENTO
International acronym — SALT
International agreements — ENTENTES
International easing of tensions — DETENTE
International org. — UNESCO
International service club members — GYROS
International understanding — ENTENTE
International writer's group — PEN
Interoceanic passage site — PANAMA
Interpret — DEFINE, EXPLAIN, READ
Interpreted — TRANSLATED
Interrogated — ASKED
Interrogated sharply — CROSS QUESTIONED
Interrogative utterances — EHS
Intersect — CONNECT, CROSS, CROSSCUT, CRISSCROSS, MEET
Intersection maneuver — U TURN
Interstice — AREOLA, CELL, GAP
Interstices — SPACES
Intertwine — LACE
Intertwined: Var. — INLACED
Interval — RECESS
Intervale — GLEN
Intervals — RESTS
Intervening, in law — MESNE
Interview — QUESTION
Interviewee's pause — ERS
Interviewer on "60 Minutes" — SAFER
Interweave — RADDLE
Interweaves — BRAIDS
Intestinal obstruction — ILEUS
Intestinal: Comb. form — ENTERO
Intimate — FRIEND, PAL
Intimate gatherings — COTERIES
Intimidate — AWE, COW, DAUNT, OVERAWE, SCARE
Intl. alliance — NATO
Into — INSIDE
Intolerant one — BIGOT
Intoned — CHANTED, SUNG
Intoxicating — HARD, HEADY
Intoxicating liq. — ALC
Intoxication — JOY
Intramolecular — INNER
Intransitive verb — NEUTER
Intrepid — HEROIC
Intrepidity — VALOR
Intricacies — INS AND OUTS
Intricate — ELABORATE
Intrigue — CABAL
Intrinsically — PER SE
Introduce — PRESENT
Introduces — INSERTS
Introduces oxygen — AERATES
Introduction — LEAD IN
Introductory to a book — PREFACE
Introverted — RETICENT
Intrude on — INTERVENE, TRESPASS
Intruded — HORNED IN
Intuit — FEEL, GRASP, KNOW, SENSE
Intuition — INSIGHT, SENSE, SIXTH SENSE
Intuitive — WISE
Intuitive good judgement — HORSE SENSE
Inuit — ESKIMO
Inuit's home — IGLOO
Inuit: Abbr. — ESK
Inundate — BURY, COVER, DROWN, ENGULF, FLOOD
Inundated — FLOODED
Inundation — DELUGE
Inure — HARDEN
Invade — ENTER
Invalid — NULL
Invalidated — NULLED
Invalidates — ANNULS
Invasion — ATTACK
Invasion beach of WW II — OMAHA
Invective — TIRADE
Inveighed — RAILED
Inveigle — LURE, TEMPT
Invent — COIN, CONCOCT, DESIGN, MAKE UP, ORIGINATE
Invent extender — ORIAL
Invent, as a phrase — COIN
Invented — CREATED
Invention — PATENT
Invention germ — IDEA
Inventive Whitney — ELI
Inventor Elias — HOWE
Inventor Howe — ELIAS
Inventor Nikola — TESLA
Inventor of a sign language — EPEE
Inventor of bone china — SPODE
Inventor of dynamite — NOBEL
Inventor of farm machinery — DEERE
Inventor of glazed pottery — LUCA
Inventor of radio — DE FOREST
Inventor of road paving — MCADAM
Inventor of the bicycle — STARLEY
Inventor of the diving bell — EADS
Inventor of the phonograph — EDISON
Inventor of the revolver — COLT
Inventor of the telegraph — MORSE
Inventor of vulcanized rubber — CHARLES GOODYEAR
Inventor Pliny — EARLE
Inventor Singer — ISAAC
Inventor Tesla — NIKOLA
Inventor Whitney — ELI
Inventor who had his ups and downs — OTIS
Inventor who laid it on the line — ALEXANDER BELL
Inventor's monogram — TAE
Inventor's protection — PATENT
Inventor's safeguards — PATENTS
Invents — CREATES
Inverness boy — LADDIE
Invert — UPEND
Inverted — UPSIDE DOWN
Investigate — PROBE, RESEARCH
Investigated — EXAMINED
Investigation — PROBE
Investigative gp. — CIA
Investigators — PANEL, PROBERS
Investment — STAKE
Investment in the U.S. — T BOND
Investment return — YIELD
Investor's guide — DOW JONES AVERAGES

Investor's purchase — STOCKS AND BONDS
Investor's reading matter — FINANCIAL PAGES
Invests with power — CROWNS
Invigorate — LIVEN
Invigorates — BRACES
Invigorating — FRESH, TONIC
Invigoration — PEP
Invincible "Mother" — NATURE
Invisible emanations — AURAE
Invitation — BID
Invitation letters — RSVP
Invitation to a duel — SLAP
Invitation to a hitchhiker — HOP IN
Invite — ASK, ATTRACT, BID, ENTICE
Invited — ASKED, REQUESTED
Invited one — GUEST
Invites — ASKS, REQUESTS
Inviting word — LETS
Invocational figure — ORANT
Invoices — BILLS
Involuntary contractions — SPASMS, TICS
Involuntary motion — TIC
Involuntary residents — INMATES
Involve — ENMESH, ENTAIL
Involve necessarily — ENTAIL
Involved — ENTAILED
Involved necessarily — ENTAILED
Involved with — INTO
Involves as a result — ENTAILS
Involving a virus — VIRAL
Involving the kneecap — PATELLAR
Inward — ENTAD, INNER, INSIDE
Inward, anatomically — ENTAD
Iodine — HATLO GIRL
Ionesco and Ormandy — EUGENES
Ionian gulf — ARTA
Ionian island — CORFU
Ionium, for one — ISOTOPE
Ionization measure — RAD
Iota — JOT, WHIT
IOU of a sort — SCRIP
IOU signer — OWER
IOU's acknowledgment — DEBT
Iowa campus site — AMES
Iowa city — AMES, WATERLOO
Iowa college — COE
Iowa college town — AMES
Iowa commune — AMANA
Iowa lake — STORM
Iowa state tree — OAK
Iowa State's site — AMES
Iowa town — CLARINDA
Ipse _____ — DIXIT
IQ test creator — BINET
IQ test name — BINET
IRA for one — NEST EGG
Ira Levin's "_____ Before Dying" — A KISS
Iran before 1935 — PERSIA
Iran's capital: Var. sp. — TEHRAN
Iran, formerly — PERSIA
Irangate figure — OLIVER NORTH
Irani money — RIAL
Iranian archeological site — SUSA
Iranian coin — RIAL, TOMAN
Iranian money — RIALS
Iranian port — ABADAN
Iranian province — FARS
Iranian river — ATREK
Iranian ruler, once — SHAH
Iranian sweet — CHOCOLATE-HERAN
Iraq city — AMARA
Iraq leader — SADDAM
Iraq's neighbor — SYRIA
Iraqi city on the Tigris — KUT
Iraqi exports — DATES
Iraqi neighbors — SAUDIS
Iraqi port — BASRA
Iraqi province — BASRA
Iraqi river — TIGRIS
Iraqi seaport — BASRA
Irate — MAD, RILED
Irate pop singer in Arkansas? — HOT SPRINGSTEEN
Ire. county — CLARE
Ireland — ERIN
Ireland poetically — HIBERNIA
Ireland's De Valera — EAMON
Ireland's former name — -EIRE
Ireland, to a Gael — EIRE
Ireland, to Gaels — EIRE
Ireland, to Spenser — IRENA
Irene _____ of "Roots" — CARA
Irene and Nolan — RYANS
Irene Dunne role — MAMA
Irene of "Fame" — CARA
Irene or Vernon — CASTLE
Irene's bird — DOVE
Irenic — CALM
Iridescent gem — OPAL
Iridescent stone — OPAL
Iris layer — UVEA
Iris species — ORRIS
Iris-family members, for short — GLADS
Irish — ERSE
Irish _____ — SETTER
Irish _____ — STEW
Irish accent — BROGUE
Irish apricot — POTATO
Irish author — BEHAN
Irish bay — DONEGAL, GALWAY
Irish breakfast? (Seuss) — GREEN EGGS AND HAM
Irish capital — TARA
Irish castle — TARA
Irish city — CORK, DUBLIN, TRALEE
Irish coastal islands — ARAN
Irish county — ARMAGH, CLARE, CORK, KERRY, ULSTER
Irish county or TV doctor — KILDARE
Irish cry — ARRA
Irish dagger — SKEAN
Irish dances — JIGS, REELS
Irish dog — SETTER
Irish dramatist — YEATS
Irish dramatist John _____ — SYNGE
Irish dramatist: 1923-64 — BEHAN
Irish English — BROGUE
Irish euphemism — BEGORRA
Irish exclamation — ARRA
Irish export — LACE, LINEN
Irish Gaelic — ERSE
Irish goblin — POOKA
Irish gods' mother — ANU
Irish imp — LEPRECHAUN
Irish island group — ARAN
Irish islands — ARAN, SHANK
Irish isles — ARAN
Irish king Brian _____ — BORU
Irish lake — ERNE
Irish lake and river — ERNES
Irish language — CELT
Irish lass — COLLEEN
Irish national emblem — SHAMROCK
Irish nationalist Robert: 1778-1603 — EMMET
Irish Neptune — LER
Irish novelist — MOORE
Irish patriot — EMMET
Irish playwright Brendan — BEHAN
Irish poet — YEATS
Irish poet and dramatist William — YEATS
Irish port — DUBLIN
Irish port of call — COBH
Irish province — ULSTER
Irish rebel — O MORE
Irish river — ANNALEE, ERNE, NORE
Irish Rose lover — ABIE
Irish sea god — LER
Irish Sea isle — MAN
Irish seaport — SLIGO, TRALEE
Irish staples — BELFASTENERS
Irish sweetheart — GRA
Irish terriers, e.g. — PETS
Irish writer — BECKETT, JOYCE, SHAW
Irish writer-teacher — SEAN O FAOLAIN
Irishman or Welshman — CELT
Irk — ANNOY
Irks — VEXES

Iron-containing pigment — HEME
Iron — NUMBERED GOLF CLUB, PRESS
Iron and Bronze — AGES
Iron and Stone — AGES
Iron block — ANVIL
Iron chancellor — OTTO VON BISMARCK
Iron collar — GARROTE
Iron cross — MEDAL
Iron Curtain — BORDER
Iron for Watson — MASHIE
Iron or shovel lead-in — STEAM
Iron or shovel preceder — STEAM
Iron out — SOLVE
Iron surfaces — SOLES
Iron waste — SLAG
Iron, long ago — YREN
Iron: Comb. form — FERRI, FERRO
Iron: Pref. — SIDERO
Iron: Prefix — SIDERO
Ironclad ship of 1862 — MONITOR
Ironer — PRESSER
Irons of films — JEREMY
Ironstone and limonite — ORES
Ironstone and tinstone — ORES
Ironstone, e.g. — ORE
Irony — SATIRE
Iroquoian — ONEIDA, SENECAN
Iroquoian group — ERIES, HURONS, ONEIDA
Iroquoian Indians — ERIES
Iroquois — MINGO
Iroquois Indians — SENECAS
Irradiate — SHED
Irrational number — SURD
Irregular — ERODED, EROSE, UNEVEN
Irregularly edged — EROSE
Irregularly notched — EROSE
Irreligious — PAGAN
Irremediable — HOPELESS
Irresistibelles — SIRENS
Irresolute — UNCERTAIN, WISHY WASHY
Irreverent — BRAZEN
Irreversible — FATAL
Irrevocable — FIRM
Irrigate — WATER
Irritable — EDGY, FRETFUL, ON EDGE, TESTY
Irritable mystery writer? — CROSS MACDONALD
Irritate — ANNOY, IRK, RILE, RUB THE WRONG WAY, VEX
Irritated — IRED, IRKED, PEEVED
Irritated state — SNIT
Irritates — CHAFES, GRATES, PEEVES, ACERBATES
Irritating — ACRID
Irritation — ITCH, RASH
IRS agent — T MAN
IRS month — APR
Irv of the 50's Yankees — NOREN
Irving and Carter — AMYS
Irving Berlin song, 1925 — ALWAYS
Irving work — ASTORIA
Irving's 1048 transportation? — BERLIN EXPRESS
Irwin of golf — HALE
Irwin Shaw novel — THE YOUNG LIONS
Is — EXISTS
Is a ham — EMOTES
Is active — MOVES
Is adequate — DOES
Is allowed: Lat. — LICET
Is annoyed — RESENTS
Is beholden — OWES
Is bested or worsted — LOSES
Is borne — RIDES
Is brilliant — STARS
Is burdensome — TRIES
Is busy and active — HUMS
Is concerned — CARES
Is consistent — JIBES
Is contrite — REPENTS
Is dependent on — RELIES
Is employed in Valenciennes — TATS
Is extremely angry — FOAMS AT THE MOUTH
Is frugal — STINTS
Is he guilty of monkey business? — ORGAN GRINDER
Is human — ERRS
Is important — MATTERS, RATES
Is in arrears — OWES
Is in debt — OWES
Is in fear of — DREADS
Is in store for — AWAITS
Is inclined — LEANS
Is indebted — OWES
Is indolent — LOLLS
Is intrepid — DARES
Is kind and generous — HAS A HEART OF GOLD
Is lacking — NEEDS
Is located — SITS
Is next to — ABUTS
Is not, colloquially — ISNT
Is obsequious — GROVELS
Is of use — AIDS
Is on cloud nine — TREADS ON AIR
Is out of sorts — AILS
Is part of the scene — IN ON
Is pliable — BENDS
Is profitable — PAYS
Is rueful — REPENTS
Is solicitous — CARES
Is suffering — AILS
Is unable to — CANNOT, CANT
Is under the weather — AILS
Is useful — AVAILS
Is worthy of — MERITS
Is: Fr. — EST
Isaac _____, violin virtuoso — STERN
Isaac Walton's delight — NIBBLE
Isaac Wise, e.b. — RABBI
Isaac's firstborn — ESAU
Isaac, Wayne or fig — NEWTON
Isherwood for short — CHRIS
Ishmael's captain — AHAB
Ishmael's mother — HAGAR
Isinglass — MICA
Isl. S. of Australia — TAS
Islam's Supreme Being — ALLAH
Islamic call to prayer — AZAN
Islamic decree — IRADE
Islamic deity — ALLAH
Islamic devil — EBLIS
Islamic god — ALLAH
Islamic judge — CADI
Islamic leader — CALIPH
Islamic leader from the Golden St.? — CALIF
Islamic princes — EMEERS
Island — CONEY
Island also called Rapa Nui — EASTER
Island city — MONTREAL
Island country — BAHAMAS
Island dance — HULA
Island due south of Manila — PANAY
Island east of Java — BALI
Island formed by deposits — DELTA
Island greeting — ALOHA
Island group — FAROE
Island group in the St. Lawrence river — THOUSAND
Island group in W Atlantic — BERMUDA
Island group off Myanmar — ANDAMAN
Island in a palindrome — ELBA
Island in New York Bay — STATEN
Island in New York harbor — ELLIS
Island in the Aegean — SAMOS
Island in the Baltic — AALAND
Island in the British West Indies — NEVIS
Island in the Cen. Cyclades — DELOS
Island in the Greater Antilles — CUBA
Island in the harbor — ELLIS

Island in the Inner Hebrides — IONA
Island in the Near group — ATTU
Island in the Netherlands Antilles — SABA
Island in the Philippines — LEYTE
Island in the W Pacific — OCEAN
Island in the West Indies — GRENADA
Island instrument, for short — UKE
Island nation — JAPAN
Island near Bay of Naples — CAPRI
Island near Italy — ELBA
Island near Luzon, P.I. — ALABAT
Island near Mull — IONA
Island near New Guinea — ROOKE
Island near Venezuela — ARUBA
Island of exile — ELBA
Island of Ireland — ARAN
Island of leis — OAHU
Island of song — BALI, CAPRI
Island of Sumatra — NIAS
Island of the Cyclades — IOS
Island of the Inner Hebrides — IONA
Island off Gotham — STATEN
Island off SE coast of China — TAIWAN
Island off Sumatra — NIAS
Island off the N.J. coast — STATEN
Island off Venezuela — ARUBA
Island staple — BREADFRUIT
Island welcome — ALOHA
Island: Comb. form — NESO
Islands in Galway Bay — ARA
Islands near Galway Bay — ARAN
Islands off Galway — ARANS
Islands off Portugal — AZORES
Islands off Sicily — EGADI
Islands off the Fla. coast — BIMINI
Islands off the Irish coast — ARANS
Islands S of Sicily — MALTA
Isle in the Irish Sea — MAN
Isle of _____ — ELY
Isle of _____ — MAN
Isle of _____, England — ELY
Isle of exile — ELBA
Isle of Man capital — DOUGLAS
Isle of Man cat — MANX
Isle of Man city — DOUGLAS
Isle of Man coin — PENCE
Isle of Man native — GAEL
Isle of song — BALI
Isles off Galway's coast — ARAN
Islet — AIT, EYOT
Isolate — ENISLE
Isolate, as Napoleon — ENISLE
Isolated — ALONE, APART
Isolated elevation — MESA
Isolated rock — SCAR
Isolated, in a way — INCOMMUNICADO
Isolates — MAROONS
Isole _____ (isles off Sicily) — EOLIE
Isomeric — ALLO
Isr. airline — EL AL
Israel — ZION
Israel's Abba — EBAN
Israel's airline — EL AL
Israel's desert — NEGEV
Israel's Eban — ABBA
Israel's Golda — MEIR
Israel's Yitzhak — SHAMIR
Israeli airline — EL AL
Israeli ambassador to U.S.: 1982-83 — ARENS
Israeli born — SABRA
Israeli breakfast food? — HAIFARINA
Israeli burp gun — UZI
Israeli chief — BEGIN
Israeli city — LOO
Israeli coin — AGORA
Israeli dance — HORA
Israeli desert — NEGEV
Israeli greeting or farewell — SHALOM
Israeli hill fortress — MASADA
Israeli hot spot — NEGEV
Israeli lang. — HEB
Israeli native — SABRA
Israeli P.M. Eshkol: 1063-69 — LEVI
Israeli port — ACRE, EILAT, ELATH, HAIFA
Israeli region — NEGEV
Israeli round dances — HORAS
Israeli seaport — ACRE, EILAT, HAIFA
Israeli statesman — EBAN
Israeli statesman Abba — EBAN
Israeli strip — GAZA
Israelis — SABRAS
Israelite leader — MOSES
Israelite's escape route — RED SEA
Israelites' camp, before David / Goliath — ELAH
Issue — COPY, PROGENY, SEND
Issue forth — EMANATE
Issue violently — ERUPT
Issued — EMITTED, EXUDED
Issued an edict — ORDERED
Issues — EMANATES
Istanbul native — TURK
Isthmus — NECK
Isthmus or monkey — KRA
It "talks" — MONEY
It beats the deuce — TREY
It boasts a delta — NILE
It can be chopped liver — PATE
It can follow six — TEEN
It carries a lot of weight — SCALE
It converts trash to ash — BURNER
It could be electric — EEL
It could be packed or tried — CASE
It crosses Hollywood — VINE
It did Cleopatra in — ASP
It dines on eucalyptus leaves — KOALA
It evokes sympathy — PATHOS
It falls mainly on the plain — RAIN
It follows a long March — APRIL
It follows beach, ski, surf and tennis — BUM, BALL
It follows printemps — ETE
It follows sieben — ACHT
It follows that — ERGO
It gits along — DOGIE
It goes before beauty — AGE
It goes with eye or can — OPENER
It goes with time — STANDARD
It has 21 dots — DIE
It has 30 men and 2 women — CHESS SET
It has a string attached? — KITE
It has a tercet — SESTINA
It has an eye, but it sees not — NEEDLE
It has its ups and downs — YOYO
It has seven vertebrae — NECK
It has staying power? — CORSET
It has the shakes — ASPEN
It holds the catch — CREEL
It hung on Tara's wall — HARP
It includes algebra and calculus — MATH
It is said, in France — ONDIT
It is said: Fr. — ONDIT
It is shot — POOL
It means the world to Juan — EL MUNDO
It multiplies by dividing — AMOEBA
It opens sesame — ESS
It repeats itself — HISTORY
It runs from a graveyard to a river — WALL STREET
It soars at shores — ERN
It sometimes calls — DUTY
It sometimes says "Welcome" — MAT

It starts with "Marley was dead.." — A CHRISTMAS CAROL
It takes two to dance this — TANGO
It tans sans sun — HIDE
It usually loves company — MISERY
It verges on Virgo — LEO
It wasn't built in a day — ROME
It's a sin to tell _____ — A LIE
It's all around us — AIR
It's all in Rhine's mind — ESP
It's as good as a miss — A MILE
It's been split — ATOM
It's below a sop. — ALT
It's between koph and sin — RESH
It's between the U.S. and Eur. — ATL
It's clear to me — I SEE
It's considered offensive — T FORMATION
It's east of Calif. — NEV
It's flexed by a kneeler — GENU
It's for reel! — MOVIE
It's full of letters — TYPE-WRITER
It's heard from a herd — LOW
It's human to do this — ERR
It's in one era — out the other — FAD
It's love-love at the start — SET
It's lox when smoked — SALMON
It's Luik, in Flemish — LIEGE
It's mad in March? — HARE
It's mightier than the sword — PEN
It's no use to Kojak — COMB
It's not a moving picture — STILL LIFE
It's nothing to Graf — LOVE
It's now C.I.S. — USSR
It's often cast — DIE
It's often private — SECTOR
It's often smashed — ATOM
It's on tap — BEER
It's provided by O.R. personnel — TLC
It's quarry — HIDER
It's required of vassals — FEALTY
It's sometimes greased — PALM
It's sometimes noire — BETE
It's sometimes petty — CASH
It's sometimes ragged — EDGE
It's sometimes saved — BACON
It's sometimes sufficient — WORD TO TO THE WISE
It's sometimes vicious — CIR-CLE
It's stuck on ham — CLOVE
It's the same to a Roman — IDEM
It's to the left of the Rive Droite — SEINE
It's used on a cue tip — CHALK
It's useless if pointless — PENCIL
It's west of Curacao — ARUBA
It. city — ATRI, SIENA
It. resort — LIDO
It. rice dish — RISOTTO
It. sculptor — PISANO
Italia capital — ROMA
Italia's capital — ROMA
Italia's major city — ROMA
Italia's second largest city — MILANO
Italian angels' instruments — ARPAS
Italian art center — SIENA
Italian artist Guido — RENI
Italian astronomer — GALILEO
Italian Baroque painter — RENI
Italian beach resort — LIDO
Italian beachhead: Sept. 1943 — SALERNO
Italian bell town — ATRI
Italian bread? — LIRE
Italian car — FIAT
Italian card game — SCOPA
Italian cheese — ROMANO
Italian chest of the Renaissance — CASSONE
Italian city — TURIN
Italian city noted for cheese — PARMA
Italian city on the Po — TURIN
Italian coin — LIRA
Italian coin of yore — SCUDO
Italian commune — ASTI, PARMA
Italian composer Antonio — ROSSINI
Italian composer: 1623-69 — CESTI
Italian condiment — TAMARA
Italian conductor — ARTURO TOSCANINI
Italian crunchy munchy? — FLORENCELERY
Italian currency — LIRA
Italian dance — TARANTELLA
Italian dessert — SPUMONI
Italian dictator — BENITO MUSSOLINI
Italian dough — PASRA
Italian dramatist-poet Ugo — BETTI
Italian eateries — PIZZERIAS
Italian epic poet — TASSO
Italian equivalent of a caudillo — DUCE
Italian fare — BREAD STICKS
Italian folk dance — TARANTELLA
Italian food staple — PASTA
Italian great operatic tenor — CARUSO
Italian host — OSTE
Italian innkeeper — OSTE
Italian interjection — ALO
Italian inventor-physicist: 1745-1827 — VOLTA
Italian island — CAPRI, ISCHIA, LIDO
Italian jet set? — NAPLES PLANES
Italian lake — COMO
Italian magistrate — DOGE
Italian meal ender — TORTONI
Italian moon — LUNA
Italian mother — MADRE
Italian mouse — TOPO
Italian navigator — COLUMBUS
Italian noble family — ESTE
Italian nobleman — CONTE
Italian noblewoman Lucretia — BORGIA
Italian painter — LEONARDO DAVINCI
Italian painter, circa 1500 — RAPHAEL
Italian peak — ETNA
Italian philosopher: 1866-1952 — CROCE
Italian physicist — ROSSI
Italian playwright — LUIGI PIRANDELLO
Italian poet: 1798-1837 — LEOPARDI
Italian port on Adriatic — BARI
Italian prima donna — DIVA
Italian princely family — ESTE
Italian pronoun — EGLI, ESSA
Italian range — APENNINE, APENNINES
Italian real-estate tycoon — MILANDOWNER
Italian resort — LIDO
Italian river — ADIGE, ARNO
Italian saint Philip _____ — NERI
Italian three — TRE
Italian town near Ancona — IESI
Italian university city — BARI
Italian violin maker — AMATI
Italian white wine — SOAVE
Italian wine center — ASTI
Italian wine city — ASTI
Italian wine district — ASTI
Italian wine region — ASTI
Italian wine-producing commune — ASTI
Italian writer Umberto _____ — ECO
Italy's "City of a Hundred Towers" — PAVIA
Italy's golden age — TRECEN-TO
Italy's Sophia — LOREN
Itch — YEN

Itching — EAGER
Itchy — ANTSY, EAGER
Item — ARTICLE
Item for a Butterfly — PARASOL
Item for a dress shirt — STUD
Item for a high stepper — STILT
Item for a toxophilite — TARGET
Item for Cio-Cio San — PARASOL
Item for Gretzky — SKATE
Item for Jack and Jill — PAIL
Item for Miss Muffet — WHEY
Item for Rumpelstiltskin — SPINNING WHEEL
Item for some surgeons — TREE
Item for stringing — BEAD
Item from a Brit's garden — VEG
Item in a chest — TOOL
Item in a dark room — NEGATIVE
Item in a holiday basket — EASTER EGG
Item in a nursery? — SEEDLING
Item in a scale — NOTE
Item in a trunk — TIRE
Item in Nicklaus' bag — IRON
Item in the "house that Jack built" — MALT
Item in the black — ASSET
Item near a tub — BATHMAT
Item not to be exposed — FILM
Item not to be washed — LINEN
Item of Japanese dress — OBI
Item of nostalgia — OLDIE
Item of ownership — ASSET
Item of value — ASSET
Item on a banderilla — BARB
Item on a French menu — ROTI
Item on a G.I. medal — OAK LEAF
Item on a grocery list — OLEO
Item on Pierre's Yule tree — ANGE
Item sought by straphangers — SEAT
Item spent in Praha — HALER
Item stored in a buttery — ALE
Item to be lent — EAR
Item underfoot? — SOLE
Item used by glaziers — PANE
Item used in Carver experiments — PEANUT
Itemize — DETAIL, LIST
Items ab gallinis — OVA
Items for a CPA — NOS
Items for Corot and Miro — PALETTES
Items in booths — PHONES
Items in Santa's pack — TOYS
Items of apparel — SHIRTS
Items on a bireme — OARS
Items on old desks — INK WELLS
Items on tap — ALES
Items sold in a deli — BAGELS
Items subject to decay — TEETH
Iterate — ECHO, RESTATE
Iterative Samoan naval base — PAGO PAGO
Itin. items — RTES
Itinerant cowboys, mod style — SADDLE TRAMPS
Itinerant salesman — PEDDLER
Itinerant set — JET
Itinerary — ROUTE
Itinerary abbr. — RTE
Its banks are bonnie — LOCH LOMOND
Its cap. is Dover — DEL
Its cap. is Madison — WIS
Its capital is Alencon — ORNE
Its capital is Bamako — MALI
Its capital is Barnaul — ALTAI
Its capital is Beauvais — OISE
Its capital is Brussels — BRABANT
Its capital is Hue: var. — ANAM
Its capital is Luanda — ANGOLA
Its capital is Lyon — RHONE
Its capital is Roma — ITALIA
Its chief town is Portoferraio — ELBA
Its customers paint, sculpt, etc — ART SHOP
Its jaws give pause — SHARK
Its motto is "Fidelity, Bravery, Integrity" — FBI
Its symbol is a lion — MGM
Its symbol is Au — GOLD
Its symbol is Pb — LEAD
Its symbol is X — CHI
Its tower is leaning — PISA
Its: Fr. — SES
Itsy _____ — BITSY
Itty bitty — WEE
Ivan and Boris — TSARS
Ivan and Peter — CZARS, TSARS
Ivan epithet — TERRIBLE
Ivan of tennis — LENDL
Ivan or Nicholas — TSAR
Ivan or Peter — TSAR
Ivan Petrovich Voinitsky — UNCLE VANYA
Ivan was one — TSAR
Ivan, for one — TSAR
Ivanhoe's bride — ROWENA
Ivanhoe's lady — ROWENA
Ivory — ANY PIANO KEY
Ivory ink — ENCRE
Ivory source — AFRICA, TUSK
Ivory tower — RETREAT
Ivory, to Octavian — EBUR
Ivory-towered — IDEAL
Ivy foliage — VINE LEAF
Ivy League college — BROWN
Ivy League school — YALE
Ivy League university — YALE
Ivy Leaguer — YALIE
Ivy Leaguers — ELIS
Ivy's clingers — TENDRILS
Iwo _____ — JIMA
IX x VI — LIV
Izaak Walton's basket — CREEL
Izzard — ZED

J

J, soundwise — NOISY BIRD
J. Baker and M. Hess — DAMES
J. Davis was its pres. — CSA
J. Irving hero — GARP
J. Lincoln's "Captain _____" — ERI
J. Wilbrand's discovery: 1863 — TNT
J.B. Rhine specialty — ESP
J.B. Rhine subj. — ESP
J.C. Oates book — THEM
J.D. holder — ATT
J.D. Salinger lass — ESME
J.F. Cooper heroine — CORA
J.F. Cooper's "The _____" — DEERSLAYER
J.F.K. commanded one — PT BOAT
J.F.K. sights — SSTS
J.F.K. visitor — SST

J.F.K. visitor — SST
J.F.K.'s favorite chair — ROCKER
J.J. or Mary — ASTOR
J.R. Ewing's hat — STETSON
J.R. Ewing's interest — OIL
J.R. or Bobby — EWING
J.W. Booth's M.D. — MUDD
Jab — POKE
Jabbar, et al. — CENTERS
Jabbed — POKED
Jabber — YAP
Jabiru and jay — BIRDS
Jabs and hooks — LEFTS
Jacaranda — TREE
Jack-in-the-pulpit, e.g. — ARUM
Jack and Jill's container — PAIL
Jack Benny's instrument — VIOLIN
Jack Frost's bite — NIP
Jack Frost's canvas — PANE
Jack London hero — EDEN
Jack Nasty — SNEAK
Jack of clubs — PAM
Jack of nursery rhymes — SPRAT
Jack of old films: 1903-78 — OAKIE
Jack or Josephus — DANIELS
Jack or Julie — LONDON
Jack or Robert — FROST
Jack Palance TV series — BRONK
Jack preceder — FLAP
Jack Sprat's diet — LEAN
Jack Yellen's question — AINT SHE SWEET
Jack's giant, e.g. — OGRE
Jack's need — PLAY
Jack- _____ — TARS
Jack-in-the-box — TOY
Jack-in-the-pulpit — FLOWER
Jack-in-the-pulpit family — AROID
Jack-of-all-trades — FACTOTUM, HANDYMAN
Jackal-headed god — ANUBIS
Jackal — FAG, LACKEY, DRONE
Jackal's kin — WOLF
Jackanapes — PUP, UPSTART
Jackass — FOOL
Jackdaw — CROW
Jacket — MACKINAW, WINDBREAKER
Jacket feature — LAPEL
Jacket or collar — ETON
Jacket or laced leader — STRAIT
Jacket part — SLEEVE
Jacket style — ETON
Jacket type — ETON
Jacket, cap and collar — ETONS
Jackets and caps — ETONS
Jackets and collars — ETONS
Jackie of "The Paleface" — SEARLE
Jackie's daughter — CAROLINE
Jackie's first child — CAROLINE
Jackie's second — ARI
Jackie's sister — LEE
Jackie, Joan or Judy — COLLINS
Jackknife — DIVE
Jackknife, e.g. — DIVE
Jackrabbits — HARES
Jackson and Smith — KATES
Jackson's first Secy. of War — EATON
Jackstay — ROPE
Jacky — TAR
Jacob _____, social reformer — RIIS
Jacob's brother — ESAU
Jacob's first wife and namesakes — LEAHS
Jacob's parent — ISAAC
Jacob's spouse — LEAH
Jacob's third son — LEVI
Jacob's twin — ESAU
Jacob's vision — LADDER
Jacob's-sword — IRIS
Jacobi of "I, Claudius" — DEREK
Jacques' black — NOIR
Jacques' friend — AMI
Jacques' girlfriend — AMIE
Jacta _____ est (The die is cast) — ALEA
Jacutinga and tinstone — ORES
Jade — NAG, TIRE
Jaded — BORED, WORN
Jaeger — SKUA
Jaeger's weapon — RIFLE
Jaffa's land: Abbr. — ISR
Jaffe or Barrett — RONA
Jag — COG, NICK, SPUR
Jagged — EROSE
Jagger — MICK
Jaguar — CAT
Jai _____ — ALAI
Jai alai — GAME
Jai alai ball — PELOTA
Jai alai basket — CESTA
Jai alai racquets — CESTAS
Jai-alai sports palace — FRONTON
Jail, in Scotland — TOLLBOOTH
Jailbird — CON
Jake La _____ of ring fame — MOTTA
Jalopy — CRATE
Jalousie — BLIND
Jam — BIND, MASH
Jam ingredient — CAR
Jam that's not sweet — SNARL
Jamaica's P.M.: 1980-89 — SEAGA
Jamaican cult member — RASTA
Jamaican export — RUM
Jambalaya base — RICE
Jamboree — GALA
James _____ Garfield — ABRAM
James _____ Jones — EARL
James and Tommy — AGEES
James Baldwin opus: 1963 — THE FIRE NEXT TIME
James Bond foe — SMERSH
James Clavell novel — SHOGUN
James Fenimore Cooper heroine — CORA
James Herriot, for short — VET
James Jones's middle name — EARL
James Joyce group of short stories — DUBLINERS
James Joyce work — EXILES
James Joyce's correspondence? — IRISH MAIL
James Mason role — NEMO
James of "Brian's Song" — CAAN
James of "The Seventh Veil" — MASON
James of the screen — CAAN
James of TV — ARNESS
James Stewart court drama — ANATOMY OF A MURDER
James Whitcomb _____ — RILEY
James Wright's predecessor — ONEILL
Jamie of TV — FARR
Jammed — FULL
Jams; pickles — SCRAPES
Jan of the Met — PEERCE
Jan. I need — REST
Jane _____, soap-opera actress — ELLIOT
Jane Eyre and Emma — HEROINES
Jane Fonda's Oscar-winning role in "Klute" — BREE
Jane Grey's title — LADY
Jane of fiction — EYRE
Jane or Peter — FONDA
Jane or Zane — GREY
Jane, to Peter — SIS
Jangle — BICKER
Janis of rock — IAN
Janitor — PORTER
Jannings and Ludwig — EMILS
Jannings of the screen — EMIL
January ordeal — EXAM
January phenomenon — THAW
January store event? — WHITE SALE
January, in Cordoba — ENERO
January, in Juarez — ENERO
January, in Seville — ENERO
January, to Juan — ENERO

Japan — NIPPON
Japan or Siam follower — ESE
Japan's chief island — HONSHU
Japan's chief religion — SHINTO
Japan's greatest port — OSAKA
Japan's largest island — HONSHU
Japanese-American — NISEI, ISSEI
Japanese aborigine — AINU
Japanese admiral, et al. — ITOS
Japanese and Javanese, e.g. — ASIANS
Japanese apricot — UME
Japanese bar order — SUSHI
Japanese beverage — SAKE
Japanese brazier — HIBACHI
Japanese caviar ad — TOKYO ROES
Japanese clog — GETA
Japanese coin — RIN
Japanese creature thriller — RODAN
Japanese cult — SHINTO
Japanese currency — SEN
Japanese dancing girl — GEISHA
Japanese drama — NOH
Japanese dramas — NOHS
Japanese emperor — HIROHITO
Japanese emperor's title — TENNO
Japanese export — CAMERA
Japanese feudal warrior — SAMURAI
Japanese fish dish — SUSHI
Japanese food plants — UDOS
Japanese foot covering — TABI
Japanese galley utensils — POT SAM PANS
Japanese gateway — TORII
Japanese greeting — BANZAI
Japanese gumbo ingredient — TOKYOKRA
Japanese immigrant — ISSEI
Japanese immigrant to U.S. — ISSEI
Japanese island — KYUSHU
Japanese legislature — DIET
Japanese measure — SHO
Japanese merchant ship — MARU
Japanese money — YEN
Japanese money of account — RIN
Japanese mountain — ASO
Japanese national park — ASO
Japanese natives — AINUS
Japanese news agency — DOMEI
Japanese P.M.: 1964-72 — SATO
Japanese P.M.: 1982-87 — NAKASONE
Japanese plant — UDO
Japanese poetic style — HAIKU
Japanese porcelain ware — IMARI
Japanese port — OTARU, YAWATA
Japanese pottery center — YAWATA
Japanese religion — SHINTO
Japanese salad plant — UDO
Japanese sashes — OBIS
Japanese seaport — OSAKA
Japanese seaport or dog — AKITA
Japanese sock — TABI
Japanese statesman — ITO, SATO
Japanese straw mats — TATAMI
Japanese stringed instrument — KOTO
Japanese suicide — KIRI
Japanese tree — UPAS
Japanese verse form — TANKA
Japanese volcano — ASAMA
Japanese warrior, of a sort — NINJA
Japanese woman diver — AMA
Japanese wooden clog — GETA
Japanese wrestling — SUMO
Japanese-style sock — TABI
Jape — GAG, JEST, JOKE, QUIP
Jar — JUG, OLLA, URN
Jar of antiquity — AMPHORA
Jar or box: Abbr. — CRTN
Jar used for home canning — MASON
Jar used for preserving foods — MASON
Jardiniere — URN
Jargon — ARGOT, CANT, LINGO
Jarry's "Ubu _____" — ROI
Jasey — WIG
Jasmine — FLOWER
Jasmine, e.g. — TEA
Jason's command — ARGO
Jason's craft — ARGO
Jason's helper — MEDEA
Jason's quest — THE GOLDEN FLEECE
Jason's ship — ARGO
Jason's transport — ARGO
Jason's vessel — ARGO
Jason's wife — MEDEA
Jasper — QUARTZ
Jati, for example — CASTE
Jaundice — ENVY
Jaunt — TRIP
Jaunty — PERT, RAKISH
Java container — COFFEEPOT
Javanese carriage — SADO
Javanese chiefs — RAJAS
Javanese ruler — RAJA
Javelins — SPEARS
Jawaharlal _____ — NEHRU
Jawaharlal of India — NEHRU
Jay — ALAN LERNER
Jay Silverheels role — TONTO
Jay's cousin — PIE
Jay's folks — LENOS
Jay, the comedian — LENO
Jayhawk state — KANSAS
Jazz — BOP, SWING
Jazz artist of note — ILLINOIS JACQUET
Jazz artist of note — JELLY ROLL MORTON
Jazz artist of note — WILD BILL DAVISON
Jazz artist Zoot — SIMS
Jazz clarinetist Jimmie _____ — NOONE
Jazz composition — RAG
Jazz dance — STOMP
Jazz entertainer Crothers — SCATMAN
Jazz form — BEBOP
Jazz genre — BEBOP
Jazz great — ELLA
Jazz group — COMBO
Jazz music — JIVE
Jazz musician's engagement — GIG
Jazz nonsense — SCAT
Jazz pianist Tatum — ART
Jazz queen — ELLA
Jazz singer Simone — NINA
Jazz style — BOP, SCAT
Jazz trumpeter Al — HIRT
Jazz variety — BLUES, BOP
Jazz, for one — ERA
Jazzman's job — GIG
Jazzy dance — STOMP
Jazzy rhythm — BEBOP
Je ne _____ quoi — SAIS
Jealous — ENVIOUS, WARY
Jean Harlow, e.g. — PLATINUM BLONDE
Jean Kerr's "Lunch _____" — HOUR
Jean's cloth — DENIM
Jean's fabric — DENIM
Jeanne d'Arc, e.g.: Abbr. — STE
Jeanne d'Arc, et al. — STES
Jeanne of "State Fair" — CRAIN
Jeanne of the movies — CRAIN
Jeans material — DENIM
Jeans' alternative — KHAKI
Jedi's furry friend — EWOK
Jeep mfr. — AMC
Jeer — GIBE
Jeer for the team — BOO
Jeff Bridges movie — TRON
Jeff Davis's orig. — CSA
Jeff's pal — MUTT
Jefferson and Paine, e.g. — DEISTS
Jefferson was one — DEIST
Jefferson's bill — TWO
Jefferson's home — MONTI-CELLO
Jefferson's vice-president — BURR
Jehoshaphat's father — ASA

Jehoshaphat's predecessor — ASA
Jejune — ARID, BARE
Jejunum appendage — ILEUM
Jell — SET
Jellied garnish — ASPIC
Jelly ingredient — AGAR, PECTIN
Jelly to Jacques — GELEE
Jelly used as a garnish — ASPIC
Jennet — ASS
Jennies — ASSES
Jennifer O'Neill film: 1971 — SUMMER OF FORTY TWO
Jenny — ASS
Jenny Lou Carson's "_____ Me Go, Lover" — LET
Jenny of birdland — WREN
Jeopardy — RISK
Jeremy _____ — IRONS
Jerk — LOUSE, SCHMO, YANK
Jerky, e.g. — MEAT
Jerome K. Jerome's "Three Men in _____" — A BOAT
Jerome, of the opera — HINES
Jerry Mathers role — BEAVER CLEAVER
Jerry's Anne — MEARA
Jerry-built — CHEAP, FLIMSY
Jersey — SHIRT
Jersey expression — MOO
Jerusalem's Mosque of _____ — OMAR
Jerusalem: Var. — SION
Jessica Tandy role — MISS DAISY
Jester — FOOL, MIME, WAG
Jests — SPOOFS
Jet-engine housing — POD
Jet — SPURT
Jet engine — RAM JET
Jet receiver — TOON
Jet set — ELITE
Jet set transport — PLANE
Jet setters' carriers — SSTS
Jet stream — WIND
Jet's route — AIRWAY
Jet-assisted plane maneuvers, for short — JATOS
Jet-speed unit — MACH
Jeté — LEAP
Jets — SPURTS
Jettison — DUMP
Jettisoned goods — LIGAN
Jetty — PIER
Jeune fille — DEMOISELLE, MISS
Jew — HEBREW
Jeweled band — TIARA
Jeweled headpiece — TIARA
Jeweler's abbr — CTS
Jeweler's aid — LOUPE
Jeweler's chisel — SCAUPER
Jeweler's lens — LOUPE
Jeweler's need — LOUPE
Jeweler's stock — GEMS
Jeweler's unit — KARAT
Jeweler's weight — CARAT
Jewelry — RINGS
Jewelry designer Peretti — ELSA
Jewelry fastener — CLASP
Jewelry items — CHAINS, EARBOB
Jewelry: Slang — ICE
Jewels — GEMS
Jewish calendar entry — ADAR
Jewish ceremonial dinner — SEDER
Jewish festival — PURIM
Jewish group in Iberia — SEPHARDIM
Jewish holiday eve — EREB
Jewish month — ADAR
Jewish month — ADAR, ELUL, NISAN, TEBET
Jewish month after AV — ELUL
Jewish religious exposition — MIDRASH
Jewish sect — HASID
Jewish title of learning — RABBI
Jewish village — SHTETL
Jezebel's deity — BAAL
Jezebel's god — BAAL
Jezebel's husband — AHAB
JFK "birds" — SSTS
JFK abbr. — ARR
JFK abbreviation — ARR
JFK aircraft — SST
JFK airline — PAN AM
JFK sights — SSTS
JFK speedsters — SSTS
JFK visitors — SSTS
Jib — SAIL
Jibe — AGREE, JELL
Jibed — SNEERED
Jibing — SNEERING
Jidda natives — ARABS
Jiff — SEC
Jiffy — SEC
Jiffy: Colloq. — SEC
Jig — DANCE
Jigger — SHOT
Jiggle — JERK
Jigsaw — PUZZLE
Jigsaw puzzle — GAME
Jihad — HOLY WAR
Jill or John of films — IRELAND
Jillian and Reinking — ANNS
Jillian and Sheridan — ANNS
Jillian or Miller — ANN
Jim Dale role — BARNUM
Jim or Kitchener — LORD
Jim Ryun's run — MILE
Jim Varney role — ERNEST
Jim who sang about Leroy Brown — CROCE
Jim-dandy — A ONE, FINE
Jimmy — LEVER, PRY
Jimmy Carter's middle name — EARL
Jimmy Nelson's canine dummy — FARFEL
Jimmy or Dixie — CARTER
Jimmy or James — DEAN
Jimmy who played "Lindy" — STEWART
Jingle — TUNE
Jingly February outing — SLEIGH RIDE
Jinxes — HOO DOOS
Jipijapa item — PANAMA
Jipijapa product — HAT
Jitterbug — LINDY
Jittery — TENSE
Jo's boys — LITTLE MEN
Jo's sister — AMY
Joan Collins miniseries — SINS
Joan of Arc triumphed here — ORLEANS
Joan of Arc, et al. — MARTYRS
Joan of art — MIRO
Joan or Marian — MAID
Joan Sutherland specialties — TRILLS
Joan Sutherland's title — DAME
Joan Sutherland, for one — DIVA
Joan Van _____ — ARK
Joanne _____ of the films — DRU
Joanne of films — DRU
Joanne of Logan, W.Va — DRU
Job — LINE, POST, POSITION
Job for an emcee — INTRO
Job for Spade — CASE
Job O. Henry had — TELLER
Job of TV's Teddy Z — AGT
Job securities — TENURES
Job seeker — APPLICANT
Job's observation — IMPATIENT
Job, to a jazz player — GIG
Job; position — BERTH
Jock — ATHLETE
Jockey Cordero — ANGEL
Jockey Eddie — ARCARO
Jockey of note — STEVE CAUTHEN
Jockey Turcotte — RON
Jockey's garb — SILKS
Jockey's whip — BAT
Jockey, at times — RATER
Jockeys' wear — SILKS
Jocose — COMIC, WITTY
Jocular — FACETIOUS, JOLLY
Jocund — GAY, MERRY
Joe E. Brown 1939 movie warning — BEWARE SPOOKS
Joe Friday portrayer — WEBB
Joe Montana's job — PASSER
Joe Orton play — LOOT
Joe Palooka's bride — ANN
Joe Palooka's manager — WALSH
Joe Penner pitch — WANNA BUY A DUCK
Joel or Zane — GREY

Joel, of "Cabaret" — GREY
Joeys — KANGAROOS
Jog — TROT
Jog the memory — REMIND
Jogged — RAN
Jogger's problems — CHARLEY HORSES
Jogging gait — TROT
Johanna Spyri character — HEIDI
John _____ Garner — NANCE
John _____ Jones — PAUL
John _____ Whittier — GREENLEAF
John Adams — SECOND PRESIDENT
John and Audrey's grasslands? — HAY MEADOWS
John Belushi domestic film — ANIMAL HOUSE
John Boy Walton's sister — ERIN
John Brown's dog — RAB
John Buchan hero — GREEN-MANTLE
John Curry's milieu — RINK
John Denver album — AERIE
John Doe's "cousin" Richard — ROE
John Dos Passos novel — MANHATTAN TRANSFER
John Drew co-star — REHAN
John Duncan was one — UTE
John Evelyn was one — DIARIST
John Fletcher's Rx? — GO TO BED SOBER
John Ford 1952 film, "The _____ Man" — QUIET
John French _____: American painter — SLOAN
John Gielgud film — TIME AFTER TIME
John Gielgud's title — SIR
John Glenn's former org. — NASA
John Herzfeld TV film: 1987 — DADDY
John Jacob _____ — ASTOR
John Jacob or Mary — ASTOR
John Keats, e.g. — ODIST
John L. Lewis's group in the 30's — CIO
John Law — OFFICER
John McCormack song subject — MOTHER MACHREE
John Milton's Rx? — FEAST AND REVELRY
John or Bo — DEREK
John or Jane — DOE
John or Maureen — OHARA
John Paul II — POPE
John Paul II's title — HOLINESS
John Paul Jones captured this — SERAPIS
John Paul's title: Abbr. — SSD
John Paul, for one — POLE
John Philip's folks — SOUSAS
John Q. Adams' VP — JOHN CALHOUN
John Ritter's dad — TEX
John Travolta musical — GREASE
John Wayne film — HONDO
John Wayne film: 1953 — HONDO
John Wayne movie: 1969 — TRUE GRIT
John Wellington Wells' profes-sion — SORCERER
John who wed Pocahontas — ROLFE
John Wilkes Booth, e.g. — ACTOR
John's PGA stint? — COOKS TOUR
John, in Cardiff — EVAN
John, in Wales — EVAN
Johnny _____ — REB
Johnny Appleseed was one — PIONEER
Johnny of N.F.L. fame — UNITAS
Johnny of the C.S.A. — REB
Johnny Reb's org. — CSA
Johnny's bandleader — DOC
Johnny's here — NBC
Johnnycake — BREAD
Johnson and Knotts — DONS
Johnson of "Laugh-In" — ARTE
Johnson of "The Front Page" — HILDY
Johnson's "_____ Man in His Humour" — EVERY
Joie de vivre — ELAN, GUSTO
Join — ADD, ENLIST, ENTER, UNITE, WED
Join a cause — ENLIST
Join a meeting — ATTEND
Join ends — SPLICE
Join forces with — SIDE
Join the army — ENLIST
Join together — ANNEX
Join with thread — SEW
Joined — ENTERED, SPLICED
Joined in a common cause — ALLIED
Joined securely — MORTISED
Joined together for sports — TEAMED
Joined up: Abbr. — ENL
Joiner of a sort — AND
Joiner's groove — RABBET, SEAM
Joiners — UNITERS
Joining of a sort — SEAM
Joins — SPLICES, UNITES
Joins metallically — WELDS
Joins permanently — WELDS
Joint — ANKLE, ARTHRON, ELBOW, KNEE, SEAM
Joint or cap — KNEE
Joint or switch — TOGGLE
Joint part — TENON
Joint partaker — SHARE
Joint projection — TENON
Joint with a cap — KNEE
Joint: Comb. form — ARTHRO
Jointed feelers — PALPI
Joints — KNEES
Joist — STUD
Joker — CARD, RIBBER, WAG
Joker Jay — LENO
Joker, maybe — CARD
Jokester — BANTERER
Jolly boat — YAWL
Jolly Roger feature — CROSS-BONES
Jolson and Hirt — ALS
Jolson relative — SONNY BOY
Jolson song hit: 1920 — AVALON
Jolson topper — YOU AINT HEARD NOTHIN YET
Jolt — JAR
Jonathan — APPLE
Jonathan Livingston _____ — SEAGULL
Jonathan Livingston, for one — SEAGULL
Jonathan Winters, e.g. — COMEDIAN
Jones' prize: 1779 — SERAPIS
Jones's partner — DOW
Jong — ERICA
Jongg lead-in — MAH
Joplin compositions — RAGS
Joplin creation — RAG
Joplin work — RAG
Joppolo's post — ADANO
Jordan feat — SLAM DUNK
Jordan neighbor — SYRIA
Jordan River state — UTAH
Jordan target — NET
Jordan's Amman — CAPITAL
Jordan's neighbor: Abbr. — SYR
Jordan's queen — NOOR
Jordan's tongue — ARABIC
Jorge of baseball — ORTA
Jorum — JUG
Jose Luis of tennis — CLERC
Jose Maria _____, Spanish painter — SERT
Jose's aunt — TIA
Jose's uncles — TIOS
Joseph Lincoln's "Cap'n _____" — ERI
Joseph's grandmother — REBEKAH
Joseph's pride — COAT
Josh — RIB
Joshed — BANTERED
Joshua's cohort — CALEB
Josip Broz — TITO
Jostle — BUMP, SHOVE
Jostled — ELBOWED
Jostles — POKES, SHOVES

Jot — ATOM, ENTER, IOTA, MITE, TITTLE, WHIT
Jot down — NOTE
Jotted down — NOTED
Jounce — BUMP
Jourdan role in "The Swan" — TUTOR
Journal — CAHIER, PAPER
Journal attachment — ESE
Journal ending — ESE
Journalist — SCRIBE
Journalist Adolph — OCHS
Journalist Bernstein — CARL
Journalist Bly — NELLY
Journalist Jacob — RIIS
Journalist Joseph — ALSOP
Journalist Pyle — ERNIE
Journalize — ENTER
Journals — DIARIES
Journey — TRAVEL, TRIP
Journey by wagon — TREK
Journey for Juvenal — ITER
Journey stages — LEGS
Journey's _____ — END
Joust — TILT
Joust standards — PENNONS
Jousted — TILTED
Jouster's weapon — LANCE
Jousting weapon — LANCE
Jousting wear — ARMOR
Jousts — TILTS
Jove, to Juvenal — GOD
Joy — DELIGHT
Joy Adamson's lioness — ELSA
Joy ride — SPIN
Joyce and Stritch — ELAINES
Joyce Carol Oates work — THEM
Joyce Kilmer subject — TREE
Joyce Kilmer topic — TREE
Joyce's "_____ Livia Plurabelle" — ANNA
Joyce's land — ERIN
Joyful — GLADSOME
Joyful tune — LILT
Joyless — GRIM
Joyner-Kersee, for one — RACER
Joyous — GLAD
Joyous, in Strasbourg — GAI
Jr. for example — DESC
Jr. High, e.g. — SCH
Jr.'s junior — SOPH
Jr.'s sib — BRO, SIS
Jrs.' elders — SRS
Juan and Quixote — DONS
Juan Carlos of Espana — REY
Juan Carlos's realm — SPAIN
Juan Carlos's spouse — REINA
Juan Carlos, one — REY
Juan Domingo _____ — PERON
Juan or Carlos — DON
Juan or Salvador — SAN
Juan's assent — SISI
Juan's eight — OCHO
Juan's January — ENERO
Juan's mother in Byron's "Don Juan" — INEZ
Juan's new daughter — NINA
Juan's river — RIO
Juan's spouse — EVITA
Juan's uncles — TIOS
Juarez jar — OLLA
Juarez resident's neighbor — EL PASOAN
Jubal _____ of the C.S.A. — EARLY
Jubal's invention — ORGAN
Jubilation — GLEE
Jubilee — GALA
Judah Ben- _____ — HUR
Judah's second son: Gen. 38: 4 — ONAN
Judd Hirsch role — ALEX
Judd Hirsch series — TAXI
Judd Hirsch vehicle — TAXI
Judd Hirsch's TV show — TAXI
Judean king — HEROD
Judge — ARBITER, DEEM, RATE, RATER
Judge a case — TRY
Judge again — RETRY
Judge for Dred Scott — TANEY
Judge Priest's creator — COBB
Judge served by Samuel — ELI
Judge the worth — ASSAY
Judge's bench — BANC
Judge's concern — LAWS
Judge's demand — ORDER
Judge's determination — BAIL
Judge's directive — COURT ORDER, ORDER IN THE COURT
Judge's judgments — SENTENCES
Judge's wear — ROBE
Judgelike — SOBER
Judgement — DOOM, ESTIMATE
Judges' garb — ROBES
Judges' seats — BANCS
Judicial — LEGAL
Judicial action — APPEAL
Judicial assertion — DICTA
Judicial decrees — ARRETS
Judicial disqualification — RECUSAL
Judicial garb — ROBE
Judicial garments — ROBES
Judicial seating — BANCS
Judicial writ — ELEGIT, TALES
Judiciary document — WRIT
Judicious — SAGE
Judy Garland flick — MEET ME IN ST LOUIS
Judy's daughter — LIZA
Judy's girl — LIZA
Jug — EWER
Jug handles — EARS
Jug lug — EAR
Juggle — RIG
Juice: Prefix — OPO
Juicers — REAMERS
Juicy East Coast city? — ORANGE NEW JERSEY
Juicy fruits — ORANGES
Jujitsu and judo — ARTS
Juju — FETISH
Jujube — DATE
Jujube or loquat — FRUIT
Jukebox — NICKELODEON
Jul. and Aug. — MOS
Julep enhancement — MINT
Julep ingredient — MINT
Julia of "Man of LaMancha" — RAUL
Julia Ward _____ — HOWE
Julia Ward or Elias — HOWE
Julian — CALENDAR
Julian of "The Red and the Black" — SOREL
Julie Andrews film: 1981 — SOB
Juliet or Cordelia — HEROINE
Juliet's emotion — AMORE
Juliet's family name — CAPULET
Juliette Low's org. — GSA
Julio Iglesias, at home — SENOR
July farm journal entry — HOW DRY I AM
July Fourth sight — SKY-ROCKET
July hrs. — DST
Jumble — HASH, HODGE-PODGE, OLIO, MEDLEY
Jumble together — CONFUSE
Jumbles — HASHES
Jumbo — GIANT
Jump — LEAP
Jump bail — FLEE
Jump on ice — AXEL
Jump rope — SKIP
Jump suit — COVERALL
Jump the track — DERAIL
Jumped — LEAPT
Jumpers do it — SOAR
Jumping bean — SEED
Jumping insect — FLEA
Jumpy noblemen? — LORDS ALEAPING
Junction — JOINT
Juncture — SEAM
June 15th, e.g. — IDES
June 6, 1944 — DDAY
June anniversary — DDAY
June birthstone — PEARL
June bug — DOR
June celebrant — DAD
June grads — SRS
June heroes — DADS
June honorees — DADS
June setting — ALTAR
June VIP — BRIDE, DAD
June words — I DO
June, 1944 event — DDAY
Jungfrau, e.g. — ALP
Jungle alerts — ROARS

Jungle denizen — LION, PARROT
Jungle film of 1955 — SIMBA
Jungle grass — POA
Jungle jaunt — SAFARI
Jungle queen — SHEENA
Jungle sound — ROAR
Jungle trek — SAFARI
Jungle vine — LIANE
Junior — SON
Junior miss — LASS
Junior's expletive — GEE
Junior's imprecation — DARN
Juniper — CEDAR
Juniper of the Bible — RETEM
Junk — TRASH
Junk mail usually — THIRD CLASS
Junk part — SAIL
Junked jalopies — CRATES
Junket — TOUR, TRIP
Junkmen — BRUISED CAR DEALERS
Juno, e.g. — DEA
Juno, to Cato — DEA
Junta — CABAL
Jupati — PALM
Jupiter — JOVE
Jupiter, e.g. — PLANET
Jurassic division — LIAS
Juridic — LEGAL
Jurisprudence — LAW
Juror's group — PANEL
Juror, in theory — PEER
Jury — PANEL
Jury list — PANEL
Jury member — PEER
Jury panel — VENIRE
Jury summons — VENIRE
Jury-rigged — HAYWIRE
Jurymen — PEERS
Jus soli — RIGHT OF LAND
Just a _____ — SEC
Just a taste — SIP
Just average — SOSO
Just deserts — MEEDS
Just great — SUPER
Just like ewe? — OVINE
Just managed, with "out" — EKED
Just off the press — HOT
Just out — NEW
Just out of reach — SO NEAR YET SO FAR
Just plain pennies? — COMMON CENTS
Just so — TO A T
Justice Burger — WARREN
Justice Frankfurter — FELIX
Justice Hugo — BLACK
Justice of the peace — SQUIRE
Justice Warren — EARL
Justification — WARRANTY
Justification for existence — RAISON D ETRE
Justified, as margins — EVENED
Justifies — DEFENDS
Justin Kaplan subject — TWAIN
Jutland natives — DANES
Jutlander — DANE
Juvenal work — SATIRE
Juvenile — YOUNG
Juvenile delinquent residence? — YOUTH HOSTILE
Juvenile infatuation — PUPPY LOVE
Juxtapose — ABUT

K

K-S connection — LMNOPQR
K and C — RATIONS
K-O connection — LMN
K.C.-N.Y.C. direction — ENE
K.D. of country music — LANG
Ka _____, Hawaiian cape — LAE
Kabuki costume adornment — OBI
Kabuki prop — FAN
Kabuki, for example — DRAMA
Kabul canine — AFGHAN HOUND
Kachina, e.g. — DOLL
Kaffee _____ — KLATSCH
Kafka heroine — OLGA
Kahn man — OTTO
Kaiser — RULER
Kalahari and Kara Kum — DESERTS
Kalahari or Thar — DESERT
Kalashnikov, for one — RIFLE
Kale's relative — CHARD
Kaleidoscopic — LABILE, MOBILE, MOTLEY
Kaline and Simmons — ALS
Kálmán operetta — SARI
Kalmar-Ruby question — WHOS SORRY NOW
Kampala is here — UGANDA
Kampala is its capital — UGANDA
Kan. city — IOLA
Kandinsky's output — ART
Kane director — WELLES
Kane, to Welles — PART
Kaneohe and Kawaihae — BAYS
Kanga's child, et al. — ROOS
Kanga's creator — MILNE
Kanga's kin — ROOS
Kansas capital — TOPEKA
Kansas flag motto — AD ASTRA PER ASPERA
Kansas native — JAYHAWK
Kansas or Massachusetts cabbage — COLESLAWRENCE
Kansas Senator — DOLE
Kant's concern — EGO
Kanten — AGAR
Kaplan of TV — GABE
Kaput — ALL UP, BROKEN, DEAD, EXTINCT
Karate blow — CHOP
Karate blow — CHOP
Karate expert — BLACK BELT
Karate trophy — BELT
Karate's cousin — JUDO
Kareem's team — LAKERS
Karen's 1934 nemesis? — THE BLACK CAT
Karenina — ANNA
Karenina or Christie — ANNA
Karloff film: 1940 — THE APE
Karloff role — MUMMY
Karma — FATE
Karras and Haley — ALEXES
Karras of TV — ALEX
Kashmir's capital — SRINAGAR
Kassel river — FULDA
Katarina Witt feat — AXEL
Katarina Witt's leap — AXEL
Kate and H. Allen — SMITHS
Kate Nelligan movie, 1985 — ELENI
Kate of "Atlantic City" — REID
Kate's TV friend — ALLIE
Kathleen _____, actress on "Knots Landing" — NOONE
Kathleen Battle, for one — DIVA
Katmandu citizen — NEPALESE
Katmandu is here — NEPAL
Katmandu is its capital — NEPAL
Katmandu locale — NEPAL

Katmandu's continent — ASIA
Kauai greeting — ALOHA
Kauai hi — ALOHA
Kauai mementos — LEIS
Kay of song — ARMEN
Kay Thompson character — ELOISE
Kayak — CANOE
Kayo — END
Kayo or lulu — ONER
Kazakh and Kirghiz — SSRS
Kazakh-Uzbek border sea — ARAL
Kazan — ELIA
Kazan of Hollywood — ELIA
Kazan resident — TATAR
Keaton — DIANE
Keaton "The General" — MOVIE
Keaton and Sawyer — DIANES
Keaton of "Annie Hall" — DIANE
Keaton or Crabbe — BUSTER
Keaton or Sawyer — DIANE
Keats creation — ODE
Keats feats — ODES
Keats or Yeats — POET
Keats output — ODES, POETRY
Keats poem — ODE
Keats subject — GRECIAN URN
Keats title opening — ODE ON
Keats wished to bare these — ALL NAKED TRUTHS
Keats, for example — POET
Keatsian game — ODE
Keatsian output — ODES
Keatsian work — ODE
Kebab choice — LAMB
Kedrova of "Zorba the Greek" — LILA
Keel-shaped part — CARINA
Keel — BOARD, CENTERBOARD, KEELSON
Keel over — FAINT, SWOON
Keelbills — ANIS
Keeling — ALIST
Keen — ACUTE, ALERT, EAGER, SHARP
Keen desire — EAGER
Keen pain — STING
Keen-eyed — ACUTE, PERCEPTIVE, SHARP
Keened — WAILED
Keener from Kerry — BANSHEE
Keening sound — WAIL
Keenness — ACUMEN
Keenness of perception — ACUMEN
Keep _____ (persevere) — AT IT
Keep _____ (watch) — TABS ON
Keep _____ on — AN EYE
Keep _____ on — THE LID
Keep _____ on (watch) — AN EYE, TABS
Keep _____: (hold off) — AT BAY
Keep a rein on — CONTROL
Keep afloat — BUOY
Keep an _____ the ground — EAR TO
Keep an _____ the ground; stay informed — EAR TO
Keep an eye on — GUARD, WATCH
Keep at — ENDURE, GRIND, PERSIST
Keep at it — PERSIST
Keep away from — SHUN
Keep back — HOLD
Keep company (with) — CONSORT
Keep from harm — PRESERVE
Keep going effortlessly — COAST
Keep in custody — DETAIN
Keep in reserve — STORE
Keep intact — PRESERVE
Keep mum — BUTTON ONES LIP
Keep one's cool — ACCEPT
Keep one's distance — AVOID
Keep one's head above water — ENDURE, FLOAT
Keep quiet! — SHH
Keep score — TALLY
Keep scoreless — BLANK
Keep the home fires burning — STOKE
Keep watch on — SPY
Keep within bars — RESTRICT
Keeper — GUARD, JAILER, TURNKEY
Keeper of an elephant — MAHOUT
Keeper of birds — AVIARIST
Keeper of pigs — SWINEHERD
Keeper, to inmates — SCREW
Keeping in view — EYEING
Keeps — RETAINS
Keeps costs low — SKIMPS
Keeps in check — CURBS
Keeps plugging — STRIVES
Keepsake — RELIC, SOUVENIR, TOKEN
Keeve — TUB
Kefauver — ESTES
Keg — CASK, VAT
Keg stoppers — BUNGS
Kegler's lane — ALLEY
Kegler's milieu — LANES
Kegling — BOWLING
Kegs carrier — TRUCK
Keister — FANNY, PRAT, REAR
Keith and Hunter — IANS
Keith of film — BRIAN
Kelep — ANT
Keller or Hayes — HELEN
Kelly and Krupa — GENES
Kelly and Raymond — GENES
Kelly film: 1952 — SINGING IN THE RAIN
Kelly forte — SONG AND DANCE
Kelly of W.W. II fame — COLIN
Kelly or Tierney — GENE
Kelly's cartoon — POGO
Kelly's creature — POGO
Kelly/Reynolds musical: 1952 — SINGING IN THE RAIN
Kelp, for one — ALGA
Kemo _____, Tonto's "trusty scout" — SABE
Kemo _____, Tonto's pal — SABE
Kemper, in K.C. — ARENA
Kemper, in Kansas City — ARENA
Ken — KNOWLEDGE
Ken of "Thirtysomething" — OLIN
Kenesaw Mountain _____ of baseball fame — LANDIS
Kennedy and Koppel — TEDS
Kennedy arrs. — SSTS
Kennedy customer — PASSENGER
Kennedy Library designer — PEI
Kennedy location — AIRLINE TERMINAL
Kennedy matriarch — ROSE
Kennedy or Knight — TED
Kennel — POUND, SHELTER
Kennel adjunct — RUN
Kennel cacophony — BARKS
Kennel caution? — STEP ON NO PETS
Kennel creature — POODLE
Kennel cry — YELP
Kennel din — YAPS
Kennel problem — FLEAS
Kennel sound — YAP, YIP
Kennel sounds — GNARS
Kensington Park vehicles — PRAMS
Kent's girlfriend — LANE
Kenton — STAN
Kentucky capital — FRANKFORT
Kentucky college town — BEREA
Kentucky Derby prize — ROSES
Kentucky Derby winner: 1935 — OMAHA
Kentucky Derby winner: 1955 — SWAPS
Kentucky garden creatures? — BLUE GRASSHOPPERS
Kentucky grass — BLUE
Kenya export — TEA
Kenya's capital — NAIROBI
Kenyan organization of the 1950's — MAU MAU
Kenyatta — JOMO

Kepi features — VISORS
Kept — HELD
Kept — RETAINED
Kept a tryst — MET
Kept back — DETAINED
Kept going — RAN ON
Kept in bondage — ENSLAVED
Kerchief — SCARF
Kermes — GRAIN
Kermis — FAIR
Kermit — FROG
Kermit as a kid — TADPOLE
Kern and Robbins — JEROMES
Kern musical — ROBERTA
Kern show — SUNNY
Kernel — CORE, GRAIN, PITH, SEED, STONE
Kerouac's "Big _____" — SUR
Kerr or Hersholt — JEAN
Kerr role — ANNA
Kerry's land — EIRE
Kersenneh — ERS
Kersey — FABRIC
Kesey and Rosewall — KENS
Kestrel — FALCON
Ketch-like craft — GALIOTS
Ketch tippers — GALES
Kett of the Comics — ETTA
Kettle — TEAPOT
Kettle and Bell — MAS
Kettle emission — STEAM
Kettle of fish — MESS
Kew Gardens in London — PARK
Key — BASAL, CAY, ISLE, ISLET, PITCH, SKELETON
Key _____ — LARGO
Key _____ pie — LIME
Key battle in Normandy — ST LO
Key dice throw — SEVEN
Key letter — BETA, PHI
Key men in the military — CADRE
Key of Beethoven's Fifth — C MINOR
Key of Beethoven's Seventh — A MAJOR
Key pie ingredients — LIMES
Key signature — B FLAT
Key to heredity — DNA
Key watched o'er them — RAMPARTS
Key work — ANTHEM
Key, in Cannes — CLE
Keyboard — CLAVIER
Keyboard instrument — CELESTA, ORGAN
Keyed — INDEXED
Keyhole — SLOT
Keyhole snoop — PEEPER
Keynote — ESSENCE, THEME
Keys' kin — ISLES
Keystone comedy missiles — PIES
Keystone State founder — PENN
Keystone State's eponym — PENN
KGB predecessor — NKVD
Khabarovsk's river — AMUR
Khachaturian — ARAM
Khaki-colored cotton twill — CHINO
Khakis — JEANS
Khan — TITLE
Khan's namesakes — ALYS
Khartoum residents — SUDANESE
Khartoum's country — SUDAN
Khartoum's land — SUDAN
Khartoum's river — NILE
Khayyam — OMAR
Khayyam and namesakes — OMARS
Khayyam and Sharif — OMARS
Khedive — RULER
Khirghiz range — ARAI
Khomeini's country — IRAN
Khomeini, for one — IRANI
Khrushchev, et al. — NIKITAS
Kibitz — BUTT IN
Kibitz, in a way — IMPOSE
Kick — BOOT, PUNT, PROPEL
Kick (someone) upstairs — PROMOTE
Kick around — ABUSE, MISUSE, MALTREAT
Kick downstairs — DEMOTE
Kick off — START
Kick or step starter — SIDE
Kick out — BUMS RUSH, DISPEL, EXPEL, OUST
Kickback — BRIBE, PERCENTAGE, SHARE
Kicked off — BOOTED
Kicker's asset — TOE
Kicker's nightmare — BLOCKED KICK
Kicking's companion — ALIVE
Kicks a football — PUNTS
Kicks a pigskin — PUNTS
Kid — GOAT, JEST, JOSH, RIB
Kid _____ of jazz fame — ORY
Kid around — CRACK A JOKE
Kid sister's garb — HAND ME DOWN
Kid's game — TAG
Kidnap — ABDUCT, CAPTURE, STEAL
Kidnap in Nanking — SHANGHAI
Kidney related — RENAL
Kids' hero of radio and early TV — CAPTAIN MIDNIGHT
Kids' play — TAG
Kids' sport event — THREE LEGGED RACE
Kiel or Suez — CANAL
Kiel, e.g. — CANAL
Kigali is its capital — RWANDA
Kilauaea dffusian — LAVA
Kilimanjaro sight — SNOWS
Kill, as a bill — VETO
Killarney lass — COLLEEN
Killer whale — ORCA
Killer, in London — RIPPER
Killjoy's admonitions — DONTS
Kills flies — SWATS
Kills time — POTTERS
Killy's sport — SKIING
Kilmer last words — A TREE
Kilmer opus — TREES
Kilmer poem — TREES
Kilmer subject — TREE
Kilmer title — TREES
Kilmer's ending — A TREE
Kilmer's ideal — TREE
Kiln — OAST, OVEN
Kiln for hops — OSAT
Kilt — FILIBEG, SKIRT
Kilt country — SCOTLAND
Kilt feature — PLEAT
Kiltie's dagger — DIRK
Kim Basinger movie: 1987 — NADINE
Kimono accessory — OBI
Kimono adjuncts — OBIES
Kimono sash — OBI
Kimono wrappers — OBIS
Kin — RELATED
Kin of "By Jove" — EGAD
Kin of "drats" — EGADS
Kin of a dalmatic — ALB
Kin of a parvis — STOA
Kin of a sieva — LIMA
Kin of an asor — LYRE
Kin of aves — RDS
Kin of bravo — OLE
Kin of calends — IDES
Kin of cock-and-bull stories — FIBS
Kin of daboias — ASPS
Kin of etc. — ET AL
Kin of floribundas — TEA ROSES
Kin of fulmars — ERNS
Kin of Houri — SIREN
Kin of hydria — EWER
Kin of hydriae — EWERS
Kin of kerplunk — SPLAT
Kin of least — MEREST
Kin of Micmacs — SACS
Kin of morganatic marriage — MESALLIANCE
Kin of nix — NOPE
Kin of P.D.Q. — ASAP
Kin of paraments — ALBS
Kin of peristyles — ATRIA
Kin of pine martens — SABLES
Kin of rhoncus in the bronchus — RALE
Kin of savannas — VELDTS
Kin of secs. and mins. — HRS
Kin of strathspeys — REELS
Kin of tchus and pfuis — BAHS

Kin of Tennyson's venison — KEATS MEATS
Kin of the edges of ledges — EAVES
Kin of the shaddock — GRAPEFRUIT
Kin of to explain — ID EST
Kin of togae — STOLAE
Kin of tombolos — REEFS
Kin of Tonys — OBIES
Kin of vibrissae — SETAE
Kin of viols — REBECS
Kin of W.W. II landing craft — LCI
Kin to "drat" — DANG
Kin to a hero — HOAGY
Kin to an English horn — OBOE
Kin to the ides — NONES
Kin to ukase — IRADE
Kin to velvet — PANNE
Kind — GENRE, ILK, SORT, TYPE
Kind of a race — DRAG
Kind of accompaniment — CHAPERONAGE
Kind of acid — AMINO, BORIC, FOLIC, OLEIC
Kind of acid used in poison gas — PRUSSIC
Kind of admiral — REAR
Kind of age — TEEN
Kind of algebra — BOOLEAN, LINEAR
Kind of American — AFRO
Kind of angle — ACUTE
Kind of antenna — DISH, RABBIT EARS
Kind of apple — ROME
Kind of arch — OGEE
Kind of arch? — MATRI
Kind of bag — TOTE
Kind of bag or ball — BEAN
Kind of bag, bank or bar — SAND
Kind of ball — RUBBER
Kind of band — ONE MAN
Kind of bank — DATA, ENTRY, SOIL
Kind of bar — SALAD
Kind of barn or port — CAR
Kind of barrel — PORK
Kind of basil — SWEET
Kind of basin — TIDAL
Kind of bass — BIG MOUTH
Kind of battery — SOLAR, STORAGE
Kind of beam — LASER
Kind of bean — LIMA, PINTO
Kind of bear — POLAR
Kind of beaver — EAGER
Kind of bee — QUILTING
Kind of beer — DRAFT
Kind of bet — ACROSS THE BOARD
Kind of bicycle — TANDEM
Kind of bike — DIRT
Kind of bird — EARLY
Kind of blanket — WET
Kind of blond — ASH
Kind of blueberry — RABBIT EYE
Kind of board — TOTE
Kind of board or walker — FLOOR
Kind of boarder — STAR
Kind of boat? — GRAVY, PIG
Kind of bog in Wareham, Mass: — CRANBERRY
Kind of bond — BAIL
Kind of bonsai — MING TREE
Kind of boom — SONIC
Kind of bopper — TEENY
Kind of bore — TIDAL
Kind of bottom or face — FALSE
Kind of box — BALLOT, MITER
Kind of box or joint — MITER
Kind of bracelet — ANKLE
Kind of brake — DISC
Kind of bran — OAT
Kind of bread — GLUTEN, RYE, SOURDOUGH
Kind of break on TV — STA
Kind of breath — BATED
Kind of bridge — COVERED
Kind of brother — LAY
Kind of brown — SIENNA
Kind of Buddhism — ZEN
Kind of bug — LITTER
Kind of bug or fly — ASSASSIN
Kind of bulb — FLASH
Kind of bull — PAPAL
Kind of buoy — NUN
Kind of bus — MINI
Kind of buster — SOD
Kind of button — PUSH
Kind of cake or tart — TEA
Kind of candle — VOTIVE
Kind of cap — BERET
Kind of car — ARMORED, COUPE, PROWL, SEDAN
Kind of car or maid — PARLOR
Kind of card — CREDIT, GREETING, HONOR
Kind of card or union — POSTAL
Kind of case — FEDERAL
Kind of case or flight — TEST
Kind of cat — SCAREDY
Kind of caterpillar — TENT
Kind of charge — DEPTH
Kind of chart — PIE
Kind of cheese — BRIE, EDAM
Kind of chemical dye — AZO
Kind of chest or dog — SEA
Kind of china — BONE
Kind of ck. — CERT
Kind of clam — RAZOR
Kind of cleft or flute — ALTO
Kind of clock or table — TIME
Kind of cloth or paint — OIL
Kind of club — GLEE
Kind of coal or coat — PEA
Kind of coal or pump — JET
Kind of coat — TRENCH
Kind of code — AREA, DRESS, MORSE, ZIP
Kind of coffee — DRIP
Kind of collision — MIDAIR
Kind of color — LOCAL
Kind of column — DORIC
Kind of comb or bear — HONEY
Kind of combat — HAND TO HAND
Kind of comfort — CREATURE
Kind of committee — AD HOC
Kind of computer — ANALOG
Kind of consciousness or book — CLASS
Kind of conservation — SOIL
Kind of cook — SHORT ORDER
Kind of cord — RIP
Kind of cotton — PIMA
Kind of cotton cloth — CALICO
Kind of crab — SOFTSHELL
Kind of cracker — ANIMAL, SAFE, SODA
Kind of cross — MALTESE, TAU
Kind of current — INSHORE
Kind of daboias — ASPS
Kind of dam — WEIR
Kind of dance — TOE
Kind of dancer — GO GO, TOE
Kind of Danish — PRUNE
Kind of deck — POOP
Kind of decorator — INTERIOR
Kind of deed — TITLE
Kind of deer — ROE
Kind of derby — ROLLER
Kind of design — INTERIOR
Kind of desk — ROLLTOP
Kind of dictum — OBITER
Kind of diet — NO SALT
Kind of distance — METRIC
Kind of dive — CRASH, NOSE
Kind of dollars — EURO, PETRO
Kind of door — GATE
Kind of door or screen — SMOKE
Kind of dorm — COED
Kind of down — EIDER
Kind of dragon — SNAP
Kind of dress — SHEATH
Kind of driver — SLAVE
Kind of drop — TEAR
Kind of dropper — EAVES
Kind of drum — BONGO, SNARE
Kind of duck or sisal — BAHAMA
Kind of dunk — SLAM

Kind of dye — ANILINE, AZO
Kind of ear — TIN
Kind of eared seal — OTARY
Kind of eclipse — SOLAR
Kind of editor or hall — CITY
Kind of elec. key — IGN
Kind of embroidery — EYELET
Kind of energy — SOLAR
Kind of engine — DIESEL, INLINE, MULE
Kind of estate — REAL
Kind of exam — ORAL
Kind of expression — PAINED
Kind of eye or eel — ELECTRIC
Kind of eye or hand — GLAD
Kind of facts — BARE
Kind of fee — ADMISSION
Kind of fence — RAIL
Kind of fever — LASSA
Kind of fine china — BONE
Kind of fir or cypress — SHASTA
Kind of fish or dance — SWORD
Kind of fish or flower — GLOBE
Kind of fisherman — EELER
Kind of flakes or snow — CORN
Kind of flight — SOLO
Kind of flight or pilot — TEST
Kind of floor — INLAID
Kind of flush — ROYAL
Kind of food — FAST
Kind of food or music — SOUL
Kind of foot or head — HOT
Kind of friendship — PLATONIC
Kind of frog? — LEAP
Kind of frost — HOAR, PERMA
Kind of fugue — TONAL
Kind of furnace — BLAST
Kind of game or walk — BOARD
Kind of garden — TRUCK
Kind of geometry — SOLID
Kind of German silver — ALBATA
Kind of gin — SLOE
Kind of glass — HOUR, OPERA
Kind of glass or lamp — OPAL
Kind of glass or table — PIER
Kind of grand slams — VOLES
Kind of grapes — SOUR
Kind of grind — DRIP
Kind of grinder — ORGAN
Kind of guard — NOSE
Kind of guidance — PARENTAL
Kind of hairdo — AFRO
Kind of hall — MESS
Kind of hat — FEDORA
Kind of heating — SOLAR
Kind of helmets — PITH
Kind of help — HIRED
Kind of highway — INTERSTATE
Kind of history — CASE, ORAL
Kind of hitter — SWITCH
Kind of hog — WART
Kind of hole or note — KEY
Kind of holiday — ROMAN
Kind of house — ALPHA FRAME, PENT, PREFAB
Kind of husky — SIBERIAN
Kind of ingenuity — YANKEE
Kind of ink — INDIA
Kind of insect — ANT, BORER, PISMIRE
Kind of inspection — ON SITE
Kind of iron — FLAT
Kind of iron or shovel — STEAM
Kind of jack or suit — UNION
Kind of jacket — ETON
Kind of jam — RASPBERRY
Kind of jazz — BOP, DIXIELAND
Kind of jet — GAS
Kind of jockey — DISC
Kind of joint — SEAM
Kind of jump — BROAD
Kind of jury — PETIT
Kind of kale — COLLARD
Kind of kettle — TEA
Kind of kitchen — EAT IN
Kind of knot — GRANNY
Kind of lantern — CHINESE
Kind of larceny — PETIT
Kind of leather — TOOLED
Kind of license — POETIC
Kind of light — STOP
Kind of light or bulb — FLASH
Kind of lily — CALLA, SEGO, TIGER
Kind of line — PLUMB
Kind of line to sign — DOTTED
Kind of lot — SAND
Kind of lottery — RAFFLE
Kind of lover or keeper — BOOK
Kind of maid — METER
Kind of mail — BULK
Kind of mail boat — PACKET
Kind of majority — SIDED
Kind of man — YES
Kind of man or boss — STRAW
Kind of man or mat — DOOR
Kind of market — EURO, FLEA
Kind of marm or master — SCHOOL
Kind of master or hunter — HEAD
Kind of measure — CUBIC
Kind of metabolism — BASAL
Kind of mgr. — ASST
Kind of minister or mover — PRIME
Kind of mirror — FULL LENGTH
Kind of miss — NEAR
Kind of money — SEED
Kind of monkey — GREASE
Kind of monster — GILA
Kind of mortgage — CHATTEL
Kind of moss — PEAT
Kind of moth — LUNA, YUCCA
Kind of mother — DEN
Kind of muffin — BRAN
Kind of music — BEPOP, FOLK
Kind of musical note — OPEN TONE
Kind of nail — BOX
Kind of neck blow — RABBIT PUNCH
Kind of nose — PUG, ROMAN
Kind of oak — RED
Kind of oil — CASTOR, LINSEED
Kind of opera — SOAP
Kind of orange — NAVEL
Kind of oven — GLOST
Kind of owl — BARN
Kind of palm — NIPA, SAGO
Kind of pants? — SMARTY
Kind of paper — TAR
Kind of paper or box — SAND
Kind of particle or ray — BETA
Kind of partner — SENIOR
Kind of party — STAG
Kind of performance — REPEAT
Kind of period or home — REST
Kind of phobia — XENO
Kind of phone or drum — EAR
Kind of physics — META
Kind of picker — NIT
Kind of pickle — DILL
Kind of picnic — TAILGATE
Kind of pie — KEY LIME, MINCE, PECAN
Kind of pie or board — CHESS
Kind of pigeon — HOMING
Kind of pile — ATOMIC
Kind of pitch — SALES
Kind of pitcher — RELIEF
Kind of pity or praise — SELF
Kind of plaintiff — USEE
Kind of plan — GAME
Kind of plane — TANGENT
Kind of plane or dynamics — AERO
Kind of plank — GANG
Kind of plant — EGG
Kind of plasm — ECTO
Kind of plaster — SHIN
Kind of plate — FASHION
Kind of play — ONE ACT
Kind of play or power — HORSE
Kind of player — ROLE
Kind of plum, for short — GAGE
Kind of pocket or power — AIR
Kind of poker — LIARS, STUD

Kind of pole — TOTEM
Kind of pony — POLO
Kind of pool — KELLY
Kind of porridge — PEASE
Kind of post — PARCEL
Kind of pottery — WARE
Kind of price — ASKING
Kind of prize — DOOR
Kind of prize or post — DOOR
Kind of processing — DATA
Kind of prof. — ASST
Kind of propeller — SCREW
Kind of pudding — COTTAGE
Kind of pump — SUMP
Kind of race — HARNESS, RAT, RELAY
Kind of rags — GLAD
Kind of rally — PEP
Kind of ray — GAMMA
Kind of reaction — DELAYED
Kind of recall — TOTAL
Kind of relief — BAS
Kind of remark — SNIDE
Kind of remark or stick — POINTED
Kind of renewal — URBAN
Kind of resin — UREA
Kind of resistance — PASSIVE
Kind of resort — LAST
Kind of review — RAVE
Kind of rhyme — NURSERY
Kind of ring — BRASS
Kind of rock — PUNK
Kind of rock or candy — HARD
Kind of rocket — RETRO
Kind of role — DUAL
Kind of room — REC
Kind of room or dancer — TAP
Kind of room, for short — REC
Kind of rug — AREA, BEAR SKIN
Kind of S.D.I. weapon — ASAT
Kind of sail — LATEEN
Kind of salt or wit — ATTIC
Kind of salts — BATH
Kind of sauce — SOY
Kind of saxophone — ALTO
Kind of scene — MOB
Kind of sch. — ELEM
Kind of school — NORMAL, PREP
Kind of school, for short — PREP
Kind of school: Abbr. — ELEM
Kind of scope or meter — ANEMO
Kind of scout — EAGLE
Kind of screw — LAG
Kind of sea duck — EIDER
Kind of seal — EARED
Kind of season — RAINY
Kind of servant — CIVIL
Kind of shadow — EYE
Kind of shelter — HUTCH
Kind of ship — TALL
Kind of ship accommodation — CABIN CLASS
Kind of shirt — HAIR, POLO
Kind of shirt or suit — SWEAT
Kind of shoe — ELEVATOR, PUMP
Kind of shooter — PEA
Kind of shoppe — MALT
Kind of shot — LONG, MUG, SLAP
Kind of shovel — STEAM
Kind of show — LATE, PANEL, RAREE
Kind of shrimp — PRAWN
Kind of sided — LOP
Kind of signal — SMOKE, TURN
Kind of skirt — HOOP, MAXI, MINI
Kind of sole — DOVER
Kind of song — TORCH
Kind of soup — MOCK TURTLE, PEA, TOMATO
Kind of sphere or phyte — TROPO
Kind of sphere? — ATMO
Kind of spirit — EVIL
Kind of split — BANANA
Kind of spoon — RUNCIBLE
Kind of spread — JAM, OLEO
Kind of squash — ACORN
Kind of squeak? — PIP
Kind of staircase — SPIRAL
Kind of star — NOVA
Kind of statesman — ELDER
Kind of steak — T BONE
Kind of steamer — TRAMP
Kind of stick — POGO
Kind of stock — PREFERRED
Kind of stone — STEPPING
Kind of stone or post — MILE
Kind of store: Abbr. — DEPT
Kind of story — FISH, SOB, TALL
Kind of street — ONE WAY, TWO WAY
Kind of stroke — SIDE
Kind of strut — OLEO
Kind of success or monkey — HOWLING
Kind of sugar — MAPLE
Kind of surgeon — NEURO, ORAL
Kind of sweater — TURTLENECK
Kind of synthetic textile fiber — OLEFIN
Kind of system — METRIC, STEREO
Kind of table — END, PIER
Kind of tactics — SCARE
Kind of talk or pitch — SALES
Kind of tank — GAS
Kind of tape — VIDEO
Kind of tax — HEAD
Kind of tea — PEKOE
Kind of team — FARM
Kind of tense — PAST
Kind of terrier — SKYE
Kind of test — ACID, ORAL
Kind of therapy — SERO
Kind of tide — NEAP, PERIGEAN
Kind of tie — BOW
Kind of tiger — PAPER
Kind of tire — SPARE
Kind of titmouse — TUFTED
Kind of toast — MELBA
Kind of ton — MEGA, METRIC
Kind of tooth — SWEET
Kind of total insurance — UMBRELLA POLICY
Kind of towel — BATH
Kind of town — ONE HORSE
Kind of toy — JUMPING JACK
Kind of training — ON THE JOB
Kind of transit — RAPID
Kind of tray — ASH
Kind of tree — EBOE
Kind of triangle — SCALENE
Kind of trip — EGO
Kind of trombone — VALVE
Kind of truck — TWO TON
Kind of trumpet — AIDA
Kind of TV show — TALK
Kind of V.P. — ASST
Kind of verb: Abbr. — IRR
Kind of virus — RNA
Kind of wagon or pot — TEA
Kind of walk — CAKE
Kind of warfare — CHEMICAL
Kind of watch — STOP
Kind of wave — TIDAL
Kind of wave or wing — DELTA
Kind of way — MID, THRU
Kind of well — ARTESIAN
Kind of well or way — STAIR
Kind of whale — SCARG
Kind of wind — ONSHORE, TRADE, WOOD
Kind of window — CASEMENT, DORMER
Kind of wine — ROSE
Kind of wine or salad — DANDELION
Kind of wit — NIT
Kind of worker — WHITE COLLAR
Kind of worker's protest — SLOWDOWN
Kind of works or light — GAS
Kind of wreath — FLORAL
Kind of wrench — ALLEN
Kind of wrestling — ARM, SUMO
Kind of year — LUNAR
Kind of yell — REBEL
Kind RNs give this — TLC
Kind words from a critic — RAVE

Kind words from Clive Barnes — RAVE
Kind, in Calais — SORTE
Kind: Fr. — SORTE
Kindergartener — TOT
Kindle — START
Kindled — LIT
Kindled again — RELIT
Kindling — TINDER
Kinds of ammo — BBS, SHOT
Kinds of mate, politically — RUNNING
Kine — CATTLE
Kinetic — LIVELY
King-sized sandwich — HERO
King — CHARLEMAGNE, LOUIS, RULER, TSAR
King _____ — COLE
King _____ — KONG
King after Ethelred — ALFRED
King and Ladd — ALANS
King and Newton — WAYNES
King and Queen — RULERS
King and Thicke — ALANS
King Arthur's address — CAMELOT
King Arthur's birthplace — TINTAGEL
King Arthur's father — UTHER
King Arthur's final home — AVALON
King Arthur's killer — MODRED
King Arthur's nephew — GAWAIN
King Arthur's resting place — AVALON
King beater — ACE
King Birendra's land — NEPAL
King Cole, et al. — NATS
King Cotton's bundles — BALES
King Hassan's country — MOROCCO
King Ibn _____ — SAUD
King in I Kings — ASA
King James Version — BIBLE
King Kong, e.g. — APE
King Lear's dog — TRAY
King Minos was one — CRETAN
King of ancient Egypt — MENES, RAMSES I
King of ancient Persia — XERXES I
King of Aragon — PEDRO
King of beasts — LION
King of cheeses — BRIE
King of comedy — ALAN
King of Crete — MINOS
King of France — ROI
King of hearts — CARD
King of Hollywood — VIDOR
King of Israel — AHAB
King of Jordan — HUSSEIN
King of Judah — AMON, ASA
King of Judea — HEROD
King of Mommur — OBERON
King of Monaco — RAINIER
King of Norway — OLAV
King of Persia — DARIUS
King of Phrygia — MIDAS
King of Sardinia: c. 1238-49 — ENZIO
King of Scotland: 1124-53 — DAVID
King of Siam's song for Wall St.? — A PUZZLEMENT
King of Spain — REY
King of Sweden — GUSTAV
King of the Huns — ATLI, ATTILA
King of the Meccans: 1953-64 — SAUD
King of Tyre — HIRAM
King or Hagman — LARRY
King or Milne — ALAN
King or Queen — HONOR
King or queen, e.g. — CARD
King Sisters — QUARTET
King toppers — ACES
King who called for a horse — RICHARD THE THIRD
King who lost the colonies — GEORGE THE THIRD
King who married often — HENRY THE EIGHTH
King with the golden touch — MIDAS
King's o.k. — SOLOMONS SEAL
King's predecessors — ALA
King's proxy — REGENT
King's staff — SCEPTER
King's successor, in Vegas — ICE
King: Fr. — ROI
King: Sp. — REY
Kingdom — EMPIRE, REALM
Kingdom east of Babylonia — ELAM
Kingdom in the SW Pacific — TONGA
Kingdoms — REALMS
Kingfish — CERO, HAKU
Kingfisher — BIRD
Kingly — REGAL
Kingly address — SIRE
Kings of the road — HOBOS
Kingsley of letters — AMIS
Kingsley or Hur — BEN
Kingsley title from "Twelfth Night" — WESTWARD HO
Kingsley's "_____ White" — MEN IN
Kingsley's "The Sands of _____" — DEE
Kingston _____ — TRIO
Kingston group — TRIO
Kingston trio hit: 1962 — SCOTCH AND SODA
Kingston Trio's bad lad — TOM DOOLEY
Kingston, for one — TRIO
Kink — KNOT
Kinky comic? — CURL REINER
Kinshasa is its capital — ZAIRE
Kinski role: 1979 — TESS
Kinsman — SIB
Kinsman, for short — REL
Kinsman: Abbr. — REL
Kiosk — STALL
Kiosks' cousins — BOOTHS
Kipfels — ROLLS
Kipling electrician's problem? — LIGHT THAT FAILED
Kipling hero — DIN
Kipling lad — KIM
Kipling words — A RAG
Kipling's "Soldiers _____" — THREE
Kipling's birthplace — BOMBAY
Kipling's Danny — DEEVER
Kipling's Kim — OHARA
Kipling's novel — KIM
Kipling's python — KAA
Kipling's Rikki-tikki _____ — TAVI
Kipling's unfortunate Danny — DEEVER
Kippers herring — CURSE
Kirghiz capital — FRUNZE
Kirghiz range — ALAI
Kirghiz Range mountains — ALAI
Kirghizian mountains — ALAI
Kiribati Islands capital — TARAWA
Kiribati's capital — TARAWA
Kirk of song — LISA
Kirk's journey? — TREK
Kirk's title: Abbr. — CAPT
Kirsch — BRANDY
Kirstie from Wichita — ALLEY
Kirstie of "Cheers" — ALLEY
Kismet — DOOM, FATE, LOT
Kiss — BUSS
Kiss of peace — PAX
Kiss sculptor — RODIN
Kiss's companion — TELL
Kissel and Opel — CARS
Kisser — PAN
Kisses' companions — HUGS
Kist — CHEST
Kit — GEAR, OUTFIT, SET, SUPPLIES, TOOL
Kit contents — TOOLS
Kit of kitten — YOUNG RABBIT
Kit, the frontiersman — CARSON
Kitchen — GALLEY, LARDER, PANTRY, ROOM
Kitchen add-on — ETTE
Kitchen annex — ETTE
Kitchen appliance — BEATER, TOASTER
Kitchen attraction — AROMA
Kitchen commander — COOK
Kitchen emanation — AROMA

Kitchen ender — ETTE
Kitchen equipment — CORER
Kitchen extension — ETTE
Kitchen finish — ETTE
Kitchen fixtures — OVENS, SINKS
Kitchen follower — ETTE
Kitchen gadget — CORER, EGG TIMER, OPENER, RICER
Kitchen girl of song — DINAH
Kitchen implement — RICER
Kitchen item — JAR
Kitchen items — POTS
Kitchen measures — CUPS
Kitchen must — OVEN
Kitchen product — HEAT
Kitchen sieve — COLANDER
Kitchen specialty — AROMA
Kitchen spice — MACE
Kitchen square — TILE
Kitchen staple — OLEO, SODA
Kitchen tag-on — ETTE
Kitchen tool — BLENDER, PARER
Kitchen utensil — MASHER, PEELER, RICER, OPENER
Kitchen wear — APRONS
Kitchen wrap — FOIL
Kitchenware — POTS
Kite — BOX
Kite follower — TAIL
Kite part — TAIL
Kite's cousin — ELANET
Kites — FLYING COLORS
Kith — FRIEND
Kitling — KITTEN
Kitt from S.C. — EARTHA
Kitten's comment — MEW
Kitten's cry — MEOW
Kitten's loss — MITTEN
Kitten's sound — MEW
Kitties — POTS
Kittiwake — GULL
Kittle — TICKLE
Kitty — POOL, RESERVE FUND
Kitty starters — ANTES
Kitty sweetener — ANTE
Kiwi's cousin — MOA
Kiwi's extinct kin — MOA
Kiwi, emu or moa, e.g. — RATITE
Klaxon — HORN
Klee's medium — ART
Klemperer role — KLINK
Klingon foe — KIRK
Klomath weed — EDLA
Klondike's territory — YUKON
Klutz — NERD
Klutz's exclamation — OOPS
Klutzes — CLODS
Klutzy — INAPT
Knack — ART, FORTE, GIFT, HANG, TALENT
Knacks — FLAIRS
Knapsack — BAG, POKE, SADDLEBAG
Knave — CHEAT, JACK, VARLET
Knave of clubs — PAM
Knave's loot — TARTS
Knaves — ROGUES
Knawel or spurry — WEED
Knead — FASHION, FOLD, MASSA, MASSAGE, PRESS, SHAPE
Kneaded mixtures — DOUGHS
Knee — GENU, JOINT
Knee-hole placement — DESK
Kneecap — PATELLA
Knell — PEAL, RING, TOLL
Knesset's country — ISRAEL
Knew — FORESAW
Knick-nack — ORNAMENT, TRIFLE
Knicks and Nets — CAGERS
Knicks' coach — RILEY
Knievel — EVEL
Knife edge — BLADE
Knife handle — HAFT
Knife man — BOWIE
Knife of yore — SNEE
Knight — HORSEMAN, LORD, PRINCE, SIR
Knight fight — TILT
Knight wear — ARMET, ARMOR
Knight's arm — LANCE
Knight's best friend? — STEED
Knight's calling — ERRANTRY
Knight's skullcap — COIF
Knight's title — SIR
Knight's transport — STEED
Knight's weapon — LANCE, POLE AX
Knight's wear — MAIL
Knight's wife — DAME
Knightley's bride — EMMA
Knightly title — SIR
Knightly weapons — MACES
Knights — SIR GERAINT, SIR GALAHAD, SIRS
Knights of "Star Wars" saga — JEDI
Knights of Columbus — ORDER
Knigt of the road — HOBO
Knit — CROCHET, GATHER, HOOK, PURL
Knitted Afghan works — BLANKET
Knitted cotton fabric — LISLE
Knitted shawl of wool — AFGHAN
Knitter's concern — STITCH
Knitter's need — YARN
Knitting needle — ROD
Knitting pattern, from the Scots — ARGYLE
Knitting stitch — PURL
Knitware — CARDIGANS
Knives: Slang — SHIVS
Knob on a pipe organ — STOP
Knobbed — NODAL
Knobby — NODAL
Knock — RAP, TAP
Knock _____ cocked hat — IN TO A
Knock about — WANDER
Knock down — FLATTEN, LEVEL, SMASH
Knock from a steed — UNHORSE
Knock off — WASTE
Knock over a joint — HEIST
Knock to pieces — CHIP
Knock-knock question — WHOS THERE
Knockabout — SLOOP
Knockabout comedy — FARCE
Knocked for a loop — UPENDED
Knocked over — TOPPLED
Knockout blow — SUNDAY PUNCH
Knockout combination — ONE TWO
Knockout of a place — ARENA
Knockout stuff — ETHER
Knocks — RAPS
Knocks down — SMITES
Knocks for a loop — STUNS
Knocks out — FLATTENS
Knoll — HILL, MOUND
Knot again — RETIE
Knot for ties — WINDSOR
Knot in cotton — NEP
Knot in wood — GNAR, KNAR
Knot type — GRANNY
Knot units — SEA MILES
Knotty — NODOSE
Know by cognition — INTUIT
Know by hunch — INTUIT
Know-how — ABILITY
Know: Archaic — WIST
Knowing — AWARE, SCIENT
Knowledge — LORE
Knowledge acquisition — LEARNING
Knowledge: Comb. form — NOMY
Knowledgeable — UP ON
Knows _____ (is hip) — THE SCORE
Knows, in a way — KENS
Knox and Dix — FORTS
Knox and Ord — FORTS
Knoxville footballer — VOL
Knuckle sandwich — PUNCH
Koala — MONKEY BEAR
Koch and colleagues — MAYORS
Kohlrabi — CABBAGE
Kojak — THEO
Kojak and a Huxtable — THEOS

Kojak and a young Huxtable — THEOS
Koko's weapon — SNEE
Kokoon — GNU
Kol _____ (He. prayer) — NIDRE
Kolinsky, e.g. — FUR
Komatik, e.g. — SLED
Komatiks — SLEDS
Kon _____ — TIKI
Kon-Tiki Museum city — OSLO
Kon-Tiki worshiper — INCA
Kon-Tiki, et al. — RAFTS
Kong's first love — WRAY
Konigsberg's philosopher — KANT
Konrad's epithet — ALTE
Kooks — ZANIES
Kopell of "Love Boat" — BERNIE
Koppel — TED
Koppel of "Nightline" — TED
Koppel or Danson — TED
Koppel or Knight — TED
Koppel's namesakes — TEDS
Koran chapter — SURA
Korbut and Petrova — OLGAS
Korchnoi's winning word — MATE
Korda's elephant boy — SABU
Korea — CHOSEN
Korea's Syngman — RHEE
Korean — ASIAN
Korean border river — YALU
Korean boundary river — YALU
Korean G.I. — ROK
Korean seaport — INCHON, PUSAN
Korean soldier — ROC
Korean, for one — ASIAN
Kosher — GENUINE, PERMITTED, RIGHT
Kovacs and Ford — ERNIES
Kovacs and namesakes — ERNIES
Kowalski portrayer: 1947 — BRANDO
Kowtow — BOW
Kraken's habitat — SEA
Krakow natives — POLES
Kramden's vehicle — BUS
Krantz best seller — SCRUPLES
Kravchenko's "_____ Freedom" — I CHOSE
Krazy _____ — KAT
Krazy _____ of comics — KAT
Kringle's burden — TOYS
Kristofferson — KRIS
Krona spender — SWEDE
Kronborg Castle features — MOATS
Kruegerrand — COIN
Kruegerrand's makeup — GOLD
Kruger and Graham — OTTOS
Krypton — SUPERMANS PLANET
Kublai Khan follower — MONGOL
Kubrick film: 1962 — LOLITA
Kudos — FAME, GLORY, HONOR
Kukla's friend — FRAN, OLLIE
Kumquat's shape — OVAL
Kumquat, i.e. — TREE
Kung fu's kin — KARATE
Kura tributary — ARAS
Kurosawa epic — RAN
Kurosawa film: 1985 — RAN
Kuwaiti chief — EMIR
Kuwaiti chieftain — EMIR
Kuwaiti head — EMIR
Kuwaiti title — EMIR
Kvetch — STEW
Ky. college — BEREA
Ky. college town — BEREA
Ky. fort — KNOX
Ky.'s neighbor — ILL
Kyd was one — DRAMATIST
Kyd work — DRAMA
Kyle of football fame — ROTE
Kyoodle — YAP
Kyoto cummerbund — OBI
Kyoto ship — MARU
Kyushu seaport — OITA
Kyushu volcano — ASO

L

L-Q connection — MNOP
L-Q filler — MNOP
L + I — FIFTY ONE
L in roman numerals — FIFTY
L plus L, in roman numerals — CEE
L x W — AREA
L, M and S — SIZES
L-o-n-g times — EONS
L-o-o-n-g stretches — EONS
L-P connection — MNO
L-Q tie — MNOP
L. L'Amour's "The Haunted _____" — MESA
L.A. campus — USC
L.A. eleven — RAMS
L.A. phenomenon — SMOG
L.A. to Reno dir. — NNW
L.A. wintertime — PST
L.A.'s state — CALIF
L.A.-to-Las Vegas dir. — NNE
L.A.-to-San Diego dir. — SSE
L.A.P.D. member — TEC
L.B.J. beagle — HER, HIM
L.B.J.'s "_____ Poverty" — WAR ON
L.B.J.'s birth month — AUG
L.B.J.'s first Supreme Court appointee — FORTAS
La _____ tar pits — BREA
La _____, Milan — SCALA
La _____, Milano's opera house — SCALA
La _____, Spanish seaport — CORUNA
La _____, Trinidad — BREA
La _____, Wisconsin — CROSSE
La _____: French explorer — SALLE
La Boheme — MIMI
La Boheme composer — PUCCINI
La Douce — IRMA
La femme — ELLE
La Gallienne and Gabor — EVAS
La Guardia's neighbor — SHEA
La Mediterranee, e.g. — MER
La predecessor — TRA
La rienda: the _____ in Spain — REIN
La Scala city, to natives — MILANO
La Scala harp — ARPA
La Scala highlight — ARIA
La Scala hit — ARIA
La Scala offering — AIDA
La Scala opera unit — SCENA
La Scala's city — MILAN
La Scala's home — MILAN
La, la predecessor — TRA
La-di-da — SNOBBY
La-di-da — TOO TOO
La-la lead-in — OOH
La. Senator: 1948-87 — RUSSELL LONG
Lab burner — ETNA
Lab container — VIAL
Lab dish — PETRI

Lab equipment — VIAL
Lab feature — X RAY
Lab heater — ETNA
Lab items — VIALS
Lab measures — CCS
Lab procedure — TEST
Lab tube — PIPET
Lab vessels — ETNAS
Lab wire loops — OESES
Laban's eldest daughter — LEAH
Label — MARK, STICKER, TAG
Label again — RETAG
Label anew — RETAG
Labels — TAGS
Labine namesakes — CLEMS
Labor — BIRTH, STRAIN, TOIL, WORK
Labor (struggle) — HEAVE
Labor follower — ITE
Labor for — TRY TO
Labor gp. — ILO
Labor group — CIO, ILO, UNION
Labor hard — MOIL
Labor leader Conboy: 1870-1928 — SARA
Labor leader Eugene _____ — DEBS
Labor leader George — MEANY
Labor org. — ILA, WFTU
Labor org. founded in 1886 — AFL
Labor resource — POOL
Laboratory — STUDIO
Laboratory burners — ETNAS
Laboratory dish — PETRI
Laboratory heater — ETNA
Laboratory phenomenon — ONE CELLED ORGANISM
Laboratory salt — BORATE
Laboratory worker, for one — EXPERIMENTALIST
Labored — FORCED, STRAINED
Labored breath — PANT
Laborer of old — ESNE
Laborer once — ESNE
Laborers of yore — ESNES
Laborious — HARD, TOUGH, TOILSOME, UPHILL
Labyrinth — MAZE, WINDING
Lace — MESH, NET, WEB
Lace edge — PICOT
Lace edging of tiny loops — PICOTS
Lace from Belgium — MECHLIN
Lace holders — AGLETS
Lace into — ASSAIL, FLAIL, SCOLD
Lace shade — ECRU
Lace, in Italy — TRINA
Laced, as a racket — STRUNG
Lacedaemon — SPARTA
Lacelike fabrics — NETS
Lacelike pattern — KNOTTING
Lacerate — CUT, REND, RIP, TEAR
Lacerates — TEARS
Laceration — GASH
Lachrymá — TEAR
Lachrymal drop — TEAR
Lachrymal liquid — TEAR
Lachrymal secretion — TEAR
Lachrymation — CRYING, TEARING
Lachrymose — TEARY
Lack — ABSENCE, DEARTH, NEED, WANT
Lack of accord — DISUNITY
Lack of energy — LANGOUR
Lack of health — MALAISE
Lack of maturity — NONAGE
Lack of purpose — ANOMIE
Lack of restraint — ABANDON
Lack of strength — WEAKNESS
Lack of vigor — ANEMIA
Lackadaisical — CAREFREE, DULL, LAZY
Lackaday! — ALAS
Lacked — HAD NOT, NEEDED
Lackey — MENIAL, PAWN
Lacking — OUT OF, SANS
Lacking a breastbone — ASTERNAL
Lacking a key — ATONAL
Lacking aroma — ODORLESS
Lacking breadth — NARROW
Lacking complications — EASY
Lacking courage — CRAVEN
Lacking emotion — ASEPTIC, STONY
Lacking ethics — AMORAL
Lacking foundation — BASELESS
Lacking heft — LIGHT
Lacking imagination — TRITE
Lacking in freedom — EARTHBOUND
Lacking in richness — LEAN
Lacking in strength — WEAK
Lacking intrepidity — NONHEROIC
Lacking reverence — IMPIOUS
Lacking sense — INANE
Lacking slack — TAUT
Lacking substance — TRITE
Lacking vigor — ANEMIC, EFFETE
Lacking vitality — ANEMIC, ATONY
Lackluster — BLAND, DULL, FLAT
Lacks — DEARTHS, NEEDS
Laconian clan — OBE
Laconian serf — HELOT
Laconic — BRIEF, TERSE
Lacoste and Auberjonois — RENES
Lacoste and Descartes — RENES
Lacoste of tennis — RENE
Lacoste of tennis fame — RENE
Lacquer — GLAZE, PAINT
Lacquer ingredient — ELEMI
Lacquered metalware — TOLE
Lacrimator — TEAR GAS
Lacrimose — TEARY
Lacta _____ est: the die is cast — ALEA
Lacuna — GAP
Lacunae — GAPS
Lad's friend — LASS, LASSIE
Lad's pal — GAL
Lad, in Lyon — GARS
Ladd film — SHANE
Ladd or Mowbray — ALAN
Ladder part — RUNG
Ladder rung — SPOKE
Ladder steps — RUNGS
Laders' org. — ILA
Lades — STOWS
Ladies — MADAMES
Ladies in Berlin — FRAUS
Ladies in Leon — DAMAS
Ladies of Lisbon — DONAS
Ladies of Spain — SENORAS
Ladies of Spain, for short — SRAS
Ladles out — SPOONS
Lady Bird's successor — PAT
Lady Bird, for one — TEXAN
Lady Chaplin — OONA
Lady Churchill, to friends — CLEM
Lady flier — AVIATRIX
Lady Hamilton — EMMA
Lady Hamilton's love — NELSON
Lady in Granada — SENORA
Lady in the chair — CASSIOPEIA
Lady lambs — EWES
Lady love — GIRL FRIEND
Lady Luck reigns here — RENO
Lady of "The Sun Also Rises" — BRETT
Lady of Lahore — RANI
Lady of Lisbon — DONA
Lady of Spain — DONA, SENORA, SENORITA
Lady of Spain: Abbr. — SRA, DAMA
Lady of the house — MADAM
Lady or Dame — PEERESS
Lady Penelope Devereux — STELLA
Lady Windermere had one — FAN
Lady with a fan — WINDERMERE
Lady's address — MADAM
Lady's bloke — GENT

Lady's fancy headcovering — MOBCAP
Lady's maid — ABIGAIL
Lady's man — LORD
Lady, in Berlin — FRAU
Ladyfinger — CAKE
Ladylike — FEMALE
Lafayette College site — EASTON
Lager — BEER
Lager beer — PILSNER
Lager head — FOAM
Lager holder — KEG
Lager's relative — ALE
Laggard — TRIFLER
Lagniappe — PLUS
Lagomorph — HARE
Lagomorph exes? — SPLIT HARES
Lagomorphs — RABBITS
Lagoon — BOG, POND
Lagoon shapers — ATOLLS
Lagoon surrounder — ATOLL
Lagoon's island — ATOLL
Lahore garb — SAREE
Lahore lilt — RAGA
Lahr — BERT
Lahr and Convy — BERTS
Lahr or Ayres — LION
Lahr or Parks — BERT
Lahr part — LION
Lahr role — LION
Lahr, of the movies — BERT
Lahti resident — FINN
Laic — CIVIL, LAY
Laid off — FIRED
Laid-back — CALM, EASY, RELAXED
Lair — DEN
Laird — OWNER
Laird of "The Lodger" — CREGAR
Laissez _____ — FAIRE
Laissez-faire — LAX, LOOSE
Lait topper — CREME
Laity — FLOCK, FOLD
Lake — POND
Lake _____, N.H. vacation spot — SUNAPEE
Lake _____: Mississippi river source — ITASCA
Lake Champlain feeder — SARANAC
Lake Erie bay — PUTIN
Lake Erie port — TOLEDO
Lake in a cirque — TARN
Lake in cen. New York — ONEIDA
Lake in Finland — ENARE
Lake in N Finland — INARI
Lake in NW Soviet Union — ONEGA
Lake in Oregon — CRATER
Lake in Roma — COMO
Lake in Scotland — LOCH
Lake in SE Africa — NYASA
Lake Indian — ERIE
Lake Ladoga region — KARELIA
Lake Maggiore town — STRESSA
Lake near a temple of Diana — NEMI
Lake near Novgorod — ILMEN
Lake near Reno — TAHOE
Lake near Yosemite — MONO
Lake Ontario port — OSWEGO
Lake or Perry — COMO
Lake port — ERIE
Lake Titicaca locale — PERU
Lake trout — TOGUE
Lake Victoria, e.g. — HEADWATERS
Lake, in Roma — LAGO
Lake, source of the Blue Nile — TANA
Lake: Sp. — LAGO
Lakshmi — SRI
Lalique or Lacoste — RENE
Lalo's "Le Roi _____" — DYS
Lama — MONK
Lamarr of films — HEDY
Lamarr of Hollywood — HEDY
Lamb — ELIA, YEAN
Lamb cut — RACK
Lamb for Lucullus — AGNUS
Lamb of pork fame — ELIA
Lamb or mutton — MEAT
Lamb product — ESSAY
Lamb topper — EPI
Lamb's-quarters — WEED
Lamb's "Essay of _____" — ELIA
Lamb's dam — EWE
Lamb's mother — DAM
Lamb's nom de plume — ELIA
Lamb's parent — EWE
Lamb's pen name — ELIA
Lamb's pseudonym — ELIA
Lamb's word — MAA
Lambaste — CREAM, THRASH
Lambda followers — MUS
Lamblike — GENTLE, MEEK, MILD
Lambs mamas — EWES
Lame — POOR, THIN, WEAK
Lamebrain — SIMP
Lamebrained — INANE
Lamebrains — SAPS
Lament — BEWAIL, DIRGE, MOAN, MOURN, REGRET
Lament — REPENT, SIGH, WAIL, WEEP
Lamentable — GRIEVOUS
Lamentations — PLAINTS
Lamented — CRIED
Lamenter — RUER
Laments — KEENS
Laments, long ago — MONES
Lamina — COVER, SHINGLE
Laminar — STRATAL
Laminated rock — SHALE
Lammermoor lady — LUCIA
Lamp dweller? — GENIE
Lamp for openings — KLIEG
Lamp fuel — OIL
Lamp in Liverpool — TORCH
Lamp resident — GENIE
Lampblack — SOOT
Lampoon — PARODY, SPOOF
Lampooner's works — SATIRES
Lampoons — SATIRES
Lamprey — EEL
Lamprey fisherman — EELER
Lanai party — LUAU
Lanais — VERANDAHS
Lancaster — BURT
Lance — CUT
Lancelot's love — ELAINE
Lancelot's son — GALAHAD
Lanchester and namesakes — ELSAS
Land-locked Asian country — LAOS
Land — ALIGHT
Land a haymaker — KAYO
Land areas — TERRENES
Land based newt — EFT
Land broker — REALTOR
Land dealer — REALTOR
Land fit for cultivation — ARABLE
Land holdings — ESTATES
Land map — PLAT
Land mass — ASIA
Land measure — ACRE, ROD
Land of Brian Boru — EIRE
Land of curry cuisine — INDIA
Land of fighting gamecocks — CAROLINA
Land of King Mongkut — SIAM
Land of Leonardo — ITALY
Land of Liberty: Abbr. — USA
Land of Nod — SLEEP
Land of plenty — GOSHEN
Land of Qum — IRAN
Land of sand — DESERT
Land of the eisteddfod — WALES
Land of the Great Wall — CHINA
Land of the Incas — PERU
Land of the Midnight Sun — NORWAY
Land of the Orient — ASIA
Land of the rising sun and lowering dollar — JAPAN
Land of the sunrise — ORIENT
Land owned absolutely in feudal days — ALOD
Land plot — ACRE
Land unit — ACRE
Land unit in Canada — ARPEN
Land west of Nod — EDEN
Land's end — SPIT
Land, in Roma — TERRA
Land: Abbr. — TER
Landau or phaeton — AUTO
Landed — ALIT

Landed estate — MANOR
Landed manor — ESTATE
Landed proprietors — ESQUIRES
Landers, et al. — ANNS
Landing craft — LST
Landing fields — AIRSTRIPS
Landing ship, for short — LSD
Landlocked country — LAOS
Landlocked land — LAOS
Landlord — LEASER, OWNER
Landlord of old — HOST
Landlord's income — RENT
Landlord's lessee — RENTER
Landlord's sign — TO LET
Landlords — LEASERS
Landlords' take — RENTS
Landmark — BEACON
Landmark in Sicily — ETNA
Landon — ALF
Landon and a TV alien — ALFS
Landon of Kansas — ALF
Lands End (cape) locale — NWT
Lands in Texas — SPREADS
Landscape — SCENE
Landscaping item — SHRUB
Landslide debris — SCREE
Lane — PATHWAY
Lanes gp. — PBA
Lanes' locale — ALLEY
Lanford Wilson's "Serenading _____" — LOUIE
Lang. — GER
Langley or Lackland: Abbr. — AFB
Language — DIALECT, JARGON
Language expert — LINGUIST
Language in Katmandu — NEPALESE
Language of ancient Iberians — BASQUE
Language of Cato — LATIN
Language of Helsinki — FINNISH
Language of India — TAMIL
Language of northern Thailand — LAO
Language of Pakistan — URDU
Language of Picasso — ESPANOL
Language of the Algonquians — CREE
Language spoken in Spain — BASQUE
Language teachers' org. — ETA
Languid — INERT, SLOW
Languish — DROOP, WILT
Languor — DROWSINESS
Lank — LEAN, THIN
Lanky — SLIM, TALL
Lanky monkey of SE Asia — LANGUR
Lanky one — BEANPOLE
Lanolin source — WOOL
Lansbury role — MAME
Lanyards — ROPES
Lanza role — CARUSO
Lao-_____, famed Taoist — TSE
Lao-tse's way — TAO
Lao or Mao follower — TSE
Laos locale — ASIA
Laotian money — ATS
Laotian, for one — ASIATIC
Lap — LICK, SEAT
Lap robe — THROW
Lap up — SLURP
Lapdog, for short — PEKE, POM
Lapel — REVERS
Lapel flower — CARNATION
Lapel grabbers — BORES
Lapidate — PELT
Lapin — RABBIT FUR
Lapis chaser — LAZULI
Laps up — LICKS
Lapsang Souchong — TEA
Lapse — SLIP
Lapwing — PEWIT
Lar and siamang — APES
Larboard — PORT
Larboard side of a ship — PORT
Larceny — FRAUD, THEFT
Lard — SUET
Larder location — PANTRY
Lardlike — SUETY
Lardner's "_____ Ike" — ALIBI
Large-mouthed fish — BASS
Large — AMPLE, BIG, GREAT, HUGE, ROOMY
Large American cat — OCELOT
Large amount — GOB, MASS, SCAD
Large antelope — ELAND
Large Asiatic deer — RUSAS
Large barges — SCOWS
Large basket — PANNIER
Large beetle — UANG
Large birds — RAVENS
Large bodies of water — SEAS
Large book — TOME
Large book size — FOLIO
Large bovine — YAK
Large brown bear — KODIAK
Large bundle — BALE
Large cask — TUN
Large cisterns — VATS
Large city on the Chang Jiang — HANJING
Large clams — GAPERS
Large constrictor — ABOMA
Large container — CRATE, TANK, VAT
Large cross — ROOD
Large deer — WAPITI
Large delicious flat fish — HALIBUT
Large dog — TOWSER
Large drinking bowl — JORUM
Large drinking vessels — JORUMS
Large expanse — OCEAN
Large fish — COBIA
Large forearm bone — ULNA
Large fragment of a glacier — SERAC
Large handkerchief or scarf — BANDANNA
Large hauler, for short — SEMI
Large instrument — BASS DRUM
Large joint of beef — BARON
Large kangaroo — EURO
Large knife — SNEE
Large land mass — ASIA
Large lizard — IGUANA, UTA
Large lot — ACRE
Large lunch — HERO
Large mackerel — WAHOO
Large molding — TORE
Large moldings — TORI
Large moth — LUNA
Large New Zealand parrot — KEA
Large number — ARMY, HORDE, SCAD
Large numbers — DROVES
Large ocean liner — LEVIATHAN
Large packages — BALES
Large pear — BOSC
Large person — GIANT
Large pitcher — EWER
Large quantities — MASSES, REAMS, TONS
Large quantity — MASS, SLEW
Large retriever — CHESA-PEAKE
Large rodent — PACA
Large round number, for short — THOU
Large sea duck — EIDER
Large seaweed — KELP
Large shoe width — EEE
Large showy flowers — DAHLIAS, IRISES
Large shrimp — SCAMPI
Large source of income in Fla. — TOURISM
Large South American snake — ABOMA
Large sport fish — CERO
Large tangelo — UGLI
Large tank forces — ARMADAS
Large throng — HORDE
Large tool — LATHE
Large tremors — EARTHQUAKES
Large truck — SEMI
Large trunk — AORTA
Large umbrella — GAMP
Large vat for bleaching cloth — KIER
Large vessel — VAT
Large violin — BELL FIDDLE

Large wardrobes — ARMOIRES
Large white duck — PEKIN
Large white gannet — SOLAN
Large white goose — SOLAN
Large works — TOMES
Large, convex moldings — TORI
Large, graceful tree — ELM
Large, striped cat — BENGAL TIGER
Large-eyed lemur — LORIS
Large-leafed house plant — URALIA
Large-scale — WIDE
Large: Comb. form — MACRO
Largely — AMPLY, MAINLY
Largess — CHARITY
Largest asteroid — CERES
Largest book size — FOLIO
Largest city of Jordan — AMMAN
Largest continent — ASIA
Largest inner planet — EARTH
Largest lake — SUPERIOR
Largest lake in Iran — URMIA
Largest land mass — EURASIA
Largest lesser Sunda Island — TIMOR
Largest mammal — WHALE
Largest natural lake in Wales — BALA
Largest of seven — ASIA
Largest of the Galapagos — ISABELLA
Largest pit viper — BUSHMASTER
Largest planet — PLUTO
Largo like spiritual — GOING HOME
Lariat — LASSO, RIATA, ROPE
Lariat eye — HONDA
Lariat feature — NOOSE
Lariats — LASSOS, RIATAS, ROPES
Lark — WARBLER
Larks' cousins — PIPITS
Larry _____, harmonica virtuoso — ADLER
Larry of the Celtics — BIRD
Larry or Luther — ADLER
Larry Shur comedy, with "The" — NERD
Larry Shur play, with "The" — NERD
Larry Shur subject — NERD
Larry, _____ and Curly of comical fame — MOE
Lars Porsena was one — ETRUSCAN
Larson cartoon, with "The" — FAR SIDE
Larva — MAGGOT
Las Vegas lure — CASINO
Las Vegas natural — SEVEN
Las Vegas offering — CRAPS
Las Vegas posting — ODDS
Las Vegas sign — NEON
Las Vegas types — GAMBLERS
Lascaux area — CAVE
Lascivious looks — LEERS
Lash out — DECRY
Lashed — ROPED
Lashes — CILIA
Lasorda's predecessor at L.A. — ALSTON
Lass — GIRL
Lass who got an A — HESTER
Lass whom Cantor knew — SUSIE
Lassen Peak — VOLCANO
Lassie and Benji, e.g. — PETS
Lassitude — ENNUI, STUPOR
Lasso — LARIAT, RIATA, ROPE
Lasso end — NOOSE
Lasso knots — NOOSES
Lasso part — NOOSE
Lassos — RIATAS
Last — END, ENDURE, KEEP, OMEGA
Last but not _____ — LEAST
Last degree — NTH
Last entry in list — ETC
Last exams — FINALS
Last Hawaiian queen — LILIUOKALANI
Last innings — NINTHS
Last letter — ZEE
Last letter, in London — ZED
Last month — DECEMBER
Last mount Moses climbed — NEBO
Last name of a spy — — HARI
Last of a familiar hebdomad — SATURDAY
Last of a Hemingway title — TREES
Last of a Latin trio — AMAT
Last of the highway — ROADS END
Last of the Mohicans — UNCAS
Last of the teens — NINE
Last Shah of Iran — PAHLAVI
Last supper — MAUNDY
Last syllable — ULTIMA
Last testament — WILL
Last word — AMEN, ENDER, LATEST
Last word of "Ulysses" — YES
Last word of Genesis — EGYPT
Last word of Missouri's motto — ESTO
Last word of Mo.'s motto — ESTO
Last words, often — ET AL
Last year's jr.'s — SRS
Last, for short — ULT
Last-ditch — FINAL
Last: Abbr. — ULT
Lasting beginning — EVER
Lasting forever — AGELONG
Lasting into the wee hours — LATE
Lasting only a short time — EPHEMERAL
Lat. Amer. Christmas item — PINATA
Lat. list shortener — ET AL
Lat. music — SALSA
Latch — CATCH
Latch part — HASP
Latched — HASPED
Late — RECENT, TARDY
Late Art Deco illustrator — ERTE
Late bloomer — ASTER
Late chanteuse — PIAF
Late Chinese Chairman — MAO
Late Chinese VIP — CHOU
Late choreographer — AILEY
Late great jazz pianist — TATUM
Late nibbles — MIDNIGHT SNACKS
Late night flight — REDEYE
Late show, usually — RERUN
Late TV fare — RERUNS
Late, in Lyon — TARD
Late, late TV fare — MOVIE
Latency — HINT
Latent — HIDDEN
Later — ANOW
Lateral — SIDE
Lateral surface — SIDE
Latest possible time — THE ELEVENTH HOUR
Latest reports — NEWS
Latest thing — RAGE
Latest: Prefix — NEO
Lathe-adjusting device — SET OVER
Lathe spindle — MANDRIL
Lather — FOAM, SUDS
Lathered — SOAPY
Lathered up — SOAPY
Latin American beat — SALSA
Latin American country — PANAMA
Latin American dance music — SALSA
Latin American dances — SALSAS
Latin beat — SALSA
Latin boy — PUER
Latin case — ABLATIVE
Latin catchall — ETAL
Latin class word — AMO
Latin conjugation starter — AMO
Latin dance — CHA CHA, SAMBA, TANGO
Latin farewell — VALE
Latin greeting — AVE
Latin I verb — AMO
Latin I word — AMAS, AMAT, AMO
Latin laws — LEGES
Latin lesson verb — AMAT

Latin lesson word — AMAS
Latin name for a British isle — HIBERNIA
Latin or Greek — FOREIGN LANGUAGE
Latin Quarter dances — CANCANS
Latin speakers' facial features? — ROMAN NOSES
Latin teacher's command — PARSE
Latin trio member — AMAS
Latin verb for February 14 — AMAS
Latin, for law — JUS
Latin-American dance — TANGO
Latin: sic — THUS
Latino music — SALSA
Latitude measurements — DEGREES
Latrine in London — LOO
Latter-day — NEO
Latter part of life — OLD AGE
Lattice — TRELLIS
Latticework — TRELLIS
Latticework for a rambler — TRELLIS
Latvian — LETT
Latvian capital — RIGA
Latvian city — RIGA
Latvian seaport — RIGA
Laud — EXTOL, PRAISE
Laudatory verses — ODES
Lauder of note — ESTEE
Laugh — CHUCKLE
Laugh _____ — RIOTS
Laugh at — DERIDE
Laugh in derision — SNORT
Laugh lightly — TITTER
Laugh off — DISMISS
Laugh, in Lyon — RIRE
Laugh-getters — JOKES
Laughable — ABSURD, COMICAL, RISIBLE
Laughed in a way — CACKLED
Laughed nervously — TITTERED
Laughing — CHUCKLE, HOWL, RIANT
Laughing creature — HYENA
Laughing jack-asses — KOOKABURRAS
Laughing sounds — HAS
Laughingstock — FOOL
Laughs at — MOCKS
Laughs heartily — ROARS
Laughs uproariously — HOWLS
Laughter — MIRTH
Laughter's sound — HAHA
Laughter, in Lyon — RIRE
Launch — BOAT, HURL, INITIATE
Launch vehicle — ROCKET
Launching area — PAD
Launder — WASH
Laundered — CLEAN, NATTY
Launderette machine — DRIER
Laundromat feature — DRYER
Laundry cycle — PREWASH, RINSE
Laundry employee — PRESSER
Laundry equipment — DRYER
Laundry machine — MANGLE
Laundry residue — LINT
Laundry unit — LOAD
Laundry worker — PRESSER
Laurel-derived spice — BAYLEAF
Laurel — STAN
Laurel and Hardy, e.g. — PALS
Laurel foilage — WREATH
Laurentian Mountains locale — CANADA
Laurie of "Twin Peaks" — PIPER
Laurie or Oakley — ANNIE
Lava-lava — KILT
Lavalava — PAREU
Lavalier — PENDANT
Lavatory — BASIN
Lave — POUR
Lave in England — TUB
Lavender — OLD LACES PAL
Lavender and frangipani — ODORS
Laver or Stewart — ROD
Laves — BATHS
Laves lightly — RINSES
Lavin role — ALICE
Lavished affection on — DOTED
Lavishes love on — DOTES
Law breaker — SPEEDER
Law governing payroll deductions for Soc. Sec. — FICA
Law grp. — ACLU
Law matters — CASES
Law of the Middle Ages — CURFEW
Law partner — ORDER
Law student's concern — BAR EXAMINATIONS
Law's companion — ORDER
Law's partner — ORDER
Law, in Lyons — LOI
Law-abiding — ABLE
Law-book material — STATUTES
Lawbreaker — FELON
Lawful — JUST, LEGAL, LICIT, RIGHT
Lawful: Lat. — LICET
Lawgiver — SOLON
Lawless — UNRULY
Lawmaker — SENATOR
Lawman — COP
Lawn — GRASS
Lawn cleaners — RAKERS
Lawn game from Italy — BOCCI
Lawn jumpers — GRASSHOPPERS
Lawn liner — SOD
Lawn pest — MOLE
Lawn tennis award — DAVIS CUP
Lawn tool — EDGER
Lawn trimmer — EDGER
Lawn worker — RAKER
Lawrence _____: Mr. T — TERO
Lawrence relationships — SONS AND LOVERS
Lawrence's other half — GORME
Lawrence, in Sweden — LARS
Laws — STATUTES
Laws or statutes — ENACTMENTS
Lawsuits — CASES
Lawyer Darrow — CLARENCE
Lawyer's charge — FEE
Lawyer's concern — CLIENT
Lawyer's document — BRIEF
Lawyer's fee — RETAINER
Lawyer's org. — ABA
Lawyer's place — BAR
Lawyer's plan? — GET ON YOUR CASE
Lawyer's suit — CASE
Lawyer's thing — RES
Lawyer's work — CASELOAD
Lawyer, for short — ATTY
Lawyers' holdalls — BRIEFCASE
Lawyers: Abbr. — ATT
Lax — SLACK
LAX advisory — ETD
LAX notice — ARR
Lay — PUT, SET
Lay _____ (flatter) — IT ON
Lay an egg — BOMB
Lay aside — TABLE
Lay away — STORE
Lay bare — STRIP
Lay churchman — ELDER
Lay doggo, in London — HID
Lay down the law — DICTATE, GOVERN
Lay it on — FLATTER
Lay off — LET GO
Lay on in plenty — REGALE
Lay or leather attachment — ETTE
Lay out — CHART
Lay up — STORE
Layer — COAT, HEN, PLY, TIER
Layer: Comb. form — STRATI
Layered coifs — SHAGS
Layers — LAMINAE, STRATAS, TIERS
Layfayette college's town — EASTON
Laying by — HOARDING
Laymen — LAICS
Lays bare — STRIPS
Lazes — IDLES
Laziness — SLOTH
Lazy — OTIOSE
Lazy _____ — SUSAN

Lazy and Hayward — SUSANS
Lazy assent — YEAH
Lazy girls — SUSANS
Lazy ones — SLUGS
Lazy people — IDLERS
Lazy Susan — TRAY
Lazybones — IDLER
Lb. or gal. — AMT
Lb. or oz. — WGT
Le _____ of spydom — CARRE
Le _____: French port — HAVRE
Le Carre character — SPY
Le Carre's Russian spy — KARLA
Le Dernier _____ — CRI
Le Gallienne and Gabor — EVAS
Le Harvres river — SEINE
Lea herd — COWS
Leach title from "Henry VIII" — A KILLING FROST
Lead — GUIDE
Lead _____ (slow vehicle in CB lingo) — PEDAL
Lead astray — SEDUCE
Lead into another — SEGUE
Lead monoxide — MASSICOT
Lead or bit — ROLE
Lead ore — GALENA
Lead pellets — SHOT
Lead the way — PACE
Lead up to a leer — OGLE
Lead, perhaps — ROLE
Lead-in to choo or plunk — KER
Lead-pipe cinch — SNAP
Leader — HEAD, RULER
Leader after Kerensky — LENIN
Leader of a Mass. rebellion: 1786-87 — SHAYS
Leader of the CSA — DAVIS
Leader of the Green Mountain Boys — ETHAN ALLEN
Leaders like Mussolini — DUCES
Leadership — HIGH COMMAND
Leading — ON TOP
Leading comic in vaudeville — TOP BANANA
Leading ladies — HEROINES
Leading lady — STAR
Leading lady from Italy — LOREN
Leading lady in Lahore — RANEE
Leading lyric-dramatic tenor — DOMINGO
Leading man — HERO
Leading parts in duets or trios — PRIMOS
Leading player — STAR
Leading position in a race — FRONT END
Leading, as a role — STELLAR
Leads an active social life — STEPS OUT
Leaf-stem angles — AXIALS
Leaf angles — AXILS
Leaf area — AREOLA
Leaf base — STIPEL
Leaf cutter — ANT
Leaf eater — APHIS
Leaf gatherers — RAKERS
Leaf of a manuscript — FOLIO
Leaf on an axis — BRACT
Leaf opening — STOMA
Leaf part — STEM
Leaf pest — APHIS
Leaf pore — STOMA
Leaf veins — MIDRIBS
Leafless — BARE
Leaflet — TRACT
Leaflet, to a botanist — FOLIOLE
Leaflets — FLIERS
Leaflike plant part — BRACT
Leafstalk-enclosing sheath — OCREA
Leafy lettuce — COS
Leafy spot — TREE TOP
Leafy vegetables — KALE
League of Nations' first home — GENEVA
League or Legion — AMERICAN
League results — STANDINGS
Leah's son — LEVI
Leak — DIVULGE, DRIP
Leak-proofer — GASKET
Leaked through — SEEPED
Leaking — DRIPPY, SEEPY
Leaking radiator's sound — SISS
Leaks slowly — SEEPS
Lean-to — SHED
Lean — CANT, SLIM, TILT
Lean and sinewy — WIRY
Lean as a rake — BONY
Lean one — SCRAG
Lean to one side — HEEL
Lean toward — TEND
Lean, haggard — GAUNT
Leander's friend — HERO
Leander's love — HERO
Leandro's amorosa — ERO
Leandro's girl — ERO
Leaned — LISTED
Leaned (on) — DEPENDED
Leaner — SCRAWNIER, THINNER
Leaning — ATILT
Leaning to one side — ALIST
Leaning tower town — PISA
Leans — TENDS
Leap — POUNCE, SPRING
Leap frog — GAME
Leap, like some lovers — ELOPE
Leapin _____ — LENA
Leaping amphibian — TOAD
Lear production — ALL IN THE FAMILY
Lear's daughter — REGAN
Lear's devoted companion — FOOL
Lear's faithful companion — KENT
Lear's loyal follower — KENT
Lear's youngest — REGAN
Learn by _____: memorize — ROTE
Learn by heart — MEMORIZE
Learned — VERSED
Learned bit by bit — GLEANED
Learned lot — LITERATI
Learned Muslim group — HIRAM
Learned ones — PUNDITS
Learned skills — ART
Learners' loci — CLASSROOMS
Learning — ERUDITION, LORE
Learning center in Columbus, O. — OSU
Learning centers — COLLEGES
Learning inst. — SCH
Learning method — ROTE
Lease — RENT, LET
Lease again — RELET, RERENT
Lease signer — RENTER, TENANT
Lease to a new tenant — RELET
Lease-holder's fee — RENT
Leased property — RENTAL
Leases — CHARTERS, RENTS
Leash — TETHER
Leashes — TETHERS
Least abundant — RAREST
Least batty — SANEST
Least believable excuse — LAMEST
Least colorful — PALEST
Least common — RAREST
Least difficult — EASIEST
Least expensive cruise accommodations — STEERAGE
Least favorably — AT WORST
Least forth-right — SLIEST
Least furnished — BAREST
Least generous — NEAREST
Least important — MEREST
Least interesting — DRIEST
Least likely — LAST, SLIMMEST
Least messy — NEATEST
Least of the litter — RUNT
Least original — TRITEST
Least perilous — SAFEST
Least polite — RUDEST
Least possible — BAREST
Least tanned — WHITEST
Leather cleaner — SADDLE SOAP
Leather padding for armor — CUIRIE
Leather process — TANNING
Leather strap — THONG

Leather with a napped surface — SUEDE
Leather worker — TANNER
Leather worker's need — AWL
Leather worker's tool — AWL
Leatherneck — MARINE
Leave-taking — ADIEU
Leave — DEPART, EMBARK, EXIT, VACATE
Leave _____ unturned — NO STONE
Leave a caboose — DETRAIN
Leave alone — SPARE
Leave behind — BEAT
Leave for good — BURN ONES BRIDGES
Leave high and dry — ABANDON, MAROON, STRAND
Leave in a hurry — TAKE A POWDER
Leave in the lurch — DESERT
Leave no doubt — MAKE CLEAR
Leave off — CEASE, WAIVE
Leave one's native land — EMIGRATE
Leave one's party — BOLT
Leave out — OMIT, SKIP
Leave port — SAIL
Leave rolling in the aisle — SLAY
Leave the straight and narrow — ERR
Leave undone — OMIT
Leaven — RAISE
Leavening agent — YEAST
Leaves — GOES, PAGES
Leaves collateral for — HOCKS
Leaves forlorn — BEREAVES
Leaves off — DESISTS
Leaves out — OMITS
Leaves the track — DERAILS
Leaves' home? — TREE
Leaving port — ASEA
Leavings — ORTS
Leb.'s neighbor — SYR
Lebanese sect — DRUSE
Lebanese trees — CEDAR
Lebanon's capital — BEIRUT
Leblanc's hero — LUPIN
Leblanc's Lupin — ARSENE
Lech Walesa, for one — POLE
Lecher's look — LEER
Lecherous — GOATY
Lechwe's cousin — ELAND
Lection — EPISTLE
Lecture — TALK
Lecturer — DOCENT
Lecturer's aid — GRAPH
Lecturers' aides-memoire — NOTES
Led astray — DECOYED
Lederhosen — PANTS
Ledger entries — EXPENSES, POSTINGS
Ledger entry — DEBT, DEBIT
Ledger item — DEBIT, ENTRY
Lee in "Funny Face" — RUTA
Lee J. Cobb role — LOMAN
Lee J. or Ty — COBB
Lee or Grant — GENERAL
Lee or Jones — SPIKE
Lee surrendered to Grant at — APPOMATTOX
Lee's daughter — SUSAN STRASBERG
Lee's men — REBS
Leed's river — AIRE
Leek-green gemstone — PRASE
Leek — ONION
Leer at — OGLE
Leered at — OGLED
Leers lasciviously — OGLES
Lees — DREGS
Leesee's payment — RENT
Leeward island — ANGUILLA, SABA
Leeward isle — MONTSERRAT
Leeway — ROOM
Left — DEPARTED, HAD GONE, WENT
Left after taxes — NET
Left an airplane — DEBARKED
Left Bank river — SEINE
Left hastily — SKIPPED
Left in the lurch — DESERTED
Left out — OMITTED
Left-hand page — VERSO
Left-hander — SOUTHPAW
Leftie — SOUTHPAW
Leftover — ORT
Leftover dish — HASH
Leftover shipmates — ODDLOTS
Leftovers — ORTS, REST
Leftovers from a TV roast — SPARE RIBS
Leftward — APORT
Leg-foot connection — ANKLE
Leg — SUPPORT
Leg bone — FIBULA, TIBIA
Leg bones — FEMURA, TIBULAE
Leg joints — ANKLES, KNEES
Leg of lamb — GIGOT
Leg part — CALF, SHIN
Leg up — BOOST
Leg wear — HOSE
Leg-of-mutton, e.g. — SLEEVE
Leg: Comb. form — SCEL
Legal action — PLEA
Legal agt. — ATT
Legal attachments — LIENS
Legal claim — LIEN
Legal claim holder — LIENOR
Legal contract — LEASE
Legal deeds — ACTA
Legal document — LEASE, TITLE
Legal documents — DEEDS, WRIT
Legal eagle — LEGIST
Legal holding — LIEN
Legal instrument — DEED, LEASE, WILL
Legal locales — VENUES
Legal matter — TORT, RES
Legal order — WRIT
Legal org. — ABA
Legal paper — WRIT
Legal ploy — PLEA
Legal point — RES
Legal proceedings — HEARINGS
Legal profession as a whole — LAW
Legal prohibition — BAN
Legal recipient of security — BAILEE
Legal rep. — ATTY
Legal restraint — ESTOP
Legal right — DROIT
Legal site — VENUE
Legal successor — HEIR
Legal suit — PLEA
Legal tender from Sec. Bentsen — T NOTE
Legal tender in Bulgaria — LEV
Legal thing — RES
Legal wrong — TORT
Legalis homo — ADULT
Legally responsible — LIABLE
Legally supervised one — PAROLEE
Legatee — HEIR
Legato — SMOOTH
Legend — BALLAD, CODE, KEY, MYTH, SAGA, TALE
Legendary automaton — GOLEM
Legendary bird — ROC
Legendary Casey Jones, for one — ENGINEER
Legendary Gaelic hero — OSSIAN
Legendary galley — ARGO
Legendary gold maker — MIDAS
Legendary Greek — AJAX
Legendary Greek hero — IDAS
Legendary Greta — GARBO
Legendary king of Crete — MINOS
Legendary magician — MERLIN
Legendary tale — FABLE
Legendary twins — ROMULUS AND REMUS
Legendary victims of the Romans — SABINES
Legged it fast — RAN
Legging — PUTTEE
Leghorn — FOWL
Legion — MANY
Legionnaire, e.g. — VET
Legions — HORDES
Legislate — ENACT

Legislation for the needy — POOR LAWS
Legislative body — SENATE
Legislative body in Czarist Russia — DUMA
Legislative get-togethers? — BLOC PARTIES
Legislative group — BLOC
Legislative sittings — SESSIONS
Legislator — SOLON
Legislator, at times — ENACTOR
Legislatures — GOVERNING BODIES
Legitimate — LEGAL
Legless creature — APOD
Leglin — PAIL
Legs — GAMS
Legumes — BEANS, PEAS
Leguminous plant — SENNA
Legware — HOSE
Lehar specialty — OPERETTA
Lehmann or Lenya — LOTTE
Leibman or Howard — RON
Leibman TV role — KAZ
Leiden footwear — SABOTS
Leinsdorf or Korngold — ERICH
Leister — SPEAR
Leisure — EASE
Leisure activity — SPORT
Leisure pursuits — GAMES
Leisurely — SLOW
Leisurely stroll — PASEO
Leisurely walk — STROLL
Leitmotif — IDEA
Lely or Klee — ARTIST
Lemieux's target — NET
Lemon additive — ADE
Lemon and lime additives — ADES
Lemon and orange additives — ADES
Lemon attachment — ADE
Lemon follower — ADE
Lemon on wheels — EDSEL
Lemon or lime follower — ADE
Lemonlike fruit — CITRON
Lemons — PILLS
LEMs creator — NASA
Lemur of Sri Lanka — LORIS
Lena or Marilyn — HORNE
Lenard's "Winnie _____ Pooh" — ILLE
Lend — IMPART
Lend _____ (listen) — AN EAR
Lend _____ (pay attention) — AN EAR
Lend a hand — AID, ASSIST
Lend- _____ — LEASE
Lendl and namesakes — IVANS
Lendl and Wilander, at times — ACERS
Lendl's arena — COURT
Lendl's milieu — COURT
Lendl, at times — ACER
Lendl, of the courts — IVAN
Lends a helping hand — ASSISTS
Length — EXTENT, REACH, SPAN
Length measure — INCH, MIL
Length of cloth — BOLT
Length of rope — HANK
Length times width, often — AREA
Length units — FEET
Length x width — AREA
Lengthen — ELONGATE, PROLONG, STRETCH
Lengthwise — ALONG
Lengthy — TALL
Lenient — EASY
Lenient towards — SOFT ON
Leningrad's famous ballet company — KIROV
Leningrad's river — NEVA
Lenni _____, Delaware Indian — LENAPE
Lennon was one — BEATLE
Lennon's "_____ Do You Sleep?" — HOW
Lennon's widow — YOKO, ONO
Lennon's wife — ONO
Lens-shaped edible seeds — LENTILS
Lent a hand — AIDED
Lent, in Lille — CAREME
Lenten event — PALM SUNDAY
Lenten symbol — ASHES
Lentil, in Koln — LINSE
Lento — SLOW
Lenya of "The Three Penny Opera" — LOTTE
Leo Constellation — LION
Leo Gorcey assent — YEAH
Leo of films — GENN
Leo's hideaway — LAIR
Leo's pride — MANE
Leo's ruff — MANE
Leo, for one — LION
Leo, Pius and John — POPES
Leon _____, Russian artist-set designer — BAKST
Leon Bismark Beiderbecke — BIX
Leonard _____: Roy Rogers — SLYE
Leonardo da _____ — VINCI
Leone or Madre — SIERRA
Leonine group — PRIDE
Leonine locks — MANE
Leonine outbursts — ROARS
Leonine pad — LAIR
Leopold of Belgium — KING
Leopold or Mischa — AUER
Leopold's co-defendant — LOEB
Leos and Toms — MALES
Lepidopteran — MOTH
Lepidopterist's favorite opera — MADAME BUTTERFLY
Leporid — HARE
Leporine group — HARES
Leprechaun-land — EIRE
Lermontov's "_____ of Our Time" — A HERO
Lerots — DORMICE
Leroy Anderson's "_____ of the Ball" — BELLE
Leroy Paige, familiarly — SATCHEL
Les _____ Unis — ETATS
Les Etats- _____ — UNIS
Les femmes — ELLES
Les Folies Bergere, for one — REVUE
Lesage hero _____ Blas — GIL
Lesage's Blas — GIL
Lese majesty — TREASON
Lesions — SORES
Leslie Caron film — LILI
Leslie Caron role — LILI
Leslie King became one — FORD
Lesotho capital — MASERU
Less — MINUS
Less alternative — MORE
Less apt to bolt — TAMER
Less brackish — SALTIER
Less brilliant — PALER
Less colorful — PALER
Less cooked — RARER
Less cordial — ICIER
Less deceitful — TRUER
Less desiccated — SAPPIER
Less desirable — WORSE
Less difficult — EASIER
Less done — RAWER
Less dry — WETTER
Less energetic — LAZIER
Less experienced — RAWER
Less familiar — ODDER
Less ferocious — TAMER
Less frequent — RARER
Less friendly — ICIER
Less gregarious — SHIER
Less humid — DRIER
Less interesting — DRIER
Less like Junior's room — TIDIER
Less lucid — NUTTIER
Less modern — OLDER
Less original — STALER
Less plentiful — SPARSER
Less polluted — PURER
Less populated — SPARSER
Less prevalent — RARER
Less refined — RUDER
Less risky — SAFER
Less slovenly — NEATER
Less stocky — SLIMMER
Less superficial — DEEPER
Less svelte — SLIM
Less tart — SWEETER
Less than a crowd — TWO

Less than less — LEAST
Less than lg. — MED
Less trained — RAWER
Less trite — NEWER
Less unruly — TAMER
Less used — NEWER
Less well cooked — RARER
Less well done — RARER
Lessee — TENANT
Lessen — ABATE, ALLEVIATE, DECREASE, EBB
Lessen — REDUCE, WANE
Lessen in value — DEPRECIATE
Lessened — ABATED
Lesser — MINOR
Lesser of two _____ — EVILS
Lessor's income — RENT
Let — LEASE, RENT
Let _____ (bettor's expression) — IT RIDE
Let _____ (stet) — IT STAND
Let down — RELAP
Let fall — DROP
Let forth — EMIT
Let go — RELEASE, RELEASED, UNLOOSE
Let go until later — PUT IT ON ICE
Let in — ADMIT
Let it stand — STET
Let loose — RELEASE, SING
Let off — CLEAR, EMIT
Let oneself go — WENT TO SEED
Let out — EASED
Let out conditionally — PAROLED
Let stand — STET
Let the cat out of the bag — DISCLOSE
Let up — ABATED, EASE, EASED, RELENT
Let up a bit — EASED
Let up on — RELENT
Let well enough alone — AVOID
Lethargic — INERT, LOGY, STUPOR
Lethargy — SOPOR
Lets — ALLOWS, RENTS
Lets fall — DROPS
Lets go — UNCLASPS, RELEASES
Lets off — EMITS
Lets up — ABATES, EASES
Lett's neighbors — ESTHS
Letter-shaped beam — H BAR
Letter — DISPATCH, MESSAGE, NOTE
Letter abbr. — ATTN, ENC
Letter additions — PSS
Letter after ar — ESS
Letter afterthoughts: Abr. — PSS
Letter before aitch — GEE
Letter carrier — MAILMAN
Letter drop — CHUTE
Letter embellishment — SERIF
Letter from Athens — ETA
Letter from Greece — ETA, PSI
Letter from Paul — EPISTLE
Letter from Plato — ETA
Letter grade — CEE
Letter of a kind — REPLY
Letter on a locket: Abbr. — INIT
Letter opener — DEAR, SIR
Letter patterns — STENCILS
Letter recipient, often — SIR
Letter sign-off word — TRULY, YOURS
Letter starters — DEARS
Letter stroke — SERIF
Letter writer's abbr. — PPS
Letter's concern — RENT
Letter's ending — REGARDS
Letter-container — ENVELOPE
Letterman's show — LATE NIGHT
Letters — EPISTLES
Letters — ESSES, EFFS, ELS, EXES, MAIL
Letters at Calvary — INRI
Letters for day six — TGIF
Letters from Athens — ETAS
Letters from Greece — OMEGAS, RHOS, XIS, ZETAS
Letters from Paul — ROMANS
Letters in a package — COD
Letters in Einstein's famous equation — EM, CEE
Letters of credit? — IOU
Letters of the cross — INRI
Letters on a carrier — USS
Letters on a chasuble — IHS
Letters on a ship's bow — USS
Letters that make the "angels" sing — SRO
Letting in air — DRAFTY
Letts' neighbors — ESTHS
Lettuce — COS
Lettuce lovers — RABBITS
Lettuce type — COS
Lettuce variety — COS
Leucothea, as a mortal — INO
Levant — OSCAR
Levant vessel — SAIC
Levantine garment — CAFTAN
Levantine ketch — SAIC
Levee — DIKE
Levee load — BALE
Level — EVEN, PLANAR
Level a Hereford house — RASE
Level in Leipzig — UBEN
Level link — STAIR
Level off (with "out") — FLATTEN
Level to the ground — RASE
Level up, in a way — SHIM
Level, in Leeds — RASE
Level-headed — CALM, SANE
Leveled — EVENED
Leveler of a sort — SHIM
Leveling a flat — RAISING
Levels — EVENS, TRUES
Levels, in Toronto — RASES
Levene and Levenson — SAMS
Lever on a loom — TREADLE
Levered — PRIED
Leverets — HARES
Leviathans of the sea — WHALES
Levin or Gershwin — IRA
Levin, the author — IRA
Levitate — RISE
Levitated — AROSE
Levy — IMPOSE
Lew of tennis — HOAD
Lew Wallace's "Ben" — HUR
Lew who played Dr. Kildare — AYRES
Lewd — BAWDY
Lewd look — LEER
Lewd material for short — PORN
Lewd one — LECHER
Lewis and Weems — TEDS
Lewis Carroll work — JABBERWOCKY
Lewis or Belafonte — SHARI
Lewis or Ezra — STONE
Lewis or Weems — TED
Lewis's partner — CLARK
Lewis-Young song of 1928 — LAUGH CLOWN LAUGH
Lexicon from Brit. — OED
Leyte capital — TACLOBAN
Leyte's island neighbor — SAMAR
LGs counterparts — RGS
Lhasa _____ — APSO
Lhasa _____ (Tibetan dog) — APSO
Lhasa is its capital — TIBET
Lhasa priest — LAMA
Lhasa's country — TIBET
LI + LI — CII
Li'l Abner's Daisy _____ — MAE
Li'l Abner's son — ABE
Liability — DEBT
Liability's opposite — ASSET
Liana — VINE
Liana, e.g. — VINE
Libations — DRINKS
Libel — SLUR
Liberace and Nero — PIANISTS
Liberal follower — ARTS
Liberal group at college — ARTS
Liberals — LEFT
Liberals in Canada — GRITS
Liberate — DELIVER, RESCUE
Liberate from bondage — EMANCIPATE
Liberated — FREE
Liberation — RELEASED
Liberian group — GBE
Liberian people — GOLA

Libertine — RAKE, ROUE
Libertine's looks — OGLES
Libertines — RAKES
Liberty — FREEDOM
Libra symbol — SCALES
Librarian's concern — ANA
Librarian's device — DATER
Library equipment — DATER
Library gadgets — DATERS
Library listings — TITLES
Library nook — CARREL
Library reference — TITLE
Library treasures: Abbr. — MSS
Libretto — TEXT
Libya's Gulf of _____ — SIDRA
Libya's neighbor — CHAD
License — AUTHORIZE, CERTIFICATE, PERMIT, WARRANT
License plate — TAG
Licenses — PERMITS
Licentious — LEWD
Lichen — MOSS
Lick — WASH
Licked up — LAPPED
Lid — COVER
Lidos — POOLS
Lids — HATS
Lie — PALTER
Lie adjacent to — ABUT
Lie at anchor — RIDE
Lie dormant — SLEEP
Lie in wait — LURK
Liege river — MEUSE
Lienee's obligation — PAYMENTS
Lieu — STEAD
Lieutenant's insignia — BARS
Lieutenant, to a private — SIR
Life form study: Abbr. — BIOL
Life guard, at times — SAVER
Life histories — PASTS
Life of Riley — EASE
Life or thought starter — AFTER
Life preserver — MAE WEST
Life principle — ANIMA
Life recap — BIO
Life stories, briefly — BIOS
Life story, for short — BIO
Life's work — CAREER
Life, in Nice — VIE
Life-preserver stuffing — KAPOK
Lifeboat crane — DAVIT
Lifeguard is here — ON THE BEACH
Lifeless — INERT
Lifeless, old style — AMORT
Lifeline, e.g. — ROPE
Lifelong pursuit — CAREER
Lifesaver — JOHNNY ON THE SPOT
Lifesaver of myth — INO
Lifesaving fluid — PLASMA
Lifetime — AGE, DAY
Lifetime occupation — CAREER
Lifetime, to Livy — AETAS
Lifework — CAREER
Lift — HEIST, HOIST
Lift with a crane — HOIST
Lifted — UPHEAVED
Lifted with effort — HOVE
Lifting machine — CRANE
Lifts — GLOMS
Lifts for skiers — T BARS
Lifts up — REARS
Ligated — TIED
Ligatures — TIES
Light-switch positions — ONS
Light — LAMP
Light _____ under — A FIRE
Light amplifier — LASER
Light anchor — KEDGE
Light axe — TOMAHAWK
Light blow — PAT
Light breezes — AIRS
Light Brigade attack — CHARGE
Light brown — TAWNY
Light browns — BRANS
Light carriage — TRAP
Light color — ECRU, PASTEL
Light disperser — PRISM
Light entertainment — REVUE
Light for Paul Revere — LANTERN
Light foundation garment — CORSELET
Light gas — NEON
Light giver — LAMP
Light into — ASSAIL
Light lead-in — TWI
Light lines — RAYS
Light metal — ALUMINUM
Light on the Great White Way — NEON
Light or shine starter — MOON
Light orange shade — APRICOT
Light rays — SUNBEAMS
Light refractor — PRISM
Light role on TV — ANGELA
Light ropes for a boat's anchor — RODES
Light satirical drama — FARCE
Light shade — TINT
Light sketch — PASTEL
Light source — LAMP
Light source — NEON
Light stroke — DAB
Light submachine gun — STEN
Light tan — ECRU
Light theatrical fare — REVUE
Light touches — DABS, PATS
Light undergarment, shift — SYMAR
Light undergarments — LINGERIE
Light weight — OUNCE
Light wood — BALSA
Light wood used for floats — BALSA
Light yellow — LEMON
Light, in Lugo — LUZ
Light-amplification device — LASER
Light-brown color — HAZLE
Light-brown thin material — KHAKI
Light-bulb unit — WATT
Light-fingered — SLY
Light-footed — AGILE, SPRY
Light-headed — GIDDY
Lighten — ALLAY
Lightened — EASED
Lighter-than-air airship — BLIMP
Lighthouse, as on Greek island — PHARE
Lighting fixture — LAMP
Lighting unit — LUMEN
Lightless — DARK
Lightly wash — RINSE
Lights out — TAPS
Lightweight champ Carlos: 1960 — ORTIZ
Lightweights — NINNIES
Ligurian Sea port — IMPERIA
Like — CHOOSE, DESIRE, ENJOY, FANCY, ILK
Like — NEAR, SIMILAR
Like "Halloween" — EERIE
Like _____ (floundering) — A FISH OUT OF WATER
Like _____ (in a pod) — PEAS
Like _____ (of bricks) — A TON
Like _____ (probably) — AS NOT
Like _____ from the blue — A BOLT
Like _____ out of hell — A BAT
Like a _____ lard — TUB OF
Like a bad actor — HAMMY
Like a basset — LOP EARED
Like a basso — DEEP
Like a bionic man — WIRED
Like a bishop's headdress — MITRAL
Like a boiler factory — NOISY
Like a bower — LEAFY
Like a bright night — STARLIT
Like a bugbear — SCARY
Like a bump on _____ — A LOG
Like a bungee jumper's cord — ELASTIC
Like a calla lily — AROID
Like a castoff — UNWANTED
Like a cereal grass — OATEN
Like a certain bucket — OAKEN
Like a certain old bucket — OAKEN
Like a certain ranger — LONE
Like a chatterbox — TALKY

Like a cheering crowd — AROAR
Like a cheetah — FLEET
Like a chimney — SOOTY
Like a chimney sweep — SOOTY
Like a chimney sweep's clothes — SOOTY
Like a church mouse — POOR
Like a clarinet — REEDY
Like a cocktail "lady" — PINK
Like a coin — TWO SIDED
Like a crazy hombre — LOCO
Like a crone — ANILE
Like a desert spot — OASEAN
Like a diadem — JEWELLED
Like a Disney dog — SHAGGY
Like a Dives — RICH
Like a dividing wall or membrane — SEPTAL
Like a dog-chased cat — TREED
Like a downpour — TORRENTIAL
Like a fawn or stag — CERVAINE
Like a filibuster's voice — HOARSE
Like a firebrand — HOT HEADED
Like a flapper's hair — BOBBED
Like a flue — SOOTY
Like a forearm bone — ULNAR
Like a gala — FESTAL
Like a galley — OARED
Like a ghost — ASHEN
Like a ghost story — EERY
Like a harrow — TINED
Like a hedgehog — SPINY
Like a hibernal glaze — SLEETY
Like a jaybird? — NAKED
Like a julep — MINTY
Like a king — REGAL
Like a King novel — EERIE
Like a layer of tissue — TELAR
Like a leader of men — BOLD
Like a ledger — LINED
Like a links hazard — SANDY
Like a lot — ADORE
Like a Maltese cross: Var. — PATEE
Like a March hare — MAD
Like a mixed bag — ASSORTED
Like a monkey's tail — PREHENSILE
Like a moonless night — INKY
Like a moose stag — ANTLERED
Like a mosaic — PIECED
Like a mountain goat — AGILE
Like a new car — SHINY
Like a niche — RECESSED
Like a nobleman — DUCAL
Like a noted office — OVAL
Like a peacock — PROUD
Like a perspiring horse — SWEATY
Like a photo lens — APERTURED
Like a pin — NEAT
Like a posted letter — STAMPED
Like a praline — NUTTY
Like a pride of lions — A ROAR
Like a Puccini product — ARIOSO
Like a queenly home — PALATIAL
Like a quidnunc — NOSY
Like a quodlibet — MOOT
Like a rain forest — HUMID
Like a rascal — SCAMPISH
Like a rat's eyes — BEADY
Like a red spruce — CONED
Like a road full of furrows — RUTTY
Like a row of — PINS
Like a rugged bug? — SNUG
Like a runt — PUNY
Like a sachet — SCENTED
Like a schooner — MASTED
Like a Shetland — WOOLEN
Like a silent night — STILL
Like a skeleton — BONY
Like a snowy slope — SKIABLE
Like a solarium — SUNLIT
Like a street after sleet — ICY
Like a switch-hitter — AMBIDEXTROUS
Like a tabby — AGILE
Like a Tate display — ARTISTIC
Like a tennis player's compliment? — BACK HANDED
Like a tip, at times: Abbr. — INCL
Like a tireme — OARED
Like a tonsure — SHAVEN
Like a torte — RICH
Like a wall of ivy — VINY
Like a warm friendly host — GENIAL
Like a wet hen — IRATE, MAD
Like a workaholic — BUSY AS A BEE
Like ABC — SIMPLE
Like Adam and Eve before the fall — SINLESS
Like Africa's veld — GRASSY
Like Albee's Alice — TINY
Like an anchoress — LONE
Like an anchoret — LONE
Like an angry babe? — UP IN ARMS
Like an angry perfumer? — INCENSED
Like an Annie Oakley — ON THE HOUSE
Like an antelope — FLEET
Like an ascetic's existence — MONASTIC
Like an aster — RADIAL
Like an Easter outfit — DRESSY
Like an edited manuscript — PRINTABLE
Like an egg — OVATE
Like an empty tank — GASLESS
Like an honest piano? — UPRIGHT
Like an igloo's roof — DOMED
Like an oak leaf — LOBATE
Like an oboe's sound — REEDY
Like an old woman — ANILE
Like an otary — EARED
Like an owl — WISE
Like an ox — STRONG
Like angry Clara Bow? — FIT TO BE TIED
Like angry Ma Kettle? — BOILING OVER
Like angry Mr. Burns? — ALL FIRED UP
Like ante-bellum South — RURAL
Like Apley — LATE
Like April, proverbially — SHOWERY
Like Archie Bunker — BIASED
Like argon — INERT
Like argon or krypton — INERT
Like Arthur's table — ROUND
Like Australia or Hispaniola — SEAGIRT
Like autumn leaves — SERE
Like bearded grain — AWNED
Like Ben Jonson — RARE
Like betting partners' feelings? — MUTUEL
Like Bo Peep's sheep — LOST
Like Bogart's falcon — MALTESE
Like Bonnie and Clyde — LAWLESS
Like breeze-kissed water — RIPPLY
Like Brown's walls — IVIED
Like bubble baths — SUDSY
Like Bunyan's tales — TALL
Like Burgess's cow — PURPLE
Like Caesar's Gaul — TRISECTED
Like Capp's Abner — LIL
Like Casey's Mets — AMAZIN
Like Cassius' look — LEAN
Like cats in the 40's — HEP
Like certain gates — PEARLY
Like certain maidens — FAIR
Like certain pies — DEEP DISH
Like certain wines — SEC
Like Chablis — SEC
Like checks or cash — BANKABLE
Like college walls — IVIED
Like corraled cattle — ALL BOXED IN
Like crackerbarrel philosophy — HOMESPUN
Like Croesus — RICH
Like crudites — RAW

Like crumbly earth — MARLE
Like custard — EGGY
Like Daffy Duck — ALISP
Like daisies — RAYED
Like dark clouds — OMINOUS
Like draft beer — ON TAP
Like dross — RECREMENTAL
Like E.T. — ALIEN
Like eggs baked with Gruyère cheese — A LA SUISSE
Like England, in days of old — MERRIE
Like fairy-tale stepmothers — CRUEL
Like falling off _____ — A LOG
Like falling off a log — EASY
Like fertile land — LOAMY
Like fish eyes — GLASSY
Like foam — CREAMY
Like foo yong — EGGY
Like forks — TINED
Like Franklin's "Richard" — POOR
Like Fred Astaire — DEBONAIR
Like fresh toast — CRISP
Like G.W.'s wooden teeth — FALSE
Like good beef — TENDER
Like good cheese — AGED
Like good news — ELATING
Like Gray's herd — LOWING
Like Grendel — OGRISH
Like hair needing an antimacassar — OILY
Like heaven's gates — PEARLY
Like Horace's poems — ODIC
Like Hume's tomes — DEEP
Like Humpty Dumpty — OVAL, OVATE
Like Iago — EVIL
Like Iago's purse — TRASHY
Like iambic pentameter — CADENT
Like ideal fishing country — STREAMY
Like iron — HARD
Like ivy — CREEPY
Like Jack Sprat's fare — LEAN
Like Jane Pauley — TELEGENIC
Like Jason's quests — FLEECY
Like Judy Tenuta — COMICAL
Like junk mail, perhaps — UNREAD
Like Kate in Act V — TAMED
Like Kate, as a wife — TAMED
Like King Cole — OLD
Like krypton — INERT
Like lava — MOLTEN
Like Leo — MANED
Like lions or zebras — MANED
Like little pitchers — EARED
Like London in 1666 — AFIRE
Like long-winded orators — GASSY
Like Macaulay Culkin in a 1990 film — ALONE
Like Maine woodlands — PINY
Like Maine woods — PINEY
Like many an attic — DUSTY
Like many bathrooms — TILED
Like many modern people — NEUROTICS
Like many needs of the needy — UNMET
Like many pastures in Vermont — STONY
Like many U.K. drinks — ICELESS
Like marchers of March 17th — IRISH
Like Marquand's Apley — LATE
Like McCullers's cafe — SAD
Like Melville's Ahab — OBSESSED
Like minded — KINDRED
Like Miniver Cheevy — LEAN
Like molasses — SLOW
Like Mom's kitchen — HOMEY
Like Monday's child — FAIR
Like monsoon weather — RAINY
Like most churches — STEEPLED
Like most sandals — TOELESS
Like most soap — SCENTED
Like Mother Hubbard's cupboard — BARE
Like much modern music — ATONAL
Like Mutt — SHORT
Like neon — INERT
Like Nero Wolfe — OBESE
Like new bills — CRISP
Like Nike — WINGED
Like Niobe's tears — SALINE
Like O'Neill's "Ile" — ONE ACT
Like October's birthstone — OPALINE
Like old news — STALE
Like old style garments — LACED
Like old sweaters — RAVELLED
Like ones in a wallet — FILLERS
Like part of a grandfather clock — PENDULAR
Like patchwork — PIECED
Like Paul Pry — NOSY
Like peanut brittle — NUTTY
Like peas in _____ — A POD
Like Pegasus — ALATE, ALAR
Like Picasso's guitarist — OLD
Like pie — EASY
Like Pisa's tower — ALOP, ATILT
Like potatoes and pasta — STARCHY
Like pottery material — EARTHEN
Like Princess Di — SHY
Like prom suits — RENTED
Like prophets Hosea, Joel, et al. — MINOR
Like prying Parker — NOSY
Like quail eggs — SPECKLY
Like Robinson Crusoe — MAROONED
Like Roger? — JOLLY
Like rusty parts — SQUEAKY
Like saps in spring — RUNNY
Like school tablets — LINED
Like seersucker — CRINKLED
Like September in a 1937 song — RAINY
Like Shakespeare's Wives of Windsor — MERRY
Like Shangri-La's horizon — LOST
Like Shelley's works — LYRICAL
Like short pastry — CRISP
Like Sidney Greenstreet — OBESE
Like Skelton's angry wife? — SEEING RED
Like snakeskin — SCALY
Like some alleles — DOMINANT
Like some baskets — OSIERED
Like some beavers — EAGER
Like some beef — RARE
Like some beverages — ICED
Like some birds — RARE, SONGLESS
Like some bloomers — LATE
Like some bombs — SMART
Like some books — SEWN
Like some cakes — ICED
Like some campus buildings — IVIED
Like some cars — USED
Like some causes — LOST
Like some cement — PRECAST
Like some cereal — OATEN
Like some chair seats — CANED
Like some churches — SPIRED
Like some coats — BELTED
Like some crystals — BIAXIAL
Like some dentistry — PAINLESS
Like some detergents — LATHERY
Like some diets — BLAND
Like some evergreens: Comb. form — PINI
Like some excuses — LAME
Like some fish — EARED
Like some floors — TILED
Like some fractions — REDUCIBLE
Like some fruit — DRIED
Like some gases — INERT
Like some grapes — SEEDLESS, SOUR
Like some halls — IVIED

Like some happenings — FREAK
Like some Hitchcock villains — PSYCHOTIC
Like some horses — DAPPLED, SHOD
Like some hose — MESH
Like some hoves — CLOVEN
Like some jewelry — GOLD FILLED, PASTE
Like some juleps — MINTY
Like some manuscripts — TYPED
Like some meats — FATTY
Like some minds — CLOSED
Like some MP's — TITLED
Like some note paper — LINED
Like some novelists — VERBOSE
Like some numbers — ODD
Like some Oriental music — ATONAL
Like some paper — LINED
Like some pates — BALD
Like some peanuts — SALTED
Like some pickings — SLIM
Like some pretzels — SALTY
Like some prunes — STEWED
Like some rags — GLAD
Like some roads or plots — TWISTY
Like some rocks — MOSSY
Like some roofing material — SLATY
Like some roots — TILED
Like some rustic cottages — LATTICED
Like some sale prices — ROCK BOTTOM
Like some seals — EARED
Like some skirts — GORED, MINI, SHORT
Like some soup — WATERY
Like some stares — ICY
Like some stories — TALL
Like some strawflowers — DRIED
Like some talkers — GLIB
Like some telecasts — LIVE
Like some tires — STUDED
Like some trains — OVER-CROWDED
Like some transit — RAPID
Like some university walls — IVIED
Like some vaudeville shows — TWO A DAY
Like some vault locks — TIMED
Like some vegetables — LEAFY
Like some verbs: Abbr. — IRR
Like some walls — IVIED, PANELED
Like some weather — NASTY
Like stadiums at touchdown time — AROAR
Like stickum — GLUEY
Like stilts — BIRDLEGGED
Like street talk — SLANGY
Like Suckling's "fond lover" — PALE
Like Sue of song — SWEET
Like Sue of songdom — SWEET
Like sumo competitors — BULGING
Like Sushi — RAW
Like Swiss cheese — HOLEY
Like Swiss scenery — ALPINE
Like talc — POWDERY
Like tanks — ARMORED
Like tea in summer — ICED
Like that old bucket — OAKEN
Like the angry clockmaker? — TICKED OFF
Like the best top soil — LOAMIEST
Like the Dead Sea — SALINE, SALTY
Like the edelweiss — ALPINE
Like the Egyptian Apis — BULL HEADED
Like the Eiger — STEEP
Like the fabled — PIED
Like the fabled piper — PIED
Like the fairy-tale duckling — UGLY
Like the first rinse — SOAPY
Like the flu — VIRAL
Like the Fourth of July — AMERICAN
Like the Gobi — ARID
Like the grapes of Aesop — SOUR
Like the north side of trees — MOSSY
Like the oak leaf — EROSE
Like the old bucket of song — OAKEN
Like the otary — EARED
Like the owl and the pussycat — ASEA
Like the racing set — HORSY
Like the Reaper — GRIM
Like the Roman Forum — RUINED
Like the Sahara — ARID, SANDY
Like the sun — RAYED, SOLAR
Like the top of Fuji — SNOWY
Like the webs we weave — TANGLED
Like the White Rabbit — LATE, TARDY
Like uncorked soda water — FLAT
Like Uriah Heep — SERVILE
Like Verdi's music — ARIOSO
Like very much — ADORE, GO FOR
Like virgin territory — UNEXPLORED
Like watery ketchup — RUNNY
Like weak coffee — WATERY
Like Willie Winkie — WEE
Like wind and glaciers — EROSIVE
Like wind and rain — EROSIVE
Like worms or eels — APODAL
Like xenon — INERT
Likeable — NICE
Likeable one — IKE
Likelihood — CHANCE
Likely — APT, PRONE
Likely (to) — APT
Likely: Abbr. — PROB
Liken — COMPARE
Likeness — IMAGE
Likeness: Prefix — ICONOS
Likes — TAKES TO
Likewise — ALSO, DITTO
Liking — FONDNESS
Lil E. _____, 1992 Derby winner — TEE
Lilac or orchid, e.g. — COLOR
Lilaceous plant — SEGO, SMILAX
Lilies — SEGOS
Lille lily — LIS
Lille's dept. — NORD
Lillian or Dorothy — GISH
Lillian Russell attribute — HOURGLASS FIGURE
Lilliputian — TEENY, TINY, WEE
Lilliputian hallmark — TININESS
Lilting Lily — PONS
Lilting melodies — AIRS
Lily — ALOE
Lily family emollient — ALOE
Lily genus — CALLA
Lily in Lille — LIS
Lily Maid of Astolat — ELAINE
Lily of opera fame — PONS
Lily of Utah — SEGO
Lily plant — ALOE
Lily plant — SEGO
Lily type — SEGO, WATER
Lily variety — CALLA
Lily, in Lyon — LIS
Lily, the diva — PONS
Lily-family member — CAMASS
Lily-white — PURE
Lima land — PERU
Lima, for example — BEAN
Limb — ARM, ORGAN
Limb bandage — SPICA
Limb supporter — BOLE
Limbs — ARMS, LEGS
Limbs of the Devil — IMPS
Lime additive — ADE
Lime and lemon drinks — ADES
Lime's cousin — CITRON
Limelight — SPOT
Limelight one — STAR
Limerick poet Edward — LEAR
Limerick starter — THERE
Limericks man — LEAR
Limit — STINT

Limited — LOCAL, NARROW
Limited in range — NARROW
Limited item — EDITION
Limited time — STINT
Limitless — LARGE
Limits — ENDS
Limits of scope — AMBIT
Limn — DRAW
Limnite and hematite — ORES
Limo laundromat — CARWASH
Limo users, often — VIPS
Limoges item — SAUCER
Limp — FALTER, HOBBLE
Limp as _____ — A RAG
Limpid — CLEAR
Lin. portion — SEG
Linc. is one — CTR
Lincoln and Ribicoff — ABES
Lincoln and Vigoda — ABES
Lincoln bills — FIVES
Lincoln Center number — ARIA
Lincoln Center offering — OPERA
Lincoln namesakes — ABES
Lincoln of the silents — ELMO
Lincoln or Maxwell — CAR
Lincoln or Rockefeller — CENTER
Lincoln's "Cap'n _____" — ERI
Lincoln's late cousin — EDSEL
Lincoln's law partner — HERNDON
Lincoln's son — TODD
Lincoln's st. — NEB
Lincolns' unpopular kin — EDSELS
Linda Lavin role — ALICE
Linda Lavin's TV hit — ALICE
Linda of TV — EVANS
Linda or Dale — EVANS
Linda Ronstadt hit — YOURE NO GOOD
Linden and Roach — HALS
Linden or Holbrook — HAL
Linden or March — HAL
Linden trees — TEILS
Lindens — LIMES
Lindstrom and Zadora — PIAS
Lindstrom of TV — PIA
Lindy or bunny chaser — HOP
Line — QUEUE, RULE
Line for adjusting a sail — SHEET
Line from Tennyson — RIFT WITHIN THE LUTE
Line made by sewing — SEAM
Line of _____ — DEMARCATION
Line of color — SLASH
Line of products — GOODS
Line of sight — HORIZON
Line of soldiers — RANK
Line of two feet — DIMETER
Line of verse — STICH
Line on a football field — GOAL
Line on a weather map — ISOBAR
Line on Form 1040 — WAGES
Line out — DRAFT
Line to prevent overloading of ships — PLIMSOLL
Line up — ALIGN, AROW, ARRAY
Lineal — FAMILY, RACIAL
Linear diagram — GRAPH
Linear measure — ROD
Linear measures — FEET
Linear unit — ROD
Lined up — AROW
Lined with mother-of-pearl — NACRED
Lineman — END, GUARD, WIREMAN
Lineman's call in tennis — FAULT
Linen — TOILE
Linen closet item — SHEET
Linen fabric — DAMASK
Linen fabrics — TOILES
Linen marking — HERS
Linen or whisky — IRISH
Linen tape — INKLE
Linen tape or thread — INKLE
Liner — SHIP
Liner schedules — SAILINGS
Lines drawn to attract sunshine — ISOHELS
Lines of cliffs — SCARPS
Lines on maps: Abbr. — LATS
Lineup on a fine report card — AAAA
Ling-Ling and Hsing-Hsing — PANDAS
Ling-Ling or Yong-Yong — PANDA
Ling-Ling, e.g. — PANDA
Ling. unit — SYL
Linger — STAY, TARRY
Linger aimlessly — LOITER
Lingerie — FINERY, UNDERWEAR, UNDIES
Lingerie boutique? — UNDERCOVER
Lingerie item — BRA, NEGLIGEE
Lingerie listing — BRA
Lingers — STAYS
Lingo — JARGON, SLANG
Linguini — PASTA
Linguist Chomsky — NOAM
Linguistic blooper — SLIP OF THE TONGUE
Linguistic root — RADIX
Lining for a raincoat — SNAP IN
Link — CATENATE, COMBINE
Link or lock lead-in — INTER
Link up — DOCK
Link's score — PAR
Linked — YOKED
Linked group — GANG
Linking together — INCATENATION
Linkletter or Carney — ART
Links — WEDS
Links area — TEE
Links cry — FORE
Links figure — CADDY
Links gadget — TEE
Links goal — PAR
Links hazard — TRAP
Links hazard, with trap — SAND
Links letters — PGA
Links org. — PGA
Links platform — TEE
Links prop — TEE
Links situations — LIES
Links standard — PAR
Links target — GREEN
Links tools — CLUBS
Links tyro — DUFFER
Links user — GOLFER
Links VIP — PRO
Links' assn. — PGA
Linksman Snead — SAM
Lint-collecting material — SERGE
Linton Heathcliff's wife — CATHY
Linus' expletive — RATS
Lion on the screen — LAHR
Lion portrayer — LAHR
Lion's pad — DEN, LAIR
Lion's pride — MANE
Lion's share — MOST
Lion's warning — ROAR
Lioness in "Born Free" — ELSA
Lionize — EXALT
Lionized — FETED
Lions — CELEBRITIES
Lions, Tigers, Cubs — TEAMS
Lip — EDGE, RIM, SASS
Lip service? — KISS
Lip: Comb. form — LABIO
Lippizan, e.g. — STEED
Lippo Lippi's title — FRA
Lipton's business — TEA
Liq. methane for shipment — LNG
Liquefied — MOLTEN
Liquefy — MELT
Liqueur flavoring — ANISE
Liqueur ingredient — ANISE
Liquid container — CARAFE, EWER
Liquid fat — OLEIN
Liquid gold — OIL
Liquid holder — EWER
Liquid meas. — GAL
Liquid measure — GALLON, OUNCE, SHOT
Liquid measure, in Leeds — LITRE

Liquid measures — DRAMS, PINTS
Liquid portion of a fat — OLEIN
Liquid sealer — GASKET
Liquid-crystal display: Abbr. — LCD
Liquidated Russian: 1953 — BERIA
Liquidated, with "in" — CASHED
Liquor container — FLASK
Liquor for a baba — RHUM
Lisbon lady — SENHORA
Lisbon misters — SENHORES
Lisle, for one — THREAD
Lisp — PRATTLE
Lissome — AGILE, LITHE, SVELTE
List — ROLL
List component — ITEM
List ender — ETC, ET AL
List ender: Abbr. — ETC
List extender — ETC
List of appointments — DATES
List of candidates — NOMINEES, SLATES
List of files — CARD
List of maps symbols — KEY
List of mistakes — ERRATA
List of persons — ROTA
List parts — ITEMS
Listen — ATTEND, HEAR, HIST
Listen carefully — HEARKEN
Listen in — EAVESDROP
Listen! — HARK
Listener's choice — MONO
Listeners — AUDITORS, EARS
Listening device — EAR
Listens to — HEEDS
Lister, e.g. — PLOW
Listless — LOGY
Liston the pug — SONNY
Lists — CAREENS
Lit — AGLOW, IGNITED
Lit or light starter — MOON
Lit up — AGLOW, SMILED
Litchi, e.g. — NUT
Liter lead-in — KILO
Literacy monogram — RLS
Literally — WORD FOR WORD
Literary — LETTERED
Literary and musical congress — MOD
Literary collections — ANAS
Literary composition — OPUS
Literary conflict — AGON
Literary contest — AGON
Literary device — IRONY
Literary form — ODE
Literary inits — RLS
Literary lioness — ELSA
Literary memorabillia — ANA
Literary monogram — GBS, RLS, TSE
Literary oddments — ANAS
Literary opus — ESSAY
Literary org. — PEN
Literary patchwork — CENTO
Literary production — OPUS
Literary ridicule — SATIRE
Literary scraps — ANA
Literary shrine — STRATFORD
Literary sketch — CAMEO
Literary work — SHORT STORY
Literate — TUTORED
Literature — BLURBS
Literature Nobelist, 1947 — GIDE
Lithe — AGILE, SVELTE, WILLOWY
Lithograph — PRINT
Lithoid objects — STONES
Litigant — SUER
Litigant's activity — SUING
Litigate — SUE
Litigated — SUED
Litigious people — SUERS
Litter — DEBRIS
Litter member — PUPPY
Litter members — PUPS, RUNT
Litter of pigs — FARROW
Litter's littlest — RUNT
Litter's smallest — RUNT
Littery — DIRTY, MESSY
Little Big _____ — HORN
Little big horn — SAX
Little bit — MITE, IOTA
Little bone — OSSICLE
Little by little: Fr. — PEU A PEU
Little chap — TYKE
Little child — TOT
Little corn grower — TOE
Little devil — IMP
Little fellow — TAD
Little foxes — KITS
Little hooter — OWLET
Little Iodine's creator — HATLO
Little island: Brit. — AIT
Little knot — NODULE
Little land — ISLET
Little league fans — DADS
Little lie — FIB
Little meadow denizen — VOLE
Little one — TAD, TOT, TYKE
Little ones — BABIES
Little or Frye — APER
Little people — ELVES, PIXIES, TROLLS
Little piggies — TOES
Little puff — WISPS
Little Rachel — RAE
Little Red Hen's words — NOT I
Little Red Hen, once — PUL-LET
Little sea pike — SPET
Little who made it big — APER
Little women — GIRLS
Little, e.g. — APER
Little, for examle — MIMIC
Little, in Dundee — SMA
Little, in Lanark — SMA
Little, in Lille — PETIT
Littoral — SHORE
Littoral area — COAST
Littoral phenomena — TIDES
Liturgical book — MISSAL
Liturgical readings — LESSONS
Liturgical singer — CANTOR
Liturgical vestment — ALB
Liturgy — RITE, WORSHIP
Liv Ullmann's 1984 autobiography — CHOICES
Live — ARE, EXIST
Live coal — EMBER
Live high off the hog — PROSPER
Live in peace — COEXIST
Live oak — ENCINA
Live on — SUBSIST
Live wire — DOER
Lived — RESIDED, WERE
Liveliness — ALACRITY
Lively — ACTIVE, AGILE, ANIMATED, NIMBLE, SPIRITED
Lively dance — FLING, GALOP, JIG, REEL, STOMP
Lively horse — STEED
Lively Israeli dance — HORA
Lively Latin bombshell — CHARO
Lively numbers — ALLEGROS
Lively party — BASH
Lively Spanish dances — BOLEROS
Lively times — ERAS
Lively tunes — LILTS
Lively wit — ESPRIT
Lively, in music: Abbr. — ANIM
Lively; juicy — RACY
Liven — ANIMATE
Liven up — ANIMATE, MOVE
Liver's companion — ONIONS
Liveright's publishing partner — BONI
Liverpudlian Starr — RINGO
Livers — RESIDERS
Livestock — CATTLE, OXEN
Livestock feed — STOVER
Livestock food — MASH
Livestock shelters — BARNS
Livid — BLACK AND BLUE
Livid with rage — IRATE
Living near the ground, as insects — EPIGEAL
Living quarters — HOME
Living room — PARLOR
Living room feature — SOFA
Living room item — SOFA
Livorno ladies — SIGNORAS
Livy or Ovid — ROMAN
Livy's field — AGER

Livy's language — LATIN
Livy's love — AMOR
Lixivium — LYE
Liz or Robert — TAYLOR
Liz Taylor role — CLEO
Liza Minnelli film: 1977 — NEW YORK NEW YORK
Liza or Mizar — STAR
Lizard — ANOLE, SKINK
Lizard fish — ULAE
Lizard of Egypt — ADDA
Lizard: Comb. form — SAUR
Lizardlike salamander — EFT
Lizzie _____ — BORDEN
Lizzie's weapon — AXE
LL.D. holder — ATTY
Llama country — ANDES
Llama land — PERU
Llama territory — ANDES
Llama's cousin — ALPACA
Llama's habit — PERU
Llama's kin — CAMELS
Llamas roam here — PERU
Llamas' locale — ANDES
Llamas' milieu — ANDES
Lloyd — FRANK WRIGHT
Lloyd or Paul of baseball — WANER
Lloyd or Pinter — HAROLD
Lloyd or Ryan — NOLAN
Lo or chow follower — MEIN
Lo! to Lucretius — ECCE
Load — CARGO
Load the dice — RIG
Load to capacity — SATURATE
Loaded, as a cannon — SHOTTED
Loading zones — PIERS
Loads — MUCH
Loaf — DOG IT
Loaf ends — HEELS
Loafed — IDLED
Loafers — IDLERS, SHOES
Loafs — IDLES
Loam — LOESS
Loam and marl — SOILS
Loam lumps — CLODS
Loamy deposit — LOESS
Loamy soil — LOESS
Loan — ADVANCE
Loaned, for a price — RENTED
Loathe — ABHOR, DESPISE, HATE
Loathed — DETESTED, HATED
Loathsome — NASTY
Lob or mob follower — STER
Lobby furniture — DIVANS
Lobby sign — SRO
Lobe — NODE
Lobe dangler — EARRING
Loblollies — PINES
Lobo — TIMBERWOLF
Lobo group — PACK
Lobster boat — DORY
Lobster claw — CHELA
Lobster coral — ROE
Lobster limbs — CLAWS
Lobster part — CLAW
Lobster pot — CREEL, TRAP
Lobster traps — POTS
Lobster's feeler — PALP
Lobster's shell — MAIL
Local deity, in Roman myth — NUMEN
Local expression — IDIOM
Local levy — STATE TAX
Local plants — FAUNA
Local Semitic deity — BAAL
Locale — AREA, SITE, SPOT
Locale for Hogan's Heroes — STALAG
Locale for Mrs. Leonowens — SIAM
Locale for musical slaughter — TENTH AVENUE
Locale for simple pleasures — ARCADIA
Locale of "As You Like It" — ARDEN
Locale of "Cheers" — BAR, BOSTON
Locale of "Kiss Me Kate" — PADUA
Locale of 1944 movie — ADANO
Locale of Beauvais — OISE
Locale of Cardiff — WALES
Locale of Diamond Head — OAHU
Locale of Koko Head — OAHU
Locale of Mt. Everest — NEPAL
Locale of Pago Pago — SAMOA
Locale of Rainbow Bridge — UTAH
Locale of San Marino — ITALY
Locale of the Prado — MADRID
Locale of Uinta Mountains — UTAH
Locale of William the Conqueror's tomb — CAEN
Locales — SITES
Locales for Manet and Monet — ATELIERS
Localities — AREAS, SPOTS
Locality — AREA
Located — SITED
Located farthest within — INNERMOST
Located next to — ADJOINING
Location — AREA, REAR, SITE, SITUS
Location in a Stendhal title — PARMA
Location of Livingston — ZAMBIA
Location of the Mariana Trench — PACIFIC
Location of the Rose Bowl — PASADENA
Location of Zeno's city — ITALY
Location: Abbr. — PSN
Locations — AREAS, SITES
Loch _____ — LOMOND
Loch _____ monster — NESS
Loch in Scotland — ETIVE
Loch of note — NESS
Loch without a key? — NESS
Loci — SITES, SPOTS
Lock — CURL, TRESS
Lock accessory — HASP
Lock horns — TANGLE
Lock of hair — TRESS
Lock opener — KEY
Lock out — DEBAR
Lock part — BOLT, HASP, STRIKE
Lock stock and barrel — ALL
Lock trademark — YALE
Lock up — EMBAR
Lockbox — VAULT
Locked on — FROZEN
Locked up — PENT
Locked waterway — CANAL
Locker — TRUNK
Locker art — PIN UP
Locker room V.I.P. — TRAINER
Lockhart or Allyson — JUNE
Lockjaw — TETANUS
Lockjaw symptom — TRISMUS
Lockless? — SHORN
Lockmaker Linus — YALE
Locks — HAIR, TRESSES
Locks of Mich. and Ont. — SOO
Locks, of sorts — TRESSES
Lockups — JAILS
Loco — OUT OF ONES HEAD
Locomotive — DIESEL
Locomotive men: Abbr. — ENGRS
Locomotive's forerunner — COWCATCHER
Locomotive, e.g. — CHEER
Locust — ACACIA, CICADA
Locust bean — CAROB
Lode — VEIN
Lodes of material — ORES
Lodestar — POLARIS
Lodestone — MAGNET
Lodge — CABIN, INN
Lodge brother — MOOSE
Lodge income — DUES
Lodge letters — AFAM
Lodge member — ELK, MOOSE
Lodger — GUEST
Lodging payment — RENT
Lodging places — HOSTELS
Lodgings — ROOMS
Loewe's partner — LERNER
Loft — ATTIC, GARRET, HAYBARN, MANSARD
Loftier — TALLER
Loftiest — TALLEST
Loftiness — EMINENCE

Lofty — AERIAL, ANDEAN
Lofty abode — AERIE
Lofty Celtic — BIRD
Lofty church tower — STEEPLE
Lofty dwelling — AERIE
Lofty lair — AERIE
Lofty mountain — ALP
Lofty nest — AERIE
Lofty retreat — AERIE
Log — ENTER
Log cabins? — ROUGH HOUSES
Log rolling contest — ROLEO
Logan or Raines — ELLA
Logged — ENTERED
Logger's gear — AXES
Logger's travois — SLED
Logging debris — SLASH
Logic — REASON, SENSE
Logic or graphic beginning — GEO
Logistics — STRATEGY
Logo — EMBLEM
Logo in journalism — MASTHEAD
Logogriph — ANAGRAM
Logomachize — DEBATE
Logrolling contest — ROLEO
Logy — DULL
Lohengrin's bride, et al. — ELSAS
Lohengrin's wife — ELSA
Loin — FLANK
Loire Valley attraction — CHATEAU
Lois or Abbe — LANE
Lois or primrose — LANE
Loiter — DALLY, LAG
Loiterer — LAGGARD
Loki raised her — HEL
Loki's daughter — HEL
Loki's daughter — NEL
Loll about — LAZE
Lollapalooza — BEAUT, ONER
Lollipop, for one — SHIP
Lollobrigida, et al. — GINAS
Loman or Lear — ROLE
Lombard city — MILAN
Lombardy capital — MILAN
Lombardy lake — COMO
Lombardy town — LODI
Lombok neighbor — BALI
London apartment — FLAT
London area — SOHO
London art gallery — TATE
London bishop's hat — MITRE
London bishop's headdress — MITRE
London borough — EALING
London bridge — TOWER
London broil — STEAK
London cleaning woman — CHAR
London dandy — TOFF
London demolition crew — RASERS
London diaper — NAPKIN
London district — SOHO
London docker — MATEY
London doctors' street — HARLEY
London elevators — LIFTS
London film center — SOHO
London gallery — TATE
London hero — EDEN
London local — PUB
London lockup — GAOL
London monument — NELSON
London newspaper — EVENING STANDARD
London novel — MARTIN EDEN
London novel — THE SEA WOLF
London nursemaid — NANNY
London repast — TEA
London restaurant district — SOHO
London ringer? — BIG BEN
London river — THAMES
London so'long — TATA
London statue — EROS
London street — FLEET
London streetcar — TRAM
London taverns — PUBS
London trolleys — TRAMS
London's _____ Circus — PICCADILLY
London's _____ Common — WIMBLEDON
London's _____ Row — SAVILE
London's _____ Square — KENSINGTON, SOHO, TRAFALGAR
London's Burlington _____ — ARCADE
London's Mayfair — DISTRICT
London's Old _____ — VIC
London's Pall _____ — MALL
London's prov. — ONT
London's restaurant area — SOHO
London's WW II siege — BLITZ
Londoner's coin — BOB
Londoner's lift — ELEVATOR
Lone — ONLY
Lone Ranger's faithful friend — TONTO
Lone Ranger's pal — TONTO
Lone Star officer — RANGER
Lone Star sch. — UTEP
Lone Star State athlete — OILER
Long-commute spot — EXURB
Long-legged — RANGY, SPINDLESHANKS
Long-time congressmen — POLS
Long — ACHE, TALL, YEARN
Long _____ the law — ARM OF
Long after — ENVY
Long ago, long ago — ERST
Long and lean — LANK, SPARE
Long and lean — LANKY
Long and slender — LINEAR, REEDY
Long bout — SEIGE
Long day's journey — TREK
Long division word — INTO
Long dry spells: Var. — DROUTH
Long fish — GAR
Long follower — AGO
Long for — ACHE, HOPE, PINE, YEARN
Long in the tooth — AGED, OLD
Long Island or Puget — SOUND
Long Island town — ISLIP
Long John Silver's pet — MACAW
Long loaf of bread — BATON
Long march — TREK
Long march souvenir — SORE FEET
Long narrative — SAGA
Long narrative poem — EPIC
Long necktie — FOUR IN HAND
Long of La. — HUEY
Long of Louisiana — HUEY
Long overblouse — TUNIC
Long period — EON
Long period of time — EON, AEON
Long running B'way musical — ANNIE, EVITA
Long running TV talk show — FACE THE NATION
Long scarfs — STOLES
Long seat — SETTEE
Long series of wanderings — ODYSSEY
Long series of woes — ILIAD
Long shot, at times — SPOILER
Long skirt, for short — MAXI
Long sleeper — RIP
Long spear — PIKE
Long spell — SIEGE
Long stemmed American Beauties? — TALL GIRLS
Long stories — SAGAS
Long story — SAGA
Long successor on "Cheers" — ALLEY
Long tales — SAGAS
Long term IOU — LIEN
Long time — A MONTH OF SUNDAYS, AGES, EONS, YEARS
Long wandering — ODYSSEY
Long way off — AFAR
Long while — EON
Long winded — WORDY
Long, deep bow — SALAAM

Long, easy stride — LOPE
Long, long periods — EONS
Long, long tale — SAGA
Long, long time — EON, AGES, YEARS
Long, narrow cut — SLIT
Long, sidekick — LAT
Long, slender cigar — PANATELA
Long, thick locks — MANE
Long, untapered cigars — CORONAS
Long-armed ape, for short — ORANG
Long-beaked fish — GARS
Long-billed bird — IBIS
Long-eared creatures — HARES
Long-eared dogs — COCKER SPANIELS
Long-faced — MOROSE, SAD
Long-horned antelope — ELAND
Long-lasting — CHRONIC
Long-legged bird — OSTRICH, STILT
Long-legged shore bird — AVOCET
Long-legged wildcat — SERVAL
Long-legged, long-necked wading bird — HERON
Long-limbed — LEGGY
Long-lived — OLD
Long-loved Lucille — BALL
Long-run musical/film — GREASE
Long-running musical — EVITA
Long-snouted animals — TAPIRS
Long-stemmed beauty — ROSE
Long-stemmed blooms, to Hans — ROSEN
Long-tailed blackbird — ANI
Long-tailed parrot — MACAW
Long-winged seabird — PETREL, SHEARWATER
Long. crossing — LAT
Longed — ACHED, YEARNED
Longed for — PINED
Longest day of the year — SOLSTICE
Longest French river — LOIRE
Longest modern note — BREVE
Longest river in Europe — VOLGA
Longest river in France — LOIRE
Longest sentence — LIFE
Longest standing — OLDEST
Longest Swiss river — AAR
Longfellow hero — REVERE
Longfellow loser — MILES STANDISH
Longfellow town — ATRI
Longfellow's bell town — ATRI
Longfellow's tree — CHESTNUT
Longhorn, e.g. — STEER
Longing — ACHE, DESIRE, HOPEFUL, YEN
Longings — YENS
Longitudinal body segments — SOMITES
Longs for — YEARNS
Longshoreman — LADER
Longshoreman's derrick — STEEVE
Longshoremen's org. — ILA
Longstreet's choice — CSA
Longwinded — WINDY
Loni's ex-husband — BURT
Lonigan or Terkel — STUDS
Looie's aide — SARGE
Look after — MIND, OVERSEE, SEE TO, TEND
Look alikes — TWEEDLEDUM AND TWEEDLEDEE
Look back — MUSE
Look daggers at — GLARE, GLOWER
Look down on — SCORN
Look everywhere — COMB
Look for — SEEK
Look for _____ (seek backing) — A SPONSOR
Look for fingerprints — DUST
Look furtively — PEEK
Look into — INSPECT, PROBE
Look of disdain — SNEER
Look out! — FORE
Look over — CHECK, PERUSE, SCAN
Look over quickly — SCAN
Look through the keyhole — SPY ON
Look toward — FACE
Look toward the sun — SQUINT
Look up to — ADMIRE, ESTEEM
Look what the wind _____ in! — BLEW
Look-alike — RINGER, TWIN
Looked askance — SKEWED
Looked at the books — AUDITED
Looked lasciviously — LEERED
Looked narrowly — PEERED
Looked over the joint — CASED
Looked over, as a yegg — CASED
Looked over, in advance — CASED
Looked searchingly — PEERED
Looked through keyholes — SPIED
Looker — EYER
Looking — GAZING
Looking at — EYEING
Looking forward to — AGOG
Lookout spots — CROWS NESTS
Looks — PEERS, SEES
Looks after — TENDS
Looks at — EYES
Looks hard upon — STARES AT
Looks intently — PEERS
Looks obliquely — SQUINTS
Looks over — EYES
Looks within — INTROSPECTS
Loom bar — EASER
Loomed — TOWERED
Looms — APPEARS
Loony — BATTY
Loop — NOOSE, TAB
Loop for Captain Lynch — NOOSE
Loop loopers — ELS
Loop the loop, for example — STUNT
Loop trains — ELS
Looped handle — ANSA
Looplike structure — ANSA
Loos and Louise — ANITAS
Loos or Bryant — ANITA
Loos' "_____ Like I" — A GIRL
Loose — AT EASE, SLACK, UNTIED
Loose change — CENTS, COIN
Loose coins — SPARE CHANGE
Loose dress — SHIFT
Loose end — THREAD
Loose garment — SMOCK
Loose head lettuce — BIBB
Loose overcoat — RAGLAN
Loose robe — CAFTAN
Loose tangled bunch — MOP
Loosely woven cotton — ETAMINE
Loosen — EASE, RELAX, SLACK, UNDO, UNTIE
Loosen a strap — UNLASH
Loosen as a knot — UNDO
Loosen up — UNBUTTON
Loosen, in one way — UNSNAP
Loosened — UNTIED
Looseness — LAXITY
Loot — BOOTY, SPOILS, SWAG
Loot for a conquistador — ORO
Loot for Cortés — ORO
Lop-eared dog — SPANIEL
Lope — FROLIC, STRIDE
Lopez opus — NOLA
Lopsided — ASKEW, ATILT
Loquacious — GLIB
Loquacious taxi driver — GABBY CABBY
Lord _____ Wimsey — PETER
Lord and master — LIEGE
Lord Darnley's birthplace — LEEDS
Lord High everything else — POOHBAH
Lord Mountbatten's wife — EDWINA

Lord of evil — SATAN
Lord of the ring — ALI
Lord protector of England — CROMWELL
Lord Wimsey's alma mater — ETON
Lord's wife — LADY
Lord, for one — TITLE
Lord, in Judaism — ADONAI
Lordly — DUCAL
Lorelei — SIREN
Lorelei Lee's creator — LOOS
Lorelei's home — RHINE
Lorelei's river — RHINE
Lorelei, for one — TEMPTRESS
Lorenzo Lamas role — LANCE
Lorenzo or Moss — HART
Lorenzo's bride — JESSICA
Loretta of "M*A*S*H" — SWIT
Lorgnette — EYEGLASS
Lorna Doone's John — RIDD
Lorna Doone's lover — RIDD
Lorry fuel — PETROL
Los _____ — ALAMOS
Los _____, CA — ALTOS
Los Angeles airport acronym — LAX
Los Angeles eleven — RAMS
Los Angeles players — RAMS
Los Angeles problem — SMOG
Los Angeles suburb — MONTEBELLO
Lose _____(miss out) — ONES TURN
Lose a lap — STAND, RISE
Lose an opportunity — MISS THE BUS
Lose color — FADE
Lose control — SNAP
Lose energy — TIRE
Lose enthusiasm for — SOUR ON
Lose for the moment — MISLAY
Lose force — WANE
Lose fur — SHED
Lose ground — LAG BEHIND
Lose intensity — ABATE
Lose interest — PALL
Lose nerve — CHICKEN
Lose no time — HIE
Lose out on a risky trip — MISADVENTURE
Lose vigor — FLAG
Loser — ALSO RAN
Loser of a fabled race — HARE
Loser to a tortoise — HARE
Loser to D.D.E. — AES
Loser to H.S.T. — TED
Loser to R.M.N. in 1972 — GSM
Loser to the Allies: 1945 — AXIS
Loser to Truman — DEWEY
Loser's remark — WAIT TILL NEXT YEAR
Loser, proverbially — WEEPER
Losers' helpers — DIETS
Loses a lap — STANDS
Loses balance — TIPS
Loses color — PALES
Loses feathers — MOLTS
Loses hair — BALDS
Loses in pinball — TILTS
Loses traction — SKIDS
Loses weight — DIETS
Losing color — FADING
Losing regimens — DIETS
Loss — DEFEAT, YIELD
Loss of ability to make decisions — ABULIA
Loss of hair — BALDNESS
Loss of hope — DESPAIR
Loss of speech — ALALIA
Loss of status — DEMISE
Lost-article checker — TRACER
Lost — AT SEA
Lost cause — GONER
Lost color — PALED
Lost feathers — MOLTED
Lost heat — COOLED
Lost one's standing — SLID
Lost Paradise — EDEN
Lost soul — GONER
Lost to DDE — AES
Lost turgor — WILTED
Lot — FATE
Lot or spot — SITE
Lot size — ACRE
Lot's refuge — ZOAR
Lot's sister: Gen. 11:29 — ISCAH
Lot, plot or spot — AREA
Lotharios — ROMEOS
Lotion — SALVE
Lotion additive — ALOE
Lotion for men — AFTER SHAVE
Lotion ingredient — ALOE
Lotion of a type — CALAMINE
Lots — RAFTS
Lots and lots — REAMS
Lots of hot air — BLAHS
Lots of money — WADS
Lots of sailors — GOBS
Lotte Lenya vehicle — THREEPENNY OPERA
Lottery — POOL
Lotto's kin — BINGO
Lotto's relative — BINGO, KENO
Lou Gehrig portrayer — COOPER
Lou Grant portrayer — ASNER
Loud — NOISY
Loud guffaw — ROAR
Loud horn — KLAXON
Loud kiss — SMACK
Loud ringing of bells — PEAL
Loud warning signals — KLAXONS
Loud-voiced one — STENTOR
Loudmouth — BRAGGART
Loudness units — SONES
Loudonville, NY college — SIENA
Louella Parsons rival — HEDDA HOPPER
Louganis, e.g. — DIVER
Lough _____, in Eire — ERNE
Louis — ROBERT STEVENSON
Louis _____ of the N.B.A. — ORR
Louis _____, 19th cen. insurgent — RIEL
Louis and Frazier — JOES
Louis and Gerald — NYES
Louis Armstrong's alias — SATCHMO
Louis challenger — CONN
Louis et Henri — ROIS
Louis Jourdan's piquet partner, in 1958 film — GIGI
Louis L' _____, Sackett creator — AMOUR
Louis of "The Steve Allen Show" — NYE
Louis Quatorze, e.g. — ROI
Louis Riel, for example — CANADIAN
Louis XIV and XV — ROIS
Louis XIV and XVI — ROIS
Louis XIV, for one — ROI
Louis XIV, par example — ROI
Louis XV, e.g. — ROI
Louis, Louis, Louis, et al. — ROIS
Louis, the champion — JOE
Louise and George — LAKES
Louise and Turner — TINAS
Louise, for one — LAKE
Louisiana cuisine — CREOLE
Louisiana Indians — ADAI
Louisiana state flower — MAGNOLIAS
Louisiana's "Kingfish" Long — HUEY
Louisville/New York vector — ENE
Lounge — LOLL
Lounge about — LOLL
Lounge furniture — SOFAS
Lounge idly — LOAF
Lounge plants — FERNS
Lounged — LOLLED
Lounges — LOLLS
Lounging terrace, island style — LANAI
Loup _____: werewolf — GAROU
Loupe — LENS
Lourdes landlord's income — RENTE
Lourdes phenomenon — MIRACLE
Lourdes, e.g. — SHRINE
Lout — CLOD
Louver — SLAT

Louvre displays — ART, CANVASES
Louvre treasure — NIKE
Lovable — DEAR, GOOD, SWEET
Love — ALL CONQUEROR
Love _____ — AFFAIR
Love affair — AMOUR, TRYST
Love apple — TOMATO
Love feast — AGAPE
Love god — EROS
Love letter abbr. — SWAK
Love missive — VALENTINE
Love of Uncas — CORA
Love or hate — EMOTION
Love poem — SONNET
Love seat, e.g. — SOFA
Love song — BALLAD
Love story — ROMANCE
Love, Dean Martin style — AMORE
Love, for Luigi — AMORE
Love, hate, fear, etc. — EMOTIONS
Love, in Livorno — AMORE
Love, in Madrid — AMOR
Love, in Paris — AMOUR
Love, in Roma — AMORE
Love, in Rome — AMORE
Love, Italian style — AMORE
Love, Latin style — AMOR
Love, Spanish style — AMOR
Love, to Juan — AMOR
Love, to Luigi — AMORE
Love-in- _____ (buttercups) — A MIST
Love-letter letters — EXES
Love-struck — SMITTEN
Lovebird — PARROT
Loved one — IDOL
Loved ones — DEARS
Lovelace's first love — HONOUR
Lovelorn person's problem — ACHE
Lovely — PULCHRITUDINOUS
Lovely lasses — PERIS
Lovely woman — HOURI
Lover — BEAU, ROMEO
Lover of Aeneas — DIDO
Lover's hideaway — LANE
Lover's longing — ACHE
Lover's quarrel, perhaps — ADO
Loverly marksman — AMOR
Lovers' date — TRYST
Loves of Luis — AMORS
Loveseats — SOFAS
Lovesick — GAGA
Lovesick welder's task? — CARRY A TORCH
Loving — FOND, KIND
Loving meeting — TRYST
Loving term — DEARIE
Loving touch — CARESS
Low-mileage used car — DEMO
Low — BASE, FLAT, HUMBLE, LEVEL, MOO, SQUAT
Low and Thomas — SETHS
Low bench — STOOL
Low blow — FOUL
Low bow — SALAAM
Low card — TREY
Low comedy — SLAPSTICK
Low cupboard — HUTCH
Low deck — ORLOP
Low digits — TOES
Low in rank — PLAIN
Low key — MUTED
Low land — BOG
Low level literature — TRIPE
Low man — BASSO
Low place — LEA
Low point — NADIR
Low ranking cards — TWOS
Low sand hills in England — DENES
Low spot — DALE
Low tide — NEAP
Low voice — ALTO, BASS
Low wet land — SWALE
Low, droning sound — HUM
Low, heavy carts — DRAYS
Low, moist place — SWALE
Low-cal word — LITE
Low-cost — CHEAP
Low-cut shoes — PUMPS
Low-down — DIRT
Low-fat spreads — OLEOS
Low-lying stretch of land — SWALE
Low-lying tracts — VALES
Low-profile colonizer — ANT
Low-value playing cards — TREYS
Low-volume sound — MURMUR
Lowdown — INFO
Lowell or Teasdale — POET
Lowell Thomas' milieu — RADIO
Lower — DEBASE, DEMEAN, DEMIT, NETHER, SINK
Lower a spar — REEF
Lower California — BAJA
Lower in rank — DEGRADE, DEMOTE
Lower in status — PLAYING SECOND FIDDLE
Lower Saxony port — EMDEN
Lowered — DEMOTED
Lowers — DEBASES
Lowest — BOTTOM
Lowest depths — PITS
Lowest female voice — ALTO
Lowest high tide — NEAP
Lowest level — ROCK BOTTOM
Lowest of four decks — ORLOP
Lowest point — NADIR, ROCK BOTTOM
Lowland — SWALE
Lowliest member of a production crew — GOFER
Lowlife — HEEL
Lowly — MENIAL
Loyal — TRUE
Loyal adviser — MENTOR
Loyal subject — LIEGE
Loyalty Islands port — TADINE
Lozenge — DROP, PASTILLE
LP interruptor? — MNO
LP, e.g. — REC
Lt. Cable's love in "South Pacific" — LIAT
Lt. Col's group — BATT
Lt. Col. North, to friends — OLLIE
Lt. Joseph Cable's love — LIAT
Luanda native — ANGOLAN
Luanda resident — ANGOLAN
Luanda's locale — ANGOLA
Luanda's site — ANGOLA
Luandan — ANGOLAN
Luang Prabang's land — NEAR
Luau dish — POI
Luau food — POI
Luau inst. — UKE
Luau instrument, for short — UKE
Luau neckwear — LEIS
Luau specialty — POI
Lubricate — GREASE, OIL, WAX
Lubricated — GREASED, OILED
Lubricator — OIL CAN
Lucas' "The _____ Strikes Back" — EMPIRE
Luce mistress — ADRIANA
Luciano coin — LIRA
Lucid Liquid, Fla. — CLEARWATER
Lucie's dad — DESI
Lucifer — SATAN
Lucille of comedy — BALL
Lucinda's country — ANGOLA
Lucine of the opera — AMARA
Luck of the Irish — CESS
Luck, in Livorno — SORTE
Lucky number — SEVEN
Lucky number to some — SEVEN
Lucky strikes — FLUKES
Lucky stroke — BREAK
Lucrative line — GOLDMINE
Lucrezia Borgia's brother — CESARE
Lucrezia of the opera — BORI
Lucubratory pabulum — FOOD FOR THOUGHT
Lucy _____, the bride of Lammermoor — ASHTON
Lucy Ball and others — REDHEADS
Lucy lover — DESI

Lucy or Skelton — REDHEAD
Lucy Van _____, in "Peanuts" — PELT
Lucy's co-star — DESI
Lucy's friend — ETHEL
Lucy's man — DESI
Ludicrous — ABSURD
Ludicrous act — ANTIC
Ludicrous failure — DEBACLES
Ludlum's "The _____ Ultimatum" — BOURNE
Ludwig _____ van der Rohe — MIES
Ludwig and Jannings — EMILS
Lug — TOTE
Lug of a jug — EAR
Luge — SLED
Luge lover — SLEDDER
Luggage — BAGS, VALISES
Luggage IDs — TAGS
Luggage item — GRIP, STEAMER TRUNK
Lugged — TOTED
Lugged jug — EWERS
Lugosi — BELA
Lugubrious — SAD
Lugworm — LOB
Luigi's enough — BASTA
Luigi's love — AMORE
Luke in "The Dukes of Hazzard" — WOPAT
Lukewarm — TEPID
Lulu — ONER, PIP
Lulus — CORKERS
Lulus or kayos — ONERS
Lumber carriers — SLEDS
Lumber cutting tool — RIFT SAW
Lumbering boats — ARKS
Lumberjack's tool — AXE, BROAD AX, CHAINSAW
Lumberjacks — HEWERS
Lumberman — HEWER
Lumbermen or beetles — SAWYERS
Lumbers — STAGGERS
Luminaries — STARS
Luminary — STAR
Luminous circle — CORONA
Luminous radiation — AURA
Lummox — OAF
Lump of earth — CLOD
Lump of gold — NUGGET
Lump together — CLOT
Lumpy — CHUNKY, NODULAR
Lumpy masses — GLOBS
Lunar calendar periods — EPACTS
Lunar feature — RILLE
Lunar landscape feature — CRATER
Lunar New Year in Asia — TET
Lunar New Year in Vietnam — TET
Lunar plain — MARE
Lunar-solar calendar gap — EPACT
Lunch — EAT
Lunch or munch — EAT
Lunch time for many — NOON
Luncheon ending — ETTE
Luncheon follower — ETTE
Luncher — EATER
Lunchmeat emporium — DELI
Lung menace — SMOG
Lunge forward — THRUST
Lupine look — LEER
Lupino and Cantor — IDAS
Lupino and others — IDAS
Lupino or Tarbell — IDA
LuPone musical — EVITA
LuPone role — EVITA
LuPone's hit role — EVITA
Luray attraction — CAVERN
Lurch — CAREEN, LEAP, REEL, ROLL
Lurched — CAREENED
Lure — BAIT, DRAW, ENTICE
Lured — DECOYED, LED ON
Lures — BAITS
Lurker among coral reefs — MORAY
Lush — SOFT
Lusitania's undoer — UBOAT
Lust — CRAVE
Luster — GLOSS, POLISH, SHEEN
Lusterless — DRAB, MATTE
Lustrous — GLOSSY, NITID, SILKY
Lustrous bast fiber — RAMIE
Lustrous black — RAVEN
Lustrous fabric — LAME, PANNE, SATIN
Lustrous fiber — RAMIE
Lustrous gems — OPALS
Lustrous mineral — BLENDE, SPAR
Lustrous velvet — PANNE
Lusty looks — LEERS
Luther or Stella — ADLER
Luxurious — POSH
Luxury — EASE, FRILL
Luxury item — FUR
Luzon native — URSA
Luzon peak — IBA
Luzon river — AGNO
Lycee pupil — ELEVE
Lycee, par exemple — ECOLE
Lyceum — HALL
Lydia's capital — SARDIS
Lying-in — BIRTH
Lymph knot — NODE
Lynda Johnson _____ — ROBB
Lynn _____, top bridge player — DEAS
Lynn's sister — VANESSA
Lynn, from Ky. — LORETTA
Lynn, of baseball fame — FRED
Lynx — BOBCAT
Lyra star — VEGA
Lyre of yore — ASOR
Lyre-holding muse — ERATO
Lyre-playing Muse — ERATO
Lyric — ODE
Lyric poem — EPODE, ODE
Lyrical literature — ODES
Lyrical offering — ODE
Lyricist Evans — REDD
Lyricist Green — ADOLPH
Lyricist Hammerstein — OSCAR
Lyricist Harbach — OTTO
Lyricist of "Porgy and Bess" — IRA GERSHWIN
Lyricist Sammy — CAHN
Lyrics — SONG
Lyrist — POET
Lysander's love — HERMIA

M

M-1 rifle — GARAND
M*A*S*H character — RADAR
M*A*S*H name — ALDA
M*A*S*H role — RADAR
M*A*S*H star — ALDA
M, soundwise — KANSAS AUNT
M. Atget's companion — CAMERA
M. Butterfly's binders — OBIS
M. Clair — RENE
M. Coty — RENE
M. Descartes — RENE
M. Jackson offering — ALBUM
M. Lacoste — RENE

M. Lupin — ARSENE
M. Zola — EMILE
M.D. Zaharias — BABE
M.D.'s associates — RNS
M.D.'s org. — AMA
M.I.T. degree — SCD
M.I.T. grads — EES
M.I.T., R.P.I. et al. — INSTS
M.J. Ward plumber's supply — THE SNAKE PIT
Ma and Pa — PARENTS
MA senator — TED
Ma tante's writing implement — PLUME
MA teams — PATRIOTS, RED SOX
Macabre — EERIE, EERY
Macadam stickum — TAR
Macadam surface — TARMAC
Macadamia — NUT
Macadamized — PAVED
Macaroni — PASTA
Macaroni or vermicelli — PASTA
Macaroni product — RIGATONI
Macaroon ingredient — ALMONDS
MacArthur hailed from here — ARKANSAS
Macaw — ARA, PARROT
Macaws — ARAS
Macbeth — SCOT
Macbeth title — THANE
Macbeth was one — THANE
Macbeth's victim — DUNCAN
MacDonald branch, e.g. — SEPT
MacDonald's co-star — EDDY
MacDonald's McGee, to friends — TRAV
MacDonald's partner — EDDY
MacDonald's spread — FARM
MacDonald-Eddy movie — ROSE MARIE
MacDonald-Eddy offerings — DUETS
MacDonalds, et al. — CLANS
MacDowell's "_____ Wild Rose" — TO A
Macduff's title — THANE
Macduff, e.g. — CLAN
Macduff, for one — SCOT
Mace — CLUB
Mace, e.g. — SPICE
Macedonian town — EDESSA
Macerate — RET
MacGraw and Baba — ALIS
MacGraw and others — ALIS
MacGraw, et al. — ALIS
Machiavellian — CRAFTY, SLY
Machinate — PLOT
Machine — TOOL
Machine disruptor — MONKEY WRENCH
Machine for cleaning cotton — WILLOW
Machine for hurling missles — CATAPULT
Machine guns — BRENS
Machine part — CAM, GEAR, ROTOR
Machine preceder — SLOT
Machine shop item — LATHE
Machine tool — LATHE, PLANER
Machine unit — COG
Machine's stationary part — STATOR
Machinery parts — CAMS, STATORS
Macho — MALE
Macho category — MALE
Macho fellows — HE MEN
Macho male — HE MAN
Macho matches — DUELS
Macho type — HE MAN
Machree of songdom — MOTHER
Machu Picchu — RUINS
Machu Picchu native — INCA
Machu Picchu residents — INCAS
Mack and Lewis — TEDS
Mackerel — SHAD
Mackerel family fish food — TUNA
Mackerel's kin — CERO, SAUREL
Mackinaw, e.g. — COAT
Mackle — BLUR
MacLaine role — IRMA
MacNelly comic strip — SHOE
Mâcon's stream — SAONE
Macrocosm — WORLD
Maculas — SPOTS
Macushi — AROON
Mad — INSANE, SORE
Mad about — EAGER
Mad about the guy — GAGA
Mad as _____ hen — A WET
Mad as a _____ — HATTER
Mad as a wet hen — ENRAGED, IRATE, SORE
Mad Hatter's party guest — DORMOUSE
Mad rushes to nowhere — RAT RACES
Mad scramble — RAT RACE
Mad. Ave. creations — ADS
Mad. follower — AVE
Madagascar island group — ALDABRA
Madagascar lemur — INDRI
Madagascar mammal — TENREC
Madagascar's largest carnivore — FOSSA
Madalyn Murray _____ — OHAIR
Madam, in Milano — SIGNORA
Madame — MAAM
Madame Chiang Kai-shek's brother — SOONG
Madame Chiang Kai-Shek, nee _____ — SOONG
Madame de _____ belle-lettrist — STAEL
Madame de _____: French wit — STAEL
Madame de _____: French writer — STAEL
Madcap — RASH
Madden — IRE
Maddens — DERANGES
Made a big to-do — FUSSED
Made a boo-boo — ERRED
Made a bovine sound — LOWED
Made a buzzing sound — WHIRRED
Made a choice — OPTED
Made a dash for — SPED
Made a deal — SOLD
Made a decision — OPTED
Made a distribution — ALLOTTED
Made a dog sound — SNARLED
Made a hole in one — ACED
Made a living — EARNED
Made a mistake — ERR, ERRED
Made a perfect serve — ACED
Made a selection — OPTED
Made a sound — PEEPED
Made a surprise foray — RAIDED
Made a swap — TRADED
Made a wish — HOPED
Made amends — ATONED
Made an endeavor — ASSAYED
Made angry — IRED
Made another draft — REWROTE
Made available, as time — FREED UP
Made believe — PRETENDED
Made beloved — ENDEARED
Made bubbly — AERATED
Made certain, with "up" — SEWN
Made circles or ovals — LOOPED
Made coffee — PERKED
Made corvine sounds — CAWED
Made do, with "out" — EKED
Made dull — HEBETATED
Made duplicate scores — TIED
Made equal — EVENED
Made even — ALINED
Made eyes at — OGLED
Made from a certain grain — OATEN
Made from clay — CERAMIC
Made fun of — GIBED
Made go — SENT
Made good — ATONED

Made haste — RAN
Made indirect reference to — ALLUDED
Made Jonathan feel hollow? — CORED
Made jottings — NOTATED
Made known — AIRED, NOTIFIED
Made lawful — ENACTED
Made less objectionable — SUGAR COATED
Made like Paul Pry — SNOOPED
Made merry — REVELED
Made more comfortable — EASED
Made Morse signals — SENT
Made nasal sounds — SNORED
Made of a certain cereal grass — OATEN
Made of grain — OATEN
Made plans in secret — PLOTTED
Made possible — ENABLED
Made public — AIRED
Made reference (to) — ALLUDED
Made the grade — PASSED
Made to order — CUSTOM, TAILORED
Made to order kin — CLONE
Made to pay for misdeed — FINED
Made tracks — FLED, HARED, HIED, TORE
Made up of — CONSIST
Made with yeast — RAISED
Made yarn — SPUN
Made zzz's — SNORED
Made, with "out" — EKED
Made-up — INVENTED
Madeleine — CAKE
Madeline from Boston — KAHN
Mademoiselle — ELLE, MISS
Madhouse — BEDLAM
Madison Ave. come-on — TEASER
Madison Ave. copywriters — AD SMITHS
Madison Ave. drive — CAMPAIGN
Madison Ave. product — ADS, SLOGAN
Madison Ave. workers — ADMEN
Madison Avenue come-on — TEASER
Madison Avenue productions — ADS
Madison or Monroe — JAMES
Madonna's motto? — IMMATERIAL
Madras garb — SARI
Madras money — RUPEE
Madre's brother — TIO
Madre's sister — TIA
Madrid abode — CASA
Madrid king — REY
Madrid mamas — SRAS
Madrid miss — SENORITA
Madrid misters — SENORS
Madrid Mr. — SNR
Madrid Mrs. — SRA
Madrid museum — PRADO
Madrid promenade — PRADO
Madrid's Fifth Ave. — PRADO
Madrigal — CAROL, LYRIC
Madrigal syllable — TRA
Madrilene flavoring — TOMATO
Madrilenian staple — SPANISH RICE
Mae — WEST
Mae and Adam — WESTS
Mae West — LIFE PRESERVER
Mae West role — LIL
Mae's overture — COME UP AND SEE ME SOMETIME
Maecenas — PATRON
Maelstrom — VORTEX
Maestro — MASTER
Maestro Bruno — WALTER
Maestro De Waart — EDO
Maestro Klemperer — OTTO
Maestro Koussevitzky — SERGE
Maestro Lombard — ALAIN
Maestro Riccardo — MUTI
Maestro's wand — BATON
Mafeking fighter — BOER
Mafia heaters — GATS
Mag. chiefs — EDS
Mag. group — EDS
Magazine — PERIODICAL
Magazine contents — AMMO
Magazine feature — COVER STORY
Magazine for military stores — DEPOT
Magazine for the fashionable — ELLE
Magazine publisher — HEARST
Maggot — LARVA
Magi gift — MYRRH
Magi headbands — DIADEMS
Magic — RUNE
Magic incantation — RUNE
Magic Johnson was one — LAKER
Magic maker — GENIE
Magic, Kareem, Larry, et al. — NBA
Magical conveyance — CARPET
Magical word — PRESTO
Magician Henning — DOUG
Magician's interjection — POOF
Magician's word — PRESTO
Maginot, for one — LINE
Magistrate — JUDGE
Magistrate of old Venice — DOGE
Maglie and Mineo — SALS
Maglie of baseball fame — SAL
Magna _____ — CARTA
Magna cum _____ — LAUDE
Magnani, et al. — ANNAS
Magnanimous — BIG, GENEROUS
Magnate — BARON
Magnesia, by another name — BITTER EARTH
Magnet — DRAW, LURE
Magnetic — ATTRACT
Magnetic amplifier, for short — MASER
Magnetism — ATTRACTION
Magnetism measurement — OERSTED
Magnetize — ATTRACT
Magnetized — ATTRACTED
Magnets to guys — GALS
Magnificent — PALATIAL
Magnificent attire — REGALIA
Magnified map detail — INSET
Magnifier — LENS
Magnify — RISE
Magnifying glass used by jewelers — LOUPE
Magnitudes — SIZES
Magnum _____ — OPUS
Magpie — CHATTERBOX, PIET
Magpie's cousins — CROWS
Maguey center in Mexico — APAM
Mah-jongg piece — TILE
Maharashtra city — POONA
Mahatma — SAGE
Mahler's "Das Lied von der _____" — ENDE
Mahogany — SAPELE
Mai _____ (cocktail) — TAI
Mai _____ (drink) — TAI
Mai _____ (rum drink) — TAI
Maid — LASS
Maid in Japan — AMAH
Maid of _____ — HONOR
Maid of Orleans — JOAN
Maid or butler — SERVANT
Maid, in France — FILLE
Maid, in Marseilles — BONNE
Maiden-name preceder — NEE
Maiden — DAMSEL, FIRST, GIRL, LASS, VIRGIN
Maiden in Muslim paradise — HOURI
Maiden name — NEE
Maiden, in old literature — DAMSEL
Maiden, of lore — DAMSEL
Maiden, often in distress — DAMSEL
Maids' reading matter? — METERS
Mail — ARMOR, SEND
Mail abbr. — GPO
Mail again — RESEND
Mail boat — PACKET

Mail carrier's way — ROUTE
Mail centers: Abbr. — POS
Mail class — THIRD
Mail out again — RESEND
Mail rtes. — RFDS
Mail-oriented — POSTAL
Mail: Fr. — POSTE
Mailbox — DROP
Mailbox opening — SLOT
Mailed — SENT, POSTED
Mailer or Lear — NORMAN
Mailer's "_____ and the Dead" — THE NAKED
Mails — SENDS
Main — DUCT
Main _____ — EVENT
Main _____ — STREAM
Main arteries — AORTAE, AORTAS
Main artery — AORTA
Main artery-related — AORTAL
Main channels — ARTERIES
Main course in U.S. — ENTREE
Main course of a meal — ENTREE
Main dishes — ENTREES
Main idea — GIST
Main line — AORTA
Main or square — SAIL
Main point — GIST
Main road, for one — ARTERY
Main side of a coin — OBVERSE
Main Street feature — STORE
Main Street store — DRUG
Main vein — MOTHER LODE
Main, Elm or Church — STREET NAME
Maine bay — CASCO
Maine bay or river — SACO
Maine college town — ORONO
Maine or Ohio or Utah, etc. — STATE OF THE UNION
Maine river — SACO
Maine seaport — BATH
Maine Senator William _____ — COHEN
Maine tree — PINE
Maine university town — ORONO
Mainland America, for short — CONUS
Maintain — ASSERT, AVER, CLAIM, HAS, KEEP, KEEP UP
Maintain against attack — DEFEND
Maintain ownership of — HAVE AND HOLD
Maison room — SALLE
Maison section — SALLE
Maize — CORN
Maj Strasser — VEIDT
Majestic — AUGUST
Majestic — EPIC, EPICAL, REGAL
Majestic monogram — HIH
Major _____: chief steward — DOMO
Major artery — AORTA
Major Barbara's creator — SHAW
Major chaser — ETTE
Major division in biology — GENERA
Major ending — ETTE
Major follower — ETTE
Major Hoople's "drat" — EGAD
Major Hoople's cry — EGAD
Major Hoople's name — AMOS
Major Hoople's oath — EGAD
Major Hoople's word — EGAD
Major Houlihan of "M*A*S*H" — HOT LIPS
Major leaguers — PROS
Major musical work — OPUS
Major network — ABC
Major or minor constellation — CANIS, URSA
Major part — BULK
Major parts of the brain — CEREBRA
Major portion — BULK
Major swaps — BIG DEALS
Major vessel — AORTA
Major-domo — BUTLER
Majorca country — SPAIN
Majorca's capital — PALMA
Majorette's need — BATON
Majorette's wand — BATON
Majoris or Minoris — URSAE
Majority — MOST
Majority of September births — VIRGO THE VIRGIN
Majors and Grant — LEES
Majors or Marvin — LEE
Majors or Meriwether — LEE
Majors, et al. — LEES
Make — CREATE
Make _____ (get rich) — A MINT
Make _____ at (flirt) — A PASS
Make _____ at (try) — A STAB
Make _____ buck — A FAST
Make _____ for oneself — A NAME
Make _____ in (progress) — A DENT
Make _____ in: reduce — A DENT
Make _____ of — A GO
Make _____ of — A MEAL
Make _____ of — A NOTE
Make _____ scarce — ONESELF
Make _____ tail of — HEAD OR
Make _____ the right direction — A MOVE IN
Make _____: a good impression — A HIT
Make a _____ of: jumble — A HASH
Make a _____: try — STAB
Make a basket — WEAVE
Make a big showing — PUT UP A FRONT
Make a blooper — GOOF
Make a bow — TIE
Make a call — PHONE
Make a call upon — VISIT
Make a choice — OPT, VOTE
Make a clean break — SNAP
Make a dent — IMPRESS
Make a door ajar — OPEN
Make a *faux pas* — ERR, PULL A BONER
Make a fist — CLENCH
Make a forceful impression — CUT A WIDE SWATH
Make a fuss over — ENTHUSE
Make a gaff — ERR
Make a getaway — FLY THE COOP
Make a guess — ESTIMATE
Make a hit — SCORE
Make a hole in one — ACE
Make a killing — CLEAN UP
Make a larger margin — INDENT
Make a law — ENACT
Make a living, as wages — EARN
Make a long cut — SLIT
Make a mockery of — SNEER AT
Make a new half-hitch — RETIE
Make a new inventory — RELIST
Make a new requisition — REORDER
Make a new seam — RESEW
Make a play — WOO
Make a pompous speech — ORATE
Make a quick visit — POP IN
Make a recension — EDIT
Make a run — SCORE
Make a selection — APPOINT, OPT
Make a smooth transition — SEGUE
Make a sweater — KNIT
Make a trade — SWAP
Make a wage — EARN
Make a web — SPIN
Make adjustments — ALTER
Make agree, for short — SYNCH
Make amends — ATONE
Make amends? — EDIT
Make an associate — COOPT
Make an attempt — TRY
Make an error — SLIP
Make an impression — AWE, DENT

Make an oral error — MISSTATE
Make argyles — KNIT
Make as if — PRETEND
Make as profit — NET
Make away with — ROB
Make baby food — PUREE
Make believe — DREAM
Make beloved — ENDEAR
Make better — AMEND, HEAL
Make by official action — ENACT
Make certain — ASSURE
Make crunchy — CRISPEN
Make defamatory statements about — LIBEL
Make do — COPE, EKE, SURVIVE
Make do, with "out" — EKES
Make doilies — TAT
Make dough — EARN
Make drinkable — DESALT
Make effective — ENABLE
Make eyes at — OGLE
Make faces — MUG
Make fast — LASH
Make fast, as a rope — BELAY
Make firm — CEMENT
Make fit — QUALIFY, READY
Make for — FAVOR
Make friendly — DISARM
Make fun of — DERIDE, MOCK, RIDICULE
Make fun of, old style — JEST AT
Make furrows — STRIATE
Make good — ARRIVE
Make good _____ of — USE
Make good on a pledge — KEEP ONES WORD
Make greater — WIDEN
Make happy — ELATE
Make haste — HIE
Make haste — RUSH, TEAR
Make healthy — CURE
Make heavy going — SLOG
Make heavy work of — PLOD
Make imperfect — MAR
Make incisions — SCORE
Make ineffective — DISABLE
Make inquiry — ASK
Make interesting — ENLIVEN
Make into law — ENACT
Make into thread — SPIN
Make it — ARRIVE
Make jagged — INDENT
Make joyful — GLADDEN
Make jubilant — ELATE
Make known — AIR
Make lace — TAT
Make law — ENACT
Make leather — TAN
Make less difficult — EASE
Make less toxic — SAFEN
Make level — TRUE
Make like — IMITATE
Make limp, damp and messy — BEDRAGGLE
Make mad — DERANGE
Make mentally uncertain — CONFUSE
Make merry — JEST, REVEL
Make messy — MUSS
Make money — EARN
Make more precipitous — STEEPEN
Make more profound — DEEPEN
Make more substantial — FATTEN
Make more suitable — ADAPT
Make more tolerable — AMELIORATE
Make more useful — ADAPT
Make nervous — UNDO
Make nervous — UNDO
Make nervous, with "on" — GRATE
Make off — FLEE, SPLIT
Make off in the night — ELOPE
Make one's way — WEND
Make orderly — ALINE
Make out — SPOT
Make over — REDO
Make over, as a dress — RESTYLE
Make parallel — ALINE
Make picots — TAT
Make plans — ARRANGE
Make possible — ENABLE
Make red blue — DYE
Make restitution — ATONE
Make shipshape again — REFIT
Make sounds of mirth — CHORTLE
Make sport of — ROAST, SCOFF
Make suitable — BEFIT
Make sure, for short — VER
Make sweaters — KNIT
Make the _____ of it — BEST
Make the copy right — EDIT
Make the rounds — PATROL
Make tipsy — BESOT
Make tracks — HARE, HASTEN, HIE, SCOOT, TEAR
Make uniform — EVEN
Make up — INVENT
Make up (for) — ATONE, COMPENSATE, RECOUP
Make use of — EXERT
Make very angry — INCENSE
Make warm — CHAFE
Make water — PEE
Make wavy — CRIMP
Make weary — TIRE
Make well — CURE, HEAL
Make white sugar — REFINE
Make worse — AGGRAVATE
Make-believe — PRETEND, SHAM
Make-up — ROUGE
Make-up lady Lauder — ESTEE
Maker of pots and pans — TINSMITH
Maker of valuable violins — AMATI
Maker of verses — METRIST
Makers of hills — ANTS
Makes a choice — OPTS
Makes a choice of — SELECTS
Makes a droning sound — HUMS
Makes a funny — PUNS
Makes a hook shot — SINKS
Makes a mistake — ERRS
Makes a point — SCORES
Makes a record of — ENTERS
Makes a statement — AVERS
Makes a sweater — KNITS
Makes a try — STABS
Makes airtight — SEALS
Makes amends — ATONES
Makes angry — IRES
Makes available — OPEN UP
Makes away with — STEALS
Makes beloved — ENDEARS
Makes better — AMENDS, ENHANCES
Makes clothing — SEWS
Makes depressed — SADDENS
Makes do, with "out" — EKES
Makes edging — TATS
Makes equitable — EVENS
Makes fast — SECURES
Makes flawless — PERFECTS
Makes fun of — TEASES
Makes garment adjustments — ALTERS
Makes glass — FRITS
Makes happy — ELATES
Makes hide into leather — TANS
Makes lace — TATS
Makes like — APES
Makes lovable — ENDEARS
Makes merry — REVELS
Makes mistakes — ERRS
Makes money — EARNS
Makes muffins — BAKES
Makes mufflers — KNITS
Makes obeisance — — BOWS
Makes packages — WRAPS
Makes possible — ENABLES
Makes ready — ALERTS
Makes right — CORRECTS
Makes sound again — HEALS
Makes strips — SHREDS
Makes tea — STEEPS
Makes the grade — PASSES
Makes thread — SPINS
Makes tracks — HIES
Makes up — ATONES
Makes yarns — SPINS
Makeup — MASCARA
Makeup maker — ESTEE

Makeup master Westmore — PERC
Makeup of a magazine — FORMAT
Makeup of fine lawns — KENTUCKY BLUE GRASS
Making a choice — OPTING
Making do, with "out" — EKING
Making iridescent — OPALIZING
Making no progress — IN A RUT
Making sheepish sounds — BAAING
Making tracks — HARING
Mal de _____ — TETE
Maladies — DISEASES, ILLS
Malady — AILMENT
Malaga — GRAPE
Malaga Miss: Abbr. — SRTA
Malaise — THROB
Malarial fever — AGUE
Malarial malaise — AGUE
Malarkey — HOT AIR, ROT
Malay boats — PROAS
Malay canoe — PROA
Malay craft — PROA
Malay daggers — KRISES
Malay garment — SARONG
Malay gibbon — LAR
Malay isl. gp., now Indonesian — NEI
Malay island — TIMOR
Malay money — TICAL
Malay outrigger — PROA
Malay sesame — BENNE
Malay title of respect — TUAN
Malayan boat — PROA
Malayan craft — PROA
Malayan dagger — CREESE
Malayan gibbon — LAR
Malayan outrigger — PROA
Malayan state — PERAK
Malaysian bird — PENANG
Malaysian state — PERAK
Malcolm-Jamal Warner's TV role — THEO
Malcontent — UNHAPPY
Malden and Marx — KARLS
Malden or Marx — KARL
Male — BOY, MANLY
Male "at eve" — STAG
Male abbr. — MASC
Male animal — STAG
Male ant — ANER
Male aoudad — RAM
Male ballet dancer — DANSEUR
Male bear — BOAR
Male cat — GIB, TOM
Male deer — STAGS
Male duck — DRAKE
Male escort — GIGOLO
Male falcon — TERCEL
Male goose — GANDER
Male hawk: Var. — TERCEL
Male honeybee — DRONE
Male issue — SON
Male kangaroo — BOOMER
Male mergansers — DRAKES
Male only — STAG
Male persons — HES
Male raccoon — BOAR
Male seal's surrounders — HAREM
Male spouse — HUSBAND
Male swan — COB
Male sweetheart — BEAU
Male swine — BOAR
Malediction — CURSE, BAN
Malefaction — CRIME
Malefaction, in law — TORT
Malefactor — MISDOER
Malefic — EVIL
Malevolence — SPITE
Malevolent — EVIL
Malevolent forces — EVILS
Mali neighbor — NIGER
Malice — HATE, SPITE, VENOM
Malicious — SNIDE
Malicious and sly — SNIDE
Malicious burning — ARSON
Malicious glance — LEER
Malicious gossip — DIRT, SCANDAL
Malicious little creatures — HOBGOBLINS
Malicious look — LEER
Malign — LIBEL, SMEAR, TRADUCE
Maligned auto — EDSEL
Maligns — DEFAMES, SLANDERS
Malines, e.g. — NET
Malkovich and Davidson — JOHNS
Mall — WALK
Mall merchants — JEWELERS
Mall of yore — AGORA
Mall sites — STORES
Mall transaction — SALE
Mall units — SHOPS, STORES
Mallard — DUCK
Mallard's milieu — POND
Malle medium — CINEMA
Malleable — PLIANT
Mallet — GAVEL
Mallorca or Ibiza — ISLE
Mallorca or Menorca — ISLA
Mallorca, for one — ISLA
Malmo man — SWEDE
Malmo native — SWEDE
Malmo's land — SWEDEN
Malodorous — FETID, OLID
Malpractice — FAULT
Malt-drying units — OASTS
Malt drink — ALE, BEER, BREWAGE, LAGER
Malt ender — ESE
Malt infusions — ALES
Malt kin — OAST
Malt oven — OAST
Malted brews — ALES
Maltreat — ABUSE, MISUSE
Maltreaters — ABUSERS
Mam, in ancient Rome — VIR
Mama bear, in Taxco — OSA
Mama's boy — SISSY
Mama's imperative — DONT
Mama's mate — PAPA
Mama's title — MRS
Mamie's man — IKE
Mamie's successor — JACKIE
Mammal — BEAST
Mammal from Argentina to the southern U.S. — ARMADILLO
Mammon — WEALTH
Mammoth — ENORMOUS, GIANT
Mammoth has three — EMS
Man-at-arms — WARRIOR
Man — BIPED, STAFF
Man _____ — O WAR
Man about town — DANDY, FOP
Man and Capri — ISLES
Man and Pines — ISLES
Man and Wight — ISLES
Man at home — BATTER
Man at the altar — GROOM
Man at the mike — EMCEE
Man at the plate: Abbr. — BATT
Man for the moment — JOHNNY ON THE SPOT
Man Friday, for short — ASST, AIDE
Man from Big D — TEX
Man from Canea — CRETAN
Man from La Mancha — SENOR
Man from Lamar — TRUMAN
Man from Malaga — SENOR
Man from Managua — LATIN
Man from Marietta — OHIOAN
Man from Mars — ALIEN
Man from Riga — LETT
Man from Sana — YEMENI
Man from Shiraz — IRANI
Man from Stockholm — SWEDE
Man from the far east — ASIAN
Man has seven — AGES
Man in a box — BATTER
Man in a shell — OAR
Man in need — YEARNER
Man in the paddock — TRAINER
Man in the van of a clan — THANE
Man is one — MAMMAL
Man not born of woman — ADAM
Man of ciphers — CODER
Man of degree — DENTIST
Man of God — CLERIC
Man of great wealth — NABOB

Man of heredity? — GENE
Man of history/ship of song — ROBERT E LEE
Man of integrity — HONEST JOHN
Man of La Mancha — SENOR
Man of La Mancha, e.g. — SPANIARD
Man of maniac parts? — BORIS KARLOFF
Man of many opinions — POLLSTER
Man of means — FAT CAT
Man of poetry — ODIST
Man of rank — SIR
Man of rank in Turkey — PASHA
Man of Tabriz — IRANI
Man of the cloth — PADRE, PARSON
Man of the hour — HERO, IDOL
Man of the hour, 1914 — KAISER
Man of the house — PAPA
Man of the North: Abbr. — ESK
Man of the road — HOBO
Man of the soil — PEASANT
Man of Titograd — MONTENEGRIN
Man of war — BATTLESHIP
Man of war? — HENRY SHRAPNEL
Man of weighty cantos — EZRA POUND
Man on a tylopod — CAMELEER
Man on the Ark — SHEM
Man on the beat — COP
Man on the go — NOMAD
Man on the moon — ARMSTRONG
Man on the move — NOMAD
Man or beast — CREATURE
Man or boy — MALE
Man or Wight — ISLE
Man out for blood? — DRACULA
Man unredeemed — OLD ADAM
Man who is not Jewish — SHEGETZ
Man who would be A. King? — CLOWN PRINCE
Man with a mike — EMCEE
Man with a Plan — GEORGE C MARSHALL
Man with dough — BAKER
Man without a country — NOLAN
Man's — HIS
Man's best friends — DOGS
Man's man — VALET
Man's name — ERNEST, IAN, IRA
Man's name meaning "steadfast": Abbr. — EUST
Man's nickname — GIL, NED, SYD, TIM, TINO, TINY
Man's septet, to W.S. — AGES
Man's slipper — ROMEO
Man, e.g. — BIPED
Man, for one — BIPED, ISLE
Man, to Caesar — VIR
Man, to Marcello — UOMO
Man-eater — TIGER
Man-friendly beetle — LADYBUG
Man-hater — CYNIC
Man-like — ANDROID
Man-made object — ARTIFACT
Man-of-the-hour, Cockney style — ERO
Man-shaped beer mugs — TOBIES
Manacle — BIND
Manacles — IRONS
Manada member — HORSE
Manage — COPE
Manage others — BOSS
Managed — COPED, RAN
Management change — RESHUFFLE
Manager — BOSS, STEWARD
Manager of the _____ — YEAR
Manages — RUNS
Manages efficiently — RUNS A TIGHT SHIP
Manatee — SEACOW
Manchurian border river — AMUR
Manchurian port — DARIEN
Mancinelli's "_____ e Leandro" — ERO
Mandarin — ORANGE, TANGERINE
Mandarin and temple — ORANGE
Mandarin orange-grapefruit hybrids — TANGELOS
Mandarin's residence — YAMEN
Mandarins — ORANGES
Mandate — COMMAND, FIAT, EDICT
Mandates — LAWS, ORDERS
Mandatory — NEEDED
Mandible — JAW
Mandlikova of tennis — HANA
Mandolin's kin — LUTES
Mane site — NAPE
Manet's "_____ Boat" — IN A
Manet's "In _____" — A BOAT
Manet's "Olympia", e.g. — NUDE
Maneuvered — JOCKEYED
Maneuvered militarily — DEPLOYED
Manfred von Richthofen — THE RED BARON
Manful — BRAVE
Manger — CRIB
Manger occupant? — DOG
Mangle — IRON, TEAR
Mangle user — IRONER
Mangles — PRESSES
Mango part — NAK
Manhattan and Roanoke — ISLANDS
Manhattan College team — JASPERS
Manhattan or Martinique — ISLAND
Manhattan school — HUNTER COLLEGE
Manhattan, e.g. — ISLAND
Manhole — HATCH
Mania — CRAZE, URGE
Maniac lead-in — ONIO
Manicurist's implement — FILE
Manicurist's work surface — NAIL
Manifest — EVINCE, OVERT
Manikin — MIDGET
Manilow's "_____ Want to Walk Without You" — I DONT
Maniple — BAND, FANON
Manipulate — GERRYMANDER, HANDLE, RIG
Manipulate redistricting — GERRYMANDER
Manitoba's neighbor: Abbr. — NDAK
Manitoban Indian — CREE
Mankind — WORLD
Mann's "Der _____ in Venedig" — TOD
Manna — AID, FOOD
Mannequins — MODELS
Manner — CUSTOM, FORM, MIEN, MODE, STYLE
Manner of speaking — IDIOM, TONE, WAY
Manner, in Marseille — SORTE
Mannered — FORMAL
Mannerly — CIVIL
Manners — AIRS
Manolete's concern — EL TORO
Manor dweller — LAIRD
Manor follower — IAL
Manor or baron attachment — IAL
Mans the tiller — STEERS
Mans the wheel — STEERS
Mansard — ROOF
Mansard extension — EAVE
Mansard feature — EAVES
Mansard, for one — ROOF
Manse — PARSONAGE
Manservant — VALET
Mansion — HOUSE
Manta — CLOTH
Mantas — RAYS
Mantel — LEDGE, ROBE, SHELF
Mantelpiece — LEDGE
Mantilla — SCARF

Mantles for Madrileños — CAPAS
Mantra words — OMS
Mantua money — LIRE
Manual arts — TRADES
Manual laborer — GRIP
Manual measure — HAND SPAN
Manuel de _____, Spanish composer — FALLA
Manufacture — MAKE
Manufactured — MADE
Manufactured items — WARE
Manufacturer of fighters — BOEING
Manufacturers' org. — NAM
Manumit — FREE
Manuscript — FOLIO
Manuscript mark — STET
Manuscript matter — TEXT
Manuscript notation — STET
Manuscript reference: Abbr. — LSC
Manx tongue — ERSE
Many _____ (often) — A TIME
Many a title starter — THE
Many ages — EONS
Many centuries — EON
Many condos — APTS
Many eras — EON
Many ft. — YDS
Many land sales? — LOTS
Many millennia — EONS
Many mos. — YRS
Many of these are golden — OLDIES
Many sided figure — POLYGONS
Many stadiums — OVALS
Many times — OFTEN
Many, many eras — EON
Many, many moons — EON
Many-colored — MOSAIC
Many-headed serpent of classical mythology — HYDRA
Many-legged creature — CENTIPEDE
Many-sided — COMPLEX
Many: Comb. form — MULTI
Mañana — TOMORROW
Mao _____-tung — TSE
Mao follower — TSE
Maori canoe — WAKA
Maori sweet potato — KUMARA
Maori war dance — HAKA
Map — CHART, PLAT
Map abbr. — LAT, MTS, RTE
Map abbreviations — AVES, STS
Map addition — INSET
Map blowup — INSET
Map collection — ATLAS
Map copier — PANTOGRAPH
Map details — INSETS
Map feature — INSET
Map information — ROUTE
Map letters — RTE
Map line: Abbr. — LAT
Map maker — MERCATOR
Map maker's abbr. — PAC
Map out — PLAN
Map out details — DESIGN
Map part — INSET
Map routes — RDS
Map sections — INSETS
Map sector — RTE
Map segment — INSET
Map source — ATLAS
Maple genus — ACER
Maple seed — SAMARA
Maple tree genus — ACER
Maple tree taps — SPILES
Maples — ACERS
Maples' fruit — SAMARA
Maquillage items — ROUGES
Mar — DAMAGE
Mar slightly — DENT
Mar. 15, in Milano — IDI
Mar. 17th VIP — ST PAT
Mar. follower — APR
Mar. vessel — STR
Marabou — STORK
Maral — DEER
Marat's colleague — DANTON
Marathon — RACE
Marathon man — RACER
Marathon man Salazar — ALBERTO
Marathon measures — MILES
Marathon participant — RACER
Marathon winner: 1972 Olympics — SHORTER
Marathoner Allison _____ — ROE
Marathoner Markova — OLGA
Maraud — LOOT, RAID
Maravich of the NBA — PISTOL PETE
Marble — AGATE, AGGIE, MIB, TAW
Marble flower — POPPY
Marble markings — VEINS
Marble piece — SLAB
Marble shooter — TAWER
Marc — RESIDUE
Marceau's forte — MIME
Marceau, for one — MIME
Marcel — WAVE
Marcel _____, film director — CARNE
Marcel Marceau role — BIP
Marcel Marceau's clown — BIP
Marcel Marceau's forte — MIME
Marcel Marceau, e.g. — MIME
Marcel Marceau, notably — MIME
Marcellus' mother — MATER
March — PARADE, STEP, STRIDE, TRAMP
March (along) — TROOP
March _____ — HARE
March 15, for one — IDES
March 15, in Milano — IDI
March 15, to Caesar — IDES
March 15th, to Nero — IDES
March and Belgian — HARES
March coins? — DIMES
March date — IDES
March division — TRIO
March man — SOUSA
March neighbor — APRIL
March of _____ — DIMES
March past — PARADE
March shopper's woe — BLOWIN IN THE WIND
March sign — ARIES
March site in Alabama — SELMA
March symbol — LAMB
March time — IDES
March, et al.: Abbr. — MOS
Marched en passe — TROOPED
Märchen — TALE
Marchetti of pro football — GINO
Marching-band glockenspiels — BELL LYRES
Marco — POLO
Marco Polo was one — TRAVELER
Marcus Aurelius's M.D. — GALEN
Marcus Porcius _____ — CATO
Mardi _____ — GRAS
Mardi Gras city, for short — RIO
Mardi Gras follower — LENT
Mardi Gras sequel — LENT
Mardi Gras V.I.P. — REX
Mardi Gras, e.g. — CARNIVAL
Mare's nest — HOAX
Mares' morsels — OATS
Margaret _____ — ROSE
Margaret Daniel, _____ Truman — NEE
Margaret Mead worked here — SAMOA
Margaret Mead's island — SAMOA
Margaret Mitchell opus — GONE WITH THE WIND
Margaret of tennis fame — COURT
Margaret, who studied Samoa — MEAD
Margarines — OLEOS
Margarita base — TEQUILA
Margery of rhyme — DAW
Margin — EDGE
Margin for error — LEEWAY
Margin of victory — A NOSE
Marginal note — APOSTIL
Marginalia — NOTES
Margot Fonteyn's title — DAME
Maria — ANNA ALBERGHETTI
Maria _____, former queen — THERESA

Maria _____: 1941 song — ELENA
Maria or Monica — SANTA
Maria von Trapp's title — BARONESS
Maria's "West Side Story" friend — ANITA
Marian, for one — MAID
Marianne or Henry — MOORE
Marianne or Thomas — MOORE
Marie Antoinette, for one — REINE
Marie Dressler role — TUGBOAT ANNIE
Marie Louise de la Ramee — OUIDA
Marie Saint, et al. — EVAS
Marie Wilson role — IRMA
Marijuana — GANJAH
Marijuana relative — HASHISH
Marina area — PIER
Marina sights — MASTS, PIERS, YACHTS
Marinara ingredient — TOMATO
Marinate — SOAK, STEEP
Marine — NAVAL
Marine animal — SEAL
Marine apodes — EELS
Marine area — OPEN SEA
Marine barker — SEAL
Marine carnivore — SEAL
Marine clinger — LIMPET
Marine crustacean — BARNACLE
Marine fish — SAUREL, SCAD, SEAHORSE
Marine flyers — ERNES
Marine hazard — REEF
Marine miles — KNOTS
Marine mollusk — ASTARTE, SEA SNAIL, TRITON
Marine navigation — BUOYS
Marine or Signal — CORPS
Marine painter — HOMER
Marine snail genus — OLIVA
Marine vegetation — SEA BEETS
Marine whirlwind — WATERSPOUT
Mariner — SEAMAN
Mariner's direction — NNE
Mariner's greeting — AHOY
Mariners — TARS
Mariners "Halt!" — AVAST
Mariners concern — LEE TIDE
Marion chaser — ETTE
Marionette — PUPPET
Marionette maker — SARG
Marionette's cousin — HAND PUPPET
Marisa Berenson's grandmother — ELSA SCHIAPARELLI
Marital — CONNUBIAL
Marital breakup short of divorce: Abbr. — SEPN
Marital state? — POST DATING
Maritime — SEA
Maritime alert — SOS
Maritime larceny — PIRACY
Maritime: Abbr. — NAV
Marius, to Sulla — ENEMY
Marjoram, e.g. — MINT
Mark — TARGET
Mark birds for identification — BAND
Mark cattle again — REBRAND
Mark down — CUT, REDUCE, SLASH
Mark for omission — KILL
Mark of approval — SEAL
Mark of approval in kindergarten — GOLD STAR
Mark of excellence — GOLD STAR
Mark of office — SEAL
Mark off — SELL
Mark on an office memo — INITIAL
Mark or union — TRADE
Mark over a vowel — MACRON
Mark time — AWAIT
Mark Twain lived here — ELMIRA
Mark up — HIKE, RAISE
Marked by boisterous roughness — WOOLLY
Marked by coarseness — SORDID
Marked by regularity — ORDERED
Marked with stripes — LINEATE
Marked, as mahogany — ROED
Marker — CHALK, IOU
Marker, for short — IOU
Markers — IOUS
Market — SELL
Market and Main — STREETS
Market bulls — BUYERS
Market feature — STALL
Market on the rise — BULL
Market on Wall Street — NYSE
Market or circus — FLEA
Market places, in Sparta — AGORAE
Market quant. — STK
Market tote — BAG
Market town near Caen — ST LO
Marketplace — AGORA
Marketplace locations — STALLS
Marketplace of old — AGORA
Markey and Bagnold — ENIDS
Marks — NOTICES
Marksman — CRACK SHOT, SHOOTIST
Marley was one — GHOST
Marley, to Scrooge — PARTNER
Marlon Brando film — A STREETCAR NAMED DESIRE
Marmalade — ORANGE
Marmalade ingredient — RIND
Marmalade tree — SAPOTE
Marmara, e.g. — SEA
Marmoset — MONKEY
Marner of fiction — SILAS
Marner or Lapham — SILAS
Maroon — ENISLE
Marple or Havisham — MISS
Marquand's "H.M. Pulham, _____" — ESQ
Marquand's "Late George" — APLEY
Marquand's detective — MR MOTO
Marquand's George — APLEY
Marquand's Mr. _____ — MOTO
Marquand's Oriental sleuth — MOTO
Marquand's proper person — BOSTONIAN
Marquand's sleuth — MOTO
Marquee — CANOPY
Marquee element — NEON
Marquis de _____ — SADE
Marquis Mehitabel, for one — CAT
Marquise de Sevigne specialty — LETTER
Marquisette — LENO
Marriage — UNION
Marriage counsler? — MAKEUP ARTIST
Married — WED
Married life — MATRIMONY
Married to a Bratislavan? — CZECHMATED
Married woman — FEME COVERT, MATRON
Married woman, in Madrid — SENORA
Marries in haste — ELOPES
Marrow — CORE, HEART
Marrow: Prefix — MYELO
Marry — HITCH, WED, WIVE
Marry again — REWED
Marry in haste — ELOPE
Marry modestly — ELOPE
Marry on Maui? — WALK DOWN THE ISLE
Marry secretly — ELOPE
Mars — ARES, DEFACES
Mars neighbor — TERRA
Mars, to Sophocles — ARES
Mars: Comb. form — AREO
Mars: Prefix — AREO
Marseillaise: Fr. — SONG
Marseilles money — SOUS

Marseilles Mrs. — MME
Marsh — BOG, PEN, SWAMP
Marsh and West — MAES
Marsh bird — RAIL, SNIPE, SORA, STILT
Marsh birds — CRAKES
Marsh denizen — EGRET
Marsh elder — IVA
Marsh gas — METHANE
Marsh growth — REED, SEDGES
Marsh hens — COOTS
Marsh marigold — COWSLIP
Marsh of mystery — GAIL
Marsh plant — REED
Marshal Dillon — MATT
Marshal Wyatt — EARP
Marshal's men — POSSE
Marshall had one — PLAN
Marshall Plan agcy. — ECA
Marshall Plan initials — ERP
Marshes — FENS
Marshy — PALUDAL
Marshy area — BOG
Marshy areas — SWALES
Marshy body of water — BAYOU
Marshy place — FEN
Marshy tract — AGLET
Marsupial extra — POUCH
Marsupial, colloquially — ROO
Mart part — STORE
Marta of the movies — TOREN
Marten — SABLE
Martha of comedy — RAYE
Martha of the movies — RAYE
Martha of the screen — HYER
Martha's Vineyard: Abbr. — ISL
Martha, the comedienne — RAYE
Martial operations — SIEGES
Martian — ALIEN
Martian, for example — ALIEN
Martian, for one — ALIEN
Martian: Comb. form — AREO
Martin and Astor — MARYS
Martin and Charlie — SHEENS
Martin and Jones — DEANS
Martin Luther — KING
Martin or Allen — STEVE
Martin or Charlie — SHEEN
Martin or Randall — TONY
Martin Smith's "_____ for a Gypsy" — CANTO
Martin Van _____ — BUREN
Martin Waldseemuller, e.g. — MAPPER
Martin's "_____ Amore" — THATS
Martin's 1986 accident — SHORT CIRCUIT
Martin's pal — ROWAN
Martin, et al. — DINOS
Martin, to friends — DINO
Martinelli of the screen — ELSA
Martinet — RAM ROD
Martingale — REIN
Martini embellishment — OLIVE
Martini ingredient — OLIVE
Martini served with pickled onion — GIBSON
Martinique capital — ILE DE FRANCE
Martinique peak — PELEE
Martinique snuff — MACCABOY
Martinique volcano — PELEE
Martinique, et al. — ILES
Martinique, for one — ILE
Martinique, Grenada, et al. — WINDWARD ISLANDS
Martinique, is one — ILE
Martyred president — KENNEDY
Marvelous — COOL, NIFTY
Marvin and Grant — LEES
Marvin and Majors — LEES
Marvin or Peggy — LEE
Marx Brothers howler — A DAY AT THE RACES
Marx's "_____ Kapital" — DAS
Mary _____ Lincoln — TODD
Mary _____, fictional ship — DEARE
Mary and Dean — MARTIN
Mary Ann Evans' nom de plume — GEORGE ELIOT
Mary Baker and Nelson — EDDYS
Mary Baker's kin — EDDYS
Mary had one — LAMB
Mary Janes — SHOES
Mary Livingstone's mate — BENNY
Mary Martin stage hit: 1966 — I DO I DO
Mary Martin's Broadway hit: 1966 — I DO I DO
Mary or John Jacob — ASTOR
Mary or Marianne — MOORE
Mary Roberts Rinehart book — TISH
Mary Stuart's realm — SCOTLAND
Mary Tyler _____ — MOORE
Mary's chaser — LAMB
Mary's TV friend — RHODA
Maryland athlete — ORIOLE
Maryland team — TERPS
Marzipan ingredient — ALMOND
Mas' mates — PAS
Masai Mara antelope — TOPI
Mascagni flirt — LOLA
Mascagni heroine — LOLA
Mascara neighbor — ORAN
Mascara recipient — EYELASH, LASH
Mascara site — EYELASH
Masculine — MALE, VIRILE
Masefield heroine — NAN
Masefield's "_____ Harker" — SARD
Mash — BLEND, CRUSH, FLATTEN
Masher's grimace — LEER
Mashes grapes — STOMPS
Mashhad money — RIAL
Mashie and niblick — IRONS
Mashie, for one — IRON
Mask — CONCEAL, FACADE
Masked man's companion — TONTO
Mason and Plummer — ACTORS
Mason's activity — LEVELING
Mason's aide — STREET
Mason's Della, et al. — STREETS
Mason's gear — TROWELS
Mason's job — CASE
Mason's medium — STONE
Mason's tool — TROWEL
Mason's wedge — SHIM
Mason-Dixon line — BOUNDARY
Masonic doorkeeper — TILER
Masonic tools — HODS
Masons' burdens — HODS
Mass celebrants' robes — ALBS
Mass meeting to arouse enthusiasm — RALLY
Mass of fine particles — FLOC
Mass of hair — MOP
Mass outer vestment — CHASUBLE
Mass. cape — ANN
Mass. motto word — ENSE
Mass. or Va., e.g. — COMM
Mass: Suffix — OME
Massachusetts cape — ANN, COD
Massachusetts fish — COD
Massachusetts prep school — ANDOVER
Massachusetts university — TUFTS
Massage — RUB
Massenet heroine — MANON
Massenet opera — MANON, THAIS
Massenet oratorio — EVE
Massenet's "_____ de Lahore" — LEROI
Massenet's contemporary — LALO
Massenet's forte — OPERA
Massenet's tragic heroine — MANON
Massey — ILONA
Massey, et al. — ILONAS
Massive mammals, for short — RHINOS
Mast appendage — SPRIT
Mast crosspiece — FID
Mast on a sailboat — SPAR
Mast spar — SPRIT
Mast support — STAY

Master and skeleton — KEY
Master of "Jeopardy" — TREBEK
Master of a Dublin domicile — HIMSELF
Master of authority — CHIEF
Master of ceremonies — EMCEE
Master of love ballads — MATHIS
Master of stride piano "nickname" — FATS
Master of two "Rs" — LITERATE
Master stroke — COUP
Master, in India — SAHIB
Master, in Madras — SAHIB
Master, in Malaysia — TUAN
Master, in Mexico — AMO
Master, in Swahili — BWANA
Masterpiece in marble — PIETA
Masters' "_____ Anthology" — SPOON RIVER
Masterson — BAT
Masterstrokes — FEATS
Masthead names — EDITORS
Masticate — CHEW
Masticates — CHEWS TO BITS
Mastroianni's money — LIRE
Mat. day — WED
Mata _____ — HARI
Mata, the spy — HARI
Matador — TORERO
Matador chaser — TORO
Matador's cloth — MULETA
Matador's rival — TORO
Match — BOUT, CONTEST, MEET, PAIR
Match for Manolete? — RAGING BULL
Match king Kreuger — IVAR
Match part — SET
Matched collection — SET
Matched pieces — SET
Matched set — PAIR
Matched-furniture group — SUITE
Matches — AGREES, PITS
Matches, in poker — SEES
Matching pairs — MATES
Matchless — INIMITABLE
Matchstick of yore — FUSEE
Mate — SPOUSE, YOKE FELLOW
Mate for maam — SIR
Mate of rajah — RANEE
Mated — PAIRED
Matelot's milieu — MER
Material — CREPE, GOODS
Material for 36 keys — EBONY
Material for fedoras — FELT
Material for mending a broken heart? — TICKER TAPE
Material for some mills — ORE
Material formed by weaving — CLOTH
Material joiner — SEAM
Material wealth — MAMMON
Materialize — APPEAR
Matériel — GEAR
Maternal kin — ENATES
Maternally related — ENATE
Math formulated by Archimedes — CALCULUS
Math function — SUBTRACTION
Math is his forte — CPA
Math subj. — ALG
Math subject — GEOM, TRIG
Math term — INTO, SECANT
Math type — TRIG
Math. course — ALG
Math., for one — SCI
Mathematical conjecture — THEOREM
Mathematical exercise — CUBING
Mathematical term — SINE
Mathematically validated — PROVEN
Matinee _____ — IDOL
Matisse — HENRI
Matisse or Pétain — HENRI
Matisse, the painter — HENRI
Matlock of TV — BEN
Matriculants — STUDENTS
Matriculate — ATTEST, CERTIFY, ENROL, ENTER
Matriculated — ENROLLED, ENTERED
Matriculates — ADMITS
Matriculating — ENTERING
Matrix — CAST, DIE, MINT, MOLD
Matron — DAME, DOWAGER, LADY, GRANDMOTHER
Matron, in Managua — SENORA
Matronly ladies — DOWAGERS
Matt Dillon's _____ City — DODGE
Matt of "Gunsmoke" — DILLON
Matte — DULL
Matted — KNOTTED, RAVELED, SNARLED, TANGLED
Matter — AFFAIR, CONTENT, ELEMENT, MEDIUM
Matter's superior — MIND
Matter, in law — RES
Matter-of-fact — DRY, PROSE, STRICT
Matter: Law — RES
Matterhorn or Jungfrau — ALP
Matterhorn's locale — ALPS
Matterhorn, e.g. — ALP
Matterhorn, for one — ALP
Matthau-Jackson hit — HOUSE CALLS
Matthew and Joan: Abbr. — STS
Matthew Vassar, e.g. — BREWER
Matthew, in Madrid — MATEO
Mattock — PICKAX
Mattress problem — SAG
Mattress supports — SLATS
Matty or Felipe — ALOU
Mature — ADULT, AGE, GROW, OF AGE, RIPE
Mature — RIPEN, VERSED
Mature as wine — AGE
Matured — ADULT, AGED, DEVELOPED, MELLOWED, RIPE
Matures — AGES, FORMS
Maturing — RIPENING
Maturing additives — AGERS
Maturing agents — RIPENERS
Maturing factor — AGER
Maturity — ADULTHOOD, RIPENESS
Maud — SHAWL
Maude portrayer — BEA
Maudlin — MUSHY, SAPPY, TIPSY
Maugham book — CAKES AND ALE
Maugham character — SADIE
Maugham opus — CAKES AND ALE
Maugham tale — RAIN
Maugham title from "Twelth Night" — CAKES AND ALE
Maugham's "_____ Ale" — CAKES AND
Maugham's "British Agent" — ASHENDEN
Maugham's "The Razor's _____" — EDGE
Maugham's Miss Thompson — SADIE
Maui dance — HULA
Maui fete — LUAU
Maui garland — LEI
Maui howdy — ALOHA
Maul — BATTER, BEAT, PAW, SLEDGE
Mauna _____ — LOA
Mauna _____ — LOA
Mauna _____, Hawaiian peak — KEA
Mauna Loa output — LAVA
Mauna Loa's site — MAUI
Maureen and Jean — STAPLETONS
Maureen and John — OHARAS
Maureen or John — OHARA
Maureen or Scarlett — OHARA
Maureen's daughter — MIA
Maureen's home — ERIN
Maurice and Laurence — STERNES
Maurice or Edith — EVANS
Mauritius casualty — DODO
Mausoleum — TOMB
Mauve — LILAC
Mavens — EXPERTS
Maw — GULF

Maw! Where's the R.I. road map? — PAW TUCKET
Mawkish — CORNY, HOKEY
Mawkish sentimentality — MUSH
Mawkishness — SMARM
Max _____, author of "Zuleika Dobson" — BEERBOHM
Max or Buddy — BAER
Max or Buddy of pugilism — BAER
Max Sr. and Max Jr. — BAERS
Max, Buddy and Bugs — BAERS
Max. — ULT
Maxilla, e.g. — BONE
Maxim — ADAGE, MOTTO, PROVERB, SAW
Maxim de Winter's estate — MANDERLEY
Maximally — AT BEST
Maxims — SAWS
Maximum — MOST, TOP, UTMOST
Maxwell and Lanchester — ELSAS
Maxwell and Oakland — AUTOS
Maxwell Anderson drama — WINTERSET
Maxwell Anderson play — SATURDAYS CHILDREN
Maxwell Anderson play, "High _____" — TOR
Maxwell contemporary — REO
Maxwell or Lanchester — ELSA
May — EDNA OLIVER, MONTH
May and Stritch — ELAINES
May birthstone — AGATE, EMERALD
May honoree — MOM
May it be so! — AMEN
May or Cod — CAPE
May or Stritch — ELAINE
May queen? — MOM
May Sarton's "_____ Are Now" — AS WE
May Witty, e.g. — DAME
May, e.g. — MONTH
Mayan and Mundane — ERAS
Mayan language — MAM
Mayan or Mundane — ERA
Maybe — PER CHANCE, PERHAPS
Mayday! — SOS
Mayo and Yaqui — RIOS
Mayor, in Marseilles — MAIRE
Maze — PUZZLE
Mazo _____ Roche — DE LA
Mazuma — DO RE MI, GELT
MBA course — ECON
MBA's study — ECON
McAuliffe's reply — NUTS
McAuliffe's succinct reply — NUTS
McBride and McKerrow — BALLERINAS
MCC plus CCCI — MDI
McCarthy and others — EUGENES
McCarthy's friend — SNERD
McCarthy's rival — SNERD
McClellan adversary — LEE
McClurg and Brickell — EDIES
McCormack's model mom? — MOTHER MACHREE
McCormick's idea — HARVESTER
McCowen or Guinness — ALEC
McDowall of "Planet of the Apes" — RODDY
McEnroe's winners — ACES
McEntire of country music — REBA
McEntire of song — REBA
McGinniss title from "Macbeth" — FATAL VISION
McGrew's lady — LOU
McGuffey's book — READER
McKellen and Fleming — IANS
McKinley's birthplace — NILES
McKinley's Ohio birthplace — NILES
McKinley's opponent — BRYAN
McMahon and Murrow — EDS
McMahon and Muskie — EDS
McMahon's drawn-out word — HERES
McMillan's wife — SALLY
McNeil of Tennis — LORI
McQueen or Allen — STEVE
McQueen or Martin — STEVE
MD's "Immediately!" — STAT
MD's group — AMA
MD's org. — AMA
MD's tools — XRAYS
Md.'s inst. — USNA
Md.'s neighbor — DEL
Mdse. — GDS
Me- _____ (coat-tails policy) — TOOISM
Me. city — SACO
Me. location — NNE
Me. storm — NOREASTER
Mea _____ — CULPA
Meadow — LEA, SWALE
Meadow sounds — BAAS
Meadowlands — LEAS
Meadowlands events — TROTS
Meadowlands team — NETS
Meadows — LEAS
Meadows or Mansfield — JAYNE
Meadowsweet — SPIRAEA
Meager — LENTEN, SCANT, SPARSE
Meal — REPAST
Meal in the military — MESS
Meal lead-in — OAT
Meal starter — OAT
Meal, in Paris — REPAS
Meals — BOARD
Mealtime prayer — GRACE
Mean — DENOTE, PETTY
Mean little child — BRAT
Meander — ROAM, ROVE, WANDER
Meaning — IMPORT, SENSE, TENOR
Meaningless — INANE
Means — AGENCY, AVENUE, CAPITAL
Means justifier? — END
Means of access — DOOR, KEY
Means of identification — LABEL
Means to ends — MEASURES
Means' counterparts — ENDS
Means' partner — WAYS
Meant — DENOTED
Meant for — PERFECT
Meantime — INTERIM
Meara and Jackson — ANNES
Meara or Murray — ANNE
Meara's partner — STILLER
Meas. equaling 3.7854 liters — GAL
Meas. of area — SQ IN
Meas. of revolution — TPI
Measure — ASSESS, GAGE, INDEX, METER, RULER
Measure — STEP, TAPE
Measure for milk — PINT, QUART
Measure for wire — MIL
Measure of area — ARE
Measure of capacitance — FARAD
Measure of capacity — LITER
Measure of distance — MILE
Measure of Galahad's strength — TEN
Measure of lgth. — RDS
Measure of movement in marching — BEAT
Measure round the body — GIRTH
Measure the depth of water — PLUMB
Measure, with "out" — METE
Measured — TIMED
Measured amounts — DOSES
Measured portion — CUP
Measured quantity — DOSE
Measured tread — PACE
Measured, with "up" — SIZED
Measurement from side to side — BREADTH
Measures of lgth. — YDS
Measures of weight: Abbr. — GRS
Measures of wt. — TNS
Measures partner — WEIGHTS
Measures, in Monaco — METERS
Measuring device — GAUGE, METER

Measuring instruments — CALIPERS
Measuring, in a sense — SIZING
Meat and vegetables — FOOD
Meat carver's board — TRENCHER
Meat choice — LOIN
Meat cut — BRISKET, CHOP, LOIN
Meat dish — STEW, VEAL
Meat dish with vegetables — STEW
Meat entree — ROTI
Meat for scaloppine — VEAL
Meat on a stick — KABOB
Meat pie — PASTY
Meat-and-vegetables combo — IRISH STEW
Meatheads — NERDS
Mecca for scuba divers — ARUBA
Mecca for turiste — TREVI
Mecca trek — HADJ
Mecca trekker — ARAB
Meccans' deity — ALLAH
Meccawee, e.g. — ASIAN
Meccawee, for one — ASIAN
Mechanical pitcher? — DWIGHT WOODEN
Mechanical repetition — ROTE
Mechanical worker — ROBOT
Mechlin — LACE
Med. checkup — EXAM
Med. course — ANAT
Med. facility — HOSP
Med. personnel — MDS
Med. school course — ANAT
Med. students subj. — ANAT
Med. subject — ANAT
Med. suffix — ITIS
Medal designation — VALOR
Medal winner — HERO
Meddle — INTRUDE, NOSE
Meddled — NOSED
Meddler — BUSYBODY
Meddler in others' affairs — POLYPRAGMATIST
Meddlers — BUSYBODIES
Medford, Mass. campus — TUFTS
Media for newsperson — PRESS
Media meeting — PRESS CONFERENCE
Media member — RADIO, NEWSMAN
Media network — NBC
Media people — PRESS
Medial sounds — INLAUTE
Mediators, occasionally? — IRE CUTTERS
Medic — DOC
Medic for Fido — VET
Medic's burden — STRETCHER
Medical amounts — DOSES
Medical chemical science — ALCHEMY
Medical facility — CLINIC
Medical grp. — APA
Medical machine — SCANNER
Medical measure — DOSE
Medical org. — AMA
Medical pics — XRAYS
Medical suffix — EMIA, OSIS
Medical treatment: Suffix — IATRIC
Medical: Comb. form — HEMAT, OMA, ITIS
Medicate — DOSE
Medicated lotion — CALAMINE
Medicated lozenges — TROCHES
Medici protege: 15th century — POLLAIUOLO
Medicinal herb — ALOE
Medicinal mixture — POTION
Medicinal plant — SENNA
Medicinal root — SENEGA
Medicinal root bark or S.C. mountain — SASSAFRAS
Medicine amount — DOSAGE
Medicine man — SHAMAN
Medics — DOCS
Medics, at times — SEDATERS
Medieval club — MACE
Medieval domestic — ESNE
Medieval fabric — ACCA
Medieval helmet — ARMET
Medieval Italian coin — TARI
Medieval laborer — ESNE
Medieval land tenure — SOCAGE
Medieval lyric poem — LAI
Medieval merchant guild — HANSE
Medieval narrative poem — LAI
Medieval Russian ruler — RURIK
Medieval soldier — SLINGER
Medieval song — LAI
Medieval town WNW of Trieste — AGLAR
Medieval underclass — SERFS
Medieval verse forms — SESTINAS
Medieval war clubs — MACES
Mediocre — SECOND CLASS, SOSO
Mediocre mark — CEE
Meditate — BROOD, MUSE
Meditative discipline — ZEN
Mediterranean boat — DHOW, FELUCCA
Mediterranean class chicken — LEGHORN
Mediterranean evergreen — CAROB
Mediterranean flower — MUSKROSE
Mediterranean island — CRETE
Mediterranean lubricant? — ELBA GREASE
Mediterranean nation — TUNISIA
Mediterranean plant — ANISE
Mediterranean port — ORAN
Mediterranean port of Italy — GENOA
Mediterranean republic — MALTA
Mediterranean resort — NICE
Mediterranean seaport — ACRE, MALAGA
Mediterranean vessel — XEBEC
Mediterranean weight — ROTL
Medium — PSYCHIC
Medium culture — AGAR
Medium for Melville — NOVEL
Medium for Velazquez — OILS
Medium midpoint — AVERAGE
Medium's state — TRANCE
Medium, for short — ESP
Medium, half — MEZZO
Medley — MELANGE, OLIO, STEW
Médoc, for one — VIN
Meek beast — LAMB
Meek one — LAMB
Meek's partner in comics — EEK
Meerschaum — PIPE
Meet expenses — AFFORD
Meet one's gaze in a haze — LOOM
Meet the need — AVAIL
Meeting halfway — REACHING A COMPROMISE
Meeting leader — CHAIR
Meeting outline — AGENDA
Meeting place — HALL
Meeting place of yore — AGORA
Meeting schedule — AGENDA
Meeting, for short — SESS
Meeting: Abbr. — SESS
Meets — SITS
Meets halfway — SPLITS THE DIFFERENCE
Meets the challenge — RISES TO
Mega or mono ending — LITH
Mehitabel's friend — ARCHY
Mehitabel, for one — CAT
Mehta, for one — MAESTRO
Meir of Israel — GOLDA
Meistersinger Hans: 1494-1576 — SACHS
Mel and Ed of baseball — OTTS
Mel and Mont — BLANCS
Mel Brooks film — BLAZING SADDLES
Mel Brooks Western: 1973 — BLAZING SADDLES
Mel of baseball — OTT
Mel of baseball, et al. — OTTS
Mel of the Giants — OTT
Melancholy — BLUE, SAD, SOMBER

Melancholy poem — ELEGY
Melancholy, to Milton — DREAR
Melanese garments — SULUS
Melange — OLIO
Melba and Sutherland — DAMES
Melba or Roger — MOORE
Melba specialty — ARIA
Melbourne rush hour — AUSTRALIAN CRAWL
Melbourne's state — VICTORIA
Meld — UNITE
Meld in hand — POINTS
Melding card game — PINOCHLE, RUMMY
Meleager's father — OENEUS
Melee — BRAWL, FIGHT, RAMPAGE, RIOT, SCRAP
Melina Mercouri movie — NEVER ON SUNDAY
Melkarth — BAAL
Mellow — AGE, RIPE
Mellowed — AGED
Mellows — AGES
Melodeon — ORGAN
Melodic — ARIOSE
Melodies — ARIAS
Melodious — ARIOSE
Melodious passages — CANTABILES
Melodrama cries — AHAS
Melodramatic — OVERDONE
Melodramatize — EMOTE
Melody — AIR, THEME, TUNE
Melon — CANTALOUPE
Melon cover — RIND
Melon: Var. — CASAVA
Melonlike fruit — PAPAYA
Melons or gourds — PEPOS
Melt — RENDER
Melted — DISSOLVED
Melted cheese dish — FONDUE
Melts — SAD, THAWS
Melvil Dewey's occupation — LIBRARIAN
Melville book — MARDI, OMOO
Melville captain — AHAB
Melville novel — OMOO
Melville opus — OMOO
Melville title — OMOO
Melville work — TYPEE
Melville's "_____ Dick" — MOBY
Melville's animal — WHALE
Melville's captain — AHAB
Member of a barbershop quartet — TENOR
Member of a brass band — CORNETTIST
Member of a brotherhood — ELK
Member of a certain sect — DRUSE
Member of a discussion group — PANELIST
Member of a family, for short — DAD
Member of a French dozen — JUNI
Member of a Middle Eastern sect — DRUSE
Member of a pool — STENO
Member of a priestly Jewish tribe — LEVITE
Member of a Scottish band — PIPER
Member of a second-century ascetic sect — ESESENE
Member of a Siouan tribe — OTOE
Member of a sorority — SISTER
Member of a US political party, circa 1834 — WHIG
Member of Cong. — SEN
Member of highest court in ancient Athens — DICAST
Member of legislature — SENATOR
Member of Suffix — ITE
Member of the bar — COUNSEL
Member of the brass — TUBA, CORNETIST
Member of the chorus — ALTO
Member of the clergy — RABBI
Member of the crew — OAR
Member of the deer family — MOOSE
Member of the faculty — PROF
Member of the family — MAMA
Member of the flock — EWE
Member of the gourd family — WATERMELON
Member of the herd — STEER
Member of the high command — GENERAL
Member of the human race — PERSON
Member of the legislature — WHIP
Member of the string section — VIOLA
Member of the wedding — GROOM, USHER
Member of the winds — OBOIST
Member of the woodwinds — CLARINET
Members of a flock — EWES
Members of a jazz band — SIDEMEN
Members of a Shoshonean tribe — UTES
Members of a Sicilian org. — MAFIOSI
Members of a wagon train — SETTLERS
Members of the armed forces — STRIPERS
Members of the British peerage — LORDS
Members of the CD — AMBS
Members of the choir — TENORS
Members of the fourth estate — EDITORS
Members of the highest social class — UPPER TEN
Members of the peerage — BARONS, EARLS
Membership — CLUB
Membership fees — DUES
Membrane — FILM, LAYER
Memento — KEEPSAKE, RELIC, SOUVENIR, TOKEN
Mementoes of a wounded knee? — SCABS
Memo addenda — PSS
Memo from a bored stripteaser — SAME OLD GRIND
Memo taker — STENO
Memo to a dilatory chess player? — GET A MOVE ON
Memo to a gabby vintner — PUT A CORK IN IT
Memo to a hasty seamstress — GIVE IT A RIP
Memo to a lazy galena miner — GET THE LEAD OUT
Memo to a waiting taxidermist — DO YOUR STUFF
Memoir — DIARY
Memorabilia — ANA
Memorable actor — CLIFT
Memorable actor Erwin — STU
Memorable actor Peter — LORRE
Memorable actress — TERRY
Memorable actress from Canada — LILLIE
Memorable author of children's tales — SEUSS
Memorable Belgian muscian — BREL
Memorable cartoonist Peter — ARNO, REA
Memorable cellist Jacqueline du _____ — PRE
Memorable Chaplin film — LIMELIGHT
Memorable collections — ANAS
Memorable comedian Danny — KAYE
Memorable comedian Harold — LLOYD
Memorable conductor Walter — BRUNO
Memorable court star — ASHE
Memorable couturier — DIOR
Memorable cowardly lion — LAHR

Memorable crossword editor — WENG
Memorable Egyptian leader — SADAT
Memorable English actress — URE
Memorable English official in India — YALE
Memorable guitarist — SEGOVIA
Memorable hostess — MESTA, PERLE
Memorable impresario Hurok — SOL
Memorable Israeli political leader — MEIR
Memorable jazz artist Zoot _____ — SIMS
Memorable jogger James — FIXX
Memorable Kipling poem — BOOTS
Memorable Lahr — BERT
Memorable Lombard — CAROLE
Memorable melodic Marvin — GAYE
Memorable Merman — ETHEL
Memorable mission — ALAMO
Memorable modern dancer Jose _____ — LIMON
Memorable name in tennis — ASHE
Memorable New Zealand detective-story writer — MARSH
Memorable newsman Huntley — CHET
Memorable period — ERA
Memorable pianist — LIBERACE
Memorable poet — NASH
Memorable Romanian violinist — ENESCO
Memorable Ruth — BABE
Memorable sayings — ANA
Memorable singer Edith — PIAF
Memorable surrealist — DALI
Memorable target: 12/7/41 — USS ARIZONA
Memorable teacher of drama at Yale — EATON
Memorable time period — ERA
Memorable Tinseltown tattletale — HEDDA HOPPER
Memorable toastmaster George — JESSEL
Memorable Turkish chief — AHMED
Memorable TV mini-series — ROOTS
Memorable U.S. tennis champ — ASHE
Memorable violinish Mischa — ELMAN
Memorable violinist — ELMAN
Memorable Welles role — KANE
Memorable Yale — ELIHU
Memorandum — REMINDER
Memorial — CRYPT, MARKER, MONUMENT, SHRINE, STONE
Memorial Day race — INDY
Memorize — KEEP, LEARN, RETAIN
Memory jogger — LIST
Memory loss — AMNESIA
Memory or Drury — LANE
Memphis deity — PTAH
Men from Mars, for short — ETS
Men in uniform — GUARDS
Men of Adana, Bursa, etc. — TURKS
Men of Glasgow — SCOTS
Men of Odense — DANES
Men of Warsaw — POLES
Men or den follower — IAL
Men with a yen — YEARNERS
Men, e.g. — BIPEDS
Menace — IMPEND, THREAT, THREATEN
Menace with reata — VEILED THREAT
Menaces for mariners — REEFS
Menachem's co-Nobelist for Peace: 1978 — ANWAR
Menage a _____ — TROIS
Menagerie — ZOO
Menages — HOUSEHOLDS
Mend — HEAL
Mend a seam — SEW
Mend socks — DARN
Mendacious — FALSE
Mended — DARNED
Mended a tear — TAPED
Mended socks — DARNED
Mended, in a way — PIECED
Mendelssohn oratorio — ELIJAH
Mendelssohn's birthplace — HAMBURG
Mends — HEALS, SEWS
Menelaus' wife — HELEN
Menhaden — POGY
Menhaden or minnow — BAIT FISH
Menial — LOWLY, TOADY
Menjou of many movies — ADOLPHE
Menlo Park family — EDISONS
Menlo Park genius — EDISON
Menlo Park ID — TAE
Menlo Park inits. — TAE
Menlo Park monogram — TAE
Menlo Park name — ALVA, EDISON
Menlo Park wizard — THOMAS A EDISON
Mennonite — AMISH
Mennonite group — AMISH
Mennonite sect — AMISH
Menotti character — AMAHL
Menotti hero — AMAHL
Menotti heroine — AMELIA
Menotti role — AMAHL
Menotti's "_____ Goes to the Ball" — AMALIA
Menotti's first name — GIAN
Mens _____ in corpore sano — SANA
Mental deficient — IDIOT
Mental faculties — WITS
Mental flash — IDEA
Mental images — VISIONS
Mental inventions — FIGMENTS
Mental keenness — ACUMEN
Mental picture — IMAGE
Mental shock — TRAUMA
Mental telepathy — ESP
Mentally alert — AGILE
Mentally obscure — HAZY
Menthaceous plants — OREGANOS
Mention — REFER
Mentioned — CITED
Mentioned for honors — CITED
Mentioned lead-in — AFORE
Mentions — CITES
Mentor — GURU, TUTOR
Mentor of Luke Skywalker — YODA
Menu — CARTE
Menu adjective — GARNI
Menu beverage — COCOA
Menu choice — SALAD
Menu course — SALAD
Menu entree — SWISS STEAK
Menu favorite — IRISH STEW
Menu item — ENTREE, FOOD, SOUP
Menu meats — ROTIS
Menu offering — ENTREE
Menu phrase — ALAMODE
Menuhin's teacher — AUER, ENESCO
Mephistopheles — SATAN
Mercantile — COMMERCIAL
Mercator item — MAP
Mercator works — MAPS
Mercenary — HIRED, VENAL
Merchandise — LINE, SELL, WARES
Merchandise symbols: Abbr. — TMS
Merchandiser's warning — AS IS
Merchandising promotions — SALES
Merchandizes — SELLS
Merchant — DEALER, HANSE, SELLER, TRADER
Merchant gilds — HANSAS
Merchant ship — ARGOSY, OILER, PACKET
Merchant ships — ARGOSIES
Merchantman — GALLEON

Merci, in Mainz — DANKE
Merciful — FORGIVING
Merciless — CRUEL, IRON
Mercury — MESSENGER OF MYTH, PLANET
Mercury's staff — CADUCEUS
Mercury's winged sandals — TALARIA
Mercury, in alchemy — AZOTH
Mercutio's nemesis — TYBALT
Mercy — LENITY
Mere — SCANT
Mere handful — WISP
Mere indication — WISP
Mere ostentation — PRETENSE
Merely — JUST
Merengue, e.g. — DANCE
Merganser — ROBIN, SMEW
Merge — MELD
Mergers — UNIONS
Merges — BLENDS
Mérida state — LEGATO
Merino — WOOL
Merino mama — EWE
Merit — EARN
Meriwether and Majors — LEES
Merkel of the movies — UNA
Merlin and Ole — OLSENS
Merlin's magic — WIZARDRY
Mermaid or Mitre — TAVERN
Merman and Waters — ETHELS
Merrill or Wilbur — POET
Merrily — GAILY
Merrimack foe — MONITOR
Merriment — GLEE, MIRTH
Merry — RIANT
Merry as a grig — CHEERFUL
Merry month, in Munchen — MAI
Merry old monarch — COLE
Merry sounds — HAHA
Merry young girls — PEATS
Merry, in Metz — GAI
Merry, to a Basque — ALAI
Merry-Andrew — DROLL, FOOL
Merry-go-round — RIDE
Merry: Fr. — GAI
Meryl Streep, for one — ACTRESS
Mesa — BUTTE, PLATEAU, TABLELAND
Mesabi activity — MINING
Mesabi output — ORES
Mesabi products — ORES
Mesabi range ore — IRON
Mescal — CACTUS, PEYOTE, YUCCA
Mescal source — AGAVE
Mesh — INTERLOCK, NET
Mesh fabric — LENO
Meshed fabric — LENO
Meshlike — NETTY
Mesmerized — IN A TRANCE
Mesozoic or Cenozoic — ERA
Mess — DISORDER, KETTLE OF FISH
Mess hall fare — CHOW
Mess hall queues — CHOW LINES
Message — CABLE, MEMO
Message medium — TELEX
Message of a sort — WIRE
Message: "I acknowledge" — ROGER
Messages — NOTES
Messenger of the gods — HERMES
Messy ones — SLOBS
Mesta, the hostess — PEARL
Met — SAT
Met bass-baritone — ESTES
Met diva Mitchell — LEONA
Met extras, for short — SUPES
Met highlight — ARIA
Met man — BASSO
Met offering — OPERA
Met or Net, e.g. — PRO
Met solo — ARIA
Metal-bending tool — SWAGE
Metal-working tools: Var. — SUAGES
Metal alloy — BRASS
Metal balls used in petanque — BOULES
Metal bar — INGOT
Metal bolt — RIVET
Metal deposit — LODE
Metal dross — SLAG
Metal fastener — BRAD, RIVET
Metal flask — CANTEEN
Metal fusion process — SPOT WELDING
Metal mix — ALLOY
Metal pattern for machinery — TEMPLATE
Metal pin — RIVET
Metal plate — COKETIN
Metal refuse — SCORIA
Metal shavings — FILINGS
Metal structural unit — I BEAM
Metal used for trays — TOLE
Metal wedge — SHIM
Metal worker — WELDER
Metallic — TINNY
Metallic disk — PATEN
Metallic element — ERBIUM
Metallic fabric — LAME
Metallic paint job? — COAT OF MAIL
Metallic wrap — TINFOIL
Metalliferous veins — LODES
Metallurgical objective? — BRASS TACKS
Metallurgical worth? — ONES WEIGHT IN GOLD
Metalware — TOLE
Metalware of a type — TOLE
Metalwork machine — LATHE
Metalworking tool — ANVIL
Metaphor's cousin — SIMILE
Metaphoric word for a close call — EYELASH
Metaphysical being — ENS
Metaphysical writer — DONNE
Mete — ALLOCATE
Mete out — ALLOT
Mete out justice — AVENGE
Meted out — DOLED
Meteor — COMET
Meteorites — BOLIDES
Meteorological areas — HIGHS
Meteorological line — ISOBAR
Meter lead-in — ALTI
Meter or scope starter — PERI
Meth. — SYST
Method — MODE, SYSTEM, WAY
Method of dyeing cloth — BATIK
Method of natural childbirth — LAMAZE
Methodical — EXACT
Methodist man — WESLEY
Methusalan — OLD
Methuselah's claim to fame — AGE
Methuselah's father — ENOCH
Methuselah, to Enoch — SON
Meticulous — EXACT
Metric acre — ARE
Metric amt. — KILO
Metric distances: Abbr. — KMS
Metric foot — IAMB
Metric land unit — ARE
Metric measure — ARE, LITER, METER, STERE
Metric surface measure — ARE
Metric thousand — KILO
Metric unit — HECTARE, LITER
Metric unit of capacity — LITER
Metric units — STERES
Metric units, inverse — FEET
Metric weight — GRAM
Metric weight unit — TONNE
Metrical feet — ANAPESTS, IAMBS, PAEONS
Metrical foot — SPONDEE
Metrical stresses — BEATS
Metrodome, for one — ARENA
Metronome — TIMER
Metropolis — CITY
Metropolitan offering — OPERA
Metropolitan thrush — DIVA
Mets stamping ground — SHEA
Mets' home — SHEA
Mettle — NERVE
Mex. ladies — SRAS
Mex. misses — SRTAS
Mexican — AZTEC
Mexican actress — DEL RIO
Mexican baker's product — TORTILLA
Mexican basket grass — OTATE
Mexican beach resort — CANCUN

Mexican Christmas pottery — PINATA
Mexican city — TAXCO
Mexican coat — PONCHO
Mexican coins — PESOS
Mexican desert — SONORA
Mexican dish — TAMALE
Mexican empire — MAYAN
Mexican estate — FINCA
Mexican fare — TACOS
Mexican Indian — TECA
Mexican lad — NINO
Mexican liquor — SOTOL
Mexican money — PESO
Mexican Mrs. — SRA
Mexican nosh — TACO
Mexican peninsula — YUCATAN
Mexican president 1851-53 — ARISTA
Mexican resort town — CANCUN
Mexican room — SALA
Mexican sandal — HUARACHE
Mexican sandwich — TACO
Mexican standoff — TIE
Mexican state — SONORA
Mexican tribute to Terpsichore — HATDANCE
Mexican tykes — NINOS
Mexican War president — POLK
Mexican wraps — SERAPES
Mexican's moola — DINERO
Mexican's O.K.'s — SISIS
Mexico's _____ of Tehuantepec — ISTHMUS
Mexico's tourist expense — HIDDEN COST
Meyerbeer's bottom line? — THE PROFIT
Mezzo-soprano Marilyn — HORNE
Mezzo Frederica Von _____ — STADE
Mezzo Petina — IRRA
Mezzo Stevens — RISE
MGM lion — LEO
Mia Farrow role — ROSEMARY
Miami acquisition — TAN
Miami arena — ORANGE BOWL
Miami inst. — STU
Miami's bay — BISCAYNE
Miami's bowl — ORANGE
Miami's county — DADE
Miami's N.B.A. team — HEAT
Miasma — REEK
Micawber's boss — HEEP
Mice, pigs or bears of fiction — THREE
Mich. city — FLINT
Michael Caine movie — ALFIE
Michael Caine role, 1966 — ALFIE
Michael Gartner's department — NEWS
Michael Gilbert mystery — LONG JOURNEY HOME
Michael J. _____ — FOX
Michael J. Fox movie — BACK TO THE FUTURE
Michael Jackson hit — BAD
Michael of Royal Ballet fame — SOMES
Michael or Gabriel — ARCHANGEL
Michael or Lena — OLIN
Michael Redgrave film: 1946 — THE CAPTIVE HEART
Michael Romanov, e.g. — TSAR
Michael Shalhoub today — OMAR SHARIF
Michaelmas daisies — ASTERS
Michelangelo masterpiece — PIETA
Michelangelo painting — SISTINE CHAPEL
Michelangelo work — PIETA
Michelangelo's is in the Vatican — PIETA
Michener book — IBERIA
Michener opus — ALASKA, IBERIA
Michigan city — LANSING, TROY
Michigan college — ALBION, ALMA
Michigan fresh water lake — HURON
Michigan State player — SPARTAN
Michigan tulip town — HOLLAND
Michigan's capital — LANSING
Mick's group — STONES
Mickey and Minnie — MICE
Mickey's pal — PLUTO
Mickey's pet — PLUTO
Micmac's cousin — SAC
Micraner, e.g. — ANT
Microbe — GERM
Microcircuit — CHIP
Microfilm sheet — FICHE
Microorganism — GERM
Microscope parts — LENSES
Microscopic — TEENY
Microwave device — LASER, OVEN
Microwave, e.g. — OVEN
Mid-European — SLAV
Mid pts. — CTRS
Mid-alphabet trio — MNO
Mid-May or mid-July — IDES
Mid-orchestra locale — ROW M
Mid-season baseball classic — ALL STAR GAME
Mid. East land — SYR
Midday — NOON, NOONTIME
Midday nap — SIESTA
Midday snooze — SIESTA
Middle — HUB
Middle ear part — EARDRUM
Middle East bigwig: Var. — AMIR
Middle East chieftains — EMEERS
Middle East inn — IMARET
Middle East liquor — RAKEE
Middle East native — IRANI
Middle East neighbors — JORDAN AND ISRAEL
Middle East peninsula — SINAI
Middle East prince — EMIR
Middle east ruler — EMEER
Middle East waters — RED SEA
Middle eastern fiddle — REBAB
Middle Eastern titles — AMIRS
Middle finger — MEDIUS
Middle linesman — CENTER
Middle manager's hope — ROOM AT THE TOP
Middle name of a July 16, 1962, dropout — ROSS
Middle nameless: Abbr. — NMI
Middle of Q.E.D. — ERAT
Middle of the road — CENTER
Middle point — MEDIAN
Middle section — WAIST
Middle: Comb. form — MEDI
Middleweight champion: 1923-26 — GREB
Middling — SOSO
Mideast airline — EL AL
Mideast bigwig — EMIR
Mideast bread — PITA
Mideast canal — SUEZ
Mideast capital — BEIRUT
Mideast chieftain — EMEER
Mideast country — IRAQ
Mideast country: Abbr. — ISR
Mideast desert — NEGEV
Mideast father — ABBA
Mideast gulf — ADEN
Mideast hotspot — IRAN, IRAQ
Mideast land — IRAN
Mideast mogul — AMEER
Mideast nation — IRAN
Mideast notable — EMIR
Mideast officers — AGAS
Mideast org. — PLO
Mideast org., once — UAR
Mideast peninsula — SINAI
Mideast port — ADEN
Mideast port and gulf — ADEN
Mideast potentate — EMIR
Mideast rep. — SYR
Mideast ruler — EMIR
Mideast support org. — PLO
Mideast title — AMIR, EMIR
Mideast trouble spot — IRAN
Mideastern capital — BEIRUT, SANAA
Mideastern city and gulf — ADEN
Mideastern org. — PLO

Midge — GNAT
Midget, in Marseille — NABOT
Midi meadow — PRE
Midi midwife — ACCOUCHEUSE
Midi seasons — ETES
Midianite defeated by Gideon — OREB
Midianite King — REBA
Midler or Davis — BETTE
Midlothian — SCOT
Midnight assembly — SABBAT
Midnight rider — REVERE
Midnight rider of fame — PAUL REVERE
Midnight snack attack — RAID
Midpoint — CENTER
Midpt. — CEN, CTR
Midterm, for one — EXAM
Midway attraction — RIDE
Midwest airport — OHARE
Midwest Indian — OTOE
Midwest mkt. — CME
Midwestern Pulitzer poet — CARL SANDBURG
Midwestern state — IOWA
Midwestern state: Abbr. — IND
Mielziner and Stafford — JOS
Mielziner design — SCENE
Mien — AIR, ASPECT
Miff — PEEVE, RANCOR, RILE
Miffed — SORE
Mighty fleet — ARMADA
Mighty Mike — TYSON
Mighty mite — ATOM, ION
Mighty mite in a computer — CHIP
Mighty one — TITAN
Mighty trees — OAKS
Mignon lead-in — FILET
Migrates — TREKS
Miguel or Manuel — SAO
Miguel's share — PARTE
Mike or Ann — TODD
Mike Tyson's milieu — BOXING RING
Mike's complement — AMP
Mike's pal — PAT
Mikhail's lady — RAISA
Mil. address — APO
Mil. awards — DSCS, DSOS
Mil. banners — SDTS
Mil. command — ATTN
Mil. cops — MPS
Mil. decoration — DSM, DSOS
Mil. educational institution — OTS
Mil. gp. on call — RES
Mil. group — USNR
Mil. hooky — AWOL
Mil. installation — AFB
Mil. man — NCO
Mil. men — GIS
Mil. metal — DSC
Mil. officer — COL
Mil. officers — CPTS
Mil. rank — PFC
Mil. scouting expedition — RECON
Mil. student — CAD
Mil. title — NCO, SGT
Mil. training grp. — ROTC
Mil. transports — LCS
Mil. truant — AWOL
Mil. unit — RGT
Mil. vehicles — LCTS
Mil. weapon — ABM, ICBM
Milady — DAME
Milan landmark — LA SCALA
Milan man — SIGNORE
Milan money — LIRE
Milan moolah — LIRA
Milan museum — BRERA
Milan's La _____ — SCALA
Milanese moola — LIRE
Milano money — LIRA, LIRE
Milano's country — ITALIA
Milano's subway — METRO
Mild — MODERATE
Mild cigar — CLARO
Mild disorders — AILMENTS
Mild expletive — DARN, DRAT, GOSH, HECK
Mild expletive in Ireland — ARRA
Mild expletives — EGADS
Mild flavor — VANILLA
Mild imprecation — DARN IT
Mild interjection — EGAD
Mild laugh — TITTER
Mild medicinal beverage — TISANE
Mild oath — DRAT, EGAD, GOSH
Mild oath, old style — PARDI
Mild reproofs — TUTS
Mildew — MOLD, ROT, SMUT
Miler Andersson — ARNE
Miler Jim — RYUN
Miler Sebastian _____ — COE
Miler's footwear? — RUNNING SHOES
Miles of films — VERA
Miles of the movies — VERA
Miles or Zorina — VERA
Milestone for mountain climbers — TREELINE
Milieu atmosphere — AMBIENCE
Milieu for a troupe member — STAGE
Milieu for le juge — BANC
Milieu for Levine — MET
Milieu for star of "Nana" — CINEMA
Milieu for the Wallendas — CIRCUS
Milieu of "Mother Courage" — STAGE
Milieu's mood — AMBIANCE
Milieu: Abbr. — ATM
Milion: Prefix — MEGA
Militant campus org. — SDS
Military abbr. — RGT
Military alliance of WW II — AXIS
Military area — SECTOR
Military assistant — AIDE
Military assts. — ADCS
Military attache — AIDE
Military ceremony — REVIEW
Military command — AT EASE, HALT
Military decoration — BLUE MAX, DSC, IRON CROSS
Military decoration — NAVY CROSS, PURPLE HEART
Military entity — UNIT
Military force — UNIT
Military group — UNIT
Military hat — KEPI
Military headdress — SHAKO
Military headware — KEPI
Military informer — SPY
Military initials — USN
Military insignia — EAGLE, STAR
Military inst. — OTS
Military installation — FORT
Military instructor — SERGEANT
Military locations — BASES
Military macaw — ARA
Military meal, alas — MESS
Military mixups — SNAFU
Military necessity — AMMO
Military org. — ROTC
Military rank: Abbr. — CINC, NCO
Military regime — JUNTA
Military salute — SALVO
Military staff person — AIDE
Military standbys — RESERVES
Military station — POST
Military station under the Raj — CANTONMENT
Military storage building — ARMORY
Military student — CADET
Military subdivisions — UNITS
Military topper — SHAKE
Military trainee — CADET
Military truancy, briefly — AOL
Military unit: Abbr. — DET
Military vehicle — TANK
Military zone — SECTOR
Milk containers — PAILS
Milk measure in Manchester — LITRE
Milk of _____ — MAGNESIA
Milk of human kindness — SYMPATHY
Milk producer — DAIRY COW
Milk source — DAIRY
Milk sugar — LACTOSE
Milk train — LOCAL
Milk, in Metz — LAIT
Milk, in Paris — LAIT

Milk-white — CHALKY
Milk: Comb. form — LACT, LACTO
Milkfishes — AWAS
Milkmaid's seat — STOOL
Milkman — VENDOR
Milksop — SISSY, WIMP
Milky — TAME
Milky Way — GALAXY
Milky Way sphere — NOVA
Mill — PLANT
Mill fodder — GRIST
Mill input — GRIST
Mill product — STEEL
Milland or Charles — RAY
Milland-Kelly film of 1954 — DIAL M FOR MURDER
Millay and Milton — POETS
Millay's middle — ST VINCENT
Millay, the poet — EDNA
Milldams — WEIRS
Millennia — EONS
Miller — MOTH
Miller and Blyth — ANNS
Miller or Landers — ANN
Miller's daughter — LUISA
Miller's Loman, for one — SALESMAN
Miller's salesman — LOMAN
Miller's Willie — LOMAN
Millet — GRAIN
Millet masterpiece (with "The") — ANGELUS
Millet subject — GLEANERS
Millet's "Man With the _____" — HOE
Millet, e.g. — GRAIN
Millie Perkins role — ANNE FRANK
Milliner's relative — HATTER
Milliners make them — HATS
Millinery item — TOQUE
Million chaser — AIRE
Million follower — AIRE
Millions of years — EONS
Millo or Mitchell — DIVA
Millpond — DAM
Mills of the high Cs — ERIE
Mills of the opera — ERIE
Mills or Reed — DONNA
Millstone bar — RYND
Milne marsupial — ROO
Milne's Winnie — POOH
Milquetoasts — WIMPS
Milt. branch — UNSR
Milt. personnel — WACS
Miltie or Sam — UNCLE
Milton Caniff's pilot hero Steve _____ — CANYON
Milton's "Regent of the Sun" — URIEL
Milwaukee shortstops? — VAT OF BREWERS
Mime-dancer Parenti — NOEL
Mime — APER
Mime Marcel — MARCEAU
Mimeograph inventor — EDISON
Mimic — APE, APER
Mimic a whirlybird — HOVER
Mimicked — APED
Mimics — APES
Mimosa genus — INGA
Mince — CHOP
Mince pie ingredient — SUET
Minced oath — DRAT
Minced, maybe — OATH
Mind — BRAIN, HEED, INTELLECT, OBEY, REASON
Mindanao's Tasadays, e.g. — SUBTRIBE
Mindful — AWARE
Mindless — ASININE, INANE, SILLY, STUPID
Minds — CARES FOR, TENDS
Minds the baby — SITS
Minds the store — TENDS
Mine access — ADIT
Mine areas — SEAMS
Mine car — TRAM
Mine disasters — CAVEINS
Mine entrance — ADIT, MY FRONT DOOR, STULM
Mine exits — ADITS
Mine features — ORES
Mine field — LODE
Mine find — LODE, ORE
Mine finds — ORES
Mine line — ORE
Mine openings — ADITS
Mine output — ORE
Mine owner, e.g. — CLAIMANT
Mine passages — ADITS
Mine product — ORE
Mine shaft — PIT
Mine vein — LODE
Mine worker — CAGER
Mine yield — ORE
Mine, in Marne — AMOI
Mine, in Metz — AMOI
Mined products — ORE
Mineo or Maglie — SAL
Mineo, et al. — SALS
Miner — COAL PORTER
Miner of a sort? — GOLD DIGGER
Miner's bonanza — LODE
Miner's find — ORE
Miner's nail — SPAD
Miner's need — LAMP
Miner's target — ORE
Miner's way in — ADIT
Mineral — MICA
Mineral baths town in France — DAX
Mineral deposit — PLACER
Mineral deposits — LODES
Mineral fiber: Abbr. — ASB
Mineral in quartz — SILICA
Mineral oil — KEROSENE
Mineral resembling feldspar — WERNERITE
Mineral spring — SPA
Mineral springs? — STEEL SPIRALS
Mineral: Comb. form — LITE
Mineral: Suff. — LITE
Minerals — ORES
Minerals having topazlike crystals — BERYLLONITES
Minerals' hardness-scale inventor — MOHS
Miners' stakeouts — CLAIMS
Minerva or Venus — DEA
Minestrone ingredient — BEANS
Minestrone, et al. — SOUPS
Ming nurse — AMAH
Mingle — ADMIX, BLEND
Mini or maxi — SKIRT
Mini racing car — KART
Miniature maelstroms — EDDIES
Miniature ornamental structure — WALLETTE
Miniature scene — DIORAMA
Minim — DROP
Minimal — LEAST
Minimally — AT LEAST
Minims, in music — HALFNOTES
Minimum — LEAST
Mining city in Montana — BUTTE
Mining tool — GAD
Mining waste — TAILINGS
Minion — LACKEY, PET
Miniscule — TRIVIA
Miniskirt maker's dearth — WANT OF QUANT
Minister to — TEND
Ministry member — CLERIC
Miniver Cheevy's love — MEDICI
Miniver title — MRS
Miniver's status — MRS
Mink and sable — FURS
Mink's cousin — OTTER
Mink's kin — OTTERS
Mink's relative — OTTER
Minn. city — WINONA
Minn. neighbor — NDAK, SDAK, WIS
Minn. range — MESABI
Minn. Siouans — IOWAS
Minn.'s St. _____ College — OLAF
Minneapolis suburb — EDINA
Minnesota Fats' game — POOL
Minnesota first basemen? — CRIB FULL OF TWINS
Minnesota twins — ENS
Minnie of the Opry — PEARL
Minnow — MIDGET
Minnow man? — REGINALD GUPPY

Minoans horne — CRETE
Minor — VENIAL
Minor Augury? — LITTLE OMEN
Minor falsehoods — FIBS
Minor insult — DIG
Minor league team — FARM
Minor leagues — BUSH
Minor minor — TOT
Minor or Major — CANIS
Minor place? — ASIA
Minor prohibition — NONO
Minor prophet — AMOS, HOSEA
Minor Prophet and namesakes — MICAHS
Minor tantrum — SNIT
Minor tiff — SPAT
Minor, but notable role — CANEO
Minor-league baseball team — FARM
Minos, e.g. — CRETAN
Minotaur's island — CRETE
Minotaur's milieu — CRETE
Mins. multiples — HRS
Minstrel — BARD, SINGER
Minstrel's instrument — LUTE
Minstrel's offering — LAY
Minstrel's song — LAY
Minstrels — BARDS
Minstrels' repertoire — LAYS
Mint — BASIL, COIN
Mint _____ — JULEP
Mint drink — JULEP
Mint stamp — UNUSED
Minty spice — SAGE
Minuet — DANCE
Minuet or mambo — DANCE
Minuet's cousin — GAVOT
Minus — LESS, SUBTRACT
Minus wool — SHORN
Minuscular — TEENY
Minute — SMALL, TEENY, TINY
Minute amount — IOTA
Minute amount, in Scotland — HAET
Minute men of 1776 — IDOLS
Minute opening — PORE, STOMA
Minute particle — ATOM, IOTA
Minute quantity — DROP
Minutiae — TRIVIA
Minx — HUSSY, SNIP
Miquelon, par example — ILE
Mirabile _____ — DICTU
Miracle response — AWE
Miracle sight — CANA
Mirador — ORIEL
Mire — EMBOG, MUD
Mirror — APE, GLASS
Mirror feedbacks — IMAGES
Mirror of reflection — IMAGE
Mirror reflection — IMAGE
Mirror, in a way — ECHO
Mirroring — APING
Mirth — GLEE
Mirthful — RIANT
Mirthful Martha — RAYE
Misanthrope — HATER
Misbehave — ACT UP
Miscalculate — ERR
Miscellaneous — OLIO
Miscellaneous items — SUNDRIES, VARIA
Miscellanies — OLIOS
Miscellany — OLIO
Mischa of music — ELMAN
Mischa on violin — ELMAN
Mischa or Leopold — AUER
Mischief-makers — IMPS, RASCALS
Mischievous — ELFIN, NAUGHTY
Mischievous bowman — EROS
Mischievous child — ELF
Mischievous miss — GAMINE
Mischievous Olympian — ATE
Miscomputes — ERR
Miscue — ERR, ERROR, SLIP
Miscued — ERRED
Miscues — ERRS, SLIPS
Misdid — ERRED
Misemploy — ABUSE
Miserable — ABJECT
Miserable person — WRETCH
Miseries — WOES
Miserly — CLOSE, TIGHT
Misery — WOE
Misfortunates — EVILS, ILLS, VENDETTAS
Mishaps — ACCIDENTS
Mishmashes — OLIOS
Misinformant — LIAR
Misinformers — LIARS
Misjudged — ERRED
Mislays — LOSES
Mislead — DELUDE, FOOL
Mislead the mind — DELUDE
Misleading clue — RED HERRING
Misogynist — HATER
Misogynist's attitude — SEXISM
Misogynist's emotion — HATE
Mispickel — ORE
Mispickel and others — ORES
Mispickel is one — ORE
Mispickel or cinnabar — ORE
Misplace — LOSE
Misplaced — LOST
Misplay — ERR, FLUFF
Misplays — ERRORS
Misprint — TYPO
Misrepresent — BELIE
Miss _____ — THE BOAT
Miss _____ of "Dallas" — ELLIE
Miss America, e.g. — CONTEST
Miss Cinders — ELLA
Miss Cinders of the comics — ELLA
Miss Clare of "Bleak House" and others — ADAS
Miss Dinsmore — ELSIE
Miss Dinsmore of fiction — ELSIE
Miss Doone — LORNA
Miss Durbeyfield — TESS
Miss Eyre — JANE
Miss Gardner, et al. — AVAS
Miss Gilbert of "Little House ..." — MELISSA
Miss has two — ESSES
Miss Havisham's niece — ESTELLA
Miss Hogg — IMA
Miss Hogg of Tex. — IM A
Miss Hogg, et al. — IMAS
Miss Kett — ETTA
Miss Kett and others — ETTAS
Miss Kett of the comics — ETTA
Miss Kett's namesakes — ETTAS
Miss Louise, et al. — TINAS
Miss Minnelli — LIZA
Miss Muffet's chaser — SPIDER
Miss Muffet's quaff — WHEY
Miss O'Grady — ROSIE
Miss Piggy's "Me"? — MOI
Miss Piggy's passion — KERMIT
Miss Quested in "A Passage to India" — ADELA
Miss Raines — ELLA
Miss Thompson — SADIE
Miss Velez — LUPE
Miss. or Mo., e.g. — RIV
Miss. river bridge — EADS
Misses — LACKS
Misshape — DEFORM
Missile description — AIR TO AIR
Missile from Cupid — ARROW
Missile home — SILO
Missile housing — SILO
Missile of a sort, for short — TNW
Missile type — MIRV
Missing — ABSENT, LOST
Missing recruits — AWOLS
Missing ring — COURT OF APS
Missing, in Roma — ASSENTE
Mission — ERRAND
Missionaries of Charity founder — TERESA
Missionary Junipero — SERRA
Mississippi Native American — CHOCTAW
Mississippi nickname — BAYOU
Mississippi Riv. boats — STRS
Mississippi River city — ALTON
Mississippi River sight — LEVEE
Mississippi River source — ITASCA
Missive — LETTER
Missouri bird? — HANNIBALDEAGLE
Missouri campus town — ROLLA
Missouri feeder — OSAGE

Missouri pres. — HST
Missouri river feeder — PLATTE
Missouri tributary — PLATTE
Missouri's nickname — SHOW ME STATE
Misstatement — LIE
Mist — STEAM
Mist, Manchester style — ROKE
Mistake — ERROR
Mistake in printing — ERRATUM
Mistaken — OFF BASE
Mistakes — SLIPUPS
Mister, in Barcelona — SENOR
Mister, in Berlin — HERR
Mister, in Bonn — HERR
Mister, in Ems — HERR
Mister, in Malaysia — TUAH
Mister, in Mexico — SENOR
Mister, in Oviedo — SENOR
Mistreat — ABUSE
Mistreated — WRONGED
Mistress Gwyn and namesakes — NELLS
Mistress of la casa — AMA
Misty — HAZY
Mistypes — ERRS
MIT grads — CES, EES, ENGS
MIT workroom — LAB
Mitch Miller plays it — OBOE
Mitchell mansion — TARA
Mitchell plantation — TARA
Mite — DRAM
Mite or tick — ACARID
Miter — HAT
Mites — ACARI
Mitigate — TEMPER
Mitigated — ALLAYED, EASED
Mitigation — RELIEF
Mitt — PAW
Mitterrand's "palais" — ELYSEE
Mitty or Cronkite — WALTER
MIV halved — DII
Mix — BLEND, STIR
Mix a salad — TOSS
Mix smoothly — BLEND
Mix together — BLEND
Mix-up — CHAOS
Mixer — SELTZER
Mixers' frozen assets — CUBES
Mixes — BLENDS
Mixes anew — RETOSSES
Mixes up — ADDLES
Mixing implement — AGITATOR
Mixture — AMALGAM, BLEND, OLIO
Mixture of bran and hot water for horses — MASH
Mixture of sand and clay — LOAM
Miyoshi of "Flower Drum Song" — UMEKI
Mme. Bovary — EMMA
Mme. Chiang's maiden name — SOONG
Mme. Curie — MARIE
Mme. Gorbachev — RAISA
Mme. Karenina — ANNA
Mme., in Madrid — SRA
Mme., in the USA — MRS
MN city — MPLS
Mnemonic — MEMORY
Mo or Stu — UDALL
Mo-town — DET
Mo. for hobgoblins — OCT
Mo. for Kringle — DEC
Moa, kiwi or emu, e.g. — RATITE
Moab is here — UTAH
Moans — LAMENTS
Moat — DITCH
Moats — FOSSES
Mob — CROWD
Mob units — GANGS
Mobile artist — CALDER
Mobile beginning — AUTO
Mobile cart with wheels — DOLLY
Mobile home's relative — VAN
Mobile home, once — TEPEE
Mobile home? — TEEPEE
Mobile person — ALABAMAN
Mobile socialities — JETSET
Mobile's place — ALABAMA
Mobster — THUG
Mobutu _____ Seko, Zaire's leader — SESE
Moby Dick — GREAT WHITE WHALE
Moby Dick's hunter — AHAB
Moby Dick's pursuer — AHAB
Moby Dick's seeker — AHAB
Moccasin — PAC
Moccasin material — DEERSKIN
Mocha stone — AGATE
Mock — DERIDE, FLEER, JAPE, SNEER
Mock blow — FEINT
Mock, old style — DORRE
Mocked — GIBED, JEERED
Mockery — DERISION, FARCE, JEERING, JOKE
Mockery — SPORT, TRAVESTY
Mockingly — TONGUE IN CHEEK
Mod ending — ULAR
Mod hair style — AFRO
Mod hairdo — AFRO
Mod music — ROCK
Mod music talk — RAP
Mod musical — HAIR
Mod's Christmas present — LOOT
Mod's place — PAD
Mode — CRAZE, MANNER, STYLE
Model — DRESSED TO KILL, SHAPE, TYPE
Model _____ de la Fressange — INES
Model A — FORD
Model Carol — ALT
Model de la Fressange — INES
Model Macpherson, et al. — ELLES
Model of perfection — PARAGON
Model-airplane material — BALSA
Model-airplane wood — BALSA
Model/actress Cheryl — TIEGS
Models or puzzles — POSERS
Models, at times — COVER GIRLS
Modem medium — PHONE
Modena money — LIRA
Moderate — ABATE, EASE
Moderate gallop — CANTER
Moderate reds — CERISES
Moderately slow, to Muti — ANDANTE
Moderately well — SOSO
Moderates — EBBS
Moderator — CHAIR, LEADER, SPEAKER
Modern — NEW
Modern art movement of 1919 — DADA
Modern artist Fernand — LEGER
Modern artist from Spain — DALI
Modern defenses: Abbr. — ABMS
Modern French composer — LALO
Modern French compo ser Erik — SATIE
Modern frontier — SPACE
Modern Greek vernacular — ROMAIC
Modern lead-in — ULTRA
Modern music form — RAP
Modern painter Max _____ — ERNST
Modern sleeping surface — WATERBED
Modern Teutonic lang. — NHG
Modern times — TODAY
Modern: Pref. — NEO
Modernist — NEO
Modernize — UPDATE
Modest and reserved — DEMURE
Modest and shy person — SHRINKING VIOLET
Modesty, in Madrid — RESERVA
Modified — TONED
Modified leaf — BRACT
Modified, with "down" — TONED
Modifier — ADVERB
Modifies — ALTERS

Modify — ADAPT, ALTER, AMEND
Modify for usage — ADAPT
Modify text — EDIT
Modify to suit — ADAPT
Modigliani's "The Rose _____" — NUDE
Modish — CHIC
Modiste's outfit for a stripper — STRING ENSEMBLE
Modus operandi — WAY
Moe, Curly or Larry — STOOGE
Moffo and Pavlova — ANNAS
Mogul — CZAR, NABOB
Mogul empire capital — DELHI
Mohammed _____ Pahlavi — REZA
Mohammed's daughter — FATIMA
Mohammed's favorite wife — AYESHA
Mohammedan faith — ISLAM
Mohammedan fasting period — RAMADAN
Mohammedan magistrate — CADI
Mohammedan mystic — SUFI
Mohammedan officer — DIWAN
Mohammedan prince — AMEER
Mohammedan successor — CALIPH
Mohave phenomenon — SANDSTORM
Mohawk months — MOONS
Moira of ballet fame — SHEARER
Moira Shearer, for one — REDHEAD
Moist — ASOP, DAMP, DEWY, WET
Moist and chilly — DANK
Moist camise? — SWEATY SHIRT
Moist land areas — SWALES
Moisten — WASH, WET
Moisten the turkey — BASTE
Moistened — BEDEWED
Moistens, as a turkey — BASTES
Moisture — DEW
Moisture of morning — DEW
Mojave — DESERT
Mojave monster — GILA
Mojave plants — DESERT PALMS
Molampsus or Mopsus — SEER
Molars — TEETH
Molasses — TREACLE
Molasses confection — TAFFY
Mold — SHAPE
Moldable — PLASTIC
Moldboard — BLADE
Molder — ERODE
Molding — OGEE, OVOLO
Molding angle — ARRIS
Molding edge — ARRIS
Molding style — OGEE
Molding type — OGEE
Moldovan city to Romanians — CAHUL
Moldy — MILDEWED
Mole — BEAUTY SPOT, NEVUS, RODENT, SPY
Mole's color — TAUPE
Mole, for one — DIGGER
Molecule parts — ATOMS
Moleskin-colored — TAUPE
Moll's companion — GANGSTER
Moll's weapon — GAT
Mollification — APPEASEMENT
Mollifies — SOOTHES
Mollify — EASE
Molls' men — HOODS
Mollusk or atomic particle — LEPTON
Mollusk with eight arms — OCTOPUS
Molly, of radio — GOLDBERG
Mollycoddle — COSSET
Mollycoddled — SPOILT
Molokai greeting — ALOHA
Molotov cocktails and such — GRENADES
Molt — SHED
Molten rock — LAVA
Molten rock within the earth — MAGMA
Molybdenite and bauxite — ORES
Mom's are best — PIES
Mom's mate — DAD, POP
Mom's prohibitions — NONOS
Mom's title — MRS
Moment — JIFFY
Moment-of-truth man — TORERO
Momentous — EARTH SHATTERING
Momentum — SPEED
Mommy's sister — AUNTY
Mon. follower — TUES
Mon., to Tues. — YEST
Mona _____ — LISA
Mona and Kirk — LISAS
Monaco attraction — MONTE CARLO
Monad — ONE, UNIT
Monads — ATOMS
Monarch — SULTAN
Monarch butterfly's look-alike — VICEROY
Monarch's personal stamp — GREAT SEAL
Monastery head — ABBOT
Monastery man — FRA
Monastery men — PRIORS
Monastic of the first century — ESSENE
Monastic officer — PRIOR
Monastic symbol — COWL
Monastic title — DOM
Monceau, par example — PARA
Monday chore — WASH
Monday in Madrid — LUNES
Monday night TV fare — FOOTBALL
Monday, in Marseille — LUNDI
Monday, Tuesday and Doris — DAYS
Mondrian, for one — ARTIST
Monet or Debussy — CLAUDE
Monetary unit of France — FRANC
Monetary unit of India — CRORE
Monetary unit of Laos — KIP
Monetary unit of Panama — BALBOA
Monetary unit of Siam — BHAT
Money — CASH
Money dispenser — AUTOMATED TELLER
Money exchange premium — AGIO
Money for Shylock — DUCATS
Money holder — TILL
Money holders — TELLERS
Money in Callao — SOL
Money in Delhi — RUPEE
Money in Dortmund — GELD
Money in Ecuador — SUCRES
Money in Haiti — GOURDE
Money in India — RUPEE
Money in Iran — RIALS
Money in Istanbul — LIRA
Money in Kuwait — DINAR
Money in Madrid — PESETA
Money in Malaga — PESETA
Money in Manchester — PENCE
Money in Mannheim — GELD
Money in Mecca — RIAL
Money in Mexico — PESO
Money in Milano — LIRA, LIRE
Money in Monterey — PESO
Money in München — GELD
Money in Oman — RIAL
Money in Oslo — ORE
Money in Prague — HALER
Money in Santander — PESETA
Money in the bank — ASSET
Money in the form of bills — CASH
Money of a sort — LOAN
Money of Iceland — KRONA
Money of the Mid-East — DINAR
Money or record subject — CHANGER
Money player — PRO
Money pooled for a specific purpose — KITTY
Money recipient — PAYEE
Money source — MINT

Money to spring someone from jail — BAIL
Money's worth at beauty salon? — FACE VALUE
Money-makers — MINE, MINTS
Moneybags — FAT CAT
Moneyed — RICH
Moneymakers for TV — ADS
Mongol — TATAR
Mongol conquerer — BABAR
Mongol tent — YURT
Mongol, for one — ASIAN
Mongolia or Hebrides — OUTER
Mongolia's _____ Bator — ULAN
Mongolian desert — GOBI
Mongolian tent — YURT
Mongoose — URVA
Mongoose's enemies — COBRAS
Mongoose's prey — RAT
Mongrel — CUR
Moniker — NAME
Moniker for one on the lam — ALIAS
Monitor lizard — URAN, VARAN
Monk — FRIAR
Monk or monkish — MONASTIC
Monk's abode — CELL
Monk's cowl — AMICE
Monk's room — CELL
Monk's title — FRA
Monk's wear — COWLS
Monkey — BABOON
Monkey's cousin — LEMUR
Monkeyshine — PRANK
Monkeyshines — ANTICS
Monks — FRAS
Monks, in Metz — MOINES
Monocle — LENS
Monogram — INIT
Monogram for Elizabeth II — HRH
Monogram for Jim Hawkins creator — RLS
Monogram in ancient Rome — SPQR
Monogram of "The Waste Land" poet — TSE
Monogram of a suffragette — SBA
Monogram of an e.e.c. contemporary — TSE
Monogram of Garfield's successor — CAA
Monogram of House Speaker Mr. Sam — STR
Monogram of Mr. Hyde's creator — RLS
Monogram of Prufrock's creator — TSE
Monogram of the "Ozymandias" poet — PBS
Monogram of the 21st V.P. — TAH
Monogram of the author of "The Killers" — EMH
Monogram part: Abbr. — INIT
Monogram unit — INITIAL
Monograms on many exports — USAS
Monologist Mort — SAHL
Monologue — SOLO
Monologue, for example — SOLO
Monopoly, for one — GAME
Monosoki — SLED
Monotonous — DULL, HUMDRUM, SING SONG
Monotonous recital — LITANY
Monotonously — IN A RUT
Monotony — DRABNESS, SAMENESS
Monroe film 1953 — NIAGARA
Monsieur, in Barcelona — SENOR
Monster — LEVIATHAN, OGRE
Monster of Greek myth — CHIMERA
Monster type — GILA
Monster's loch — NESS
Monster: Prefix — TERAT
Mont _____ — BLANC
Mont Blanc buddy — AMI
Mont Blanc's range — ALPS
Mont Blanc, for one — ALP
Mont Blanc, par example — ALPE
Mont, in the Alps — BLANC
Mont.'s neighbor — ALTA
Montague's offspring — ROMEO
Montana and others — PASSERS
Montana or Marino — PASSER
Montana target — END
Montana's capital — HELENA
Montana's state appellation — TREASURE
Monte Carlo number — TRENTE
Monterey Bay city — SEASIDE
Monterey's neighbor — CARMEL
Monterrey Mrs. — SRA
Montezuma, for one — AZTEC
Montgomery's state — ALABAMA
Month after Nisan — IYAR
Month after Shebats — ADARS
Month before Nisan — ADAR
Month for Independence Day — JULY
Month in Milano — MESE
Month in Pamplona — ENERO
Month of the Jewish year — ADAR
Month or eclipse — LUNAR
Monthly collection — RENTAL
Monthly outlay — RENT
Months, to Pocahontas — MOONS
Monticello, for one — ESTATE
Montmartre morn — MATIN
Montparnasse's city — PARIS
Montpelier is its cap. — VER
Montreal baseball player — EXPO
Montreal player — EXPO
Montreal pro — EXPO
Montreal's prov. — QBC
Montreal's province — QUEBEC
Monts _____, French range — DORE
Monty Hall's specialty — DEAL
Monument — STELE
Monument marker — STELE
Monument site in India — AGRA
Monumental — EPIC
Monumental stone — STELE
Moo — LOW
Moo like a cow — LOW
Mooch — CADGE
Mooched — CADGED
Moocher — SPONGER
Mooches — BUMS
Mood — BLUES, WHIM
Moody tennis player? — HELEN
Moola — BREAD, DINERO, DO RE MI, GELT, LUCRE
Moon buggies — LEMS
Moon craft, for short — LEM
Moon feature — CRATER
Moon goddess — LUNA, SELENE
Moon jumper? — COW
Moon man #2 — ALDRIN
Moon of Jupiter — EUROPA
Moon or Spoon — RIVER
Moon over Modena — LUNA
Moon spacecraft — APOLLO
Moon stage — PHASE
Moon valley — RILLE
Moon vehicles — LEMS
Moon's aspect — PHASE
Moon's plain — MARE
Moon-oriented — LUNAR
Moon-struck — MAD
Moon: Comb. form — SELEN, SELENO
Moonfish — OPAH
Moonshiner's machine — STILL
Moonstone's cousin — ADULARIA
Moor — HEATH
Moore's "_____ Rookh" — LALLA
Moore's TV boss — ASNER
Mooring cable — HAWSER
Moorish _____ (tropical fish) — IDOL

Moorish city, port of Algeria — ORAN
Moors — HEATHS
Moot — IFFY
Mop — SWAB
Mop up — ABSORB, SWAB
Mop up aids — PAPER TOWELS
Moped — MOONED, MINIBIKE
Moppet — DOLL, TOT
Moppets — TADS
Mopsus and Calchas — SEERS
Mopsus or Melampus — SEER
Moraine — ESKER
Moral — ETHICAL
Moral code — EHTIC
Moral customs — MORES
Moral flaws — BLOTS
Moral nature — ETHOS
Moral precept — ETHIC
Moral principles — ETHICS
Moral standard — ETHIC
Moral system — ETHIC
Morale — HOPE
Morally corrupt — ROTTEN
Moran or Gray — ERIN
Morass — BOG, FEN
Moratorium — BAN, RESPITE
Moray — EEL
Moray fisherman — EELER
Moray or conger — EEL
Morays — EELS
Morbid state: Suffix — IASIS
More "now" — NEWER
More accurate — NICER
More agile — SPRIER
More aloof — ICIER
More alternative — LESS
More ancient — OLDER
More appealing — CUTER
More apt to happen — LIKELIER
More ashen — PALER
More balanced — SANER
More bizarre — ODDER
More bohemian — ARTIER
More cautious — WARIER
More certain — SURER
More chichi — ARTIER
More closefisted — NEARER
More comely — PRETTIER
More comfortable — EASIER
More comical — DROLLER
More compact — DENSER
More compendious — TERSER
More competent — ABLER
More concise — SHORTER
More confident — SURER
More contemptible — VILER
More contrite — SORRIER
More corpulent — FATTER
More courageous — GAMER, STOUTER
More cowardly — YELLOWER
More crafty — SLIER
More crowded — DENSER
More daffy — BATTIER
More delicate — LACIER
More demure — SHIER
More depressed — BLUER
More desperate — DIRER
More despicable — BASER
More difficult to find — RARER
More dilatory — SLOWER
More discerning — SAGER
More disgusting — VILER
More dishonest — SHADIER
More dismal — SORRIER
More docile — TAMER
More downcast — SADDER
More downhearted — BLUER
More dreadful — DIRER
More drippy, as paste — RUNNIER
More eccentric — ODDER
More eldritch — EERIER
More embarrassed — REDDER
More exceptional — RARER
More exposed — BARER, BARREN
More extensive — LARGER
More facile — EASIER
More factual — TRUER
More faithful — TRUER
More fashionable — TRENDIER
More feeble — LAMER
More fitting — SEEMLIER
More flashy — SPORTIER
More fleshy — FATTER
More foxy — SLIER
More frequently — OFTENER
More friable — CRISPER
More frigid — ICIER
More fun to be with — JOLLIER
More furtive — SLIER
More glacial — COLDER
More glittering — STARRIER
More gooey — ICKIER
More grubby — DIRTIER
More guileful — SLIER
More hurtful — SORER
More ignoble — BASER
More immediate — NEARER
More imposing — TALLER
More in the open — AIRIER
More inane — SILLIER
More indigent — POORER
More inexperienced — RAWER
More inferior — BASER, WORSE
More innocent — NAIVER
More inquisitive — NOSIER
More insolent — CHEEKIER
More intrepid — GAMER
More inventive — CLEVERER
More irascible — TESTIER
More irate — ANGRIER
More ironic — WRIER
More jittery — TENSER
More joyous — GAYER
More judicious — FAIRER, SANER
More kindhearted — NICER
More lawnlike — GRASSIER
More learned — SAGER
More leisurely — SLOWER
More like a Felix Unger — NEATER
More like a fox — SLYER
More like Arbuckle — FATTER
More like Felix Unger — TIDIER
More like Poe's midnight — DREARIER
More like silk — SOFTER
More like Wilt — TALLER
More lithe — SPRYER
More lively — GAYER
More loyal — TRUER
More lucid — CLEARER, SANER
More macabre — EERIER
More malicious — MEANER
More mature — OLDER, RIPER
More meager — SCANTIER, SPARSER
More obese — FATTER
More obtuse — DENSER
More ominous — DIRER
More optimistic — RESIER
More opulent — RICHER
More or _____ — LESS
More or less — ABOUT
More or Mann — THOMAS
More osseous — BONIER
More particular — NICER
More pious — HOLIER
More pixilated — NUTTIER
More pleasant — NICER
More pleased — HAPPIER
More plump — FLESHIER
More poky — SLOWER
More positive — SURER
More precious — DEARER
More precipitous — STEEPER
More prickly — THORNIER
More qualified — ABLER
More rankled — SORER
More rational — SANER
More reasonable — SANER, SOBERER
More recent — NEWER, LATER
More recondite — DEEPER
More refined — NICER
More relaxed — LOOSER
More reprehensible — VILER
More resentful — SORER
More reticent — — SHIER
More reticulate — NETTIER
More revealing — BARER
More ripe — OLDER
More rule-conscious — STRICTER
More sagacious — WISER
More sapient — WISER
More scarce — RARER
More scary — EERIER
More seasoned — OLDER
More severe — STERNER

More shipshape — TIGHTER
More sizable — LARGER
More skinny — BONIER
More sophisticated — SUAVER
More spacious — LARGER, ROOMIER
More spooky — EERIER
More strange — ERRIER
More suspicious — LEERIER
More swift of foot — FLEETER
More tender — SORER
More than a few — SEVERAL
More than odd — EERIE
More than one actress? — POLY BERGEN
More than one spouse — POLYGAMY
More than one stout — ALES
More than one: Comb. form — PLURI, MULTI
More than pleasantly plump — FAT, OBESE
More than pleasingly plump — OBESE
More than pudgy — OBESE
More than thin — GAUNT
More threatening — DIRER
More timid — SHIER
More trendy — NEWER
More tricky — SLYER
More trite — STALER
More uncouth — RUDER
More unctuous — OILIER
More underhanded — SLYER
More unfavorable — WORSE
More unpleasant — WORSE
More unusual — ODDER, RARER
More upset — SORER
More vast — HUGER
More ventilated — AIRIER
More veridical — TRUER
More viscid — ICKIER
More weird — EERIER
More's partner — LESS
More, in Madrid — MAS
More: It. — PIU
Moreno — RITA
Moreover — AGAIN, ALSO, TOO
Morgan — HORSE
Mork was one — ALIEN
Mork's home — ORK
Mork's planet — ORK
Morley of "60 Minutes" — SAFER
Morley's "Kitty _____" — FOYLE
Mormons' state — UTAH
Morning deposit — DEW
Morning eye-opener — ALARM
Morning hrs — AMS
Morning line — ODDS
Morning mist — DEW
Morning moisture — DEW
Morning prayer — MATINS
Morning song — MATIN
Mornings, for short — AMS
Mornings: Abbr. — AMS
Moroccan coastal area — IFNI
Moroccan district — IFNI
Moroccan mountains — ATLAS
Moroccan nursery tale? — PETER RABAT
Moroccan sluggers? — RABATTERS
Morocco range — RIF
Morocco's capital — RABAT
Morose — SAD
Morris or Garfield — CAT
Morrow in Stuttgart — MORGEN
Morse "E" — DOT
Morse and area — CODES
Morse character — DIT
Morse code characters — DITS
Morse code signals — DAHS, DITS
Morse code sound — DIT
Morse contribution — CODE
Morse signal — SOS
Morse symbol — DASH, DIT, DOT
Morse, for one — CODE
Morse-code word — DAH
Morsel — BITE, BIT, ORT, TASTE
Morsel — ORT
Morsel for a chickadee — SEED
Morsel for a duck — BREAD
Morsel for an elephant — PEANUT
Morsel for Trigger — OAT
Morsels — ORTS
Mort from Montreal — SAHL
Mortar beater — RAB
Mortar carriers — HODS
Mortar companion — PESTLE
Mortar ingredient — SAND
Mortar men's get-together — CEMENT MIXERS
Mortar-mixing tool — RAB
Mortarboard attachment — TASSEL
Mortarboard trim — TASSEL
Mortarboards — CAPS
Mortars' partners — PESTLES
Mortgage (claim) — LIEN
Mortgage paper — DEED
Mortgage, e.g. — LIEN
Mortgage, for example — LIEN
Mortgages — LIENS
Mortician's favorite Saint-Saëns work? — DANSE MACABRE
Mortiferous — FATAL
Mortify — DISGRACE
Mortimer — SNERD
Mortimer, the dummy — SNERD
Mortise match — TENON
Mortise's partner — TENON
Mos. and mos. — YRS
Mosaic — FRISOLEE
Mosaic piece — SMALTO
Mosaic tiles — TESSERAE
Mosaic, for example: Var. — ENLAY
Mosconi ploy — MASSE
Moscow denial — NYET
Moscow negative — NYET
Moscow salad bar serving? — RUSSIAN DRESSING
Moscow square — RED
Moscow thumbs-down — NYET
Moscow's Gorky _____ — PARK
Mosel feeder — SAAR
Mosel River city — TRIER
Mosel River feeder — SAAR
Mosel tributary — SAAR
Moses brother — AARON
Moses' law — TORAH
Mosey — ANKLE, STROLL
Mosey along — ANKLE
Moslem — ISLAMIC
Moslem "brain trust" — ULEMA
Moslem bigwig — AGHA
Moslem chief — RAIS
Moslem concept — FANA
Moslem fasting month — RAMADAN
Moslem holy man — IMAM
Moslem judge — CADI
Moslem leader — AGHA
Moslem leaders — IMAMS
Moslem magistrate — SADI
Moslem nobleman's bailiwick — EMIRATE
Moslem of the Philippines — MORO
Moslem priest — IMAM
Moslem prince — AMEER, AMIR, EMEER, EMIR
Moslem rulers — AGAS, EMEERS, EMIRS
Moslem sacred dress — IHRAMS
Moslem scholar — ULEMA
Moslem scriptures — KORAN
Moslem title — AGHA
Moslem tower — MINARET
Moslem VIP — AGA
Moslem's greeting — SALAAM
Mosque tower — MINARET
Mosquito genus — AEDES
Mosquito netting around a bed — CANOPY
Moss gathering nonentity — A ROLLING STONE
Moss or Gray — HART
Mosshorn, e.g. — STEER
Most abashed — REDDEST
Most abject — MEANEST
Most abundant — RIFEST
Most abundant Atlantic Coast fish — MENHADEN

Most adorable — CUTEST
Most adventurous — RASHEST
Most agreeable — NICEST
Most aloof — ICIEST
Most ancient — OLDEST
Most arid — DRIEST
Most ashen — PALEST
Most attenuated — RAREST
Most August babies — LEOS
Most authentic — REALEST
Most balanced — SANEST
Most bashful — SHIEST
Most bizarre — ODDEST
Most bleak — RAWEST
Most Bohemian — ARTIEST
Most brave — STOUTEST
Most capable — ABLEST
Most carefree — BLITHEST
Most certain — SUREST
Most cherished — DEAREST
Most civilized — WILDEST
Most clearheaded — SANEST
Most clever — SMARTEST
Most comfortable — COZIEST
Most corpulent — FATTEST
Most crafty — SLIEST
Most cunning — ASTUTEST, CANNIEST, CUTEST, WILIEST
Most curious — ODDEST
Most curt — SNIPPIEST
Most desirable — BEST
Most despicable — VILEST
Most diminutive — WEEST
Most distorted — WRIEST
Most domestic — TAMEST
Most Draconian — STERNEST
Most feeble — LAMEST
Most flamboyant — SHOWIEST
Most foul — DIRTIEST
Most foxy — SLIEST
Most frosted — ICIEST
Most fuliginous — SOOTIEST
Most gigantic — LARGEST
Most greasy — OILIEST
Most hair-raising — EERIEST
Most harsh — SEVEREST
Most healthy — HALEST
Most heroic — BRAVEST
Most humble — LOWLIEST
Most ignoble — BASEST
Most important — TOP DRAWER
Most important component — LINCHPIN
Most indolent — IDLEST, LAZIEST
Most ineffective — LAMEST
Most ineffectual — FEEBLEST
Most inferior — WORST
Most insensitive — DEADEST
Most ironic — WRIEST
Most joyful — MERRIEST
Most lacking in warmth — ICIEST
Most lively — GAYEST
Most loyal — TRUEST
Most melancholy — SADDEST
Most melodious — SWEETEST
Most minute — FINEST
Most miserly — CLOSET
Most modern — LATEST
Most of Switzerland — ALPS
Most of the U.K. — GTBR
Most otiose — IDLEST
Most pallid — PASTIEST
Most peculiar — ODDEST
Most populous African city — CAIRO
Most precious — DEAREST
Most prolific writer, for short? — ANON
Most protracted — LONGEST
Most proximate — NEAREST
Most prudent — CANNIEST
Most prying — NOSIEST
Most rapid — SWIFTEST
Most rational — SANEST
Most reasonable — SANEST
Most recent — LATEST
Most recent newswise — HOTTEST
Most recent: Comb. form — NEO
Most reliable — SANEST
Most rigid — HARDEST, SEVEREST
Most secure — SAFEST, TIGHT-EST
Most self-esteemed — PROUDEST
Most sensible — WISEST
Most sere — DRIEST
Most sharp — KEENEST
Most shoddy — CHEAPEST
Most shrewd — SLIEST
Most sick — ILLEST
Most simple — MEREST
Most simple; least — MEREST
Most sluggish — SLOWEST
Most smokers — INHALERS
Most sophisticated — COOLEST
Most sordid — BASEST
Most spiteful — MEANEST
Most straightforward — SINCEREST
Most strained — TENSEST
Most strict — STERNEST
Most suitable for Sprat — LEANEST
Most tender — SOREST
Most tense — EDGIEST, SHORTEST
Most uncommon — RAREST
Most unimportant — LEAST
Most unique — RAREST
Most unkind — CRUELEST
Most unusual — ODDEST, RAREST
Most up-to-date — NEWEST
Most vapid — STALEST
Most venerable — OLDEST
Most virtuous — PUREST
Most wan — PALEST
Most wary — CAGIEST
Most weird — EERIEST
Most wily — SLIEST
Most wrathful — ANGRIEST
Mosul language — KURDISH
Mosul man — KURD
Mote — ATOM
Motel room — UNIT
Motet anagram — TOTEM
Moth attraction — FLAME
Moth type — LUNA
Moth's glossa — TONGUE
Moth-eaten — DATED
Mother-in-law of Ruth — NAOMI
Mother — MATRON
Mother _____ — NATURE
Mother _____, Nobelist for Peace — TERESA
Mother _____, U.S. saint — SETON
Mother Astaire's daughter — ADELE
Mother Cooper's son — GARY
Mother doesn't like this title — MADAM
Mother Goose entry — RHYME
Mother Hubbard — DRESS
Mother Hubbard's quest — BONE
Mother Hubbard, for one — GOWN
Mother of "Dennis the Menace" — ALICE
Mother of Aeneas — VENUS
Mother of Apollo — LETO
Mother of Castor — LEDA
Mother of Castor and Pollux — LEDA
Mother of Constantine the Great — HELENA
Mother of Dionysus — SEMELE
Mother of Elizabeth I — ANNE BOLEYN
Mother of Eos — THEIA
Mother of Eris — HERA
Mother of Helen of Troy — LEDA
Mother of Hermes — MAIA
Mother of Ishmael — HAGAR
Mother of Liza Minnelli — JUDY GARLAND
Mother of Louis XIV — ANNE OF AUSTRIA
Mother of Marie Antoinette — MARIE THERESA
Mother of Minos — EUROPA
Mother of Nero — AGRIPPINA
Mother of Orestes — CLYTEMNESTRA
Mother of Presidents — VIRGINIA

Mother of Proserpina — CERES
Mother of the Gorgons — CETO
Mother of the Nereids — DORIS
Mother on Mother's Day? — PRIMA DONNA
Mother Saarinen's son — EERO
Mother Seton's mainstay — FAITH
Mother superior — ABBESS
Mother's admonition — NONO
Mother's advice — EAT UP
Mother's brother — UNCLE
Mother's day honoree — MATRON
Mother's Day treats, perhaps — SUNDAY MATINEES
Mother's forte, for short — TLC
Mother's helper — AUPAIR GIRL, BABY SITTER, SITTER
Mother's relatives — ENATES
Mother, in Marseilles — MERE
Mother, in Paris — MERE
Mother-of-pearl — NACRE
Mother-of-pearl source — ABALONE
Mother: Comb. form — MATRI
Motherly — MATERNAL
Mothers, certainly — MARVELS
Mothers: Colloq. — MAMMIES
Mothers: Lat. — MATERS
Moths — EGGERS, MILLERS
Motif — CONCEPT, FIGURE, THEME
Motilal or Jawaharlal — NEHRU
Motion picture heavy — VILLAIN
Motionless — AT REST, INERT
Motivates — IMPELS
Motivating force — ANIMUS
Motivation — CAUSE
Motive — CAUSE, DESIRE
Motor — ENGINE
Motor flop — EDSEL
Motor fuels — OCTANES
Motor homes, for short — RVS
Motor readings — RPMS
Motor sound — PING
Motorcade vehicle, for short — LIMO
Motorcycle-bicycle hybrid — MOPED
Motorcyclist's need — HELMET
Motorist's asso. — AAA
Motorist's concern — SPEED LIMIT
Motorist's expense — TOLL
Motorist's stop — DINER
Motorists' org. — AAA
Motorists' worry — DETOURS
Motorized bike — MOPED
Motorized vehicle — CAR
Motorman? — RUDOLPH DIESEL
Motorways — ROADS
Motown — DETROIT
Motown product — AUTO
Motown's Franklin — ARETHA
Mott St. hors d'oeuvre — EGGROLL
Mottled — DAPPLED, PIED
Motto for a dieter — THINK SHRINK
Motto of California — EUREKA
Motto's relative — ADAGE
Moulin Rouge dance — CANCAN
Mounds — HEAPS, PILES
Moundsman who starts a game — STARTING PITCHER
Mount — STEED
Mount _____ College — UNION
Mount _____ Observatory — PALOMAR
Mount _____, Alaska volcano — KATMAI
Mount _____, Calif.: Observatory site — PALOMAR
Mount _____, Colo. — ETNA
Mount _____: Texas peak — ORD
Mount a new "As You Like It" — RESTAGE
Mount a soapbox — ORATE
Mount an assault — STORM
Mount associated with Moses — SINAI
Mount Churchill locale — ALASKA
Mount Desert Island's park — ACADIA
Mount in Tasmania — OSSA
Mount in Thessaly — OSSA
Mount of _____, near Jerusalem — OLIVES
Mount Santo _____, Philippines — TOMAS
Mount St. _____ — HELENS
Mount the soapbox — ORATE
Mount Vernon's river — POTOMAC
Mountain _____ — DEW
Mountain ash — ROWAN
Mountain ashes, to Virgil — ORNI
Mountain chain — RIDGE
Mountain chains — SIERRAS
Mountain clothing? — HIGH JUMPER
Mountain crest — ARETE
Mountain curve — ESS
Mountain deity — OREAD
Mountain detritus — SCREE
Mountain feature — CRAG
Mountain in Crete — IDA
Mountain in NE Greece — ATHOS
Mountain in Thessaly — OSSA
Mountain lake — MERE, TARN
Mountain mint — BASIL
Mountain near Edom — HOR
Mountain nymph — OREAD
Mountain on Crete — IDA
Mountain panther — COUGAR
Mountain pass — COL, GHAT
Mountain passes — COLS
Mountain peak — TOR
Mountain peak in Calif. — SHASTA
Mountain pool — TARN
Mountain range in NW Wyoming — TETON
Mountain range in Utah — UINTA
Mountain range of central Asia — ALTAI
Mountain ridge — ARETE
Mountain spine — ARETE
Mountain, in Frankfurt — BERG
Mountain, to Marcellus — MONS
Mountain: Comb. form — ORO, OREO
Mountain: Ger. — ALPE
Mountain: Prefix — OREO
Mountaineer's hazards — CHASMS
Mountaineering descent — ABSEIL
Mountainous ride — ARETE
Mountebank's forte — TRICK
Mounted — ASTRIDE, SCALED
Mounted "The Tempest" — STAGED
Mounted policeman — TROOPER
Mountie's command — WHOA
Mourn — ACHE, GRIEVE, LAMENT, SUFFER
Mourn for — REGRET
Mourned aloud — KEENED
Mourner's garb — SACK CLOTH
Mournful exhalation — SIGH
Mournful sound — KNELL
Mournful tunes — DIRGES
Mourns — RUES
Mouse or fish — SHINER
Mouselike — SHY
Mousse — DESSERT
Mouth or pipe — ORGAN
Mouth playing instrument — HARMONICA
Mouth, colloquially — TRAP
Mouth, to a zoologist — STOMA
Mouth: Comb. form — ORI, STOME
Mouthful — BITE, GULP, SLICE, TASTE
Mouthing off — LIP
Mouthlike opening — STOMA
Mouthpiece of a sort — SHYSTER
Mouthpieces — SHYSTERS

Mouths — ORA, VOICES
Mouths off to — SASSES
Mouths, to Brutus — ORA
Mouths: Lat. — ORA
Mouthward — ORAD
Move — BUDGE, RELOCATE, SHIFT, YIELD
Move _____ (use great effort) — HEAVEN AND EARTH
Move along — GET ON
Move along the runway — TAXI
Move back — RECEDE
Move backward and forward — WAGGLE
Move briskly — HUM
Move by small degrees — INCH
Move cargo — UNLOAD
Move crab-wise — SIDLE
Move decisively — CROSS THE RUBICON
Move deeply — STIR
Move edgewise — SIDLE
Move forward — MAKE HEADWAY
Move furtively — CREEP
Move furtively — SLINK
Move in a circle — GYRE
Move in a crowd — SWARM
Move in a spiral — GYRE
Move like a certain crustacean — SIDLE
Move like a crab — SIDLE
Move like a snake — SLITHER
Move muscles — FLEX
Move sideways — CRAB
Move sinuously — SLINK, SNAKE
Move slowly — CRAWL, INCH
Move slowly, with "along" — INCH
Move smoothly — GLIDE
Move stealthily — SLINK
Move swiftly — FLIT, ZOOM
Move through mud — SLOG
Move through water — SLOSH
Move to a higher level — RAISE
Move to another country — EMIGRATE
Move unsteadily — WOBBLE
Move up and down — SEESAW
Move with confidence — STRIDE
Move without power — COAST
Moved a painting — REHUNG
Moved ahead — ADVANCED
Moved back and forth — SEE SAWED
Moved in a curved course — ARCED
Moved sideways — SLUED
Moved slowly — CREPT, EDGED, TRICKLED
Moved smoothly — SLID
Moved suddenly — DARTED
Moved with haste — RAN
Movement of people — MIGRATION
Movement to unify Cyprus and Greece — ENOSIS
Mover — VANMAN
Mover to another country — EMIGRE
Mover's vehicle — VAN
Movers — GOERS
Moves — STIRS
Moves deeply — STIRS
Moves erratically — CAREENS
Moves furtively — SLINKS
Moves quickly — ZIPS
Moves rapidly — PELTS, TROTS
Moves the furniture again — REARRANGES
Moves with grace — LOPES
Moves, like a river — FLOWS
Movie — CINEMA, FILM, FLICK, THEATER
Movie canine — ASTA, LASSIE
Movie channel — HBO
Movie critic Judith — CRIST
Movie dog — ASTA
Movie enhancer — BACK-GROUND MUSIC
Movie great — STAR
Movie highlights of the 30's — TEMPLES DIMPLES
Movie house, in Madrid — CINE
Movie lion — ELSA
Movie Messala — BOYD
Movie mogul — CZAR
Movie monogram — RKO
Movie of 1930 — ANIMAL CRACKERS
Movie of 1931 — MONKEY BUSINESS
Movie of 1937 — A DAY AT THE RACES
Movie or record of past years — OLDIE
Movie pooch — ASTA
Movie star of the 30's — NORMA SHEARER
Movie studio initials — RKO
Movie thriller in 1977 — THE CAR
Movie units — REELS
Movie vamp — BARA
Movie western — OATER
Movie whale — ORCA
Movie-maker Mack's relations — SENNETTS
Movie-theater treat — POPCORN
Movies — CINE, CINEMA
Movies, in Barcelona — CINES
Movies, in Cannes — CINE
Moving — DRIVING, GOING, MOTIVATING, TOUCHING
Moving about — ASTIR
Moving at a high speed — BARRELING
Moving experience? — TRANSFER
Moving forward — PROGRESSIVE
Moving machinery pieces — CAMS
Moving on a seasonal basis — MIGRATORY
Moving part — ROTOR
Moving vehicles — VANS
Mowbray or Thicke — ALAN
Mower attachment — EDGER
Mower paths — SWATHS
Mowgli's python — KAA
Mozart opera: 1781 — IDOMONEO
Mozart opera: 1787 — DON GIOVANNI
Mozart opera: 1791 — DIE ZAUBERFLOTE
Mozart portrayer in "Amadeus" — HULCE
Mozart's "_____ fan tutte" — COSI
Mozart's "_____ Pastore" — IL RE
Mozart's birthplace: Jan. 27, 1756 — SALZBURG
Mozart's bride in 1782 — CONSTANZE WEBER
Mozart's middle name — AMADEUS
Mozart's was music — FORTE
MP's concern — AWOL
MP's quarry — AWOL
Mr. _____ of "Wind in the Willows" — TOAD
Mr. America's source of pride — PHYSIQUE
Mr. Anybody — JOHN DOE
Mr. Arnaz — DESI
Mr. Chips' star — DONAT
Mr. Claus racetrack — SANTA ANITA
Mr. Connery's chess pieces? — SEANS PAWNS
Mr. Coolidge, et al. — CALS
Mr. Dithers to Dagwood — BOSS
Mr. Domino — FATS
Mr. Dooley's creator — DUNNE
Mr. Fixit's — REPAIR SHOP
Mr. Flintstone — FRED
Mr. Franklin — BEN
Mr. Frost — JACK
Mr. Gander's wife, perhaps? — MRS GOOSE
Mr. Gantry — ELMER
Mr. Harriman — AVERELL
Mr. Heap — URIAH
Mr. in Milano — SIG
Mr. Kefauver — ESTES
Mr. Kovacs — ERNIE
Mr. Oop — ALLEY
Mr. Preacher — REV

Mr. Rochester's beloved — EYRE
Mr. Sharif — OMAR
Mr. Spock of TV — NIMOY
Mr. Spock's father in "Star Trek" — SAREK
Mr. Spock, of "Star Trek" — NIMOY
Mr. T's group — A TEAM
Mr. T's outfit — THE A TEAM
Mr. Wallach, et al. — ELIS
Mr. Welles — ORSON
Mr. Winterhalter — HUGO
Mrs. Archer in "The Maltese Falcon" — IVA
Mrs. Arrowsmith — LEORA
Mrs. B.'s question — HOW DO I LOVE THEE
Mrs. Bumstead — BLONDIE
Mrs. Burt Reynolds, once — LONI
Mrs. Cantor — IDA
Mrs. Charles — NORA
Mrs. Charles of fiction — NORA
Mrs. Clinton — HILLARY
Mrs. Dick Tracy — TESS
Mrs. Donahue — MARLO
Mrs. Dukakis — KITTY
Mrs. Ford, _____ Bloomer — NEE
Mrs. from Madrid — SRA
Mrs. Gorbachev — RAISA
Mrs. Gustav Mahler — ALMA
Mrs. Helmsley — LEONA
Mrs. Henry Wood's melodrama — EAST LYNNE
Mrs. Irving Berlin — ELLIN
Mrs. Lennon — ONO
Mrs. Leonowens — ANNA
Mrs. Leopold Bloom — MOLLY
Mrs. Lincoln's family — TODDS
Mrs. Lincoln's maiden name — TODD
Mrs. Lindbergh — ANNE
Mrs. Lopez and Mrs. Mendez — SENORAS
Mrs. Luce — CLARE
Mrs. Marcos — IMELDA
Mrs. McKinley — IDA
Mrs. Miller's naive daughter — DAISY
Mrs. Nick Charles — NORA
Mrs. Rochester's kin — EYRES
Mrs. Ross's claim to fame — SEWING
Mrs. Schwarzenegger — MARIA
Mrs. Shakespeare — ANNE
Mrs. Skelton's favorite color — RED
Mrs. Sprat's fare — FAT
Mrs. Sprat's no-no — LEAN
Mrs. Sprat's preference — FAT
Mrs. T. S. Eliot, et al. — ESMES
Mrs. Thatcher, for one — TORY
Mrs. Trump — IVANA
Mrs. Van Buren, nee — HOES
Mrs. Vernon Castle — IRENE
Mrs. Warner's nickname — LIZ
Mrs. Weller's boy — SAM
Mrs. Zaharias — BABE
Mrs., in Avila — SRA
Mrs., in Madrid — SRA
Mrs., in Metz — MME
Ms. accompaniment, usually — SASE
Ms. Fabray, to friends — NAN
Ms. Fitzgerald — ELLA
Ms. Gardner — AVA
Ms. Hogg — IMA
Ms. Kett — ETTA
Ms. Meyers — ARI
Ms. Oyl — OLIVE
Ms. people — EDS
Ms. Shire of "Rocky" films — TALIA
Ms. Verdugo — ELENA
Ms. West — MAE
Ms. Zadora — PIA
Mss. amenders — EDS
Mss. workers — EDS
Mt. _____, Italy — BRE
Mt. Etna's city — CATANIA
Mt. Hood's loc. — ORE
Mt. Ida maiden — OREAD
Mt. McKinley's location — ALASKA
Mt. Rushmore site — S DAK
Mt. Rushmore's state — S DAK
Mt. Vesuvius — VOLCANO
Mt. Wilson glass — LENS
Mtg. — SESS
Muammar al-Qadhafi's realm — LIBYA
Mubarek's capital — CAIRO
Much about nothing — ADO
Much heard — STALE
Much married clarinetist and bandleader — SHAW
Much or many — FAR
Much puzzled bird — EMU
Much used article — THE
Much wived Henry — VIII
Much, in music — MOLTO
Much-used article — THE
Mucilage — EPOXY, GLUE, GUM, PASTE, RESIN
Muckraker Tarbell — IDA
Mud _____ (gallinule) — HEN
Mud dauber — WASP
Mud eel — SIREN
Mud hole — PUDDLE
Mud-slinger — LIBELER
Muddied — ROILED
Muddies the waters — ROILS
Muddle — MESS, SNAFU
Muddle with drink — BESOT
Muddled situation, G.I. style — SNAFU
Muddles — JUMBLES
Muddlin — SOSO
Muddy or Ethel — WATERS
Muddy residue — SILT
Mudslinging fumarole — SALSE
Mudville fans' fanner — CASEY
Mudville non-hero — CASEY
Mudville strikeout victim — CASEY
Muezzen — CRIER
Muezzin's call to prayer — AZAN
Muff — BOTCH, ERR, SLIP, TRIP
Muffed — BLEW
Muffet frightener — SPIDER
Muffet's nemesis — SPIDER
Muffin — BRAN, BUN, GEM, ROLL
Muffin ingredient — BRAN
Muffle — COVER, DEADEN, HOOD
Muffled — DIM, MUTED, SOFT, SUBDUED
Muffler — BOA, CRAVAT, SCARF
Muffler menace — RUT
Mufflers — SCARFS
Muffles — MUTES
Mug fillers — ALES
Mugger repellent — MACE
Muggers on the boards — HAMS
Muggy — CLOSE, DAMP, HUMID, MOIST
Muggy day index: Abbr. — THI
Mugs — BEAKERS, FACES, STEINS, TOBIES
Muhammad's birthplace — MECCA
Mulberry bark — TAPA
Mulct — FEE, FINE, PENALTY
Mule "on the Erie Canal" — SAL
Mule of songdom — SAL
Mule's cousin — BURRO, HINNY
Mull Island neighbor — IONA
Mull over — MUSE
Mulled drink — TODDY
Mulligan or Irish — STEW
Mulligan, e.g. — STEW
Mulligrubs — COLIC
Mulliniks of baseball — RANCE
Multi-axled truck — SEMI
Multiheaded giant — BRIAREUS
Multinational defense org. — NATO
Multiplies — ADDS TO, DOUBLES, INCREASES
Multipurpose bean — SOY
Multitalented person — JACK OF ALL TRADES
Multitude — HORDE
Multitudes — ARMIES
Mum — DUMB, MUTE, QUIET, SILENT
Mumble — GROUSE, MURMUR, MUTTER

Munch — EAT, GNAW, NIBBLE, NOSH
Munch or brunch — CHUMP, EAT
Munchausen story — YARN
Munchausen type — LIAR
Munchausen, e.g. — BARON
Munchausen, for one — LIAR
Munched — ATE, GORGED
Mundane — EARTHLY, PROSY, SENSUAL, WORLDLY
Muni or Simon — PAUL
Munich Mr. — HERR
Munich's river — ISAR
Municipal — CITY, CIVIC, LOCAL
Municipal council member — ALDERMAN
Municipal maps — PLATS
Municipal problem — TRASH
Municipalities — CITIES
Munitions, for short — AMMO
Munity — PRIVILEGE
Munro's pseudonym — SAKI
Munson of "G.W.T.W." — ONA
Munster man — TEUTONIC
Muralist Jose' Maria — SERT
Muralist Rivera — DIEGO
Murder, arson, burglary, etc. — FELONIES
Muriel Spark's "Memento _____" — MORI
Murkiness — HAZE
Murmur lovingly — COO
Murmured fondly — COOED
Murphy or Murray — EDDIE
Murphy's _____ — LAW
Murray and West — MAES
Murray or Howard — KEN
Murray or Kesey — KEN
Murrow's "_____ Now" — SEE IT
Murrow's "You are _____" — THERE
Mus. adaption — ARR
Mus. mark — STAC
Muscat's capital — OMAN
Muscat's country — OMAN
Muscat-eer? — OMANI
Muscle — BRAWN, SINEW, TENSOR, THEWS
Muscle _____, Ala. — SHOALS
Muscle protein — ACTIN
Muscle type — TENSOR
Muscleman — BODYGUARD, THUG
Muscleman Steve — REEVES
Muscovite, for one — ORE
Muscovites — REDS
Muscovites' council — SOVIET
Muscovites' land — RUSSIA
Muscular fitness — TONE
Muscular pain — TETANY
Muse — CHEW, ERATO, REFLECT
Muse for Marceau — ERATO
Muse for Pindar — ERATO
Muse for Sappho — ERATO
Muse number — NINE
Muse of bridal songs — ERATO
Muse of history — CLIO
Muse of love poetry — ERATO
Muse of lyric poetry — ERATO
Muse of poetry — ERATO
Musette — OBOE
Museum — WAX
Museum contents — ART
Museum display — OPART
Museum guide — DOCENT
Museum offering — OPART
Museum piece, perhaps — OIL
Museum staff members — RESTORERS
Mushroom — MOREL
Mushroom caps — PILEI
Mushroom, in Madrid — SETA
Musial — STAN
Musial and Laurel — STANS
Musial namesakes — STANS
Musial or Getz — STAN
Musial or Laurel — STAN
Musial's team — CARDINALS
Music and dance — ARTS
Music award — GRAMMY
Music beats, from the German — TAKTS
Music characters — NOTES
Music for Shankar — RAGA
Music hall — ODEUM, ODIUM, OSEON
Music halls — ODEA
Music in the background — MUZAK
Music industry acronym — ASCAP
Music machine — PIANOLA
Music maker's org. — ASCAP
Music man Ringo — STARR
Music of the common people — FOLK
Music performed at a party — GIG
Music syllable — TRA
Music systems — STEREOS
Music teacher's remark — PRACTICE
Music to an actor's ear — APPLAUSE
Music to Bo Peep's ears? — BLEATS
Music to Manolete's ears — OLES
Music to the matador's ear — OLE
Music type — BOP
Music's Paul — SIMON
Musical — MELODIOUS
Musical "sweet potatoes" — OCARINAS
Musical "thoroughfare" — TIN PAN ALLEY
Musical "very" — ASSAI
Musical about songbirds — DREAM GIRLS
Musical acuity — EAR
Musical adaptations: Abbr. — ARRS
Musical aptitude — EAR
Musical arranger — ADAPTER
Musical breaks — RESTS
Musical chord — MAJOR, TRIAD
Musical classic — OPERA
Musical combos — TRIOS
Musical comedy of 1923 — RUNNING WILD
Musical composition — CANTATA, ETUDE, OPUS, PIECE
Musical composition — RONDO, WORK
Musical composition for nine — NONET
Musical critic Taylor — DEEMS
Musical Della — REESE
Musical Diamond — NEIL
Musical direction — LARGO, LENTO, OTTAVA
Musical direction — PIU, SEGUE
Musical direction word — ASSAI
Musical drama — OPERA
Musical ending — CODA
Musical epilogue — CODA
Musical event — CHORALE
Musical exercise — ETUDE
Musical fanfare — FLOURISH
Musical finale — CODA
Musical Flack — ROBERTA
Musical for care — SOMEONE TO WATCH OVER ME
Musical form — DIRGE
Musical Fountain — PETE
Musical from Berlin — ANNIE GET YOUR GUN
Musical from Shavian play — MY FAIR LADY
Musical Gluck — ALMA
Musical group — BAND, CHOIR, COMBO, OCTET, SYMPHONY
Musical group — TRIAD, TRIO
Musical heirloom — STRAD
Musical heroine — HATTIE
Musical highlight — ARIA
Musical inspired by T.S. Eliot — CATS
Musical instrument — LYRE, SPINET, STRING, VIOLIN
Musical instrument for short — SAX
Musical interval — FIFTH, OCTAVE, REST, TRITONE
Musical introduction — PRELUDE
Musical Kazan — LAINIE
Musical locale — BROADWAY
Musical marchers — BANDS

Musical McCartney — PAUL
Musical measures — BARS
Musical mixture — MEDLEY
Musical Moore — MELBA
Musical movements — ALLEGROS
Musical Nelson — OZZIE
Musical notational sign — NEUME
Musical notes — RES, SOLS, TIS
Musical number — DUET
Musical offering — ARIA
Musical on Broadway — CATS
Musical paces — TEMPI
Musical part — CODA, TENOR
Musical passage — CODA
Musical pattern — SCORE
Musical pauses — RESTS
Musical performance — RECITAL
Musical piece — CODA, ETUDE, RONDO
Musical platform — BANDSTAND
Musical prelude — VORSPIEL
Musical production — REVUE
Musical quality — TONE
Musical refrain — LALA, RONDO
Musical response/opposed to a faker? — ANTIPHONY
Musical revue of 1949 — ALL FOR LOVE
Musical rhythm — SWING
Musical role: 1977 — ANNIE
Musical round — CANON
Musical sections — CODAS
Musical sense — EAR
Musical Shaw — ARTIE
Musical Shore — DINAH
Musical show — REVUE
Musical sign — CLEF, REST, SHARP
Musical sound — TONE
Musical stand — PODIUM
Musical star Gwen — VERDON
Musical suite — PARTITA
Musical syllables — FAS, LALAS, LAS, SOLS, TRAS
Musical symbol — CLEF, NOTE, REST, SHARP
Musical talent — EAR
Musical term — SLUR
Musical threesome — TRIO
Musical tone — CHIME
Musical transition — SEGUE
Musical unit — NOTE
Musical Waller — FATS
Musical Wilder — ALEC
Musical work — MOTET, OPUS
Musically smooth — LEGATO
Musician — PIPER
Musician Herb — ALPERT
Musician Lanin — LESTER
Musician misplaces a mug — LEONARD BERN
Musician Paul — LES
Musician Puente — TITO
Musician's asset — EAR
Musician's engagement — GIG
Musician's gift — EAR
Musician's must — EAR
Musician's talent — EAR
Musician's transition — SEGUE
Musicians Kipnis and Buketoff — IGORS
Musicologist Taylor — DEEMS
Musket or cannon follower — EER
Musketeer — ARAMIS
Musketeer's foil — EPEE
Muskmelon — CANTALOUPE
Muslim call to prayer — AZAN
Muslim cap — TAJ
Muslim charmer — HOURI
Muslim code — AMIR
Muslim decree — IRADE
Muslim deity — ALLAH
Muslim dignitary — AMEER
Muslim doctrine — TAUHID
Muslim faith — ISLAM
Muslim general — AGA
Muslim God — ALLAH
Muslim holymen — IMAMS
Muslim journey — HEGIRA
Muslim judge — CADI
Muslim judge: Var. — KADI
Muslim leader — AGA, EMIR
Muslim moneybags — EMEER
Muslim of the Philippines — MORO
Muslim prayer leader — IMAM
Muslim priest — IMAM
Muslim prince — AGHA, AMIR, EMIR
Muslim princes — EMIRS
Muslim queen in India — BEGUM
Muslim ruler — AGHA, AMEER, AMIR
Muslim rulers: Var. — REIS
Muslim sacred book — AL KORAN
Muslim saint — PIR
Muslim scholar — IMAM
Muslim title — AMIR
Muslim VIP — AGHA
Muslim's faith — ISLAM
Muslim's sacred book — KORAN
Muss — TOUSLE
Muss the coiffure — TOUSLE
Mussel genus — UNIO
Mussolini was one — FASCIST
Mussolini's title — IL DUCE
Mussorgsky vocal composition — SONG OF THE FLEA
Mussorgsky's "Pictures _____ Exhibition" — AT AN
Mussulman — MOSLEM
Must — HAS TO
Must for a camper — CAN OPENER
Mustard-family plant — RADISH
Muster — GATHER
Muster out, British style — DEMOB
Mute — SILENT
Muted hue — PASTEL
Muted trumpet sound — WAWA
Muti's opinion of skat — CRAZY RHYTHM
Mutineer — REBEL
Mutt — CUR
Mutt and Jeff, e.g. — PAIR, PALS
Mutt to Jeff — PAL
Mutt's friend — JEFF
Mutt, in Dixie — FEIST
Mutter complaints — GRUMBLE
Mutton chops — WHISKERS
Mutual influence — INTERACTION
Mutuality of support — INTERDEPENDENCE
Mutuel-window employee, e.g. — SELLER
My gal _____ — SAL
My, to monsieur — MON
Myanmar — BURMA
Myopic herbivore — RHINO
Myrna — LOY
Myrna from Montana — LOY
Mysost or pecorino — CHEESE
Mysterious — EERIE
Mysterious material — ESOTERICA
Mystery — ENIGMA, SECRET
Mystery award — EDGAR
Mystery needs — CLUES
Mystery writer Foley — RAE
Mystery writer Howard — ENGEL
Mystery writer John Dickson — CARR
Mystery writer Josephine — TEY
Mystery writer Marsh — NGAIO
Mystery writer Michael — INNES
Mystery writer Sheridan Le _____ — FANU
Mystery writer Wahloo — PER
Mystery writer's award — EDGAR
Mystery writer's prize — EDGAR
Mystery's Gardner, et al. — ERLES
Mystic ascetic — SUFI
Mystic character — RUNE
Mystic formula — MANTRA
Mystic playing card — TAROT
Mystic teachers — GURUS
Mystical mark — RUNE

Mystify — PUZZLE
Mystiques — AURAS
Myth — FICTION
Mythic coffer — PANDORAS BOX
Mythic goddess — HERA
Mythical animals — UNICORNS
Mythical archer — EROS
Mythical beast — YALE
Mythical birds — ROCS
Mythical creature — FAUNS
Mythical flyer — ROC
Mythical flyer in Amerind lore — THUNDERBIRD
Mythical founder of "Iliad" city — TROS
Mythical Greek hunter — ORION
Mythical hunter — ORION
Mythical many-eyed monster — ARGUS
Mythical meanie — OGRE
Mythical Muslim maiden — HOURI
Mythical piper — RUNE
Mythical poem — RUNE
Mythical seductress — CIRCE
Mythical siren — CIRCE
Mythical sisters — FATES
Mythical Spartan queen — LEDA
Mythological creature — ROC
Mythological Egyptian bird — PHOENIX
Mythological elephant carrier — ROC
Mythological enchantress — MEDEA
Mythological twin — REMUS
Mythological weeper — NIOBE
Mythology — LEGENDS
Mythomaniac — LIAR

N

N as in _____ — NAN
N Nigerian city — KANO
N Norway denizen — LAPP
N Oklahoma city — TIPI
N Oklahoma town — ENID
N-S connection — OPQR
N. Amer.-Eur. connection — ATL
N. Ireland Protestant — ORANGE MAN
N.A. border canals — SOO
N.A.A.C.P., e.g. — ASSN
N.B.A. player with the Kings — SPARROW
N.B.A. stringbean — SOL
N.C. college — ELON
N.C.A.A.'s rival — AAU
N.C.O. — SGT
N.E. natives — YANKS
N.E. times — ESTS
N.E. university — URI
N.F.L. "zebras" — REFS
N.F.L. scores — TDS
N.F.L.'s _____ Bay Buccaneers — TAMPA
N.H. campus — KEENE
N.H. city — KEENE
N.H.L. great — ORR
N.H.L. team — TORONTO
N.H.L. whistler — REF
N.J. city — HOBOKEN
N.J. five — NETS
N.J. township — TEANECK
N.L. arbiter — UMP
N.L. home-run leader: 1947-52 — KINER
N.L. M.V.P. 1952 — SAUER
N.L. team — REDS
N.M. Indian — SIA
N.M.U. member — SEAMAN
N.R.C. concern — ATOM
N.T. book — HEB
N.Y. city — OLEAN
N.Y. city on the Mohawk — UTICA
N.Y. Giant great, TV sportscaster — FRANK GIFFORD
N.Y. stage award — OBIE
N.Y. subway — IRT
N.Y. time — EST
N.Y. time in winter — EST
N.Y. time, at times — DST
N.Y. winter time — EST
N.Y. winter time — EST
N.Y.-N.J. river — RAMAPO
N.Y.-to-Bos. dir. — ENE
N.Y.-to-Boston dir. — ENE
N.Y.C. artists' area — SOHO
N.Y.C. dept. — HRA
N.Y.C. museum — MOMA
N.Y.C. river — EAST, HARLEM
N.Y.C. subway — IND
N.Y.C. subway line — IRT
N.Y.C. subway syst. — BMT
N.Y.P.D. order — APB
N.Y.S.E. abbr. — PFD, STKS
N.Y.S.E. item — STK
N.Y.S.E. membership — SEAT
N.Y.S.E. unit — SHARE
N.Y.S.E.'s birth: 1792 — BUTTONWOOD AGREEMENT
N.Y.U.'s hue — VIOLETS
N.Z. native — MAORI
N.Z. or Aussie W.W.I soldier — DIGGER
N.Z. songbird — KIRI TE KANAWA
N.Z. tunas — EELS
Nab — ARREST, COLLAR, NAIL
Nabbed — COLLARED, RAN IN
Nabob — CHIEF, LORD
Nabokov book — ADA
Nabokov book: 1957 — PNIN
Nabokov character — LOLITA
Nabokov hero — PNIN
Nabokov heroine — ADA
Nabokov novel — ADA, DAR, PNIN
Nabokov nymphet — LOLITA
Nabokov title — ADA
Nabors — JIM
Nacelle — BOAT
Nacre — MOTHER OF PEARL
Nag — HASSLE, RIDE
Nag, in a way — HENPECK
Nahuati — AZTEC
Nail — FASTEN, SPAD
Nail board — EMERY
Nail for a plummet — SPAD
Nail or old plane — SPAD
Nail polishes — ENAMELS
Nail shaper — FILE
Nail's partner — TOOTH
Naive — INNOCENT, SIMPLE
Naldi of the movies — NITA
Naldi of the silents — NITA
Name — APPOINT, DUB, ENTITLE, NOMEN
Name — TITLE
Name akin to Louis — ALOIS
Name anew — RETITLE
Name assumed by Celia, "As You Like It" — ALIENA
Name callers, and worse — ABUSERS
Name dropper — SNOB
Name famous in fiction — EYRE
Name for a carrottop — RED
Name for a colleen — ERIN

Name for a dalmatian — SPOT
Name for a daredevil — EVEL
Name for a Dublin lass — ERIN
Name for a fille — RENEE
Name for a Fräulein — ILSE
Name for a lamb — ELIA
Name for a Moscow miss — OLGA
Name for a poodle — FIFI
Name for an amateur radio operator — HAM
Name for an Irish lass — ERIN
Name for Madame — RENEE
Name for Monsieur — RENE
Name for office — NOMINATE
Name for three English rivers — AVON
Name giver — EPONYM
Name in a Beethoven opus — ELISE
Name in circus lore — RINGLING
Name in cosmetics — ESTEE
Name in couture — DIOR
Name in early cars — OLDS
Name in elevators — OTIS
Name in fashion — DIOR, GUCCI
Name in IQ testing — BINET
Name in movie lore — INCE
Name in pugilism — ALI
Name in puppetry — SARG
Name in railroad lore — CASEY JONES
Name in the history of US journalism — OCHS
Name in tractors — DEERE
Name in TV ratings — NIELSEN
Name meaning "God's protector" — ANSEL
Name meaning "graceful one" — ANNE
Name meaning "man" — ENOS
Name meaning farmer — CARL
Name meaning noble friend — ALVINO
Name meaning princess — SARA
Name meaning watchdog — IRA
Name of 12 Egyptian monarchs — RAMESES
Name of 12 popes — PIUS
Name of 14 popes — CLEMENT
Name of 8 kings of Siam — RAMA
Name of a blotter, perhaps — ALIAS
Name of fame in mysteries — NERO
Name of fame in Sweden — NOBEL
Name of friend of D'Artagnan — ATHOS, ARAMIS
Name of many popes — PIUS
Name of three English rivers — OUSE
Name of three Ottoman rulers — OSMAN
Name often in Vegas lights — NEWTON
Name on early cars — OLDS
Name on farming equipment — DEERE
Name on Japanese ships — MARU
Name source — EPONYM
Name the price — QUOTE
Name to an office — APPOINT
Name to remember — ALAMO, MAINE
Name, _____ and serial number — RANK
Named — CHRISTENED
Nameless — UNSUNG
Namely — TO WIT
Names — DUBS
Names on the marquee — STARS
Namesakes of a "Golden Girl" — BEAS
Namesakes of a Caesar — SIDS
Namesakes of a Christie — AGATHAS
Namesakes of a Cobb — TYS
Namesakes of a comic King — ALANS
Namesakes of a Darling girl — WENDYS
Namesakes of a Dickens tot — TIMS
Namesakes of a Ford — EDSELS
Namesakes of a Gilbert & Sullivan princess — IDAS
Namesakes of a Grant — LEES
Namesakes of a King — ALANS
Namesakes of a king of Judah — ASAS
Namesakes of a literary Auntie — MAMES
Namesakes of a Marx brother — ZEPPOS
Namesakes of a nymph — ECHOS
Namesakes of a Roosevelt — ELEANORS
Namesakes of a Sommer — ELKES
Namesakes of a Spanish queen — ENAS
Namesakes of a Stowe character — EVAS
Namesakes of a Stowe heroine — EVAS
Namesakes of a sunken Mary — DEARES
Namesakes of a Uris hero — ARIS
Namesakes of actor Navarro — RAMONS
Namesakes of actress Sothern — ANNS
Namesakes of Adam's third son — SETHS
Namesakes of an acting Albert — EDDIES
Namesakes of brown bears — KARENS
Namesakes of Cadmus's daughter — INOS
Namesakes of Chinese leader — MAOS
Namesakes of designer Schiaparelli — ELSAS
Namesakes of designer Simpson — ADELES
Namesakes of Dorothy's dog — TOTOS
Namesakes of FDR's dog — FALAS
Namesakes of Israel's Eban — ABBAS
Namesakes of the Darlings' dog — NANAS
Namesakes of the first Mrs. Copperfield — DORAS
Namesakes of TV's Foxx — REDDS
Namesakes of violinist Bull — OLES
Namesakes of Wolfe, the sleuth — NEROS
Namesakes of Zerah's son: I Chron. 2:6 — DARAS
Namibia, once: Abbr. — SWA
Nana — NURSE
Nana hero — NATA
Nana to Wendy — PET
Nancy and Mary — ASTORS
Nancy Lopez requirement — TEE
Nancy or Clint — WALKER
Nancy Walker character — IDA
Nancy's man — RON
Nanette's caution — NONO
Nanki-_____ of "The Mikado" — POO
Nanking nursemaid — AMAH
Nanny — DOE
Nanny has three — ENS
Nanny's carriage — PRAM
Nanny's goat — BILLY
Nanny's vehicle — PRAM
Nantes negative — NON
Nantes night — NUIT
Nantes-to-Angers dir. — ENE
Naos — CELLA
Nap-raiser — TEASEL
Nap — DOZE, PILE, REST, SLEEP
Nap noisly — SNORE
Nap, in Nayarit — SIESTA
Nap-raising plant — TEASEL
Napalm — JELLY
Nape drape — SCARF
Napery — LINEN

Napkin — CLOTH
Napkin material — DAMASK
Napoleon _____, "The Man from U.N.C.L.E." — SOLO
Napoleon and Alexander: Abbr. — EMPS
Napoleon slept here: 1814 — ELBA
Napoleon victory site — LODI
Napoleon victory site: 1806 — JENA
Napoleon won here: 1796 — LODI
Napoleon's "birthplace"? — BAKERY
Napoleon's downfall — WATERLOO
Napoleon's forced retreat — ELBA
Napoleon's marshal — NEY
Napoleon's marshall and family — NEYS
Napoleon's place? — PASTRY SHOP
Napoleon, e.g. — EXILE
Napoleon, twice — EXILE
Napoleonic battle site: 1806 — JENA
Napoleonic marshal — NEY
Napoleonic victory site — LODI
Napoli dish — PASTA
Napoli night — NOTTE
Napoli or Milano — CITTA
Napped noisily — SNORED
Napped, as fabrics — FRIEZED
Nappy leather — SUEDE
Naps — DOZES, SIESTAS
Narc's prey — DOPER
Narcissus' love — ECHO
Narcotics — OPIATE
Nard — SALVE
Naris — NOSTRIL
Narrate anew — RETELL
Narrated — TOLD
Narrative — SAGA, TALE
Narrative poem — EPOS
Narrative poem by Byron — LARA
Narrator of a Chaucer tale — NUN
Narrow — NEAR
Narrow channel — STRIA
Narrow cut — SLIT
Narrow fillet — ORLE
Narrow furrow — STRIA
Narrow groove — STRIA
Narrow inlet — RIA
Narrow line forming a boundary — EDGE, FRINGE, RIM
Narrow minded — SMALL
Narrow neck of land — SPIT
Narrow notch — SLOT
Narrow opening — SLIT
Narrow passage — STRAIT
Narrow pew — SLIP
Narrow racing boat — SCULL
Narrow shelves — LEDGES
Narrow street — ALLEY
Narrow stretch of land — NECK
Narrow strip of wood — LATH
Narrow strip used in shipbuilding — RIBBAND
Narrow the eyes — SQUINT
Narrow urn — VASE
Narrow valleys — GLENS
Narrow walk — PATH
Narrow water passages — STRAITS
Narrow-minded — INSULAR
Narrow: Comb. form — STENO
Narrowing of a corporeal passage — STENOSIS
Narrowly defeated, with out — NOSED
Nary a body — NO ONE
Nary a person — NO ONE
Nary a soul — NO ONE
NASA approvals — AOKS
NASA cart — LEM
NASA lunar program — APOLLO
NASA rocket — AGENA
NASA space capsules — RKTS
NASA space probe — MARINER
NASA's Armstrong — NEIL
NASA's Sheppard — ALAN
Nasal — RHINAL
Nasal bone — VOMER
Nasal cavity — SINUS
Nasal passages — NARES
Nasal sounding — REEDY
Nasal: Comb. form — NASI
NASCAR vehicle — RACER
Nascent — RISING
Nash specialty — VERSE
Nashville campus — FISK
Naso of Rome — OVID
Nassau attraction — CASINO
Nasser's successor — SADAT
Nastase of tennis — ILIE
Nastase of the courts — ILIE
Nastase's nickname — NASTY
Nasty — MEAN, SNIDE
Nasty glances — LEERS
Nasty kid — BRAT
Nasty looks — LEERS
Nasty nickname for a chubby — FATSO
Nasty one — MEANIE, MEANY, RAT
Nasty remark — BARB
Nat "_____" Cole — KING
Nat and Natalie — COLES
Nat King Cole hit — MONA LISA
Nat or Lana — TURNER
Nat. travel org. — NTA
Natal native — ZULU
Natal seaport — DURBAN
Natalie and Nat King — COLES
Natalie Wood's sister — LANA
Natasha's cohort — BORIS
Nathan Hale's alma mater — YALE
Nathan, the patriot — HALE
Nathaniel, to friends — NATE
Nation — COUNTRY, KINGDOM, LAND
Nation born May 24, 1933 — ERITREA
Nation's foes — WETS
Nation: Comb. form — ETHNO
National _____ — DEBT
National character — ETHOS
National flag — UNION JACK
National guard — MILITIA
National hero of Hungary — ARPAD
National leader — INTER
National network of public television: Abbr. — PBS
National Park in Canada — BANFF
National Park in SW Alberta — JASPER
National Park in Wyoming — YELLOW STONE
National songs — ANTHEMS
National symbol — FLAG
Nationality: Abbr. — AMER
Nationwide mil. instruction — UMT
Native — ENDEMIC
Native ability — TALENT
Native American — CREE, KIOWA, OTOE, REE, SAC
Native American — UTE
Native American of puzzle fame — OTO
Native Americans of northeastern Arizona — HOPIS
Native born Israeli — SABRA
Native Canadian — CREE
Native dance — HULA
Native dog — DINGO
Native Egyptians — COPTS
Native land — HOME
Native of — ITE
Native of a city in SE France — ARLESIAN
Native of a S Iraq port — BASRAN
Native of Aberdeen — SCOT
Native of Asmara — ERITREAN
Native of Australia — MAORI
Native of Borneo — DAYAK
Native of Granada — ANDALUSIAN
Native of Hawaii — ISLANDER
Native of Isfahan — IRANI
Native of Israel — SABRA
Native of Jugoslavia — SERB
Native of Kuwait — ARAB
Native of Lahti — FINN
Native of Luzon — IGOROT

Native of Muscat — OMANI
Native of Natal — ZULU
Native of New Zealand — MAORI
Native of Oran — ALGERIAN
Native of Pakistan — SINDI
Native of Penang — MALAY
Native of Peru — INCA
Native of Qatar — ARAB
Native of Riga — LETT
Native of Riyadh — ARAB
Native of SE Idaho city — POCATELLAN
Native of Tehran — IRANI
Native of the highlands — SCOT
Native of the Orient — ASIAN
Native of W Alaska — ALEUT
Native of Zagreb — CROAT
Native of: Suffix — ITE
Native roofing — THATCH
Native ruler in Africa — AMEER
Native servant of Crusoe — FRIDAY
Native to the sea — MARINE
Native: Comb. form — OTE
Native: Suffix — ITE
Natives in northern Scandinavia — LAPPS
Natives of Benin City — EDOS
Natives of Bergen — NORWEGIANS
Natives of Cardiff — WELSH
Natives of Ecbatana, e.g. — MEDES
Natives of Esfahan — IRANIS
Natives of Riga — LETTS
Natives of Tampere — FINNS
Natives of the Arctic — ESKIMOS
Natives of Valletta — MALTESE
Natives of: Suffix — ITES
Natives: Suffix — ITES, OTES
Nativity — BIRTH
Nativity scene — CRECHE
Nativity suffix — ITE
Natl. cultural subsidy gp. — NEA
NATO member — USA
NATO, e.g. — PACT
NATO, for one — PACT
Natterjack — TOAD
Natty — SPIFFY
Natural ability — TALENT
Natural environment — HABITAT
Natural fabric — WOOL
Natural fertilizer — GUANO
Natural gas component — ETHANE
Natural gift — TALENT
Natural habitat — HOME
Natural height — STATURE
Natural resources — ORES
Natural satellite of a planet — MOON
Natural talent or gift — DOWER
Naturalist Fossey, et al. — DIANS
Naturalist John — MUIR
Naturalistic — LIFELIKE
Naturally — SIMPLY
Naturalness — EASE
Nature's nobleman's offering (M. Tupper) — HEART IN
Nature: Comb. form — PHYSI
Naught — NIL
Naughty — BAD
Nautical "cease" — BELAY
Nautical "halt" — AVAST
Nautical "stop" — AVAST
Nautical chain — TYE
Nautical command — ALEE, AVAST
Nautical cry — AVAST, SHIP AHOY
Nautical direction — ABEAM, ALEE, APORT, SBE
Nautical distance — SEAMILE
Nautical greeting — AHOY
Nautical hoisting device — CAPSTAN
Nautical miles per hour — KNOTS
Nautical miles: Abbr. — KTS
Nautical position — ASTERN
Nautical rope — HAWSER
Nautical spar — SPRIT
Nautical term — ABEAM, ALEE
Nautical term — ALEE
Nautical VIP — BOSUN
Nautilus commander — NEMO
Nav. craft — LST
Nav. off. — ENS, ADM
Nav. officer — ENS
Nav. officers — CDRS
Nav. officials — CPOS
Navaho's home — HOGAN
Navajo dwellings — HOGANS
Naval C.I.A. — ONI
Naval construction worker — SEABEE
Naval forces — ARMADA
Naval hazard of mythology — SIREN
Naval historian — MAHAN
Naval initials — USS
Naval NCO — CPO
Naval noncom — SEAMAN
Naval off. — CDR, ENS
Naval officer — CPO, ENSIGN
Naval officer Hopkins: 1718-1802 — ESEK
Naval ship — CARRIER, SHE
Naval unit — FLOTILLA
Naval vessel — SUB
Naval VIP's — ADMS, CNOS
Navigation aid — SONAR
Navigation hazard — REEF
Navigational aid — LORAN
Navigational problem — SANDBAR
Navigational system — LORAN
Navigator's aide — SEXTANT
Navigator's concern — ROUTE
Navigator's need — COMPASS
Navigators Islands, today — SAMOA
Navratilova rival — GRAF
Navratilova's competitor — EVERT
Navy bigwig: Abbr. — ADM
Navy builder — SEABEE
Navy coffee — MUD
Navy constructor — SEABEE
Navy four striper — CAPTAIN
Navy man: Abbr. — ADM
Navy or lima — BEAN
Navy ship initial — USS
Navy woman — WAVE
Navy's C.I.A. — ONI
Navy's nonsense — TOSH
Navy-yard area — PIER
Naysayer — DENIER
Nazimova — ALLA
Nazimova of silents — ALLA
Nazis — BROWN SHIRTS
NBA Hall of Famer Thurmond — NATE
NBA nickname of fame — DR J
NBA setting — ARENA
NBA superstar Larry — BIRD
NBA team — NETS
NBA whistler — REF
NBA's Archibald or Thurmond — NATE
NBA's Birdsong — OTIS
NBA's Bol — MANUTE
NBA's Miami _____ — HEAT
NBA's Unseld — WES
NBC show — TODAY
NBC's rival — CBS
NCO — MSGT, SFC, SGT, SSGT
NCO York, e.g. — SGT
NCO, familiarly — SARGE
NCOs — SGTS
NE capital — BOS
NE Italian city — ESTE
NE N.J. city — LODI
Ne plus _____ — ULTRA
Ne plus ultra — ACME
Ne'er do well — LOSER
Ne'er-do-wells — IDLERS
Neap and ebb — TIDE
Neap or ebb — TIDE
Neapolitan fruit? — CAPRICOT
Near East chieftain — EMIR
Near East gulf — ADEN
Near East ketch — SAIC
Near East name — OMAR
Near Eastern coin — DINAR
Near enough to shoot at — IN RANGE
Near Group island — ATTU
Near Islands member — ATTU
Near or Far — EAST

Near sightedness — MYOPIA
Near the deck — ALOW
Near the fantail — ASTERN
Nearby — CLOSE, NIGH
Nearby, poetically — ANIGH
Nearer — CLOSER
Nearly — ALMOST
Nearness — PROPINQUITY
Neat as _____ — A PIN
Neat, in the Highlands — SNOD
Neath's opposite — OER
Neb — BEAK
Neb. neighbor — KAN
Nebr. neighbor — KAN
Nebraska city — OMAHA
Nebraska governor Kay — ORR
Nebraska's capital — LINCOLN
Nebraskan city — OMAHA
Nebraskan Indian — OTOES
Nebraskan Native American — OMAHA
Necessities — NEEDS
Necessity for a screwdriver — VODKA
Necessity for big business — BANK CREDIT
Necessity for skiing — SNOW
Neck area — NAPE
Neck artery — CAROTID
Neck hair — MANE
Neck jewelry — BEADS
Neck part — NAPE
Neck piece — FICHU
Neck-and-neck — EVEN
Necklace fastening — HASP
Necklace gem — PEARL
Necklace part — CLASP, PEARLET
Neckline shapes — VEES
Necklines — VEES
Neckpiece — SCARF
Necktie — ASCOT
Neckties — CRAVATS
Neckwear — ASCOTS, CRAVAT, TIES, SCARF
Neckwear accessory — TIETAC
Neckwear for Sen. Simon — BOWTIES
Nectar collector — BEE
Nectares — SWEET
Nectarine — PEACH
Ned of radio news — CALMER
Nedda's husband — CANIO
Need — WANT
Need a breather — PANT
Need for a Perry Mason client — ALIBI
Need greens for them — SALADS
Needing a diet — ROTUND
Needing a washer — DRIPPY
Needle — RIB, TWIT
Needle cases — ETUIS
Needle feature — EYE
Needle holders — ETUIS
Needle part — ETE
Needle shaped — ACERATE
Needle: Comb. form — ACU
Needlefish — GAR
Needlework loop — BRIDE
Needs — REQS
Needy — POOR
Negates — ANNULS
Negation in Nurnberg — NEIN, NICHT, NIE
Negative conjunction — NOR
Negative connective — NOR
Negative contraction — DONT, ISNT
Negative horse? — NEIGHSAYER
Negative imperative — DO NOT
Negative joiner — NOR
Negative particles — ANIONS
Negative prefix — NON
Negative Presidential role — VETOER
Negative replies — NOS
Negative terminal — ANODE
Negative terminals — CATHODES
Negative votes — NAYS
Negatively charged ion — ANION
Negatively charged particle — ANION
Negatives — NOTS
Negev and Nefud — DESERTS
Neglect — IGNORE, OMIT, OVERSIGHT
Neglect of duty — OMISSION
Negligent — CARELESS, REMISS, SLACK
Negotiate — TREAT
Negri of films — POLA
Negri silents — POLA
Nehru, e.g. — INDIAN
Neigh — BRAY
Neighbor of a humerus — ULNA
Neighbor of Afghanistan — IRAN
Neighbor of Ala. — FLA
Neighbor of Alta. — MONT
Neighbor of Arg. — URU
Neighbor of Aust. — GER
Neighbor of Braz. — ARG
Neighbor of Caen — ST LO
Neighbor of Canada — MAINE
Neighbor of Esth. and Pol. — LITH
Neighbor of Greece — ALBANIA
Neighbor of Hades — EREBUS
Neighbor of Hung. — AUST
Neighbor of Iraq: Abbr. — SYR
Neighbor of Isr. — SYR
Neighbor of Ky. — IND
Neighbor of Latvia — ESTH
Neighbor of Leyte — SAMAR
Neighbor of Libya — CHAD
Neighbor of Md. — DEL
Neighbor of Metz — NANCY
Neighbor of Mex. — USA
Neighbor of Mich. — ONT
Neighbor of Minn. — NDAK, SDAK
Neighbor of Minneapolis — EDINA
Neighbor of Mont. — ALTA, SDAK
Neighbor of Nebr. — WYO
Neighbor of Nepal — INDIA
Neighbor of Nev. — CALIF
Neighbor of Nigeria — BENIN
Neighbor of Norw. — SWED
Neighbor of old Palestine — EDOM
Neighbor of Ont. — MINN
Neighbor of Oreg. — COLO
Neighbor of Padua — ESTE
Neighbor of Para. — BOL
Neighbor of Perugia — ASSISI, SPOLETO
Neighbor of Philadelphia — CAMDEN
Neighbor of Phoenix — MESA
Neighbor of Que. — ONT
Neighbor of Russia — UKRAINE
Neighbor of Scorpius — ARA
Neighbor of Silver Springs — OCALA
Neighbor of Syr. — ISR, LEB
Neighbor of Thailand — LAOS
Neighbor of Tibet — NEPAL
Neighbor of Turkey — IRAN
Neighbor of Twelve Oaks — TARA
Neighbor of Venice — LUDINE, PADUA
Neighbor of Wis. — MINN
Neighbor of Wyo. — MONT
Neighbor of Zaire — UGANDA
Neighbor or the radius — ULNA
Neighbor to Fin. — USSR
Neighbor's child? — BRAT
Neighborhood — AREA, NECK OF THE WOODS
Neighborhood — ENVIRONS, LOCALE
Neighborhood gathering — BEE
Neighborly — NEAR
Neighborly talk — CHAT
Neighbors of the radii — ULNAE
Neil Shicoff is one — TENOR
Neil Simon comedy — CALIFORNIA SUITE
Neil Simon play and TV success — THE ODD COUPLE
Neil Simon product — PLAY
Neil's 1935 merchant? — DIAMOND JIM

Neither animal nor vegetable — MINERAL
Neither Dem. or Rep. — IND
Neither fem. nor neut. — MASC
Neither fish _____ fowl — NOR
Neither his nor hers — ITS
Neither oui nor non — PEUTETRE
Neither's companion — NOR
Neither's partner — NOR
Neither's tagalong — NOR
Nellie _____ — BLY
Nellie _____, first American governor, 1924 — ROSS
Nelson and Springfield — RICKS
Nelson of the movies — EDDY
Nemesis' realm — EVIL
Nemo or Kangaroo: Abbr. — CAPT
Nemo's record — LOG
Nene cry — HONK
Neon — GAS
Neon and xenon — GASES
Neon's job — SIGN ILLUMINATOR
Neon, et al. — GASSES
Neophyte — TYRO
Nepal native — ASIAN
Nepal's neighbor — INDIA
Neph., for one — REL
Nephric — RENAL
Nephrite — GREENSTONE, JADE
Nepotism — BIAS
Neptune's scepter — TRIDENT
Neptune's spear — TRIDENT
Nerd — SAP
Nero or O'Toole — PETER
Nero Wolfe author — STOUT
Nero's 905 — CMV
Nero's cover-up — TOGA
Nero's M, today — 1000
Nero's nephew — NEPOS
Nero's salutation — AVE
Nero's teacher — SENECA
Nero's tongue: Abbr. — LAT
Nerve — BRASS, CHEEK
Nerve cell — NEURON
Nerve cell part — AXON
Nerve cell process — AXON
Nerve network — RETE
Nerve: Comb. form — NEUR
Nerves of _____ — STEEL
Nervous — ANTSY, EDGY, NELLY
Nervous ailments — TICS
Nervous disorder — CHOREA
Nervous laugh — TITTER
Nervous Nellie — FIDGETER
Nervous, Australian style — TOEY
Nervously — UNEASILY
Nervy — GAME
Ness for one — LOCH
Nest — AERIE
Nest alert — PEEP
Nest egg — STORE
Nest egg funds — IRA
Nest egg inits. — IRA
Nest eggs — ASSETS
Nest eggs: Abbr. — IRAS
Nest noise — CHIRP
Nest of pheasants — NIDE
Nest-building fish — ACARA
Nested boxes, from Japan — INRI
Nesting places — BRANCHES
Nestle — CUDDLE
Nestling hawk — EYAS
Nestlings' cries — PEEPS
Net — SEINE
Net locale — COURT
Net nicker — LET
Net on a schooner — SEINE
Net, in business — CLEAR
Neth. neighbor — GER
Neth. town — EDE
Netherland's city — LEIDEN
Netherland's East Indies — INDONESIA
Netherland's town — EDE
Netherlandish — DUTCHY
Netherlands' export — EDAM, TULIP
Netherworld — HADES
Netman Arthur — ASHE
Netman Budge — DON
Netman Camporese — OMAR
Netman Connors — JIMMY
Netman from D.C. — HAROLD SOLOMON
Netman Lendl — IVAN
Netman Nastase — ILIE
Netman of note — ASHE
Netman Wilander — MATS
Netman Yannick's family — NOAHS
Nets and Mets — TEAMS
Nets, Mets and Jets — TEAMS
Netted — CLEARED
Netter Nastase — ILIE
Netting — MESH
Nettle — ANNOY, IRK, PEEVE, RILE, WORRY
Nettles — GRATES
Network — CHAIN, GRID, RETE, WEB
Network letters — CBS
Network monogram — CBS
Network or knitwork — MESH
Networks — RETIA, WEBS
Neural — DORSAL, NERVE
Neural networks — RETIA
Neurons' junction point — SYNAPSE
Neurosis — HYSTERIA
Neurosurg. reading — EMG
Neutral — EVEN
Neutral shade — ECRU
Neutralized an asp — DEFANGED
Nev. neighbor — CAL, CALIF
Nev. resort — TAHOE, RENO
Nev.'s neighbor — ARIZ
Nevada blast — A TEST
Nevada city — ELKO
Nevada Indian — MOHAVE, PAIUTE
Nevada lode — COMSTOCK
Nevada mecca — RENO
Nevada resort — RENO
Nevada resort area — TAHOE
Nevada tourist center — RENO
Nevada town — ELKO
Nevada's second city — RENO
Neve — FIRN, SNOW FIELD
Never — A MONTH OF SUNDAYS
Never _____ moment — A DULL
Never _____! — AGAIN
Never before a horse — CART
Never before, in Bonn — NIE
Never boiler — A WATCHED POT
Never buy a pig in one! — POKE
Never, in Nüremberg — NIE
Never, to a poet — NEER
Nevertheless — AFTER ALL, EVEN SO
Nevertheless — IN A WAY
Nevus — MOLE
New — ADDITIONAL, FRESH, EXTRA, FURTHER, LATE
New _____, Conn. — HAVEN
New beginning — NEO
New broom — CLEAN SWEEPER
New Brunswick island — CAMPOBELLO
New car calamity — DENT
New coalition after the first failed — RE ALLIANCE
New Deal agcy. — NRA, RFC
New Deal org. — NRA
New Deal prog. — WPA
New Delhi delicacy — INDIAN CURRY
New England cape — ANN, COD
New England eleven, familiarly — PATS
New England fisherman's boat — DORY
New England prep school — ANDOVER
New England state — MAINE
New England's contribution — ROAST TURKEY
New Guinea city — RABAUL
New Guinea gulf — HUON
New Guinea islands — ARU
New Guinea port — LAE, MORESBY

New Guinea sea — CORAL
New Guinea strait — TORRES
New Guinea, to Indonesians — IRIAN
New Guinean city — LAE
New Haven institution — YALE
New Haven name — ELI
New Haven students — ELIS
New Haven, City of _____ — ELMS
New Hebrides island — EFATE
New in Nürnberg — NEU
New Jersey airport — NEWARK
New Jersey athlete — NET
New Jersey cagers — NETS
New Jersey city — NEWARK
New Jersey five — NETS
New Jersey port — CARNEY
New Jersey pros — NETS
New Jersey sinker — DOUGHNUT
New Jersey town — LODI
New Mexican art colony — TAOS
New Mexican brick — ADOBE
New Mexico gulch — ARROYO
New Mexico Pueblo Indian — KERES
New Mexico resort — TAOS
New Mexico town — TAOS
New mom or pop — NAMER
New Netherland landowners — PATROONS
New on the job — GREEN
New or Old city of India — DELHI
New Orleans athlete — SAINT
New Orleans eleven — SAINTS
New Orleans event — MARDI GRAS PARADE
New Orleans Fountain — PETE
New Orleans institution — TULANE
New Orleans player — SAINT
New Orleans pro — SAINT
New Persia — IRAN
New pilot's feat — SOLO
New productions of old plays — REVIVALS
New Rochelle campus — IONA
New Rochelle college — IONA
New Rochelle school — IONA
New Rochelle, NY college — IONA
New securities offering — ISSUE
New student — FROSH
New Testament book — ACTS, MARK
New Testament letter — EPISTLE
New title for Schwarzkopf — SIR
New versions of old movies — REMAKES
New wine — MUST
New world org. — OAS
New World rodent — DEGU
New Year Festival in Vietnam — TET
New Year's Eve relative — FATHER TIME
New Year's Eve visitor — FATHER TIME
New Year's Eve word — SYNE
New Year's word — AULD
New York and San Diego — SEAPORTS
New York canal — ERIE
New York City Ballet's Peter Martins, e.g. — DANE
New York City brownstone house feature — STOOP
New York City nickname — GOTHAM
New York City river — EAST
New York flag feature — STATE COAT OF ARMS
New York Governor: 1932-42 — LEHMAN
New York iceman — RANGER
New York island — FIRE
New York lake or river — ONEIDA
New York player — GIANT, JET
New York prison — SING SING
New York river — HUDSON
New York silverware city — ONEIDA
New York State bird — BLUEBIRD
New York State spa — SARATOGA
New York town on Great South Bay — ISLIP
New York's nickname — EMPIRE STATE
New York's rialto — BROADWAY
New York's Tuesday — WELD
New York, the _____ state — EMPIRE
New York, to some — THE BIG APPLE
New Zealand bird — KIWI
New Zealand discoverer — TASMAN
New Zealand native — MAORI
New Zealand parrots — KEA, KAKA
New Zealand sheep-killer — KEA
New Zealand statesman: 1878-1943 — COATES
New Zealand symbol — KIWI
New Zealand tree — RATA
New Zealander — MAORI
New, to Juan — NUEVO
New-born — NEONATAL
New: Abbr. — ORIG
New: Comb form — NEO
New: Comb. form — NEO
New: Prefix — NEO
Newborn's outfit — LAYETTE
Newcomer — GREENHORN, STRANGER
Newcomer in January — YEAR
Newel — POST
Newf., e.g. — ISL
Newfangled — MODERN
Newfoundland's nosh — ORT
Newfoundlander's narrow lane — DRANG
Newhart and Hope — BOBS
Newly — AFRESH
Newlywed — BRIDE
Newlyweds — BRIDES AND GROOMS
Newlyweds' purchase — DINING ROOM SUITE
Newman film — THE TOWERING INFERNO
Newman or Simon — PAUL
Newman role: 1961 — HUSTLER
Newmen Pappas and Seaman — IKES
News — ADVICE, WORD
News acct. — BUL
News agency in the news — TASS
News article — STORY
News bit — ITEM
News broadcasters — CRIERS
News chief — EDITOR
News coup — SCOOP
News flash — BULLETIN
News hawker of yore: Waxer — CRYER
News information — CURRENT EVENTS
News information — SPORTS UPDATES
News information — WEATHER FORECAST
News item lead — DATELINE
News item, briefly — OBIT
News item, for short — OBIT
News items — OBITS
News nugget — ITEM
News office unit — DESK
News room unit — DESK
News round-up — RECAP
News source — LEAK
News squibb — ITEM
News staff — REPORTERS
News time — SIX
News windup — RECAP
Newscaster Huntley — CHET
Newshound's prize — SCOOP
Newsman Dan, et al. — RATHERS
Newsman Donaldson — SAM
Newsman Elie — ABEL
Newsman James _____ — RESTON

Newsman Koppel — TED
Newsman Pyle: 1900-45 — ERNIE
Newsman Rather — DAN
Newsman Roger _____ — MUDD
Newsman Sevareid — ERIC
Newspaper department — ART
Newspaper editorial, British style — LEADER
Newspaper employee, for example — STAFFER
Newspaper entry — ITEM
Newspaper feature — COMICS, ESSAY
Newspaper feature, for short — OBIT
Newspaper headline — DATELINE
Newspaper item, for short — OBIT
Newspaper listing — MASTHEAD
Newspaper notice — OBIT
Newspaper of the USSR — PRAVDA
Newspaper paragraph — ITEM
Newspaper part — BANNER
Newspaper people: Var. — EDS
Newspaper publishing family — HEARSTS
Newspaper section — SPORTS
Newspaper section, for short — ROTO
Newspaper stat. — CIRC
Newspaper story — FEATURE
Newspaper supplement — COMICS
Newspaper topper — HEADLINE
Newspaper VIPs — EDS
Newspaper's photo section, once — ROTO
Newspaperman — EDITOR
Newspapers — DAILIES
Newspapers, radio, TV, etc. — MEDIA
Newsperson — EDITOR, REPORTER
Newsstand — KIOSK
Newsy — TOPICAL
Newsy digest — RECAP
Newsy summaries — RECAPS
Newton — ISAAC
Newton or Hayes — ISAAC
Newton or Stern — ISAAC
Newts — EFTS
Next below a marquess — EARL
Next in rank to an Earl — VISCOUNT
Next to — BESIDE
Next year's grads. — SRS
Next year's soph — FROSH
Nexus — BOND
Nez _____ (American Indian) — PERCE
NFL 6-pointers — TDS
NFL player — PRO
NFL scores — TDS
NFL team — RAMS
NFL's Eubanks — WEEB
NH motto — LIVE FREE OR DIE
NHL arena — ICE RINK
NHL shutout — OOO
NHL'er — ICEMAN, SABER
Niacin is one — ACID
Niacin, e.g. — ACID
Nibble — NOSH
Nibbler — EATER
Nibbles at — PICKS
Nibelungenlied character — HAGEN
Niblick sockets — HOSELS
Nicaraguan group — RAMAS
Nicaraguan president — ORTEGA
Nicaraguan rebels — CONTRAS
Nicaraguan's nap — SIESTA
Nice — PLEASANT
Nice farewell — ADIEU
Nice man — HOMME
Nice night — NUIT
Nice nose — NEZ
Nice notion — IDEE
Nice piece of change — FRANC
Nice recreation area — PARC
Nice school — ECOLE
Nice season — ETE
Nice seasoning — SEL
Nice summer — ETE
Nice time — ETE
Nice wave — ONDE
Nicely lined up — AROW
Nicene _____ — CREED
Nicene of Apostles — CREED
Nicety — NUANCE
Niche — CORNER, HOLE
Niche objects — ICONS
Niche occupant — ICON
Nicholas Gage book — ELENI
Nicholas I and II — TSARS
Nicholas II and Ivan IV — TSARS
Nicholas II, e.g. — TSAR
Nichols hero — ABIE
Nichols' heroine — ROSE
Nicholson with a homily? — JACK IN THE PULPIT
Nicholson/Streep film, 1987 — IRON WEED
Nick — DENT, MAR
Nick and Nora's dog — ASTA
Nick and Nora's pooch — ASTA
Nick Charles — ASTAS MASTER
Nick Charles' wife — NORA
Nick Nolte film, with "The" — DEEP
Nick of the movies — NOLTE
Nick's spouse — NORA
Nickels and dimes — CHANGE
Nicklaus collection — PRIZES
Nickleby actor Roger — REES
Nickname — HANDLE
Nickname abbr. — AKA
Nickname akin to Ricky — RODDY
Nickname at the rodeo — TEX
Nickname for a carrot top — RED
Nickname for a family member — SIS
Nickname for a noncom — SARGE
Nickname for DDE — IKE
Nickname for Eddy — NEL
Nickname for Edith — EDIE
Nickname for Esther — ESSIE
Nickname for namesakes of Mrs. Kennedy — ROSES
Nickname for Teresa — TESS
Nickname for Theresa — TERRI
Nickname meaning "like a lion" — LEN
Nickname of "Land of 10,000 Lakes" — NORTH STAR
Nickname of a former N.L. slugger — KLU
Nickname of a Shakespearean prince — HAL
Nickname of hockey's Phil — ESPO
Nickname of J.F.K.'s grandfather — HONEY FITZ
Nickname, often disparaging — EPITHET
Nicoise, for one — SALAD
Nidus — NEST
Niels Bohr's subject — ATOM
Nielsen or Uggams — LESLIE
Nielsen ratings — SWEEPS
Nieuport's river — YSER
Nifty — CHIC
Niger's neighbor — CHAD
Nigerian capital — LAGOS
Nigerian city — EDE, LAGOS
Nigerian group — EFIKS
Nigerian native — ARO, IBO, EDO, NUPE
Nigerian seaport — LAGOS
Nigerian singer — SADE
Nigerian town — EDE
Niggardly — MEAN, NEAR, STINGY
Niggling — PETTY
Nigh — ANEAR
Night adventure — DREAM
Night before — EVE
Night flight — REDEYE
Night flyer — OWL
Night light — NEON, STAR
Night music? — SNORE

Night prowlers — TOMCATS
Night ray — MOONBEAM
Night sights — NEONS
Night sound — HOOT, SNORE
Night spot — DISCO
Night watchman in early London — CHARLEY
Night watchman's residence — GUARD IN APARTMENT
Night's brightest star — SIRIUS
Night, in Caen — NUIT
Night, in Koln — NACHT
Night, in Milano — NOTTE
Night, in Nantes — NUIT
Nightclub — BOITE
Nightclub activity — BALLROOM DANCING
Nightclub employee — EMCEE
Nightclubs — BISTROS, CABARETS
Nightingale and others — NURSES
Nightingale or Cavell — NURSE
Nightingale types — NURSES
Nightingale's prop — LAMP
Nightingale's symbol — LAMP
Nightingale's vessel — LAMP
Nightly noise — SNORE
Nightmares — INCUBI
Nightmarish — SCARY
Nights before — EVES
Nights before holidays — EVES
Nights preceding — EVES
Nights, to Byron — EENS
Nighttime disturbances — SNORES
Nighttime predator — OWL
Nighttime sign — NEON
Nightwear — ROBE
Nihal or Nunki — STAR
Nijinsky ballet — THE AFTERNOON OF A FAUN
Nike's reveries? — DREAMS OF VICTORY
Nikolaidi of the Met — ELENA
Nil — ZERO
Nil, in tennis — LOVE
Nile avifauna — IBISES
Nile bird — IBIS
Nile dam — ASWAN
Nile delta city — TANTA
Nile denizens, for short — CROCS
Nile green — BOA
Nile hazards — ASPS
Nile killers — ASPS
Nile ophidians — ASPS
Nile queen — CLEO
Nile reptile — ASP
Nile river capital — CAIRO
Nimbi — AURAE, HALOS
Nimble — ADROIT, AGILE, LITHE, YARE
Nimbus — AURA, HALO
Nimitz' svc. — USN
Nimrod — HUNTER
Nincompoop — DIMWIT, SAP
Nine-sided figures — NONAGONS
Nine in the sticks — BUSH LEAGUE TEAM
Nine inches — SPAN
Nine performers — NONET
Nine popes — STEPHENS
Nine saver — A STITCH IN TIME
Nine to fiver — STENO
Nine, in combinations — ENNEA
Nine, in Napoli — NOVE
Nine-part composition — NONET
Nine: Comb. form — ENNEA, ENNE
Nine: Prefix — ENNEA
Nineteenth letter — TAU
Nineveh and _____ — TYRE
Ninnies — ASSES
Ninny — ASS, BOOB
Ninny needs three — ENS
Ninth letter — IOTA
Ninth mo. — SEPT
Ninth President of the United States — HARRISON
Ninth: Comb. form — NONA
Ninut — MAGPIE
Niña and her sisters — CARAVELS
Niobe product — TEAR
Niobe's father — TANTALUS
Nip — BITE, DRAM
Nip in the bud — PINCH, STYMIE, TWEAK
Nipa palm — ATAP
Nipper's co. — RCA
Nippon ship word — MARU
Nis natives — SERBS
Nit's cousin — TWIT
Nit-pick — CARP, CAVEL, SPLIT HAIRS
Nita of the silents — NALDI
Nitid — BRIGHT
Nitrous oxide, e.g. — GAS
Nitti's nemesis — NESS
Nitty-gritty — CRUX, GIST
Nitwit — SAP
Nitwits — ASSES
Nivellate — LEVEL
Niven of Scotland — DAVID
Nixon nix, once — VETO
Nixon running mate — AGNEW
Nixon's defense secretary — LAIRD
Nixon's dog — CHECKERS
Nizer subject — LIBEL
NJ NBA team — NETS
NL homer champ: 1936-38 — OTT
NNE plus 180 degrees — SSW
No _____ — DICE
No better — WORSE
No charge — FREE
No Clowning, Sir!: 1988 Derby — WINNING COLORS
No extremist, he — MIDDLE OF THE ROADER
No foe — PAL
No genius he — MORON
No gentleman he — CAD
No good — BAD
No great shakes — SOSO
No ifs, _____ or buts — ANDS
No ifs, ands or _____ — BUTS
No ivory-tower resident he — REALIST
No longer a minor — ADULT
No longer ahead — OVERTAKEN
No longer current — DATED
No longer fresh — STALE
No longer green — RIPE
No longer in demand — PASSE
No longer on the ship — OVERBOARD
No longer present — GONE
No longer wild — TAME
No longer working: Abbr. — RET
No more than — MERE
No particular person — ANYONE
No particular place — ANYWHERE
No party pooper he — GOOD TIME CHARLIE
No place like _____ — HOME
No problem — SNAP
No rod sparer — SWITCHER
No room at the inn? — FULL HOUSE
No special place — ANY-WHERE
No spur for this poet — SAMUEL COLE
No use — IDLE
No, _____! — SIREE
No, CB terminology — NEGATORY
No, for one — DOCTOR
No, for one: Abbr. — NEG
No, in the Highlands — NAE
No, per Herr Schmidt — NEIN
No, to Ho — AOLE
No, to Tsars — NYET
No-no — TABOO, TABU
No-no for a pitcher — BALK
No-no in some diets — SALT, SPICE
No-nukes group — SANE
No-see-um — GNAT
No. 1 — PRES
No. 1 or 40, e.g. — RTE
No. 9 on a menology — SEP
Noah's eldest — SHEM
Noah's haven — ARARAT
Noah's landfall — ARARAT
Noah's numbers — TWOS

Noah's oldest — SHEM
Nobel Peace Prize co-winner: 1978 — SADAT
Nobel Peace Prize winner of 1978 — SADAT
Nobel Peace Prize winner: 1987 — ARIAS
Nobel physicist: 1943 — STERN
Nobel physicist: 1944 — RABI
Nobel physicist: 1945 — PAULI
Nobel prize winner for chemistry: 1950 — ADLER
Nobelist Bishop Desmond _____ — TUTU
Nobelist for literature: 1948 — EMOIT
Nobelist for Peace: 1958 — PIRE
Nobelist for Peace: 1987 — ARIAS
Nobelist from Poland: 1983 — WALESA
Nobelist in Chemistry: 1918 — HABER
Nobelist in Chemistry: 1922 — ASTON
Nobelist in Literature: 1923 — YEATS
Nobelist in Literature: 1938 — PEARL S BUCK
Nobelist in Literature: 1946 — HESSE
Nobelist in Literature: 1948 — ELIOT
Nobelist in Literature: 1957 — CAMUS
Nobelist in Medicine: 1906 — GOLGI
Nobelist in Physics: 1912 — DALEN
Nobelist in Physics: 1944 — RABI
Nobelist in Physics: 1959 — SEGRE
Nobelist in Physics: 1973 — ESAKI
Nobelist Lagerlof — SELMA
Nobelist Mother _____ — TERESA
Nobelist Root — ELIHU
Nobelist Walesa and namesakes — LECHS
Nobelist Wiesel — ELIE
Nobelman — EARL
Nobility — PEERAGE
Nobility level — BARONET
Noble — GRAND
Noble Ferrara family name — ESTE
Noble Italian family — ESTE
Noble of ancient Athens — EUPATRID
Noble person — SALT OF THE EARTH
Noble rank — BARONY
Noble vacillator — HAMLET
Nobleman — EARL, LORD, PEER
Nobleman — LORD
Nobleman in Chaucer's day — ERL
Noblewomen — COUNTESS
Nobodies — SMALL POTATOES
Nocturnal badger — RATEL
Nocturnal insect — MOTH
Nocturnal mammal — LEMUR
Nocturnal pest — SNORER
Nocturnal sawyers — SNORERS
Nod visitor — SLEEPER
Nod's neighbor — EDEN
Nodded — DOZED
Noddy or sooty — TERN
Nods — ERRS
Nods off — DROWSES
Nodular — LUMPY
Nodular stone — GEODE
Noel — CAROL, COWARD
Noel mother — VIRGIN MARY
Noel singers — CAROLERS
Noelis Hunter — EVAN
Noggin — BEAN, PATE
Noise — CLAMOR, DIN
Noise in the night — SNORE
Noisemaker of a sort — RATTLE
Noisemakers, paper hats, etc. — FAVORS
Noises about — BRUITS
Noisette — HAZEL
Noisy — LOUD
Noisy birds — JAYS
Noisy brawl — AFFRAY
Noisy disturbance — BROIL
Noisy grasshoppers — KATYDIDS
Noisy jets — SSTS
Noisy quarrel — SPAT
Noisy sleeper — SNORER
Noisy, mock serenade — SHIVAREE
Nol of Cambodia — LON
Nolan Ryan stat — ERA
Nom de guerre — ALIAS
Nom de plume — ALIAS
Nom de plume, of a sort — ALIAS
Nomad — ROVER
Nomadic Ethiopian — AFAR
Nomadic reindeer herders — LAPPS
Nomadic type — ROVER
Nome in 1899 — BOOM TOWN
Nome time zone: Abbr. — AST
Nominate them all? — NAME NO ONE MAN
Nominator — NAMER
Nomologist's forte — LAW
Non-barking dog — BESENJI
Non _____ — GRATA
Non compos _____ — MENTIS
Non flying bird — RHEA
Non-clerical — LAIC
Non-coms — CPOS
Non-ecclesiastic — LAIC
Non-specific list item — ETC
Nonbeliever — ATHEIST, PAGAN
Nonbeliever's viewpoint — ATHEISTIC
Nonchalant — AIRY
Noncom — NCO, SGT
Noncom — SGT
Noncommittal — GUARDED
Nonconformist — HERETIC, ICONOCLAST
None other — SAME
Nonentity — RES NIHILI
Nonetheless — ANYWAYS
Nonexistent — VOID
Noninformer — CLAM
Nonmetallic element — BORON
Nonpareil — ONER
Nonpartisan — JUST, NEUTRAL
Nonpayer — CRIME
Nonplus — STUMP
Nonplussed — FLOORED
Nonprofessionals — LAYMEN
Nonsense — BALONEY, BOSH, HOT AIR
Nonsense — HORSE FEATHERS, IDIOCY, PIFFLE, ROT
Nonsense! — BOSH, BLAH, TOSH, TRIPE
Nonsense, in Soho — CODS WALLOP
Nonsense: Slang — NERTS
Nonstandard speech — SLANG
Nonstick coating — TEFLON
Nonsuccesses — LOSSES
Nonterrestrial — ALIEN
Nonvenomous reptile — WART SNAKE
Nonwindy side — ALEE
Nonwinners at the track — MAIDENS
Noody and soot seabirds — TERNS
Nook — COVE
Nookeries — DENS
Noon — MIDDAY
Noon lead-in — AFTER
Noon, for one — HOUR
Noose — LOOP
Nope — NIX
Nope's opposite — YEAH
Nor's companion — NEITHER
Nor. money — KRONE
Nora's pet — ASTA
Nora's pooch — ASTA
Nordic, to a Nazi — ARYAN
Norfolk-New York vector — NNE
Norm — PAR

Norm's unseen wife in "Cheers" — VERA
Norm: Abbr. — STD
Norma and Charlotte — RAES
Norma Jean Baker — MONROE
Norma or Charlotte — RAE
Norma or Moira — SHEARER
Normal requirement: Abbr. — STD
Normal value — PAR
Normal: Abbr. — REG
Norman Bates place — MOTEL
Norman battle town — ST LO
Norman city — CAEN
Norman Mailer book, with "The" — DEER PARK
Norman of TV — LEAR
Norman or Mills — DIVA
Norman town — ST LO
Norman Vincent — PEALE
Normand of silents — MABEL
Normandy city — CAEN
Normandy invasion town — ST LO
Normandy W.W. II objective — ST LO
Norms: Abbr. — STDS
Norse alphabet — RUNICS
Norse capital — OSLO
Norse chieftain — ROLLO
Norse deity — ODIN, THOR
Norse epic — EDDA
Norse explorer — ERIC
Norse Fate — NORN
Norse god — ODIN, TIR
Norse god of mischief — LOKI
Norse goddess — FREYA, HEL
Norse goddess of death — HEL
Norse goddess of fate — NORN
Norse goddess of healing — EIR
Norse gods — AESIR, VANIR
Norse king: 975 AD — OLAFI
Norse love goddess — FREYA
Norse monarch — OLAF
Norse name — SVEN
Norse narratives — EDDAS
Norse poem — RUNE
Norse poems — EDDAS
Norse poetry collection — EDDA
Norse precursor of William Tell — EGI
Norse saint — OLAV
Norse tale — SAGA
Norse underworld goddess — HEL
Norse war god — TYR
Norse wife of Odin — FRIGGA
North African capital — TUNIS
North African ruler of old — DEY
North African seaport — ORAN
North American apple — WINESAP
North American Indian — CADOO, SHAWNEE
North American Indians' pipe of peace — CALUMET
North American mountain range — ROCKY
North American rail — SORA
North American skunks — POLECATS
North American tribe — OMAHA
North Atlantic menaces — ICEBERGS
North Carolina athletes — TARHEELS
North Carolina campus — ELON
North Carolina cape — FEAR
North Carolina college — ELON
North Carolina river — TRENT
North chaser — ERN
North Dakota city — MINOT
North follower — ERN
North Germanic language: Var. — FAROESE
North of the PGA — ANDY
North or South — POLE
North or south follower — ERN
North Pole helpers — ELVES
North Sea feeder — ELBE, EMS, TEES, YSER
North sea firth — TAY
North Sea tributary — ELBE, YSER
North star — POLARIS
North, in Nogales — NORTE
North, in Nuevo Laredo — NORTE
North, of Hollywood — SHEREE
Northern bear — POLAR
Northern capital — OSLO
Northern Connecticut town — TOLLAND
Northern constellation — DRACO
Northern deer — MOOSE
Northern deer family member — MOOSE
Northern diving bird — AUK
Northern European — LAPP, SCAND
Northern highway — ALCAN
Northern Indian — HINDU
Northern Islander — ALEUT
Northern native — ESKIMO
Northern New York to New Yorkers — UPSTATE
Northern nomad — LAPP
Northern sea birds — AUKS
Northern Spy — APPLE VARIETY
Northumberland river — ALN
Northwest catch — SALMON
Northwest Coast pole — TOTEM
Norw. news service — NTB
Norway in Norway — NORGE
Norway's capital — OSLO
Norway's patron saint — OLAF
Norwegian coastal feature — FIORD
Norwegian coin — ORE
Norwegian composer — GRIEG, OLSEN
Norwegian dramatist — IBSEN
Norwegian king — OLAV
Norwegian kings — OLAFS
Norwegian monarch — OLAV
Norwegian river — OTRA
Norwegian saint — OLAF
Norwegian sight — FIORD
Nos. expert — CPA
Nos. people — CPAS
Nos. person — CPA
Nose — BEAK, PROBOSCIS, SNOOT
Nose about — PRY
Nose around — ROOT
Nose feature — ALARE
Nose job: Var. — RHINO
Nose part — ALARE
Nose, in Nuremburg — NASE
Nose, of a sort — ROMAN
Nose: Comb. form — RHINO
Nosegay — POSY
Nosh — SNACK
Nosh or snack — EAT
Nosh shop — DELI
Noshed — ATE
Nosher's desire — SNACKS
Noshes — SNACKS
Nostradamus — SEER
Nostradamus' forte: Abbr. — ASTROL
Nostradamus, e.g. — SEER
Nostrils — NARES
Nosy neighbor — PEEPING TOM
Nosy one — SNOOP
Nosy Parker — SNOOP
Not "agin" in Dogpatch — FER
Not "fer" — AGIN
Not "in" — PASSE
Not _____ (better) — AS BAD
Not _____ (mediocre) — SO HOT
Not _____ (pretty good) — SO BAD
Not _____ (refuse to help) — LIFT A FINGER
Not _____ a red cent — WORTH
Not _____ eye — BAT AN
Not _____ in the world — A CARE
Not _____ you first! — IF I SEE
Not a Dem. or Rep. — IND

Not a one — NARY
Not a soul — NONE, NO ONE
Not absolved — UNVINDICATED
Not afar — ANEAR
Not against — FOR
Not any — NONE
Not any, in law — NUL
Not any, to the D.A. — NUL
Not appropriate — UNAPT
Not arisen — ABED
Not as _____ (rarely) — A RULE
Not as fat — SPARER
Not as grandiose — SMALLER
Not as many — FEWER
Not as messy — NEATER
Not as much — LESS
Not as prevalent — RARER
Not as quick — SLOWER
Not as removed — NEARER
Not as rude — NICER
Not at all — IN NO WAY, NEVER, NO HOW
Not at all, in Oahu — AOLE
Not aweather — ALEE
Not barefoot — SHOD
Not boos — RAHS
Not bright — DRAB
Not C.O.D. — PPD
Not capable — INEPT
Not care _____ — A RAP
Not Christian, Moslem or Jewish — PAGAN
Not clerical — LAIC
Not closed — AJAR
Not closed tight — AJAR
Not common — SCARCE
Not concealed — OVERT
Not confined to bed — AMBULATORY
Not counting — EXCLUDING
Not curly — LANK
Not curly, as hair — LANK
Not current — DATED
Not cut out for — UNFIT
Not dispatched — UNSENT
Not early — LATE
Not elsewhere — HERE
Not essential — EXTRANEOUS
Not even fair — POOR
Not ever, poetically — NEER
Not exactly — ALMOST
Not fancy — PLAIN
Not far at all — NEAR
Not final, in law — NISI
Not fitting — INAPT
Not fooled by — ONTO
Not for publication — OFF THE RECORD
Not forever — TEMPORAL
Not fresh — FADED
Not friendly — COOL
Not fully closed — AJAR
Not give _____ — A RAP, A FIG
Not give _____ (care not) — A RAP
Not give _____ for — A FIG
Not glossy — MATTE
Not good — BAD
Not gregarious — ASOCIAL
Not gross — NET
Not hear _____ drop — A PIN
Not hep — SQUARE
Not here — AWAY, THERE
Not here: Abbr. — ABS
Not home — AWAY, OUT
Not horiz. — VERT
Not idle — DOING, IN USE
Not illuminated — UNLIT
Not in — AWAY
Not in attendance — ABSENT
Not in commercial grade — UNDESIRED
Not in love — FANCY FREE
Not in the dark — AWARE
Not involved — UNENTANGLED
Not knowing which way to turn — UNSURE
Not kosher — SHADY, TREF
Not lean — SUETY
Not liable to — IMMUNE
Not likely — UNAPT
Not live — TAPED
Not loc. — EXP
Not many — FEW
Not marbled, as meat — LEAN
Not masc. — FEM
Not mod. — ANC
Not more — LESS
Not much on looks — PLAIN
Not new — USED, WARMED OVER
Not now — THEN
Not observed — UNSEEN
Not of the cloth — LAIC
Not on duty — INACTIVE
Not on time — BEHIND, LATE, TARDY
Not one — NARY
Not one, in Nimes — NUL
Not oral — NASAL
Not original: Abbr. — DERIV
Not out of the woods — IN DEEP WATER
Not part of a series — ONE SHOT
Not perceived by the ear — UNHEARD
Not pres. — ABS
Not pro — ANTI
Not qualified — UNFIT
Not quite — BARELY, HARDLY
Not quite N — NNE
Not really! — OH NO
Not related — UNTOLD
Not resonant — FLAT
Not sanctioned by law — ILLICIT
Not securely closed — AJAR
Not severe — EASY
Not sharp, not acute — OBTUSE
Not shiny or glossy — MATTE
Not single — DUAL
Not so — FALSE
Not so callow — MATURER
Not so colorful — PALER
Not so cordial — ICIER
Not so dumb — SLIER
Not so exciting — TAMER
Not so far away — CLOSER
Not so fresh — OLDER
Not so funny — GRAYER
Not so green — RIPER
Not so hot — TEPID
Not so inept — ABLER
Not so much — LESS
Not so nasty — NICER
Not so noble — BASER
Not so rainy — FAIRER
Not so ruddy — PALER
Not so slovenly — NATTIER
Not so sparse — DENSER
Not so trite — NEWER
Not so untidy — NEATER
Not sotto voce — ALOUD
Not spontaneous — PLANNED
Not spurious — REAL
Not subject to — SAFE
Not subject to usual rules — PRIVILEGED
Not suitable — INEPT, UNFIT
Not talking — MUM
Not taped — LIVE
Not tense — LAX
Not that — THIS
Not the least — NARY
Not theirs — OURS
Not these, not those — OTHERS
Not this — THAT
Not thrifty — UNECONOMIC
Not together — APART
Not too bright — DENSE
Not turn _____ (stay calm) — A HAIR
Not up — ABED
Not up to snuff — SECOND RATE
Not up yet — ABED
Not ventro — DORSO
Not wearing hose — BARE LEGGED
Not well — ILL
Not windward — ALEE
Not working — OFF, OUT OF ORDER
Not worth _____ of beans — A HILL
Not worth _____: useless — A FIG
Not worth a _____ — SOU
Not yet solved — UNMET
Not yet up — ABED
Not-so-fancy fur — LAPIN

Nota _____ — BENE
Notable Ali — BABA
Notable beam — LASER
Notable designer to movie stars — ADRIAN
Notable French artist-designer — ERTE
Notable Golda — MEIR
Notable Irish patriot — EMMET
Notable name in American poetry — BENET
Notable period — ERA
Notable service club — LIONS
Notable ship — BOUNTY
Notable surrealist — DALI
Notable time — ERA
Notable Watergate figure — RODINO
Notables — GREATS
Notary — CLERK
Notation — ENTRY
Notch — CRENA, NICK, SLOT
Notched — SERRATED
Notched, as a leaf — EROSE
Note from Guido — ELA
Note in old music — ELA
Note on a farmhouse door — GONE TO TOWN
Note, to key — SHARP
Notebook flaps — TABS
Notebook for an élève — CAHIER
Noted — EMINENT
Noted Alabama city — SELMA
Noted American jurist — LEARNED HAND
Noted American lawyer — BELLI
Noted athlete Jim and family — THORPES
Noted caravel — PINTA
Noted caveman — OOP
Noted cellist — CASALS
Noted Chinese family — SOONG
Noted conductor-composer — PREVIN
Noted conductor from Genoa — EREDE
Noted Czech novelist — HASEK
Noted Dadaist — ARP
Noted dancer-choreographer — TOMMY TUNE
Noted ecdysiast — LEE
Noted English potter — SPODE
Noted fighter of oil fires — ADAIR
Noted folk singer — SEEGER
Noted for its tea culture — ASSAM
Noted French engineer — EIFFEL
Noted Indian diplomat — RAU
Noted Irish playwright — SHAW
Noted journalist born in Scotland — RESTON
Noted Justice's monogram — SDO
Noted literary monograms — RLS
Noted loser — HARE
Noted movie critic — REX REED
Noted muralist — SERT
Noted muralist and family — SERTS
Noted name in baseball — REESE
Noted name in polio research — SABIN
Noted naval historian — MAHAN
Noted prep school — EXETER
Noted puppeteer — SARG
Noted Renaissance family — ESTE
Noted surrealist — DALI
Noted Swiss mathematician: 1707-83 — EULER
Noted tenor — CARUSO
Noted theater in Paris — ODEON
Noted TV journalist — BILL MOYERS
Noted U.S. architect — PEI
Noted U.S. entomologist: 1879-1943 — LUTZ
Noted U.S. surgeon: 1864-1943 — CRILE
Noted western lawman — EARP
Noted writer-director-actor Allen — WOODY
Notes — TIS
Noteworthy — EPIC
Nothing — NIL, ZERO
Nothing alternative — ALL
Nothing at all — NIL
Nothing but — ALL, ONLY
Nothing but bovines? — WHOLLY COWS
Nothing doing — NO WAY
Nothing more — JUST, MERE
Nothing more than — MERE, MERELY
Nothing to _____ (important) — SNEEZE AT
Nothing to do situation — IDLESSE
Nothing to lean on — REED
Nothing under the sun — ZILCH
Nothing whatever — NIL
Nothing, in Madrid — NADA
Nothing, in Nantes — RIEN
Nothing, in Nicaragua — NADA
Nothing, in Nice — RIEN
Notica, in Spain — AVISO
Notice — HEED, SEE, SIGHT, SPOT
Notice: Sp. — AVISO
Noticed — NOTED, REMARKED, SEEN
Notify — TELL, WARN
Notify in writing — PUBLISH
Notion — IDEA
Notion, in Nantes — IDEE
Notorious marquis — DE SADE
Notorious spy of WW I — HARI
Notorious train robber — SAM BASS
Notre _____ — DAME
Nottingham natives — BRITISH
Notwithstanding — ASIDE, DESPITE
Noun connector — AND
Noun ending — ANCE, ENCE, SION
Noun suffix — ENCE, INCE, INE, ISE
Noun-forming suffix — TION
Nourish — FEED
Nourishing — ALIMENTARY
Nourishment: Pref. — TROPH
Nous — MIND
Nouveau _____ — RICHE
Nov. 1 group — STS
Nov. 11 honoree — ST MARTIN
Nov. follower — DEC
Nova — NEW STAR
Nova _____ — SCOTIA
Nova Scotia time abbr. — AST
Nova Scotia, originally — ACADIA
Novak, of "Picnic" fame — KIM
Novak, of "Vertigo" — KIM
Novel — NEW
Novel by Charles Perrault — CINDERELLA
Novel by Ferber — GIANT
Novel by Fielding — AMELIA
Novel by Hemingway — A FAREWELL TO ARMS
Novel by Hemingway — THE SUN ALSO RISES
Novel by J.J. Rousseau — EMILE
Novel by Nabokov — ADA, LOLITA
Novel by Sinclair Lewis — ARROWSMITH, MAIN STREET
Novel by Zola — NANA
Novel drafts: Abbr. — MSS
Novel ending — ETTE, IST
Novel in "The Forsyte Saga" — TO LET
Novel need — PLOT
Novel or vital — FRESH
Novel type — ROMANCE, SAGA
Novelette — STORY
Novelist _____ Hunter — EVAN

Novelist Ambler — ERIC
Novelist Bagnold — ENID
Novelist Bellow — SAUL
Novelist Bret — HARTE
Novelist C.P. — SNOW
Novelist Clancy — TOM
Novelist Cook — ROBIN
Novelist de Queiroz — ECA
Novelist Delmar — VINA
Novelist Edwin Way _____ — TEALE
Novelist Emile — ZOLA
Novelist Eric — AMBLER
Novelist Evelyn — SCOTT
Novelist Ferber — EDNA
Novelist from Illinois — ERNEST HEMINGWAY
Novelist from Indiana — THEODORE DREISER
Novelist from New York City — HENRY JAMES
Novelist George — SAND
Novelist Glasgow — ELLEN
Novelist Grey — ZANE
Novelist Haggard's title — SIR
Novelist Hostvsky — EGON
Novelist Irwin — SHAW
Novelist Jaffe — RONA
Novelist Joyce Carol — OATES
Novelist Karmel — ILONA
Novelist Ken — KESEY
Novelist Kesey — KEN
Novelist Kingsley — AMIS
Novelist Kingsley's novelist son — MARTIN AMIS
Novelist Laurence — STERNE
Novelist Murdoch — IRIS
Novelist Rölvaag — OLE
Novelist Seton — ANYA
Novelist Troyat — HENRI
Novelist Trump — IVANA
Novelist Turgenev — IVAN
Novelist Uris and namesakes — LEONS
Novelist Waugh — ALEC
Novelist Wharton — EDITH
Novelist Zola — EMILE
Novello — IVOR
Novello of "The Lodger" — IVOR
Novello of British musicals — IVOR
November 13, e.g. — IDES
November birthstone — TOPAZ
November event — ELECTION
November exhortation — VOTE
November headache — AUTUMN LEAVES
November occasion — ELECTION DAY
Novgorod no — NYET
Novice — TIRO, TYRO
Novices, along the Thames — TIROS
Novices, British style — TIROS
Now — AT THIS POINT IN TIME
Now alternative — NEVER
NOW cause — ERA
NOW fights this bias — SEXISM
NOW goal — ERA
NOW member — WOMAN
Now's companion — HERE
Now's partner — HERE
Now, in Nogales — AHORA
Now, now! — TUT
Now, to Calpurnia — NUNC
Noxious atmospheres — MIASMAS
Noxious biblical weed — TARE
Noxious drug — OPIUM
Noxious weed — TARE
NT book — ACTS
Nuance — NICETY, SHADE, TINT
Nubbin — EAR, LUMP
Nuchal area — NAPE
Nuclear energy agcy. — AEA
Nuclear scientist — BRAUN
Nuclear trial, for short — A TEST
Nuclear units — RADS
Nucleic acid inits. — RNA
Nucleus — CORE
Nudge — PROD
Nudges — JOGS, POKE
Nudist — ADAMITE
Nudnik — PEST
Nudnik or buttinsky — NUISANCE
Nugatory — VAIN
Nugent of rock — TED
Nuisance — BORE, PEST, PILL
Nuisance insect — GNAT
Nul tiel records — PLEAS
Null's companion — VOID
Nullified — NEGATED
Nullifies — VOIDS
Nullify — CANCEL, ERASE, NEGATE, REPEAL
Nullify a correction — STET
Numb — DEADEN
Numbat's tidbits — ANTS
Number — ONE
Number 2 golf club — MID IRON
Number 3 wood — SPOON
Number at Fenway — NINE
Number before sette — SEI
Number by tens — DECIMAL
Number for a Louis — ONZE
Number for tea, tunefully — TWO
Number in a shell — EIGHT
Number in Naples — SETEE
Number of "swans a-swimming" — SEVEN
Number of Bears or Bengals — ELEVEN
Number of Little Foys — SEVEN
Number of little pigs — THREE
Number of muses — NINE
Number of original astronauts — SEVEN
Number of Padres or Pirates — NINE
Number of persons present — ATTENDANCE
Number of Seas — SEVEN
Number of small deer — ROES
Number of things — SERIES
Number of Trevi coins — TRE
Number of wise men — THREE
Number six on a die — SICE
Numbers each leaf or page — FOLIOS
Numbers game — LOTTO, LOTTERY
Numbers man — CPA
Numbers named for an Austrian physicist — MACHS
Numbers to be totaled — ADDENDS
Numbers' person — CPA
Numbers, in Nimes — UNES
Numbing blow — KAYO
Numbness: Comb. form — NARCO
Numbskull — NITWIT
Numerical ending — ETH, TEEN
Numerical prefix — HEXA, OCTA, OCTO, PENTA, TRI
Numerical suffix — ETH, ETHS, TEEN
Numero _____ — UNO
Numero uno — ADAM
Numismatic tails — REVERSE
Numismatist's prize — COIN
Numismatist's residence — OLD QUARTERS
Numskull — DOLT, DUNCE
Nun — SISTER, VOTARESS
Nun's garb, sometimes — HABIT
Nuncupative — ORAL
Nunn, for one — SENATOR
Nuptial festivities — BRIDALS
Nuptial pronouncement — I DO
Nuptial put-on — RING
Nureyev donning tights? — RUSSIAN DRESSING
Nureyev specialty — LEAP
Nureyev, for one — TATAR
Nureyev, to friends — RUDY
Nurse Barton — CLARA
Nurse shark — GATA
Nurse's assistant — AIDE
Nursemaid — NANA
Nursemaid from the East — AMAH
Nursemaid in Shanghai — AMAH

Nursery group, with "The" — THREE LITTLE PIGS
Nursery item — CRIB
Nursery items — LAYETTES
Nursery lady — MOTHER GOOSE
Nursery needs — BASSINETS, CRIBS
Nursery query — HOW DOES YOUR GARDEN GROW
Nursery rhyme duo, with "The" — CAT AND THE FIDDLE
Nursery rhyme gardener — MARY
Nursery rhyme pair — SPRATS
Nursery rhyme porridge — PEASE
Nursery sleeper — BASSINET
Nursery villain — WOLF
Nursery wear — BIBS
Nursery word — MAMA, TATA
Nursery-rhyme dwelling — SHOE
Nursery-rhyme king — COLE
Nursery-rhyme pie filler — BLACKBIRDS
Nurses' _____ — AIDES
Nurture — REAR
Nurtured — BRED
Nut — ACORN, CASHEW
Nut contents — MEATS
Nut delicacies — MEATS
Nut for soft drinks — KOLA
Nut in a chocolate bar — ALMOND
Nut type — CASHEW
Nut's companion — BOLT
Nutcracker's suite? — NEST
Nutgall product — INK
Nuthatch genus — SITTA
Nutmeg coverings — ARILS
Nutmeg derivative — MACE
Nutmeg feature — ARIL
Nutmeg product — MACE
Nutmeg State: Abbr. — CONN
Nuts — KOOKIE
Nuts' partners — BOLTS
Nuts, in Navarre — NUECES
Nutty — FLAVOR
Nutty needlework? — CRAZY QUILT
NW Argentine group — IPA
NW Belgian commune — YPRES
NW Oregon port — ASTORIA
NY summertime — DST
NY's Finger _____ — LAKES
NY's time zone — EST
Nyborg natives — DANES
NYC mass transit — IRT
NYC museum — MOMA
NYC nine — METS
NYC section — SOHO
NYC stadium — SHEA
NYC subway — IND
NYC time — EST
NYC's ocean — ATL
Nyet, for one — VETO
Nylon and rayon — POLYMERS
Nylon constituent — AMIDE
Nylons — STOCKINGS
Nymph — GIRL, MAID
Nymph who loved Narcissus — ECHO
NYS time — EST
NYSE gamble — FLIER
NYSE type — SPECULATOR
NYSE unit — SHR
NYSE watchdog — SEC

O

O'Day or Ekberg — ANITA
O'er — THRU
O'er's antithesis — NEATH
O'Flaherty product — TALE
O'Grady of song — ROSIE
O'Hara home — TARA
O'Hara's "_____ Joey" — PAL
O'Hara's "_____ to Live" — A RAGE
O'Hara's "A _____ to Live" — RAGE
O'Hara's "From the _____" — TERRACE
O'Hara's "The Hat on the _____" — BED
O'Hara's place — TARA
O'Henry's Jimmy — VALENTINE
O'Neill barber's problem? — THE HAIRY APE
O'Neill hero — ORIN
O'Neill heroine — ELECTRA
O'Neill play — ILE
O'Neill play — THE HAIRY APE
O'Neill play: 1917 — ILE
O'Neill play: 1920 — THE EMPEROR JONES
O'Neill's "_____ For the Misbegotten" — A MOON
O'Neill's "_____ Under the ..." — DESIRE
O'Neill's "The _____ Ape" — HAIRY
O'Neill's "The Great _____ Brown" — GOD
O'Neill's daughter — OONA
O'Neill's Jones — EMPEROR
O'Neill's trees — ELMS
O'Neill's Yank, e.g. — STOKER
O, U companions — AEI
O. Henry prod. — STO
O. Henry story ending — THEY ARE THE MAGI
O. Henry title word — MAGI
O. Henry's monogram — WSP
O.K. — YES
O.K. Corral figure — EARP
O.R. personnel — RNS
O.T. book — AMOS, ISAIAH, NAHUM
O.T. book — DEUT, NEH, OBAD
O.T. book — KINGS, ISA, LEV
O.T. part — DEUT
O.T. sufferer — JOB
O.T.'s 20th book — PROV
Oafs — CLODS, LOUTS
Oahu dance — HULA
Oahu farewell — ALOHA
Oahu garlands — LEIS
Oahu greeting — ALOHA
Oahu souvenirs — LEIS
Oak — PIN
Oak fruit — ACORN
Oak seed — ACORN
Oak-to-be — ACORN
Oakland players? — THE A TEAM
Oakum — HEMP
Oar — SCULL
Oar part — BLADE
Oar pin — THOLE
Oarlocks — THOLES
Oars — CREW
Oarsman — SCULLER
Oarsman's boat — SHELL
OAS member — USA
Oasis — WADI
Oasis — WATERING HOLE
Oasis wear — ABA
Oater — WESTERN
Oater actions — CHASERS
Oater challenge — DRAW
Oater chase group — POSSE
Oater group — POSSE
Oater pursuers — POSSE
Oater sidekick — PARD

Oater sounds — CLOPS
Oater star Maynard — KEN
Oater trackers — POSSE
Oaters — HORSE OPERAS, WESTERNS
Oates novel — THEM
Oates title — THEM
Oath — BOND
Oath taker — SWEARER
Oatmeal — CEREAL
Oats for Arazi, e.g. — FEED
Obclude — HIDE
Obdurate — FIRM, SET, STONY
Obedience — RESPECT
Obedient — AMENABLE
Obeisance — BOW, HOMAGE
Obelisk — SHAFT
Obese — FAT, TUBBY
Obese one's nickname — FATSO
Obey — MIND, TOE THE MARK
Obey a cheerleader — YELL
Obey a triangular sign — YIELD
Obeys a sentry — HALTS
Obfuscate — BLUR
Obi — SASH
Obi accessory — INRO
Obi's relative — SASH
Obie or Tony — AWARD
Obis — SASHES
Obit — NOTICE
Object — DEMUR, PROTEST, REMONSTRATE, THING
Object of a spring hunt — EASTER EGG
Object of Petrarch's affection — LAURA
Object of worship — DEITY, IDOL
Objection — DOUBT
Objection trifle and petty — CAVIL
Objective — AIM, END, GOAL, PURPOSE, TARGET
Objective pronoun — THEM
Objectives — AIMS, GOALS
Objects — PROTESTS
Objects officially — PROTESTS
Objects to — PROTESTS
Objet d'art — CURIO
Obligate — PLEDGE
Obligate, in a way — HOLD TO
Obligation — DEBT, DUTY, MUST, ONUS
Oblige — ASSIST, HELP
Obliged — BOUND, LIABLE
Oblique — ASLANT
Obliquely — ASLANT, SLANTWAYS
Obliquely positioned — STANDING ATHWART
Obliterate — ANNUL, ERASE, DESTRUCT
Obliterated — ERASED
Obliterations — ERASURES
Oblivion — LETHE, LIMBO
Oblong — OVAL
Obloquy — ABUSE
Obnoxious — FAULTY, FOUL, NASTY
Obnoxious child — BRAT
Oboe — REED
Oboes, clarinets, etc. — REEDS
Oboist's concern — REED
Obscene — BAWDY, BLUE, RACY, RISQUE
Obscene material — SMUT
Obscure — ARCANE, BEDIM, DIM, RUNIC, SHADE, VAGUE
Obscured — CLOUDED, HAZED
Obscures — VEILS
Obsequious — DOCILE
Obsequy — FUNERAL
Observance — CUSTOM, RITE
Observance of moral law — NOMISM
Observances — RITES
Observant — ALERT, HEEDFUL
Observant one — NOTER
Observation — COMMENT
Observation dome — BLISTER
Observation point — VIEW
Observation post — BEACON, TOWER
Observations — ESPIALS
Observatory — POST
Observe — HEED, NOTE, SEE, REGARD
Observe — SEE
Observe carefully — NOTE
Observed — EYED
Observed — NOTED, SAW, SEEN
Observer — EYER, NOTER
Observes — BEHOLDS
Observes Halloween — TREATS
Observes Yom Kippur — FASTS
Observing — EYING
Obsess — RULE
Obsess the thoughts of — HAUNT
Obsessed by — INTO
Obsession — MANIA, TIC
Obsolescent — FADING
Obsolete — PASSE, SUPERANNUATED
Obsolete auto — REO
Obstacle — SNAG
Obstacle for a sleeping princess — PEA
Obstetrix — MIDWIFE
Obstinate — HEADSTRONG, SET
Obstinate one — ASS
Obstreperous — UNRULY
Obstruct — STEM
Obstruction — SNAG
Obstructs — ARRESTS
Obtain — GAIN, GET
Obtain justly — EARN
Obtained — GOT, GOTTEN, TAKEN
Obtains — GETS
Obtrude — THRUST ON
Obtuse — CRASS, DENSE, THICK HEADED
Obvious — OPEN
Obvious, easily decided — OPEN AND SHUT
Obviously — CLEARLY
Oca or yarn — TUBER
Ocala's state abbr. — FLA
Ocarina, a la the Irish — SWEET PATATO
Occasion — EVENT
Occasion to primp — DATE
Occasional TV fare — SPECIAL
Occasionally — FROM TIME TO TIME
Occidental — WESTERN
Occlude — SHUT
Occult — ARCANE, HIDDEN
Occult initials — ESP
Occult system — CABALA
Occupation — LINE, TRADE
Occupation of a Forty-niner — PANNING
Occupation of Hillary — ATTORNEY
Occupied — IN USE, RAPT, TENANTED
Occupied with — INTO
Occur — EXIST, FOLLOW
Occur as a consequence — ENSUE
Occurrence — EVENT
Occurring at night — DARKLING
Occurring on the open sea — OCEANIC
Occurring under orders — IN THE LINE OF DUTY
Ocean — BLUE, PACIFIC
Ocean current off Ecuador — EL NINO
Ocean disturbance — TSUNAMI
Ocean flow — NEAPTIDE
Ocean greyhound — LINER
Ocean mammal — WHALE
Ocean motion — TIDE, WAVE
Ocean movement — TIDE
Ocean pollutant — OIL SLICK
Ocean route — SEAWAY
Ocean sodium chloride — SEA SALT
Ocean spume — SEAFOAM
Ocean vessel — LINER, SHIP
Ocean voyages — SEA TRIPS
Ocean, in Berlin — MEER
Ocean: Abbr. — ATL
Oceania island — COOK
Oceanography & Meteorology — SCIENCES

Oceans — TONS
Ocellus — EYE, SPOT
Ocelot — WILDCAT
Ocelot's cousin — JAGUAR
Ocotes — PINES
OCS eligibles — SGTS
Octa or penta follower — GON
Octad in a gallon — PINTS
Octagonal signal — STOP
Octave of a feast — UTAS
Octavia's husband — NERO
Octavian — EMPEROR AUGUSTUS
Octet — EIGHT
Octet plus one — ENNEAD
October birthstone — BERYL, OPAL
October flower — COSMOS
October gems — OPALS
October occasion — COLUMBUS DAY
October occasions — HALLOWEENS
October sign — LIBRA
October stone — OPAL
October victory for Yale — BLUE HEAVEN
October's month of the year — TENTH
Ocular gadget — EYECUP
Ocular pest — EYE GNAT
Ocular structure: Prefix — CILI
Oda _____ — MAE
Odalisque's home — HAREM
Odd — ERRATIC, RARE
Odd birds — ONERS
Odd Couple photographer — FELIX
Odd in Aberdeen — ORRA
Odd job — CHORE
Odd magazine? — HARPERS BIZARRE
Odd people or animals — SPLACKNUCKS
Odd, to Burns — ORRA
Odd: Scot. — ORRA
Odds and ends — CRUMBS, REMNANTS, STUFF
Odds' opposite — EVENS
Ode or elegy — POEM
Odense natives — DANES
Oder feeder — NEISSE
Oder tributary — NEISSE
Odes anagram — DOES
Odets play: 1937 — GOLDEN BOY
Odette's garb — TUTU
Odette's opposite number — ODILE
Odin's gang — AESIR
Odin's realm — VALHALLA
Odin's wife: Var. — FRIA
Odin, Balder, et al. — AESIR
Odin, Thor, et al. — AESIR
Odious — VILE
Odists — POETS
Odom of baseball — STEVE
Odom or Post — AVIATOR
Odor — AROMA, SCENT
Odorous — SMELLY
Odysseus author — HOMER
Oeillade — ODLE
Oenochoe — EWER
Oenologist's concern — AGE, YEAR
Oenologist's interest — WINE
Oenologist's word — SEC
Oenophile's attribute — NOSE
Oenophile's word — SEC
Of a 14th-century Tuscan family — MEDICEAN
Of a bacterin — VACCINAL
Of a blood vessel — AORTIC
Of a cereal — OATEN
Of a cereal grain — OATEN
Of a cereal grass — OATEN
Of a certain bone — SACRAL
Of a chemical process — SOLUTIONAL
Of a continent — ASIAN, ASIATIC
Of a district — AREAL
Of a fast period — LENTEN
Of a forearm bone — ULNAR
Of a Frankish people — SALIC
Of a Great Lake — ERIAN
Of a hereditary rank — DUCAL
Of a kind — EQUAL
Of a kittiwake — LARINE
Of a larynx opening — GLOTTAL
Of a lower social order — DECLASSE
Of a membrane — SEPTAL
Of a Mesolithic cultural stage — AZILIAN
Of a noxious atmosphere — MIASMAL
Of a pair — DYADIC
Of a pelvic bone: Comb. form — ILIO
Of a people — ETHNIC
Of a period — ERAL
Of a piece — ALIKE
Of a portion — SEGMENTAL
Of a region — AREAL
Of a religious system — CULTIC
Of a ruler — MONARCHAL
Of a seed scar — HILAR
Of a Sicilian mount — ETNEAN
Of a Sicilian volcano — ETNEAN
Of a songbird suborder — OSCINE
Of a surface — AREAL
Of a time — ERAL
Of a trunk in a trunk — AORTAL
Of a type of poem — ODIC
Of a verse form — ODIC
Of age — ADULT, RIPE
Of aircraft — AERO
Of an age — ERAL
Of an ancient Greek city — ELIAN
Of an epoch — ERAL
Of an eye part — UVEAL
Of an historic time — ERAL
Of an infectious agent — VIRAL
Of an insect's stage — PUPAL
Of ancestral descent — LINEAL
Of ancient Carthage — PUNIC
Of ancient vintage — OLD
Of ancient writing — HIERATIC
Of astounding size — ENORMOUS
Of bees — APIAN
Of birds — AVIAN
Of birth — NATAL
Of certain perennial plants — ACROGENIC
Of comparative reasoning — ANALOGIC
Of course! — SURE
Of different meanings of words — SEMANTIC
Of epic proportions — HOMERIC
Of equal value — SAME
Of flying: Comb. form — AERI
Of good stock — PUREBRED
Of grubs and caterpillars — LARVAL
Of harmony — TONAL
Of hearing — AURAL, OTIC
Of heat — CALORIC
Of high mountains — ALPINE
Of high repute — FAMED
Of Icelandic works — EDDIC
Of Lamb's writing — ELIAN
Of little importance — SMALL
Of little value — CHEAP
Of long standing — ESTABLISHED
Of lunar stages — PHASIC
Of lymph glands — ADENOID
Of Mandela's culture — AFRIC
Of Mars: Comb. form — AREO
Of Mary's lamb — OVINE
Of milk — LACTIC
Of minimum clarity — MURKIEST
Of muscular vigor — TONAL
Of musical pitch — TONAL
Of musical sounds — TONAL
Of necessity — PERFORCE
Of Norse poetry — EDDIC
Of old age — SENILE
Of one mind: Abbr. — UNAN
Of or out of — SORTS
Of parrots or pigeons — AVIAN
Of Pindar's poems — ODIC
Of pitch — TONAL

Of plants and animals — BIOLOGIC
Of present month: Abbr. — INST
Of religious rites — SACRAL
Of sacred Hindu books — VEDAIC
Of sacred Hindu writings — VEDIC
Of scenic terrain — HILLY
Of ships — NAVAL
Of soil: Comb. form — AGRO
Of some voices — NASAL
Of sound quality — TONAL
Of sovereignty — REGNAL
Of space — AREAL
Of speech sounds — PHONETIC
Of symbolic reasoning — LOGISTIC
Of the ages — EONIC
Of the ankles — TARSAL
Of the Asian subcontinent — INDIC
Of the backbone — SPINAL
Of the bees — APIAN
Of the calf — SURAL
Of the cheek — MALAR
Of the cuckoopint family — AROID
Of the Dawn — EOAN
Of the ear — AURAL, OTIC
Of the early morning — MATAN
Of the earth — GEAL
Of the east — ASIATIC
Of the ego's source — IDIC
Of the intellect — NOETIC
Of the kidneys — RENAL
Of the kind mentioned — SUCH
Of the Milky Way — GALACTIC
Of the moon — SELENIC
Of the nasal cavities — SINAL
Of the North — BOREAL
Of the North wind — BOREAL
Of the nose — NARIC
Of the nostrils — NARINE
Of the number six — SENARY
Of the old school — FORMAL
Of the people of Aden — YEMENIC
Of the preceding mo. — ULTO
Of the Red Planet — AREO
Of the sciences of origins — ETIOLOGIC
Of the skull — CRANIAL
Of the soil: Comb. form — AGRO
Of the stars — ASTRAL
Of the state of the blood: Suffix — HEMIA
Of the sun — SOLAR
Of the world's heaviest metal — OSMIC
Of the: Fr. — DES
Of time — ERAL
Of tisssue — TELAR
Of vision — OPTIC
Of which — WHERE OF
Of yore — ELD
Of yore — OLDEN, PAST
Off-balance — ATIP
Off-Broadway award — OBIE
Off-course — ERRANT, AMISS
Off-limits — TABOO
Off-shore — ASEA
Off — ABSENT, AWAY
Off _____ flying start — TO A
Off course — ASTRAY, LOST
Off key — FLAT, SOUR
Off limits — TABOO
Off one's feed — ILL
Off one's rocker — BANANAS, BATS
Off ramps — EXITS
Off the beaten track — ASTRAY
Off the boat — ASHORE
Off the coast — ASEA
Off the cuff — ADLIB
Off the mark — AMISS
Off the plate — EATEN
Off the subject — BESIDE THE POINT
Off yonder — AFAR
Off-color — SPICY
Off-ramp — EXIT
Off. of _____ Intelligence — NAV
Off. outranking CPO — ENS
Off. worker — STENO
Off: Poet. — YON
Offal — TRASH
Offenbach's "_____ Parisienne" — GAITE
Offenbach's "The _____ Hoffmann" — TALES OF
Offend — REPEL
Offend the nostril — STINK
Offended — HUFFY
Offensive — NOISOME, RANCID, RUDE
Offensive ace in the hole — SECRET WEAPON
Offensive odor — FETOR
Offer — BID, DONATE, EXTEND, PROPOSE, SUBMIT, SUGGEST
Offer _____ (be unconvincing) — A THIN EXCUSE
Offer anew, as a bond issue — REFLOAT
Offer maker — TENDERER
Offer more than — OUTBID
Offered — TENDERED
Offering for thoughts — PENNY
Offers — BIDS
Offers as a reason — ADDUCES
Offhand — ADLIB
Office — DEN, POST, ROOM, STUDY
Office abbr. — ASAP
Office appliance — DATER
Office biggie — STENO
Office bigwig — BOSS
Office copy — STAT
Office copy, for short — STAT
Office dept. — PERS
Office feature — DESK
Office furniture — DESKS
Office gadget — DATER, SHARPENER
Office help — STENOS
Office holders — INS
Office machine — DATER, COPIER
Office note — MEMO
Office of the President — OVAL
Office purchase — DESK
Office stalwart — STENO
Office stamps — DATERS
Office sub — TEMP
Office VIP — BOSS
Office worker — CLERK, STENO
Office worker, for short — TEMP
Office worker, in Wassy — CLERC
Office-holders — INS
Officeholders — INS
Officer's assistant — AIDE
Officer's go-fer — ORDERLY
Officers' dining room — MESS
Officers' ed. centr. — OCS
Officers' meal — MESS
Official emblems used for documents — GREAT SEALS
Official in a whodunit — CORONER
Official language of India — HINDI
Official mark — SEAL
Official proceedings — ACTA
Official records — ACTA
Official rejection — VETO
Official rules for short — REGS
Officials in ancient Rome — AEDILES
Officiate — REFEREE
Officiate at tea — POUR
Offset worker — INKER
Offshoot — ARM, SPUR
Offshore hazard — REEF
Offspring — BROOD, ISSUE, SCION, SONS, SPRIGS
Offspring's offspring — GRANDCHILD
Offspring: Abbr. — DESC
Oft watched line — WAIST
Oft-heard — STALE
Oft-printed articles — THES

Oft-quoted author: Abbr. — ANON
Often-chewed nut — KOLA
Ogden — NASH
Ogee and Gothic — ARCHES
Ogham — RUNE
Ogive — ARCH
Ogive molding — OGEE
Oglata's home — TEPEE
Ogle — EYE, GAZE, STARE
Ogled — PEERED
Ogled like an ogre — LEERED
Ogler — EYER, FLIRT
Oglers — GOGLERS
Ogles — LEERS
Ogre — ORC
Oh dear! — ALAS
Oh me! — ALAS
Oh so proper — PRIM
OH team — REDS
Oh, yes — AHSO
Ohio and Oklahoma cities — ADAS
Ohio athlete — RED
Ohio author Zane — GREY
Ohio city — NILES, AKRON
Ohio city on the Ohio: Abbr. — CIN
Ohio college — KENT
Ohio college town — ADA
Ohio flag shape — SWALLOWTAIL
Ohio home of Warren Harding — MARION
Ohio river port — EVANSVILLE
Ohio rubber city — AKRON
Ohio senator — GLENN
Ohioan — BUCKEYE
Oil cartel — OPEC
Oil distilled from orange flowers — NEROLI
Oil field worker — RIGGER
Oil for Orly — HUILE
Oil made from orange blossoms — NEROLI
Oil of orange blossoms — NEROLI
Oil or gas — FUEL
Oil rigs — DERRICKS
Oil source — SHALE, SOYA
Oil sources — OLIVES
Oil support — EASEL
Oil well — GUSHER
Oil, in New Orleans — HUILE
Oil, watercolor, etc. — MEDIA
Oil-fire extinguisher Red _____ — ADAIR
Oil-yielding tropical tree — EBO
Oil: Comb. form — ELAIO, ELEO, OLEI
Oiler or Steeler — FOOTBALL PLAYER
Oily — OLEIC
Oily esters — OLEATES
Oily fish — SMELT
Oily goo — TAR
Oily hydrocarbon in petroleum — CETANE
Oily liquid — OLEIN
Oily resin — ELEMI
Ointment — CERATE, SALVE
Ojibway's cousin — CREE
OK Corral figure — WYATT EARP
Oka city — OREL
Oka River city — OREL
Okhotsk or Andaman — SEA
Okhotsk, e.g. — SEA
Okhotsk, for one — SEA
Okinawa island group — RYUKYU
Okinawan capital — NAHA
Okinawan city — NAHA
Okla. city — ADA, ENID, TULSA
Okla. Indian — OTOE
Oklahoma and West Virginia — BATTLESHIPS
Oklahoma city — ADA, ENID
Oklahoma Indians — OTOS, SACS
Oklahoma oil center — TULSA
Oklahoma oil city — ADA
Oklahoma outlaw — BELLE STARR
Oklahoma Sioux — OSAGES
Oklahoma town — ENID
Oklahoman — SOONER
Olajuwon of the NBA — AKEEM, HAKEEM
Olav V's capital — OSLO
Old-age nest-egg — IRA
Old-fashioned card game — OLD MAID
Old-time actor Gibson — HOOT
Old-time car — REO
Old-time dirk — SNEE
Old-time oath — EGAD
Old — AGED
Old _____, Virginia — DOMINION
Old Ace of Spades — LEE
Old African big-game gun — ROER
Old age, of old — ELD
Old autos — REOS
Old Bailey in London — COURT
Old ballroom dance — ONE STEP
Old brocade — ACCA
Old campaigners — POLITICAL HACKS
Old car — DE SOTO, NASH
Old card game — LOO
Old characters — RUNES
Old chest for valuables — ARCA
Old Chinese weight unit — LIANG
Old cloth — RAG
Old codger — DODO
Old cries of triumph — HOOS
Old dagger — SNEE
Old Dominion State — VIRGINIA
Old Dutch coin — STIVE
Old English bard — SCOP
Old English court — LEET
Old English letter — EDH
Old English letter: Var. — ETH
Old English measure — ELL
Old English W — WEN
Old Faithful — GEYSER
Old Faithful's activity — SPURTING
Old farm building — ICE HOUSE
Old fogy — DODO
Old form of enough — ENOW
Old French coin — ECU, SOU
Old French unit of area — ARPENT
Old Gaelic tongue — ERSE
Old German-French province — ALSACE
Old German coin — TALER
Old Glory — FLAG, STARS AND STRIPES
Old Glory, is one — FLAG
Old goat — LECHER
Old gold coin — FLORIN
Old grad meets classmates — REUNES
Old Greek coins — OBOLI
Old Greek marketplace — AGORA
Old hand — STAGER, VET, VETERAN
Old hat — DATED, PASSE, STALE
Old Hebrew avenger — GOEL
Old Hebrew measure — KOR
Old inhabitant of Britain — PICT
Old instrument — ASOR
Old Ir. alphabet — OGHAM
Old Irish alphabet — OGAM
Old Irish war cry — ERIN GO BRAGH
Old Ironsides — CONSTITUTION
Old Italian coin — SCUDO, SOLDO
Old jokes — CORN
Old King of Portugal called the Great — JOHN I
Old laborer — ESNE
Old laundry appliance — WRINGER
Old lemons — EDSELS
Old liner — HAS BEEN
Old lyric poem — LAI
Old maid — PRUDE, SPINSTRESS, TABBY
Old man — FOGEY
Old man, to Cicero — SENEX

Old master — PAINTER
Old McDonald vowels — EIEIO
Old movie heavy Laird — CREGAR
Old musical symbols — UTS
Old nags — JADES
Old name for a Swiss city — BASLE
Old name for Ireland — IERNE
Old name of Donetsk — STALINO
Old name of Xiamen — AMOY
Old Nick — SANTA, SATAN
Old Nick's forte — EVIL
Old Norse poem — EDDA
Old Norse poetry — EDDA
Old Norse works — EDDAS
Old or New city of India — DELHI
Old or young ending — STER
Old overshoe — GAITER
Old radio program — THE SHADOW
Old refrigerator — ICEBOX
Old Rome's port — OSTIA
Old round dances — CAROLS
Old Russian artwork — ICON
Old salt — SEADOG, TAR
Old Sci-fi TV show — LAND OF THE GIANTS
Old Scratch — DEVIL
Old Scratch himself — DEVIL, SATAN
Old shilling pieces — ORAE
Old Siamese coins — ATTS
Old Sod — ERIN
Old soldier — VETERAN
Old soldiers — VETS
Old Spanish coins — DOBLAS, ESCUDOS, REALS
Old Spanish sherry — XERES
Old steps — STELAE
Old stone tools — EOLITHS
Old strongbox — ARCA
Old sweetheart — FLAME
Old terms of address — SIRRA, SIRRAS
Old Testament aboriginal giant — ANAK
Old Testament book — AMOS, ESTHER, EZRA, HOSEA
Old Testament book — PROVERBS
Old Testament sufferer — JOB
Old Tex. units of length — VARAS
Old time actress Ada — REHAN
Old time entertainment — SILENTS
Old time instrument — ASOR
Old timer — VETERAN
Old times, old style — ELD
Old tongue — ERSE, LATIN
Old Turkish coin — ASPER
Old unit of length — BARLEYCORN
Old US rifle — YAGER
Old verb endings — ETHS
Old weapons — PIKESTAFFS
Old wearer of an albatross — MARINER
Old wives tale — SUPERSTITION
Old woman — CARLINE
Old woman's dwelling — SHOE
Old woman's home — SHOE
Old World herb — TANSY
Old World lizards — AGAMA
Old, withered woman — CRONE
Old, worn clothes — RAGS
Old-fashioned — DATED, FUSTY, PASSE, QUAINT
Old-fashioned oaths — EGADS
Old-fashioned person — FUDDY DUDDY
Old-fashioned traveling pouch — CARPETBAG
Old-time days — BYGONE
Old-time dill — ANET
Old-time verb ending — ETH
Old-timer — VETERAN
Old-womanish — ANILE, FUSSY
Old: Abbr. — ANC
Olden Quechua speaker — INCA
Older — ELDER
Older brother of Moses — AARON
Older section of Middle East city — CASBAH
Oldest existing city in the world — DAMASCUS
Oldest settler in the west — SUN
Oldest sister: Fr. — AINEE
Oldest street in L.A. — OLVERA
Oldtime auto — REO
Oldtime rhymer — OMAR
Ole _____, Norwegian composer — OLSEN
Ole _____: Norwegian violinist — BULL
Ole of "Hellzapoppin" — OLSEN
Ole's kin — RAH
Oleaginous — OILY
Oleander — SHRUB
Oleander's color — PINK AND WHITE
Oleg _____, clown in "Moscow Circus" — POPOV
Olent oleoresin — ELEMI
Olent seed — ANISE
Oleo coloring — ANATTO
Oleo, to a Brit — MARGE
Olfactory inputs — ODORS
Olfactory stimulus — ODOR
Olga, Masha, and Idrina — THREE SISTERS
Oligophrenia — IDIOCY
Oligophrenic — MORON
Olio — STEW
Olive branch — CHILD
Olive drab — UNIFORM
Olive family member — ASH
Olive genus — OLEA
Olive or sunflower product — OIL
Olive product — OIL
Olive shade — PEA GREEN, STONE GREY
Olive-branch — EMBLEM, PEACE
Oliver in "Tommy" — REED
Oliver Stone product — FILM
Oliver Twist character — FAGIN
Oliver Twist's entreaty — MORE
Oliver's opponent turned friend — ROLAND
Oliver's request — MORE
Oliver's sidekick — STAN
Oliver's wicked tutor — FAGIN
Olivet — PEARL
Olivia Newton-John's grandfather — MAX BORN
Olivia of the Met — STAPP
Olivia's clown — FESTE
Olivier's title — LORD
Olla podrida — STEW
Olla, e.g. — STEW
Ollie's friend — FRAN
Ollie's pal — STAN
Olpe — FLASK
Olympian — ARES, HERA
Olympian Bruce _____ — JENNER
Olympian deity — HERA
Olympian deity, in a way — ATHENE
Olympian goddess — HERA
Olympian hawk — ARES
Olympian Heiden — ERIC
Olympian Korbut — OLGA
Olympian queen — HERA
Olympian Spitz, et al. — MARKS
Olympian Zatopek — EMIL
Olympian's vehicle — SLED
Olympians — DEITIES
Olympic brat — ATE
Olympic champ in the butterfly stroke — MEAGHER
Olympic competitor — ATHLETE
Olympic emblem — TORCH
Olympic event — RACE
Olympic events — DASHES
Olympic hawk — ARES, MARS
Olympic prize — MEDAL
Olympic runner, of a sort — LUGE
Olympic site: 1960 — ROME

Olympic skater Bonnie — BLAIR
Olympic slalom star: 1984 — MAHRE
Olympic sleds — LUGES
Olympic sprinter Lewis — CARL
Olympic Stadium player — EXPO
Olympic star Comaneci — NADIA
Olympic's Comaneci — NADIA
Olympicist Jesse — OWENS
Olympics contender — ATHLETE
Olympics contestants — ATHLETES
Olympics host country in 1988: Abbr. — KOR
Olympics prize — GOLD MEDAL
Olympics site of 1988 — SEOUL
Olympus — HEAVEN, SKY
Omaha Bch. vessel — LST
Omaha Beach craft — LST
Oman — SULTANATE
Oman coin — RIAL
Omani — ARAB
Omani money — RIALS
Omar from Alexandria — SHARIF
Omar Khayyam — POET
Omar Sharif role — CHE
Omar's productions — TENTS
Ombudsman — NEGOTIATOR
Omega — END, LAST
Omega preceder — ZETA
Omega's antithesis — ALPHA
Omega's partner — ALPHA
Omelet base for Brutus — OVA
Omelet makers — EGGS
Omelet starts — EGGS
Omen — HARBINGER, SIGN, TOKEN
Omens — PORTENTS, PREMONITIONS
Ominous — SINISTER, THREATENING
Omission — ERASURE
Omissions — ELISIONS
Omit — BYPASS, ELIDE, EXCEPT, SKIP
Omit a syllable — ELIDE
Omits — MISSES
Omni or Kemper — ARENA
Omni or mini follower — BUS
Omni, e.g. — ARENA
Omni, for one — ARENA
Omnibus — READER
Omnipotent — MIGHTY, UNLIMITED
Omsk coin — KOPEK
On — ATOP
On _____ — A PAR
On _____ (active) — THE GO
On _____ (at variance) — THE OUTS
On _____ (busy) — THE GO
On _____ (carousing) — A TEAR
On _____ (hot) — A ROLL
On _____ (in reserve) — ICE
On _____ (nervous) — EDGE
On _____ (sailing) — THE BRINY
On _____ and ... (honest) — THE UP
On _____ with (even) — A PAR
On _____ with: equal to — A PAR
On _____: instantly — A DIME
On _____: not under contract — SPEC
On _____: speaking for — BEHALF OF
On a close play: "Macbeth" — OUT I SAY
On a cruise — ASEA
On a level — EVEN
On a lower plane — BELOW THE HORIZON
On a miscue: "Julius Caesar" — OH HATEFUL ERROR
On a par — EVEN
On a par, to Pierre — EGAL
On a slant — ATILT
On any and all occasions — EVERYTIME
On call — READY
On cloud nine — ELATED, CHEERFUL
On coming — APPROACHING
On display — OPEN
On duty — WORKING
On fire — ABLAZE
On foot — APIED
On guard — ALERT, DUTY, WARY
On hand — ACCESSIBLE
On having an effect — CAUSER
On high — SOARING
On horseback — ASTRIDE
On in years — AGED, OLD
On key — TUNED
On land — ASHORE
On land, to a sailor — ASHORE
On occasion — SOMETIMES
On one's _____ — MIND
On one's own — SOLO
On one's toes — ALERT
On one's uppers — POOR
On pins and needles — ATINGLE, EAGER
On set — START
On the _____ (alternatively) — OTHER HAND
On the _____ (sailing) — BRINY
On the _____ (unfriendly) — OUTS
On the _____ my tongue — TIP OF
On the _____: fleeing — LAM
On the Adriatic — AT SEA
On the back of a tow truck — ON THE HOOK
On the ball — ALERT, SHARP
On the beach — ASHORE
On the bias — SLANTED
On the blink — BUSTED
On the bounding main — ASEA
On the briny — ASEA
On the calm side — ALEE
On the Coral — ASEA
On the deep — ASEA
On the dot — EXACT
On the double — FAST
On the gaudy side — SHOWY
On the go — ACTIVE
On the house — FREE
On the latch — OPEN
On the level — EVEN, FAIR
On the Ligurian — ASEA
On the lookout — ALERT
On the main — ASEA
On the mother's side — ENATE
On the move — AFOOT
On the ocean — ASEA
On the payroll — EARNING
On the QE2 — ABOARD
On the qui vive — ALERT
On the Red — ASEA
On the road — AWAY, TOURING
On the rocks — ICED
On the safe side — ALEE
On the shady side of — PAST
On the shelf — ATOP
On the sheltered side — ALEE
On the ship — ABOARD
On the showy side — LOUDISH
On the side of — FOR
On the summit — ATOP
On the trail of — AFTER
On the up and up — LEGIT
On the wane — EBBING
On the waves — ASEA
On the way — ENROUTE
On the way out — OBSOLESCENT
On the way to — BOUND
On this side: Prefix — CIS
On time — PROMPT
On to — ESSES
On top of — OVER
On top of the heap — BEST
On-air — SPOKEN
On/off device — TOGGLE SWITCH
Onagers — ASSES
Onagers, French style — ANES
Onassis — ARI
Onassis nickname — ARI
Once-powerful Persian — MEDE

Once _____ a time .... — UPON
Once _____ blue moon — IN A
Once again — ANEW, TWICE
Once around the oval — LAP
Once around the track — LAP
Once known as — NEE
Once more — AGAIN, ANEW
Once more, in Dogpatch — AGIN
Once or twice — RARELY
Once, once — ERST
Once-overs and more — OGLES
Oncoming — CLOSE
One- _____, like Odin — EYED
One-celled animal — AMOEBA
One-piece dress — CHEMISE
One _____ — SIDED
One _____ (child's game) — O CAT
One _____ (sandlot game) — O CAT
One _____ customer — TO A
One _____ time — AT A
One accepted for a job — HIREE
One after another — SERIATIM
One and only fish — SOLE
One and the same — DITTO
One anxious to please the boss — EAR BANGER
One at _____ — A TIME
One at Roanoke, e.g. — SETTLER
One at the Waughs — ALEC
One beyond hope — GONER
One billionth: Prefix — NANO
One born August 22 — LEO
One casting ballot — VOTER
One cause of trysts — AMOUR
One connected with: Suffix — AST
One day — SOMETIME
One dedicated to a religious life — OBLAT
One end of a needle — EYE
One enjoying caramels — CHEWER
One Eve had three — FACES
One Eve's grandsons — ENOS
One eyed god — ODIN
One for the books — CPA
One for the Gipper — PEP TALK
One Grande — RIO
One having a tryst — MEETER
One having legal title — OWNER
One having spats — SQUABBLER
One hundred makes a gridiron — YARDS
One hundred yrs. — CEN
One in a roll book — ATTENDEE
One in a thousand — PEARL
One in an unruly mob — RIOTER
One in arrears — OWER
One in the "noonday sun" — MAD DOG
One is Superior — LAKE
One kind of maniac — EGO
One kind of race — RAT
One kind of test — ACID
One kind of will — IRON
One leaving a will — TESTATOR
One less than septi- — HEXA
One liner — QUIP
One living on another — PARASITE
One man performance — SOLI
One man's flight — SOLO
One more time — AGAIN
One needing an att. — DEF
One not dry behind the ears — GREENY
One of 100 — SENATOR
One of 15 in Eurasia: Abbr. — SSR
One of 52 — TREY
One of a `40's singing group — INKSPOT
One of a cap'n's aides — BOSUN
One of a central Caucasian people — OSSET
One of a colorful trio — RED
One of a Columbus trio — NINA
One of a Disney trio — PIG
One of a dozen — UNIT
One of a Dumas trio — ARAMIS
One of a famous seven — DOC
One of a Gaelic people — SCOT
One of a kind — LONE
One of a Kipling trio — A RAG
One of a Latin trio — AMO
One of a Michelangelo trio — PIETA
One of a Nixon sextet — CRISIS
One of a pair — MATE
One of a rabbit trio — MOPSY
One of a required three — OUT
One of a sea-going trio — NINA
One of a slapstick trio — MOE
One of a traffic trio — STOP
One of a trio at the races — SHOW
One of a Vegas twosome — DIE
One of an unau's two — TOE
One of Athena's names — ALEA
One of Byron's names — NOEL
One of Charlie's angels — JACLYN SMITH
One of Disney's dogs — LADY, PLUTO, TRAMP
One of Eve's children — ABEL
One of Father Damien's parishioners — LEPER
One of fifty-two — TREY
One of fifty: Abbr. — TENN
One of Gunther's subjects — ASIA
One of Henry's Catherines — PARR
One of Hollmann's loves — STELLA
One of Isaac's sons — ESAU
One of Jacob's sons — ASHER
One of Job's friends — ELIHU
One of Joseph's brothers — ASHER
One of Judy's daughters — LORNA
One of Jupiter's conquests — LEDA
One of last year's frosh — SOPH
One of LBJ's dogs — HAM
One of Lyons' rivers — SAONE
One of Manhattan's rivers — EAST
One of many — ITEM
One of Nader's men? — RAIDER
One of Oberon's subjects — FAIRY
One of our armed forces — USAF
One of Ovid's names — NASO
One of Pooh's friends — ROO
One of R.E. Lee's men — REB
One of Rebekah's boys — ESAU
One of Samuel's sons — ABIA
One of Santa's crew — ELF
One of Santa's eight — DASHER
One of Santa's reindeer — DANCER, PRANCER
One of scriptural names for Deity — ELOI
One of seven — ASIA
One of Seven Deadly Sins — AVARICE
One of seven original astronauts — GRISSOM
One of Seven Sages of Greece — BIAS, SOLON
One of Seven Virtues — JUSTICE
One of several early U.S. satellites — RELAY
One of several Pharaohs — RAMESES
One of Shakespeare's last — THE WINTERS TALE

One of Texas heroes — JAMES BOWIE
One of Thalia's sisters — ERATO
One of the "Little Women" — AMY
One of the 12 tribes of Israel — ASHER
One of the 3 B's — JSB
One of the 3 R's — ARITH
One of the 400 — ASTOR
One of the Aesir — ODIN
One of the ages — TEEN
One of the Aldas — ALAN
One of the Aleutians — ATTU, ATKA
One of the Allens — STEVE, WOODY
One of the Andersons — LONI
One of the Andreanofs — ATKA
One of the Andrews Sisters — MAXINE
One of the Argonauts — IDAS
One of the Barrymores — ETHEL, JOHN
One of the bears — MAMA, URSA, POLAR
One of the believers — THEIST
One of the blinds of a horse — WINKER
One of the brasses — HORN
One of the British Isles — MAN
One of the Brontës — ANNE, EMILY
One of the Canary Islands — PALMA
One of the Carolinas — SOUTH
One of the Carolines — TRUK
One of the Chaplins — SYD
One of the Cole family — NAT
One of the common people — PLEB
One of the courses — SOUP
One of the Cratchits — TIM
One of the Dakotas — TETON
One of the Darling children — WENDY
One of the Days — DORIS
One of the de Milles — AGNES
One of the Deans — DIZZY
One of the Dioscuri — CASTOR
One of the Dorsey brothers — TOMMY
One of the downs — EIDER
One of the Dryads — ERATO
One of the EEC — ITAL
One of the Fab Four — LENNON
One of the Farrows — MIA
One of the fates — ATROPOS
One of the feds — T MAN
One of the finches — WAXBILL
One of the Finger Lakes — SENECA
One of the Fitzgeralds — ELLA
One of the Flintstones — WILMA
One of the Fords — EDSEL
One of the Forsytes — IRENE
One of the Four Horsemen — DEATH
One of the Furies — ALECTO
One of the Gandhis — INDIRA
One of the Giants — LEE
One of the Gorgons — MEDUSA
One of the Guthries — ARLO
One of the hemispheres — EASTERN
One of the Horae — IRENE
One of the Huxleys — ALDOUS
One of the Huxtables — DENISE, THEO
One of the Inner Hebrides — SKYE
One of the Jackson Five — TITO
One of the Jacksons — JESSE, KATE
One of the Johnson's beagles — HIM
One of the Johnsons — ARTE
One of the Joneses — GRACE
One of the Keatons — DIANE
One of the Kellys — GENE
One of the Kennedys — EUNICE
One of the Lauders — ESTEE
One of the Leewards — SABA, ST KITTS
One of the Lennons — ONO
One of the Marches — AMY
One of the Marxes — KARL
One of the Masseys — ILONA
One of the media — PRESS, RADIO
One of the Moluccas — CERAM
One of the Monty Python troupe — CLEESE
One of the Moores — DEMI
One of the Murphys — EDDIE
One of the Muses — CLIO
One of the musical B's — BACH
One of the Near Islands — ATTU
One of the Norns — URD
One of the Perons — EVITA
One of the Philippines — CEBU
One of the Pillars of Hercules — ROCK OF GIBRALTAR
One of the Pointer Sisters — ANITA
One of the rappers — DRE
One of the Redgraves — LYNN
One of the Reindeer people — LAPP
One of the Reiners — ROB
One of the robber barons — ASTOR
One of the Rover Boys — SAM
One of the Saarinens — EERO, ELIEL
One of the San Juan Islands — ORCAS
One of the Santas — ANITA
One of the seals — SEA LION
One of the senses — TOUCH
One of the seven hills of Rome — PALATINE
One of the seven prismatic colors — INDIGO
One of the seven sins — SLOTH
One of the Shaws — ARTIE
One of the Simpsons — BART, OJ
One of the Sitwells — EDITH
One of the Society Islands — TAHITI
One of the Starrs — RINGO
One of the stooges — MOE, SHEMP
One of the Three Musketeers — ATHOS
One of the tides — EBB
One of the titans — CRONUS
One of the Trumps — BLAINE
One of the Turners — LANA, NAT, TINA
One of the Waughs — ALEC, EVELYN
One of the Wilsons — FLIP
One of the Windward Islands — TAHITI
One of the Wise Men — GASPAR
One of triplets — TRIN
One of Uncle Remus's gang — BRER RABBIT
One of Uranus's moons — ARIEL
One of us — HUMAN
One of Woody's children — ARLO
One on the payroll — EARNER
One on the watch — ESPIER
One on the way up — COMER
One opposed — ANTI
One or more — ANY
One outside the Muslim faith — GIAOUR
One over par — BOGEY
One point of view — VERSION
One quart, roughly — LITER
One result of thinking — PLAN
One road to take — LOW
One seeded fruit — ACHENE
One side of a coin: Abbr. — OBV, TAILS
One side of a letter — PAGE
One sided — ASKEW
One sock to another — MATE
One spoon — UNIT

One spot — ACE, BUCK
One stripe G.I.'s — PFCS
One that eats: Comb. form — PHAGE
One that provokes mirth — SCREAM
One third of IX — III
One thousand — MIL
One to distrust — LIAR
One trillion — TERA
One Tuesday — WELD
One type of photograph — X RAY
One under bogey — PAR
One versed in disputation — POLEMIST
One versed in literature — SAVANT
One way not to be seen — IN THE ALTOGETHER
One way of looking at things — BACKWARDS
One way or another — BY HOOK OR CROOK
One way to cook eggs — SUNNY SIDE UP
One way to jump in the lake — FEET FIRST
One way to reach second — SLIDE
One way to save gas — BUS
One way to serve meals — FAMILY STYLE
One way to stand — PAT
One weber per square meter — TESLA
One who avoids detection — ELUDER
One who babbles — PRATTLER
One who bells the cat — DARER
One who calls a cab — HAILER
One who corrupts — DEBASER
One who designs flags — VEXILLOGRAPHER
One who dies for a cause — MARTYR
One who excels at table conversation — DEIP-NOSOPHIST
One who gives back — RESTORER
One who has an aversion to work — ERGOPHOBE
One who has insight — SEER
One who has poor penmanship — CACOGRAPHER
One who hates marriage — MISOGAMIST
One who is the center of attention — LION
One who likes dogs — CYNOPHILIST
One who makes sparks fly — WELDER
One who nullifies — NEGATOR
One who owns or controls wealth — CAPITALIST
One who practices sorcery — WITCH
One who prods — URGER
One who ruminates — MUSER
One who stores grain — ENSILER
One who studies ants — MYRMECOLOGIST
One who ties shoes — LACER
One who toes the line — HEWER
One who treats with disdain — SNUBBER
One with a bug gun — SPRAYER
One with a gun for a run — STARTER
One with a plan — INTENDER
One with eagle eyes — ERNE
One with potential — COMER
One with pressing duties? — IRONER
One year's record — ANNAL
One's behavior — MIEN
One's college — ALMA MATER
One's companion — ALL
One's husband or wife — SPOUSE
One's in Lily — UNES
One's lifework — CAREER
One's own: Comb. form — IDIO
One's own: Prefix — IDIO
One's pledged word — TROTH
One's sibling's daughters — NIECES
One's strong point — FORTE
One's total assets — ESTATE
One, in Ayr — ANE
One, in Berlin — EIN, EINE
One, in Dumfries — ANE
One, in France — UNE
One, in Frankfurt — EIN
One, in Koln — EINE
One, in Malaga — UNA
One, in Paris — UNE
One, in Spain — UNA
One, to a Fraulein — EINE
One, to a Scot — AIN
One, to Burns — ANE
One, to Fritz — EINE
One- _____ (correlating uniquely) — TO ONE
One- _____ mind — TRACK
One-armed bandit — SLOT
One-billionth: Comb. form — NANO
One-celled creatures — AMOEBAS
One-dish meal — STEW
One-eyed god — ODIN
One-horned fish — UNIE
One-horse — PETTY, SMALL
One-liner — GAG, JOKE
One-month president — HARRISON
One-named singer — CHARO
One-night stand — GIG
One-note — MONOTONE
One-seeded fruit of the elm — SAMARA
One-seeded fruit: Var. — AKENE
One-seeded winged fruit — SAMARA
One-sided — ASKEW, UNILAT-ERAL
One-sided win — ROUT
One-tenth — TITHE
One-third of a 1970 film title — TORA
One-time bloomer — CENTURY PLANT
One-time conductor of the Cleveland Orchestra — SZELL
One-time silver screen star — BARA
One-time TV host — PAAR
One-time Washington hostess — MESTA
One-time wedding word — OBEY
One: Ger. — EINE
Onefold — SIMPLE, SINGLE
Oner — BEST
Onerous — HEAVY
Ones — PERSONS
Ones who got away — ESCAPEES
Ones, to Burns — ANES
Onion — LEEK
Onion or hyacinth — BULB
Onion's kin — LEEK
Onion-flavored rolls — BIALYS
Only — MERE
Only _____ a customer — ONE TO
Only now and then — RARELY
Only sure cure for baldness — HAIR
Only's companion — ONE
Only, in Bonn — NUR
Onset — START
Onsets — ATTACKS
Ontario Bay — HUDSON
Ontario canal system — TRENT
Ontario Indian — CREE
Ontario neighbor — MANITOBA
Ontario river — SEVERN, TRENT
Ontario tribe member — CREE
Ontario tribesmen — CREES
Ontario's sister lake — ERIE
Onto — HEP
Onus — BLAME, DUTY
Onward — AHEAD, FOURTH
Oodles — LOTS, OCEANS, SCADS, TONS

Oohs and _____ — AHS
Oolong — TEA
Oolong and souchong — TEAS
Oolong brewer — TEAPOT
Oolong or Pekoe — TEA
Oomph — ELAN, PEP
Oont — CAMEL
Oop's abode — CAVE
Oop's girl — OOLA
Oop's homeland — MOO
Oop's mate — OOLA
Oops! — UH OH
Oopsies — OH OHS
Ooze — EXUDE, SEEP, SEEPAGE, SLIME
Ooze out — EXUDE
Oozed — SEEPED
Oozes — SEEPS
Op _____ — CIT
Op. cit. relative — IBID
Opacity — FOG
Opacity causing impairment of vision — CATARACT
Opal finish — INE
Opal or onyx — STONE
Opalescent — PEARLY
Opaque — DENSE, DULL, SHADY
OPEC country — IRAN
OPEC export — CRUDE
OPEC member — QATAR
OPEC moguls — EMIRS
OPEC unit — BBL
OPEC, for example — CARTEL
OPEC, for one — CARTEL
Opel or Citroën — AUTO
Open — AJAR, OVERT, REMOVE, UNBAR, UNDO
Open a _____ worms — CAN OF
Open a bit — AJAR
Open a book — READ
Open a bottle — DECAP
Open a lock (illegally) — PICK
Open a soda bottle — UNCAP
Open and above board — HONEST
Open areas — GAPS
Open as a package — UNTIED
Open door — WELCOME
Open drains — KENNELS
Open entryways — ATRIA
Open for all to see — OVERT
Open grating — GRILLE
Open ocean — OUTSEA
Open onto — ADJOIN
Open patios — ATRIA
Open porch — RAMADA
Open portico, in ancient Rome — XYST
Open shelter — RAMADA
Open spaces — RANGES
Open the ginger ale — UNCAP
Open to attack — VULNERABLE
Open to bribery — VENAL
Open to contravention — OPPOSABLE
Open up — UNZIP
Open upland, in England — WOLD
Open weave fabric — LENO
Open, as a sleeping bag — UNROLL
Open, tartlike pastries — FLANS
Open-air — OUTDOOR
Open-book exam? — AUDIT
Open-eyed — AGOG, ASTARE
Open-handed blow — SLAP
Open-hearted — FRANK
Opened the throttle — RACED
Opener — KEY
Opener of many doors — PASSKEY
Opening — SLOT
Opening in the head — NARIS
Opening letters — ABCDE
Opening maneuver — GAMBIT
Opening maneuver to gain advantage — GAMBIT
Opening music, for short — INTRO
Opening night event — PARTY
Opening of a sort — PORE
Opening word — SESAME
Openings — VENTS
Opens — UNSHUTS
Opens, in a way — BROADENS
Opera "extra" — SPEARMAN
Opera by Beethoven — FIDELIO
Opera by Bellini — NORMA
Opera by Bizet — CARMEN
Opera by d'Erlanger — TESS
Opera by Donizetti — LUCREZIA BORGIA
Opera by Giordano — FEDORA
Opera by Gounod — FAUST
Opera by Handel — NERO, SERSE
Opera by Puccini — LA BOHEME
Opera by Rossini — WILLIAM TELL
Opera by Salieri — ATAR
Opera by Verdi — OTELLO
Opera by Weber — OBERON
Opera heroine — AIDA, MIMI
Opera highlight — ARIA
Opera house feature — TIER, PIT
Opera house reed — OBOE
Opera member — BASSO
Opera of a sort — SOAP
Opera overture — SINFONIA
Opera part — SCENA
Opera role — ELSA, TONIO
Opera singer Simon _____ — ESTES
Opera singer turned director — SILLS
Opera star — DIVA
Opera star Ponselle — ROSA
Opera text writer — LIBRETTIST
Opera trailer — TION
Opera wear — CAPE, TOP HATS
Opera's Maria — CALLAS
Opera's Ponselle — ROSA
Opera's Stevens — RISE
Operate — HANDLE, RUN
Operated — RAN
Operated a loom — WOVE
Operates — RUNS
Operatic Eugen — ONEGIN
Operatic highlight — ARIA
Operatic Merriman — NAN
Operatic prince — IGOR
Operatic role — AIDA
Operatic showstopper — ARIA
Operatic soli — ARIAS
Operatic solo — ARIA
Operation by an obstetrician — CAESAREAN
Operetta by Noel Coward, 1922 — BITTER SWEET
Operetta master — LEHAR
Operettist — LEHAR
Operose — INTENT
Ophidian — ASP
Ophthalmologist — OCULIST
Opinion — TENET, VIEW, VOICE
Opossum shrimp — SCHIZOPOD
Opp. of civ. — MIL
Opp. of NNW — SSE
Opp. of SSW — NNE
Opp. of WNW — ESE
Opp. of WSW — ENE
Oppenheim sleuth — SLANE
Oppidan — CIVIC
Opponent — ANTI, FOE, RIVAL
Opponent — RIVAL
Opponent of Ike — AES
Opponent of Luther — ECK
Opponents — ANTIS
Opponents of Reps. — DEMS
Opportune — TIMELY
Oppose — ANTI, COMBAT, FACE, RESIST
Opposed — AVERSE
Opposed to — ANTI
Opposing — ANTI, RESISTANT
Opposing monopolies — ANTITRUST
Opposing positions — SIDES
Opposite — POLAR
Opposite camp — ENEMY
Opposite of "odi" — AMO
Opposite of "yeah" — NOPE
Opposite of apteral — ALAR
Opposite of apterous — ALAR
Opposite of aweather — ALEE
Opposite of broadside — END ON
Opposite of da — NYET

Opposite of dele — STET
Opposite of ectasis — SYSTOLE
Opposite of eso — EXO
Opposite of ext. — INT
Opposite of hawed — GEED
Opposite of helter-skelter — ORDERED
Opposite of ja — NEIN
Opposite of lowest point — ZENITH
Opposite of nadir — APEX
Opposite of neg. — POS
Opposite of NNW — SSE
Opposite of nope — YEP
Opposite of outer — INNER
Opposite of Pos — NEG
Opposite of Post — PRE
Opposite of saludos — ADIOS
Opposite of sml. — LGE
Opposite of surfeits — STARVES
Opposite of vive — ABAS
Opposite of wax — WANE
Opposite of weather — ALEE
Opposite of WSW — ENE
Opposite the middle of a ship's side — ABEAM
Opposite: Prefix — CONTRA
Opposites — ANTONYMS
Opposition votes — NAYS
Oppositionist — ANTI
Oppresses — MISTREATS
Oppressive — BITTER, DIRE, HOT
Oppressor — DESPOT
Opprobrium — SHAME
Opt — CHOOSE, ELECT
Optic cover — EYELID
Optic membrane: Comb. form — IRIDO
Optical device — LENS
Optical glass — LENS
Optical illusion — MIRAGE
Optical instruments — SCOPES
Optical maser — LASER
Optical projector — ENLARGER
Optician's product — LENS
Opticians' products — LENSES
Optimally — AT BEST
Optimism — HOPE
Optimistic — ROSY, SANGUINE, UPBEAT
Optimum — CREST
Option — CHOICE
Optometrist's concern — LENS
Optometrist's favorite song? — I ONLY HAVE EYES FOR YOU
Opulence — WEALTH
Opulent — LAVISH, RICH
Opus — PIECE, WORK
Or _____ — ELSE
Or _____: otherwise — ELSE
Or else, in music — OSSIA
OR procedure — SURGERY
Ora pro _____ — NOBIS
Ora pro nobis — PRAY FOR US
Oracle — SEER
Oracle locale — DELPHI
Oracle worker — SEER
Oral — PAROL, SPOKEN
Oral-vaccine man — SABIN
Orale — FANON
Orally — ALOUD
Orange-red gems — SARDS
Orange — GROVE, NAVEL
Orange and lemon beverages — ADES
Orange Bowl site — MIAMI
Orange extract — JUICE
Orange follower — JUICE
Orange gem — BALAS
Orange or grapefruit _____ — PEEL
Orange peel — RIND
Orange variety — NAVEL
Orange-brown butterflies — ELFINS
Orange-red chalcedony — SARD
Orange-shipping city in Fla. — OCALA
Orange-yellow — OCHRE
Orange-yellows — SAFFRONS
Orarion — STOLE
Orator, at times — RAVER
Oratorio highlight — ARIA
Oratorio part — ARIA
Oratory — CHAPEL
Orb — SPHERE
Orbicular object — SPHERE
Orbit point — APOGEE, APSIS
Orbital high point — APOGEE
Orchard — GARDEN
Orchard output — APPLE
Orchard pest — APHID
Orchard unit — ACRE
Orchard, for example — GALA
Orchestra member — BASSOONIST, REED
Orchestra sec. — STR
Orchestra section — REEDS
Orchestra tuners — OBOES
Orchestral instruments — VIOLAS
Orchestrate — SCORE
Orchestrate anew — RESCORE
Orchid derivatives — SALEPS
Orchid tubers — SALEP
Ordains — ENACTS
Order _____ (agenda) — OF THE DAY
Order back — REMAND
Order from a catalogue — SEND AWAY
Order from Delbert Mann — CUT
Order from Hunter — FREEZE
Order member — ELK
Order of angels — CHERUBS
Order of magnitude — ESTIMATE
Order on Wall Street — SELL
Order out — EAT IN
Order to a broker — SELL
Order to a fly — SHOO
Order to follow — COME
Order's partner — LAW
Order, of a sort — EDICT
Order: Comb. form — TAXO, TAXY
Ordered — BADE, COMMANDED
Ordered around — BOSSED
Orderly — AIDE, NEAT, REGULAR, TIDY
Orders — BIDS, FIATS, MANDATES
Orders off the premises — EVICTS
Ordinal number ending — ETH
Ordinal suffix — ETH
Ordinary — BANAL, ROUTINE, SO SO, USUAL
Ordinary writing — PROSE
Ordinary, commonplace person: Br. — LUG
Ordnance items — GUNS
Ordnance: Abbr. — ORDN
Ore — MINERAL
Ore sources — MINES
Ore store — LODE, MINE
Ore vein — LODE
Oregon and Santa Fe — TRAILS
Oregon bay — COOS
Oregon city — SALEM
Oregon coast cape — ARAGO
Oregon nickname — WEBFOOT
Oregon or Santa Fe: Abbr. — TRL
Orel's river — OKA
Org. — ASSN, SYST
Org. dating from 1897 — PTA
Org. for boys — BSA
Org. for Brownies — GSA
Org. for Couples — PGA
Org. for Koop — AMA
Org. for Pei or Wright — AIA
Org. for retirees — AARP
Org. for Snead — PGA
Org. for Sondheim, et al. — ASCAP
Org. for Spock — AMA
Org. for teachers — NEA
Org. for the rah-rah people — NCAA
Org. for Trevino, et al. — PGA
Org. for Tway — PGA
Org. founded in 1910 — BSA
Org. founded in 1915 — KKK
Org. founded in 1949 — NATO
Org. Hoover headed — FBI
Org. of creative people — ASCAP
Org. of Tin Pan Alley — ASCAP
Org. opposing the Brady bill — NRA

Org. to protect animals — SPCA
Organ _____ — GRINDER
Organ having a series of steam whistles — CALLIOPE
Organ knobs — STOPS
Organ part — STOP
Organ stop — SALICET
Organa of "Star Wars" — LEIA
Organic — NATURAL
Organic acid — AMINO
Organic chemical compound — ENOL
Organic compound — AMINE, ENOL, ESTER, NITRILE
Organic salt — ESTER
Organic vessel — VAS
Organization for high-I.Q. folk — MENSA
Organizational regulation — BYLAW
Organza — TRIM
Orgs. — ASSNS
Oribi's hue — TAN
Oriel component — WINDOWPANE
Orient — ASIA, EAST
Orient expresser — POLO
Oriental — ASIAN, EASTERN
Oriental bigwigs — AGAS
Oriental butter — GHEE
Oriental calculators — ABACI
Oriental desire? — JAPANESE YEN
Oriental greeting — SALAAM
Oriental holidays — TETS
Oriental inn — SERAI
Oriental legumes — SOYAS
Oriental nannies — AMAHS
Oriental nurse — AMAH
Oriental principle — TAO
Oriental shrine — TAA
Oriental skiff — SAMPAN
Oriental staple — RICE
Oriental tea — CHA
Oriental units of weight — TAELS
Oriental VIP — AGA
Oriental waist wrapper — OBI
Oriental weight — TAEL
Orientals — ASIANS
Orientate — ADJUST
Oriente native — CUBAN
Origin — GERM
Origin of a drive — TEE
Origin: Suffix — ENE
Original — FIRST
Original garden locale — EDEN
Original inhabitant — ABORIGINE
Original words — TEXT
Original: Comb. form — PROTO
Originally called — NEE
Originate — ARISE, CREATE, ISSUE, RISE, STEM
Originated — AROSE, STEMMED
Originates — ARISES
Originator of Impressionism — MANET
Origins — ROOTS
Orison — PRAYER
Orkney shed — SKEO
Orlando of diamond fame — CEPEDA
Orleans's river — LOIRE
Ornament — STUD
Ornament made of ribbons — ROSETTE
Ornament silverware — CHASE
Ornamental — FANCY, FRILLY
Ornamental band of a sort — ARMLET
Ornamental bauble of glass — BEAD
Ornamental charm — AMULET
Ornamental evergreen shrub — TOYON
Ornamental loop — PICOT
Ornamental mat made of lace — DOILY
Ornamental pink — CARNATION
Ornamental shrub — MAGNOLIA, OLEANDER
Ornamental strip — EDGING
Ornamental stud — AGLET
Ornamental style — DECOR
Ornamental trim on a shirt — JABOT
Ornamental wreath — CORONET
Ornate — BAROQUE
Ornate wardrobe — ARMOIRE
Ornate wood finish — GOLD LEAF
Ornery — BLUNT
Ornithologist's favorite ballet? — THE FIREBIRD
Orphan of fame — ANNIE
Orphan's new parent — ADOPTER
Orpheus's instrument — LYRE
Orsk's river — URAL
Ort — BIT, CRUMB, SCRAP
Orthodontist's degree — DMD
Orthodoxy — FAITH
Orwell prediction for 1984 — BIG BROTHER
Orwell's old school — ETON
Orwellian citizen — KPROLE
Orwellian relative — BIG BROTHER
Ory of jazz — KID
Oryxes — ELANDS
Osaka Bay point — KOBE
Osaka's Island — HONSHU
Oscar-winner Rainer — LUISE
Oscar _____ Sanchez: 1987 Nobel winner — ARIAS
Oscar and Tony — AWARDS
Oscar de la _____ — RENTA
Oscar or Edgar — AWARD
Oscar-winner Kline — KEVIN
Oscar-winner of 1987 — CHER
Oscar-winning Anouk — AIMEE
Oscar-winning film — CHARIOTS OF FIRE
Oscar-winning film: 1979 — KRAMER VS KRAMER
Oscar-winning Goldie — HAWN
Oscars' kin — TONYS
Oscillate — SWAY, WEAVE
Oscillated — SWUNG
Oscitant — SLEEPY
Osculate — KISS
Osier — WAND
Osiris' wife — ISIS
Oslo _____ — FJORD
Oslo coin — ORE
Oslo toast — SKOAL
Osmium or uranium — ELEMENT
Osprey's home — AERY
Osprey's quarters — AERIE
Ospreys' kin — ERNES
OSS follower — CIA
Ossa and Ida: Abbr. — MTS
Osseous — BONY
Osso buco base — VEAL
Ossuary — URN
Ossuary holding — BONES
Ostentatious display: Colloq. — RITZ
Ostracize — BAN
Ostracized — BANNED
Ostrich feather-trimmed "Eugenie" — HAT
Ostrich kin — EMU
Ostrich or emu — RATITE
Ostrich relatives — EMUS
Ostrich's cousin — EMU, RHEA
Ostrich's kin — EMU
Ostrich's relative — EMU, MOA
Ostro or Visi follower — GOTH
OT books — CHRON
Otalgia — EAR ACHE
Otary — SEA LION
Othello or Iago — ROLE
Othello's "ancient" — IAGO
Othello's two-faced friend — IAGO
Othello's underling — IAGO
Other — ADDED, ELSE, FURTHER, MORE
Other name of Lalitpur, Nepal — PATAN
Other than: Prefix — NON
Other women in Mexico — OTRAS
Other women, to El Cid — OTRAS
Other, in Chile — OTRA
Other, to Orozco — OTRO
Other: Comb. form — ALLO
Others, in Oviedo — OTROS

Others, to Ovid — ALII
Otherwise — BESIDES, ELSE, IF NOT
Otherwise known as — ALIAS
Otherwordly — SUPERNATURAL
Otic — AURAL
Otic organ — EAR
Otiose — DULL, IDLE, USELESS
Otoe relative — OSAGE
Otologist's concern — EARS
Ott or Torme — MEL
Ottawa chief — PONTIAC
Ottawa's country — CANADA
Ottawa's province — ONT
Otter — HURON
Otto _____ Bismarck — VON
Otto I's dom. — HRE
Otto's realm: Abbr. — HRE
Otto, nove, _____ — DIECI
Ottoman — SOFA
Ottoman dynasty founder — OSMAN
Ottoman Empire bigwigs — AGAS
Ottoman Empire follower — OSMAN
Ottoman Empire founder — OTHMAN
Ottoman governors — BEYS
Ottoman officers — AGHAS
Ottoman officials — DEYS
Ottoman peasant — RAYA
Ottoman ruler — SULTAN
Ottoman ruler of old — DEY
Ottoman VIP — AGA
Ottomans — SEATS
Oubliette — DUNGEON
Ouch — PAIN
Ought to — SHOULD
Oui, oui, on Oviedo — SISI
Ouija — BOARD
Ounces — SNOW LEOPARD
Ouph — ELF
Our largest bone — FEMUR
Ouse tributary — URE
Ousel — DIPPER
Oust — DEPOSE, EJECT, EXPEL
Ouster — REMOVAL
Ousts — EVICTS
Out-and-out — WHOLLY
Out-of-doors — ALFRESCO
Out — NOT IN
Out _____ (no longer available) — OF PRINT
Out _____ limb — ON A
Out and away — BY FAR
Out and out — TOTAL
Out at the elbows — SEEDY
Out for — AFTER
Out forerunner — SHUT
Out like a light — ASLEEP
Out of _____ (cross) — SORTS
Out of _____ (discordant) — SYNC
Out of _____ (disjointed) — SYNC
Out of _____ (grumpy) — SORTS
Out of bed — RISEN
Out of breath — WINDED
Out of control — AMOK
Out of court — EXCURIA
Out of fashion — PASSE
Out of funds — BROKE
Out of jail, conditionally — PAROLED
Out of kilter — AWRY
Out of line — ASKEW
Out of order — KAPUT
Out of place — UNFIT
Out of port — ASEA
Out of practice — RUSTY
Out of shape — UNFIT
Out of sight — CONCEALED, HIDDEN
Out of sorts — CROSS, CURT, SHORT
Out of style — DATED
Out of the elements — INDOORS
Out of the house — ABROAD
Out of the labor mkt. — RET
Out of the ordinary — AS IF, RARE, UNUSUAL
Out of the way — AFIELD, ASIDE
Out of the wind — ALEE
Out of this world — REMOTE
Out of town — AWAY
Out of whack — AMISS, ALOP
Out of work — IDLE
Out on _____ — A LIMB
Out on a _____ — LIMB
Out on a limb — TREED
Out score — BEAT
Out with — TELL
Out, in Edam — UIT
Out-of-date — PASSE
Out-of-the-way — REMOTE
Outback bird — EMU
Outbreak — RIOT
Outbuilding — SHED
Outburst — SALLY
Outburst from Etna — ERUPTION
Outcast — PARIAH
Outcome — ISSUE, RESULT, UPSHOT
Outcry — BAWL
Outcry at the Omni — HOORAY
Outdated — PASSE, STALE
Outdated: Abbr. — OBS
Outdid — TOPPED
Outdistance — LOSE
Outdo — BEST, EXCEL
Outdoes — CAPS
Outdoor military entertainment — TATTOO
Outdoor storage fee — YARDAGE
Outdoorsman — CAMPER
Outer coating — RIND
Outer ear parts — TRAGI
Outer edges — RIMS
Outer garments — CAPES, COATS, JACKET
Outer rim — EDGE
Outer space — ETHER
Outer space, once — ETHER
Outer surfaces — COATS
Outer: Abbr. — EXT
Outer: Comb. form — ECT
Outer: Prefix — ECTO, EXO
Outfielder's feat — SHOESTRING CATCH
Outfit — ENSEMBLE, EQUIP
Outfit for baby? — WET SUIT
Outfit for Odette or Odile — TUTU
Outfits — RIGS
Outflowing branch of a lake — EFFLUENT
Outguess — PSYCH
Outhouse — PRIVY
Outing — EXCURSION
Outlander — ALIEN, STRANGER
Outlandish — OUTRE
Outlaw — RENEGADE
Outlaw Starr — BELLE
Outlaws — BADMEN
Outlay — COST
Outlet — VENT
Outlet for N.Y. horse players — OTB
Outline — PLAN
Outline sharply — LIMN
Outlines — SKETCHES, TRACES
Outlook — ASPECT
Outlying — REMOTE
Outmoded — BYGONE, DATED, PASSE
Outmoded companion — CHAPERON
Outpour from Vesuvius — LAVA
Outpouring — EFFUSION
Output's opposite — INTAKE
Outputs — YIELDS
Outrageous — DAMNABLE
Outrigger — PROA
Outside: Comb. form — ECTO, EXO
Outside: Prefix — ECT, EXO, EXTRO
Outsider — ALIEN
Outspoken — VOCAL
Outstanding review — RAVE
Outta _____! — SIGHT
Outward — ECTAD, ECTAL
Outward appearance — AIR
Outward moving muscle — EVERTOR

Outwit — ELUDE, EVADE
Outwitted — ELUDED
Ova — EGGS
Oval circuit — LAP
Ovation's demand — ENCORE
Oven — KILN, OAST
Oven emanation — AROMA
Oven for annealing glass — LEHR
Oven setting — BAKE
Oven used to anneal glass — LEHR
Ovens — OASTS
Over — ABOVE, ATOP, DONE, ENDED
Over 100 — OLD
Over 65 — SPEEDING
Over a toy? — ATOP
Over again — ANEW
Over all — ATOP
Over and above — ELSE, PLUS
Over and done with — PAST
Over and over — OFTEN
Over there — ACROSS
Over there, of yore — YOND
Over with — ENDED
Over yonder — THERE
Over, to an Odist — OER
Over, to Dickinson — OER
Over, to Fritz — UBER
Over: Comb. form — HYPER
Over: Ger. — UBER
Over: Prefix — EPI
Overact — EMOTE
Overall — TOTAL
Overbearing — RUDE
Overburden — TASK
Overcharges — SOAKS, STINGS
Overcoat — PARKA, RAGLAN
Overcome — BEAT
Overcome easily — ROUT
Overcome reserve — BREAK THE ICE
Overcomes — AWES
Overcomes hostility — DISARMS
Overconsumers? — HOGS
Overdo — EXHAUST
Overdoes — STRAINS
Overdue — LATE
Overdue debts — ARREARS
Overeat — GORGE, STUFF
Overflow — FLOAT
Overgrown with shrubbery — BUSHY
Overhangs — EAVES
Overhead — ATOP, ALOFT
Overhead door locale — GARAGE
Overhead expense — RENT
Overhead rail lines — ELS
Overhead railways — ELS
Overindulge — SATE
Overindulge, in a way — TOPE
Overjoyed — ELATED
Overlays — CEILS
Overlays with gold — GILDS
Overload with work — SWAMP
Overloads — JAMB
Overlook — FORGET, IGNORE, OMIT
Overlooked, as an offense — CONDONED
Overly — TOO
Overly adorned — ORNATE
Overly aggressive — PUSHY
Overly bright — GLARY
Overly enthusiastic — GAGA
Overly enthusiastic one — MANIAC
Overly prim one — PRISS
Overly sentimental — MUSHY, SOUPY
Overnight bivouac — ETAPE
Overplayed — EMOTED
Overpoured the milk — SPILT
Overpriced, informally — OUT OF SIGHT
Overrate — MISPRAISE
Oversaw — RAN
Overseas — ABROAD
Overseas addresses for G.I.s — APOS
Overseas addresses, for short — APOS
Oversees — RUNS
Oversentimental — SAPPY
Overshadow — ECLIPSE
Overshoe — GALOSH
Overshoes — GAITERS
Oversight — OMISSION
Oversize shoe width — EEEE
Oversized — HORSY
Overstuff — SATIATE
Oversupply — GLUT
Overt — OPEN
Overthrow — DEPOSE, DOWNFALL, OUST
Overthrows first base — ERRS
Overture — PRELUDE
Overture follower — ACT I
Overture used by "The Lone Ranger" — WILLIAM TELL
Overturn — CAPSIZE, UPEND, UPSET
Overused — HACKNEYED, TRITE
Overwhelm — AWE, BLITZ
Overwhelmed — ENGULFED
Overwhelmed — FLOORED
Overwhelmed, in a way — AWED
Overwhelms — AWES, STUNS
Overwhelms with wonder — AMAZES
Overwrought — FRANTIC
Overzealous dieters — STARVERS
Overzealous worker — EAGER BEAVER
Ovid's "it was" — ERAT
Ovid's "you love" — AMAS
Ovid's eggs — OVA
Ovid's omelet base — OVA
Ovid's others — ALIA
Ovine call — BAA
Ovine noises — BLEATINGS
Ovine parents — EWES
Ovine sound — BAA
Ovules — SEEDS
Owen Josephus _____ — ROBERTS
Owens of the Olympics — JESSE
Owing — DUE, IN DEBT
Owl's shipmate — PUSSY
Owl's utterance — HOOT
Owlish — WISE
Owlish comment — HOOT
Own — HAS, HAVE, HOLD
Own up — ADMIT TO
Own up to — ADMIT
Own, to Burns — HAE
Owned — HAD
Owner — HOLDER
Owner of Asta — NORA
Owner of real estate — LAND HOLDER
Owner's document — DEED
Owning much land — ACRED
Owns — HAS
Owns: Ger. — EIGEN
Ox — BISON
Ox attachment — IDE
Ox of Celebes — ANOA
Ox of puzzledom — ANOA
Ox, in Osnabruck — OCHS
Oxen don't laugh at these? — YOKES
Oxen of Asia — YAKS
Oxen restraints — YOKES
Oxen yoke parts — SKEYS
Oxeye or English — DAISY
Oxford — SHOE
Oxford cinchers — LACES
Oxford college — ORIEL
Oxford fellows — DONS
Oxford Group's concern — MORALS
Oxford sweaters — ROLLNECKS
Oxford tutor — DON
Oxford, for one — SHOE
Oxheart — CHERRY
Oxidative — AEROBIC
Oxidized — RUSTED
Oxidizes — RUSTS
Oxygen discoverer — JOSEPH PRIESTLEY
Oyster shell — SHUCK
Oyster's creation — PEARL
Oyster's home — BED
Oysters' hues — ECRUS
Oz creature — LION
Oz dog — TOTO
Oz visitor — TOTO
Ozark's "encore" — AGIN
Ozzie and Harriet — NELSON

P

P-U connection — QRST
P. Benchley's filmed novel: 1977 — THE DEEP
P.A.'s promotional gimmicks — HYPE
P.C. Wren's "Beau _____" — GESTE
P.C. Wren's "Beau _____" — GESTE
P.D. alert — APB
P.D.Q. — ASAP, PRESTO
P.D.Q., updated — ASAP
P.G.A. tourer — PRO
P.G.A.'s Lee _____ — ELDER
P.I. timber tree — ACLE
P.L.O.'s Arafat — YASIR
P.M. of Japan "1964-72" — SATO
P.O. — COP
P.O. decisions — RTES
P.O. item — LTR, PCL, STP
P.O. stamp — CANC
P.O.W. camp of W.W. II — STALAG
P.R. man's concern — IMAGE
PA port — ERIE
Pa's — DADS
Pa. city — ALTOONA
Pa. port — ERIE
Pablo's love — AMOR
Pablo's uncle — TIO
Pabulum — FOOD
Pac-10 power — UCLA
Pac-Man's home — ARCADE
Pac. counterpart — ATL
Pac.'s partner — ATL
Pace — TEMPO
Pace car — STARTER
Pace for Solti — LENTO
Pacer — TROTTER
Pacers or Packers — TEAM
Pachinko — GAME
Pachyderm — ELEPHANT
Pachysandra — PLANT
Pacific — IRENIC
Pacific _____ — RIM
Pacific garlands — LEIS
Pacific goose — NENE
Pacific Island — FIJI
Pacific island group — FIJI, MARIANAS
Pacific islands — OCEANIA
Pacific nations — ASIANS
Pacific Ocean discoverer — BALBOA
Pacific Ocean major island — GUAM
Pacific palm — NIPA
Pacific pinnipeds — SEA LIONS
Pacific porgy — TAI
Pacific rainbows — STEELHEAD TROUT
Pacific staples — EDDOES
Pacific state — HAWAII
Pacific trading shell — COWRIE
Pacify — ALLAY, APPEASE, SOOTHE
Pacino and Hirt — ALS
Pacino and Kaline — ALS
Pacino and Smith — ALS
Pacino film — DOG DAY AFTERNOON
Pack — STOW
Pack a pipe — TAMP
Pack animal — MULE
Pack away — STORE, STOW
Pack down — TAMP
Pack fruit with the best on top — DEACON
Pack in the hold — STEVE
Pack in tightly — TAMP
Pack of cards — DECK
Pack of Pachyderms — HERD
Pack pipe tobacco — TAMP
Pack tightly — STIVE
Package — ENCASE
Package cotton — BALE
Package deceptively — DEACON
Packager of a kind — CANNER
Packed away — STOWED
Packed cotton — BALED
Packed the fruit in jars — CANNED
Packer — CASER
Packet — STEAMBOAT
Packing a Colt — ARMED
Packing a rod — ARMED
Packs away — STOWS
Packs down tightly — TAMPS
Pad — CRIB, TABLET
Pad of sorts — FLAT
Padding in packing — DUNNAGE
Paddle — OAR, PROPEL
Paddle's relative — OAR
Paddock dweller — MARE
Paddock parent — MARE, SIRE
Paddock sound — SNORT
Paddock treats — EATS
Paddock youngsters — FOALS
Paddy product — RICE
Paddy wagon — VAN
Paddy Wagon's load — SUSPECTS
Paderewski — IGNACE
Paderewski's middle name — JAN
Padlock — FASTEN
Padlock parts — HASP
Padlocks — SHUTS
Padres' French kin — ABBES
Padres' late owner — KROC
Pads — TABLETS
Padua frescoes, e.g. — GIOTTOS
Paducah's river — OHIO
Paean — HYMN
Paella ingredient — RICE
Paella part — RICE
Paer wrote 43 of these — OPERAS
Pagan image — IDOL
Pagans — HEATHENS
Page — LEAF
Page instrn. — PTO
Page number — FOLIO
Page of a book — LEAF
Page size — OCTAVO
Pageant — SHOW
Pager — BEEPER
Pago Pago location — SAMOA
Pago Pago native — SAMOAN
Pago Pago person — SAMOAN
Pagoda — SHRINE
Pahlavi was one — SHAH
Pahlavi, et al. — SHAHS
Pahlavi, for one — SHAH
Pahlevi's namesakes — RIZAS
Pahoehoe, e.g. — LAVA
Paid attention to — HEEDED
Paid by service — IN KIND
Paid for a hand — ANTED
Paid the cost — DEFRAYED
Paid to play — ANTEED
Paid up — ANTED
Paige, the pitcher — SATCHEL
Pail — BUCKET
Pain — ACHE, CRAMP, PANG, SMART
Pain in the neck — BORE
Pain in the neck — PEST
Pain killer — AGENT
Pain relievers — OPIATES
Paine's creed — DEISM
Paine's pamplet, "Common _____" — SENSE
Pained exclamations — OWS
Painful — ACHY, SORE
Painful areas — SORES
Painful mistakes — BONERS
Painful spots — SORES
Painful things — SORES
Pains — EFFORTS
Painstaking — EXACT, DILIGENT

Paint — COAT, COLOR, DEPICT, EMBELLISH, PRIMER
Paint — SKETCH, STAIN, TINT
Paint again — REDO
Paint binders — CASEINS
Paint by pressure — SPRAY
Paint ingredient — LAC
Paint layers — COATS
Paint on Suncays — DAUB
Paint remover — TURPENTINE
Paint solvent — ACETONE
Paint stand — EASEL
Paint the town red — MAKE A NIGHT OF IT, REVE
Paint with a gun — SPRAY
Paint-factory employee — TONER
Paint: Comb. form — PICTO
Painted — COVERED, DECORATED
Painted _____ — DESERT
Painted lady — BUTTERFLY
Painted leopard — OCELOT
Painted metalware — TOLE
Painted or Mojave — DESERT
Painted tinplate — TOLE
Painted up — ROUGED
Painter _____ Borch — TER
Painter Andrea del _____ — SARTO
Painter Chagall — MARC
Painter Claude _____, né Gelée — LORRAIN
Painter Dufy — RAOUL
Painter Edward _____: 1780-1949 — HICKS
Painter Ernst — MAX
Painter Fernand's family — LEGERS
Painter Grabar — IGOR
Painter Hieronymus — BOSCH
Painter Joan _____ — MIRO
Painter Jose Maria — SERT
Painter leaves behind a fifth of N.Y.C. — THOMAS GAINS
Painter Lichtenstein — ROY
Painter Matisse — HENRI
Painter Max — ERNST
Painter Neiman — LEROY
Painter of "Arrangement in Grey and Black" — WHISTLER
Painter of "Aurora" — RENI
Painter of "Christian World" — WYETH
Painter of "Descent from the Cross" — RUBENS
Painter of "Haystack" — MONET
Painter of "Les Demoiselles d'Avignon" — PICASSO
Painter of "Olympia" — MANET
Painter of "Persistence of Memory — DALI
Painter of "St. Francis in Ecstasy" — BELLINI
Painter of "Stag at Sharkey's" — BELLOWS
Painter of "Starry Night" — VAN GOGH
Painter of "Tenant Farmer" — WYETH
Painter of "The Bath" — BONNARD
Painter of "The Dance" — MATISSE
Painter of "The Death of Marat" — DAVID
Painter of "The Feast of St. Nicholas" — STEEN
Painter of "The Fife Player" — MANET
Painter of "The Lacemaker" — VERMEER
Painter of "The Potato Eaters" — VAN GOGH
Painter of American Indians — CATLIN
Painter of ballerinas — DEGAS
Painter of dancers — DEGAS
Painter of limp watches — DALI
Painter of melted watches — DALI
Painter of murals — RIVERA
Painter of waterlilies — MONET
Painter Picasso — PABLO
Painter Winslow — HOMER
Painter Wyeth — ANDREW
Painter's boards — PALETTES
Painter's choice — ENAMEL
Painter's medium — TEMPERA
Painter's need — EASEL
Painter's paste — GESSO
Painter's perches — LADDERS
Painter's prop — EASEL
Painter's subject — NUDE
Painter-engraver Albrecht — DURER
Painter-engraver from Bologna — RENI
Painter-writer Kokoschka — OSKAR
Painters — ARTISTS
Painters' gear — LADDERS
Painters' gear — LADDERS
Painting — ART, LANDSCAPE, OIL
Painting and poetry, e.g. — ARTS
Painting exhibit — SALON
Painting on plaster — MURAL
Painting style — GENRE
Paintings in the Louvre — COROTS
Pair — BRACE, DUAD, DYAD
Pair for Tell — BOW AND ARROW
Pair makers — DUAD
Pair of matched horses — SPAN
Pair on an angelus — ALAE
Paired — DOUBLED, MATCHED, YOKED
Paired horses — SPAN
Paired, as socks — MATED
Pairs — DUOS, SETS, TWOS
Paisano in Rome — PAL
Paisley native — SCOT
Paiute — AMERINDIAN
Pakistan's neighbor — IRAN
Pakistani city — LAHORE
Pakistani coin — RUPEE
Pakistani language — URDU
Pakistani port — KARACHI
Pakse's land — LAOS
Palace — MANSION
Palace in Paris — ELYSEE
Palace VIP — PRINCESS
Paladin — KNIGHT
Palais social events — BALS
Palatable — SAPID, SAVORY, TASTY
Palate lobes — UVULAS
Palatine — SOLDIER
Palaver — CHATTER
Palazzo d'_____, at Varese — ESTE
Pale — ANEMIC, ASHEN, ASHY, PASTY, WAN
Pale blue-green — AQUA
Pale blusher — LIGHT ROUGE
Pale color — TINT
Pale green — ALOES
Pale hero — WHITE KNIGHT
Pale purple — LILAC, ORCHID
Pale shades of beige — ECRUS
Pale tan — ECRU
Pale yellow — MAIZE
Pale yellow: Comb. form — OCHRO
Paleo — OLD
Paleozoic, for one — ERA
Paler — PASTIER
Palermo's country — SICILY
Palermo's neighbor — CARINI
Pales — FADES
Palestra — ARENA, WORK OUT
Palimony — ALLOWANCE
Palindrome part — ERE I SAW
Palindrome word — ERE
Palindrome's first word — MADAM
Palindromic — ARA
Palindromic belief — TENET
Palindromic constellation — ARA
Palindromic craft — KAYAK
Palindromic emperor — OTTO
Palindromic French quisling — LAVAL
Palindromic Indian — OTO
Palindromic man — OTTO

Palindromic names — ANNA, OTTO, NAN
Palindromic nicknames — NANS
Palindromic nitwit — BOOB
Palindromic parrot — ARARA
Palindromic preposition — ERE
Palindromic sheep — EWE
Palindromic signal receiver — RADAR
Palindromic time — NOON
Palindromic title — MAAM, MADAM
Palisade — CORRAL
Pall — COVER
Pallets — BEDS
Palliate — MASK, SMOOTH
Pallid — ASHEN, WAN, WASHY
Palm — ARECA, NIPA
Palm beach shade — TAN
Palm cockatoo — ARARA
Palm fruit — DATE, COCONUT
Palm leaf — FROND, OLA
Palm leaf: var. — OLA
Palm of the hand — VOLA
Palm product — DATE
Palm reader — SEER
Palm Springs mayor and family — BONOS
Palm Springs mayor Sonny — BONO
Palm starches — SAGOS
Palm Sunday beast — ASS
Palm tree stem — CAUDEX
Palmas or Vegas — LAS
Palmer — ARNIE
Palmer and McKay — JIMS
Palmer club — BRASSIE
Palmer of baseball — JIM
Palmer of the links — ARNIE
Palmer peg — TEE
Palmer's need — DRIVER
Palmer's org. — PGA
Palmist's concern — LIFELINE
Palmist's interest — LINES
Palo _____ — ALTO
Palo singer? — ALTO
Palomar — MOUNT
Palpable — TANGIBLE
Palpably sticky substance — GOO
Palpate — FEEL
Palsy-walsy — CHUMMY
Palter — LIE
Paltry — POOR, SORRY
Palustrine plant — REED
Pamlic Sound feeder — NEUSE
Pampas — PLAIN
Pampas rope — RIATA
Pamper — COSSET, MOLLYCODDLE
Pamper in Africa? — MALI CODDLE
Pamper: Irish — COSHER
Pampered — BABIED
Pamphlet — TRACT
Pamplona encouragements — OLES
Pamplona sight — TORO
Pan-fry — SAUTE
Panacea — CURE, NOSTRUM, REMEDY
Panache — STYLE, ELAN
Panama — CANAL
Panama hat material — JIPAJAPA
Panamanian breakfast food — GRANOLA PALMA
Panamanian coins — BALBOAS
Panamanian province — DARIEN
Panay inhabitant — ATI
Panay native — ATI
Panay seaport — ILOILO
Pancake mix — BATTER
Pancakes' enhancer — SIRUP
Panda's cousin — RACCOON
Pandas — WAHS
Pandora's escapees — ILLS
Panegyric — ELONGE
Panegyrics — PRAISES
Panel — JURY
Panel member — JUROR
Panel piece — STILE
Panel strip — SPLAT
Panfry — SAUTE
Pang — THROE
Pangs — ACHES
Panhandle — BEG
Panhandle State — WVA
Panic — FUNK, SCARE, TERROR
Panic and run — BOLT
Panoply — ARRAY
Panorama — SCENE, VIEW
Pant — HEAVE
Panting — AGASP
Pantomime pastimes — CHARADES
Pantry — LARDER
Pantry assortment — CANS
Pantry item — LARD
Pantry stock — SUGAR
Pants section — SEAT
Pantyhose shade — ECRU
Pantywaist — SISSY
Papa Bear of football — HALAS
Papa Bear, e.g. — SIRE
Papa Hemingway — ERNEST
Papal cape — FANON, ORALE
Papal court — CURIA, HOLY SEE
Papal edict — BULL
Papal garment — ORALE
Papal name — PIUS
Papal vestment — FANON, ORALE
Papas from Greece — IRENE
Paper ball — WAD
Paper cut eight from a sheet — OCTAVO
Paper fasteners — STAPLES
Paper holder — CLIP
Paper material — PULP
Paper measure — REAM
Paper money — ONES, SCRIP
Paper money: Abbr. — SCR
Paper or board lead-in — WALL
Paper quantity — REAM
Paper size — POTT
Paper type — CARBON
Paper-mulberry bark — TAPA
Paperback, sometimes — REPRINT
Paperboy's cry — EXTRA
Paperhanger's need — PASTE
Papier- _____ — MACHE
Papini subject — CRISTO
Papua New Guinea town — LAE
Par _____ — AVION, NORM
Par excellence — A ONE
Parabasis — ODE
Parable — STORY
Parabolas — ARCS
Parachutes, with "out" — BAILS
Parachutist — SKY TROOPER
Parachutist's decent — DROP
Parade — MARCH
Parade confetti — TICKER TAPE
Parade element — UNIT
Parade hat — SHAKO
Parade item — FLOAT
Parade music — MARCH
Parade or bonnet leader — EASTER
Paradiddle — DRUM BEAT
Paradigm — MODEL, STANDARD
Paradigms or paragons — IDEALS
Paradise — EDEN
Paragon — IDEAL, IDOL, MODEL, NONESUCH
Paragram — PUN
Paragraph — PASSAGE
Paraguay's capital — ASUNCION
Paraguayan tea — MATE
Parallel to level ground: Abbr. — HOR
Paralyze with fear — PETRIFY
Paramount workplace — LOT
Paraphernalia — GEAR, TACKLE
Paraphrase — TRANSLATE
Parasite — FLEA
Paravane — OTTER
Parcel marking — HANDLE WITH CARE
Parcel of land — ACRE
Parcel out — ALLOCATE, DOLE, METE
Parcel's partner — PART
Parceled (out) — METED
Parch — SEAR
Parched — ARID, SERE
Pardon — AMNESTY, REMIT

Pare — TRIM
Pared — PEELED
Parent — DAD
Parent to child — REARER
Parent's concern — SCHOOL
Parent, in Dogpatch — MAW
Parental admonition — NONE OF YOUR LIP
Parental admonition — NONO, DONT
Parental meal time command — EAT IT
Parental reproof — NONO
Parental siblings — AUNTS
Pares — PEELS
Pares down — REDUCES
Parhelion — SUNDOG
Pariah — LEPER
Parings — RINDS
Paris airport — ORLY
Paris and D.C. subways — METROS
Paris aportioned her — HELEN
Paris divider — SEINE
Paris green spot — PARC
Paris greens? — SALADE
Paris season — ETE
Paris springtime — MAI
Paris suburb — ISSY
Paris subway — METRO
Paris university — SORBONNE
Paris's _____ Neuf — PONT
Paris's home town — TROY
Paris's rival — ROMEO
Paris-to-Orlèans dir. — SSW
Parish in Bermuda — PAGET
Parish priest — CURATE
Parishioner's word — AMEN
Parishioners' places — PEWS
Parisian color — FRENCH BLUE
Parisian expletive — MON DIEU
Parisian greeting — BON JOUR
Parisian head — TETE
Parisian hen — POULE
Parisian landmark — EIFFEL TOWER
Parisian money lender? — LEFT BANKER
Parisian nights — NUITS
Parisian pancake — CREPE
Parisian parent — MAMAN
Parisian pates — TETES
Parisian poser — MODELE
Parisian possessive — SES
Parisian recreation area — PARC
Parisian season — ETE
Parisian's "Are you there?" — ALLO
Parisian's "Eureka!" — VOILA
Parisian's consent — OUI
Parisian's donkey — ANE
Parisian's high school — LYCEE
Parisian's pal — AMI
Parisian's plug — BONDE
Parisian's shelter — ABRI
Parisienne — ELLE
Parisienne's maidservant — BONNE
Parisienne's poet — EGALE
Park — COMMON, GARDEN, GRASS, PLAZA, WOODLAND
Park Chung _____, S Korean President — HEE
Park in Colorado — ESTES
Park in Oslo — FROGNER
Parka — ANARAK
Parka features — HOODS
Parka piece — HOOD
Parka's British cousin — ANDORAK
Parker of "Daniel Boone" — FESS
Parking lot fixture — METER
Parking place — GARAGE, DRIVEWAY
Parking violation penalty — FINE
Parkway — ROAD
Parkway sign — EXIT
Parlance — IDIOM
Parley — SPEAK
Parleys — CONFABS
Parliament figure — LORD
Parlor furniture — DIVAN
Parlor piece — ROCKER, SETTEE, SOFA
Parnassian number — NINE
Parnassus figure — MUSE
Parodies — SPOOFS
Parody — SKIT
Parotitis — MUMPS
Paroxysm — FIT, SPELL
Parquet circle — PARTREE
Parrot — APE, ECHO, KEA, MACAW
Parrot — LORY
Parrot fish — LORO
Parrot's activity — ECHOING
Parrot's mandible covering — CERE
Parrot, often — ECHOER
Parroted — APED
Parrots — APERS, APES
Parrots or pigeons — AVIAN
Parry — AVERT, EVADE, FEND, STOP, WARD
Parse — DISSECT
Parsees' sacred writings — AVESTA
Parsees, e.g. — SECT
Parseghian — ARA
Parseval — AIRCRAFT
Parsifal composer — WAGNER
Parsimonious — FRUGAL
Parsley relative — ANISE
Parsley, to a chef — GARNI, GARNISH
Parson bird — TUI
Parson's place — MANSE
Parsonage — CLERGY, MANSE
Parsons' homes — MANSES
Parsons, et al. — ESTELLES
Part — ROLE, SEVER
Part company — DIVORCE
Part follower — ITION
Part OAS — ORG
Part of — ABA
Part of — INTO
Part of "G.W.T.W." — GONE
Part of "I Remember Mama" — SCENE
Part of "to be" — ARE
Part of a 3-piece suit — VEST
Part of a 747 — ENGINE
Part of a ball team — CATCHER
Part of a barn — MOW
Part of a barrel — HOOP
Part of a basilica — NAVE
Part of a bassoon — REED
Part of a bird's bill — CERE
Part of a book — INDEX, SPINE
Part of a boot or shoe — VAMP
Part of a bottle — NECK
Part of a bout — ROUND
Part of a bowling alley — LANE
Part of a bridle — REIN
Part of a C.S.A. hero's signature — E LEE
Part of a Caesarian trio — VIDI
Part of a calix — SEPAL
Part of a cart — AXLE
Part of a castle — KEEP
Part of a cheer — HIP
Part of a china set — DISH
Part of a Chinese acre — MOU
Part of a church — APSE
Part of a city silhouette — SKY-SCRAPER
Part of a clan — SEPT
Part of a coat — LAPEL
Part of a college course — LECTURE
Part of a colon — DOT
Part of a column — ORRO
Part of a comet — TAIL
Part of a constellation — STAR
Part of a dagger — HILT
Part of a daily dozen — SITUPS
Part of a dart — SHAFT
Part of a dictionary — INDEX
Part of a dollar — CENT
Part of a drama — ACT
Part of a film — REEL
Part of a flight — STAIR
Part of a flower — STAMEN
Part of a foot — INCH, INSTEP, TOE
Part of a full house — PAIR
Part of a Gallic question — PARLEZ VOUS
Part of a gateleg — TABLE TOP
Part of a GI's address — APO

Part of a golf club — TOE
Part of a golf course — GREEN
Part of a hammer — CLAW
Part of a hammerhead — PEEN
Part of a hand — PINKY
Part of a hat trick — GOAL
Part of a highlander's garb — PLAID
Part of a hippogriff — STAG
Part of a Hunan dinner — RICE
Part of a journey — LEG
Part of a lamp — HARP
Part of a lasso — NOOSE
Part of a Latin dance — CHA
Part of a leg — CALF, SHIN
Part of a letterhead: Abbr. — ADR
Part of a locomotive — CAB
Part of a London building — STOREY
Part of a loom — EASER
Part of a maison — SALLE
Part of a mart — STORE
Part of a microscope — LENS
Part of a midsummer night? — DREAM
Part of a min. — SEC
Part of a mine shaft — SUMP
Part of a mirror — FOIL
Part of a monogram, for short — INIT
Part of a morning glory — TENDRIL
Part of a Moscow mule — VODKA
Part of a necklace — BEAD
Part of a network show — COMMERCIAL
Part of a news broadcast — RECAP
Part of a news story — DATELINE
Part of a P.C. Wren title — GESTE
Part of a parrot's beak — CERE
Part of a part — SEG
Part of a pedestal — DADO
Part of a pie — PIECE
Part of a pilot light — FLAME
Part of a place setting — KNIFE, TEASPOON
Part of a plant — ROOT
Part of a play — ACT
Part of a Playbill lead — SCENE I
Part of a potpurri — PETAL
Part of a pound — OUNCE
Part of a Presley autograph — ARON
Part of a pump — TOE
Part of a puppet — STRING
Part of a race — HEAT, LAP
Part of a radio code — DIT
Part of a ratchet — PAWL
Part of a ream: Abbr. — SHT
Part of a refrain — LALA
Part of a revue — SKIT
Part of a riel — SEN
Part of a rigging — SPAR
Part of a rosary — BEAD
Part of a rose — PETAL, STEM
Part of a royal flush — ACE
Part of a rusty nail — SCOTCH
Part of a sales force — WOMAN
Part of a sandal — STRAP
Part of a school day — RECESS
Part of a seafood platter — FISH CAKES
Part of a semi — TLR
Part of a sentence — CLAUSE, WORD
Part of a shandy — ALE
Part of a ship's bow — HAWSE
Part of a shoe — HEEL, INSOLE
Part of a skyline — DOME, TOWER
Part of a soap — EPISODE
Part of a song — VOCAL
Part of a Spanish explorer's name — DE LEON
Part of a stage — APRON
Part of a stair — TREAD
Part of a staircase — STEP
Part of a Stein line — A ROSE
Part of a stop-motion device — FALLER
Part of a stove — OVEN
Part of a suit — VEST
Part of a teapot — SPOUT
Part of a text — LESSON
Part of a ticket order: Abbr. — SASE
Part of a tool chest — SCREW-DRIVER
Part of a trident — PRONG
Part of a turbine — STATOR
Part of a TV broadcast — VIDEO
Part of a TV set — SCR
Part of a TV transmission — AUDIO
Part of a twin set — CARDI-GAN
Part of a violin — CHIN REST
Part of a Waikiki welcome — LEI
Part of a watch mechanism — DETENT
Part of a wave — CREST
Part of a week, in Madrid — DIA
Part of a whole — UNIT
Part of a wooden chair leg — TENON
Part of a worm's body — SOMITE
Part of A.D. — ANNO
Part of A.E.S. — EWING
Part of A.L.U. — ARITH
Part of AC — ALT
Part of AEF — FORCE
Part of AES — ADLAI
Part of AFL — AMERICAN
Part of Afr. — ETH
Part of ALF — ALIEN
Part of AMA — MED, ASSN
Part of an academic year — SEMESTER
Part of an acre, in Yugoslavia — RALO
Part of an act — SCENE
Part of an actor's wardrobe — CRAVAT
Part of an arrow — BARB
Part of an athletic shoe — CLEAT
Part of an eastern church — BEMA
Part of an engine — BOILER
Part of an estate — MANOR
Part of an eye — UVEA
Part of an opera — SCENA
Part of an orange — RIND
Part of an oratorio — ARIA
Part of an ounce — DRAM
Part of an x and o game — TAC
Part of Asia Minor — AEOLIS
Part of AWOL — ABSENT, LEAVE
Part of B.A. — ARTS
Part of b.l.t. — TOMATO
Part of BA — ARTS, ARTS I
Part of badminton — NET
Part of BLT — TOMATO
Part of Borg's game — LOB
Part of BPOE — ELKS
Part of Broadway — MUSICAL
Part of BTU — UNIT
Part of Caesar's boast — VICI
Part of Caesar's trio — VENI
Part of CARE — RELIEF
Part of CBS — SYST
Part of CEO — EXEC
Part of China — TIBET
Part of CINC — CDR
Part of CNN — CABLE
Part of COL — COST
Part of CPA — ACCT, CERT
Part of D.C. — DISTRICT
Part of DEW — EARLY
Part of DIY — DO IT
Part of DNA — ACID
Part of DSM — MEDAL
Part of E.I. DuPont — IRENEE
Part of E.R.A. — EQUAL
Part of E.T.A. — ARRIVAL
Part of EAP — ALLAN, ARON, EDGAR, POE
Part of EDP — DATA
Part of EEC — EUR
Part of EEO — EQUAL
Part of Einstein's $e = mc^2$ — MASS
Part of enigma — ASHORE, DOES A
Part of EST — TIME

Part of ETA — ARR
Part of ETO — THEATER
Part of Europe: Abbr. — AUS
Part of FCC — FEDERAL
Part of FDR — DELANO
Part of France — ILE
Part of FRS — SYSTEM
Part of G.A.R. — ARMY OF
Part of G.P.A. — AVERAGE
Part of GB — ENG
Part of GBS — SHAW
Part of GMT — MEAN
Part of GNP — GROSS
Part of Greater London — PENGE
Part of GWTW — GONE WITH
Part of H.C.L. — COST
Part of H.R.E. — EMPIRE, HOLY, ROMAN
Part of H.R.H — HER, ROYAL
Part of HHH — HUBERT
Part of Hibernia — EIRE
Part of Hispaniola — HAITI
Part of HOMES — ERIE, HURON, ONT
Part of HRE — EMP
Part of HRH — HER, ROYAL
Part of i.e. — EST
Part of i.o.u. — OWE
Part of I.T.T. — TEL
Part of IRA — ACC
Part of IRS — REVENUE
Part of ITT — TEL
Part of KKK — KLAN
Part of KP — KITCHEN
Part of KY motto — UNITED WE STAND
Part of LL.B — LAWS
Part of M-G-M's motto — ART IS
Part of M.I.T. — INST, TECH
Part of Manhattan — HARLEM
Part of many place names — GLEN, SANTA
Part of Marshall Islands — RALIK
Part of MGM — MAYER
Part of Miss Muffet's meal — CURDS
Part of Montana's shoe — CLEAT
Part of Morse code — DOT
Part of Moslem law — SUNNA
Part of mpg — GAL
Part of MPH — PER
Part of Muslim prayers — RAKA
Part of MVP — MOST
Part of N.A. — AMER
Part of N.A.A.C.P. — ASSN, COLORED
Part of N.A.S. — NAVAL
Part of N.B. — BENE
Part of N.B. — NOTA
Part of N.C.O. — NON
Part of N.E.A. — EDUC
Part of NAACP — ASSN
Part of NASA — SPACE
Part of NCAA — ATH
Part of North America — CANADA
Part of Notre Dame stadium — TIER
Part of NOW — WOMEN
Part of NRA — INIT
Part of NSW — WALES
Part of NYC — NEW
Part of NYSE — EXCHANGE
Part of O.D. — OLIVE
Part of OAS — AMER, ORG
Part of old glory — STAR
Part of one's daily dozen — PUSH UPS
Part of OPEC — ORG
Part of overhead — RENT
Part of Paris — LEFT BANK
Part of PC — COMPUTER
Part of Pegasus — STAR
Part of pewter — TIN
Part of PGA — PRO
Part of Public Broadcasting _____ — NETWORK
Part of Q.E.D. — QUOD, ERAT
Part of QED — ERAT
Part of R & R — REC
Part of r.b.i. — RUNS
Part of R.I.P. — PACE, INST
Part of r.p.m. — PER
Part of R.S.V.P. — SIL
Part of R.W.E. — WALDO
Part of RCMP — POLICE
Part of RI — RHODE
Part of Roman name — NOMEN
Part of ROTC — TNG
Part of RPI — INST
Part of RPM — PER, REVS
Part of RSVP — SIL
Part of RV — REC
Part of SAT — TEST
Part of SBA — SMALL
Part of Screen _____ Guild — ACTORS
Part of shandy — ALE
Part of SLR — LENS
Part of some street scenes — GASLAMP
Part of some tarts — FRUIT
Part of Spain — ARAGON
Part of SPCA — SOC
Part of speech — NOUN
Part of SSS — SYS
Part of SST — SUPER
Part of SW — WAVE
Part of SWAK — KISS
Part of T.A.E. — ALVA
Part of T.G.I.F. — ITS
Part of TAE — ALVA, THOS
Part of TGIF — FRI
Part of the Asian skyline — PAGODA
Part of the brain — THALAMUS
Part of the conspiracy — IN ON
Part of the Constitution — ARTICLE
Part of the country scene — BARN
Part of the ear — LOBE
Part of the eye — CORNEA, IRIS, RETINA, UVEA
Part of the farm — ACRE
Part of the forearm — ULNA
Part of the former USSR — ARMENIA
Part of the holiday check-out snarl — LADIES WAITING
Part of the invisible spectrum — INFRARED
Part of the iris — UVEA
Part of the La. Purchase — IOWA
Part of the leg — SHIN
Part of the lunar landscape — CRATER
Part of the Marshall Islands — RALIK
Part of the middle — CENTER
Part of the opposition — ANTI
Part of the psyche — SUPEREGO
Part of the retina — FOVEA
Part of the rural landscape — SILO
Part of the school yr. — SEM
Part of the skyline — CLOCK TOWER, SPIRE, TOWER
Part of the stomach of a ruminant — OMASUM
Part of the street scene — CAR, BUS
Part of the UK — ENG
Part of the United Kingdom — BRITAIN
Part of TID — TER
Part of TLC — CARE
Part of TLC — CARE
Part of TNT — TRI
Part of to be — ARE
Part of TSE — ELIOT
Part of TV — TELE
Part of TVA — TENNESSEE VALLEY
Part of U.A.R. — ARAB
Part of U.S.A. — AMER, STATES
Part of U.S.S.R. — UKR
Part of UCLA — CALIF
Part of UFO — FLYING
Part of UHF — ULTRA
Part of UK — WALES
Part of UNICEF — FUND
Part of UNLV — LAS
Part of USA — AMER, UNITED
Part of USMA — ACAD
Part of USMC — STATES
Part of USNA — ACAD

Part of USSR — SOVIET, UNION
Part of VCR — CASSETTE
Part of VOA — VOICE
Part of Volga-Baltic Waterway — NEVA
Part of YMCA — ASSN
Part with — SELL
Part-time military gp. — USAR
Part-time workers for short — TEMPS
Partake — SHARE
Partake of — RECEIVE
Partake of brunch — EAT
Parted — SPLIT
Parthenope, for one — SIREN
Parti-colored horse — PIEBALD
Parti-colored — VARIED
Partial — HALF, ONE SIDED
Partial: Comb. form — MERI
Partiality — BIAS, TASTE
Partially open — AJAR
Partible — DIVISIBLE
Participate — ENTER
Participate in a langlauf — SKI
Participated at Henley — ROWED
Participated in a track event — HURDLED
Participial ending — ING
Particle — ATOM, FRAGMENT, ION, SCRAP, WHIT
Particle item — ISOTOPE
Particle of fire — SPARK
Particle piece — SHRED
Particle, in Scotland — STIM
Particular — ITEM, OWN, SOLE
Particularized — DETAILED
Partita — SUITE
Partition on a ship — FIREWALL
Partitions — SEPTA
Partly — SEMI
Partly open — AJAR
Partly submerged — AWASH
Partner — MATE
Partner for a fee — TAXI DANCER
Partner for billed — COOED
Partner for turn — TOSS
Partner of "see" — SAW
Partner of 'earty — ALE
Partner of abet — AID
Partner of above — BEYOND, OVER
Partner of aid — ABET
Partner of bounds — LEAPS
Partner of cool and collected — CALM
Partner of cry — HUE
Partner of dearest — NEAREST
Partner of dribs — DRABS
Partner of get set and go — READY
Partner of kicking — ALIVE
Partner of means — ENDS
Partner of neither — NOR
Partner of odds — ENDS
Partner of Old Lace — ARSENIC
Partner of onions — LIVER
Partner of order — LAW
Partner of pass — FAIL
Partner of promise — LICK
Partner of reason — RHYME
Partner of Rogers and Powell — ASTAIRE
Partner of seek — HIDE
Partner of sm. and med. — LRG
Partner of starts — FITS
Partner of the caped crusader — ROBIN
Partner of time — TIDE
Partner of to — FROM
Partner of void — NULL
Partner of ways — MEANS
Partner of wide — FAR
Partner of wiser — OLDER
Partner to — IN ON
Partners — MATES
Partners of cleaners — DYERS
Partners of Dads — MAS
Partners of ifs or ands — BUTS
Partners of needles — PINS
Partners of reels — RODS
Partridge mother — HEN
Parts of a $ — CTS
Parts of a Becker game — SETS
Parts of a bushel — PECKS
Parts of a cen. — YRS
Parts of a clan — SEPTS
Parts of a contract — TERMS
Parts of a horse's collar — HAMES
Parts of a mi. — RDS
Parts of a nasus — NARES
Parts of a necklace — BEADS
Parts of a physical — STRESS TESTS
Parts of a polygon — SIDES
Parts of a pound — PENCE
Parts of a relay race — LAPS
Parts of a service — SAUCERS
Parts of a solution — STEPS
Parts of a sort: Abbr. — POTS
Parts of a text — EXTRACTS
Parts of a three-piece suit — TROUSERS
Parts of a ton — LBS
Parts of a trip — LEGS
Parts of airfields — STRIPS
Parts of an act — SCENES
Parts of an auto engine — TAPPETS
Parts of books — SPINES
Parts of circles — ARCS
Parts of days, for short — AMS
Parts of dols. — CTS
Parts of elevens — ONES
Parts of feet — HEELS
Parts of fortifications — BASTIONS
Parts of hammers — PEENS
Parts of hrs. — SECS
Parts of infinitives — TOS
Parts of irises — AREOLAS
Parts of joules — ERGS
Parts of juleps, sazeracs, etc. — SPIRITS
Parts of La France — ILES
Parts of legs — SHINS
Parts of mins. — SECS
Parts of months — DAYS
Parts of pitchers — EARS
Parts of potions — DOSES
Parts of psyches — IDS
Parts of pumps — SOLES
Parts of QEDs — ERATS
Parts of quarters — CENTS
Parts of ships' bows — HAWSES
Parts of soft palates — UVULAE
Parts of sonnets — SESTETS
Parts of speech — NOUNS
Parts of speech — NOUNS
Parts of the lunar landscape — RILLS
Parts of the string section — CELLI
Parts of the suburban scene — TOWNS
Parts of wads — BILLS
Parts of young leaves — STIPELS
Party — BASH, SOIREE
Party _____: wet blanket — POOPER
Party beverage — FRUIT PUNCH
Party decorations — BALLOONS
Party extra — STAG
Party fare — DIPS
Party favorite — NOMINEE
Party give-away — FAVOR
Party giver — HOST
Party goodies — DIPS
Party handout — FAVOR
Party leader? — EMCEE
Party loner — STAG
Party man — PARTISAN
Party member, for short — DEM
Party mixture — DIP
Party pastimes — GAMES
Party person, for short — POL
Party pro — POL
Party spread — PATE
Party tidbit — CANAPE
Party to — IN ON
Party treat — DIP
Party type — STAG
Parvenu — SNOB
Pas de _____ — DEUX
Pas de deux, e.g. — DUET

Pas seul — SOLO
Pasadena — CITY OF ROSES
Pascal — BLAISE
Pasch — EASTER
Pasquinade — SATIRE
Pass — ELAPSE, ENACT, GAP
Pass a law — ENACT
Pass between Idaho and Montana — TARGHEE
Pass by — SKIP
Pass by a gridder — LATERAL
Pass catchers — ENDS
Pass judgment — SENTENCE
Pass laws — ENACT
Pass lightly — BRUSH
Pass off as genuine — FOIST
Pass out — SWOON
Pass over — ELIDE, FORGO, OMIT
Pass over lightly — SCAN
Pass quickly — FLIT
Pass receiver — END
Pass rushers — ENDS
Pass the hat — BEG
Pass up — OMIT, WAIVE
Pass, as a law — ENACT
Passable — DECENT, SOSO
Passage — FARE, TRANSIT
Passage for ventilation — AIR SHAFT
Passage into a fort — SALLYPORT
Passages — VIAS
Passageway — ACCESS, AISLE, ARTERY
Passageway for a plane — AIRLANE
Passageway, of a kind — AISLE
Passbook holder — SAVER
Passbook notation — WITHDRAWAL
Passbook owner — SAVER
Passé — DATED, OUT OF STYLE, OUTDATES
Passed — ELAPSED, WENT BY
Passed back and forth — BANDIED
Passed the time — BIDED
Passed up — MISSED
Passed, as time — ELAPSED
Passenger — FARE
Passenger vehicle — AUTOBUS
Passer, often — QUARTERBACK
Passer-by — WITNESS
Passerby: Abbr. — TRAN
Passerine songbird — OSCINE
Passerines — ORIOLES
Passes — GOES BY
Passing craze — FAD
Passing fancy — FAD
Passing marks — CEES
Passing through a portal — ENTERING
Passion — MANIA
Passive — STOIC
Passover bread — MATZO
Passover custom — SEDER
Passover meal — SEDER
Passover wafer — MATZO
Passport adjunct — VISA
Past — AGO, OVER
Past and future — TENSES
Past cabinet member — MEESE
Past due — LATE
Past one's prime — OVER THE HILL
Past or future — TENSE
Past or present — TENSE
Past working hours — OVERTIME
Pasta — NOODLES
Pasta base — SEMOLINA
Pasta choice — ZITI
Pasta dish of curved fluted pieces — RIGATONI
Pasta favorite — LASAGNA
Paste — GLUE, PUNCH, SLUG
Paste made from sesame seeds — TAHINI
Pasteboard — CARD, KRAFT
Pastel — CRAYON, PALE, TINT
Pasternak character — LARA
Pastiche — OLIO
Pastimes — GAMES
Pastor or priest — CLERIC
Pastor's place — MANSE
Pastoral African — MASAI
Pastoral paths: Abbr. — LNS
Pastoral people of Kenya — MASAI
Pastoral poem — IDYLL
Pastoral pooch? — SHEPHERD
Pastoral sound — BAA
Pastoral staffs — PEDA
Pastrami provider — DELI
Pastrami purveyor, for short — DELI
Pastries — TARTS
Pastry — CAKE, DANISH, PIE, TART
Pastry for serving meat — PATTY SHELL
Pastry fried in deep fat — RISSOLE
Pastry items — TARTS
Pastry plus — PIE A LA MODE
Pastry tray item — BABA AU RHUM, ECLAIR, TART
Pastry type — SCONE, TART
Pasture — LEA
Pasture creature — NANNY
Pasture forage — RED TOP
Pasture grass — HERBAGE
Pasture grazer — EWE
Pasture growth — RYE GRASS
Pasture land — ACREAGE
Pasture livestock for a fee — AGIST
Pasture parent — EWE
Pasture sound — MAA
Pastures — LEAS
Pasty — ASHEN, GRAY
Pat — CARESS, DAB
Pat or Daniel — BOONE
Pat or Debby — BOONE
Pat or Richard — BOONE
Pataella area — KNEE
Patch — DARN, MARK, MEND
Patch of land — PLAT
Patch up a painting — RESTORE
Patch up a road — RETAR
Patchin Place resident: 1923-62 — E E CUMMINGS
Patchwork — OLIO
Patchy — PIED
Pate covers — RUGS
Pate de _____ gras — FOIE
Patella — KNEECAP
Patella locations — KNEES
Patella site — KNEE
Patent — CHARTER, COPYRIGHT, PERMIT
Patent beginning — IDEA
Patent notice — CAVEAT
Patent pronouncement? — IMPENDING
Pater pauses — ERS
Paternally related — AGNATE
Paters — DADS
Path — ORBIT, ROUTE
Path for Pluto — ORBIT
Path lead-in — OSTEO
Pathet _____, Communist group — LAO
Pathogen — GERM
Pathogenic bacterium, for short — STAPH
Pathological — MORBID
Patient bill clerk? — GRACE PERIOD
Patient helper — NURSE
Patina — SHEEN
Patio — TERRACE
Patio cooker — GRILL
Patio event — BARBECUE
Patio gear — SPIT
Patio item — GRILL
Patio pest — ANT
Patisserie item — TARTE
Patisserie purchase — PETIT FOUR
Patois — ARGOT, LINGO
Patola — SARI
Patriarchic — SENIOR
Patricia of films — NEAL
Patrick Dennis's aunt — MAME
Patrick, the patriot — HENRY
Patrilineal — AGNATE
Patrilineal clan in old Rome — GENS
Patrimony — SHARE
Patriot's target — SCUD
Patriotic colors — RED WHITE AND BLUE
Patriotic date — THE FOURTH OF JULY
Patriotic initials — USMA

Patriotic org. — DAR, SAR
Patriotic relative — UNCLE SAM
Patriotic seamstress — ROSS
Patriotic song — ANTHEM
Patriotic superhero — CAPTAIN AMERICA
Patriotic symbol — STARS AND STRIPES
Patron saint — ELMO
Patron saint of England — GEORGE
Patron saint of Erin — PATRICK
Patron saint of France — DENIS
Patron saint of Norway — OLAF
Patroness of France since 1922 — JEANNE
Patronizes — SHOPS AT
Patsy — TOOL
Patten or huarache — SANDAL
Patten's cousin — SABOT
Patten, e.g. — SANDAL
Patter — LINGO
Pattern — CONSTELLATION, DESIGN, MODEL, TEMPLET, TYPE
Pattern of perfection — IDEAL
Pattern on some stamps — MOIRE
Pattern or mold — TEMPLATE
Patterned cloth for a kilt — TARTAN
Patterns used in decorating — STENCILS
Patterns: Abbr. — DIAGS
Patti Lupone role — EVITA
Patty Duke _____ — ASTON
Patty Duke's real name — ANNA
Paucity — DEARTH
Paul — LES
Paul Bunyan's companion — BABE
Paul Bunyan's cook — OLE
Paul Hogan role — CROCODILE DUNDEE
Paul McCartney band — WINGS
Paul Newman film: 1989 — BLAZE
Paul Newman role, 1960 — ARI
Paul or Brown — LES
Paul or Nan ending — ETTE
Paul or Nicholas — SAINT
Paul Revere, for one — RIDER
Paul Scott subject — INDIA
Paul Scott's "The _____ Quartet" — RAJ
Pauline's nemesis — PERILS
Pauline's woes — PERILS
Pause, in music — REST
Pause, in Pisa — RESTA
Pauses — RESTS, STOPS
Pavarotti's paese — ITALIA
Pavarotti, for one — TENOR
Pavers' targets — ROADS
Paving material — ASPHALT, MACADAM, TAR
Paving material of yore — COBBLESTONES
Paving stone — SETT
Pavlova — ANNA
Paw — FOOT
Pawl engager — RATCHET
Pawn — HOCK, SELL, TOOL, TRADE
Pawn's superior — PIECE
Pawnbroker — LENDER, UNCLE
Pawnbrokers: Slang — UNCLES
Pawned — HOCKED
Pawnee's friend — OTOE
Pawnees' neighbors — OTOS
Pawns — THINGS DEPOSITED IN PLEDGE
Pawpaw? — CLASPED HANDS
Pay — DEFRAY, EXPEND, REMIT, SALARY
Pay (with "up") — ANTE
Pay _____ — SCALE
Pay attention — HEED, LISTEN
Pay attention to — HEED
Pay dirt — ORE
Pay homage — KNEEL
Pay in full — SETTLE
Pay out — SPEND
Pay the bills — REMIT
Pay the check — TREAT
Pay to play — ANTE
Pay tribute — HONOR
Pay up — ANTE
Payable — DUE
Payable now — DUE
Paycheck recipient — EARNER
Payed to play — ANTED
Paying customers — GATE
Payment — FEE
Payment for Charon — OBOL
Payment for Perry Mason — FEE
Payment on delivery — COD
Paymt. records — RCTS
Paynim — PAGAN
Payoff — GET AT, REWARD
Pays — REMITS
Pays attention — HEEDS, LISTENS
Pays in — ANTES
Pays the pot — ANTES
Pays up — SETTLES
PBJ alternative — BLT
PBS series — NOVA
PC add-ons — CRTS
PDQ — ASAP
Pea or sharp follower — SHOOTER
Pea petals — ALAE
Pea shells — PODS
Peace — SERENITY
Peace _____, R.I. — DALE
Peace co-Nobelist, 1901 — PASSY
Peace goddess — IRENE
Peace Nobelist in 1978 — SADAT
Peace Nobelist John R. _____: 1946 — MOTT
Peace Nobelist Walesa — LECH
Peace Nobelist Wiesel — ELIE
Peace Nobelist, 1946 — MOTT
Peace Nobelist: 1987 — ARIAS
Peace offer — OLIVE BRANCH
Peace pipe — CALUMET
Peace Prize co-Nobelist: 1911 — ASSER
Peace prize donor — NOBEL
Peace symbol — DOVE
Peace, in Haifa — SHALOM
Peace-loving — DOVISH
Peace-pipe item — TRUCE
Peaceful — IRENIC
Peaceful bird — DOVE
Peaceful harmony — AMITY
Peaceful Indian tribe in Manitoba — CREE
Peaceful periods — CALMS
Peaceful, in Pau — COI
Peacekeeper — LAWMAN
Peacemaker? — OLIVE BRANCH
Peach _____ — MELBA
Peach mutations — NECTARINES
Peach or Piggy — MISS
Peach part — PIT
Peach peels — EPICARPS
Peachtree street's city — ATLANTA
Peachy-keen — SUPER DUPER
Peacock — PAON
Peacock and Eye — LOGOS
Peacock plumage spots — OCELLI
Peacock spots — OCELLI
Peacock's feather decor — OCELLUS
Peacock's pride — TRAIN
Peak — ACME, ALP, CREST, TOP
Peak in the Valais Alps — LEONE
Peak in Thessaly — OSSA
Peak of perfection — ACME, PINK
Peak point — APEX
Peak sometimes called Tacoma — RANIER
Peaked — DRAWN, SHARP
Peaked Zebulon — PIKE
Peaked-cap wearer — HIM COURIER
Peaks — APEXES
Peaks of pique — SNITS
Peaky — PALE
Peal — BANG, CLANG, DIN
Peale appeal — SERMON
Pealed — RANG

Peanut place — GALLERY
Peanut, down south — GOOBER
Peanuts — GOOBER PEAS
Peapod — HULL, HUSK
Pear-shaped instruments — LUTES
Pear — FRUIT
Pear variety — BOSC
Pear, in Pamplona — PERA
Pear-shaped bottle in a lab — ALUDEL
Pear-shaped fruit — FIG
Pearl — BEAD, DROPLET
Pearl blue — METAL
Pearl Buck heroine — OLAN
Pearl Buck's "The _____": 1936 — EXILE
Pearl divers — AMAS
Pearl mosque site — AGRA
Pearl of Antilles — CUBA
Pearl of comedy — MINNIE
Pearl source — OYSTER
Pearl's "Won't you come home, _____" — BILL BAILEY
Pearls are cast before them — SWINE
Pearly — CREAMY, MILKY, WHITE
Pearly portals — GATES
Peary base in Greenland — ETAH
Peary's discovery: 1909 — NORTH POLE
Peasant — COMMONER, PLEBIAN, SERF
Peasant of India — RYOT
Peat source — BOG
Pebble — GRAVEL, ROCK, STONE
Pebbles's mother on TV — WILMA
Pecan — NUT
Pecan confection — PRALINE
Pecans and filberts — NUTS
Pecans, e.g. — NUTS
Peccaries — SWINE
Peck — DAB, NICK, POKE, RAP, TAP
Peck role — AHAB
Peck's partner — HUNT
Pectoral — CHEST, THORACIC
Peculate — STEAL
Peculiar — ODD
Peculiar phrase — IDIOM
Peculiar to one: Comb. form — IDIO
Pecuniary — MONETARY
Pedal arch — INSTEP
Pedal pusher — BIKER
Pedals — TREADLES
Pedants — DIDACTS
Peddle — HAWK, FLOG, VEND
Pedestal occupant — IDOL
Pedestal part — DADO
Pedestrian — HIKER
Pedestrian bullfighters — TOREROS
Pediatrician? — NURSERYMAN
Pedicure fanatics? — CLIPTO-MANIACS
Pedicurist's concern — TOENAIL
Pedigree — BIRTH, STRAIN
Pedigreed animal — PUREBRED
Pedro's "Positively!" — SI SI
Pedro's aunt — TIA
Pedro's friend — AMIGO
Pedro's pal — AMIGO
Pedro's son — NINA
Pedro's uncle — TIO
Pedro's water — AGUA
Pee Wee — REESE
Pee Wee and Jimmy of baseball — REESES
Pee Wee or Della — REESE
Peek-a-boo — SHEER
Peek — GLANCE, LOOK
Peel — PARE, SCALE
Peeled — PARED
Peeled off — FLAKED
Peelers target — RIND
Peels — STRIPS
Peep — TWEET
Peep show — RAREE
Peephole — EYE, EYELET, PINHOLE
Peeping Tom — OGLER, STARER
Peer — EQUAL, LIKE, MATCH, TWIN
Peer between a viscount and marquess — EARL
Peer Gynt's mother — ASE
Peer's domain — EARLDOM
Peer's mother — ASE
Peerage — ELITE, NOBILITY
Peerage members — BARONS
Peerage types — DAMES
Peerless — ONLY
Peerless, in Paris — SANSPAREIL
Peers — EARLS
Peers, collectively — BARONAGE
Peeve — ANNOY, MIFF, PIQUE, VEX
Peeved — SORE
Peevish — FRETTY
Peevish state — SNIT
Peewee — BIRD
Peewee or Della — REESE
Peewit or pipit — BIRD
Peg — PIN, SPIKE, STAPLE
Peg for Palmer — TEE
Peg for Pete — TEE
Peg for Snead — TEE
Peggy and Spike — LEES
Peggy Lee hit — FEVER
Peggy Lee's "_____ Good Day" — ITS A
Peignoir — KIMONA, NIGHTIE, ROBE
Peking board game — CHINESE CHECKERS
Peking idol — MAO
Peking supermarket group? — CHINESE CHECKERS
Peking's province — HOPEH
Pekingese lunacy? — CHINESE CRACKERS
Pekoe and oolong — TEAS
Pekoe, e.g. — TEA
Pelage — COAT, FUR, HAIR, WOOL
Pelagic — MARINE
Pelagic bird — ERN
Pelagic predator — ERNE
Pelagic soarers — ERNES
Pelagic whale — SEI
Pele's forte — SOCCER
Pelé's gp., once — ASL
Peleg's father: Gen. 10:25 — EBER
Pelf — CAPITAL, MONEY
Pelican features — BEAKS
Pell- _____ (in a jumble) — MELL
Pellucid — CLEAR
Peloponnesian region — ACHAEA
Peloponnesus — MOREA
Pelted — PEPPERED
Pelts — HIDES
Pelvic bones — PUBES, SACRA
Pelvis part — ILIUM
Pen — CORRAL, WRITE
Pen and paper place — STATIONERY STORE
Pen contents — INK
Pen name of a mystery writer — QUEEN
Pen name of Mary Ann Evans — ELIOT
Pen parts — NIBS
Pen point — NIB
Pen resident — PIG
Pen talks — OINKS
Pen's mate — COB
Pen's pals — COBS
Pen-shaped, pointed instruments — STYLI
Penalize — AMERCE, DISCIPLINE, PUNISH
Penalizes — FINES
Penalty — COST
Penalty for not paying — FORFEIT
Penang person — ASIAN
Penates' partners — LARES
Pencil "Helmet" — ERASER
Pencil ends — ERASERS
Pencil part — ERASER
Pendant jewel — DROP
Pendants — LAVALIERES
Pending — UP IN THE AIR

Pendulous fold of skin — DEWLAP
Pendulous part of a dog's ear — LEATHER
Pendulum's partner in a Poe title — PIT
Penetrates — ENTERS
Peninsula of Southwest Europe — IBERIAN
Penitent — ATONER
Penitent's activity — RUING
Penitent's emotion — SHAME
Penitential season — LENT
Penn _____, village on Keuka Lake, N.Y. — YAN
Penn or Connery — SEAN
Penn pronoun — THEE
Penn Station builder — REA
Penn, to Pennsylvania — EPONYM
Penn. and 5th — AVES
Penn. and Grd. Ctrl. — STNS
Penn/Duvall film — COLORS
Penned — WROTE, YARDED
Pennies or Carpathians: Abbr. — MTNS
Pennon — STREAMER
Pennsylvania bird? — LANCASTERN
Pennsylvania isle — PRESQUE
Pennsylvania port — ERIE
Penny — CENT
Penny _____ — ANTE, ARCADE
Penny dreadful or shilling shocker — NOVEL
Penny in Soho — COPPER
Penny pincher — MISER
Penny, to a Brit — COPPER
Penpoints — NIBS
Pens — COOPS, STIES
Pension layaways — IRAS
Pension plan for short — IRA
Pensioners — RETIREES
Pentacle — MEDAL, STAR
Pentagon material? — BRASS
Pentangles — STARS
Pentateuch — BIBLE, TORAH
Pentateuch scroll -TORAH
Penthouse — AERIE
Penthouse adjuncts — TERRACES
Penthouse perhaps — AERY
Penthouse, in a way — AERIE
Penthouses on peaks — AERIES
Penultimate chess call — MATE
Penultimate Greek letter — PSI
Penultimate Hebrew letter — SHIN
Penultimate rounds — SEMIS
Penurious — INDIGENT, NEEDY
Penury — NEED, WANT
Penzance resident? — PIRATE
Penzance's peninsula — CORNWALL
Peon — HELOT, SLAVE
Peon's mite — PESO
Peony — FLOWER, RED
People — FOLK, MEN
People born July 21-Aug. 22 — LEOS
People generally — THEY
People hard to take — PILLS
People of central Europe — POLES
People of Europe — SERBS
People of Gotham — NEW YORKERS
People of Graz — STYRIANS
People of great courage — SPARTANS
People of Pisa: Abbr. — ITALS
People of SW China — LOLO, YIS
People of the Platte — OTOES
People of Tralee — IRISH
People with like interests — BIRDS OF A FEATHER
People with petitions — ASKERS
People, en masse — LAITY
Pep _____ — RALLY
Pep-rally cry — RAH
Pepe Le _____ of cartoons — PEW
Pepe Le _____: Boyer "Algiers" role — MOKO
Pepe Le Moko's milieu — CASBAH
Peppard and pals — A TEAM
Pepper — PELT
Pepper missing? (Hanford) — WHERES WALDO
Pepper picker — PIPER
Pepper plants — KAVAS
Peppermint candy — CANE
Peppery — HOT
Pepsin and papain — ENZYMES
Pepys — SAMUEL
Per — EACH
Per _____ — DIEM
Per _____ (yearly) — ANNUM
Per diem — DAILY
Per person — EACH
Perambulates — WALKS
Perceived — SENSED
Perceived in a way — SENSATE
Percent of iceberg above water — TEN
Percentage gift — TITHE
Perception — SENSE
Perceptive powers — WITS
Perch — BAR, FISH, POLE, ROOST
Perch for a redwing — REED
Perchance — PERHAPS
Perched — ALIT, ROOSTED
Percheron — DRAFT HORSE
Percheron's repast — OATS
Perches — ROOSTS
Perching place — LEDGE
Percolate — DRIP, FILTER, SEEP
Percussion drum — KETTLE
Percussion instrument — TRIANGLE
Perdition — RUIN
Perdu — FORLORN, HIDDEN
Perdure — LAST
Pere's wife — MERE
Peregrinate — ROAM, ROVE
Peregrine — ALIEN, FALCON
Perfect — AOK, IDEAL
Perfect "10" — IDEAL
Perfect number — TEN
Perfect place — EDEN
Perfect rating — TEN
Perfect score — ACE
Perfect scores — TENS
Perfect serve — ACE
Perfecta or exacta — BET
Perfectly simple — OPEN AND SHUT
Perfectly, with "to" — A TEE
Perforate — BORE, DRILL
Perforated plate — STENCIL
Perform — ACT, EXECUTE
Perform a christy — SKI
Perform a cool caper — STREAK
Perform a wedeln — SKI
Perform brilliantly — SPARKLE
Perform Christies — SKI
Perform Gregorian chants — INTONE
Perform in a think tank — IDEATE
Perform peripeteia, in a way — DO AN ABOUT FACE
Perform successfully — CARRY OFF
Performance repetition — RERUN
Performances after performances — ENCORES
Performed — ACTED
Performed a role — PLAYED
Performed diligently — PLIED
Performed improperly — MISDONE
Performed one's work — PLIED
Performed the oath of office — SWORE IN
Performer — ACTOR, ARTISTE
Performer, in Perugia — ATTORE
Performers — CAST
Performs — ACTS, DOES
Perfume — ATTAR, CENSE, ESSENCE, ESTER
Perfume additives — IRONIES
Perfume anime — ELEMI
Perfume bottle — PHIAL
Perfume bottles — VIALS
Perfume containers — VIALS
Perfume dispenser, Brit. style — ATOMISER
Perfume essence — NEROLI

Perfume ingredient — ATTAR, ESTER, IRONE
Perfume measure — DRAM
Perfume oil — ATTAR, NEROLI
Perfume resin — ELEMI
Perfumed — SCENTED
Perfumed powder — SACHET
Perfumer's concern — AROMA
Perfumes — ESSENCES
Perfumes the air — CENSES
Perfuse — COAT
Pergola — ARBOR, GAZEBO
Perhaps — MAYBE
Peri chaser — SCOPE
Pericles and Cicero — ORATORS
Pericles's land — TYRE
Peridot — JEWEL
Perigee of the moon — APSIS
Perils — DANGERS
Perimeter — EDGE
Period — ERA, DOT, FULL STOP
Period after a sentence — TIME
Period in classical mythology — GOLDEN AGE
Period of calm — LULL
Period of church division — GREAT SCHISM
Period of duty — TOUR
Period of penitence — LENT
Period of power — DAY
Period of time — ERA
Period part — EPOCH
Period piece — ART
Periodic growth, as of funds — ACCRUAL
Periodic visitor — COMET
Periodical, for short — MAG
Periods — DOTS, ERAS, SPELLS
Periods for Aries and Taurus — APRILS
Periods of abstinence — FASTS
Periods of note — ERAS
Periods of prosperity — UPS
Periods of time — ERAS, WEEKS
Peripheral — OUTER
Periphery — EDGES
Periwinkle — SNAIL
Perjure — TELL A LIE
Perjurer — LIAR
Perk — BONUS, EXTRA
Perk up — LIVEN
Perk up a straight edge — STROP
Perkins of the theater — OSGOOD
Perkins or Sagan — CARL
Perky — HAPPY
Perle of Washington — MESTA
Perlman forte — VIOLIN
Perlman of "Cheers" — RHEA
Perlman or Howard — RON
Perm term — WAVY
Permanent — FIXED
Permanent commitment? — I DO
Permeable parts of trees — SAPWOODS
Permeate — ENTER, IMBUE, INVADE
Permissible — ALLOWABLE, LICIT
Permission — GREEN LIGHT, LEAVE
Permit — ALLOW, LET, PASS, SUFFER
Permitted — ALLOWED
Pernicious — EVIL
Pernod flavoring — ANISE
Pernod ingredient — ANISE
Peron and Gabor — EVAS
Peron namesakes — EVITAS
Peron's land: Abbr. — ARG
Perot — ROSS
Perpendicular distance — ALTITUDE
Perpetrate — COMMIT, ENACT
Perpetually — EVER
Perpetually, to Poe — EER
Perplex — BEMUSE, STUMP
Perplexed — AT SEA
Perron parts — RISERS
Perry and Della's creator — ERLE
Perry locale — ERIE
Perry Mason matter — CASE
Perry Mason specialty — CASE
Perry Mason's concern — CLIENT
Perry or James — MASON
Perry's creator — ERLE
Perry's Della — STREET
Perry's favorite Street — DELLA
Perry's sidekick — DELLA
Pers. cards — IDS
Persea and poon — TREES
Persevere — COPE, HANG IN, INSIST, LAST
Persevered — HUNG ON
Persevering — SEDULOUS
Pershing command, for short — AEF
Pershing's gp — AEF
Persia now — IRAN
Persia, after 1935 — IRAN
Persia, today — IRAN
Persian — CAT, RUG
Persian — PARSI
Persian carpet — HAMADAN
Persian dialect — PARSI
Persian elf — PERI
Persian fairy — PERI
Persian Gulf country — IRAN
Persian Gulf diet observers? — KUWAIT WATCHERS
Persian Gulf emirate — QATAR
Persian Gulf sight — TANKER
Persian language — PAHLAVI
Persian or Siamese — CAT
Persian poet — OMAR
Persian supernatural — PERI
Persian title — MIRZA
Persian unit of length — ZAR
Persian VIP — SHAH
Persian's ancient foe — MEDE
Persian, for example — CAT
Persians of yore — MEDES
Persians' foes — MEDES
Persist — LAST
Persistent attack — SIEGE
Persistent attempts to gain control — SIEGES
Persistent searchers — FERRETS
Person — ONE
Person at the helm — PILOT
Person from Barcelona — CATALAN
Person from outer space — ALIEN
Person from Paisley — SCOT
Person from Pakistani — ASIAN
Person from Penzance — PIRATE
Person from Ponca City — SOONER
Person from Wales — CELT
Person in a race for space — ADVERTISER
Person of interest — BANK TELLER
Person of prominence — NABOB
Person of the cloth — CLERIC
Person on probation — PAROLEE
Person who estimates — RATER
Person with a speech problem — STAMMERER
Person's post-practice announcement — IMPERFECT
Persona — CAST
Persona non _____ — GRATA
Personage — CHIEF
Personal force, in Hinduism — KARMA
Personal property policies — FLOATERS
Personal quirk — TIC
Personal: Comb. form — IDIO
Personalities — EGOS
Personals — ADS
Personate — ACT
Personification of England — JOHN BULL
Personification of evil — SATAN
Personification of reckless ambition — ATE
Personify — MIRROR
Personnel — STAFF
Personnel concern — ABSENTEEISM

Personnel cutback for economy reasons — RIF
Personnel list — ROSTER
Persons — BEINGS, ONES
Persons or things — ONES
Perspire — DRIP, EGEST
Persuade — COAX, SELL, URGE
Persuader's request — TAKE MY WORD
Pert — BOLD, SASSY, SAUCY
Pert one — MINX, SNIP
Pert. to Reykjavik — ICEL
Pertaining to a belief: Var. — CREDAL
Pertaining to a cenotaph — STELAR
Pertaining to a certain pope — SISTINE
Pertaining to a leaf stem — NODAL
Pertaining to a pig — PORCINE
Pertaining to ankle bones — TARSAL
Pertaining to birds — AVIAN
Pertaining to farming — AGRARIAN
Pertaining to grandparents — AVAL
Pertaining to hearing — AUDILE
Pertaining to John Paul — PAPAL
Pertaining to Mars — AREAN
Pertaining to still water — LENTIC
Pertaining to the eye — OCULAR
Pertaining to the instep — TARSAL
Pertaining to the nostrils — NARINE
Pertaining to the open seas — PELAGIC
Pertaining to the Vatican — PAPAL
Pertaining to: Suffix — INE
Pertinent — APROPOS
Perturb — DISTURB
Perturbed — UPSET, VEXED
Peruke — WIG
Peruse — CON, READ, SCAN
Peruse again — REREAD
Perused — READ
Peruvian — INCA
Peruvian indian — INCA
Peruvian Native — INCA
Peruvian plant — OCA
Peruvian post? — LIMA MAIL
Peruvian, perhaps — ANDEAN
Peruvians — INCAS
Pervade — HAUNT
Pervading attitude — NORM
Pesky insect — GNAT
Pessimistic — DISMAL
Pessimistic, Exchange style — BEARISH
Pester — HARASS, TEASE
Pestered — RODE
Pesticide letters — DDT
Pestiferous insect — GNAT
Pet _____ — PEEVE
Pet name — HON
Pet of FDR — FALA
Pet of the Charles' household — ASTA
Pet peeves — HATES
Pet's peeve — FLEA
Pet's perch — LAP
Pet. unit — GAL
Petain and Matisse — HENRIS
Petal perfume — ATTAR
Petard — BOMB, GRENADE
Pete Seeger instrument — BANJO
Pete's 1955 insignia — THE ROSE TATTOO
Peteman — YEGG
Peteman's purchase — NITRO
Peter and a Wolfe — NEROS
Peter and Alexander — TSARS
Peter and Mary's friend — PAUL
Peter Benchley's short coat? — SHARKSKIN JACKET
Peter Cottontail's pace — HIPPETY HOP
Peter Jennings network — ABC
Peter Lind Hayes-Robert Allen opus — LILAC CHIFFON
Peter or Ivan — TSAR
Peter or Nicholas — TSAR
Peter or Paul — APOSTLE, TSAR
Peter out — FADE, WANE
Peter Pan pirate — SMEE
Peter Pan role — SMEE
Peter Rabbit's sibling — MOPSY
Peter the Great — TSAR
Peter the Great, for one — TSAR
Peter who played Henry II — OTOOLE
Peter Wimsey's creator — SAYERS
Peter's daughter — BRIDGET FONDA
Peter, of "The Maltese Falcon" — LORRE
Peter, Paul and Mary song — MORNING TRAIN
Peter, Paul and Mary, e.g. — TRIO
Peter, Paul and Nicholas — TSARS
Peter, Paul or Nicholas — TSAR
Peter, the pianist — NERO
Petite pup — PEKE
Petition — APPEAL, ENTREATY, REQUEST, SUE
Petitioned — SUED
Petitioners — SUERS
Petitions — ASKS, BEGS
Petrarch's beloved — LAURA
Petrels' cousins — FULMARS
Petri-dish filler — AGAR
Petri dish contents — AGAR
Petrify — SCARE
Petro producer assn. — OPEC
Petrocelli of baseball — RICO
Petrol-station accessory — TYRE
Petrol — GAS
Petroleum-cartel inits. — OPEC
Petroleum — NAPHTHA, OIL
Petruchio's activity — TAMING
Petruchio's Katharina — SHREW
Pets popular with children — HAMSTERS
Pettifogger — SHYSTER
Petty — MEAN
Petty crooks — CHISELERS
Petty officer — BOSN, BOSUN
Petty officer in the Navy: Abbr. — BOSN
Petty officers — YEOMEN
Petty people — MEANIES
Petty prince — SATRAP
Petty quarrel — TIFF
Petty tyrant — SATRAP
Petulant — CROSS, SPLEENY, SULKY, TESTY
Petulant person — WASP
Pew accessory — KNEELER
PFC's — GIS
Pfc. superior — CPL
PG or R — RATING
PG or X — RATING
PGA player — PRO
PGA stop — DORAL
PGA's Crenshaw — BEN
PGA's Snead — SAM
Ph.D. applicant — TESTEE
Phalarope — SEASNIPE
Phanlanges' locales — TOES
Phantasm — DREAM, SPECTER
Phantasmal — EERIE
Phantoms — EIDOLA
Pharaoh's talisman — SCARAB
Pharmacist in London — CHEMIST
Pharmacist's abbr. for salve — UNG
Pharmacist's guide: Abbr. — USP
Pharynx tissues — ADENOIDS
Phase — STEP
Phaseolus limensis — LIMA BEANS
Phases — FACETS
PhDs — DRS
Pheasant brood — NIDE
Pheasant's nest — NIDE
Phi _____ Kappa — BETA
Phi followers — CHIS
Phil Silvers role — BILKO
Phil the Fiddler's creator — ALGER
Philadelphia eleven — EAGLES

Philadelphia Orchestra conductor, emeritus — MUTI
Philadelphia suburban complex — MAINLINE
Philadelphia university — TEMPLE
Philadelphia's Spectrum — ARENA
Philanderer — FLIRT
Philanthropist in education — YALE
Philatelic item — STAMP
Philatelic term — HINGE
Philatelic unit — PANE
Philatelist's prize — STAMP
Philatelist's sheet — PANE
Phileas Fogg on film — NIVEN
Philip Nolan, for one — EXILE
Philippine beast? — MANILA ANIMAL
Philippine dictator — MARCOS
Philippine dwarf — AETA
Philippine fetish — ANITO
Philippine fort — COTA
Philippine idol — ANITO
Philippine island — LEYTE, LUZON, MINDANAO, PANAY
Philippine island — PANAY, SAMAR
Philippine Island natives — ATIS
Philippine Moslem — MORO
Philippine native — AETA, IGOROT, MORO
Philippine palm — SALAK
Philippine port — DAVAO
Philippine textile — SABA
Philippine timber tree — ACLE
Philippine town or tree — DAO
Philippine volcano — APO
Philippine's palm — NIPA
Philippines sea — SULU
Phillip Johnson's org. — AIA
Phillips University site — ENID
Philly paraders — MUMMERS
Philly's transit system — SEPTA
Philo, the sleuth — VANCE
Philodendron's family — ARUM
Philomel — NIGHTINGALE
Philosopher — SAGE
Philosopher _____ Hsi — CHU
Philosopher Descartes — RENE
Philosopher Jose _____ y Gasset — ORTEGA
Philosopher, usually — SAGE
Phiz — MUG
Phlegm finish — ATIC
Phlegmatic — STOLID
Phlox genus — JACOBS LADDER
Phobia starter — AGORA
Phobias — DREADS, FEARS
Phocid — SEAL
Phoebes — PEWEES
Phoebus — SOL
Phoebus — SUN
Phoenician capital — TYRE
Phoenician city — TYRE
Phoenician goddess — ASTARTE
Phoenician letter — SADHU
Phoenician local deities — BAALIM
Phoenician love goddess — ASTARTE
Phoenician name of Dido — ELISSA
Phoenician vessel — TRIREME
Phoenix neighbor — MESA
Phoenix renewal site — ASHES
Phoenix source — ASHES
Phoenix's N.B.A. team — SUNS
Phoenix's remains — ASHES
Phoenix's source of rebirth — ASHES
Phone — CALL, DIAL, RING, RING UP
Phone caller, at times — DIALER
Phone company abbr. — ATT, ITT
Phone feature — DIAL
Phone or cycle starter — MEGA
Phone or scope lead-in — MICRO
Phone user — CALLER
Phoned — RANG
Phones — CALLS
Phonetic — VOCAL
Phonetic elision — SLUR
Phonetically smooth — LENE
Phonograph inventor — EDISON
Phonograph record — DISC
Phony — BOGUS, SHAM
Phony medicine — PLACEBO
Phooey! — PAH, RATS
Photo — SNAP
Photo attachment — STAT
Photo developer — HYPO
Photo developer's substance — TONER
Photo finish? — MATTE, STAT
Photo finisher — GENIC
Photocopies — STATS
Photocopy for short — STAT
Photog. abbr. — ENL
Photog. image — NEG
Photog.'s measure — F STOP
Photograph — SNAP
Photographed — SHOT
Photographer Adams — ANSEL
Photographer Arbus: 1923-71 — DIANE
Photographer Morath — INGE
Photographer's abbr. — ENL
Photographer's command — SMILE
Photographer's need — FILM
Photographer's request — SAY CHEESE
Photographer's surface — MATTE
Photographer's test print — PROOF
Photographic developer compound — AMIDOL
Photographs — SHOTS
Photographs of a sort — STILLS
Photolab abbr. — ENL
Photos — PIX, SNAPS
Photos from Merthyr Tydfil? — PRINTS OF WALES
Photosynthetic plants — ALGAS
Phrase — PASSAGE
Phrase of understanding — I SEE
Phrase on a shop sign — AND UP
Phrase on many dietary foods — LESS SALT
Phrase welcomed by Mom — BACK TO SCHOOL
Phrontistery — DEN
Phrontistery product — IDEA
Phyle — TRIBE
Phylum of insects, spiders and crustaceans — ARTHROPODA
Phylum of one-celled animals — PROTOZOA
Physical exam — STRESS TEST
Physical makeup — CONSTITUTION
Physical trainer at times — MASSAGER
Physician: Comb. form — IATRO
Physicians' org. — AMA
Physicist Bohr — NIELS
Physicist from Hungary — TELLER
Physicist Georg Simon — OHM
Physicist Isidor Isaac — RABI
Physicist Niels — BOHR
Physicist's deg. — MSC
Physicist's particle — ATOM
Physics Nobelist: 1922 — ASSTON
Physics Nobelist: 1944 — RABI
Physics preceder — ASTRO
Physiologist Jacques — LOEB
Physiotherapist — MASSEUR
Pi and Sigma separator — RHO
Pi followers — RHOS
Pi's follower — RHO
Piaget subject — CHILD
Pianist at Rick's Cafe — SAM
Pianist Balogh — FERNO
Pianist Blake — EUBIE
Pianist Claudio from Chile — ARRAU
Pianist Cliburn — VAN
Pianist Davis — IVAN
Pianist Frankie — CARLE
Pianist from N.Y.C. — PETER NERO
Pianist Gilels — EMIL

Pianist Myra — HESS
Pianist Nero — PETER
Pianist Oscar and family — LEVANTS
Pianist Pete — NERO
Pianist Peter — NERO
Pianist Rosalyn — TURECK
Pianist Rubinstein — ARTUR
Pianist son of Rudolf Serkin — PETER
Pianist Templeton — ALEC
Pianist Von Alpenhelm — ILSE
Piano exercises — SCALES
Piano expert — TUNER
Piano features — KEYS
Piano infant — SPINET
Piano keys — IVORY
Piano man — TUNER
Piano piece — CHOPSTICKS, NOCTURNE, NOLA
Piano piece for Lopez — NOLA
Piano specialists — TUNER
Piano standard — NOLA
Piano technician — TUNER
Piano virtuoso Art — TATUM
Piano wood — EBONY
Piano's ancestor — CLAVIER
Piazza — TERRACE
Picador pleaser — OLE
Picador's target — TORO
Picardy bloomers — ROSES
Picaresque person — RASCAL
Picasso contemporary — DALI
Picasso or Casals — PABLO
Picasso prop — EASEL
Picasso's latest stand? — EASEL
Picayune — PUNY
Piccadilly Circus statue — EROS
Piccadilly figure — EROS
Piccolo — FLUTE
Piccolo man of song — PETE
Pick-me-up — TONIC
Pick — ELECT, SELECT
Pick at — HASSLE, NIBBLE
Pick for a role — CAST
Pick on — ANNOY, NAG, TEASE
Pick or wit beginning — NIT
Pick out — CULL
Pick over — SORT
Pick pockets — STEAL
Pick up the bill — TREAT
Pick up the check — TREAT
Pick up the tab — HOST, PAY, TREAT
Picked dandelions — WEEDED
Pickerel — WALLEYE
Picket — STAKE
Pickford's Academy Award winner — COQUETTE
Pickle — BRINE, DILL
Pickle bath — BRINE
Pickle choice — DILL
Pickle flavoring — DILL
Pickle fluid — BRINE
Pickle herbs — DILLS
Pickle mixture — BRINE
Pickle type — DILL
Pickles — JAMS
Pickling ingredient — ALLSPICE
Pickling potion — BRINE
Pickling substance — BRINE
Pickpocket's prize — WALLET
Pickpockets: Slang — DIPS
Picks on — TEASES
Picks out — SELECTS
Picks up the tab — TREATS
Pickwick or Pepys — SAMUEL
Picnic — OUTING
Picnic buttinsky — ANT
Picnic device — COOLER
Picnic featuring ice-cream — SOCIAL
Picnic intruder — ANT
Picnic participants — ANTS
Picnic pests — ANTS, GNATS
Picnic playwright — INGE
Picnic site — LEA
Picnicker's tote — HAMPER
Pico de _____ — ANETO
Picot — LOOP
Picot feature — LOOP
Pictorial presswork — ROTO
Picture — FILM, IMAGE, IMAGINE, MOVIE, PORTRAIT, SCENE
Picture challenge — SMILE
Picture or humor ending — ESQUE
Picture or Roman follower — ESQUE
Picture portrayal — DIAGRAM
Picture puzzle — REBUS
Picture tube — KINESCOPE
Picturesque — SCENIC
Picturesque in its simplicity — IDYLLIC
Picturesque, as a setting — SCENIC
Piddling — MEASLY
Piddling amount — FEW
Pie _____ mode — A LA
Pie crust ingredient — LARD
Pie fancier — HORNER
Pie ingredients — PECANS
Pie portion — WEDGE
Pie's relative — ANNA
Pie, ice, yellow or dud — LEMON
Pie, in Pisa — TORTA
Pie-mode connection — A LA
Piebald — MOTTLED
Piebald penny — PINTO
Piece — HUNK
Piece de resistance — ROAST
Piece for nine — NONET
Piece for Price — ARIA
Piece of advice — TIP
Piece of cake — CINCH, LAYER, SLICE
Piece of change — COIN
Piece of china — PLATE
Piece of cultivated land — GLEBE
Piece of earth — ASIA
Piece of fired clay — TILE
Piece of furniture — COT, SETTEE
Piece of hardware — T NUT
Piece of jewelry — BANGLE, EARDROP
Piece of land — PLAT, TRACT
Piece of legislation — ACT
Piece of luggage — VALISE
Piece of material — PATCH
Piece of music — ETUDE, SONG
Piece of paper — SHEET
Piece of pine — SLAB
Piece of turf — SOD
Piece of wisdom — PEARL
Piece together — PATCH
Pieces of furniture — DESKS
Pieces of pottery — SHARDS
Pied-a-_____ — TERRE
Pied Piper's river — WESER
Piedmont province — ASTI
Piedmontese citizen — TORINESE
Piedmontese city — ASTI
Piedmontese province — ASTI
Pier — ANTA
Pier of Hollywood: 1932-71 — ANGELI
Pier wrks.' union — ILA
Pier, of a sort — ANTA
Pierce — PENETRATE, STAB
Pierce Arrows — AUTOS
Pierce of "M*A*S*H" — ALDA
Pierce, in a TV series — ALDA
Piercing — KEEN, SHRILL
Piercing cry — SCREAM
Piercing tools — AWLS
Pierre or Marie — CURIE
Pierre's aunt — TANTE
Pierre's dreams — REVES
Pierre's friend — AMIE
Pierre's girlfriends — AMIES
Pierre's head — TETE
Pierre's notion — IDEE
Pierre's pal — AMI
Pierre's rifle-range — TIR
Pierre's state — SOUTH DAKOTA
Pierre's State: Abbr. — SDAK
Pierre's sweetheart — CHERIE
Pierre's that — CELA
Pierre's woman — FEMME
Pierrot of song — AMI
Pierrot's Pierrette, perhaps — AMIE
Piers — ANTAS
Pietermaritzburg local — NATAL
Piffle — BILGE
Piffling — MEASLEY
PIG — IRON, LATIN, TAIL
Pig _____ poke — IN A

Pig or fan follower — TAIL
Pig pens — STIES
Pig's cousin — PECCARY
Pig's digs — STY
Pig's home — STY
Pig, in Paris — PORC
Pigboat — SUB
Pigeon-_____ — TOED
Pigeon-coop kin — DOVE-COTE
Pigeon call — COO
Pigeon carrier — HOMING
Pigeon coop — COTE
Pigeon of a sort — STOOL
Pigeon sounds — COOS
Pigeon's home — COTE
Pigeonhole — NOOK
Piggeries — STIES
Piggery — STY
Piggy bank coin — PENNY
Piggy or Peach — MISS
Piggy or penny — BANK
Piglet's mama — SOW
Pigment for Constable — OCHRE
Pigment for Gainsborough — OCHRE
Pigment for paint — OCHER
Pigmented pirate? — BLUE BEARD
Pigpen — STY
Pigskin — FOOTBALL
Pigsticker — POCKETKNIFE
Pigtail — BRAID, PLAIT
Pilaf base — RICE
Pilaf ingredient — RICE
Pilaster — ANTA
Pilasters — ANTAE
Pilatus, e.g. — ALP
Pilchard — SARDINE
Pile — NAP
Pile — STACK
Pile one on another — STACK UP
Pile together — AMASS
Pile up — AMASS, STACK
Piled up — HEAPED
Piles — NAPS
Pilfer — FILCH, STEAL
Pilgrim becomes golfer? — ARNIE PALMER
Pilgrimage — TOUR
Pilgrimage to Mecca — HADJ
Pili or macadamia — NUT
Pill for a chill — TABLET
Pill for veterinary use — BOLUS
Pillage — WASTE
Pillager — LOOTER
Pillar like — STELLAR
Pillbox — HAT
Pillow — CUSHION
Pillow cover — SHAM
Pillow filling — KAPOK
Pillow stuffing — DOWN
Pillow's quality — SOFTNESS
Pillowcases — SLIPS
Pilot — AVIATOR, STEER
Pilot sans instructor — SOLO
Pilot's aid: Abbr. — ATC, RADAR
Pilot's device: Abbr. — DME
Pilot's direction — ALEE
Pilot's manuever — LOOPS
Pilot's milieu — SKY
Pilot's place — HELM
Pilot's records — LOGS
Pilot's residence — ALOFT
Pilotless planes — DRONES
Pilots — NAVIGATORS
Pilsner, e.g. — BEER
Pin — DOWEL
Pin a label on — TAG
Pin down — BIND, HOLD
Pin for golfers — TEE
Pin point — SPOT
Pina _____ (rum drink) — COLADA
Pinafore — APRON
Pinafore part — BIB
Pinafore, for one — HMS
Pinafores — APRONS
Pinball-game ender — TILT
Pincers — PLIERS
Pinch — NAB, TWEAK
Pinch hit — REPLACE
Pinch pennies — STINT
Pinched — NABBED, RAN IN
Pinches — NIPS
Pinchpenny — MISER
Pindar creation — ODE
Pindar notably — ODIST
Pindaric productions — ODES
Pindling — PUNY
Pine — YEARN
Pine cone — STROBILE
Pine for — MISS
Pine fruit — CONES
Pine native to Oregon or California — JEFFREY
Pine or nose — CONE
Pine product — RESIN
Pine strategy? — SIGHCHOLOGY
Pine tree emission — RESIN
Pine Tree state — MAINE
Pine, e.g. — SOFT WOOD, TREE
Pine-tar product — RETENE
Pineapples — ANANAS
Pined — LONGED, ACHED
Pines and balsams — FIRS
Pinetree State's school at Orono — MAINE U
Pining person — YEARNER
Pinion — GEAR
Pink — STAB
Pink bird — FLAMINGO
Pink Panther, e.g. — JEWEL
Pinkham — LYDIA
Pinkish shade — CORAL
Pinkish-red — ROSY
Pinlike? — NEAT
Pinna — EAR
Pinna's pendant part — EARLOBE
Pinnacle — ACME, APEX, PEAK, SUMMIT
Pinned — ATTACHED
Pinned down — NAILED
Pinniped — SEAL
Pinniped's fur — SEALSKIN
Pinnule — FIN
Pinocchio offense — LIE
Pinocchio's undoing — NOSE
Pinochle ploy — MELD
Pinochle tallies — MELDS
Pinstripes color — OXFORD GRAY
Pinta's sister ship — NINA
Pintail duck — SMEE
Pintails — SMEES
Pinto — HORSE
Pinto's gait — LOPE
Pinto, for one — BEAN
Pintquart? — BOUND VOLUMES
Pinup girl — CUTEY
Pinza namesakes — EZIOS
Pinza of "South Pacific" — EZIO
Pinza of opera fame — EZIO
Pinza replacement, Tajo — ITALO
Pioneer Daniel — BOONE
Pioneer film producer: 1864-1948 — SELIG
Pioneer in development of celluloid — HYATT
Pioneer opera composer — PERI
Pioneer's tool — FROE
Pioneered — LED
Pioneering labor leader — DEBS
Pious jargon — CANT
Pious partisan woman: Abbr. — STE
Pious talk — CANT
Piously — DEVOTEDLY
Pip — SEED
Pip or pippin — SEED
Pipe — BRIAR
Pipe bends — ELLS
Pipe elbows — ELLS
Pipe joint — ELL, TEE
Pipe part — STEM
Pipe type — BRIAR
Piper's garb — KILTS
Piper's son — TOM
Pipes used to carry fluids downwards — PARTISANS
Pipistrelles — BATS
Pipkins — POTS
Pippin — APPLE, SEED
Piquancy — SPICE, TANG, WIT, ZEST
Piquant — LIVELY, RACY, SPICY
Pique — GOAD, IRE, SNIT
Piqued — IRATE

Piquet bonuses — PICS
Piranha — CARIBE
Pirate Captain _____ — KIDD
Pirate flag — JOLLY ROGER
Pirate in "Peter Pan" — SMEE
Pirate with a long name? — JOHN SILVER
Pirates or Padres count — NINE
Pirates plunder — LOOT
Pirates, for example — PREYERS
Pirates, perhaps — LOOTERS
Pirogue — CANOE
Pirouette — PIVOT, TURN
Pisa attraction — TOWER
Pisa divider — ARNO
Pisa's river — ARNO
Pisa-to-Leghorn dir. — SSW
Pisa-to-Verona dir. — NNE
Pisan — ITALIAN
Piscator — ANGLER
Piscatorial amor — SCALE
Pisces follower — ARIES
Piscine pens — AQUARIUMS
Piscivorous bird — ERN
Piscivorous fliers — ERNES
Pish! — FIE
Pismire — ANT
Pistachio — NUT
Pistol — GUN, ROSCOE
Pisum sativum — PEA
Pit — ABYSS
Pit _____ — A PAT
Pit remover — STONER
Pit vipers — CUPRUM HEADS
Pitcairn, for one — ISLAND
Pitch — HURL, TAR, TONE, TOSS
Pitch from Clemens — SLIDER
Pitch heavily at anchor — HAWSE
Pitch in — AED
Pitch pipe, e.g. — TUNER
Pitch pro — TUNER
Pitch-dark — BLACK, INKY
Pitchblende and bauxite — ORES
Pitched in — AIDED
Pitcher — EWER
Pitcher _____ Blue — VIDA
Pitcher adjuncts — EARS
Pitcher Alejandro — PENA
Pitcher Darling — RON
Pitcher feature — RIM
Pitcher Harder — MEL
Pitcher Hershiser — OREL
Pitcher Labine — CLEM
Pitcher Luis — TIANT
Pitcher of a sort — RELIEF
Pitcher Paige — SATCHEL
Pitcher parts — EARS
Pitcher Ryan — NOLAN
Pitcher Saberhagen — BRET
Pitcher schoolboy — ROWE
Pitcher Swan — CRAIG
Pitcher Warren family — SPAHNS
Pitcher with ears — EWER
Pitcher's bag — ROSIN
Pitcher's fault — BALK
Pitcher's favorite game — NO HIT
Pitcher's goals — WINS
Pitcher's handles — EARS
Pitcher's lug — EAR
Pitcher's milieu — BULLPEN
Pitcher's mound miscue — BALK
Pitcher's objective — STRIKE
Pitcher's place — MOUND
Pitcher's plate — SLAB
Pitcher's ploy — SPITBALL
Pitcher's specialty — THROW
Pitcher's throw — FASTBALL
Pitchers — EWERS
Pitchers' bane — ERRORS
Pitchers' targets — PLATES
Pitchfork part — TINE
Pitching error — BALK
Pitching stars — ACES
Pitching stats. — ERAS
Pitchman's aides — SHILLS
Pitchman's lines — SPIELS
Pitchman's talk — SPIEL
Pitfall — SNARE, TRAP
Pith — CORE
Pith helmet — TOPEE
Pithy remark — MOT
Pithy saying — MOT
Pithy sayings — EPIGRAMS
Pitiful — PATHETIC, SORRY
Pitiless — STONY
Pitman's workplace — SAWMILL
Pits — ABYSMS
Pittance — IOTA, MITE
Pittsburgh athlete — STEELER
Pittsburgh eleven — STEELERS
Pittsburgh intake — ORE
Pittsburgh player — STEELER
Pittsburgh product — STEEL
Pittsburgh slugger, turned announcer — KINER
Pittsburgh team — STEELERS
Pituitary _____ — GLAND
Pituitary hormone, initials — ACTH
Pivot — SLUE
Pivotal — POLAR
Pivotal areas — HEARTLANDS
Pixie — SPRITE
Pixies — ELVES
Pixilated — DAFT, LOOPY
Pixy — ELF
Pizazz — ELAN, PEP, ZING
Pizza pieces — SLICES
Pizza topping — PEPPERONI
Pizzaro victims — INCAS
Pizzaro's gold — ORO
Pizzaro's landing place — PERU
Pizzaro's quest — ORO
Pizzeria appliances — OVENS
Pizzeria necessity — OVEN
Pizzicato — NOTE
Placard — SIGN
Placate — APPEASE
Place — AREA, LAY, LIEU, SITE, SITUATE, SPOT
Place above — SET OVER
Place again — RESET
Place apart — ENISLE
Place at table — SEAT
Place for a "steak-out" — PATIO
Place for a beezer — GRINDSTONE
Place for a bite — DELI
Place for a bovine — LEA
Place for a bracelet — ANKLE
Place for a casquette — TETE
Place for a chapeau — TETE
Place for a cheap meal — EATERY
Place for a chicken — POT
Place for a coin — SLOT
Place for a cookout — PATIO
Place for a dance — BARN
Place for a dart game — PUB
Place for a delayed project — BACK BURNER
Place for a Devil to cool his heels? — PENALTY BOX
Place for a dip — POOL
Place for a discussion — ROUND TABLE
Place for a fence sitter — MID-DLE OF THE ROAD
Place for a future Lt. — OCS
Place for a garden tool — SHED
Place for a grill — PATIO
Place for a hat or a shoe — TREE
Place for a horseshoe — HOOF
Place for a mashie or niblick — GOLF BAG
Place for a medal — CHEST
Place for a P.T.A. — SCH
Place for a padlock — HASP
Place for a plant — SILL
Place for a posy — LAPEL, VASE
Place for a prompter — IN THE BACKGROUND
Place for a putee — LEG
Place for a ring — EARLOBE
Place for a roast — OVEN
Place for a simple French meal — BISTRO
Place for a wedding — ALTAR
Place for a young falcon — AERIE
Place for affairs? — STATE
Place for an eleve — ECOLE
Place for an inscription — FLY LEAF
Place for avions — ORLY
Place for baby — KNEE

Place for butts — ASHTRAY
Place for Caesar's calceus — PES
Place for casquettes — TETES
Place for change — SLOT
Place for chow — MESS
Place for cuddling — LAP
Place for eats — DINER
Place for experiments, for short — LAB
Place for fans — ARENA
Place for fish — TANK
Place for matches — ARENA
Place for matriculants — CLASSROOMS
Place for men — YMCA
Place for one's savings — PIGGY BANK
Place for prayer — ALTAR
Place for taking of vows — ALTAR
Place for the Burgermeister? — GERMANTOWN
Place for valuables — TILL
Place for worship, to a poet — FANE
Place for would-be its — OCS
Place for Zeno — STOA
Place in a cabinet — FILE
Place in a new setting — REHOUSE
Place in another pew — RESEAT
Place in Congress — SEAT
Place in office — ELECT
Place in space — EARTH
Place next to — APPOSE
Place not to be caught — OFF BASE
Place of confusion — BABEL
Place of debate — FORUM
Place of exile — ELBA
Place of innocence — EDEN
Place of interest? — BANKS
Place of Mead studies — SAMOA
Place of nether darkness — EREBUS
Place of origin suffix — ESE
Place of refuge — SANCTUARY
Place of worship — ALTAR, HOUSE OF GOD
Place offering welcome relief — OASIS
Place or door — MAT
Place or welcome — MAT
Place reliance on — DEPEND
Place selling Jersey juice — DAIRY
Place side by side — APPOSE
Place strategically — DEPLOY
Place that's ahum — HIVE
Place the racers — SEED
Place to anchor — PORT
Place to be in the morning — CAROLINA
Place to caulk — SEAM
Place to eat, drink and be merry — CAFE
Place to eat, Mexican style — CASA
Place to go beyond — PALE
Place to hobnob all night in disguise — MASKED BALL
Place to place tokens — SLOT
Place to play blackjack — RENO
Place to remember — ALAMO
Place to schuss — SLOPE
Place to see a Turner — TATE
Place to see Giotto paintings — ASSISI
Place to stop, look and listen — RR CROSSING
Place to worship — CHAPEL
Place where jays prey — NEST
Place where one hangs his hat — HOME
Place where one's heart is — HOME
Place: Comb. form — TOPO
Placed — LAID
Placed a bet — GAMBLED
Placed in a heavenly area — SPHERED
Placed the white ball — TEED UP
Placer material — ORE
Places — LOCI, PUTS, STEADS
Places for coins — SLOTS
Places for cold cuts — DELIS
Places for liners — PIERS
Places for loafers — FEET
Places for matériel — ARSENAL
Places for murals — WALLS
Places for orchestras, at one time — PITS
Places for parishioners — PEWS
Places for pennies — SLOTS
Places for place settings — MATS
Places for races — OVALS
Places for schussing — SLOPES
Places for tons and poker — HEARTH
Places for valuables — TILLS
Places for: Suffix — ORIA
Places named for ancient Ilium — TROYS
Places of respite — OASES
Places of safety — ASYLA
Places of worship — CHAPELS
Places to say "I do" — ALTARS
Placid — SERENE
Placket — SLIT
Plague — HARASS
Plaid — TARTAN
Plaid or ship — TARTAN
Plaid shawl — MAUD
Plain — CLEAR, EVIDENT
Plain spoken and abrupt — BLUNT
Plainer — PURER
Plains Amerinds — OTOES
Plains animal — BISON
Plains dwelling, of old — TEPEE
Plains home — TEPEE
Plains Indian — ARIKARA, KIOWA, OSAGE, OTOE
Plains Indian dwellings: Var. — TIPIE
Plains Indian shelter — TEPEE
Plains of South America — LLANOS
Plaint of a Bo-Peep sheep? — IM LOST
Plaintiff — SUER
Plaintive poem — ELEGY
Plaintive, in music — DOLOROSO
Plan — INTEND, INTENT, MAP, SCHEME, SYSTEM
Plan for a movie — SCENARIO
Plan in detail — CHART
Plan of action — PROPOSAL
Planate — EVEN
Plane curve — PARABOLA
Plane landings — ARRIVALS
Plane personnel — CREW
Plane preceder — AERO
Plane route — AIRLANE
Plane tree — SYCAMORE
Planet — EARTH, MARS
Planet or city starter — INNER
Planet paths — ARCS
Planetarium in Chicago — ADLER
Planetary rulers in a 1968 movie — APES
Planets — ORBS
Plank — BOARD
Plank curve — SNY
Plankton part — DIATOM
Plankton snare — D NET
Planned undertaking — PROJECT
Plant — FLORA, MILL, SEED, SOW
Plant again — RESEED
Plant also called germander — BETONY
Plant beginning — SEED
Plant branch — STOLON
Plant bristles — AWNS
Plant disease — EDEMA
Plant fluid — SERUM
Plant food: Comb. form — SERO
Plant fungus — ERGOT, UREDO
Plant juices — SAPS
Plant life — BIOTA
Plant membrane — SEPTA
Plant of the Canary Islands — DRAGON TREE
Plant of the genus Brassica — TURNIP

Plant of the heath family — ERICA
Plant of the legume family — SENNA
Plant of the lily family — SOTOL
Plant of the milkweed family — STAPELIA
Plant of the nightshade family — TOMATO
Plant of the umbel family — ANISE
Plant on the Mojave — CACTUS
Plant openings — STOMATA
Plant organs — SPORES
Plant part — ROOT, STEM, TAPROOT
Plant pest — APHID
Plant pests — APHIS
Plant pouch — SAC
Plant problem — EDEMA
Plant product — SEED
Plant protuberance — NODE
Plant resembling spinach — ORACH
Plant sometimes called toadflax — LINARIA
Plant starter — SEEDBED
Plant stem — BINE
Plant stipule — OCREA
Plant swelling — EDEMA
Plant with a fragrant root — ORRIS
Plant with arrow-shaped leaves — ARUM
Plant with silky catkins — PUSSY WILLOW
Plant's adaptation to a new milieu — ECESIS
Plant: Comb. form — PHYLO
Plantae's counterpart — ANIMALIA
Plantain lily — HOSTA
Plantain, in Spain — LLANTEN
Plantation — MANOR
Plantation employee — OVERSEER
Plantation hand — BALER
Planted — SEEDED, SOWN
Planted a mike — BUGGED
Planted grass — SODDED
Planter — SEEDER
Planter's punch ingredient — RUM
Planting tools — SEEDERS
Plants — SOWS
Plants of the bellflower family — LOBELIAS
Plants with tough fibers — HEMPS
Plants with two seed leaves, for short — DICOTS
Plants' branches — RAMI
Plaque — SLAB
Plasm start — ECTO
Plaster — LATH
Plaster of Paris — GESSO
Plaster painting — FRESCO
Plaster the walls — CEIL
Plaster tool — SPATULA
Plaster-backing strips — LATHS
Plastic source — VINYL
Plastic wrap — SARAN
Plastron (fencing) — PAD
Plat — MAP
Plate — CHINA, DINNER, DISH
Plate preceder — BOILER
Plate scraping — ORT
Plate, for Strawberry — HOME
Plated type of saurus — STEGO
Platelike part — LAMELLA
Platen — ROLLER
Plates of a type — PATENS
Plates with metal — CHROMES
Platform — DAIS, STAGE
Plath ploys — SIMILES
Plath work — ARIEL
Platinum — VARIETY OF BLONDE
Platinum blonde Jean — HARLOW
Plato and Hippocrates, e.g. — GREEKS
Plato dialogue — ION
Plato's mart — AGORA
Plato's porch — STOA
Plato's shopping plaza — AGORA
Plato's symposium topic — EROS
Plato, for one — ATHENIAN
Plato, to Aristotle — TEACHER
Platte valley Indian — OTOE
Platter — DISC
Platter's for a DJ — LPS
Plaudit — PRAISE
Plausible — TENABLE
Play — ACT, DRAMA
Play _____ (lie low) — POSSUM
Play _____ (share) — A PART
Play a fife — TOOTLE
Play a flute — TOOTLE
Play a horn — BLOW
Play a part — ACT
Play a role — PRETEND
Play about Miss Thompson — RAIN
Play around — PHILANDER
Play at — FAKE
Play backer — ANGEL
Play based on Maugham tale — RAIN
Play beginning — ACT I
Play by _____ — EAR
Play by Agatha Christie — THE MOUSE TRAP
Play by E.E. Cummings — HIM
Play by ear — FAKE
Play by O'Neill — ILE
Play by play — ASIDE
Play by Turgenev — A MONTH IN THE COUNTRY
Play calling — HUDDLE
Play division — SCENE
Play end — FINAL CURTAIN
Play for a fool — DUPE
Play for time — STALL
Play interlocutor — ASK
Play it again — REPRISE
Play it by ear — AD LIB, WING IT
Play like a filly — FRISK
Play lookout — ABET
Play mates? — CAST
Play midsection — ACT II
Play on words — PUN
Play opener — ACT I
Play out — TIRE
Play part — ACT, SCENE
Play part, in Paris — ACTE
Play people — CAST
Play pranks — HORSE AROUND
Play rm. — REC
Play segment — SCENE
Play start — SCENES
Play the diaskeuast — EDIT
Play the flute — TOOTLE
Play the host — TREAT
Play the lead — STAR
Play the part of — ENACT
Play the voyeur — OGLE
Play to the balcony — EMOTE
Play tricks — JAPE
Play tricks by sleight of hand — JUGGLE
Play unit — SCENE
Play with fire — BURN ONES FINGERS
Play-gun ammo — PEAS
Play-thing — TOY
Playa clay — ADOBE
Playbill — POSTER
Playbill heading — ACT I
Playbill listing — CAST
Playboys of yore — RAKES
Played a child's game — HID
Played a kazoo — TOOTED
Played a part — ACTED
Played a pipe — BLEW
Played a trumpet — BLEW
Played detective — SLEUTHED
Played it again — RERAN
Played the ham — EMOTED
Played the tape again — RERAN
Player able to bargain — FREE AGENT
Player behind home plate — CATCHER
Player in "The Boys of Summer" — REESE

Player in Naismith's game — CAGER
Player not on the first team — SCRUB
Player of tough blonde roles — SHEREE NORTH
Player piano — PIANOLA
Player's org. — PGA
Player's script — LINES
Players at Rose Bowl game — BAND
Playful — GAMESOME
Playful act — ANTIC
Playful mammal — OTTER
Playful musical passages — SCHERZO
Playful personality — SPRITE
Playful prank — MON-KEYSHINE
Playful river animal — OTTER
Playful swimmer — OTTER
Playgoer's choice — DRAMA
Playground — PARK
Playground attraction — SEESAW, SLIDES
Playground feature — MONKEY BARS
Playground features — SLIDES
Playground item — SLIDE
Playground time — RECESS
Playing card — NINE, TAROT, TREY
Playing card symbol — SPADE
Playing cards of a kind — TAROTS
Playing engagements — TOURS
Playing field for Montana — GRID
Playing marble — AGGIE, AGATE, MIB, STEELIE
Playing or recording engagement — GIG
Playlet — ONE ACTER, SKIT
Playmates? — CAST
Plays a child's game — HOP SCOTCHES
Plays a guitar — STRUMS
Plays a horn — BLOWS
Plays a part — ACTS
Plays a sidewalk game — HOPSCOTCHES
Plays for time — STALLS
Plays roulette — BETS
Plays the host — GREETS
Plays the lead — STARS
Plays the snoop — NOSES
Plays trencherman — EATS
Plays tug of war — PULLS
Plays voyeur — OGLES
Plays with fire — TEMPTS FATE
Plaything — TOY
Playthings — TOPS, TOYS
Playtime — RECESS
Playwright — AUTHOR
Playwright Arthur Wing — PINERO
Playwright born in Columbus, Miss. — TN WILLIAMS
Playwright Connelly — MARC
Playwright Elmer — RICE
Playwright Howe — TINA
Playwright Jones — LEROI
Playwright King — LARRY
Playwright Ionesco — EUGENE
Playwright Noel — COWARD
Playwright O'Casey — SEAN
Playwright of "Bus Stop" — INGE
Playwright Pirandello — LUIGI
Playwright Rattigan — TER-ENCE
Playwright Rice — ELMER
Playwright Simon — NEIL
Playwright Sir Arthur _____ Pinero — WING
Playwright William — INGE
Playwright's ploy — ASIDE
Plaza accomodation — SUITE
Plaza girl — ELOISE
Plea — APPEAL, ENTREATY, PRAYER, REQUEST
Plea at sea — SOS
Plea ploy — COP
Plea to a departing one — WRITE
Plea to Bill Bailey — WONT YOU COME HOME
Pleach — INTERLACE, PLAIT
Plead — BEG, ENTREAT
Pleas heard in court — ALIBIS
Pleasant — MERRY, NICE, SWEET
Pleasant and cheerful — ALL SMILES
Pleasant Island, today — NAURU
Pleasant place for a picnic — GLADE
Please — AGREE, GRATIFY, HUMOR
Please nemesis — AVENGE
Please with savory food — TICKLE THE PALATE
Please, in Berlin — BITTE
Please, in Potsdam — BITTE
Please: Ger. — BITTE
Pleased — GLAD
Pleases me — DOES MY HEART GOOD
Pleasing — NICE
Pleasing to the eye — WINSOME
Pleasingly zaftig — PLUMP
Pleasurable — HEDONIC
Pleasure craft — YACHT
Pleasure Island sounds — BRAYS
Pleasure, in Paris — GRE
Pleasures — AMUSEMENT
Pleat — CREASE, FOLD
Plebe — CADET
Plebiscite — VOTE
Plebiscites — REFERENDA
Pledge — AVOW, OATH, PAWN, VOW
Pledge or risk — PAWN
Pledged — PROMISED, SWORE
Pledged word — TROTH
Pledges — OATHS, SURETIES
Pledget — SWAB
Pleistocene Age — ICE
Pleistocene is one — EPOCH
Plenary — ENTIRE, FULL
Plenteous — RIFE
Plentiful — AMPLE, RIFE
Plenty — LOTS
Plenty, to poets — ENOW
Plenty: Lat. — COPIA
Plenum — SPACE
Plethora — EXCESS, GLUT, PLENTY, SURFEIT
Pleven or Coty — RENE
Pleven or Lévesque — RENE
Plexus — RETE, TANGLE
Pliable — MALLEABLE
Pliant — FLEXIBLE
Plied with potions — DOSED
Plies the needle — SEWS
Plight — JAM, PICKLE, STATE
Plighted vows — TROTHS
Plimsoll — SNEAKER
Plimsoll mark — LINE
Plinth — SOCLE
Pliny the Younger, for one — ORATOR
Plod — SLOG
Plodding one — TRUDGER
Plods through clods — SLOGS
Plot — CHART, CONNIVE
Plot devices — TWISTS
Plot feature — TWIST
Plot line — SCENARIO
Plots of land — PARCELS
Plottage — AREA
Plotted — CONSPIRED
Plotter exposed by Esther — HAMAN
Ploverlike bird of Asia — COURSER
Plow name — DEERE
Plow part — SHARE
Plowed acreage — TILLAGE
Plowman John — DEERE
Plowman's benefactor — DEERE
Ploy — STRATAGEM
Pluck — GRIT, METTLE, PICK
Plucky — GAMY
Plug up — STOP
Plugs on the TV — ADS
Plum — DAMSON, SLOE
Plum for gin — SLOE
Plum for the jet set — SST
Plum role — LEAD
Plumb bob — SINKER
Plumb's Cinders — ELLA
Plumber's concern — AIR TRAP
Plumber's gadget — PLUNGER

Plumber's technique — SWEAT
Plumber's tool — SNAKE
Plumber, at times — FILER
Plumbers' cables — SNAKES
Plumbers' concern — DRIPS
Plumbing parts — STEMS
Plumbing problem — DRIP
Plume — EGRET
Plumed avion — EGRET
Plumed bird — EGRET
Plumed hat — SHAKO
Plumed hat wearer — CYRANO
Plumed military hat — SHAKO
Plumlike fruit — SLOE
Plummeted — SANK
Plump one — PUDGE
Plump red-breast? — ROUND ROBIN
Plump roasting fowl — CAPON
Plumped up — FATTENED
Plunder — FORAGE, HARRY, LOOT, SACK
Plundered — LOOTED
Plunderer — LOOTER
Plunderers — RANSACKERS
Plunders — LOOTS
Plunge — DIVE
Plunges — DROPS
Plunk — DROP, PLOP
Plunk preceder — KER
Pluperfect, e.g. — TENSE
Plural abbreviation — ETAL
Plus — AND
Plus factor — ASSET
Plus for hitters: Abbr. — RBI
Plus item — ASSET
Pluto's creator — DISNEY
Pluto's realm — HADES
Pluto, to Cleo — OSIRIS
Pluto, to Plato — HADES
Ply — FEED, PROVIDE
Ply the blue pencil — EDIT
Ply the needles — KNIT
PM's — AFTS
PMs — NTS
Pneumatic tooter — AIRHORN
Po tributary — ADDA
Poacher's pitfall — MANTRAP
Pocahontas' John, et al. — ROLFES
Pocatello's state — IDAHO
Pochards — SMEES
Pochette — KIT
Pock — MARK
Pocket bread — PITA
Pocket contents — KEYS
Pocket fillers — COINS
Pocket money — PETTY CASH
Pocket opening — SLIT
Pocket pager — BEEPER
Pocket piece of yore — GOLD COIN
Pocketbook — PURSE
Pocketwatch accessory — FOB
Poconos pool — TARN
Poculiform item — CUP
Pod denizens — PEAS
Pod occupant — PEA
Pod or corn lead-in — TRI
Pod pickings — PEAS
Pod population — PEAS
Pod unit — PEA
Pod vegetable — OCRA, PEA
Podded plant — PW
Podiatrist concern — INSTEP
Podium — DAIS
Pods for soup — OKRA
Pods of flax — BOLLS
Poe and Guest — EDGARS
Poe bird — RAVEN
Poe character — PYM
Poe exterminator's quarry? — THE GOLD BUG
Poe house — USHER
Poe Lizette — REESE
Poe maiden — ANNABEL
Poe poem — THE RAVEN
Poe subject — RAVEN
Poe tale — THE GOLD BUG
Poe's "always" — EER
Poe's "Annabelle _____" — LEE
Poe's "gold bug" — SCARAB
Poe's "Raven" lady — LENORE
Poe's "The _____ of the Perverse" — IMP
Poe's bird — RAVEN
Poe's croaker — RAVEN
Poe's middle name — ALLAN
Poe-tic birds — RAVENS
Poem — VERSE
Poem by Mary Dow Brine — SOMEBODYS MOTHER
Poem by Tennyson — DORA
Poem by William Carlos Williams — THESE
Poem of lament — ELEGY
Poem of repetitive rhymes — RONDEAU
Poem part — CANTO
Poems — ODES
Poems with epic themes — EPOS
Poet-novelist May — SARTON
Poet — BARD, ODIST
Poet _____ de Lisle — LECONTE
Poet _____ Manley Hopkins — GERARD
Poet Alighieri — DANTE
Poet Carl — SANDBURG
Poet Crane — HART
Poet Dickinson — EMILY
Poet Edgar — GUEST
Poet Edgar/Outlaw Belle — GUEST STARR
Poet Ezra — POUND
Poet Garcia _____ of Spain — LORCA
Poet Ginsberg — ALLEN
Poet Jones — LEROI
Poet Khayyam — OMAR
Poet laureate after Shadwell — TATE
Poet Lazarus — EMMA
Poet Lizette Woodworth _____ — REESE
Poet Lowell — AMY
Poet Marianne — MOORE
Poet McKuen — ROD
Poet Merriam — EVE
Poet Millay — EDNA
Poet of "Book of Songs" — HEINE
Poet of "Endymion" — KEATS
Poet of "The Turtle " — NASH
Poet of ancient Greece — HESIOD
Poet Ogden — NASH
Poet or Nobelist's title — LAUREATE
Poet or tact ending — ICAL
Poet Pound — EZRA
Poet Sandburg — CARL
Poet Seeger — ALAN
Poet Shapiro — KARL
Poet Shelley — PERCY
Poet Stephen Vincent — BENET
Poet Teasdale — SARA
Poet Thomas — DYLAN
Poet W.H. — AUDEN
Poet Walter _____ Mare — DE LA
Poet who was Flaubert's mistress — COLET
Poet William _____ Bryant — CULLEN
Poet Wylie — ELINOR
Poet's before — ERE
Poet's concern — METER
Poet's contraction — EER
Poet's dawns — MORNS
Poet's even — EEN
Poet's ever — EER
Poet's frequently — OFT
Poet's muse — ERATO
Poet's preposition — OER
Poet's time of day — EEN
Poet's vehicle — ODE
Poet's word — EER, ERE
Poet, master of the couplet — POPE
Poet-novelist Wylie — ELINOR
Poet/novelist Harte — BRET
Poetic adverb — NEER
Poetic before — ERE
Poetic composition — EPIC
Poetic contr. — EEN
Poetic contraction — EEN, EER, NEER
Poetic contraction — OER, TWEEN
Poetic division — STANZA
Poetic foot — IAMB
Poetic form — ELEGY, ODE
Poetic never — NEER
Poetic preposition — OER
Poetic saga — EPOS

Poetic sundown — EENS
Poetic time — EEN
Poetic twilight — EEN
Poetic type of year — YESTER
Poetic verb — OPE
Poetic word — EEN
Poetic work — ODE
Poetic, a la Keats — ODIC
Poetical ploy — SPEECH
Poetical word — OER
Poetically before — ERE
Poetically below — NEATH
Poetically bereft — LORN
Poetically forever — EER
Poetically perpetual — ETERN
Poetry buff? — METER READER
Poetry form — EPOS
Poetry ingredient — METER
Poetry muse — ERATO
Poetry unit — VERSE
Poets Sexton and Marx — ANNES
Poi ingredient — TARO
Poi prerequisite — TARO
Poilu's cap — KEPI
Poilu's term for his foe — BOCHE
Point — CUSP, DOT, SPOT
Point Barrow dwellings — IGLOOS
Point blank — BLUNT
Point in a certain space orbit — APOLUNE
Point in an orbit — APSIS
Point in moon's orbit nearest earth — PERIGEE
Point of a mariner's compass — RHUMB
Point of chief interest — CLOU
Point of concentration — FOCUS
Point of land — SPIT
Point of view — ANGLE, SLANT, STAND
Point on a stem — NODE
Point on the Isle of Man — AYRE
Point on the nose — ALARE
Point out — REFER
Point the finger at — ACCUSE, BLAME
Point winning tennis serve — ACE
Point-blank — DIRECT
Pointed — ACUTE
Pointed a gun — AIMED
Pointed arch — OGEE, OGIVE
Pointed ends — CUSPS
Pointed remark — BARB
Pointer — HINT
Pointer's best point — SCENT
Pointer's clue — SCENT
Pointers — INPICATORS
Pointillist Georges — SEURAT
Pointillist's prop — EASEL
Pointing to the Zenith — PERPENDICULAR
Pointless — IDLE, INANE
Points for Fonteyn — TOES
Points in orbit — APOGEES
Poise — BALANCE
Poison — BANE, INFECT, TAINT, TOXIN
Poison for Nero? — WOLFES-BANE
Poison from castor beans — RICIN
Poison ivy or sumac — RHUS
Poison ivy's cousin — SUMAC
Poison oak — SUMAC
Poison plant — SUMAC
Poison sumac — SHRUB
Poisonous arachnid — SCORPION
Poisonous fungi — AMANITAS
Poisonous mushroom — AMANITA, TOADSTOOL
Poisonous plant — SUMAC
Poisonous powder — PARIS GREEN
Poisonous protein in the castor bean — RICIN
Poisonous sap tree — UPAS
Poisonous shrub — SUMAC
Poisonous snakes — ASPS, MAMBAS
Poisonous white-spored fungus — AMANITA
Poisons — BANES
Poisonwood — SUMAC
Poitier-Cosby film — LETS DO IT AGAIN
Poitier-Steiger movie — IN THE HEAT OF THE NIGHT
Poivre's table-mate — SEL
Poke — JAB, NUDGE
Poke contents — A PIG
Poke fun at — DERIDE, RIB
Poke occupant — PIG
Poked around — ROOTED
Poked fun at — RODE
Poker-faced — STOIC
Poker — STUD
Poker "dues" — ANTE
Poker arbiter — HOYLE
Poker choice — STUD
Poker fee — ANTE
Poker game — SEVEN CARD STUD
Poker hand — PAIR
Poker holding — PAIR
Poker money — ANTE
Poker move — RAISE
Poker payment — ANTE
Poker place for low rollers? — PENNY ANTEROOM
Poker play — DRAW
Poker player's stake — ANTE
Poker ploys — CALLS, RAISES
Poker pot — KITTY
Poker pots — ANTES
Poker stake — ANTE
Poker term — ANTE, SEE
Pokes fun at — RIBS
Pokeys — STIRS
Poky — SLOW
Poky vessel — SLOW BOAT
Pol's pursuit — VOTE
Pol. officer — INSP
Pol. subdivision — TERR
Poland China — SWINE
Poland China's enclosure — STY
Poland's Lech — WALESA
Polanski '79 film — TESS
Polar explorer — BYRD
Polaris — STAR
Polaris and Canopus — F STARS
Pole in Scottish sport — CABER
Pole near a teepee — TOTEM
Pole or Serb — SLAV
Pole, e.g. — SLAV
Polecat of a type — FERRET
Polecat's relative — FERRET
Poles for some clowns — STILTS
Police action — RAID
Police blotter abbr. — AKA
Police bulletin — APB
Police cordon — NET
Police device — RADAR
Police files — DOSSIERS
Police officer, at times — NAB-BER
Police officers — INSPECTORS
Police science — CRIMINOLOGY
Police team — RIOT SQUAD
Police-report inits. — AKA
Policeman — COP, OFFICER, PATROLMAN
Policeman becomes landscape painter? — JOHN CON-STABLE
Policeman's round — BEAT
Policeman, at times — CAPTOR
Policy — COURSE, METHOD, PRACTICE
Policy allowing other than official beliefs — TOLERATION
Polish-Czech region — SILESIA
Polish — BUFF, BURNISH, CLEAN, ENHANCE, RUB, SCOUR
Polish astronomer: 1473-1543 — COPERNICUS
Polish boundary river — ODRA
Polish city — KRAKOW
Polish manually — HAND RUB
Polish national dance — MAZURKA
Polish or ploy — FINESSE
Polish partner — SPIT

Polish pianist _____ Paderewski — IGNACE
Polish seaport — GDYNIA
Polish writer of sci-fi fame — LEM
Polish's companion — SPIT
Polished — ELEGANT
Polished shoes to Claude? — RAINS SHINES
Polisher — FACER
Polishes — SHINES UP
Polishing aid — SANDPAPER
Polishing machine — REELER, WAXER
Polishing powder — ROUGE
Polishing stone — PUMICE
Polit. party — REP, DEMO
Polite — CIVIL, CORDIAL, ELEGANT, FORMAL
Polite — GALLANT, REFINED
Polite address — MAAM
Polite addresses to ladies — MAAMS
Polite bloke — GENT
Polite denial — NO SIR
Polite entreaty, old style — PRITHEE
Polite form of address — MAAM
Polite interruption — AHEM
Polite term of address — MADAM
Polite, in German — BITTE
Politesse — COURTESY
Political — NATIONAL, PARTISAN, STATE
Political alliance — BLOC, ENTENTE
Political boss's henchman — HEELER
Political campaign orgs. — PACS
Political cartoonist — NAST
Political contest — SENATE RACE
Political exile — EMIGRE
Political group — BLOC, CAUCUS, PARTY
Political leader Khmer _____ — ROUGE
Political monogram — GOP
Political party principles — PLANKS
Political perk — LULU
Political policy — LINE, PARTY LINE
Political pollster — HARRIS
Political position — MIDDLE OF THE ROAD
Political talkfest — FILIBUSTER
Politician — DIPLOMAT, SENATOR
Politician Harold from Minnesota — STASSEN
Politician Sonny — BONO
Politician's support gp. — PAC
Politician's uniform — PARTY DRESS
Politician's weapon? — MUD
Politico Landon — ALF
Politico's patronage — PORK BARREL
Polka _____ — DOTS
Polka follower — DOT
Poll follower — STER
Polled — SHORN
Pollen source — RAGWEED
Pollock's kin — COD
Polloi leader — HOI
Pollster's unit — SAMPLE
Pollutant — SMOG
Pollution problem — SMOG
Polly Holliday TV role — FLO
Polly to Tom — AUNT
Polly, Betsy and Em — AUNTS
Pollyanna's outlook — ROSY
Polo — MARCO
Polo Grounds here — OTT
Polo mount — PONY
Polo or Ping-Pong — SPORT
Polo play — HIT IN
Polo player's purchase — MALLET
Polo players' gear — MALLETS
Polo's namesakes — MARCOS
Poloists' needs — PONIES
Polonaise — DANCE
Polonius hid behind this — ARRAS
Poly follower — ESTER
Poly's partner — ROLY
Polyantha, e.g. — ROSE
Polygon — SQUARE
Polynesia grouping — ATOLLS
Polynesian anulet — TIKI
Polynesian apparel — GRASS SKIRT
Polynesian bark cloth — TAPA
Polynesian cloth — TAPA
Polynesian dance — HULA
Polynesian drinks — KAVAS
Polynesian fruit — FEI
Polynesian garment — PAREU
Polynesian island — SAMOA
Polynesian oven — UMU
Polynesian spirit — ATUA
Polynesian's supernatural force — MANA
Polytechnique student — ELEVE
Polytheistic — PAGAN
Polytheists — PAGANS
Pomander — CASE
Pomeranian's place — LAP
Pomme de _____ (potato) — TERRE
Pommel — BUMP, KNOB
Pompeii heroine — IONE
Pompeii tourist attraction — RUINS
Pompeii's blanket — ASHES
Pompeii's pall — ASHES
Pompey's head — CAPUT
Pompon — BALL OF WOOL, DAHLIA
Pompous — TURGID
Ponce de _____ — LEON
Ponce de Leon's discovery: Abbr. — FLA
Ponce de Leon's quest — FOUNTAIN OF YOUTH
Ponchielli ballet music — DANCE OF THE HOURS
Poncho blankets — SERAPES
Poncho's relative — RUANA
Pond — BASIN, LAGOON, POOL
Pond bloom — LOTUS
Pond denizen — EGRET
Pond duck — MALLARD
Pond life — ALGA
Pond plant — ALGA
Pond product — ALGAE
Pond topper — SCUM
Ponder — BROOD, MUSE
Pondered — MULLED, MUSED
Ponderosa apparel — CHAPS
Ponderosa man — HOSS
Ponderosity — WEIGHT
Ponerology topics — EVILS
Pongee — FABROC
Pongee color — TAN
Pongid — APE
Ponies — TROTS
Ponies or beans — PINTOS
Ponies up — ANTES
Ponselle — ROSA
Ponselle and Raisa — ROSAS
Ponselle of opera fame — ROSA
Pont — FLOAT
Pont du Gard locale — NIMES
Pont du Gard site — NIMES
Pont on Huon Gulf — LAE
Ponti's partner — LOREN
Ponti's Sophia — LOREN
Ponti's wife — LOREN
Pontiac Silverdome team — LIONS
Pontiac was one — OTTAWA
Pontiff — POPE
Pontiff's garb — ORALE
Pontifical cape — ORALE
Pony — BANGTAIL, TROT
Pony _____ — EXPRESS
Pony buggies — TRAP
Pony's gait — TROT
Pooch — PUP, WHELP
Pooch of pictures — ASTA
Pooch's name — FIDO, SPOT
Poodle hair care? — CLIP SERVICE
Poodle size — TOY
Pooh's pal — CHRISTOPHER ROBIN
Pooh-pooh — SCORN
Pool — BASIN, LAGOON, POOL
Pool adjunct — CABANA

Pool ball — CUE, EIGHT
Pool game — EIGHT BALL
Pool growth — ALGA
Pool member — STENO
Pool member, for short — STENO
Pool owner's need — FILTER
Pool person — STENO
Pool problems — ALGAS
Pool shark — MINNESOTA FATS
Pool shot — CAROM, MASSE
Pool specialty — BACKSTROKE
Pool stick — CUE
Pool stroke — CRAWL
Pool table felt — BAIZE
Pool worker — STENO
Pool worker, for short — STENOG
Poolside furniture — CHAISE
Poona's locale — INDIA
Pooped — ALL IN, TIRED
Pooped: bushed — ALL IN
Poor — BROKE
Poor Clare — NUN
Poor golf shot — SLICE
Poor grade — DEE
Poor in quality: Slang — BUM
Poor loser — SORE HEAD
Poor one — HAVE NOT
Poor surfer — HODAD
Poorer — WORSE
Poorest, most underdeveloped countries — FOURTH WORLD
Poorly drained — SEEPY
Poorly educated — UNREAD
Poorly lit — DIM
Poorly played whist — BUMBLE PUPPY
Poorly structured — MISMADE
Pop — COLA, DAD, DADDY, SODA
Pop artist Jasper — JOHNS
Pop author? — ANON
Pop canine craze — BEAGLE-MANIA
Pop category — COLAS
Pop flavor — COLA
Pop flavoring — COLA
Pop investments — IRAS
Pop off — SPLIT
Pop or op — ART
Pop singer Jackson _____ — BROWNE
Pop singer Mitchell — JONI
Pop singer Nina _____ — SIMONE
Pop singer Vicki — CARR
Pop vocalist Jerry — VALE
Pop-top — TAB
Pop-ups, usually — OUTS
Pop. Bible — GID
Pope John Paul's robes — ALBS
Pope John XXIII's "_____ in Terris" — PACEM
Pope's "Essay _____" — ON MAN
Pope's crown — TIARA
Pope's hat — MITER
Pope: 847-855 — LEO IV
Popeye character — WIMPY
Popeye's "fuel" — SPINACH
Popeye's _____ Pea — SWEE
Popeye's creator — SEGAR
Popeye's muscle-builder — SPINACH
Popeye's Swee' _____ — PEA
Popeye, to Pipeye — UNCLE
Popinjay — DUDE
Popish Plot fabricator — OATES
Poplar — ABELE, ASPEN
Poplar's — ABELES
Poplars — ALAMOS, ASPENS
Poppins, in Beijing — AMAH
Pops outlawed? — BAND IN BOSTON
Pops' conductor — WILLIAMS
Pops' mates — MAS, MOMS
Popular — ABELE, WELL LIKED
Popular aperitif — LIR
Popular aquarium fish — TETRA
Popular bag — GRAB
Popular biscuits — ENGLISH MUFFINS
Popular board game — SCRABBLE
Popular cookie — OREO
Popular cuisine — CHINESE
Popular dance of the 1930s — SHAG
Popular drink — COLA
Popular emcee on TV — MERV
Popular fabric — SERGE
Popular fast foods — FRENCH FRIES
Popular Ferber novel — SO BIG
Popular figure — IDOL
Popular flavoring — COLA
Popular fries — POTATOES
Popular fur — LAPIN
Popular gin mixer — TONIC
Popular golfer — PALMER
Popular hair style — PONYTAIL
Popular health food — YOGURT
Popular hop — LINDY
Popular house plant — AFRICAN VIOLET
Popular imaginary figure — GNOME
Popular investments — IRAS
Popular Irish ballad — DANNY BOY
Popular Italian sauce — PESTO
Popular jacket — BLAZER
Popular libation — MARTINI
Popular meal starter — TOMATO SOUP
Popular munchie — JELLY BEAN
Popular name for popes — PIUS
Popular name in Moscow — IVAN
Popular name in Oslo — OLAF, OLAV
Popular name in Paris — RENE
Popular nestegg — IRA
Popular novel of 1881 — THE PRINCE AND THE PAUPER
Popular nut — ALMOND
Popular opera — AIDA
Popular pad — CONDO
Popular pasta sauce — PESTO
Popular PBS program — NOVA
Popular pie — MINCE
Popular plants — BEGONIAS
Popular play by Neil Simon — PLAZA SUITE
Popular poem — THE RAVEN
Popular pool stroke — AUSTRALIAN CRAWL
Popular pop — COLA
Popular recorder, for short — VCR
Popular salad — TUNA
Popular sandwich fish — TUNA
Popular scent — LILAC
Popular skirt — MINI
Popular song of the past — OLDIE
Popular soup — ONION
Popular souvenir — T SHIRT
Popular spuds — IDAHO POTATOES
Popular street name — MAIN
Popular style of cooking — CAJUN
Popular thirst quencher — ADE
Popular TV game show — WHEEL OF FORTUNE
Popular TV show — TODAY
Popular TV soap — GENERAL HOSPITAL
Popular uncle — SAM
Popular uprising — EMEUTE
Populate — INHABIT
Populated — PEOPLED
Population statistic — BIRTH
Porcelain — CHINA
Porcelain ware — CHINA, LIMOGES
Porch — STOA, TERRACE, VERANDA
Porch adjuncts — DOOR STEP
Porch, in Hawaii — LANAI
Porch, to Plato — STOA
Porches — VERANDAHS
Porcine parent — SOW
Porcupine's protection — SPINES
Pore over — SCAN
Porgy — SCUP
Porgy's woman — BESS
Pork and veal — MEATS
Pork bellies, in hand — ACTUALS

Pork cut — LOIN
Porker — PIG
Porker's pads — STIES
Porker's place — STY
Porker's plaint — OINK
Porkpie — HAT
Porky patriot? — NICOLAS CHAUVIN
Porky's feature — SNOUT
Porous — SPONGY
Porous item — SPONGE
Porsena — LARS
Port city in Hokkaido — OTARU
Port city of N Chile — ARICA
Port city of Yemen — ADEN
Port east of Algiers — TUNIS
Port follower — FOLIO
Port for Pompey — OSTIA
Port in Egypt — SAID
Port in Libya — HOMS
Port in W Germany — EMDEN
Port in Yemen — ADEN
Port NE of Gibraltar — MALAGA
Port near Cadiz — ROTA
Port near Gibraltar — MALAGA
Port of Aug. 3, 1492 — PALOS
Port of Israel — ELATH
Port of Jordan — AQABA
Port of NW Israel — ACRE
Port of S Italy — NAPLES
Port of Scotland — OBAN
Port of Spain — ROTA
Port of Spain's island — TRINIDAD
Port of SW Scotland — AYR
Port of Yemen — ADEN
Port on Frisco Bay — OAKLAND
Port on Illinois River — PEORIA
Port on the Adriatic — BARI
Port on the Loire — NANTES
Port on the Whangpoo — SHANGHAI
Port on the Yellow River — SIAN
Port on W coast of Hokkaido — OTARU
Port or hock — WINE
Port side — LEFT
Port side when sailing south — EAST
Port, for short — RIO
Port-au-Prince native — HAITIAN
Port-au-Prince's country — HAITI
Port-au-Prince's land — HAITI
Portable — COMPACT, HANDY, MOVABLE
Portable arms — TOMMYGUNS
Portable bed — COT
Portable berths — COTS
Portable boat — KAYAK
Portable chair — SEDAN
Portable light — LAMP, LANTERN
Portable platform in a warehouse — PALLET
Portable seats — CAMP STOOLS
Portable shelter — TENT
Portable trough — HOD
Portable trough for mortar — HOD
Portable video camera — MINICAM
Portage — TRANSFER
Portal — DOOR, ENTRY, GATE
Portal part — JAMB
Portals — GATES
Portend — BODE, OMEN
Portend, old style — OSSE
Portent — OMEN, THREAT
Portents — SIGNS
Porter — ALE, COLE
Porter and stout — ALES
Porter novel — SHIP OF FOOLS
Porter opus — SONG
Porter products — TUNE
Porter's "_____ Magnifique" — CEST
Porter's "In the _____ of the Night" — STILL
Porter's "You're the _____" — TOP
Porter's shrew — KATE
Porterhouse — STEAK
Porters — ALES
Portfolio — CASE
Portho's passes — BOTTES
Portia saved his skin — ANTONIO
Portia's waiting woman — NERISSA
Portico — STOA
Portico for Pericles — STOA
Portico in ancient Greece — STOA
Porticos for Pericles — STOAE
Porticos, to Plato — STOAS
Portion — PARCEL, PIECE, SEGMENT, SHARE
Portion of a portion — DOSE
Portion of food — RATIO
Portion of the pie — SLICE
Portion: Abbr. — AMT
Portions of an ellipse — ARCS
Portly — FAT
Portly U.S. President — TAFT
Portmanteau word — SMOG
Portnoy's creator — ROTH
Portoferraio's island — ELBA
Portrait — IMAGE, PICTURE
Portrait sculpture — BUST
Portray — DRAW, SKETCH
Portray in words — LIMN
Portray on stage — ENACT
Portray verbally — DELINEATE
Portrayer of Disraeli — ARLISS
Portrayer of Gypsy Rose Lee, 1962 — NATALIE WOOD
Portrayer of many O'Neill protagonists — ROBARDS
Portrayer of western villains — ELAM
Portugal's shrine — OUR LADY OF FATIMA
Portuguese cape — ROCA
Portuguese city — BRAGA, EVORA
Portuguese coin — ESCUDO
Portuguese colony of China — MACAU
Portuguese enclave in China — MACOA
Portuguese harbor city — OPORTO
Portuguese king — REI
Portuguese money — REIS
Portuguese resort — ESTORIL
Portuguese seaport — OPORTO
Posada — INN
Pose — SIT
Posed — MODELED, SAT
Posed for a picture — SAT
Poseidon's weapon — TRIDENT
Poser — MODEL
Poses — SITS
Poses for a portrait — SITS
Posh — ELEGANT, RITZY
Posh party — BASH
Posh, beauty parlor — SALON
Posit — SUPPOSE
Position — CAPACITY, LOCATION, PLACE, SEAT
Position — STANCE, STAND
Position again — REORIENT
Position Jackie Robinson usually played — SECOND
Position, in golf — STANCE
Positions for Strange — LIES
Positive — CERTAIN, SURE
Positive answer — YES
Positive pole — ANODE
Positive quantity — PLUS
Positive responses — AMENS, AYES
Positive terminal — ANODE
Positive terminal on a battery — PLUS
Positive thinker — PEALE
Positive votes — YESES
Positive word — YES
Positive, in a way — DOGMATIC
Positively a nocturnal lemur — AYEAYE
Positively as is — NO IFS ANDS OR BUTS
Posnet — BASIN

Possess — HAVE, OWN
Possessed — HELD, OWNED
Possesses — HAS, OWNS
Possessing flavor — SAPID
Possession — ASSET
Possessions — ESTATE
Possessive — OURS, YOUR
Possessive adjective — THEIR
Possessive pron. — YRS
Possessive pronoun — HERS, OURS
Possessor — OWNER
Possible Easter topper — TOQUE
Possible port in a storm — INLET
Possible sky sight, for short — UFO
Possible tree — ACORN
Post — BERTH, END, ENTER, SHAFT
Post chaise — COACH
Post exchange — CANTEEN
Post for harbor houses — STILTS
Post of politesse — EMILY
Post office offering — STAMP
Post office posting — REWARD
Post office purchase — STAMP
Post offices? — STAMPING GROUNDS
Post on a ship — BITT
Post station in India — DAK
Post used in air races — PYLON
Post-bath powder — TALC
Post-grad degree — DOCTOR-ATE
Post-grad-deg. — SCD
Post-prandial quaff — PORT
Post-prandial sound — BURP
Post-W.W.II assn. — NATO
Postage stamp unit — PANE
Postage unit — STAMP
Postal abbr. — RFD
Postal sect. — RLO
Postcard note — LINE
Poster — SIGN
Posterior — REAR
Postern — GATE
Posters — PLACARDS
Postgrad degrees in public works — MCES
Postman's creed word — NOR
Postpone — DEFER, DELAY, HOLD OVER, TABLE
Postponed — DELAYED
Postponement — DEFERRAL
Postpones — LAYS OVER
Postprandial offering — MINT
Posts — MAILS
Posts a letter — MAILS
Postulate — ASSERT
Postulates — POSITS
Posy pottery — VASE
Pot-au-_____, meat and vegetable dish — FEU
Pot adjunct — HANDLE
Pot base — CROCK BOTTOM
Pot builder — ANTE
Pot filler — ANTE
Pot for a Mexican stew — OLLA
Pot for a spicy stew — OLLA
Pot for posies — VASE
Pot herb — POKE
Pot or double follower — BOILER
Pot pie — STEW
Pot scrubbers need — CLEANSER
Pot starters — ANTES
Pot sweetener — ANTE
Pot-au-feu — STEW
Pot-scrubbers — SOAP PADS
Potassium nitrate — NITER
Potato — TUBER
Potato _____ — CHIPS
Potato features — EYES
Potato pancake — LATKE
Potato's partner — MEAT
Potato, informally — SPUD
Potatoes' companion — MEAT
Potatoes, e.g. — TUBERS
Potboiler's product — TRIPE
Poteen — WHISKEY
Potent — STRONG
Potent pill — NITRO
Potential blossom — BUD
Potential bride's response — YES
Potential cpl. — PFC
Potential hot spot — TENDER BOX
Potential juror — TALESMAN
Potential queen — PAWN
Pother — ADO
Pother — STIR
Potherb — LOVAGE, SEAKALE
Pothers — STEWS
Potion — DOSE
Potion portion — DOSE
Potok's "My Name Is Asher _____" — LEV
Potok's "The _____" — CHOSEN
Potpourri's output — ODOR
Potpurri — OLIO
Potpurri: Abbr. — MISC
Pots again — REPLANTS
Potted — TINNED
Potter's need — KILN
Potters' Jemima _____ — PUDDLE DUCK
Pottery fragment — SHARD
Pottery tree — CARAIPI
Potty — PETTY, TRIVIAL
Pou _____ (vantage point) — STO
Pouch — SAC
Pouch-shaped — SACCATE
Poulettes? — FRENCH HENS
Poultry pen — COOP
Poultry purchase — CAPON
Pounce — DESCEND
Pound — BEAT, PELT
Pound division — CANTO
Pound in Paris — LIVRE
Pound or Stone — EZRA
Pound prospects — STRAYS
Pound sound — ARF, YELP
Pound, in Bayreuth — PFUND
Pound, the poet — EZRA
Pounds — HAMMERS
Pour — DECAMT, RAIN CATS AND DOGS, TEEM
Pour forth — SPEW
Pour molten metal into a mold — CAST
Pour oil on troubled waters — CALM
Pour out — SPEW
Pour out slowly — EXUDE
Pour wine from a bottle — DECANT
Pourboire — TIP
Pours — RAINS
Pours out, as a crowd — STREAMS
Pousse-_____ — CAFE
Pouter's look — MOVE
Pouters' pads — COTES
Pow-wows — CONVENTIONS
Pow! — WHAM
Powder — TALC
Powder and shot, for short — AMMO
Powder for baby — TALC
Powder ingredient — TALC
Powders — TALCS
Power — DINT, SINEW, STRENGTH
Power agency — REA
Power failure — OUTAGE
Power for a side-wheeler — STEAM
Power measurement — WATT
Power of Hollywood — TYRONE
Power of the mind — WIT
Power play — ELITIST
Power producer — FUEL OIL
Power proj. of 1933 — TVA
Power role in a 1940 film — ZORRO
Power source — ATOM, FUEL, STEAM
Power to influence — LEVERAGE
Power tool — BANDSAW
Power tower — PYLON
Power up — START
Powerful — HARDY, MIGHTY, POTENT, STRONG
Powerful beam — LASER
Powerful bloc — OPEC
Powerful bomb — ATOM

Powerful explosive — AMATOL
Powerful letters — TNT
Powerful political group — MACHINE
Powerful punch — BLOW
Powerful redolence — REEK
Powerful spotlight — KLIEG
Powers of Hollywood — MALA
Poznan to Germans — POSEN
Practical — USUAL, UTILE
Practical intelligence — HORSE SENSE
Practical joke — PRANK, JAPE
Practical joke: Slang — RIB
Practical joker — JAPER
Practical lessons from fables — MORALS
Practice — PLY, USAGE, USE, WARM UP
Practice game — WORKOUT
Practice piece for Previn — ETUDE
Practice quiz — PRETEST
Practice upon — IMPOSE
Practice witchcraft — HEX
Practiced — TRAINED
Practiced diligently — PLIED
Practiced for a bout — SPARRED
Practices of yoga — ANGAS
Practices to excess — OVERTRAINS
Practitioner — DOER
Practitioner of Hindu philosophy — YOGIN
Praenomen sharer — NAMESAKE
Pragmatic — EMPIRIC, SKILLED
Pragmatic person — REALIST
Prague exile — BOUNCED CZECH
Prague natives — CZECHS
Prague, in Prague — PRAHA
Prague, to a Czech — PRAHA
Prairie — MEADOW
Prairie schooner — WAGON
Prairie wolf — COYOTE
Praise — APPLAUD, COMMEND, EXALT, EXTOL, LAUD
Praise for Pavorotti — BRAVO
Praise in words alone — LAUD
Praised with enthusiasm — RAVED
Praline morsels — PECANS
Pram — BUGGY
Pram pushers — NANAS
Pram wheel — TYRE
Prance — STRUT
Pranced — TROD
Prancer — STRUTTER
Prank — CAPER, DIDO, ESCAPADE, GAG, JOKE, LARK
Prank ending — STER
Prankster — CUTUP
Prate — BABBLE, JABBER
Pravda founder — LENIN
Prawns — SHRIMPS
Prayer — AVE, ORISON
Prayer beads — ROSARY
Prayer ending — AMEN
Prayer endorsements — AMENS
Prayer form — LITANY
Prayer sessions — NOVENAS
Prayerful insect? — MANTICE
Praying _____ — MANTIS
Praying _____, beneficial insect — MANTIS
Praying figure — ORANT
Pre-abattoir pen — STOCK YARD
Pre-Aztec in Mexico — TOLTEC
Pre-divorce arrangement — LEGAL SEPARATION
Pre-Easter time — LENT
Pre-election competition — CAUCUS RACE
Pre-holiday time — EVE
Pre-Renaissance — MEDIEVAL
Pre-schooler — TOT
Pre-1866 Tokyo — EDO
Pre-1918 German rulers — KAISERS
Pre-cancellation rating curve — SAG
Pre-college exam — SAT
Pre-concert musicians — RETUNERS
Pre-croakers — TADPOLES
Pre-storm condition — CALM
Pre-teen — LAD
Pre-war — ANTEBELLUM
Preacher — PARSON
Preacher of a type — EVANGELIST
Preacher's stand — PULPIT
Preachment — TENET
Preakness and Belmont — RACES
Preakness and Belmont winner, 1955 — NASHUA
Preakness pick — HORSE
Preamble — PREFACE
Precarious — TOUCH AND GO
Precarious perch — LIMB
Precarious position — IN HOT WATER
Precarious position — ON THE ROPES
Precarious position — OUT ON A LIMB
Precarious position — UP THE CREEK
Precarious spot — THIN ICE
Precautionary comment — JUST IN CASE
Precede in time — PREDATE
Preceded — LED
Preceded Reagan — CARTER
Preceded Woodrow Wilson — TAFT
Precedent setter, in court — TEST CASE
Preceder of band or line — WAIST
Preceder of easter — NOR
Preceder of French hens — THREE
Preceder of meter — SPHERO
Preceders of febreros — ENEROS
Preceders of xi's — NUS
Precedes "ocho" — SIETE
Precedes automne — ETE
Precedes cure — EPI
Precedes Donald or Arthur — MAC
Precedes end or leaf — LOOSE
Precedes in time — ANTEDATES
Preceding nights — EVES
Preceding, of old — AFORE
Precept — CANON, TENSE
Precinct — BEAT
Precious — CUTE, DEAR
Precious fiddle — STRAD
Precious gem — PEARL
Precious ones — DEARIES
Precious optimist? — HOPE DIAMOND
Precious stone — GEM, RUBY
Preciousness — WORTH
Precipice — CRAG
Precipice: Scot. — LINN
Precipitate — RASH
Precipitate reorganizations — SHAKE UPS
Precipitated — SLEETED
Precipitation — RAIN, SLEET
Precipitation: amounts of rain — TRACES
Precipitous — SHEER, STEEP
Precipitous rock — SCAR
Precise — NEAT, NICE, TIDY
Precisely — EXACTLY, SPANG, STRICTLY, TO A T
Precisely — TO A TEE, TO THE LETTER
Preciseness in style — PURISM
Preclude — OBVIATE
Preclude legally — ESTOP
Precludes — BARS
Precocious — CLEVER, FAST
Precooks — PARBOILS
Predatory bird — SHRIKE
Predatory dolphins — ORCAS
Predecessor of CIA — OSS
Predicament — CRISIS, FIX, NODE, PLIGHT
Predicament — SCRAPE, SPOT
Prediction — ORACLE
Predilection — TASTE
Predisposed — BIASED
Predominant — UPMOST

Predominate — REIGN
Preeminent crossword editor Margaret _____ — FARRAR
Preemptive bridge bid — SHUT OUT
Prefaces — PROEMS
Preferences — TASTES
Preferred — CARED TO
Preferred agreement — IN BLACK AND WHITE
Preferred seating — DAIS
Prefix denoting size — DEMI
Prefix for adroit — MAL
Prefix for angle or corn — TRI
Prefix for center — EPI
Prefix for circle or final — SEMI
Prefix for date or room — ANTE
Prefix for form — AERI
Prefix for Martian study — AERO
Prefix for mum or kin — MINI
Prefix for physics — META
Prefix for plus or sense — NON
Prefix for present — OMNI
Prefix for puncture — ACU
Prefix for sphere — ATMO
Prefix for the European boot — ITALO
Prefix for thesis — SYN
Prefix for vinegar — ACETO
Prefix in "nose" words — NASI
Prefix in medicine — NEURO
Prefix meaning "four" — TETRA
Prefix meaning "half" — HEMI
Prefix with angle — TRI
Prefix with bus or car — MINI
Prefix with cast or type — TELE
Prefix with cede or cept — INTER
Prefix with chance — PER
Prefix with China or European — INDO
Prefix with chord or meter — OCTA
Prefix with coastal or mural — INTRA
Prefix with color or corn — TRI
Prefix with corn — UNI
Prefix with cycle — TRI
Prefix with cycle or plane — TRI
Prefix with dynamics — AERO
Prefix with eminent — PRE
Prefix with form or corn — UNI
Prefix with form or cycle — UNI
Prefix with form or verse — UNI
Prefix with god or lune — DEMI
Prefix with grade or flex — RETRO
Prefix with gram and logue — IDEO
Prefix with gram or graph — AERO
Prefix with gram or meter — MILLI
Prefix with gram or type — TELE
Prefix with lead or guide — MIS
Prefix with light or night — TWI
Prefix with morph or carp — ENDO
Prefix with mural or state — INTRA
Prefix with phone or bucks — MEGA
Prefix with plane or dynamics — AERO
Prefix with plasm — ECTO
Prefix with pod — TRI
Prefix with pod or stere — DECA
Prefix with practice — MAL
Prefix with print or play — MIS
Prefix with puncture — ACU
Prefix with rail or tone — MONO
Prefix with science or present — OMNI
Prefix with sect — TRI
Prefix with sked or skid — NON
Prefix with sol and stat — AERO
Prefix with sphere — HEMI
Prefix with tank or trust — ANTI
Prefix with verse or form — UNI
Prehensile organ — TENTACLE
Prehistoric — PRIMITIVE
Prehistoric stone implement — CELT
Prehistoric tool — CELT
Preholiday time — EVE
Prejudice — BIAS
Prelim race — HEAT
Prelim. calculations — ESTS
Preliminary coat — PRIMER
Preliminary impression — PROOF
Preliminary outline — DRAFT
Preliminary plan — IDEA
Preliminary races — HEATS
Prelims — HEATS
Prelude to a duel — SLAP
Prelude to an invention — IDEA
Preludes — OVERTURES
Premarital status — SINGLE
Premature — EARLY, UNTIMELY
Prematurely hatched — ALTRICIAL
Premed class — ANAT
Premed course — ANAT
Premed subj. — ANAT
Premier of South Africa, 1910-19 — BOTHA
Preminger — OTTO
Preminger and Bismark — OTTOS
Preminger or Kruger — OTTO
Premise — THESIS
Prenuptial bashes — BACHELOR PARTIES
Preobrajenska and Spessivtzeva — OLGAS
Preoccupied — TAKEN
Preoccupied with — INTO
Preoccupied with something — LOST IN IT
Preoccupy — ABSORB, ENGAGE, ENGROSS, OBSESS
Prep cap — BEANIE
Prep school principal — HEADMASTER
Prep. school type — ACAD
Prepandial beverage — APERTIF
Prepare — DRAFT, EQUIP, FIX, MAKE, READY
Prepare a canvas — SIZE
Prepare another draft — REEDIT
Prepare apples for pies — PEEL
Prepare by heat — FRIT
Prepare copy jointly — COEDIT
Prepare eggs — SHIRR
Prepare fish — BONE
Prepare flax — RET
Prepare for "The Mikado" — REHEARSE
Prepare for a bout — TRAIN
Prepare for a task — TRAIN
Prepare for action — STRETCH
Prepare for an opening — REHEARSE
Prepare for exam — CRAM
Prepare for gift-giving — WRAP
Prepare for printing — EDIT
Prepare for shipping — ENCASE
Prepare for the prom — PRIMP
Prepare for war again — REARM
Prepare leftovers — REHEAT
Prepare metal for coating — ANODIZE
Prepare potatoes — PEEL
Prepare soda water — AERATE
Prepare the neighborhood for yuppies — GENTRIFY
Prepare the table — SET
Prepare to braise — SEAR
Prepare to drive — TEE UP
Prepare to make a new model — RETOOL
Prepare turkey — ROAST
Prepared — SET
Prepared anew — REARMED
Prepared apples — CORED
Prepared apples for baking — PEELED
Prepared cherries — PITTED

Prepared fish — SCALED
Prepared for a clutch — NESTED
Prepared for a date — PREENED
Prepared for a final — STUDIED
Prepared for painting — SANDED
Prepared for refinishing — SANDED
Prepared lyonnaise — ONIONED
Prepared potatoes — DICED, RICED
Prepared potatoes, in a way — RICED
Prepared prunes — STEWED
Prepared the way for — LED UP TO
Prepared to fire again — RELOADED
Prepared to pray — KNELT
Prepared to propose — KNEELED
Prepares flax — RETS
Prepares for later use, as a meal — PRECOOKS
Prepares for publication — EDITS
Prepares for publication/Communist deeds — REDACTS
Preparing for military inspection — GIING
Preponderance — MOST
Preposterous — FARCICAL
Preppy, e.g. — TEEN
Preprandial prayer — GRACE
Preprandial reading — MENUS
Prerequisite for a certain run — HIT
Prerequisite of rank — TITLE
Pres. advisory gp. — NSC
Pres. and prem. — HDS
Pres. Arthur's middle name — ALAN
Pres. monogram — DDE
Pres. or C.E.O. — EXEC
Pres. title — CIC
Pres. Wilson was one — PHD
Presage — BODE, OMEN
Presbyter — ELDER
Preschoolers — TOTS
Prescribed amount — DOSE
Prescribed, as food — DIETETIC
Prescribes — ORDAINS
Prescribing punishment — PENAL
Prescription abbrs. — CCS
Prescription datum — DOSE
Prescription for Greek tragedy? — OEDIPUS RX
Prescription unit — DOSE
Presence — SPIRIT
Present — GIFT, HERE, NONCE
Present and bus preceder — OMNI
Present day — NEW
Present purpose — NONCE
Present time — TODAY
Presentable — FIT
Presentation, for short — DEMO
Presently — ANON, SOON
Presents — CITES
Presents with restraint — UNDERSTATES
Preserve — CAN, CORN, CURE, PICKLE, SALT, SAVE
Preserve, in a way — BOTTLE, CAN, CORN
Preserved — ON ICE
Preserves — CANS, SALTS, SMOKES
Preserves, as beef — CORNS
Preset — TIMED
Preside — CHAIR
Preside at a dinner — EMCEE
Preside at tea — POUR
Presided — SAT
Presided over — CHAIRED
President (U.S.) 1845-49 — POLK
President and Vice-President: 1953 — EISENHOWER NIXON
President and Vice: 1945 — ROOSEVELT TRUMAN
President Bongo of Gavon — OMAR
President from Plains — CARTER
President of Albania — ALIA
President of France: 1954-59 — COTY
President of Mali: 1960-68 — KEITA
President, at times — VETORER
President: father or son — ADAMS
Presidential assistant — AIDE
Presidential confidante — INSIDER
Presidential initials — HSS
Presidential monogram — HST, DDE
Presidential name — ABE, IKE
Presidential nickname — ABE, IKE
Presidential office — OVAL
Presidential power — VETO
Presidential privilege — VETO
Presidential selections — CABINET
Presidential snake? — BUSHMASTER
Presidio — FORT
Presley hit set to Poulton music — LOVE ME TENDER
Presley's "Blue _____ Shoes" — SUEDE
Presley's birthplace — TUPELO
Presley's middle name — ARON
Press — CRUSH, FLATTEN, FORCE, IRON, PUSH
Press — SMOOTH, URGE
Press for payment — DUN
Press forward — SURGE
Press. meas. — PSI
Pressed — IRONED
Pressed charges — SUED
Presses — URGES
Presses into grains — RICES
Pressing — EXIGENT
Pressing need — IRON
Pressman's need — PRINTERS INK
Pressman, at times — INKER
Pressure units — TORRS
Prestidigitation — LEGERDEMAIN, MAGIC
Prestidigitator — JUGGLER
Prestidigitator's tool? — MAGIC WAND
Presume — DARE
Presumptuous — ARROGANT
Pretend — FEIGN, LET ON
Pretend to — PROFESS
Pretended disdain for the unattainable — SOUR GRAPES
Pretender — HUMBUG, IMPOSTER
Pretense — CHARADE, POSE, SHAM, VENEER
Pretension — VENEER
Pretensions — AIRS
Pretentious — ARTY, CHI CHI
Pretentious display — RITZ
Pretoria's land Abbr. — RSA
Pretoria's locale — TRANSVAAL
Prettify — ADORN
Pretty _____ picture — AS A
Pretty child — DOLL
Pretty girl — PERI
Pretty silly — GAGA
Pretty soft — CUSHY
Pretty verses — POESIES
Pretty woman — PERI
Prevail — OBTAIN
Prevailed upon — INDUCED
Prevailing — USUAL
Prevailing current of activity — MAINSTREAM
Prevailing direction — GRAIN
Prevailing mania — FUROR
Prevailing taste — STYLE
Prevalent — DOMINANT, POPULAR
Prevaricated — LIED
Prevaricates — LIES
Prevaricators — LIARS
Prevent — AVERT, BAR, DETER
Prevent from doing — DETER

Prevent legally — ESTOP
Prevented from entering — LOCKED OUT
Preventers — AVERTERS
Previous — EARLIER, PRIOR
Previous customer? — PRIOR BUYER
Previously — ERE NOW
Prevost heroine — MANON
Prewedding surprise — SHOWER
Prexy's stand-in — VEEPEE
Prey — GAME
Preys for jays — NESTS
Priam's home — TROY
Pribilof Islands visitors — SEALS
Price — COST, FIGURE, RATE, RESULT
Price again — RETAG
Price come-ons — LEADERS
Price cutter, for one — SLASHER
Price tag — COST
Priceless violin — AMATI
Prices — COSTS, RATES
Prick — BRIAR, JAG
Prickle — STING
Prickly — WIRY
Prickly heat, et al. — WOES
Prickly pear — CACTI, TUNA
Prickly plants — CACTUS, THISTLES
Prickly seedcases — BURRS
Prickly: Comb. form — ECHINO
Pricks — PRODS
Pride — EGO
Pride of Adolph Ochs: 1896 et seq. — THE NY TIMES
Pride of Philip II — ARMADA
Pride sound — ROAR
Prides' dens — LAIRS
Prie-dieu user — KNEELER
Pried — NOSED, SNOOPED
Pried's prides — MANES
Pries — NOSES
Priest of the East — LAMA
Priest saying Mass, e.g. — VENERATOR
Priest's garment — ALB
Priest's home: Abbr. — RECT
Priest's scarf — AMICE
Priest's vestments — ALBS
Priestly robes — ALBS
Priestly vestment — ALB, ORALE
Priestly wear — ORALE
Priests' neckcloths — AMICES
Prig — BLUENOSE
Prill or pyrite — ORE
Prim and proper — STAID
Prima donna — DIVA
Primary — FIRST, MAIN
Primary locations — POLLS
Primary offerings — SLATES
Primate — APE
Primatologist Fossy — DIAN
Prime-time time — NINE
Primer dog — SPOT
Primer's relative — READER
Primitive — EARLY
Primitive hunting method — SPEARING
Primitive plants — ALGAE
Primitive: Comb. form — PALAE
Primo Carnera — BOXER
Primordial goo — SLIME
Primp — PREEN
Primrose kin — FUCHSIA
Prince Charles's sister — ANNE
Prince Edward Island — PROVINCE
Prince Harry's aunt — ANNE
Prince of _____ — WALES
Prince of Broadway — HAL
Prince of darkness — SATAN
Prince of opera — IGOR
Prince Phillip, e.g. — CONSORT
Prince Valiant's son — ARN
Prince Valiant's wife — ALETA
Prince, perhaps? — FROG
Princely — REGAL
Princely name — ANDREW
Princely name in Florence — MEDICI
Princely Punjab title — RAJA
Princes in Java — RAJAS
Princess-prodder — PEA
Princess Di's niece — BEA
Princess Margaret's nephew — PRINCE CHARLES
Princess of myth — IOLE
Princess of Wales — DIANA
Princess perturber — PEA
Princess tester — PEA
Princess tormentor? — PEA
Princess, e.g. — PHONE
Princeton, to N.Y.C., e.g. — EXURB
Principal — MAIN, MAJOR
Principal dancer at the Paris Opera — ETOILE
Principal joints — HIPS
Principal meat dish — ENTREE
Principal part of a country — MAINLAND
Principal race of Norse gods — AESIR
Principal role — LEAD
Principal's cousin — RECTOR
Principle — ETHIC, ISM, TENET
Principle of good conduct — ETHIC
Principle of minimized hypotheses — OCCAMS RAZOR
Principles of behavior — ETHICS
Prink — ADORN, WINK
Print measures — ENS
Print money — ENGRAVE
Print style: Abbr. — ITAL
Printed announcement — NOTICE
Printed page — LEAF
Printemps follower — ETE
Printer of a sort — LASER
Printer's "Let be" — STET
Printer's bodkin — AWL
Printer's comments — STETS
Printer's cross stroke — SERIF
Printer's direction — CUT, DELETE
Printer's directive — STET
Printer's dot — BULLET
Printer's mark — CARET, STET
Printer's measures — ENS
Printer's mistakes — ERRATA
Printer's order — DELE
Printer's roller — INKER
Printer's setting — LOWER CASE
Printer's type excess — OVERSET
Printers' errors — ERRATA
Printing-machine operators — PRESSMEN
Printing abbr. — ITAL
Printing errors — ERRATA
Printing press pioneer — HOE
Printing style — ITALICS
Printing term — DELE
Prinze role, once — CHICO
Prior — ABBEY
Prior nights — EVES
Prior to — ANTE, ERE
Prior to a golfer's warning? — FORE
Prior to Prior — ERE
Prior, poetically — ERE
Prioritized — RANKED
Priscilla Mullins' love — ALDEN
Prism extension — ATIC
Prisoner — JAILBIRD
Prisoner's ordeal — THIRD DEGREE
Prisoners — INMATES
Prissy — FUSSY
Priv. debts — IOUS
Private _____ — EYE
Private chamber — SANCTUM
Private eye — TEC
Private eye task — TAIL
Private eye, at times — TRAILER
Private eye, for short — TEC
Private teacher — TUTOR
Privation — HARDSHIP, LOSS, NEED
Privilege of the President — VETO
Privileges — PERKS
Privileges, briefly — ITS
Privileges: Abbr. — RTS
Privy to — IN ON
Privy to the deal — IN ON
Prize — PLUM, REWARD, VALUE
Prize fight — BOUT
Prize money — PURSE

Prize won by Lama — NOBEL
Prized — VALUED
Prized possession — GEM
Prized violin, for short — STRAD
Prizes at SRO shows — SRO
Prizes on the hill — SEATS
Prizewinning short story: 1843 — THE GOLD BUG
Pro — FOR, OLD HAND
Pro _____ — RATA
Pro _____ — TEM
Pro _____ (for the nonce) — TEM
Pro _____ (for the time being) — TEM
Pro _____ (proportionately) — RATA
Pro _____ (set up in advance) — FORMA
Pro follower — RATA
Pro shop wares — TEES
Pro vote — AYE
Pro's adversary — CON
Pro's foes — ANTI
Pro's opposite — ANTI
Probability — ODDS
Probe deeply — DELVE
Probes — TESTS
Probing devices — SEEKER, SONDES
Problem at the United Nations — LANGUAGE BARRIER
Problem for a diplomat — PROTOCOL
Problem for cats — FLEAS
Problem for Cyrano — NOSE
Problem for King Lear — OLD AGE
Problem gas — METHANE
Problem in the Mideast — TERRORIST
Problem or pain — HEADACHE
Problematic — IFFY, MOOT
Problems — CARES
Problems for Job — SORES
Proboscis — NOSE
Proboscis monkeys — NOSE APES
Procacious — PERT
Proceed — COME, WEND
Proceed to what follows, in music — SEGUE
Proceed with turn and twists — MEANDER
Proceeded — WENT
Proceeded toward a target, with "in" — HOMED
Proceeding correctly — ON THE RIGHT TRACK
Proceedings — ACTA
Proceeds — FEE
Proceeds at a snail's pace — CRAWLS
Process chemically — CURE
Process leather — CURE, TAN
Process of grading products, in Britain — TRIAGE
Process of mountain formation — OROGENY
Process: Suffix — ATION
Processed for printing — INKED
Processes: Suffix — SES
Procession of cars — AUTOCADE
Proclaims loudly — BLARES
Proclamation — EDICT
Procrastinate — DELAY
Procrastinated — STALLED
Procrastinating newswoman? — LESLIE STALL
Procrastinator's word — LATER
Procrastinator, in a way — SHIRKER
Procreate — FATHER
Prod — EGG, GOAD, NUDGE, URGE
Prod into action — GOAD
Prodded — POKED, URGED
Prodded, with "on" — EGGED
Prodding by Polynesian hostess? — HAVE SAMOA
Prodding person — URGER
Prodigious — HUGE, TITANIC
Prods to action — SPURS
Produce — MAKE
Produce young from eggs — HATCH
Produce, as a musical — STAGE
Produced — BEGOTTEN, MADE, STAGED
Produced interest — EARNED
Produced milk — LACTATED
Producer — MAKER
Producer Hayward — LELAND
Producer of inertia — OPIATE
Producer of raga's — SITAR
Producer Ponti — CARLO
Producer Sir Alexander — KORDA
Producer Wallis — HAL
Producing sound — PHONIC
Product for overseas sale — EXPORT
Product from seaweed — AGAR
Product of a lorimer — SPUR
Product of a Spanish pine — CONO
Product of Fall River, Massachusettes — TEXTILES
Product of Keats — ODE
Product of Lodes — ORES
Product of Tampa — CIGAR
Product of the Dakotas — WHEAT
Product used in baking — YEAST
Production measure — OUTPUT
Production segments — ACTS
Products of means? — ENDS
Products of the stars — RECORDS
Prof's concoction — EXAM
Prof's deg. — EDD
Prof's protection — TENURE
Prof. travel agt. — CTC
Profess — ASSERT, AVOW
Professes — AVOWS
Profession — METIER
Professional charge — FEE
Professional man — OCCULIST
Professional moniker — PEN NAME
Professional trainee — INTERN
Professional's customer — CLIENT
Professions — CAREERS
Professor's goal — TENURE
Proffered — TENDERED
Proficient — ABLE, ADEPT
Profit — AVAIL, EARN, GAIN, USE
Profit chaser — EER
Profit on the court? — MAKE A NET GAIN
Profit's offset — LOSS
Profitable things, in high finance — PLUMS
Profited — GAINED
Profound — DEEP
Profound respect — AWE
Profound sleep — SOPOR
Profoundness — DEPTH
Profundity — DEPTH
Profuse — LAVISH, LUSH
Profusely disordered — A RIOT
Progenitor — PARENT
Progeny — BROOD, ISSUE
Prognosticator — SEER
Prognosticator's card — TAROT
Program — AGENDA
Program list — AGENDA
Program problem — BUG
Programmed life — RUT
Prohibit — BAN, DEBAR, FORBID, VETO
Prohibited — ILLICIT, OUTLAWED, TABU, TABOO
Prohibition — TABOO, TABU
Prohibition tipple — HOME-BREW
Prohibitionist — DRY
Prohibitionists' foes — WETS
Project director — MASTERMIND
Projectile — BULLET, ROCKET
Projecting edges — EAVES
Projecting rim — FLANGE
Projecting window — ORIEL
Projection — OVERHANG
Projection of Saturn's rings — ANSA
Projects — IMPELS

Proliferate — TEEM
Prolific author, for short — ANON
Prolixity — VERBIAGE
Prolong — DELAY, PRESERVE
Prolonged attack — SIEGE
Prom adornments — BELLES
Prom goer — TEEN
Prom queen's date — ESCORT
Prom-night item — CORSAGE
Promenade — MALL, PASEO
Promenade in ancient Greece — STOA
Prometheus' theft — FIRE
Prominent — IMPORTANT
Prominent Gable features — EARS
Prominent Ohio name — TAFT
Promise in marriage — BETROTH
Promise of fidelity — VOW
Promise to pay, for short — IOU
Promises — VOWS
Promising — ROSY
Promising one — COMER
Promising people — COMERS
Promising words — I DO
Promologist's spray — ALAR
Promontory — NESS, SPIT
Promontory signal — OMEN
Promos — ADS
Promotes the status quo — LETS SLEEPING DOG LIE
Promotes with pride — BOOSTS
Promotion — BUILD UP
Promotional personnel — SALES FORCE
Prompt — CUE, ON TIME, URGE
Prompted — CUED
Prompter's activity — CUING
Prompter's words — CUES
Promulgate — ISSUE
Prone — APT
Prone — APT, FLAT, FACE DOWN
Prong — TINE
Pronged — TINED
Pronghorn — DEER
Prongs — TINES
Pronoun — HER, ITSELF, ONESELF
Pronoun for a calico cat — SHE
Pronoun for femmes — ELLES
Pronoun for Hans — ICH
Pronoun for Penn — THOU
Pronoun for the Andrea Doria — ESSA
Pronounce judgment — SENTENCE
Pronounced indistinctly — SLURRED
Pronouncement — DICTUM
Pronouncements — DICTA

Pronto — ASAP
Pronto, for short — ASAP
Proof — ASSAY
Proof of innocence — ALIBI
Proofreader's "keep" — STET
Proofreader's direction — STET
Proofreader's directions — NPS
Proofreader's mark — CARET
Proofreader's word — DELE, STET
Prop — BRACE
Prop (up) — SHORE
Prop for Cagney? — GAT
Prop for Neptune — TRIDENT
Prop man's concern — LAMP
Prop up — SHORE
Prop, e.g. — AID
Propaganda, often — LIES
Propel a canoe — PADDLE
Propel a randan — OAR
Propelled a gondola — POLED
Propelled a punt — POLLED
Propelled a randon — OARED
Propelled a scull — OARED
Propeller — ROTOR
Proper — DUE, KOSHER, PRIM, STAID
Proper _____ — NOUN
Proper and fitting — DECENT
Proper pistol handling — GUN ETIQUETTE
Properly — DULY
Property — ESTATE
Property charge — LIEN
Property listing — RENTAL
Property of value — ASSET
Property receiver — ALIENEE
Property tax in Britain — RATES
Property transfer — DEMISE
Property, e.g. — ASSET
Property, for one — ASSET
Prophesy — DIVINE, VATICINATE
Prophet — AMOS, SEER
Prophet from Tekoa — AMOS
Prophet rebuked by an ass — BALAAM
Prophet's docks? — SEERS PIERS
Prophetic — VATIC
Prophetic signs — OMENS
Prophets — SEERS
Propiety — DECENCY
Propitiatory bribe — SOP
Proponents — ISTS
Proportion — RATIO, SCALE
Proposal — OFFER, OVERTURE
Propose — BROACH, OFFER, POSE, SUGGEST
Propose _____: drink to — A TOAST
Propose for office — NOMINATE
Proposes a toast — DRINKS
Proposition — LEMMA, THESES

Propound — POSE, PROPOSE
Propounded — PROPOSED
Propounds — POSES
Proprietor — OWNER
Propriety — DECORUM
Props for TV weathermen — MAPS
Props. — ESTS
Propulsion device — OAR
Propulsion unit — OAR
Prosaic — DULL, LITERAL
Proscription — TABOO
Prosecutor's need — EVIDENCE
Prosecutors, for short — DAS
Prospect — CHANCE, HOPE, SCENE, VISTA
Prospector — MINER
Prospector's find — ORE
Prospector's quest — ORE
Prospector's sight? — DIAMOND IN THE ROUGH
Prospectors' objectives — ORES
Prosperity — WEAL
Prospero's brother — ANTONIO
Prospero's servant — ARIEL
Prospero's spirit — ARIEL
Prospero, e.g. — EXILE
Prosperous baker's situations? — IN THE DOUGH
Prosperous states — WEALS
Protagonist — HEROINE
Protagonist, usually — HERO
Protect — DEFEND, GUARD, SHELTER
Protect from heat — INSULATE
Protect, in a way — INSULATE
Protected direction — ALEE
Protected from gunfire — ARMORED
Protected, at sea — ALEE
Protection — EGIS, SHELTER
Protection for a loafer — TOE PLATE
Protection for Hulk Hogan — MAT
Protection for locks — HAIRNETS
Protection in cold weather — EARMUFFS
Protective bank — BERM
Protective coating — TIN
Protective cover — APRON
Protective covering — BANDAGE
Protective following — REAR GUARD
Protective pal? — BUDDY SYSTEM
Protective wall — PARAPET
Protector — GUARDIAN
Protector of Joshua's spies: Var. — RANCHAB
Protein — ZEIN
Protein acid — ALANINE

Protein assembly director — RNA
Protein hormone — ACTH
Protein source — MEAT, MILK
Protein-rich vegetables — PEAS
Protest — DENY
Protest action — SIT IN
Protest singer-songwriter Phil _____ — OCHS
Protest, in a way — DEMONSTRATE
Protestant denom. — BAP
Protestant org. — NCC
Prototype — MODEL
Protozoan — AMOEBA
Protozoans — MONADS, STENTORS
Protract — DEFER, EXTEND, PROLONG
Protracted attack — SIEGE
Protrude — JUT
Protruding rock — SCAR
Protruding, as from water — EMERSED
Protuberance — NODE
Protuberances — BULGES, NOSES
Proud possessor — OWNER
Prove deficient — FAIL
Prove durable — STAND UP
Prove out — WASH
Prove wearisome — TIRE
Prove, in law — AVER
Proved to be trustworthy — TRIED
Proven — TESTED
Provencal dance — FARANDOLE
Provencal love song — ALBA
Provencal pronoun — TOI
Provencal summer — ETE
Provencal troubadour's love song — ALBA
Provence city — ARLES
Provence pronoun — ELLE
Proverb — ADAGE
Proverbial backbreaker — STRAW
Proverbial company — TWO
Proverbial dirt hider — RUG
Proverbial heirs — MEEK
Proverbial kingdom-loser — NAIL
Proverbially "lucky" people — IRISH
Proverbs — SAYINGS
Provide — AFFORD
Provide (with) — ENDUE
Provide food — CATER, SERVE
Provide funds — ENDOW
Provide guidance — PILOT
Provide new weapons — REARM
Provide party food — CATER
Provide service — CATER
Provide spoken commentary — NARRATE
Provide the provender — FEED
Provide viands — CATER
Provide weaponry — ARM
Provided a banquet for a fee — CATERED
Providence university — BROWN
Providential — HEAVEN SENT
Provides new weapons — REARMS
Provides props — SHORES UP
Providing weapons — ARMING
Province in N Spain — ALAVA
Province in NE China, old style — HOPEH
Province in South Africa — NATAL
Province of NE Spain — TARRAGONA
Province of Piedmont — ASTI
Province of SE China — HUNAN
Province of SW Spain — HUELVA
Provincial — BUCOLIC, LOCAL, PAROCHIAL, REGIONAL
Provision in a contract — CLAUSE
Proviso — CLAUSE
Provo plant — SEGO
Provoke — TEASE, TEMPT
Provoked — IRED, RILED
Provokes — INCITES
Provokes — INSTIGATES, IRES, STIRS
Provost — HEAD
Prow — BOW
Prowl after prey — RAVEN
Prowler — THIEF
Proximal's opposite — DISTAL
Proximate — NEAR
Proxy — AGENT
Prtg. — LITH
Prude — PRIG, PURIST
Prudent — WISE
Prudhoe bay output — OIL
Prufrock's "Do I dare to eat _____?" — A PEACH
Prufrock's creator — ELIOT
Prufrock's creator — ELIOT
Prufrock's trade — POET
Prune — SNIP, TRIM
Prune: Scot. — SNED
Prunelle flavoring — SLOE
Prunes — CLIPS, LOPS
Prunes a fruit tree severely — DEHORNS
Prurient — LEWD
Prussian cavalry man — UHLAN
Prussian lancer — UHLAN
Pry — LEVER, NOSE, SNOOP
Prying — NOSY
Prying into other's affairs — NOSING
Prying ones — SNOOPS
Psalm — ODE
Psalm verse ender — SELAH
Psalmic pause — SELAH
Pseudo — FALSE
Pseudo butter — OLEO
Pseudologist — LIAR
Pseudomaniacs — LIARS
Pseudonym — ALIAS, NAME
Pseudonym of Dickens — BOZ
Pseudonym, of a sort — ALIAS
Pshaw kin — PISH
Psst! — AHEM
Psych. neurosis — HYS
Psyche component — EGO
Psyche element — EGO
Psyche's beloved — EROS
Psyche's lover — EROS
Psyche's opposite — SOMA
Psyched up — READY
Psychedelic initials — LSD, PCP
Psyches — EGOS
Psychiatric concerns — IDS
Psychiatric treatment: Abbr. — ECT
Psychiatrist's favorite veggie? — COUCH POTATO
Psychiatrist's remark — RELAX
Psychiatrist's song — JUNG AT HEART
Psychic affinity — TELE
Psychic emanation — AURA
Psychic's metier — ESP
Psychics — SEERS
Psychoanalyst's clue — FREUDIAN SLIP
Psychological selves — EGOS
Psychological test — BINET
Psychologist Alfred — BINET
PT or U — BOAT
Pt. of A & P — ATL
Pt. of a circle — SEG
Pt. of E.T.A. — ARR
Pt. of NATO — ATL
Pt. of speech — ADV
Pt. of U.S.A. — AMER
Pt. of U.S.N. — NAV
PTA group — LADIES
PTA members — MAMAS
Pts. for Bears — TDS
Pts. of a day — HRS
Pts. of cents. — YRS
Pts. of dollars — CTS
Pub — TAVERN
Pub beverages — ALES
Pub drink — ALE, STOUT
Pub game — DARTS
Pub missle — DART
Pub offerings — ALES
Pub orders — ALES, PINTS
Pub pastime — DARTS
Pub pints — ALES
Pub portions — PINTS
Pub potables — ALES

Pub potion — ALE
Pub serving — STOUT
Pub sign — ALE
Pub-game item — DART
Pub. co. pileup — MSS
Public-utility magnate of the 30's — INSULL
Public — OVERT
Public _____ No. 1 — ENEMY
Public assistance — WELFARE
Public conveyance — TAXI
Public Enemy _____ — NO 1
Public Health agcy. — SGO
Public meetings — FORUMS
Public notices — OBITS
Public official — MAYOR
Public plugs — ADS
Public records book — LIBER
Public spirited — CIVIC
Public square — PLAZA
Public square in a town — PLAZA
Public storehouse — ETAPE
Public supervisor of accounts: Abbr. — COMPT
Public transport — COMMON CARRIER
Public TV — PBS
Public uproars in England — FURORS
Public utility, for short — ELEC
Public warehouse — ETAPE
Publication — DAILY
Publication head — EDITOR
Publication unit — ISSUE
Publicist — ADMAN, SOLON, WRITER
Publicity — EXPOSURE
Publicized — AIRED
Publicizes — BEAT THE DRUM FOR
Publish — ISSUE, PRINT
Publish in installments — SERIALIZE
Published — AIRED
Published with the news first — SCOOPED
Publisher Murdoch — RUPERT
Publisher's outlet — BOOK CLUB
Publisher's payment — ROYALTY
Publishers — ISSUERS
Publishing name of fame — OCHS
Pubs — LOCALS
Puccini heroine — MIMI, TOSCA
Puccini opera — LA TOSCA, MADAME BUTTERFLY
Puccini opera: 1926 — TURANDOT
Puccini prelude — OVERTURE
Puccini products — OPERAS
Puccini work — OPERA
Puccini's "_____ Anglica" — SUOR
Puccini's "La _____" — TOSCA
Puccini's Floria — TOSCA
Puck — IMP
Puckered material — SEER SUCKER
Puckerels — IMPS
Puckish — ELFIN
Pudding ingredient — TAPIOCA
Puddinglike sweet — BLANCMANGE
Puddings and pies — DESSERTS
Pueblo dweller — HOPI, ZUNI
Pueblo Indian — HOPI, ZUNI
Pueblo material — ADOBE
Puente of music — TITO
Puerto _____ — RICO
Puerto Rico city — PONCE
Puerto Rico, for one — COMMONWEALTH
Puff — CHUG
Puff adder — VIPER
Puff and Draco — DRAGONS
Puff out — BLOAT
Puff up — BLOAT, SWELL
Puffed up — PROUD
Puffin's cousin — AUK
Puffing adder — HOGNOSE
Pug — DOG, SPRITE
Puget Sound port — TACOMA
Puget Sound site — TACOMA
Pugilist — BOXER
Pugilist's quest — TITLE
Pugilistic enforcer — FIST
Pugs and poodles — DOGS
Puissance — POWER
Puissant — POTENT
Puissant spondulicks — ALMIGHTY DOLLAR
Pulchritude — BEAUTY, GRACE
Pulitzer author Morrison — TONI
Pulitzer awards — PRIZES
Pulitzer biographer: 1963 — EDEL
Pulitzer poet Anne — SEXTON
Pulitzer Prize author: 1970 — STAFFORD
Pulitzer Prize biographer — EDEL
Pulitzer Prize journalist Arthur _____ — KROCK
Pulitzer Prize playwright: 1953 — INGE
Pulitzer Prize poet Dugan — ALAN
Pulitzer prize winner of 1957 — AGEE
Pulitzer prize-winner Glasgow, 1942 — ELLEN
Pulitzer winner — AGEE
Pull — TOW, YANK
Pull one's leg — TEASE
Pull strings — TIE
Pull the trigger — FIRE
Pull through — RECOVER
Pull to pieces — SHRED
Pull together — COOPERATE
Pull up stakes — MOVE
Pull, in politics — CLOUT
Pulled — TOWED
Pulled a boner — GOOFED
Pulled back — RECOILED
Pulley — WHEEL
Pullman car — SLEEPER
Pullover — SWEATER
Pulls up — BRAKES
Pullulate — SPROUT, TEEM
Pulmonary cavities — AIRSACS
Pulpit in early churches — AMBO
Pulpit, of old — AMBO
Pulpits — ROSTRA
Pulpits of yore — AMBOS
Pulpy fruit — ATES
Pulsated — THROBBED
Pulse — THROB
Pulse, in music — TAKT
Pulverize — MILL
Pulvers rank — ENSIGN
Puma — CAT
Pumice source — LAVA
Pummels — THUMPS
Pump — SHOE
Pump feature — GAS
Pump iron — EXERT
Pump or platform — SHOE
Pump part — SOLE
Pump up — AERATE
Pump width — EEE
Pump, in Peru — BOMBA
Pumpernickel ingredient — RYE
Pumping material — IRON
Pumpkin eater of rhyme — PETER
Pumpkin, for one — PEPO
Pumps lack — STRAP
Pumps or scuffs — SHOES
Pun responses — MOANS
Pun, perhaps — GROANER
Punch — JAB
Punch and _____ — JUDY
Punch bowl adjunct — LADLE
Punch drinker's essential — LADLE
Punch the clock — ARRIVE
Puncheon — KEG, SLAB
Punchinello — CLOWN
Punching tools — AWLS
Punchpoke — KNITTED SOCKS
Punctilio — NICETY
Punctual — PROMPT
Punctuation mark — COLON, DASH, PERIOD
Puncture — CUT, HOLE
Pundit — SAGE, SAVANT, SWAMI
Pung and luge — SLEDS
Pungency — TANG
Pungent — ACRID, RACY, TANGY

Pungent Arabian coffee — MOCHA
Pungent bulb — ONION
Pungent herb — LEEK
Pungent sauce made from peppers — TABASCO
Pungle up — ANTE
Punish — AMERCE
Punish informally — SETTLE ONES HASH
Punisher — AVENGER
Punishment, in Prussia — STRAFE
Punitive persons — SADISTS
Punjab bigwig — RAJA
Punjab prince — RAJAH
Punjab princess — RANEE, RANI
Punjabi policeman's club — LATHI
Punkie — GNAT
Punt pusher — POLE
Punta _____, Chile — ARENAS
Punta _____, Fla. — RASSA
Punta del _____ — ESTE
Punted — POLED
Punter's need — POLE
Punty — ROD
Punty or mandrel — ROD
Puny ones — RUNTS
Pupil — FRESHMAN, LEARNER, SCHOLAR, STUDENT
Pupil cover — CORNEA
Pupil of Socrates — PLATO
Pupil transport — BUS
Pupil's place? — IRIS
Pupil's reward — STAR
Pupil, in Paris — ELEVE
Pupils' locales — IRISES
Pupils, in Paris — ELEVES
Puppet — TOOL
Puppeteer Baird — BIL
Puppeteer Bil — BAIRD
Puppeteer Lewis — SHARI
Puppeteer of the 30's — SARG
Puppeteer Tony — SARG
Puppeteers Bil and Cora — BAIRDS
Pur. slips — RECS
Purcell's "_____ and Aeneas" — DIDO
Purchase — BUY
Purchase consideration — COST
Purchasing agents to Peter? — SELLERS BUYERS
Purdah prop — VEIL
Pure — CHASTE, INNOCENT AS A LAMB, UNMIXED
Pure (or impure) fiction — LIES
Pure _____ driven snow — AS THE
Pure air — OZONE
Pure and refreshing air — OZONE
Pure joy — GLEE
Pure, in Parma — FINO
Pure, refreshing air — OZONIC
Puree spread — PATE
Purely by accident — UNINTENTIONALLY
Purge — RID
Purify — CLEAN
Purin is one — FESTIVAL
Puritan — BLUENOSE, PRIG
Purlieus — AREAS
Purloin — STEAL
Purple dyestuff — ORCEIN
Purplish gray — SLATE
Purplish red — MUREX
Purport — CLAIM
Purportedly psychic phenomena — PSIS
Purpose — END, INTENT, REASON
Purpose of a hansa — TRADE
Purpose of the DEW line — DEFENSE
Purposeful parties — SOIREES
Purposes — SAKES, USES
Purr-fect Broadway show — CATS
Purse item — COMB, TISSUE
Pursue — CHASE, SEEK
Pursue stealthily — STALK
Pursued by tracking — STALKED
Pursues — HUNTS
Pursues ardently — WOOS
Pursuing — AFTER
Pursuit — CHASE, HUNT, QUEST
Pursuit of precision — PURISM
Pursuit with troops — DRAGONNADE
Purvey — SUPPLY
Purveyed — CATERED
Purveyor of goodies — CANDY STORE
Pusan's locale — KOREA
Push against — JOSTLE
Push ahead — PROPEL
Push along — URGE
Push away — REPEL
Pushes — PROMOTES
Pushes with force — SHOVES
Pushover — SETUP
Pussyfoot around — SNEAK
Put-in-Bay's lake — ERIE
Put-on — FEIGN, SHAM
Put-ons — HOAXES
Put — LAY, PLACE, PUT, SET, STATE
Put _____ (show off) — ON AIRS
Put _____ to (stop) — AN END
Put _____ writing — IT IN
Put 2 and 2 together — ADD
Put a fence around — ENCLOSE
Put a play on again — RESTAGE
Put a stop to — PREVENT
Put across — CONVEY, GET AT
Put an _____: (squelch) — END TO
Put an _____: (stop) — END TO
Put an edge on — HONE
Put an end to — ANNUL, STOP
Put aside — SAVE, STOW
Put at rest — CALM, HUSH
Put away — STASH, STORE, STOW
Put away for future use — LAY UP
Put back — REPLACE, RESTORE
Put back in shape — RESTORE
Put by — STASH
Put down — BERATE, DEMOTED, LAID, LAY
Put down a new lawn — RESOD
Put down macadam — PAVE
Put film into a camera — LOAD
Put forth — APPLY
Put forth — EXERTED
Put forth energy — EXERT
Put forward — TENDER
Put in a good word for — REFER, REWROTE
Put in a hiding place — SECRETE
Put in a pet — IRK
Put in a silo — STORED
Put in for — REQUEST
Put in jeopardy — PERIL
Put in order — ALIGN, ALINE
Put in order, with "up" — TIDIES
Put in place — INSTALLED, SET
Put in power — ELECT
Put in the hold — STOWED
Put in the oven again — REHEAT
Put in the post — MAIL TO
Put into a carton — ENCASED
Put into action — EXERT
Put into close quarters — CABINED
Put into law — ENACT, ENACTED
Put into office — ELECTS
Put into practice — USED
Put into service — USE
Put into words — VOICE
Put off — DEFER
Put on — ACT, AIRS, AN ACT, DON
Put on — ENACT, STAGE, STAGED, WORE
Put on a jury — IMPANELLED
Put on a new finish — REGLAZE

Put on a new label — RETAG
Put on a new road top — RETAR
Put on a pedestal — ADORE
Put on a second coat — REPAINT
Put on board — LADE
Put on broadway — STAGED
Put on cargo — LADED
Put on cloud nine — ELATE
Put on guard — ALERT
Put on ice — DEFER
Put on plays — STAGE
Put on poundage — GAIN
Put on sale — MARKETED
Put on the air — TELEVISE
Put on the block — AUCTION
Put on the market — SELL
Put on the pan again — REFRY
Put on the payroll — HIRE
Put on the sidelines — BENCH
Put on weight — GAINED
Put on years — AGED
Put one's feet down — TROD
Put one's finger on — ISOLATE
Put out — EVICT, EMIT, OUST
Put out of reach — PROHIBIT
Put out of work — IDLES
Put out pounds — SPEND
Put out to pasture — RETIRE
Put plants in temporary beds — HEEL IN
Put pressure on — URGE
Put pressure on again — REEXERT
Put someone's _____: Irritate — NOSE OUT OF JOINT
Put the bite on — BORROW, REQUEST
Put the heat on — PRESSURE
Put the whammy on — HEXED
Put this up or chase flies — SCREENED PORCH
Put through a blender — PUREE
Put through the mill — GROUND
Put to flight — ROUT
Put to high a price on — OVERCHARGE
Put to rest — LAIN
Put to shame — BEST
Put to the test — PROVE
Put to the torch — LIT
Put to use — APPLY
Put together — CALM
Put two and two together — ADDED UP
Put up — ERECTED, POST
Put up a picture — HANG
Put up money — ANTED
Put up with — ENDURE, STOOD
Put-in-Bay hero — PERRY
Put-in-Bay's state — OHIO
Putrefy — ROT
Puts 2 and 2 together — ADDS
Puts a new cover on a book — RECASES
Puts a stop to — HALTS
Puts away — EATS
Puts down — DEMEANS, LAYS
Puts down for the count — KOS
Puts down in bridge — SETS
Puts down stakes — STAYS
Puts forth — POSES
Puts in — ANTES
Puts in office, old style — ENSTALLS
Puts in plain words — SPELLS OUT
Puts in reserve — ICES
Puts in the book — ENTERS
Puts into effect — ADOPTS
Puts on — ACTS, DONS
Puts on a show — STAGES
Puts on freight — LADES
Puts on the payroll — HIRES
Puts on, as a play — STAGES
Puts the finisher on — ZAPS
Puts the kibosh on — ENDS, VETO, ZAPS
Puts the lid back on — RESEALS
Puts to flight — ROUTS
Puts to rout — DEFEATS
Puts to use — APPLIES
Puts together — COMPILES
Puts two and two together — ADDS
Puts up — ERECTS
Puts up with, Elizabethan style — BROOKS
Putter — CLUB, IRON
Putting on one's clothes — ATTIRING
Putting position — AWAY
Putting salt in one's coffee, e.g. — BOOBOO
Puzzle — MYSTERY
Puzzle causing anger — CROSS WORD
Puzzle out — SOLVE
Puzzle theme, Italian style — AMORE
Puzzle variety — ACROSTIC
Puzzle with pictures — REBUS
Puzzle word — ACROSS
Puzzler's aid — CLUE
Puzzler's favorite Anglo-Saxon — ESNE
Puzzling nasty remarks? — CROSS WORDS
Puzzling problem — POSER
Pygmy — DWARF, ELF, GNOME, PIXY
Pygmy antelope — ORIBI
Pyknic — OBESE
Pyle of TV — GOMER
Pyle portrayer — NABORS
Pyle, the columnist — ERNIE
Pylonlike — CONED
Pyramid — MEMORIAL
Pyramid, e.g. — TOMB
Pyrenees chamois — IZARD
Pyrenees nation — ANDORRA
Pyrenees peak — ANETO
Pyrennes republic — ANDORRA
Pyrexia — FEVER
Pyrite — FOOLS GOLD
Pyromaniac's ploy — ARSON
Pyromaniacs — FIREBUGS
Pyrotechnic props — ROMAN CANDLES
Pyroxene variety — AUGITE

Q

Q followers — RST
Q, soundwise — LINE OF PERSONS
Q-U bridge — RST
Q-U connection — RST
Q-U linkage — RST
Q-V connection — RSTU
Qatar coin — RIYAL
Qatar ruler — EMIR
QB Brian — SIPE
QB Tarkenton — FRAN
QB's goals — TDS
QE2, for one — LINER
QED word — ERAT
Qt. components — PTS
Qty. — AMT
Qua _____ (here and there, in Napoli) — ELA

Qua non lead-in — SINE
Quack — CACKLE, FAKER
Quack medicine — NOSTRUM
Quad edifice — DORM
Quadragesima — LENT
Quadrangle — TETRAGON
Quadruped's foot — PES
Quaestor's cousin — EDILE
Quaff — DOWN, GULP, SWIG
Quagmire — BOG, MORASS
Quahog — CLAM
Quai _____, Paris — DORSAY
Quai d'Orsay locale — PARIS
Quaid film: 1988 — DOA
Quail — COWER, CRINGE
Quail flock — BEVY
Quaint — STRANGE
Quaint contraction — TIS
Quaint hotel — INN
Quaint oath — EGAD
Quake — JAR, SHAKE, SWAY, TREMOR
Quake's warning — TREMOR
Quaker colonist — PENN
Quaker color — GREY
Quaker founder — FOX
Quaker Gray — ACIER
Quaker in a grove — ASPEN
Quaker pronoun — THEE
Quaker's group — FRIENDS
Quaker's word — THEE
Quaker, for example — FRIEND
Quaking aspen — TREE
Qualified — ABLE
Qualifiers — TESTS
Qualifies — FITS
Qualify — CERTIFY, PREPARE
Quality — GRADE, PRIME, VALUE
Quality Ananias lacked — HONESTY
Quality checker at the Mint? — BUCK PASSER
Quality control — STANDARD
Quality control watchdog — TESTER
Quality of being unified — ATONENESS
Quality of having limits — FINITENESS
Quality of naturalness — EARTHINESS
Quality of tone — TIMBRE
Quality; nature — SORT
Qualm — PALL, DOUBT, REGRET
Quandary — DILEMMA, FIX, KNOT, RIDDLE
Quang _____, city in Vietnam — TRI
Quant. — AMT
Quantico gp. — USMC
Quantities — AMOUNTS
Quantities of paper — REAMS
Quantities: Abbr. — AMTS
Quantity of firewood — CORD
Quantity of paper — QUIRE, REAM, SHEAF
Quantity: Abbr. — AMT
Quarantine — DETENTION
Quarrel — ARGUE, SCRAP, SPAT, TIFF
Quarrel between families — FEUD
Quarrel over a long period of time — VENDETTA
Quarrels — ROWS, SET TOS
Quarrels continually — LEADS A CAT AND DOG LIFE
Quarries — MINES
Quarry — PREY
Quart in a London pub — LITRE
Quarter — AREA, ONE FOURTH
Quarter acre — ROOD
Quarter of four — ONE
Quarterback "Golden Joe" — MONTANA
Quarterback word — HIKE
Quarterback Y.A. — TITTLE
Quarterback's count — ON ONE
Quarterback's options — LATERALS
Quarterback, at times — SCRAMBLER
Quarterback, e.g. — PASSER
Quarterback, sometimes — PASSER
Quarterbacks, at times — PASSERS
Quartermaster (mil.) — OFFICER
Quarters — BILLET
Quarters for mods — PADS
Quartet in "A Midsummer-Night's Dream" — EMS
Quartet members — BASSOS, TENORS
Quarts' counterparts — LITERS
Quartz variety — AGATE
Quay — LEVEE, PIER
Quay for the Robert E. Lee — LEVEE
Que. neighbor — ONT
Quebec city — HULL
Quebec city on the St. Lawrence — LACHINE
Quebec peninsula — GASPE
Quebec's Lé esque — RENE
Quechua — INCA
Quechuan — INCAN
Quechuan language — INCAN
Queeg's command — CAINE
Queeg's vessel — CAINE
Queen — ELIZABETH, VICTORIA, MARY
Queen _____ Land, Antarctica — MAUD
Queen Anne's Lace — CARROT
Queen city — CINCINNATI
Queen for 1,000 days — ANNE
Queen in a Shelley poem — MAB
Queen in Shakespeare — MAB
Queen of Egypt, for short — CLEO
Queen of fiction — ELLERY
Queen of Jordan — NOOR
Queen of scat — ELLA
Queen of the Antilles — CUBA
Queen of the ball — BELLE
Queen of the gods — HERA
Queen of the Nile — CLEOPATRA
Queen of the underworld — HELA
Queen of the whodunits — ELLERY
Queen's collete locale — CORK
Queen's honorees — DAMES
Queen's tenure — REIGN
Queen's workers — ANTS
Queen-like — NOBLE, REGAL
Queen: Fr. — REINE
Queenly — REGAL
Queenly address — MAAM
Queenly name in Spain — ENA
Queens' stadium — SHEA
Queens' team — METS
Queens, for one — BOROUGH
Queensland's capital — BRISBANE
Queer — FUNNY, GIDDY, ODD
Quell — REPRESS
Quench — DOUSE, SLAKE
Quench one's thirst — SLAKE
Quencher, in a way — RAIN
Queriman or tetraodont — FISH
Querimonious child — WHINER
Quern, e.g. — MILL
Querulous — WHINEY
Query — ASK
Querying sounds — EHS
Ques. complement — ANS
Ques. opposite — ANS
Quest — PURSUIT, SEEK
Quest of Indiana Jones — ARK
Question — ASK, DOUBT
Question beginner — HOW
Question closely — PUMP
Question for Bennett Cerf — WHATS MY LINE
Question for Bossy — HOW NOW BROWN COW
Question formally — DEBRIEF
Question from Bugs — WHATS UP DOC
Question intensely — GRILL
Question word — HOW, WHEN, WHO
Questionable sightings, for short — UFOS

Questioned — ASKED, CONTESTED
Questioned, in a way — CROSS EXAMINED
Questioning sounds — EHS
Questions — ASKS
Queue — BRAID, LINE
Queue cue — NEXT
Queued up — IN A LINE
Queues — LINES
Quibble — CARP
Quibbles — CAVILS
Quiche ingredient — SWISS CHEESE
Quick-witted — CLEVER
Quick — AGILE, ALERT, DEFT, KEEN, LIVELY
Quick and resourceful — AGILE
Quick drink — SNORT
Quick impression — APERCU
Quick letters — ASAP
Quick look — GLANCE, ONCE OVER, PEEK
Quick pull — JERK
Quick reads — SCANS
Quick sampling — SPOT CHECK
Quick shot — SNORT
Quick thrust with something sharp — JAB
Quick to act — ALERT
Quick to learn — APT
Quick to the helm — YAR
Quick, sharp cry — YELP
Quick, straight drink — SNORT
Quick, to a helmsman — YARE
Quick-tempered one — HOT-HEADS
Quickly — APACE, PRESTO
Quickly, for Cato — CITO
Quickly, to Titus — CITO
Quicksand — TRAP
Quid — CUD
Quid, in dogpatch — CHAW
Quidnunc's interest — LATEST
Quien _____? — SABE
Quiescence — REST, STASIS
Quiescent — AT REST, REST-ING
Quiet — HUSHED, LULL, PEACE, SILENT
Quiet area — DEN
Quiet interval — LACUNA
Quiet place at school — STUDY HALL
Quiet! — SSH
Quietude — CALM
Quill-equipped — SPINY
Quilter's necessity — NEEDLE
Quilting activity — BEE
Quince or pear — POME
Quinn role — ZORBA
Quintain — TARGET
Quintet plus two — HEPTAD
Quintillionth: Comb. form — ATTO
Quinze a _____(fifteen love): Fr. — RIEN
Quips for monologists? — ONE LINERS
Quipsters — WAGS
Quirk — KINK, TRAIT
Quislings — TRAITORS
Quit — CEASE
Quitclaim — DEED, RELEASE
Quite a few — A LOT, MANY
Quite disinterested — BORED
Quito's location — ECUADOR
Quits — GIVES UP THE GHOST
Quitter's comment — I CANT
Quiver — SHIVER
Quivering — TREMULOUS
Quivery — SHAKE
Quiz — ASK
Quiz answer — TRUE, FALSE
Quiz show M.C., e.g. — ASKER
Quo modo — HOW
Quod _____ demonstrandum — ERAT
Quoin — KEYSTONE
Quoits — GAME
Quonset — HUT
Quota — SHARE
Quote — CITE, PARAPHRASE
Quoted the raven — CAWED
Quotidian — DAILY
Quotient factor — DIVISOR
QWERTY — KEYBOARD

R

R, soundwise — PART OF TO BE
R-rated — RACY
R-V connection — STU
R-V linkup — STU
R. Carson's "Silent _____" — SPRING
R. Wilbur's "Walking to _____" — SLEEP
R.A.F. supporter — HOARE
R.b.i. is one — STAT
R.C. devotions — NOVENA
R.E. Lee soldier — REB
R.E. Lee, e.g. — GENL
R.I. rebel — EORR
R.I.P. notice — OBIT
R.J. Gatling's invention — GUN
R.L. Stevenson classic — TREASURE ISLALND
R.M.N.'s first V.P. — STA
R.R. stop — STA
Rabat natives — MOROCCANS
Rabat residents — MOROCCANS
Rabbet — GROVE
Rabbi — SCHOLAR
Rabbinical seminary — YESHIVA
Rabbit — BUNNY, EARS, BALL, HARE, JACK, LAGOMORPH
Rabbit — LAPIN, PUNCH
Rabbit ear — ANTENNA
Rabbit food, to some — SALAD
Rabbit fur — LAPIN
Rabbit of kingdom — ROGER
Rabbit of note — PETER
Rabbit or Fox — BRER
Rabbit relative — PIKA
Rabbit tails — SCUTS
Rabbit's foot — CHARM
Rabbit's tail — SCUT
Rabbitlike rodent — AGOUTI
Rabbits — HARES
Rabbitt of music — EDDIE
Rabble-rouser — FIREBRAND
Rabble — MOB
Rabble, to Rabelais — CANAILLE
Rabin's predecessor — MEIR
Raccoon-family member — PANDA
Raccoon hounds — RED-BONES
Raccoon's cousin — COATI
Raccoon's Himalayan cousin — PANDA
Raccoon's relative — COATI
Raccoonlike mammals of S. America — OLINGOS
Race — RUN, SPEED
Race against the clock — TIME
Race an engine — GUN
Race car, of a sort — HOT ROD

Race circuits — LAPS
Race course — OVAL
Race distance — MILE
Race loser of fable — HARE
Race named for a Greek plain — MARATHON
Race official — TIMER
Race participants — ENTRANTS
Race segment — LAP
Race the motor — REV
Race units — LAPS
Race winners — SLOW AND STEADY
Race-track figures — TOUTS
Race: Comb. form — ETHNO
Racecourse — TRACK
Racecourse marker — PYLON
Raced — RAN, SPED, TORE
Raced pellmell — TORE
Racehorse — MAIDEN
Racer — BANGTAIL
Racer Yarborough — CALE
Racer's vehicle — DRAGSTER
Racetrack — OVAL
Racetrack circuit — LAP
Racetrack enclosure — PADDOCK
Racetrack figures — TOUTS
Racetrack hanger-on — TOUT
Racetrack parley — TRIFECTA
Racetrack performers — PONIES
Racetrack pest — TOUT
Racetrack regulars — TOUTERS
Racetrack section — BACK STRETCH
Racetrack word — ODDS
Racetrack, e.g. — OVAL
Raceway — OVAL, TRACK
Rachel Carson subject — SEA
Rachel's rival — LEAH
Rachmaninoff — SERGEI
Racial — ETHNIC
Racial; cultural — ETHNIC
Racine tragedy: 1691 — ATHALIE
Racing car — MIDGET
Racing craft — SCULL
Racing form? — OVAL
Racing fuel — PETROL
Racing sailboats — MOTHS
Racing sled — LUGE
Racing's Seattle _____ — SLEW
Rack and _____ — PINION
Rack one's brain — THINK
Rack out — SLEEP
Rack's companion — RUIN
Rack's partner — RUIN
Racket — DIN, NOISE
Racket by a poet? — NOYES NOISE
Racket or musket ending — EER
Racket sport — SQUASH
Racks up — WINS
Racqueteer Arthur — ASHE
Racy — RIBALD
Rad — UNIT
Radames' beloved — AIDA
Radames' love — AIDA
Radar action — SCAN
Radar housing — RADOME
Radar image on the screen — BLIP
Radar images — BLIPS
Radar reading — SPED
Radar station (combat) — CIC
Radar's relative — LORAN
Raddle — SCAR
Radial — SAW, TIRE
Radial bone — ULNA
Radial or spare — TIRE
Radiance — GLOW
Radiant light — HALO
Radiant warmth — HEATER
Radiate — EMIT
Radiation dosage — REM
Radiation term — L LINE
Radiation units — RADS
Radiator — HEATER
Radiator sound — SISS
Radical art school — DADA
Radical org. in the 60's — SDS
Radii — SPOKES
Radio — WIRELESS
Radio "choke" victim — MIKE FRIGHT
Radio and TV — MEDIA
Radio annoyance — STATIC
Radio band — POLICE
Radio chain — NETWORK
Radio channels — BANDS
Radio distress signal — SOS
Radio nuisance — STATIC
Radio oldie — LUM AND ABNER, THE WHISTLER
Radio oldie — OUR GAL SUNDAY, THE THIN MAN
Radio oldie — THE FALCON, PERRY MASON
Radio operator's response — ROGER
Radio parts — TUBES
Radio plugs — ADS
Radio receiver — SET
Radio role of John Todd — TONTO
Radio talk for "T" — TANGO
Radio transmission — SIGNAL
Radio transmitter, informal — RIG
Radio V.I.P.'s — DJS
Radio's "_____ the Magician" — CHANDU
Radio's "Amos and _____" — ANDY
Radio's "Digger" — ODELL
Radio's "John's Other _____" — WIFE
Radio's "Our _____ Sunday" — GAL
Radio's Major _____ — BOWES
Radio-tube workers — AGERS
Radioactive element — RADON
Radioactive rays — BETAS
Radioman's gear — HEADSET
Radium discoverer — CURIE
Radium, e.g. — EMITTER
Radius — SPOKE
Radius neighbor — ULNA
Radon or radium — ELEMENT
Raffle — DRAW, LOTTERY
Raffle ticket — STUB
Rafsenjani's land — IRAN
Raft — FLOAT
Raft wood — BALSA
Rage — FURY, STORM
Rage onstage — EMOTE
Rages — IRES
Ragged — TATTERED
Ragged Dick's creator — ALGER
Raggedy _____ — ANN
Raggedy Ann or Andy — DOLL
Raggedy doll — ANN
Raggedy Galway rigging? — IRISH PENNANT
Raggedy one — ANDY
Ragouts — STEWS
Rags — TEASES
Rags-to-riches author — ALGER
Ragtime dance — ONE STEP
Raid — FORAGE
Raids — INROADS, MARAUDS
Rail — COOT, SORA
Rail bird — SORA
Rail family member — SORA
Rail for Susan Jaffe — BARRE
Railing — FENCE
Raillery — BADINAGE
Railroad car — HOPPER
Railroad car, in Valladolid — VAGON
Railroad employee — SIGNALMAN
Railroad engineer's dearth? — LACK OF TRACK
Railroad of song — ATCHINSON TOPEKA SANTA FE
Railroad of yesteryear — ERIE
Railroad rails beam — TIE
Rails — SORAS
Railways — ELS
Raiment — ATTIRE
Rain _____ — OR SNOW
Rain and more rain — CATS AND DOGS
Rain buckets — TEEM
Rain cats and dogs — POUR, TEEM
Rain check — STUB
Rain forest climber — LIANA
Rain forest vine — LIANA, LIANE
Rain or shine — IN ANY EVENT

Rain or sleet: Abbr. — PPTN
Rainbow — ARC, IRIS, TROUT
Rainbow color — INDIGO
Rainbow Falls' site — HILO
Rainbow goddess — IRIS
Rainbow shape — ARC
Rainbow: Comb. form — IRIDO
Rainbow: Prefix — IRID
Rainbows — IRISES
Rainbows for Noah? — ARCS
Raincheck — STUB
Raincoat — ULSTER
Rained cats and dogs — TEEMED
Rained ice — SLEETED
Rained very hard — PELTED
Rainer of "The Good Earth" — LUISE
Raines and Cinders — ELLAS
Raines or Fitzgerald — ELLA
Rainier's daily activity — SAYING GRACE
Rainy-day prize — CAB
Rainy — DAMP
Rainy vacation syndrome — CABIN FEVER
Rainy-day layaway — IRA
Rainy-day need — CAB FARE
Rainy-day stash — IRA
Raipur raiment — SARIS
Raisa's affirmatives — DAS
Raise — ERECT, REAR
Raise _____ (create a commotion) — CAIN
Raise _____ (display anger) — THE ROOF
Raise a hand — REBUFF
Raise a nap on — TEASEL
Raise a question — POSE
Raise aloft — HOIST
Raise high — LOFT
Raise high: Colloq. — SKY
Raise on high — EXALT
Raise or increase sharply — HIKE
Raise the roof — COMPLAIN
Raise trivial objections — CAVIL
Raised — BRED
Raised platform — DAIS
Raised rampart — PARAPET
Raised-letter printers — EMBOSSERS
Raises — HOISTS, RAISES, UPS
Raises cain — WHOOPS IT UP
Raises spirits — ELATES
Raison d' _____ — ETRE
Raison d'etre — ROOT
Raja _____, Indian novelist — RAO
Rajah's lady — RANEE
Rajah's mate — RANEE, RANI
Rajah's spouse — RANI, RANEE
Rajah's wife — RANI
Rake — ROUE
Rake's glance — LEER
Rake-off — CUT, SHARE
Rakes' place — TOOL SHED
Raleigh's rival — ESSEX
Rally of a sort — PEP
Ralph _____: Australian pediatrician — REYE
Ralph Rackstraw, e.g. — TAR
Ralph's name in Paris — RAOUL
Ralph, the consumer's friend — NADER
Ram — ARIES
Ram in the sky — ARIES
Ram on high — ARIES
Ram's dam — EWE
Ram's mate — EWE
Ramada — ARBOR
Ramate — BRANCHED
Ramble — AMBLE, ROAM, ROVE, WANDER
Rambler — ROSE
Rambles — STROLLS
Rambouillet — SHEEP
Rameau's "Les _____ galanates" — INDES
Ramee's pen name — OUIDA
Ramentum — SCALE
Ramp alternative at a stadium — STAIR
Ramp sign — EXIT
Rampal's instrument — FLUTE
Rampant — RIFE, WILD
Rampart — WALL
Ramparts — PARAPETS
Ramrod — DRIVE, FORCE
Rams' dams — EWES
Ramses' river — NILE
Ramshackle — RICKETY, SHAKY
Ramson — GARLIC
Ran — MANAGED, OPERATED, TORE
Ran faster than — OUT RACED
Ran in the laundry — BLED
Ran into — MET
Ran off — FLED
Ran out, like time — LAPSED
Ran second — PLACED
Ran wild — RIOTED
Ran, as dye — BLED
Ran, as Madras — BLED
Ran-tan — NOISE
Ran-tans — SPREES
Ranch animal — MERINO
Ranch components — ACRES
Ranch guests — DUDES
Ranch in Ferber's "Giant" — REATA
Ranch logo — BRAND
Ranch outside of Austin — SPREAD
Ranch unit — ACRE
Ranch worker — COWHAND
Ranchero's weapon — BOLO
Ranchers — HERDERS
Ranches gear — BRANDING IRONS
Ranchland unit — ACRE
Rancho worker — PEON
Rancid — SOUR
Rancid (Sl.) — YECHY
Rancor — GALL
Rand and Struthers — SALLYS
Rand's shrugger — ATLAS
Randan implememt — OAR
Randolph Scott films — OATERS
Random profusion of color — RIOT
Randy's rinkmate — TAI
Randy's skating partner — TAI
Ranee's garment — SAREE
Rang — TOLLED
Rang out — PEALED
Range — AREA, GAMUT, OVEN, ROAM, STOVE
Range action — HERDING
Range animal — BISON
Range creature — ANTELOPE
Range cries — BAAS
Range feature — OVEN
Range gear — RIATA
Range group — HERD
Range in the USSR — ALAI
Range in Utah — UINTA
Range including Mt. Rainier — CASCADES
Range of hills — RIDGE
Range of knowledge — KEN
Range of NE Italy — CADORE
Range of sight — KEN
Range of the peak Telpos-Iz — URAL
Range of understanding — KEN
Range rider — COWBOY
Range rope — RIATA
Range rover — STEER
Range youngster — CALF
Ranger or Wolf — LONE
Ranges — STOVES
Ranges of knowledge — KENS
Ranges of understanding — KENS
Rangoon weight — PAI
Rangoon's location — BURMA
Rangy — LANK, SLIM
Rani raiment — SARIS
Rani's spouse — RAJAH
Rani's wardrobe — SARIS
Rani's wear — SARI
Rani's wrap — SARI
Rank — CLASS, LEVEL, OLIO, RATING, STATION, STATUS
Rank above marquis — DUKE
Rank above viscount — EARL
Rank and file — SOCIETY
Rank downward — DEMOTE
Rank tennis players — SEED
Rank's companion — FILE
Rank, in tennis — SEED
Rankle — IRRITATE

Ranks athletes — SEEDS
Ransack — PROBE, RIFLE
Ransack and rob — RIFLE
Ransom — FREE, REDEEM
Rant and rage — STORM
Rant and rave — RAIL
Rant's partner — RAVE
Ranting — RABID
Ranula — CYST
Rap — PUT DOWN, SHOOT THE BREEZE
Rap for a ham? — PAN
Rap for order — GAVEL
Rap session of sorts — SEANCE
Rapid — SPEEDY
Rapid movements in music — ALLEGROS
Rapid rodent — HARE
Rapid-fire gun — STEN
Rapidity — HASTE
Rapidly — APACE, HASTILY
Rapids riders — CANOEISTS
Rapier — EPEE
Rappahannock — RIVER
Rappee — SNUFF
Rappel — DESCEND
Rappel direction — DOWN
Rapper in a courtroom — GAVEL
Raps — CHATS
Rapscallion — ROGUE
Raptor's grabber — CLAW
Rara _____ — AVIS
Rara _____: Unusual thing — AVIS
Rara avis — ONER
Rara follower — AVIS
Rarae _____ — AVES
Rarae aves — ONERS
Rare bird — ONER
Rare bird, probably — LONER
Rare green gems — EMERALDS
Rare object — CURIO
Rare object, sometimes — T BONE
Rare old porcelain vases — MINGS
Rare one, sometimes — STEAK
Rare violin — AMATI
Rarebit ingredient — ALE
Raree show type — PEEP
Rarely — ONCE IN A BLUE MOON, SELDOM
Rarely, old style — SELD
Rarin to go — ALERT
Rarin' and ready — EAGER
Ras, in Ethiopia — PRINCE
Rascal — ROGUE, SCAMP
Rascals — IMPS
Rash — HASTY, HEEDLESS, INSANE, MADCAP
Rash maitre d'? — HEADY WAITER
Rash person — HOT HEAD
Rasorial bird — CHICKEN
Rasp — GRATE
Raspberries, e.g. — ACINI
Raspberry for Strawberry — BOO
Raspberry, R. Idaeus — RED
Rat — STOOLIE
Rat _____: drum sound — A TAT
Rat catcher — TRAP
Rat- _____ — A TAT
Ratatouille — STEW
Ratchet-wheel feature — PAWL
Ratchet bar — PAWL
Ratchet part — PAWL
Rate — ASSESS
Rate highly — ESTEEM
Rate of speed — MPH
Rated at Wimbledon — SEEDED
Rather — DAN, INSTEAD
Rather like an ogre — MEANISH
Rather namesakes — DANS
Rather or Brokaw — ANCHOR
Rathskeller offering — ALE
Rathskeller order — LAGER
Ratify — ENDORSE
Rating symbols — STARS
Ratio calculation — RATE
Ratio phrase — IS TO
Ratio words — IS TO
Ration — ALLOT, SHARE
Ration: Abbr. — ALW
Rational — FAIR, SANE
Rationale — EXPLANATION, PRETEXT
Rationality — SENSES
Rations — DOLES
Ratite — EMU
Ratite bird — EMU, KIWI
Ratline — ROPE
Rats — TATTLES
Rats! — DARN, DRAT
Rattail — FILE, PIGTAIL
Rattan — PALM
Rattan workers — CANERS
Ratted — SANG
Rattletrap — HEAP
Ratty place — DIVE
Raucous — SCREECHY
Raucous fan — HOOTER
Raul's brother — FIDEL
Rave — RANT
Rave's partner — RANT
Raved about — ENTHUSED
Ravel — COMB, UNDO
Ravel's famous piece — BOLERO
Ravelings — LINT
Ravell'd-sleave knitter — SLEEP
Raven comments — CAWS
Raven of Odin — HUGIN
Ravenous — GREEDY
Ravens' cries — CAWS
Ravens' havens — NESTS
Ravens' strident cries — CAWS
Ravi Shankar's companion — SITAR
Ravi's instrument — SITAR
Ravine — ARROYO, COOMB, DELL, WADI
Ravine in Africa — WADI
Ravine that is often dry — WADI
Ravioli — PASTA
Raw-silk shade — ECRU
Raw material — STAPLE
Raw materials — ORES
Raw metal — ORE
Raw vegetables, dressed — SALAD
Raw-boned animal or person — SCRAG
Rawboned — LEAN, SPARE
Rawboned one — SCRAG
Rawboned person — SCRAG
Ray — BEAM, GLEAM, SKATE, SUGAR ROBINSON
Ray Charles hit — NO ONE
Ray Charles instrument — PIANO
Ray from Pen Argyl — ALDO
Ray of Hollywood — ALDO
Ray of light — BEAM
Ray of movie fame — ALDO
Rayed flowers — DAISIES
Raymond and Aaron — BURRS
Raymond in Seville — RAMON
Rayon maker's solvent — ACE-TONE
Raze — DEMOLISH
Razee — PRUNE
Razor sharpener — STROP
Razor's edge — STROP
RBI or ERA — STAT
RBI, e.g. — STAT
Re fields: Comb. form — AGRO
Re stars: Prefix — ASTERI
Reach — GET AT
Reach a higher level — RISE
Reach blindly — GROPE
Reach by radio — RAISE
Reach the depths — HIT BOTTOM
Reach, goalwise — ATTAIN
Reached — GOT AT
Reached a sum — ADDED
Reached ground — ALIT
Reaches — GETS TO
Reaches across — SPANS
Reaches port — GETS HOME
React to mal de mer — RETCH
React to ragweed — SNEEZE
Reactance — IMPEDANCE
Reacted to cold or fear — GOOSE FLESHED
Reaction to a sweet treat — YUMMY
Reactions to solar plexus punches — OOFS
Reactor part — CORE

Read — PERUSE, PERUSED
Read a meter — SCAN
Read by a gypsy — TEA LEAF
Read hastily — SCAN
Read in haste — SCAN
Read on the run — SKIM
Read quickly — SCAN
Read rapidly — SCAN
Read studiously (with "over") — PORE
Read with interest — PORE
Read, with "over" — PORED
Reader's retreat — DEN
Readied the port — DECANTED
Readied the presses — INKED
Readies an oven — PREHEATS
Readies champagne — ICES
Readily available — ON HAND, ON TAP
Readily molded — WAXY
Reading direction — VIDE
Reading matter, for short — MAG
Reading, to Oscar Wilde — GAOL
Reads hurriedly — SCANS
Reads over — PERUSES
Reads rapidly — SCANS
Ready — ALERT, ALL SET, PREPARE, SET
Ready at the bar — ON TAP
Ready for a siesta — TIRED
Ready for anything — GAME
Ready for business — OPEN
Ready for eating — RIPE
Ready for mailing — STAMPED
Ready for Morpheus — DROWSY
Ready for picking — RIPE
Ready for printing — INKED
Ready for publication — EDIT
Ready for rest — TIRED
Ready for the ball — GOWNED
Ready for use — ON TAP
Ready to be drawn — ON TAP
Ready to belt one — AT BAT
Ready to buy — IN THE MARKET FOR
Ready to eat — RIPE
Ready to eat — RIPE
Ready to go — SET
Ready to pick — RIPE
Ready to say "Cheese" — POSED
Ready to take off — FUELED
Ready, in Remedios — LISTO
Ready-made — PREFAB
Reagan and Colman — RONALDS
Reagan cabinet member — MEESE
Reagan's Attorney General — MEESE
Reagan's first Secretary of State — HAIG
Reagan's middle name — WILSON
Reagan's second Attorney General — MEESE
Real _____ agent — ESTATE
Real author of Baron Munchausen's tales — RASPE
Real easy — SNAP
Real estate — ACRE, LAND
Real estate parcel — LOT
Real follower — ESTATE
Reality — FACT, TRUTH
Realize — EARN, KNOW
Really big weights — MEGATONS
Really enjoy, slangily — EAT UP
Really go up — SKY
Really involved with — INTO
Really likes — ADORES
Really run — HUM
Realm — DUCHY, EMPIRE, KINGDOM
Realm of a biblical queen — SHEBA
Realm of Boreas — NORTH
Realm of Croesus — LYDIA
Realm of Helios — SUN
Realm of Morpheus — SLEEP
Realtor's offering — LOTS
Realtor's term — CONDO
Realty notice — TO LET
Realty sign — FOR SALE
Realty units — LOTS
Reaphook — SICKLE
Rear — RAISE
Rear Admiral — RANK
Rear, to Popeye — AFT
Reared — BRED
Rearward — AFT
Reason — CAUSE
Reason for a detour — ROAD CLOSED
Reason for a traffic pileup — ROAD OBSTRUCTION
Reason out — EDUCE
Reason to dial 911: Abbr. — EMER
Reason to say "Gesundheit" — SNEEZE
Reasonable — SANE
Reasoned out — EDUCED
Reasoning — LOGIC
Reasons — DEDUCES
Reb's foe — YANKEE
Rebate — DISCOUNT
Rebecca Crawley, _____ Sharp — NEE
Rebekah's son — ESAU
Rebel — ARISE, RISE
Rebel in "Henry VI, Part 2" — CADE
Rebel's cry — UNITE
Rebelled — AROSE
Rebellion leader: 1786-87 — SHAYS
Rebellious — DEFIANT
Reboant — AROAR
Rebounded — CAROMED
Rebuff — SLAP, SNUB
Rebuffed — SCORNED
Rebukes severely — TELLS OFF
Rebut — REFUTE
Rec. measures — TSPS
Rec. of brain waves — EEG
Recall reason — DEFECT
Recall the past — REMINISCE
Recall, in London — RUB UP
Recant — REVERSE, UNSAY
Recap — SYNOPSIS
Recapture — REGAIN
Recede — EBB, FADE
Receded — WANED
Receipts — GATE
Receipts, for example — INFLOW
Receive a windfall — INHERIT A MILLION
Receive as one's due — REAP
Receive readily — ACCEPT
Receive warmly — HUG
Receiver — RADIO
Receiver of "Fighter of the Century" award — ALI
Receiver of checkout checks — CASHIER
Receiver of money — PAYEE
Recent — LATE
Recent arrival — NEWCOMER
Recent, to a geologist — CENE
Recent: Comb. form — CAENO, CENE
Recent: Prefix — NEO
Recently — LATELY
Receptacle — CONTAINER
Receptacles for coal — BINS
Reception — SALON, TEA
Reception beverage — TEA
Reception hall — SALON
Reception room — SALA
Receptive — ALERT, KEEN
Recess — APSE, NICHE
Recess periods — PLAYTIMES
Recesses — ALCOVES
Recessional — HYMN
Recherché — CHOICE, RARE
Recipe abbr. — TSP
Recipe amount — TSP
Recipe amts. — TSPS
Recipe direction — STIR
Recipe meas. — TBS
Recipe verb — STIR
Recipe words — FOR FLAVOR
Recipient — DONEE
Recipient of a bid — OFFEREE
Recipient of recognition — HONOREE
Recipients of gifts — DONEES
Reciprocate — REPAY
Recital — SOLO, TALE

Recital bonus — ENCORE
Recitals at Luther's Inn — TALES OF HOFFMANN
Reckless — RASH
Reckless daring — ELAN
Reckless Olympian — ATE
Reckon — OPINE
Reckon with — HANDLE
Reckoning — TALE
Recline awkwardly — SPRADDLE
Reclined — LAIN
Recluse — LONER
Reclusive — EREMITIC
Recognition of merit — ACCOLADE
Recognized — KNOWN
Recoil — KICK, KICK BACK, WINCE
Recolored — DYED
Recolors — DYES
Recommendation — WORD OF ADVICE
Recompense — PAYMENT, REWARD
Recompensed — REWARDED
Recon aircraft — AWACS
Reconcile — ADAPT
Reconciled — ATONED
Reconciles — MEDIATES
Recondite — DEEP, ESOTERIC
Recondite matters — ESOTERICA
Reconnaissance groups — SEARCH PARTIES
Record — DISC, DISK, FILE, INSCROLL, TAPE
Record again — RETAPE
Record band — TRACK
Record company — LABEL
Record for a DJ — DEMO
Record holder — ALBUM, SLEEVE
Record in advance — PRETAPE
Record in writing — NOTE
Record of a single year — ANNAL
Record player moving arm — PICKUP
Record player needles — STYLI
Record players — STEREOS
Record sets — ALBUMS
Record spinner — DEEJAY
Record-album designation — SIDE ONE
Recorded — TAPED
Recorded anew — RESTAMPED
Recorded item — ENTRY
Recorded proceedings — ACTA
Recorded, in a way — TAPED
Recorder — SCRIBE
Recording process — TAPING
Recording ribbon — TAPE
Recording star of "Chicago" — SINATRA
Recording star of "Hot Diggety" — COMO
Recording star of "Mule Train" — LANE
Recording unit — CASSETTE
Records — DISCS, ENTERS, FILES
Recount — ITERATE, TELL
Recover from a wassail — SOBER UP
Recover property from a fire — SALVAGE
Recovery — RALLY
Recreate — RELAX
Recreation spot — RIVERSIDE PARK
Recruit — ENLISTEE, PLEBE, TRAINEE
Rect. divider — DIAG
Rect. figure — OBL
Rectangles — OBLONGS
Rectangular column — ANTA
Rectangular pier — ANTA
Rectifier — DIODE
Rectifies — AMENDS
Rectify — AMEND
Rector — PASTOR
Rector's residence — MANSE
Rectory — MANSE
Rectrix — FEATHER
Recumbent — ABED, PRONE
Recuperate from — GET OVER
Recuperates — HEALS
Recur persistently — HAUNT
Recurring annually — ETESIAN
Recurring art themes — MOTIFS
Red — SOVIET
Red _____ — CENT
Red _____ (night flight) — EYE
Red _____ (southern African shrubs) — ELSES
Red _____ beet — AS A
Red 1 or Blue 5 — DYE
Red admiral — BUTTERFLY
Red and Black — SEAS
Red and Coral — SEAS
Red and fire insects — ANTS
Red and White, e.g. — SEAS
Red and Yellow — SEAS
Red antelope — IMPALA
Red apple, for short — MAC
Red Army leader — MAO
Red Army? — ANTS
Red as _____ — A BEET
Red as a _____ — BEET
Red Baron, e.g. — ACE
Red bird — TANAGER
Red Bordeaux — MEDOC
Red brown — SEPIA
Red bug — CHIGGER
Red chalcedony — SARD
Red Cross mission — RELIEF
Red Cross supply — SERUM
Red crystal mineral — RUTILE
Red deer — HART
Red deer female — HIND
Red denial — NYET
Red dye — EOSIN
Red dyes — MADDERS
Red dyestuff — EOSIN
Red entries — LOSSES
Red faced — FLUSHED
Red gem — GARNET
Red giant or white dwarf — STAR
Red horse with white patches — ROAN
Red ink entry — DEBIT, LOAN
Red ink item — DEBIT
Red ink producer — DEBTOR
Red lead for paint — MINIUM
Red leader? — INFRA
Red letters — USSR
Red light — STOP
Red man — CREE
Red news feeder — TASS
Red onlooker? — RUBY-STANDER
Red or Black — SEA
Red or Coral — SEA
Red or Dead — SEA
Red or Ross — SEA
Red or White — SEA
Red or White team — SOX
Red orbiter — MARS
Red ore — IRON
Red pigs — DUROCS
Red planet — MARS
Red Planet people — MARTIANS
Red quartz — SARD
Red Queen's advice to Alice — FASTER FASTER
Red refusal — NYET
Red Riding Hood's "grandma" — WOLF
Red Sea country — YEMEN
Red Sea craft — SAICS
Red Sea gulf — SUEZ
Red Sea republic — YEMEN
Red seaweed — DULSE
Red shade — CERISE
Red soil — LATERITE
Red Sox catcher — PENA
Red Square figures — LENIN
Red star in Scorpius — ANTARES
Red tabby cat — MARMALADE
Red table wine — CLARET
Red tape — FORMS
Red wine — MEDOC
Red winter apple — ESOPUS
Red's Rose — PETE
Red, Black and Yellow — SEAS
Red, in heraldry — GULES
Red, in Marseille — ROUGE
Red, serrated crest of a rooster — COXCOMB
Red, White and blue — SEAS

Red-backed sandpiper in winter plumage — PURRE
Red-haired clown — BOZO
Red-hot — NEW
Red-hot parents? — MAMAS
Redactor — EDITOR
Redacts — EDITS, EMENDS
Redbreast — ROBIN
Redcoats, to Minutemen — ENEMIES
Redd — FOXX
Redden — BLUSH
Reddening — ABLUSH
Reddish-brown — ROAN, RUST
Reddish colored American breed of swine — DUROC
Reddish dye — EOSIN
Reddish hog — DUROC
Reddish parasite plants — PINESAPS
Reddish purple — ANEMONE
Reddish-brown hue — SEPIA
Reddish-yellow — TITIAN
Reddish-yellow dyes — ANNATTOS
Redecorate — REDO
Redeem — EXCHANGE, FULFILL, KEEP, RECOVER
Redeem — REGAIN, SAVE
Redeemer — SAVIOR
Redford film — THE HOT ROCK
Redford is one — BLOND
Redford movie, with "The" — STING
Redford role — THE SUNDANCE KID
Redford, e.g. — BLOND
Redford-Newman movie, with "The" — STING
Redheaded nickname — RUSTY
Redness of the skin — ERUBESCENCE
Redolence — ODOR, SCENT
Redolences — AROMAS, ODORS
Redolent root — ORRIS
Reds or whites — WINES
Reduce — DECREASE, DEDUCT, LESSEN, PARE
Reduce costs — CUT CORNERS
Reduce sail — REEF
Reduce the importance of — CUT DOWN TO SIZE
Reduce to extremities for lack of a necessity — FAMISH
Reduce to poverty — PAUPERIZE
Reduced — DIETED, EXERCISED, PARED
Reduced estimate — EST
Reduced in value — DEBASED
Reduced the sail area — REEFED
Reduced to low status — DECLASSE
Reduces — DIETS, SLIMS
Redwood — TREE
Reed instrument — OBOE
Reed or Harrison — REX
Reed or Morgan — REX
Reed weaver — CANER
Reef companion — CORAL
Reeking — FETID
Reeky — OLID
Reel — SPOOL
Reel in — WIND
Reel of film — SPOOL
Reels partner — RODS
Reese — PEEWEE
Reese and Street — DELLAS
Reese or Street — DELLA
Ref's cousin — UMP
Ref's decision — TKO
Ref. book — DICT, ENC
Ref. tome — ENCYC
Ref. work — ENCYC
Ref.-book word — IBID
Refer to — ALLUDE
Referee — JUDGE
Reference bk. — ENC
Reference book — ALMANAC, ATLAS, TOME
Reference work — ATLAS
References — ATLASES
Referendum — VOTE
Referred (to) — ALLUDED
Refers to — CITES
Refine metal — SMELT
Refine the edge — HONE
Refined — ELEGANT, SMELTED, URBANE
Refined grace — ELEGANCE
Refined ore — METAL
Refinement — CLASS
Refinery refuse — DROSS
Refines — PURIFIES
Reflect — BEND
Reflected deeply — PORED
Reflection — IMAGE
Reflective glow — SHEEN
Reflective quality — SHEEN
Reflexive pronoun — ITSELF
Reformer Jacob _____ — RIIS
Reformer who started a fashion trend — BLOOMER
Refract — DIVIDE
Refrain — VERSE
Refrain in old songs — DERRY
Refrain syllable — TRA, TRALA
Refrain syllables — LAS, TRAS
Refrain word — TRA
Refresh — BATHE
Refreshed — BRACED
Refreshing dessert — SHERBET
Refreshment — SODA
Refrigerant — FREON
Refs' kin — UMPS
Refuge — HAVEN, SHELTER
Refugee from a beauty parlor — HAG
Refurbished — RENOVATED
Refusal — NEGATION
Refusal, in Rennes — NON
Refusals — NOES
Refuse — DROSS, SCUM, TRASH
Refuse "no" for an answer — INSIST
Refuse barge — SCOW
Refuse collector — ASHMAN
Refuse to buy or use — BOYCOTT
Refuse to notice — IGNORE
Refuse to release — HOLD
Refuses to quit — HANGS ON
Refute — DENY
Regain a favorable position — RECOUP
Regains consciousness — COMES TO
Regal — IMPERIAL
Regal — ROYAL
Regal address — SIRE
Regal headdress — TIARA
Regal headpiece — TIARA
Regal perches — THRONES
Regal residence — PALACE
Regale — EAT
Regan's father — LEAR
Regan's sire — LEAR
Regard — ESTEEM
Regard highly — ADMIRE, ESTEEM
Regard with pleasure — ADMIRE
Regarding — ANENT, AS TO, IN RE
Regardless of circumstances — RAIN OR SHINE
Regards — EYES, HEEDS, RATES
Regards highly — ESTEEMS
Regatta — RACE
Regatta entrant — OAR
Regatta locale — HENLEY
Regatta participants — OARS
Regatta, for one — RACE
Regeneration — REBIRTH
Regicides, e.g. — SLAYERS
Regimen — DIET
Reginald Dwight today — ELTON JOHN
Region — AREA, PARTS, SECTOR, ZONE
Region in NE Spain — ARAGON
Region in W France — ANJOU
Region near the Rhine — ALSACE
Region north of Afr. — EUR
Region of Greece — IONIA
Region of SE Asia — ANNAM
Region of SE Europe — MACEDONIA

Region of Spain — ARAGON, CASTILE
Region of WC India — BERAR
Region to Keats — CLIME
Region, poetically — CLIME
Region-related — AREAL
Region: Abbr. — TERR
Regional flora and fauna — BIOTA
Regions — TERRITORIES
Regions in general — DEMENSES
Regions of shifting sands — REGS
Regions surrounding Athens — ATTICA
Register — LEDGER, LIST, ROSTER, SIGN UP
Register in Britain — ENROL
Register: Var. — ENROL
Registered again — REENTERED
Registered: Abbr. — REGD
Registers — ENROLLS, LISTS
Registers for two party primaries — CROSS FILES
Regress — GO BACK
Regret — LAMENT, RUE
Regretful — PENITENT
Regretful Miss of song — OTIS
Regretful one — RUER
Regretful-sounding garment — SARI
Regrets — RUES
Regrettable — SORRY
Regretted — RUED
Regretting — RUING
Regular — HABITUE, TYPAL
Regulate — DIRECT, SET
Regulate again — READJUST
Regulations — RULES
Rehab hose — DARN
Rehan and Neilson — ADAS
Rehan and others — ADAS
Rehan or Huxtable — ADA
Rehearsal — PREPARATION
Rehobeth _____ — BEACH
Reign — PREVAIL, RULE
Reign of _____: 1793-94 — TERROR
Reindeer herder — LAPP
Reindeer's kin — CARIBOU
Reine's mate — ROI
Reiner or Bernstein — CARL
Reiner or Lowe — ROB
Reiner or Sagan — CARL
Reinforced support — TBEAM
Reinforcements — RELIEF
Reinforcing strips — WELTS
Reiterative ailment half — BERI
Reiterative composition — RONDO
Reiterative fly syllable — TSE
Reiterative Kenyan tribal name — MAU
Reiterative skirt — TUTU
Reiterative syllable for Dr. Dolittle monkey — CHEE
Reject — DENY, SCRAP, SPURN
Reject disdainfully — SPURN
Reject, vegetably speaking? — TURNIP ONES NOSE
Rejected — SPURNED
Rejection of dogma — HERESY
Rejoinder — ANSWER
Rejuvenate — RENEW
Rel. of ditto — ETC
Rel. of ltd. — INC
Relapse — EBB
Relate — TELL
Relate again — RETELL
Relate to — REACT
Related — AKIN, TOLD
Related groups — SERIES
Related maternally — ENATE
Related on Father's side — AGNATE
Related on Mom's side — ENATE
Related on the mother's side — ENATE, ENATIC
Related to birds — AVIAN
Related to mama — ENATE
Relates — TELLS
Relates, with "to" — PERTAINS
Relating to — ABOUT, ANENT
Relating to a period — ERAL
Relating to an eye part — UVEAL
Relating to grades 1 to 12 — ELHI
Relating to gulls — LARINE
Relating to mites and ticks — ACARIAN
Relating to morning — MATIN, MATINAL
Relating to stakes — PALAR
Relating to the cheek — MALAR
Relating to the ear — OTIC
Relating to the mind — MENTAL
Relating to the populace — DEMOGRAPHIC
Relating to the Vatican — PAPAL
Relating to thread — FILAR
Relating to wise men — MAGIAN
Relating to: Suffix — ATIVE, ILE
Relations — KIN
Relationship — LIAISON, TIE IN
Relative — AUNT, INLAW, UNCLE
Relative acquired — INLAW
Relative by marriage — AFFINE, INLAW
Relative humidity — VAPOR
Relative of "Aroint thee!" — SCRAM
Relative of "Eureka" — O HO
Relative of "kinda" — SORTA
Relative of "Pow!" — BAM
Relative of "tut" — TSK
Relative of a b'ar — COON
Relative of a buttercup — PEONY
Relative of a clip joint — TOURIST TRAP
Relative of a crown — TIARA
Relative of a daisy cutter — LINER
Relative of a gore — INSET
Relative of a kickback — SHAKEDOWN
Relative of a lute — ASOR
Relative of a mesa — LOMA
Relative of a prom — HOP
Relative of a sheik — EMEER
Relative of a sort — INLAW
Relative of a spree — TOOT
Relative of a swamp stalker — IBIS
Relative of a twirp — DRIP
Relative of aromas — ODORS
Relative of bingo — BEANO
Relative of chocolat — VANILLE
Relative of curare — INEE
Relative of et al. — ETCS
Relative of etc. — ETAL
Relative of H.I.M. — NRH
Relative of long. — LAT
Relative of lotto — BINGO
Relative of moll or doll — BABE
Relative of nope — NAH
Relative of Rachel — RAE
Relative of rain — HAIL
Relative of rampage — RIOT
Relative of Sis — BRO
Relative of yoo-hoo — HALLO
Relative: Abbr. — DAU
Relatives — KIN, SIB
Relatives by blood — KINDRED
Relatives of ers — UHS
Relatives of sts. — AVES
Relatives of wadis — ARROYOS
Relativity suffix — IER
Relax — REST, SIT
Relax in a listless way — LOLL
Relaxation aid — BIOFEEDBACK
Relaxation of relations between nations — DETENTES
Relaxed — AT EASE, AT REST, EASED, LOOSE
Relaxing — IDLE
Relaxing of international tensions — DETENTE
Release — EMIT, FREE, LET GO, LIBERATE, UNFASTEN
Release sources — ISSUERS
Released — FREED, LET GO, LOOSED, SET FREE
Released conditionally — PAROLED

Releases — UNLOOSENS
Releases conditionally — PAROLES
Relent — BEND, SOFTEN
Relenting — MELTING
Reliable — STABLE, STOLID, TRIED
Reliable fund? — TRUST
Reliance — DEPENDENCE, TRUST
Relic — MEMENTO, RUIN
Relics — ARTIFACTS, TOKENS
Relied (on) — BANKED
Relief — DOLE
Relief org. — ARC
Relief pitcher's feats — SAVES
Relief pitchers milieu — BULL PEN
Relief pitchers, at times — SAVERS
Relief, of a sort — BAS
Relies, with "on" — BANKS
Relieve — ALLAY, ALLEVIATE, SPELL
Relieve of weapons — UNARM
Relieved — EASED
Reliever Alejandro — PENA
Relieves — ALLAYS, EASES
Relig. teaching deg. — DRE
Religieuse — NUN
Religion — FAITH
Religion of "the way" — TAOISM
Religious — HOLY
Religious acronym — INRI
Religious belief — DEISM, FAITH
Religious beliefs — THEISMS
Religious ceremonies — RITES
Religious ceremony — MASS
Religious congregation — PARISH
Religious denomination — SECT
Religious devotee — FAKIR
Religious devotion — PIETY
Religious exclamation — HOSANNA
Religious faction — SECT
Religious group — SECT
Religious image — ICON
Religious image: Var. — IKON
Religious leader — RABBI
Religious leaders — AGAS
Religious manual — CATE-CHISM
Religious picture — ICON
Religious rebel — APOSTATE
Religious recluses — EREMITES
Religious retreats for hindus — ASHRAMS
Religious rite — BAPTISM
Religious sayings — LOGIA
Religious service — MASS
Religious singer — CANTOR
Religious society of Iowa — AMANA
Religious song — PAEAN
Religious title: Abbr. — MSGR
Relinquish — ABDICATE, CEDE, CONCEDE
Relinquish control — STEP DOWN
Reliquary — SHRINE
Relish — GUSTO, LIKE, SAVOR, SPICE, ZEST
Relish-tray item — CELERY
Relished — SAVORED
Relocate — MOVE
Reluctance — HESITANCY
Reluctant — AVERSE, LOATH
Rely — COUNT ON, DEPEND, HINGE
Rely (on) — DEPEND, TRUST
REM state — SLEEP
Remain — STAY
Remain at home — STAY IN
Remain longer — OUTLAST
Remain stationary — STAND
Remain suspended — HANG
Remain undecided — PEND
Remainder — BALANCE, END, EXCESS, REST
Remainder: Fr. — RESTE
Remained dormant — SLEPT
Remained for a time — DWELLED
Remaining amt. — BAL
Remains — STAYS
Remains in a tray — ASHES
Remark — HEED
Remark from Sandy — ARF
Remark to the audience — ASIDE
Remarkable: Scot. — UNCO
Remarked — STATED
Remarque or Segal — ERICH
Rembrandt van _____ — RIJN
Rembrandt's "_____ and Cottage" — BARN
Rembrandt's birthplace — LEIDEN
Rembrandt's last name — RIJN
Remedy — CURE, MEND
Remedy Bowler, Atla. — MEDICINE HAT
Remedy of a sort — THERAPY
Remember — RECALL
Reminder — NOTE
Reminder of a sort — CUE
Remindful of Rapunzel — TRESSY
Remit — SEND
Remitted — SENT
Remnant — DREG, END, ORT, SCRAP, TAG END
Remnants — ODDMENTS, RAGS
Remodeling projects — ELLS
Remonstrates — PROTESTS
Remorse — SORROW
Remote — AFAR, FAR
Remote telecast — REMO
Remote TV broadcast — REMO
Remotely — AFAR
Remoteness — DISTANCE
Remove — DELE, DELETE, UNLOAD
Remove by cutting, erosion, melting, etc. — ABLATE
Remove certain stitches — UNSEAM
Remove from office — DEPOSE, OUST
Remove hidden mikes from — DEBUG
Remove husks — UNHULL
Remove mist — DEFOG
Remove rind — PARE, PEEL
Remove stopple — UNCOCK
Remove the cream — SKIM
Remove the goatee — SHAVE
Remove the pop-top — UNCAP
Remove the rough edges — SMOOTHEN
Remove the squeak — OIL
Remove the tape — UNSTICK
Remove to a distance — ELOIN
Remove type — DELE
Remove wrinkles — IRON
Remove, as ink or gravy — BLOT UP
Remove, in printing — DELE
Remove, to an editor — DELE
Removed — DELED, TAKEN
Removed friction — OILED
Removed grit — DESANDED
Removed snow — SHOVELED
Removed the skin — PARED
Removed the soap — RINSED
Removed, in printing — DELED
Removes the cholesterol — DEFATS
Removes the rind — PARED, PEELS
Removes, in printing — DELES
Remuda — HERD
Remunerates — PAYS
Remuneration — WAGE
Renaissance — REBIRTH
Renaissance family — ESTE
Renaissance fiddle — REBEC
Renaissance sword — ESTOC
Renan's "La _____ Jésus" — VIE DE
Rend — TEAR
Render a snake harmless — DEFANG
Render ineffective — ANNUL
Render powerless — STRAN-GLE
Renders lip service — SNIVELS
Renders powerless — DISARMS
Renders, as bacon — TRIES
Rendezvous — RETREAT, TRYST
Rendezvous of witches — SABBAT

Rene's affirmative — OUI
Rene's brainstorm — IDEE
Rene's dream — REVE
Rene's girlfriend — AMIE
Rene's high school — LYCEE
Rene's remainder — RESTE
Rene's soul — AME
Renee of silents — ADOREE
Renee's husband — MARI
Renew the edge — HONE
Renews — FRESHES
Reno "natural" — SEVEN
Reno dazzlers — NEONS
Reno game — FARO
Reno raisers — BETTORS
Reno resident — NEVADAN
Reno roller — DICER
Reno-to-Las Vegas dir. — SSE
Renoir's "The _____ Bather" — BLONDE
Renovates — REPAIRS
Renowned — FAMED
Renowned bishop — TUTU
Renowned miler — COE
Renowned Missourian — CLEMENS
Rent — LET, LEASE
Rent again — RELET
Rent gent — LESSOR
Rent payee — LESSEE
Rent payer — LESSER
Rent sharer — ROOMMATE
Rent-_____ — A CAR
Rental contract — LEASE
Rental document — LEASE
Rental sign — TO LET
Rented — LEASED
Renter — TENANT
Renter's contract — LEASE
Renter's document — LEASE
Renting agent — LESSOR
Rents out — LETS
Rep. antagonist — DEM
Rep. Les _____ from Wis. — ASPIN
Rep.'s opponent — DEM
Repair — MEND
Repair a sock again — REDARN
Repair holes in hose — DARN
Repair shop accommodation — LOANER
Repair the lawn — RESOD
Repair with a needle — DARN
Repaired — MENDED
Repairs socks — DARNS
Repast, military style — CHOW
Repeat — DUPLICATE, ECHO, RERUN
Repeated musical passages — DA CAPOS
Repeated sound — RATATAT
Repeatedly — AGAIN, OFTEN
Repeater requisite — AMMO
Repeats — ITERATES, ECHOS
Repeats again — REITERATES
Repelled a mugger — MACED
Repent — ATONE
Repentant ones — RUERS
Repenter — ATONER
Repetition — ROTE
Repetitive — ITERANT
Repetitive melody — CHANT
Repetitive sounds — TICTACS
Rephrased — AMENDED
Replace — SUPERCEDE
Replace a receiver — HANG UP
Replacement — FILL IN
Replete — SATED
Replica — COPY
Replicate — CLONE
Reply — ANSWER
Reply to "Why?" — BECAUSE
Reply to Virginia — YES
Reply, for short — ANS
Reply: Abbr. — ANS
Reporter — THE FRONT PAGE
Reporter for the "Daily Planet" — CLARK KENT
Reporter Lane — LOIS
Reporter's concern — NEWS
Reporter's coup — SCOOP
Reporter's milieu — NEWSROOM
Reporter's query — WHEN
Reporter's question — WHEN, WHERE, WHO
Reporter, at times — ASKER
Reporters' goals — SCOOPS
Reports, with "about" — BRUITS
Repose — REST
Repository — SAFE
Repository: Abbr. — STGE
Repplier work — ESSAY
Represent — ACT FOR
Represent on the stage — ENACT
Representation — DEPICTION
Representation of a sort — ICON
Representative — AGENT, ENVOY, PROXY, SURROGATE
Representative Jack from Buffalo — KEMP
Representative, for short — AGT
Represents — ENACTS
Reprieve — STAY
Reprimands — REBUKES
Repro fluid — TONER
Reproduce — CLONE
Reproduce perfectly — CLONE
Reproductions — PRINTS
Reprove — SCOLD
Reproved — REPRIMANDED
Reps. — AGTS
Reps.' rivals — DEMS
Reptile — SNAKE
Republic of Ireland — EIRE
Republic of Yemen's capital — ADEN
Republic south of Libya — CHAD
Republican monogram — GOP
Repudiates — SPURNS
Repudiations — DENIALS
Repugnance — NAUSEA
Repurchase agreement, for short — REPO
Reputation — NAME
Reputations — FAMES, ODORS
Repute — ODOR
Request — ASK, PETITION, PLEA, SEEK
Request humbly — PRAY
Request imperiously — ORDERS
Request to Gabriel — BLOW
Request to the congregation — BE SEATED
Requests — PLEAS
Requests for more — ENCORES
Requiem — DIRGE, MASS
Require — DEMAND, NEED
Required — DUE
Required: Abbr. — NEC
Requirement — NEED
Requirement for MS return — SASE
Requirements — MUSTS, NEEDS
Requires — NEEDS
Requisite — NEED, NEEDED
Res. of Riga — ESTH
Rescind — LIFT
Rescue — RECLAIM, SAVE
Rescuer of a kind — KNIGHT IN SHINING ARMOR
Rescuer of Odysseus — INO
Rescues, in a way — RANSOMS
Research ctrs. — LABS
Research fig. — STAT
Research places — LABS
Research rm. — LAB
Researcher's abbr. — NES
Reseau — MESH
Resembling — SIMILAR
Resembling a cereal grain — RICEY
Resembling a fairy tale creature: Var. — OGRISH
Resembling a narrow band — STREAKLIKE
Resembling a rodent — BATLIKE
Resembling: Suffix — OIDAL
Resentment — IRE
Reserve — SPARE
Reserve org. — USAR
Reserved — ALOOF, DEMURE, STAID, TAKEN
Reserved parking — PRIVATE
Reserves — BACKUPS, SETS APART, SPARES, STORES

Reserves for future use — STORES
Reservoir near Los Angeles — ENCINO
Reside — DWELL
Resided — DWELT
Residence — DOMICILE, HOME
Residence in sound of Bow bell — OME
Residence of early Irish kings — TARA
Residences — ABODES
Residences of a sort — TENTS
Resident — AMIDER
Resident of 333 Riverside: mid-50's — SAUL BELLOW
Resident of 570 Park Ave.: 1932-47 — WILLA CATHER
Resident of a sort — INMATE
Resident of ancient Crete — KEFTIAN
Resident of Belgrade — SERB
Resident of Latvia — LETT
Resident of N Iran — KURD
Resident of: Suffix — ITE
Resident: Suffix — ITE
Residential district in Boston — BACK BAY
Residents of Oklahoma City — SOONERS
Residents of: Suffix — ERS, ITES
Residue — ASH, LEES
Residue from pressed grapes — MARC
Resign — STEP DOWN
Resign, as an office — VACATE
Resilience — BOUNCE, ELASTICITY, SNAP
Resiliency — TONE
Resilient — FLEXIBLE
Resin — ELEMI, LAC
Resin ingredient — MELAMINE
Resin used in perfumes — TOLU
Resinous — RETENE
Resinous substance — LAC
Resinous tree — PINE
Resins — LACS
Resistance — DEFIANCE, OPPOSITION, PROTEST
Resistance unit — OHM
Resisted — OPPOSED
Resolute — DETERMINED, GRITTY
Resolution time for Jose — ENERO
Resolution vehicle — MOTION
Resonant — OROTUND, TUNED
Resonant sound — BONG
Resort — CHANCE, FREQUENT, SPA, TURN TO
Resort for the punctilious? — NICE
Resort in Belgium — SPA
Resort in Scotland — OBAN
Resort in Sicily — ENNA
Resort in the Bahamas — NASSAU
Resort NE of Santa Fe — TAOS
Resort near Liege — SPA
Resort near Santa Fe — TAOS
Resort near Venice — LIDO
Resort of a sort — SPA
Resort of Venice — LIDO
Resort on Frenchman's Bay — BAR HARBOR
Resort to — USE
Resorts — SPAS
Resound — ECHO, RESONATE
Resounded — RANG
Resounding gaffes, in Soho — CLANGERS
Resounding sound — CLANG
Resource — ASSET, SKILL
Respect — ESTEEM
Respectable — DECENT
Respectful address — MADAM
Respecting — INRE
Respiration — RALE
Respiratory organs — LUNGS
Respiratory problem — ASTHMA
Respiratory sound — RAIL
Respire — BREATHE
Respite — LULL, TRUCE
Respond — REACT
Respond to stimuli — REACT
Responded to the alarm — AROSE
Response evokers — STIMULI
Response from Fido — WOOF
Response from Sandy — ARF
Responsibility — ONUS
Responsible — LIABLE
Responsory song after the Epistle — GRADUAL
Rest — NAP, PAUSE
Rest place for Gretel's witch — OVEN
Restatement — ITERATION
Restaurant — BRASSERIE
Restaurant bill — TAB
Restaurant busybody — TABLE HOPPER
Restaurant employee — COOK
Restaurant product — MEAL
Restauranteur Toots — SHOR
Rested — LAIN
Rested, in a way — SAT
Resting — IDLE
Resting place for some — LAIR
Resting place of a type — ROOST
Resting places — BEDS, INNS
Restitution — REFUND
Restive — EDGY, ITCHY
Restless longing — ITCH
Restless yen — ITCH
Restorative — TONIC
Restorative resort — SPA
Restore calm — PACIFY
Restore to health — HEAL
Restore to life — REVIVE
Restore, for short — REHAB
Restored bldg. — REHAB
Restrain — BRIDLE, CHECK, CURB, HOLD BACK, HOLD DOWN
Restrain — REIN, STAY
Restrain with a chain — TETHER
Restrain, in a way — TETHER
Restrainer for a yegg? — YOKE
Restrains — TETHERS
Restraint — CHECK, LEASH, TETHER
Restrict — LIMIT
Rests — PAUSES
Restylings — REDOS
Result — EFFECT, END, ENSUE, FRUIT
Result in — CAUSE
Result of "hearthburn"? — EMBERS
Result of a shaver's flub — NICK
Result of Dracula's attentions? — ANEMIA
Result of flooding — EROSION
Result of gradual decline — LYSATE
Result of many a "lost weekend" — DTS
Result of raining cats and dogs? — MUDPOODLES
Result of thrift — RICHES
Result, in Paris — EFFET
Results from — STEMS
Results of a flogging — WEALS
Results that follow naturally — COROLLARIES
Resume — RENEW
Ret. plans — IRAS
Retail outlet — DEPARTMENT STORE
Retail outlets — DRY GOODS EMPORIA
Retail outlets — MERCANTILE MARTS
Retailer — SELLER
Retailer's abbr. — MDSE
Retain — KEEP
Retained — KEPT
Retainer — FEE
Retaining wall — PILING
Retains after expenses — NETS
Retina area — YELLOW SPOT
Retinue — CORTEGE, CREW, ESCORT, TRAIN
Retire — DEPART, GO TO BED, LEAVE
Retired — ABED
Retired batters — OUTS
Retired but still holding former title — EMERITUS

Retired natator's word — SWUM
Retiree — SENIOR
Retiree of hockey fame — ORR
Retiree's concern — PENSION
Retirement accts. — IRAS
Retirement fund: Abbr. — IRA
Retiring — MEEK
Retraced one's step — BACK TRACKED
Retract — UNSAY
Retread, for one — TIRE
Retreat — DEN, GO BACK, LAIR
Retreated — BACK PEDALED
Retrospection — HIND SIGHT
Retton's score — TEN
Return part of purchase price — REBATE
Return to office — REELECT
Return to prior position — RESILE
Return to reality — COME DOWN TO EARTH
Return to the past — PUT THE CLOCK BACK
Returned from dreamland — AWOKE
Reunion and The Summit — ARENAS
Reunion et Martinique, e.g. — ILES
Reunion goer — CLASSMATE
Reunion in Dallas, e.g. — ARENA
Reuter's US cousin — UPI
Rev. talks — SERS
Reveal — BARE, DISCLOSE, LAY OPEN
Reveal or pretend — LET ON
Revealed — BARED, SHOWN
Reveals wrongdoing — PUTS THE FINGER ON
Revel — FROLIC
Revel in — ENJOY
Revel noisily — ROISTER
Revel, of a sort — CAROUSAL
Revelation — EXPOSE
Reveled — CAROUSED
Revelers — CELEBRANTS
Revelry cry of old — EVOE
Revenue — INCOME, YIELD
Revenue, in Reims — RENTE
Revenuer — AGENT
Revenuers target — STILL
Revenues, in Rennes — RENTES
Reverberate — ECHO
Reverberated — RANG
Reverberating — THUNDER-ING
Reverberation — ECHOS
Revere — ADORE, LAPEL
Revered name in Norway — OLAF
Revered objects — ICONS
Revered one — IDOL
Revered patron, for short — ST PAT
Revered things — ICONS
Reverence — AWE
Reverent fear — AWE
Reverie — DAYDREAM
Revering — ADORANT
Reversal — SETBACK
Reverse — UNDO
Reverse curve — OGEE
Reverse of par — RAP
Reversible fabric — DAMASK
Review board — PANEL
Review quickly — SCAN
Review unfavorably — PAN
Reviewed — GONE OVER
Reviews copy — EDITS
Revile — ABUSE
Revise — AMEND, EDIT
Revise copy — EDIT
Revise the text — EDIT
Revised — EDITED, REWROTE
Revised Standard Version — BIBLE
Revisers — EDITORS
Revises — EDITS, EMENDS
Revitalized — FRESHENED UP
Revival — REBIRTH
Revived — CAME TO
Revoice — ECHO
Revoke — ANNUL, CANCEL, VOID
Revoke a legacy — ADEEM
Revoke, at the bar — ADEEM
Revoked: Abbr. — CANC
Revokes — RESCINDS
Revokes, as a legacy — ADEEMS
Revokes, in bridge — RENEGES
Revolts — ARISES
Revolution loyalists — TORRIES
Revolutionary Allen — ETHAN
Revolutionary battle lake — ERIE
Revolutionary battle or aircraft carrier — BENNINGTON
Revolutionary commander or software man — GATES
Revolutionary patriot Thomas — PAINE
Revolutionary portraitist — PEALE
Revolutionary soldier Allen — ETHAN
Revolutionary symbol — RED FLAG
Revolutionary War battle — BUNKER HILL
Revolutionary War hero — HALE
Revolutionary War mercenary — HESSIAN
Revolutionary who overthrew Batista — CASTRO
Revolve — MOVE
Revolved the center — CORED
Revolver — GUN
Revolver of a sort — DOOR, ROTOR
Revolves — TURNS
Revolving machine part — ROTOR
Revolving part on a machine — ROTOR
Revue — SHOW
Revue bit — SKIT
Revved up — RACED
Reward for gallantry — SILVER STAR
Reward of a sort — RAISE
Rex _____, film critic — REED
Rex and Robert — REEDS
Rex and Walter — REEDS
Rex Ingram role — SATAN
Rex or Donna — REED
Rex or Walter — REED
Rex Reed, for short — CRIT
Reykjavik is its cap. — ICEL
Reykjavik resident — ICE-LANDER
Reys mate — TEINA
Rhapsodize — RAVE
Rhea relative — EMU
Rhea's cousin — EMU
Rhea's role in "Cheers" — CARLA
Rheostat part — WIPER
Rhett's last word — DAMN
Rhine city — BONN
Rhine feeder — AAR, ISERE, MOSEL, RAHR
Rhine siren — LORELEI
Rhine tributary — AAR, AARE, ISERE, SAONE
Rhine wine — MOSELLE
Rhine wine in Britain — HOCK
Rhino's relative — TAPIR
Rhinoceros beetle — UANG
Rhinoplasty objects — NOSES
Rhode Island bird? — NEW-PORTOLAN
Rhode Island college — BROWN
Rhode Island eleven — RAMS
Rhode Island Red — LAYER
Rhode Island Red's — HENS
Rhode Island, island — BLOCK
Rhodes of Polo Grounds fame — DUSTY
Rhodes or De Mille — CECIL
Rhodes scholar's school — OXFORD
Rhonchus — SNORE
Rhone city — ARLES
Rhone feeder — AIN, ISERE, SAONE
Rhone river augmenter — SAONE
Rhone river feeder — ISERE
Rhone Roman ruin site — ARLES

Rhone tributary — AIN, ISERE, SAONE
Rhubarb — DISPUTE
Rhum cakes — BABAS
Rhyme scheme — ABBA
Rhyme Western group — POSSE
Rhyme's partner — REASON
Rhythm — BEAT, LILT
Rhythm maker — CASTANET
Rhythm pattern — CLAVE
Rhythm, in music — METER
Rhythm, in sequence — CADENCE
Rhythm, in verse — METER
Rhythmic — CADENT, LILTING
Rhythmic cadence — LILT
Rhythmic contractions — SYSTOLES
Rhythmic Cuban dance — RUMBA
Rhythmic step — PAS
Rhythmic swing — LILT
Rhythmical — PACED
Rhythmical beat — PULSE
RI motto — HOPE
Ria — INLET
Rialto muggers — HAMS
Rialto sign — NEON
Riata loop — NOOSE
Riatas — LASSOS
Rib — COSTA, TEASE
Rib or pan — ROAST
Rib repair — PATCH
Riband — RIBBON
Ribbed fabric — FAILLE
Ribbed woolen cloth — SATARA
Ribbon — TAPE
Ribbonlike, braided fabric — GIMP
Ribicoff or Burrows — ABE
Ribonucleic acids — RNA
Ribs of leaves — VEINS
Ricardo Montalban's TV island — FANTASY
Rice-Webber hit — CATS
Rice — PILAF
Rice beverage — SAKE
Rice boiled with meat — PILAF
Rice dish — PILAU
Rice dish — PILAU, RISOTTO
Rice dishes — PILAFS
Rice drink — SAKI
Rice field — PADDY
Rice flavoring — SAFFRON
Rice or Fudd — ELMER
Rice style — PILAF
Rice, in Nice — RIZ
Rice, in Roma — RISO
Rice-Webber musical — EVITA
Rich — OPULENT
Rich cake — TORTE
Rich copper ore — PRILL
Rich gear? — TRAPS
Rich in color — GRAPHIC
Rich pastries — NAPOLEONS
Rich soil — LOAM
Rich source — LODE
Rich tapestry — ARRAS
Rich yeast cake — SAVARIN
Richard Arlen role: 1933 — CHESHIRE CAT
Richard from Philadelphia — GERE
Richard Gere film — YANKS
Richard Harris vehicle — ORCA
Richard of "The Cotton Club" — GERE
Richard of film — EGAN
Richard of the screen — EGAN
Richard Starkey — RINGO STARR
Richardson's "_____ Harlowe" — CLARISSA
Riches — LUCRE, PELF
Riches antithesis — RAGS
Richmond V.I.P. set — FFV
Richness of sound — RESONANCE
Richtofen quarry — SPAD
Rick _____, talk-show host — DEES
Rick Blaine — HUMPHREY BOGART
Rick's "gin joint" — CAFE AMERICAIN
Rick's love in "Casablanca" — ILSA
Rick's pianist — SAM
Rickey ingredients — LIMES
Rickles — DON
Ricky of "I Love Lucy" — DESI
Ricochet — BOOMERANG, CAROM
Ricwe in N. Zaire — UELE
Rid of pests — DERAT
Riddles — ENIGMA
Ride a bike — PEDAL
Ride at anchor — LIE TO
Rider — CLAUSE
Rider's attire — BOOTS
Rider's garb — HABIT
Rider's need — REIN
Rider's sport — POLO
Rides a bike — PEDALS
Rides the boards — SKIS
Ridge — ESKER, WALE
Ridge of eskers — OSAR
Ridgepole — BEAM
Ridges between ice walls — OSAR
Ridgy — TWILLED
Ridicule — DERIDE, RIDE, SCORN, TWIT
Ridiculed — SNEERED
Ridiculous — INANE, INSANE
Ridiculous rite — MUMMERY
Riding control — REIN
Rife — RAMPANT
Rife of S. Bulgaria — ARDA
Riffraff — RAGTAG, TRASH
Rifle — GARAND, ROB
Rifle part — SEAR
Rifle range at Saint-Cyr — TIR
Rifle's forerunner — MUSKET
Rift — BELCH, CHASM, CRACK, SCHISM
Rig — EQUIP, EQUIPAGE
Rig truck — SEMI
Riga man — LETT
Riga resident — LETT
Rigel or Betelgeuse — STAR
Rigel's location — ORION
Rigging pole — SPAR
Right-hand page — RECTO
Right a wrong — MAKE AMENDS
Right and left — SIDES
Right and left endings — ISTS
Right angle — ELL
Right Bank river — SEINE
Right hand — AIDE
Right of way — EASEMENT
Right on, old style — OKEH
Right tidy — IN APPLE PIE ORDER
Right to comment — SAY
Right to decide — SAY
Right to purchase in the future — OPTION
Right, in law — DROIT
Right, in Rostock — RECHT
Right-angled house extension — ELL
Right-angled to a keel — ABEAM
Right-triangle ratio — SINE
Rightful — TRUE
Rights org. — ACLU
Rigid — TAUT, STERN
Rigid adherence on nicety — PURISM
Rigid belief — DOGMA
Rigorous — SEVERE
Rigorous degree — THIRD
Rigs — SEMIS
Rile — IRK
Riled — ANGERED
Riled up — SORE
Riled, with "up" — SHOOK
Rill — STREAM
Rim — EDGE
Rim that holds crystal on watch — BEZEL
Rime — FROST
Rimple — FOLD
Rims — LIPS
Rimsky-Korsakov piece — SONG OF INDIA
Rimsky-Korsakov's "Le Coq _____" — DOR

Rin _____ — TIN TIN
Rind — SKIN
Ring — AREOLA, LARDNER
Ring around the moon? — ORBIT
Ring blows — LEFTS
Ring boundaries — ROPES
Ring decision — TKO
Ring decisions: Abbr. — KOS
Ring dog? — BOXER
Ring event — BOUT
Ring great — ALI
Ring immortal — ALI
Ring needs — MATS
Ring of light around the sun — HALO
Ring Primo — CARNERA
Ring ref's decision — TKO
Ring result — SPLIT DECISION
Ring training partner — SPARRER
Ring up — PHONE
Ring victory — TKO
Ring weapons — FISTS
Ring wearer — FINGER
Ring windup — TKO
Ring wins — TKOS
Ring-tailed animal — COATI
Ring-tailed cat — CACOMISTLE
Ringing of bells — PEALING
Ringing sound — DING DONG
Ringlet — LOCK
Ringlets — HAIRS
Ringlike — ANNULAR
Rings — CALLS
Rings of light — HALOS
Ringworm — TINEA
Rink maneuver — AXEL
Rink structures — CAGES
Rio _____ — GRANDE
Rio _____: NW Africa — DE ORO
Rio beach, for short — COPA
Rio de _____ — ORO
Rio de Janeiro's beach — COPACABANA
Rio de Janeiro's peak — SUGARLOAF
Rio Grande city — EL PASO, LAREDO
Rio Grande feeder — PECOS
Rio's mountain — SUGARLOAF
Rip — TEAR
Rip along or rip — TEAR
Rip off — ROB
Rip up — SHRED
Ripcord on a parachute — OPENER
Ripe — ODOR
Ripe old age — NINETY
Ripen — AGE, MATURE
Ripened — AGED
Ripeners — AGERS
Ripening agent — AGER
Ripening device — AGER
Ripens — AGES
Ripken of baseball — CAL
Ripped — TORE, TORN
Ripped again — RETORE
Ripped apart — TORN
Ripple — LAP
Ripple-patterned fabric — MOIRE
Ripples — PURLS
Rips — RENDS, TEARS
Rise — ASCEND, CLIMB, MOUNT, STAND
Rise Stevens forte — ARIA
Rise to one's feet — STAND
Rise up suddenly — LOOM
Rise up, like a horse — REAR
Rise, like Silver — REAR UP
Riser's adjunct — STEP
Rises — GOES UP
Risiblity — MIRTH
Rising row of seats — TIER
Rising star — COMER
Risk — JEOPARDY
Risk a ticket — SPEED
Risk everything — GO FOR BROKE
Risked a ticket — SPED
Risky N.Y.S.E. activity — SPEC
Risque — RACY
Ristorante appetizer — MINESTRONE
Ristorante repast — PASTA
Rita of the screen — GAM
Ritual — RITE
Ritualistic declaration — OATH
Rituals — SOLEMNITIES
Ritz Brothers, e.g. — TRIO
Ritzy — ELEGANT, POSH
Riv. boat: Abbr. — STR
Rival — CHALLENGER, EMULATE, ENEMY, FOE
Rival of a Sadducee — PHARISEE
Rival of George and Bill in '92 — ROSS
Rival of Martina — CHRIS
Rival of Sparta — ARGOS
Rivals of the Cornhuskers — SOONERS
River 2 miles SE of Paris — MARNE
River access, in India — GHAT
River and dam of Germany — EDER
River and department of France — OISES
River and Lake in Scotland — DOONS
River at Amiens — SOMME
River at Bangor — PENOBSCOT
River at Bath — AVON
River at Bern — AARE
River at Berne — AARE
River at Caen — ORNE
River at Florence — ARNO
River at Grenoble — ISERE
River at Leeds — AIRE
River at Orleans — LOIRE
River at Paris — SEINE
River at Pisa — ARNO
River at Rennes — ILLE
River between Maryland and Virginia — POTOMAC
River boat — BARGE
River boat wheel — PADDLE
River bottom — BED
River boundary between Germany and Poland — ODER
River Burton explored — NILE
River channel — BED
River craft — CANOE
River dam — WEIR
River dike — LEVEE
River duck — TEAL
River embankment — LEVEE
River feeding the Elbe — ELDE
River Gauche — SEINE
River ice breakup — DEBACLE
River in a Burns poem — DOOM
River in Central Africa — UELE
River in central Europe — ODER
River in central India — PURNA
River in China — LIAO
River in Corsica — GOLO
River in Devon — EXE
River in E. England — CAM
River in E. Malaysia — BARAM
River in Hades — LETHE
River in Hesse — EDER
River in Kenya — TANA
River in Lombardy — ADDA
River in N. England — TEES
River in N. France — AISNE
River in N. India — SARDA
River in N. Ireland — ERNE
River in NE England — OUSE
River in Nebraska — PLATTE
River in NW France — ORNE
River in Romania — OLT
River in SE Ontario — TRENT
River in Solway Firth — DEE
River in South Africa — VAAL
River in Southern France — TARN
River in Spain — EBRO
River in SW Maine — SACO
River in the Carolinas — PEE DEE
River in Tuscany — ARNO
River in Vietnam — MEKONG
River in W Africa — NIGER
River in W Canada — NASS
River in Yorkshire — AIRE, OUSE, URE

River in Zaire — UELE
River into Donegal Bay — ERNE
River into Lake Balkhash — ILI
River into Monterey Bay — SALINAS
River into Moray Firth — NESS
River into Solway Firth — DEE
River into the Adriatic — RENO
River into the Baltic — ODER
River into the Bay of the Seine — ORNE
River into the Caspian Sea — URAL
River into the North Sea — YSER
River into the Rhone — ISERE
River into the Seine — OISE
River island — AIT
River islands — HOLMS
River isle — AIT
River islets — AITS
River mouth — BOCA, DELTA
River mouth deposit — SILT
River near Bangkok — MUN
River near Mt. Ararat — ARAS
River near Pisa — ARNO
River near Rouen — EURE
River nymph — NAIAD, NAIS
River of "The Last Frontier" — TANANA
River of Charon — STYX
River of Devon — EXE
River of eastern Wales — WYE
River of Florence — ARNO
River of forgetfulness — LETHE
River of Hades — STYX
River of Hesse — EDER
River of Hungary — EGER
River of Ireland — ERNE, LIFFEY
River of N England — TEES
River of N France — YSER, SELLE
River of N Pakistan — RAVI
River of NE China — LIAO
River of NE Spain — EBRO
River of NW France — ORNE
River of oblivion — LETHE
River of Paraguay — APA
River of S Bulgaria — ARDA
River of S central China — YUEN
River of SE Asia — MEKONG
River of SE Ontario — KENT
River of song — AFTON, WABASH
River of Soviet Asia — LENA
River of Spain — EBRO
River of Tuscany — ARNO
River of Zaire — UELE
River or city of Maine — SACO
River or Indian — OSAGE
River or monster — GILA
River or town in Ecuador — DAULE
River past Enniskillen — ERNE
River past Notre Dame — SEINE
River plied by boatmen of song — VOLGA
River quay — LEVEE
River residence — HOUSEBOAT
River rising in the Urals — TOBOL
River sight — MILL DAM
River sources — HEADWATERS
River Styx local — HADES
River that sounds like a horse — RHONE
River through Cleveland — CUYAHOGA
River through Firenze — ARNO
River through Rome — TIBER
River to Lake Rudolph — OMO
River to Limerick — SHANNON
River to Solway Firth — DEE
River to the Adriatic — ADIGE
River to the Baltic — ODER
River to the Bay of Biscay — LOIRE
River to the Caspian — URAL
River to the China Sea — WEST RIVER
River to the Congo — UBANGI
River to the Danube — SAVA
River to the Dead Sea — JORDAN
River to the Fulda — EDER
River to the Gulf of Lions — YSER
River to the Mediterranean — NILE
River to the Mosel — SAAR
River to the North Sea — YSER
River to the Rhine — MOSEL, AAR
River to the Rhone — ISERE, SAONE
River to the Seine — OISE
River to the Severn — AVON
River to the Wash — OUSE
River two miles SE of Paris — MARNE
River, in Toledo — RIO
Riverbank — RIPA
Riverbank denizen — OTTER
Riverfront men — REDS
Riverine real estate — AITS
Rivers in Kenya and Norway — TANAS
Rivers in Scotland and England — DEES
Rivers, in Malaga — RIOS
Rivet — GRIP
Riveter of WW II fame — ROSIE
Riviera acquisition — TAN
Riviera and Seville — AUTOS
Riviera resort — NICE
Riviera season — ETE
Rivulet — RILL
Rivulet in England — BOURN
Rivulets — STREAMS
Riyadh resident — ARAB, SAUDI
Riza Khan Pahlevi, e.g. — SHAH
Riza Pahlevi, once — SHAH
RN assistants — LPNS
RN's dispense this — TLC
RN's ministrations — TLC
Roach of Hollywood fame — HAL
Road — STREET
Road _____ — HOG
Road alert — BEEP
Road base — ASPHALT
Road coat — TAR
Road cover — MACADAM
Road curve — ESS
Road curves — ESSES
Road depression — DIP
Road ending — STER
Road for sweethearts — LOVERS LANE
Road hazard — SMOG
Road lead-in — APIS
Road maneuver — U TURN
Road map abbr. — RTE
Road mishap — WRECK
Road over wet ground — CAUSEWAY
Road repair substance — TAR
Road shoulder — BERM
Road shoulders — WAYSIDE
Road sign — EATS, SLO, STOP
Road surfacing — TAR
Road to conflict — WARPATH
Road to Fairbanks — ALCAN
Road to Rome — ITER
Road vehicle alongside the Po? — TURIN CAR
Road worker — PAVER
Road, to Cicero — ITER
Road-repair substance — TAR
Road-ster? — HOBO
Roads scholar? — HOBO, HIKER
Roadside litter — EYESORES
Roadside sign — MOTEL
Roadside stopover — MOTEL
Roadster — RUNABOUT
Roadway — MACADAM
Roam about — GAD, STROLL
Roanoke Island group — SETTLERS
Roared and raged — THUNDERED
Roared for more — ENCORED
Roaring Twenties, e.g. — ERA

Roast — MEAT
Roast of roaster — PAN
Roast, in Metz — ROTI
Roast, in Reims — ROTI
Roast: Sp. — ASADO
Roasting _____ — EARS
Roasting device — SPIT
Rob of natural vigor — ETIOLATE
Rob or Carl — REINER
Rob Reiner's dad — CARL
Robber's reward — BOOTY
Robbie Burns' "do" — DAE
Robe de _____ (evening dress) — BAL
Robe for a mulier — STOLA
Robe for Cato — TOGA
Robed — VESTED
Robed scythe carrier — FATHER TIME
Robert (pere) or Alan (fils) — ALDA
Robert _____ — E LEE
Robert _____ Sherwood — EMMET
Robert _____ Warren — PENN
Robert and David — FROSTS
Robert Burns' "one" — ANE
Robert Daley best-seller — YEAR OF THE DRAGON
Robert De _____ — NIRO
Robert Frost, for one — POET
Robert Graves novel: 1944 — THE GOLDEN FLEECE
Robert Morse's Capote portrayal — TRU
Robert Nagy is one — TENOR
Robert of "Goodbye Mr. Chips" — DONAT
Robert or Alan — ALDA
Robert or David — FROST
Robert or Elizabeth of politics — DOLE
Robert or Jack — FROST
Robert or Roland — YOUNG
Robert Redford movie, with "The" — STING
Robert Stack role — NESS
Robert the Bruce, e.g. — SCOT
Robert: Var. — BOB
Roberto of boxing — DURAN
Robertson and Evans — DALES
Robeson, for one — BASS
Robin — THRUSH
Robin Cook thriller — COMA
Robin Hood and William Tell — ARCHERS
Robin of song — ADAIR
Robin's companion — BATMAN
Robin's forest? — HOODS WOODS
Robin, traditionally — HERALD
Robinson's middle — ARLINGTON
Robles and wicopies — TREES
Robot Detoo in "Star Wars" — ARTOO
Robot? — METAL WORKER
Robs of vitality — SAPS
Robt _____ — E LEE
Robust — HALE, LUSTY, STURDY
Robust person — HEALTHY
Rochester camera — KODAK
Rochester's Jane — EYRE
Rochet — SMOCK
Rock — CANDY, STONE
Rock attachment — ETTE
Rock bottom — LOWEST, NADIR
Rock cavities — VUGS
Rock drilling tool — BORING ROD
Rock fault angle — HADE
Rock fragments — GRAVEL
Rock group — CREAM, KISS, THE MONKEES
Rock group, for short — STONES
Rock group? — ORES
Rock having roelike grains — OOLITE
Rock lovers — TEENS
Rock musical — HAIR
Rock of _____ — AGES
Rock quartz — CHERT
Rock salt — HALITE
Rock sci. — GEOL
Rock star — MADONNA, PRESLEY
Rock star _____ John — ELTON
Rock star Adam — ANT
Rock star, e.g. — IDOL
Rock star-actor — STING
Rock stars — CHICAGO
Rock stars, with "The" — BEATLES
Rock temple village of India — ELLORA
Rock vocalist Billy — IDOL
Rock's Hendrix — JIMI
Rock's partner — ROLL
Rock-producer Brian — ENO
Rock: Comb. form — LITE
Rockefeller Plaza statue — ATLAS
Rocker — CHAIR
Rocker _____ John — ELTON
Rocker Adam — ANT
Rocker Ant — ADAM
Rocker Clapton — ERIC
Rocker John — ELTON
Rocker Kiki _____ — DEE
Rocker Turner — TINA
Rocket attachment — EER
Rocket cargo — PAYLOAD
Rocket or musket ending — EER
Rocket stage — AGENA
Rocket starter — RETRO
Rocket's route — ORBIT
Rocket, surface to air missile — SAM
Rockfish — GROUPERS, RASHER, RENA
Rockies crest — ARETE
Rockies range — TETON
Rockies watershed — CONTINENTAL DIVIDE
Rocking chair porch — VERANDA
Rocks — SWAYS
Rocky city? — BOULDER COLORADO
Rocky crag — SCAR
Rocky debris — SCREE, TALUS
Rocky hill — TOR
Rocky mountains — GREAT DIVIDE
Rocky outcropping — CRAG
Rocky peak — TOR
Rocky pinnacle — TOR
Rocky projection — CRAG
Rocky rubble — SCREE
Rocky slope — TALUS
Rocky summit — TOR
Rococo — FLORID
Rod — STAFF
Rod adjunct — REEL
Rod attachment — REEL
Rod Carew's weapon — BAT
Rod for curtains — TUBE
Rod Laver contemporary — ASHE
Rod of tennis — LAVER
Rod riders — HOBOS
Rod's partner — REEL
Rode a luge — SLEDDED
Rode a tandem — PEDALED
Rode the waves — SURFED
Rode the wind — KITED
Rodent — VOLE
Rodent relay? — RAT RACE
Rodeo necessity — LASSO
Rodeo performers — BRONCO BUSTERS
Rodeo restraints — ROPES
Rodeo rope — RIATA
Rodeo structure — CHUTE
Rodgers and Hammerstein musical — ALLEGRO
Rodgers and Hammerstein revelry? — CAROUSAL
Rodgers musical partner — HART
Rodgers' "There Is Nothing Like _____!" — A DAME
Rodolfo's love — MIMI
Rodomontade — BUNK, HOT AIR, RANT
Roe holders — SHAD
Roe source — SHAD
Roe v. _____ (historic case) — WADE
Roebuck's partner — SEARS
Roentgen's discovery — XRAY
Roentgenogram — XRAY

Roger _____, star of "Nicholas Nickleby" — REES
Roger Clemens's team — BOSTON RED SOX
Roger Moore TV role — SAINT
Roger of the stage — REES
Roger's follower — WILCO
Rogers and Acuff — ROYS
Rogers and Campanella — ROYS
Rogers' rye? — GINGER BREAD
Roget and Webster? — TWO GOOD FOR WORDS
Rogue — KNAVE
Roguish — ARCH
Roi's spouse — REINE
Roil — STIR UP
Role — FUNCTION, PART
Role for a "sweet young thing" — INGENUE
Role for a diva — AIDA
Role for a Shakespearean — LEAR
Role for Ben Gazzara — CAPONE
Role for E. Zimbalist Jr. — G MAN
Role for Field — RAE
Role for Leslie Caron — LILI
Role for Liz — CLEO
Role for Lord Olivier — LEAR
Role for Orson Welles — KANE
Role for Price — TOSCA
Role for Reeves — KENT
Role for Sharon Gless — ROSIE
Role for Todd or Silverheels — TONTO
Role for Welles — KANE
Role for Zimbalist Jr. — G MAN
Role in "Ariadne auf Naxos" — ECHO
Role in "As You Like It" — CELIA
Role in "Hamlet" — OSRIC
Role in "Henry V" — PISTOL
Role in "King Lear" — ALBANY
Role in "Lohengrin" — ELSA
Role in "The Iceman Cometh" — OBAN
Role in "The Odd Couple" — OSCAR
Role in "The Tempest" — ARIEL
Role in "Uncle Vanya" — SONIA
Role in a Gershwin opus — BESS
Role in Chekhov's "The Three Sisters" — MASHA
Role in Gluck's "Orfeo ed Euridice" — AMOR
Role in old TV series — ANDY
Role player — ACTOR
Roleo gear — AXES
Roles for Karloff — MONSTERS
Roles in "The Godfather" — PADRONI
Roll — CYLINDER, ROSTER, SPOOL
Roll call — ROTA
Roll call reply — HERE
Roll call response — HERE
Roll call responses — NOES
Roll for Arnold Moss — LEAR
Roll of bills — ONES, WAD
Roll of dough — WAD
Roll of money — WAD
Roll of tape — REEL
Roll of wire — COIL
Roll up — FURL
Roll up the hair again — RECURL
Roll used for sandwiches — KAISER
Roll's partner — ROCK
Roll, as a flag — FURL
Roll-call answer — ADSUM
Roll-call reply — HERE
Rolled tea — CHA, TCHA
Roller at Reno — DIE
Rollick — SPORT
Rolling in money — HEELED
Rolling restaurants — DINERS
Rolling stock — TRAINS
Rolling stone — NO MOSS GATHERER, ROVER
Rolling stones lack it — MOSS
Rolls for cream cheese and lox — BAGELS
Rolltops — DESKS
Roma or Milano — CITTA
Roma's best known fountain — TREVI
Roma's country — ITALIA
Roma's land — ITALIA
Romaine — COS
Roman _____ — NUMERAL
Roman 3001 — MMMI
Roman 502 — DII
Roman 52 — LII
Roman and pug, e.g. — NOSES
Roman army elite — PRAETORIAN GUARD
Roman attachment — ESQUE
Roman author — CATO
Roman battering team — ARIES
Roman bigwig — PRAETOR
Roman burial stone — STELA
Roman calendar date — IDES
Roman called "The Censor" — CATO
Roman Cath. title of respect — VEN
Roman Catholic devotion — NOVENA
Roman chambers — ATRIA
Roman cloak — ABOLLA
Roman conspirator — CASCA
Roman courtyards — ATRIA
Roman date — IDES, NONES
Roman day — DIES
Roman deity of crops — CERES
Roman dictator: 82-79 B.C. — SULLA
Roman emperor — NERO, OTHO
Roman emperor of 69 A.D. — OTHO
Roman emperor: A.D. 37 — CALIGULA
Roman fontana — TREVI
Roman garb — STOLA
Roman gathering places — BATHS
Roman god — JANUS, MORS
Roman god of war — MARS
Roman goddess of flowers and spring — FLORA
Roman goddess of hope — SPES
Roman goddess of the harvest — OPS
Roman goddess of war — BELLONA
Roman helmet — GALEA
Roman Hispania Peninsula — IBERIAN
Roman historian — LIVY
Roman holiday — FESTA
Roman household god — LAR
Roman in charge of games — EDILE
Roman landmark — COLOSSEUM
Roman magistrate — EDILE, PRETOR
Roman market-places — FORA
Roman meal — CENA
Roman moralist — CATO
Roman nose — NASUS
Roman official — EDILE
Roman or Christian — ERA
Roman or Hussey — RUTH
Roman patriot — CATO
Roman philosopher — CATO
Roman Pluto — DIS
Roman poet — OVID
Roman poet: A.D. 39-65 — LUCAN
Roman priest — FETIAL
Roman relative — ELITE
Roman road — ITER
Roman robe — STOLA
Roman robes — TOGAS
Roman ruins site in France — ARLES
Roman sacred shield — ANCILE
Roman statesman — CATO, CICERO
Roman times — NONES

Roman trumpets — TUBAE
Roman tyrant — NERO
Roman wall-breaching device — TEREBRA
Roman weapons — JAVELINS
Roman wear — TOGAS
Roman-calendar day — NONES
Roman-fleuve — SAGA
Romance — AFFAIR
Romance lang. — ITAL
Romance language — NEOLATIN
Romancer's offering — SERENADE
Romanian city — IASI
Romanian city and county — ARADS
Romanian coins — LEYS
Romanian monetary unit — LEU
Romans' foes in Britain: fourth century — PICTS
Romantic — EXOTIC, POETIC
Romantic flowers — ROSES
Romantic interlude — IDYL
Romantic isle — CAPRI
Romberg-Gershwin work — ROSALIE
Romberg's "_____ Alone" — ONE
Rome of Hungary — EGER
Rome's _____ of Caracalla — BATHS
Rome's famous fountain — TREVI
Rome's port — OSTIA
Rome's river — TIBER
Rome's Spanish _____ — STEPS
Rome, for one — APPLE
Romeo — GALLANT
Romeo and Juliet — SOUL-MATES
Romeo and Juliet, e.g. — ROLES
Romeo or Juliet — ROLE
Romeo or Regan — ROLE
Romeo's victim — PARIS
Romney Marsh — SHEEP
Romulus, to Remus — TWIN
Ron and Rick — ELYS
Ron Howard role — OPIE
Ron Nessen was one — PRESS SECRETARY
Ron who played Tarzan — ELY
Ron's 1932 good luck piece — SILVER DOLLAR
Roo's mother — KANGA
Rood — CROSS
Roof adjunct — EAVES
Roof beam — RAFTER
Roof edge — EAVE
Roof hanger — EAVE
Roof material — TILES
Roof ornament — EPI
Roof over one's head — PAD
Roof overhang — EAVES
Roof part — EAVE, SHINGLE
Roof projections — EAVES
Roof section — EAVE
Roof supports — RAFTERS
Roof topping — SLATE
Roof unit — TILE
Roof window — DORMER
Roof worker — TILER
Roof: Fr. — TOIT
Roofed porch — VERANDA
Roofer — SLATER
Roofing choice — SHINGLES
Roofing feature — EAVE
Roofing material — SLATE
Roofing slate — RAG
Roofing sounds — RAHS
Roofing tool — ADZE
Roofing workers — SLATERS
Roofless rooms — ATRIA
Rooftop feature — VANE
Rooftop sight — AERIAL
Rook (old world) — BIRD
Rookie — TYRO
Rookies' superiors — SARGES
Room — SPACE
Room appointments — DECOR
Room finisher — ETTE
Room for action — LEEWAY
Room for jugs and linens — EWERY
Room in a casa — SALA
Room in a chateau — SALLE
Room in a harem — ODA
Room in a maison — SALLE
Room on board — CABIN
Room recess — ALCOVE
Room styling — DECOR
Room's partner — BOARD
Room, at the hacienda — SALA
Room, in Rheims — SALLE
Room: Fr. — SALLE
Rooms in Lugo — SALAS
Rooms to _____ — LET
Roomy cars — SEDANS
Roomy dress style — TENT
Roomy film of 1967? — HOTEL
Rooney and Hardy — ANDYS
Rooney of "Sixty Minutes" — ANDY
Rooney role — ANDY HARDY
Roosevelt and Teasdale — SARAS
Roosevelt belonged to it — DEMOCRATIC PARTY
Roosevelt biographer Joseph P. — LASH
Roosevelt coin — DIME
Roosevelt's father (FDR) — JAMES
Rooster — BANTAM
Rooster feature — COMB
Root — ELIHU
Root or Yale — ELIHU
Root used as a cleanser in Mexico — AMOLE
Root vegetable — BEET
Root word — ETYMON
Rooted on — EGGED
Rooter — FAN
Rooter for the Buffalos and Rams — COLORADAN
Rooter's outcry — HOORAY, OLE, RAH
Rooter's shout — RAH
Rooter, often — SHOUTER
Rootless plant — ALGA
Rootlessness — ANOMY
Rope — RIATA, STRAND
Rope fiber — ABACA, BAST, HEMP
Rope in — DUPE
Rope ladder with rigid rungs — JACOBS
Rope or scope — TETHER
Roped — LASSOED
Roping device — RIATA
Roping gear — LARIAT
Roquefort — CHEESE
Rorem — NED
Rorem and others — NEDS
Rorem or Sparks — NED
Roric — DEWEY
Rorschach picture — BLOT
Rorschach, etc. — TESTS
Rorschach, for one — TEST
Rory _____ — OMORE
Rosaceous plant — AVENS
Rosalind Russell role — MAME
Rosary bead — AVE
Rosary unit — BEAD
Roscoe — GAT
Roscoe Coltrane's deputy — ENOS
Roscoe of the silents — ATES
Roscoe, the comedian — ATES
Roscoes — GATS
Rose — FLOWER, GARDEN, STOOD
Rose _____ — HIPS
Rose _____: Wine — DANJOU
Rose and Rozelle — PETES
Rose bowl — VASE
Rose Bowl Parade, e.g. — EVENT
Rose Bowl site — PASADENA
Rose Bowl, e.g. — OVAL
Rose Bowl, et al. — OVALS
Rose counterpart, in song — TULIP
Rose essence — ATTAR
Rose feature — THORN
Rose fragrance — ATTAR
Rose holders — VASES
Rose lover — ABIE
Rose of _____ — SHARON
Rose oils — ATTARS
Rose or nomad — RAMBLER
Rose or snake items — HIPS
Rose petal essence — ATTAR

Rose petal oil — ATTAR
Rose red spinel — BALAS RUBY
Rose's beloved — ABIE
Rose's man — ABIE
Rose, for one — PETE
Rose-lover — ABIE
Rose-red — ROSY
Rose: Comb. form — RHODO
Rosebud, e.g. — SLED
Rosemary and angelica — HERBS
Rosemary, for one — HERB
Rosette — BADGE, ORNAMENT
Rosewall of tennis, et al. — KENS
Rosey of football and TV — GRIER
Rosie's fastener — RIVET
Rosie-faced doll with a topknot — KEWPIE
Rosinante or Traveller — STEED
Ross and Barents — SEAS
Ross and Macduff — THANES
Ross and Palmer — BETSYS
Ross or Andaman — SEA
Ross or Gordon — CLAN
Ross or Rigg — DIANA
Ross Sea sight — ICEBERG
Rossellini epic film: 1946 — OPEN CITY
Rossetti's "_____ Beatrix" — BEATA
Rossetti's "Who _____ the Wind?" — HAS SEEN
Rossini opera, with "The" — THIEVING MAGPIE
Rossini or Verdi — ITALIAN
Rossini's "Count _____" — ORY
Rostand character — CYRANO
Rosten's Kaplan — HYMAN
Roster — LIST, ROTA
Rostropovich's instrument — CELLO
Rostrum — BEAK, DAIS
Rosy — PINK
Rot — DECAY, SPOIL
Rot-resistant wood — ALDER
Rota — ROSTER
Rotary-wing aircraft, for short — GIROS
Rotate — TURN
Rotate the camera — PAN
Rotating part — CAM
Rotating pieces — CAMS
Rotisserie feature — SPIT
Rotisserie part — SPIT
Rotten — LOUSY
Rotten Row figure — HORSEMAN, RIDER
Rotter — CAD, HEEL
Rotund — OBESE
Rouen relative — TANTE
Rouen roof — TOIT
Rouen room — SALLE
Rouen rooms — CHAMBRES
Rouen's river — SEINE
Roues — CADS
Rough — COARSE
Rough handler — PAWER
Rough it — CAMP
Rough rugs — SHAGS
Rough situation — LIE
Rough sketch — DRAFT
Rough spot — SCUFF
Rough time for Caesar — IDES
Rough's partner — READY
Roughage fanatics? — BRAN FLAKES
Roughen — CHAP
Roughly — OR SO
Roughrider, e.g. — TAMER
Roughvoiced — HOARSE
Roulette bet — CARRE, NOIR, ROUGE
Roulette color — NOIR, RED
Roumania's first capital — IASI
Roumanian coin — LEU
Round — ORBED
Round cheese — EDAM
Round clam — QUAHOG
Round dance — HORA, POLKA
Round figures — ORBS
Round hand script — RONDE
Round of applause — HAND
Round of cheers — SALVO
Round of duty — WATCH
Round of golf starts here — TEE
Round Table knight — LANCELOT
Round Table member — KNIGHT
Round Table title — SIR
Round up — CORRAL, HERD
Round-up abbr. — ETAL
Roundabout ways — DETOURS
Rounded lump — GLOB
Rounded molding — OVOLO
Rounded ornament — KNOP
Rounded parts — LOBES
Rounders — WASTRELS
Roundish — OVAL
Rounds of play — LAPS
Roundup — RODEO
Rouse — AWAKEN, PROD, STIR
Rouse into activity — ENERGIZE
Rouse to action — PROD
Rouser — ALARM
Rousseau classic — EMILE
Rousseau hero — EMILE
Route — PATH, ROAD
Route or road — WAY
Routine — CUT AND DRIED, ROTE
Routine condition — NORMALCY
Routine in tropical lands — SIESTA
Routine question — WHOS ON FIRST
Routines — ROTES
Rove — DRIFT, GAD, ROAM, STRAY
Rove on the wing — FLIT
Roved — WANDERED
Rover — GAD ABOUT, GOER
Rover and Fido — PETS
Rover's restraint — LEASH
Row — LINE, OAR, QUEUE, SCRAP, SPAT, TIER
Rowan tree — SORB
Rowboat feature — OARLOCK
Rowboat fulcrum — OARLOCK
Rowboat users — OARERS
Rowdy — LOUD, TOUGH, UNRULY
Rowdy free-for-all — MELEE
Rowdy group — GANG
Rowdy one — YAHOO
Rowdydow — TO DO
Rowe of Tiger fame — SCHOOLBOY
Rower — OAR
Rower's need — OAR
Rower's rig — SHELL
Rowers — OARSMEN
Rowing companions — CREW
Rowing shell — QUADRUPLE SCULL
Rows — LINES, SPATS, TIERS
Rows of seats — TIERS
Roxanne's lover — CYRANO
Roy Crane's captain — EASY
Roy Orbison hit: 1963 — IN DREAMS
Roy Rogers' horse — TRIGGER
Roy Scherer Jr. — ROCK HUDSON
Roy, the country musician — ACUFF
Royal — KINGLY, NOBLE, REGAL
Royal abbr. — HRH
Royal administrations — RULES
Royal circlet — TIARA
Royal domain — REALM
Royal fur — ERMINE
Royal headdress — DIADEM
Royal headware — TIARA
Royal house — TUDOR
Royal house: 1399-1461 — LANCASTER
Royal letters — HSH
Royal lover of yesteryear (female) — WALLIS

Royal lover of yesteryear (male) — EDWARD
Royal messenger — HERALD
Royal name in England — EDWARD
Royal name in Norway — OLAV
Royal or Windsor — BLUE
Royal owner of fabled Greek stables — AUGEAS
Royal rock snake — PYTHON
Royal ruins? — OEDIPUS WRECKS
Royal symbols — ORBS
Royal trimming — QUEEN ANNES LACE
Royce subject — LOYALTY
RPM part — REVS
RR depot — STA, STN
RR notice — ARR
RR stops — STAS, STNS
RR terminal — STA
RR timetable — SCHED
RRs of a kind — ELS
RSV's predecessor — ASV
Rte. choice — ENE
Ruark's "Poor _____" — NO MORE
Rub — BUFF, KNEAD, MASSAGE, POLISH
Rub off — ABRADE, ERASE
Rub out — DO IN, ERASE
Rub painfully — CHAFE
Rub smooth — SAND
Rub the wrong way — CHAFE
Rub with oil — ANOINT
Rub, Scot. style — DIGHT
Rubaiyat poet — OMAR
Rubbed out, gangster style — ICED
Rubbed with rubber — ERASED
Rubber port of N Brazil — MANAUS
Rubber preceder — LATEX
Rubber source — LATEX
Rubber stamp — ENDORSEMENT, PAID
Rubber tree — ULE
Rubber tube — HOSE
Rubberneck — GAWK, STARE
Rubbernecks — PEERS, STARES
Rubbing oil: Abbr. — LIN
Rubbish pile — DUST HEAP
Rubbish! — BAH, TRASH, TRIPE
Rubella — GERMAN MEASLES
Rubeola — MEASLES
Rubicund — RED
Rubik namesakes — CUBES
Rubik of the cube craze — ERNO
Rubik's cube — PUZZLE
Rubik's gadget — CUBE
Ruble unit — KOPECK
Rubric — RULE
Rubs the wrong way — RILES
Ruby and family — DEES
Ruby and Sandra — DEES
Ruby of the Silver Screen — KEELER
Ruby or Frances — DEE
Ruby Spinel — BALAS
Ruby, Sandra and 3 British rivers — DEES
Rucksack — BACKPACK
Ruckus — ROW, TO DO
Ruction — ROW
Ruddy — BURNT
Rude — BOORISH
Rude awakening — DISILLUSIONMENT
Rude one — BOOR
Rudimentary — BASAL
Rudiments — ABC
Rudolph — VALENTINO
Rudolph's asset — RED NOSE
Rudolph's high beam — NOSE
Rue — REGRET
Rue _____ Paix — DE LA
Rue and Betty's partner — BEA
Rue de la _____ — PAIX
Rue Morgue murderer — APE
Rue the day — REGRET
Rue, for example — HERB
Rueful — REPENTANT
Rueful remark — ALAS
Ruff's relation — REE
Ruffed — PIQUED
Ruffian — BULLY, BRUTE, THUG, TOUGH
Ruffle — FRILL, ROIL
Ruffled pride — PIQUE
Rug — CARPET, COVERLET, WIG
Rug for royalty — RED CARPET
Rug surface — PILE
Rugby term — RUCK
Rugby's river — AVON
Rugged fellows — HE MEN
Rugged ridge — ARETE
Rugged rock — CRAG
Rugged rocky eminence — CRAG
Rugged runabouts — JEEPS
Ruhr city — ESSEN
Ruhr metropolis — ESSEN
Ruhr rejection — NEIN
Ruhr river — EDER
Ruhr row — REH
Ruhr Valley city — ESSEN
Ruin — DOWNFALL, UNDO
Ruin's companion — WRACK
Ruin's partner — WRACK
Ruined — SPOILT, UNDONE
Ruins — DESTROYS, DOES IN
Ruisdael's occupation — PAINTER
Rule — CONTROL, DICTATE, EDICT, GOVERN, POLICY
Rule in old Bombay — RAJ
Rule of thumb — GUIDE
Rule out — EXCLUDE
Rule, for short — REG
Rule, in India — RAJ
Ruled — LINED
Ruler — DYNAST, TSAR
Ruler at Versailles, once — ROI
Ruler in Persia — SATRAP
Ruler in the East — EMIR
Ruler marking — INCH
Ruler mixed up in arts — TSAR
Ruler of Asgard — ODIN
Ruler of the underworld — HADES
Ruler who acted as barber — IVAN THE TERRIBLE
Ruler who fled: Jan. 16, 1979 — SHAH
Ruler, circa 1917 — TSAR
Ruler, in Africa — AMIR
Ruler, in Cadiz — REY
Ruler: Abbr. — EMP
Rulers — EMPERORS
Rulers whose day is done — DEYS
Rules — REIGNS
Rules authority — HOYLE
Rules expert — PARLIAMENTARIAN
Rules of right living — LAWS
Rules to follow — DOS
Ruling group — JUNTA
Rum cake — BABA
Rum or window — BAY
Rum-runner — SMUGGLER
Rum-soaked cake — BABA
Ruman of films — SIG
Rumanian city — BACAU
Rumanian coin — LEU
Rumer _____, pseudonym of British novelist — GODDEN
Ruminant — CAMEL, COW, DEER, SHEEP
Rummages about — ROUTS
Rummy — CARD GAME
Rumor — GOSSIP, HEARSAY
Rumor in Montmarte — ONDIT
Rumor mill — GRAPEVINE
Rumor spreader — ALARMIST
Rumpelteazer's creator — ELIOT
Rumple — MUSS
Rumpled — TOUSLED
Rumpus — ADO
Rumpus room, briefly — REC
Rumpuses — TODOS
Run-of-the-mill porters? — STANDARD BEARERS
Run-off deposits — SILTS
Run — CANTER, MOVE, OPERATE, TROT
Run _____ of (hit a snag) — AFOUL

Run a tab — OWE
Run after — PURSUE
Run all-out — DASH
Run away — ELOPE, FLEE
Run away fast — FLEE
Run before a gale — SCUD
Run before the wind — SCUD
Run circles around — OUTDO
Run down — SEEDY
Run for office — STAND
Run in — ARREST
Run in neutral gear — IDLE
Run in the wash — BLEED
Run its course — ELAPSES
Run like a cloud in the wind — SCUD
Run of luck — STREAK
Run off — ELOPE, FLEE, PRINT
Run off together — ELOPE
Run out — ELAPSE, EXPIRE
Run out of gas — TIRE
Run producer — SNAG
Run rife — OVERGROW
Run rings around — OUT DO
Run short — LACK
Run swiftly — SCOOT
Run the show — MANAGE
Run-in — ROW, SPAT
Run-of-the-mill — ORDINARY
Run-of-the-mill work — POTBOILER
Run-off — OVERFLOW
Runabouts — AUTOS
Runagates — HOBOES
Runaway — DESERT
Rundle — STEP
Rundown — SEEDY, TIRED
Rung — BAR, RAIL, SPOKE, STEP
Runner — NOMINEE, SCOUT
Runner of a sort — PACER
Runner on a plant — STOLON
Runner Sebastian and family — COES
Runner up — ALSO RAN
Runner's sport — TRACK
Running mate — HORSE
Running wild — A RIOT, ON A TEAR
Runs — FLOWS
Runs amok — RIOTS
Runs in neutral — IDLES
Runs of good luck — STREAKS
Runs out of gas — TIRES
Runs, in a way — BLEEDS
Runtish — PUNY
Runway — STRIP
Runyon's $100 — C NOTE
Rupert's meal maker — BROOKES COOK
Rupture — BREAK, CRACK, SPLIT
Ruptures — RENTS
Rural — COUNTRY, RUSTIC, SYLVAN
Rural apothecary? — FARMACIST
Rural area — COUNTRYSIDE
Rural baseball field — SANDLOT
Rural byway — LANE
Rural crossing — STILE
Rural dance site — BARN
Rural dwelling — LODGE
Rural events — FAIRS
Rural kin of aves — LNS
Rural location — FARM
Rural road — LANE
Rural Roman god — FAUN
Rural routes — LANES
Rural sights — BARNS
Rural sound — BAAING
Rural sound effect — MOO
Rural stopover — INN
Rural way — LANE
Ruse — DECEIT, FEINT, PLOY
Rush — DASH, HURRY, RACE, SPATE
Rush of wind — BIRR
Rush the quarterback — BLITZ
Rush wildly — CAREER
Rush-hour rarities on buses — SEATS
Rush; charge — LUNGE
Rushes — HURLS
Rushes headlong — RIPS
Russ. drink — KVASS
Russ. grasslands — STEPPES
Russ. news agency — TASS
Russ. plane — MIG
Russ. sea — ARAL
Russell and Frederic's trek — LONG MARCH
Russell role — MAME
Russet colored — BROWNISH
Russia — USSR
Russian beer — KVASS
Russian C.I.A. — KGB
Russian city — OREL
Russian co-op — ARTEL
Russian collective — ARTEL
Russian cooperative — ARTEL
Russian despot — TSAR
Russian dry measure — LOF
Russian equivalent of John — IVAN
Russian expanse — SIBERIA
Russian fare — BLACK BREAD
Russian fighter plane — MIG
Russian hemp — RINE
Russian inland sea — ARAL
Russian islands — KURILS
Russian monarch — TSAR
Russian mystic — RASPUTIN
Russian negative — NYET
Russian nobleman — BOYAR
Russian pancake — BLIN
Russian peninsula — CRIMEA
Russian pianist _____ Gabrillowitsch — OSSIP
Russian pianist Gilels — EMIL
Russian planes — MIGS
Russian press org. — TASS
Russian range — ALAI, URALS
Russian refusal — NYET
Russian river — DESNA, URAL
Russian ruler — TSAR
Russian satellite — SPUTNIK
Russian sea — ARAL, AZOV
Russian statesman: 1849-1915 — WITTE
Russian summer home — DACHA
Russian symbol — RED STAR
Russian tenor Vladmir — POPOV
Russian urn — SAMOVAR
Russian villa — DACHA
Russian village — MIR
Russian, to a Russian — COMRADE
Russian-born American violinist — HEIFETZ
Russian/Lithuanian river — NEMAN
Rust — ERODE
Rusted away — EATEN
Rustic — HOMESPUN, MOSS-BACK, PEASANT
Rustic hideaway — CABIN
Rustic path — LANE
Rustic retreat — CABIN
Rustic road — LANE
Rustic way — LANE
Rustle — STIR
Rustlers take — CATTLE
Rusty — EATEN, ERODED
Rusty-gate sound — SCROOP
Rut; habit — GROOVE
Rutabaga — TURNIP
Ruth Etting favorite — TEN CENTS A DANCE
Ruth of song — ETTING
Ruth's "sultanate" — SWAT
Ruth's mother-in-law — NAOMI
Ruth's nickname — BABE
Ruth's realm? — SWAT
Ruth's second husband — BOAZ
Ruth, to Naomi — DAUGHTER IN LAW
Ruthian clout — SWAT
Ruthless Russian czar — IVAN
Ruy Diaz de Bivar — EL CID
Ryan and Tatum — ONEALS
Ryan of Hollywood — ONEAL
Ryan or Tatum — ONEAL
Ryan's "Love Story" co-star — ALI
Ryan's daughter — TATUM
Rye bread — AWN
Rye fungus — ERGOT
Rye grass — DARNEL
Rye or wheat — BREAD
Ryuku pit viper — HABU

S

S African fox — ASSE
S Kirgiz, USSR town — OSH
S Orange, N.J. university — SHU
S Philippine island — MINDANAO
S Scottish river — ESK
S-curve — OGEE
S-shaped curves — OGEES
S-shaped decorative curves — OGEES
S-shaped molding — OGEE
S. Africa's _____ Paul Kruger — OOM
S. African town — STAD
S. American rodent — PACA
S. Korea — ROK
S. Korean president: 1948-60 — RHEE
S. Korean soldiers — ROKS
S. Vietnam's Dinh Diem — NGO
S.A. border river — PLATA
S.A. country — ECUA, VENEZ
S.A. land — URU
S.A. port, for short — RIO
S.A. rodent — PACA
S.A. snake — ABOMA
S.A. sorrels — OCAS
S.A.T.'s — EXAMS
S.D. neighbor — NEB
S.E.C. member — ALA
SA resort, for short — RIO
Saar _____, German territory — BASIN
Saarinen — EERO
Saarinen and namesakes — EEROS
Saarinen, the architect — EERO
Saber rattling — JINGOISM
Saber rattling — THREAT
Sabers' less lethal kin — EPEES
Sabin colleague — SALK
Sable — BLACK
Sabot's sound — CLOP
Sabotage — HARM
Sabots' kin — CLOGS
Sabra — ISRAELI
Sabra's lively dance — HORA
Sabra's name — RIVA
Sac — BURSA, CYST
Sac or city once sacked by Tatars — BURSA
Saccharine — SWEET
Sacher _____ — TORTE
Sacher or Linzer — TORTE
Sachet scent — LAVENDER
Sack out — RETIRE
Sackcloth — BURLAP
Sackcloth's partner — ASHES
Sacks — BAGS, FIRES
Sacrament — TROTH
Sacramento's neighbor — LODI
Sacred — HIERO, HOLY
Sacred and not to be mentioned — TABOO
Sacred article — ICON
Sacred bird — IBIS
Sacred bull — APIS
Sacred bull of Egypt — APIS
Sacred bull, to Ramses — APIS
Sacred choral compositions — MOTETS
Sacred choral piece — MOTET
Sacred Hindu writings — VEDA
Sacred hymn — PSALM
Sacred image — ICON, IDOL, IKON
Sacred Nile bird — IBIS
Sacred pictures — ICONS
Sacred place — SHRINE
Sacred song — PSALM
Sacred statues: Var. — IKONS
Sacred symbol in the land of Ra — ANKH
Sacred-cow — SAFE
Sacred: Comb. form — HIERO
Sacrifice play — BUNT
Sacrilegious conditions — DESECRATIONS
Sacro addendum — ILIAC
Sacrosanct — SECURE
Sad — WOEFUL
Sad and dreary — BLEAK
Sad notice — OBIT
Sad or ill-humored — GLUM
Sad poem — ELEGY
Sad Sack's WAC girlfriend — SADIE
Sad-eyed hound — BASSET
Sadat — ANWAR
Sadat's country — EGYPT
Sadat's namesakes — ANWARS
Sadat's predecessor — NASSER
Sadder but _____ — WISER
Saddle — RIDGE
Saddle blankets, slangy style — PANCAKES
Saddle for a second rider — PILLION
Saddle horse — MORGAN
Saddle on an elephant's back — HOWDAH
Saddle strap — GIRTH
Saddle straps, in the West — LATIGOES
Saddled Silver? — WHITE HORSE
Saddlers' products — REINS
Sadie of "Rain" — THOMPSON
Sadie's opposite number — SOL
Sadness — DOLOR
Sadr or Salm — STAR
Sadware alloy — PEWTER
Safe — VAULT
Safe and sound — UNHURT
Safe from sweet talk? — OUT OF CHARMS WAY
Safe harbors — HAVENS
Safe havens — NESTS
Safe place — HAVEN
Safe preceder — FAIL
Safe-conduct — PASS
Safecracker — YEGG
Safeguard — ENSURE
Safekeeping: Abbr. — STGE
Safest option — BEST BET
Safety — REFUGE
Safety device — FIRE EXTINGUISHER
Safety device — SMOKE DETECTOR
Safety devices — CIRCUIT BREAKERS
Safety precaution — BULLET PROOF VEST
Safety precaution — BULLET PROOFING
Saffron — DYE, SANDY
Saffron's origin — EGYPT
Saffron's use — ROLLS
Sag — DROOP, WILT
Saga? — GLORY STORY
Sagacious — ASTUTE, WISE
Sagacious saltine? — WISE CRACKER
Sagacity — BRAINS
Sagan and Reiner — CARL
Sage — SEER
Sage and savory — SPICES
Sage and thyme — MINTS
Sage of Greek myth — NESTOR
Sagebrush State: Abbr. — NEV
Sages — MAGI
Sagging — SLACK
Sagittarius — ARCHER
Sagittarius symbol — ARCHER
Sagittarius weapon — BOW
Sahara filling station — OASIS
Sahara sections — ERGS
Sahara sites — OASES
Sahara steed — CAMEL
Sahara wanderer — NOMAD
Sahara's soil — SAND
Saharan — ARID
Saharan people — NOMAD

Saharan sights — SANDS
Saharan stopover — OASIS
Saharan transport — CAMEL
Sahib is one — TITLE
Sahl from Montreal — MORT
Said — UTTERED
Said it was so — ASSERTED
Sail — CANVAS
Sail insert — GORE
Sail on water — NAVIGATE
Sail stiffener — BATTEN
Sail support — MAST, SPAR
Sailboat — SLOOP
Sailboat part — CANVAS
Sailboat rope — SHEET
Sailing — ASEA
Sailing companion — SHIPMATE
Sailing equipment — GEAR
Sailing problem — CALM
Sailing ship — BRIG
Sailing straight into a gale — IN THE WINDS EYE
Sailing vessel — KETCH, SLOOP
Sailing word — ALEE
Sailor — GOB, SEAMAN, TAR
Sailor from the East Indies — LASCAR
Sailor's bag — DITTY, SEA
Sailor's boulevard? — FLEET STREET
Sailor's chanty — SONG
Sailor's coat — REEFER
Sailor's direction — ALEE, LEEWARD
Sailor's free time — LIBERTY
Sailor's jumper — BLOUSE
Sailor's location — ABEAM
Sailor's patron saint — ELMO
Sailor's rating — ABLE
Sailor's rope — TYE
Sailor's saint — ELMO
Sailor's stir — BRIG
Sailor's stop — AVAST
Sailor's vacation — LEAVE
Sailor, e.g. — HAT
Sailor, to some — TAR
Sailors — TARS
Sailors' saint — ELMO
Sailplane — GLIDER
Saint _____ Aquinas — THOMAS
Saint _____, Arles neighbor — REMY
Saint _____, France — REMY
Saint Anthony's pig — RUNT
Saint Elmo's fire — CORONA
Saint Francis birthplace — ASSISI
Saint George saved — SABRA
Saint of Avila — TERESA
Saint of Jan. 21 — AGNES
Saint of sailors — ELMO
Saint Paul's architect — WREN
Saint Paul's birthplace — TARSUS
Saint Phillip _____ — NERI
Saint Vincent Island group — GRENADINES
Saint-_____ French port — MALO
Saint-_____, Fr. — MALO
Saint-Saëns's "_____ Macabre" — DANSE
Sainted bishop of France — REMY
Sainted mother of Constantine — HELENA
Sainted woman — BEATA
Saintly light — HALO
Saintly symbols — HALOS
Saison — ETE
Saison chaude — ETE
Saison in the sun — ETE
Sake source — RICE
Saki — MUNRO
Saki and family — MUNROS
Saki's real name — MUNRO
Sal _____, town of the Cape Verde Islands — REI
Sal of song — GAL
Sal, e.g. — GAL
Salaam preliminaries — DAR ES
Salaams — BOWS
Salacious — LEWD
Salacious look — LEER
Salacious stare — LEER
Salacity — PRURIENCE
Salad — SLAW
Salad and hotel — WALDORFS
Salad bar item — SLAW
Salad days — YOUTH
Salad dressing — RUSSIAN
Salad garnish — OLIVE
Salad green — ENDIVE
Salad herb — BORAGE, ENDIVE
Salad ingredient — CRESS, EGG, ENDIVE
Salad ingredient — RADISH, TUNA
Salad serving — SLAW
Salad topping —DRESSING
Salad veggie — CUKE
Salad years — TEENS
Salad, to disdainers — RABBIT FOOD
Saladin subject — SARACEN
Salamander — EFT, NEWT
Salamanders — TRITONS
Salami emporium — DELI
Salamis — SAUSAGES
Salary — NET, STIPEND, WAGE
Salary at fixed rate — FEE
Salary plus — PERKS
Sale abbreviation — IRR
Sale caveat — AS IS
Sale condition — AS IS
Sale labels — TAGS
Sale merchandise — AS IS
Sale reckoning — BILL
Sale reduction — DISCOUNT
Sale sign — AS IS
Sale tag warning — AS IS
Sales agt. — REP
Sales gimmick — REBATE
Sales incentive — REBATE
Sales slips — RECEIPTS
Sales techniques, for short — DEMOS
Sales transaction — TRADE IN
Salesman — CLERK
Salesman of a sort — PEDDLER
Salesman's assigned area: Abbr. — TERR
Salesman's car, frequently — DEMO
Salesman's delight — REORDER
Salesman's due — COMMISSION
Salesman's pitch — SPIEL
Salesperson — CLERK
Salient — BOUNDING
Salieri, to Mozart — RIVAL
Salina — LAKE
Saline drop — TEAR
Salinger girl — ESME
Salinger heroine — ESME
Salivate, in a way — DROOL
Salk contemporary — SABIN
Salk's subject — POLIO
Sallies — RETORTS
Sally — CHARGE, RAID
Sally _____ cake — LUNN
Sally of "All in the Family" — STRUTHERS
Sally of space — RIDE
Sally Rand specialty — FAN DANCE
Salmagundi — HASH, OLIO
Salminen of the Met — MATTI
Salmon family fish — TROUT
Salmon or Chevy — CHASE
Salome had seven — VEILS
Salome's septet — VEILS
Salome's stepfather — HEROD
Salon offering — RINSE
Salon treatment — RINSE
Salon treatment, for short — PERM
Saloon staple — ALE
Saloon swinger — DOOR
Saloonkeeper's nemesis — NATION
Saloons — BARROOMS
Salsify — OYSTER PLANT
Salt-water food fish — SAUREL
Salt — SPICE, TAR
Salt away — STASH
Salt basins of the desert — DRY LAKES
Salt Lake City athlete — UTE
Salt Lake City eleven — TRES
Salt Lake City player — UTE
Salt Lake City team — UTES
Salt Lake in Palestine — DEAD SEA
Salt lake of Asia — ARAL

Salt of a fatty acid — OLEATE
Salt of a fruit acid — CITRATE
Salt of nitric acid — NITRATE
Salt or smoke — CURE
Salt pit — VAT
Salt tree — ATLE, ATLEE
Salt water — BRINE
Salt's salute — AHOY
Salt's swig — GROG
Salt, in Nice — SEL
Salt, in Paris — SEL
Saltation — LEAP
Saltmaker of sorts — EARNER
Salton and Sargasso — SEAS
Saltpeter — NITER
Salts — TARS
Salts or Downs — EPSOM
Salty drop — TEAR
Salty solution — BRINE, SALINE
Salutation of a sort — SIRS
Salutation of a sort, for short — HELLO
Salutation to a señor — HOLA
Salutations — AVES
Salute — HAIL, SALVO
Salute a patriot? — HALE NATHAN
Salute from Caesar — AVE
Saluted — GREETED
Saluted warmly — KISSED
Salvador _____ — DALI
Salvador from Spain — DALI
Salvador or Gabriel — SAN
Salvador, the painter — DALI
Salvage — SAVE
Salvage an old shoe — RESOLE
Salvages — RECLAIMS
Salvation Army founder — BOOTH
Salve — BALM
Salver — TRAY
Salvers — TRAYS
Salvo — SALUTE
Sam and Tom — UNCLES
Sam and Vanya — UNCLES
Sam Jaffe's "Lost Horizon" role — LAMA
Sam of the links — SNEAD
Sam, from "Casablanca" — DOOLEY
Sam, Toby or Tom — UNCLE
Samara feature — ALA
Sambar — DEER
Sambar deer — MAHA
Sambar, e.g. — DEER
Same — ALIKE, DITTO
Same old stuff — NOTHING NEW UNDER THE SUN
Same, in Savoie — EGAL
Same, to Pierre — EGAL
Same: pref. — TAUTO
Samlet; skegger — PARR
Sammy Baugh's position — QUARTERBACK
Sammy Cahn creation — LYRIC
Sammy Davis hit song — THIS IS MY BELOVED
Sammy Davis Jr.'s autobiography — YES I CAN
Sammy of song — CAHN
Sammy or Danny — KAYE
Sammy or Geena — DAVIS
Samoa-oriented anthropologist — MEAD
Samoan capital — APIA
Samoan drink — AVA
Samoan island — UPOLU
Samoan port — APIA
Samovar — URN
Samovars — URNS
Sampan — SKIFF
Sample — SIP, TASTE
Sample again — RETASTE
Sample disc — DEMO
Sample record — DEMO
Sample the fare — TASTE
Sample the food — TASTE
Sample trial — TEST
Sample TV fare — PILOT
Sample: Abbr. — SPEC
Sampled — TASTED
Sampler — MODEL
Sampras of the courts — PETE
Samsun's water — BLACK SEA
Samuel _____, utilities magnate — INSULL
Samuel Finley Breese _____ — MORSE
Samuel's mentor — ELI
Samuel's teacher — ELI
Samurai — BUSHI
San _____ — JOSE
San _____ fault, California — ANDREAS
San _____ Obispo — LUIS
San _____, CA — DIEGO
San _____, CA — MATEO
San _____, Italian resort — REMO
San _____, Texas — ANGELO
San _____: Italian port — REMO
San Andreas, for one — FAULT
San Antonio cagers — SPURS
San Antonio landmark — ALAMO
San Antonio mission — ALAMO
San Antonio shrine — ALAMO
San Antonio team — SPURS
San Antonio trademark — ALAMO
San Diego nine — PADRES
San Diego suburb — LA MESA
San Diego team member — PADRE
San Diego wives, perhaps — MADRES
San Francisco athlete — GIANT
San Francisco Bay denizen — SEAL
San Francisco hill — NOB
San Francisco player — GIANT
San Francisco transportation — CABLE CAR
San Francisco's _____ bridge — GOLDEN GATE
San Francisco's 49_____ — ERS
San Jose-to-Reno dir. — NNE
San Juan of musicals — OLGA
San Luis _____ — REY
San or Don — JUAN
San Rafael's county — MARIN
Sanctified — BLESSED
Sanctified — BLEST
Sanctify — BLESS
Sanction — APPROVAL, FIAT
Sanctioned — LICIT
Sanctions — ALLOWS
Sanctuaries — ASYLA, REFUGES
Sanctuary — SHRINE
Sanctum — HAVEN, STUDY
Sanctum or circle — INNER
Sanctum preceder — INNER
Sand — SPECK
Sand bars — SHOALS
Sand box occupant — TOT
Sand dab — FISH
Sand hill — DUNE
Sand hill, in Devon — DENE
Sand ridge — REEF
Sand to Chopin — AMIE
Sand's "Elle et _____" — LUI
Sand-trap shots — BLASTS
Sandal — CLOG
Sandal feature — STRAP
Sandal strap — THONG
Sandalwood — TREE
Sandarac, e.g. — RESIN
Sandarac, for one — TREE
Sandbag — BALLAST
Sandbank — REEF, SHOAL
Sandbars — SHOALS
Sandblaster's target — GRIME
Sandbox "treats" — MUDPIES
Sandburg or Reiner — CARL
Sandburg or Sagan — CARL
Sandburg's "bucket of ashes" — PAST
Sanded down — ABRADED
Sandford actor — FOXX
Sandhurst's American counter-part — WEST POINT
Sandlot game — ONE A CAT
Sandpaper — ABRADE
Sandpipers — REES
Sandpipers' kin — TERNS
Sandra _____ O'Connor — DAY
Sandra and Bobby — DEES
Sandra and Ruby — DEES
Sandra of Hollywood — DEE
Sandwich board usage — ADS
Sandwich favorite — TUNA
Sandwich for a big eater — HERO

Sandwich letters — BLT
Sandwich meat — SALAMI
Sandwich of a sort, for short — BLT
Sandwich wrapper — SARAN
Sandy — ARENOSE
Sandy Dennis stage vehicle — ANY WEDNESDAY
Sandy hill, in Devon — DENE
Sandy ridge — ESKER
Sandy tracts in England — DENES
Sandy's caps — BEANIES
Sandy's mistress — ANNIE
Sandy's negative — NAE
Sandy's only word — ARF
Sandy's owner — ANNIE
Sandy's sound — ARF
Sandy's sounds — ARFS
Sandy's two cents — ARF
Sandy's uncle — EME
Sane — SOUND
Sang at the station — RATTED
Sang the blues — MOANED
Sang-froid — POISE
Sanguine — HAPPY, ROSY
Sanitary — CLEAN
Sans vitesse — POKILY
Sanskrit or Hindi — INDIC
Sant, to Chopin — AMIE
Santa _____ — ANITA
Santa _____ — CLARA
Santa _____, CA — ROSA
Santa _____, Calif. — ANA
Santa _____, town in S Puerto Rico — ISABEL
Santa Anna won here — ALAMO
Santa Anna's deposer — ALVAREZ
Santa Claus, for one — ELF
Santa Fe and Chisholm — TRAILS
Santa has one — LIST
Santa helper — ELF
Santa in "Miracle on 34th Street" — GWENN
Santa's bane — SOOT
Santa's closing words — TO ALL A GOOD NIGHT
Santa's crew — ELVES
Santa's eye signal — WINK
Santa's sounds — HO HO
Santa's time — YULE
Santa's transport — SLED
Santa, e.g. — ELF
Santha Rama _____ — RAU
Santiago backdrop — ANDES
Santiago is its capital — CHILE
Santiago specie — PESO
Santo _____, Philippine university — TOMAS
Sao _____ — PAULO
Sap — DRAIN, DELETE, EXHAUST, WEAKEN
Sap source — TREE
Sapient — SANE, WISE
Sapins — FIRS
Sapor — TASTE
Sapphira's co-conspirator — ANANIAS
Sapphire — GEM
Sapphire source — CEYLON
Sappho creation — ODE
Sapporo sash — OBI
Saps — NITWITS
Saragossa's river — EBRO
Sarah _____ Jewett — ORNE
Sarah _____, Met soprano — REESE
Sarah Jewett's middle name — ORNE
Sarah's slave — HAGAR
Saratoga and Ems — SPAS
Saratoga and Warm Springs — SPAS
Saratoga Springs, e.g. — SPA
Saratoga, e.g. — SPA
Saratoga, for example — SPA
Saratoga, for one — SPA
Sarawak's island — BORNEO
Sarcastic — CAUSTIC, SNIDE
Sarcastic rebuke — SLAP
Sarcastic remarks from the Deli? — SCOLD CUTS
Sardinia's capital — CAGLIARI
Sardinia's neighbors — CORSICANS
Saree wearer — RANEE, RANI
Sarge — NCO
Sari wearer — RANI
Saroyan hero — ARAM
Saroyan's "My Name is _____" — ARAM
Sartorial evasion? — SKIRTING THE ISSUE
Sartre novel — NAUSEA
SASE, sometimes — ENC
Sash — OBI
Sash for Yum-Yum — OBI
Sashay — CHASSE, STRUT
Sashay along — MOSEY
Sashes for Cio-Cio-San — OBIS
Sashes for Yum Yum — OBIS
Sashes, of a sort — OBIS
Saskatchewan capital — REGINA
Saskatchewan neighbor — ALBERTA
Saskatchewan river — CREE
Sass — INSOLENCE, LIP, MOUTH
Sassy — PERT
Sassy shaver — BRAT
Sat — POSED
Sat in session — MET
Sat, in a way — PERCHED
Satan — MOLOCH, FIEND
Satan's work — EVIL
Satchel — BAG, CASE
Satellite — MOON
Satellite launched in 1966 — ATS
Satellite launched on 12/6/66 — ATS
Satellite letters: 1962-75 — OSO
Satellite of Neptune — TRITON
Satellite of Saturn — DIONE
Satellite org. — NASA
Satellite's route — ORBIT
Satellites — MOONS
Satiate — FILL, GLUT, PALL
Satiated — CLOYED, JADED
Satiated, in Vera Cruz — HARTO
Satiates — CLOYS
Satie's namesakes — ERIKS
Satins and sables — FINERY
Satiny — SMOOTH
Satire — SPOOF, WIT
Satires' cousins — IRONIES
Satiric twist — IRONY
Satirical — IRONIC
Satirical imitation — PARODY
Satirist Freeburg — STAN
Satirist Mort — SAHL
Satirize — LAMPOON
Satisfied — CONTENT
Satisfied sound — PURR
Satisfies — PLEASES, SATES
Satisfies fully — SATES
Satisfy — APPEASE, FILL, PLEASE
Satisfy — SATE, SUIT
Satisfy a thirst — SLAKE
Satisified — SATED
Satrap — RULER
Satrap's superior — AMIR
Saturate — FILL, SOP, STEEP
Saturday, in Bonn — SAMSTAG
Saturn attachment — ALIA
Saturn features — RINGS
Saturn halos — RINGS
Saturn has a few — MOONS
Saturn's consort — OPS
Saturn's sixth moon — TITAN
Saturnalia — BLAST, ORGY
Saturnine — GLUM
Satyajit Ray's "World of _____" — APU
Satyr — DEITY
Sauce — GRAVY
Sauce for gravy — WHITE
Sauce for pasta — PESTO
Sauce for seafood — TARTAR
Sauce or soup thickener — ROUX
Saucer — DISH
Saucer-shaped disk — FRISBEE
Saucy — BOLD, FRESH, PERT
Saucy — PERT
Saucy girl — SNIP
Saucy ones — IMPS
Saudi — ARAB
Saudi Arabia capital — RIYADH
Saudi Arabia city — MECCA

Saudi Arabia region — ASIR
Saudi Arabia's sea — RED
Saudi Arabian king — IBN SAUD
Saudi capital: Var. sp. — RIAD
Saudi district — ASSIR
Saudi garb — ABA
Saudi king: 1964-75 — FAISAL
Saudi, e.g. — ARAB
Saul's grandfather — NER
Saul's kingdom — EDOM
Saul's successor — DAVID
Saul's uncle — NER
Saul's uncle and grandfather — NERS
Sault _____ Marie — STE
Sault Sainte Marie — SOO
Saunas — BATHS
Saunter — MOSEY, STROLL
Sausage ingredient — PORK
Sausage, in Soho — BANGER
Sauté — FRY
Sauterne — WINE
Sautés — FRIES
Savage — BRUTE, FERAL, FIERCE, RUDE
Savage Island — NIUE
Savage Island's other name — NIUE
Savalas — TELLY
Savalas, et al. — TELLYS
Savanna — LEA
Savanna — TREELESS TRACT
Savant — SAGE
Save — CONSERVE, HOARD, LAYAWAY, PRESERVE, SPARE
Save — RESCUE, SPARE
Saved — REDEEMED
Saver's initials — IRA
Savers, of a sort — DEPOSITORS
Saves stamps — COLLECTS
Savine — JUNIPER
Saving — EXCEPT
Savings abbr. — IRA
Savings account addn. — INT
Savings acct. — IRA, NEST EGG
Savings protectors — BANK GUARDS
Savings-acct. entry — INT
Saviour — REDEEMER
Savoir-faire — POISE, TACT
Savor — RELISH, TASTE
Savors — RELISHES
Savory — PLEASING, TASTY
Savory flavor — TANG
Savory jelly — ASPIC
Savory odor of meats cooking: obs. — FUMET
Savory tomato jelly — ASPIC
Savoy dance — STOMP
Savvies — SABES
Savvy — SMARTS
Saw — ADAGE
Saw eye to eye — AGREED
Saw of a sawfish — SERRA
Saw or law suffix — YER
Saw or store — CHAIN
Saw socially — DATED
Saw with a vertical motion — JIGSAW
Saw wood — SNORE
Saw's relative — MOTTO
Saw, in Siena — SEGO
Saw-toothed — NOTCHED
Saw-toothed ridge — SIERRA
Sawbones — DOC
Sawbucks — TENS
Sawed wood — SNORED
Sawfish feature — SERRA
Saws — ADAGES
Saws with the grain — RIPS
Sawyer of 60 Minutes — DIANE
Sax Rohmer character — DOCTOR FU MANCHU
Saxon slave — ESNE
Say — REPORT
Say "Shalom" — GREET
Say again — RESTATE
Say cheese — SMILE
Say further — ADD
Say grace — PRAY
Say Hey Willie — MAYS
Say is so — ATTEST
Say nay, in a way — VETO
Say no — REFUSE
Say thanks — PRAY
Say the rosary — PRAY
Say yes — AGREE
Say, drat — CUSS
Say-so — VOICE
Sayer's detective — LORD PETER WIMSEY
Sayer's detective, Montague _____ — EGG
Saying — ADAGE
Says — AVERS, UTTERS
SC motto — DUM SPIRO SPERO
Scab, as after a burn — ESCHAR
Scabbard — SHEATH
Scad — HEAP
Scads — ALOT
Scads of lads — BOBS
Scaffold — STAGE
Scalawags — SCAMPS
Scalding — HOT
Scale — CLIMB, SKIN, SQUAMA
Scale item — NOTE
Scale note — SOL
Scale starters — DO RE
Scale tones — SOLS
Scaleless fish — OLEO
Scaler's equipment — PITON
Scallop — CUT, PECTEN
Scalp division — PART
Scalp problem — DANDRUFF
Scalpel — KNIFE
Scaly crust — SCURF
Scam — CON
Scam — STING
Scamp — IMP, RASCAL, ROGUE
Scamper — RUN
Scampered — SPED
Scan or scam — CON
Scan the print — READ
Scand. land — NOR
Scand. nation — NOR
Scandal — DIRT, SIN
Scandal _____ — SHEET
Scandal sheet — RAG
Scandinavian — NORDIC, NORSE, SWEDE
Scandinavian capital — OSLO
Scandinavian explorer — ERIC
Scandinavian folklore figure — TROLL
Scandinavian god — ODIN
Scandinavian god of rain — THOR
Scandinavian god of victory — TYR
Scandinavian goddess — HEL
Scandinavian goddess of fate — NORN
Scandinavian king — OLAF
Scandinavian man's name — SVEN
Scandinavian measure — PUND, UNTZ
Scandinavian or the Far North — LAPP
Scandinavian rugs — RYAS
Scandinavian saint — OLAF
Scandinavian sea monster — KRAKEN
Scans — PERUSES
Scant — MEAGER, NARROW, SLIM
Scanty — SKIMPY, SPARSE
Scapegoat — PATSY
Scar — MARK
Scarab — BEETLE, CHAFER
Scarab beetle — CHAFER
Scarabaeid beetle — CHAFER
Scaramouch — FOOL, RAPSCALLION
Scarce — FEW, RARE
Scarcity — DEARTH
Scare: anagram — RACES
Scarebabes — OGRES
Scarecrow — EFFIGY
Scarecrow stuffing — STRAW
Scarecrow's quest — BRAIN
Scarecrow: Brit. — MAUMET
Scared — AFRAID
Scaredy-cat — SISSY
Scaredy-cats — SISSIES
Scarf — BOA
Scarf or necktie — ASCOT
Scarlet — RED
Scarlet and John — OHARAS
Scarlet sage — SALVIA

Scarlett — OHARA
Scarlett's home — TARA
Scarlett's love — RHETT
Scarlett's mansion — TARA
Scary — EERIE
Scary 1941 Leo Carrillo film — HORROR ISLAND
Scat singer of note — ELLA
Scat singing style — BEBOP
Scat! — BEGONE, SHOO
Scat! — SHOO
Scathe — HARM
Scatter — BESTREW, STREW
Scatter about — SEW, STREW
Scatter in different directions — DISPERSE
Scattered, in heraldry — SEME
Scattered: Fr. — EPARS
Scattered: her. — SEME
Scatters chum — BAITS
Scaup — DUCK
Scenario — PLOT
Scenarist Lehman — ERNEST
Scene — VIEW
Scene in Wagner opera — RHINE
Scene of a G.W. coup — TRENTON NJ
Scene of a Napoleonic victory — LODI
Scene of a strike — LANE
Scene of action — ARENA
Scene of cacophony — BABEL
Scene of Dec.-March rains — SAMOA
Scene of great activity — HIVE
Scene of long-run TV series — KOREA
Scene of many a strike — LANE
Scene of more than four-score erruptions — ETNA
Scene of noise and confusion — BABEL
Scene of temptation — EDEN
Scene of the crime — VENUE
Scene shifters — STAGE-HANDS
Scene-stealer, perhaps — HAM
Scenery — SETS
Scenery changer — TRIP
Scenery chewer — ACTOR, HAM
Scenes; settings — LOCALES, PANORAMAS
Sceneshifter — GRIP
Scenic canton in Switzerland — LUCERNE
Scenic Italian drive — AMALFI
Scenic New Hampshire city — KEENE
Scenic view — SCAPE
Scent — AROMA, ODOR, PATH, SMELL
Sceptre Cosmetic, La.? — BATON ROUGE
Sch. course — ENG
Sch. groups — PTAS
Sch. near Harvard — MIT
Scheduled — ON TAP, SLATED
Schedules again — RESLATES
Scheherazade's stock in trade — TALES
Scheldt feeder — LYS
Scheme — IDEA, PLAN, PLOT
Scheme for Frost — ABAA
Schiller hero — TELL
Schism — DISCORD
Schismatic group — SECT
Schisms — RENTS
Schlep — TOTE
Schlepped — TOTED
Schmaltz — CORN
Schmo — JERK, NERD
Scholar's asset — BRAIN
Scholar's deg. — BLIT
Scholars collars — ETONS
School — PREP
School allied with Kings College — ETON
School dance — HOP, PROM
School founded by Ninette de Valois — RBS
School gp. — PTA
School group — CLASS
School in St. Lo — ECOLE
School near Windsor Castle — ETON
School on the Thames — ETON
School subj. — ECON, MATH
School year part — SEMESTER
School, in Soissons — ECOLE
Schoolmate of Coleridge — LAMB
Schools of thought — ISMS
Schools of whales — GAMS
Schubert song — LIED
Schuss — SKI
Schussboomer's spot — SLOPE
Schussed — SKIED
Schwarzkopf's ordinary duds — MUFTI
Sci-fi aliens, for short — ETS
Sci-fi Author _____ Hubbard — L RON
Sci-fi horror film: 1979 — ALIEN
Sci. of rocks — GEOL
Sci. subj — GEOL
Scicoloni on screen — LOREN
Science writer Willy _____ — LEY
Scipio, to Hannibal — ENEMY
Scissors — SHEARS
Scoff — JEER
Scold — BERATE, CHIDE, NAG, REBUKE
Scold vehemently — BERATE
Scolded — RATED
Scolds — RANTS
Scone movers — TEACARTS
Scorch the steak — SEAR
Scorches — SEARS
Score — GRADE, GROOVE, MARK, SCRATCH, TALLY
Score dir. — RIT
Score for Steffi — ADIN
Score minus one — NINETEEN
Score the game — CALCULATE
Scored the furniture — MARRED, NICKED
Scores in cricket — ONS
Scoria — SLAG
Scot's not — NAE
Scot's small, sturdy workhorse — GARRON
Scot's veto — NAE
Scotch admixture — SODA
Scotsman's negative — NAE
Scott — FRANCIS KEY
Scott Joplin favorites — RAG-TIME
Scott Joplin's forte — RAGTIME
Scott or John — GLENN
Scott Turow book — ONEL
Scottish dish — HAGGIS
Scottish explorer — RAE
Scottish family group — CLAN
Scottish fishing boat — BALDIE, TROW
Scottish folk hero — ROB ROY
Scottish goblet — TASS
Scottish hillside — BRAE
Scottish lake or river — AWE
Scottish miss — LASS
Scottish negatives — NAES
Scottish poet Hew _____: 1792-1878 — AINSILE
Scottish seaport — AYR
Scottish seaside resort — OBAN
Scottish title — LAIRD
Scottish turndowns — NAES
Scottish uncle — EME
Scoundrel — CUR, KNAVE, ROUE
Scoundrels — CADS, VILLAINS
Scourge of serge — LINT
Scout badge — MERIT
Scow chow — MESS
Scowls — POUTS
Scrabble piece — TILE
Scram! — BLOW, GIT
Scrap for Fido — ORT
Scrap of food — ORT
Scrape — ABRADE
Scrape together — RAKE
Scraped one's shins — BARKED
Scraps that Spot gets into — ORTS
Scrawny — THIN
Scream — HOWL, SCREECH, WAIL
Screams — YELLS
Screams in the comics — EEKS
Screams of laughter — SHRIEKS

Screen — NETTING
Screen for sizing ore — TROMMEL
Screen part — PANEL
Screen's Sommer — ELKE
Screenwriter Diamond — IAL
Scribes — PENS
Scriptural mysticism — CABALA
Scrooge's clerk — CRATCHIT
Scrounge — CADGE
Scrub — CANCEL
Scrub a mission — ABORT
Scrubbed a mission — ABORTED
Scruff — NAPE
Scruffs — NAPES
Scrutinize — SCAN
Scrutinized — PROBED
Scud component — FLYING CLOUD
Scuffle, e.g. — HOE
Scull — OAR
Sculled — OARED
Sculler — OARSMAN
Sculptor Jo _____: 1883-1952 — DAVIDSON
Sculptor Nadelman — ELIE
Sculptured forms — BUSTS
Scurvy fighters — LIMES
Scuttle — RUN, SCURRY
Scuttlebutt — RUMOR
SE Asia capital — HANOI
SE Asia native — SHAN
SE Asian — THAI
Sea — OCEAN
Sea and wild — OATS
Sea anemone — CORAL
Sea anemone or hydra — POLYP
Sea animal — ORC
Sea barrier — DIKE
Sea bird — AUK, ERN, SKUA, TERN
Sea bird — PETREL
Sea birds — ERNES, ERNS, TERNS
Sea biscuit — HARDTACK
Sea call — AHOY
Sea cow — MANATEE
Sea dog — TAR
Sea dogs — SALTS
Sea duck — EIDER, POCHARD, SCOTER
Sea eagle — ERN, ERNE
Sea east of the Caspian — ARAL
Sea flower — ANEMONE
Sea flyers — ERNES
Sea foam — SPUME
Sea food — SCALLOPS
Sea fowl — EIDER
Sea god — LER, NEPTUNE
Sea holly — ERYNGO
Sea in Soviet central Asia — ARAL
Sea in the W Pacific — SULU
Sea lettuce, et al. — ALGAE
Sea lion, e.g. — OTARY
Sea mammal — WHALE
Sea moss — ALGA
Sea near Antarctica — ROSS
Sea near Bermuda — SARGASSO
Sea nymph — GALATEA
Sea nymphs — NEREIDS
Sea of _____ — AZOV
Sea of Japan port — AKITA
Sea of Soviet Central Asia — ARAL
Sea of the Philippines — SULU
Sea or Islands — AEGEAN
Sea or land chaser — SCAPE
Sea or land follower — SCAPE
Sea personification: Irish myth — LER
Sea pheasants — SMEES
Sea route — LANE
Sea sight — ERN
Sea snail — WINKLE
Sea spray — SPIN DRIFT
Sea swallow — TERN
Sea swooper — ERNE
Sea to which the Po flows: Abbr. — MEDIT
Sea trout — SMELT
Sea urchins — ECHINI
Sea vessel — SHIP
Sea water, e.g. — BRINE
Sea wolf — PIRATE
Sea, in Sweden — MER
Sea, to Debussy — MER
Sea-going flyer — ERN
Sea-urchin features — SPINES
Sea: Fr. — MER
Seabees' motto — CAN DO
Seabird — AUK, ERN, GANNET, TERN
Seabiscuit's grandsire — MAN O WAR
Seaboard — COAST
Seacoast — STRAND
Seadog — SALT, TAR
Seadog's potation — GROG
Seafood — CHINOOK SALMON, MAINE LOBSTER, ROE
Seafood — SOFT SHELLED CRAB
Seafood choice — EELS
Seafood delicacy — ROE, SHAD
Seafood items — ROE, SHRIMP
Seafood on the half shell — CLAMS CASINO
Seafood order — CLAMS
Seafood style — SCAMPI
Seafood treats from Maine — LOBSTERS
Seafood, for some — EELS
Seafood? — NAVY BEAN
Seagoer — SALT
Seagoing shout — AVAST
Seagoing vessel — OCEAN LINER
Seagull — ERNE, MEW
Seal — SCOTCH TAPE, SEA LION, SHUT OFF, SIGNET
Seal group — HERD
Seal, in Paris — SCEAU
Sealer — CAULK, PUTTY
Sealing agent — LUTE
Sealing rings — GASKETS
Sealing with heat — SEARING
Seam — JOINT
Seam features — WELTS
Seaman — MARINER, SAILOR, SALTS, TAR
Seaman in a gig — ROWER
Seaman's "Stop!" — AVAST
Seaman's favorite Debussy work? — LA MER
Seaman's rope — TYE
Seaman's saint — ELMO
Seamen — SAILORS
Seamstress — SEWER, TAILOR
Seamstress benefactor Howe — ELIAS
Seamstress Betsy — ROSS
Seamstress in "La Bohème" — MIMI
Seamstress's insert — GUSSET
Seamstress, at times — SHIRRER
Sean Connery role — BOND
Séance intermediary — MEDIUM
Séance phenomena — TRANCES
Séance sound — RAP
Séance sounds — MOANS
Séances with talkative medium? — RAP SESSIONS
Seaport in Algeria — ORAN
Seaport in Brittany — BREST
Seaport in Israel — ACRE
Seaport in N Japan — SITKA
Seaport in NW Germany — EMDEN
Seaport in SE China — AMOY
Seaport in Yemen — ADEN
Seaport of Athens, on Saronic Gulf — PIRAEUS
Seaport of Guam — APRA
Seaport of SE France — MARSEILLES
Seaport of SW Spain — CADIZ
Seaport on the Adriatic — BARI
Seaport on the Elbe river — HAMBURG
Sear — SCATHE
Sear milk — SCALD
Search — FRISK
Search for — HUNT, SEEK
Search for "dirt" — SNOOP
Search for food — FORAGE
Search for gold — PAN
Search for shells — COMB
Search high and low — SCOUR

Search into — DELVE
Search out — SEEK
Search party near the Oval Office? — EASTER EGG HUNT
Search widely — SCOUR
Searches — FERRETS
Searches (out) — FERRETS
Searches for — SEEKS
Searches for prey — RAVENS
Searches thoroughly — COMBS
Sears Tower adjective — TALLEST
Seas, in Paris — MERS
Seasame Street grouch — OSCAR
Seasame Street regular — ERNIE
Seashell — CONCH
Seashore — COAST
Seashore cookouts — CLAM-BAKE
Seashore feature — BREAKER, DUNES, LIFE GUARD
Seaside — SHORE
Seaside basin — MARINA
Seaside cities — PORTS
Seaside resort of Scotland — OBAN
Season — ACCENT, FALL, FLAVOR, SALT, SPICE
Season in Tours — ETE
Season shoots — SPRING SPROUTS
Season, in a way — MARINATE
Seasonal greeting — MERRY CHRISTMAS
Seasonal pie — MINCE
Seasonal song — CAROL
Seasonal songs — NOELS
Seasonal toast — WASSAIL
Seasonal tree topper — STAR
Seasonal visitor — SANTA
Seasonal visitor, in London — FATHER CHRISTMAS
Seasoned — SALTED
Seasoned hands — PROS
Seasoned with a certain herb — SAGY
Seasoning — SALT, SPICE
Seasoning amplifier, for short — MSG
Seasoning for Bardot — SEL
Seasoning herbs — BASILS
Seasoning plant — SALTERY
Seasons anew — RESALTS
Seasons, in Pau — ETES
Seat — SETTLE
Seat for a judge — BANC
Seat for a sermon — PEW
Seat in a bay window — CAROL
Seat in a British theater — STALL
Seat of ancient Irish kings — TARA
Seat of ancient Kings — TARA
Seat of Clearwater Co., Idaho — OROFINO
Seat of Essex Co., Mass. — SALEM
Seat of fortitude? — INTESTINE
Seat of justice — BENCH
Seat of power — THRONE
Seat of Wayne Co., Utah — LOA
Seat, in old Rome — SELLA
Seat, in Siena — SEDE
Seater — USHER
Seats — INSTATES
Seats for judges — BANCS
Seats of a sort — STOOLS
Seattle _____ — SLEW
Seaver and Selleck — TOMS
Seaver and Sneva — TOMS
Seaver's first team — METS
Seawater — BRINE
Seaweed — AGAR, ALGA, KELP
Seaweed product — AGAR
Seaweed substance — AGAR
Seaweeds — ALGAE
Seaworthy — SNUG
Seaworthy boat of the New England coast — DORY
Sec.-largest planet — SAT
Secede — SPLIT
Seckel's kin — BOSC
Seckel, for one — PEAR
Seckels — PEARS
Seclude — ISOLATE
Seclude, as a jury — SEQUESTER
Secluded place — RECESS
Secluded spot — DELL, GLEN
Secluded valleys — DELLS, GLENS
Seclusion — ISOLATION
Second-hand car, e.g. — TRADE IN
Second-rate singer's residence? — A LITTLE FLAT
Second — ABET, NATURE OR THOUGHT
Second at Kentucky Derby — PLACE
Second caliph — OMAR
Second cen. date — CLI
Second city of Tunisia — SFAX
Second epic of Homer — ODYSSEY
Second fairy-tale word — UPON
Second in a Greek series — BETA
Second largest Asian body of water — ARAL SEA
Second largest Belgian city — OSTEND
Second largest city in Nevada — RENO
Second letter — BETA
Second looeys — SHAVETAILS
Second magnitude star in Ursa Major — DUBHE
Second man — CAIN
Second name — EVE
Second notes — RES
Second of five orders of British nobility — MARQUIS
Second of two — LATTER, OTHER
Second or sixth president — ADAMS
Second part of Adage by Bayly — HEART GROW FONDER
Second rate — GAUDY
Second showing — RERUN
Second sight, for short — ESP
Second son — ABEL
Second string — SUBS
Second team — SCRUBS
Second tel. line — EXT
Second test — RETRIAL
Second time around, TV style — RERUN
Second to none — PERFECT
Second transfers — RESALES
Second word of a fairy tale — UPON
Second-hand — USED
Second-hand transaction — RESALE
Second-rate — SHABBY
Second-rate race horses — HAY BURNERS
Secondary route — SIDE ROAD
Secondary statute — BYLAW
Secondhand — USED, WORN
Seconds, e.g. — ASSISTERS
Secret — ARCANE, CRYPTIC
Secret agent — OPERATIVE, SPY
Secret communications — CODES
Secret doctrine — CABALA
Secret retreat — LAIR
Secret service in Russia — NKVD
Secret service of Israel — MOSSAD
Secret sightings — ESPIALS
Secret society — CABAL, KLAN
Secret society, Italian style — CAMORRA
Secret: Prefix — CRYPT
Secretariat — OFFICE
Secretary — DESK, SCRIBE
Secretary between Day and Root — HAY
Secretary of State Jim — BAKER

Secretary of State: 1961-69 — RUSK
Secretary of the Interior: 1956-60 — SEATON
Secretary of the Interior: 1961-69 — UDALL
Secrete — CACHE, HIDE
Secreted — CACHED
Secretes — STOWS
Secretive — HUSH HUSH, QUIET
Secretly — ASIDE
Sect — CULT, PARTY
Sect follower — ARIAN
Sectarian — PARTISAN
Section — AREA, PIECE
Section eight — DISCHARGE
Section of a document — CLAUSE
Section of a liner in the good ole days — STEERAGE
Section of a Pound poem — CANTO
Section of Fez — KASBAH
Section of film — REEL
Section of L.A. — BEL AIR
Sections — AREAS
Sections for pulpits — CHANCELS
Sector — AREA
Secular — CARNAL, CIVIL, LAIC, LAY
Secular cantata — SERENATA
Secular French clergyman — ABBE
Secularize — LAICIZE
Secure — ATTACH, BOLT, FASTEN, SAFE, TIGHTEN
Secure a sail — TRICE
Secure with ropes — FRAP
Secure, in a way — LOCKUP
Secured — BOUND, LASHED
Secures by fitting into a groove — DADOS
Securing device — LATCH
Securities — STOCKS
Security — BAIL, GAGE
Security devices — BURGLAR ALARMS, PADLOCKS
Security exchange area — PIT
Security guards — WATCH-DOGS, BURGLAR ALARMS
Security person — BODY-GUARD
Security trouble — LEAK
Security vehicles — POLICE PATROL CARS
Sedan — CAR
Sedan shelter — ABRI
Sedan summers — ETES
Sedans — AUTOS
Sedans for execs. — LIMOS
Sedate — PRIM, STAID
Sedative — AMYTAL, OPIATE
Sedentary — INACTIVE, SESSILE
Sediment — DREG, LEES, SILT
Sediment-laden — SILTY
Sediments — RESIDUA
Seduce — ENTICE, INVITE, LURE, TEMPT
Seductive — LURING
Seductive tricks — WILES
Seductively beautiful woman — HOURI
Seductress — VAMP
See — ESPY, NOTE, UNDER-STAND
See at _____ — A GLANCE
See eye to eye — AGREE
See holder — PRELATE
See how it fits — TRY ON
See in the mind's eye — ENVI-SION
See red — BLOW ONES STACK, HIT THE CEILING
See red — THROW A FIT
See red? — OWE
See the sights — TOUR
See to — TEND
See you later — CIAO
See you later, Pierre! — TATA
See's — PERCEIVES
Seed — OVULE, SPORE
Seed appendage — ARIL
Seed coat — ARIL, TESTA
Seed coating — ARIL
Seed corn — PLANT
Seed cover — ARIL, POD
Seed coverings — ARILS, TESTA
Seed envelope — ARIL
Seed holder — POD
Seed husk — BRAN
Seed of a peach — PIT
Seed of a sort — SPORE
Seed or pip of a grape — ACINUS
Seed parts — ARILS
Seed plant dust — POLLEN
Seed planter — SOWER
Seed scars — HILA
Seed used for flavoring food — SESAME
Seed: Comb. form — SPORI
Seeded players delight — BYE
Seedless raisin — CURRANT
Seeds again — RERANKS
Seeds, in tennis — RANKS
Seedy — TACKY
Seedy Manhattan area — BOWERY
Seeger or Fountain — PETE
Seeing red — AFIRE, ANGRY, SORE
Seeing that — SINCE
Seek (updated) — AND YOU SHALL FIND
Seek a politician's ear — LOBBY
Seek ambitiously — ASPIRE
Seek an answer — ASK
Seek compassion — ACHE
Seek redress — SUE
Seek to attain — ASPIRE
Seek to learn — ASK
Seek's companion — HIDE
Seeker of subversives: 1938-44 — DIES
Seeking into — ASKING
Seem — APPEAR
Seemann's milieu — MEER
Seemed to radiate — EXUDED
Seemingly harmless person — SNAKE IN THE GRASS
Seemly — DECENT, MEET
Seems — APPEARS
Seen from the Mississippi — LEVEE
Seen in the Seine — ILES
Seep — OOZE
Seep through — OOZE
Seepage — OSMOSIS
Seeping — OOZY
Seer reading matter — PALM
Seer's ledger statement? — PROPHET AND LOSS
Seer's reading material — PALM
Seer's stock in trade — OMENS
Seers — ORACLES
Sees eye to eye — HITS IT OFF
Sees momentarily — GLIMPSES
Sees red — STEAMS
Sees to — TENDS
Seesaw — TEETER
Seesaw sitter in a rhyme — ESAU
Seethe — BOIL, FRY, FUME, STEW
Seethes — FERMENTS
Seething — ABOIL
Segal's "Oliver's _____" — STORY
Segmented novel — SERIAL
Segments — PARTS
Segovia's companion — GUI-TAR
Segovia's instrument — GUITAR
Segovia's music — CLASSICAL
Segregate — SEPARATE
Seine — NET
Seine feature — ILES
Seine feeder — EURE, ISERE, MARNE, OISE, YVONNE
Seine land masses — ILES
Seine river sight — QUAI
Seine sight — BATEAU
Seine sights — ILES
Seine site, informally — PAREE
Seine terrain — ILE
Seine tributary — AUBE, MARNE, OISE
Seines — NETS
Seis, _____, ocho — SIETE
Seize — APPREHEND, GRAB, TAKE
Seize by the neck — SCRUFF
Seize for payment, for short — REPO

Seize power illegally — USURP
Seized — RIGID
Seized first — PREEMPTED
Seized suddenly (with up) — SNAPPED
Seizes — NABS, NIPS
Seizes by force — WRESTS
Seizes power — USURPS
Selassie — HAILE
Seldom — ONCE IN A BLUE MOON, RARELY
Seldom found today — RARE
Seldom seen — RARE
Select — CULL, OPT, TAB
Select, as a jury — PANEL
Selected — CHOSEN, OPTED
Selection — CHOICE
Selection at a Chinese eatery — EGG FOO YOUNG
Selection for Sutherland — ARIA
Selene's realm — MOON
Seles of tennis — MONICA
Self — EGO
Self-approval — VANITY
Self-assured — COCKY
Self-centered — SELFISH
Self-conceits — EGOS
Self-confidence — POISE
Self-conscious — BASHFUL
Self-control — WILL
Self-defense — JUDO
Self-defense system — KARATE
Self-employed movie exhibitor — INDIE
Self-esteem — EGO, PRIDE
Self-help author Wayne _____ — DYER
Self-image — EGO
Self-important — VAIN
Self-important person — ASS
Self-interest — EGO
Self-multiplies: Abbr. — SQS
Self-portrait? — EGO
Self-reliant — FREE
Self-respect — AMOUR PROPRE
Self-satisfied — SMUG
Self-service item — GAS
Self-service restaurant — AUTOMAT
Self-starter? — ONE
Selfish one — EGOIST, HOG, MEANIE
Selfish person — HOG
Selfish sort — USER
Sell — VEND
Sell hot tickets — SCALP
Sell in a forceful way — HUSTLE
Sell or tell — RETAIL
Sell tickets for a quick buck — SCALP
Sell tickets illegaly — SCALP
Selleck — TOM
Selleck and Smothers — TOMS
Seller — CADGER, VENDOR
Seller of candles — CHANDLER
Seller of cloth, in England — DRAPER
Seller of goods in the street — HUCKSTER
Seller's conflict — PRICE
Seller's notices — ADS
Seller's patter? — SALES TALK
Sellout notice — SRO
Sellout sign — SRO
Selves — EGOS
Semanticist's concern — LANGUAGE
Semaphores on a RR — SGLS
Semblance — GUISE
Semblances — IMAGES
Semester, e.g. — TERM
Semi-aquatic animals — EFTS
Semi-opaque projection curtain — SCRIM
Semicircular building projection — APSE
Seminar — CLINIC
Seminarian's degree — THD
Semiprecious gem — TOURMALINE
Semiprecious stone — ONYX, OPAL
Semis, e.g. — RIGS
Semisheer fabric — VOILE
Semisolid — GEL
Semisweet liqueur — EAU
Semitic fertility goddess — ASTARTE
Semitic language — ARAMAIC
Sen. Bradley was one — KNICKERBOCKER
Sen. Feinstein of Calif. — DIANNE
Sen. Kefauver — ESTES
Sen. Thurmond — STROM
Senate "cadet" — PAGE
Senate action — CENSURE
Senate votes — YEAS
Senator Bob — DOLE
Senator from Delaware — BIDEN
Senator from Kansas — DOLE
Senator from Maine — COHEN
Senator from Ohio — GLENN
Senator from Tennessee — GORE
Senator in the American Hall of Fame — CHOATE
Senator Kefauver — ESTES
Senator Moynihan — DANIEL
Senator Thurmond — STROM
Senator who went to space — GARN
Senator, for example — SOLON
Senator, for one — SOLON
Send — DIRECT, ISSUE, MAIL, REMIT, SHIP
Send a second reminder — RENOTIFY
Send abroad — EXPORT
Send again — RESHIP
Send away — DISMISS
Send back a manuscript — REJECT
Send for — SUMMON
Send forth — EMIT
Send in payment — REMIT
Send money — WIRE
Send packing — OUST
Send payment — REMIT
Send spiritually — TELEPORT
Send the wrong way — MISDIRECT
Send to _____ (shun) — COVENTRY
Send to Coventry — SHUN
Send up a rocket — ALERT
Send word — WRITE
Sends a telegram — WIRES
Sends a wireless — RADIOS
Sends back to custody — REMANDS
Sends back to the Hill — REELECTS
Sends forth — EMANATES, ISSUES
Sends off — MAILS, SHIPS
Sends out — EMITS
Sends soaring — LOFTS
Seneca, Cayuga, etc. — FINGER LAKES
Senectuous — AGED
Senegal city — DAKAR
Senegal's capital — DAKAR
Senior — DEAN, ELDER
Senior Chinese leader — DENG
Senior citizens — OLDSTERS
Senior event — PROM, REUNION
Senior member — DOYEN
Senior on the Seine — AINE
Sennacherib, for one — ASSYRIAN
Senor's blankets — SERAPES
Senor's residence — CASA
Senor's response — SI SI
Senor's shawl — SERAPE
Senor, stateside — MISTER
Senora's house — CASA
Senorita's chaperone — DUENNA
Senorita's fingernails — UNAS
Senorita's kisses — BESOS
Sens's colleagues — REPS
Sensational — LURID
Sense — FEEL, LOGIC, REASON
Sense of humor — WIT
Sense of ill-being — MALAISE
Sense of taste — PALATE
Sense organ — EAR
Sense sounds — HEAR
Sensed — FELT
Senseless — INANE

Senses — FEELS
Sensible — SANE
Sensitive — THIN SKINNED
Sensitive spots — RAWS
Sensitivity of a film — SPEED
Sensitivity to musical tone — EAR
Sensualist — SYBARITE
Sensualists — EPICURES
Sensuous — EROTIC
Sent along — RELAYED
Sent away for — ORDERED
Sent back — REMANDED
Sent back: Abbr. — RETD, RTD
Sent for — ORDERED
Sent pictures — TELEVISED
Sent: Abbr. — DLD
Sentence — DOOM
Sentence segment — CLAUSE
Sentence subjects — NOUNS
Sentence using all the alphabet — PANGRAM
Sentence-divider — COLON
Sentence-filling cliche — AS A MATTER OF FACT
Sentence-filling cliche — BE THAT AS IT MAY
Sentence-filling cliche — BUT IN ANY EVENT
Sentences — SENDS UP
Sentient — AWARE
Sentimental in a cheap way — MAUDLIN
Sentimentalize — EMOTE
Sentries in the street — GUARDIAN ANGELS
Sentry's call — HALT
Sentry's cry — HALT
Sentry's remark — HALT WHO GOES THERE
Sentry's words — HALTS
Señora Perón — EVA
Señorita's snack — NACHO
Seoul G.I. — ROK
Seoul native — KOREAN
Seoul soldier — ROK
Separate — DETACH, DISCRETE, DIVERGE, ISOLATE, PART
Separate differing ingredients — UNMIX
Separate the wheat from the chaff — WINNOW
Separated — APART
Separately — EACH
Separately, in music — ASUE
Separates — PARTS
Separation of married couple — DIVORCE
Sept. 13, 1977 — ROSH HASHANAH
Sepulcher — ENTOMB
Sequel — UPSHOT
Sequence — SERIES, STRING
Sequential — SERIAL
Sequesters — SECLUDES
Seraglio — HAREM, SERAI
Seraglio chamber — ODA
Serai — IMARET, INN
Serape — SHAWL
Seraph's song: Var. — PEAN
Serb or Croat, e.g. — SLAV
Serb or Czech — SLAV
Serb or Sorb — SLAV
Sere — DRY
Serenata — ODE
Serene — CALM, PEACEFUL, TRANQUIL
Serengeti sight — ELAND
Serenity — PEACE
Serf — HELOT
Serf of yore — ESNE
Serge scourge — LINT
Sergeant York's home state — TENN
Series in Sevilla — SERIE
Series of boat races — REGATTA
Series of book copies: Abbr. — PTG
Series of eight — OCTAD
Series of steps — STAIR
Series opener — ABCDE
Serious — ARDENT, EARNEST, GRAVE, GRIM, PENSIVE
Serious — SEDATE, SOBER, SOMBER
Serious play — DRAMA
Serious reading — TEXTBOOK
Serious-minded — STAID
Serjeants' _____ London — INN
Serling and namesakes — RODS
Serling of TV — ROD
Sermon subject — TEXT
Sermon's preface — TEXT
Sermons — TALKS
Serpent — PYTHON
Serpent follower — INE
Serpent: Comb. form — OPHIO
Serpentine — SNAKE
Serpents — ASPS
Serpico on the screen — PACINO
Sert work — MURAL
Serum — FLUID
Servant — MAID, RETAINER
Servant to Cleopatra — IRAS
Servants, e.g. — HELP
Serve — ACT, AID, ASSIST, DISH, HELP, PERFORM
Serve a winner — ACE
Serve as a model — SIT
Serve drinks — POUR
Serve impeccably — ACE
Serve sugar cubes — TONG
Serve the soup — LADLE
Serve with verve — ACE
Served a winner — ACED
Served for a point — ACED
Served in a mess — MEALS
Served perfectly — ACED
Served to perfection — ACED
Served well — ACED
Served with parsley, to a chef — GARNI
Server — TRAY
Server of café and vin — GARCON
Server's edge on the court — AD IN
Serves as an example — TYPIFIES
Serves perfectly — ACES
Serves well — ACES
Service — AGENCY, BENEFIT, DUTY, WEAR
Service call — LET
Service club — LIONS
Service gp. — ORT
Service group — LIONS
Service initials — USN
Service monogram — USCG
Service org. — YWCA
Service person at Lackland base — WAF
Service recreation areas — CANTEENS
Service trucks — UTES
Service women of WW II — WAAC, WAC
Serviceable — UTILE
Servicemen, for short — GIS
Services for canonical hours — TERCES
Servile one — GROVELER
Serving for another — SUBSTITUTE
Serving of bacon — RASHER
Serving perfectly — ACING
Serving soup — LADLING
Serving spoon — LADLE
Servings of fresh corn — EARS
Sesame — BENNE, TIL, TEEL
Sesame seeds — TILS
Sesame St. sponsor — ECV, CTW
Sesame Street dweller — ERNIE
Sesbania — AGATI
Sessions for Borg — SETS
Sestina, e.g. — POEM
Set-to — SPATS, TIFF
Set — GEL, LAID, SCENE, SOLIDIFIED
Set _____ (prepare to snare) — A TRAP
Set a price — ASK
Set a time — HOUR
Set about — BEGIN
Set against — AVERSE
Set apart — SECLUDE
Set apart funds — EARMARK
Set aside — ISOLATE, PIT, SAVE

Set aside for future use — MOTHBALL
Set at odds — SPLIT
Set back — RECESS
Set boundaries — LIMIT
Set down — LAND
Set down (situate) — PLACE
Set down (writing) — NOTE
Set down, as a choreographer's score — NOTATE
Set firmly — IMBED
Set foot — TROD
Set from margin — IDENT
Set in order — NEATEN
Set into motion — ACTUATE
Set new boundaries — REDEFINE
Set of maps — ATLAS
Set of rows — TIER
Set of steps over a fence — STILE
Set of ten — DECADE
Set of three — TERN
Set off — DETONATE, LIGHT
Set on a pedestal — ADORE
Set or group — CLASS
Set out — ARRAY, START
Set right — TRUE
Set straight — ALIGN
Set systems — ROTES
Set to trip — ACOCK
Set up — ERECT
Set up for golf — TEED
Set upon — ASSAIL, ASSAILED
Setae — BRISTLES
Setbacks — REVERSALS
Seth's son — EON
Sets against — OPPOSES
Sets aside — SAVES
Sets down — PLACES
Sets of beliefs — CREEDS
Sets of runes — FUTHARCS
Sets of three — TERNS
Sets of type — FONTS
Sets on — ASSAILS
Sets one's sights too high — MISAIMS
Sets the theme — KEYNOTES
Sets type — COMPOSES
Setting — LOCALE
Setting apart — INSULATING
Setting for "Cheers" — BAR
Setting for "Hogan's Heroes" — STALAG
Setting for "The King and I" — SIAM
Setting for a Christie classic — THE ORIENT EXPRESS
Setting for M*A*S*H — KOREA
Settings — BACKDROPS
Settings — LOCALES
Settings for Coe — OVALS
Settle — ARRANGE, SAG
Settle a score — AVENGE
Settle a tab — REPAY
Settle down — DESCEND, SIT
Settle snugly — NESTLE
Settled — ALIT, LOCATED
Settled down: Abbr. — NSTD
Settled for the night — ROOSTED
Settled to earth — ALIT
Settlement in Greenland — ETAH
Settlement of a kind — COLONY
Seural stroke — DOT
Seurat unit — DOT
Seuss villain — GRINCH
Sevareid — ERIC
Sevareid and Blore — ERICS
Seven _____ — SEAS
Seven to Luigi — SETTE
Seven, in old Rome — VII
Seven, in Spain — SIETE
Seven-week period in Judaism — ONER
Seven-year period — TEENS
Seventeenth letter — RHO
Seventh Greek letter — ETA
Seventh sign — LIBRA
Seventh son of a seventh son — SEER
Seventh sons — SEERS
Sever — REND
Sever the anchor cable and depart — CUT AND RUN
Several — SOME
Several Danish kings — ERICS
Several divisions — ARMY
Severe — HARSH, SPARTAN, STRICT
Severe test — CRUCIBLE, ORDEAL
Severe test of reliability — ACID
Severed — CUT
Severinsen — DOC
Severity — RIGOR
Severn feeder — AVON
Severn tributary — AVON
Sevilla matrons — SENORAS
Sevilla province town — OSUNA
Sevilla savants — SABIOS
Sevres silk — SOIE
Sevres summer — ETE
Sew — MEND, STITCH
Sew loosely — BASTE
Seward city — NOME
Seward Peninsula city — NOME
Seward's folly — ALASKA
Sewed quickly — RAN UP
Sewer worker in "The Honeymooners" — CARNEY
Sewer's aid — THREADER
Sewing case — ETUI
Sewing devices — NEEDLES
Sewing item — THREAD
Sewing machine attachment — HEMMER
Sewing need — NEEDLE
Sewing or cooking term — BASTE
Sex — GENDER
Sex classification — GENDER
Sexual — GAMIC
Sgt. — NCO
Sgt. Friday's show — DRAGNET
Sgt. or cpl. — NCO
Sgt. Snorkel's dog — OTTO
Sgt.'s superiors — LTS
Sgt.'s underling — PVT
Sgt., for one — NCO
Shabby — DOWN AT THE HEELS, MEAN
Shabby — OUT AT THE ELBOWS
Shabby — RATTY, SEEDY, TORN
Shabby — THE WORSE FOR WEAR
Shack — HUT
Shackle — BIND, TIE
Shackles are put on chain gangs? — CONSTRAINS
Shad _____ — ROE
Shad delicacy — ROE
Shad's is highly prized — ROE
Shade — NUANCE, TINT, VISOR
Shade giver — ELM
Shade of beige — ECRU
Shade of blonde — ASH
Shade of blue — ALICE, AQUA, CYAN, NAVY, ROYAL
Shade of blue — SLATE, TEAL
Shade of blue-green — TEAL
Shade of brown — SEPIA, TAUPE
Shade of difference — NUANCE
Shade of green — ALOES, DRAKE, FOREST, NEVA
Shade of green — LIME, NILE, OLIVE
Shade of light blue — CIEL
Shade of pink — CORAL
Shade of red — CERISE
Shade of rose — BEGONIA
Shade of tan — ECRU, TAWNY
Shade of white — SNOW
Shade provider — ELM
Shade tree — ELM
Shade tree of the SW U.S. — CHINA BERRY
Shaded walk — ALLEE
Shades — HUES, TINTS, TONES, UMBRAS
Shades of blue — INDIGOS
Shades of difference — NUANCES
Shades of red — SCARLET
Shadlike fish — ALEWIFE
Shadow — TAIL, TRAIL
Shadow of death — GLOOM
Shadowbox — SPAR
Shadowed — TAILED
Shadows — HOUNDS

Shadows, to Jeanne — OMBRES
Shadowy — UNDEFINED
Shady accomplice — SHILL
Shady business — RACKETS
Shady ones — ELMS
Shady places — ARBORS
Shady promenades — MALLS
SHAEF sector — ETO
Shaft of light — BEAM
Shafts — RAYS
Shaggy — HIRSUTE
Shaggy dog — PULI
Shah — RULER
Shah _____ -ed-Din: 19th century — NASR
Shah's pelf — RIALS
Shaitan — DEVIL
Shake — JAR
Shake _____ — A LEG
Shake a drink — SLOSH
Shake a leg — HIE
Shake a stick at — POINT
Shake down — EXTORT
Shake hands with — GREET
Shakers' companions — MOVERS
Shakes a leg — RUSHES
Shakes a little — JOGGLES
Shakes up — UNNERVES
Shakespeare — BARD
Shakespeare contemporary — PEELE
Shakespeare opus — SONNET
Shakespeare or Burns — BARD
Shakespeare or Homer — BARD
Shakespeare's "_____ of Athens" — TIMON
Shakespeare's Arden — FOREST
Shakespeare's ghostwriter? — BACON
Shakespeare's Katharine, for one — SHREW
Shakespeare's merchant — ANTONIO
Shakespeare's Moor — OTHELLO
Shakespeare's river — AVON
Shakespeare's shrew — KATE
Shakespeare's Sir _____ Belch — TOBY
Shakespeare's sprite — ARIEL
Shakespeare, allegedly — BACON
Shakespeare, for one — BARD
Shakespearean baddie — IAGO
Shakespearean forest — ARDEN
Shakespearean girl — CELIA
Shakespearean Halloween play? — COMEDY OF TERRORS
Shakespearean king — LEAR
Shakespearean lawyer — PORTIA
Shakespearean play — MEASURE FOR MEASURE
Shakespearean prankster — ARIEL
Shakespearean ruler — LEAR
Shakespearean setting — ARDEN
Shakespearean sprite — ARIEL
Shakespearean theater — GLOBE
Shakespearean tinker — SLY
Shakespearean tragedy — HAMLET
Shakespearean villain — IAGO
Shaking — AGUISH
Shallops and shells — BOATS
Shallot's cousin — ONION
Shallot's pungent kin — GARLIC
Shallow box — FLAT
Shallow vessel — PATEN
Sham — BOGUS, PRETENSE
Shame — ABASH, CHAGRIN, GUILT, PITY, REGRET
Shame _____! — ON YOU
Shampoo produce — LATHER
Shamrock country — ERIN
Shamrock land — ERIN
Shams — PRETENSES
Shamus — TEC
Shanghai servant — AMAH
Shangri-la — EDEN
Shangri-la head — LAMA
Shangri-la, for one — UTOPIA
Shank — CRUS
Shankar — RAVI
Shankar composition — RAGA
Shankar plays it — SITAR
Shankar specialty — RAGA
Shankar's companion — SITAR
Shankar's instrument — SITAR
Shankar, for one — SITARIST
Shankar, the sitarist — RAVI
Shanks — CRURA
Shantung province port: Ger. — TSINGTAU
Shanty — SHED
Shape — FORM, MOLD
Shape of a famous office — OVAL
Shape of a hogan — CONE
Shape of skier's tow bar — TEE
Shaped like a certain D.C. office — OVAL
Shaped like an egg — OVATE
Shaped like an oak leaf — EROSE
Shapeless lumps — BLOBS
Shapely letter — ESS
Shapes — FORMS
Shaping — FORGING
Shaping tool — ADZE, PLANE
Shard — PIECE
Share — CUT, LOT
Share in a venture — STAKE
Share the marquee — COSTAR
Share top billing — COSTAR
Share with others — DIVVY UP
Shared by two or more — JOINT
Shared in — PARTOOK
Sharif — OMAR
Sharif or Bradley — OMAR
Sharif or Khayyam — OMAR
Sharif, et al. — OMARS
Shark — CHEAT, FRAUD
Shark film — JAWS
Shark's hitchhiker — REMORE
Sharklike fish — CHIMAERA
Sharks hang out here — POOL-ROOM
Sharon of "Cagney and Lacey" — GLESS
Sharp — ABRUPT, ACUTE, ASTRINGENT, BARBED
Sharp — CLEAR, COLD, IN FASHION, IRRITABLE
Sharp — KEEN, ON THE BALL, PRECISELY, RAZOR EDGE
Sharp — SPIKED, WITTY
Sharp a customer — CHEAT
Sharp and biting — ACID
Sharp and harsh — ACRID
Sharp as _____ — A TACK
Sharp as a bayonet — ACUTE
Sharp as a tack — KEEN
Sharp cactus — THORNY
Sharp comeback — RIPOSTE
Sharp crested ridge — ARETE
Sharp cry — YELP
Sharp curve — ESS
Sharp decline — SLUMP
Sharp flavor — TANG
Sharp humor — WIT
Sharp mountain ridges — ARETES
Sharp of "Vanity Fair" — BECKY
Sharp on a piano — BLACK KEY
Sharp pain — PANG
Sharp plant part — BARB
Sharp projections — FANGS
Sharp remark — BARB
Sharp ridge — ARETE, ARRIS
Sharp ridge on a glacier — SERAC
Sharp speech — UNKIND
Sharp taste — TANG
Sharp tasting — BITTER
Sharp turndown — TAILSPIN
Sharp turns — ZIGS
Sharp-cornered — ANGULAR
Sharp-crested mountain ridge — ARETE
Sharp-eyed — KEEN
Sharp-sighted — ALERT
Sharp-tongued — TART
Sharp-witted — SHREWD
Sharp: Comb. form — OXY
Sharp; biting; cold — NIPPY
Sharpen — HONE, STROP, WHET
Sharpen a razor — HONE

Sharpen again — REHONE
Sharpened — ACTUATED, HONED
Sharpens — WHETS
Sharper — NATTIER
Sharpie — BOAT
Sharpies — ROGUES
Sharply hit ball — LINER
Sharpness — ACUMEN
Sharpshooter Oakley of yore — ANNIE
Shasta, for one — DAM
Shastri of India — LAL
Shatter — SMASH
Shattered — BROKE
Shave — SHEAR, PARE
Shave off — PARE
Shaver — LADS
Shavers of the ring — ERNIE
Shavian forte — WIT
Shavian monogram — GBS
Shaving mishap — NICK
Shaving need — LATHER
Shaw of "Pajama Game" — RETA
Shaw title starter — ARMS
Shaw's "_____ and the Man" — ARMS
Shaw's Captain _____ — BRASSBOUND
Shaw's phonetic spelling of "fish" — GHOTI
Shawn and others — TEDS
She-bear: Sp. — OSA
She — FEMALE
She betrayed Samson — DELILAH
She comes out — DEB
She disposes, for Tey — PYM
She gives money for a molar — TOOTH FAIRY
She grins and bares it — ECDYSIAST
She has a ball at a ball — BELLE
She knows roses — STEIN
She looked after Cinderella — FAIRY GODMOTHER
She lost her sheep — BO PEEP
She loved Launcelot — GUINEVERE
She loved Narcissus — ECHO
She may have a sobrina — TIA
She may wear a chador — RANI
She nag-nag-nagged — XANTHIPPE
She played Lucy Ricardo — BALL
She played Mame — ANGELA
She played Nora Charles — LOY
She pulled a switch on a witch — GRETEL
She rescued Odysseus at sea — INO
She rhymes with miss — SIS
She scats with cats — ELLA
She sings "Liebestod" — ISOLDE
She starred in the role of "Anna Bolena" — CALLAS
She turned men into swine — CIRCE
She twice played Elizabeth — BETTE
She was "all tears" — NIOBE
She was "The Barefoot Contessa" — AVA
She was Edna Garrett — RAE
She was Norma Rae — SALLY FIELD
She was Tosca on TV in 1955 — LEONTYNE PRICE
She wrote "Little Women" — LOUISA MAY ALCOTT
She wrote "Three Weeks" — GLYN
She wrote "Women Who Run With the Wolves" — ESTES
She, in Frankfurt — SIE
She, in Paris — ELLE
She, in Roma — ELLA
She, in Sedan — ELLE
She, in Siena — ESSA
She-bear, in Sevilla — OSA
Shea denizens — METS
Shea player — MET
Shea Stadium item — HOME PLATE
Sheep before first shearing — TEG
Sheep's product — WOOL
Sheepcote matriarchs — EWES
Sheepish comment — BLEAT
Sheepshank — KNOT
Sheer — ABRUPT, FILMY, STEEP, TRANSPARENT, UTTER
Sheer folly — IDIOTRY
Sheet — NAPPE
Sheet fabrics — PERCALE
Shell-shaped vessels — CONCHAE
Shelly opus — ODE
Shelter — HAVEN, HOUSING, REFUGE, SHIELD
Shelter for doves — COTE
Shelter of a sort — AWNING
Sheltered, to a salt — ALEE
Shelters of a type — ABRIS
Shepherd prophet — AMOS
Sheridan's "The _____ for Scandal" — SCHOOL
Sheriff's asst. — DEP
Shield — ARMOR, COVER, EGIS, GUARD, MASK
Shields — SCREENS
Shin and Zen — SECTS
Shinbone — TIBIA
Shindig — BASH
Shine — GLITTER, GLOW
Shining example — GEM
Shins — TIBIAS
Shinto shrine gateway — TORII
Shinto temple — SHA
Shinto temple gateway — TORII
Shiny — GLOSSY, LUSTROUS, WAXED
Shiny fabric — SATEEN, SATIN
Ship-shaped napkin holder — NEF
Ship — LINER
Ship again — RESEND
Ship area — AFT
Ship decks — ORLOPS
Ship deserters — RATS
Ship dimension — BEAM
Ship feature — HULL
Ship hazard — REEF
Ship initials — HMS
Ship of myth — ARGO
Ship of the desert — CAMEL
Ship part — HAWSE, HOLD, KEEL
Ship powered by oars — BIREME
Ship powered by sail — SLOOP
Ship section — AFT
Ship steward — PURSER
Ship that brought Miss Liberty to the U.S. — ISERE
Ship that picked up Glenn — NOA
Ship to remember — MAINE
Ship with Columbus — NINA
Ship worm — BORER
Ship's accommodations — STATEROOMS
Ship's backbone — KEEL
Ship's backward movement — STERNWAY
Ship's bow — PROW
Ship's bow area — HAWSE
Ship's captain — MASTER
Ship's chain — TYE
Ship's company — CREW
Ship's complement — CREW
Ship's contents — CARGOS
Ship's course — ENE, ESE, SSE
Ship's craft — LONGBOAT
Ship's crane — DAVIT
Ship's deck — ORLOP
Ship's diary — LOG
Ship's levels: Abbr. — DKS
Ship's officer — BOSUN, MATE, PURSER
Ship's petty officer — BOSN
Ship's position — ALEE
Ship's prison — BRIG
Ship's spine — KEEL
Ship's spoor? — WAKE
Ship's tackle — HALYARD
Ship's tender — PINNACLE
Ship's tiller — HELM
Ship's unsteady action — YAWING
Ship's wheel — HELM
Ship's, in Posey — KEELS

Ship-shaped clock — NEF
Ship-shaped table utensil — NEF
Shipboard crane — DAVIT
Shipbuilder's peg — TRENAIL
Shipbuilders strip of wood — BATTEN
Shipbuilders' timber — TEAK
Shipbuilding peg — TRENAIL
Shipfitter — ERECTOR
Shipment from Iraq — DATES
Shipment from Saudi Arabia — OIL
Shipped — SENT
Shipper's abbr. — CAF
Shipping abbr. — CAF, TBL
Shipping hazard — SHOAL
Shipping room item — CRATE
Shipping wts. — GTS
Ships — BOATS
Ships diary — LOG
Ships entryways — GANGPLANKS
Ships' afts — STERNS
Ships' cargo spaces — HOLDS
Ships' companies — CREWS
Ships' entryways — GANGPLANKS
Ships' records — LOGS
Ships, to poets — KEELS
Shipshape — NEAT, TRIM
Shipworm — BORER
Shipwreck — HULK
Shipwreck remains — HULK
Shipwrecked king of "The Tempest" — ALONSO
Shipwrecked sailor — CRUSOE
Shiraz locale — IRAN
Shirk — DODGE, EVADE, NEGLECT
Shirking responsibility — TRUANT
Shirley Jones sitcom, with "The" — PARTRIDGE FAMILY
Shirley McLaine roll — IRMA
Shirley Temple's first husband — AGAR
Shirley's pal — LAVERNE
Shirley's partner on TV — LAVERNE
Shirt — BLOUSE
Shirt fastener — STUD
Shirt or trigger — HAIR
Shirt size — TALL
Shish-kebab holder — SKEWER
Shiva's wife — KALI
Shivaree — DIN
Shiver — SHAKE
Shivers — JITTERS
Shoal — BANK, REEF
Shoals — SHALLOWS
Shoat's cote — STY
Shock — ASTOUND, JOLT, STUN, SURPRISE, TRAUMA
Shock of corn — STAND
Shocked — AGHAST, STARTLED
Shocked sound — GASP
Shocking — UGLY
Shocking report — SCANDAL
Shocking swimmer? — EEL
Shoddy — POOR
Shoe feature — INSOLE, TOE
Shoe grip — CLEAT
Shoe insert — TREE
Shoe leather — SOLES
Shoe musts — SOLES
Shoe or family — TREE
Shoe or suit starter — SNOW
Shoe part — HEEL, INSTEP, SOLE, TOE CAP
Shoe salesman, at times — LACER
Shoe shaper — LAST
Shoe size — EEE, NINE, TEN A, TEN E
Shoe style — PUMP
Shoe type — T STRAP
Shoe width — EEE
Shoe width for Big Foot? — EEE
Shoe-box ltrs. — EEE
Shoe-factory worker — TREER
Shoe-front reinforcement — TOECAP
Shoemaker — COBBLER
Shoemaker's help — ELVES
Shoemaker's helper — ELF
Shoemaker's nail — BRAD
Shoemakers' forms — LASTS
Shoemakers' helpers — ELVES
Shoemaking specialist — BARRER
Shoes for "Magic" — SNEAKERS
Shoes of a sort — SABOTS
Shoestring — LACE
Shofar, e.g. — HORN
Shogun — RULER
Shogunate capital — EDO
Shone — RAYED
Shoo — SCAT
Shoo-in — PET
Shook a leg — HIED
Shoot — SPEAR, TWIG
Shoot down — DISCREDIT
Shoot fireworks in the sky — PROPEL
Shoot from ambush — SNIPE
Shoot from cover — SNIPE
Shoot from plant roots — RATOONS
Shoot off — FIRE
Shoot or boot — FIRE
Shoot the breeze — CHAT, GAS, RAP
Shoot the works — GO FOR BROKE
Shooter — TAW
Shooters, in marbles — TAWS
Shooting exercise — SKEET
Shooting gallery — RANGE
Shooting marbles — TAWS
Shooting sport — SKEET
Shoots holes in — DEBUNKS
Shoots in the direction of — FIRE AT
Shop — MERCHANT
Shop window sign — OPEN
Shopkeeper — RETAILER
Shoplift — ROB
Shopper stopper — SALE
Shopper's concern — PRICE
Shopper's delight — SALE
Shopper's homemade aid — LIST
Shopper's magnet — SALE
Shopper's mecca — MART
Shopper's need — LIST
Shopper's special — SALE
Shoppers' arenas — MALLS
Shoppers' concerns — PRICES
Shoppers' magnet — SALE
Shoppers' meccas — SALES
Shoppers' need — BAG, LIST
Shoppers' paradise — MALL
Shoppers' stop — MALL
Shopping area — ARCADE
Shopping area for Xanthippe — AGORA
Shopping bags — TOTES
Shopping center — MALL, MART
Shopping list dozen — EGGS
Shopping list entry — ITEM
Shopping list notation — ITEM
Shopping place — MART
Shoptalk — ARGOT
Shore — DINAH, SEASIDE, STRAND
Shore _____ — LEAVE
Shore bird — AVOCET, ERN, ERNE, PLOVER, RAIL, TERN
Shore dinner item — MUSSEL, ROE
Shore dinner tidbit — SCALLOP
Shore flyer — ERNE
Shore of song — DINAH
Shore stalker — HERON
Shore structure — PIER
Shore up an entryway? — PROPAGATE
Shore-related — LITTORAL
Shorebird — ERN, ERNE, WADER
Shoreline — SEASIDE
Shoreline feature — INLET
Shoreline peril — SHOAL
Shorelines — COASTS
Shores (up) — PROPS
Short-billed birds — SORAS
Short-billed rail — CRAKE, SORA
Short-haired dog — DALMATIAN

Short-legged horse — COB
Short-tailed parrot — LORY
Short — SHY
Short _____ (little attention) — SHRIFT
Short _____ (quick work) — SHRIFT
Short and not so sweet — CURT
Short and plump — PUDGY
Short and sharp — TERSE
Short and sweet — BRIEF, TERSE, TO THE POINT
Short break — CATNAP
Short commercials — ADS
Short cut — CREW
Short distance — STEP
Short dog — POM
Short drink in a pub — TOT
Short drive — SPIN
Short estimate — EST
Short farewell — BYE
Short farm vehicle — TRAC
Short fiber — NOIL
Short haircuts — BOBS
Short jackets — ETONS
Short lawsuit? — BRIEFCASE
Short legged horses — COBS
Short letter — NOTE
Short lines to fasten nets — NORSELS
Short lives? — BIOS
Short memos — JOTS
Short message — NOTE
Short noncom? — SGT
Short of the ready — HARD UP
Short on looks — UGLY
Short order — OMELET
Short piece of music — ARIETTA
Short plane trip — HOP
Short plant stalk — STIPE
Short play — I ACT
Short press bios — OBITS
Short race — DASH
Short ride — SPIN
Short skirt — TUTU
Short smoke: Slang — CIG
Short snorts — NIPS
Short sock — ANKLET
Short spade — SPUD
Short spelling of "gauge" — GAGE
Short story — WEEKLY
Short story: Fr. — CONTE
Short surplice — COTTA
Short swim — DIP
Short tail — SCUT
Short tempered — TESTY
Short term of endearment — HON
Short textile fibers — NOIL
Short time — TWO SHAKES
Short trip — EXC
Short trips — HOPS
Short wave — PERM
Short window drapery — VALANCE
Short, musical composition — SONATINA
Short-fused ones — HOT-HEADS
Short-lived — FADING
Short-spoken — ABRUPT
Short-timer — FLY BY NIGHT
Shortage — NEED, WANT
Shortages — DROUGHTS
Shortchanges — SWINDLES
Shorten — CLIP
Shorten sails — REEF
Shortened a sail — REEFED
Shortened form, for short — ABBR
Shortened versions: Abbr. — ABRS
Shortening — LARD
Shortest day phenomenon — WINTER SOLSTICE
Shortest route — BEELINE
Shorthairs — CATS
Shorthand experts — STENOS
Shorthand notebook — STENOPAD
Shorthand pro — STENO
Shorthand taker for short — STENOG
Shorthand whiz — STENO
Shorthander — STENO
Shorthorns — CATTLE
Shortly — ANON
Shorts — BERMUDAS
Shortstop — INFIELDER
Shoshone Falls site — IDAHO
Shoshonean — HOPI, UTE
Shoshoneans of Colo. — UTES
Shot — DONE
Shot follower — CHASER
Shot for Snead — CHIP
Shot in billiards — CAROM
Shot in the arm — BOOST
Shot on the ice — SLAP
Shot or dragon predecessor — SNAP
Shot two under par on a hole — EAGLED
Shot, as of liquor — SNORT
Shotgun sport — SKEET
Should's cousin — WOULD
Shoulder — BEAR, CARRY
Shoulder blade — SCAPULA
Shoulder part — BLADE
Shoulder piece — STOLE
Shoulder to elbow bones — HUMERI
Shoulder warmer — SHAWL, STOLE
Shoulder wrap — STOLE
Shoulder: Comb. form — OMO
Shout — YELL
Shout after final curtain — AUTHOR
Shout at the opera — ENCORE
Shout for help — YELL
Shout of derision — YAH
Shout of joy — HOORAY
Shouted — CLAMORED
Shove off — DEPART
Show — MOVIE
Show a movie — SCREEN
Show amazement — PANT
Show approval — APPLAUD, CLAP, NOD
Show avarice — COVET
Show biz acronym — ASCAP
Show biz award — OBIE
Show biz talk — BREAK A LEG
Show boredom — YAWN
Show business, with "the" — STAGE
Show car — DEMO
Show contempt — SNEER
Show delight — CLAP, GRIN
Show excessive fondness — DOTE
Show excitement — PANT
Show fatigue — NOD
Show fear — COWER, CRINGE
Show for "Hawkeye" — MASH
Show from a show — SPIN OFF
Show gratitude — THANK
Show happiness — EXULT
Show in — USHER
Show indecision — WAVER
Show indignation — RESENT
Show muscle — FLEX
Show of temper — TANTRUM
Show off — GRANDSTAND, PREEN
Show passion — EMOTE
Show pluck — DARE
Show reverence — KNEEL
Show signs of wear — ERODE
Show sorrow — RUE
Show stomach discomfort — RETCH
Show suppressed anger — SMOLDER
Show surprise — GASP
Show the way — USHER
Show up — APPEAR
Show up again — REAPPEAR
Show up for the 15th — REUNE
Show weariness — PANT
Show-biz medium — STAGE
Show-off — HOT DOG
Showboat — SPLURGE
Showcases — DISPLAYS
Showed a film again — RERAN
Showed an old TV program — RERAN
Showed concern — CARED
Showed empathy — CARED
Showed interest — SAT UP
Showed mercy — SPARED
Showed nerve — DARED
Showed partisanship — SIDED

Showed pleasure — SMILED
Showed respect — SALUTED
Showed reverence — ADORED
Showed the movies again — RERAN
Showed the way — LED
Showed up — CAME
Shower — POUR, RAIN
Shower ice — SLEET
Showered — RAINED
Showers frigidly — SLEETS
Showery month — APRIL
Showing clearly — EVINCING
Showing composure — POISED
Showing corrosion — EATEN
Showing homage — OBEISANT
Showing no partiality — UNBIASED
Showing: Abbr. — DEMO
Showmaker's tool — AWL
Shows clemency — SPARES
Shows disdain — SCORNS
Shows of bad temper — SNITS
Shows scorn — SNEERS
Shows, western style — RODEOS
Showy — ARTY, ORNATE
Showy clothing — FINERY
Showy embellishment — AURUM PLATING
Showy fan palms — TALIPOTS
Showy flowers — DAHLIAS
Showy houseplant — CALLA
Showy lily — SEGO
Showy plant — PHLOX
Showy shrubs — AZALEAS
Shreads of threads — LINT
Shred — TEAR UP
Shredder — TEARER
Shrewd — ASTUTE, CUTE, FOXY, PERSPICACIOUS, WILY
Shrewd manner — CAGINESS
Shrieks — SCREAMS, YELLS
Shrill — HIGH, LOUD, STRIDENT, TREBLE
Shrill barks — YIPS
Shrill cry, as of an owl — SCREECH
Shrill outcries — SHRIEKS
Shrill sounds — SHRIEKS
Shrimp — RUNT
Shrimp dish — SCAMPI
Shrimp relative — PRAWN
Shrimp's cousin — PRAWN
Shrimp, on a trattoria menu — SCAMPI
Shrine Bowl team — WEST
Shrine Bowl teams — EASTS
Shrine sight — RELIC
Shrine site in Portugal — FATIMA
Shrine to remember — ALAMO
Shrink — WINCE
Shrinking one — CRINGER
Shrinks back — RESILES
Shrivels — WILTS, WIZENS
Shriver and Dawber — PAMS
Shriver of tennis — PAM
Shriver shot — ACE
Shroud cite — TURIN
Shrove Tuesday follower — LENT
Shrovetide follower — LENT
Shroyer role — ENOS
Shrub — ALTER
Shrub of the heath family — AZALEA
Shrub of the rose family — SPIREA
Shrub related to the roses — SPIREA
Shrubby tree — SUMAC
Shrubby wasteland — HEATH
Shrubs for a warm region — MIMOSA
Shucks! — RATS
Shuffle along — AMBLE
Shun — AVOID, ELUDE, IGNORE
Shunned — OSTRACIZED
Shunned, in a big way — BOYCOTTED
Shunning spirits — ON THE WAGON
Shuns — ESCHOWS
Shur play, with "The" — NERD
Shut — CLOSE
Shut down — CEASE
Shut in — CORRAL
Shut out — DEBAR
Shut tight — BOLT, SEALED
Shut up — COOP, TRAPPED
Shuts out — DEBARS
Shutter parts — SLATS
Shutters — BLINDS
Shuttle operators — NASA
Shuttle phase — REENTRY
Shy — BASHFUL, MODEST, START, TIMID
Shy away — CRINGE, START
Shy Pilgrim — ALDEN
Shylock, e.g. — USURER
Siam coin — TICAL
Siam or Japan follower — ESE
Siamangs — APES
Siamese — CAT, THAI
Siamese coins — BAHTS, TICALS
Siamese measure — NGAN, RAI
Sian is its capital — SHENSI
Sib — SIS
Sibelius and Nurmi — FINNS
Sibelius tone poem, with "The" — SWAN OF TUONELA
Sibelius's countrymen — FINNS
Sibelius, composer — JEAN
Siberian antelope — SAIGA
Siberian city — OMSK
Siberian landscape — STEPPE
Siberian log hut — ISBA
Siberian river — AMUR, LENA
Siberian sled dog — SAMOYED
Siberian snowstorm — PURGA
Siberian supernatural practitioner — SHAMAN
Siberian tribesman — TATAR
Sibilant aside — PSST
Sibilant sound — HISS
Sibilate — HISSING
Sibiliant letter — ESS
Sibling for sis — BRO
Sibling's daughters — NIECES
Sibling, for short — BRO
Siblings: Abbr. — BROS
Sibyl — ORACLE
Sic — THUS
Sicilian center — ENNA
Sicilian city — ENNA
Sicilian code of silence — OMERTA
Sicilian landmark — ETNA
Sicilian peak — ETNA
Sicilian port — MESSINA
Sicilian resort — ENNA
Sicilian sight: Var. — AETNA
Sicilian smoker — ETNA
Sicilian spa — ENNA
Sicilian volcano — ETNA
Sicily's capital — PALERMO
Sicily's harbor — PALERMO
Sicily's hot wind — SIROCCO
Sick and tired — FED UP
Sick to one's stomach — QUEASY
Sick: Ger. — KRANK
Sicken — AIL, UPSET
Sickens — AILS
Sickest — ILLEST
Sickle — MOW
Sid's co-star — IMOGENE
Side — BRIM
Side arm — PISTOL
Side by side — ABREAST
Side dish — COLE SLAW, SLAW
Side line — BRANCH
Side meat — BACON
Side of a triangle — LEG
Side of ship, of old — BOAR
Side order — SALAD
Side petals — ALAE
Side petals, in botany — ALAE
Side show to leave one scratching — FLEA CIRCUS
Side view of a human head — PROFILE
Side with — SUPPORT
Side-by-side, at sea — ABEAM
Side-kick — PAL
Side-step — PARRY
Sideboard — BUFFET
Sideboard display — TEA SET
Sideboard: Fr. — DESSERTE
Sideburns — HAIR
Sideburns locale — CHEEK
Sidekick — CHUM, PAL

Sideline — BENCH
Sidepiece of a door — JAMB
Sidereal — STARRY
Siderite — ORE
Siderite or stibnite — ORE
Sides of cricket fields — OFFS
Sides of cricket wickets — ONS
Sideshow entertainer — FIRE EATER
Sideshow pitchman becomes gameshow host — BOB BARKER
Sideslip — SKID, SLUE
Sidestep — DODGE, ELUDE
Sidestepped — DUCKED, EVADED
Sidesteps — EVADES
Sidetrack — DETOUR, PIGEONHOLE, SHUNT
Sidewalk — PATH
Sidewalk eateries — CAFES
Sidewalk eatery — CAFE
Sidewalk grass trimmers — EDGERS
Sidewalk site — CAFE
Sidewall, e.g. — TIRE
Sidewinder — SNAKE
Sidewinders and Skybolts — MISSILES
Siding — BOARDS
Siding bolts — PAWLS
Sidled — EDGED
Sidney Kingsley play: 1934 — MEN IN WHITE
Sieben follower — ACHT
Siecle — AGE
Siege Perilous — SEAT
Siegfried: Ger. — HERO
Sienna — PIGMENT
Siepi, Hines, et al. — BASSI
Sierra _____ — LEONE, MADRE
Sierra Nevada peak — WHITNEY
Sierra Nevada resort — TAHOE
Sierra Nevada's locale — SPAIN
Siesta — NAP
Sieve — SIFT
Sieve boiled food — PUREE
Sievelike vessels — LEACHES
Sif's husband — THOR
Sift — SCREEN, SIEVE
Sifter — SIEVE
Sigh — MOAN
Sigh for Yorick — ALAS
Sigher's word — ALAS
Sighing phrase — AH ME
Sight along the Ganges — GHAT
Sight and smell — SENSES
Sight at Agra — TAJ MAHAL
Sight at Ipanema — CABANA
Sight attachment — SEER
Sight enhancer — EYEGLASS
Sight follower — SEER
Sight from a schooner — WHITE CAPS
Sight from Cleveland — ERIE
Sight from the League of Nations — LAKE GENEVA
Sight from Warwick Castle — AVON
Sight in Kyoto — PAGODA
Sight in the country — SILO
Sight of Knight's fights — LISTS
Sight organs — EYES
Sight, in Sedan — VUE
Sight-related — OPTIC
Sightless — BLIND
Sights at Shaker Heights — ESTATES
Sights at Stowe — SLOPES
Sigil — SEAL
Sigma — ESS
Sigma _____ (frat of sondom) — CHI
Sigma follower — TAU
Sigma preceder — RHO
Sigma upsilon separator — TAU
Sigmoid — CURVE
Sigmoid molding — OGEE
Sign — INK, JUST MARRIED
Sign a lease — RENT
Sign at a crossing — SLOW
Sign away — WAIVE
Sign for a seer — OMEN
Sign for another hitch — REUP
Sign for Churchill — VEE
Sign gas — NEON
Sign in — PEN
Sign in the theatre — EXIT
Sign language — AMESLAN
Sign of a cold — SNEEZE
Sign of a doctor — SHINGLE
Sign of a hit — SRO
Sign of a sort — OMEN
Sign of an overused hammock — SAG
Sign of approval — NOD
Sign of assent — NOD
Sign of disapproval — HISS, THUMBS DOWN
Sign of endearment — CARESS
Sign of healing — SCAB
Sign of illness — SYMPTOM
Sign of pleasure — GRIN
Sign of shame — STIGMA
Sign of sorrow — TEAR
Sign of sorts — HEX
Sign of spring — MAY POLE, ROBIN
Sign of the blues — GLOOMINESS
Sign of the future — OMEN
Sign of the Ram — ARES
Sign of the times — NEON
Sign of the Zodiac — ARIES, LIBRA
Sign of triumph — VEE
Sign on a door — ENTER, PRIVATE
Sign on a staff — CLEF
Sign on sale merchandise — AS IS
Sign on the _____ line — DOTTED
Sign on the staff — CLEF
Sign seen throughout the world — COLA
Sign that's fine or malign — OMEN
Sign to delight angels — SRO
Sign up — ENROL, ENTER, JOIN
Sign up for service — ENLIST
Sign, in a way — INK
Sign-language developer — EPEE
Sign-language pioneer — EPEE
Signal — CUE, FLARE
Signal fire — FLARE
Signal flare — FUZEE
Signal of rejection — THUMBS DOWN
Signal of the approach of something — HERALD
Signal to attract attention — PST
Signaled — WAVED
Signals — CUES, FLARES, GESTURES
Signals for silence — PSTS
Signature — JOHN HENRY
Signed — INKED
Signed and sealed transfer — DEED
Signed up — ENTERED
Signed up as a G.I. — ENL
Signed vouchers — CHIT
Signer as owner — ENDORSER
Signet — SEAL
Significance — PITH
Significant times — ERAS
Signified — DENOTED
Signifies assent — NODS
Signify — FLAG, WAVE
Signify agreement — NOD
Signifying a maiden name — NEE
Signoret film: 1967 — GAMES
Signs — INKS, OMENS
Signs a contract — INKS
Signs of a hit — SROS
Signs of approval — NODS
Signs of healing — SCABS
Signs of sorrow — TEARS
Signs of Spring — BLOSSOMS
Signs of suffrage — BALLOTS
Signs on — HIRES
Signs up — ENLISTS, JOINS
Signs used in printing — FISTS
Signs, in a way — INKS
Sigurd's steed — GRANI
Sikh's coin — RUPEE
Sikorsky — IGOR
Sikorsky and Stravinsky — IGORS
Silas _____, diplomat — DEANE

Silas Marner apparatus — LOOM
Silas Marner's foundling — EPPIE
Silence — GAG, HUSH
Silent — PLACID, TACIT
Silent comedian — HARPO MARX
Silent one — CLAM
Silent screen star — NEGRI
Silent vamp Negri — POLA
Silents' Theda — BARA
Silenus, e.g. — SATYR
Silesian river — ODER
Silex — SILICA
Silhouette — PROFILE, SHADOW
Silica gem — OPAL
Silicates — MICAS
Silk-stocking class — ELITE
Silk — TULLE
Silk compound — SERICIN
Silk fabric — SATIN, SENDAL, SHANTUNG, TRAM
Silk fabric of yore — SAMITE
Silk fabrics — MOIRES
Silk from Assam — ERIA
Silk hat — OPERA
Silk makers — ERIAS
Silk, in Savoie — SOIE
Silken — SERIC, SOFT
Silkworm — ERI, ERIA
Silkworm of Assam — ERIA
Sill — LEDGE
Sillographers' creations — SATIRES
Silly — ASININE, INANE
Silly goose — TWIT
Silly laugh — TITTER
Silly one — ASS
Silly ones — GEESE
Silly people — GEESE, SAPS
Silly smile — SIMPER
Silo — GRANARY
Silo contents — FODDER
Silt and sand — ALLUVIA
Silty spot — DELTA
Silver — LONE RANGERS HORSE
Silver _____ — SCREEN
Silver and china — TABLEWARE
Silver braid — ORROS
Silver center in N.Y. — ONEIDA
Silver coin of Turkey — ASPER
Silver dollar — CARTWHEEL
Silver in Seville — PLATA
Silver or Trigger — MOUNT
Silver pesos — DUROS
Silver salmon — COHO
Silver sidekick — PARROT
Silver source — MINE
Silver Springs neighbor — OCALA
Silver State city — RENO
Silver: Comb. form — ARGENT
Silverheels role — TONTO
Silvers from Brooklyn — PHIL
Silvers or Spitalny — PHIL
Silvertip — BEAR
Silverware item — TEASPOON
Silverweed — TANSY
Silvery — ARGENT
Silvery fishes — SMELTS
Silvery white — ARGENT
Silvery-white ice — RIME
Simba — LION
Simba's call — ROAR
Simba's sound — ROAR
Simian — APE
Similar — ALIKE, LIKE, PARALLEL
Similar to a common cornichon? — TYPICKLE
Similar: Prefix — HOMEO
Similarities — ANALOGIES
Similarity — PARALLEL
Simile — PARALLEL
Simile words — ASA
Similitude — ANALOGY
Simmer in summer — BOIL
Simmer spot — BACK BURNER
Simoleons — MOOLA
Simon _____ (elimination game) — SAYS
Simon _____, St. John the Divine carver — VERITY
Simon does it — SAYS
Simon objective — SIMPLE
Simon of the opera — ESTES
Simon or Diamond — NEIL
Simon pure — REAL
Simon's "_____ Suite" — PLAZA
Simon's sporty slob — OSCAR
Simone of song — NINA
Simone's smoke — TABAC
Simones school — ECOLE
Simper — SMIRK
Simple — EASY, MERE, NAIVE
Simple addition — ELL
Simple one — SIMON
Simple organisms — MONADS
Simple organisms: Var. — AMEBES
Simple plant — ALGA
Simple Simon met him — PIEMAN
Simple Simon's pal — MORON
Simple song — DITTY
Simple sugars — OSES
Simple wind instrument — OCARINA
Simple's companion — PURE
Simple-hearted — SINCERE
Simple-minded — FOOLISH
Simpletons — GEESE
Simplicity — EASE
Simply — ONLY
Simpson and Starr — BARTS
Simulacrum — IMAGE, MATCH, TWIN
Simulate — MAKE BELIEVE, PERSONATE, POSTURE
Simulated gold — ORMOLU
Simulates — FEIGNS
Simultaneous occurrence — SYNCHRONY
Sin — EVIL, TRESPASS, VIOLATION
Sin city — SODOM
Sin site — EDEN
Sinatra contemporary — COMO
Sinatra film: 1954 — SUDDENLY
Sinatra's cohorts — CLAN
Sinbad and Popeye — SEAFARERS
Sinbad's transport — ROC
Since — AGO
Since, in Stuttgart — SEIT
Sincere — HEARTY, HONEST, REAL
Sincere appreciation — HEARTFELT THANKS
Sinclair Lewis to friends — RED
Sine _____ (indefinitely) — DIE
Sine qua _____ — NON
Sine qua non — IDEALS
Sinew — TENDON
Sinful — EVIL
Sing — TRILL
Sing _____ — ALONG
Sing gently — CROON
Sing in a way — YODEL
Sing like a bird — TRILL
Sing like Bing — CROON
Sing like Ella — SCAT
Sing lustily — TROLL
Sing wordlessly — HUM
Sing, as a lullaby — CROON
Sing-along — SONGFEST
Singapore's continent — ASIA
Singe — BURN, CHAR, SCORCH
Singer-actress Lotte — LENYA
Singer-song writer ("Piano Man") — BILLY JOEL
Singer — BARD, DIVA, MUSICIAN
Singer Acuff — ROY
Singer Adams — EDIE
Singer Al B. _____ — SURE
Singer and Soviet river — LENAS
Singer Anita — BAKER, ODAY
Singer Baker — ANITA
Singer Barbara — MANDRELL
Singer Brewer — TERESA
Singer Brooks — GARTH
Singer Burl — IVES
Singer Campbell — GLEN
Singer Cantrell — LANA
Singer Cassidy — SHAUN
Singer Clapton — ERIC
Singer Cole — NAT
Singer Connie — STEVENS

Singer Coolidge — RITA
Singer Davis — MAC
Singer Debby — BOONE
Singer Della — REESE
Singer Diana — ROSS
Singer Easton — SHEENA
Singer Ed — AMES
Singer Edith — PIAF
Singer Falana — LOLA
Singer Feliciano — JOSE
Singer Frankie — LAINE
Singer Franklin — ARETHA
Singer from Australia — REDDY
Singer Guthrie — ARLO
Singer Helen — REDDY
Singer Horne — LENA
Singer Houston — WHITNEY
Singer Jagger — MICK
Singer James — ETTA
Singer James or Jones — ETTA
Singer Janet Baker's title — DAME
Singer Janis — IAN
Singer Jerry — VALE
Singer Joan — BAEZ
Singer Joanna — NEEL
Singer John — ELTON
Singer Johnny — CASH
Singer Judd — NAOMI
Singer Julius — LAROSA
Singer Kay — ARMEN
Singer Kiki — DEE
Singer Kirk — LISA
Singer Kitt — EARTHA
Singer Kristofferson — KRIS
Singer Laine — CLEO
Singer Larry — GATLIN
Singer Lenya — LOTTE
Singer Logan — ELLA
Singer Lopez — TRINI
Singer Lorna — LUFT
Singer Lou from Chicago — RAWLS
Singer Lucine — AMARA
Singer Luft — LORNA
Singer Manchester — MELISSA
Singer McEntire — REBA
Singer Mel — TORME
Singer Mitchell — JONI
Singer Moreno — RITA
Singer Natalie's dad — NAT
Singer Newton — WAYNE
Singer Newton-John — OLIVIA
Singer Nixon — MARNI
Singer of "God Bless America" fame — SMITH
Singer of "I Am Woman" fame — REDDY
Singer of "Over the Rainbow" fame — GARLAND
Singer of "Stop the Music" fame — ARMEN
Singer of opera — DIVA
Singer Osmond — MARIE
Singer Page — PATTI
Singer Paul — ANKA
Singer Paul from Ottawa — ANKA
Singer Peerce — JAN
Singer Perry — COMO
Singer Petina — IRRA
Singer Petula — CLARK
Singer Ponselle — ROSA
Singer Rawls — LOU
Singer Ray or Bob — EBERLE
Singer Redding — OTIS
Singer Reese — DELLA
Singer renowned for her Gilda — GALLICURCI
Singer Richard _____ -Bennet — DYER
Singer Richie from Alabama — LIONEL
Singer Robert of "The Most Happy Fella" — REEDE
Singer Ronstadt — LINDA
Singer Ross — LANNY
Singer Simon — CARLY
Singer Stevens — KAYE
Singer Stuart — ENZO
Singer Sullivan — KATHIE
Singer Sumac — YMA
Singer Sumac and namesakes — YMAS
Singer Susan — ANTON
Singer Tennille — TONI
Singer Teresa — BREWER
Singer Torme — MEL
Singer Travis — RANDY
Singer Tucker — TANYA
Singer Tucker, et al. — TANYAS
Singer Turner — TINA
Singer Turner and namesakes — TINAS
Singer Vallee — RUDY
Singer Vic — DAMONE
Singer Vikki — CARR
Singer Vikki from El Paso — CARR
Singer Warwick — DIONNE
Singer Willie — NELSON
Singer Yma — SUMAC
Singer, comedienne Martha — RAYE
Singer-actor Burl — IVES
Singer-actress Cara — IRENE
Singer-actress Kirk — LISA
Singer-actress Lena — HORNE
Singer-composer from Canada — ANKA
Singer-guitarist Axton — HOYT
Singers on the briny — SIRENS
Singers' syllables — TRAS
Singes — SEARS
Singing and dancing — ARTS
Singing barber — FIGARO
Singing brothers — AMES
Singing group — CHORALE, CHORUS, SEXTET, TRIO
Singing insect — WASP
Singing King — COLE
Singing syllable — TRA
Singing syllables — LALA
Singing Turner — TINA
Singing voice — ALTO, BASS, TENOR
Single — ONE, ONLY, UNAL
Single pers. — INDIV
Single star — UNMARRIED ACTOR
Single thing — UNIT
Single unit — ONE
Single-celled organism — MONAD
Single-edged Philippine knife — BOLO
Single-masted vessel — SLOOP
Single-seeded fruit — ACHENE
Singlehanded — LONE
Singles — ONES
Singles and doubles — HITS
Singles champ at Wimbledon: 1939 — BOBBY RIGGS
Singles champ at Wimbledon: 37-38 — DONALD BUDGE
Singles champ at Wimbledon: 59-60 — MARIA BUENO
Singles star — TENNIS CHAMPION
Singles to female singles — MISSES HITS
Singles, in Mexico — UNOS
Singleton — ONE
Sings like Columbo — CROONS
Sings lustily — TROLLS
Sings, in a way — CROONS
Singsong speech — CANT
Singular — ODD, RARE
Singular performance — ARIA
Singular reflexive — ONESELF
Singultus — HICCUPS
Sinister or ugly — ILL LOOKING
Sink — BASIN, IMMERSE, SAG
Sink down gradually — SETTLE
Sink part — TRAP
Sink spot — DRAIN
Sink's alternative — SWIM
Sinker — DONUT, LEADY
Sinkiang staple — RICE
Sinking gradually — LAPSING
Sinking ship leaver — RAT
Sinless — PURE
Sinn Fein homeland — ERIN
Sinned — ERRED
Sinner — DEBTOR
Sinner turned saintly — ATONER
Sino-Russian river — AMUR
Sins — ERRS, VICES
Sinuous — WAVY
Sinuous Eastern dance — NAUTCH
Sinus — CAVITY

Sinus cavities — ANTRA
Sinuses — ANTRA, CAVITIES
Siouan — OTO, OTOE
Siouan Indian — OTOE, PONCA
Siouan of Okla. — OTO
Siouan people — OSAGE, OTO, OTOE
Siouan speaker — OSAGE, OTOE
Siouan tongue — OSAGE
Siouan tribe — DAKOTA, MISSOURI
Siouan tribesman — OTOE
Sioux — DAKOTAS, OMAHAS, OTO, OTOE
Sioux member — OTOE
Siphonaptera members — FLEAS
Siqueiros work — OBRA
Sir _____ Dolin of ballet fame — ANTON
Sir _____ Guinness — ALEC
Sir _____ Newton — ISAAC
Sir _____ Richardson — RALPH
Sir Arthur _____ Doyle — CONAN
Sir Arthur Wing — PINERO
Sir Christopher, the architect — WREN
Sir Francis — DRAKE
Sir Galahad's mother — ELAINE
Sir George _____ — SOLTI
Sir Geraint's wife — ENID
Sir Henry Irving, e.g. — ACTOR
Sir Henry Wotton's Rx — A WELL CHOSEN BOOK
Sir of Lord — TITLE
Sir Thomas — MORE
Sir, in Delhi — SAHIB
Sir, in India — SAHIB
Sir, in Santiago — SENOR
Sire — BEGAT, BEGET, BREED, FATHER
Sire, Biblical style — BEGET
Siren — ALLURER, ATTRACTER, ENTICER
Siren signals — ALARMS
Sirius in Canis Major — DOG STAR
Sirius or Vega — STAR
Sirocco — WIND
Sis or bro. — REL
Sisal — HEMP
Siskel's partner — EBERT
Sissified — PRISSY
Sissy of films — SPACEK
Sissy, the actress — SPACEK
Sister — NUN
Sister of Ares — ERIS
Sister of Calliope — ERATO
Sister of John and Lionel — ETHEL
Sister of Santa — PINTA, NINA, MARIA
Sister's daughter — NIECE
Sisters — NUNS
Sisters of Ares — ERIS
Sit — POSE
Sit for a portrait — POSE
Sit like a slouch — SLUMP
Sit on — SQUELCH
Sit still for — POSE
Sitar solos — RAGAS
Sitarist Shankar — RAVI
Sitcom starring Sherman Hemsley — AMEN
Site for a contest — ARENA
Site for a drum — EAR
Site for light bites — SNACK-BAR
Site for lots of bucks — RODEO
Site for Sir Flinders — RUINS
Site in the news: 12/7/41 — PEARL HARBOR
Site of "Potemkin" revolt — ODESSA
Site of 1952 olympics — OSLO
Site of 1962 Kennedy-Kruschev confrontation — CUBA
Site of 1987 Brititsh Open — MUIRFIELD
Site of a 1431-43 council — BASLE
Site of a biblical splashdown — ARARAT
Site of a civil rights march — SELMA
Site of a Liza Doolittle triumph — ASCOT
Site of Alabama State U. — MONTGOMERY
Site of an 1836 battle — ALAMO
Site of an ancient wonder — RHODES
Site of an architectural master-piece — AGRA
Site of ancient olympic games — ELIS
Site of Basra — IRAQ
Site of Beersheba — ISRAEL
Site of Bhutan — ASIA
Site of Cardinal Wolsey's mansion — ESHER
Site of cave temples in India — ELLORA
Site of Christ's first miracle — CANA
Site of first opera, 1611 — TURIN
Site of Fort McIntosh — LAR
Site of Funafuti — TUVALU
Site of Gray's herd — LEA
Site of Hells Canyon — IDAHO
Site of Hercules' lion slaying — NEMEA
Site of Humayun's tomb — DELHI
Site of India's National Defense Academy — POONA
Site of Iowa State College — AMES
Site of Jan. 1 event — ORANGE BOWL, ROSE BOWL
Site of Kampala — UGANDA
Site of Kinabalu — BORNEO
Site of King Arthur's palace — CAMELOT
Site of Knights' fights — LISTS
Site of Kubla Khan's garden — XANADU
Site of La Scala — MILAN
Site of Marina City — CHICAGO
Site of Mumtaz Mahal's tomb — AGRA
Site of Phillips University — ENID
Site of Rainbow Bridge National Monument — UTAH
Site of rods and cones — RETINA
Site of shootings, May 4, 1970: Abbr. — KSU
Site of St. Columba's abbey — IONA
Site of Stanford Univ. — PALO ALTO
Site of T. Moore's harp — TARA
Site of Taj Mahal — AGRA
Site of Teheran — IRAN
Site of the Alhambra — GRANADA
Site of the first Olympics — ELIS
Site of the Krupp works — ESSEN
Site of the Louvre — PARIS
Site of the Taj Mahal — AGRA
Site of Twain's remains — ELMIRA
Site of Vance A.F.B. — ENID
Site of Vientiane — LAOS
Site of Washburn collete — TOPEKA
Site, WW II conference — TEHRAN
Site: Abbr. — LOC
Sites along the Atlantic — SEASHORES
Sites for gladiators — ARENAE
Sits — MEETS
Sits for — POSES
Sits in — ATTENDS
Sitter's creation — LAP
Sitter's feature — LAP
Sitting Bull's enemy — CUSTER
Sitting Bull's social group? — INDIAN CLUB
Sitting Bull, for example — CHIEF
Sitting duck — PATSY, PREY
Sitting face to face — VIS A VIS
Sitting pretty — ON TOP
Situate — POSIT

Situation — CASE, PLACE, SETUP
Situation controlled — IN HAND
Situation inducing warmth — FIRESIDE ROMANCE
Sitwell — EDITH
Sitwell character — ELISA
Six-line poem — SESTET
Six-sided body — CUBE
Six bells on the midwatch — THREE AM
Six follower — TEEN
Six ft. measurement — FTH
Six hearts, e.g. — BID
Six line stanzas — SESTET
Six made a drachma — OBOLS
Six on a die — SICE
Six or seven trailer — TEEN
Six or wolf — PACK
Six popes and Edgar Douglas — ADRIANS
Six, in dice — SICE
Six-line stanzas — SESTETS
Six-sided state — UTAH
Six-time N.L. home-run leader — OTT
Six: Prefix — HEXA
Sixteenth & thirteenth Gr. letters — PI AND NU
Sixth century date — DVII
Sixth Jewish month — ADAR
Sixth Jewish month in civil calendars — ADAR
Sixth letter — ZETA
Sixth minor prophet — MICAH
Sixth or common follower — SENSE
Sixth president — ADAMS
Sixth sense, for short — ESP
Sixties protest group — SDS
Sixty minutes in Siena — ORA
Sixty-six, for one — ROUTE
Sizable — LARGE
Size of paper — POTT
Sized up — EYE, CASED, MEASURED
Sizzle — FRY
Sizzling serves — ACES
Skagerrak feeder — OTRA
Skate blade — RUNNER
Skate feature — BLADE
Skate parts — EDGES
Skater Babilonia — TAI
Skater Babilonia and namesakes — TAIS
Skater Gardner — RANDY
Skater Hamilton — SCOTT
Skater Heiden — ERIC
Skater Katarina — WITT
Skater Sonja — HENIE
Skater with two golds — WITT
Skater's surface — ICE
Skaters Heiden and Flaim — ERICS
Skating headwear? — ROLLER DERBY
Sked posting — ETA
Skedaddle — DART, FLEE, SCOOT
Skedaddles — SCOOTS
Skeedaddled — FLED
Skeet feat — HIT
Skeletal — SKINNY
Skeleton — BONES
Skeleton crew — CADRE
Skeleton in the closet — SCANDAL
Skeleton key — PASSKEY
Skelton — RED
Skelton's _____ Kadiddlehopper — CLEM
Skelton's script-writing wife — EDNA
Skep — HIVE
Skep builders — BEES
Sketch — DRAW, DELINEATE, SKIT
Sketch again — REDRAW
Sketched — DRAWN, DREW
Sketches, in a way — DRAFTS
Skewbald — PIED
Skewed — ALOP
Skewer — ROAST, SPIKE, SPIT
Ski course — SLALOM
Ski lift — T BAR
Ski maneuver — STEM
Ski race — SLALOM
Ski report words — CORN SNOW
Ski resort — ASPEN
Ski resort fixtures — T BARS
Ski resort in Colorado — ASPEN
Ski resort in Utah — ALTA
Ski resort in Vermont — STOWE
Ski slope bump — MOGUL
Ski stick — POLE
Ski transports — T BARS
Ski turn — STEM
Ski wood — ASH
Ski-lodge offering — TODDY
Skid — FISHTAIL, SLIDE, SLUE
Skid-row affliction — DTS
Skid-row clientele — HOBO
Skid-row denizens — WINOS
Skid-row problem — DTS
Skidded — SLID
Skiddoo — GO AWAY, LEAVE, SHOO
Skidmore, Owings and Merrill — PARTNERS
Skier of a sort — LANGLAUFER
Skier's convenience — T BAR
Skier's equipment — POLES
Skier's gear — POLES
Skier's lift — T BAR
Skier's manuevers — STEM TURNS
Skier's milieu — SLOPE
Skier's Saint — BERNARD
Skier's transport — LIFT, T BAR
Skier's turn — ESS, TELEMARK
Skiers' org. — NSA
Skiers' paradise, to the French — ALPES
Skies — WELKINS
Skiff — DINGHY
Skiing center — ASPEN
Skiing champ Phil — MAHRE
Skiing descents — SLALOMS
Skiing turn — ESS
Skill — ART
Skilled — ABLE, ADEPT
Skilled partisan — POLEMIST
Skilled penman — SCRIBE
Skilled performers — ARTISTES
Skilled persons — ADEPTS
Skilled practitioners — ADEPTS
Skilled tradesmen — ARTISANS
Skillet — FRYER, PAN, SPIDER
Skillful — DEFT
Skillfully crafted — WELL MADE
Skim — GLIDE, SCRAPE
Skim off grease — DEFAT
Skim over — HIT THE HIGH SPOTS, SCAN
Skim through papers — BROWSE, SCAN
Skimpy — SCANT, SLIM, SPARE, STINGY
Skin — COAT, DERMA, FUR, HIDE, HULL, PARE, PELT, POD
Skin ailment — TINEA
Skin disease — TINEA
Skin exfoliation — SCURF
Skin flick — NUDIE
Skin furrow — STRIA
Skin Granny Smiths — PARE APPLES
Skin irritation — AMATE, UREDO
Skin layer — DERM
Skin of a tangerine — PEEL
Skin opening — PORE
Skin or slick preceder — OIL
Skin problem — ACNE, RASH
Skin tone — TAN
Skin-deep — SHALLOW
Skin: Comb. form — DERM
Skinflint — MISER
Skinflinty — CHEAP
Skinny — THIN
Skinny follower — DIP
Skins: Comb. form — DERMA
Skip — OMIT
Skip a syllable — ELIDE
Skip these on a rainy day — PUDDLES
Skipjack — BONITO
Skipped out — FLEW THE COOP

Skipped over — ELIDED
Skipped town — FLED
Skipper — MASTER
Skipper obsessed by a whale — AHAB
Skipper's order — LIE TO
Skipper, often — PILOT
Skips — OMITS
Skips over — ELIDES, OMITS
Skirmish — BATTLE
Skirt — AVOID, BYPASS, EVADE, HULA
Skirt addition — FLOUNCE
Skirt features — GORES, HEM, SLITS
Skirt fold — PLEAT
Skirt inset — GODET, GORE
Skirt openings — SLITS
Skirt shape — ALINE
Skirt style — A LINE, MIDI, MINI
Skirt type — A LINE
Skirt's eye-catchers — SLITS
Skirt-shorts hybrid — CULOTTES
Skirted the basket — RIMMED
Skirts in Sevilla — SAYAS
Skittered — SLID
Skittish — EDGY
Skittles' partner — BEER
Skives — PARES
Skivvies' old cousins — BVDS
Skoal and cheers — TOASTS
Skoal, e.g. — TOAST
Skoal, to a Berliner — PROSIT
Skulk — SLINK
Skulked — CREPT
Skulks — SNEAKS
Skull — CRANIUM
Skull part — AKKRA
Skull protrusion — INION
Skull protuberance — INION
Skunk — POLECAT
Skunk river city — AMES
Skunk's cousin — POLECAT
Skunk's relative — POLECAT
Sky altar — ARA
Sky Bear — URSA
Sky blue — AZURE
Sky enigma — UFO
Sky floater — BLIMP
Sky jockey — AERONAUT
Sky King's plane — SONGBIRD
Sky pastries? — PIES
Sky pilot's distance unit — AIRMILE
Sky sight — COMET
Sky sightings: Abbr. — UFOS
Sky-blue translucent — TURQUOISE
Sky-high — LOFTY
Sky: Comb. form — URAN, URANO
Skylight sight — SPIRE
Skyline site — SPIRE
Slab — CHUNK
Slack part of a sail — SLAB
Slack-jawed — AGAPE
Slacken — FLAG, REMIT
Slackened — EASED
Slackening: mus. — RIT
Slackens — EASES
Slacks — PANTS
Slacks' supporters — BELTS
Slag — DROSS, LAVA
Slain, Boleyn style — BEHEADED
Slalom manuevers — ZIGS
Slalom obstacle — GATE
Slalom turn — ESS
Slam — BANG, WHAM
Slammer — HOOSEGOW, JAIL, POKEY
Slammer springer — BAIL
Slammin' Sam and family — SNEADS
Slammin' Sam of golf — SNEAD
Slander — ASPERSE, DEFAME, SMEAR
Slander or defame — CALUMNIATE
Slandered — TRADUCED
Slang — LINGO
Slang for "good" — BAD
Slangy affirmative — YEP
Slangy assents — YEPS
Slangy denials — NAHS
Slangy negations — NOPES
Slangy negative — IXNAY, NO HOW, NOPE
Slangy negatives — NAHS
Slangy no — NAW
Slangy refusal — NAH
Slangy street greeting — GIVE ME SOME SKIN
Slangy suffix — AROO
Slangy suffixes — EROOS
Slangy turndown — NOPE
Slant — BEVEL, BIAS, SKEW, TILT
Slant a certain way — UPTILT
Slant, as news — COLOR
Slanted — ATILT, LEANT
Slanted letter — ITALIC
Slanted type: Abbr. — ITAL
Slanting — ASLOPE, ATILT
Slanting type — ITALIC
Slants — SLOPES
Slants a nail — TOES
Slanty type, for short — DIAG
Slap it on — SLATHER
Slap on — DAUB
Slaphappy — SILLY
Slapping sounds — SPLATS
Slapstick staples — PIES
Slash with a cavalry weapon — SABRE
Slashed — SLIT
Slat — LATH
Slate black — COLOR
Slate of court cases — DOCKET
Slats — SPLINES
Slattern — SLUT, TROLLOP
Slaughter — ENOS
Slaughter on the diamond — ENOS
Slaughterhouse — ABATTOIR
Slav — CROAT, CZECH, SERB
Slavanic sprite — VILA
Slave of old — HELOT
Slaver — DROOL
Slavery — GRIND, TOIL
Slaves — ESNES, SERFS
Slaves of yore — ESNES
Slaves to decorum — PRUDES
Slaw — SALAD
Slay 'em — WOW
Slayer of Achilles — PARIS
Slayer of Castor — IDAS
Sleazy — THIN
Sled — COASTER, LUGE, PUNG
Sled pullers — DOG TEAMS
Sleek — OILY
Sleep — REST
Sleep abbr. — REM
Sleep fitfully — TOSS
Sleep inducer — OPIATE, SANDMAN
Sleep inducer of a sort — BORE
Sleep lightly — DOZE, DROWSE
Sleep like _____ — A LOG, A TOP
Sleep meas. — REM
Sleep phenomenon: Abbr. — REM
Sleep problem — APNEA
Sleep study initials — REM
Sleep, food, etc. — NEEDS
Sleep, with "eye" — SHUT
Sleeper — TIE
Sleeper's activity, for short — REM
Sleeping accommodations — BED ROLLS
Sleeping car — PULLMAN
Sleeping with flowers? — A BED OF ROSES
Sleeps noisily — SNORES
Sleepy — TIRED
Sleepytime pal? — MISTER SANDMAN
Sleeve style — RAGLAN
Sleeve type — SET IN
Sleeveless garments — VESTS
Sleeveless jacket — VEST
Sleeveless wrap — CAPE
Sleighs, e.g. — RIDES
Sleight of hand — MAGIC
Slender — LEAN, REEDY, SLIM
Slender and sharp — ACEROSE
Slender as _____ — A REED
Slender bristle — AWN
Slender craft — CANOES
Slender finials — EPIS

Slender nail — BRAD
Slender sea creatures — EELS
Slender thread — FILAMENT
Slept like _____ — A LOG
Sleuth Charlie — CHAN
Sleuth Lupin — ARSENE
Sleuth of dime novel fame — NICK CARTER
Sleuth Spade — SAM
Sleuth Vance — PHILO
Sleuth with a "number one son" — CHAN
Sleuth Wolfe — NERO
Sleuth's quest — CLUE
Slew — RAFT, SCADS
Slice — CARVE, PARE, SEVER, SHAVE
Slice of bacon — BARD
Slice of the pie — SHARE
Sliced off sharply — SHEARED
Slices — CUTS
Slick — GLIB
Slick, with or without pics — MAG
Slicker — CHEAT
Slicks, e.g. — MAGS
Slide — SLIP
Sliding bolt — PAWL
Sliding piece of machinery — CAM
Slight — MERE, THIN, TINY
Slight advantage — EDGE, TOE HOLD
Slight altercation — SPAT
Slight breeze — WAFT
Slight burn — SINGE
Slight coloration — TINGE
Slight lead — EDGE
Slighter — LESS
Slightest — LEAST
Slightly open — AJAR
Slightly purplish-gray — SLATY
Slightly risqué — RACY
Slightly sarcastic — SNIDE
Slightly tapering — TERETE
Slights — SLURS
Slip-ups — BOOBOOS
Slip — ERROR, GLIDE, LAPSE, SKID, STUMBLE
Slip away — ELOPE, ESCAPE
Slip by — ELAPSE
Slip case — COVER
Slip noose knots, in angling — TURLES
Slip of paper containing a name — LABEL
Slip, another way — LISP
Slip-ons — MOCS
Slip-up — ERR, LAPSE
Slipped away — ELAPSED
Slipped up — ERRED
Slipper — MULE, ROMEO
Slippery — EELY
Slippery catch — EEL
Slippery one — EEL
Slippery stuff — SLIME
Slippery surface — ICE
Slips — ERRS
Slips away — ELAPSES
Slithery one — EEL
Slithy creatures — TOVES
Slivovitz — BRANDY
Slogan — MOTTO
Slogan for Dutch cheese — GOUD AEN OUGHT TO EAT
Slope — BANK, GRADE, PITCH, SLANT, TILT
Sloped — TILTED
Slopes — ESCARPS
Slopes course — SLALOM
Sloping letters — ITALICS
Sloping runways — RAMPS
Slops — SWILL
Slot machine no-no — SLUG
Slot machine sign — TILT
Sloth or envy — SIN
Sloth, e.g. — SIN
Slothful — IDLE, INDOLENT
Sloths — AIS
Slouch — SLUMP
Slough — MORASS
Slough of Despond, e.g. — MORASS
Sloughs off — SHEDS
Sloven — FRUMP
Slovenly one — SLOB
Slovenly woman — SLATTERN
Slow-witted — DENSE
Slow — IMPEDE
Slow a steed — REIN
Slow and steady — RACE-WINNER
Slow boats — TUBS
Slow down — EASE
Slow flow — OOZE
Slow flower in January — MOLASSES
Slow goer — SNAIL
Slow motion symbol — SNAIL
Slow mover — LAGGER, SNAIL
Slow pacifist? — TURTLE DOVE
Slow to re-think — OPINION-ATED
Slow, dull one — FOGY
Slow, musically — LENTO
Slow, to Solti — LENTO
Slow-cooking utensil — BEAN-POT
Slow: Mus. — TARDO
Slowed up — BRAKED
Slower than the hand — THE EYE
Slower, in mus. — RIT
Slowing: Mus. abbr. — RIT
Slowly crumbles — DECAYS
Slowly or rapidly, e.g. — ADVERB
Slowly, to Bernstein — LENTO
Slowly, to Solti — LENTO
Slowly, with breadth and dignity — LARGO
Slowpoke — SNAIL
Slows down — BRAKES
Slows the horses — REINS IN
Sludge — MUD
Slued: anagram — DUELS
Slug at a bar — SNORT
Slug the ball — SMASH
Sluggard — SLOWPOKE
Slugged — BOPPED
Slugger Hank — AARON
Slugger in Hall of Fame — KINER
Slugger Mel — OTT
Slugger Slaughter — ENOS
Slugger Van Slyke — ANDY
Slugger's destination — HOME
Slugger's need — BAT
Slugger's stat — RBI
Slugging percentage, for one — STATISTIC
Sluggish — DROUSY, LOGY
Sluggish, in Sicilia — INERTE
Sluggishness — INERTIA, STAGNATION
Slugs — BOPS
Slumber music — LULLABIES
Slumbers — SLEEPS
Slumgullion — STEW
Slur over — ELIDE
Slur, in music — GLIDE
Sly — FOXY, WILY
Sly artifices — WILES
Sly as _____ — A FOX
Sly look — LEER
Sly one — FOX, SNEAK
Sly person? — STONE
Sly role — RAMBO
Sly's "Rocky" co-star — TALIA
Slyly derisive — SNIDE
Slyly disparaging — SNIDE
Slyly malicious — SNIDE
Slyly sarcastic — SNIDE
Smack — SWAT
Smacking of the nautical life — SALTY
Small — LIL, LITTLE, MEAGER, PETITE, PETTY
Small — PUNY, RUNTY, WEE
Small "small" — LIL
Small _____ (youngsters) — FRY
Small 18th century table — CHEVERET
Small active bird — TOMTIT
Small African dog — BASENJI
Small amount — ATOM, DAB, DRAM, MITE, MODICUM
Small amount — PARTICLE, PINCH, SNIP, SPOT, TAD, TRACE
Small amount of liquor — SHOT
Small amounts — DRAWS, DRIBLETS, MODICUMS
Small anchors — KEDGES
Small and glittery — BEADY

Small animal, to Burns — BEASTIE
Small antelope — ORIBI
Small antelope of Somaliland — BEIRA
Small appliance — TOASTER
Small armadillos — PEBAS
Small arrow — DART
Small barracuda — SPET
Small barrels — KEGS
Small bay — INLET
Small bead from the deep — SEED PEARL
Small bed — COT
Small bill — ONE
Small binocular — OPERA GLASS
Small bird — KITE, TOMTIT, WREN
Small birds — FINCHES, WRENS
Small birds of prey — EAGLETS
Small blisters — BLEBS
Small boat — CANOE, DORY
Small boat of the Pacific — BANCA
Small boats: Var. — DINGIES
Small bodies of land: Var. — ILOTS
Small bodies of water — PONDS
Small bone — OSSICLE
Small bottle — CRUSE, VIAL
Small boy — TAD
Small branch — SPRIG, TWIG
Small British farm — CROFT
Small brooks — RILLS
Small brown birds — WRENS
Small buffalo of Celebes — ANOA
Small bullets — SLUGS
Small cactus — MESCAL
Small carriage — FIACRE
Small carriage, British style — WAGGONETTE
Small case — ETUI
Small case: Var. — ETWEE
Small casks — KEGS
Small cavity — AIRSAC, AREOLE, FOLLICLE
Small centipede — EARWIG
Small change — CENT, COINS
Small change? — CTS
Small child — TAD
Small children — TOTS
Small cities — TOWNS
Small coach — FIACRE
Small cobra — ASP
Small coin — CENT
Small coin — SOU
Small coin of Israel — MIL
Small coin of Shakespeare's time — TESTON
Small combos — TRIOS
Small computer — MINI
Small container — VIAL
Small contribution — MITE
Small cormorani — SHAG
Small crown — CORONET
Small cut — SNIP
Small dab — WAD
Small dear — ROE
Small decorative jug — TOBY
Small decorative mat: var. — DOYLEY
Small delicacies — BITS
Small dog, for short — PEKO
Small donkey — BURRO
Small drink — DRAM, SIP, SNORT
Small drum — BONGO, TAMBOURINE
Small drums — SNARE, TABORS
Small eel — SNIG
Small egg — OVULE
Small error — LAPSE
Small evergreen tree — TITI
Small featured role — CAMEO
Small finches — SERINS
Small fish — SPRAT
Small fleet — FLOTILLA
Small flock — COVEY
Small fly — GNAT
Small food fish — SMELT
Small fresh-water fish — DACES, DARTER
Small fruit — FIG
Small generator — MAGNETO
Small glass vials — AMPULS
Small greenish finch — SERIN
Small group of stars — ASTERISM
Small heaters — ETNAS
Small herring — SPRAT
Small hill — RISE
Small hollow — FOSSA
Small horse — BIDET
Small ice mass — CALF
Small insect — GNAT
Small instruments — PICCOLOS
Small interstices — AREOLES
Small island — EYOT
Small island: Br. — EYOT
Small islands — ISLES
Small isle in river — EYOT
Small isle off Australia — THURSDAY
Small kitchen knives — PARERS
Small kite — ELANET
Small land area — ISLET
Small land mass — ISLE, ISLET
Small landing field — AIRSTRIP
Small letter — LOWER CASE
Small liquid measure — MINIM
Small lizard — EFT, GECKO
Small mark — FLECK
Small measure — DRAM, INCH, OUNCE
Small meat pie — PASTY
Small monkey — TITI
Small municipality — TOWN
Small musical combo — TRIO
Small nail — BRAD
Small narrow space — INTERSTICE
Small newspaper — TABLOID
Small night birds — OWLETS
Small one — MITE
Small opening — PORE, STOMA
Small opening in a plant — STOMA
Small particle — ATOM, SHRED
Small penguin — ADELIE
Small pet — LAP DOG
Small piano — SPINET
Small pie — TARTLET
Small piece — SLIVER
Small pike perch — SAUGER
Small pit — AREOLE
Small planets — ASTEROIDS
Small point of land — SAND SPIT
Small porch — STOOP
Small quaffs — NIPS
Small quantities — IOTAS, TOTS
Small quantity — DRIB, DROP
Small racing vehicles — KARTS
Small rattlesnake — SIDE WINDER
Small ringlike areas — AREOLAS
Small rodent — VOLE
Small role for a big star — CAMEO
Small role in a movie or play — BIT
Small rowboat — DORY
Small rug — MAT
Small sailboat — CAT, YAWL
Small salamander — NEWT
Small salmon — COHO
Small sandpipers — PEEPS
Small sea birds — TERNS
Small serving dish — NAPPIE
Small shark — TOPE
Small shelters — SHEDS
Small shoot — SPRIG
Small shoulder wrap — CAPELET
Small silverfish — SMELT
Small snake — ASP
Small sofa — SETTEE
Small songbird — WREN
Small souvenir — FAVOR
Small spaces — AREOLAE
Small sphere — GLOBULE
Small spiny mammal — TENREC
Small sponge cakes — LADY FINGERS
Small spot — DOT
Small spring — SEEP
Small springs — SEEPS
Small stores item — SOAP
Small stream — RILL
Small sturdy dogs — PUGS
Small sturgeons — STERLETS

Small suckers — LEMON DROPS
Small sum of money — MITE
Small talk — PRATTLE
Small tapering fish — BLENNY
Small things — FRY
Small thread — FIBRIL
Small trucks — PICKUPS
Small uprights — SPINETS
Small valise — GRIP
Small valley — GLEN
Small vessels — VIALS
Small wave — RIPPLE
Small weight — GRAM
Small weight: Abbr. — GRAM
Small Western pine — PINON
Small whale — SEI
Small wheel on a swivel — CASTOR
Small wheeled vehicle — CART
Small whirlpool — EDDY
Small whirlpools — EDDIES
Small, brightly-colored freshwater fish — GUPPY
Small, long-haired dog — MALTESE, POMERANIAN
Small, medieval shields — ECUS
Small, medium or large — SIZE
Small, noisy bird — CHIPPING SPARROW
Small, round window — OEIL DE BOEUF
Small, shallow countainer — CUPEL
Small, spiny fish — STICKLEBACK
Small, sturdy dog — PUG
Small-fry — PEANUT
Small-minded — PETTY
Small-time — PENNY ANTE
Small: Scot. — SMA
Small: Suffix — ETTE
Smaller — TINIER
Smaller than usual stock package — ODD LOT
Smallest — LEAST, TEENIEST, WEEST
Smallest amount — LEAST
Smallest of the apes — GIBBONS
Smallest of the Cyclades — DEL, DELOS
Smallest of the litter — RUNT
Smallest unit of speech — PHONE ME
Smallpox — VARIOLA
Smart — BRAINY, CHIC, NEAT
Smart _____ — ALECK
Smart curing utensils — SURGICAL INSTRUMENTS
Smart one — ALECK
Smart remark — REPLY
Smart set — TON
Smarten — IMPROVE
Smartly dressed — NATTY
Smash — SHATTER, WRECK
Smash sign — SRO
Smasheroo — BLOCKBUSTER
Smashing party — BASH
Smattering — SLIGHT
Smear — BLUR, DAUB
Smell _____ (suspect) — A RAT
Smell and taste — SENSES
Smell this — A RAT
Smell, in Sheffield — ODOUR
Smells — ODORS
Smells like an old stogie — REEKS
Smelt — FUSE
Smelter fodder — ORE
Smelter input — ORES
Smelter's materials — ORES
Smelting refuse — DROSS
Smeltry leavings — SLAGS
Smeltry stocks — ORES
Smetana's "The _____ Bride" — BARTERED
Smew — DUCK
Smew's cousin — ERNE
Smidgen — DAB, BIT, IOTA
Smile — BEAM, GRIN
Smile enhancer — DENTIST
Smiled — BEAMED
Smiling — RIANT
Smirch — SMEAR, SMUDGE, SOIL
Smirk — GRIN, LEER
Smite — HIT, SLAP
Smith and Jolson — ALS
Smith and Pacino — ALS
Smith or Bede — ADAM
Smith or Fleming — IAN
Smith or Jones, at times — ALIAS
Smith's block — ANVIL
Smith's device — FORGE
Smithereens — ATOMS
Smithsonian — INSTITUTION
Smithsonian, for short — INST
Smithy — FORGE
Smitten — STRUCK
Smocking — STITCHING
Smoke _____ — DETECTORS
Smoke and ash — TREE
Smoke meat — CURE
Smoke-eaters, en masse — FIRE DEPARTMENTS
Smoked delicacy — LOX
Smoked salmon — LOX, NOVA
Smoker's accessory — ASHTRAY
Smoker's selection — CHEROOT
Smoker's worry — TAR
Smokes — CIGARS
Smokey — BEAR
Smoky haze — SMOG
Smoky peak — ETNA
Smooth — EVEN, GLIB, PAVE
Smooth and connected in music — LEGATO
Smooth and glossy — SATINY
Smooth and pallid — WAXEN
Smooth and white — ALABASTER
Smooth as a billiard ball — BALD
Smooth as glass — SLICK
Smooth gaits — LOPES
Smooth gauze — LISSE
Smooth musical passages — LEGATO
Smooth ruffled feathers — SQUARE THE BEEF
Smooth sound — LENE
Smooth spoken — SUAVE
Smooth tongued — SUAVE
Smooth transitions, in music — SEGUES
Smooth, musically — LEGATO
Smooth-barked tree — BEECH
Smooth-faced — SHAVEN
Smooth-scaled lizard — SKINK
Smooth-talking — ELOQUENT
Smooth: Comb. form — LEIO
Smoothed — EASED, PLANED
Smoothed concrete in a pavement — LUTED
Smoothly, in music — LEGATO
Smooths — EASES, EVENS
Smooths wood — SANDS
Smother — STIFLE
Smothers brothers — TOM AND DICK
Smudge — BLUR, SOIL, SPOT
Smudged — BLOTTED, SOILED
Smug expression — GRIN
Smuggled — STOLEN
Smut, for short — PORN
Smut, tersely — PORN
Smuts, e.g. — BOER
Smyrna export — FIGS
Snack — BITE, EAT, NOSH
Snack shops — DELIS
Snack-bar drink — MALTED
Snacked — ATE
Snacks — EATS, NOSHES
Snacks served aboard Concorde? — FAST FOODS
Snaffle — BIT
Snafu — MIXUP
Snag sufferer — HOSE
Snail's pace — SLOW
Snail's speed — SLOW
Snake — ADDER, ASP, COPPERHEAD
Snake eyes at Vegas — ONES
Snake feeder — SALMON RIVER
Snake mackerel — ESCOLAR
Snake oil, ostensibly — CURE
Snake river flopper — EVEL
Snake sound — HISS
Snake, for one — APOD
Snakebirds — DARTERS
Snakebite antidote — GUACO
Snakelike condition — APODIA

Snakes — ASPS, RATTLERS
Snaky curve — ESS
Snaky sea food — EELS
Snaky shape — ESS
Snappish — CURT, TESTY
Snappy comeback — BARB
Snaps — PICS
Snapshots — PICTURES
Snare — NET, GIN, TRAP
Snare and kettle — DRUM
Snare, for one — DRUM
Snares — NOOSES
Snares by trickery — ENTRAPS
Snarl — ENTANGLE, GNAR, TANGLE
Snatch — GRAB, NAB
Snatches — SWIPES
Snazzy — NIFTY, POSH
Snead sport — GOLF
Snead's need — IRON
Sneak around — LURK
Sneaked — STOLE
Sneaker — SHOE
Sneaky ones — ELUDERS
Sneaky Pete — WEASEL
Snee's partner — SNICK
Sneer — SCOFF
Sneezer's supply — TISSUES
Snick-or- _____ — SNEE
Snick and _____ — SNEE
Snick's partner — SNEE
Snick-a- _____ — SNEE
Snide — CATTY
Sniggled — EELED
Sniggler — EELER
Sniggler's catch — EELS
Sniggler's prey — EELS
Sniggler's snag — EEL
Snigglers for wrigglers — EELER
Snip — CUT
Snipe's habitat — SHORE
Snippet — MORSEL
Snippy rejoinder — SASS
Snips once more — RECUTS
Snit — PET
Snitch — STOOLIE, TATTLE
Snobbish — UPPITY
Snobbish attitudes — AIRS
Snoek — FISH
Snood — NET
Snoodlike — NETTY
Snooker stick — CUE
Snooker, e.g. — POOL
Snookers — FOILS
Snoop — NOSE, PRY
Snoop's sobriquet — NOSY
Snooped — PRIED
Snoops — NOSES
Snoopy — NOSEY
Snoopy one — PRIER
Snoopy, for example — BEAGLE
Snooze — CATNAP, DOZE, NAP
Snoozed — SLEPT
Snoozes — NAPS
Snoozing — ASLEEP
Snopper — PRIER
Snorri story — EDDA
Snorri Sturluson's work — EDDA
Snortlike expression — HUMPH
Snout — NOSE
Snouty mammal — TAPIR
Snow field — NEVE
Snow house — IGLOO
Snow in Firenze — NEVE
Snow item: Var. — SKEE
Snow leopard — OUNCE
Snow removers — PLOWS
Snow runner — SKI
Snow vehicle — SLED
Snow, in Scotland — SNA
Snow, in Sedan — NEIGE
Snow-sport conveyor — SKILIFT
Snowcapped peak — ALP
Snowy — NIVAL
Snra. counterpart — MRS
Snub — CUT, SLIGHT
Snubbed — COLD SHOULDER
Snuff box — MULL
Snug apparel — VESTS
Snug as a bug in _____ — A RUG
Snug bug's location — IN A RUG
Snug fitting garment for acrobats — LEOTARD
Snug retreats — NESTS
Snug, in Scotland — COSH
Snugged in — EMBAYED
Snuggle — NESTLE
Snuggle down — NESTLE
Snuggly — COMFY
So-so grade — CEE
So — THUS
So _____: amen — BE IT
So be it — AMEN
So far — AS YET
So long — ADIEU, TATA
So long, in England — TATA
So long, in Paris — ADIEU
So long, senor — ADIOS
So much, to Verdi — TANTO
So so — AVERAGE
So what _____ is new? — ELSE
So-called — ALLEGED
Soak — RET, SATURATE, STEEP
Soak flax — RET
Soak flax or lumber — RET
Soak food in seasoning — MARINATE
Soak in water — RET
Soak meat for flavor — MARINATE
Soak through — OOZE
Soak, as flax — RET
Soaked in liquid — MACERATED
Soaking medium — BATH
Soaks — RETS, SATURATES, STEEPS
Soaks flax — RETS
Soaks hemp — RETS
Soap additives — LYES
Soap ingredient — ALOE, LYE
Soap opera need — SPONSOR
Soap opera, for example — SERIAL
Soap opera, for short — SER
Soap operas — SERIALS
Soap plant — AMOLE
Soap segment — EPISODE
Soap source — AMOLE
Soap substitute — AMOLE
Soapbox — CRATE
Soapbox demagogue — RANTER
Soapbox oration — LECTURE
Soapstone — TALC
Soapstone, e.g. — TALC
Soaring — ALOFT
Soars in the air — GLIDES
Sob sister — BLEEDING HEART
Sob's sister — MOAN
Sobbed — WEPT
Soberly — GRAVE
Sobrins's relative — TIA
Sobriquet for Clemenceau — TIGRE
Sobriquet for Hemingway — PAPA
Sobriquet for Mr. Edison — MR AC
Sobs — CRIES
Soc. or org. — ORIGIN
Socagers, e.g. — TENANTS
Soccer great — PELE
Soccer movement — KICK
Soccer name of fame — PELE
Soccer superstar — PELE
Soccer team — ELEVEN
Soccer's Black Pearl — PELE
Social — BEE, FRIENDLY, PLEASANT, TEA
Social affair — TEA
Social affair: Fr. — BAL
Social asset — POISE
Social beginning — ANTI
Social blunder — GAFFE
Social character — ETHOS
Social classes — STRATA
Social climber's credo — GET AHEAD
Social climbers — SNOBS
Social disintegration — ANOMIE
Social division — CLIQUE
Social dud — BOOR
Social event — SOIREE
Social events — TEAS
Social figure Pearl — MESTA
Social functions — TEAS
Social gathering — PARTY
Social insects — ANTS, WASPS
Social organization — CLUB

Social plus — TACT
Social position — STATE
Social rank — CLASS
Social reformer Jacob _____ — RIIS
Social sci. — ECON
Social services employee — CASE WORKER
Social sideliner — WALL-FLOWER
Social standing — CASTE
Social stratum — CASTE
Social type — GENTLEMEN
Social wisdom — TACT
Socialite's daughter — DEB
Societal group — CASTE
Society — CIRCLE, ELITE, MONDE, PEOPLE
Society bow — DEBUT
Society bud — DEB
Society buds, for short — DEBS
Society division — CASTE
Society gal — DEB
Society lass — DEB
Society musician? — BALL PLAYER
Society newcomer — DEB
Society of film and television editors: Abbr. — ACE
Society word — NEE
Society-page item — NUPTIALS
Society-page word — NEE
Sock — HOSE, PUNCH, SLIPPER
Sock _____: (teen party) — HOP
Sock exchange — BOUT
Sock it _____! — TO ME
Sock or buck ending — EROO
Sock or smack trailer — EROO
Sock part — TOE
Sock pattern — ARGYLE
Socko reviews — RAVES
Socks — ARGYLES, HOSE
Socks, to Chelsea — PET
Socrates milieus — STOAS
Socrates pupil — PLATO
Socratic letters — ETAS
Sod — TURF
Soda — POP
Soda fountain orders — MALTS
Soda jerk's brews — MALTS
Soda, for one — ANTACID
Soda, often — CHASER
Sodden — SOGGY
Sodom citizen — LOT
Sofa — COUCH, DIVAN
Sofas — SETEES
Sofia coins — LEVS
Sofia's country — BULGARIA
Sofia's land, for short — BULG
Sofia's predecessor — ENA
Soft-soaps — SWEET TALKS
Soft — DOWNY, FLUFFY, LOW, MUTED
Soft and crumbling, as bricks — SAMEL
Soft and fluffy — DOWNY
Soft breeze — AURA
Soft cheese — BRIE
Soft color — PASTEL
Soft drink — COLA, CREAM SODA, SODA
Soft drink tycoon Candler — ASA
Soft earth — SAND
Soft fabric — TWEED, VELURE
Soft food — PAP
Soft food for invalids — PAP
Soft French cheese — BRIE
Soft light — DIM
Soft lines — FLOWING
Soft material — SILK
Soft mineral — TALC
Soft mud — OOZE
Soft palate — VELUM
Soft plumage — DOWN
Soft protection — PADDING
Soft sheer fabric — PINA
Soft shoe — MOC
Soft sounds — COOS
Soft synthetic — ORLON
Soft throws — LOBS
Soft touches — TAPS
Soft wood — BALSA
Soft, light wool — CASHMERE
Soft, rushing sound — WHISH
Soft, thin muslin — MULL
Soft-colored — PALE
Soft-palate projection — UVULA
Soft-shell clams — STEAMERS
Soft-shoe dance — TAP
Soft: It. — DOLCE
Soften — MELT, RELENT
Soften, in color — TONE
Softened — MUTED
Softened the sound, with "down" — TONED
Softened the tone of — MUTED
Softening — MELTING
Softens — TAMES
Softly — GENTLY
Soggy — MOIST
Soggy ground — MIRE
Soho blackjack — COSH
Soho clothespins — PEGS
Soho coin, for short — SOV
Soho digs — PAD
Soho domestic — CHAR
Soho flooring — LINO
Soho hoodlum — YOB
Soho houseworkers — CHARS
Soho lean-to — OUTSHOT
Soho matinee idol — ERO
Soho partner — FLAT
Soho streetcar — TRAM
Soho truck — LORRY
Soho vehicle — LORRY
Sohrab to Rustum — SON
Soil — EARTH, LOAM
Soil of a type — LOAM
Soil scientist — AGRONOMIST
Soil turner — HOE
Soil: Comb. form — AGRO, GEO
Soil: Pref. — AGRO
Soiled — DIRTY
Soissons seasoning — SEL
Soissons seasons — ETES
Soissons summers — ETES
Sojurn — RESIDE, STAY, VISIT
Sol — HELIOS
Sol do connectors — LA TI
Sol followers — LAS
Sol or space lead-in — AERO
Sol or stat starter — AERO
Solace — AID, HELP
Solan — GOOSE
Solans — GEESE
Solanum melongena — EGGPLANT
Solar deity — ATEN
Solar disc — ATEN
Solar disc of Amenhotep — ATEN
Solar phenomena — SUNSPOTS
Solar system member — PLANET
Solar year — EPACT
Solar year excess — EPACT
Solar-lunar year difference — EPACT
Solarity — ONE
Solarium — SUN ROOM
Sold moonshine — BOOT-LEGGED
Sold, in Paris — VENDU
Solder — JOIN
Soldier — GI JOE
Soldier from London — TOMMY
Soldier from the Marine Corp — GYRENE
Soldier in "King Henry V" — NYM
Soldier of WWI — DOUGH-BOY
Soldier's field, for one — ARENA
Soldier's post exchange — CANTEEN
Soldier's sack — COT
Soldier's vacation — LEAVE
Soldiers in Seoul — ROKS
Sole — ONLY
Sole of a plow — SLADE
Solemn — SAD, STAID
Solemn act — RITE
Solemn promise — OATH
Solemnity — RITE
Solicit — SEEK
Solicited — ASKED, SOUGHT
Solicitor — SUITOR
Solicits — ASKS

Solicitude — CARE
Solid — FIRM
Solid as _____ — A ROCK
Solid hit review — RAVE
Solid metal shaft — AXLE
Solid pattern in lace making — TOILE
Solid rain — SLEET
Solidago — GOLDEN ROD
Solidarity — POWER
Solidifies — GELS, SETS
Solidify — GEL
Soliloquy words — TO BE
Solipsistic person — EGOIST
Solitary — ALONE, LONE, ONE
Solitary, as a hermit — EREMITIC
Solitary: Comb. form — EREMO
Solitude — ISOLATION
Solitudinarian — HERMIT, ALONE
Solo — ALONE
Solo for Sills — ARIA
Solo for Sutherland — ARIA
Solo of "Star Wars" — HAN
Solomon — SAGE
Solomon, to David — SON
Solomonic — WISE
Solomonic seasoning? — SAGE
Solomonic to the nth degree — WISEST
Solos — ARIAS
Solothurn's river — AARE
Solti's beat — TEMPO
Solti's need — BATON
Soluble salt from potash — ALKALI
Solute — FREE
Solution — ANSWER
Solution finder — SOLVER
Solve — CRACK, UNRAVEL
Solve a "weighty" problem — REDUCE
Solve, as a puzzle — WORK
Solve, with "out" — DOPE
Solvent — ACETONE, ALDOL, SOUND
Solver's favorite ox — ANOA
Solves a mystery — BREAKS THE CASE
Solway Firth tributary — EDEN
Somber — DULL, GRAY
Somber or meager — LENTEN
Sombre — SAD
Some — ANY, SEVERAL
Some advice from T. Roosevelt — CARRY A BIG STICK
Some ancient Greeks — DORIANS
Some ants — CARPENTERS
Some are "educated" — GUESSES
Some are a trois — MENAGES
Some are British — ISLES
Some are fine — ARTS
Some are flying — COLORS
Some are frayed or frazzled — NERVES
Some are hooked — RUGS
Some are inflated — EGOS
Some are knights — ELKS
Some are loose — ENDS
Some are Roman — NOSES
Some are scrambled — EGGS
Some are stuffed — SHIRTS
Some are tight — ENDS
Some are wild — OATS
Some aviator's talent — SKYWRITING
Some Balinese roofing — THATCH
Some become knights — ELKS
Some Bethlehem buildings — IRON WORKS
Some bills — ONES, TENS
Some bookstore customers — BROWSERS
Some Brit. lords — MPS
Some buoys — NUNS
Some cards — ACES
Some carriers — MAILMEN
Some cases — TORTS
Some census data — AGES
Some chemical compounds — HALIDES
Some cocktails — MARTINIS
Some cod — LING
Some coll. buildings — DORMS
Some coll. linemen — LGS
Some collars — ETONS
Some collectors items — STAMPS
Some comprehension — IDEA
Some cords — VOCAL
Some cover-ups — BIBS
Some cuts of meat — ROUNDS
Some Dadaist works — ARPS
Some displaced persons — EMIGRES
Some do get the hang of it — GLIDER
Some do it twice — THINK
Some drillers — OILMEN
Some drums — SNARES
Some eateries — TEAROOMS
Some Europeans — DANES
Some exams — ORALS
Some exercises — SITUPS
Some fancy dives — GAINERS
Some fashion wear — DIORS
Some Feds — G MEN
Some females weapon of defense — MACE
Some fighters — LIGHT HEAVY WEIGHTS
Some floor layers — TILERS
Some footballers — ENDS
Some form-sheet data — SIRES
Some freethinkers — AGNOSTICS
Some G.I. togs — ODS
Some gallery displays — NUDES
Some Ghanaians — ASHANTIS
Some guards — LINEMEN
Some head coverings — TOUPEES
Some heels — STILETTOS
Some huts — LEANTOS
Some is common — SENSE
Some July 4th salutes — EXPLOSIONS
Some July babies — LEOS
Some kids components — PUPPY DOGS TAILS
Some kids components — SNIPS AND SNAILS
Some knots — SHEEP SHANKS
Some leagues — MINOR
Some learn by this — ROTE
Some legal writs — MISES
Some legislatures — DIETS
Some legumes — PEAS
Some lilies — SEGOS
Some M.I.T. grads — EES, ENGS
Some marsupials, for short — ROOS
Some members of the reed section — OBOISTS
Some N.F.L. linemen — RTS
Some N.Y.C. trains — ELS
Some NCO's — SGTS
Some necklines — VEES
Some nerve you've got — OPTIC
Some objets d'art — VIRTU
Some of Chopin's output — ETUDES
Some of the Apodes — EELS
Some of the haves — OWNERS
Some of the Iroquoians — ONEIDAS
Some of these are precious — METALS
Some office work — CLERICAL
Some oranges — OSAGES
Some organic compounds — AMIDES
Some paintings — OILS
Some parties — STAGS
Some pavements — ASPHALT
Some penultimate words — ET TU
Some photo-copies, for short — STATS
Some pilots — AIRMEN
Some Princetonians — COEDS
Some propositions in logic — MODALS
Some putti — CUPIDS
Some radio buffs — CBERS
Some ratites — EMUS
Some receivers — ENDS
Some records, for short — LPS
Some Renoir paintings — NUDES

Some Russian planes — MIGS
Some salad days — TEENS
Some sari wearers — RANIS
Some seamen, for short — ABS
Some seines — COD NETS
Some senior citizens — RETIREES
Some Shelley products — ODES
Some shoe leather — SUEDE
Some small dogs, for short — PEKES
Some Spanish murals — SERTS
Some teams — NINES
Some teeth — MOLARS
Some tournaments — OPENS
Some trunks — TORSI
Some TV fare — RERUNS
Some TV showings — REPEATS
Some uniforms — MONKEY SUITS
Some units of length — MILS
Some upperclassmen: Abbr. — SRS
Some Virginians — LEES
Some Vivaldi compositions — CONCERTI
Some voters — MEN
Some votes — NOES
Some weekdays: Abbr. — FRIS
Some wheys — SERA
Some winter storms — SNOWINS
Some women's fashions — A LINES
Some woodworkers — STAINERS
Some workers' lot — HARD LABOR
Some writing — PROSE
Some Yalies — COEDS
Some Yalies today — COEDS
Some, in Seville — UNOS
Some, in Spain — UNOS
Somebody — CELEB, ONE, PERSONAGE
Somehow — SOMEWAY
Someone _____ (another's) — ELSES
Someone else — ANOTHER
Someone else's kid — BRAT
Someone not to catch — TARTAR
Somersault — FLIP, ROLL
Somerset stream — EXE
Something extraordinary: Brit. — ONER
Something fluffed — LINE
Something for clock punchers — TIMECARDS
Something frail — WISP
Something gratis — FREEBEE
Something isolated — ISLAND
Something made up — COINAGE
Something Mississippi has — ESSES
Something of value — ASSET
Something required — A MUST
Something stated — PAROL
Something supplemented — ADD ON
Something to behold — SPECTACLE
Something to boast about — FEAT
Something to break — CAMP
Something to eat — RED MEAT
Something to eschew — NO NO
Something to keep on — SHIRT
Something to lend — EAR
Something to read — NEWSPAPER
Something to serve — TERM
Something to shed — COAT
Something to wear — CAPE, DRESS
Something to wish upon — STAR
Something wildly amusing — RIOT
Sometime — EVENTUALLY, SOON
Sometime frosh wear — BEANIES
Sometime in the future — LATER
Sometime legislative act — REPEAL
Sometime name for Ireland — EIRE
Sometime place for frogs — THROAT
Sometimes — EVERY NOW AND THEN
Sometimes baked, for dessert — ALASKA
Sometimes it's clear — COAST
Sometimes it's in the neck — PAIN
Sometimes it's true — GRIT
Sometimes they come in wheels — CHEESES
Sometimes they're double — TAKES
Sometimes they're loose — ENDS
Sometimes they're shady — DEALINGS
Sometimes with crossbones — SKULL
Sometimes, it's common — SENSE
Somewhat — MILDLY, RATHER, SORT OF
Somewhat eccentric — ODDISH
Somewhat moist — DAMP
Somewhat reckless — WILDISH
Somewhat, in music — POCO
Somewhat: Suffix — ISH
Somewhere dark — AGES
Somme seasons — ETES
Somme summers — ETES
Sommelier's dearth? — SHORT OF PORT
Sommer from Berlin — ELKE
Sommer of the screen — ELKE
Sommers, in Somme: Fr. — ETES
Somnambulist — SLEEPWALKER
Somnolent — DOZY, GROGGY, SLEEPY
Son — BOY, LAD
Son _____ — IN LAW
Son _____ gun — OF A
Son in "Desire Under the Elms" — EBEN
Son of _____ — A GUN
Son of a famous Henry — EDSEL
Son of Aeolus — SISYPHUS
Son of Agamemnon — ORESTES
Son of an unc. — NEPH
Son of Anchises: Var. — ENEAS
Son of Andromeda — PERSES
Son of Aphrodite — EROS
Son of Apollo — ION
Son of Claudius — NERO
Son of Cush — SEBA
Son of Daedalus — ICARUS
Son of Eric the Red — LEIF
Son of Gad — ERI
Son of Hera — ARES
Son of Indira — RAJIV
Son of Isaac — ESAU
Son of Jacob — ASHER, LEVI
Son of Jerahmeel — OREN
Son of Judah — ONAN
Son of Lamech — NOAH
Son of Launcelot — SIR GALAHAD
Son of Lot — MOAB
Son of Mary, Queen of Scots — JAMES I
Son of Odin — BRAGI, THOR, TYR
Son of Peleg, in Genesis — REU
Son of Scrooge's clerk — TIM
Son of Seth — ENOS
Son of Venus — AMOR
Son of Vulcan — CACUS
Son of Zeus — ARES
Son of Zeus and Hera — ARES
Son of Zibeon — ANAH
Son, in Soissons — FILS
Son, in Sonora — HIJO
Sonata — LARGO
Sonata movement — RONDO
Sonata part — RONDO
Sondheim-Styne musical — GYPSY
Song-_____ man — AND DANCE
Song _____, Vietnamese fishing port — CAU

Song Al Jolson made famous — SWANEE
Song by Andrew Lloyd Webber — THE MUSIC OF THE NIGHT
Song for a broker's day? — SUNRISE SUNSET
Song for blue-chip stocks? — YOURE THE TOP
Song for Domingo — ARIA
Song for late Oct. 1929? — ILL GET BY
Song for Marilyn Mims — ARIA
Song for market tip that bombed? — I APOLOGIZE
Song for Norman or Mills — ARIA
Song for Sutherland — ARIA
Song for Te Kanawa — ARIA
Song for two — DUET
Song from "A Chorus Line" — AND
Song from "Ain't Misbehavin'" — YOUR FEETS TOO BIG
Song from "Casablanca" — AS TIME GOES BY
Song from "Hans Christian Anderson" — THUMBELINA
Song from "West Side Story" — MARIA
Song hit of 1934 — STARS FELL ON ALABAMA
Song in "A Chorus Line" — ONE
Song in "Let 'Em Eat Cake": 1933 — MINE
Song in a Lansbury musical — MAME
Song of 1925 — DONT BRING LULU
Song of 1933 — ITS ONLY A PAPER MOON
Song of joy — PAEAN
Song of joyful praise — PAEAN
Song of Norway? — OSLO SOLO
Song of praise — CAROL, HYMN, PAEAN
Song of sorrow — DIRGE
Song of the 1930's — ALONE
Song of the Aegean sailor? — RHO RHO RHO YOUR BOAT
Song or gab ending — FEST
Song popular during WW I — ROSES OF PICARDY
Song related — CHORAL
Song sounds — TRAS
Song syllable — TRA
Song thrush — MAVIS
Song, often golden — OLDIE
Song, to Mozart — LIED
Song, to Schubert — LIED
Song-and-dance cat? — CHEETAH RIVERA
Songbird — LARK, SERIN, VIREO, WREN
Songbird London — JULIE
Songbird Smith — KATE
Songbird Turner — TINA
Songlike — ARIOSE
Songlike and flowing in style — CANTABILE
Songs — CHANTS, VOCALS
Songs for two — DUETS
Songs of Lisboa — FADOS
Songs, to Schubert — LIEDER
Songster — WREN
Songstress McEntire — REBA
Songstress Nina — SIMONE
Songstress Patti — LABELLE
Songstress Steber — ELEANOR
Songwriter guitarist Don — MCLEAN
Songwriter Gus — KAHN
Songwriter Harold — ARLEN
Songwriter Jule — STYNE
Songwriter Sammy and family — CAHNS
Songwriter Sammy, et al. — CAHNS
Songwriter's citrus queen — TANGERINE
Songwriter's org. — ASCAP
Songwriter's stringbean Sara — LONG TALL SALLY
Songwriter's Tarzan type — NATURE BOY
Sonic bounce — ECHO
Sonnet part — SESTET
Sonny and Chastity — BONOS
Sonny of the ring — LISTON
Sonny Shroyer role — ENOS
Sonny's sibling — SIS
Sonny, the mayor — BONO
Sonoma neighbor — NAPA
Sonoma snack — TACO
Sonora Indian — YAQUI
Sonora is one — ESTADO
Sonora sandwich — TACO
Sonoran Mrs. — SRA
Sonorous guffaw — LOUD BELLOW
Sons — MALES
Sons and daughters — HEIRS
Soon — ANON
Soon parters — A FOOL AND HIS MONEY
Soon-to-be alums — SRS
Sooner _____: eventually — OR LATER
Sooner St. — OKLA
Sooner than — ERE
Sooner than, poetically — ERE
Sooners — OKLAHOMANS
Soot — GRIME
Soot; smutch — GRIME
Sooth follower — SAYER
Soothe — ALLAY, LULL
Soothe the throat — GARGLE
Soothes — CALMS
Soothing application — BALM
Soothing remedy — SALVE
Soothing salves — BALMS
Soothing succulent — ALOE
Soothing word — THERE
Soothsayer — SEER
Sop — BRIBE
Sop up — BLOT
Sopherim — SCRIBES
Sophia's spouse — CARLO
Sophisticated — SMART, URBANE
Sophisticated rockets: Abbr. — MIRVS
Soporifics — OPIATES
Soprano Aprile of the Met — MILLO
Soprano Berger — ERNA
Soprano Clamma — DALE
Soprano Eames — EMMA
Soprano Elinor — ROSS
Soprano Farrell — EILEEN
Soprano Gluck — ALMA
Soprano Grist — RERI
Soprano Kiri Te Kanawa, e.g. — MAORI
Soprano Lehmann — LILLI
Soprano Lucine — AMARA
Soprano Lucrezia — BORI
Soprano Marton — EVA
Soprano Mills — ERIE
Soprano Mitchell — LEONA
Soprano Moffo — ANNA
Soprano Petina — IRRA
Soprano Ponselle — ROSA
Soprano role in "Orfeo ed Euridice" — AMOR
Soprano Rysanek — LEONIE
Soprano Sarah of the Met — REESE
Soprano Scotto — RENATA
Soprano Shade — ELLEN
Soprano Souez — INA
Soprano Stratas — TERESA
Soprano Sylvia — SASS
Soprano Tebaldi — RENATA
Soprano Wilma — LIPP
Sopranos Hunter and Shane — RITAS
Sops — PLACEBOS
Sora — RAIL
Sorcerer's spell — VOODOO
Sorcerers' stock-in-trade — SPELLS
Sorceress — LAMIA
Sorceress encountered by Odysseus — CIRCE
Sorceresses — SIBYLS
Sorcery — MAGIC
Sorcery belief: Var. — OBIA
Sordid — SEAMY
Sordino — MUTE
Sordor — DIRT, DREGS, LEES
Sore — ABRASION, ACHY, IRATE

Sorority headwear? — SISTER HOODS
Sorrel of fiction and Green of finance — HETTYS
Sorrel's kin — ROAN
Sorrels — OCAS
Sorrow — DOLOR, REMORSE, WOE
Sorrow, in Sonora — DOLOR
Sorrowful — TRISTE
Sorrowful troupe? — DOWN-CAST
Sort — CATALOG, GRADE, ILK, KIND
Sort of court — MOTEL
Sort of friend — FAIR WEATHER
Sort of key — AIT
Sort of ship or story — TALL
Sort of: Suffix — ISH
Sortie — RAID
SOS! — MAYDAY
Sot — DRINKER
Sothern — ANN
Sothern namesakes — ANNS
Sotomayer's country — CUBA
Sotto voce — UNDER ONES BREATH
Sou'easter — WIND
Soubise, e.g. — SAUCE
Soubrettes — MAIDS
Souchong — TEA
Sought coal — MINED
Sought intercession — PRAYED
Sought morays — EELED
Sought office — RAN
Souk — BAZAAR
Soul — ANIMA
Soul chaser: Abbr. — BRO
Soul group — LTD
Soul or life — ANIMA
Soul, in Paris — AME
Soul, in Rouen — AME
Sound — CLICK, HALE, INTACT, SANE
Sound — TONE, VALID
Sound an alarm — SIGNAL
Sound barrier — MUFFLE
Sound effect — ECHO
Sound equipment — STEREO
Sound frequencies — HERTZ
Sound from a barnyard — MAA
Sound from a campanile — DONG
Sound from a ewe — BAA
Sound from a meadow — BLEAT
Sound from a poupee — MAMAN
Sound from a stable — SNORT
Sound from a stall — SNORT
Sound from Sandy — ARF
Sound from Socks — PURR
Sound from Tabby — PURR
Sound from the belfry — PEAL
Sound from the byre — MOO
Sound from the crowd — ROAR
Sound from the lion's den — ROAR
Sound from the meadow — LOW
Sound from the nest — PEEP
Sound from the pasture — MOO
Sound from the phone — TING A LING
Sound heard at stadiums — RAH
Sound Humpty Dumpty made — SPLAT
Sound in body — HALE
Sound in the night — SNORE
Sound loudly — BLARE
Sound made by Big Ben — BONG
Sound measurements — SONES
Sound near Olympia, Wash. — PUGET
Sound of a chick — PEEP
Sound of a wind instrument — BLAST
Sound of audience appreciation — ROAR
Sound of chicks — PEEP
Sound of delight — WHEE
Sound of disapproval — RASPBERRY, TSK
Sound of disgust — PSHAW
Sound of displeasure — UGH
Sound of exertion — PANT
Sound of laughter — HA HA
Sound of mind — SANE
Sound of rebuke — TUT
Sound of regret — SIGH
Sound of relief — SIGH
Sound of satisfaction — AHH, PURR
Sound of speed, in the comics — VOOM
Sound of terror — SCREAM
Sound off — BAY, BOAST, ORATE
Sound proofing, for example — DEADENER
Sound quality — TONE
Sound reasoning — LOGIC
Sound receptor — EAR
Sound recording — TAPE
Sound reproduction systems — STEREOS
Sound seeking attention — AHEM
Sound seeking silence — HIST, TST
Sound system — AUDIO, STEREO
Sound system for a sub — SONAR
Sound's partner — SAFE
Sound, to a TV repairman — AUDIO
Sound, usually in triplicate — RAH
Sound: Comb. form — SONI, SONO
Sound: Prefix — PHONO
Sounded an alarm — WARNED
Sounded harshly — BRAYED
Sounded kittenish — MEWED
Sounded like a bovine — MOOED
Sounded like a sheep — BLEATED
Sounded like bacon frying — SIZZLED
Sounded the bell — RANG
Sounding like an oboe — REEDY
Sounding like Niagara — AROAR
Soundness of mind — SANITY
Soundness, to Skinner — SANITY
Sounds — TONES
Sounds at a shower — AHS
Sounds at Babel — DIN
Sounds distressed — MOANS
Sounds from a cat — PURRS
Sounds from a Nanny — MAAS
Sounds from Leo — ROARS
Sounds from Sandy — ARFS
Sounds from Santa — HO HO HO
Sounds from the beyond — RAPS
Sounds from the herd — LOWS
Sounds heard on a midnite dreary — RAPS
Sounds in the street — SIRENS
Sounds indicating trouble — UH OH
Sounds made by Lassie — YELP
Sounds of a pride — ROARS
Sounds of activity — HUMS
Sounds of delight — OHS
Sounds of discovery — AHAS
Sounds of disgust — UGHS
Sounds of distaste — UGHS
Sounds of glee — HAHA
Sounds of hesitation — ERS
Sounds of laughter — HAHAS
Sounds of merriment — HA HA
Sounds of rejection — UGHS
Sounds of rooting — RAHS
Sounds of surprise — AHAS, AHS, OHOHS, OHS
Sounds of time — TICKS
Soup — BISQUE, BROTH, GUMBO, STEW
Soup accompaniment — SALTINE
Soup herb — BASIL
Soup ingredients — PEAS
Soup scoop — LADLE

Soup server — LADLE
Soup vegetable — OKRA
Soup vegetable: Var. — OCRA
Soup veggies — LEEKS
Soupcon — DRAM, TRACE
Soupcons — TINGES, TRACES
Soupy — SALES
Sour — ACERB, ACIDY, TART, VINEGARY
Sour ale — ALEGAR
Sour in taste — ACERB
Sour or sweet ending — ISH
Sour-ball — CANDY
Sour-tasting — ACERB
Source — FONT, ORIGIN, ROOT
Source of a perfume ingredient — CIVET
Source of agar-agar — KELP
Source of an oil — OLIVES
Source of annoyance — TRIAL
Source of basalt — LAVA
Source of chocolate — CACAO
Source of coconut oil — COPRA
Source of constant irritation — THORN IN THE FLESH
Source of danger — THREAT
Source of emetine — IPECAC
Source of energy — SUN
Source of energy, mod style — SYNFUEL
Source of First Amendment — THE BILL OF RIGHTS
Source of harm — BANE
Source of igneous rock — MAGMA
Source of income — WORK
Source of indigo — ANIL
Source of light — SUN
Source of mohair — ANGORA
Source of Popeye's strength — SPINACH
Source of protein — BEAN, YOLK
Source of roe — SHAD
Source of rubber — LATEX
Source of Samson's strength — HAIR
Source of supply — SPRING
Source of the Blue Nile — TANA
Source of the Ewing fortune — OIL
Source of the Mississippi — ITASCA
Source of vexation — SORE
Source of Vitamin B — NIACIN
Source of warmth — HEATER
Sources — FOUNTS
Sources of Archers' bows — YEWS
Sources of income — RENTS
Sources of wisdom — ORACLES
Sourdough — MINER
Sourdough's concern — CLAIM
Sourdough's holdings — CLAIMS
Sourdough's sack — POKE
Sourdough's tract — CLAIM
Soured — BAD
Sourpuss — CRAB
Sousa composition — WASHINGTON POST MARCH
Sousa product — MARCH
Sousa sobriquet — MARCH KING
Sousa sound — OOMPAH
Sousaphone, for one — HORN
South Africa's Bishop — TUTU
South African — BOER
South African assembly — RAAD
South African city — DURBAN
South African coin — RAND
South African language — BANTU
South African money — RAND
South African pen for animals — KRAAL
South African province — NATAL
South America prairie — PAMPA
South American capital — LIMA, QUITO
South American Indian — CARIB
South American land, Spanish style — BRASIL
South American mountain range — ANDES
South American nation — PERU
South American parrots — ARAS
South American peaks — ANDES
South American range — ANDES
South American region: Abbr. — GUI
South American rodent — PACA
South American tanager — TENI
South American timber tree — APAS
South American ungulate — TAPIR
South Bend team — IRISH
South Bend varsity — IRISH
South Carolina and Georgia in 1861 — SECEDERS
South Carolina college — CLEMSON
South Carolina county — AIKEN
South Carolina fort — SUMTER
South Carolina island — EDISTO
South Carolina state tree — PALMETTO
South Dakota capital — PIERRE
South Dakota college — HURON
South Dakota town — CUSTER
South Dakota, the _____ State — COYOTE
South European — SLAV
South European dormice — LEROTS
South Italian port — NAPLES
South Korea capital — SEOUL
South Korean port — PUSAN
South of Ore. — CAL
South of the border — JOINT
South of the border foot kicker — MEXICAN HAT DANCE
South Pacific boat — PROA
South Pacific craft — PROA
South Pacific export — COPRA
South Pacific setting — BALI
South Pole constellation — APUS
South Sea Island — BORNEO
South Sea Isle — BALI
South Seas staple — POI
South Vietnam port — DANANG
South: Comb. form — AUSTRO
Southampton shindigs — DOS
Southeast Asian resident — THAI
Southern — AUSTRAL
Southern African fox — CAAMA
Southern bros. — BRERS
Southern charm feature — DRAWL
Southern constellation — APUS, ARA, HYDRA, LEPUS
Southern corn dish — GRITS
Southern dish — GRITS
Southern hominy — GRITS
Southern sounds — DRAWLS
Southern st. — FLA
Southern tree decor — MOSS
Southerner — NATIVE
Southfork family — EWINGS
Southpaws — LEFTHANDERS, LEFTIES
Southwest Conf. team — SMU
Southwest Indian — HOPI, UTE
Southwest lake or river — SABINE
Southwest landscape features — MESAS
Southwest stewpot — OLLA
Southwest wind — AFER
Southwestern copse — MOTTE
Southwestern evergreen — ATLE
Southwestern hills — LOMAS
Southwestern plain — LLANO
Southwestern poplar — ALAMO

Southwestern porridge — ATOLE
Southwestern promenade — ALAMEDA
Southwestern stewpot — OLLA
Souvenir — PENNANT
Sov. unit — SSR
Sovereign — CZAR, KING, QUEEN, RULER
Sovereign decree — ARRET
Sovereigns — SIRES
Sovereignties — EMPIRES
Sovereignty — CROWN, THRONE
Soviet abbr. — SSR
Soviet ballet company — KIROV
Soviet city on the Om — OMSK
Soviet co-op — ARTEL
Soviet collective — ARTEL
Soviet committees — PRESIDIA
Soviet cooperative — ARTEL
Soviet earth orbiter — SPUTNIK
Soviet inland sea — ARAL
Soviet Lake or sea — ARAL
Soviet mountain range — ALAI, URAL
Soviet plane — MIG
Soviet press agcy. — TASS
Soviet press org. — TASS
Soviet range — URALS, ALTAI
Soviet republic — TATAR
Soviet river — CHU
Soviet river to the Volga — KAMA
Soviet sea — ARAL, AZOV, CASPIAN
Soviet space dog — LAIKA
Soviet state, for short — SSR
Soviet veto — NYET
Soviet workers' collective — ARTEL
Soviet workers' cooperative — ARTEL
Sow — SEED
Sow and hoe — FARM
Sow chow — MAST
Sow seeds — PLANT
Sow sound — OINK
Sow: Var. — YILT
Sown; strewn: Fr. — SEMEE
Soybean product — OIL
Sp. blanket — SERAPE
Sp. explorer — DE SOTO
Sp. ladies — SRAS
Sp. lady — SRTA
Sp. matron — SRA
Sp. misses — SRTAS
Sp. mistress — DUENA
Sp. painter's works — GOYAS
Sp. poet-playwright: Federico Garcia _____ — LORCA
Sp. primate's city — TOL
Sp. queen — ENA
Sp. rice dish — PAELLA
Sp. wife — SRA
Spa on the Avon — BATH
Spa, in New York State — SARATOGA
Space-related — AREAL
Space-vehicle boosters — SATURNS
Space — AREA, ELBOW ROOM, GAP, ROOM
Space above the earth — ETHER
Space Age acronym — NASA
Space Agency — NASA
Space agency's interest — MARS
Space contract — LEASE
Space filler — SHIM
Space for passing — WAY
Space is the last one — FRONTIER
Space monogram — NASA
Space on the face of a bird — LORE
Space or sol preceder — AERO
Space or sphere starter — AERO
Space or stat start — AERO
Space org. — NASA
Space travelers — ASTRONAUTS
Spacecraft — APOLLO
Spacecraft's freight — PAYLOAD
Spacek's "_____ Man" — RAGGEDY
Spaces — AREAS, GAP
Spaces between birds' eyes and beak — LORA
Spaceship? — SAUCER
Spacious — BROAD, ROOMY
Spacious suburban lot — ACRE
Spade — SAM
Spade of whodunit — SAM
Spade, et al. — SAMS
Spaded anew — REDUG
Spades or clubs — SUIT
Spadille, sometimes — ACE
Spaghetti and ravioli — PASTAS
Spaghetti associate — MEAT BALLS
Spaghetti western — FILM
Spain and Portugal — IBERIA
Spain's "Nile" — EBRO
Spain's El _____ — CID
Spain's last queen — ENA
Spain's longest river — EBRO
Spain's peninsula — IBERIA
Spain's spring — VENERO
Spall — FLAKE
Spall of paint — CHIP
Span member — MULE
Span of time — YEARS
Spangle — SEQUIN
Spaniard's greeting — HOLA
Spanish anesthetic — ETER
Spanish answer to the Louvre — PRADO
Spanish article — LOS
Spanish artist — SERT
Spanish aunt — TIA
Spanish baby boys — NENES, NINOS
Spanish belle — MAJA
Spanish card suit — OROS
Spanish cellist Casals — PABLO
Spanish chaperone — DUENNA
Spanish city — ELCHE
Spanish coin — PESETA
Spanish commander of a castle — ALCAYDE
Spanish commune — YESTE
Spanish composer: 1729-83 — SOLER
Spanish cousin of nil — NADA
Spanish custard — FLAN
Spanish dance — BOLERO, FLAMENCO
Spanish deictic — ESTOS
Spanish demonstrative — ESTA
Spanish dessert — FLAN
Spanish dollar — DURO
Spanish flower — DALIA
Spanish gentleman — DON, SENOR
Spanish girl's nickname — NITA
Spanish gold — ORO
Spanish gypsies — GITANOS
Spanish ice skating figures — OCHOS
Spanish inns, English style — PARADORS
Spanish island — ISLA
Spanish James — DIEGO
Spanish jar — OLLA
Spanish key — LLAVE
Spanish king — REY
Spanish ladies — DAMAS, DONAS
Spanish liqueur — ANIS
Spanish Main booty — ORO
Spanish men — SENORES
Spanish miss: Abbr. — SRTA
Spanish movie house — CINE
Spanish muralist — SERT
Spanish nobleman — DON
Spanish number — SIETA
Spanish or Western — OMELET
Spanish painter and designer — SERT
Spanish painter Joan — MIRO
Spanish painter, born 1904 — DALI
Spanish playwright — LORCA
Spanish poet Federico Garcia _____ — LORCA
Spanish port — CADIZ
Spanish port NE of Gibraltar — ADRA
Spanish pot — OLLA
Spanish pronoun — ESO, ESTA

Spanish pronunciation mark — TILDE
Spanish queen: 1906-31 — ENA
Spanish residences — CASAS
Spanish river — EBRO
Spanish room — SALA
Spanish seaport — ADRA
Spanish sherry category — FINO
Spanish shovel — PALA
Spanish silver — PLATA
Spanish singer — CHARO
Spanish step — PASO
Spanish Steps locale — ROME
Spanish stews — OLLAS
Spanish streams — RIOS
Spanish surrealist — DALI
Spanish surrealist Joan — MIRO
Spanish title — DON, SENOR
Spanish to Spanish — ESPANOL
Spanish treasure — ORO
Spanish wave — OLA
Spanish weight unit — ARROBA
Spanish weights — ONZAS
Spanish wine measures — COPAS
Spanish wines — SHERRIES
Spanish wolf — LOBO
Spanish woman's title — DONA
Spanker or jigger — SAIL
Spanky of "Our Gang," e.g. — RASCAL
Spanning — ASTRIDE
Spar — MAST, SPRIT
Spare — LEAN, TIRE
Spare or retread — TIRE
Spare rib, once — EVE
Sparing, as with praise — CHARY
Spark — LIVEN
Spark, a la grampa — SPOON
Sparkle — GLEAM, GLISTEN
Sparkling — GLITTERY, SMELT
Sparkling wine — ASTI
Sparks frantic message — SOS
Sparks of filmdom — NED
Sparks or Beatty — NED
Sparks or Calmer — NED
Sparks or Rorem — NED
Spars — BOOMS
Spartacus or Turner — SLAVE
Spartan magistrate — EPHOR
Spartan queen — LEDA
Spartan serf — HELOT
Spartan slave — HELOT
Spasm — THROE
Spasmodic sound — HIC
Spasmodic twitch — TIC
Spasms — TICS
Spat — TIFF
Spate — ONRUSH
Spates — TORRENTS
Spatiate — RAMBLE, ROVE
Spawn — SPORE
Spayed — UNSEXED
SPCA doctor — VET
Speak — UTTER
Speak against — GAINSAY
Speak at length — PERORATE
Speak candidly — TALK TURKEY
Speak confidently — AVER
Speak formally — ORATE
Speak hoarsely — RASP
Speak like a fishwife? — CARP
Speak poorly of — DEMEAN
Speak up — VOICE
Speak with assurance — AVER
Speak with conviction — AVER
Speak words not in the script — AD LIB
Speakeasy — BAR
Speaker — ORATOR, TRIS
Speaker component — TWEETER
Speaker of baseball — TRIS
Speaker of Cooperstown — TRIS
Speaker of Indo-European — ARYAN
Speaker of the Diamond — TRIS
Speaker of the House: 1801-07 — MACON
Speaker on the dais — ORATOR
Speaker's place — DAIS
Speaker's platform — DAIS
Speaker's prop — LECTERN
Speaker's spot — DAIS
Speaking two languages — BILINGUAL
Speaks harshly — RASPS
Speaks imperfectly — LISPS
Speaks indistinctly — SLURS
Speaks loudly and irrationally — RANTS
Speaks with forked tongue — FIBS
Spear — LANCE
Spear for Neptune — TRIDENT
Special — SALE
Special article — FEATURE
Special being — ONER
Special containers — PODS
Special dress — REGALIA
Special editions — EXTRAS
Special efforts — PAINS
Special forces wear — BERET
Special help for Elsie — COWHAND
Special language — LINGO
Special performance — GALA
Special person — ONER
Special position — NICHE
Special talent — BENT
Special times — ERAS
Special vocabulary — LINGO
Specialist in bel canto repertory — LUCIANO PAVAROTTI
Specialized circus trainers — FLEA TAMERS
Specially fitted — TAILORED
Specially made — CUSTOM BUILT
Specialty — AREA, METIER
Specialty in music — HI FI
Specialty of some sharks — USURY
Species — SORT
Species group — MALES
Species of hickory — PECAN
Species of sub-unit — GENUS
Species of wheat — EMMER
Specific-gravity scale — BAUME
Specific heat: Abbr. — SPHT
Specified — GIVEN
Specifies — DESIGNATES, DETAILS
Specify — CITE
Specimen — SAMPLE
Specimen of cloth — SWATCH
Speck — DOT
Speck — IOTA
Speck of dust — MOTE
Speckled — SPOTTY
Specks — DOTS, IOTAS, MOTES
Spectacle — EXTRAVAGANZA, SCENE, SHOW, SIGHT
Spectacular "Ben" — HUR
Spectator's spot — STANDS
Specter — GHOST
Spectral — SPOOKY
Spectral classification: astron. — OSTAR
Spectral shade — VIOLET
Spectrum producer — PRISM
Spectrum's rival — OMNI
Speculate — BET, GUESS, WAGER
Speculate in stocks — SCALP
Speculate in tickets — SCALP
Speculations — THEORIES
Sped — RACED, TORE
Sped along — TORE
Speech assn. — SAA
Speech characteristics — TWANGS
Speech defect — LISP
Speech fault — LISP
Speech flaw — LISP
Speech hesitations — ERS
Speech impediments — LISPS
Speech imperfections — LISPS
Speech phone — SOUND
Speech problem — LISP
Speechifies — ORATES
Speechify — IRATE, ORATE
Speechless — MUM, OUT OF WORDS
Speed — DASH, HIE, RATE, RIP
Speed contest — RACE
Speed it up! — HURRY
Speed meas. — IPS
Speed rate, for short — RPS
Speed reads — SCANS
Speed trap device — RADAR

Speed units — BAUDS
Speed: Abbr. — VEL
Speed: Comb. form — TACHO
Speeder's penalty — FINE
Speedily — APACE, FAST, FLEET, HASTY
Speediness — HASTE
Speedometer fig. — MPH
Speeds — TEARS
Speeds away — RACES OFF
Speeds up — REVS
Speedy — FAST, FLEET, RAPID
Speedy Atl. flyer — SST
Speedy communiques: Abbr. — NLS
Speedy descent — SWOOP
Speedy plane: Abbr. — SST
Speedy planes, for short — SSTS
Speer was jailed here — SPANDAU
Spell — CHARM, CURSE, HEX
Spell of work — STINT
Spellbind — ENTRANCE, ORATE
Spellbinder — ORATOR
Spellbound — AGOG
Spelling _____ — BEE
Spelling contests — BEES
Spelling or sewing affair — BEE
Spells a movie star — STANDS IN
Spelunker's milieu — CAVE
Spelunking locale — CAVE
Spelunking sites — CAVES
Spencer of film — TRACY
Spencer or Dick — TRACY
Spend it in Milan — LIRA
Spend money as if it grew on trees — WASTE
Spend money like water — SPLURGE
Spend the summer — ESTIVATE
Spends time in idle reverie — MOONS
Spendthrift — WASTER
Spent — TIRED
Spent foolishly — WASTED
Spew forth — EGEST
Spew lava — ERUPT
Sphere — ARENA, ORB
Sphere of work — AREA
Sphere or tactic lead-in — CHEMO
Sphere preceder — HEMI
Sphere starter — ATMO, IONO
Sphere to fear when pooling? — EIGHT
Spherical body — ORB
Spheroid-like — OBLATE
Spherule — BEAD
Sphragistic item — SIGIL
Spice — ZEST
Spice in a curry — CUMIN
Spice the wine — MULL
Spice used in curry powder — TURMERIC
Spick-and-span — CLEAN
Spicy — HOT
Spicy dessert? — GINGER BREAD
Spicy drink — TODDY
Spicy Italian condiment — TAMARA
Spicy Italian mixture — TAMARA
Spicy rootstock — GINGER
Spicy sausage — SALAMI
Spicy scent — AROMA
Spicy snack — NACHO
Spicy stew of game — CIVET
Spider flower — CLEOME
Spider in the kitchen — PAN
Spider's invitation — COME INTO MY PARLOR
Spider's parlor — WEB
Spider, in Spain — ARANA
Spielberg — STEVEN
Spiffily togged out — NATTY
Spigot — TAP
Spike — NAIL
Spike of corn — EAR
Spike the punch — LACE
Spiked shield boss — UMBO
Spikelet used in bouquets — CLOUD GRASS
Spiker's sport — VOLLEYBALL
Spiking the punch — LACING
Spile — STAKE
Spill — SLOP
Spill the beans — BLAB, LET ON, RAT, TELL
Spill wiper, on TV — ROSIE
Spillane sleuth — MIKE HAMMER
Spilled the beans — GAVE AWAY, SANG
Spills the beans — TELLS
Spin — BIRL, REVOLVE, TURN, TWIRL, WHIRL
Spin a log — BIRL
Spindle — HASP
Spindle on a cart — AXLE
Spindles — AXLES
Spine — RIDGE
Spine of a book — BACK
Spines — THORNS
Spinks of the ring — LEON
Spinnaker — SAIL
Spinnaker, for one — SAIL
Spinnakers and spankers — SAILS
Spinner — LURE, TOP
Spinning — AREEL, AWHIRL
Spinning apparatus — COILER
Spinning devices — GYROS
Spinning wheel adjunct — SPINDLE
Spins — ROTATES
Spiny shrub — FURZE
Spiny, flowered shrub — GORSE
Spiral — COIL
Spiral — HELIX, LOOP
Spiral groove — THREAD
Spiral shape — HELICAL
Spiral, often — PASS
Spirals — COILS
Spire — STEEPLE
Spire ornament — EPI
Spirit — ELAN, HAUNT, PEP
Spirit of a culture — ETHOS
Spirit of evil — SATAN
Spirit, in Siena — BRIO
Spirited — SPUNKY
Spirited dance — SAMBA
Spirited equine — STEED
Spirited horse — ARAB
Spirited movement — PRANCE
Spirited song — LILT
Spirited tune — LILT
Spiritual advisors — GURUS
Spiritual force — NUMEN
Spiritual mentor — GURU
Spiro _____ — AGNEW
Spit out, as lava — SPEW
Spite — MALICE, VENOM
Spiteful — CATTY, NASTY
Spitfires, e.g. — AIRPLANES
Spitzlike dog — AKITA
Splash — DAUB, SLOSH
Splash haphazardly — SLOSH
Splash of color — RIOT
Splash paint — SPLATTER
Splashes of color — RIOTS
Splendid — FINE
Splendor — POMP
Splenetic — CRABBY
Splice — UNITE
Spliced film, etc. — EDITED
Spline — SLAT
Splint — LATH
Splinter — SLIVER
Split — CLEFT, REND, RIVE, RIVEN
Split apart — RIVE
Split asunder — REND
Split hairs — QUIBBLE
Split in earth's crust — GREAT RIFT VALLEY
Split in earth's crust — SAN ANDREAS FAULT
Split off — DIVERGE
Split the difference — SHARE
Split the loot: Slang — WHACK UP
Split up — SHARED
Splits apart — RENDS
Splitting up — DIVORCING
Splotch — BLOB, BLOT, STAIN
Spoil — DECAY, DEFACE, MAR, MILDEW, PAMPER, ROT
Spoil — STAIN, SULLY, TAINT
Spoil rotten — PAMPER
Spoiled — RUINED
Spoils — BOOTY, ROTS
Spoke — SAID
Spoke dovishly — COOED

Spoken — ORAL
Spoken evidence — PAROL
Spoken exam — ORAL
Spoken from memory — RECITED
Spoken with a twang — NASALLY
Spokes — RADII
Spokesman — VOICE
Spoliate — ROB
Sponge — CADGE, MOOCH
Sponge out — ERASE
Sponge spicle — OXEA
Sponged off — SWABBED
Sponger — FREE LOADER
Spongers — DEADBEATS
Spongy — SOFT
Sponsors — FINANCES
Sponsorship — EGIS
Spontaneous remark — ADLIB
Spoofs, in a way — ROASTS
Spookier — CREEPIER, EERIER
Spooks cry — BOO
Spooks' den — CIA
Spooky-sounding lake — ERIE
Spooky — EERIE
Spool — REEL
Spools — REELS
Spoon or spinner — LURE
Spoon or tune follower — FUL
Spoon-bender Geller — URI
Spoonerized dinner drink — CULLEDMIDER
Spoonerized dinner entree — TOASTRURKEY
Spoonerized dinner extra — BOTHISCUITS
Spoonerized dinner favorite — YANDIEDCAMS
Spoonerized side dish — STESTNUTCHUFFING
Spoonerized Thanksgiving dinner item — PIPPEDWHATA-TOES
Spoonerized theme holiday — DANKSGIVINGTHAY
Spoors — SCENTS
Spore — SEED
Spore cases of ferns — SORI
Spore cluster — SORUS
Spore clusters — SORI
Spore sacs — ASCI
Spore-case cluster — SORI, SORUS
Sport — FUN, PLAY
Sport fish — CERO
Sport for Boitano — ICE SKATING
Sport for ringers — HORSE SHOES
Sport of princes — POLO
Sport spot — ARENA
Sport with chukkers — POLO
Sport; ridicule — FUN
Sported — WORE
Sporting — ATHLETIC
Sporting fish — CERO
Sporting pumps — SHOD
Sporting sight — ARENA
Sporting sound — RAH
Sports area, for short — GYM
Sports areas — ARENAS
Sports center — ARENA
Sports competitions — MEETS
Sports event — C TEST, MEET, OPEN
Sports event of Arthurian times — TILT
Sports info — STATS
Sports man — REF
Sports news — RESULTS
Sports off. — UMP
Sports official — LINEMAN
Sports official: Abbr. — REF
Sports org. — NBA, NCAA, NFL, NRA
Sports palace — ARENA
Sports place — DOME
Sports-oriented — ATHLETIC
Sportscaster Barber — RED
Sportscaster Cross — IRV
Sportscaster Howard — COSELL
Sportscasting commentator's forte — COLOR
Sportsman — HUNTER
Sportsman Bruce — JENNER
Sportsmanlike — CLEAN
Sportsmanship — HONESTY
Sporty — FLASHY
Spot — ESPY, LOCALE, LOCATE
Spot for a barbecue — PATIO
Spot for a beret — TETE
Spot for a bracelet — ANKLE
Spot for a shot — BAR
Spot for an arras — WALL
Spot for an oilman? — GETTYS BURG
Spot for books — SHELF
Spot for desert dates — OASIS
Spot in Sherwood Forest — GLADE
Spot or mark, in Madrid — PINTA
Spot to stop on — DIME
Spote — SEED
Spotlight — FEATURE
Spotlight color — AMBER
Spots — DETECTS, SEES
Spots for berets — TETES
Spots for lounge lizards — SETTEES
Spots for slots — DOORS
Spots for swimmers — POOLS
Spots for trash — ASHBINS
Spotted — EYED, FOUND, SEEN
Spotted cats — JAGUARS, LEOPARDS, MARGAYS
Spotted cavy — PACA
Spotted racers — CHEETAHS
Spotty — UNEVEN
Spousal symbols — GOLD RINGS
Spouse — CONSORT, MATE, PARTNER, WIFE
Spouse of Martin Luther King — CORETTA SCOTT
Spouse of Zeus — HERA
Spouse's family member — INLAW
Spouses — MATES
Spout off — RANT
Sprain applications — ARNICAS
Sprang from — AROSE
Sprat's garb? — HERRING-BONE SUIT
Sprawl — SLUMP
Spray — ATOMIZE, HOSE, MIST
Sprayed — HOSED
Sprays a houseplant — MISTS
Spread — ACREAGE, FEAST, OLEO, RAN, STREW
Spread hay — TED
Spread out — SPACED, SPLAY
Spread out, in a way — SPRAWL
Spread over — COVER
Spread rapidly — MUSHROOM
Spread seed — SOWED
Spread unchecked — RAGED
Spread widely — STREW
Spreads — OLEOS, PATES
Spreads about — SCATTERS
Spreads alfalfa — TEDS
Spreads hay — TEDS
Spreads nitrates — FERTILIZES
Spreads on thickly — SLATHERS
Spreads rumors — NOISES
Spree — BINGE, CAROUSAL, FLING, TEAR, TOOT
Sprees — LARKS
Sprig — BRANCH, SHOOT, TWIG
Sprightly — AGILE, LIVELY, PERT
Spring — DART, FONT, LEAP, WELL
Spring back — REVERSE
Spring beauty — FORSYTHIA
Spring beauty — IRIS
Spring bloom — IRIS, LILY OF THE VALLEY, TULIP
Spring bloom — VIOLET
Spring bloom from Bermuda — EASTER LILY
Spring bloomer — IRIS
Spring break — RECESS
Spring flower — IRIS, PANSY, VIOLET
Spring flowers — IRIDES
Spring forward or fall back — RESET
Spring harbinger — ROBIN
Spring holiday — EASTER
Spring in Soissons — MAI

Spring mo. — APR
Spring months — APRILS
Spring morning phenomena — DEWS
Spring observation — LENT
Spring parts — COILS
Spring phenomenon — THAW
Spring sporting event, for short — NBA PLAYOFFS
Spring training league — GRAPEFRUIT
Spring up — GROW
Spring, e.g. — SEASON
Springbell — HERB
Springe, e.g. — TRAP
Springfield — RIFLE
Springlike — MILD
Springs — SPAS
Springs or Sunday — PALM
Springs that may bring some zings — SPAS
Springsteen's "Born in the _____" — USA
Springsteen, popularly — THE BOSS
Springsteen, with "The" — BOSS
Springtime — APRIL
Springtime phenomena — BUDS
Springy, in a way — SPRY
Sprinkle — RAIN, SPLATTER, WET
Sprint — TROLL
Sprinted — RACED, TORE
Sprinter's concern — START
Sprinter, perhaps — TRACKMAN
Sprints — DARTS, RACES
Sprite — ELF, ELVE, PIXY
Sprite and satellite — ARIELS
Sprite-ly — ELFIN
Sprites — IMPS
Spritzer item — SODA
Sprout: Var. — CION
Sprouters — SEEDS
Sprouting spring — GEYSER
Sprouts — GROWS
Spruce — NEATEN, PINE, SMARTEN, TRIM
Spruce tree — NORWAY
Spruces up — TIDYS, TRIGS
Spry — AGILE, SMART
Spud — TATER
Spud's bud — EYE
Spume — MIST
Spume forth — EJECT
Spumescent — FOAMY
Spumous — FOAME
Spunk — GRIT
Spunky — NERVY
Spur — ROWEL
Spur accessory — ROWEL
Spur and heel of Italy's "boot" — APULIA
Spur wheels — ROWELS
Spurious — PSEUDO
Spurious imitation — SHAM
Spurious wing — ALULA
Spurn — REPEL
Spurry or henbit — WEED
Spurs — STIMULI
Spurt — GUSH
Spurt up — ERUPT
Spy of 1780 — ANDRE
Spy on — WATCH
Spy Penkovsky — OLEG
Spy portrayed by Greta — MATA
Spy's means of contact — CODE
Spyri girl — HEIDI
Sq., for one — RECT
Squabble — DISPUTE, HASSLE, ROW, SPAT
Squad car item — SIREN
Squalid — FOUL
Squama — SCALE
Squander — LOSE, WASTE
Square-tipped cigars — CHEROOTS
Square — CORNY, EVEN
Square column — ANTA
Square dance — HOEDOWN
Square feet — AREA
Square follower — ROOT
Square foot: Abbr. — SQ FT
Square near Fifth Avenue — WASHINGTON
Square of Manhattan — TIMES
Square off — DEFY
Square one — START
Square pillar — PIER
Square's properties — SIDES
Square-root signs — RADICALS
Squared — TRUED
Squared away — PAID
Squared off — ANTI
Squared stones — ASHLARS
Squarely — SPANG
Squash — PEPO, SQUELCH
Squash implement — BAT
Squash variety — ACORN, WINTER
Squash, for example — PEPO
Squash, for one — SPORT
Squat broad-mouthed jar — KORO
Squatter — NESTER
Squatter in 1889 — SOONER
Squawk — BLAT, CROAK, CRY, SCREECH
Squawk box — SPEAKER
Squeaky sound — PEEP
Squeal — EEK, HOWL, RAT, SCREAM
Squealed — RATTED, TOLD ON
Squealers — RATS
Squealers of a sort — CANARIES
Squealers, to a Brit. — NARKS
Squeals — RATS
Squeamish — COY, MODEST, PRIM
Squeeze — ELBOW, HUG
Squeeze box — CONCERTINA
Squeeze out — EXTRUDE
Squeeze-play sign in the Bronx — YANKEE GO HOME
Squeezed by — EKED
Squeezed orange — JUICE
Squelch — STIFLE
Squelched — SAT ON
Squelches — SITS ON
Squid's clutches — TENTACLES
Squid's defense — INK
Squid's squirt — INK
Squiffed — LOADED, OILED, STONED
Squint — PEER
Squinted — PEERED
Squire, in "The Rivals" — ACRES
Squire-to-be — PAGE
Squirrel away — STASH, STORE
Squirrel nest — DREY
Squirrel or beaver — RODENT
Squirrel, for one — NUTTER
Squirrels' nest — DRAY
Squirrels' nests: Var. — DREYS
Sri _____ — LANKA
Sri Lanka's continent — ASIA
Sri Lankan — TAMIL
Sri Lankan aborigine — VEDDA
Sri Lankan native — VEDDAH
Sri Lankan seaport — NEGOMBO
SRO ticketholder — STANDEE
SST's, e.g. — APS
SST, e.g. — AERO
SST, for one — PLANE
St. _____ — l'Ecole, Fr. West Point — CYR
St. _____ — NICK
St. _____, W. Indies — KITTS
St. Columba's isle — IONA
St. Francis of _____ — ASSISI
St. Francis' hometown — ASSISI
St. George's form — DRAGON
St. John followers — ACTS, BAPTISTS
St. John's bread — CAROB
St. Lawrence River peninsula — GASPE
St. Lo seasons — ETES
St. Louis base of yore — BROWN BAG
St. Louis bridge — EADS
St. Louis bridge builder — EADS
St. Louis runs — CARDINAL POINTS
St. Louis-Little Rock vector — SSW
St. Nick — SANTA
St. Patrick's Day color — IRISH GREEN
St. Patrick's land, for short — EIRE

St. Paul's designer — WREN
St. Petersburg resident — TSAR
St. Petersburg-born actor: 1906-72 — GEORGE SANDERS
St. Philip _____ — NERI
St. Teresa of _____ — AVILA
Stab in the back — BETRAY
Stability — PERMANENCE
Stabilize again — RESET
Stabilized — STEADIED
Stabilizing agent — AGAR
Stable — BARN, LOYAL
Stable breeders — STUDS
Stable creatures — PONIES
Stable dwellers — MARES
Stable fables? — PONY TALES
Stable food — HAY
Stable mates — MARES
Stable sound — NEIGH, SNORT, SWISH
Stable staple — OATS
Stableman, in India: Var. — SICE
Stablemates — MARES
Stabler's first team — RAIDERS
Stabler's nickname — THE SNAKE
Stabler, using his left — PASSER
Stack — HEAP, NEST, PILE
Stack for burning — PYRE
Stack of corn — RICK
Stack of wood — CORD
Stack role — NESS
Stack stuff — HAY
Stack the deck — CHEAT
Stacked, in a way — NESTED
Stacks — HEAPS
Stacks the cards — CHEATS
Stadium — ARENA, FIELD
Stadium area — TIER
Stadium cheers — RAHS
Stadium crowd — FANS
Stadium displeasure — BOOS
Stadium feature — TIER
Stadium in Atlanta — OMNI
Stadium section — TIER
Stadium shape — OVAL
Stadium shout — RAH
Stadium sound — RAH
Stadt on the Rhein — KOLN
Staff — CREW, MAN, WAND
Staff in music — STAVE
Staff mem. — ASST
Staff member — AIDE
Staff of life — BREAD
Staff people — AIDES
Staff symbol — CLEF, NOTE
Staff worker — AIDE
Staff: Abbr. — PERS
Staffed — MANNED
Staffer — AIDE, EMPLOYEE
Stag — BUCK, BULL, COCK, MALE
Stag adornment — ANTLER
Stag attendees — MEN
Stag horn — ANTLER
Stag or stallion — MALE
Stag party guest — MALE
Stag party sign — FOR MEN ONLY
Stage-door loser? — JOHNNY COME LATELY
Stage — ENACT
Stage _____ (facetious tribute) — A ROAST
Stage award — OBIE
Stage curtain — ARRAS
Stage decor — SET
Stage designer Bernstein — ALINE
Stage device — ASIDE
Stage direction — ENTER, EXIT, SOLUS
Stage elevator — LIFT
Stage fright — HAM
Stage honors — OBIES
Stage illuminator — FOOT-LIGHT
Stage in a scale — RUNG
Stage in lunar cycle — PHASE
Stage lines — ASIDES
Stage manager's concern — PROPS
Stage name for Mr. Iskowitz — CANTOR
Stage offering — DRAMA
Stage part — ROLE
Stage play — DRAMA
Stage portion — APRON
Stage presence — ACTOR
Stage prop — CURTAIN
Stage remark — ASIDE
Stage requisite — PROP
Stage setting — BACKDROP, SCENERY
Stage shows — ACTS
Stage signal — CUE
Stage whisper — ASIDE
Stage whisper from Elsie? — ASIDE OF BEEF
Stage, in Sevilla — ETAPA
Stagecoach company — WELLS FARGO
Staged effects — THEATRICS
Stagehand — GRIP
Stagehand's concern — PROP
Stages — PHASES, STEPS
Stagger — REEL, TOTTER
Staggered — REELED
Staggering — AREEL
Staggers — REELS
Staghorn _____ — CORAL
Stagnant — INERT
Stagnation — STASIS
Stags and bucks — MALES
Staid — SEDATE
Stain — BLOT, DYE, TAINT
Stain, of old — TASH
Stained — MACULATE
Stainers' containers — VATS
Stainless — HONEST, PURE
Stains, old style — SOILURES
Stair part — RISER
Stair post — NEWEL
Staircase part — LADDER
Staircase post — NEWEL
Stairway part — RISER
Stairway post — NEWEL
Stake — ANTE, BET
Stakes for sword practice — PELS
Stalactite look-alike — ICICLE
Stale — TRITE
Stalemate — DRAW
Stalk — FOLLOW, HUNT, STEM, TRACK
Stalk of bananas — STEM
Stalk units — EARS
Stalked — PREYED
Stalker in a salt marsh — EGRET
Stall — KIOSK, LOGE
Stallone feature — CHEST
Stallone film — FIST
Stallone role — RAMBO
Stallone's nickname — SLY
Stallone, to friends — SLY
Stamina — ENERGY
Stamp — BRAND
Stamp a document — ENFACE
Stamp a passport — VISE
Stamp collecting — PHILATELY
Stamp of the 1960's — FIVE CENT
Stamp out — QUELL, SCOTCH
Stamp sheet — PANE
Stamp unit — PANE
Stan and Ollie, e.g. — PALS
Stan's foil — OLLIE
Stan's partner — OLLIE
Stanches — STEMS
Stanchion — POST
Stand — BEAR
Stand _____: show reverence — IN AWE
Stand by — BACK
Stand credit for (a bill) — FOOT
Stand for a Degas — EASEL
Stand for Frank or Joseph Stella — EASEL
Stand for Seurat — EASEL
Stand in an Atelier — EASEL
Stand in the way — IMPEDE
Stand one in good _____ — STEAD
Stand or tank add-on — ARD
Stand out — STAR
Stand pat — STAY
Stand stock-still — FREEZE
Stand the _____ (take abuse) — GAFF
Stand the gaff — ENDURE
Stand the test — HOLD TRUE, PASS MUSTER
Stand up — ARISE
Stand up for — UPHOLD

Stand up to — FACE
Stand up to — OPPOSE
Stand well — RATED
Stand-in for Standish — ALDEN
Standard — GAUGE, NORM, NORMAL
Standard & Poor's 500 — STOCK INDEX
Standard bearer — CORNET
Standard measure — UNIT
Standardized mental picture — STEREOTYPE
Standards of perfection — IDEALS
Standing — ON END, RANK
Standing rule — BYLAW
Standing start — OUT
Standings — RANKS
Standish — MILES
Standish stand-in — ALDEN
Standoff — TIE
Standoff's ending — ISH
Standoffish — ALOOF, COLD
Standouts — ONERS
Standouts in an orchestra — SOLOISTS
Stands in the way — IMPEDES
Stands still — STOPS
Stands the gaff — ENDURES
Stands up to — FACES
Standstill — CESSATION
Stanford and E.B. — WHITES
Stanford's neighbor — PALO ALTO
Stanley to Livingstone " ... I _____" — PRESUME
Stannum — TIN
Stans partner — OLLIE
Stanwyck film: 1945 — CHRISTMAS IN CONNECTICUT
Stanza of six lines — SESTET
Stapes locale — EAR
Star — IDOL
Star assemblage — CLUSTER
Star cluster — NEBULA
Star gazers, in Hollywood — OGLERS
Star in "Cactus Flower" — HAWN
Star in "Rumba" — RAFT
Star in "The Serpent" — ALDA
Star in "Yanks" — GERE
Star in Aquila — ALTAIR
Star in Cetus — MIRA
Star in Cygnet — DENEB
Star in Draco — ADIB
Star in Lyra — VEGA
Star in Perseus — ALGOL
Star in the whale — MIRA
Star of "48 Hours" — NOLTE
Star of "Barney Miller" — LINDEN
Star of "Blume in Love" — SEGAL
Star of "Bombshell" — HARLOW
Star of "Moonstruck" — CHER
Star of "Nana," Anna _____ — ATEN
Star of "The Bank Dick" — FIELDS
Star of "The Invisible Man" — RAINS
Star of "The Kid" — CHAPLIN
Star of "Two by Two" — KAYE
Star of Cygnus — DENEB
Star or Ranger — LONE
Star or stone starter — LODE
Star quality — TALENT
Star shaped — ASTRAL
Star's award — OSCAR
Star's bit part — CAMEO
Star's car — LIMO
Star's minor role — CAMEO
Star's part — LEAD, TITLE ROLE
Star, moon, gold, etc. — DUST
Star-crossed actors? — TRAGEDIANS
Star-crossed whaler — AHAB
Star-shaped — STELLATE
Star: Comb. form — ASTRO, ASTERO
Starch — STIFF
Starch plants — ARROW ROOTS
Starchy foodstuff — SALEP
Starchy root — TARO
Stare-downs — EYE CLASHES
Stare — GAPE, GAZE, OGLE
Stare amorously — OGLE
Stare at — EYE
Stare in wonder — GAPE
Stare open-mouthed — GAPE
Stare, in a way — OGLE
Stared slack-jawed — GAPED
Stares — GAPES, OGLES
Stares in wonder — GAPES
Starfish arms — RAYS
Staring — AGAPE
Staring open-mouthed — AGAPE
Stark — SPARTAN
Stark naked — NUDE
Starlet's dream — ROLE
Starr of football fame — BART
Starred — SHONE
Starring roles — LEADS
Starry — ASTRAL
Stars and Bars — FLAG
Stars and Stripes, for example — BOAT
Stars' companion — STRIPES
Start — BEGIN, DEBUT, INAUGURATE, ORIGIN
Start — OUTSET, SET IN, SET OFF
Start a card game — DEAL
Start a new paragraph — INDENT
Start anew — REOPEN
Start for Ballesteros — TEE
Start for climax — ANTI
Start for potent or present — OMNI
Start forward suddenly — JACK RABBIT
Start of "Home, Sweet Home" — MID
Start of "The Raven" — ONCE UPON A
Start of a 1936 best seller's title — GONE
Start of a C. Moore classic — TWAS
Start of a carol — ADESTE
Start of a child's chant — EENY
Start of a count — ONE
Start of a D.H. Lawrence title — LADY
Start of a Dickens title — A TALE
Start of a Dostoyevsky title — CRIME
Start of a Hardy title — FAR
Start of a Hemingway title — ACROSS
Start of a hole — TEE
Start of a hymn — NEARER
Start of a journey — STEP
Start of a kindergarten chant — ABCD
Start of a mighty oak — ACORN
Start of a pencil game — TIC
Start of a quip — A FREE-LOADER IS A
Start of a quote — THE FICKLENESS
Start of a reply to Virginia — YES
Start of a saying — THERE IS
Start of a Shakespearean title — MUCH, ALLS
Start of a Shelley question — IF WINTER COMES
Start of a soliloquy — TO BE
Start of a speech — LADIES
Start of a Step-quote — HAVEE
Start of a toast — HERES
Start of a two-line verse — GOD IN
Start of a W.S. title — ALLS
Start of a Williams title — CAT ON
Start of a Wolfe title — OF TIME
Start of a Yale song — BOOLA
Start of an O'Neill title — DESIRE
Start of Caesar's boast — VENI
Start of Caesar's message — VENI
Start of corner or pillar — CATER
Start of eighth century — DCCI

Start of Hamlet's soliloquy — TO BE
Start of Idaho's title — ESTO
Start of Mass. motto — ENSE
Start of motto of N.C. — ESSE
Start of quote, with "As" — ALL LOOKS YELLOW
Start of something big? — ONSET
Start of the handwriting on the wall — MENE
Start of the Hebrew alphabet — ALEF
Start of the reign of Tiberius — XIV
Start the bidding — OPEN
Start the steak — SEAR
Start to bloom — BUD
Start to riches, for some — RAGS
Started — BEGUN
Started suddenly — SHIED
Started the set — SERVED
Starter for alike and alive — LOOK
Starter for bag, bar and bank — SAND
Starter for stone or storm — SAND
Starters — SEEDS
Starting golfer — TEER
Starting point — ORIGIN
Startle — ALARM
Startles — SCARES
Starts a voyage — SETS SAIL
Starts to weaken — STIRS
Starve — SUFFER
Stash — HIDE, STOW
Stash away — HOARD
Stashed away — SAVED
Stat. for a slugger — RBI
Stat. for Brett — RBI
Stat. for Gooden — ERA
Stat. for Saberhagen — ERA
State — AVER, SAY, UTTER
State adjoining Ill. — IND
State an equivalence — EQUATE
State as a fact — AVER
State as true — AVER
State bird of Hawaii — NENE
State firmly — AVER
State flower of Indiana — PEONY
State flower of La. — MAGNOLIA
State flower of N.H. — LILAC
State flower of Tenn. — IRIS
State flower of Texas — BLUE BONNET
State flower of Utah — SEGO
State flowers of New Mexico — YUCCAS
State forcefully — ASSERT
State founder — PENN
State in Austl. — NSW
State in detail — EXPOUND
State in E India — ORISSA
State in Mexico — TABASCO
State in NE India — ASSAM
State in St. Lo — ETAT
State motto of Rhode Island — HOPE
State motto of Texas — FRIENDSHIP
State named for Honeycutt's pal? — IOWA
State of agitation — SNIT
State of being all tuckered out — EXHAUSTION
State of being level — FLATNESS
State of bodily tissues — TONUS
State of extreme delight — ECSTACY
State of France — ETAT
State of lawlessness — ANOMIE
State of mind — MOOD
State of NE Brazil — CEARA
State of NE India — ASSAM
State of neglect — DESUE-TUDE
State of pine forests — MAINE
State of the moon — PHASE
State of W.J.C.'s mom? — VIRGINIA
State of well-being — EUPHORIA
State off. — GOV
State official — SENATOR
State or angle lead-in — TRI
State police — TROOPER
State positively — ASSERT
State proposed by the Mormons: 1849 — DESERET
State south of NJ — DEL
State subdivision — COUNTY
State tree of Tex. — PECAN
State under oath — DEPONE
State VIP — GOV
State with assurance — ASSERT
State without proof — ALLEGE
State, in Paris — ETAT
State, in Sedan — ETAT
State: Abbr. — TENN
Stated again — RETOLD
Statehouse — CAPITAL
Stately — LOFTY
Stately abodes — MANORS
Stately carriage — CAROCHE
Stately flower — PHLOX
Stately potato? — IDAHO
Stately residence — MANSION
Stately tree — ELM
Stately woman — JUNO
Statement — REMARK
Statement by a certain advertis-er? — IM PERSONAL
Statement from Liberace — I LOVE A PIANO
Statement in a confessional? — IM PENITENT
Statement made by Alice — A CAT MAY LOOK AT A KING
Statement of belief — CREED
Statement of religious belief — CREDO
Statement of understanding — I SEE
Statements of opinions on any subject — CREEDS
States — ASSERTS, AVERS
States firmly — AVERS
States of pique — SNITS
States positively — AVERS
Statesman — SOLON
Statesman Hammarskjold — DAG
Statesman Motilal- _____ of India — NEHRU
Statesman Root — ELIHU
Statesman Stevenson — ADLAI
Static — NOISE
Static acronym in ham radio — QRN
Stating — UTTERING
Stating over — ITERATING
Station — BASE, DEPOT, POST, RANK, TERMINAL
Station _____ — WAGON
Station, in Paris — GARE
Station, in Sedan — GARE
Stationary — STABILE
Stationery — PAPER
Stationery feature — LETTER-HEAD
Stationery item — ERASER
Stationery item: Abbr. — ENV
Stats for Maury Wills — SBS
Stats for Ryan and Clemens — ERAS
Stats for Seaver — ERAS
Stats for Strawberry — RBIS
Statuary — TORSOS
Statue — ACT, FIGURE
Statue in the Duomo at Florence — PIETA
Statue, of a sort — TORSO
Stature — PRESTIGE
Status — RANK, RANKING
Status _____ — QUO
Status reached by Streep — STARDOM
Status seeker — SOCIAL CLIMBER
Statute — ACT, ENACTMENT
Statutes — LAWS
Staunch supporter — BOOST-ER
Stave — SLAT
Stay — BIDE
Stay cool — KEEP ONES SHIRT ON

Stay stationary, as a ship — LIE TO
Stayed — REMAINED
Stays to the end — SITS OUT
Stays with till the end — SEES OUT
Stays within the budget — AFFORDS
Stead — LIEU
Stead, with "in" — LIEU
Steadfast — FIRM, FIXED
Steadfast one — DIEHARD
Steadiness on deck — SEA LEGS
Steady — REGULAR
Steady Eddie of pitching fame — LOPAT
Steady income — WEEKLY SALARY
Steak cut — T BONE
Steak house specification — RARE
Steak order — RARE
Steak preparation — RARE
Steak variety — LONDON BROIL
Steal — THIEVE
Steal ransom security — KIDNAP
Steal silently — CREEP
Steal, slangily — GLOM
Steals away — DECAMPS
Steals, old style — NIMS
Stealthy — FURTIVE
Steam — RAGE, VAPOR
Steam bath — SAUNA
Steam, for example — VAPOR
Steamed — IRATE
Steamed pudding — DUFF
Steamed up — IRATE
Steaming — HOT, MAD
Steamroom apparel — TURKISH TOWELS
Steamy places — BATHS
Stearin, for one — ESTER
Steatite — TALC
Steber role — ELSA
Steed — HORSE
Steed feature — MANE
Steel — HARDEN
Steel City of the Ruhr — ESSEN
Steel girder — I BEAM
Steel mill worker — STRANDER
Steel plow pioneer — DEERE
Steel rods used by carpenters — NAILSETS
Steel splint, in armor — TASSE
Steel structural column — LALLY
Steel substance — WOOL
Steel, in St. Lo — ACIER
Steeler coach and family — NOLLS
Steeler Lynn — SWANN
Steep — SOAK
Steep cliff — CRAG
Steep hill — BUTTE
Steep slope — SCRAP
Steep slopes — ESCARPS
Steep, as tea — BREW
Steep, in a pickling solution — MARINATE
Steep, rugged rock — CRAG
Steeple — SPIRE, TOWER
Steeple adornment — EPI
Steeple occupants — BELLS
Steeplechase, e.g. — RACE
Steeps — BREWS, RETS
Steer — PILOT
Steer clear of — EVADE, SHUN, SKIP
Steer sound — LOW
Steerage — CONTROL
Steering station — HELM
Steffi of tennis — GRAF
Steiger and Serling — RODS
Stein — MUG
Stein filler — LAGER
Stein subject — ROSE
Stein's predecessor? — EIN
Steinbeck character — OKIE
Steinbeck novel — SWEET THURSDAY
Steinbeck opus — OF MICE AND MEN
Steinbeck protagonist — OKIE
Steinbeck siren — ABRA
Steinbeck's "_____ With Charley" — TRAVELS
Steinway for golf's Gary? — PLAYER PIANO
Stellar hunter — ORION
Stellar phenomena — NOVAE
Stem — ARREST
Stem cutters — SNIPPERS
Stem growth — NODE
Stem joint — NODE
Stem of a gladiolus — CORM
Stem part — PITH
Stem protrusion — NODE
Stem running underground: Bot. — STOLON
Stem: Suffix — OME
Stench — SMELL
Stencil — MARK
Stendhal's "Le Rouge _____ Noir" — ET LE
Stengel follower — ESE
Stengel's monicker — CASEY
Stengel's wife — EDNA
Steno — SECY
Steno's error — TYPO
Steno's need — PAD
Stenos slip — TYPO
Step — GAIT
Step _____ (hustle) — ON IT
Step face — RISER
Step heavily — STOMP
Step on — TROMP
Step on it — HIE
Step out into traffic — JAYWALK
Step up to the plate — BAT
Step-down — REDUCE
Step-in — GARMENT
Stephen, the poet — SPENDER
Steppe — PLAIN
Steppe abode — YURT
Stepped — TROD
Steppes location — RUSSIA
Steps along the Ganges — GHAT
Steps down — RESIGNS
Steps to a graduate degree — ORALS
Steps to success — RUNGS
Stere — CUBIC METER
Stereo choice — HIFI
Stereo speaker — WOOFER
Stereotyped — CORNY, TRITE
Stereotypical pirate — PEGLEG
Sterile — PURE
Sterling North book: 1963 — RASCAL
Stern — ABAFT, DOUR, GRIM, HARD
Stern fiddler — ISAAC
Stern law-giver — DRACO
Stern's opposite — STEM
Sternward — AFT
Steroid, for example — HORMONE
Stertorous sound — SNORE
Stetson wearer — JOHN WAYNE
Stettin's river — ODER
Steve — STOW
Steve Allen role — BENNY GOODMAN
Steve Cauthen holds them — REINS
Steve of the comics — CANYON
Steve or Woody — ALLEN
Stevedore's group — ILA
Stevedores' org. — ILA
Steven's modifier — EVEN
Stevenson classic — TREASURE ISLAND
Stevland Morris from Saginaw — WONDER
Stew — RAGOUT, SNIT
Stew _____ — POT
Stew ingredient — ONION
Stew pot — OLLA
Stewart and Serling — RODS
Stewart and Taylor — RODS
Stewart in Harvey — DOWD
Stewart or Joseph — ALSOP
Stewart's "_____ Coaches Waiting" — NINE
Stewart, for one — CLAN
Stewed — DRUNK
Stewing pot — OLLA
Stewpot — OLLA
Stews — FRETS

Stich specialty — ACE
Stick — ADHERE, COHERE
Stick out — PROJECT
Stick out like _____ thumb — A SORE
Stick to — ADHERE
Stick together — CEMENT
Stick up for — AID
Stick with these — GLUES
Stick's on — PASTES
Sticks (to) — CLINGS
Sticks out like a _____ — SORE THUMB
Stickum — PASTE
Stickup — HEIST
Sticky — GUMMY, PASTY, TACKY
Sticky stuff — GOO, RESIN
Stiff — RIGID
Stiff collar — ETON
Stiff cotton fabric — WIGAN
Stiff hair — SETA
Stiff hairs — SETAE
Stiff, in Soissons — RAIDE
Stiff-upper-lip type — STOIC
Stiffens — TENSES UP
Stiffer — LAMER
Stiffly proper — PRIM
Stifle — CHOKE
Stifles — GAGS
Stigma — BLOT, BRAND, ONUS
Stigmatize — TAINT
Still — EVEN, INERT, YET
Still hungry — UNSATED
Still on the shelf — UNREAD, UNSOLD
Still waters — DEEP RUNNERS
Stiller's partner — MEARA
Stilt, e.g. — WADER
Stimulate — INSPIRE, ROUSE, URGE, WHET
Stimulated — TURNED ON
Stimulator — TONIC
Stimulus — DRIVE, GOAD, SPUR
Sting — SCAM, SMART
Sting operators? — BEES
Stinger — BARB, BITE, SMART, WASP
Stinging — BARBED
Stinging ant — KELEP
Stinging remark — BARB
Stings — SMARTS
Stingy — NEAR
Stint — TASK
Stipend — FEE
Stipulation in a contract — ARTICLE
Stir — ADO, AGITATE, FUSS, MOVE
Stir until foamy — MILL
Stir up — AGITATE, RILE
Stir-fry pan — WOK
Stirs — MOVES
Stirs up — ROILS
Stitch — SEW
Stitch again — RESEW
Stitch for Defarge — PURL
Stitch up — SEW
Stitched — SEWN
Stitches again — RESEWS
Stoat — ERMINE
Stock-market term — AT PAR
Stock — BREED, BUTT, CACHE, GOODS, HAN-DLE, INVENTORY
Stock — SELECTION, WARES
Stock clothing — READY MADES
Stock exchange abbr. — AMEX
Stock exchange area — PIT
Stock exchange membership — SEAT
Stock Exchange position — SEAT
Stock exchange: Fr. — BOURSE
Stock farmer — RANCHER
Stock in trade — GOODS
Stock unit — SHARE
Stock up — AMASS, PILE
Stockade — BOMA
Stockholm gnome — NISSE
Stockholm native — SWEDE
Stockholm prize — NOBEL
Stocking fabric — LISLE
Stocking features — SEAMS
Stocking mishap — SNAG
Stocking shade — ECRU
Stocking stuff — SILK
Stocking stuffer — SANTA
Stocking supports — GARTERS
Stocking yarn — NYLON
Stockings — HOSE
Stockpile — AMASS, HOARD
Stocks, bonds, etc. — HOLDINGS
Stocky — BEEFY
Stodgy — DULL
Stoic — ZENO
Stoical — COOL
Stoker's count — DRACULA
Stole — BOA, WRAP
Stole second base — SLID
Stolen — HOT
Stolen goods? — HOT STUFF
Stolen sockeye? — POACHED SALMON
Stoles — BOAS
Stomach — GUT
Stomach ache: Comb. form — COELI
Stomach churners — ACIDS
Stomach strengthener — SITUP
Stomped — TRAMPED
Stone — PEBBLE, ROCK
Stone broke — POOR
Stone cavity — GEODE
Stone for Suetonius — LAPIS
Stone hurling device — ONAGER
Stone landmark — CAIRN
Stone lined with crystals — GEODE
Stone marten — SABLE
Stone memorial — STELE
Stone monument — MT RUSHMORE, STELA
Stone or iron — AGE
Stone paving block — SETT
Stone pillar — STELA, STELE
Stone used for vessels in old Roma — MURRA
Stone vases — URNS
Stone worker — MASON
Stone: Comb. form — LITHO
Stone: Suffix — LITE
Stonecrop-family plant — ORPINE
Stones as garden art — ROCK WORK
Stonewall's boys — REBS
Stoneware, in Limoges — GRES
Stoneworker — MASON
Stood — ENDURED
Stood for a second term — RERAN
Stood for office — RAN
Stood out — SHONE
Stood up — AROSE
Stooge name — MOE
Stooge with Larry and Curly — MOE
Stool pigeon — RAT, WEASEL
Stoop — BEND, BOW, CROUCH
Stop — ARREST, CEASE, HALT
Stop _____ — ON A DIME
Stop at the meter — PARK
Stop by — VISIT
Stop for a tourist — MOTEL
Stop for gas and repairs (in racing) — PIT
Stop on _____ — A DIME
Stop or go — VERB
Stop temporarily — PAUSE
Stop work for lunch — PAUSE
Stop, at sea — AVAST
Stop, in Montmarte — ARRET
Stop, in Montreal — ARRET
Stop, to a sailor — AVAST
Stopcock — SPIGOT
Stopover for a tourist — MOTEL
Stopped — ENDED
Stopped the squeak — OILED
Stopped unexpectedly — STALLED
Stopper — BRAKE, CORK, PLUG
Stoppered the wine bottle — CORKED
Stops — ARRESTS, BELAYS, HALTS
Stops in the action — TIME OUTS
Stops, in a way — FLAGS

Stopwatch — TIMER
Stopwatch device — RESET
Storage area — ATTIC, BIN, CLOSET, SHED
Storage boxes — SAFES
Storage building — WAREHOUSE
Storage cribs — BINS
Storage holder for grain — SILO
Storage place — BIN, BOX, CHEST, CELLAR
Storage space — ATTIC, DRAWER
Storage structure — SILO
Store — MART
Store a car — GARAGE
Store department — MENS
Store employee — CLERK
Store event — SALE
Store fodder — ENSILE
Store for hats — MILLINERY
Store for tools — HARDWARE
Store of knowledge — LORE
Store promotion — SALE, WHITE SALE
Store sign — OPEN
Store up — AMASS, BANK
Store window sign — OPEN, SALE
Stored away — LAID IN
Stored fodder — ENSILED
Storehouse — ARSENAL
Storehouse, of a sort — ARSENAL
Storekeepers — RETAILERS
Stores, on the farm — ENSILES
Storied — FAMED
Storied canal — ERIE
Storied pachyderm — BABAR
Storied sleeper — RIP
Stories — TALES, YARNS
Storing away — SAVING
Storm — ATTACK, RAGE, RAVE
Storm and Gordon — GALES
Storm at vocally — RANT
Storm centers — EYES
Storm direction — SEAWARD
Storm haven — PORT
Storm of Hollywood — GALE
Storm or rainwear — SOUWESTER
Storm part — EYE
Storm trooper — BROWN SHIRT
Storm warning — ALARM
Storm, in Normandy — ORAGE
Stormed — RAGED
Stormed about — RAMPAGED
Storms in Oklahoma, early 30's — DUST
Stormy petrels, e.g. — SIGNS
Story — ACCOUNT, FABLE, FLOOR, LEGEND
Story — LIE, MYTH, PLOT, TALE, YARN
Story above — ATTIC
Story beginner — ONCE
Story in batiment — ETAGE
Story lines — PLOTS
Story starter — ONCE
Story time heavy — OGRE
Story villain — OGRE
Storybook elephant — BABAR
Storybook rabbit — BRER
Storytellers — FIBBERS, RELATERS
Stound — ACHE
Stout — ALE, THICK
Stout choices — ALES
Stout cord — TWINE
Stout detective Wolfe — NERO
Stout hero — NERO
Stout relatives — ALES
Stout's Wolfe — NERO
Stout-hearted — BRAVE
Stove feature — OVEN
Stove parts — BURNERS
Stovepipes and pillboxes — HATS
Stow — PUT AWAY
Stow away — STASH
Stow cargo — LADE
Stowe book — DRED
Stowe character — EVA, TOPSY
Stowe heroine — EVA
Stowe or Vail — SKI RESORT
Stowe's ice-crosser — ELIZA
Stowe's Little _____ — EVA
Stowe's little heroine — EVA
Stowe's Simon — LEGREE
Stowed cargo — LADED
Straddlers — HOES
Strads' precursors — REBECS
Strafe — RAKE
Straggle — LAG, SPRAWL, TRAIL
Straggles — SPRAWLS
Straight — DIRECT, LINEAR, NEAT
Straight _____ arrow — AS AN
Straight edge — RULER
Straight half of a comedy team — ABBOTT
Straight razor honer — STROP
Straight thinking — LOGIC
Straight up — NEAT
Straight, at the bar — NEAT
Straight: Comb. form — ORTH
Straight: Pref. — ORTH
Straighten — ALIGN, ALINE
Straightened — EVENED
Straightens — ALINES, LEVELS
Straightforward — DIRECT, HONEST
Straights of _____, Michigan — MACKINAC
Strain — ACHE, STRAIN, SIEVE
Strained — TAXED
Strained vegetables — PUREE
Strainer — SIEVE
Strains — TAXES, TRIES
Strains the brain — RACKS
Strait — INLET, NARROW
Strait outlet? — LACED
Straitlaced one — PRUDE
Strand — BEACH, MAROON, SHORE
Strand of hair — LOCK
Strands — SHORES
Strange — ALIEN, EERIE, EERY, WEIRD
Strange ducks — SCREWBALLS
Strange need — TEE
Strange or Kite — GOLFER
Strange to say — ODDLY
Strange, in Soho — RUM
Strange: Comb. form — XENO
Stranger — OUTSIDER, TEES
Strangers — ALIENS
Straphanger Boone — STANDING PAT
Straphangers — STANDERS
Strapped — NEEDY
Strasbourg season — ETE
Strasbourg's river — ILL
Strata — LAYERS
Stratagem — GAMBIT, PLAN, PLOY
Strategic Mideast "Strip" — GAZA
Strategic port in W.W. II — LAE
Stratford _____ Avon — UPON
Stratford's prov. — ONT
Stratford's river — AVON
Stratford's stream — AVON
Stratton Porter's first name — GENE
Stratum — LAYER, SEAM, TIER, VEIN
Stratum; level — TIER
Strauss opera — ARIADNE AUF NAXOS
Strauss's "_____ Italien" — AUS
Strauss's "_____ Rosen-kavalier" — DER
Strauss's "Die _____ ohne Schatten" — FRAU
Stravinsky — IGOR
Stravinsky "Spring" thing — RITE
Stravinsky ballet score — AGON
Stravinsky's "_____ of Spring" — RITE
Stravinsky's "Card _____" — PARTY
Stravinsky's "Le _____ du Printemps" — SACRE
Stravinsky's "Spring" thing — RITE
Stravinsky's "The _____ of Spring" — RITE
Straw hat — BOATER, KATY
Straw in the wind — OMEN
Strawberry — FRAISE

Strawberry and others — METS
Strawberry of baseball — DARRYL
Strawberry's patch, once — SHEA
Strawberry's turf — SHEA
Strawberry, for one — ACHENE
Strawberry, in Strasbourg — FRAISE
Straws in the wind — SIGNS
Stray — DRIFT, ERR, ROAM, ROVE
Stray calf — DOGIE
Stray tom — ALLEY CAT
Strayed — ERRED
Strayed from the topic — DIGRESSED
Straying — ERRANT
Strays — ERRS
Streak in marble — VEIN
Streaked — SPED
Stream — CREEK, POUR, RIA
Stream deposit — SILT
Streaming with sunshine — GLOWING
Streamlined — SLEEK
Streams — FLOWS
Streams of sunlight — RAYS
Streep — STAR
Street-smart and knowing — HEP
Street and seed — SESAMES
Street divider — ARROW
Street in a horror film — ELM
Street in Rouen — RUE
Street in Tokyo — GINZA
Street map abbr. — AVE
Street musician's instrument — HURDY GURDY
Street name — ELM
Street noise — BEEP
Street of blues — BASIN
Street of high finance — WALL
Street of puppets — SESAME
Street or seed — SESAME
Street rebellions — RIOTS
Street show — RAREE
Street sign — ONE WAY, SLO, SLOW, STOP
Street sound — BEEP, HORN, SIREN
Street sound of old — CLOP
Street talk — SLANG
Street toughs — HOODS
Street urchin — GAMIN
Street waif — GAMIN
Street where Holmes lived — BAKER
Street's boss — MASON
Street, in Paris — RUE
Streetcars — TRAMS
Streeter's "_____ Mable" — DERE
Streets, in Strasbourg — RUES
Streetwise — ONTO
Streisand film — NUTS
Streisand recording — PEOPLE
Streisand role in "Hello, Dolly!" — LEVI
Strength — FORTE, MIGHT, POWER, SINEW
Stress — ACCENT, TENSION
Stressed — ACCENTED
Stresses — TENSIONS
Stretch — COVER, TAUTEN
Stretch out — WIDEN
Stretch the neck — CRANE
Stretch transport — LIMO
Stretch, in a way — MAKE DO
Stretched for a better look — CRANED
Stretched tight — TAUT
Stretcher — LITTER
Stretches the budget — EKES
Stretches tightly — STRAINS, TAUTENS
Stretches, with "out" — EKES
Stretching muscle — TENSOR
Strew — SCATTER
Strew with unwanted articles — LITTER
Strict — HARSH
Strict — SEVERE
Strictness — RIGOR
Stride — GAIT, HEADWAY, PACE, STRIDE, WALK
Stride piano — JAZZ
Strident — HARSH
Strife — COMBAT, CONFLICT
Strike — HIT, SLAP, SMOTE
Strike _____ (hit the mark) — A NERVE
Strike a word — CANCEL
Strike back — RETALIATE
Strike breakers — GOONS
Strike callers — UMPIRES
Strike discovery — OIL
Strike it out — DELE
Strike makers — BOWLERS
Strike out — DELE, DELETE, ERASE, FAN
Strike out wildly — FLAIL
Strike sharply — BANG, RAP
Strike up the band — PLAY
Strikebreaker — SCAB
Strikeout artist Nolan — RYAN
Strikes again — REZAPS
Strikes that please mine owners — ORES
Striking — ARRESTING, SALIENT
Striking out — FANNING
String — CORD, LINE, SEQUENCE, THREAD, TWINE
String beans — SCRAGS
String instruments — CELLI, CELLOS, LUTES
String section — CELLOS
String tie — BOW
Stringed instrument — GRAND PIANO, HARP, GUITAR
Stringed instrument — LUTE, LYRE, VIOL, VIOLA
Stringed instrument of old — LUTE
Stringed instruments — BANJOS, CELLOS
Stringed toy — YOYO
Stringent — RIGID, SEVER
Strip — PEEL, WELT
Strip _____ — TEASE
Strip bare — SKIN
Strip blubber — FLENSE
Strip of land between rivers — DOAB
Strip of leather — THONG, WELT
Strip of wood — LATH, SLAT
Strip off — PEEL
Strip on a shoe — WELT
Strip, in Madrid — TIRA
Striped cloth — MADRAS
Striped quartz — AGATE
Stripes — STRIAE
Stripes from strokes — WEALS
Stripling — LAD
Stripped-down camper? — NUDIST
Stripped — BARED, DENUDED, EXPOSED, PEELED
Strips, in a way — DIVESTS
Striptease dancer — PEELER
Stritch or May — ELAINE
Strive — ESSAY
Strive to equal — EMULATE
Strives against — RESISTS
Strobile — CONE
Strode — TROD
Stroke for Ivan Lendl — LOB
Stroke from Graf — LOB
Stroke of luck — FLUKE
Stroke on a violin — UPBOW
Stroke play game — GOLF
Stroke the wrong way — ANNOY, RUFFLE
Strokes gently — PATS
Strokes lovingly — CARESSES
Strokes of fortune — CASTS
Strokes with affection — PATS
Stroll — SAUNTER
Stroma — HYPHAE, TISSUE
Strong _____ ox — AS AN
Strong alkaline solution — LYE
Strong beam — LASER
Strong blow — ONER
Strong box of old — ARCA
Strong breeze — GALE
Strong brew — ALE
Strong brown paper — KRAFT
Strong coffee — ESPRESSO
Strong cord — ROPE
Strong cotton thread — LISLE
Strong desire — PASSION, THIRST, URGE
Strong drink — GIN

Strong drink for short — USQUE
Strong fiber — RAMIE, SISAL
Strong opinions — BIASES
Strong outburst — SPATE
Strong point — FORTE
Strong synthetic — NYLON
Strong Vt. horse — MORGAN
Strong winds — GALES
Strong-arm — FORCE
Strong-scented herb — RUE
Strongboxes — SAFES
Stronghold of Hereward the Wake, 1070-71 — ELY
Strongholds — POSTS
Strongly audible — LOUD
Strongly flavored — GAMY
Strontium-90 — FISSION
Strop — HONE
Stropped — HONED
Strops — WHETS
Struck — SMIT, SMOTE
Struck a Philistine — SMOTE
Struck forcefully — SMOTE
Struck out — FANNED
Structural — ANATOMIC
Structural bar — I RAIL
Structure component — I BEAM
Structure on a predella — ALTAR
Structure projecting into water — JETTY
Strudel — PASTRY
Struggle — RESIST
Struggle against (something) — FIGHT IT
Struggle for — CONTEND
Struggle to overcome problems, etc. — COPE
Struggled — STRIVEN
Struggled awkwardly — FLOUNDERED
Struggles — EFFORTS
Struggles for breath — GASPS
Strut proudly — SWAGGER
Sts. — RDS
Stu of films — ERWIN
Stu of the screen — ERWIN
Stuart queen — ANNE
Stub — NUB
Stubborn — HARDHEADED
Stubborn animal — MULE
Stubborn as _____ — A MULE
Stubborn as a mule — HEAD-STRONG
Stubbornly willful — FROWARD
Stubby Kaye role — NICELY NICELY
Stuck — ADHERED, GLUED, MIRED
Stuck around — REMAINED, STAYED
Stuck in a bog — MIRED
Stuck in the mud — MIRED
Stuck-up — HOITY TOITY, SNOOTY
Student at the Sorbonne — ELEVE
Student gp. — NSA
Student monitors — PREFECTS
Student of Socrates — PLATO
Student ordeals — EXAMS
Student roster — HONOR ROLL
Student society — FRAT
Student transport — BUS
Student's assignments — THEMES
Student's blooper — BONER
Student's concern — EXAM, GRADE
Student's course grades, usually — AVERAGES
Student's howler — BONER
Student's problem — EXAM
Student's quest: Abbr. — CRS
Student's trial — EXAM
Student, hopefully — LEARNER
Student, in St Lo — ELEVE
Students goal — DEGREE
Students' fund — DOLLARS FOR SCHOLARS
Students' instructions — LESSONS
Students' ponies — TROTS
Students, ideally — LEARNERS
Studied hard — BONED,PORED
Studies — DENS
Studies for exams — CRAMS
Studio item — EASEL
Studio scenery — SETS
Studio structures — SETS
Studious — ACADEMIC
Study — CON, DEN, LEARN, PERUSAL, PERUSE, READ
Study (with "over") — PORE
Study for Horowitz — ETUDE
Study hard — PORE
Study method — ROTE
Study of body motions — KINESICS
Study of evil spirits — DEMONOLOGY
Study of place names — TOPONYMY
Study pieces — ETUDES
Study up on — CRAM
Study, ponder — CONSIDER
Stuff — CRAM
Stuff for troubled waters — OIL
Stuff one is made of — METAL
Stuff oneself — GORGE
Stuff with cotton — PAD
Stuffed _____ (kishke) — DERMA
Stuffed footstool — HASSOCK
Stuffed shirt — PRIG
Stuffed shirt's cousin — JACKANAPES
Stuffed to the gills — FED UP
Stuffing for a quilt — BATT
Stuffs — CRAMS
Stuffy — PRIM
Stumble-bunny — SLOB
Stumble — TRIP
Stumbles — ERRS
Stumbling block — PITFALL
Stumbling blocks — SNAGS
Stumper — BAMBOOZLER
Stun — BEDAZZLE, DAZE, FLOOR
Stung — BITTEN, NETTLED
Stunned — AGOG, DAZED
Stuns — DAZES
Stunt — FEAT, RETARD, TRICK
Stuntman Knievel — EVEL
Stunts for a second banana — PRAT FALLS
Stupefy — BEMUSE, STUN
Stupid person — KNUCKLE-HEAD
Stupor — COMA
Stupor: Comb: form — NARCO
Stuporous — NARCOSE
Sturdy — BEEFY, FIRM, LUSTY, ROBUST
Sturdy shoe — BROGAN
Sturdy stocking material — LISLE
Sturdy trees — OAKS
Sturm und _____ — DRANG
Stutter — HESITATE
Sty cry — OINK
Sty dwellers — PIGS
Sty occupant — SOW
Sty sound — OINK
Sty youngsters — STOATS
Style — MANNER, MODE, PANACHE
Style again — REDO
Style for a stoa — IONIC
Style of column — DORIC
Style of furniture — ADAM
Style of pinafore — TIER
Style of some footwear — TOELESS
Style period — REGENCY
Style; taste: Fr. — GOUT
Styles of the hour — FADS
Styles; kinds — GENRES
Stylish — CHIC, DRESSY, MOD
Stylish accessories — GLASSES
Stylographs — PENS
Styptic — ALUM
Styptic-pencil ingredient — ALUM
Suable slander — LIBEL
Suave — OILY, SMOOTH, URBANE
Suave British actor: 1906-72 — SANDERS
Suave, glib person — SMOOTHIE
Sub — U BOAT
Sub _____ (secretly) — ROSA

Sub finder — SONAR
Sub sensor — SONAR
Sub's "ears" — SONAR
Subarctic evergreen forests — TAIGA
Subdivisions — SECTS
Subdued — MUTED, TAMED
Subdues a shrew — TAMES
Subj. for medicos — ANAT
Subject — COURSE, POINT, PRIMER, TEXT, THEME
Subject for a herpetologist — REPTILE
Subject for entomologists — ANTS
Subject for Gertrude Stein — ROSE
Subject for Handel — MESSIAH
Subject for head or heart — ACHE
Subject for Keats — URN
Subject for Margaret Mead — SAMOA
Subject for William Blake — TIGER
Subject matter — TOPIC
Subject matters — NOUNS
Subject of a Cantor song — SUSIE
Subject of a famed 1897 editorial — SANTA
Subject of a long Frost poem — HIRED MAN
Subject of a Peter Weiss play — MARQUIS DE SADE
Subject of a Shelley lyric — SKYLARK
Subject of a Wedekind play — SPRING AWAKENING
Subject of a Wilde ballad — GAOL
Subject of Boyle's law — GAS
Subject of Philosopher Croce — DANTE
Subject of Plato's Symposium — EROS
Subject to plantation — ERODE
Subject under discussion — TOPIC
Subjects for Steinbeck, in a way — MEN AND MICE
Subjoin — AFFIX
Subjugate — ENSLAVE
Sublease — RELET, RENT
Subleased — RELET
Submachine gun — BREN
Submarine detector — SONAR
Submarine equipment — SONAR
Submarine manuever — CRASH DIVE
Submerge — SINK
Submerged — SANK
Submergence — DUNK
Submerges — SWAMPS
Submerges again — REFLOODS
Submit — OBEY, OFFER
Submitted a tax return — FILED
Subordinate Claus? — ELF
Subordinate duty — DAEMON
Subordinate rulers — SATRAPS
Subordinate to — UNDER
Subordinated — BELOW, UNDER
Subs at bridge — SITS IN
Subs detector — SONAR
Subs heading — SSE
Subscribe again — RENEW
Subscribe to — SANCTION
Subsequent — NEXT
Subsequently — AFTER, LATER, SINCE
Subside — EBB, SETTLE, WARMS
Subsided — ABATED
Subsides — EBBS
Subsidiary group — RUMP
Subsidy — AWARD, GRANT, PENSION
Subsist — ENDURE
Subsisted — LIVED ON
Subspecies — ECOTYPE
Substance — HOLE, MATTER, MEAT, TENOR
Substances for Strads — ROSINS
Substantial — STURDY
Substantiate — UPHOLD
Substantive — ACTUAL, MEATY
Substitute — EXCHANGE, PROXY, SURROGATE
Substitute for John — JACK
Substitute money — SCRIP
Substitute soap producer — AMOLE
Substitutes — REPLACES
Substitutes: Abbr. — ALTS
Subterfuge — EVASION, RUSE
Subterranean passage — MINE
Subtle details — NICETIES
Subtle sarcasm — IRONY
Subtlety — ART
Subtly nasty — SNIDE
Subtropical grasslands — SAVANNAS
Suburb of Honolulu — AIEA
Suburb of Liege — ANS
Suburb of Paris — ISSY
Suburb of Philadelphia — PAOLI
Suburb of Pittsburgh — ETNA
Suburb of Rabat — SLA
Suburban expanse — LAWN
Suburbanite's concern — YARD
Subvert — SAP
Subway coins — TOKENS
Subway fare — TOKEN
Subway gate — STILE
Subway need — TOKEN
Subways — METROS
Succeed — PREVAIL
Succeed initially — BREAK THE ICE
Succes d'estime — PRESTIGE
Success — HIT
Successful — ON TOP
Successful searcher — FINDER
Successful songs — HITS
Successively — AROW, IN TURN
Successor to Ramses I — SETI
Succinct — BRIEF, CONCISE, SHORT, TERSE
Succor — ABET, AID
Succotash ingredient — CORN
Succotash item — CORN, LIMA
Succulent — JUICY
Succulent fowl — CAPON
Succulent plant — ALOE
Succumb — YIELD
Succumb to wanderlust — ROAM
Succumbs to Cupid's arrow — HEAD OVER HEELS IN LOVE
Such: in prescriptions — TAL
Suchlike — SIMILAR
Suck — DRAW, SIP
Suck up — LAP
Sucker — PATSY
Suckling's output — POESY
Suction — VACUUM
Sudan river — PIBOR
Sudan's _____ mountains — MARRA
Sudan's neighbor — CHAD
Sudanese neighbor — CHAD
Sudden — ABRUPT
Sudden bright star — NOVA
Sudden burst of energy — SPASM
Sudden burst of voltage — SURGE
Sudden bursts of activity — SPASMS
Sudden contractions — SPASMS
Sudden dash — BOLT
Sudden descent — SWOOP
Sudden fright — START
Sudden gushes — SPURTS
Sudden inclination — IMPULSE
Sudden insight expressions — AHAS
Sudden jump — START
Sudden outpouring — SPATE
Sudden rainstorms — SPATES
Sudden rushes — SPATES
Sudden thrust — LUNGE
Suddenly — ASTART, PRESTO
Sudra and Vaisya — CASTES
Sudra, for one — CASTE
Suds — BEER, ETCHERS
Sue _____ Langdon — ANE
Sue for payments — DUN
Suede lead-in — ULTRA
Suer — PLAINTIFF

Suet — FAT, TALLOW
Suffer — AIL, ACHE, LET
Suffer defeat — LOSE
Suffered — AILED
Suffers — ACHES
Suffers from — AILS
Suffice — LAST
Sufficient — AMPLE
Sufficient for a poet — ENOW
Sufficient, to Keats — ENOW
Sufficiently cooked — DONE
Suffix akin to "ile" — ESE
Suffix for Annam or Assam — ESE
Suffix for baby or old — ISH
Suffix for ballad or profit — EER
Suffix for boy — ISH
Suffix for buck — EROO
Suffix for Canton — ESE
Suffix for Capri — OTE
Suffix for cash or cloth — IER
Suffix for cult or strict — URE
Suffix for fix or flirt — ATION
Suffix for hip or gang — STER
Suffix for inchoative verbs — ESCE
Suffix for Jersey or Brooklyn — ITE
Suffix for kitchen or luncheon — ETTE
Suffix for major or leather — ETTE
Suffix for mod or nod — ULE
Suffix for musket or canon — EER
Suffix for photo — GENIC
Suffix for poet — ICS
Suffix for Rock — ETTES
Suffix for simple — TON
Suffix for usher or major — ETTE
Suffix for young or old — STER
Suffix forming inchoative verbs — ESCE
Suffix meaning "realm" — RIC
Suffix of block — AGE
Suffix to some ships' names — MARU
Suffix used by physicists — IUM
Suffix used with gab or song — FEST
Suffix with Adam or Edom — ITE
Suffix with Boswell or Burns — IANA
Suffix with cash or cloth — IER
Suffix with cigar — ETTE
Suffix with depend — ENT
Suffix with diet — ETIC
Suffix with differ — ENT
Suffix with dull — ARD
Suffix with hip or tip — STER
Suffix with idol or lion: Brit. — ISE
Suffix with iron or myth — ICAL
Suffix with Johnson or journal — ESE
Suffix with lob and mob — STERS
Suffix with malt — OSE
Suffix with mother or father — HOOD
Suffix with persist — ENCE
Suffix with poly — ESTER
Suffix with rend or vend — ITION
Suffix with ripe or near — NESS
Suffix with Siam — ESE
Suffix with slander and thunder — OUS
Suffix with tact or diet — ICIAN
Suffix with Tartar — EAN
Suffix with verb — OSE
Suffix with young or old — STER
Suffixes for professionals — ERS
Suffixes used in medical terms — OMAS
Suffixes with attend and appear — ANCES
Suffixes with convention and auction — EERS
Suffixes with lemon and lime — ADES
Suffocation — APNEA
Suffrage pioneer — CATT
Suffragette Carrie Chapman _____ — CATT
Suffragette Elizabeth Cady _____ — STANTON
Suffuse — BATHE
Sugar _____ — CANE
Sugar and spice group — GIRLS
Sugar Bill — SWEET WILLIAM
Sugar Bowl noise — ROAR
Sugar cane knives — MACHETES
Sugar daddy pickups — TABS
Sugar Ray, e.g. — BOXER
Sugar source — BEET, CANE, MAPLE
Sugar's partner — SPICE
Sugar, e.g. — STAPLE
Sugar: Suffix — OSE
Sugared — SWEET
Sugarless _____ — GUM
Sugarloaf — MOUNTAIN
Sugarplum, e.g. — TREAT
Sugary — SWEET
Sugary ending — OSE
Suggest — OPINE, POSIT
Suggest: volunteer — PROFER
Suggestion — CLUE, HINT, IDEA
Suggestive look — LEER
Suggestive of an Eden dweller — ADAMIC
Suggestive of the first man — ADAMIC
Sui _____ (unique) — GENERIS
Suit — BEFIT
Suit _____ T — TO A
Suit beneficiary — USEE
Suit card — HEART
Suit companions — BLOUSES
Suit fabric — DENIM, TWEED
Suit feature — LAPEL, VEST
Suit for Belli — TORT
Suit material — SERGE
Suit of clothes — DUDS
Suit or atoll — BIKINIS
Suit parts — VESTS
Suit sprucer — DRY CLEANER
Suit style — TAILORED
Suit to _____ — A TEE
Suit to a tee — TAILOR
Suit with propriety — BECOME
Suitable — APT
Suitable position — NICHE
Suitcase marker — DOGTAG
Suitcase of old — CARPETBAG
Suited to _____ — A TEE
Suitor — BEAU
Suits — BEFITS
Suits to _____ — A TEE
Sulawesi seaport — MANADO
Sulfide mixtures — MATTES
Sulking — IN A PET
Sulks — POUTS
Sulky — CART
Sulky puller — PACER
Sullen — DOUR, GLUM, MOODY
Sullen look — GLOWER
Sullen; unsmiling — DOUR
Sullied, in Scotland — SMIT
Sullivan and Ames — EDS
Sullivan and Koch — EDS
Sullivan and Wynn — EDS
Sullivan song, with "The" — LOST CHORD
Sully — DEFAME, SOIL, STAIN, SPOT, TAINT
Sultan — RULER
Sultan's decree — IRADE
Sultan's or sheik's domain — EMIRATE
Sultan's son in "The Arabian Nights" — AHMED
Sultanate — OMAN
Sultry — HUMID
Sum — TOTAL
Sum and substance — CONTENT, GIST
Sum total — ALL
Sum total: Abbr. — AMT
Sum: Abbr. — AMT
Sumac — DOGWOOD
Sumac from Peru — YMA
Sumac genus — RHUS
Sumatra — ISLAND
Sumatran primates — ORANGS
Sumerian moon god — NANNA
Summa _____ laude — CUM
Summa cum _____ — LAUDE

Summarize — DIGEST, RECAP, WRAP UP
Summary — BRIEF, CONSPECTUS, EPITOME, RECAP
Summation, for short — RECAP
Summer along the Seine — ETE
Summer beach phenomena — CROWDS
Summer beverage — ADE
Summer coat — TAN
Summer color — TAN
Summer concerns — GARDENS
Summer cool — ADE
Summer coolers — ADES
Summer danger — HEAT STROKE
Summer drink — ADES, ICE TEA
Summer flounder — FLUKE
Summer forecast — HOTTER, HUMID
Summer holiday — THE FOURTH OF JULY
Summer hours — EDT
Summer house — GAZEBO
Summer in Phila. — EDT
Summer in the Midi — ETE
Summer mo. — JUL
Summer month in Buenos Aires — ENERO
Summer outing — PICNIC
Summer problem — HEAT WAVE
Summer quaff — LIMEADE
Summer refresher — ICE TEA
Summer refreshers — ADES
Summer refreshments — ADES
Summer resort — CAMP
Summer retreat — CAMP
Summer shade — TAN
Summer shader — TREE
Summer shades — TANS
Summer shoe — SANDAL
Summer sporting event — WIMBLEDON
Summer time in Milwaukee — CDT
Summer time zones — EDSTS
Summer time, in Fla. — EDT
Summer treat — WATERMELON
Summer treats — ICES
Summer TV fare — RERUN
Summer vacation site — CAMP
Summer wear — BERMUDA SHORTS, SHORTS
Summer wear to Shelley and Huey? — LONG SHORTS
Summer, in Monaco — ETE
Summer, in Paris — ETE
Summer: Fr. — ETE
Summers, along the Riviera — ETES
Summers, in Aix — ETES
Summers, in Soissons — ETES
Summers, on the Seine — ETES
Summertime in NY — EDT
Summertime refresher — ICED TEA
Summerville namesakes — SLIMS
Summery — LIGHT
Summit — ACME, ALP, APEX, APOGEE, CREST
Summit — PINNACLE, TIP TOP
Summon — BECKON, CALL, PAGE, MUSTER
Summon an actress? — PAGE GERALDINE
Summon up — ROUSE
Summon, in a way — PAGE
Summoned — PAGED
Summoned the butler — RANG
Summons — EVOKES
Summons for Dan? — QUAYLE CALL
Summons, old style — CLEPE
Sump — PIT
Sumpter — PACK
Sumptuous — COSTLY, DELUXE, PLUSH, RICH
Sumptuous meal — FEAST
Sumptuous repast — FEAST
Sumptuousness — LUXE
Sums — TOTALS
Sun-rooms — SOLARIA
Sun belt state, for short — FLA
Sun City, Ariz. — SUBURB
Sun disk — ATEN
Sun hat — TOPEE
Sun helmets — TOPIES
Sun parlors — SOLARIA
Sun rooms — SOLARIA
Sun shade — RED, TAN
Sun shine? — TAN
Sun's output — RAYS
Sun-dried brick — ADOBE
Sun-powered — SOLAR
Sun-tanned — BROWN
Sun-visor — EYESHADE
Sun. event — SER
Sun. follower — MON
Sun. homily — SER
Sun. speech — SER
Sun: Comb. form — HELIO, SOLI
Sun: Prefix — FOLLOWER
Sunbather's goal — TAN
Sunbather's objective — TAN
Sunbathes — TANS
Sunbeam — RAY
Sunburned — RED
Sundance Kid's girl — ETTA
Sundance or Cisco — KID
Sunday before Easter — PALM
Sunday dinner treat — RIB ROAST
Sunday go to meeting — CLOTHES
Sunday performer in Mexico — MATADOR
Sunday seating — PEW
Sunday seats — PEWS
Sunday section, for short — ROTO
Sunday service — MASS
Sunday song — PSALM
Sunday speech: Abbr. — SER
Sunday-go-to-meeting clothes — SUIT
Sunder — REND, SEVER
Sundry — ASSORTED, VARIED
Sunfish genus — MOLA
Sunflower or heliotrope — TURNSOLE
Sunflower product — OIL
Sunflowers — JERUSALEM ARTICHOKES
Sung(960-1270 A.D.) — DYNASTY
Sunglasses to some — SHADES
Sunglasses: colloquially — SHADES
Sunken court — AREAWAY
Sunken fences — HAHA
Sunlight — DAY
Sunny side of a mountain — ADRET
Sunnybrook, for one — FARM
Sunrise direction — EAST
Sunrise, poetically — MORN
Sunrise, to Shelley — MORN
Sunscreen acronym — PABA
Sunscreen ingredient — ALOE
Sunscreen stuff — ALOE
Sunset — EVE
Sunset _____ — STRIP
Sunset, e.g. — BLVD
Sunshade — PARASOL
Sunshine state city — OCALA
Sunshine State natives — FLORIDIANS
Sunstroke — ICTUS
Sunup — DAWN
Sunup area — EAST
Sup — DINE
Super — A ONE
Super bowl M.V.P. 1990 — MONTANA
Super Bowl XVIII site — TAMPA
Super fan — BUFF
Super fiddle — AMATI
Super sandwich — HERO
Super serve — ACE
Super used cars — CREAM PUFF
Super! — GREAT, NIFTY, TIPTOP
Super- _____: fabulous — DUPER
Super-sandwich — HERO
Superb — PRIMO
Superb violin — AMATI

Supercilious — SNOBBY, SNOOTY, UPPITY
Superficial — SHALLOW
Superficial brilliance — GILT
Superficial charm — VENEER
Superficial polish — VENEER
Supergiant in Scorpio — ANTARES
Superhighway feature — ON RAMPS
Superintended — OVERSAW
Superior — A ONE, PAR EXCELLENCE, PREEMINENT
Superior coffee — MOCHA
Superior in a monastery — ABBOT
Superior in quality — FINE
Superior in rank — ABOVE
Superior iron alloy — STEEL
Superior of sgts. — LTS
Superior planet — JUPITER
Superior quality — DE LUXE
Superior ratings — BETTER, CHOICE, HIGH GRADES
Superlative ending — EST
Superlative for Snow White — FAIREST
Superlative maker — EST
Superlative suffix — EST
Superlatively bad — WORST
Superlatives for the heavens — STARRIEST
Superman portrayer — REEVE
Superman's girl — LOIS
Superman's ID — KENT
Superman's planet — KRYPTON
Superman's wear — CAPE
Superman, at the movies — REEVE
Supermarket choices — OLEOS
Supermarket employee — BAGGER
Supermarket giveaway — BAG
Supermarket item — BAG
Supermarket lineup — CANS
Supermarket staple — OLEO
Supernal craft: abbr. — UFO
Supernatural — MAGIC
Supernatural being — GENIE
Supernatural power — MANA
Supernatural spirit — GENIE
Superstar — IDOL
Superstar, often — IDOL
Supervene — ENSUE
Supervise — OVERSEE, RUN
Supervised — OVERSAW
Supervisor — OVERSEER
Supine — INERT, PRONE
Supped — ATE, DINED
Supplant — SUPERCEDE
Supple — ELASTIC
Supplement — ADD, APPENDIX
Supplement with effort — EKE
Supplementary — ADDED
Supplemented, with "out" — EKED
Supplements — ADDS
Suppliant — ASKER
Supplicant — PLEADER
Supplicate — PRAY
Supplied manpower — STAFFED
Supplied troops again — REARMED
Supplied with weapons — ARMED
Supplies — STORES
Supply — EQUIP, LEND, PROVIDE
Supply again — REFIT
Supply food commercially — CATER
Supply new weapons — REARM
Supply party food — CATER
Supply prepared food — CATER
Supply weapons — ARM
Supply with oxygen — AERATE
Supply with weapons — ARM
Support — ABET, TRUSS
Support — BRACE
Support for Michelangelo — SCAFFOLD
Support for Soyer — EASEL
Support of a sort — SPLINT
Support of Kings — ROYALISM
Support stick — CANE
Support, in Sedan — APPUI
Supported — AIDED
Supported in a dispute — SIDED
Supporter of spectacles — EARS
Supporter of: Comb. form — CRAT
Supporting — FOR, PRO, PROPPING UP
Supporting beams — RAFTERS
Supporting framework — TRESTLE
Supporting structure — PIER
Supporting timbers — GIRDERS
Supports — BACKS, ENDORSES, PROPS, TRESTLES
Supports for Sargent — EASELS
Supports of sorts — CRUTCHES
Supports, in medicine — SPLINTS
Supports, of sorts — FULCRA
Suppose — ASSUME, OPINE
Supposed fountain-of-youth isle — BIMINI
Supposed to be such — REPUTED
Supposes — PRESUMES
Suppositions — IFS
Suppress — ELIDE, QUASH
Suppress again — RESTIFLE
Supra — ABOVE
Supreme Being — ALLAH
Supreme being, to the Sioux — GREAT SPIRIT
Supreme Court figure — NINE
Supreme Court's concern — LAW
Supreme Egyptian god — AMEN RA
Supreme self: Brahma — ATMAN
Suprised sound — GASP
Sure — CERTAIN
Surety money receivers — BAILEES
Surface — FACET
Surface dirt — GRIME
Surface flaw — DENT
Surface for Gretzky — ICE
Surface lusters — SHEENS
Surface protection — FILM
Surfaces — ARISES
Surfeit — EXCESS, OVERFLOW, PLETHORA
Surfeits — CLOYS, SATES, SATIATES
Surfer's place — SEA
Surfer's surface — CREST
Surgical instrument — XYSTER
Surgical knife — LANCET
Surinamese pidgin language — SRANAN
Surly — CRUSTY, GRUFF, RUDE
Surly, churly chap — CUR
Surmise — GUESS, IMAGINE, INFER
Surmounting — ATOP
Surname — FAMILY
Surpass — ECLIPSE, EXCEL, TOP
Surpass in firepower — OUTGUN
Surpass in scope — OUTRANGE
Surpassed — TOPPED
Surpassed in audacity — OUTDARED
Surpasses — CAPS, EXCELS
Surprise attack — RAID
Surprise from Francis Mahon — RAID
Surprised — STARTLED
Surprised exclamation — OHS
Surprised sound — OOH
Surrealist from Spain — DALI
Surrealist Salvador — DALI
Surrender — CEDE
Surrender, as land — CEDE
Surreptitious — COVERT
Surrey town famed for chickens — DORKING

Surround — CIRCLE, CONFINE, ENCLOSE, ENVIRON, RIM
Surrounded — AMID
Surrounded by — AMID, AMIDST, AMONG
Surroundings — MILIEU, SCENERY
Surrounds — GIRDS
Survey — EXAMINE, MAP, OVERLOOK, POLL, SCAN
Surveying instrument — ALIDADE
Surveying method — STADIA
Surveyor — EYER
Surveyor president — WASHINGTON
Surveyor's instrument — TRANSIT
Surveyor's map — PLAT
Survival — RELIC
Survive, with "out" — EKE
Survives — EXISTS
Surviving traces — RELICS
Susa was its capital — ELAM
Susan of "L.A. Law" — DEY
Susan Strasberg film of 1973 — TOMA
Susann novel, with "The" — LOVE MACHINE
Susann title — ONCE IS NOT ENOUGH
Sushi ingredient — RICE
Sushi tidbit — TUNA
Susiana — ELAM
Suspend — HANG
Suspended — HUNG
Suspension — DELAY, FAILURE
Suspension of hostilities — PEACE
Suspicion — HUNCH
Suspicious — LEERY
Sussex napery item — SERVIETTE
Sustain — BOLSTER, CARRY, PROP, UPHOLD
Sustenance — ALIMENT
Sutherland songs — ARIAS
Sutherland specialty — ARIA
Sutherland, for one — DIVA
Sutured — SEWN
Suva is its capital — FIJI
Suzeraine — KING
Svc. branch — USN
Svelte — LITHE, SLIM, THIN, TRIM
Sverige neighbor — NORGE
SW Asian country — ISR
SW Connecticut city — DANBURY
SW New Hampshire city — KEENE
SW New Jersey port — CAMDEN
SW New York city — OLEAN
SW Nigerian city — EDE
Swab — MOP, SPONGE, WIPE UP
Swabber — TAR
Swabbie — GOB
Swaddle — WRAP
Swag — FESTOON
Swag of any sort — BOODLE
Swagger — PRANCE, ROISTER, STRUT
Swaggerer — BLADE
Swain — BEAU, LOVER, SUITOR
Swain's song — SERENADE
Swallow — INGEST
Swallow greedily — GULP
Swallow one's pride — EAT CROW
Swallow up — ABSORB, ENGROSS, ENGULF
Swallow's prey — GNAT
Swallowed — ATE
Swallows hastily — BOLTS
Swallows, as flattery — LAPS UP
Swam — BACK STROKED
Swamp — BOG, FEN, MARSH, MORASS, ROUT
Swamp birds — RAILS
Swamp denizen — TOAD
Swamp stalker — EGRET
Swamp trees — SPLASH PINES
Swampy locale — MARSH
Swampy tract — EVERGLADE
Swan — CYGNET
Swan genus — OLOR
Swan or band member: Abbr. — TPTR
Swan's victim — LEDA
Swank — CHIC, POSH
Swanky — PLUSH, POSH
Swann's creator — PROUST
Swann's wife — ODETTE
Swap — EXCHANGE, TRADE
Swapped — TRADED
Swaps — TRADES
Sward — GRASS, SOD, TURF
Swarm — TEEM
Swarmed — TEEMED
Swarms — HORDES, TEEMS
Swarthy — BLACK, DARK, DUSKY
Swashbuckling TV swordsman — ZORRO
Swatch — SAMPLE
Swathe — BIND, WRAP
Sway — WAVE
Sway, in a way — TEETER
Swayed — TEETERED
Sways — ROCKS
Swear — AFFIRM, AVER, CURSE, PROFANE, VOW
Swear anew — REPLEDGE
Swears — ATTESTS
Swears to — ATTESTS
Sweat and tears, e.g. — EGESTA
Sweater size — LARGE
Sweater style — PULLOVER
Sweater type — CARDIGAN
Sweaterman? — EARL OF CARDIGAN
Sweden's largest lake — VANERN
Sweden's martyred Palme — OLOF
Sweden's monetary unit — KRONA
Swedish actress — OLIN
Swedish actress May — BRITT
Swedish astronomer Anders _____ — CELSIUS
Swedish author Munthe — AXEL
Swedish explorer Hedin — SVEN
Swedish island in the Baltic — ALAND
Swedish name for Turku — ABO
Swedish philanthropist — NOBEL
Swedish pile rug — RYA
Swedish poet Hansson — OLA
Swedish port — MALMO
Swedish rock group — ABBA
Swedish rug — RYA
Swedish seaport — MALMO
Swedish turnip — RUTABAGA
Sweep — EXPANSE, OAR
Sweep away — WHISK
Sweep's target — SOOT
Sweeping — RADICAL
Sweet _____ — PEA
Sweet cherry — BING
Sweet course — DESSERT
Sweet drinks — SODAS
Sweet girl of song — SUE
Sweet liqueur — CREME, CREME DE CACAO
Sweet ones — LAMBS
Sweet or crowder chaser — PEA
Sweet potato — YAM
Sweet potatoes' relatives — YAMS
Sweet sixteen, e.g. — AGE
Sweet spire — ITEA
Sweet syrup used in the East — DIBS
Sweet talk — LINE
Sweet treat — TOFFEE
Sweet treats from Boston — CREAM PIES
Sweet wine — PORT, MARSALA, SAUTERNE, TOKAY
Sweet wine from Spain — MALAGA
Sweet, seedy fruit — WATER-MELON
Sweet-and-Sour — SAUCE
Sweeten — SUGAR
Sweeten the pot — ANTE
Sweetened the pot — ANTED

Sweetener — SUGAR
Sweetheart — LASS, TURTLE-DOVE
Sweetheart in gangland — MOLL
Sweethearts — FLAMES, GIRLS, LOVERS , HONEYS
Sweetie — HON
Sweetmeat — CANDY, TAFFY
Sweetsop — ATES
Sweetsop or soursop — ANONA
Swell — DILATE, EXPAND, NIFTY, OKAY
Swell place? — SEA
Swell shindig — BLAST
Swell the pot — RAISE
Swell, in Soho — PLIM
Swelling — NODE
Swelling in plant swells — EDEMA
Swelter — PERSPIRE, SWEAT
Sweltering — DAMP
Sweltry — TORRID
Swenson of "Benson" — INGA
Swept back — ANGLED
Swerve — SKEW, VEER, YAW
Swerved — SHEERED
Swerving — VEERING
Swift — BRISK, FAST, FLEET, RAPID
Swift Atl. plane — SST
Swift Australian bird — EMU
Swift brute — YAHOO
Swift creature — HARE
Swift hunting dog — AFGHAN
Swift jet — SST
Swift plane, for short — SST
Swift's "A Tale of a _____" — TUB
Swift's forte — SATIRE
Swift: Abbr. — FST
Swiftly — APACE
Swig — GULP
Swim — BATHE
Swim alternative — SINK
Swim meet event — BREAST STROKE
Swim's alternative — SINK
Swimmer — NATATOR
Swimmer Louganis, et al. — GREGS
Swimmer's bane — CRAMPS
Swimmer's measure — LAP
Swimmers — BATHERS, NATATORS
Swimmers in the altogether — SKINNY DIPPERS
Swimming — NATANT
Swimming actress — ESTHER
Swimming aids — FINS
Swimming method — STROKE
Swimming stroke — AUSTRALIAN CRAWL
Swimming, in heraldry — NAIANT
Swimming-pool cover — TARP
Swimmmer's count — LAPS
Swimsuit parts — BRAS
Swimsuit top — BRA
Swindle — DUPE, FLEECE, GYP, RAMP, SCAM
Swindled — BUNCOED, ROGUED
Swindles — CHEATS, CONS, RIPS OFF, SCAMS
Swine breed — DUROC
Swines confines — STY
Swing about — SLUE
Swing around — SLUE
Swing bandleader Rey — ALVINO
Swing expert — PRO
Swing followup — SHIFT
Swing's King — BENNY
Swingers of the 40's — HEPCATS
Swingy rythm — LILT
Swiped — LIFTED
Swirl — EDDY
Swirl around — EDDY
Swirled — EDDIED
Swiss _____ — CHARD
Swiss artist — KLEE
Swiss canton — URI
Swiss canton (former spelling) — BASLE
Swiss capital — BERN
Swiss cheese features — HOLES
Swiss city — BERNE
Swiss city on the Aare — BERN
Swiss city on the Rhine — BASEL
Swiss Guard duty — VATICAN
Swiss hero — TELL
Swiss house — CHALET
Swiss lake or city — LUCERNE
Swiss linear unit — ELLE
Swiss mathematician: 1707-83 — EULER
Swiss mountain — ALP
Swiss mountain group — ADULA
Swiss Nobel physicist Wolfgang _____ — PAULI
Swiss painter Paul — KLEE
Swiss psychiatrist and family — JUNGS
Swiss resort on the Rhine — SIOW
Swiss river — AAR, AARE
Swiss scenery — ALPS
Swiss sight — ALPS
Swiss singing — YODEL
Swiss sledder — LUGER
Swiss statesman: 1845-1928 — ADOR
Swiss stream — AARE
Swiss town — AARAU
Swiss town near Zurich — USTER
Swiss veggie — CHARD
Swiss waterway — AAR
Swiss-born French revolutionary — MARAT
Swit role in M*A*S*H — NURSE
Switch — BOUGH, HANDLE, LEVER, WHIP
Switch endings — EROOS
Switch engines — MULES
Switch or smash ender — EROO
Switch position — OFF, ON
Switch positions — ONS
Switch settings — OFFS
Switchblade: Slang — SHIV
Switches tracks — SHUNTS
Swiveled — SPUN
Swiveling wheel — CASTER
Swivets — SNITS, STEWS
Swizzle — STIR
Swizzle stick — STIRRER
Swollen — DISTENDED, TUMID
Swoons — FAINTS
Sword — EPEE
Sword conqueror — PEN
Sword handle — HAFT
Sword handles — HILTS
Sword of a kind — EPEE
Sword play — DUEL
Sword section — HILT
Sword with a blunted edge — EPEE
Sword's conqueror — PEN
Sword, for a Coldstream guard — SABER, SABRE
Sword-shaped — ENSATE
Sword-shaped, as a leaf — ENSATE
Swordfish feature — SERRA
Swords — RAPIERS
Swordsman — FENCER
Sybarite's delight — EASE
Sycamore — PLANE
Sycamore summit — TREETOP
Sycophant — TOAD, TOADY, YES MAN
Sycophant's reply — YES
Sycophant's response — YES
Sycophants' oft-used words — YESES
Sydney-to-Lord Howe Island dir. — ENE
Syllabic stress — ARSIS
Syllogistic — LOGICAL
Sylvan deity — SATYR
Sylvan sight — LEA
Sylvan spring sound — CHIRP
Symbol — EMBLEM, MARK, SIGN, TOKEN
Symbol at Austin — LONE STAR
Symbol for teletype — TTY

Symbol in music — CLEF
Symbol of a sort — LOGO
Symbol of a town meeting — GAVEL
Symbol of ease and luxury — CLOVER
Symbol of feminine curiosity — FATIMA
Symbol of France — Marianne
Symbol of goodness — HALO
Symbol of greed — MIDAS
Symbol of industry — ANT, BEE
Symbol of loftiness — EVEREST
Symbol of luxury — ERMINE
Symbol of manly youth and beauty — APOLLO
Symbol of official status — SEAL
Symbol of peace — DOVE
Symbol of purity — SNOW
Symbol of redness — BEET
Symbol of sadness — TEAR
Symbol of silence — CLAM
Symbol of slimness — REED
Symbol of slowness — SNAIL
Symbol of sudden heaviness — TON OF BRICKS
Symbol of tidiness — PIN
Symbol of triumph — VEE
Symbol of Wales — LEEK
Symbol on a staff — CRISSCROSS
Symbol on the dollar bill — PYRAMID WITH ONE EYE
Symbol or easiness — PIE
Symbolic bird — EAGLE
Symbolic Englishman — JOHN BULL
Symbolic ID — LOGO
Symbolic leaf — MAPLE
Symbolic ring — HALO
Symbolic showbiz city — PEORIA
Symbolic small college — SIWASH
Symbolic wear — ROBE
Symbolized — MEANT
Symbols for Niobe — TEARS
Symbols of authority — MACES
Symbols of celebrity status — RED CARPET
Symbols of hardness — NAILS
Symbols of industry — BEES
Symbols of modesty — VIOLETS
Symbols of Nazi tyranny — SWASTIKAS
Symbols of slimness — REEDS
Symbols of the spurious — TIN STARS
Symbols of toughness — NAILS
Symmetric — EVEN
Sympathetic — TENDER
Sympathetic attention — EAR
Sympathize with someone — CONDOLE
Sympathized — CARED
Sympathy — PITY
Symph. offering — SEL
Symptoms indicating a disease — SYNDROME
Syn., often — DEF
Synagogue — SHUL
Synagogue enclosures — ARKS
Synchro — SELSYN
Syncopated music — RAGTIME
Syncope — FAINT
Syndicated feature — GOSSIP COLUMN
Synge or O'Casey work — DRAMA
Synopsis — BRIEF
Synthetic fabric — ARNEL, NYLON, ORLON, RAYON
Synthetic fiber — ARNEL, DACRON, ORLON, RAYON
Synthetic material — ACETATE
Synthetic rubber — NEOPRENE
Synthetic sapphires — BOULES
Synthetic silk — NYLON, RAYON
Syr. leader — ASSAD
Syr. neighbor — ISR
Syracuse player — ORANGEMAN
Syria's president — ASSAD
Syria, formerly — ARAM
Syria, long ago — ARAM
Syrian — DAMASCENE
Syrian city — ALEPPO
Syrian city, to the French — ALEP
Syrian hub — ALEPPO
Syrian president — ASSAD
Syrian sect member — DRUSE
Syrian shrub — RETEM
Syrian statesman — ASSAD
Syrup providers — MAPLES
Syrup source — SAP, SORGO
System of belief — CREDO, ISM
System of courts — BAR
System of exercises — YOGA
System of India — CASTE
System of moral values — ETHIC
System of tenets — DOGMA
System or plexus — SOLAR
Systematic — ORDERED
Systems of navigation — LORANS
Systems of signals — CODES

T

'Tisn't's vulgar cousin — TAINT
T-bar rider — SKIER
T-bone — STEAK
T-man's quarry — COINER
T-men — FEDS
T-X connection — UVW
T-X splitter — UVW
T-bill payout — INT
T-man — FED
T-shirt size — SMALL
T-X connection — UVW
T. Gray opus — ELEGY
T. Williams play — SUDDENLY LAST SUMMER
T.A.E. — EDISON
T.H. Benton's "Self-portrait With _____" — RITA
T.L.C. givers — RNS
T.L.C. providers — RNS
T.N. Page's "In _____ Virginia" — OLE
T.S. and George — ELIOTS
T.S. Eliot inspired musical — CATS
T.S. Eliot subjects — CATS
T.S. Eliot's "Sweeney _____" — ERECT
T.V.A. constructions — DAMS
Tab — TAG
Tabard — COAT
Tabasco — SAUCE
Tabby — CAT
Tabby terrifies him — AELUROPHOBE
Tabby's tidbit — CATNIP
Table-talk item — ANA
Table — SHELVE
Table base — TRESTLE
Table Bay is one — INLET
Table d' _____: menu offering — HOTE
Table decor — MATS

Table extenders — LEAVES
Table for Tacitus — MENSA
Table fowl — PHEASANT
Table game — PING PONG
Table items — SILVERWARE
Table land — MESA
Table linen — NAPERY
Table of contents — INDEX
Table on a predella — ALTAR
Table plate for a hot dish — TRIVET
Table scraps — MEAL TIME SPATS, ORTS
Table setting — LENOX CHINA
Table shaker — SALT
Table spread — OLEO
Table staple — SALT
Table support — LEG
Table wine — CLARET
Table-d'hote inclusion — SHERBET
Table-talk — CHAT
Tableland — MESA
Tableland in the West — MESA
Tablet — PAD
Tableware — CRUETS
Taboo — BAN, SACRED
Taboo items — DONTS
Taboo thing — NO NO
Taboos — BANS
Tabor — DRUM
Tabriz coin — RIAL
Tabriz location — IRAN
Tabriz native — IRANI
Tabriz's site — IRAN
Tabula _____ — RASA
Tabulate — COUNT, TALLY
Tabulates — TALLIES
Tach reading — RPM
Tachometer readout — RPM
Tacit — SILENT
Tack — BASTE, FASTEN
Tack for a racer — SADDLE
Tack room item — BRIDLE
Tacked on — ADDED
Tackle — GEAR, HAVE AT
Tackle items — HOOKS
Tackled — HAD AT
Tackled the quarterback — SACKED
Tacks on — ADDS
Tacks up a hem — BASTES
Tacmahac — BALSAM
Taco dip — SALSA
Tact — KNACK
Tact, for one — ASSET
Tactical unit — BRIGADE
Tactics — PLOYS
Tactless — GAUCHE
Tad — SHAVER
Tadpole, for one — LARVA
Tadzhik or Turkmen: Abbr. — SSR
Tael — LIANG
Taffeta — FABRIC
Taffrail's locale — AFT
Taffy — CANDY
Taft's home turf — OHIO
Tag — LABEL
Tag data — PRICE
Tag end — REAR
Tag-along's words — ME TOO
Tag-team victories — PINS
Tags for PFC's — IDS
Tags for trying — AGLETS
Tahiti togs — SARONGS
Tahitian woman — WAHINI
Tahoe, for one — LAKE
Tail — SHADOW
Tail of a fox — BRUSH
Tail of a meteor — ITE
Tail's tail, at times — ENDER
Tailed — SHADOWED
Tailer, often — SEWER
Tailing — WASTE
Tailless cat — MANX
Taillike — CAUDAL
Tailor — ALTER, SARTOR
Tailor sometimes — ALTERER
Tailor's concern — SEAM
Tailor's dearth — NEED OF TWEED
Tailor's job — ALTERATION
Tailoring problem — FIT
Tails' alternative — HEADS
Taint — STAIN, VITIATE
Taints — CORRUPTS
Taipei airport code — TAI
Taiwan brew — OOLONG
Taiwan's capital — TAIPEI
Taiwan, once — FORMOSA
Taj _____ — MAHAL
Taj Mahal's locale — AGRA
Taj Mahal, for one — TOMB
Taj Majal site — AGRA
Taj site — AGRA
Tajo of the Met — ITALO
Tajo or Balbo — ITALO
Take — GRAB, SEIZE, SNATCH, STEAL, USURP
Take _____ — A BOW
Take _____ (accept accolades) — A BOW
Take _____ (alternate) — TURNS
Take _____ (relax) — TEN
Take _____ (rest) — A NAP
Take _____ (snooze) — A NAP
Take _____ (taste) — A SIP
Take _____ (the lamb) — IT ON
Take _____ (through the fight) — A DIVE
Take _____ (undergo risks) — A DARE
Take _____ the chin — IT ON
Take _____ the lam — IT ON
Take _____ view of — A DIM
Take _____: look slyly — A PEEK
Take a _____: scram — POWDER
Take a big chance — RISK LIFE AND LIMB
Take a bow! — CONGRATULATIONS
Take a break — REST
Take a cab — RIDE
Take a chair — SIT
Take a chance — DARE
Take a drive — MOTOR
Take a flier — RISK
Take a good look — STARE
Take a hand in a card game — SIT IN
Take a powder — TALC
Take a role — ACT IN
Take a second shot at — RETRY
Take a shot — FIRE
Take a spill — SLIP
Take a turn for the better — IMPROVE
Take advantage of — USE
Take after — RESEMBLE
Take another look — RESEE
Take apart — SEPARATE, UNDO
Take as one's own — ADOPT
Take away — DEDUCT, ERASE
Take away the natural vigor — ETIOLATE
Take away, in law — ADEEM
Take back — RECANT, RESCIND
Take back on — REHIRE
Take care — BEWARE
Take care of — MIND, SEE TO
Take charge — LEAD
Take command — LEAD
Take down a peg — DEMOTE
Take exception — DEMUR
Take five — REST
Take flight — FLEE
Take flight to unite — ELOPE
Take for _____ — A RIDE
Take for granted — ASSUME, PRESUME
Take forty winks — DOZE
Take from the top — SKIM
Take heed — MIND
Take hold — BITE
Take home — NET
Take in — LEARN
Take in sail — REEF
Take into account — CONSIDER
Take into one's arms — HUG
Take it easy — COAST, DRIFT, IDLE, LOAF
Take it easy — REST, SLOW DOWN
Take it on the _____ — LAM
Take measures with junior — BOX THE EARS
Take money for — VEND

Take off — DEDUCT, DOFF, ERASE, REMOVE
Take off — SPLIT, SKIM, SOAR
Take off the top — SKIM
Take offense — RESENT
Take on — EMPLOY, HIRE
Take on cargo — LADE, LOAD
Take on freight — LADE
Take on help — HIRE
Take one's ease — SIT
Take one's own sweet time — DILLY DALLY
Take one's time — DALLY
Take out — DELETE, ERASE
Take out order — TO GO
Take out, in printing — DELE
Take over — SEIZE
Take over the coals — ROAST
Take panes with one's work — GLAZE
Take part in a speed contest — RACE
Take pleasure in — RELISH
Take steps — ACT
Take steps, in a way — STRIDE
Take stock — SURVEY
Take ten — REST
Take testimony from — HEAR
Take the _____ (testify) — STAND
Take the bait — REACT
Take the bat — HIT
Take the bull by the horns — EXPLOIT
Take the cake — OUTSHINE
Take the consequences — FACE THE MUSIC
Take the cruise — SAIL
Take the gloomiest possible view — PESSIMISTIC
Take the helm — PILOT, STEER
Take the honey and run? — ELOPE
Take the lead — STAR
Take the stick — STEER
Take the stump — ORATE
Take the sun — BASK
Take the trolley — RIDE
Take the veil — RETIRE
Take the wheel — STEER, DRIVE
Take to a higher court — APPEAL
Take to court — SUE
Take to task — BERATE, CHIDE, SCOLD
Take to the hills — FLEE
Take to the slopes — SKI
Take to the stump — ORATE
Take turns — ROTATE
Take umbrage — RESENT
Take under consideration — HEAR
Take up a hem — ALTER
Take up quarters — RESIDE
Take wing — SAIL
Take without asking — ANNEX
Take-charge person — SPARKPLUG
Take-in — DUPE
Take-out order — DELETE
Taken _____ (amazed) — ABACK
Taken _____ (surprised) — ABACK
Taken aback — AMAZED
Taken along — TOTED
Taken away — REMOVED
Taken care of — SEEN TO
Taken for _____ A RIDE
Takeoff — SEND UP
Takeoff group — GOERS
Takeoff specialist — APER
Takeout counter order — TO GO
Takeover attempt — COUP
Takeover song? — YOU BELONG TO ME
Takes _____ view of: frowns on — A DIM
Takes a break — RECESSES, RESTS
Takes a chance — BETS, DARES
Takes a false step — TRIPS
Takes a flat — RENTS
Takes a mate — WEDS
Takes a powder — SCRAMS
Takes a powder? — TALCS
Takes a seat — SITS
Takes a siesta — NAPS
Takes a spouse — WEDS
Takes action — DOES
Takes advantage of — USES
Takes affect — TELLS
Takes back — RECANTS
Takes care of — MINDS, SEES TO, TENDS
Takes down a peg — ABASES
Takes five — RESTS
Takes forty winks — REPOSES
Takes great interest in — DOTES
Takes in — VIEWS
Takes it all — HOGS
Takes it easy — RESTS
Takes notice — SEES, SITS UP
Takes off — BOLTS, SOARS
Takes off the cream — SKIMS
Takes on — HIRES
Takes on anew — REHIRES
Takes on cargo — LADES
Takes out — DELES
Takes ten — NAPS, RESTS
Takes the blue ribbon — WINS
Takes the check — TREATS
Takes the edge — DULLS
Takes the helm — HEADS, STEERS
Takes the subway, British style — TUBES
Takes the trouble — CARES
Takes to court — SUES
Takes to the sky — SOARS
Takes wing — SOARS
Taking a dip — SWIMMING
Taking a guess — SURMISING
Taking five — RESTING
Taking part — IN ON
Taking the lead — SPEAR-HEADING
Taking the waters, in a way — CRUISING
Taking to court — SUING
Taking up of water by soil — INSOAK
Tale — STORY
Tale of Troy — ILIAD
Tale opener — ONCE
Tale teller — INFORMER
Tale twister — LIAR
Talent — FLAIR, FORTE, GIFT, KNACK, SKILL
Talent, for one — ASSET
Talented — ABLE
Talented in a number of ways — VERSATILE
Talented lady — ARTISTE
Talents — CAPABILITIES, GIFTS
Tales — YARNS
Talia Shire film: 1986 — RAD
Talisman — AMULET
Talk — CONFER
Talk aimlessly — CHATTER
Talk back — SASS
Talk foolishly — DROOL
Talk frankly — RAP
Talk gibberish — RAVE
Talk impudently — SASS
Talk inanely — DROOL
Talk incessantly — NATTER
Talk nonsense — DROOL, GAS
Talk on and on — PRATE
Talk out of — WANGLE
Talk show host — EMCEE
Talk show hostess — JOAN RIVERS
Talk show pioneer — PAAR
Talk thoughtlessly — BLAB
Talk up — SPEAK
Talk wildly — RANT
Talk, at times — IDLE
Talk, in a way — JAW
Talk, mod style — RAP
Talk-show mascot? — MERVS GRIFFIN
Talkative — CHATTY, GLIB
Talkative bird — MYNA
Talked too much — RAN ON
Talkies — FLICKS
Talking bird — MYNA
Talking horse of TV — MR ED
Talks — PARLEYS
Talks back — SASSES
Talks foolishly — PIFFLES
Talks hot air — GASSES
Tall — LOFTY
Tall and thin — LANKY
Tall Asiatic tree — ACLE

Tall beer glass — SCHOONER
Tall cap — MITER
Tall flightless bird — EMU
Tall marsh plants — CATTAILS
Tall story — ATTIC, YARN
Tall summer drink — ICED TEA
Tall tale — LIE, YARN
Tall tollers — GRANDFATHER CLOCKS
Tall veldt grazer — GIRAFFE
Tall, ornamental grasses — GAMAS
Tallahassee inst. — FSU
Tallahassee time — EST
Talleyrand's "Affair" — XYZ
Tallies — SCORES
Tallinn is its capital — ESTONIA
Tallinn native — ESTONIAN
Tallinn native: Abbr. — ESTH
Tally — SCORE
Tallyho drivers — TOOLERS
Talon — CLAW
Talus — SCREE
Tam o'Shanter — CAP
Tam-tams — GONGS
Tamale topping — SALSA
Tamarau's relative — BISON
Tamarisk — SHRUB
Tamarisk tree — ATLE
Tame — SUBDUE
Tamein's kin — SARIS
Tamiroff — AKIM
Tamp — PLUG, STOP
Tampa Bay — INLET
Tampa industry — CIGAR
Tampa's neighbor — SARASOTA
Tampa-to-Miami dir. — SSE
Tamper — MONKEY WITH
Tamper with — RIG
Tampered with checks — KITED
Tan — ECRU, SOAK
Tan shade — BEIGE
Tangent — LINE
Tangential — ASIDE
Tangible — SOLID, TACTILE
Tangle — ENSNARL, SNARE, SNARL
Tangle in — ENSNARE
Tangled — MATTED
Tangled stuff — MATTED MATTER
Tangles — ENSNARLS
Tangles up — ENSNARLS
Tanglewood event — CONCERT
Tangy — PUNGENT, TART
Tank — JAIL
Tank contents — WATER
Tank filler — GAS
Tankard — MUG
Tanker — OILER
Tanker or tender — SHIP
Tanned leather — SUEDE
Tanned skin — SUEDE
Tannenbaum — TREE
Tannenbaum topper — ANGEL, STAR
Tanning — BEATING
Tanning energy — RAYS
Tanning equipment — SUN LAMPS
Tanning locale — SHORE
Tantalize — TEASE
Tantalized — TEASED
Tantalizer — TEASER
Tantalizes — TEMPTS
Tantalizing riddle — TEASER
Tantalum — METAL
Tantamount — EQUAL
Tantara — BLARE
Tante's husband — ONCLE
Tante, in Spain — TIA
Tantrum's in public — SCENES
Taoism founder — LAO TSE
Taos buildings — ADOBES
Tap — FAUCET
Tap brew — BEER
Tap dancer Coles — HONI
Tap dancers, breezily — HOOFERS
Tap word — HOT
Tap, in a keg — SPIGOT
Tape holder — CASSETTE
Tape over — ERASE
Taper — LESSEN
Taper off — ABATE
Tapered trouser for women — CAPRI PANTS
Tapers and torches — LIGHTS
Tapestry — ARRAS
Tapioca plant — CASAVA
Tapioca source — CASSAVA
Tappet — CAM
Taproom — SALOON
Taproom spats — BAR ROWS
Taps gently — DABS
Tar — SAILOR, SALT
Tar the driveway again — RETOP
Tar's quaff — GROG
Tar's unit of distance — SEA MILE
Tar's yes — AYE
Tara native — CELT
Taradiddle — FIB
Taragon — HERB
Tarantella — DANCE
Tarawa — ATOLL
Tarbell, e.g. — MUCKRAKER
Tarboosh — FEZ, HAT
Tardigrade — WATERBEAR
Tardy — LATE
Tares' partner — TREATS
Target — GOAL
Target area — RANGE
Target competition — SKEET
Target for Gooden — MITT
Target for Gretzky — GOAL
Target for Ness — CAPONE
Target for Smiley — MOLE
Target in archery — CLOUT
Target in horseshoes — STAKE
Targets for Testaverde — ENDS
Tarheel of North Carolina — NATIVE
Tariff at customs — DUTY
Tarkington hero — PENROD
Tarkington's "_____ and Sam" — PENROD
Tarkington's "In the _____" — ARENA
Tarkington's "The Magnificent _____" — AMBERSONS
Tarkington's Adams — ALICE
Tarn river locale — FRANCE
Tarn's hue — AQUA
Taro preparation — POI
Taro root — EDDO
Taro rootstocks — EDDOS
Tarot suit — CUPS
Tarried — ABIDE, BIDED
Tarry — BIDE, DELAY, DROOP, LINGER
Tarry — LAG
Tarsus — ANKLE
Tart — ACID, SOUR
Tart ice — SORBET
Tart taste — TANG
Tartan — FABRIC, PLAID
Tartan designations — CLANS
Tartan pattern — SETT
Tartan wearers — CLANS
Tartan wraps — PLAIDS
Tartar formed in wine casks — ARGOL
Tarts and trifles — DESSERTS
Tarzan's rope — LIANA
Tarzan, et al. — APEMEN
Tarzan, to Ken Maynard — STEED
Task — JOB, STINT
Taskmaster — MARTINET
Tasks — STINTS
Tasman — ABEL
Tasmania, e.g. — ISLAND
Tassel — FRINGE
Tasso heroine — ERMINIA
Tasso's birthplace — SORRENTO
Tasso's patron — ESTE
Taste — SIP, TRY
Taste in general — FLAVOR
Taste with delight — SAVOR
Taste-bud stimulator — AROMA
Tasteless — STALE, VAPID
Tasty — SAPID
Tasty mollusk — ABALONE
Tasty tidbits — MORSELS
Tasty tubers — YAMS
Tatadiddler — LIAR
Tatami — MAT
Tatami material — STRAW
Tate offering — ART
Tate treasures — ART
Tater — SPUD

Tatter — SHRED
Tatterdemalions — RAGAMUFFINS
Tattered — RAGGY
Tatters — RAGS, SHREDS
Tattle — REVEAL
Tattle tail — TALE
Tattled — TOLD
Tattoo standard — MOM
Tatum and Blakey — ARTS
Tatum and Carney — ARTS
Tatum or Ryan — ONEAL
Tatum's dad — RYAN
Taught — SCHOOLED
Taunt — GIVE, TEASE, TWIT
Taunt to an early motorist — GET A HORSE
Taurus neighbor — ARIES
Taut — TENSE
Tavern — BAR, INN, PUB
Tavern drink — ALE
Tavern specialty — ALE
Taverns — BARS
Tawdry — CHEA, GARISH
Tawdry art — KITSCH
Tax — ASSESS, SCOT
Tax expert, for short — CPA
Tax for each member of a household — POLL
Tax men — ASSESSORS
Tax or dental compound — STENT
Tax or draft dodger — EVADER
Tax org. — IRS
Tax paid in medieval England — GELD
Tax shelters — IRAS
Tax, in Torino — TASSA
Tax-deferred acct. — IRA
Taxable item — INCOME
Taxco money — PESO
Taxi drivers — CABBIES
Taxi fee — FARE
Taxi riders — FARES
Taxi, in Turin — TASSI
Taxing initials? — IRS
Taxing org. — IRS
Taxis — CABS
Taxonomic categories — GENERA
Taxonomic terms — GENRA
Taxpayers' bane — AUDIT
Taylor Caldwell novel — MELISSA
Taylor of films — ROD
Taylor or Adoree — RENEE
Taylor, for fans — LIZ
Tbilisi native — GEORGIAN
Tbsp. units — TSPS
Tchaikovsky favorite, with "The" — NUTCRACKER SUITE
Tchaikovsky's "_____ Onegin" — EUGENE
Tchaikovsky's "Capriccio _____" — ITALIEN
Tchaikovsky's "Marche _____" — SLAV
Tchr. — INSTR
Tchrs. gp. — NEA
TCU rival — SMU
TD's yield six of these — PTS
Te Kanawa, for one — MAORI
Tea-leaf readers — SEERS
Tea — CHA
Tea cake — SCONE
Tea from spray's first three leaves — PEKOE
Tea leaf readers — SEERS
Tea party adjunct — URN
Tea party setting — BOSTON
Tea server — SAMOVAR
Tea source — THEA
Tea treats — SCONES
Tea type — BOHEA, OOLONG, PEKOE
Tea V.I.P. — POURER
Tea variety — CHA
Tea-party party — POURER
Teach new skills — RETRAIN
Teach, for one — PIRATE
Teacher — COACH, MENTOR
Teacher's deg. — EDB
Teacher's goal — TENURE
Teacher's homework item — TEST PAPER
Teacher's in an ecole — MAITRES
Teacher's need — CHALK
Teacher's org. — NEA
Teacher's pet — MOLLY CODDLE
Teacher's pet? — APPLE POLISHER
Teacher's present — APPLE
Teacher's project — EXAM
Teacher's surprise — QUIZ
Teachers at times — RATERS
Teachers in an ecole — MAITRES
Teachers' _____ — PET
Teachers' gp. — NEA
Teaching — TENET
Teaching deg. — EDD
Teaching method — ROTE
Teal — DUCK
Team — CLUB, CREW, SQUAD
Team anagram — MEAT
Team cheered in Salt Lake City — UTES
Team jacket — BLAZER
Team lists — ROSTERS
Team mates — OXEN
Team number — NINE
Team of shipmates — CREW
Team that's almost bare? — EXPOS
Teamaker for the Tsar — SAMOVAR
Teammate — ALLY
Teams — SIDES
Teams of horses — SOANS
Teamster rig — SEMI
Teamsters — HAULERS
Tean — SIDE
Teaneck's time — EST
Teapot feature — SPOUT
Tear — BOLT, DASH, RACE, REND, RENT, RIP
Tear _____ — DUCT
Tear again — RERIP
Tear apart — REND, RIVE
Tear away — UPROOT
Tear dabber — HANKIE
Tear down — RAZE
Tear gas, e.g. — IRRITANT
Tear homophone — TIER
Tear into pieces — REND
Tear to pieces — REND
Tear's companion — WEAR
Tear's mate — WEAR
Tear's partner — WEAR
Tear-jerker — ONION
Tearful comedienne Pitts — ZASU
Tearful mother — NIOBE
Tearful one of myth — NIOBE
Tearful timber — WEEPING WILLOW
Tears — LACHRYMAE, RIPS
Teas maker — KETTLE
Teasdale — SARA
Teasdale and others — SARAS
Tease — BAIT, NEEDLE, PESTER, RAG, RIB
Tease — KID
Tease — RIDE, TWIT
Tease good-naturedly — KID
Tease, in a way — COMB
Teased — NEEDLED, RIBBED, RODE
Teased constantly — RODE
Teasel — BURR
Teases — RIDES, TWITS
Teases good-naturedly — BANTERS
Teaset part — CUP
Teatime goody — SCONE
Teatime refreshment — SCONE
Teatro San Carlo offerings — OPERAS
Tec Lupin — ARSENE
Tech. space — LAB
Technic — STUDY
Tecs' terriers — ASTA
Tecumseh's tribe — SHAWNEE
Ted Danson role — SAM
Ted Danson's show — CHEERS
Teddy — BEAR
Teddy, for example — STEP IN
Tedious — DRAB, DULL, TIRESOME
Tedious ones — BORES
Tedious, to Highlanders — DREE
Tediously iterant — REPETITIVE
Tediously verbose — LONG WINDED

Tee-hee: titter — SNICKER
Tee follower — HEE
Tee leader — ESS
Tee preceder — ESS
Tee toters — GOLFERS
Teed off — IRED, IRATE, PEEVED
Teeming — ASWARM, RIFE
Teems — SWARMS
Teen-ager, figuratively — SAPLING
Teen detective of fiction — DREW
Teen follower — AGER
Teen problem — ACNE
Teen's bane — ACNE
Teen's woe — ACNE
Teenage status symbol — BOMBER JACKET
Teenager — MINOR
Teenager's bane — ACNE
Teenager's woe — ACNE
Teener's hangout — DISCO
Teer — DAUB
Tees off — RILES
Teeter — SEESAW
Teeter-totter — SEESAW
Teeth — MOLARS
Teetotal — ABSTAIN
Tehees — SNIGGERS
Teheran citizen — IRANI
Teheran coin — RIAL
Teheran inhabitants — IRANIS
Teheran resident — IRANI
Teheran runner — PERSIAN RUG
Tehuantepec — ISTHMUS
Teiid — LIZARD
Tel _____ — AVIV
Tel Aviv dances — HORAS
Telegram — WIRE
Telegram period — STOP
Telegraph — SEND
Telegraphed — WIRED
Telegraphs — MORSES
Teleost fish — EEL
Telephone — CALL
Telephone answer — ALLO
Telephone booths — KIOSKS
Telephone button — HOLD
Telephone greeting — HELLO
Telephone pole, for one — PYLON
Telephone response, for some — ELLO
Telephone sound — BUSY SIGNAL
Telephone-book item — NUMBER
Telescope — GLASS
Telescope inventor — GALILEO
Telescope operators — SPYERS
Telescope part — LENS
Television feature — NEWS
Television lifeline — CABLE
Television's Howser — DOOGIE
Tell — NARRATE, RELATE
Tell _____ the judge — IT TO
Tell a whopper — LIE
Tell about being tardy? — RELATE
Tell all — SPILLER
Tell and Hood — ARCHERS
Tell it like _____ — IT IS
Tell or Hood — ARCHER
Tell the truth — LEVEL
Tell's canton — URI
Tell, for one — ARCHER
Teller of fish stories — LIAR
Teller of tall tales — ANANAIS, LIAR
Teller's area — CAGE
Teller's items — ONES
Telling it like it is — BEING LOGICAL
Telling it like it is — MAKING SENSE
Telling it like it is — STATING FACTS
Telling it like it is — USING REASON
Telling lead — HEADSTART
Tells — RELATES
Tells or sells — RETAILS
Tells tall tales — FIBS
Telltale mark — SCRATCH
Telltale sign — SCAR
Telly on the telly — KOJAK
Telpher, e.g. — CAR
Telstar and Sputnik — SATELLITES
Temerarious — UNRULY
Temerity — RASHNESS
Temp. type — FAH
Tempe ed. inst. — ASU
Temper — ANNEAL, MOOD
Temper tantrums — TIRADES
Temperance — SOBRIETY
Temperate — SOBER
Tempers — ANNEALS
Tempers steel — FORGES
Tempest — GALE, STORM
Tempest loci — TEAPOT
Tempestuous — WINDY
Templar portrayer — MOORE
Templar sobriquet — SAINT
Temple — PAGODA, SHUL
Temple in Thailand — WAT
Temple's good ship — LOLLIPOP
Templeton — ALEC
Tempo — PACE
Temporarily — FOR THE TIME BEING
Temporarily supply — LEND
Temporary arrangement — RENTING
Temporary beginner — CON
Temporary cessation of breathing — APNEA
Temporary condition — SPELL
Temporary property holder — BAILEE
Temporary quiet — LULL
Temporary respiratory stoppage — APNOEA
Temporary stops in journeys — LAYOVERS
Temporary teacher in Torino? — ITALIAN SUB
Temporary use — LOAN
Temps, at times — STENOS
Tempt — ENTICE
Temptation site — EDEN
Tempted — BAITED, LED ON
Tempting — WINSOME
Tempting dangler — CARROT
Temptress — SIREN
Tempts — ENTICES
Ten — FIVE TWOS
Ten C-notes — GRAND
Ten commandments verb — SHALT
Ten decibels — BEL
Ten mills — CEBT
Ten percenter — AGENT
Ten-sided figure — DECAGON
Ten-speed — BIKE
Ten: Comb. form — DECA, DEC, DECI
Ten: Prefix — DECA
Tenacious dog — TERRIER
Tenant — LESSEE, RENTER, RESIDENT
Tenant farmer in India — RYOT
Tenant in the feudal days — VASSAL
Tenant lead-in — LIEU
Tenant of a type — ROOMER
Tenant's concern — LEASE, RENT
Tenant's contract — LEASE
Tenant's quest — LEASE
Tenants — LESSEES
Tend — SEE TO
Tend the garden — RAKE
Tend the roast — BASTE
Tend to separate — PELLATE
Tended a border — EDGED
Tendencies — BENTS
Tendency — TREND
Tender — DELICATE, EXTEND, GENTLE, KIND, LOVING
Tender — OFFER, SORE
Tender passion — AMOR
Tender places — SORES
Tender spots — SORES
Tender touch — CARESS, PAT
Tenderhearted one — SOFTY
Tenders — OFFERS
Tending to grow dim — FADY
Tending to rust — EROSIVE
Tendon — SINEW
Tendrils — CURLS
Tends — SEES TO

Tends to — CARES FOR
Tenet of M.L. King — WE SHALL OVERCOME
Tenfold — DENARY
Tenn. athlete — VOL
Tenn. eleven — VOLS
Tenn. neighbor — ALA
Tenn.'s Albert — GORE
Tennessee _____ Ford — ERNIE
Tennessee's largest city — MEMPHIS
Tennessee's Senator and family — GORES
Tennille — TONI
Tennis ace? — POINT OF NO RETURN
Tennis call — AD IN
Tennis call — NET
Tennis cry — LET
Tennis divisions — SETS
Tennis great — ASHE, BORG
Tennis great of 1920's and 30's — MOODY
Tennis great Rod — LAVER
Tennis great Trabert — TONY
Tennis match part — SET
Tennis name of fame — ASHE, EVERT
Tennis necessity — NET
Tennis notable Vic _____ — SEIXAS
Tennis opener — SERVE
Tennis org. — USTA
Tennis player — NETMAN
Tennis player Helen — JACOBS
Tennis player's sitcom? — ANYTHING BUT LOVE
Tennis player, at times — SERVER
Tennis prodigy — CHANG
Tennis round — SET
Tennis score — FIFTEEN
Tennis serves — ACES
Tennis shot — LOB
Tennis standout — IVAN LENDL
Tennis star of the 1930's — LOTT
Tennis stratagem — LOB
Tennis stroke — LOB
Tennis teacher — PRO
Tennis term — AD IN, ALL, LET, LOB, SET
Tennis units — SETS
Tennis VIP — ASHE
Tennis winners — ACES
Tennis' Rod — LAVER
Tennyson crossed it: 1892 — BAR
Tennyson heroine — ISOLT, MAUD
Tennyson poem — MAUD
Tennyson title — LORD
Tennyson's "The _____ of the King" — IDYLLS
Tennyson's Arden et al. — ENOCHS
Tennyson's Rx — RING IN THE NEW
Tenor Bergonzi — CARLO
Tenor John, of the opera — ALER
Tenor Mario _____ Monaco — DEL
Tenor or alto — VOICE
Tenor Vinay — RAMON
Tenor Vladimir — POPOV
Tense — EDGY, TAUT
Tense for Thucydides — AORIST
Tension — STRESS
Tent — CANVAS, SHELTER, TARPAULIN
Tent beds — COTS
Tenth letter of the Greek alphabet — KAPPA
Tenth of a sen — RIN
Tenth part of an ephah — OMER
Tentmaker of literature — OMAR
Tenuous — ETHEREAL
Tenuous and thin — FRAIL
Tenure — TERM
Tepee toddler — PAPOOSE
Tepid — WARM
Tequila country: Abbr. — MEX
Tequila with orange juice — SUNRISE
Tequila? — THE GULP OF MEXICO
Teraph — IDOL
Teraphim — IDOLS
Tergenev heroine — ELENA
Tergenev's birthplace — OREL
Terhune canine — LAD
Term for a worm — ERIA
Term in a card game — BYE
Term in music — MAJOR
Term in printing — EM
Term in trigonometry — COSINE
Term of address, with "your" — LADYSHIP
Term of endearment — BABE, BABY, SUGAR
Term projects — PAPERS
Term with two meanings — DOUBLE ENTENDRE
Term-end test — FINAL
Term. — STA
Termagant — SHREW
Terminal man — PORTER
Terminal of a cell — ANODE
Terminate — CEASE, END, EXPIRE, LAPSE
Terminated — ENDED
Terminator — ENDER
Terminer's partner — OYER
Terminus — END
Terms in math — SINES
Terms of a sale — AS IS
Terra _____ — COTTA, FIRMA
Terra _____: pottery material — COTTA
Terra alba — GYPSUM
Terra follower — FIRMA
Terrapin — EMYD
Terrapin suffix — EMYD
Terret — RING
Terrible — AWFUL, DIRE
Terrible Ivan — TSAR
Terrible tsar — IVAN
Terrible, in Soho — ORRID
Terrible: Slang — GOD AWFUL
Terrier film star — ASTA
Terrier or stew — IRISH
Terrier type — CAIRN, SKYE
Terriers — AIREDALES
Terrific bargain — STEAL
Terrific! — GREAT, SUPER, WOW
Terrified — SCARED
Terrifies — AWES
Territory — REGION
Terrorized — COWED
Terry or Drew — ELLEN
Terse — LACONIC
Tertiary division — NEOCENE
Tertiary Period epoch — EOCENE
Tess, to Hardy — HEROINE
Tessellate — TILED
Tessie of music hall fame — OSHEA
Test — QUIZ, TRIAL, TRY
Test answers — TRUES
Test choice, sometimes — TRUE
Test for flavor — TASTE
Test for gold — ASSAY
Test of patience — TRIAL
Test the fit — TRY ON
Test type — ACID
Test, in Tours — ESSAI
Testator's appointee — EXECUTOR
Testers — TRIERS
Testified — DEPOSED
Testifies — AVERS
Testify — AVER, DEPONE
Testify to — WITNESS
Testing places, for short — LABS
Testy one — CRAB, CRANK
Testy person — EXAMINER
Testy, in Tiverton — SNARKY
Tête-à-tête — CHAT
Tête _____ — A TETE
Tête covering — BERET
Tête topper — BERET, TAM
Tether — HOBBLE, LEASH
Tetra minus one — TRI
Teutonic goddess — ERDA
Teutonic gods — AESIR
Teutonic war god — TIU
Tevye portrayer — TOPOL
Tex-Mex condiment — SALSA

Tex-Mex treat — TAMALE
Tex. campus — SMU
Tex. city — PAMPA
Tex. coll. — SMU
Tex. neighbor — OKLA
Tex. school — SMU
Tex. shrine — ALAMO
Texan's stewpot — OLLA
Texan's topper — STETSON
Texas athlete — ASTRO
Texas border city — EL PASO
Texas city — AUSTIN, WACO
Texas cottonwood — ALAMO
Texas critters — LONGHORNS
Texas flag colors — RED WHITE AND BLUE
Texas Island — PADRE
Texas leaguer, for one — HIT
Texas leaguers? — ASTROS
Texas longhorn — STEER
Texas nine — RANGERS
Texas oilmen, at times — REFINERS
Texas Panhandle city — AMARILLO
Texas players — ASTROS
Texas port of entry — EL PASO, LAREDO
Texas ranches — SPREADS
Texas shrine — ALAMO
Texas sites — DERRICKS
Texas symbol — LONE STAR
Texas team — ASTROS, OILERS
Texas town of song — LAREDO
Texas trial? — LAREDO ORDEAL
Texas university — RICE
Text explanations — GLOSSARIES
Text set to music — ORATORIO
Textbook insert — ERRATA
Textile city in N France — AMIENS
Textile dealer — MERCER
Textile fiber — RAYON
Textile lubricant — OLEIN
Textile measure — YARD
Textile tinters — DYERS
Textile worker — DYER
Textile-machine devices — EVENERS
Texts of a play — SCRIPTS
Tey's "_____ Farrar" — BRAT
Thai coin — BAHT
Thai language — LAO
Thai money — BAHT
Thai or Lai — ASIAN
Thai or Tibetan — ASIAN
Thai river — MEKONG
Thai temples — WATS
Thai's neighbor — LAO
Thai, e.g. — ASIAN
Thailand's neighbor — LAOS
Thailand, formerly — SIAM
Thailand, once — SIAM
Thais and Tibetans — ASIANS
Thais, e.g. — ASIANS
Thalassic expanse — SEA
Thalia or Euterpe — MUSE
Thalia's sister — ERATO
Thames Tugboat slogan — THE TOWER OF LONDON
Thane's group — HARD
Thanes — LAIRDS
Thank you — MAAM
Thankful — GLAD
Thanks _____! — A LOT
Thanks, to Pierre — MERCI
Thanksgiving Day repasts — TURKEY DINNERS
Thanksgiving decorations? — CORNAMENTS
Thanksgiving dinner treat — CRANBERRY SAUCE
Thanksgiving dinner treat — OYSTER STUFFING
Thanksgiving fare — GOBBLER
Thanksgiving tradition — PARADE
That — AS IF
That certain something — AURA
That girl — SHE
That guy's — HIS
That is — ID EST
That is, to Nero — ID EST
That is, to Tacitus — ID EST
That is: Lat. — ID EST
That man — HIM
That many — NO LESS
That Menlo Park man — EDISON
That old ratite bird — EMU
That ship — SHE
That that is — REALITY
That which produces change — ALTERNANT
That's a fact — DATUM
That's a moray — EEL
That, in Paris — CELA
That, in Tijuana — ESO
That, in Toledo — ESE
That, in Tours — CELA
That, to Sophia — ESO
That: Fr. — CELA
That: It. — CHE
Thatched beach shelter — RAMADA
Thatcher is one — TORY
Thatching grass — ICHU
Thaumaturgy — MAGIC
Thaw — DEICE, MELT
Thawed — MELTED
The "Bohemian Girl" — ARLINE
The "cruellest month," to T.S. Eliot — APRIL
The "good guy" — HERO
The "gray cells" — BRAIN
The "it" game — TAG
The "March King" — SOUSA
The "Music Man" was one — DRUMMER
The "Mysterious East" — ORIENT
The "N" in NB — NOTA
The "p" in music — SOFT
The "punch" in a planter's punch — RUM
The "Rolling _____" — STONES
The "Roof of the World" — TIBET
The "Swedish Nightingale" — LIND
The "tiger in your tank"? — GAS
The _____ (rock group) — WHO
The _____ (Springsteen) — BOSS
The _____ - _____ the land — FAT OF
The _____ 500 — INDY
The _____ Baltimore" — HOTL
The _____ Boys — BEACH
The _____ Brothers of song — AMES
The _____ Brothers, pop group — ISLEY
The _____ deadly sins — SEVEN
The _____ Isle — EMERALD
The _____ layer — OZONE
The _____ Marbles — ELGIN
The _____ of March — IDES
The _____ of two evils — LESSER
The _____ the Apostles — ACTS OF
The _____ Truth": Grant/Dunne classic — AWFUL
The _____, of rock fame — WHO
The _____, TV rescuers — A TEAM
The 19th president — HAYES
The 23rd Hebrew letter — TAV
The 4077th, for short — MASH
The 60's or 70's — DECADE
The A in BA — ARTS
The Adamsons' pet — ELSA
The Aesir, e.g. — GODS
The Altar — ARA
The Altar constellation — ARA
The Athens of America — BOSTON
The Author with Kipling — RUDYARD
The bagpipe is a _____ instrument — WIND
The Baisyas, for one — CASTE
The Bambino or Iron Horse — YANKEE
The Bard's Kate — SHREW

The Bard's river — AVON
The Bard's stream — AVON
The Baskervilles' dog — HOUND
The Beatles' meter maid — RITA
The Bee Gees, e.g. — TRIO
The Beerys — NOAHS
The bench — RESERVES
The best — A ONE, TOPS
The better part — MOST
The Big _____ of basketball — EAST
The birds — AVES
The bishop of Rome — POPE
The boss calls it — TUNE
The bottom line — NET
The bottom line, to Blass — HEM
The boyfriend, perhaps — STEADY
The bread spread — OLEO
The Brown Bomber — LOUIS
The Buckeyes — OSU
The candidates — SLATE
The caped crusader — BATMAN
The cast — ACTORS
The Chaneys — LONS
The Charles' dog — ASTA
The Charles' pet — ASTA
The Charles' terrier — ASTA
The Charles' wirehair — ASTA
The cheaper spread — OLEO
The check — TAB
The choice part — ELITE
The clear sky — ETHER
The Clintons' alma mater — YALE
The color of money — GREEN
The conclusion — WINDUP
The Crimson Tide — ALABAMA, BAMA
The Dark Con. — AFR
The Dark Cont. — AFR
The Darlings' dog — NANA
The demos — MASSES
The Devil — OLD NICK
The dewlap of cattle — JOWL
The dirt under one's feet — EARTH
The divine Miss? — MIDLER
The Dodgers' Hershiser — OREL
The double helix — DNA
The Doughboys, for short — AEF
The draft: Abbr. — SSS
The Duchess of York, for one — REDHEAD
The Duke of Hollywood — WAYNE
The Duke, formerly — MORRISON
The Earl of Chatham — PITT
The earth's _____ — AXIS
The Ebro, for one — RIO
The elusive Himalayan — YETI
The Emerald Isle — HIBERNIA
The end — FINIS, OMEGA
The end of joy and humor — OUS
The enemy — FOE
The Eternal City — ROME
The exercise of power — ACT
The facts: Colloq. — SCORE
The family — KIN
The Father of Microbiology — LEEUWENHOEK
The Feast of the Lots — PURIM
The Few, to WSC — RAF
The final result — BOTTOM LINE
The first lady — EVE
The first man: Scand. myth. — ASK
The first Mrs. Copperfield — DORA
The first musical "B" — BACH
The first Nellie Forbush — MARY MARTIN
The first true gramophone artist — ENRICO CARUSO
The flower that never grows old — AGERATUM
The Fonz of "Happy Days" — WINKLER
The Foul Fiend — SATAN
The Four _____, singing group — LADS
The Four Hundred — ELITE
The Fourth Estate — PRESS
The fourth Musketeer — DARTAGNAN
The fourth planet — MARS
The Friendly islands — TONGA
The full range — GAMUT
The Furies — ERINYES
The Furies of myth — DIRAE
The gate — TAKE
The girl who's back in town — LULU
The Golden Tenor — CARUSO
The good earth — SOIL
The good life — CAKES AND ALE
The good old days — PAST
The good ole days — YORE
The Gorgons and Graces — TRIOS
The Grande — RIO
The Grande and Ebro — RIOS
The Grateful _____ of rock — DEAD
The great commoner — PITT
The Great White Way — NEONS
The Greatest — ALI
The greatest amount — MOST
The Green Wave — TULANE
The Hague location: Abbr. — NETH
The halls of ivy — ACADEME
The Hawkeyes — IOWA
The Hawks fly here — OMNI
The head: Lat. — CAPUT
The headman, for short — SUPER
The heart of the matter — GIST
The Henley racer — BOAT
The Henley, e.g. — REGATTA
The horror of Gomorrah — VICE
The House of Lords — PEERAGE
The house, to Pedro — LA CASA
The Hunter — ORION
The infamous Marquis de _____ — SADE
The Invisible Man of 1933 — RAINS
The islanders, e.g. — ICEMEN
The Italian Stallion — ROCKY
The Kingston _____ — TRIO
The Kremlin's first lady — RAISA
The largest continent — ASIA
The last word — AMEN
The latest — NEW
The latest info on actor Tom? — CRUISE NEWS
The latest thing — FAD, RAGE
The law — COPS
The law's reach — ARM
The Law, to Mr. Bumble — ASS
The lawn at dawn, often — DEWY
The Leaning Tower's city — PISA
The least bit — RAP
The letter v? — CENTER OF GRAVITY
The libido — EROS
The life of Riley — EASE
The lifeline of Egypt — NILE
The like — KIND
The limit of one's strength — TETHER
The limit, at times — SKY
The limit, to some — SKY
The Lone Eagle — LINDY
The Lone Eagle's monogram — CAL
The Lorelei's river — RHINE
The Louvre's Mona — LISA
The low-fat spread — OLEO
The luck of the Irish — CESS
The lunar landers — NASA
The Lunts' milieu — STAGE
The Magi, e.g. — TRIO
The majority — MOST
The makings of a potpourri — PETALS

The man behind Bunker — LEAR
The man for all seasons — MORE
The Man of a Thousand Faces — LON
The maples — ACER
The March King and family — SOUSAS
The March King's family — SOUSA
The McCoys, to the Hatfields — FOES
The Mets stadium — SHEA
The mind: Comb. form — NOO
The moon has four — PHASES
The Moor of Venice — OTHELLO
The movies — SCREEN
The naked truth? — NUDISM
The National Pastime — BASEBALL
The nether world — HADES
The New Yorker founder — ROSS
The night before — EVE
The night has a thousand — EYES
The Nile has one — DELTA
The Nile, as a god — HAPI
The nominees — SLATE
The Norse gods — AESIR
The north wind personified — BOREAS
The number seven — HEPTAD
The O'Grady girl — ROSIE
The O'Hara home — TARA
The O'Haras' abode — TARA
The O'Haras' mansion — TARA
The Ohre, in Germany — EGER
The old _____ (Ireland) — SOD
The Old _____, Hawthorne's home — MANSE
The old sod — EIRE, ERIN
The one with the mike — EMCEE
The ones chosen — ELECTEES
The Orient Express, e.g. — TRAIN
The original "Vanessa" — STEBER
The other woman, Roman style — ALTERA
The ox of Celebes — ANOA
The pair — BOTH
The Pearly _____ — GATES
The Pentagon, for one — EDIFICE
The Pentateuch — TORAH
The people — THEY
The Pequod's captain — AHAB
The piper's son — TOM
The Plain People — AMISH
The poker plant — TRITOMA
The pokey — STIR
The powers that be — THEM
The present — NONCE, NOW
The President? — CABINET MAKER
The price to pay — COST
The price to play — ANTE
The priest, not the beast — LAMA
The problem in Hamelin — RATS
The rainbow — IRIS
The rainbow's _____ gold — POT OF
The Ram — ARIES
The Red Baron, e.g. — ACE
The Red Cross needs it — PLASMA
The red planet — MARS
The Red Raiders — COLGATE
The Reindeer people — LAPPS
The remaining September births — LIBRA THE SCALES
The rest — OTHERS
The ring has a main one — EVENT
The rite things to say — IDOS
The Rivoli, for one — LA RUE
The road to Rome — ITER
The Rock of Gibraltar, of old — CALPE
The Rolling _____ — STONES
The Rolling Stones, for one — ROCK BAND
The Rome of Hungary — EGER
The same — DITTO, IDEM
The same: Lat. — IDEM
The Sargossa, for one — SEA
The Say Hey Kid — MAYS
The Schnozz — DURANTE
The score — EVEN
The second — ANOTHER
The Seine, to Spaniards — SENA
The serious musical stage — OPERA
The Seven _____ — SEAS
The sky over Paris — CIEL
The slammer — STIR
The smart set — TON
The Smothers Brothers, for one — DUO
The South of France — MIDI
The sovereign of a nation — KING
The Speaker's prop — GAVEL
The state, to Yves — ETAT
The steppes don't have one — TREE
The Stooges, for example — TRIO
The Street Singer's theme song — MARTA
The street, in Paris — GLAZIERS, LA RUE
The substance of trees — WOOD
The Summit in Houston — ARENA
The sun — SOL
The sun, for one — STAR
The Sunshine St. — FLA
The supreme self, in Hinduism — ATMAN
The Supremes, e.g. — TRIO
The sweetsop — ATES
The T in R.O.T.C. — TNG
The Taj Mahal, e.g. — TOMB
The Tentmaker — OMAR
The Terrible one — IVAN
The Terrible tsar — IVAN
The Thames, at Oxford — ISIS
The theater's Burrows — ABE
The thing here — THIS
The third deadly sin — ENVY
The Third Man — ABEL
The time being — NONCE
The time to be in Paris — APRIL
The transept crosses it — NAVE
The triumph of winning — JOY
The Trump friend? — MARLA
The U.S.A., for one — REPUBLIC
The Ugly American, in Mexico — GRINGO
The underground, in London — TUBE
The unused W.J.C.? — NEW DEMOCRAT
The upper hand — MASTERY
The uraeus — ASP
The vanquished — LOSER
The Venerable _____ — BEDE
The very best — A ONE, CREAM OF THE CROP
The Village People hit — YMCA
The Vistula, to Poles — WISLA
The void — SKY
The Wars of the _____ — ROSES
The water, in France — LEAU
The way there — ROUTE
The way to the altar — AISLE
The way up — HITCH YOUR WAGON TO A STAR
The way up — STAIRS
The way, in China — TAO
The West — OCCIDENT
The whipped cream? the cherry? — SUNDAE BEST
The White House is her Everest — HILLARY
The white poplar — ABELE
The Wicked Wasp of Twickenham — POPE
The wild blue yonder — ETHER
The Wizard of Menlo Park — EDISON
The woad plant — PASTEL
The works — ALL, ENTIRETY

The world over — UNDER THE SUN
The world, according to Shakespeare — STAGE
The written word — PROSE
The Yokums' creator — CAPP
The, in Thiers — LES
Theater-in-the-round — ARENA
Theater — ARENA, DRAMA, STAGE
Theater area — PIT
Theater areas — AISLES
Theater award — OBIE, TONY
Theater booth — LOGE
Theater boxes — LOGES
Theater critic Barnes — CLIVE
Theater curtain — DROP
Theater district — RIALTO
Theater employee — TICKET SELLER, USHER
Theater follower — GOER
Theater forestage — APRON
Theater gp. — ANTA
Theater grouping — RIALTO
Theater honor — OBIE
Theater latecomer — STANDEE
Theater lighting expert Jennifer — TIPTON
Theater location — LOGE
Theater of old — ODEON
Theater offering — DRAMA
Theater org. — ANTA
Theater part — AISLE
Theater seats — LOGES
Theater section — LOGE
Theater sign — EXIT, SRO
Theater that Gilbert and Sullivan made famous — SAVOY
Theater-district restaurateur — SARDI
Theater-goer's choice — DRAMA
Theatrical — HISTRIONIC
Theatrical "Auntie" — MAME
Theatrical award — TONY
Theatrical backer from Rome? — ITALIANGEL
Theatrical circuit, for short — RKO
Theatrical first name — MAE
Theatrical lover — ABIE
Theatrical offerings of a sort — MELODRAMAS
Theatrical org. — AFTRA, ANTA
Theatrical sketch — SKIT
Theca — CASE
Theca inhabitant — SPORE
Theda — BARA
Theda contemporary — POLA
Theda of movie fame — BARA
Theda of silents — BARA
Theda's colleague — POLA
Thee, in Tours — TOI
Their Acropolis is a tourist's must — ATHENIANS
Their job causes lots of interest — LOAN SHARKS
Theirs, in Tours — LEUR
Thematic letter herein — ESS
Theme — MOTIF, TOPIC
Theme of "South Pacific" song — A DAME
Theme of this puzzle — CROSSWORD
Theme song of Vincent Lopez — NOLA
Then, in Paris — ALORS
Then, to Etienne — ALORS
Then, to Pierre — ALORS
Theo's cousin — TED
Theol. degree — BSL, THM
Theologian advocating strict conformity — LEGALIST
Theologian's deg. — STB
Theological — HOLY
Theology deg. — STB
Theology study — DIVINITY
Theoretical — PURE
Theories — APSES
Theories: Abbr. — SYSTS
Therapy — CURE
There are 100 in D.C. — SENS
There are two in mathematics — EMS
There ought to be _____ — A LAW
There's no place like it — HOME
There's one in every suit — ACE
There's one on this page — DIAGRAM
There: Sp. — AHI
Thereabouts — OR SO
Thereby hangs a tail? — SHIRT
Therefore — ERGO, HENCE
Therefore, in Toulouse — AINSI
Therefore, to a Shakespeare clown — ARGAL
Therm. reading — TEMP
Thermal units: Abbr. — BTUS
Thermometer fluid — MERCURY
Thermonuclear threat — H BOMB
Thermoplastic resin — SARAN
Thermos bottle — FLASK
Thesaurus — LEXICON
Thesaurus compiler — ROGET
Thesaurus man — ROGET
Thesaurus name — ROGET
Thesaurus wd. — SYN
These are called — MANY
These are proper or common — NOUNS
These are sometimes round — ROBINS
These give ade — LIMES
These go to a higher court — APPEALS
These have keys — PIANOS
These have ups and downs — HEMS
These make flights — STAIRS
These make one walk tall — STILTS
These make some love N.Y. — SHOWS
These may lead to lead — ADITS
These may produce speiss — ORES
These or those: Fr. — CES
These produce six pts. — TDS
These sometimes come in a pack — LIES
These sometimes fly? — TEMPERS
These, in Inveraray — THAE
These, in Thiers — CES
These, in Tours — CES
These, to Rene — CES
These: Fr. — CES
Theseus' ship — DELIAS
Thesmothetes' milieu — SENATE
Thespian — ACTOR, HISTRIO
Thespian Hagen — UTA
Thespian milieu — STAGE
Thespian or thesmothete — ENACTOR
Thespian Thomas — MARLO
Thespian's quest — ROLE
Thespians — ACTORS
Thespians' org. — AEA
Thessalian peak — OSSA
Thessaly mountain — OSSA
Thessaly peak — OSSA
Theurgy — MAGIC
They — PERSONS
They accept wagers — TAKERS
They are in some boots — HOBNAILS
They are often split — HAIRS
They await the time — BIDERS
They call K's — UMPS
They came bearing gifts — MAGI
They can take a yoke — OXEN
They can't be choosers — BEGGARS
They come along for "deride" — JEERERS
They cross the plate — SCORERS
They do the dirty work — BULLDOZERS
They elude dreamers — REALITIES
They fled to wed — ELOPERS
They follow an animal's trail — TRACKERS
They fool people — DELUDERS
They fought the Iroquois — ERIES

They get cooked with vegetables — SWISS STEAKS
They get the job done — WORKFORCE
They go in and out — DOORS
They go to and fro — COMMUTERS
They go to blazes? — HOSES
They have a hold on things — PAPER CLIPS
They have Attic salt — WITS
They have baleen — WHALES
They heap haystacks — PILERS
They lived in Chichén Itzá — MAYAS
They loop the loop — ELS
They make barbed remarks — NEEDLERS
They make bundles — BALERS
They make stars shine — SPOTLIGHTS
They make up a score — NOTES
They may be split — HAIRS
They often blow — FUSES
They oversee sgts. — LTS
They provide the goods — SUPPLIERS
They pull in pushers — NARCS
They put on coats — PAINTERS
They rank above viscounts — EARLS
They remit — SENDERS
They resume in September — SCHOOL DAYS
They shellac — STAINERS
They sing so low — BASSI
They sit above nks. — HDS
They sometimes bounce mgrs. — UMPS
They span hybrid gestation — COVERED BRIDGES
They surround Banff — CANADIAN ROCKIES
They take a pasting — TEETH
They use gins to get skins — SNARERS
They usually have a cause — REBELS
They vend — PEDDLERS
They watch the Grizzlies and Bobcats — MONTANANS
They were: Lat. — ERANT
They work a ship — CREW
They wrote in runes — NORSE
They're all in the family — INLAWS
They're almost grads — SRS
They're in the know — INSIDERS
They're made in Vegas — ODDS
They're often billowed — SAILS
They're often exploded — MYTHS
They're sometimes grand — PARENTS
They're sometimes grim — REAPERS
They're used in baseball — BATS
They're used in Dodger's forte — BATS
They've had it — GONERS
They, in Lyon — ILS
They, in Paris — ILS
They, in Roma — ESSE
They: Fr. — ILS
Thibodaux, La. campus — NSU
Thick — BROAD, DENSE, FAT, LUSH
Thick double-breasted jacket — REEFER
Thick piece — SLAB
Thick slice — SLAB
Thick slice, as of bread — SLAB
Thick soup — PORRIDGE, PUREE
Thick, long locks — MANE
Thick-flexing muscles — ILIACI
Thick-set — STOCKY
Thick-set shrubs — GORSE
Thick-skinned vegetarian, for short — RHINO
Thicke or Bates — ALAN
Thicken — CLOT
Thickener — AGAR
Thickening agent — CORNSTARCH
Thickens — GELS
Thickest — DENSEST
Thicket — BOSCAGE, BOSK, COPSE
Thickets of small trees — COPSES
Thickheaded — DENSE
Thickly populated — DENSE
Thief — CROOK, HEISTER, PILFERER
Thief, to Tevye — GANEF
Thigh bone — FEMUR
Thimblerig — CHEAT
Thin — SLENDER, SPARSE
Thin and slender — LANKY
Thin as _____ — A RAIL
Thin bit of pastry — WAFER
Thin broth — GRUEL
Thin cloth — VOILE
Thin coating — FILM
Thin coin — DIME
Thin layer — LAMINA, SHEET
Thin metal disk — PATEN
Thin nail — BRAD
Thin one's nickname — SLATS
Thin pancakes — BLINI, CREPES
Thin plate — LAMINA
Thin porridge — GRUEL
Thin salmon — KELT
Thin sheet — LAMINA
Thin silk fabric — A LA MODE
Thin silk for hoods — A LA MODE
Thin slice — SHAVE
Thin soup — BROTH
Thin surface — VENEER
Thin wedge — SHIM
Thin wire nails — BRADS
Thin wooden strip — SLAT
Thin, flat bread — PITA
Thin-skinned — TESTY
Thine, in Château-Thierry — ATOI
Thine, in Rouen — ATOI
Thine, to Therese — ATOI
Thine: Fr. — ATOI
Thing off the old block — CHIP
Thing often dropped — NOTE
Thing to attorneys — RES
Thing, in court — RES
Thing, in law — RES
Thing, to Tiberius — RES
Thingamajig — DOODAD, GIZMO
Things afoot — IRONS IN THE FIRE
Things similar in function — ANALOGS
Things that are "In" — FADS
Things to be done — AGENDA
Things to be learned — ABCS
Things to count — NOSES
Things to know, with "the" — ROPES
Things to roll up — SLEEVES
Things to see — SIGHTS
Think — DEEM, IDEATE
Think ahead — PLAN
Think of — CONCEIVE
Think the world of — ADORE
Think-tank members — IDEA MEN
Think-tank output — IDEA
Think-tank type — IDEA MAN
Thinker sculptor — RODIN
Thinks back — REMEMBERS
Thinks highly of — ESTEEMS
Thinly spread — SPARSE
Thinner — BONIER
Third-party payer — DRAWEE
Third — BASEMAN OR DEGREE
Third and fourth words of a soliloquy — OR NOT
Third deadly sin — LUST
Third degree? — PHD
Third King of Judah — ASA
Third leg — CANE
Third letter — CEE, GAMMA
Third of a Latin trio — AMAT
Third of thrice — ONCE
Third person: It. — CAINO
Third Reich salute — HEIL
Third Reich secret police — GESTAPO
Third son — SETH

Third tier of schooling — HIGHER EDUCATION
Third, at the track — SHOW
Third: Comb. form — TRIT
Thirst quenchers — ADES
Thirsty substance — SORBENT
Thirteen witches — COVEN
Thirties movie star Hopkins — MIRIAM
Thirty, in Tours — TRENTE
This and no more — ONLY
This and that — BOTH
This answer has three — ESSES
This could a tale unfold — ET AL
This could be a skeleton — KEY
This could use polish — NAIL
This doth murder another's sleep — SNORE
This features Achilles' wrath — ILIAD
This for that — SWAP
This goes with something — ELSE
This golfer has an army — ARNIE
This has a pompom — TAM
This has a soffit — EAVE
This holds water — CARAFE
This is a challenge to find — SECLUDED BEACH
This is often grande — RANCHO
This is paid to heroes — HOMAGE
This is silly! — INANE
This leads to lodes— ADIT
This look brings hisses — LEER
This makes Rover no rover — LEASH
This may be a little Scottish — SMA
This may be floppy — DISC
This may be posted — STAIR
This may lead to lead — ADIT
This might be a garden — ARENA
This might be slippery — ELM
This month: Abbr. — INST
This must go through — MAIL
This often runneth over — BRIMMER
This place — HERE
This place only: Var. — NES
This sometimes needs a fix — PRE
This sometimes thickens — PLOT
This spot — HERE
This woman, in Madrid — ESTA
This won't fill a filly — OAT
This, in Madrid — ESTO
This, in Oviedo — ESTA
This, in Seville — ESTA
This, in Spain — ESTO
This, in Toledo — ESTO
This, in Tours — CET
This, to a torero — ESTA
This, to Caesar — HIC
This, to Felipe — ESTA
This, to Jose — ESTO
This, to Juan — ESTO
This, to Pedro — ESTO
This: Sp. — ESTA
Thither and _____ — YON
Thomas and Babilonia — SKATERS
Thomas and Condé — NASTS
Thomas girl — MARLO
Thomas Gray et al. — ELEGISTS
Thomas had this? — DOUBT
Thomas or Bradshaw — TERRY
Thomas or Robin — HOOD
Thomas, the cartoonist — NAST
Thomasina or Grimalkin — CAT
Thompson from Des Moines — SADA
Thompson of "Family" — SADA
Thompson or Hawkins — SADIE
Thong — STRAP
Thor's father — ODIN
Thor's wife — SIF
Thoreau subject — WALDEN POND
Thorn — BARB
Thorn as on a rose — ACULEUS
Thorn in the side — PESTER
Thornburgh's predecessor — MEESE
Thornlike projection — SPINA
Thorns — BARB
Thornton Wilder play — THE LONG CHRISTMAS DINNER
Thorny — SPINY
Thorny bunch — ROSES
Thorny bush — BRIAR
Thorny plant — ROSE
Thorny tree — LIME
Thorny twig — BRIER
Thorough — TOTAL
Thoroughbred — PURE
Thoroughfares: Abbr. — STS
Thoroughgoing — ARRANT
Those against — ANTIS
Those Frenchmen — ILS
Those halls of ivy — ACADEME
Those in favor — YEAS
Those in power — INS
Those making reparation — ATONERS
Those making sacrifices — OFFERERS
Those ninas — ESAS
Those not of the clergy — LAICS
Those on whom payment orders are issued — DRAWEES
Those opposed — ANTIS
Those owed — PAYEES
Those ready to graduate: Abbr. — SRS
Those two — BOTH
Those who evaluate manuscripts — READERS
Those who exploit — USERS
Those with endurance — STAYERS
Those with telephonitis? — CALLING BIRDS
Those, in Oviedo — ESOS
Those, in Tijuana — ESOS
Thou-shalt-nots — NONOS
Though, to Tacitus — ETSI
Thought — BELIEF, IDEA, OPINED
Thought, in Toulon — IDEE
Thought, to Pascal — PENSES
Thought: Comb. form — IDEO
Thought: Prefix — IDEO
Thoughtful — ATTENTIVE, KIND, PENSIVE
Thousand: Comb. form — KILO
Thraldom — SLAVERY
Thrall — ESNE, SLAVE
Thrall of puzzledom — ESNE
Thralls and helots — SERFS
Thrash — BASTE, DRUB, LARRUP, TAN
Thrashed — CANED, TANNED
Thrashes — TANS
Thread — STRING
Thread a needle — REEVE
Thread holder — SPOOL
Thread unit — SPOOL
Thread: Comb. form — NEME
Thread: Prefix — NEMAT
Threadbare — SEEDY, WORN
Threadlike — FILAR, FILOSE
Threads — DUDS, FIBERS, TOGS
Threat — MENACE
Threaten — IMPEND
Threaten, in a way — MAKE A FIST
Threatened feeling — PARANOIA
Threatening — DIRE
Threatening alternative — OR ELSE
Threatening situation — SCARE
Three _____ Island — MILE
Three _____ match — ON A
Three bagger — TRIPLE
Three bases — TRIPLE
Three days till T.G.I.F. — TUE
Three feet, e.g. — LENGTH
Three games of bridge — RUBBER

Three handed card game — SKAT
Three legged — TRIPODAL
Three legged stand — TRIVET
Three minus twice — ONCE
Three piece outfit — SUIT
Three pronged spear — TRIDENT
Three ring setting — BIG TOP
Three scruples — DRAM
Three sheets to the wind — TANKED, TIGHT
Three spot — TREY
Three steps and a shuffle — CHA CHA
Three times a day, in Rx's — TID
Three to Luigi — TRE
Three toed sloths — AIS
Three tsps. — TBS
Three wheeled cabs in the Far East — TRISHA
Three wise men — MAGI
Three, at the Trevi — TRE
Three, for Ms. Loren — TRE
Three, in a way — DREI
Three, in Dresden — DREI
Three, in Madrid — TRES
Three, in Munich — DREI
Three, in Toledo — TRES
Three, in Torino — TRE
Three, in Venice — TRE
Three, Roman style — III
Three, to a couple — CROWD
Three, to a Teuton — DREI
Three, to Fritz — DREI
Three, to Pavarotti — TRE
Three-base hit — TRIPLE
Three-card game — MONTE
Three-digit starter for a dialer — AREA CODE
Three-handed card game — SKAT
Three-horse shay — TROIKA
Three-piece suits items — VESTS
Three-spotted card — TREY
Three-time singles champ at Wimbledon — CHRIS EVERT
Three-toed treeclimbers — SLOTHS
Three: Prefix — TRI
Threefold — TRINE, TRIPLE
Threesome — TRINE, TRIO
Threnody — DIRGE
Threshing instrument — FLAIL
Threshold — EDGE, SILL
Threw out of bed? — DEBUNKED
Threw with force — HOVE
Thrice the champ — ALI
Thrice: Prefix — TRIS
Thrift-shop transaction — RESALE
Thrifty — FRUGAL
Thrifty one — PENNY PINCHER
Thrill — ELATE, SEND
Thrill ride — LOOP THE LOOP
Thrills — ELATES
Thrip or cockchafer — INSECT
Thrips, e.g. — INSECT
Thrive — PROSPER
Thriving — LUSH
Throat growth — TONSIL
Throat of a bird — CRAW
Throat sounds — AHEMS
Throat specialist's request — SAY AH
Throat: Comb. form — DERO
Throb — ACHE, PULSATE
Throbbed — PULSED
Throe — SPASM
Throes — PANGS
Thrombi — CLOTS
Thrombus — CLOT
Throne claimants — PRETENDERS
Throne of Israel contender: I Kgs.16 — TIBNI
Throng — CROWD, HORDE, HOST, MOB, SWARM
Throttle — STRANGLE
Through — OVER, VIA
Through with effort — HEAVE
Through: Prefix — DIA
Through; for each — PER
Throughgoing — ALL OUT
Throw — CAST, HURL, PEG, TOSS
Throw a party — HOST
Throw a tantrum — RANT
Throw about — STREW
Throw away — DISCARD
Throw back — REPEL
Throw in the towel — QUIT
Throw mud — SMEAR
Throw off — DROP
Throw off the track — DERAIL
Throw out — EJECT, EXPEL
Throw out bait at the end of a fishing line — CAST
Throwing mud — SMEARING
Throws — CASTS
Throws out — EJECTS, EVICTS
Thrust — LUNGE, STAB, SHOVE
Thrust forward — OBTRUDE
Thrusting sword — ESTOC
Thug — GOON
Thumb one's nose at — MOCK
Thumb through — SKIM
Thumb-raising film critic — EBERT
Thumbnail sketch — BRIEF
Thumbs-up — YES
Thummim's biblical companion — URIM
Thump, in Scotland — SOSS
Thumped — SMOTE
Thundering — AROAR, CRASHING
Thunderous — AROAR
Thunderstruck — AWED
Thurible — CENSER
Thurify — CENSE
Thurman of baseball — MUNSON
Thurmond — STROM
Thurs. chaser — FRI
Thurs. follower — FRI
Thus — ERGO
Thus far — YET
Thus spake an optomistic meteorologist — CLEARLY
Thus spake Arthur Guinness — FOR THE RECORD
Thus spake Beverly Sills — ONLY WITH NOTES
Thus spake Cyrano — VERY NASALLY
Thus spake Edgar Bergen, with "in": — DOUBLE TALK
Thus spake Gray's herd — WITH LOW VOICES
Thus spake peace conferees — DISARMINGLY
Thus spake Thackeray's Becky — MOST SHARPLY
Thus spake the umpire — AT A HIGH PITCH
Thus spake Venus de Milo — OFFHANDEDLY
Thus, in a quote — SIC
Thus, in Toledo — ASI
Thus, to Titus — SIC
Thwack — SLAM
Thwart — IMPEDE, FOIL, SPIKE, STOP, STYMIE
Thyroid cartilage projection — ADAMS APPLE
Thyroid, i.e. — GLAND
Thyself — THOU
Tiant — LUIS
Tiara — CROWN
Tiber feeder — NERA
Tiber tributary — NERA
Tiberius tongue — LATIN
Tibet's capital — LHASA
Tibet's neighbor — NEPAL
Tibetan animal — MASTIFF
Tibetan antelope — SEROW
Tibetan bearers — SHERPAS
Tibetan beast — YAK
Tibetan beasts of burden — YAKS
Tibetan capital — LHASA
Tibetan gazelle — GOA
Tibetan guide — SHERPA
Tibetan holy man — LAMA
Tibetan leader — LAMA
Tibetan monk — LAMA
Tibetan priest — LAMA
Tibetan terrier, Lhasa _____ — APSO
Tibetan trailblazer — YETI

Tibeto-Burman people — NOSU
Tibia — SHIN
Tibia's locale — SHIN
Tic — SPASM
Tic- _____ -toe — TAC
Tic-toe center — TAC
Tic-toe connector — TAC
Tick — CREDIT
Tick off — RILE
Tick, e.g. — ACARID
Ticked off — HET UP, IRATE, RECITED, SORE
Ticker — HEART
Ticker _____ — TAPE
Ticker on Wall Street — TAPE
Ticket — DUCAT
Ticket agent's headache — NO-SHOW
Ticket assignment — SEAT
Ticket end — STUB
Ticket holder's guarantee — SEAT
Ticket order enc. — SASE
Ticket parts — STUBS
Ticket remainder — STUB
Ticket scalper, for short — SPEC
Tickets — CITES
Tickle — ITCH
Tickle pink — ELATE
Tickle the fancy — AMUSE
Ticks off — RILES
Tidal bore — EAGRE
Tidal flood — BORE, EAGRE
Tidal surge — RIP
Tidal wave — AIGRE, EAGRE
Tidbit for a horse — OAT
Tidbit for Dobbin — OAT
Tidbit for Hansel — OAT
Tidbit for horse — OAT
Tidbit for Toto — ORT
Tidbits — MORSELS
Tide — NEAP
Tide type — NEAP
Tidewater — STRAND
Tidings — NEWS
Tidy — NEAT, ORDERLY
Tidy sum — PILE
Tie — ASCOT, BIND, DRAW, RELATION, WINDSOR
Tie down — LASH
Tie down securely — LASH
Tie fabrics — FOULARDS
Tie for the races — ASCOT
Tie on — ATTACH
Tie on a boot — LACE
Tie tack — STUD
Tie the knot — WED
Tie the knot, on short notice — ELOPE
Tie the shoes over — RELACE
Tie together — SPLICE
Tie up — TRUSS
Tie up the boat — MOOR
Tie, as a certain knot — WED
Tie-breaking contest, e.g. — PLAYOFF
Tied — EVEN, EVEN STEVEN, EVENED, HELD, ROPED
Tied the knot — WED
Tied up — EVEN, TRUSSED
Tiegs or Ladd — CHERYL
Tiered centerpiece — EPERGNE
Tiered sleeping spots — BUNKBEDS
Tierney flick of '44 — LAURA
Tierney title role: 1944 — LAURA
Tierney-Webb movie, 1944 — LAURA
Tierra del Fuego native — ONA
Tierra del Fuego's land — ARGENTINA
Tierra firma — DARIEN
Tiers — RANKS, ROWS
Ties — CRAVATS, EVENS, EVENS UP, TWINES
Ties a quick knot — ELOPES
Ties the knot — WEDS
Ties the knot again — REWEDS
Ties up — EVENS
Ties up traffic — SNARLS
Ties up, as property — ENTAILS
Tiff — ROW, SPAT
Tiffin — LUNCH
Tiffin treats — TEACAKES
Tiger's locale — ASIA
Tigerish, in a way — STRIPED
Tigers and Cubs — NINES
Tigers' tracks — SPOORS
Tight-fisted — MISERLY, NARROW
Tight — FRUGAL, STINGY
Tight and defensive — ENDS
Tight curls — FRIZ
Tight shutter — CLAM
Tight situation — BIND
Tight spot — BIND, DILEMMA
Tight squeezes — BEARHUG
Tightened the shoelaces — RETIED
Tightens, as a drum — FRAPS
Tightly sealed — HERMETIC
Tightwad — PIKER
Tijuana Brass man — ALPERT
Tijuana dish — TACO
Tijuana good-bye — ADIOS
Tijuana shout — OLE
Tijuana tender — PESO
Tijuana tidbit — TACO
Tijuana tie — MEXICAN STANDOFF
Tijuana tomorrows — MANANAS
Tijuana treat — TACO
Til — SESAME
Tile — DRAIN
Tile used in a game — DOMINO
Till — PLOW
Till now — AS YET
Till the soil — PLOW
Tilled the soil — HOED
Tilt — CAREEN, HEEL, INCLINE, JOUST, LEAN
Tilt, slant — LIST
Tilted — ASLOPE, LEANED, SLANTED
Tilting — ALIST, ALOP, ASLANT
Tilting board — SEESAW
Tilting weapons — LANCES
Tim and Victoria — HOLTS
Tim McCoy's horse — PAL
Tim of the Angels — FOLI
Timber — WOOD
Timber tree — ASH
Timber tree of Central America — EREDO
Timber trees — ASHES
Timber trees of the south — GEORGIA PINES
Timber unit — TON
Timber wolf — LOBO
Timberlane of fiction — CASS
Time — ERA, SPAN
Time _____ — LAG
Time _____ again — AND
Time _____ half — AND A
Time and again — AFTEN
Time co-founder — HADDEN
Time division — EON
Time follower — SLOT, TIDE
Time for Alice, Allegra & Edith — CHILDRENS HOUR
Time for malt beverages: Abbr. — OCT
Time in D.C. — EST
Time in NYC — EST
Time in Wyo. — MST
Time long past — YORE
Time Machine author — WELLS
Time of day — NOON, TEN TO ONE
Time of fasting — LENT
Time of one's life — BALL
Time of your life — CHILDHOOD
Time off — LEAVE
Time or figure preceder — FATHER
Time out — BREATHER
Time past — YORE
Time period — AGE, DECADE, EON, EPOCH, ERA
Time period — HOUR, TERM, YEAR
Time piece? — ERA, GRANDFATHER CLOCK
Time sectors — ERAS
Time segs. — HRS
Time served — TERM
Time slots — ERAS

Time sound — TICK TOCK
Time span — YEAR
Time to do the laundry — WASHDAY
Time to eat, Mr. Ruth! — CHOW BAMBINO
Time yet to come — FUTURE
Time zone abbr. — EST, PST
Time zone letters — CST, EDT
Time's companion — TIDE
Time-saver — TOOL
Time: Abbr. — MIN
Time: Comb. form — CHRON
Timekeeper — METRONOME
Timeless — ETERNAL
Timeless beauty — AGELESS
Timely — EARLY, PREMATURE, TIDY
Timely prod? — MOMENT OF THE SPUR
Timely ultimatum — NOW OR NEVER
Timepiece — CLOCK, DIAL, WATCH, WRISTWATCH
Timepiece features — MINUTE HANDS
Timer — SUNDIAL
Timer button — RESET
Times — MULTIPLY
Times for wages — PAYDAYS
Times gone by — PASTS
Times poetic beginning — OFT
Times Sq. sign — SRO
Times to remember — ERAS
Timesaving route — SHORT-CUT
Timetable abbr. — ERR
Timetable, briefly — SKED
Timetable, for short — SKED
Timid — UNHEROIC
Timid person — CREAM PUFF
Timon and Nestor — GRECIANS
Timorous — SCARED
Timothy — GRASS
Timothy and family — LEARYS
Tin can — DESTROYER
Tin horn — BRAGGART
Tin Lizzie — CRATE
Tin men? — SOLDIERS
Tin Pan _____ — ALLEY
Tin Pan Alley acronym — ASCAP
Tin Pan Alley name — ROGERS
Tin Pan Alley org. — ASCAP
Tin Pan Alley regretter — OTIS
Tin Pan or bowling — ALLEY
Tin plate — BOX
Tin worker — TINKER
Tine — PRONG
Tinge — CAST
Tinhorn's game — POKER
Tinker in "A Midsummer-Night's Dream" — SNOUT
Tinker's target — EVERS
Tins — CANS
Tint — COLOR, SHADE
Tinted — DYED
Tintinnabular sound — DONG
Tintinnabulate — RING
Tiny — MINUTE, WEE, WEENSY
Tiny _____ — TIM
Tiny amount — DAB, IOTA, TAD
Tiny arachnid — MITE
Tiny bit — ATOM, IOTA
Tiny blossom — FLORET
Tiny bodies that aid coagulation — PLATELETS
Tiny chorine — PONY
Tiny colonizers — ANTS
Tiny creature — MITE
Tiny farmers — ANTS
Tiny Greek island — DELOS
Tiny margin — HAIR
Tiny morsels — BITS
Tiny object — MITE
Tiny one — MITE
Tiny openings — STOMATA
Tiny particle — ATOM
Tiny space — AREOLE
Tiny spot — SPECK
Tiny spots — FLECKS
Tiny thing — MOTE
Tiny Tim's verb — BLESS
Tiny, in Aberdeen — SMA
Tiny, in Troon — SMA
Tiny, to a Glaswegian — SMA
Tip — APEX, CAREEN, END, LEAD, POINTER, STEER
Tip givers at the Big A — TOUTERS
Tip over — UPSET
Tip the derby — UNHAT
Tip: Comb. form — ACRO
Tipped — ON END
Tipped a topper — DOFFED
Tipped off — CLUED
Tipper Gore, _____ Aitcheson — NEE
Tippler — BIBBER, TOPPER
Tipplers — SOTS
Tipples — NIPS, SWIGS
Tippy boat — CANOE
Tips — CANTS, SLANTS, ENDS
Tips off — WARNS
Tipster — TOUT
Tipsy — SAUCED
Tiptop — APEX
Tirade — HARANGUE, INVECTIVE, REPRIMAND
Tirades — DIATRIBES, JEREMIADS
Tire-gauge reading — PSI
Tire — SPARE
Tire feature — BEAD, TREAD
Tire imprint — TREAD
Tire out — WEARY
Tire type — RADIAL
Tired man, in Le Mans — DUC
Tired of — FED UP
Tired of it all — JADED
Tired's companion — SICK
Tired, in poesy — AWEARY
Tired-looking — DRAWN
Tireless vehicle — SLED
Tires — FAGS, IRKS
Tiresome ones — BOORS
Tiresome person — BORE
Tiresome person grew old — PILLAGED
Tiresome speeches — SCREEDS
Tiresome-sounding animal — BOAR
Tisane — TEA
Tissue — SHEER, TELA
Tissue exam — BIOPSY
Tissue layer — TELA
Tissue: Comb. form — HISTO
Tit for tat — QUID PRO QUO
Titan — CRONUS
Titan in lexicography — WEBSTER
Titan of Phobos — MOON
Titan who fathered Prometheus — IAPETUS
Titania's spouse — OBERON
Titania, for one — FAIRY
Titanic — SHIP
Titanium dioxide — ANATASE
Titanium dioxide mineral — ANATASE
Tithe — TENTH
Titi or sapota — TREE
Titicaca, for one — LAKE
Titillates — AMUSES
Title — EARL, JOT, NAME, SIR
Title Christie held — DAME
Title Columbus held — ADMIRAL
Title created by James I — BARONET
Title Drake held — SIR
Title for a Benedictine — DOM
Title for a gov. or amb. — EXC
Title for a Romanov — TSAR
Title for Alec Guinness — SIR
Title for Cécilie: Abbr. — STE
Title for Dracula? — BLOOD COUNT
Title for Eliz. II — HSM
Title for Eve? — FIRST LADY
Title for G.H.W.B. — CIC
Title for Gielgud — SIR
Title for Jeanne — SAINTE
Title for Joan Sutherland — DAME
Title for John Gielgud — SIR
Title for Macbeth — THANE
Title for Margot Fonteyn — DAME
Title for Mother? — WOMAN OF THE YEAR

Title for mujer or madre — SRA
Title for Olivier — LORD
Title for one of the Perons — SENORA
Title for Paul Kruger — OOM
Title for Pompadour — MADAME
Title for Sellers' Clouseau: Abbr. — INSP
Title for Shaw's Barbara — MAJOR
Title for some madrileñas — SENORA
Title for Tweed — BOSS
Title given to Olivier — LORD
Title holder — CHAMPION
Title in India — RAJAH
Title in old India — SAHIB
Title in the Near East — PASHA
Title in Trabzon — AGA
Title in Turkey — EMIR
Title last held by Nicholas — TSAR
Title Liszt held — ABBE
Title Mac held — SCAP
Title Macbeth held — THANE
Title of respect — SAHIB, SIR
Title Pinero had — SIR
Title, for short — MLLE
Title, in Kuwait — EMIR
Title, in Tours — DUC
Titled — CAPTIONED
Titled nobleman — LORD
Titles of respect in India — SRIS
Tito — BROZ
Tito's real name — BROZ
Titter — TEE HEE
Tittle — IOTA
Tittles — JOTS
Titus, the conspirator — OATES
Tizzy — SNIT, STEW, TWITTER
TLC dispensers — RNS
TLC giver — NURSE
TLC providers — RNS
TNT mixture — AMATOL
To-do — BROUHAHA, ROW, STIR
To _____ (exactly) — A TEE
To _____ (his own) — EACH
To _____ (ideal) — A TEE
To _____ (it may concern) — WHOM
To _____ (just so) — A TEE
To _____ (perfectly) — A TEE
To _____ (precisely) — A TEE
To a degree — IN SO FAR, KIND OF, PARTLY
To a moderate degree, in a way — SORTA
To a position upon — ONTO
To acquire greater status — ACCRUE
To act in harmony — CONFORM
To an extent — IN SO FAR
To and _____ — FRO
To and fro — DEBATE
To assert dogmatically — LAY DOWN
To be alive — EXIST
To be born, in Brest — NAITRE
To be done — CHORE
To be paid — DUE
To be silent: Lat. — TACERE
To be sure — INDEED
To be, in Aix — ETRE
To be, in Blois — ETRE
To be, in Boulogne — ETRE
To be, in Madrid — ESTAR
To be, in Paris — ETRE
To be, to Bernadette — ETRE
To be, to Caesar — ESSE
To be, to Virgil — ESSE
To be: Fr. — ETRE
To be: Lat. — ESSE
To be: Sp. — SER
To begin with — FOR STARTERS
To believe, in Bretagne — CROIRE
To bend: Fr. — PLIER
To boot — AS WELL
To bring about — EFFECT
To crush by beating — MASH
To date — SO FAR
To deposit — LAY
To do — COMMOTION, HASSLE
To drink, in Dijon — BOIRE
To execute — EFFECT
To get by begging — CADGE
To go, in Paris — ALLER
To go: Fr. — ALLER
To great lengths — FAR AND WIDE
To have, in LeHavre — AVOIR
To have, in Paris — AVOIR
To influence — AFFECT
To irritate — RANKLE
To join, to Jeanne — UNIR
To jump incorrectly in ballet — HEAVE
To laugh, in Evian — RIRE
To laugh, in Nice — RIRE
To live, to Livy — ESSE
To love, in Brest — AIMER
To love, in Paris — AIMER
To love, Spanish style — AMAR
To me: Fr. — AMOI
To move — STIR
To no purpose — IN VAIN
To one side — ASIDE
To pieces — APART
To place in order — RANK
To play, Italian style — GIOCARE
To rob with violence — RAMP
To say nothing of — LET ALONE
To shelter — LEEWARD
To speak: Sp. — HABLAR
To stir or excite, old style — GOG
To subdue in chess — MATE
To such extent — IN SO FAR
To the _____ (fully) — HILT
To the _____ degree — NTH
To the contrary — BUT
To the left — APORT
To the limit — UTMOST
To the point — AD REM, APT, COGENT, CONCISE
To the point, in law — AD REM
To the point: Lat. — AD REM
To the rear — ABAFT, ASTERN
To the right — GEE
To the sheltered side — ALEE
To the side — APART
To them, stones have souls — ANIMISTS
To think, of yore — TROW
To this place — HERE
To throw with force — HURL
To trifle with — PLAY
To twist or run into knots — KINK
To use, to Nero — UTOR
To venture, in Versailles — OSER
To what extent — WHATSOEVER
To what place — WHITHER
To wit — NAMELY
To work against — OPPOSE
To write in ciphers: It. — CIFRARE
To you, to Alain — ATOI
To's companion — FRO
To's opposite — FRO
To's partner — FRO
To, to Burns — TAE
Toady — FAWN
Toast start — HERES
Toast topper — OLEO
Toast topping — ORANGE MARMALADE
Toast, Scandinavian style — SKOAL
Toasted — DRANK TO
Toastmaster — EMCEE
Toastmasters, for short — MCS
Tobacco pipe — BRIAR
Tobacco plug — QUID
Tobago's neighbor — TRINIDAD
Toboggans — SLEDS
Toby — MUG
Toby's cousin — STEINS
Tocsin — ALARM
Tocsins — ALERTS
Today — NOW, NOWADAYS
Today, in Rome — OGGI
Todd and Ritter of films — THELMAS
Toddle — STROLL
Toddler — TOT

Toddlers' perches — LAPS
Toe _____ (conform) — THE LINE
Toe the line — OBEY
Toe troubler — CORN
Toe woe — GOUT
Toe, e.g. — DIGIT
Toe: Scot. — TAE
Toes the mark — OBEYS
Toff — GENT
Toga — GARB
Toga wearer — ROMAN
Together — COUPLED, EN MASSE, JOINTLY
Together again — REUNITED
Together musically — A DUE
Together with — AND
Together with that — TOO
Together with: Prefix — SYN
Together, at the Met — A DUE
Together: Mus. — A DUE
Togetherness — UNITY
Togged for graduation — ROBED
Toggery — APPAREL
Togo's neighbor — GHANA
Togs — DUDS
Toil — LABOR, SLAVE, SLOG
Toile — FABRIC
Toiled mightily — LABORED
Toiler of long ago — ESNE
Toiler of yore — ESNE
Toiletries case — ETUI
Toiletries case: var. — ETWEE
Toils — NETS
Token — SIGN, SLUG
Token of friendship — KEEPSAKE
Token of respect — SALUTE
Token taker — SLOT
Token, sometimes — CAR FARE
Tokens of defiance — GAGES
Tokyo from Shanghai — ENE
Tokyo once — EDO
Tokyo potation — SAKE
Tokyo quaff — SAKE
Tokyo rock garden group? — JAPANESE BEETLES
Tokyo sash — OBI
Tokyo street — GINZA
Tokyo tipple — SAKE
Tokyo's Broadway — GINZA
Tokyo, formerly — EDO
Tokyo, long ago — EDO
Tokyo, once — EDO
Tolbooth — JAIL
Told a tale — SPUN
Told all — SANG
Told all to the fuzz — SANG
Told on: Slang — RATTED
Told tall tales — LIED
Toledo Mrs. — SRA
Toledo toast — SALUD
Toledo towers — TORRES
Toledo's lake — ERIE
Toledo, in Spain — CIUDAD
Tolerably — SOSO
Tolerance — LEEWAY
Tolerant — BROAD MINDED
Tolerate — ABIDE, ALLOW, BROOK, STAND
Tolerated — STOOD
Tolerates — ABIDES, BEARS
Tolkien creature — ENT
Tolkien forest denizen — ENT
Tolkien tree — ENT
Tolkien tree creatures — ENTS
Tolkien tree giants — ENTS
Tolkien tree warriors — ENTS
Tolkien villain — ORC
Tolkien's Fangorn et al. — ENTS
Tolkien's tree — ENT
Tolkien's tree people — ENTS
Tolkien's tree shepherds — ENTS
Toll — SLAVE
Tolled — RANG
Tolstoi, et al. — LEOS
Tolstoy — LEO
Tolstoy and Gorcey — LEOS
Tolstoy epic — WAR AND PEACE
Tolstoy title word — WAR
Tom cared about this voter? — DEMOCRAT
Tom Collins — DRINK
Tom Hanks film: 1984 — SPLASH
Tom Joad, e.g. — OKIE
Tom of "A Few Good Men" — CRUISE
Tom of the PGA — KITE
Tom Sawyer's aunt — POLLY
Tom Selleck role — MAGNUM PI
Tom Watson's org. — PGA
Tom's father — PIPER
Tom's friend in "Typee" — TOBY
Tom, Dick and Harry, e.g. — MEN, TRIO
Tom, Dick or Harry — MALE, NAME
Tom, the General — THUMB
Tomato blights — EDEMAS
Tomato disease — EDEMA
Tomatoes — LOVE APPLES
Tomboy — JO
Tommie of Gil Hodge's Mets — AGEE
Tommy and John Stewart's factory? — STEELEMILL
Tommy follower — ROT
Tommy guns? — STENS
Tommy of baseball — AGEE
Tommy of links fame — ARMOUR
Tommy's gun — STEN
Tommyrot — NONSENSE
Tomorrow, to Tiberius — CRAS
Ton components — LBS
Ton preceder — WON
Tonal inflection — CADENCE
Tone — NOTE
Tone or gram beginner — MONO
Toned down — SOFTENED
Tones down — TAMES
Tones on a scale — LAS
Tongue twister verb — SELLS
Toni, of ballet fame — LANDER
Tonic — ELIXIR
Tonic's companion — GIN
Tonic-producing plant — ALOE
Tonsorial service — SINGE
Tonsorial summons — NEXT
Tonsorial tool — COMB
Tonsorial worry area — HAIRLINE
Tonto's horse — SCOUT
Tonto's mount — SCOUT
Tony _____, Sinatra role — ROME
Tony La _____: BB mgr. — RUSSA
Tony of A.L. fame — OLIVA
Tony of the "Twins" — OLIVA
Tony Pena's glove — MITT
Tony's cousin — OBIE
Tony's daughter — JAMIE LEE CURTIS
Tony's pet, in "Baretta" — COCKATOO
Tony's relative — OBIE
Tony-winner Gregory — HINES
Tony-winner Tammy — GRIMES
Tony-winning choreographer — KIDD
Too — ALSO, AS WELL, OVERLY
Too abstruse — OVER ONES HEAD
Too bad! — ALAS
Too big — OVERLARGE
Too fervent — OVEREAGER
Too many cooks — BROTH SPOILERS
Too much, for Therese — TROP
Too often told — OLD
Too sweet — CLOYING
Toodle-oo — TATA
Took a break — RESTED
Took a chair — SAT
Took a chance — BET, DARED, GAMBLED, RISKED
Took a chance — SKATED ON THIN ICE
Took a Concorde — FLEW
Took a dim view — SCOWLED
Took a gamble — DARED
Took a licking and left — STAMPED OUT
Took a load off — SAT
Took a match to — LIT
Took a new survey — REPOLLED
Took a plane — FLEW

Took a rest — RECESSED
Took a siesta — RESTED
Took a whiff — SMELLED
Took an excessive share — HOGGED
Took an oath — SWORE
Took apart — UNDID
Took by stealth — BAGGED
Took care of — MINDED, SAW TO
Took charge — BOSS
Took command — LED
Took five — RESTED
Took flight — RAN
Took for granted — ASSUMED
Took in a scam — STUNG
Took leave — WENT
Took notice — SAT UP
Took off — BOLTED, DEPARTED, WENT
Took off like a rabbit — HARED
Took on — ADOPTED, ASSUMED, STOOD UP TO
Took out — DELED
Took part in — SHARED
Took part in a langlauf — SKIED
Took part in a relay — RAN
Took testimony — HEARD
Took the bait — BIT, BIT AT
Took the blue ribbon — WON
Took the bus — RODE
Took the challenge — DARED
Took the exam over — RESAT
Took the helm — PILOTED
Took the tube at Waikiki — SURFED
Took the waters — BATHED
Took to court — SUED
Took to the cleaners — FLEECED
Took turns, British style — SPELT
Took umbrage — RESENTED
Tool box — CHEST
Tool box item — AWL, PLIERS
Tool chest item — SCREW
Tool for a pair — TWO HAND SAW
Tool for Archimedes — LEVER
Tool for Bunyan — AXE
Tool for strawberries — HULLER
Tool or insect — BORER
Tool part connecting blade with handle — TANG
Tool used to bend wire — PLIERS
Tool with jaws — VISE
Toolbox item — NAIL, PLIERS
Toolchest item — BRAD
Tools for preparing potatoes — PEELERS
Tools set — KIT
Toolshed item — RAKE
Toot — BEEP
Toot the horn — BEEP
Tooters — HORNS
Tooth — CANINE, FANG, MOLAR
Tooth decay — CAVITIES
Tooth doctor — DENTIST
Tooth filling — INLAY
Tooth or dog — CANINE
Tooth problem — CARIES
Tooth prominence — CUSP
Tooth repair — FILLING, INLAY
Tooth specialists' gp — NDA
Tooth surface — MENSA
Tooth tissue — GUM
Tooth: Comb. form — DENTI, ODONT
Tooth: Prefix — DENTO
Toothed — SERRATED
Toothed bar — RATCH
Toothed tools — SAWS
Toothed wheels — GEARS
Toothed: Comb. form — ODON
Toothless — EDENTATE
Toothless, in Calais — EDENTE
Toothsome — TASTY
Toots — SPREES
Top — ACME, APEX, ZENITH
Top authority — TSAR
Top card — ACE
Top corporate mgrs. — CEOS
Top defense gp. — NSC
Top dog — BEST OF THE WURST, BOSS
Top dog, in bus. — CEO
Top drawer — A ONE
Top floors — ATTICS
Top grade — A ONE, CLASS A, ELITE
Top gun — ACE
Top Kick — SARGE
Top level business gps. — MGTS
Top limit — CAP
Top money horse of 1950 — NOOR
Top of a suit — ACE
Top of an Abbé — TETE
Top of the cake — ICING
Top of the line — BEST
Top of the world — EVEREST
Top pitcher — ACE
Top quality — PREMIUM
Top rating for a bond — AAA
Top rating, for some — TEN
Top ratings — A ONES
Top, for one — TOY
Top-drawer — ELITE
Top-flight fliers — ACES
Top-hat wearer — FRED ASTAIRE
Top-notch — A ONE
Top-notch performer — STANDOUT
Top-of-the-line — BEST
Top-rate — A ONE
Topee material — SOLA
Toper — SOT, SOUSE
Toper's malady — DTS
Topgallant — MAST
Topic — TEXT
Topic for biol. class — RNA
Topic of an Emerson essay — ART
Topical — LOCAL
Topical in philately — ANIMALS
Topics — THEMES
Topmast support — FID
Topmost — ELITE
Topped off a cake — ICED
Topper — HAT, LID
Topper, in bridge — ACE
Toppings for a Madrid burger — SPANISH ONIONS
Topple — UPEND
Tops — A ONE, ACES, LIDS, SUPERB
Tops 212 degrees — BOILS
Tops in cheeriness — GAYEST
Tops in orderliness — NEATEST
Tops: Abbr. — SUPERL
Topsoil — EARTH
Topsy's friend — EVA
Topsy-turvy — CHAOTIC
Toque blanche wearer — CHEF
Toque wearers — CHEFS
Torch — BURN
Torchiere — LAMP
Tore — DASHED, SPED
Tore down — RASED, RAZED
Tore into — HAD AT
Toren of "Casbah" — MARTA
Torero's milieu — BULLRING
Tormé — MEL
Tormé and Blanc — MELS
Torment — AGONY, GNAW, TEASE, TORTURE
Tormentor — SADIST
Torn or Taylor — RIP
Tornadoes — TWISTERS
Toronto gallery, for short — AGO
Toronto's prov. — ONT
Toronto's river — DON
Torpedo craft — EBOAT
Torpid — INERT
Torpidity — INERTIA
Torquemada's claim to fame — TORTURE
Torrefy — PARCH
Torsk — COD
Torso feature — HIP
Tortoise — TURTLE
Tortoise's competition — HARE
Tortoise's rival — HARE
Tortosa's river — EBRO
Tosca — FLORIA
Tosca's "Vissi d' ______" — ARTE
Toscanini — ARTURO
Toscanini, notably — MAESTRO
Toss — FLING, THROW

Toss a party — HOST
Toss about — BANDY
Toss back and forth — BANDY
Toss out — EVICT
Toss with effort — HEAVE
Tossed — THREW
Tossed about, as waves — VEXED
Tossed greens — SALAD
Tossed item — SALAD
Tossed off, as an exam — ACED
Tosspots — SOTS
Tot — DRAM
Tot up — ADD
Tot's "little piggy" — TOE
Tot's "stomach" — TUM TUM
Tot's need — BIB
Tot's spot — MEASLE
Tot's toe — PIGGY
Tot's transportation — STROLLER
Tot's tummy trouble — COLIC
Total — ADD, ADD UP, SUM
Total wipeout — MASSACRE
Totals — ADDS, SUMS
Totals: Abbr. — AMTS
Tote — LUG
Tote board info — ODDS
Tote board numbers — ODDS
Tote laboriously — SCHLEP
Toted — CARRIED
Totem — ICON
Totipalmate birds — PELICANS
Tots — ADDS
Tots transports — TRIKES
Totted up — ADDED
Totter — REEL
Toucan's pride — BEAK
Touch — ABUT
Touch a base runner — TAG OUT
Touch clumsily — PAW
Touch down — LAND
Touch gently — CARESS
Touch ground — LAND
Touch lightly — BRUSH, DAB
Touch lovingly — CARESS
Touch of color — TINT
Touch off — BEGIN
Touch on — ABUT
Touch or taste — SENSE
Touch up — ENHANCE
Touch upon — ABUT
Touch-and-go — HASTY
Touchdown — LANDING
Touched — CONTACTED, FELT
Touched down — ALIT
Touched ground — ALIT
Touched lightly — PATTED
Touches gingerly — DABS AT
Touches upon — ABUTS
Touching — UPON
Touchstone — TEST
Touchy — CROSS, TESTY
Tough — DURABLE, FIRM, HARD, HARD BITTEN
Tough actor — MR T
Tough and cohesive — TENACIOUS
Tough bast fiber — HEMP
Tough cloth — DENIM
Tough fabric — DENIM
Tough guy — BRUISER
Tough luck — DISTRESS
Tough query — POSER
Tough question — POSER
Tough spinners — HARD TOPS
Tough trip — TREK
Tough wood — ASH
Tough, elastic wood — ASH
Toughen — ANNEAL, INURE
Toughens — STEELS
Toulouse-Lautrec painting locale — CABARET
Toupee — PERIWIG
Tour — RIDE, TRAVEL
Tour de force — STUNT
Tour golfers — PROS
Tour of duty — STINT
Tour starter — GRAND
Tourist attraction — RUIN
Tourist spots — INNS, SIGHTS
Tourist stopover — INN
Tourist transport — BUS
Tourist vessel — CRUISE SHIP
Tourist's aid — MAP
Tourist's help — MAP
Tourist's interest — SIGHTS
Tourists — FARERS
Tourn. won five times by J. Nicklaus — PGA
Tournament advance, of a kind — BYE
Tournament favorites — SEEDS
Tournament of a sort — OPEN
Tours of duty — SHIFTS
Tours tooter? — FRENCH HORN
Tours' river — LOIRE
Touse or towse — ADO
Touses or towses — ADOS
Tout — TOOT
Tout le _____ — MONDE
Tout le _____ (everyone) — MONDE
Tout's subject — WAGER
Tow colored — BLOND
Toward shelter — ALEE
Toward ship's stern — ABAFT
Toward the center — INTO, INWARDS
Toward the mouth — ORAD
Toward the stern — AFT
Towel — NAPKIN
Towel salesgirl? — TERRY CLOTH
Towel sign — HIS
Towel word — HERS, HIS
Toweled — WIPED
Toweling — TERRY
Tower — REAR, SOAR
Tower above — EXCEED
Tower city of yore — BABEL
Tower for an escapist — IVORY
Tower name — SEARS
Tower near the Seine — EIFFEL
Tower of Bombay — MINAR
Tower of India — MINAR
Tower of London warders — BEEFEATERS
Tower town — PISA
Tower used in air races — PYLON
Towering — LOFTY, TALL
Towers over — DWARFS
Towing rope — HAWSER
Town crier — GOSSIP
Town ENE of Lucknow, India — GONDA
Town in central Mozambique — SENA
Town in E Mexico — APAM
Town in E Sardinia — IERZU
Town in Fairfax County, Va. — LORTON
Town in Gelderland — EDE
Town in Greenland — ETAH
Town in Iraq — AMA
Town in Mass. — AYER
Town in Mozambique — SENA
Town in N India — MANDI
Town in N.J. or Cal. — LODI
Town in Nigeria — KANO
Town in Norway — NES
Town in Shakespeare title — VERONA
Town near Ancona, Italy — IESI
Town near Des Moines — ADEL
Town near Liege — SPA
Town near Manchester, N.H. — DERRY
Town near Omaha Beach — ST LO
Town near Padua — ESTE
Town near Reagan's ranch — OJAI
Town near Sacramento — IONE
Town near Steubenville, Ohio — ADENA
Town near Windsor Castle — ETON
Town NNW of Baghdad — SAMARRA
Town of the Big Red — ITHACA
Town on Buzzards Bay — ONSET
Town on Cape Cod — TRURO
Town on Philadelphia's main line — PAOLI
Town on the Thames — ETON
Town on the Vire River — ST LO
Town or county in Ontario — DUNDAS

Town or village — PLACE
Town S of Oviedo, Spain — LENA
Town S.E. of Brussels — YVOIR
Town south of Albuquerque — BELEN
Town SW of Padua — ESTE
Town W of Zurich — AARAU
Town west of Gauguin's birthplace — ANET
Town WSW of Caen — ST LO
Towns in Ark. and Pa. — ENOLAS
Towns in Conn. and Md. — EASTONS
Townshend _____: 1767 — ACTS
Toxic — POISONOUS
Toxic substance in a snake's fluid — VENOM
Toxophilite's forte — ARCHERY
Toy for baby — RATTLE
Toy or weirdo — YO YO
Toy shop purchase — YO YO
Toy-pistol ammo — CAP
Toys to Timothy? — BOTTOM STOPS
Tra _____ — LALA
Tra follower — LALA
Trabea — TOGA
Trace — SCINTILLA, TINGE
Traces — HINTS, REMNANTS
Trachea — DUCT
Track — OVAL
Track action — WAGER
Track athelete — MILER, SPRINTER
Track branch — SPUR
Track circuits — LAPS
Track devotees — BETTORS
Track down — FIND
Track employee — STARTER
Track entrant — RACER
Track event — DASH, MEET, RACE
Track figure — BETTOR, TOUT
Track meet entrant — SPRINTER
Track meet event — DASH, HUNDRED YARD DASH
Track of a ship — WAKE
Track of the pack — SPOOR
Track of waves, left by a ship — WAKE
Track official — HANDICAPPER
Track pace — TROT
Track shape — OVAL
Track sustaining military tank — TREAD
Track tipster — TOUT
Track trial — HEAT
Track word — ODDS
Track workers — STABLEMEN
Tracked, like a hound — SCENTED
Trackman — ATHLETE
Tracks by a canal — TOWPATHS
Tract — AREA, EXPANSE, RANGE, STRETCH, ZONE
Tract of land — PATCH
Tract of wasteland — HEATH
Tractable — TAMR
Traction device — CLEAT
Tractor adjunct — DISC, PLOW, TRAILERS
Tractor-trailers — RIGS
Tracts of land — PARCELS
Tracy and Hepburn, quite often — COSTARS
Tracy to Beatty — ROLE
Tracy's lady — TESS
Tracy's Trueheart — TESS
Trade — BARTER, SWAP
Trade center — MART
Trade mark — LABEL
Trade mark, for short — LOGO
Traded with — DEALT
Trademark — LOGO
Trademark for a type of acoustic guitar — DOBRO
Trademark, for short — LOGO
Trader — BUYER, PLIER
Trades — DEALS
Trades man, e.g. — PLYER
Trading area — MART
Trading center — MART
Trading place: Abbr. — MKT
Tradition — CUSTOM, USAGE
Tradition at Trevi — WISH
Tradition or surgeon — ORAL
Traditional — DAILY
Traditional customs — MORES
Traditional dessert — PLUM PUDDING
Traditional knowledge — LORE
Traditional newlywed — JUNE BRIDE
Traditional story — LEGEND
Traduce — REVILE
Trafalgar or Washington — SQUARE
Traffic — TRADE
Traffic circles in New England — ROTARIES
Traffic nightmare — GRIDLOCK
Traffic no-no's — U TURNS
Traffic problem — SNARL
Traffic sign — SLOW, STOP, YIELD
Traffic stopper — RED LIGHT, SIREN
Traffic ticket — TAG
Traffic tie-ups — JAMS
Traffic turns — LEFTS
Tragedy by Euripides — MEDEA
Tragi — EARLETS
Tragic epic — ILIAD
Trail — LAG, PATH, PUG, SCENT
Trail in the jungle — SPOOR
Trail marker — CAIRN
Trail of a wild animal — SPOOR
Trailblazer — PIONEER
Trailer — SEMI
Trailing — AREAR
Train — EDUCATE, SCHOOL
Train a tyro — BREAK IN
Train bearers — RAILS
Train components — CARS, BOXCARS
Train conductor's gift? — FANTASTIC RAILROAD TIE
Train for many N.Y. commuters — LIRR
Train sound — CHOO
Train stop — DEPOT
Train tracks — RAILS
Train trailer — CABOOSE
Train, in Spain — TREN
Train, to Jose — TREN
Trained in the ring — SPARRED
Trained sailors, for short — ABS
Trainer Dundee of boxing — ANGELO
Trainer's aid, often — ICE
Training drills — LAPS
Trainman — ENGINEER
Traitor — RENEGADE
Traject — CAST, TOSS
Trajectory — ARC
Tralee county — KERRY
Tralee's land — EIRE
Tram filler — ORE
Tram load — ORE
Trammel material — MESH
Trammel of a sort — LEASH
Tramp — BUM, DRIFTER, HOBO, SLOG, TRUDGE
Trample — STEP ON
Trample or tread — STEP ON
Trampled — TROD
Tramplers — TREADERS
Tramps — HOBOS
Trams — STREETCARS
Trance — SPELL, STUPOR
Trances — COMAS
Tranquility — PEACE, REPOSE
Tranquilize — BECALM, SOOTHE
Tranquilizes — SERENES
Trans-central chord — DIAMETER
Transaction — DEAL, SALE
Transactions — DEALINGS
Transactions of public business — AFFAIRS
Transcript — COPY
Transduce — CONVERT
Transfer — CEDE
Transfer document — DEED
Transfer property — SELL
Transfer, for short — DECAL
Transferable picture — DECAL

Transferred, as property — DEDEED
Transferred, as sovereignty, by death — DEMISED
Transfers — DECALS
Transfixed — PINNED
Transform — CHANGE, REMAKE
Transfuse — CHARGE, ENDUE, IMPREGNATE, PERMEATE
Transgress — ERR
Transgresses — BREAKS THE LAW, SINS
Transgression — SIN
Transient things — EPHEMERA
Transit patron — USER
Transit trails — RAILROAD TRACKS
Transitions — SEGUES
Translated into Ovid's tongue — LATINED
Translating device — CODER, DECODER
Translator's challenge — IDIOM
Transmission of graphics — PHOTO TELEGRAPHY
Transmit — CARRY, CONVEY, ISSUE, SEND
Transmit rotary motion — CRANK
Transmitted — SENT
Transp. to the Hamptons — LIRR
Transparent — LUCID, SHEER
Transparent curtain — SCRIM
Transplants of a kind — ALIENS
Transport — DELIGHT, TOTE
Transport for a London baby — PRAM
Transport for Bob — SLED
Transport for Heyerdahl — RAFT
Transport for Hiawatha — CANOE
Transport for Tarzan — LIANA
Transport for Tom Sawyer — RAFT
Transport for VIP — LIMO
Transport protectors? — FERRY GOD MOTHERS
Transport to Staten Island — FERRY
Transport: Var. — ENTHRAL
Transportation acronym — AMTRAK
Transportation charge — FARE
Transportation for short trips — HELICOPTERS
Transportation organization — AIRLINE
Transportation sharers — CAR POOLERS
Transportation to a coven — BROOMSTICK
Transported — SENT
Transports — SENDS, TOTES
Transude — OOZE, SEEP
Transuded — SEEPED
Trap — AMBUSH, DECOY, ENSNARE, NET, SNARE
Trap or drum — SNARE
Trap or prize — BOOBY
Trapdoor — PITFALL
Trapeze artists, e.g. — FLIERS
Trapp family saga — THE SOUND OF MUSIC
Trapped — SNARED, TREED
Trapper — SNARER
Trapper's collection — HIDES
Trapper's prize — PELT
Trapper's take — PELT
Trapper's trophy — PELT
Trappist cheese — OKA
Traps — SETUPS
Trapshooting sport — SKEET
Trash-cans-on Thames — DUSTBINS
Trash or thresh — FLAIL
Trattoria beverage — CAPPUCCINO
Trattoria brew — ESPRESSO
Trattoria food — PASTA
Trattoria offering — PASTA
Trattoria sauce — PESTO
Trattoria specialty — PASTA
Trattoria staple — FETTUCCINE, PASTA
Trattoria treat — PIZZA PIE
Trauma — HURT
Traumatize — HARM
Travail — LABOR
Trave — CROSSPIECE
Travel — GET AROUND, TOUR
Travel agency specialties — TOURS
Travel agent's org. — ASTA
Travel agent? — JOURNEYMEN
Travel bag — SATCHEL
Travel by car — MOTOR
Travel hazard — FOG
Travel money — FARE
Travel permit — VISA
Travel plan — ITINERARY
Travel systems: Abbr. — RRS
Travel to and from work — COMMUTE
Travel with — MINGLE
Traveled on Trigger — RODE
Traveler — FARER
Traveler to Oz — TOTO
Traveler's aid — MAP
Traveler's choice — RAILROAD
Traveler's helpers — ATLASES
Traveler's Midwest mecca — OHARE
Traveler's need — PASSPORT
Traveler's need at times — PASSPORT
Traveler's rests — INNS
Traveler's rider — LEE
Traveler's stopover — MOTEL
Traveler, at times — UNPACKER
Travelers — FARES
Travelers' rests — INNS
Travelers' stops — INNS
Traveling salesman — DRUMMERS
Traveling tinker — CAIRD
Traveling, as a knight — ERRANT
Travelled by air — FLEW
Traveller to Lee — HORSE
Travels by bus — RIDES
Travels swiftly — JETS
Travels, in a way — MOTORS
Travesty — FARCE
Travolta hit — SATURDAY NIGHT FEVER
Trawl — NET
Tray for a bank teller — CASH DRAWER
Tray type — ASH
Tread wearily — PLOD
Treads and risers — STAIRWAY
Treads the boards — ACTS
Treas. agcy. — IRS
Treasure — VALUE
Treasure _____ — TROVE
Treasure chaser — CHEST
Treasure follower — TROVE
Treasure or hope — CHEST
Treasure seeker of a sort — PEARL DIVER
Treasure State capital — HELENA
Treasurer's problem — DEBT
Treasures from ancient China — MING VASES
Treasury note — BOND
Treasury's Fort — KNOX
Treat for an Apso — BONE
Treat for Fido — ORT
Treat leftovers — REHEAT
Treat under glass — PHEASANT
Treat with contempt — SCORN
Treat's partner — TRICK
Treated — DOSED
Treated a charley horse — MASSAGED
Treated tire — RECAP
Treated with caustic — LYED
Treated with salt — BRINED
Treated wrongfully — HARMED
Treatise on trees — SILVA
Treatises — TRACTS
Treats — HANDLES
Treats for gourmets — PATES
Treats for kitty — CATNIPS
Treats for Rover — BONES
Treats for tots — LOLLYPOPS
Treats inadequately — SCANTS
Treats with CO2 — AERATES
Treats with disdain — SNUBS
Treaty — ALLIANCE, COVENANT, PACT

Treaty between nations — PACT
Treaty of _____: 1814 — GHENT
Treaty of a sort — ENTENTE
Treaty org. — NATO
Treaty site: 1925 — LOCARNO
Tree-lined passage — ALLEE
Tree — ASH, CORNER, ELM
Tree akin to the breadfruit — UPAS
Tree angle — AXIL
Tree dweller — APE
Tree frog — HYLA
Tree fruit — PINECONE
Tree house — NEST
Tree in an O'Neill title — ELM
Tree juice — SAP
Tree lined walk — ALAMEDA
Tree of C. America — EBO
Tree of life location — EDEN
Tree of the birch family — ALDER
Tree of the olive family — ASH
Tree of the rose family — SORB
Tree part — LIMB
Tree shrew — TANA
Tree trunk — BOLE
Tree yielding sweet sap — MAPLE
Tree-lined walk — ALLEE
Tree-of-life site — EDEN
Tree: Comb. form — DENDRI
Treeless plain — PAMPA, TUNDRA
Treeless plains — STEPPES
Treeless tracts — STEPPES
Trees — MAPLES, OAKS
Trees in an O'Neill title — ELMS
Trees of the pine family — FIRS
Trees or nuts — HAZELS
Trees with glossy leaves — MADRONAS
Treetop residence — NEST
Treetop sight — NEST
Trek power — OXEN
Trek to Mecca — HADJ
Trek vehicle — WAGON
Trekked — HIKED
Trellis pieces — LATHS
Trellis treatments — VINES
Tremble — QUAKE
Tremble anew — RESHAKE
Trembling trees — ASPENS
Trembly tree — ASPEN
Tremolo — TRILL
Trench in the W Pacific — MARIANA
Trenchant — ACUTE, BITTER, CAUSTIC, DULL, EDGED, KEEN
Trenchant wit — SATIRE
Trencherman — EATER
Trenches around Elsinore — MOATS
Trend — TIDE
Trendy — MOD
Trendy food — SUSHI
Trendy one — MOD
Trendy thing — FAD
Trenet's "La _____" — MER
Trenton's time — EST
Trepidation — FEAR
Tres _____ — BIEN
Trespasses — INFRINGES
Tress — CURL, LOCK
Tresses — CURLS, HAIRS
Trevanian's "The _____ Sanction" — LOO
Trevanian's "The Summer of _____" — KATYA
Trevi coins — LIRE
Trevi throw-in — LIRA
Trevino gadgets — TEES
Trial — ORDEAL, TEST
Trial effort — FLING
Trial TV program — PILOT
Trial witness, of a sort — DEPOSER
Trial's companion — ERROR
Trial's partner — ERROR
Trials — TESTINGS, TESTS
Trials, in the Old Testament — PLAGUES
Triangle — DELTA
Triangle sides, a la the Irish? — HYPATEN USES
Triangular inset — GORE
Triangular sail — JIB
Triangular shape — DELTA
Tribal emblem — TOTEM
Tribal symbol — TOTEM
Tribe near Hudson Bay — CREE
Tribe of Israel — ASHER
Tribe of the Niger Delta — IBO
Tribulations — WOES
Tribunal — BAR, FORUM
Tributary of the Danube — ENNS
Tributary of the Vistula — SAU
Tributary verses — ODES
Tribute — HOMAGE, TOAST
Trice — MOMENT, SPLIT SECOND
Trick — DUPE, FOOL, RUSE
Trick ending — ERY, STER
Trick victim, sometimes — APRIL FOOL
Trick's alternative — TREAT
Trickery — HANKY PANKY
Trickle — DRIP, SEEP
Trickle through — SEEP
Trickled — DROPPED, RAN, SEEPED
Trickles — SEEPS
Trickles out — LEAKS
Tricky drawback — CATCH
Triclinium meal — CENA
Tricolor hue — BLEU
Tricorn — HAT
Trident and Titan — MISSILES
Trident prongs — TINES
Tridents — SPEARS
Tried — PROVED, TESTED
Tried and true — FAITHFUL
Tried out — USED
Tried to equal or surpass — EMULATED
Tried's partner — TRUE
Tries anew — REHEARS
Tries out — TESTS
Tries to lose weight — DIETS
Trieste three — TRE
Trieste wine measure — ORNA
Trifle — DOIT, SOU, TRINKET, TOY
Trifle and strudel — DESSERTS
Trifled — TOYED
Trifler — TOYER
Trifles — TRIVIA
Trifling amount — SOU
Trifling sum — GROAT
Trig function — COSINE, SINE
Trig ratio — SINE
Trigger, e.g. — HORSE
Trigonometric function — COSINE, SINE
Trigonometric ratios — SINES
Trigonometric term — COSINE
Trikes cousin — TWO WHEELER
Trilbies — FEET
Trill — WARBLE
Trilling or Hampton — LIONEL
Trillion: Comb. form — TERA
Trim — CROP, LOP, PRUNE, SPRUCE
Trim a photo — CROP
Trim anew — RECLIP
Trim for state robes — ERMINE
Trimmed — EDGED
Trimmed with mink — FURRED
Trinculo or Yorick — JESTER
Trinidad combo — STEEL BAND
Trinity — TRIAD
Trinket — BAUBLE, GEWGAW
Trinkets: Var. — GEEGAWS
Trio from Oslo — AHA
Trio item, with blood and tears — SWEAT
Trio less one — DUO
Trio of trios — NONET
Trio plus five — OCTET
Trio, with Vishnu and Shiva — BRAHMA
Trip — MISSTEP
Trip merchant — TRAVEL AGENT
Trip taken for pleasure — JUNKET
Trip type — EGO
Triple Crown race — PREAKNESS
Triple Crown winner: 1977 — SEATTLE SLEW

Triple this for a wine — EST
Triplet — TRIN
Tripod — STAND
Tripoli ruler of old — DEY
Tripper — VOYAGER
Tripper-upper — SNAG
Trippet — CAM
Tripping tunes — LILTS
Trips — MISSTEPS, STUMBLES
Trips to the plate — AT BATS
Trips to the wardrobe? — CLOTHES ENCOUNTERS
Tripura or Orissa — STATE
Tristan's love — ISOLDE
Tristian da _____ Islands — CUNHA
Tristram Shandy's creator — STERNE
Trite — BANAL, CORNY, INSIPID, STALE
Triton — NEWT
Triton's daughter — PALLAS
Tritons — EFTS
Triumph — WIN
Triumphant cry — AHA
Triumphant exclamation — AHA
Triumphed — WON
Triumphed, board-wise — MATED
Triumphs for Tyson: Abbr. — KOS
Triumphs over — BEATS, DEFEATS
Triumverate — TROIKA
Trivial — INANE, SMALL
Trivial errors — LAPSES
Trod the boards — ACTED, SURF
Troilus or Cressida — ROLE
Trojan — ILIAN
Trojan city — ILION
Trojan hero — AJAX
Trojan hero: Var. — ENEAS
Trojan priest of legend — LAOCOON
Trojan prince killed by Achilles — HECTOR
Trojan tale — ILIAD
Trojan war epic — ILIAD
Trojan War hero — AJAX
Trojan War site — TROY
Trolley — TRAM
Trolley noise — CLANGS
Trolley sound — CLANG
Trolley terminals — CAR-BARNS
Trolley unit — CAR
Trollop — SLUT
Trolls — GNOMES
Trombone feature — SLIDE
Trombone, to a jazzman — TRAM
Trompe l' _____ — OEIL
Trondheim natives — NORSE
Trondheim toast — SKOAL
Troop assemblage — MUSTER
Trooper in Canada — RCMP
Troopers' trap — RADAR
Troops — ARMY
Troops that protect from behind — REAR GUARD
Trophy — CUP
Tropical American bird — ANI
Tropical American fruit — SWEETSOP
Tropical American palm — CHONTA
Tropical American tree — CACAO, SENNA
Tropical armadillo — TATOUAY
Tropical bird — TOUCAN
Tropical climber — LIANA
Tropical cuckoo — ANI
Tropical dog — ALCO
Tropical eel — MORAY
Tropical fruit — BANANA, DATE, MANGO, PAPAYA
Tropical grass — SUGARCANE
Tropical herb — CANNA
Tropical herbaceous plants — SESAMES
Tropical palm — ARECA
Tropical snake — BOA
Tropical storm — CYCLONE
Tropical timber tree — AMARILLO
Tropical tree — AKEE, APA, EBONY, LIME, PALM
Tropical tubers — TAROS
Tropical vine — LIANA
Tropical wildcat — EYRA
Trot — JOG, PONY
Trot or canter — GAIT
Trot or gallop — GAIT
Trotter — HORSE
Trotter's route — OVAL
Trotter's tooth — TUSH
Trouble — AIL, CARE, EFFORT, WOE
Trouble-making deity — ERIS
Troubled — UPSET
Troubled South African area — SOWETO
Troublemaker in Troy — PARIS
Troublemakers, cockney style — ELLERS
Troubles — ADOS, AILS, CARES, ILLS, PERTURBS
Troublesome — ONEROUS
Trounce — THRASH
Trounced, with "down" — MOWN
Troupe member — ACTOR
Troupial — ORIOLE
Trouser line — INSEAM
Trouser's part — LEG
Trousers — SLACKS
Trousers fold — PLEAT
Trousseau item — SLIP
Troy, N.Y. campus — RPI
Troy, N.Y. inst. — RPI
Troy, to Ajax — ILION
Troy, to Homer — ILION
Truant's game? — HOOKEY
Truck compartment — CAB
Truck half — SEMI
Truck part — AXLE
Truck-stop brew — JAVA
Truck-stop offering — HASH
Truck-stop sights — TRAILERS
Truckee city — RENO
Trucker's compartments — CABS
Trucker's rig — SEMI
Trucker's stop — DINER
Trucking rig — SEMI
Truckman's stop — DINER
Trudeau cartoon — DOONESBURY
Trudge — PLOD
Trudge through water — WADE
Trudges — SLOGS
True — ACTUAL, VALID
True _____? — OR FALSE
True grit — SAND
True to the cause — LOYAL
True's partner — TRIED
True, in Ayr — LEAL
True-blue — LOYAL
Trued up — ALINED
Truism — AXIOM
Truly — INDEED
Truman's birthplace — LAMAR
Trumpet blasts — TANTARRAS
Trumpet call — BLARE
Trumpet sound — BLARE
Trumpeter — SWAN
Trumpeter Al — HIRT
Trumpeter Al and family — HIRTS
Trumpeter and whistling — SWANS
Trumpeter from New Orleans — HIRT
Trumpeter Herb — ALPERT
Trumpeter Miles — DAVIS
Trumpeter perch — MADO
Trumpeter swan genus — OLOR
Trumpeter Wynton — MARSALIS
Trumpeter's accessory — MUTE
Trumpeters' needs — MUTES
Trumpets' cousins — CORONETS
Trumpets' rels. — CORS
Truncate — LOP
Trunk — CHEST, TORSO
Trunk item — JACK, SPARE TIRE
Trunk, to a sculptor — TORSO
Trunks — TORSOS
Truro sight — DUNES
Trust, with "on" — RELY
Trustee — AGENT

Trustful — RELIANT
Trusting — RELIANT
Trustworthy — SINCERE
Trustworthy one — OLD FAITHFUL
Truth — FACT, VERACITY
Try — ATTEMPT, ENDEAVOR, EFFORT
Try — SAMPLE, TEST
Try anew — REHEAR
Try for — AIM
Try for a ringer — TOSS
Try hard — EXERT
Try out — TEST
Try tenting — CAMP
Try to get along — FEND
Try to rip — TEAR
Trying experience — ORDEAL
Trying journey — TREK
Trying time — CRISIS
Tryon novel, with "The" — OTHER
Tryon's "The _____" — OTHER
Tryst — DATE, RENDEZVOUS
Trysted under a June moon, 1925 — SPOONED
Tsar — TITLE
Tsar's proclamation — UKASE
Tsars — AUTOCRATS
Tsk! — FIE
Tso-lin of Manchuria and family — CHANGS
TU-144's — SSTS
Tub plant — ALOE
Tuba or trumpet — INSTRUMENT
Tube lights — NEONS
Tubular weather vane — WINDSOCK
Tuck — FOLD
Tuck away — STOW
Tuck's associate — NIP
Tuck's pal — NIP
Tuck's partner — NIP
Tuck's title — FRIAR
Tucked in — ABED
Tucker's tag-along — BIB
Tuckered out — ALL IN
Tucson's time — MST
Tudor symbol — ROSE
Tuesday — WEEKDAY, WELD
Tuesday of NYC — WELD
Tuft — CREST
Tufted alga — SEABEARD
Tufty mass — FLOC
Tug's tow — SCOW
Tugs — PULLS
Tulip tree — POPLAR
Tully of Rome — CICERO
Tulsa's st. — OKLA
Tumblebug — SCARAB
Tumbler — ACROBAT, GLASS
Tumbles — SPILLS
Tumbles about — WELTERS
Tumbrel — CART
Tumescence — LUMP
Tumid — PUFFY
Tumuli — MOUNDS
Tumult — ADO, CHAOS, DIN, RIOT
Tumults — RIOTS, UPROARS
Tumultuous — HECTIC
Tun — CASK
Tuna kin — SKIPJACK
Tuna type — YELLOW FIN
Tunas — BONITAS
Tundra denizens — ELKS
Tundra dweller — SEBERIAN
Tundra hairdresser? — STYLING MOOSE
Tundra transport — SLED
Tune — AIR, DITTY, LILT
Tune for Pavarotti — ARIA
Tune for Pete Seeger — FOLK-SONG
Tuneful — ARIOSO
Tuneful Turner — TINA
Tunes — AIRS
Tunes — AIRS, SONGS
Tunes in — DIALS
Tunic of the eye — UVEA
Tunis ruler — BEY
Tunisian capital — TUNIS
Tunisian city (tain't photocopy) — SFAX
Tunisian port — SFAX
Tunisian rulers — DEYS
Tunisian titles — DEYS
Tunnel — SHAFT
Tunney and Kelly — GENES
Tupelo hero — ELVIS
Turaegs' region — SAHARA
Turbot's cousin — BRILL
Tureen accessory — LADLE
Tureen adjunct — LADLE
Tureen need — LADLE
Tureen server — LADLE
Tureen's companion — LADLE
Turf — GRASS, SOD
Turf, in general — SODGRASS
Turgenev heroine — ELENA
Turgenev relative — ELENA
Turgenev's birthplace — OREL
Turhan _____, 40's film actor — BEY
Turin, in Turin — TORINO
Turk Murphy's milieu — JAZZ
Turk. city — ADANA, EDIRNE
Turk. ruler — AGA
Turk. title — PASHA
Turkey-like bird of S.A. — CURASSOW
Turkey — FLOP
Turkey choice — LEG
Turkey dinner side dish — PEAS
Turkey's highest point — ARARAT
Turkey's neighbor — IRAN
Turkey's President: 1938-50 — INONU
Turkeys — FLOPS
Turkic people — TATARS
Turkish — OSMANLI
Turkish capital — ANKARA
Turkish chiefs — AGAS, AGHAS, BEYS
Turkish city — ADANA
Turkish city founded by the Romans — ADANA
Turkish city on the Seyhan — ADANA
Turkish coins — LIRAS
Turkish decree — IRADE
Turkish dignitary — PASHA
Turkish flag — ALAI
Turkish headwear — FEZZES
Turkish honorary title — PASHA
Turkish honorific — PASHA
Turkish hospice — IMARET
Turkish inn — IMARET
Turkish leader Kemal — ATATURK
Turkish liquor — RAKI
Turkish metropolis — ANKARA
Turkish money — LIRAS
Turkish money of old — ASPER
Turkish officer — PASHA
Turkish officials — AGAS
Turkish regiment — ALAI, ALAR
Turkish river — ARAS
Turkish royal court — DIVAN
Turkish statesman — INONU
Turkish title — AGA, PASHA
Turkish title of honor — AGHA
Turkish title of respect — EFFENDI
Turkish topper — FEZ
Turkish V.I.P. — EMIR
Turkish weight units — OKES
Turkmen turf — ASIA
Turkoman of Bukhara — ERSAR
Turku to a Swede — ABO
Turmeric — REA
Turmoil — STIR UP, UPROAR
Turn — BEND, CHANGE, CURVE, PIVOT, ROTATE
Turn — SWING, SWIVEL, TWIRL
Turn _____ ear — A DEAF
Turn _____ new leaf — OVER A
Turn adrift — UNMOOR
Turn around — ROTATE
Turn aside — AVERT, DETER, PARRY
Turn aside by advice — DISSUADE
Turn away — AVERT
Turn away from — ALIENATE
Turn back — REPEL, RESIST
Turn bad — SOUR
Turn down — DENY, FOLD
Turn inside out — INVERT, EVERT
Turn left — HAW
Turn of events — RESULT
Turn out — EVICT
Turn outward — EVERT

Turn outward, as feet — SPLAY
Turn over — REVERSE
Turn over a new leaf — AMEND
Turn pale — WHITEN
Turn right — GEE
Turn thumbs down — DENY
Turn up — UNEARTH
Turn up one's nose — SNEER
Turn up with a spade — DELVE
Turn's companion — TOSS
Turn's partner — TOSS
Turn, in Toledo — TANDA
Turn-around misfit? — ROUND PEG IN A SQUARE HOLE
Turncoat — RENEGADE, SCAB
Turndown — REFUSAL
Turned away — AVERTED
Turned into money — CASHED
Turned off — SHUT
Turned on an old car — CRANKED
Turned right — GEED
Turned stool pigeon — SANG
Turned up — RETROUSSE
Turned white — PALED
Turner — LANA
Turner and Cantrell — LANAS
Turner and Danson — TEDS
Turner and Louise — TINAS
Turner and Sinatra — TINAS
Turner memoirs — I TINA
Turner namesakes — LANAS
Turner of TV — TED
Turner or Cole — NAT
Turner or Koppel — TED
Turner or Louise — TINA
Turner's orig. — CIA
Turnery — LATHE
Turnery gear — LATHE
Turning machine — LATHE
Turning point — CRISIS
Turning point for a ballerina — TOE
Turning points — CRISES
Turning prefix — ROTO
Turnip, e.g. — ROOT
Turnip, for short — BAGA
Turnkey — WARDER
Turnkeys — JAILERS, KEEPERS
Turnover — TART
Turnpike — ROAD
Turnpike sign — EXIT, YIELD
Turns down — NOES
Turns outward — EVERTS
Turns right — GEES
Turns thumbs down — NIXES
Turow's law school book — ONE L
Turpentine component — PINENE
Turquoise hue — AQUA
Turret — MINARET
Turtle living in fresh water — TERRAPIN
Turtles' shells — CARAPACES
Tuscan commune — SIENA
Tuscan province — SIENA
Tuscany art city — SIENA
Tuscany city — PISA
Tuscany town — SIENA
Tush — BUTTOCKS
Tushingham and Moreno — RITAS
Tusk material — IVORY
Tusked whale — NARWAL
Tusker — BOAR
Tussis — COUGH
Tussle — SCRAP
Tut! — TSK
Tut's cousin — TSK
Tut, now — MUMMY
Tutelary god — LAR
Tutor — COACH, INFORM
Tutti-frutti — CONFECTION, SUNDAE
Tuttle of radio and TV — LURENE
Tutu — SKIRT
TV _____ cards — IDIOT
TV accolade — EMMY
TV actor Robert — ITO
TV actress Anderson — LONI
TV actress Garber — TERRI
TV actress Williams — CARA
TV adjunct — VCR, VHS
TV alien — ALF
TV and night club star — JOAN RIVERS
TV antenna device — ROTATOR
TV appendage — ANTENNA
TV awards — CLIOS
TV backdrop — OLEO
TV bee — MAYA
TV cartoon character — SMURF
TV choices — CHANNELS
TV clown — BOZO
TV comedian Louis and family — NYES
TV comic sings country? — TIM CONWAY TWITTY
TV commercial — SPOT
TV deletion — BLEEP
TV detective and family — LACEYS
TV diner owner — MEL
TV dragon — OLLIE
TV extraterrestrial — ALF
TV fare — SOAP
TV feature — NEWS
TV film critic — EBERT
TV Foxx — REDD
TV game show — PASSWORD
TV good guys, with "The" — A TEAM
TV Hit — MASH
TV host — REGIS
TV host Collins — GARY
TV host Convy — BERT
TV interruption — BULLETIN
TV letters — ABC
TV moderator Moore — GARRY
TV morning show — TODAY
TV network — NBC
TV network logo — TBS
TV network's concern — RATINGS
TV newsman — RATHER
TV newsman Pressman — GABE
TV offering — HBO
TV part — TELE
TV personality Alistair — COOKE
TV pioneer — BAIRD
TV police drama of 1967 — NYPD
TV predecessors: Abbr. — RDOS
TV producer Norman — LEAR
TV program recorder — VCR
TV reception problem — SNOW, TVI
TV review — REHASH, SURVEY
TV revuenue sources — ADS
TV role for Alvin Childress — AMOS
TV role for Kate Jackson — AMANDA
TV science series — NOVA
TV serials — SOAPS
TV series — CHINA BEACH
TV series of 1956-61 — YOU BET YOUR LIFE
TV series with John Neville — GRAND
TV Sheriff Andy Taylor's son — OPIE
TV show — SPECTACULAR
TV sleuth — CANNON
TV sleuth who blew his cover? — NAKED CITY DETECTIVE
TV sound signal — AUDIO
TV specialty — SOAP OPERA
TV spokesperson — NARRATOR
TV spoof — SOAP
TV spy film of 1980 — SHE
TV star Bob — NEWHART
TV star Daly — TYNE
TV street — SESAME
TV summer fare — RERUN
TV supervisor — PRODUCER
TV tabloid exposé headline? — IVE GOT A SECRET AGENT
TV Tarzan — ELY
TV term — SOAP
TV trial run — PILOT
TV's "_____ Rock" — COP
TV's "_____ -12" — ADAM
TV's "_____ Baltimore" — HOTL
TV's "_____ Bunch" — BRADY
TV's "_____ Indiana" — EERIE
TV's "_____ Lucy" — I LOVE

TV's "_____ Street" — SESAME
TV's "_____ World Turns" — AS THE
TV's "Green _____" — ACRES
TV's "Head of the _____" — CLASS
TV's "I Married _____": 1987 — DORA
TV's "Just the Ten _____" — OF US
TV's "Kate and _____" — ALLIE
TV's "L.A. _____" — LAW
TV's "One Day _____ Time" — AT A
TV's "The _____ Show" — GONG
TV's "The Captain and _____" — TENNILLE
TV's "Tic _____ Dough" — TAC
TV's "Trials of _____ O'Neill" — ROSIE
TV's "You _____ There" — ARE
TV's Anderson — LONI
TV's Arledge — ROONE
TV'S Arthur — BEA
TV's Barnaby Jones — EBSEN
TV's Burnett — CAROL
TV's Carter — NELL
TV's Charlotte — RAE
TV's Daly — TYNE
TV's Dan — RATHER
TV's Denise Huxtable — BONET
TV's Donahue — PHIL
TV's Erin — MORAN
TV's finest hours — PRIME TIME
TV's Graff — ILENE
TV's Griffin — MERV
TV's Headroom — MAX
TV's Higgins — JOEL
TV's Jack — PAAR
TV's Johnson — ARTE
TV's Kaplan — GABE
TV's Lou Grant — ASNER
TV's Mary Richards: Abbr. — MTM
TV's Matlock — BEN
TV's Merlin — OLSEN
TV's Meyers — ARI
TV's Moran — ERIN
TV's Norman — FELL
TV's Paladin — BOONE
TV's Ramsey et al. — HECS
TV's Rivera — GERALDO
TV's Rivers — JOAN
TV's Roseanne — BARR
TV's Sawyer — DIANE
TV's Selleck — TOM
TV's Sharkey et al. — CPOS
TV's talking horse — MR ED
TV's Tarzan — ELY
TV's Vigoda — ABE
TV's vocal equine — MR ED
TV's White — VANNA
TV's Winfrey — OPRAH
TV, to some — TUBE
TVA project — DAM
TVA structure — DAM
Twaddle — DRIVEL, NONSENSE, SLIPSLOP
Twain biographer — PAINE
Twain hero — HUCKLEBERRY FINN
Twain's "_____ Diary" — EVES
Twain's Finn — HUCK
Twain's grave site — ELMIRA
Twangy — NASAL
Twangy speech sounds — NASALS
Tweed Ring's nemesis — NAST
Tweed tributary — YARROW
Tweed's nemesis — NAST
Tweed, for one — BOSS
Tweeter — SPEAKER
Tweety-Bird's query? — WAS IT A CAT I SAW
Tweezer — PINCERS
Twelfth Jewish month — ELUL
Twelve — DOZEN, MIDNITE, NOON
Twelve doz. — GRO
Twelve months — YEAR
Twelve months: Abbr. — YRS
Twelve or tricks — SLAM
Twelve-month chart — CALENDAR
Twelve: Prefix — DODECA
Twenties exclamation — HOTCHA
Twentieth letter — UPSILON
Twenty-four hour periods, usually — SOLAR DAYS
Twenty quires — REAM
Twenty's ordinal suffix — ETH
Twenty-first letter — PHI
Twenty-four hour period — SOLAR DAY
Twenty-fourth letter — OMEGA
Twenty-second letter — CHI
Twenty-third letter — PSI
Twerp's cousin — NERD
Twerp, British style — NIT
Twerps — NITWITS
Twice CCLI — DII
Twice CDLI — CMII
Twice DCCLI — MDII
Twice LXXVI — CLII
Twice MI — MMII
Twice ten — SCORE
Twice the speed of sound — MACH II
Twiggy — THIN
Twill weave fabric — TOILE
Twilled cotton cloth — CHINO
Twilled fabric — SERGE
Twin — DUAL
Twin brother of Romulus — REMUS
Twin crystal — MACLE
Twin of Jacob — ESAU
Twin of sorts — CLONE
Twin stars — CASTOR AND POLLUX
Twine source — HEMP
Twinge — ACHE, PANG
Twinkle of an eye — SPLIT SECOND
Twinkled — SHONE
Twinkletoed — AGILE
Twins — PAIR
Twins of Astronomy — CASTOR AND POLLUX
Twins of Legend — ROMULUS AND REMUS
Twins of sports — TEAM IN MINNESOTA
Twins star — MINNESOTA PLAYER
Twirl — SPIN
Twirling rods — BATONS
Twist — COIL, CURL, OLIVER, SKEW, WRAP
Twist of fiction — OLIVER
Twist someone's arm — PERSUADE
Twist's kin — FRUG
Twisted — BENT, ENTWINED
Twists — WRING
Twists around — SLUES
Twit — TAUNT
Twit, to a Brit — NIT
Twitch — JERK, PULL, TIC
Twits, to Brits — NITS
Two — DUAD
Two _____ equals five — INTO TEN
Two base hit — DOUBLE
Two bells and 200 hours, e.g. — TIMES
Two English monarchs — ELIZABETHS
Two fortnights — MONTH
Two Greek philosophers — ZENOS
Two hrs. before midnight — TEN PM
Two masted sailboat — YAWL
Two of a kind — PAIR
Two or more: Abbr. — SEV
Two per oboe — REEDS
Two pints — QUART
Two points for any eleven — SAFETY
Two quartets — OCTET
Two story, two unit building — DUPLEX
Two thousand pounds — ONE TON
Two wives of Henry VIII — ANNES
Two words in a Perry Mason title — THE CASE
Two- _____ (macho) — FISTED
Two-by-four — LUMBER
Two-cents plain item, once — SODA
Two-cupped garment — BRA
Two-faced — INSINCERE

Two-faced god — JANUS
Two-handed card game — ECARTE
Two-legged — BIPEDAL
Two-legged animal — BIPED
Two-masted sailing vessel — SCHOONER
Two-master — BRIG
Two-piece outfit — PANTS SUIT
Two-seated carriage — LANDAU
Two-seeded plants — DICOTE
Two-step — DANCE
Two-syllable foot — IAMB, TROCHEE
Two-tiered galley — BIREME
Two-time opponent of Dwight — ADLAI
Two-to-one joint — ANKLE
Two-toed sloth — UNAU
Two-way — STREET
Two-way journeys — ROUND TRIPS
Two-way radio devotee — CBER
Two-way radio word — OVER
Two-wheeled carriage — HANSOM
Two-wheeled transport — RICKSHAW
Two-wheeler — BICYCLE
Two-wheeler of India — TONGA
Two-year-old male red deer — SPAY
Two-year-old sheep — TEGS
Twofold — BINAL, DUAL, DUPLE
Twos — PAIRS
Twosomes — DUOS
Twosomes: Abbr. — PRS
Twyla, the choreographer — THARP
Tybalt's slayer — ROMEO
Tycoon — MOGUL, TITLE
Tycoon Donald — TRUMP
Tycoon J. Paul — GETTY
Tycoon, for one — NABOB
Tyke protector — BIB
Tyke's parent — DADA
Tyler Moore, et al. — MARY
Tympanum's locale — EAR
Tyne or John — DALY
Typ. notation — ITAL
Typanic membrane — EARDRUM
Type designer and family — BODONIS
Type face: Abbr. — ITAL
Type font — ROMAN
Type measure — EMS, ENS
Type of acid — AMINO
Type of aircraft — STOL
Type of amphora — DIOTA
Type of amplifier — HI FI
Type of apple — ROME
Type of arch — OGEE
Type of art — DADA
Type of audience — CAPTIVE
Type of bag — TOTE
Type of bank account — JOINT
Type of barbershop — UNISEX
Type of bath — SPONGE
Type of beam — LASER
Type of bean — SOYA
Type of beer — ROOT
Type of benefit — FRINGE
Type of bible: Abbr. — ERV
Type of bike — TANDEM
Type of book — HARDCOVER
Type of bracelet or anklet — BANGLE
Type of bread — PITA
Type of brick — ADOBE
Type of bug or buffalo — WATER
Type of business person — CAREER WOMAN
Type of button — PANIC
Type of car — CABLE, SEDAN
Type of cat — ALLEY
Type of chair — SWIVEL
Type of cheese — PIMENTO
Type of chest — CEDAR
Type of church residence — DEANERY
Type of cigar — CHEROOT, CLARO
Type of clam or grass — RAZOR
Type of clause — ESCAPE
Type of clock — ALARM
Type of cloth — LOIN
Type of coat — ULSTER
Type of coat or shirt — POLO
Type of code — AREA
Type of collar — ETON
Type of committee — AD HOC
Type of computer — ANALOG
Type of coral island — ATOLL
Type of cracker — SODA
Type of cross or knight — PAPAL
Type of curve — ESS
Type of daisy — SHASTA
Type of dance — POLKA, WALTZ
Type of dancer — GOGO, TAP
Type of deck — POOP
Type of dive or song — SWAN
Type of dollars or mart — EURO
Type of dot — POLKA
Type of drum — SNARE
Type of dwelling — IGLU
Type of dynamo — MAGNETO
Type of eclipse — LUNAR
Type of engagement — NAVAL
Type of engine — TURBINE
Type of English jacket or terrier — NORFOLK
Type of exam — ORAL
Type of fern — MAIDENHAIR
Type of fertilizer — GUANO
Type of flare — SOLAR
Type of flycatcher — PEWEE
Type of fuel — DIESEL
Type of gas — TEAR
Type of grape — IVES
Type of guidance, in aerospace — INERTIAL
Type of haircut — BOB
Type of hairdo — AFRO
Type of Haitian rum — TAFIA
Type of hammer — PAUL, SLEDGE
Type of hat — PANAMA
Type of herring — SPRAT
Type of hit — SMASH
Type of home — MANSE
Type of horse — PACER
Type of hosp. room — EMER
Type of hound — TALBOT
Type of house — PREFAB
Type of hydrate — CHLORAL
Type of infection, for short — STAPH
Type of inlaid woodwork — TARSIA
Type of jar — MASON
Type of jazz singing — SCAT
Type of jerk — KNEE
Type of jet engine — ION
Type of jockey — DISC
Type of juice — GRAPE
Type of Latin — MEDIEVAL
Type of law — BLUE
Type of leather — SUEDE
Type of life insurance — TERM
Type of light — KLIEG
Type of maid — METER
Type of mail — AIR
Type of master — TASK
Type of metaphysical writer — POET
Type of missile: Abbr. — SSM
Type of mobility — UPWARD
Type of molding — OGEE
Type of molecule — LIGAND
Type of moss — LICHEN, PEAT
Type of moth — EGGER
Type of muffin — CORN
Type of muscle — RETENTOR, TENSOR
Type of musical composition — ARIOSO
Type of musical show — REVUE
Type of mystery — PROCE-DURAL
Type of nail — BRAD, SPAD
Type of nerve — OPTIC
Type of orange — NAVEL, OSAGE
Type of orange — OSAGE
Type of palm — DATE
Type of pansy — VIOLA
Type of paper — TERM
Type of payment: Abbr. — PIK
Type of phobia — AGORA
Type of pie — PECAN
Type of pinafore — TIER
Type of piper — PIED

Type of poker — STUD
Type of poker for tennis players? — DEUCES WILD
Type of power — SOLAR
Type of precis — RECAP
Type of print — GLOSSY
Type of prof — ASST
Type of promotion, cost-free — WORD OF MOUTH
Type of protest — FAST
Type of pump — SLING
Type of railroad car — DINER
Type of relationship — PLATONIC
Type of religious meditation — ZEN
Type of reporter — STRINGER
Type of riddle — REBUS
Type of rifle — CARBINE
Type of rocket — TWO STAGE
Type of roof — HIP
Type of room or chamber — ANTE
Type of rug — ORIENTAL, SHAG
Type of sail — LATEEN
Type of sandwich, for short — BLT
Type of saw — SABER
Type of scarf — ASCOT
Type of school, for short — PREP
Type of school: Abbr. — SEM
Type of screw hook — PIGTAIL
Type of seal — EARED
Type of sermon — IGNIS AND BRIMSTONE
Type of setter — IRISH
Type of shark — MAKO
Type of ship not in: 12/7/41 — AIRCRAFT CARRIER
Type of show — COMEDY, DRAMA, LATE
Type of shrub — ALISO
Type of singing: Abbr. — RECIT
Type of skirt — A LINE, MAXI, MINI
Type of sleeve — SET IN
Type of sleeve or sail — LEGO-MUTTON
Type of soil — LOAM
Type of space — AERO
Type of spaghetti sauce — MARINARA
Type of spring tide — PERIGEAN
Type of stealer — SCENE
Type of stem — CULM
Type of store — OUTLET
Type of sugar — MALTOSE
Type of surgeon — NEURO
Type of table — END
Type of tanker — OILER
Type of tea — PEKOE
Type of terrier — SKYE
Type of test — ORAL
Type of testimony — SWORN
Type of tide — NEAP
Type of time — RAG
Type of toothpaste — GEL
Type of tournament — OPEN
Type of tower — IVORY
Type of trial — OYER
Type of trip — EGO
Type of truck — PANEL
Type of tuna — ALBACORE
Type of type — AGATE, ELITE, ROMAN
Type of type, for short — ITAL
Type of type: Abbr. — ITAL
Type of vaccine — SALK
Type of vb. — IRR
Type of volcanic crater — MAAR
Type of vote — NAY
Type of wax — SEALING
Type of weight: Abbr. — CBAL
Type of wooden bench — SETTEE
Type size — ELITE, PICA
Type style — ELITE, ITALIC, ROMAN
Type type — AGATE, ELITE, PICA
Typeface style — RONDE
Typeface: Abbr. — ITAL
Types — SORTS
Types of engravings — LINE CUTS
Typesetter — PRINTER
Typesetter's concern: Abbr. — PTG
Typesetter's cue — STET
Typesetter's word — DELE
Typesetting machine, for short — LINO
Typewriter bar — SPACER
Typewriter key — SET
Typewriter lever — KEY
Typewriter part — PLATEN
Typewriter roller — PLATEN
Typhon — MONSTER
Typical — NORMAL
Typical librarian — BIBLIOPHILE
Typical Randolph Scott film — OATER
Typifies — REPRESENTS
Typify — TOKEN
Typing service? — A TOUCH OF CLASS
Typist task — SET TABS
Typo, e.g. — ERROR
Typos — ERRORS
Tyr, Balder et al. — AESIR
Tyrannical — DEMANDING
Tyrant in "2001" — HAL
Tyre companion — SIDON
Tyre monarch — HIRAM
Tyro — BEGINNER, NOVICE
Tyro's typing technique — HUNT AND PECK
Tyrolean refrain — YODEL
Tyrolean song — YODEL
Tyrone Power movie — THE SUN ALSO RISES
Tyrrhenian sea island — ELBA
Tyson weapon — FIST
Tyson's title — CHAMP
Tzara's cult — DADAISM

U

U or hairpin — TURN
U preceders — AEIO
U's companions — AEIO
U-235, to uranium — ISOTOPE
U. of Arkansas at Fayetteville player — RAZORBACK
U. of Maine site — ORONO
U. of Maryland athlete — TERP
U. of Md. athlete — TERP
U. of New Mexico team — LOBOS
U. of Puget Sound site — TACOMA
U.F.O. crew — ETS
U.K. auto — MOTORCAR
U.K. award — DSO, OBE
U.K. lawmakers — MPS
U.K. legislative branch — COMMONS
U.K. pound fraction — PENCE
U.K. service women — WAAF
U.K. stirs — GAOLS
U.K. unit of length — METRE
U.N. agency — ILO
U.N. arm — ILO
U.N. body — ILO

U.N. chief: 1962-71 — U THANT
U.N. labor body — ILO
U.N.'s Trygve and kin — LIES
U.N.'s U _____ — THANT
U.N.'s U in 1970 — THANT
U.S. architect's org. — AIA
U.S. Army off. — LT GEN
U.S. Army security gp. — CMP
U.S. author Alice _____: 1851-1911 — EARLE
U.S. ballistic missile — THOR
U.S. Cabinet department — INTERIOR
U.S. conductor-composer — ENGEL
U.S. cultural org. — NEA
U.S. currency — DOL
U.S. dancer-choreographer: 1931-89 — AILEY
U.S. draft agcy. — SSS
U.S. election routine — DEMOCRATIC PROCESS
U.S. emblem — EAGLE
U.S. film critic-author — AGEE
U.S. flag designer — REID
U.S. flight org. — NAA
U.S. flyers once — AAF
U.S. Grant's adversary — R E LEE
U.S. Grant's contemporary — R E LEE
U.S. Grant's counterpart — R E LEE
U.S. Grant's opposite, R. _____ — E LEE
U.S. Grant's rival — R E LEE
U.S. labor leader — ABEL
U.S. labor relations org. — NLRB
U.S. lexicographer-educator: 1869-1946 — NEILSON
U.S. locksmith — YALE
U.S. mil. award — DSC
U.S. missile — SAM
U.S. missiles — NIKES
U.S. money — DOLS
U.S. money unit — DOL
U.S. motor capital — DET
U.S. novelist-poet — ROBERT NATHAN
U.S. Open champ: 1976 — PATE
U.S. Open golf champ: 1927 — ARMOUR
U.S. Open golf champ: 1959 — CASPER
U.S. Open singles champ: 1972 — NASTASE
U.S. Open winner: 1977 — GREEN
U.S. painter: 1871-1951 — SLOAN
U.S. poet who wrote "The Bridge" — HART CRANE
U.S. publisher: 1858-1935 — OCHS
U.S. reconnaissance satellite — SAMOS
U.S. research rocket — AEROBEE
U.S. satellite — OGO
U.S. skater David _____ — SANTEE
U.S. space agency — NASA
U.S. Special Forces unit — A TEAM
U.S. spy ctr. — CIA
U.S. spy ctr. — CIA
U.S. statesman DeWitt — CLINTON
U.S. trade org. — FTC
U.S. weather satellite — ESSA, TIROS
U.S. wellness org. — NIH
U.S. wine valley — NAPA
U.S.-Can. defense org. — NORAD
U.S.-Canadian canals — SOO
U.S.A. last! 1946 — ASSAULT
U.S.A. units — ECHS
U.S.A.'s best customer — CANADA
U.S.A.F. Academy cadet — DOOLIE
U.S.A.F. decoration — DFC
U.S.A.F. member — AIRMAN
U.S.A.F., e.g. — SER
U.S.C. rival — UCLA
U.S.N. biggie — ADM
U.S.N. officer — CPO
U.S.N. personnel — CPOS
U.S.N. VIP — ADM
U.S.N.A. part — NAV
U.S.S.R. city — OREL
U.S.S.R. inland body of water — ARAL SEA
U.S.S.R. lake — ARAL
U.S.S.R. monetary unit — RUBLE
U.S.S.R. news agency — TASS
U.S.S.R. range — ALAI
U.S.S.R. river — LENA
U.S.S.R. subdivision — OBLAST
U.S.S.R. town — AZOV
U.S.S.R. workers collective — ARTEL
Ubangi feeder — UELE
Ubangi river feeder — UELE
Ubangi tributary — UELE
Ubiquitous abbr. — ETC
Ubiquitous author — ANON
Ubiquitous bags — TOTES
Ubiquitous bean — SOY
Ubiquitous catchall — ET AL
Uca — CRAB
Uffizi treasures — ARTE
UFO passenger — ALIEN
Uganda's capital — KAMPALA
Ugandan exile — AMIN
Ugandan exile Amin — IDI
Ugandan hostage-rescue site — ENTEBBE
Ugandan name — IDI
Ugarte — PETER LORRE
Ugly things — EYESORES
Uh huh, Pablo! — SI SI
Uh-huh — YEAH
Uhlan's weapon — LANCE
UK auto — MOTORCAR
UK award — DSO, OBE
UK country — ENG
UK language — ENG
UK network — BBC
UK pound fraction — PENCE
UK service women — WAAF
UK unit of length — METRE
Uke ridge — FRET
Ukr. et al., once — SSRS
Ukr. or Lith. — SSR
Ukraine native — ODESSAN
Ukraine seaport — ODESSA
Ukrainian initials — SSR
Ukrainian legislatures — RADAS
Ulcer — CANKER
Ullmann — LIV
Ullmann/Kelly/Albert tuber crop? — FORTY CARROTS
Ulna — BONE
Ulnae's neighbors — RADII
Ulster town — ANTRIM
Ultimate — EVENT, EVENTUAL, FINAL
Ultimate asst. for mom? — LIVE IN MAID
Ultimate degree — NTH
Ultimate in seasonal decoration — TREE TRIMMING ART
Ultimate warning — RED ALERT
Ultimatum word — ELSE
Ultra — TOO TOO
Ultraconservative — DIEHARD
Ululate — HOWL
Ulyanov — LENIN
Ulysses Grant's first name — HIRAM
Umberto _____ — ECO
Umbra — SHADOW
Umbrella — PARASOL
Umbrette's relative — HERON
Ump's call — BALL, FOWL, OUT, SAFE
Ump's colleague — REF
Ump's cousin — REF
Ump's cry — PLAY BALL, SAFE
Ump's kin — REF
Ump's relative — REF
Umpire's command — BATTER UP
Umpire's cry — SAFE
Umpteen years — AEONS
Ums' cousins — ERS
UN affiliate — ILO
UN agency — ILO
UN Agriculture Agcy. — FAO

UN initials — USSR
UN member — USSR
Unable to choose — TORN
Unabridged — UNCUT, ENTIRE
Unaccented — LENE
Unaccompanied — ALONE
Unadorned — BARE, STARK
Unadulterated — PURE
Unaffected — NATURAL
Unaffiliated writer — FREE-LANCE
Unaided — ALONE
Unaided efforts — BOOT STRAPS
Unalaska native — ALEUT
Unaltered — SAME
Unanimity — ACCORD
Unanimously — TO A MAN
Unappreciative one — INGRATE
Unaspirated — LENE
Unaspirated consonant — LENE
Unassuming — MODEST, SHY
Unattractive — UGLY
Unauthorized disclosure — LEAK
Unavailing — IDLE
Unbalanced — SHAKY
Unbarred, to Keats — OPED
Unbeliever — INFIDEL
Unbend — THAW
Unbending — IRON, RIGID
Unbends — THAWS
Unbiased — FAIR
Unbiased employer: Abbr. — EOE
Unbounded joy — GLEE
Unbranded cattle — MAVERICKS
Unbridled — LAWLESS
Unbroken horse — BRONCO
Unburden — EASE
Unc's mate — AUNTY
Uncanny — EERIE, EERY
Uncanny, to a Scot — UNCO
Uncap — OPEN
Uncas' beloved — CORA
Uncertainty — BAFFLEMENT, INDECISION
Uncertainty — PERPLEXITY, PUZZLEMENT
Unchanged — PAT, SAME
Unchic shoe — SABOT
Uncivil — RUDE
Uncle _____ (one of the Gumps) — BIM
Uncle Miltie — BERLE
Uncle of early TV — MILTIE
Uncle of fiction — REMUS
Uncle of Joseph — ESAU
Uncle or aunt: Abbr. — REL
Uncle Tom's abode — CABIN
Uncle, in Avila — TIO
Uncle, in Scotland — EME
Uncle: Dial. — EME
Unclean — GERMY
Unclear — VAGUE
Uncles, in Toledo — TIOS
Unclockable — TIMELESS
Unclose — OPE
Unclose is one for counsel — ANAGRAM
Uncloses, to a poet — OPES
Uncloses: Poet. — OPES
Uncluttered — NEAT
Uncollectables — DEBTS
Uncommitted — NEUTRAL
Uncommon — ODD, RARE, SPARSE
Uncommon sense, for short — ESP
Uncomplimentary gossip — DIRT
Uncompromising — AUSTERE, WOOL DYED
Unconcealed — OVERT
Unconcerned — CARELESS
Unconfident — TIMID
Unconfined — LOOSE
Uncontrolled — WILD
Unconventional — OUTRE
Uncooked — RAW
Uncool collegian — NERD
Uncorks — OPENS
Uncouth — COARSE, CURT, IMPOLITE, RUDE
Uncouth person — YAHOO
Uncover — DETECT, REVEAL
Uncovered — BALD, BARED, DETACHED
Unction — FERVOR
Unction flask — AMPUL
Unctuous — SMUG
Uncultivated — FALLOW
Undaunted — BRAVE
Undecked, power driven boat — LAUNCH
Undefiled — PRISTINE
Under — BELOW
Under _____ (burdened) — A STRAIN
Under age — MINOR
Under an Adm. — CAPT
Under full legal age — MINOR
Under guidance — IN TOW
Under oath — SWORN
Under poorest circumstances — AT WORST
Under sail — ASEA
Under the covers — ABED
Under the influence — STONED
Under the weather — ILL, OFF ONES FEED
Under this cover — HEREIN
Under, asea — ALOW
Under, poetically — NEATH
Undercoat — PRIME
Undercover — SECRET
Undercover agt. — NARC
Undercover operation — STING
Undercover org. — CIA
Undercut — ERODE
Underdeck area — ALOW
Undergarment — CORSET
Undergarments — SLIPS, TEDDIES
Undergo — ENDURE
Undergoes — ENDURES
Undergoing vertigo — AREEL
Undergrad from college — SOPH
Undergrad of a sort — COED
Underground chamber — CAVERN
Underground dwellers — MOLES
Underground man — COAL MINER
Underground seed — PEANUT
Underground vault — CATACOMB
Underground water tank — CISTERN
Underhanded — SNEAKY
Underhanded people — SNEAKS
Underlets — SUB RENTS
Underling of yore — ESNE
Undermines — SAPS
Underneath — BELOW
Underpinning — LEG
Underscore — ACCENT
Underseas inst. — SDR
Undersized pickpocket? — SHRIMP DIP
Understand — FATHOM, GET, READ, SEE
Understandable — CLEAR
Understanders phrase — I SEE
Understanding — KEN
Understanding reply — I SEE
Understanding sounds — OHS
Understanding words — I SEE
Understands — READS, SEES
Understands thoroughly — FATHOMS
Understood — DUG, KNOWN, SEEN
Understood, mod style — DUG
Undertake — SET OUT
Undertaker's purchase — HEARSE
Undertones — AURAS
Undertow — RIPTIDE
Underwater plant — EELGRASS
Underway — AFOOT
Underwear — BVD
Underwear type — THERMAL
Underworld — HADES
Underworld god — DIS
Underwriter — BACKER
Undesired audio signal — HUM
Undetermined quantity — SOME
Undeveloped cotton pod — BOLLY

Undeveloped state — EMBRYO
Undiluted — NEAT
Undiminished — MERE
Undisciplined freedom — LICENSE
Undisguised — BARE
Undivided — ONE
Undo — ERASE, LOOSEN, NEGATE, RUIN
Undo the seams — RIP APART
Undoes — OPENS
Undraped — NUDE
Unduly — TOO
Unduly anxious — OVEREAGER
Undying dying words — ETTU
Unearth — DETECT, DIG UP, MINE
Unearthly — EERIE, EERY, GHOSTLY, PHANTOM
Unearthly glow — AURA
Uneasy — RESTLESS
Unelected president — FORD
Unemployed — IDLE, OTIOSE
Unencumbered — FREE
Unending — ENDLESS, ETERNAL
Unenlightened — BENIGHTED
Unequal: Comb. form — ANISO
Unequaled — SOLE
Unerring — PERFECT, SURE
Unescorted — ALONE, LONE
Uneven — EROSE, ODD
Unexcelled — BEST
Unexciting — TAME
Unexpected — ABRUPT
Unexpected disclosure — EYE OPENER
Unexpected hitch — SNAG
Unexpected hits — SLEEPERS
Unexpected winnings — JACKPOT
Unexplored region — FRONTIER
Unfailing — RIGHT
Unfaltering — STEADY
Unfamiliar — STRANGE
Unfeeling — COLD AS ICE
Unfettered — LOOSE
Unfilled — EMPTY
Unfinished — ROUGH, RUDE
Unfinished sculpture — TORSO
Unflappable — CALM, POISED, SERENE
Unflattering epithet — FATSO
Unfolded — OPEN
Unfolds, to poets — OPES
Unforgiving — STERN
Unfortunate — HAPLESS
Unfortunates of W.W. II — DPS
Unfreeze — DE ICE, THAW
Unfriendly — HOSTILE
Unfruitful — ARID
Unfurnished — BARE
Ungallant — RUDE
Ungentlemanly one — CAD
Unger portrayer — CARNEY
Unguent — SALVE
Unguent plants — ALOES
Unguentary drosophila — FLY IN THE OINTMENT
Unguiculate — CLAWED
Unguis — HOOF
Ungulate feature — HOOF
Unhappy — SAD
Unharmed — SAFE
Unhealthy looking — SALLOW
Unheard of — OBSCURE
Unhearing — DEAF
Unheeding — DEAF, RASH
Unhinged — DOTTY, MAD
Unhitch — LOOSE
Unhurt — SAFE
Unicorn in the King James Bible — REEM
Unification Church follower, informally — MOONIE
Uniform — EVEN
Uniform feature — EPAULET
Uniform in Paris — EGAL
Unimaginative — DRY, EARTHBOUND, STAID
Uninterested — NOT INTO
Uninteresting — DRY
Uninteresting secondhand garment? — DULL CASTOFF
Union — ACCORD
Union action — STRIKE
Union chapter — LOCAL
Union General — MEADE
Union General George Gordon — MEADE
Union General president — GRANT
Union initials — CIO
Union leader John _____ Lewis — LLEWELLYN
Union letters — CIO
Union member — WORKER
Union minimum wages — SCALE
Union or Victoria — STATION
Union unit — STATE
Union's foe: Abbr. — CSA
Unions — LABOR
Unique — LONE, RARE, SOLE
Unique fellow — ONER
Unique individual — ONER
Unique person — ONER
Unique thing — ONER
Unique: Comb. form — IDIO
Unisex gown of old Greece — TUNIC
Unison — HARMONY
Unisonally — AS ONE
Unit — ONE
Unit equivalent to 3.26 light years — PARSEC
Unit for a physicist — ERG
Unit of angular measurement — RADIAN
Unit of area — ACRE
Unit of capacitance — FARAD
Unit of conductance — MHO
Unit of elec. current — AMP
Unit of electric current — AMPERE
Unit of electrical resistance — OHM
Unit of electricity — FARAD
Unit of energy — ERG, RAD
Unit of force — DYNE, NEWTON
Unit of heat — CALORIE
Unit of illumination — PHOT
Unit of land measure — ARE
Unit of length — METRE, MIL
Unit of length equal to 30 inches — PACE
Unit of local government in old Greece — DEME
Unit of loudness — BEL, SONE
Unit of luminous intensity — NIT
Unit of magnetic flux density — TESLA
Unit of progress — STEP
Unit of resistance — OHM
Unit of sound — DECIBEL
Unit of time — DAY
Unit of usefulness — UTIL
Unit of volume — STERE
Unit of weight — GRAM
Unit of work — ERG
Unite — BIND, FEDERATE, JOIN, SPLICE
United — AS ONE, ONE, WED
United _____ Emirates — ARAB
United Nations' mission — PEACE
Unites — FUSES, WEDS
Units — ONE
Units of capacity — LITERS
Units of elec. — AMPS
Units of elec. current — AMPS
Units of force — DYNES
Units of loudness — SONES
Units of measure for printers — ENS
Units of power — WATTS
Units of resistance — OHMS
Units of wood — CORDS
Units of work — ERGS
Units of wt. — TNS
Units on space vehicles — LEMS
Unity — ONENESS
Univ. at Fort Worth — TCU
Univ. course — ECON
Univ. degrees — AAS, ABS, BAS
Univ. entrance test — SAT
Univ. for engineers — MIT
Univ. of Maryland athlete — TERP
Univ. of Nevada town — RENO
Univ. offerings — BAS
Universal lady — MOTHER NATURE
Universe — WORLD

Universe: Comb. form — COSMO
University — ACADEME
University at New Haven, Conn. — YALE
University award — DEGREE
University city in Sweden — LUND
University in Nashville — FISK
University in Nova Scotia — ACADIA
University in Oxford, Ohio — MIAMI
University in Paris — SORBONNE
University in Quebec City — LAVAL
University near Atlanta — EMORY
University of Ghana site — ACCRA
University of Maine campus — ORONO
University of Maine locale — ORONO
University of Maine site — ORONO
University officer — REGENT
University official — DEAN
University or playwright — RICE
University subdivisions — COLLEGES
Unkempt — MESSY, SEEDY
Unkempt abodes — STIES
Unknown chap — MAC
Unknown Jane — DOE
Unknown Richard — DOE
Unlace — LOOSE
Unlatches a door, in poesy — OPES
Unlearned — GROSS
Unless — BUT
Unless in law — NISI
Unless: law — NISI
Unlikely — A GHOST OF A CHANCE
Unlit — DARK
Unload — SHED
Unlock, in poetry — OPE
Unlock, to Byron — OPE
Unlocks — OPENS
Unlucky — ILL STARRED
Unlucky bettor's loss — SHIRT
Unlucky or unwell — ILL
Unmarried — ELIGIBLE
Unmarried woman — MISS
Unmatched — UNIQUE
Unmedicated pill — PLACEBO
Unmixed — PURE
Unnamed person — ANONYM
Unnatural — FORCED
Unnatural; stiff — LABORED
Unnerve — DAUNT
Unnerved — SHAKEN
Uno + uno — DOS
Uno e due — TRE
Uno is one — NUMERO
Uno plus due — TRE
Uno y uno — DOS
Unobstructed — OPEN
Unoccupied — IDLE, VACANT
Unoriginal — BANAL, STERILE
Unorthodox religion — CULT
Unorthodoxy — HERESY
Unpackaged — LOOSE
Unpaid debt — ARREAR
Unpin — LOOSEN
Unpleasant sound — SPLAT
Unpleasantly plump — OBESE
Unpolished — RUDE
Unpolluted — PURE
Unpopular monogram — IRS
Unportrayed parent — WHISTLERS FATHER
Unpreposing lady — PLAIN JANE
Unprincipled — AMORAL
Unprized possession — WHITE ELEPHANT
Unprocessed — RAW
Unrealistic pursuit — CHASING RAINBOWS
Unrefined — BRUTE, CRASS
Unrelated — APART, SEPARATE
Unrelenting — STERN
Unrelenting, as a will — IRON
Unresolved — UP IN THE AIR
Unrestrained — HEARTY
Unrestrained sentimentality — TREACLE
Unrestricted: despotic — ARBITRARY
Unruffled — CALM, POISED, SEDATE, SERENE, SMOOTH
Unruly bunch — MOB
Unruly head of hair — MOP
Unruly mob — RIOTERS
Unruly offspring — BRATS
Unsavory — SHADY
Unscramble — DECODE
Unscrambles a secret message — DECODES
Unscrupulous — VENAL
Unscrupulous one — ROGUE
Unscrupulous person — USER
Unscrupulous real estate agent? — BLOCK MARKETEER
Unseal: Poetic — OPE
Unseasoned — RAW
Unseat — DEPOSE, THROW
Unseen — HIDDEN
Unseld of the NBA — WES
Unselfish one — ALTRUIST
Unsettled — SHAKEN
Unshaken — STEADY
Unsightly — UGLY
Unskilled one at sports — HACKER
Unsophisticated — NAIVE
Unsparing, reproving one — DUTCH UNCLE
Unspecified degree — NTH
Unsplit straw for hats — YEDDA
Unspoiled — PRISTINE
Unspoken — NONORAL
Unsqueaks — OILS
Unstable — LABILE
Unsteady — TOTTERY
Unsteady light — FLARE
Unstinting — ALL OUT
Unsubstantial — AERIAL, AIRY
Unsubstantial ship? — WINDY JAMMER
Unsuitable — DUSE, INAPT
Unsuitable pair — MISMATCH
Unsullied — CHASTE, PURE
Unsupported assertion — SAY SO
Unsure — WEAK
Unswerving look — STARE
Untamed — WILD
Untamed environment — WILDERNESS
Untethered — FREED, LOOSE
Unthinking — RASH
Untidy — CARELESS, MESSY, MUSSY, SLOPPY
Untidy handwriting — SCRAWL
Untidy one — SLOB
Untidy person — SLOVEN
Unties — LOOSENS
Until now — AS YET, TO DATE
Untouchables, for one — CASTE
Untried — NEW
Untroubled — SERENE
Untrue — FALSE
Untrustworthy — SLIPPERY AS AN EEL
Unused — IDLE, INACTIVE, VACANT
Unusual — ODD, RARE, STRANGE
Unusual bloke — ONER
Unusual condition — NOR-MALITY
Unusual people — ONERS
Unusual shoe width — EEE
Unusual thing — FREAK, ODDITY
Unusual: Abbr. — SPEC
Unveils — BARES
Unwary — RASH
Unwavering — STEADY
Unwelcome look — LEER
Unwelcome pest — LICE
Unwholesome — PRURIENT
Unwilling — AVERSE, LOATH
Unwind — OPEN, RELAX
Unwise — FOOLISH
Unworldly — NAIF
Unworn — NEW
Unwrap — OPEN
Unwritten — ORAL

Unwritten test — ORAL
Unyielding — FIRM, HARD, HEADSTRONG, IRON
Unyielding — IRONBOUND, STONY
Unzipped — OPENED
Up — RISEN, ARISEN
Up _____ (cornered) — A TREE
Up a _____ (stymied) — TREE
Up a tree — CORNERED
Up and _____ — AT EM
Up and about — ASTIR, RISEN
Up close — NEAR
Up for _____ — GRABS
Up in arms — SORE
Up in the air — ALOFT
Up in years — AGED
Up in: Prefix — EPI
Up straight — ERECT
Up the ante — RAISE
Up to — ABLE
Up to now — SO FAR, YET
Up to one's eyes — BUSY
Up to standard — ETHICAL
Up to that time — UNTIL
Up to the _____ — EARS
Up to the ears — ENGROSSED
Up to the time — UNTIL
Up, in poker — RAISE
Up-and-coming — EAGER
Up-to-date — MOD
Up-to-date chap — MOD
Up: Comb. form — ANO
Upanishad — ISHA
Upas or yew — TREE
Upbeat — CHEERY
Upbeats, in music — ARSES
Upbraid — RATE
Upbraided — SCOLDED, RAILED
Update — RENEW, REVISE
Update a factory — RETOOL
Updated: Prefix — NEO
Updike protagonist — RABBIT ANGSTROM
Updike title word — RABBIT
Updike's "Rabbit _____" — REDUX
Updike's "Rabbit, _____" — RUN
Updike's "The Same _____" — DOOR
Upgrade — ENHANCE, SLOPE
Upgrades the text — AMENDS
Upheave — RISE
Upholstery material — TABARET
Upland water: Pl. — TARNS
Uplift — BOOST, EDIFY, ELATE, INSPIRE
Uplifted — BUOYED
Uplifting fellow? — OTIS
Uplifts — ELATES
Upolu island group — SAMOA
Upolu native — SAMOAN
Upolu seaport — APIA
Upon — ATOP, ON TO
Upon, in poesy — OER
Upped — RAISED
Upper atmosphere layer — OZONE
Upper case — CAPS
Upper crust — ELITE
Upper garment — HALTER
Upper house — AERIE, SENATE
Upper limit — CAP
Upper regions of space — ETHER
Upper stage rocket — AGENA
Upper throat — GULA
Upper, to Fritz — OBER
Uppers and lowers — BERTHS
Uppishness — HIGH HORSE
Uppity character — SNOB
Uppity one — SNOB
Uppsala's country — SWEDEN
Upright — ERECT, ON END
Upright and grand — PIANOS
Upright support — PILLAR
Uprising — REVOLT
Uproar — ADO, DIN, RIOT
Uproot — GRUB
Ups the ante — RAISES
Upset — ROIL, UNDID
Upset musician during recital? — DISCONCERTS
Upset state — SNIT
Upsets — DISARRAYS
Upside down or wedding — CAKE
Upsilon follower — PHI
Upstairs — ABOVE
Upstanding — HONEST
Uptight — TAUT, TENSE
Uptown district, New York — HARLEM
Upward: Comb. form — ANO
Ur. neighbor — ARA
Uraeus — ASP
Uraeus symbol — ASP
Uraie — ASPS
Uranus satellite — ARIEL
Urban area — GHETTO
Urban clothing? — CITY SLICKER
Urban dweller — CIT
Urban dwelling — BROWN-STONE, TENEMENT
Urban haze — SMOG
Urban noisemaker — JOHN HAMMER
Urban pollution — SMOG
Urban problem — ARSON
Urban rails — ELS
Urban railways — ELS
Urban transports — ELS, TAXIS
Urban youth subculture — HIP HOP
Urbane — SUAVE
Urbane; cool — POISED
Urbanity — SAVOIR FAIRE
Urchin — IMP, TAD
Urge — SPUR, YEN
Urge Fido to attack — SIC
Urge forward — IMPEL
Urge on — IMPEL, SPUR
Urge to attack — SIC
Urge toward — IMPEL
Urged a saddle horse on — KNEED
Urgency — HASTE
Urgent — CRITICAL
Urgent request — APPEAL
Urges — YENS
Uriah Heep and others — CLERKS
Uris hero — ARI
Uris or Trotsky — LEON
Uris's "_____ 18" — MILA
Urn — SAMOVAR
Urn for tea — SAMOVAR
Urn of Russian origin — SAMOVAR
Ursid — BEAR
Ursine females in Avila — OSAS
Ursula Andress film — SHE
Ursula Andress role — SHE
Uruguay's capital — MONTEVIDEO
Us (Fr.) — NOUS
US Army Special Forces member — GREEN BERET
US author James — AGEE
US capitalist and art patron — ARMAND HAMMER
US currency — DOL
US Govt. org. — REA, AEC
US guided missile — TALOS
US med. group — AMA
US missile — TITAN
US money — DOL
US narcs — DEA
US national symbol — UNCLE SAM
US Navy engineer — SEABEE
US Open champion _____ Irwin — HALE
US president's title — CINC
US reformer — RIIS
US satellite — TIROS
US soldiers — GIS
US space rocket — AGENA
US submarine — TRIDENT
US theater org. — ANTA
US troops — GIS
US writer — POE
Us, in Augsburg — UNS
Us, to Ovid — NOS
US-Can. canals — SOO
USA officers — LTS
Usable — FIT
Usage — TREATMENT
Usage recorder — METER
Use — AVAIL, DEPLETE, EMPLOY, WIELD
Use a baton — LEAD
Use a blender — PUREE, STIR

Use a blue pencil — EDIT
Use a bubble pipe — BLOW
Use a bucket — LADE
Use a certain fork — TUNE
Use a credit card — SPEND
Use a crosscut — SAW
Use a curling iron — CRIMP
Use a death ray — ZAP
Use a dirk — STAB
Use a divining rod — DOWSE
Use a driver — TEE OFF
Use a gimlet — BORE
Use a gin — TRAP
Use a harvester — REAP
Use a hose — WET
Use a ladder — CLIMB
Use a loom — WEAVE
Use a ray gun — ZAP
Use a scythe — REAP
Use a shuttle — TAT
Use a snifter — SIP
Use a stiletto — STAB
Use a straw — SIP
Use a strop — HONE
Use a teapot — STEEP
Use a tuffet — SIT
Use a wrong name — MISNOMER
Use an auger — BORE, DRILL
Use an eraser — RUB
Use an oar — PROPEL
Use an old phone — DIAL
Use antifreeze — DEICE
Use as a prop — LEAN ON
Use as example — CITE
Use carbon — COPY
Use certain language — CUSS
Use extra energy — STRAIN
Use finger paints — SMEAR
Use for the first time — CHRISTEN
Use force — STRONGARM
Use gum elastic — ERASE
Use maxilla and mandible — CHEW
Use physical force — STRONGARM
Use pressure — EXERT
Use sandpaper — ABRADE
Use scissors — SNIP
Use scythes — REAP
Use the car — MOTOR
Use the food processor — GRIND
Use the hose — WATER
Use the kiddie pool — WADE
Use the marina — MOOR
Use the oven — BAKE
Use the phone — DIAL
Use the tub — BATHE
Use the VCR — TAPE
Use up — CONSUME, SPEND
Use white out — ERASE
Use your brain — THINK
Used-car deal — RESALE
Used — RESALE, WORN
Used a birchbark — CANOED
Used a chisel — GOUGED, TOOLED
Used a driver, with "off" — TEED
Used a gimlet — BORED
Used a Jacuzzi — BATHED
Used a lasso — ROPED
Used a lever — PRIED
Used a lever: Var. — PRISED
Used a mangle — IRONED
Used a muddler — STIRRED
Used a net — SEINED
Used a paddle — ROWED
Used a pencil — DREW
Used a plane — SHAVED
Used a prie-dieu — KNELT
Used a seine — FISHED
Used a shuttle — RODE, TATTED, WOVE
Used a sieve — SIFTED
Used a Singer — SEWED
Used a spade — DUG, GARDENED
Used a stopwatch — TIMED
Used a straddler or scuffle — HOED
Used a T square — ALINED
Used a tandem — BIKED
Used a treadle — PEDALED
Used an atomizer — SPRAYED
Used an auger — REAMED
Used an ottoman — SAT
Used clothing — HAND ME DOWN
Used color — DYED
Used diligently — PLIED
Used in footnotes: Abbr. — IBID
Used item — HAND ME DOWN
Used items — OLD CLOTHES
Used light beam — LASED
Used oars — ROWED
Used to be — WAS
Used Trump's airline — SHUTTLED
Used up — GONE, SPENT
Used wheels — RODE
Used without an oarlock — PADDLE
Used, as clothing — WORN
Useful — UTILE
Useful bit of Latin — ETC
Useful chap — HANDY ANDY
Useful item — TOOL
Useful lad — HANDY ANDY
Useful quality — ASSET
Useful thing — ASSET
Useless — FUTILE
Useless plant — WEED
User of a prayer wheel — LAMA
User of spads and brads — NAILER
Uses a come-on — BAITS
Uses a compactor — CRUSHES
Uses a crawl — SWIMS
Uses a dabber — INKS
Uses a dipstick — DOWSES
Uses a discus — HURLS
Uses a gin — SEEDS
Uses a kitchen appliance — DICES
Uses a letter opener — SLITS
Uses a radar — SCANS
Uses a reference — LOOKS UP
Uses a shaker — SALTS
Uses a shuttle — TATS
Uses a straw — SLURPS
Uses a towel — DRIES
Uses a whetstone — HONES
Uses a whisk — BEATS
Uses plastic — OWES
Uses radar — SCANS
Uses scissors — SNIPS
Uses the car — MOTORS
Uses the library — READS
Uses the tiller — STEERS
Uses Yule decor — TINSELS
Usher — ESCORT
Usher or Major ending — ETTE
Usher's beat — AISLE
Usher's milieu — AISLE
Usher's offering — SEAT
Usher's path — AISLE
Usher's work station — AISLE
Ushers — SEATERS
Ushers — SEATS
Using — WITH
Using a word processor — WRITING
Using up — SPENDING
USMA frosh — PLEBE
USMA grads — LTS
USMA locale — WEST POINT
USMA site — WEST POINT
USMA, e.g. — ACAD
USMC grads — LTS
USMC vessels — LSTS
USN aviation officers — NFOS
USN construction expert — SEABEE
USN man: Abbr. — CPO
USN monogram — MSTS
USN officer — ADM
USN rank — ENS
USN ranking — CPO
USN ship — SUB
USN type — GOB
USNA grad — ENS
USNA graduate — RANK
USSR agency — TASS
USSR city — OREL
USSR city on the Irtysh — OMSK
USSR news org. — TASS
USSR news service — TASS
USSR plane — MIG
USSR range or river — URAL
USSR's neighbor — PRC
Ust-_____, U.S.S.R. plateau — URT

Usti _____ Labem, Czechoslovak city — NAD
Ustinov or Nero — PETER
Ustinov's autobiography — DEAR ME
Usual openers — PAIR
Usual reaction to prolixity — BOREDOM
Usual vacation — TWO WEEKS WITH PAY
Usual, natural condition — NORMALCY
Usurers — LOANSHARKS
Usurers' deals — LOANS
Usurp — ARROGATE, COMMANDEER, SEIZE, WREST
Utah Beach vessel — LST
Utah bird? — LOGANNET
Utah city — PROVO
Utah national park — ZION
Utah range — UINTA
Utah resort — ALTA
Utah river — UINTA
Utah ski area — ALTA
Utah ski resort — ALTA
Utah state flower — LILY, SEGO
Utah's flower — SEGO
Utah's Jake _____ — GARN
Utah's lily — SEGO
Utah's state flower — SEGO
Utensil on a pencil — ERASER
Utensil worshipers ? — PANTHEISTS
Utility measuring device — METER
Utility vehicle — JEEP
Utilization — USAGE
Utilize — USE
Utilizer — APPLIER
Utmost — MAX, NTH, VERIEST
Utmost degree — NTH
Utmost extent — LIMIT
Utmost group — NTH
Utopia — EDEN
Utopia man — MORE
Utopian — EDENIC, IDEAL
Utopian abodes — EDENS
Utopian place — LAND OF MILK AND HONEY
Utopias — EDENS
Uttar _____, India — PRADESH
Utter — EXPRESS, SAY, SHEER, VOICE
Utter a poem — RECITE
Utter confusion — CHAOS
Utter defeat — ROUT
Utter disdain — SCORN
Utter inadvertently — BLURT
Utter joy — BLISS
Uttered — ORAL
Utterly beat — TROMP
Utters monotonously — DRONES
Utters without thinking — BLATS
Utters, in Br'er Fox jargon — SEZ
Uvula — LOBE
Uzbek corn mix? — SUCCOTASHKENT

V

V-e-r-y impressed — AGOG
V-shaped fortifications — REDANS
V.I. airport designation — STT
V.I.P. — CELEB
V.I.P.'s — EXECS
V.I.P., maybe — CELEB
V.P. — MONDALE
V.P. after Hubert — SPIRO
V.P. John _____ Garner — NANCE
V.P. to F.D.R. — HST
V.P. under G.R.F. — NAR
V.P.: 1925-29 — DAWES
Vacancy — EMPTY
Vacancy sign — TO LET
Vacant — BLANK, INANE
Vacate — LEAVE
Vacation for a soldier — LEAVE
Vacation island in the Atlantic — ARUBA
Vacation site — CAMP
Vacation spot — SPA
Vacation times — SUMMERS
Vacation: lull — RESPITE
Vacationer's choice — CAMP
Vacationer's transport — LINER
Vacillate — REEL, WAVER, WHIFFLE, WOBBLE
Vacillates — WAVERS, YOYOS
Vacuity — VOID
Vacuous — EMPTY, INANE, SILLY
Vacuum — CLEAN
Vacuum tube — DIODE, TRIODE, TETRODE
Vacuum tube: Comb. form — TRON
Vacuums, in a way — CLEANS
Vader of "Star Wars" — DARTH
Vagabond — HOBO, STRAYER, TRAMP
Vagrant — FLOATER, HOBO
Vague — LOOSE
Vague Donatello? — MUDDY TURTLE
Vague or Miles — VERA
Vagus, e.g. — NERVE
Vain — IDLE
Vain person — POP IN JAY
Vain: Ger. — EITEL
Vainglory — POMP
Valdez accident residue — OILY GOO
Valediction — ADIEU
Valence lead-in — AMBI
Valentine — CARD
Valentine message — I LOVE YOU
Valentine motif, Greek style — EROS
Valentine symbol — HEART
Valentino — RUDOLPH
Valentino? — A WOLF IN SHEIKS CLOTHING
Valerie Harper role — RHODA
Valerie Harper sitcom — RHODA
Valiant — HEROIC
Valiant or Igor — PRINCE
Validate — SEAL, VERIFY
Validates a will — PROBATES
Valise — SATCHEL
Vallee namesakes — RUDYS
Valletta native — MALTESE
Valletta personnel — MALTESE
Valletta's island — MALTA
Valletta's land — MALTA
Valley — DALE, GLEN
Valley _____ — FORGE
Valley cut by rainwater — GULLY
Valley in California — NAPA
Valley on the moon — RILLE
Valley, to a poet — VALE
Valor — ARETE
Valor; manliness — ARETE
Valor; virtue — ARETE
Valorous one — HERO
Valuable — COSTLY
Valuable belonging — ASSET
Valuable Brazilian tree — SATINE

Valuable furs — MINKS, SABLES
Valuable N.Z. trees — TOTARAS
Valuable possession — ASSET
Valuable quality — ASSET
Valuable seaweed — KELP
Valuable steed — ARAB
Valuable vases — MINGS
Valuable violin — AMATI
Valuable violins, for short — STRADS
Valuation: Abbr. — EST
Value — PRICE
Valued possessions — ASSETS
Valued seashells — CONCHS
Valued violin — AMATI
Values — ESTEEMS
Values highly — ESTEEMS
Valve rod — TARPET
Vamoose! — SCRAM
Vamp Bara of the Silents — THEDA
Vamp of Broadway and namesakes — LOLAS
Vamp of song — LOLA
Vampire — LAMIA
Vampire costume adjunct — CAPE
Vamps — ENTICERS
Van — LEAD, MOVER
Van Diemen's Land — TASMANIA
Van Dine's Vance — PHILO
Van Druten's "_____ Camera" — I AM A
Van Gogh milieu — ARLES
Van Gogh painted here — ARLES
Van Gogh painted its bridge — ARLES
Van Gogh slept here — ARLES
Van Gogh studio site — ARLES
Van Gogh's "Bridge at _____" — ARLES
Van Gogh's "Room at _____" — ARLES
Van Lewton's first horror film, 1942 — CAT PEOPLE
Van of "Johnny Eager" — HEFLIN
Van Pelt and Ricardo — LUCYS
Van's antonym — REAR
Vance AFB city — ENID
Vandal, e.g. — MARRER
Vandyke and goatee — BEARDS
Vandyke location — CHIN
Vandyke's brother — GOATEE
Vandyke's relative — GOATEE
Vandyke, e.g. — BEARD
Vane dir. — SSE
Vane heading — WSW
Vane reading — ENE
Vanessa's sister — LYNN REDGRAVE
Vanish like vapor — EVANESCE
Vanishing table item — ASHTRAY
Vanity case — ETUI
Vanity source — EGO
Vanquish — ROUT, WORST
Vanquished one — LOSER
Vanquishes — DEFEATS
Vanquishes — DEFEATS
Vantage point — PERCH
Vanuatu's former name: Abbr. — NHEB
Vanzetti's partner — SACCO
Vapid — INANE
Vapid verbiage — GOBBLEDYGOOK
Vapor — GAS, MIST, STEAM
Vapor — STEAM
Vapor: Comb. form — ARI, ATMO
Vaquero's relative — RANCHERO
Vaquero's rope — REATA
Varese's Palazzo d' _____ — ESTE
Vargueno, e.g. — DESK
Variable — CHOPPY
Variable star — MIRA, NOVA
Variable stars — NOVAE
Variant chemical compound — ISOMER
Variant spelling of a Rumanian city — JASSY
Variation of Alice — ALYS
Variation of baseball — SOFTBALL
Variegated — PIED
Variegated, as some quartz — JASPER
Variety — TYPE
Variety headline word — HIX
Variety of apple — BALDWIN
Variety of cabbage — KALE
Variety of chalcedony — ONYX, SARD
Variety of garnet — ALMANDINE
Variety of melon — HONEYDEW
Variety of orange — MANDARIN
Variety of pear — BOSC
Variety of quartz — PRASE
Variety show — REVUE
Variety show of a type — REVUE
Various — ASSORTED
Various species of swallows — MARTIN
Varlet — CAD
Varmint — PEST
Varnish — SHELLAC
Varnish base — ELEMI
Varnish ingredient — ELEMI, LAC, MASTIC, RESIN
Varnish resin — LAC, ELEMI
Varro and Vulgar — ERAS
Vary — ALTER
Vase — URN
Vassals — LIEGES
Vast amount — SEA
Vast desert — SAHARA
Vast holdings — EMPIRES
Vast land mass — ASIA
Vast plain of NE Nigeria — BORNU
Vatic input — OMEN
Vatic sign — OMEN
Vatican figure — POPE
Vatican governing body — CURIA
Vatican guard's nationality — SWISS
Vatican name — PIUS
Vatican office — PAPACY
Vatican resident — JOHN PAUL II
Vatican residents — POPES
Vatican sculpture — PIETA
Vatican tribunal — ROTA
Vatican VIP — POPE
Vaticinator — SEER
Vaudeville features — ACTS
Vaudeville offerings — SKITS
Vaudeville performance — SKIT
Vaudeville prop of yore — STRAW HAT
Vaudeville's Eddie — FOY
Vaughan or Caldwell — SARAH
Vault — LEAP, SAFE
Vaulted areas — APSES
Vaunts — BRAGS
Vauxhall gardens — LONDON
VCR button — RESET
VCR insertion — TAPE
VCR setting — REW
Veau de _____ — RIS
Veda inherent — HINDU
Veep Barkley — ALBEN
Veer — SLUE, SWAY
Veered, as a ship — YAWED
Vega or Rigel — STAR
Vega's constellation — LYRA
Veganova — FIXED STARS
Vegas "arm" — DEALER
Vegas "money" — CHIPS
Vegas attraction — SLOTS
Vegas device — ONE ARMED BANDIT
Vegas lead-in — LAS
Vegas machine — SLOT
Vegas numbers — LINE
Vegetable for soup — OKRA
Vegetable plate items — BRUSSELS SPROUTS
Vegetable pod — HULL
Vegetable-oil component — OLEIN
Vegetables of the gourd family — SQUASHES
Vegetables, for short — CUKES
Vegetarian ophidian? — GRASS IN THE SNAKE

Vegetate — GROW
Veggie holders — PEAPODS
Vehement desire — MANIA
Vehicle for baby — STROLLER
Vehicle for Barbra and Carol — HELLO DOLLY
Vehicle for the Beatles — YELLOW SUBMARINE
Vehicle for winter Olympics — LUGE
Vehicles — AUTOS, CARS
Vehicles for ETs? — UFOS
Vehicles with runners — SLEDS
Vehicular kibitzers — BACK SEAT DRIVER
Veil — COVER
Veiled dancer — SALOME
Vein — AORTA, LODE
Vein location — LODE
Vein of ore — LODE
Vein yield — ORE
Vein's glory — ORE
Veins — VENAE
Veldt animal — ELAND
Veldt antelopes: Var. — KOODOOS
Veldt creature — ELAND
Veldt family — PRIDE
Veldt ungulates — GNUS
Velez of old flicks — LUPE
Velo or hippo ending — DROME
Velocity — RATE
Velvet follower — EEN
Velvetlike clothes — PANNES
Velvety fabric — PANNE
Venal person's gain — BRIBE
Vend — SELL
Vending machine — AUTOMAT
Vending machine feature — SLOT
Vendition — SALE
Vendition condition — AS IS
Venerable — HOAR
Venerable musical comedy — IRENE
Venerable, of yore — OLDE
Venerate — ADORE
Venerated — ESTEEMED, REVERED
Venerates — REVERES
Venetian craft — GONDOLA
Venetian magistrate — DOGE
Venetian officials, of old — DOGES
Venetian resort — LIDO
Venetian sea — ADRIATIC
Venezuelan city — CORO
Venezuelan copper center — AROA
Venezuelan mining town — AROA
Venezuelan perennial? — CARACASPARAGUS
Venezuelan prairie — LLANO
Venezuelan river — ARO
Venice beach — LIDO
Venice bridge — RIALTO
Venice canals — RII
Venice of the north — STOCKHOLM
Venice's Bridge of _____ — SIGHS
Venison — DEER
Venom — HATE
Venom component — VENIN
Venomous — ASPISH
Venomous insect — SCORPION
Venomous lizard — GILA
Venomous noisemaker — RATTLER
Venomous snake — COBRA, COPPERHEAD
Venomous viper — ADDER
Venous fluid for Aphrodite — ICHOR
Venous fluid of the gods — ICHOR
Vent — HOLE
Vent hole — SPIRACLE
Vent or view leader — PRE
Ventilate — AIR
Ventilate thoroughly — AIR OUT
Ventilated — AIRED
Ventilating passageway — INTAKE
Ventilation — AIR
Ventilation area — AIRSHAFT
Ventilation shafts — AIR WELLS
Venture — RISK
Ventured — DARED
Ventures — DARES, RISKS
Venturesome — BOLD
Venturous one — DARER
Venue — SITE
Venus _____ — DE MILO
Venus de _____ — MILO
Venus de Milo's loss — ARMS
Venus flytrap — PLANT
Venus or Juno — DEA
Venus's island — MELOS
Venus, to Vergil — DEA
Vera Cruz — MEXICO
Veranda — LANAI, PORCH
Veranda, in Hawaii — LANAI
Verb attachment — OSE
Verb ending — ING, OSE
Verb ending of yore — ETH
Verb endings — ATES
Verb for innocent or guilty — PLEAD
Verb for Robert Burns — LOE
Verb suffix — ISE
Verb used with thou — DOEST
Verb-forming suffix, British style — ISE
Verbal — LINGUAL, ORAL, PAROL, VOCAL
Verbal abuse — INVECTIVE
Verbal barbs — GIBES
Verbal composition — POEM
Verbal connection — HASNT
Verbal contraction — SHANT
Verbal dig — SLAP
Verbal endings — INGS
Verbal evidence, with "by" — PAROL
Verbal exams — ORALS
Verbal miscue — SLIP OF THE TONGUE
Verbal sally — RIPOSTE
Verbal suffix — ESCE
Verbal truncations — APOCOPES
Verbose — WORDY
Verboten — TABU
Verdant — GRASSY, GREEN
Verdi heroine — AIDA
Verdi opera — AIDA, ERNANI, OTELLO, SIMON BOCCANEGRA
Verdi product, full of froth? — SOAPY OPERA
Verdi work — AIDA
Verdi's "Pace, pace mio _____!" — DIO
Verdi's "Pace, pace mio dio!" — ARIA
Verdi's Egyptian opera — AIDA
Verdi's equivalent to Romeo — RADAMES
Verdi's philanderer? — GIGOLETTO
Verdi's princess — AIDA
Verdon of "Sweet Charity" — GWEN
Vereen of musicals — BEN
Vereen's horn? (Isadora) — BENS TRUMPET
Verge — EDGE, RIM
Verge on — ABUT
Vergil opus — AENEID
Vergil's epic: Var. — ENEID
Verified item — FACT
Verify — FACT, PROVE
Verily — INDEED, YEA
Veritable — REAL
Verlaine's birthplace — METZ
Vermicelli or tortellini — PASTA
Vermin — MICE
Vermont export — SYRUP
Vermont ski resort — STOWE
Vernacular — ARGOT
Verne captain — NEMO
Vernon's partner — IRENE
Verona's river — ADIGE
Veronese question — WHO IS SILVIA
Veronica of "Hill Street Blues" — HAMEL
Veronica, of old flicks — LAKE
Versa's partner — VICE
Versatile — ALL AROUND
Versatile athlete? — JOCK OF ALL TRADES

Versatile liver — RILEY
Versatile one — JACK OF ALL TRADES
Verse division — STANZA
Verse forms — ODES
Verse measures — FEET
Verse starter — UNI
Versed — LEARNED
Verses — ODES
Versification — POESY
Versifier Nash — OGDEN
Versifier: Var. — RIMER
Versifiers — POETS
Verso's opposite — RECTO
Vertical leap in ballet — ENTRECHAT
Vertical pinball machine — PACHINKO
Verticil — WHORL
Vertiginous — AREEL, DIZZY, GIDDY
Verve — DASH, ELAN, ENTHUSIASM, SPIRIT, VIGOR, ZEST
Verve, flair — PANACHE
Verve, in Venezuela — BRIO
Very — EXTREMELY
Very active — TURBULENT
Very angry — IREFUL
Very bitter — ACRID
Very black — EBON
Very bright heavenly body — N STAR
Very cold — GELID
Very commonplace — BANAL
Very dry — BRUT, SERE
Very early bird? — CROW MAGNON
Very excessively — SUPER ABUNDANTLY
Very fast — RAPID, SPEEDY
Very foolish — MORONIC
Very funny person — SCREAM
Very funny story — SCREAM
Very hard — STEELY
Very hungry — FAMISHED
Very important people — STARS
Very important person — MOGUL
Very inactive — UNCONSCIOUS
Very large quantity — OCEAN
Very large: Comb. form — MEGA
Very light brown — ECRU
Very light weight: Abbr. — CGM
Very little money — SHOE STRING
Very long time — EON
Very loud — EARSPLITTING, STENTORIAN
Very loyal — TRUE BLUE
Very obstinate — STUBBORN AS A MULE
Very old — HOARY
Very old: Abbr. — ANC
Very pleased with oneself — PROUD AS A PEACOCK
Very poorly — NEEDY
Very proper — PRIM
Very rarely — ONCE IN A BLUE MOON
Very rarely — ONCE IN A LIFETIME
Very respectful — DEFERENTIAL
Very sad story — TEAR JERKER
Very salty — BRINY
Very secure — TIGHT AS A DRUM
Very silly — APISH
Very slow movement — SNAILS PACE
Very small — TEENY, TEENSY
Very small bits — PARTICLES
Very small country singer? — MINI PEARL
Very small creature — MITE
Very small pin — LILL
Very small town — MUDHOLE
Very softly: Mus. dir. — PPP
Very soon — SHORTLY
Very sour — ACRID
Very tall man from Cracow? — A SIX FOOT POLE
Very tense — ELECTRIC
Very tiny — WEE
Very unconventional one — BEATNIK
Very unusual — RARE
Very, in music — ASSAI
Very, in Verdun — TRES
Very, in Versaille — TRES
Very, to Verdi — ASSAI, MOLTO
Very, very short time — NSEC
Very: French — TRES
Vesicle — CYST
Vespid — WASP
Vespidae family members — HORNETS
Vessel — SHIP, SAIL SHIP
Vessel for a hypodermic solution — AMPULE
Vessel for Ham — ARK
Vessel with a long, sharp prow — SETTEE
Vessel: Abbr. — STR
Vestal virgin, for one — PRIESTESS
Vested garment — SUIT
Vestibule — ENTRY, FOYER, HALL
Vestibules — ANTEROOMS
Vestige — FRAGMENT, HINT, PIECE, RELIC
Vestige — SIGN, TRACE
Vestige — TRACE
Vestiges — RUINS
Vestigial vendors — ICEMEN
Vestment — ALB, AMICE, ROBE
Vestment for the clergy — ALB
Vestments worn at the neck — AMICES
Vestry — CHAPEL
Vestry garb — ALB
Vesuvius rival — ETNA
Vet — EX GI
Vet's day — NOV 11
Vetches — TARES
Veteran actor Robert — DONAT
Veteran of the seas — SALT
Veterans — OLDSTERS
Veto? — UPSET THE APPLE CART
Vetoes — KILLS
Vex — ACERBATE, ANGER, OFFEND, PEEVE
Vex — NETTLE, PESTER, RILE, ROIL
Vex verily — DRIVE UP THE WALL
Vex verily — GET ONES DANDER UP
Vex verily — RUFFLE FEATHERS
Vexations — WEARIFUL
Vexed — IRATE, SORE
Vexes — IRES
Vexillum, e.g. — PETAL
VFW member — VET
Via — PER
Via speech — ORALLY
Vial — CRUET
Viaud's pen name — LOTI
Viaud's pseudonym — LOTI
Vibrant — ALIVE
Vibration — TREMOR
Vibrato — TRILL
Vic's radio wife — SADE
Vice follower — VERSA
Vice-president Aaron and family — BURRS
Vice-president Garner — JOHN NANCE
Vichy marshal — PETAIN
Vichy premier: 1940-44 — PETAIN
Vichy resources — EAUX
Vichy VIP of WW II — LAVAL
Vichyssoise — SOUP
Vicinage — AREA
Vicinity — AREA
Vicious eel — MORAY
Vickers or Domingo — TENOR
Vicki Baum novel, later a movie — GRAND HOTEL
Vicount's superior — EARL
Victim — GOAT, PREY
Victim of Roman aggression: 290 B.C. — SABINE
Victimizes, with "on" — PREYS
Victims of pushers — ADDICTS
Victims of the conquistadores — INCAS

Victor Borge, for one — DANE
Victor Herbert hit — SWEETHEARTS
Victor Herbert operetta: 1922 — ORANGE BLOSSOMS
Victor Herbert sequel? — NICE MARIETTA
Victor Hugo title starter — LES
Victor Hugo's wife — ADELE
Victor Laszlo in "Casablanca" — PAUL HENREID
Victoria _____ — REGINA
Victoria and Catherine II: Abbr. — EMPS
Victoria and Reichenbach — FALLS
Victoria Cross — DECORATION
Victoria of filmdom — PRINCIPAL
Victoria's consort — ALBERT
Victoria's consort, to friends — BERTIE
Victoria's son — EDWARD
Victoria, e.g. — CARRIAGE
Victoria, for one — FALLS
Victorian expletives — DRATS
Victorian oath — EGAD
Victors fog? — DAZE OF GLORY
Victory — WIN
Victory goddess — NIKE
Victory margin — NOSE
Victory sign — VEE
Victory spoils — TROPHIES
Victory, in Berlin — SIEG
Victuals — CHOW, EATS
Vicuna's cousin — LLAMA
Vicuna's habitat — ANDES
Vidal — GORE
Videlicet — TO WIT
Video artist _____ June Paik — NAM
Video display unit — TERMINAL
Vie — COMPETE
Vienna river — DANUBE
Vienna, to an Austrian — WIEN
Vienna, to Fritz — WIEN
Vienna, to Hans — WIEN
Vienna, to the Viennese — WIEN
Vienna-to-Graz dir. — SSW
Vientiane's country — LAOS
Vientiane's locale — LAOS
Vier — CONTENDER
Viet _____ — CONG, NAM
Vietnam city — HANOI
Vietnamese monetary unit — DONG
Vietnamese new year — TET
Vietnamese port — DANANG
Vieux _____ New Orleans' French quarter — CARRE
View — SCENE, SEE
View from a range — FOOTHILLS
View from crow's nest — SEA RIM
View from River Gauche — SEINE
View from Windsor Castle — ETON
View lasciviously — OGLE
Viewers' staple — TELEVISION NEWS
Viewpoint — SLANT
Views quickly — SCANS
Vigeland Museum city — OSLO
Vigil — WATCH
Vigilant — ALERT
Vignette — SKETCH
Vigoda and Burrows — ABES
Vigor — BIRR, PEP
Vigor combined with style — FLAIR
Vigor's partner — VIM
Vigor, in Verona — BRIO
Vigorous — HALE, ROBUST
Vigorously — AMAIN
Viking Ericson — LEIF
Viking god — ODIN
Viking invader of France — ROLLO
Vikings — NORSE
Vilified — SMEARED
Vilipends — SLURS
Villa d' _____ — ESTE
Villa d' _____ in Tivoli — ESTE
Villa Maria College site — ERIE
Village — BURG, DORP
Village community in Russia — MIR
Village near Colon, Panama — PORTOBELLO
Village near Minneapolis — EDINA
Village near Nazareth — CANA
Village SW of Cedar Rapids — AMANA
Village SW of Minneapolis — EDINA
Villain's contortion — SNEER
Villain's greeting — HISS
Villain's grimace — LEER
Villain's look — LEER
Villain's smile — LEER
Villain, in oaters — BLACK HAT
Villainous glance — LEER
Villainous looks — SNEERS
Villainous one — FIEND
Villainous Vader — DARTH
Villains — ROGUES
Villains trademark — SNEER
Villanelle, for one — POEM
Villatic — RURAL
Ville V.I.P. — MAIRE
Villein, at one time — SERF
Villeins — BONDSMEN
Vilnius is its cap. — LITH
Vince, to Gomer — SARGE
Vincent — NORMAN PEALE
Vincent Lopez theme — NOLA
Vincent van _____ — GOGH
Vincente's daughter — LIZA MINNELLI
Vindicates — AVENGES
Vine — LIANA
Vine fruit for short — CUKE
Vine of the bean family — VETCH
Vine offshoot — TENDRIL
Vine support — TRELLIS
Vinegar — ACETO, ACETUM
Vinegar bottle — CRUET
Vinegar container — CRUET
Vinegar dregs — MOTHER
Vinegar Joe — STILLWELL
Vinegar: Prefix — ACETO
Vinegary — ACERB, ACETIC
Vinegary: Comb. form — ACETO
Vingt _____ card game — ETUN
Vino center — ASTI
Vintage — CHOICE
Vintage auto — EDSEL, REO
Vintage car — NASH, REO
Vintner's 252 gallons — TUN
Vintner's apparatus — PRESSER
Vintner's gear — PRESS
Vintner's holding — WINERY
Vintner's vessel — VAT
Violate — RAVAGE
Violations — INFRACTIONS
Violent — RABID
Violent anger — RAGE
Violent one — BATTERER
Violent people — TARTARS
Violent Sahara winds — SIMOOMS
Violent start — ULTRA
Violent struggles — AGONIES
Violet shade — MAUVE
Violet start — ULTRA
Violetta — LA TRAVIATA
Violin bow — STICK
Violin maker — AMATI
Violin maker Nicolo — AMATI
Violin part — NECK
Violin's predecessor — REBEC
Violinist born in Russia — STERN
Violinist Bull — OLE
Violinist Isaac — STERN
Violinist Jack — BENNY
Violinist Joseph — SZIGETI
Violinist Kavafian — ANI
Violinist Ma — YOYO
Violinist Milstein — NATHAN
Violinist Mischa — ELMAN
Violinist Stern — ISAAC
Violinist Ughi — UTO
Violinist's need — RESIN
VIP — BIGGY
VIP at Lincoln Center — MEHTA

VIP from Michigan — LEVIN
VIP in a choir — CHANTER
VIP in baseball — MANAGER
VIP in newspaper work — EDITOR
VIP in the suburbs — GARDENER
VIP of old Venice — DOGE
VIP's stretch — LIMO
VIP, with "his" — NIBS
Viperous — ASPISH
Vipers — ASPS
Vipers defense — VENOM
Viracocha worshiper — INCA
Viral skin ailment — HERPES
Vireo — GREENLET
Virgilian wrath — IRE
Virginal — CHASTE
Virginia _____ — REEL
Virginia bird? — CULPEPEREGRINE
Virginia born president — TAYLOR
Virginia dance — REEL
Virginia Senator John _____ — WARNER
Virginia willow — ITEA
Virginia willow genus — OSIER
Virginia's governor: 1717-49 — GOOCH
Virile — MACHO
Virile fellow — HEMAN
Virile one — HEMAN
Virile: Abbr. — MASC
Virtue or number — CARDINAL
Virtuosity — SKILL
Virtuous — CHASTE, MORAL
Virulent — RABID
Visayan island — CEBU
Viscid — STICKY
Viscount or baron — PEER
Viscount Templewood — HOARE
Viscous — SLIMY, STICKY
Viscous mud — SLIME
Viscous substance — SLIME
Vise — CLAMP
Vishnu avatar — RAMA
Vishnu incarnate — RAMA
Visigoth king — ALARIC
Visigothic king — ALARIC
Vision — FORESIGHT
Vision start — TELE
Visionaries — DREAMERS
Visionary — FANTAST, IDEAL, SEER
Visionary — SEER
Visionary plan — SCHEME
Visions — SIGHTS
Visit — DROP BY, DROP IN, SEE
Visit casually — RUN IN
Visit habitually — HAUNT
Visit Vail — SKI
Visiting — DROPPING BY, STOPPING IN
Visitor — CALLER, GUEST
Visitor from Mars — ALIEN
Visitor to Wonderland — ALICE
Visitors from Mars — ALIENS
Visored cap of a type — KEPI
Visorless cap — BERET
Vistas — VIEWS
Vistula tributary — SAN
Visual — OCULAR
Visual aid — GRAPH
Visualization — IMAGE
Visualize — SEE, IMAGINE, PICTURE
Vita, for short — BIO
Vitae — BIOS
Vital fluid — SAP
Vital Manhattan activity — ADVERTISING
Vital stat. — AGE
Vital statistic — AGE, DEATH
Vital vessel — AORTA
Vitality — ELAN, PULSE
Vitalize — ANIMATE
Vitalizes, with "up" — PEPS
Vitamin A source — CARROT
Vitamin letters — RDA
Vitamin qty. — RDA
Vitamin unit — RDA
Vitiates — DEBASES
Vittles — EATS
Vituperation — ABUSE
Vituperative harangue — TIRADE
Vituperative one — ABUSER
Viva voce — ALOUD, ORAL, ORALLY
Viva voce examination — ORAL
Vivacity — BRIO
Vive _____! — LE ROI
Vive's opposite — ABAS
Vivid reddish orange — VERMILION
Vivien Leigh film: 1940 — WATERLOO BRIDGE
Vivify — ANIMATE
Vixen — BATTLE AX
Vixen's home — DEN
Vizier's superior — AGA
VOA agcy. — USIA
VOA's org. — USIA
Vocal — ORAL
Vocal group — CHOIR
Vocal one — SAYER
Vocal pauses — ERS
Vocal thumbs down — HISS
Vocal vote — AYE
Vocalist — ALTO
Vocalist Cantrell — LANA
Vocalist James — ETTA
Vocalist Paul — ANKA
Vocalist Vikki — CARR
Vocalize — SING
Vocalize, Swiss style — YODEL
Vocalized — INTONED
Vocation — METIER
Vociferate — YELL
Vociferous — STRIDENT
Vogue — FASHION
Voice — THROAT
Voice of Charlie and Mortimer — EDGAR
Voice over — DUB
Voice range — ALTO
Voice vote — AYE
Voice vote — YEA
Voice-over people — NARRATORS
Voiced — SONANT, UTTERED
Voiceless — APHONIC
Voiceless sound — SURD
Voiceless sound in German — ICHLAUT
Voices insolence — SASSES
Void — NEGATE
Voight's comical Dink — PETEY
Voila! — THERE
Vol. measures — CCS
Volatile — NON, UNSTABLE
Volcanic ash — LAVA
Volcanic crater — MAAR
Volcanic flow — LAVA
Volcanic matter — ASH
Volcanic mountain — ETNA
Volcanic peaks — CONES
Volcanic product — SLAG
Volcanic rock — BASALT
Volcano feature — CRATER
Volcano in Italy — ETNA
Volcano in Martinique — PELEE
Volcano near Catania — ETNA
Volcano on Martinique — PELEE
Volcano product — SLAG
Volcano's output — LAVA
Vole of the meadows — FIELD MOUSE
Volga branch — OKA
Volga tributary — OKA
Volleys — SALVOS
Vols' home — TENN
Volstead Act opponent — WET
Volstead Act supporter — DRY
Voltaire opus — CANDIDE
Voltaire was one — DEIST
Voltaire's forte — SATIRE
Voluble — FLUENT, GLIB
Volume — TOME
Volume units — STERES
Volunteer for svc. — ENL
Volunteer from Bristol? — TENNESSEE ERNIE FORD
Volunteer State hit list? — TOP TENNESSEE
Volunteer State: Abbr. — TENN
Volunteer: Abbr. — ENL
Volunteers in Service To America — VISTA

Voluptuous woman — HOURI
Volvo competitor — SAAB
Von Richthofen's title — BARON
Von Stroheim — ERICH
Von Weber Opera — OBERON
Voracious eels — MORAYS
Voracious fish — BARRACUDA
Voracity — GREED
Vortex — EDDY
Vote — AYE, NAY
Vote count — RETURNS
Vote for — AYE
Vote in — ELECT
Vote into office — ELECT
Vote nay — OPPOSE
Vote of assent — PLACET
Vote out of office — UNSEAT
Vote to accept — ADOPT
Voted in — ELECTED
Voted into office — ELECTED
Voter — ELECTOR
Voter's choice — NAY
Voting into law — ENACTMENT
Voting list — BALLOT
Vouch for — ENDORSE
Voucher — CHIT
Voucher for food — CHIT
Vous _____ — ETES
Vow — OATH, SWEAR
Vow at the altar — I DO
Vow taker — CELIBATE
Vowed — SWORE
Vowel sequence — AEIOU, AEIO
Vowel sound — SCHWA
Vowel trio — AEI
Vows of Jan. 1 — RESOLUTIONS
Vox _____ — POPULI
Voyage — SAIL, TRIP
Voyeurs — EYERS
VP or treas. — EXEC
Vronsky's beloved — ANNA
Vt. granite center — BARRE
Vu lead-in — DEJA
Vulcan — SMITH
Vulcan's milieu — ETNA
Vulgar — COARSE, CRUDE, LOWBRED
Vulgar and Mundane — ERAS
Vulgar blokes — MUCKERS
Vulgar; cheap — TATTY
Vulgarian — BOUNDER
Vulgarized — DEGRADED
Vulnerable car parts — FENDERS
Vulnerable part of the elbow — CRAZY BONE
Vulture or shark, e.g. — PREDATOR

W

W African country — GHANA
W Austrian native — TIROLEAN
W Rumanian city — ARAD
W Samoa's capital — APIA
W Texas city — ODESSA
W Ukrainian river — SERET
W. German state — HESSE
W. Hemisphere org. — OAS
W. Hoffman play: 1985 — AS IS
W. Indies volcano — PELEE
W. Paley presided here — CBS
W.C. and Johnny's pocket money? — HANDY CASH
W.J. Bryan specialty — ORATION
W.J.C. at age 32 — GOVERNOR
W.J.C.'s half brother. O.K.! — ROGER
W.J.C.'s latest alma mater? — ELECTORAL COLLEGE
W.J.C.'s town of expectation? — HOPE
W.W. I aircraft — TRIPLANE
W.W. I poster man — FLAGG
W.W. II agency — OPA
W.W. II area — ETO
W.W. II boats — PTS
W.W. II bomber — STUKA
W.W. II coalition — AXIS
W.W. II craft — LST
W.W. II entity — AXIS
W.W. II German bomber — STUKA
W.W. II HQ acronym — SHAEF
W.W. II India-Burma road — LEDO
W.W. II journalist — PYLE
W.W. II landing craft — LST
W.W. II medal — DSC
W.W. II menace — UBOAT
W.W. II mil. woman — WAAC
W.W. II naval base — EMDEN
W.W. II riveter — ROSIE
W.W. II Service org. — USO
W.W. II soldiers — GIS
W.W. II souvenir — LUGER
W.W. II sphere of action — ETO
W.W. II tanks — SHERMANS
W.W. II theater — ETO
Wacko — ZANY
Wacky — LOCO
Wacky — LOONY, MAD
Wacky, Brit style — POTTY
Waco, Tex., University — BAYLOR
Wad — BUNDLE
Waddle — SWAY
Wade — SLOSH
Wade through — READ
Wade's opponent of note — ROE
Wader — RAIL
Wader in the Everglades — EGRET
Waders — HERONS
Wadi — RAVINE
Wading bird — CRANE, EGRET, HERON, IBIS, RAIL
Wading bird — SORA, SNIPE
Wafer — DISK
Waft — FLOAT
Wag — CARD
Wage earner — CONTRACTOR, ELECTRICIAN
Wage earner — NUCLEAR ENGINEER, STONE MASON
Wage earner — UPHOLSTERER
Wager — BET, LAY
Wagers — ANTES, BETS
Waggish — DROLL
Wagner heroine — ELSA, ISOLDE, SENTA
Wagner heroine, princess of Brabant — ELSA
Wagner opera — GOTTERDAMMERUNG
Wagner TV role — HART
Wagner's "_____ fliegende Holländer" — DER
Wagner's "_____ und Isolde" — TRISTAN
Wagner's "Tristan und _____" — ISOLDE
Wagner's advice to Elsie the cow? — LOW AND GRIN
Wagner's earth goddess — ERDA
Wagner's first wife — MINNA

Wagner's short-order cook? — FRYING DUTCHMAN
Wagner, the "Flying Dutchman" — HONUS
Wagnerian figure — ERDA
Wagnerian god — WOTAN
Wagnerian goddess — ERDA
Wagnerian heroine — ELSA
Wagnerian role — ERDA
Wagnerian yuppie? — TOWN HOUSER
Wagon — DRAY
Wagon after wagon — CARAVAN
Wagon of yore — CONESTOGA
Wagon on runners — PUNG
Wagon parts — AXLES
Wagon tongue — POLE
Wagon-wheel holder — AXLE
Wagons- _____: Fr. sleeping cars — LITS
Wags the tongue — GABS
Wahoo — ELM
Waif — GAMIN, STRAY
Waikiki welcome gift — LEI
Wail — HOWL, YOWL
Wailed — KEENED
Wailing spirit of Gaelic myth — BANSHEE
Wainscot panel — PANE
Waist cincher — BELT, SASH
Waistbands — SASHES
Waistcoat — VEST
Wait — BIDE
Wait _____: be patient — AND SEE
Wait awhile — BIDE
Wait between flights — LAYOVER
Wait on — SERVE
Waiter's assistant — BUSBOY
Waiter's burden — TRAY
Waiter's delight — TIPPER
Waiter's offering — MENU
Waiter's tote — TRAY
Waiters' formations — LINES
Waiting group — LINE
Waiting-room exercise — WALKING THE FLOOR
Waiting-room word — NEXT
Waits on — SERVES
Waits upon — ATTENDS
Waive one's decision — REJECT
Waive one's rights — CEDES
Wakashan people of Vancouver Island — AHT
Wake — AROUSE, ROUSE, STIR, WATCH
Wake up — RISE
Wake-up summons — REVEILLE
Wakefield man — VICAR
Wakefield's clergyman — VICAR
Waken — RISE, ROUSE
Wakened — ARISEN, ROUSED
Wakes up — ROUSES
Walden, e.g. — POND
Walden, for one — POND
Waldorf-Astoria muralist — SERT
Walesa — LECH
Walesa and friends — POLES
Walesa is one — POLE
Walesa of Poland — LECH
Walesa's people — POLES
Walesa, for one — POLE
Walk — ALLEE, TRAMP, TREAD
Walk _____ (be happy) — ON AIR
Walk about aimlessly — RAMBLE
Walk back and forth — PACE
Walk between trees — ALLEE
Walk down the aisle — WED
Walk heavily — PLOD
Walk on — TREAD
Walk quietly — TIPTOE
Walk the floor — PACE
Walk wearily — PLOD
Walk with a heavy step — STAMP
Walk with long steps — STRIDE
Walk-ons? — SOLES
Walked — PACED, TROD
Walked casually — SASHAYED
Walked in water — WADED
Walked on — TROD
Walked triumphantly — STRODE
Walked unsteadily — TODDLED
Walked upon — TROD
Walker or Wightman — CUP
Walker under an umbrella? — DRY PEDESTRIAN
Walker: abbr. — PED
Walkie-talkies — RADIOS
Walking — AFOOT
Walking _____ (elated) — ON AIR
Walking manner — GAIT
Walking papers — DISMISSAL, PINK SLIP
Walking shoes — FLATS
Walking stick — CANE
Walks arrogantly — STRIDES
Walks awkwardly — SHAMBLES
Walks back and forth — PACES
Walks haltingly — LIMPS
Walks in water — WADES
Walks like a peacock — STRUTS
Walks sinuously — SLINKS
Walks through water — WADES
Walkway — PATH
Wall bracket for candles — SCONCE
Wall climber — IVY, VINE
Wall decoration — DADO, MURAL
Wall hanging — ARRAS
Wall material — PLASTER
Wall ornament — PINUP
Wall painting — MURAL
Wall recess — NICHE
Wall St. abbr. — AMEX, RTS
Wall St. acronym — AMEX
Wall St. deg. — MBA
Wall St. exchange — OTC
Wall St. fixture — NYSE
Wall Street — MANHATTAN
Wall Street abbr. — RTS
Wall Street acronym — AMEX
Wall Street bull session? — RALLY
Wall Street deals — TRADES
Wall Street doc. — CTF
Wall Street figure — BROKER
Wall Street meeting places — BOARDROOMS
Wall Street order — BUY, SELL
Wall Street pessimist — BEAR
Wall Street ploy — STOCK SPLIT
Wall street symbol — BEAR
Wall Street term — NO PAR
Wall Street type — BROKER
Wall Street unit — STOCK
Wall supports — STUDS
Wallace of silents — REID
Wallace's running mate: 1968 — LEMAY
Wallach — ELI
Wallach and Whitney — ELIS
Wallach or Whitney — ELI
Wallach or Yale — ELI
Wallaroo — EURO
Wallboard — PANEL
Walled city near Segovia — AVILA
Waller or Domino — FATS
Wallet bill — ONE
Wallet contents — ONES, TENS
Wallet fillers — ONES
Wallet items — ONES
Wallet stuffers — ONES
Wallop — BELT
Wally _____ of baseball fame — PIPP
Walnut or pecan — TREE
Walnut product — OIL
Walrus's remark — THE TIME HAS COME
Walston on TV — MARTIAN
Walt _____ Disney — ELIAS
Walt Kelly character — POGO
Walt Kelly's opossum — POGO
Walt Whitman poem — O CAPTAIN MY CAPTAIN
Walter _____ Disney — ELIAS
Walter _____ Mare — DE LA
Walter and Uta — HAGENS
Walter Mitty player — KAYE
Walter of Hollywood — ABEL
Walter or Uta — HAGEN
Walter's ponies of brandy? — SCOTTS TOTS

Waltz — DANCE
Waltz or foxtrot — BALL-ROOM DANCE
Waltz portion — STEP
Wampum — BEADS
Wan — ASHEN, ASHY, PALE, PALLID, PEAKED
Wand — ROD
Wander — GAD, RANGE, ROAM, ROVE, STRAY
Wander about — ROVE
Wander freely — ROVE
Wander idly — GAD
Wander stealthily — PROWL
Wandered — ROAMED
Wandered about idly — GADDED
Wandered aimlessly — ROVED
Wanderer — NOMAD
Wandering — ERRANT, MEANDERING
Wandering aimlessly — MEANDERING
Wandering cowboy's milieu — LONE PRAIRIE
Wandering dog — ROVER
Wandering star — PLANET
Wanders about — GADS
Wane — ABATE
Waned — EBBED
Waned's partner — WAXED
Wanes — EBBS
Wang Lung's wife in "The Good Earth" — ELAN
Wangle — FALSIFY
Wanness — PALLOR
Want — NEED
Want _____ — ADS
Want badly — CRAVE
Wanted poster abbr. — AKA
Wanting — NEEDY
Wanton — AIRY
Wanton look — LEER
Wapiti — ELK
Wapiti leather — ELK SKIN
Wapner's wrap — ROBE
War — COMBAT
War club — MACE
War correspondent Ernie — PYLE
War cry in 1898 — REMEMBER THE MAINE
War god — ARES, MARS
War horse — CHARGER
War memento — SCAR
War of 1776 — REVOLUTIONARY
War theater, for short — NAM
War to end war — ARMAGEDDON
War whoops — YELLS
War's antonym — PEACE
War, to Sherman — HELL
War-horse — LEADER
Warble — SING, TRILL
Warbler — BIRD
Warbler and roller — CANARIES
Warbucks — DADDY
Warbucks' ward — ANNIE
Ward healer?: Var. — INTERNE
Ward heeler — POL
Ward heelers — POLS
Ward off — AVERT, REPEL
Ward VIP — NURSE
Wardens — CONTENDERS
Warder — TURNKEY
Wardrobe — ARMOIRE, ATTIRE, OUTFIT
Wards off — FENDS
Warehouse — DEPOT, ENTREPOT, ETAPE
Warehouse fee: Abbr. — STOR
Warehoused — STOWED
Wares — GOODS
Warhol and others — ANDYS
Warhol film: 1970 — TRASH
Warhol forte — POP ART
Warhol or Griffith — ANDY
Warhorse — STEED
Warlike — HOSTILE
Warlike tribe of the Southern Plains — COMANCHE
Warlock — WIZARD
Warm — HEAT
Warm and comfy — TOASTY
Warm mountain wind: Var. — FOHN
Warm overcoats — ULSTERS
Warm Springs, for example — SPA
Warm up — DRILL
Warm up an oven — PREHEAT
Warm weather toppers — PANAMA HATS
Warm welcome — GLAD HAND
Warm-blooded — ARDENT, RASH
Warmed up — HEATED
Warmish — TEPID
Warms again — REHEATS
Warms up again — REHEATS
Warmth — ARDOR, HEAT
Warn — ALERT, ADVISE, CAUTION, NOTIFY
Warning — CAVEAT, COUNSEL, NOTICE, TOCSIN
Warning from a whippet — GNAR
Warning initials — TNT
Warning periods — ALERTS
Warning sign — DO NOT ENTER, DONT LITTER
Warning sign — NO PARKING, NO SMOKING
Warning sign — ON OR OFF, DANGER, HIGH VOLTAGE
Warning signal of old — ALARUM
Warning signals — SIRENS
Warning sound — ALARM, ALERT, BEEP
Warning sound from the engine — PING
Warning sounds from Fido — GRRS
Warning to an equivocator — DO NOT MINCE WORDS
Warns — ALERTS
Warns — CAUTIONS
Warp — MISSHAPE, TWIST
Warp yarn — ABB
Warplane compartments — BOMB BAYS
Warrant — MERIT
Warrant off. — BOSN
Warrant officers — BOSUNS
Warrant server — ARRESTER
Warrant-officer — NCO
Warranty — BOND
Warred — FOUGHT
Warren Beatty film — REDS
Warren Beatty role — DICK TRACY
Warren Beatty's sister — SHIRLEY MACLAINE
Warren females — DOES
Warren Moon was one — OILER
Warren of the Supreme Court — EARL
Warsaw emoter? — POLISH HAM
Warsaw man — POLE
Warsaw Mrs. — PANI
Wartime friend — ALLY
Wartime inits. — OSS
Warty amphibians — TOADS
Warwick, to Houston — AUNT
Wary — ALERT, LEERY
Was a model — POSED
Was a party to — ABETTED
Was able to — COULD
Was ahead — LED
Was altruistic — SHARED
Was at the ready — HAD ON TAP
Was aware of — KNEW
Was babbling — PRATED
Was bested — LOST
Was carried along — RODE
Was checkmated — LOST
Was concerned — CARED
Was contingent — DEPENDED
Was curious — NOSED, WONDERED
Was defeated — MET ONES WATERLOO
Was destructive — HARMED
Was eminent — SHONE
Was first — LED
Was flirtatious — OGLED
Was foolishly fond — DOTED
Was human — ERRED
Was in arrears — OWED
Was in debt — OWED

Was in front — LED
Was in one — KNEW
Was in session — SAT
Was in the audience — ATTENDED
Was in the red — OWED
Was indebted — OWED
Was influential — COUNTED
Was insolent — SASSED
Was intrepid — DARED
Was left on base — DIED
Was literate — READ
Was merciful — SPARED
Was mistaken — ERRED
Was nostalgic — ACHED
Was nosy — SNOOPED
Was not well — AILED
Was obligated — HAD TO
Was out of sorts — AILED
Was overfond — DOTED
Was overly fond, with "on" — DOTED
Was overworked — SLAVED
Was prepared — WONDERED
Was rash, a la the Irish? — ACTED IMPATUOUSLY
Was sorry for — RUED
Was too fond of (with "on") — DOTED
Was too permissive — DOTED
Was under the weather — AILED
Was up to here with — HAD IT
Was very attractive — LOOKED LIKE A MILLION
Was wary — TOOK CARE
Was wrong — ERRED
Wash — BATHE, LAVE, LAUNDER
Wash basin of yore — LAVER
Wash cycle — RINSE
Wash or wild starter — HOG
Wash out — RINSE
Wash out, as impurities — ELUTE
Wash Tubbs and Captain _____ — EASY
Wash. cape — ALAVA
Wash. figure — SEN
Wash. funding agcy. — SBA
Wash. title — SEN
Wash. VIP — PRES
Washbowl — BASIN
Washday aids — SOFTENERS
Washday batch — LAUNDRY
Washed — BATHED
Washed out — FADED
Washed up — KAPUT
Washer cycle — RINSE, SPIN
Washer setting — RINSE
Washer's swasher — AGITATOR
Washes — LAVES
Washes out — RINSES
Washes out suds — RINSES
Washing dishes, e.g. — CHORE
Washing utensil — RINSER
Washington and Cleveland, e.g. — PRESIDENTS
Washington art gallery — FREER
Washington aspic? — MOUSEATTLE
Washington bill — ONE
Washington players — REDSKINS
Washington portraitist — PEALE
Washington sound — PUGET
Washington V.I.P. — SEN
Washington's _____ Theater — ARENA
Washington's bill — ONE
Washington, for example — GENERAL
Washington, for one — STATE
Washout — BUST
Washroom, for short — LAV
Washstand items — EWERS
Washup facilities — BATHS
Washup place — BATH
Washy start — WISHY
Wasn't steady — TEETERED
WASP's gift to Mom? — A STUNNING YELLOW JACKET
Wassail — DRINK
Wassail drink — ALE
Wassail quaff — ALE
Waste — RUIN
Waste allowance — TARE, TRET
Waste allowance — TRET
Waste away — WEAR
Waste maker — HASTE
Waste producer — HASTE
Waste time — DILLY DALLY
Wasted time — IDLED, POTTERED
Wasteland — DESERT
Wasting tears — CRYING OVER SPILT MILK
Wat Tyler was one — REBEL
Watch — TEND, VIEW, VIGIL
Watch activator — SPRING
Watch comms. — OGS
Watch one's weight — DIET
Watch out! — HANG ON TO YOUR HAT
Watch over — TEND
Watch part — MOVEMENT, STEM
Watch pendant — FOB
Watch pocket — FOB
Watch site — WRIST
Watch the baby — SIT
Watch the weight — DIET
Watch your _____! — STEP
Watch, for example — TIME-PIECE
Watchdog's warning — SNARL
Watched the kids — SAT
Watcher — EYER
Watches — EYES, TICKERS
Watchful — ALERT
Watchful guardian — ARGUS
Watchful ones — EYERS
Watching — SAT
Watchwords — SLOGANS
Water — ADAMS ALE
Water barriers — DAMS, DIKES
Water bird — EGRET, ERNE, SWAN
Water body east of the Caspian — ARAL
Water buffalo — ARNA
Water buffalo's cousin — ARNA
Water buffaloes — CARABAOS
Water carrier — HOSE
Water cock — KORA
Water craft — STEAMBOATS
Water frozen in the Weser — EIS
Water jugs — EWERS
Water lilies' milieu — POND
Water nymph — NAIAD
Water pictures — EWERS
Water pipes — HOOKAHS
Water places — SPAS
Water plant — ALGA
Water plants — ALGAE
Water scorpion — NEPA
Water sound — SWASH
Water strider, e.g. — BUG
Water vessel — EWER
Water wheel — NORIA
Water's edge — SHORE
Water, e.g. — LIQ
Water, in Evian — EAU
Water, in Madrid — AGUA
Water, in Mexico City — AGUA
Water, in Oviedo — AGUA
Water, in Paris — EAU
Water, in the Rio Grande — AGUA
Water, to Juan — AGUA
Water-closet — PRIVY
Water-color — PIGMENT
Watercourse — RACE
Watercourse, Cajun style — BAYOU
Watercourse, of a kind — WADI
Watered silk — MOIRE
Waterfall — CASCADE
Waterford's country — EIRE
Waterfront inn — BOTEL
Waterfront locations — DOCKS
Waterfront scene — PIER
Watering place — OASIS, SPA
Watering spots — OASES, SPAS
Watering system — SPRINKLER
Waterloo — RUIN
Waterloo marshal — NEY
Waterloo name — NEY

Waterloo winner — BRITISH
Waterloo's location — IOWA
Waterloo's state — IOWA
Waterproof canvas, for short — TARP
Waterproof coat — SLICKER
Waters — ETHEL
Waters or Kennedy — ETHEL
Waterway — CANAL
Waterways: Sp. — RIOS
Waterwheel — NORIA
Waterwitch — DOWSE
Watery — THIN
Watery phenomenon — EDDY
Watson discovery — DNA
Watson's 5's, 7's, etc. — IRONS
Watson's cry — FORE
Watt power — STEAM
Wattle tree of Australia — BOREE
Wattlebird — IAO
Watts' fuel — STEAM
Watts' instrument — PIANO
Waugh or Clunes — ALEC
Waugh or Templeton — ALEC
Waugh or Wilder — ALEC
Wave — BREAKER, RIPPLE
Wave breakers — PROWS
Wave crest — WHITE CAP
Wave motion — CHOP
Wave on the Costa del Sol — OLA
Wave on the Ebro — OLA
Wave side to side — WAG
Wave, in France — ONDE
Wave, in Paris — ONDE
Wave, in Venice — ONDA
Wave: Fr. — ONDE
Waver — TEETER
Wavered — SWAYED
Waves — SEA
Wavy-patterned silk — MOIRE
Wavy, in heraldry — ONDE
Wax source — CARNAUBA
Wax stertorous — SNORE
Wax: Comb. form — CER, CERO
Wax: Sp. — CERA
Waxed, old style — CERED
Waxen — PALE
Waxes wroth — RAGES
Waxlike: Comb. form — CER
Waxy substance — SEALANT
Way — AVENUE, CUSTOM, HABIT, MANNER, MEANS
Way — METHOD, ROUTE
Way from the heart — AORTA
Way in — DOOR, ENTRY
Way in or out — GATE
Way lead-in — THRU
Way of learning, with "by" — ROTE
Way of thinking — BELIEF
Way off base — ALL WET
Way out — DOOR, EGRESS, EXIT
Way to "spoil the child" — SPARE THE ROD
Way to address a British peer — MILORD
Way to address the queen — MAAM
Way to America for many an immigrant — STEERAGE
Way to be taken — ABACK
Way to go: Abbr. — RTE
Way to look — ALIVE
Way to Oz — YELLOW BRICK ROAD
Way to pay — CASH
Way to run — AMOK
Way to send a letter — AIRMAIL
Way to stand — PAT
Way to the altar — AISLE
Way to the highway — RAMP
Way up — STAIR
Way way away — AFAR
Way: Abbr. — SYST
Wayfarers — TRANSIENTS
Waylay — AMBUSH
Wayne hit film — HATARI
Wayne's was green — BERET
Ways — MODES, ROADS
Ways out — DOORS
Ways up — ASCENTS
Wayside hotels — INNS
Wayward — ERRANT, ROVING
WBA victory — TKO
WCTU members, for instance — DRYS
We, to Luciano — NOI
Weak — FEEBLE, FRAIL, SPINELESS
Weak-eyed worm hunter — MOLE
Weaken — DISABLE, FALTER, SAG, SAP
Weaken gradually — SAP
Weakened — SAPPED
Weakens — SAPS
Weakest excuse — LAMEST
Wealth — MEANS
Wealthy — MONIED
Wealthy person — NABOB
Wean — ABLACTATE
Weapon — GUN, LANCE, TOOL
Weapon for Artemis — EPEE
Weapon for Athos — EPEE
Weapon for D'Artagnan — RAPIER
Weapon of a sort — GAT
Weapon of old — TOMA-HAWK
Weapon of yore — BROADSWORD
Weapon suppliers — ARMERS
Weapon that makes a comeback — BOOMERANG
Weapon, for Napoleon — ARME
Weapon, in Mons — ARME
Weapon, in Toledo — ARMA
Weaponless — UNARMED
Weaponry — ARMS
Weapons hole — SILO
Weapons manufacturers — ARMORERS
Weapons repository — ARMORY
Weapons store — ARSENAL
Weapons supplier — ARMER
Weapons, of old — SNEES
Wear — ADORN
Wear away — ERODE
Wear down — TIRE
Wear out — ERODE, DO IN
Wear well — LAST
Wear with an air — SPORT
Wear's associate — WASH
Wearing — ATTIRED
Wearing a label — TAGGED
Wearing garments — CLAD
Wearing shoes — SHOD
Wearisome — OPEROSE
Wears — FRAYS, HAS ON
Wears out — TIRES
Weary — PALL
Weary looking — DRAWN
Weary Willies — VAGS
Weasel — STOAT
Weasel at times — STOAT
Weasel out — DUCK
Weasel's cousin — MINK, OTTER
Weasel's kin — OTTER
Weasel's relative — MARTEN
Weasellike mammal — STOAT
Weather Bureau group — WBO
Weather delay at Fenway — RAINOUT
Weather forecast — CLEAR, COOL, FAIR, RAIN
Weather forecaster — METEOROLOGIST
Weather indicator — BAROMETER
Weather map area — LOW
Weather map line — ISOBAR
Weather map storm belt — SQUALL LINE
Weather norms: Abbr. — STP
Weather outlook — CALM
Weather phenomenon — SMOG
Weather probe — SONDE
Weather satellite — TIROS
Weather vane — COCK
Weather word — CLOUDY, COOL, FAIR, RAIN
Weather word — SLEET, SLEETY, SMOG, SNOW
Weather word — STORM, WET
Weather, to Wordsorth — CLIME
Weathercock — VANE
Weatherman's abbr. — TEMP

Weatherman's August warning — GET OUT OF TOWN
Weatherman's concern — ELEMENTS
Weave — KNIT
Weave together — ENTWINE
Weave wickerwork — WALE
Weaver bird, formerly — ORIOLE
Weaver role on "Gunsmoke" — CHESTER
Weaver's device — SHUTTLE
Weaver's pattern — BROCADE
Weaver's reeds — SLEYS
Weaving need — LOOM
Weaving term — BEAM
Web-footed marsupial — YAPOK
Web — SNARE
Webber-Rice musical — EVITA
Weber State College site — OGDEN
Weber's "Freischutz" — DER
Webfooted mammal — OTTER
Weblike membrane — TELA
Weblike tissue — TELA
Webster entry — WORD
Webster or Clay — ORATOR
Webster, the lexicographer — NOAH
Wed — JOIN, ONED, UNITE
Wed on the run — ELOPE
Wedding-cake units — TIERS
Wedding announcement word — NEE
Wedding day event — RECEPTION
Wedding dress material — SATIN
Wedding gown epilog — TRAIN
Wedding gown feature — TRAIN
Wedding night serenade — SHIVAREE
Wedding party member — PAGE
Wedding principal — BRIDE
Wedding words — I DO
Wedding write-up word — NEE
Wedding-gown aisle sweeper — TRAIN
Wedge — AXE
Wedge shaped — CUNEATE
Wedged — IMPACTED
Wedgelike stopper — CHOCK
Wedges for wheels — TRIGS
Wedgwood — CHINA
Weds hastily — ELOPES
Weds in haste — ELOPES
Wee — ITSY, LITTLE, TEENY, TINY
Wee antelope — DIKDIK
Wee bit — DRAM
Wee fellow, in Eire — MAN EEN
Wee hoarders of legend — LEPRECHAUNS
Wee one — TOT
Wee, in Dundee — SMA
Weed — HOE
Weed in a garden, e.g. — EYESORE
Weed killer — HOE
Weeded — HOED
Weedless garden — EDEN
Weedy grass — DARNEL
Week enders — SUNDAYS
Weekday abbr. — THUR
Weep — SOB
Weep aloud — SOB
Weeper's sound — SOB
Weeping, in Paris — EPLORE
Weeps — SOBS
Weepy — TEARFUL
Weevil feature — SNOUT
Weigh — GAUGE
Weigh down — TAX
Weighed by lifting — HEFTED
Weighed down — LADEN
Weighing devices: Abbr. — SCS
Weight — BURDEN, CARAT, HEFT, LOAD, MASS
Weight abbr. — LBS
Weight allowance — TARE, TERE, TRET
Weight lifter — JACK
Weight measures, in London — CWTS
Weight measures: Abbr. — LBS
Weight unit — OUNCE, TON
Weight watcher's concern — DIET
Weight, in Asia — TAEL
Weights of India — SERS
Weighty — GRAVE
Weighty book — TOME
Weighty volume — TOME
Weighty works — TOMES
Weimar Republic's first president — EBERT
Weir — DAM, FENCE
Weird — EERIE, EERY, STRANGE
Weirdness quality — EERINESS
Weirdo — KOOK
Weisshorn, for one — ALP
Welcome _____ — MAT
Welcome forecast — FAIR
Welcome order to a G.I. — AT EASE
Welcome reply — YES
Welcome sign — ENTER
Welcome weather word — SUNNY
Welcomed — HOSTED
Welcoming item — MAT
Weld, et al. — TUESDAYS
Welder of a kind — SOLDERER
Welfare — WEAL
Welkin — SKY
Well briefed — UP ON
Well done, Beverly — BRAVO
Well follower — BRED
Well mannered — POLITE
Well regarded — NOTED
Well then, Guillaume — ALORS
Well ventilated — AIRY
Well versed — INFORMED
Well, he's no John Wayne — IS RICH LITTLE
Well, now! — AHA
Well-balanced — SANE
Well-being — HEALTH
Well-bred — CIVIL, POLITE
Well-dressed — CHIC
Well-groomed — NEAT
Well-guarded receptacle — STRONGBOX
Well-heeled — IN THE MONEY
Well-instructed — TRAINED
Well-knit femme of fiction? — MADAME LAFARGE
Well-known — NOTED
Well-known dame — NOTRE
Well-known degree — NTH
Well-known grandmother visitor — RED RIDING HOOD
Well-known Hollywood family — GABOR
Well-known quadrennial runner — STASSEN
Well-known uncle — SAM
Well-known White House name — ALICE
Well-mannered — POLITE
Well-off — AFFLUENT
Well-recognized — KNOWN
Well-suited — ABLE
Well-to-do — HEELED
Well-to-do travelers — JETSET
Well-wisher — FAN
Well-worn track — RUT
Welladay! — ALACK, ALAS
Welles and Bean — ORSONS
Welles of "Citizen Kane" — ORSON
Welles role in "The Third Man" — LIME
Welles role in 1941 — KANE
Welles' role — KANE
Welling up — SURGE
Wellington — BOOT
Wellington _____ — KOO
Wellington's alma mater — ETON
Wellington's school — ETON
Welsh-bred dog — CORGI
Welsh canine — CORGI
Welsh dog — CORGI
Welshman's name — EVAN
Welt — MARK
Weltanschauung — ETHOS
Welty mailman's story? — WHY I LIVE AT THE PO

Welty product — TALE
Welty's "Why I Live at _____" — THE PO
Wend — DEPART
Wendy Darling's dog — NANA
Went — FARED
Went after congers — EELED
Went after decapods — SHRIMPED
Went ahead — PRECEDED
Went astray — ERRED
Went away — LEFT
Went back and forth like a ferry — PLIED
Went back over — RETRACED
Went by — ELAPSED
Went by cab — TAXIED
Went by car — AUTOED, MOTORED, RODE
Went down the river — BOATED
Went downhill — SLOPED
Went first — LED
Went for a good pitch — SWUNG
Went home feet first — SLID
Went in haste — TORE
Went in order — TROOPED
Went left — PORTED
Went like Jehu — SPED
Went limp — SAGGED
Went on a spree — LARKED, PAINTED THE TOWN RED
Went out with — DATED
Went past — OVERSHOT
Went sniggling — EELED
Went to a higher court — APPEALED
Went to bat for — DEFENDED
Went to extremes — OVERDID
Went to the bottom — SANK
Went under — SANK
Went up the Irrawaddy? — ROWED TO MANDALAY
Went white — PALED
Went wrong — ERRED
Wenzel — KNAVE
Wept — CRIED
Were compatible — GOT ALONG
Were in harmony — GOT ON
Wernher von _____ — BRAUN
Wertmüller of films — LINA
West and Murray — MAES
West coast 10 — PAC
West coast athlete — RAM
West coast capital — SALEM
West Coast fort — ORD
West coast lineman — RAM
West coast nine — PADRES
West Coast pitchers? — HOST OF ANGELS
West coast player — LAKER
West coast players — RAMS
West coast shrub — SALAL
West coast univ. — UCLA
West from the east — MAE
West German port — EMDEN
West German river — EDER
West German seaport — KIEL
West German state — SAAR
West German town — EPE
West hemisphere org. — OAS
West Indian fetish — OBEAH
West Indian form of belief — OBEAH
West Indian island — ARUBA
West Indian native — CARIB
West Indian product — RUM
West Indian resort group — BAHAMAS
West Indian sorcery — OBEAH
West Indies island — ARUBA, HAITI
West Indies island chain — GRENADINES
West Indies islands — ANTILLES
West of Eng. — IRE
West of fame — MAE
West of Hollywood — MAE
West of Nod — EDEN
West or Busch — MAE
West or Murray — MAE
West partner — EAST
West Point freshman — PLEBE
West Point froshs — PLEBES
West Point lower classman — PLEBE
West Point monogram — USMA
West Point mule — MASCOT
West Pointer — CADET
West Pt. grads — LTS
West Scottish resort — OBAN
West Texas river — PECOS
West Virginia city on the Ohio — WHEELING
West's bridge partner — EAST
West, to Don Quixote — OESTE
West. entente — OAS
Westchester inst. — CNR
Western — OATER
Western "monster" — GILA
Western _____ — OMELET
Western art colony — TAOS
Western Australia capital — PERTH
Western capital — BOISE, SALEM
Western chapeau — STETSON
Western eggs — OMELETS
Western entertainment — RODEO
Western exhibitions — RODEOS
Western flick — OATER
Western grp. — NATO
Western hemisphere org. — OAS
Western hemisphere range — ANDES
Western hill — MESA
Western Indian — OTOE
Western Indians — UTAHS, UTES
Western Kentucky city — PADUCAH
Western lily — SEGO
Western lizard — UTA
Western local color writer — HARTE
Western movie staple — POSSE
Western movie, to some — OATER
Western Native American — DAKOTA, OMAHA, UTE
Western New York city — OLEAN
Western novelist — GREY
Western Pacific island — GUAM
Western peak — SHASTA
Western range — SIERRAS
Western resort — RENO, TAHOE
Western resort lake — TAHOE
Western Samoa capital — APIA
Western show — RODEO
Western squatter — NESTER
Western team — UTES
Western time zone — MST
Western wine valley — NAPA
Western writer — GREY
Westernmost Aleutian — ATTU
Westernmost Aleutian island — ATTU
Westernmost country of Eur. — ICEL
Westernmost U.S. continental city — NOME
Westerns — OATERS
Westminster clock — BIG BEN
Westminster street — WHITEHALL
Westminster structure — ABBEY
Wet — ASOP, DAMP
Wet blanket — BOOR, BORE, DRAG
Wet land for growing rice — PADDY
Wet underfoot — SLOSHY
Wet, in a way — BEDEW
Wetlands — MARSHES
Wettish — MOIST
Whack — THUMP
Whacked — BELTED
Whacked — SMOTE
Whacky — LOCO
Whale herds — GAMS
Whale in the sky — CETUS
Whale of a movie — ORCA

Whale: Comb. form — CET, CETO
Whalebone — BALEEN
Whammed and jammed — BATTERED
Wharf — DOCK, JETTY, PIER
Wharton farmer — FROME
Wharton's "The _____ of Innocence" — AGE
Wharton's Ethan — FROME
Wharves — PIERS
What "is" is — VERB
What "syne" means — SINCE
What "veni" means — I CAME
What "video" means — I SEE
What "vidi" means — I SAW
What "ye faithful" do — ADORE
What 1988 was — LEAP YEAR
What a base stealer did — SLID
What a bore evokes — YAWN
What a boxing champion holds — TITLE
What a business hopes to do — EXPAND
What a Calaveras County frog does — JUMPS
What a censor deles — NO NO
What a cicerone conducts — TOUR
What a cicerone leads — TOUR
What a cobbler furnishes — SOLE
What a dibble makes — HOLE
What a hairline sometimes does — RECEDES
What a hobo rides — RODS
What a hopper sometimes takes — HEADER
What a Manx cat lacks — TAIL
What a monarch surveys — EMPIRE
What a polite tennis player is noted for? — CIVIL SERVICE
What a Scot wears under a kilt — TREWS
What a tear-jerker evokes — SOB
What Alice had — ADVENTURES
What an ampersand means — AND
What an élève attends — ECOLE
What an RSVP is — REPLY
What anarchy means — RULE
What Anne Hathaway hath — A WAY
What are contracts? — BRIDGE BIDS
What Aristophanes called "Ares' chick" — WAR
What bakers and baseball need — BATTERS
What beefy waiters get? — SIRLOIN TIPS
What Bernstein didn't have — TIN EAR
What bindweeds do — TWINE
What Boggs belts with — BAT
What Bryan was to Taft — LOSER
What bugbears do — SCARE
What celebrators make — NOISE
What Claudius's "offense" did — SMELT
What Columbus did in 1492 — SAILED
What CX means — 110
What daily life is — STRUGGLE
What Dana sailed before — MAST
What de speeders pay? — DEFINES
What dejeuners satisfy — APPETITES
What disgust quarterbacks — INTERCEPTIONS
What dog days are — SCORCHERS
What dreidels do — SPIN
What Earth does — ROTATES
What ecdysiasts do — STRIP
What Ed Norton uncovered — MANHOLES
What elms provide — SHADE
What esse means — TO BE
What exactly is a brief? — UNDERGARMENT
What fans do — ROOT
What foes called supporters of M. Stuart — PAPISTS
What gandy dancers do — LABOR
What ghosts do — HAUNT
What gofers run — ERRANDS
What golfer did seems cruel? — SHOT A BIRDIE
What good breakfasts do — STICK TO THE RIBS
What gossips get, with "an" — EARFUL
What grammarians do — PARSE
What hairdressers do — TEASE
What hawks do — SOAR
What he says goes — SIMON
What Hitler preached — NAZISM
What i.e. stands for — ID EST
What is a talesman? — STORYTELLER
What is Equity — ACTORS GROUP
What it costs nothing to be — POLITE
What it's all about? — HOKEY POKEY
What Jack Horner found — PLUM
What jogger W.J.C. is to Hillary? — RUNNING MATE
What Juan washes with — AGUA
What kings hold — SWAY
What larvae do — PUPATE
What lawyers are called to — BAR
What Lot's wife did — LOOKED
What M.L. King advocated — NONVIOLENCE
What makes for success — COMMITMENT
What Mark got stuck with? — CLEOPATRAS NEEDLE
What mins. add up to — HRS
What misers do — HOARD
What Molly Bloom said finally — YES
What Mom would like Junior to do — MIND
What Monday morning quarterbacks discuss — INTROSPECT
What most spectacles have — RIMS
What Mr. America pumps — IRON
What Muses do — INSPIRE
What Ness put people under — ARREST
What Nichols makes — FILMS
What not to put before a horse — CART
What nudniks do — PESTER
What one swallow doesn't make — A MEAL
What opportunists make — HAY
What pitchers have — EARS
What politicos may do at N.J. convention? — SEA CAUCUS
What pom-pom girls elicit — RAHS
What quibblers split — HAIRS
What rash dieters lose — STAMINA
What Sandburg called "a bucket of ashes" — PAST
What Shea is to the Mets — HOME
What Simon does — SAYS
What Siskel and Ebert do — RATE
What snakes do — COIL
What socks come in — PAIRS
What some doors do — OPEN IN
What some grapes become — RAISINS
What some orators do — STRIKE A POSE

What some reporters do — ROVE
What some subscribers do — RENEW
What SOS indicates — DISTRESS
What spellbinders do — ORATE
What Stan tries to do to Oliver? — FOOL HARDY
What tachometers rec. — RPMS
What teetotums do — SPIN
What the "poor dog" had — NONE
What the angry clone was? — BESIDE HIMSELF
What the brave deserve — FAIR
What the irate raise — ROOF
What the K.P. peel — SPUDS
What the O'Neill iceman doth — COMETH
What they throw in Spain? — EL TORO
What this does twice — ABUTS UPON
What this is — CLUE, CROSSWORD PUZZLE
What time does to wounds — HEALS
What to do between the lines — READ
What to spend in Oslo — KRONE
What to spend in Siena — LIRE
What to take a reverse in — STRIDE
What two thousand pounds comes to — ONE TON
What unions want to do — CREATE JOBS
What W.J.C. taught at the U. of Ark. — LAW
What we all want — PEACE
What's-your-name — MAC
What's happening — NEWS
What's in _____?: Shakespeare — A NAME
What's left — REST
What's more — AND
What's new, in Koln — NEU
Whatchamacallit — DINGUS
Whatever comes along — ANY PORT IN A STORM
Whatnot — ETAGERE
Wheat — SPELT
Wheat beard — AWN
Wheat bin — GRAIN HOPPER
Wheat bristle — AWN
Wheat or cotton — STAPLE
Wheat sown in autumn — WINTER
Wheat, in England — CORN
Wheat, in Spain — TRIGO
Wheedle — CAJOLE
Wheel — HELM
Wheel connector — AXLE
Wheel hub — AXLE, NAVE
Wheel of fortune — ROULETTE
Wheel on a tea wagon — CASTER
Wheel on some spurs — ROWEL
Wheel part — SPOKE
Wheel shaft — AXLE
Wheel spoke: Fr. — RAI
Wheel spokes — RADII
Wheel support — RIM
Wheel teeth — COGS
Wheel's connector — AXLE
Wheel, in Avila — RUEDA
Wheeler's companion — DEALER
Wheeler-dealer — OPERATOR
Wheelless vehicle — SLED
Wheels for a big wheel — LIMO
Wheezer's menace — SMOG
Wheezes — GASPS
Whelp — PUP
When Arbor Day comes — APRIL
When both hands are up — NOON
When Brutus became brutal — IDES
When Grundy was born — MONDAY
When Hector was a pup — PAST
When it's warm in Chile — ENERO
When light fights night — SUNDOWN
When most people sleep — IN THE SMALL HOURS
When overturned, is it a bucket seat? — PAIL
When the French fry? — ETE
When they're red they're lucky — HERRINGS
When Yazdegerd III died — DCLI
When, in Spain — CUANDO
Whence — FROM WHERE
Whence Cugat came — SPAIN
Whence many a tune has come — TIN PAN ALLEY
Whence the Pison flowed — EDEN
Whence: Lat. — UNDE
Whenever — ANYTIME
Where "The Stem Song" is often sang — ORONO
Where "Yankees" come f rom — NEW ENGLAND
Where 2nd lts. are made — OCS
Where a native will clue you in — HINTERLANDS
Where a shenango toils — PIER
Where a sled slides — SLOPE
Where Aaron died — HOR
Where Alberich struck gold — RHINE
Where Alexander defeated Darius — ISSUS
Where American Beauties flourish — ROSEBUDS
Where Anna Leonowens taught — SIAM
Where Anna met the King — SIAM
Where Anna went — SIAM
Where Arequipa is — PERU
Where Arthur held court — ROUND TABLE
Where Ashtabula is — OHIO
Where baby rocks — TREETOP
Where Baghdad is — IRAQ
Where Baluchi is spoken — IRAN
Where Bedouins bed down — OASES
Where benedicts are created — ALTAR
Where Bhutan is — ASIA
Where boards are formed — SAWMILL
Where Bond meets Nunn — SENATE
Where boxeurs compete — ARENES
Where Braves visit Mets — SHEA
Where Buckeyes play — OHIO
Where buyers and sellers meet — EMPORIUM
Where Cain settled — NOD
Where camels caravan — SAHARA
Where Canterbury is — KENT
Where cattle low — LEA
Where certain noggins might appear — CAMEOS
Where Chanticleer rules — ROOST
Where charity begins — HOME
Where Charon labored — STYX
Where Columbus started — PALOS
Where concert musicians relax — GREEN ROOM
Where Congress meets, with "the" — CAPITOL
Where Conn. stops — MASS
Where Cowboys and Redskins meet — GRIDIRON
Where Daniel was cast — DEN OF LIONS
Where Duccio painted — SIENA
Where Ferdinand shops? — BULL MARKET

Where filets are often ruined — PATIOS
Where Frontenac governed — CANADA
Where gauchos ride — LLANO
Where George got free drinks? — MARTHAS VINEYARD
Where Gideon defeated Midian — ENDOR
Where grapefruit grows — GROVES
Where Greek met Greek — STOA
Where GUM is — MOSCOW
Where have you ____? — BEEN
Where Hercules slew the Hydra — LERNA
Where Hobart is: Abbr. — TAS
Where Horatius kept the bridge — TIBER
Where Isabella ruled — SPAIN
Where Joan of Arc was tried — ROUEN
Where Joppolo commanded — ADANO
Where Katmandu is — NEPAL
Where Laos is — ASIA
Where Leghorn is — ITALY
Where llamas roam — ANDES
Where MacArthur shops? — GENERAL STORE
Where Machu Picchu is — PERU
Where Malaga is — SPAIN
Where Marco Polo traveled — ASIA
Where most of this is — BELOW NORMAL
Where most of this is — BESIDE ONES SELF
Where most of this is — OVER A BARREL
Where Muscat is — OMAN
Where Niamey is — NIGER
Where not to fall — OVERBOARD
Where not to make a change — MIDSTREAM
Where O'Hara dwelled — TARA
Where oboli were spent — AGORA
Where or way starter — ANY
Where papers are printed — PRESSROOM
Where part of this is — UNDER SHIRT
Where people go for the Gophers — MINNESOTA
Where Perry triumphed — ERIE
Where Qum is — IRAN
Where ramblers bloom — ROSE GARDENS
Where Red Hill towers — MAUI
Where Regina is — CANADA
Where Rene goes barefoot? — PARC
Where Reykjavik is: Abbr. — ICEL
Where royalty can usually be found — IN A DECK
Where Saul saw a seeress — ENDOR
Where Saul saw a witch — ENDOR
Where Scarlett grew up — TARA
Where seals come up for air — BLOW HOLE
Where sheeted shieks' shamble? — SAHARA
Where Sikkim is — ASIA
Where speech was an impediment — BABEL
Where Stein held forth — PARIS
Where suits are pressed? — LAW COURTS
Where Tabriz is — IRAN
Where Tanumafili is King — SAMOA
Where the Adige flows — ITALY
Where the Ambrosian Library is — MILAN
Where the Amur flows — ASIA
Where the antelope play — RANGE
Where the chicken gets — TO THE OTHER SIDE
Where the Crimson Tide rolls — ALABAMA
Where the eagle has landed — AERIE
Where the Ebro flows — SPAIN
Where the end of this is — ABOVEBOARD
Where the heart is — HOME
Where the Indus flows — ASIA
Where the jet set may get wet — RIVIERA
Where the Liffey flows — EIRE
Where the Miami flows — OHIO
Where the Pison flowed — EDEN
Where the Pnyx is — ATHENS
Where the proceeds go — TILL
Where the Shannon flows — ERIN
Where the Shroud is — TURIN
Where the Styx flows — HADES
Where the sun rises — EAST
Where the sun rises in Spain — ESTE
Where the surrey's fringe is — ON TOP
Where the Tiber flows — ITALY
Where there's no advancement — BLIND ALLEY
Where they plug the leeks — WALES
Where timber travels — LOG WAYS
Where Tirane is capital — ALBANIA
Where to buy an amphora — AGORA
Where to catch congers — EELERY
Where to find a cochlea — EAR
Where to find a hero — DELI
Where to find a oner? — TOP DRAWER
Where to find Andros — BAHAMAS
Where to find Bountiful — UTAH
Where to find class action — SCHOOL
Where to find Denton and Tyler — TEXAS
Where to find McKinley — ALASKA
Where to find this — NEXT TO NOTHING
Where to find Wailuku — MAUI
Where to get dessert for Thanksgiving — BAKERY
Where to get wurst — DELI
Where to give a rap — DOOR
Where to hang one's hat — HOME
Where to put the junk mail — ROUND FILE
Where to put your dough — OVEN
Where to see standardbreds — YONKERS
Where to soul — INWARD
Where to take it? — ON THE CHIN
Where to trade a prize bull? — STOCK EXCHANGE
Where to watch Hawks — OMNI
Where Toledans go sailing — ERIE
Where Trajan trod — ITER
Where Trevino got his start — TEE
Where two become one — ALTAR
Where Valletta is — MALTA
Where Van Gogh painted — ARLES
Where vessels nestle — COVE
Where Viña del Mar is — CHILE

Where Virgil wrote the "Georgics" — NAPLES
Where W.J.C. met H.R.C. — YALE
Where: Lat. — UBI
Wherefores' partner — WHYS
Wherever — ANY PLACE
Wherewithal — MEANS
Wherewithal — MEANS
Whether _____ — OR NOT
Whetstones — HONES
Whey — PLASMA, SERUM
Wheys — SERA
Whiff — AROMA, GUST, ODOR
Whiffenpoof cry — BAA
Whiffenpoof word — BAA
Whiffle — BLOW, TURN
Whig president — FILLMORE
While on the contrary — WHERES
While preceder — ERST
Whilom — ERST
Whilom U.A.R. entity — EGYPT
Whim — CAPRICE, FANCY
Whimper — MEWL, POUT
Whimsy — CAPRICIOUSNESS
Whine — BITCH, CRY, GRIPE, MEWL, SNIVEL, WHIMPER
Whined — CANTED, PULED
Whined tearfully — SNIVELED
Whiner — PULER
Whines — PULES
Whip — FLOG, TAN, THONG
Whip butt — CROP
Whip lash — WELT
Whip mark — WALE
Whipped potatoes — MASHED
Whippersnapper's cousin — JACKANAPES
Whips up — AROUSES
Whirl — GYRATE, SPIN
Whirl — REEL
Whirl: Ancient var. — REILL
Whirled — SPUN
Whirler — DERVISH
Whirling — AREEL
Whirlpool — EDDY
Whirlpools — EDDIES
Whirls — EDDIES, SPINS
Whirlwinds — TORNADOS, VORTEXES
Whirlybird — HELICOPTER
Whirring sound — BIRR
Whisk — BEAT
Whisker — HAIR
Whiskey measure — SHOT
Whisky drinks — SHOTS
Whisky-barrel worker — CHARRER
Whist — GAME
Whistle — FIFE, PIPE, SIREN, TOOT, TWEET
Whistle chaser — STOP
Whistler creation — ETCHING
Whistler in the kitchen — TEAKETTLE
Whistler product — ETCHING
Whistler, for one — PAINTER
Whistling swan — OLOR
Whit — IOTA
White-elephant land — SIAM
White-tailed birds — ERNES
White — ASHEN, FROSTY, IVORY, PALE, PEARLY, WAN
White _____ — LIE
White and fire — SALES
White as (pale) _____ — A SHEET
White bubbles — SUDS
White dwarfs — STARS
White elephant — ALBINO
White elephant's storage — ATTIC
White filmy variety of cloud — CIRRUS
White grape — MALAGA
White heron — EGRET
White House family: 1945-53 — TRUMANS
White House group — CABINET
White House heavyweight — TAFT
White House monogram — DDE, HST
White House name — POLK
White House nickname — IKE
White House office — OVAL
White House pet of yore — FALA
White House resident — REAGAN
White lie — FIB
White liquid — MILK
White of "Sanford and Son" — SLAPPY
White or Blue river — NILE
White or garage — SALE
White or Green of New Eng. — MTS
White or Red — SOX
White piano keys — NATURALS
White poplar — ABELE
White sale items — LINEN
White sale offering — LINEN
White sale purchase — LINEN, SHEET
White sale stuff — LINEN
White Sands' county — OTERO
White shark — MAN EATER
White spotted whales — SEIS
White sturgeon — BELUGA
White water — RAPIDS
White wine — MADEIRA, RHINE
White wine in Siena — SOAVE
White's "The _____ and Future King" — ONCE
White-faced steer — HEREFORD
White-handed gibbon — LAR
White-plumed bird — EGRET
White-sale item — SHEET
White-tailed fish eater — ERNE
White: Comb. form — ALBO
Whitecapped mountain — ALP
Whitecaps — SURF
Whiten — PALE
Whiteness, in Palma — AMPO
Whitetail — DEER
Whitewalls — TIRES
Whitewash, e.g. — PAINT
Whitewashed — LIMED
Whither — WHERE
Whitish — CHALKY
Whitish in complexion — PALE
Whitman died here: 1892 — CAMDEN
Whitman or Wilbur — POET
Whitman or Wordsworth — POET
Whitney — ELI
Whitney or Yale — ELI
Whitney's bequest — GIN
Whitney's mother — CISSY HOUSTON
Whits — IOTAS
Whittier's "_____ Muller" — MAUD
Whittier's middle — GREENLEAF
Whittle — PARE
Whittled — PARED
Whittles — PARES
Whiz by — PASS FAST
Whiz kid — BRAIN
Whiz preceder — GEE
Whizzes — PROS
Who _____? — IS IT
Who is Mrs. Steve Lawrence? — EYDIE
Who or which — THAT
Who starts the most suits? — TAILOR
Who wrote "Rob Roy" (1817)? — SCOTT
Who wrote 1000 songs plus? — WOODY GUTHRIE
Who's station — FIRST
Whodunit item — CLUE
Whodunit, e.g. — NOVEL
Whodunits: Abbr. — MYSTS
Whoever — ANYONE
Whole — ENTIRE, ONE
Whole amount — SUM
Whole lot — RAFTS
Whole number — INTEGER
Whole range — GAMUT
Whole-hearted — TRUE
Wholesalers — SUPPLIERS
Wholesales — SELLS
Whooping bird — CRANE
Whoopla — TODO
Whop — HIT

Whoppers — LIES
Whops on the head — BOPS
Why elephant visits vet in Ala.? — TUSC A LOOSA
Why is Dr. Sagan being sent to N.M.? — CARLS BAD
Why mother darns a sock? — HOLE IN ONE
Why some products fail — NONUSE
WI city — RACINE
Wicked — BAD, EVIL
Wicked Arabian port? — A DEN OF INIQUITY
Wicked, shameless woman — JEZEBEL
Wickedness — VICE
Wicker — TWIG
Wicker basket — CREEL, HAMPER, SKEP
Wicker footstool, in India — MORA
Wicker source — RATTAN
Wickerwork — WATTLE
Wickerwork branch — OSIER
Wickerwork material — OSIER
Wicket — HOOP
Wickiup's cousin: Var. — TIPI
Wide — BROAD
Wide awake — ALERT
Wide of the mark — AWRY
Wide open — AGAPE
Wide scarves — STOLES
Wide ties or knots — WINDSORS
Wide's partner — FAR
Wide-awakes — TERNS
Wide-eyed — AGOG
Wide-eyed tourist — STARER
Wide-mouthed earthen pots — OLLAS
Wide-mouthed pitcher — EWER
Widely planted African tree — AKEE
Widely prevalent — RIFE
Widely separated — ASUNDER
Widened — DILATED
Widens — BROADENS, DILATES, EXTENDS
Widespread — BROAD, PREVALENT, RAMPANT
Widespread ailment — FLU
Widgeon — SMEE
Widmark's first film role — UDO
Widow of Lennon — ONO
Widow's portion — DOWER
Widow's rights — DOWER
Width x length — AREA
Wield — PLY
Wield a baton — LEAD
Wield a diving rod — DOWSE
Wields a needle — SEWS
Wienie — REDHOT
Wiesbaden one — EINS
Wiesbaden's state — HESSE
Wiesel and Abel — ELIES
Wiesel of letters — ELIE
Wife jilted for Cleopatra — OCTAVIA
Wife of a rajah — RANI
Wife of Abraham — SARAH
Wife of Ahab — JEZEBEL
Wife of Geraint — ENID
Wife of Hercules — HEBE
Wife of Iago — EMILLIA
Wife of Jacob — LEAH
Wife of King Latinas — AMATA
Wife of Menelaus — HELEN
Wife of Osiris — ISIS
Wife of Paris — OENONE
Wife of Proetus — ANTIA
Wife of Saturn — OPS
Wife of Siva — KALI
Wife of Theban god Amen-Ra — MUT
Wife of Thor — SIF
Wife of Tyndareus — LEDA
Wife of Zeus — HERA
Wife Paris deserted for Helen — OENONE
Wife, in law — FEME
Wife, in Osnabrück — FRAU
Wife, to Caesar — UXOR
Wife: Lat. — UXOR
Wife: Law — FEME
Wifely inheritances — DOWERS
Wig style — AFRO
Wigeons — SMEES
Wight or Man, e.g. — ISLE
Wight, e.g. — ISLE
Wight, for one — ISLE
Wikiup — HUT
Wilander of tennis — MATS
Wilander winner — ACE
Wilberforce U. site — XENIA
Wilbur and Kunitz — POETS
Wilbur concern — METER
Wilbur product — POEM
Wilbur's fleabag? — THIRD RAT HOTEL
Wild — FERAL, FERINE, INSANE
Wild animal track — SPOOR
Wild asses — ONAGERS
Wild asses of central Asia — ONAGERS
Wild Bill — HICKOK
Wild blue yonder — ETHER
Wild buffalo — ANOA, ARNEE
Wild cards — JOKERS
Wild carrot — QUEEN ANNES LACE
Wild cat — EYRA, PUMA
Wild celebration — REVEL
Wild cherry tree — GEAN
Wild dog — JACKAL
Wild dog of India — DHOLE
Wild dog, Down Under — DINGO
Wild duck — TEAL
Wild game bird — PHEASANT
Wild goat — IBEX, TAHR
Wild goat of Nepal — TAHR
Wild goats — TAHRS
Wild goose — BRANT, GRAYLAG
Wild guess — SHOT, STAB
Wild hog — BOAR
Wild hogs' quartets? — BOARSOMES
Wild ox — ANOA
Wild party — BASH, BLAST, ORGY
Wild pigs — BOARS
Wild plum — SLOE
Wild revelry — ORGY
Wild rose — BRIAR
Wild rye — DARNEL
Wild sheep of N Africa — ARUI
Wild sheep of Tibet — SHA
Wild time — SPREE
Wild water — TORRENT
Wild water buffalo — ARNEE
Wild west "neckware" — NOOSES
Wild-horse catcher — LASSO
Wildcat — EYRA, OCELOT, PUMA
Wildcats — LYNXES
Wildcatters quest — OIL
Wilde of the screen — CORNEL
Wilde play — SALOME
Wilde was one — WIT
Wilde's Gray — DORIAN
Wilde's Reading — GAOL
Wilde's was Reading — GAOL
Wildebeest — GNU
Wildebeest country? — GNU ENGLAND
Wildebeest locale — AFRICA
Wilder and Barry — GENES
Wilder or Hackman — GENE
Wilder's "_____ Town" — OUR
Wilderness craft — CANOE
Wilderness Road traveler — BOONE
Wilderness shelter — CAVE
Wildlife Fed.'s concern — YSL
Wildlife preserve — GAME PARK
Wiles — ARTS
Wiley and Cecil's highways? — POSTRHODES
Wiley or Emily — POST
Wilfred Owen's "_____ et Decorum Est" — DULCE
Wilkes-_____, PA — BARRE
Will administrator: Abbr. — CTA
Will item — BEQUEST
Will of "The Waltons" — GEER
Will or Ginger — ROGERS
Will power — DRIVE
Will Rogers prop — ROPE

Will supplement — CODICIL
Will word — TESTAMENT
Will- _____ -wisp — O THE
Will-o'-the- _____ — WISP
Will/examine catkin? — TESTAMENT
William _____ Thackeray — MAKEPEACE
William _____, New England botanist — OAKES
William and Stephen Vincent — BENETS
William Carlos Williams verse epic — PATERSON
William Conrad role — CANNON
William Corcoran endowment — ART
William Cowper's hometown — OLNEY
William Gibson play — TWO FOR THE SEESAW
William Holden sky movie? — THE MOON IS BLUE
William Howard — TAFT
William Randolph — HEARST
William's aunt — ANNE
William's fruit-of-the-loom — YEATS DATES
William's joint ruler — MARY
William, to Di — SON
Williams and Ralston — ESTHERS
Williams of "Happy Days" — ANSON
Williams of baseball — TED
Williams of baseball history — TED
Williams of the "Age of Aquarius" — TREAT
Williams or Rooney — ANDY
Williams play — CAT ON A HOT TIN ROOF
Williams who plays Gladys — CARA
Willie or Horatio — NELSON
Willie Stargell, e.g. — PIRATE
Willing response — YESSIR
Willing's partner — ABLE
Williwaw — STORM
Willow — ITEA, OSIER
Willow genus — ITEA
Willow Run products — AUTOS
Willow twig — OSIER, WITHE
Willow: Fr. — SAULE
Willowy — SLIM, SVELT
Wills, of baseball — MAURY
Willys-Knight contemporary — REO
Wilson and Hines — EARLS
Wilson novel of 1915 — RUGGLES OF RED GAP
Wilt, the _____ — STILT
Wilted — DROOPED
Wimbledon champ: 1975 — ASHE
Wimbledon champion: 1956 — HOAD
Wimbledon champion: 1976-80 — BORG
Wimbledon singles champ: 1950 — BUDGE PATTY
Wimbledon singles champ: 1955 — TONY TRABERT
Wimbledon singles champ: 1960 — NEALE FRASER
Wimbledon star — BORG
Wimbledon stats — LOSSES
Wimbledon three-time champ — BORIS BECKER
Wimbledon three-time singles champ — JOHN MCENROE
Wimbledon winner of 1925 — LACOSTE
Wimbledon winner: 1975 — ASHE
Wimbledon winner: 1977 — WADE
Wimbledon winner: 1987 — CASH
Wimbledon winners — ACES
Wimbledon's Lew — HOAD
Wimp's cousin — NERD
Wimp's relatives — NERDS
Wimplike — NERDY
Wimpy one — NERD
Wimpy's friend — POPEYE
Wimsey's Bunker, for example — MAN SERVANT
Win — EARN
Win at a game — OUT PLAY
Win by _____ — A NECK, A NOSE
Win over — SWAY
Win the debate — OUT TALK
Winchester or Springfield — RIFLE
Winchester, e.g. — REPEATER
Wind — BREEZE, COIL, GALE, GUST, TRADE
Wind and weather permitting — PERHAPS
Wind breaker — JACKET
Wind dir. — NNE, ENE, ESE
Wind direction — NNE, SSE
Wind indicator — VANE
Wind instrument — FIFE, OBOE, REED, TRUMPET
Wind instrument, for short — SAX
Wind of S France — MISTRAL
Wind sound — HOWL
Wind swept — EXPOSED
Wind up — END
Wind's mournful sound — MOAN
Wind: Comb. form — ANEMO
Winder — COILER
Windfall — BOON, BONUS, FIND, PLUM
Windflower — ANEMONE
Winding of jazz fame — KAI
Winding on a bobbin — SPOOLING
Windlass — REEL
Windlass in the past — TURNEL
Windmill impeller — VANE
Windmill parts — VANES
Window division — PANE
Window dressing — DRAPE
Window feature — LEDGE, SILL
Window frames — SASHES
Window glass — PANE
Window in a liner stateroom — PORTHOLE
Window inset — PANE
Window parts — PANES, SILLS
Window section — PANE, SILL
Window unit — PANE
Window view — YARD
Window washers view — THROUGH A GLASS DARKLY
Windpipe: Comb. form — TRACHE
Winds down — ABATES
Winds up — ENDS
Windshield adjunct — WIPER
Windshield cleaner — WIPER
Windshield mechanisms — WIPERS
Windsor _____ — KNOT
Windsor Castle's neighbor — ETON
Windstorm — GALE
Windswept — BLOWN
Windway — FLUE
Windy City, for short — CHI
Windy orators — GASBAGS
Wine-producing center — ASTI
Wine — CLARET, PORT, TOKAY
Wine and dine — REGALE
Wine bottle — CARAFE, DECANTER
Wine bouquet — AROMA
Wine casks — TUNS
Wine cellars — BODEGAS
Wine center in Italy — ASTI
Wine commune — ASTI
Wine disorder — CASSE
Wine experts' comb. form — OENO
Wine flask — OLPE
Wine grape — MUSCAT, PINOT
Wine grower — VIGNERON
Wine is one — COLOR
Wine list offerings — ROSES
Wine lover's prefix — OENO
Wine pitcher — OLPE

Wine region in France — MEDOC
Wine region of Italy — ASTI
Wine storage areas — CELLARS
Wine that is dry — SEC
Wine town in Piedmont — ASTI
Wine valley — NAPA
Wine variety — TOKAY
Wine word — SEC
Wine-and-nutmeg drink — SANGAREE
Wine: Comb. form — ENO, OEN, OENO, VIN, VINO
Wine: Prefix — OENO
Wined and _____ — DINED
Wineglass leftovers — LEES
Winegrowing commune — ASTI
Winemaking process — AGING
Winery container — VAT
Winfield of baseball — DAVE
Winfrey of TV — OPRAH
Wing-ding — PARTY
Wing — ANNEX, ARM, ELL
Wing chair part — ARM
Wing support — AILERON
Wing that can't fly — ELL
Wing tip — ALULA
Wing tip, for one — SHOE
Wing, in Wassy — AILE
Wing, of a sort — ALULA
Wing, often — ANNEX
Wing, to an architect — ELL
Wing-footed — ALIPED
Wing-mounted control — AILERON
Wing-shaped — ALARY, ALATE
Wing: Comb. form — PTER, PTERO
Wing: Prefix — PTER
Winged — ALAR, ALATE, ALATED
Winged ant — ALATE
Winged child, in art — AMOR
Winged elm — WAHOO
Winged fruits of elms — SAMARAS
Winged insects — WASPS
Winged plant parasites — THRIPS
Winged: Var. — ALATED
Winglike — ALAR
Winglike parts — ALAE
Winglike petals — ALAE
Winglike structures — ALAE
Wings — ALAE, ELLS, SIDES
Wings of a sort — ELLS
Wings, for Almo — ALAE
Wings, in old Rome — ALAE
Wings, Latin style — ALAE
Wings, to Francois — AILES
Wings, to I.M. Pei — ELLS
Wings, to Livy — ALAE
Wingspread — SPAN
Wink count — FORTY
Winkle out — OUST
Winless horse — MAIDEN
Winnebago relative — OTOE
Winnebago wear: Abbr. — MOCS
Winner at Saratoga: 1777 — GATES
Winner of the British Open: 1964 — LEMA
Winner of the Nobel Peace Prize: 1984 — TUTU
Winner of two Coty fashion awards — ADOLFO
Winner's "take" — ALL
Winner's award — PURSE
Winner's chorus — RAHS
Winner's portion in a saying — ALL
Winners — ACES
Winners at the polls — INS
Winners at Wimbledon — ACES
Winners from Wilander — ACES
Winners' signs — VEES
Winnie _____ Pu — ILLE
Winnie's character — POOH
Winnie-the-Pooh's creator — MILNE
Winnie-the-Pooh's pal — ROO
Winnie-the-Pooh, e.g. — BEAR
Winning coach at Super Bowl XII — LANDRY
Winning Colors, e.g. — ROAN
Winning girl, winning play — ANNIE
Winning margin, at times — NOSE
Winning move — MATE
Winning pennant: 1979 — PIRATE FLAG
Winning, for the moment — AHEAD
Winnings — GAIN
Winnowing device — SIEVE
Wino — SOT
Wino's ailment — DTS
Winos — SOUSES
Wins at chess — MATES
Winslow Homer efforts — SEASCAPES
Winsome — NICE
Winsor heroine — AMBER
Winsor's "Forever _____" — AMBER
Winston-Salem product — TOBACCO
Winter ailment — FLU
Winter baseball attraction — HOT STOVE LEAGUE
Winter cap feature — EARFLAP
Winter forecast — SLEET
Winter fun — SLEIGH RIDE
Winter hazard — SLEET
Winter hours, to some — SLOW TIME
Winter jacket — PARKA
Winter melon — CASABA
Winter mo. — DEC, FEB
Winter month, in Madrid — ENERO
Winter Olympics site, 1952 — OSLO
Winter Palace resident — TSAR
Winter racer — ICE BOAT
Winter rigs — SLEIGHS
Winter road hazard — ICE
Winter runner — SLED, SKI
Winter sight — SNOW
Winter sport — SLEDDING
Winter sporting event — SUPER BOWL
Winter time, in NYC — EST
Winter time, in St. Louis — CST
Winter transport — SLED, SLEIGHS
Winter vehicle — SLED
Winter wear — MITTENS, SCARF
Winter weather word — SLEET
Winter white — SNOW
Winter wind in Hawaii — KONA
Winter wonderland requirement — SNOW
Winter's Jack — FROST
Wintery weather — SLEET
Wintry — HIEMAL
Wintry in a way — SLEETY
Wintry phenomenon — SLEET
Wintry precipitation — SLEET, SNOW
Wintry weather word — SLEET
Wipe — DRY
Wipe clean — ERASE
Wipe off the slate — ERASE
Wipe out — ERASE
Wipe out — ERASE
Wiped out — ERASED
Wipes away — ERASES
Wire — CABLE, TELEGRAMS
Wire grass — POA
Wire measure — MIL
Wire nail — BRAD
Wire service letters — UPI
Wire winder — SPOOLER
Wire, for short — TELEG
Wireless inventor — MARCONI
Wireless telegraphy — RADIO
Wires — MESSAGES
Wires: Abbr. — TELS
Wiretap — BUG
Wisc. neighbor — MINN
Wisconsin Indians — SAUKS
Wisconsin Native American — WINNEBAGO
Wisconsin sport? — HORSE RACINE
Wisconsinite — BADGER
Wisdom — LORE
Wisdom goddess — ATHENA

Wisdom of the ages — LORE
Wise — ASTUTE, CANNY, ON TO, SAGE
Wise _____ owl — AS AN
Wise answer — ORACLE
Wise biblical king — SOLOMON
Wise brush — SAGE
Wise elder — NESTOR
Wise guy — SMART ALECK
Wise guy? — SEER
Wise guys — KNOW IT ALLS
Wise Hindu — GURU
Wise king of Pylos — NESTOR
Wise lawgiver — SOLON
Wise man — NESTOR, SAGE
Wise men — MAGI
Wise old man — NESTOR
Wise one — GURU, MAGI, ORACLE, SAGE
Wise persons — SAGES
Wise seasoning? — SAGE
Wise, trusted adviser — MENTOR
Wisecracks — QUIPS
Wised up — ON TO
Wiser's companion — OLDER
Wished — HOPED
Wishes — DESIRES
Wishes undone — RUES
Wishful — EAGER
Wishy _____ — WASHY
Wishy-washy — BLAND, NAMBY PAMBY, THIN
Wisps of precipitation — VIRGAS
Wispy white cloud — CIRRUS
Wit — HUMOR
Wit lead-in — NIT
Wit of a sort — IRONY
Wit or pick beginner — NIT
Wit's bit — QUIP
Witch — CRONE
Witch birds — ANIS
Witch doctor of a kind — SHAMAN
Witch hazel — TREE
Witch hunt town — SALEM
Witch of _____ — ENDOR
Witch's gathering — COVEN
Witch's pet — CAT
Witch's town — ENDOR
Witchery — SPELL
Witches — HAGS
Witches work — SPELL
With — AMONG
With "at", free from restraint — LARGE
With "en", fencing term — GARDE
With "his", title — HOLINESS
With "Rio", a Ziegfeld show — RITA
With "The," 1939 Bette Davis film — OLD MAID
With "The," part of Chicago — LOOP
With _____ breath — BATED
With a side-glance — ASKANCE
With a will — TESTATE
With a zest for life — LUSTY
With an _____ (considering) — EYE TO
With an _____ the ground — EAR TO
With calmness — SERENELY
With charisma — MAGNETIC
With craft — SLILY, WILILY
With decorum — STAIDLY
With drollery — AMUSEDLY
With enthusiasm — EAGERLY
With fewer leaves — BARER
With force — AMAIN
With full force — A MAIN
With gentleness — SOFTLY
With gusto — HURT
With haste — SWIFTLY
With her, it's snip and tuck — FITTER
With high spirits — GAYLY
With humility — MEEKLY
With ice cream — ALAMODE
With indifference — ICILY
With insight — ASTUTELY
With it — AWARE, HEP, HIP, ON THE BALL
With it — MOD
With Kensington, a royal borough — CHELSEA
With Maria — SANTA
With merriment: Var. — GAYLY
With no restrictions — THE SKYS THE LIMIT
With pluck — GAMELY
With respect to — AS FOR
With severity — STERNLY
With sinful interest — EVILLY
With skill — ABLY
With the bow, in music — ARCO
With the will annexed: Abbr. — CTA
With zeal — FERVENTLY
With, in Limoges — AVEC
With, in Lyons — AVEC
With, in Tours — AVEC
With, to Cato — CUM
With: Fr. — AVEC
Withdraw — RECEDE, RENEGE, SECEDE
Withdraw by degrees — WEAN
Withdraw formally — SECEDE
Withdraw from — RENEGE
Withdrawal — RETREAT
Withdrawer — SECEDER
Withdrawn — EXIT, SHY, INGROWN
Withdrew — SECEDED
Withe — ROPE, TWIG
Wither — DECAY, DROOP, SEAR, WILT
Withered — PARCHED, SERE
Withering — SEARING
Witherspoon and Dithers — CORAS
Withheld — DENY, FORE-BORN, KEPT
Within — AMID
Within audible frequencies — SONIC
Within earshot — NEAR
Within reach — AT HAND
Within the law — LICIT
Within the prescribed area — ONSIDE
Within: Comb. form — ENDO, ENTO
Within: Pref. — ESO
Within: Prefix — ENDO, INTRA
Without — SANS
Without _____ in the world — A CARE
Without a chaser — NEAT
Without a doubt — CLEARLY
Without a notion — IDEALESS
Without a sou — BROKE
Without aberration — NORMAL
Without accompaniment — ALONE
Without blemish — UNSCARRED
Without change — AS IS
Without charge — FREE
Without company — ALONE
Without complaint — WILLINGLY
Without complications — SIMPLE
Without delay — SUMMARILY
Without doubt — DEFINITE
Without end, Bard style — EER
Without escort — ALONE
Without ethics — AMORAL
Without exception — EVERY
Without face value, as stocks — NO PAR
Without feeling — NUMB
Without foundation — FALSE
Without funds — NEEDY
Without gender — NEUTER
Without inner covering — UNLINED
Without interruption — ON END
Without letup — ON END
Without limit — ANY
Without lodgings — UNHOUSED
Without mercy — PITILESS
Without pause — ON END
Without problems — EASILY
Without profit — AT COST
Without proof — ALLEGEDLY

Without purpose — AIMLESS, IDLY
Without spirit — SOULLESS
Without warmth — COLDLY
Without, in Cannes — SANS
Without, in Weimar — OHNE
Without, in Weisbaden — OHNE
Witless — INANE
Witness — EYER, NOTER, SEE
Witness's activity — ATTESTING
Witnessed — SEEN
Witnesses — BEHOLDS, SEES
Witticism — MOT
Witty — CLEVER, FUNNY, KEEN
Witty or humorous — WRY
Witty remark — JEST, MOT
Witty saying — EPIGRAM, MOT
Wives: Law — FEMES
Wizened — SERE
Wizened one — CRONE
Wkday. — TUES
Wkly. periodical — MAG
WKRP or WJM-TV — CALL LETTERS
WNW's reciprocal — ESE
Wobbles — TEETERS
Wobbling — TEETERY
Wodehouse farewell — TATA
Wodehouse title — SIR
Wodehouse's Drones _____ — CLUB
Wodehouse's Wooster — BERTRAM
Woe — GRIEF
Woe is me! — ALAS
Woebegone — SAD
Woeful word — ALAS
Woes — EVILS, GRIEFS, ILLS, MISERIES
Wolf — LOBO
Wolf's expression — LEER
Wolf's onceover — LEER
Wolf, in a sense — ROUE
Wolfe or Stoppard — TOM
Wolfert — IRA
Wolfhound — BORZOI
Wolfish look — LEER
Wolflike animal — HYENA
Wolfram's friend — TANNHAUSER
Wolverine St. — MICH
Wolverine State — MICHIGAN
Wolves in sheeps' clothing — IMPOSTERS
Wolves, often — OGLERS
Woman hater — MISOGYNIST
Woman warden — MATRON
Woman's close-fitting jacket — SPENCER
Woman's coverup — SHRUG
Woman's domain — HOME
Woman's name meaning "peaceful" — FREDA
Woman's one-piece undergarment — TEDDY
Woman's plastic surgery song? — I FEEL PRETTY
Woman's scarf — FICHU
Woman's small hat — TOQUE
Woman's tight strapless top — BUSTIER
Woman, in law — FEME
Womanizers — ROUES
Women — SHES
Women's _____ — LIB
Women's dress glove — MITT
Women's hats or nets — CAULS
Women's magazine — ELLE
Women's wear in Agra — SARIS
Won — EARNED
Won at chess — MATED
Won in the pool — OUTSWAM
Wonder — AWE
Wonder drug — SULFA
Wonder mixed with fear — AWE
Wonder's "Ebony and _____" — IVORY
Wonder-stricken — AWED
Wonderland croquet ball — HEDGEHOG
Wonderland denizen — WHITE RABBIT
Wonderland figure — ALICE
Wonderland girl — ALICE
Wonderland tearoom? — ALICES RESTAURANT
Wonderland visitor — ALICE
Wonderment — AWE
Wonderstruck — AWED
Wong of films — ANNA MAY
Wont — HABIT
Wonts — USES
Woo — COURT
Woo with music — SERENADE
Wood-dressing tool — ADZE
Wood — LUMBER
Wood clearing — GLADE
Wood cutting tool — RIPSAW
Wood eaters — MOTHS
Wood engraver's tool — BURIN
Wood file — RASP
Wood for 36 keys — EBONY
Wood for a baseball bat — ASH
Wood for a chest — CEDAR
Wood for skis — ASH
Wood for the temple of Jerusalem — CEDAR
Wood for walking sticks — HICKORY
Wood ibis — STORK
Wood joint — TENON
Wood measure — CORD
Wood nymph — OREAD
Wood quantities — CORDAGES
Wood shaper — ADZ, ADZE
Wood sorrel — OCA
Wood thickness — PLY
Wood, the boat builder — GAR
Wood-fiber mixture — PULP
Wood-shaping tools — ADZES
Wood-splitting tool — MAUL
Wood-trimming tool — ADZE
Wood-working machine — LATHE
Wood-working machine — LATHE
Woodchopper — HEWER
Woodchopper of fable — BABA
Woodchucks — MARMOTS
Wooded — SYLVAN, TREEY
Wooden — STIFF
Wooden benches — SETTLES
Wooden legs — STILTS
Wooden Mortimer — SNERD
Wooden peg — NOG
Wooden pegs — DOWELS
Wooden pin — DOWEL
Wooden pins — PEGS
Wooden shoe — SABOT
Wooden shoes — CLOGS
Wooden stand — CRISS
Wooden stand with a curved top — CRISS
Wooden strip — LATH
Wooden strip — SLAT
Wooden-soled shoe — CLOG
Woodland deities — SILENI
Woodland deity — SATYR
Woodland dweller or deity — SYLVAN
Woodland god — SATYR
Woodpecker, old style — ECCLE
Woodpeckers — BORERS
Woodrow Wilson phrase — FOURTEEN POINTS
Woods — FORESTS
Woodshed sessions — BEATINGS
Woodshop tool — PLANE
Woodward role in 1957 — EVE
Woodwind — OBOE, CLARINET
Woodwind for short — SAX
Woodwind instrument — OBOE
Woodwinds — REEDS
Woodworkers' machine — LATHES
Woodworking cut — DADO
Woodworking machines — LATHES
Woodworking tool — LATHE
Woody — ALLEN
Woody Allen's musical request — PLAY IT AGAIN SAM
Woody fiber — HEMP
Woody or Ethan — ALLEN

Woody or Steve — ALLEN
Woody perennials — TREES
Woody plant — TREE
Woody vine — LIANE
Woody's boy — ARLO
Woody's frequent co-star — MIA
Woody's son — ARLO
Wooed — COURTED
Woof's kin — ARF
Wool — FLEECE
Wool grease — DEGRAS
Wool weight unit — TOD
Wool weights of old — TODS
Wool worker — CARDER
Wool: Comb. form — LANI
Woolen cloth — LAINE
Woolen fabric — ALPACA
Woolgathering insect? — MOTH
Woolley's game? — MONTE
Woolly — FLEECY, LANATE
Woolly animals — EWES
Woolly creatures — EWES
Woolly gamboler — EWE
Woos — COURTS
Worcester or York — SHIRE
Word — CHARGE, EXPRESSION, ORDER, TERM
Word after omni and mini — BUS
Word after see and before Sea — RED
Word after Simon — SAYS
Word after wander — LUST
Word before "Action" — CAMERA
Word before Baker — ABLE
Word before ballerina — PRIMA
Word before ear or tube — INNER
Word before low or up — LAID
Word before rata — PRO
Word before shore or side — ALONG
Word before wood — DRIFT
Word blindness — ALEXIA
Word containing no vowels — NTH
Word describing Tillie — TOILER
Word element for nine — ENNEA
Word element meaning gas — AER
Word feminizer — ETTE
Word following knighting ceremony — ARISE
Word for a certain Ranger — LONE
Word for Adenauer — ALTE
Word for bore or basin — TIDAL
Word for Felix Unger — NEAT
Word for firma or cotta — TERRA
Word for fourth and real — ESTATES
Word for hanging or shoe — TREE
Word for night and blind — SPOTS
Word for stud or strip — POKER
Word for top and hard — HATS
Word for wide or series — WORLD
Word for word — VERBATIM
Word form for external — ETC
Word form for shoulder — OMO
Word from baby — DADA
Word from Oliver Twist — MORE
Word from the Lone Ranger — AWAY
Word game — ACROSTIC
Word game: Abbr. — ANAG
Word group — PHRASE
Word heard on a roller coaster — WHEE
Word history — ETYMOLOGY
Word in a Dickens title — TALE
Word in a marriage vow — HONOR
Word in a palindrome — ERE
Word in a recipe — STIR
Word in a syllogism — ERGO
Word in a threat — ELSE
Word in co. name — BROS
Word in comparisons — THAN
Word in Kan.'s motto — ASPERA, ASTRA
Word in many place names — SANTA, PORT
Word in parenthesis — SIC
Word jugglings: Abbr. — ANAGS
Word of apology — SORRY
Word of approval — AMEN
Word of assent — AMEN, YES
Word of comfort — THERE
Word of disapproval — TUT
Word of greeting — HELLO
Word of honor — OATH, PAROLE
Word of mouth — ORAL
Word of proscription — DONT
Word of query — WHOSE
Word of regret — ALACK, ALAS, SORRY
Word of reproof — TUT
Word of warning — DONT, STOP
Word of welcome — ENTER
Word of woe — ALAS
Word often in brackets — SIC
Word on a a penny — TRUST
Word on a Biblical wall — MENE
Word on a card — NOEL
Word on a Czech's check — HALER
Word on a dollar — SERIES
Word on a dollar bill — ORDO
Word on a door — PUSH
Word on a French postcard — AVION
Word on a gas pump — OCTANE
Word on a highway sign — YIELD
Word on a receipt — PAID
Word on a rubber stamp — PAID
Word on a scholar's key — KAPPA
Word on a telegram — STOP
Word on a towel — HIS
Word on a wall — MENE
Word on a wine bottle — CRU
Word on an envelope — AVE, VIA
Word on Japanese freighter hulls — MARU
Word on Japanese ships — MARU
Word on the back of a dollar bill — ORDO
Word on the wall — MENE
Word or overused expression — CLICHE
Word play humor — PUN
Word processor tool — MOUSE
Word puzzle — ACROSTIC
Word rearrangement — ANAGRAM
Word that may stop a truck — EATS
Word to a cat — SCAT
Word to a dog — HEEL
Word to a fly — SHOO
Word to a refusenik — NYET
Word to go with whiz or whillikers — GEE
Word with act or action — CLASS
Word with aero or hippo — DROME
Word with area — CODE
Word with back or baked — HALF
Word with back or call — ROLL
Word with back or hands — BARE
Word with backed or baked — HALF
Word with bag, ball or book — HAND
Word with ball, bank or bound — SNOW

Word with basin or bore — TIDAL
Word with beat or stick — DRUM
Word with bell or waiter — DUMB
Word with belt or cap — SNOW
Word with belt or pin — SAFETY
Word with bend or jerk — KNEE
Word with bike or boat — MOTOR
Word with bill, book or boy — PLAY
Word with black or blue — BERRIES
Word with blast or cast — SAND
Word with blow or tide — LOW
Word with board or bag — TOTE
Word with boat or ship — STEAM
Word with body or brew — HOME
Word with body or way — ANY
Word with book or load — CASE
Word with bound or bottom — ROCK
Word with bound or box — ICE
Word with boy or bed — WATER
Word with branch or wreath — OLIVE
Word with bread or cake — HOT
Word with by or way — LAID
Word with caddy or cake — TEA
Word with cake or change — SHORT
Word with cakes or apples — CRAB
Word with calling or dropping — NAME
Word with cap or gown — NIGHT
Word with car or maid — PARLOR
Word with case or sack — SAD
Word with circle or sanctum — INNER
Word with city or circle — INNER
Word with city or tube — INNER
Word with close or upper — CUT
Word with cloth or chop — LOIN
Word with cloth or tear — DROP
Word with clover or rover — RED
Word with code or rug — AREA
Word with coffee or tea — SET
Word with cork or thumb — SCREW
Word with Costa or Puerto — RICAN
Word with couture or cuisine — HAUTE
Word with cover or ground — UNDER
Word with cream or grapes — SOUR
Word with dark and handsome — TALL
Word with day or night — ONE
Word with day or way — ANY
Word with deep or high — KNEE
Word with dong — DING
Word with down or out — WEAR
Word with down or up — CLOSE, SHUT
Word with down or up to — LIVE
Word with dream or line — PIPE
Word with early or late — RISER
Word with East, West or America — MIDDLE
Word with egg or pie — PLANT
Word with end or side — EAST
Word with face or fisted — TWO
Word with face or heart — LOSE
Word with fall or agent — FREE
Word with fettle — FINE
Word with fide — BONA
Word with fire or file — CROSS
Word with fish or small — FRY
Word with flat or spare — TIRE
Word with frog or lily — POND
Word with game or table — END
Word with glass or ice — SHEET
Word with goods — SOFT
Word with green or glade — EVER
Word with hand or side — OFF
Word with hard or soft — SELL
Word with hat or hand — OLD
Word with head or shell — EGG
Word with heart or face — LOSE
Word with hide or deal — RAW
Word with high or deep — KNEE
Word with horn or string — SHOE
Word with human or mill — RACE
Word with in or out — COME, SET
Word with iron or tin — WARE
Word with jack or dash — SLAP
Word with jack or stick — SLAP
Word with la, la — TRA
Word with lace or line — NECK
Word with land or sea — SCAPE
Word with left or right — WING
Word with life or entertainment — THATS
Word with lift or off — FACE
Word with light or moon — HALF
Word with line or lock — DEAD
Word with mackerel or smokes — HOLY
Word with man or mat — DOOR
Word with meat or feed — FORCE
Word with miss or beer — NEAR
Word with mobile — SNOW
Word with month or year — LUNAR
Word with motif — LEIT
Word with movie or party — GOERS
Word with mower or plant — POWER
Word with near or far — EAST
Word with night or skull — CAP
Word with off or up — TEED
Word with on or out — TRY
Word with on, off or out — TURN
Word with one or many — SIDED
Word with out or in — STAND
Word with out or off — RIP, TIME
Word with over or top — COAT
Word with over or upon — ONCE

Word with pin or fold — NINE
Word with pink or rose — MOSS
Word with platypus — DUCKBILLED
Word with polloi — HOI
Word with red or blue — COAT
Word with red or magic — CARPET
Word with rib or riff — MID
Word with ride or seed — HAY
Word with rival or enemy — ARCH
Word with roll or dirt — PAY
Word with room or wear — MENS
Word with rubber — BAND
Word with sack — KNAP
Word with said or thought — AFORE
Word with Seton or toad — HALL
Word with shoppe — OLDE
Word with shot or step — ONE
Word with side or edge — WISE
Word with side or runner — ROAD
Word with sienna or umber — BURNT
Word with soap or sell — SOFT
Word with some or any — ONE
Word with some or sale — WHOLE
Word with some or struck — AWE
Word with sprawl or renewal — URBAN
Word with squirrel or spider — RED
Word with star or stone — LODE
Word with stick or happy — SLAP
Word with suit or top — TANK
Word with sun or moon — LIT
Word with tag or tight — END
Word with term or time — LONG
Word with terra — COTTA
Word with toe and tic — TAC
Word with tray or can — ASH
Word with up or down — COME, STEP
Word with up or head — START
Word with up or off — SIGN, TEED
Word with up or on — STUCK
Word with waiter or water — HEAD
Word with water — FIRE
Word with water or tea — WAGON
Word with what or when — EVER
Word with while — ERST
Word with wide or tight — END
Word with window or wood — ROSE
Word with work or wear — IRON
Word with worth or work — NET
Word with year or frog — LEAP
Word's opposite — ANTONYM
Word-for-word — VERBATIM
Word: Comb. form — LOGUE, ONYM
Wordplay — PUN
Words and music — SONG
Words before carte — A LA
Words exclusive to a group — JARGON
Words for Nanette — NO NO
Words formed from initials — ACRONYMS
Words from a Pagliaccio — LAUGH CLOWN LAUGH
Words from a positive thinker — I CAN
Words of admonition — NO NO
Words of approval — AMENS
Words of approximation — OR SO
Words of caution — SAFETY FIRST
Words of cheer — YEAS
Words of comparison — IS TO
Words of comprehension — I SEE
Words of consent — I DO
Words of the wise — ORACLES
Words of understanding — I SEE
Words of woe — AH ME
Words on a 1939 marquee — GONE WITH THE WIND
Words on a bistro menu — A LA
Words on a check — PAY TO THE ORDER OF
Words on a French menu — A LA
Words on a street sign — SLIPPERY WHEN WET
Words on proofs — STETS
Words said at the altar — WEDDING VOWS
Words to a song — LYRICS
Words to Brute — ET TU
Words to Nanette — NO NO
Words with term or time — LONG
Wordsmen — EDITORS
Wordsworth's "_____ Abbey" — TINTERN
Wordsworth, William — POET
Wore — HAD ON
Wore well — LASTED
Work — JOB, OPUS, TOIL
Work basket — CABA
Work break item — TEABAG
Work by Erle — NOVEL
Work byproduct — SWEAT
Work dough — KNEAD
Work for — EARN
Work for money — EARN
Work group — GANG
Work hard — SLAVE
Work in a smokehouse — CURE
Work in concert — COACT
Work like a dog — TOIL
Work like a horse — SWEAT
Work of a biased composer? — PARTIAL SCORE
Work of art — STATUE
Work on a bone — GNAW
Work on a chesterfield — RELINE
Work on a doily — TAT
Work on copy — EDIT
Work on hair — TEASE
Work on leather — RETAN
Work on pumps — RESOLE
Work out by reasoning — INFER
Work periods — STINTS
Work protectors — GLOVES
Work safety agcy. — OSHA
Work segments — SHIFTS
Work the bar — TEND
Work the fields — PLOW
Work the tiller — STEER
Work too hard — OVERDO
Work unit — ERG
Work unit: Abbr. — FT LB
Work units — DYNES, ERGS
Work with the hands — KNEAD
Work with wicker — CANE
Work, in Spain — OBRA
Work, with "out" — EKE
Workbaskets — CABAS
Workbench adjunct — VISE
Workbench tool — VISE, HACKSAW, REAMER
Worked at Vegas — DEALT
Worked for — EARNED
Worked for Eileen Ford — MODELED
Worked for wages — EARNED
Worked in a regatta — OARED
Worked on — COAXED, URGED
Worked on galleys — EDITED
Worked on soles — SCALED
Worked the soil — HOED
Worker — TOILER

Worker ant — ERGATE
Worker bee — DRONE
Worker in a formicary — ERGATE
Worker of yore — ESNE
Worker on a hill — ANT
Worker who assembles machines — ERECTOR
Worker with black alloy on metal — NIELLIST
Worker with shoes, footballs, etc. — LACER
Worker's pay — WAGE
Worker's reward — RAISE
Workers — HIREES
Workers in cotton — BALERS
Workers in milk-shipping companies — ICERS
Workers on MSS. — EDS
Workers' co-op in the USSR — ARTEL
Workers' cooperative in the USSR — ARTEL
Workers' group: Abbr. — CIO
Workers' joyful letters — TGIF
Workers' org. — UAW
Workers' prot. agcy. — OSHA
Workers' rights org. — NLRB
Workers' safety org. — OSHA
Working — IN USE
Working energetically — IN THERE PITCHING
Working rule — PRECEPT
Working woman's boon — DAYCARE
Workings — INNARDS
Workmanship — ARTISTRY, SKILL
Workout — JOG
Workout spot — GYM
Workplace — SHOP
Workplace safety org. — OSHA
Workplace watchdog agcy. — OSHA
Works at the bar — TENDS
Works by a Spanish muralist — SERTS
Works by French artist Fernand — LEGERS
Works clay — KNEADS
Works for — EARNS
Works for sitar — RAGAS
Works for two — DUETS
Works hard — TRAVAILS
Works of an English landscapist — CONSTABLES
Works of art — CREATIONS
Works of Pindar — ODES
Works on the lawn — RAKES
Works out by studious effort — ELECUBRATES
Worktable, in Etaples — ETABLI
World-relief org. — CARE
World chess champion: 1960-61 — TAL
World follower, in October — SERIES
World record breaker in the butterfly stroke — MORALES
World section — ASIA
World Series preliminary — PENNANT RACE
World Series winners: 1983 — ORIOLES
World toter — ATLAS
World turner? — LOVE
World War I initials — AEF
World War II alliance — AXIS
World War II vehicle — JEEP
World's Fair site: 1970 — OSAKA
World's longest river — NILE
World's lowest lake — DEAD SEA
World's most common name — WONG
World's third largest island — BORNEO
World, to a Frenchman — MONDE
World-weary — BLASE, BORED, JADED
World-wide — GLOBAL
World-wide labor group — ILO
World: Comb. form — COSM
Worldly — URBANE
Worldly goods — ESTATE
Worldly-wise — BLASE
Worldwide — GLOBAL
Worldwide in extent — ECUMENICAL
Worldwide labor org. — ILO
Worldwide maritime gp. — IMB
Worldwide newspaper org. — UPI
Worldwide relief org. — UNRRA
Worldwide workers' org. — ILO
Worldwide: Abbr. — INTL
Wormwood, for short — BROTAN
Worn-out — ALL IN, EFFETE, SPENT, TIRED
Worn-out horses — NAGS, RIPS
Worn — EROSE
Worn away — ERODED
Worn bare — BALD
Worn down by friction — ATTRITE
Worried, of yore — CARKED
Worries — FRETS, STEWS
Worriment — CONCERN
Worry — FRET
Worry — STEW
Worse off — POORER
Worship — ADORE, HONOR, REGARD, REVERE
Worshipful one — ADORER
Worshipped — ADORED
Worshipper — ADORER
Worshipper's word — AMEN
Worst kind of straits — DIRE
Worsted — SERGE
Worsted fabric — BROADCLOTH
Wort ingredient — MASH
Worth — VALUE
Worth consideration — TENABLE
Worth or Bordoni — IRENE
Worth: Abbr. — VAL
Worthless — DUD, TRASHY
Worthless coin — SOU
Worthless stuff — TRIPE
Worthless talk — BILGE
Worthless trifles — STRAWS
Worthless writing — TRIPE
Worthwhile — GOOD
Worthy — ABLE
Worthy of honor for poetic excellence — LAUREATE
Wou-wou — APE
Wouk's "The _____ Mutiny" — CAINE
Would-be grads — SRS
Would-be officer — CADET
Would-be redhead's rinse — HENNA
Would-be assassin: 1981 — AGCA
Would-be capts. — LTS
Would-be jr. — SOPH
Wound — LESION, SNAKED
Wound mark — SCAR
Wound memento — SCAR
Wound thread — SPOOLED
Wounded — HURT
Wounds — STINGS
Wove again — RESPUN
Woven double — TWO PLY
Woven fabric — WEFT
Wow — SLAY
Wow 'em — SLAY
Wow the audience — SLAY
Wow! — OUT OF SIGHT
Wowed — AWED
Wowed 'em — SLEW
Wraith — GHOST
Wrangell-Saint _____ National Park — ELIAS
Wrangle — SPAR
Wrangled over — BICKERED
Wrangler — CATTLEMAN
Wrangler's concern — HERD
Wrangler's rope — LARIAT
Wrap — STOLE
Wrap in bandages — SWATHE
Wrap up — COMPLETE, ENCASE, END
Wrap-up abbr. — ET AL
Wrapped up — OVER
Wrapper — ROBE
Wrapping material — SARAN
Wraps — STOLES

Wraps, as in bandages — ENSWATHES
Wrath — IRE
Wrath evergreen — GALAX
Wrath: Lat. — IRA
Wrathful — IRATE
Wraths — CHOLERS
Wreck winders — BREAK CRANKS
Wreckage — DEBRIS
Wrecks — TOTALS
Wrench — TEAR
Wrenches — SPRAINS
Wrestler's needs — MATS
Wrestler's ploy — KNEEING
Wrestlers' venue — ARENA
Wrestling hold — NELSON
Wrestling manuever — TAKE-DOWN
Wrestling needs — MATS
Wrestling place — MAT
Wrestling ploy — PIN
Wrestling surface — MAT
Wrests — RENDS
Wrests from — EXACTS
Wretched — POOR, SORRY, SQUALID
Wriggler — EEL
Wriggles — EELS
Wriggly critter — EEL
Wright Brothers' Ohio home — DAYTON
Wright or Brewer — TERESA
Wright or wreck — SHIP
Wright wing — ELL
Wrigley Field flora — IVY
Wrinkle — CRIMP, RUGA
Wrinkle remover — IRON
Wrinkled — RUGATE
Wrinkles, to botanist — RUGAE
Wrists — CARPI
Writ — ORDER
Write — PEN
Write a ticket — CITE
Write at length — ENLARGE
Write in letters of gold — CHRYSOGRAPH
Write in verse — RHYME
Write music — NOTATE
Write right — AMEND
Write, in a way — INK
Writer — AUTHOR
Writer _____ Thompson Seton — ERNEST
Writer Anais — NIN
Writer Anita — LOOS
Writer Anya — SETON
Writer Ayn — RAND
Writer Balzac — HONORE
Writer Ben _____ Williams — AMES
Writer Bernard De _____ — VOTO
Writer Bernstein — CARL
Writer Bombeck — ERMA
Writer Bontemps — ARNA
Writer Bret — HARTE
Writer Calderon — ERMA
Writer Calvino — ITALO
Writer Claude — ANET
Writer Dahl — ROALD
Writer Deighton — LEN
Writer Ephron — NORA
Writer Ferber — EDNA
Writer Fleming — IAN
Writer Gardner — ERLE
Writer Gardner's namesakes — ERLES
Writer Germaine de _____ — STAEL
Writer Gertrude — STEIN
Writer Grey — ZANE
Writer Harte — BRET
Writer Havelock — ELLIS
Writer Hecht — BEN
Writer Hentoff — NAT
Writer Horatio — ALGER
Writer Jaffe — RONA
Writer James and family — AGEES
Writer John _____ Passos — DOS
Writer Jong — ERICA
Writer Kesey — KEN
Writer Kingsley — AMIS
Writer Leon — URIS
Writer Loos — ANITA
Writer Macdonald — ROSS
Writer O'Casey — SEAN
Writer of inferior verse — POET ASTER
Writer of ridicule — SATIRIST
Writer of suspense tales — INNES
Writer Ogden — NASH
Writer Rand — AYN
Writer Rogers St. Johns — ADELA
Writer Rohmer — SAX
Writer Sarah _____ Jewett — ORNE
Writer Seton — ANYA
Writer St. John — ADELA
Writer turns actor? — ISAAC ASIMOVIESTAR
Writer Vidal — GORE
Writer Wiesel — ELIE
Writer Wylie — ELINOR
Writer Yutang — LIN
Writer Zola — EMILE
Writer's _____ — CRAMP
Writer's article — PIECE
Writer's concern — TENSE
Writer's Ernest Thompson and Anya — SETONS
Writer's object, of yore — INK-STAND
Writer, of sorts — PENCIL
Writer-director Kazan — ELIA
Writes — PENS
Writes "30" — ENDS
Writes "Wish you were here" — DROPS A LINE
Writes finis to — ENDS
Writes in — ENTERS
Writing material — INK
Writing on the wall — MENE
Written acknowledgement — RECEIPT
Written assignment — THEME
Written matter — ARTICLE
Written study — TREATISE
Written up — CITED
Written, e.g. — UNORAL
Wrong — AMISS, AWRY, ERRING
Wrong place to put all your eggs — BASKET
Wrong prefix — MIS
Wrong way activity — RUB
Wrongdoings — SINS
Wrongful — EVIL
Wrongful act — TORT
Wrongful behavior — CRIME
Wrongful entry — TRESPASS
Wrongheaded — PERVERSE
Wrongs — SINS
Wrongs deliberately — SPITES
Wrongs' opposites: Abbr. — RTS
Wrote — PENNED
Wrote for another — GHOSTED
Wroth — ANGRY, IRATE
Wrought-up — IRATE
Wry — IRONIC
Wrymouths' cousins — EELS
WSC's "few" — RAF
Wt. units — LBS
Wurttemberg city — ULM
WW I mil. org. — AEF
WW I naval menace — UBOAT
WW II address — APO
WW II alliance — AXIS
WW II area — ETO
WW II battle site — ST LO
WW II cloak-and-dagger outfit — OSS
WW II craft — EBOAT, UBOAT
WW II French battle site — ST LO
WW II Gen. Bradley — OMAR
WW II general — TOJO
WW II German naval base — EMDEN
WW II gr. — OPA
WW II heroes — RAF
WW II landing craft — LSTS
WW II maritime hazards — U BOATS
WW II mil. gp. — WAAC
WW II org. — OSS
WW II plane _____ Gay — ENOLA
WW II price control agcy. — OPA
WW II sector — ETO
WW II Service org. — USO

WW II vehicles — LSTS
WW II vessels — LSTS
Wyandot's kin — ERIE
Wyandotte — CHICKEN
Wyatt — EARP
Wyatt of the West — EARP
Wyatt or Wyman — JANE
Wye follower — ZEE
Wyes' predecessors — EXES
Wyeth medium — OILS
Wyeth model — HELGA
Wyler classic — BEN HUR
Wylie or Donahue — ELINOR
Wyndham Lewis novel — TARR
Wynken, Blynken, and Nod man — EUGENE FIELD
Wynn and Asner — EDS
Wynn and Koch — EDS
Wynn and Sullivan — EDS
Wynonna Judd's mom — NAOMI
Wynonna Judd's mother — NAOMI
Wyoming mountain range — TETON
Wystan Hugh — AUDEN
Wyvern — DRAGON

X

X-rated — EROTIC, INDECENT, LEWD, PORN, STEAMY
X-rated material — EROTICA
X follower — RATED
X out — ERASE
X's for Xanthippe — CHIS
X's out — DELETES
Xanthippe's forte — NAGGING
Xanthippe's type — SHREW
Xanthippe, e.g. — SHREW
Xenon and neon — GASES
Xenon and others — GASES
Xenophobe's fear — ALIEN
Xerosis — DRYNESS
Xi follower — OMICRON
XIV x III — XLII
Xmas gift — BIKE
XV — FIFTEEN
XXVI doubled — LII
XXVI plus XXVII — LIII
XXVI x II — LII
XXX, To Pierre — TRENTE
Xylophone — MARIMBA
Xylophone's cousin — MARIMBA

Y

Y.A. Tittle was one — GIANT
Y.M.C.A. or N.A.A.C.P. — ASSN
Yacht facilities — MARINAS
Yacht flag — BURGEE
Yachting — ASEA
Yachting undergarments? — MARINA SLIPS
Yachtsman or hat — BOATER
Yahoo — BRUTE, LOUT
Yak — CHATTER, JAW
Yakety-yak — TALK ONES HEAD OFF
Yakima, Herald-Republican — DAILY
Yakked — JAWED
Yaks — GABS, GASES, SHOOTS THE BREEZE
Yaks, et al. — OXEN
Yakut river — LENA
Yakutsk locale — SIBERIA
Yakutsk's river — LENA
Yale — ELI
Yale alumni — ELIS
Yale athletes — ELIS
Yale cheers — RAHS
Yale folk — ELIS
Yale name — ELI
Yale or Root — ELIHU
Yale or Whitney — ELI
Yale student — ELI
Yale undergraduate — ELI
Yale's "_____ song" — BOOLA
Yalie — ELI
Yalie, of a sort — COED
Yalta location — CRIMEA
Yalta's area — CRIMEA
Yam — POTATO, TUBER
Yamamai's kin — ERI
Yammer — GROAN
Yammered — RANTED
Yang's counterpart — YIN
Yang's partner — YIN
Yangtze craft — SAMPANS
Yank — PULL
Yank opponents: 1862 — REBS
Yankee #8 — BERRA
Yankee Doodle's feather — MACARONI
Yankees' foes in 1776 — REDCOATS
Yanks — PULLS
Yap — BARK
Yarborough card — TREY
Yarborough's top cards — NINES
Yard — SPAR
Yard event — SALE
Yard parts — FEET
Yard sections — FEET
Yardbirds — INMATES
Yardstick — GAUGE
Yarn — TALE
Yarn balls — CLEWS
Yarn fluff — LINT
Yarn measures — LEAS
Yarn quantity — SKEIN
Yarn ravelings — LINT
Yarn spinners — LIARS
Yarn weight — DENIER
Yastrzemski — CARL
Yawls and ketches — BOATS
Yawn — GAPE
Yawn inducer — BORE
Yawn-maker — BOREDOM

Yawning — AGAPE
Yawning fissure — CHASM
Yclept — NAMED
Ye _____ Shoppe — OLDE
Ye _____ Tea Shoppe — OLDE
Yea's, e.g. — VOTES
Year Claudius I died — LIV
Year in Alexius I Comnenus's reign — MCI
Year in Claudius I's reign — LIII
Year in Henry VII's reign — MDV
Year in historian Tacitus' life — CVII
Year in Luther's time — MDI
Year in reign of Claudius — LII
Year in reign of Ethelred II — MIII
Year in reign of Henry III — MCCLIV
Year in the 11th Century — LMII
Year in the first century — LII
Year in the reign of Antoninus Pius — CLVI
Year in the reign of Henry I — MCVI
Year in the reign of Louis XII — MDVI
Year or frog — LEAP
Year or frog preceder — LEAP
Year, in Arles — ANNEE
Year, in Spain — ANO
Year, to Yves — ANNEE
Yearbook — ANNUAL
Yearling — COLT
Yearn — ACHE, HANKER, LONG, PINE
Yearn for — CRAVE
Yearned — ACHED, PINED
Yearning — ACHE, ITCH, YEN
Yearns — ACHES, PINES, COVETS, LONGS
Years and years — EONS
Yeast — FUNGI
Yeast for Vassar — BARM
Yeast Value, Kan.? — LEAVENWORTH
Yeastlike fungus — TORULA
Yeats and Keats — POETS
Yegg — SAFE CRACKER
Yegg's loot — ICE
Yegg's target — SAFE
Yegg's transport, at times — BLACK MARIA
Yell — CRY
Yelled — HOLLERED
Yellow-Journalism tidbits — SCANDALS
Yellow-skinned melons — CASABAS
Yellow — OCHRE
Yellow apple — GOLDEN DELICIOUS
Yellow bird — CANARY
Yellow bugle — IVA
Yellow cheese — CHEDDAR
Yellow dye, source — AMIL
Yellow fever mosquito — AEDES
Yellow fish — IDE
Yellow flag — IRIS
Yellow hue — OCHER
Yellow melons — CASABAS
Yellow or Black — SEA
Yellow pigments — ETIOLINS
Yellow sapphire — TOPAZ
Yellow weed — TANSY
Yellow-breasted warbler — CHAT
Yellow-fever mosquito — AEDES
Yellow-flowered shrub — GORSE
Yellow-haired — BLOND
Yellow: Pref. — XANTH
Yellowfin — TUNA
Yellowhammer St. — ALA
Yellowish-brown color — TAWNY
Yellowish pigment — OCHRE
Yellowish-brown — AMBER
Yellowish-brown European? — AMBERLINER
Yellowish-green, foolish oldsters? — PERIDOTARDS
Yellowjackets — WASPS
Yellowstone Park denizens — BEARS
Yellowstone Park sight — TOWER FALLS
Yellowstone range — TETON
Yemen capital — SANA
Yemen city — ADEN
Yemen port — ADEN
Yemen's neighbor — OMAN
Yemeni port — ADEN
Yemeni seaport — ADEN
Yemenite — ARAB
Yen — 100 — SEN
Yens — URGES
Yeoman — CLERIC
Yerby's "A Rose for _____ Maria" — ANA
Yes — AMEN
Yes _____ (ultimatum words) — OR NO
Yes words — SURES
Yes, _____! — MAAM
Yes, in a way — I DO
Yes, in her private writings — WAS ANNE FRANK
Yes, no and maybe — ANSWERS
Yes, to Yves — OUI
Yesterday — PAST
Yesterday follower — TODAY
Yesterday's eternal chaser — TODAY
Yesterday's leftovers today — HASH
Yesterday's roast, today — HASH
Yesterday's ugly duckling — SWAN
Yesterday, in Padua — IERI
Yesterday, in Paris — HIER
Yesterday, in Roma — IERI
Yesterday, to Luigi — IERI
Yesterday, to Yves — HIER
Yesteryear — AGO
Yevtushenko's "Babi _____" — YAR
Yew — SHRUB
Yew and yaupon — TREES
Yew, for one — TREE
Yiddish title of respect — REB
Yield — ASSENT, CEDE, RELENT
Yield — SUCCUMB
Yielded — CODED
Yielding — SOFT
Yielding readily — SPINELESS
Yields — CEDES, RELENTS
Yikes! — EGAD
Yippee! — RAH
Yippie Jerry — RUBIN
Yitzhak's predecessor — GOLDA
YMCA and YMHA — ASSNS
YMCA, et al. — ASSNS
Yoga posture — ASANA, SQUAT
Yoga squat — ASANA
Yogi — BERRA
Yogi of the Yankees — BERRA
Yogi or Smokey — BEAR
Yoke takers — OXEN
Yokel — BORE, RUBE
Yoko — ONO
Yonder — AFAR, THERE
Yonker's performers — TROTTERS
Yore — AGO, ELD
Yore, of yore — ELD
York and Friday Abbr. — SGTS
York or Preston — SERGEANT
York symbol — ROSE
York's river — OUSE
Yorkshire city — LEEDS
Yorkshire river — AIRE, OUSE, URE
Yorkshire town NW of Leeds — OTLEY
Yorkshire waterway — AIRE
Yorktown, CV — CARRIER
Yosemite National Park river — MERCED
You bet! — YES
You may have seen this before — RERUN
You said it! — AMEN
You, in Italia — VOI
You, now — SOLVER
Young adults — TEENS

Young animal — COLT, TEEN
Young Brinker — HANS
Young codfish — SCROD
Young cow — HEIFER
Young doe — TEG
Young Durocs — SHOATS
Young eel — ELVER
Young falcon — EYAS
Young fellow — BOY, LAD
Young food fish — SCROD
Young girl — MISSY
Young goat — KID
Young Guthrie — ARLO
Young hen — PULLET
Young herrings — BRITS
Young hog — SHOAT
Young hooter — OWLET
Young horse — COLT, FOAL
Young lady from Armentieres, for short — MLLE
Young man's fancy — BEARD
Young men — LADS
Young of "Topper" films — ROLAND
Young Oliver — TWIST
Young one — CHILD, LAD, TAD, TEEM, TOT
Young or old attachment — STER
Young or old chaser — STER
Young or old ending — STER
Young or Stack — ROBERT
Young oyster — SPAT
Young persons — TEENS
Young pest — BRAT
Young pigeon — SQUAB
Young plant — SPRIG
Young salmon — GRILSE, PARR, SMOLT
Young seals — PUPS
Young Shakespeare's river — AVON
Young sheep — TEG
Young Simpson — BART
Young socialites — DEBS
Young tag-on — STER
Young woman — GIRL, LASS
Young women, to Aussies — SHEILAS
Young zebra — COLT
Young, dull person — NERD
Young, silvery salmon — SMOLTS
Younger — JUNIOR
Younger or elder statesman — PITT
Youngest son — CADET
Youngman and others — HENNYS
Youngman of comedy — HENNY
Youngman quip — ONE LINER
Youngster — CHILD, LAD, SHAVER, TAD, TEEN
Youngster's wheels — SCOOTER
Youngsters — MOPPETS
Your highness — MAAM
Your majesty! — SIRE
Your, in Hanover — IHRE
Your, of yore — THINE
Your: Fr. — TES
Yours and mine — OURS
Yours in Brittany — ATOI
Yours, in Tours — ATOI
Yours: Fr. — ATOI
Yousekevitch of ballet fame — IGOR
Youth — LAD, TEEN
Youth goddess — HEBE
Youth gp. — BSA
Youth org. — BSA, YMCA
Youthful — YOUNG
Youthful berry pickers — HANSEL AND GRETEL
Youthful period — TEENS
Yucatan capital — MERIDA
Yucatec — MAYA
Yucca — PLANT
Yucca's kin — SOTOL
Yuccalike plant — SOTOL
Yuck! — UGH
Yugoslav island in the Adriatic — BUA
Yugoslav native — SERB
Yugoslav of fame — TITO
Yugoslav port, SE of Trieste — FIUME
Yugoslav statesman — TITO
Yugoslavia's neighbor — ITALY
Yugoslavia's sea — ADRIATIC
Yukon Territory capital — WHITEHORSE
Yukon, e.g. — TERR
Yule-tree hanger — ICICLE
Yule — CHRISTMAS TIME
Yule quaff, for short — NOG
Yule singers — CAROLERS
Yule songster — CAROLER
Yule tree trim — TINSEL
Yule tune — DECK THE HALLS
Yule tune — JOY TO THE WORLD
Yule tune — THE FIRST NOEL
Yule visitor — SANTA
Yuletide decoration — MANGER, TINSEL
Yuletide guests — MAGI
Yuletides — NOELS
Yum-Yum's sash — OBI
Yummy dessert — LEMON CHIFFON PIE
Yurt or marquee — TENT
Yves' dream — REVE
Yves' world — MONDE

Z

Zachary Taylor — PRESIDENT
Zagreb people — CROATS
Zaire's western neighbor — CONGO
Zane Grey locale — MESA
Zany — COMIC
Zanzibar duo — ZEES
Zapped, as bugs — SPRAYED
Zaps — ZINGS
Zasu of the movies — PITTS
Zeal — ARDENCY, ARDOR
Zealot — DIEHARD, FANATIC
Zealous — EAGER, EARNEST
Zebu feature — HUMP
Zedong of China — MAO
Zeeland native — DANE
Zenana — HAREM
Zenana — HAREM
Zenith — ACME, APEX, SUMMIT
Zenith's opposite — NADIR
Zeno — STOIC
Zeno follower — STOIC
Zeno of _____, Greek philosopher — ELEA
Zeno's "classroom" — STOA
Zeno's city — ELEA
Zeno's home — ELEA
Zephyr — BREEZE
Zeppelin, e.g. — AIRSHIP
Zero — AUGHT, NAUGHT, NIL
Zero in — AIM
Zero to Agassi — LOVE
Zest — ELAN, GUSTO
Zestful — TANGY
Zeta follower — ETA
Zetetic person — SEEKER
Zetetics — SEEKERS

Zeus' consort — HERA
Zeus' partner — HERA
Zeus' wife — HERA
Zeus's mother — RHEA
Zeus, to Nero — JOVE
Zeus, to Zeno — DEITY
Zhivago's lady — LARA
Zhivago's love — LARA
Zhivago's portrayer — SHARIF
Ziegfeld — FLO
Zig — VEER
Zigzag car race — SLALOM
Zilch — NIL, NONE, NOTHING, ZERO
Zimbalist's teacher — AUER
Zinc producer — SMELTERY
Zing — DASH, ELAN
Zingers — RETORTS
Zion — HILL
Zip — NIL, ZERO
Zip over the surface — SKIM
Zippy — ENERGETIC
Zips — SCOOTS
Zircon is one — GEMSTONE
Zither of yore — ASOR
Zodiac division — SIGN
Zodiac sign — CRAB, RAM, LEO, LIBRA
Zodiac symbol — RAM
Zodiacal animal — RAM
Zodiacal sign — LEO
Zoe _____: 1935 Pulitzer winner for drama — AKINS
Zola — EMILE
Zola and Berliner — EMILES
Zola character — NANA
Zola heroine — NANA
Zola novel — NANA
Zola opus — NANA
Zone — AREA, BELT, REGION, SECTOR, WARD
Zonk out — NAP
Zoo attractions — PANDAS
Zoo attractions, for short — HIPPOS
Zoo equipment — CAGES
Zoo favorite — APE, LLAMA, PANDA
Zoo feature — CAMEL
Zoo simian — ORANG
Zoo sound — ROAR
Zoo structure — AVIARY
Zoo's powerful veggie eater — RHINO
Zookeeper? — STRAW BOSS
Zool. suffix — INI
Zoological stalks — PEDICLES
Zoological suffix — ACEA
Zoom or contact — LENS
Zoomed — BARRELED
Zooms — ZIPS
Zoophagan — MEAT EATER
Zoot Sims instrument — SAX
Zorba's creator — KAZANTZAKIS
Zorba's quaff — OUZO
Zori — SANDAL
Zorina — VERA
Zoroastrian — PARSEE, PARSI
Zoroastrian Bible — AVESTA
Zoroastrians' sacred book — AVESTA
Zorro's mark — ZEE
Zounds — EGAD
Zsa Zsa's sister — EVA, MAGDA
Zubin Mehta's need — BATON
Zubin Mehta, for one — BATONEER
Zucchetto, e.g. — CAP
Zuider _____ — ZEE
Zulu dialect — NGONI
Zwei follower — DREI
Zwei preceder — EINE
Zygote — CELL
Zzzzzz — SNORE

SUPPLEMENTS

CLUES BEGINNING WITH NUMERALS

000 — ZEROS
007 — AGENT
007 adversary — GOLDFINGER
007 nemesis — JAWS
007, for one — AGENT
1 or 66 — RTE
1 or 66: Abbr. — RTE
1st Century Roman emperor — OTHO
1st year doe — FAWN
1.555 grms. — PST
2-nation pen. — KOR
2-part sultanate — BRUNEI
2/3 of a famous "fleet" — PINTA, SANTA MARIA
3 bears' visitor — GOLDILOCKS
3 minutes of boxing — ROUND
3rd generation male — GRANDSON
3rd-century date — CCI
3/7 of the "Deadly Sins" — PRIDE ANGER SLOTH
3.26 light years — PARSEC
4th Century martyr saint — ELMO
5-lepta piece — OBOL
5th digit — MINIMUS
"6 Rms _____ Vu," 1972 play — RIV
6 winged angel — SERAPH
6th sense, for short — ESP
6th century date — DII
6th sense — ESP
6/6/44 — D DAY
7th planet from the sun — URANUS
7th sunday after Easter — PENTECOST
7-time Norris Trophy winner — ORR
9mm automatic weapons — STENS
9mm submachine gun — STEN
10th cen. English saint — DUNSTAN
10th inning cause — TIE
11th cen. biblical commentator — RASHI
11th cen. Danish king of England: Var. — KNUT
12 months — YEAR
13th Greek letters — NUS
14 liner — SONNET
9 to 5ers' end of the week abbr. — TGIF
9 to 5ers' pet letters — TGIF
9 to 12 year olds — PRETEENS
12/24 and 12/31 — EVES
15th of March — IDES
16th cen. dramatist-poet George — PEELE
16th letter of a certain series — AYIN
17th cen. Dutch painter — STEEN
17th cen. Dutch painter Jan — STEEN
17th cen. Dutch painter Gerhard _____ Borch — TER
17th cen. explorer La _____ — SALLE
17th cen. robe — SIMAR
17th cen. Scottish mapmaker — ADAIR
18th cen. diplomat-lawyer Silas — DEANE
18th cen. English composer — ARNE
18th cen. secular cantata — SERENATA
18th Century English poet — GRAY
18th U.S. president — GRANT
19th cen. Canadian rebel — RIEL
19th cen. French illustrator — DORE
19th cen. humorist Bill, et al. — NYES
19th cen. Polish composer-pianist — CHOPIN
19th cen. war — CIVIL
19th Century essayist — ELIA
19th Century French composer — LALO
20 cigarettes — PACK
20th Hebrew letter — RESH
20th letter of Hebrew alphabet — RESH
21-gun salute — SALVO
24-carat canary? — GOLD FINCH
24 carat indicating pure _____ — GOLD
27th US president — TAFT
30's youth agcy. — CCC
34th Street "miracle" store — MACYS
37th president — NIXON
45 degrees of arc — OCTANT
49, to Hadrian — XLIX
51st psalm — MISERERE
'56 Wimbledon champion and family — HOADS
56, in old Rome — LVI
19th, 20th, or 21st — CEN
60's character — BEATNIK
60's Pop star Bobby — RYDELL
'60's slogan — FLOWER POWER
62, to Caesar — LXII
100% — ALL
100 Centimes — FRANC
100 centimos — PESETA
100 dinars — RIAL
100 dollar bill portrait — FRANKLIN
100-year celebrations — CENTENNIALS
100 yrs. — CEN
100 yrs. — CENTURY
100 make a pound — PENCE
102 — CII
103 to Caesar — CIII
104, Roman style — CIV
111, to Caesar — CXI
200 milligrams — CARAT
212 degrees in Germany? — BERLIN POINT
500 mile race — INDY
506, to Nero — DVI
551, Roman style — DLI
551 — DLI
551 to Caesar — DLI
552 — DLII
601, to Cato — DCI
604 to Caesar — DCIV
$1,000 bleachers? — GRAND STAND
$1,000 — GRAND
1002 — MII
1006, to Ovid — MVI
1007 — MVII
1019 to Cato — MXIX
1051, in Pompeii — MLI
1051 — MLI
1101 to Caesar — MCI
1492 ship — NINA
1501 to Brutus — MDI
1501, in the Forum — MDI
1502, in old Rome — MDII

1504, in old Rome — MDIV
1550, to Fabius — MDL
1600 Penn. Ave. res. — PRES
1800 mile river important in Indian history — INDUS
1803 US acquisition from France — LA PURCHASE
1833 George Sand novel — LELIA
1849 US event — CA GOLDRUSH
1853 war site — CRIMEA
1862 battle site — SHILOH
1904's "The Garden of _____" — ALLAH
1917 Pulitzer winner Ernest — POOLE
1919 Triple Crown winner — SIR BARTON
1920 dance — CHARLESTON
1920 U.S. Open Champion — BILL TILDEN
1923 Nobel Literature winner — YEATS
1926 channel-swimmer Gertrude — EDERLE
1928 song — YOURE THE CREAM IN MY COFFEE
1929 disaster — WALL STREET CRASH
1929 Nobel writer — MANN
1932 Crawford film — RAIN
1934 Nobelist, et al. — UREYS
1934 Norma Shearer flick — RIPTIDE
1937 Triple Crown winner — WAR ADMIRAL
1938 Nobelist in physics — FERMI
1939 hit set to Ravel music — THE LAMP IS LOW
1940 Jack Benny flick — LOVE THY NEIGHBOR
1942 Preakness winner — ALSAB
1943 Bogart film — SAHARA
1944 Allied victory town — ST LO
1944 Nobelist for physics — RABI
1945 Conference site — YALTA
1947 film about a chicken farmer — THE EGG AND I
1947 Nobelist in literature — GIDE
1948 Evelyn Waugh novel — THE LOVED ONE
1950 John Ford western — WAGON MASTER
1950 Nobelist for chemistry — ALDER
1952 Ferber fiction — GIANT
1953 Oscar winner — SINATRA
1954 Oscar winner — KELLY
1954-1977 alliance: Abbr. — SEATO
1955 Kentucky Derby winner — SWAPS
1956 Marilyn Monroe movie — BUS STOP
1956 Noel Coward comedy — NUDE WITH VIOLIN
1957 Bergman movie — WILD STRAWBERRIES
1957 Literature Nobelist — CAMUS
1957 Pulitzer winner — AGEE
1957 song, "Let It _____" — BE ME
1958 Pulitzer novelist — AGEE
1958 Pulitzer novelist James — AGEE
1958 Pulitzer winner — AGEE
1959 Open champ's piano? — BOLT UPRIGHT
1965 AL batting champ — OLIVA
1965 Rhodesian pol. statement — UDI
1965 Selma-Montgomery walk — FREEDOM MARCH
1966 Fonda-Robards midweek movie? — ANY WEDNESDAY
1966 U.S. Open Tennis Champion — MARIA BUENO
1966 U.S. Open Tennis Champion — FRED STOLLE
1968 Neil Simon opus — PLAZA SUITE
1969 space target — MOON
1970's fad — PET ROCK
1971 Clint Eastwood film — PLAY MISTY FOR ME
1972 Woody Allen film — PLAY IT AGAIN SAM
1973 Masters money for Art? — WALLPAPER
1975 Wimbledon champ — ASHE
1976 Andrew Lloyd Webber musical — EVITA
1977 Frankenheimer Sabbath thriller? — BLACK SUNDAY
1974 Wilder-Burstyn 4th day comedy? — THURSDAYS GAME
1978 Nobel laureate — ISAAC BASHEVIS SINGER
1979 Broadway musical hit — EVITA
1981 Academy Award winner — CHARIOTS OF FIRE
1981 Warren Beatty film — REDS
1982 Disney film — TRON
1983 Peace Nobelist Walesa — LECH
1984 Oscar winner — AMADEUS
1984, et al.: Abbr. — YRS
1986 World Series sight — SHEA
1987 Kevin Bacon movie — LEMON SKY
1987 Vietnam movie — HAMBURG HILL
1988 name in the news — SIMON
1988 name in the news — ROBERTSON
1988 name in the news — DUKAKIS
1988 name in the news — JACKSON
1988 name in the news — BABBITT
1988 name in the news — BIDEN
1988 name in the news — DOLE
1988 name in the news — HAIG
1988 name in the news — GORE
1988 name in the news — HART
1989 play about Capote — TRU
1989 U.S. Open Tennis champion — STEFFI GRAF
2000, e.g. — YEAR
"2001" computer — HAL
2050, to Galba — MML
2104, to Cato — MMCIV
1066 or 1942 — YEAR
1776 or 1812 — YEAR
1988 or 1992 year — LEAP
5760 grains, e.g. — TROY WEIGHT
43,560 square feet — ACRE

CLUES BEGINNING WITH ANSWER BLANKS

_____ a beet — AS RED AS
_____ a boy! — ITS
_____ a can to (ousts) — TIES A
_____ a clef — ROMAN
_____ a customer — ONE TO
_____ a deal — ITS
_____ a dime — STOP ON
_____ a ghost — PALE AS A
_____ a girl! — ITS
_____ a hand — LEND
_____ a jour (be up to date) — ETRE
_____ a lifetime — ONCE IN
_____ a living — EARN
_____ a manager (dining room) — SALLES
_____ a million (very rare) — ONE IN
_____ a pin — NEAT AS
_____ a plea — COP
_____ a rail — THIN AS
_____ a ride — BUMMED
_____ a straw (seize any chance) — GRASP AT
_____ a time (singly) — ONE AT
_____ a trois (domestic triangle) — MENAGE
_____ a wet hen — MAD AS
_____ Ababa — ADDIS
_____ abet (be an accomplice) — AID AND
_____ Abner — LIL
_____ about — ON OR
_____ about (approximately) — ON OR
_____ about (circa) — ON OR
_____ about that! — HOW
_____ above (better) — A CUT
_____ above the average (better) — A CUT
_____ acceptable (proper) — SOCIALLY
_____ accepted (prevalent) — WIDELY
_____ accompli — FAIT
_____ accounts — ON NO
_____ acid — AMINO, BORIC
_____ acid (a vitamin) — FOLIC
_____ acid (oxidizing agent) — SELENIC
_____ acid: Vitamin B source — FOLIC
_____ act (pretend) — PUT ON AN
_____ Act of 1941 — LEND LEASE
_____ adagio (very slowly) — MOLTO
_____ affaire flambee — UNE
_____ age (mature) — COME OF
_____ Aires — BUENOS
_____ alai — JAI
_____ Alamos — LOS
_____ Alaska — BAKED
_____ Alegre, Brazil — PORTO
_____ alia — INTER
_____ Alighieri — DANTE
_____ all — END IT
_____ Allen — ETHAN
_____ along (moved clumsily) — LOBBED
_____ Alonzo Stagg — AMOS
_____ alt. (druggist's "every other day) — DIEB
_____ Alte: Adenauer — DER
_____ Alto, Calif. — PALO
_____ Alverio (Rita Moreno) — ROSITA
_____ America — LATIN, MISS
_____ American — ANGLO
_____ Amin — IDI
_____ amis — MES
_____ ammie — BONNE
_____ ammoniac — SAL
_____ an egg — LAID
_____ an egg (bad performance) — LAY
_____ an egg (bombs) — LAYS
_____ and anon — EVER
_____ and crafts — ARTS
_____ and downs — UPS
_____ and end all (whole) — BE ALL
_____ and ends — ODDS
_____ and Eng, original Siamese twins — CHANG
_____ and Fields, comedy team — WEBER
_____ and file — RANK
_____ and games — FUN
_____ and get it! — COME
_____ and haws — HEMS
_____ and kicking — ALIVE
_____ and Magog — GOG
_____ and penates — LARES
_____ and see — WAIT
_____ and skittles (fun) — BEER
_____ and stick — CARROT
_____ and terminer — OYER
_____ and terminer (court) — OYER
_____ and there — HERE
_____ and Thummin (Scriptural painting) — URIM
_____ and void — NULL
_____ and war — ALL IS FAIR IN LOVE
_____ angel: lost soul — FALLEN
_____ Angeles — LOS
_____ Angelico — FRA
_____ Angels — HELLS
_____ Anne de Beaupre' — STE
_____ Annie of "Oklahoma!" — ADO
_____ annum — PER
_____ anthem — NATIONAL
_____ Antilles — LESSER
_____ Antoinette — MARIE
_____ apparent — HEIR
_____ appeal — SNOB
_____ appetit — BON
_____ Appia — VIA
_____ apso — LHASA
_____ Arabia — SAUDI
_____ Arbor, Mich. — ANN
_____ area of San Francisco — BAY
_____ Ark — NOAHS
_____ arms — MEN AT
_____ arms (indignant) — UP IN
_____ around (cuts up) — HORSES
_____ as a beet — AS RED
_____ as a picture — PRETTY
_____ as a pin — AS NEAT
_____ as a whistle — CLEAN
_____ as Hades — AS HOT
_____ as molasses — AS SLOW
_____ as possible — AS SOON
_____ as soon do something — WOULD
_____ as the eye can see — AS FAR
_____ at a time — ONE
_____ at ease — ILL
_____ at the opportunity — LEAP
_____ at the switch — ASLEEP
_____ at: scorn — SNEEZE
_____ attention — STAND AT
_____ attention (heeded) — STOOD AT
_____ au rhum — BABA
_____ Auberjonois — RENE

_____ avail — TO NO
_____ avail (futilely) — TO NO
_____ average — ON AN
_____ aves — RARAE
_____ aves: unusual ones — RARAE
_____ avis — RARA
_____ Aviv — TEL
_____ away (saved) — LAID, SALTS
_____ away: moves secretly — STEALS
_____ B'rith — BNAI
_____ B. Anthony — SUSAN
_____ Baba — ALI
_____ bag — GRAB
_____ bagatelle — A MERE
_____ Baleares off Espana — ISLAS
_____ ball — FOUL, PLAY
_____ balls: walk — BASE ON
_____ banana — TOP
_____ bargain — PLEA
_____ barrel — PORK
_____ barrel (in trouble) — OVER A
_____ bars — PARALLEL
_____ Bator — ULAN
_____ Bator, formerly Urga — ULAN
_____ Bator, Mongolia — ULAN
_____ Bay, Oregon — COOS
_____ Bay, Yellow Sea inlet — KIAOCHOW
_____ be with you! — PEACE
_____ Beach, Fla. — VERO
_____ Beach, town on S Oahu — EWA
_____ beagle: lawyer — LEGAL
_____ beam — LASER
_____ beef — CORNED
_____ beer — DRAFT
_____ Bell (Emily Bronte) — ELLIS
_____ bell (seemed familiar) — RANG A
_____ bell (sound familiar) — RING A
_____ bell (sounded familiar) — RANG A
_____ Bell, Bronte pen name — ELLIS
_____ bellum — ANTE
_____ Ben Adhem — ABOU
_____ Ben Canaan, of "Exodus" — ARI
_____ bene — NOTE
_____ Benedict — EGGS
_____ Berets — GREEN
_____ Bernard — SAINT
_____ berth — LOWER
_____ Bible — DOUAY
_____ bien — TRES
_____ Bills (sign on a wall) — POST NO
_____ bird — EARLY
_____ bitsy — ITSY
_____ bitty — ITTY
_____ Blair (George Orwell) — ERIC
_____ Blanc — MONT
_____ blanche — CARTE
_____ blanket — WET
_____ bleu (bluestocking) — BAS
_____ bleu! — SACRE
_____ blot, in backgammon — HIT A
_____ bomb — ATOM
_____ Bones of fiction — BROM
_____ Boothe Luce — CLARE
_____ Borch, Dutch artist — TER
_____ Borch, Dutch painter — TER
_____ Boru — BRIAN
_____ Bovary — EMMA
_____ bow — TAKE A
_____ Box Derby — SOAP
_____ boy — ATTA, ITS A
_____ boy sandwich — POOR
_____ boys, at church — ALTAR
_____ bragh — ERIN GO
_____ Brakes, Utah National Monument — CEDAR
_____ branch (peace symbol) — OLIVE
_____ breve — ALLA
_____ breve (2/2 time) — ALLA
_____ Brinker — HANS
_____ brio — CON
_____ Brith — BNAI
_____ Brothers, 50's vocal group — AMES
_____ Brothers, dancers — STEP
_____ Brummel — BEAU
_____ buckle my shoe — ONE TWO
_____ buco (veal dish) — OSSO
_____ buco, Italian dish — OSSO
_____ Bud, a Dickens heroine — ROSA
_____ buddies — BOSOM
_____ Bueller, Broderick role — FERRIS
_____ Buena, in San Francisco Bay — YERBA
_____ buff — OPERA
_____ Burstyn — ELLEN
_____ but not least — LAST
_____ by (saves) — PUTS
_____ cabinet — CURIO
_____ caelestis; divine wrath — IRAE
_____ cake — TAKE THE
_____ Calabash — MRS
_____ Calhoun, actor — RORY
_____ California — BAJA
_____ California, peninsula in Mexico — BAJA
_____ Calloway — CAB
_____ camp: generals' assistants — AIDES DE
_____ can of worms: uncover trouble — OPEN A
_____ Canals — SOO
_____ Canals (Michigan) — SOO
_____ canem — CAVE
_____ cannon — LOOSE
_____ cantata (sung Mass) — MISSA
_____ canto — BEL
_____ cap (beret) — BASQUE
_____ capita — PER
_____ care (be wary) — HAVE A
_____ care (be watched) — HAVE A
_____ Carlo — MONTE
_____ Carlo Menotti — GIAN
_____ carol — CHRISTMAS
_____ Carpenter — KAREN
_____ carry — CASH AND
_____ carte — A LA
_____ Carte, opera company — DOYLY
_____ Cassidy, William Boyd role — HOPALONG
_____ cassis (a liqueur) — CREME DE
_____ Castle (Havana fort) — MORRO
_____ Castle, historic Cuban fort — MORRO
_____ cat — ONEO
_____ Cat (catamaran) — HOBIE
_____ catechumens — OIL OF
_____ cava — VENA
_____ cava (cor part) — VENA
_____ celebre — CAUSE
_____ cent — PER
_____ Centre, Toronto auditorium — OKEEFE
_____ champetre; garden party — FETE
_____ chance — NOT A
_____ chance (hopeless) — NOT A
_____ Chaplin, nee O'Neill — OONA
_____ chauvinism — MALE
_____ Che Guevara — ERNESTO
_____ chi (Oriental martial art) — TAI
_____ chose (a trifle) — PEUDE
_____ Christian Andersen — HANS
_____ Christie — ANNA
_____ Church Society of Iowa — AMANA
_____ circle — INNER
_____ cit, (in the place cited) — LOC

_____ citato: in the work cited — OPERE
_____ City, Calif. — CULVER
_____ Claire, stage star of the 30's — INA
_____ clay — FEET OF
_____ clear of — STEER
_____ clock (1300 hours) — ONE O
_____ clock scholar — TEN O
_____ cloth from Manila — PINA
_____ clothing — MENS
_____ coat — TRENCH
_____ cochere — PORTE
_____ code — AREA, MORSE
_____ cog (err) — SLIP A
_____ colada — PINA
_____ Cologne — EAU DE
_____ comet — HALLEYS
_____ coming (promising) — UP AND
_____ committee — AD HOC, SAT ON A
_____ companion — BOSOM
_____ Company: 18th and 19th cen. traders — EAST
_____ complex — GUILT
_____ compos mentis — NON
_____ con pollo (Spanish dish) — ARROZ
_____ Cong — VIET
_____ contendere — NOLO
_____ cook — SHORT ORDER
_____ cordiale — ENTENTE
_____ corner — AMEN
_____ corpus — HABEAS
_____ cost (regardless) — AT ANY
_____ cotta — TERRA
_____ course: eventually — IN DUE
_____ court — AUTO
_____ couture — HAUTE
_____ Cove: Hawkeye's home — CRABAPPLE
_____ Coward _____ — NOEL
_____ Creed of "Rocky" — APOLLO
_____ creek (out of luck) — UP A
_____ cricket — NOT
_____ cropper (fall) — COME A
_____ crossroads — AT A
_____ Cruces — LAS
_____ Cruces, N.M. — LAS
_____ cry — A FAR
_____ cry: long distance — A FAR
_____ culpa — MEA
_____ culpa — MEA
_____ cum laude — MAGNA, SUMMA
_____ cup (setting at a seder table) — ELIJAHS
_____ Curtain — BAMBOO
_____ d'Antibes — CAP
_____ d'Azur — COTE
_____ d'hotel — MAITRE
_____ d'oeuvre — HORS
_____ d'orchestre — VIOLE
_____ da Gama — VASCO
_____ Dagh, Bulgarian range — RILA
_____ Dame — NOTRE
_____ dance (Khachaturian) — SABRE
_____ Darya — AMU
_____ Darya (Aral Sea tributary) — SYR
_____ Dashian; Ethiopian mountain — RAS
_____ date (au courant) — UPTO
_____ David — CAMP, MOGEN, STAR OF
_____ Day — ARBOR, LABOR
_____ day (dawn) — BREAK OF
_____ Day (Sunday) — THE LORDS
_____ Day O'Connor — SANDRA
_____ day service — SAME
_____ day wonder (OTS grad. of WWII) — NINETY
_____ days' wonder — NINE
_____ days, for prayer and fasting — EMBER
_____ days, in Lent — EMBER
_____ de-mer (trepang) — BECHE
_____ de ballet — CORPS
_____ de Bearjeu, a daughter of Louis XI — ANNE
_____ de Bergerac — CERANO
_____ de boeif — ROTI
_____ de Boulogne, Paris — BOIS
_____ de Calais — PAS
_____ de Caldas, Brazilian resort — POCOS
_____ de cologne — EAU
_____ de corps. — ESPRIT
_____ de deux — PAS
_____ de foie gras — PATE
_____ de force — TOUR
_____ de France — ILE
_____ de France — TOUR
_____ de guerre — NOM
_____ de la Cite: Paris — ILE
_____ de la Plata — RIO
_____ de la Societe — OLES
_____ de Leon — PONCE
_____ de Mallorca — ISLA
_____ de menthe — CREME
_____ de Oro — RIO
_____ de Pasco, Peru — CERRO
_____ de Pascua — ISLA
_____ de plume — NOM
_____ de plume (pen names) — NOMS
_____ de Queiroz, Portuguese novelist — ECA
_____ de soie (cloth for dresses) — PEAU
_____ de tete — MAL
_____ de Triomphe — ARC
_____ de trois — PAS
_____ de veau — TETE
_____ de veau (sweatbread) — RIS
_____ de vie — EAU
_____ de vie: brandy — EAU
_____ deaf ears — FALL ON
_____ deal — ITS A
_____ deck (ducks) — HITS THE DECK
_____ Dee, Carolina river — PEE
_____ degree — NTH
_____ del Ese, Uruguay — PUNTA
_____ del Fuego — TIERRA
_____ del Rio, Cuban city — PINAR
_____ del Sol — COSTA
_____ Delgada, F. Azores — PONTA
_____ della Francesca — PIERO
_____ den Linden — UNTER
_____ des yeux (the whites of the eyes) — LE BLANC
_____ Dhabi, Eastern land — ABU
_____ Dhabi, emirate — ABU
_____ Dhabi: Arab sheikdom — ABU
_____ Diable — ILE DU
_____ diagram, in symbolic logic — VENN
_____ diem — CARPE, PER
_____ dieu — PRIE
_____ dieu: kneeling bench — PRIE
_____ dieu: praying stool — PRIE
_____ Dillon — MATT
_____ Dimitis: prayer — NUNC
_____ Dinh Diem: Vietnamese leader — NGO
_____ disant (self-styled) — SOI
_____ distant — SOI
_____ dive (throw a fight) — TAKE A
_____ dixit — IPSE
_____ do-well — NEER
_____ doble (corrida march) — PASO
_____ does it — EASY
_____ dog — LAP
_____ dog (peavey) — CANT
_____ Domingo — SANTO
_____ Domini — ANNO
_____ Domino — FATS
_____ donna — PRIMA
_____ double take — DO A

_____ down (mutes) — TONES
_____ down (softened) — TONED
_____ down (subside) — DIE
_____ down (understate) — TONE
_____ down (washed) — HOSED
_____ down cake — UPSIDE
_____ down: became quiet — PIPED
_____ down: quieted — TONED
_____ Downing Street — TEN
_____ Downs — EPSOM
_____ Downs in Surrey — EPSOM
_____ Drive, near Salerno — AMALFI
_____ du Diable — ILE
_____ du jour — CARTE
_____ du Nore, Paris — GARE
_____ du Salut — ILES
_____ du Vent — ILES
_____ Durbyfield, Hardy heroine — TESS
_____ E. Lee: Abbr. — ROBT
_____ eagle — BALD, LEGAL
_____ ear (heed) — LEND AN
_____ ear and ... — IN ONE
_____ early date — AT AN
_____ early date: soon — AT AN
_____ ears: vigilant — ALL
_____ earth — ALKALINE
_____ earth (practical) — DOWN TO
_____ ease — ILL AT
_____ ease: uncomfortable — ILL AT
_____ East — NEAR
_____ Eban — ABBA
_____ effort — A FOR, E FOR
_____ egg — NEST
_____ ego (another self) — ALTER
_____ Einsford-Hill: "My Fair Lady" role — FREDDY
_____ Eleanor Roosevelt — ANNA
_____ eleison — KYRIE
_____ Ems — BAD
_____ en scène (stage setting) — MISE
_____ En-lai — CHOU
_____ end (over) — AT AN
_____ end to — PUT AN
_____ es Salaam — DAR
_____ estate — REAL
_____ et quarante (Monte Carlo game) — TRENTE
_____ even keel — ON AN
_____ even: avenge — GET
_____ evil — SEE NO
_____ ex machina — DEUS
_____ excellency — HER
_____ Express — ORIENT
_____ extent (partly) — TO SOME
_____ extent (somewhat) — TO AN
_____ facias — SCIRE
_____ facie — PRIMA
_____ facto — IPSO
_____ fagioli (Neapolitan dish) — PASTA
_____ Fair (N.Y. 1939 event) — WORLDS
_____ Fairy: ballet role — SUGARPLUM
_____ Faithful — OLD
_____ far (to such an extent) — IN SO
_____ fatale — FEMME
_____ fatus: marsh light — IGNIS
_____ favor (Pablo's please) — POR
_____ fell swoop — IN ONE
_____ Fernando Valley — SAN
_____ fever — DENGUE
_____ fi — SCI
_____ fi, Bradbury's forte — SCI
_____ fiber — BAST
_____ fide — BONA
_____ Field, Dallas airport — LOVE
_____ Filippo Lippi — FRA
_____ fine table — SET A
_____ Finklea, aka Cyd Charisse — TULA
_____ fire (pend) — HANG
_____ firma — TERRA
_____ Fisher Hall: NYC — AVERY
_____ fixe — IDEE
_____ fixe (obsession) — IDEE
_____ flash — IN A
_____ flask (thermos prototype) — DEWAR
_____ Flow — SCAPA
_____ Flow, in the Orkneys — SCAPA
_____ Flow: Orkney Islands — SCAPA
_____ Flow: Orkney's sea basin — SCAPA
_____ fly — TSETSE
_____ fois (once, in Paris) — UNE
_____ food cake — ANGEL
_____ foot oil — NEATS
_____ for a rainy day — SET ASIDE
_____ for dinner — DRESS
_____ for one's money — A RUN
_____ for words — AT A LOSS
_____ force (by all means): Fr. — AT OUTE
_____ forces — ARMED
_____ Ford Range, Antarctica — EDSEL
_____ Forest, near London — EPPING
_____ Forest, scene of many battles — ARGONNE
_____ form — (exceptionally fine) — IN RARE
_____ fours — PLUS
_____ Fox — BRER
_____ Foxx — REDD
_____ franc of W. Afr. — CFA
_____ France — ILE DE
_____ France, famed liner — ILE DE
_____ Francisco — SAN
_____ fro (back and forth) — TO AND
_____ Fundo, city in Brazil — PASSO
_____ Galahad — SIR
_____ game — NO HIT
_____ garde — AVANT
_____ Garden, Copenhagen park — TIVOLI
_____ Gatos, Calif. — LOS
_____ Gay (WWII plane) — ENOLA
_____ Gay: historic plane — ENOLA
_____ generis (unique) — SUI
_____ gestae — RES
_____ ghanouj (Middle Eastern salad) — BABA
_____ Gibbs, country singer — TERRI
_____ Gillespie, trumpeter — DIZZY
_____ gin — SLOE
_____ gin fizz — RAMOS
_____ Girl — GIBSON
_____ girl! — ATTA
_____ glance — AT A
_____ glue — CRAZY
_____ go — LETS
_____ go bragh — ERIN
_____ good (be beneficial) — DO ONE
_____ good example — SET A
_____ Good Hope — CAPE OF
_____ Gordon — FLASH
_____ gospel (accept) — TAKE AS
_____ gossip — BACKSTAIRS
_____ Grande — RIO
_____ Grande, city in Ariz. — CASA
_____ granted (assume) — TAKE FOR
_____ grapes — SOUR
_____ gras — FOIE, MARDI
_____ grass (meadow barley) — RIE
_____ gratia — DEI
_____ gratia artis — ARS
_____ gratias — DEO
_____ grinder — ORGAN
_____ gritty — NITTY

_____ Groening: "The Simpsons" creator — MATT
_____ grudge (feel resentment) — HOLD A
_____ grudge (resent) — BEAR A
_____ guess — EDUCATED
_____ Guevara — CHE
_____ Gulf, Aegean Sea inlet — SAROS
_____ ha-Shanah (Jewish New Year) — ROSH
_____ Hague — THE
_____ Halaby (Jordan's Queen Noor) — LISA
_____ Hall University — SETON
_____ Hall, '89 NCAA finalist — SETON
_____ Hall, College, New Jersey — SETON
_____ Halles, Paris market — LES
_____ Han Mingak, S. Korea — TAE
_____ hand — LEND A
_____ hand (abjectly) — HAT IN
_____ hand (helped out) — LENT A
_____ hand (humble) — HAT IN
_____ hand (point of view) — ON ONE
_____ hand: advantage — UPPER
_____ Harbor, Guam — APRA
_____ Hari — MATA
_____ Hashana — ROSH
_____ Hassan — ABU
_____ Haute, Ind. — TERRE
_____ havoc with something — WREAK
_____ haw — HEM AND
_____ Hawkins Day — SADIE
_____ Headroom — MAX
_____ heart (cares) — HAS A
_____ Hedin, Gobi explorer — SVEN
_____ Heep — URIAH
_____ Heights — GOLAN
_____ Henri Beyle, alias Stendahl — MARIE
_____ hepatica — SAL
_____ Heyerdahl — THOR
_____ hit (single) — ONE BASE
_____ ho — GUNG
_____ hole — ACE IN THE
_____ home (out) — NOT AT
_____ Homo — ECCE
_____ homo (religious picture) — ECCE
_____ hoop — HULA
_____ Horizonte — BELO
_____ horse — TROJAN
_____ hot (soso) — NOT SO
_____ hot: mediocre — NOT SO
_____ hot: steaming — PIPING
_____ how — AND
_____ hurrah — LAST
_____ husky — SIBERIAN
_____ ice cap or bear — POLAR
_____ idol — MATINEE
_____ Ike — ALIBI
_____ image (idol) — GRAVEN
_____ impasse: deadlocked — AT AN
_____ impulse (wing it) — ACT ON
_____ in — CHIP
_____ in (meddle) — HORN
_____ in (withdraws) — CASHES
_____ in a lifetime — ONCE
_____ in a poke — A PIG
_____ in bond — BOTTLED
_____ in on (aim) — ZERO
_____ in one's belfry — A BAT
_____ in sheep's clothing — A WOLF
_____ in the bucket — A DROP
_____ in the dumps — DOWN
_____ in the neck — PAIN
_____ in the wood — AGED
_____ in the wool — DYED
_____ in years; age — GET ON
_____ in: schedule — FIT IT
_____ incognita — TERRA
_____ Indies — WEST
_____ instant (pronto) — IN AN
_____ integra — RES
_____ into (meet) — BUMP
_____ into: scolded — LAYED
_____ Irae — DIES
_____ Island — STATEN
_____ Island in the West Indies — MONA
_____ Island, off Ireland — ARAN
_____ Islands (Attu et al.) — NEAR
_____ Islands in the Bahamas — ABACO
_____ Islands, N of Cuba — BAT
_____ Isle — EMERALD
_____ isn't so — SAY IT
_____ it (amen) — SO BE
_____ it (dance, as in "L'Allegro") — TRIP
_____ it out (persevere) — GUT
_____ it over: domineered — LORDED
_____ it up — LIVE
_____ its weight in gold — WORTH
_____ jacet — HIC
_____ Jack — UNION
_____ Jahan — SHAH
_____ Janeiro — RIO DE
_____ Japanese War: 1937-45 — SINO
_____ Jemima — AUNT
_____ jiffy — IN A
_____ Jima — IWO
_____ jockey — DISC
_____ Jones Average — DOW
_____ jongg — MAH
_____ Jose — SAN
_____ Jovi, rock group — BON
_____ Juana — TIA
_____ Judgement — DAY OF
_____ judicata — RES
_____ Julius Caesar — CAIUS
_____ jump — HOP SKIP AND
_____ jure: in one's own right — SUO
_____ jury — PETIT
_____ juste (the exact word) — LE MOT
_____ Kadiddle-hopper — CLEM
_____ kebob — SHISH
_____ keel — ON AN EVEN
_____ Khan, Sir Tiger to Kipling — SHERE
_____ Khayyam — OMAR
_____ Kids — KATZENJAMMER
_____ King — A LA
_____ King Cole — NAT
_____ Kippur — YOM
_____ Kirkpatrick — JEANE
_____ knowledge (Eden landmark) — TREE OF
_____ Kong — HONG
_____ Kringle — KRIS
_____ Kutch, salt marsh in India — RANN
_____ l'oeil — TROMPE
_____ la Cité — ILE DE
_____ la Paix, Paris thoroughfare — RUE DE
_____ la vista — HASTA
_____ lace — QUEEN ANNES
_____ Lakes — GREAT
_____ Lama — DALAI
_____ land — NO MANS
_____ lane — MEMORY
_____ Lang, Superboy's friend — LANA
_____ Lanka — SRI
_____ large (mostly) — BY AND
_____ laude — CUM
_____ Law, in physics — JOULES
_____ Lazarus, "Miss Peach" cartoonist — MELL
_____ lazuli (shade of blue) — LAPIS
_____ Le Pew cartoon skunk — PEPE
_____ league, Junior circuit — AMERICAN

_____ leave it — TAKE IT OR
_____ Lee — RBT E
_____ left field — OUT IN
_____ Lehmann, German operatic soprano — LOTTE
_____ lens — CONTACT
_____ Leone — SIERRA
_____ less (diminishing) — LESS AND
_____ Levi (Yves Montand) — IVO
_____ Levy, Cohan's first wife — ETHEL
_____ libre — VERS
_____ lie (fibbed) — TOLD A
_____ light — KLIEG
_____ Lingus, Irish airline — AER
_____ lining — SILVER
_____ Lisa — MONA
_____ lively! — STEP
_____ living — EARN A
_____ living (economic index) — COST OF
_____ living: work for pay — EARN A
_____ lizard — LOUNGE
_____ Lizzy — TIN
_____ Lloyd Wright — FRANK
_____ Loa — MAUNA
_____ Locks — SOO
_____ Lomond — LOCH
_____ longa, vita brevis — ARS
_____ loose (free) — ON THE
_____ Lopez, entertainer from Dallas — TRINI
_____ loss (bewildered) — AT A
_____ loss (claims tax redress) — REPORTS A
_____ Ludwig: German biographer — EMIL
_____ Lugosi — BELA
_____ Luirc, County Cork town — RATH
_____ LXX natus (seventy years old): Lat. — ANNOS
_____ macabre — DANSE
_____ machine — VENDING
_____ made: is assured of success — HAS IT
_____ magnetism — ANIMAL
_____ Mahal — TAJ
_____ maid (servant) — LADYS
_____ majesty — LESE
_____ Major — URSA
_____ Majoris (The Great Bear) — URSA
_____ man (unanimously) — TO A
_____ man out — ODD
_____ many words — IN SO
_____ March hare — MAD AS A
_____ march on: get an advantage — STEAL A
_____ March to the Sea — SHERMANS
_____ Margret — ANN
_____ Maria Alberghetti — ANNA
_____ Marian — MAID
_____ Marie Saint — EVA
_____ Marquette — PERE
_____ Mateo, Calif. — SAN
_____ mater — ALMA
_____ mater — PIA
_____ matter of fact — AS A
_____ Mawr College, Pa. — BRYN
_____ May, in "Tobacco Road" — ELLIE
_____ me tangere — NOLI
_____ means (certainly) — BY ALL
_____ medica — MATERIA
_____ meeny ... — EENY
_____ Meir — GOLDA
_____ mell — PELL
_____ mer: cruise spoiler — MAL DE
_____ Mesta, former society hostess — PERLE
_____ metal (nickel alloy) — MONEL
_____ middling — FAIR TO
_____ mignon — FILET
_____ milk — SKIM
_____ million — ONE IN A
_____ mind (intend) — HAVE A
_____ mind (intended) — HAD IN
_____ mind (remember) — BEAR IN
_____ mind to (plans on) — HAS A
_____ Minor — ASIA
_____ Minor (the Lesser Lion) — LEO
_____ minute — A MILE A
_____ minute: soon — IN A
_____ miss — HIT OR, NEAR
_____ miss (haphazardly) — HIT OR
_____ mode — A LA
_____ Mohammad Khan: 18th cen. shah — AGHA
_____ Moines — DES
_____ Moines — DES
_____ moment (soon) — IN A
_____ monde — HAUTE
_____ monster — GILA
_____ morgana — FATA
_____ morgana: mirage — FATA
_____ moss — PEAT
_____ mosso: less rapid, in music — MENO
_____ Mountain, New Mexico peak — ELK
_____ Mountains in S. Poland — TATRA
_____ Mountains, featuring Munku-Sardyk — SAYAN
_____ movement in Botany — BROWNIAN
_____ mud in your eye! — HERES
_____ mutton — LEG O
_____ mutuel — PARI
_____ Na Na — SHA
_____ Nagy, Hungarian hero — IMRE
_____ National Park in the Cascades — CRATER LAKE
_____ New Guinea — PAPUA
_____ nibs — HIS
_____ Nicholas — SAINT
_____ nick of time — IN THE
_____ Nidre — KOL
_____ nine-tails — CAT O
_____ nisi bonum (nothing but good) — NIL
_____ noire — BETE
_____ noire: bugbear — BETE
_____ noires (anathemas) — BETES
_____ non grata — PERSONA
_____ Noster — PATER
_____ Nostra — COSA
_____ not (probably) — LIKE AS
_____ nous — ENTRE
_____ nous: between us — ENTRE
_____ nous: confidentially — ENTRE
_____ nova — BOSSA
_____ Nui (Easter Island) — RAPA
_____ number (speed ratio) — MACH
_____ nut — BETEL
_____ nut tree — KOLA
_____ nutshell (succinctly) — IN A
_____ obstat: permission to publish — NIHIL
_____ of (addressing people) — IN CARE
_____ of (replacing) — IN LIEU
_____ of Aquitaine — ELEANOR
_____ of Avon — EARL
_____ of cake (easy) — PIECE
_____ of Cleves — ANNE
_____ of colors (dazzling) — A RIOT
_____ of Congress — LIBRARY
_____ of contents — TABLE
_____ of credence — LETTER
_____ of expertise — AREAS
_____ of Fame — HALL
_____ of flux: changing — IN A STATE
_____ of Forth — FIRTH
_____ of Friends — SOCIETY
_____ of Good Feeling — ERA
_____ of Good Feeling: 1817-24 — ERA
_____ of Good Hope — THE CAPE

_____ of Habeas Corpus — WRIT
_____ of his own medicine — A DOSE
_____ of hope — A RAY
_____ of Hormuz — STRAIT
_____ of iniquity — DEN
_____ of interest — RATE
_____ of July — FOURTH
_____ of Kra in SW Thailand — ISTHMUS
_____ of luxury — LAP
_____ of Man — ISLE
_____ of March — IDES
_____ of milk and honey — LAND
_____ of mind — PEACE, STATE
_____ of mouth — WORD
_____ of no return — POINT
_____ of one's eye — APPLE
_____ of order — OUT
_____ of plenty — HORN
_____ of pottage — A MESS
_____ of quinine — OLEATE
_____ of Saint Louis — THE SPIRIT
_____ of show — BEST
_____ of the ball — BELLE
_____ of the crop — CREAM
_____ of the earth — SALT
_____ of the guard — YEOMAN
_____ of the mill — RUN OF
_____ of the Roses — WARS
_____ of the tongue — A SLIP
_____ of thousands — A CAST
_____ of thumb — RULE
_____ of voice — TONE
_____ of Wight — ISLE
_____ of: envelope notation — IN CARE
_____ off — ON AND, TEE
_____ off (angry as a golfer?) — TEED
_____ off (angry) — TEED
_____ off (drove) — TEED
_____ off (get along) — HIT IT
_____ off (irate) — TEED
_____ off (kill time) — GOOF
_____ off (repel) — FEND
_____ off (steams) — TEES
_____ off (transport) — CART
_____ off the old block — A CHIP
_____ off: parries — STAVES
_____ officianailis — ASPARAGUS
_____ on (attends) — SITS IN
_____ on (taken with) — SOLD
_____ on it: hurry — STEP
_____ on the map — A DOT
_____ on top of the world — SITTING
_____ on wheels — MEALS
_____ on: encourages — EGGS
_____ on: goad — EGG
_____ once (suddenly) — ALL AT
_____ one's knees — FALL ON
_____ one's laurels — REST ON
_____ one's leg (hoax) — PULL
_____ one's thumbs — TWIDDLE
_____ one's time — BIDE
_____ one's way — WEND
_____ one's weight — PULLS
_____ one's words — EAT
_____ opera — SOAP
_____ operandi — MODI, MODUS
_____ ordinaire — VIN
_____ ou pile (heads or tails): Fr. — TETE
_____ out — BAILS, EXES
_____ out (allot) — DOLE
_____ out (beat) — NOSED
_____ out (defeated narrowly) — NOSED
_____ out (exert) — GO ALL
_____ out (fizzles) — CONKS
_____ out (get by) — EKE
_____ out (gorge) — PIG
_____ out (got by) — EKED
_____ out (intimidate) — PSYCH
_____ out (just get by) — EKE
_____ out (made do) — EKED
_____ out (obliterated) — XED
_____ out (relax) — CHILL
_____ out (solved) — DOPED
_____ out (spent) — WORN
_____ out (squeezed) — EKED
_____ out (supplements) — EKES
_____ out (survive a storm) — RIDE IT
_____ out a win — EKE
_____ out: dwindled — PETERED
_____ out: made do — EKED
_____ out?: poker query — IN OR
_____ over (fall) — KEEL
_____ over backwards — BEND
_____ over heels in love — BE HEAD
_____ over, capsize — KEEL
_____ oxide, used in metallurgy — CHROMIC
_____ Pablo — SAN
_____ pack — FANNY
_____ paddy — RICE
_____ Palmas — LAS
_____ Pan Alley — TIN
_____ pants — SMARTY
_____ paper — LITMUS
_____ Park, Colorado resort — ESTES
_____ Park, Colorado town — ESTES
_____ Park, N.J. — MENLO
_____ Parker — NOSEY
_____ pas (blunder) — FAUX
_____ Passos — DOS
_____ passu (side by side) — PARI
_____ Patch, famous trotter — DAN
_____ Paul Kruger — OOM
_____ Paulo, Brazil — SAO
_____ Pea, small comic character — SWEET
_____ peak (hair feature) — WIDOWS
_____ Peak, Ariz. — ORD
_____ Peak, N.M. — OSHA
_____ peanuts — SALTED
_____ pectore (from the bottom of the heart) — IMO
_____ Penh — PNOM
_____ Peninsula, U.S.S.R — KOLA
_____ pentameter — IAMBIC
_____ Perce Indian — NEZ
_____ percenter — TEN
_____ perdue: casting process — CIRE
_____ Perilous (Round Table seat) — SIEGE
_____ Perpetua: Idaho's motto — ESTO
_____ person (for each) — PER
_____ phrase — COIN A
_____ pie — PIZZA
_____ pie (from head to foot) — CAP A
_____ pig's eye — IN A
_____ Pinkham — LYDIA
_____ Plaines, Ill. — DES
_____ plaisir! — AVEC
_____ plaster — MUSTARD
_____ play — FOUL
_____ plea (go to court) — ENTER A
_____ plea (legal move) — COP A
_____ plume — NOM DE
_____ podrida — OLLA
_____ poetica — ARS
_____ point: embroidery stitch — GROS
_____ poker — STUD
_____ pole — TOTEM
_____ polloi — HOI
_____ Pompela, ancient name of Asti — ASTA
_____ pool — CAR
_____ porridge — PEASE
_____ Porsena — LARS
_____ port in a storm — ANY
_____ Post — PARCEL
_____ potatoes (certain home fries) — OBRIEN
_____ powder (decamp) — TAKE A
_____ powder (flee) — TAKE A

_____ Prabang;, town in N. Laos — LUANG
_____ practice (make use of) — PUT INTO
_____ precedent — SET A
_____ precipitation — TRACES OF
_____ pro nobis — ORA
_____ processing unit (CPU) — CENTRAL
_____ profundo — BASSO
_____ prosequi (legal notice) — NOLLE
_____ public — NOTARY
_____ Public (average person) — JOHN Q
_____ pump — SUMP
_____ qua non — SINE
_____ Quarter — LATIN
_____ rabbit — BRER
_____ rain — ACID
_____ ran (loser) — ALSO
_____ Ranger — LONE
_____ Rapids, city in Minn. — COON
_____ Rapids, Michigan — GRAND
_____ Raton, Fla. — BOCA
_____ razor (philosophic rule) — OCCAMS
_____ reaction — GUT
_____ reader — LAY
_____ Rebellion — SHAYS
_____ Reekie (Edinburgh) — AULD
_____ regulation: golf term — ON IN
_____ relief — BAS
_____ renewal — URBAN
_____ restante — POSTE
_____ riches: parvenus — NOVEAUX
_____ Rio, Texas — DEL
_____ Rios, Jamaican resort — OCHO
_____ riot act — READ THE
_____ road — ONE FOR THE
_____ Rock, Australian tourist attraction — AYERS
_____ Rogers St. Johns — ADELA
_____ roll (having luck) — ON A
_____ Rookh, Thomas Moore heroine — LALLA
_____ room — REC
_____ room: (rumpus area) — REC
_____ rooms, at camp — REC
_____ roots — GRASS
_____ Rosa — SUB
_____ Royale — ISLE
_____ Royale National Park — ISLE
_____ Rud, river in Afghanistan — HARI
_____ rug — AREA
_____ rug: danced — CUT A
_____ rule (generally) — AS A
_____ run — HIT AND
_____ Ruth — BABE
_____ rye (sandwich) — HAM ON
_____ Salaam — DAR ES
_____ sale — YARD
_____ Salonga, "Miss Saigon" actress — LEA
_____ salts — EPSOM
_____ Salvador — SAN
_____ sana in corore sano — MENS
_____ Sanzio, Italian painter — RAPHAEL
_____ sapiens — HOMO
_____ Saud — IBN
_____ sax — ALTO
_____ Saxon — ANGLO
_____ say (regrettably) — SAD TO
_____ say die — NEVER
_____ scaloppine — VEAL
_____ School of painting — ASHCAN
_____ Schorer of the New York City Ballet — SUKI
_____ Scotia — NOVA
_____ Scott decision — DRED
_____ Sea (a big lake) — ARAL
_____ Sec. of the Navy (F.D.R.: 1913-20) — ASST
_____ seed: deteriorate — GO TO
_____ Semper Tyrannis: VA's motto — SIC
_____ sempre (now and always): It. — ORAE
_____ sequitur — NON
_____ Series — WORLD
_____ Service — SECRET
_____ setter — IRISH.
_____ Shan (Kirghiz range) — TIAN
_____ Shan, central Asian range — TIEN
_____ shaped curve — ESS
_____ share — LIONS
_____ share: biggest part — LIONS
_____ Shearer — NORMA
_____ shooting — SKEET
_____ shoulders above — HEAD AND
_____ show — RAREE
_____ show: pantomime — DUMB
_____ sides (everywhere) — ON ALL
_____ sides: surrounded — ON ALL
_____ signo vinces — IN HOC
_____ Simbel, Egypt — ABU
_____ sing like the birdies ... — LETS ALL
_____ six (discard) — DEEP
_____ skelter — HELTER
_____ sketch — THUMBNAIL
_____ ski — APRES
_____ skip and a jump — HOP
_____ slump (fall off) — HIT A
_____ so fast! — NOT
_____ Soleil (Louis XIV) — LE ROI
_____ song (inexpensively) — FOR A
_____ souci — SANS
_____ soup — ALPHABET
_____ soup (heavy fog) — PEA
_____ sow — AS YE
_____ space — OUTER
_____ spare — TIME TO
_____ speak — SO TO
_____ Spee — GRAF
_____ split — BANANA
_____ spot — X MARKS THE
_____ spot: fin — FIVE
_____ Spots, singing group — INK
_____ spumante — ASTI
_____ spumante: Italian wine — ASTO
_____ Square — TIMES
_____ Stadium, Milwaukee — COUNTY
_____ standstill — AT A
_____ star state — LONE
_____ State, South Africa — ORANGE FREE
_____ Ste. Marie — SAULT
_____ step — STEP BY
_____ Stevens (TV's Peter Gunn) — CRAIG
_____ stew — IN A
_____ Stoker, Dracula's creator — BRAM
_____ store by (distrust) — SET NO
_____ store: retail outlet — DRUG
_____ streak — LOSING
_____ Street — WALL
_____ strip — GAZA
_____ sugar (lump for Castro) — CUBA
_____ Sully Prudhomme, poet and Nobelist — RENE
_____ Sutcliffe, early Beatle — STU
_____ suzette — CREPE
_____ symbol — SEX
_____ synthesizer — MOOG
_____ table (dine) — SIT AT
_____ Tages: one day — EINES
_____ tai — MAI
_____ tail (cirrus cloud) — MARES
_____ tale (superstition) — OLD WIVES
_____ Tamid (synagogue lamp) — NER

_____ Taylor, musicologist — DEEMS
_____ tea — ICED
_____ tee (exactly) — TO A
_____ ten: rest — TAKE
_____ tender — LEGAL
_____ tenor McCormack — IRISH
_____ terrier — SYKE
_____ tete, Paris headache — MAL DE
_____ tetra (aquarium favorite) — NEON
_____ the beans — SPILLED
_____ the beginning — IN AT
_____ the belfry — BATS IN
_____ the better — ALL
_____ the boards (acted) — TROD
_____ the bullet — BITE
_____ the eight ball — BEHIND
_____ the face (blushing) — RED IN
_____ the fat — CHEW
_____ the finish — IN AT
_____ the gallery: seek applause — PLAY TO
_____ the gas — STEP ON
_____ the good — ALL TO
_____ the ground floor — IN ON
_____ the hills — OLD AS
_____ the hole — ACE IN
_____ the kitty — FEED
_____ the line — TOES
_____ the line (conformed) — TOED
_____ the Man — STAN
_____ the mark (obeys) — TOES
_____ the market — GLUT
_____ the mill — RUN OF
_____ the minute — UP TO
_____ the occasion — RISE TO
_____ the other — ONE OR
_____ the other (either) — ONE OR
_____ the press (brand new) — HOT OFF
_____ the Red — ERIC
_____ the Union Address — STATE OF
_____ the word — MUMS
_____ thieves — DEN OF
_____ throat — STREP
_____ through (persevered) — SAW IT
_____ thumbs: awkward — ALL
_____ Thursday — MAUNDY
_____ tide — NEAP
_____ Tiki — KON
_____ time (ever) — AT ANY
_____ time (never) — AT NO
_____ time (often) — MANY A
_____ time (singly) — ONE AT A
_____ Tin Tin — RIN
_____ tizzy — IN A
_____ to (curried favor) — PLAYED UP
_____ to (takes care of) — SEES
_____ to (tries to please) — SHINES UP
_____ to riches — RAGS
_____ to the rear! — STEP
_____ to worry! — NOT
_____ to: helpful — OF USE
_____ told (obey) — DO AS
_____ told by an idiot — A TALE
_____ ton of bricks — LIKE A
_____ towel (quit) — THROW IN THE
_____ tower — IVORY
_____ tower (cloister of sorts) — IVORY
_____ trail — VAPOR
_____ trap — SET A
_____ tree (cornered) — UP A
_____ Trench (deepest Pacific area) — MARIANA
_____ trip — EGO
_____ truly. Abbr. — YRS
_____ trump — ONE NO
_____ tube — BOOB, INNER
_____ tunnel — WIND
_____ Turn (road sign) — NO U
_____ Turner — NAT
_____ Ullah, Persian religious leader — BAHA
_____ under pressure — GRACE
_____ uno — NUMERO
_____ up (angry) — HET
_____ up (appear unexpectedly) — CROP
_____ up (be quiet) — CLAM
_____ up (completely successful) — SEWN
_____ up (confess) — OWN
_____ up (devise) — COOK
_____ up (emote) — HAM IT
_____ up (excites) — HYPES
_____ up (gets angry) — HEATS
_____ up (gives the scoop) — SMARTENS
_____ up (go for) — EAT
_____ up (got smart): Slang — WISED
_____ up (kept secret) — HUSHED
_____ up (learns) — WISES
_____ up (monopolize) — SEW
_____ up (paid) — ANTED
_____ up (preen) — SPRUCE
_____ up (relish) — EAT
_____ up (schmalzy) — HOKED
_____ up (sum) — TOT
_____ up (summed) — TOTTED
_____ up on — GANGS
_____ up on (hit the books) — BONE
_____ up the tab (pay) — PICK
_____ up the works — GUM
_____ up: assessing — SIZING
_____ up: botches — LOUSES
_____ up: cheers — PERKS
_____ up: excited — KEYED
_____ up: getting excited — KEYING
_____ uproar — IN AN
_____ urbana: Roman decrees — EDICTA
_____ Valley, Calif — IMPERIAL, NAPA
_____ Valley, Ventura Co. city — SIMI
_____ van Delft, Dutch painter — MEER
_____ Van Der Rohe — MIES
_____ Van Devere — TRISH
_____ van Kull — KILL
_____ Vanilli (dance group) — MILLI
_____ Vecchio, at Firenze — PONTE
_____ Vegas — LAS
_____ vera — ALOE
_____ Verde — MESA
_____ Verde Islands — CAPE
_____ versa — VICE
_____ victis — VAE
_____ Vieux Desert — LAC
_____ Vineyard — MARTHAS
_____ virumque cano: "Aeneid" opening — ARMA
_____ Vista — BUENA
_____ Vista Peak, Calif. — BUENA
_____ Vista, Mexican War battle site — BUENA
_____ vitae — AQUA
_____ vivant — BON
_____ vobiscum — PAX
_____ voce — SOTTO
_____ voce (orally) — VIVA
_____ voce (under the breath) — SOTTO
_____ voce: unanimously — AIRE
_____ volens (willy-nilly) — NOLENS
_____ volente — DEO
_____ volente: God willing — DEO
_____ vous plait — SIL
_____ voyage — BON
_____ walsy — PALSY
_____ War ("Big Red") — MAN O
_____ War: 1899-1902 — BOER
_____ Warren — EARL
_____ water — IN HOT

_____ water: stayed afloat — TREADED
_____ wave — HEAT, TIDAL
_____ way — MILKY
_____ Way, at Spanish Steps — APPIAN
_____ we devils — ARENT
_____ wealth — SHARE THE
_____ weather — STORMY
_____ Webster — NOAH
_____ Wednesday — ASH
_____ Wee Reese — PEE
_____ weeny — TEENY
_____ weevil — BOLL
_____ were — AS IT
_____ were (seemingly) — AS IT
_____ were (so to speak) — AS IT
_____ West — MAE
_____ West, Fla. — KEY
_____ White — SNOW
_____ Whitney — ELI
_____ whiz! — GEE
_____ Willie — WEARY
_____ Willie Winkie — WEE
_____ winks — FORTY
_____ wire — LIVE
_____ Wolfe, Stout's stout sleuth — NERO
_____ worm — ANGLE
_____ worry! — NOT TO
_____ year — LEAP
_____ year: school period — ACADEMIC
_____ years (elderly) — ON IN
_____ Yisrael (Palestine) — ERETS
_____ York, Jersey city — WEST NEW
_____ your health! — HERES TO
_____ your life — NOT ON
_____ yourself — BRACE
_____ Yutang — LIN
_____ Zagora, Bulgarian city — STARA
_____ Zeppelin — LED
_____' acte — ENTR
_____' War (racehorse) — MAN O
_____'s heart out — EAT ONE
_____, crackle and pop — SNAP
_____, Damon and Diu, India — GOA
_____, Dick and Harry — TOM
_____, esse, fui ... — SUM
_____, in Romeo — RAS
_____-a-brac — BRIC
_____-a-dire (that is to say): Fr. — CEST
_____-a gauche (a French wrench) — TOURNE
_____-a-boo — PEEK
_____-a-porter: ready-to-wear clothes — PRET
_____-about-town — MAN
_____-all (smart aleck) — KNOW IT
_____-aller (last resort) — PIS
_____-Alpine Gaul — CIS
_____-and-span — SPICK
_____-argent (silver alloy) — TIERS
_____-back chair — LADDER
_____-banc (British motor coach) — CHARA
_____-bel-Abbes, Algeria — SIDI
_____-bitsy — ITSY
_____-C.I.O. — AFL
_____-cake (child's game) — PATA
_____-cake (hand-clapping word) — PATA
_____-camp — AIDE DE
_____-China — INDO
_____-Chu school of philosophy — CHENG
_____-Coburg — SAXE
_____-cochere: entrance shelter — PORTE
_____-Coeur, basilica in Paris — SACRE
_____-Coeur, Parisian landmark — SACRE
_____-craftsy — ARTSY
_____-Cynwyd, near Philadelphia — BALA
_____-dah (affected) — LAH DI
_____-de-boeuf (small window) — OEIL
_____-de-camp — AIDE
_____-di-dah — LAH
_____-do-well — NEER
_____-do-well (wastrel) — NEER
_____-edged (of high quality) — GILT
_____-en-scene — MISE
_____-European — INDO
_____-eyed (unfaltering) — STEELY
_____-fi movie — SCI
_____-fi, Bradbury's forte — SCI
_____-fi, Verne genre — SCI
_____-Flow — SCAPA
_____-froid (calmness) — SANG
_____-frutti — TUTTI
_____-garde — AVANT
_____-hoo! — YOO
_____-in-the-wool — DYED
_____-jack, the Canada Jay — WHISKEY
_____-Japanese War — SINO
_____-jongg — MAH
_____-Kamenogorsk, U.S.S.R. city — UST
_____-King (German goblin) — ERL
_____-König (legendary goblin) — ERL
_____-kootchy — HOOTCHY
_____-la-la — OOH, TRA
_____-la-la — TRA
_____-Lease Act: 1941 — LEND
_____-liner (gag) — ONE
_____-liner (gag) — ONE
_____-Loo-ra ("Thats an Irish Lullaby") — TOORA
_____-Lorraine — ALSACE
_____-Magnon — CRO
_____-Magnon — CRO
_____-majesté — LESE
_____-Neisse Line — ODER
_____-nest (hoax) — MARES
_____-nez — PINCE
_____-nous — ENTRE
_____-on (happenings) — GOINGS
_____-pie (from head to foot) — CAP A
_____-poly — ROLY
_____-Powell of scouting — BADEN
_____-Powell, Boy Scouts founder — BADEN
_____-propre (self-esteem) — AMOUR
_____-pros — NOL
_____-Prussian War: 1866 — AUSTRO
_____-puissance (omnipotence)" Fr. — TOUTE
_____-ran (loser) — ALSO
_____-Sadr of Iran — BANI
_____-Saxon — ANGLO
_____-Simon I.Q. test — BINET
_____-ski — APRES
_____-star team — ALL
_____-surface missiles — AIR TO
_____-than thou — HOLIER
_____-the-grass — SNAKE IN
_____-Tiki — KON
_____-toed, like people or carriers — PIGEON
_____-toity — HOITY
_____-tse-tung — MAO
_____-tung, former Chinese leader — MAO TSE
_____-Urundi, Africa — RUANDA
_____-vu — DEJA
_____-Wan Konobi of "Star Wars" — OBI
_____-War of racing fame — MAN O
_____-well (idler) — NEER DO
_____-wootsy — TOOTSY
_____-wop (vocal style) — DOO
_____-Xiaoping — DENG
_____-Yat-Sen — SUN
_____-you-ma'am (pothole) — THANK
_____-yourself kit — DO IT

QUOTATIONS AS CLUES

Quotations Beginning with Words

"A _____ Blue Eyes," Hardy title — PAIR OF
"A _____ for All Seasons" — MAN
"A _____ forty is a fool indeed" — FOOL AT
"A _____ Honey" — TASTE OF
"A _____ I have won ..." — HEAVEN ON EARTH
"A _____ in one's side" — THORN
"A _____ in the Sun": Hansberry play — RAISIN
"A _____ is a Sometime Thing": 1935 — WOMAN
"A _____ of Honey" — TASTE
"A _____ of Two Cities" — TALE
"A _____ Pearls" — STRING OF
"A _____ sante!" — VOTRE
"A _____ that will live in infamy" — DATE
"A _____ the Dark,"1964 film — SHOT IN
"A _____ time saves nine" — STITCH IN
"A _____ told by an idiot" — TALE
"A _____'clock scholar" — TEN O
"A Bell for _____" — ADANO
"A Bell for Adano" author — HERSEY
"A Candle for St. _____": Godden novel — JUDE
"A Chorus Line" finale — ONE
"A Chorus Line" hit song — ONE
"A Confederacy of Dunces" author — TOOLE
"A date which will live in infamy" — FDR
"A Death in the Family" author — AGEE
"A Doll's House" creator — IBSEN
"A Doll's House" heroine — NORA
"A face that would _____ clock" — STOP A
"A Farewell to _____" — ARMS
"A Few Good _____" — MEN
"A Fish Called _____," — WANDA
"A Girl, _____ and a Gob," 1941 film — A GUY
"A grief without _____" Coleridge — A PANG
"A House _____ Home" — IS NOT A
"A House is Not _____" — A HOME
"A Lesson from _____": Fugard play — ALOES
"A Message to _____": Hubbard — GARCIA
"A Midsummer-Night's Dream" role — OBERON
"A miss _____ good as a mile" — IS AS
"A miss is as good as _____" — A MILE
"A Passage to India" director — LEAN
"A Peach of _____": 1930's song — A PAIR
"A peculiar sort of a gal" — SAL
"A Perfect Spy" author — LECARRE
"A rag and _____ ..." Kipling — A BONE
"A right jolly old _____" — ELF
"A Room of _____ Own": Woolf book — ONES
"A Room with _____" — A VIEW
"A ruddy _____ manly blood": Emerson — DROP OF
"A Sailor's Admiral" subject — HALSEY
"A Shropshire _____" — LAD
"A Small Town in Germany" author — LECARRE
"A thing of beauty is _____": — A JOY FOREVER
"A thousand _____ thy sight ..." — Watts — AGES IN
"A time to serve and _____": Swinburne — TO SIN
"A votre _____!" — SANTE
"A votre sante'!" — FRENCH TOAST
"A woman _____ as she looks": Collins — AS OLD
"A woman after _____" — MY OWN HEART
"A word to the _____" — WISE
"A Yank at _____," 1942 film — ETON
"A year and _____": — A DAY
"A" code word — ALFA
"A" to Aristotle — ALPHA
"Ab _____" — INITIO
"Abbey _____," Beatles album — ROAD
"Abdul the Bulbul _____" — AMEER
"Able was I _____ I saw Elba" — ERE
"Abou Abulbul _____" — AMIR
"About Ben Adham" poet — HUNT
"Absinthe" painter — DEGAS
"Act now _____ chance" — OR LOSE A
"Ad astra per _____" — ASPERA
"Adam _____" — BEDE
"Adriana Lecouvreur" composer — CILEA
"Aee _____ Kiss," Burns poem — FOND
"Aeneid" author — VERGIL
"Aeneid" opener — ARMA
"Aeneid" starter — ARMA
"Aeneid," for one — EPIC
"Age of Aquarius" musical — HAIR
"Age of Aquarius" show — HAIR
"Agnus _____" — DEI
"Ah, me!" — ALACK
"Ahem" alternative — PSST
"Aida" debuted here — CAIRO
"Aida" highlight — ARIA
"Aida," e.g. — OPERA
"Ain't It Awful, _____!": Hazard book — MABEL
"Ain't Misbehavin'" Carter — NELL
"Ain't Misbehavin'" composer — WALLER
"Ain't she _____?" — SWEET
"Ain't that _____?": Fats Domino hit — A SHAME
"Alas, Poor _____!" — YORICK
"Alive" author — READ
"All _____ and Heaven Too" — THIS
"All _____ Dream of You" — I DO IS
"All _____ for Christmas" — I WANT
"All _____ up" (excited) — HET
"All _____!" — ABOARD
"All _____" — OF ME
"All _____," 1984 Tomlin film — OF ME

"All About _____" — EVE
"All men are _____": Psalm 116 — LIARS
"All My _____": Miller drama — SONS
"All My Children" — SOAP OPERA
"All That Jazz" director — FOSSE
"All the President's Men" role — BOB WOODWARD
"All the Things You _____," 1939 song — ARE
"All the world's _____": Shak. — A STAGE
"All the world's a _____" — STAGE
"All together, musicians" — TUTTI
"All's Well that Ends Well" role — HELENA
"Alley _____" — OOP
"Am _____ brother's keeper?" Genesis 4:9 — I MY
"Amadeus" director — MILOS FORMAN
"Amber waves of grain"? — WHEAT
"Amores" author — OVID
"An _____ of prevention ..." — OUNCE
"An _____ Time of Hesitation": Moody — ODE IN
"An apple a _____ ..." — DAY
"An Essay on Man" author — ALEXANDER POPE
"An Essay on Projects" author: 1697 — DEFOE
"An Eye for the Dragon" author — BLOODWORTH
"Anchors _____" — AWEIGH
"And _____ bed": Pepys sign-off — SO TO
"And _____ fine seam ...: — SEW A
"And _____ I plight thee ..." — THERETO
"And _____ lies a tale" — HEREIN
"And _____"; Pepys sign-off — SO TO BED
"And all the flowers looked up _____": Chesterton — AT HIM
"And all the ships _____" — AT SEA
"And be it moon, _____ ...: Shak. — OR SUN
"And day's at the _____": Browning — MORN
"And fired the _____ heard round the world" — SHOT
"And hast thou _____ the Jabberwock?" — SLAIN
"And I Love _____" — HER
"And jeers _____": F. P. A. — AT FATE
"And leaves soul _____ little": Browning — FREE A
"And miles to go before _____": Frost — I SLEEP
"And so _____": Pepys — TO BED
"And take _____ of fate": "Macbeth" — A BOND
"And the Lord set _____ upon Cain ...": Gen. 4:15 — A MARK
"And the mome _____ outgrabe": Carroll — RATHS
"And the skys are not cloudy _____" — ALL DAY
"And then there were _____" — NONE
"And Then There Were None" author: — CHRISTIE
"And theres little _____" Kingsley — TO EARN
"And this shall be _____ unto you": Luke 2:12 — A SIGN
"And we will _____ pleasures prove": — SOME NEW
"And what _____ rare?": Lowell — IS SO
"and" symbol (&) — AMPERSAND
"Angel Arms" poet — FEARING
"Angel" Ladd — CHERYL
"Anna and the King of _____" — SIAM
"Anna and the King of Siam" star — IRENE
"Anna Christie" playwright — ONEILL
"Anne of Green _____" — GABLES
"Annie _____," 1838 song — LAURIE
"Answer yes _____" — OR NO
"Apologia Pro Vita _____" — SUA
"April is the cruellest _____ ..." — MONTH
"Arabian Nights" bird — ROC
"Are you _____ or a mouse?" — A MAN
"Arma virumque _____" — CANO
"Arrivederci _____" — ROMA
"Arrivederci" city — ROMA
"Arrowsmith" heroine — LEORA
"Ars _____, vita brevis" — LONGA
"Ars Amatoria" poet — OVID
"Ars gratia _____" — ARTIS
"Arsenic and Old Lace" star Jean — ADAIR
"Art thou a woman's _____ ...": Shak. — SON
"Artie" author — ADE
"As _____ and breathe" — I LIVE
"As leene was his horse as is _____": — A RAKE
"As you _____" — WERE
"As you sew, so shall you _____" — RIP
"Ask _____ questions ..." — ME NO
"Asleep in the _____" — DEEP
"Astrophel" author — SPENSER
"At each _____ hearer": Hamlet — EAR A
"Atlas Shrugged" author Ayn — RAND
"Auld _____ Syne" — LANG
"Auld lang _____" — SYNE
"Auntie Mame" actress — CASS
"Ay, _____ inch a King": Shak. — EVERY
"B.C." character — THOR
"Baby, It's Cold _____" — OUTSIDE
"Baby, Take _____" — A BOW
"Baby, Take _____," 1934 song — A BOW
"Back to _____ one" — SQUARE
"Bake me _____ ..." — A CAKE
"Bake me a cake _____ you can" — FAST AS
"Bald" avian — EAGLE
"Balderdash!" — ROT
"Bali _____" — HAI
"Ball and Chain" singer Joplin — JANIS
"Ballet Class" painter — DEGAS
"Bambi" character — DOE
"Bambi" fawn — GOBO
"Bananas" director-actor — ALLEN
"Banjo Eyes" — EDDIE CANTOR
"Bank _____" (old movie-house come on) — NITE
"Barbarella" director — VADIM
"Barney Miller" actor — LANDESBERG
"Barney Miller" actor Hal — LINDEN
"Batman" Adam — WEST
"Batman" e.g. — CAMP
"Battle Cry" author — URIS
"Be of good cheer; _____": Matt. — IT IS I
"Beat it!" — SCRAM
"Beau _____" — GESTE
"Beau Geste" actor J. Carrol — NAISH
"Beauty _____ the eye ..." — IS IN
"Beauty and the _____" — BEAST

"Beaux _____" — ARTS
"Bei _____ Bist Du Schoen" — MIR
"Bei Mir _____ Du Schoen" — BIST
"Bel _____" Burnford novel: 1978 — RIA
"Bel _____" by de Maupassant — AMI
"Believe _____ Not" — IT OR
"Believe it _____" — OR NOT
"Believe It or Not" — RIPLEY
"Bell of _____" — ATRI
"Bellefleur" author — OATES
"Ben _____" — HUR
"Ben- _____" — HUR
"Benevolent" ones — ELKS
"Bent" actor — GERE
"Beowulf" or "Poema del Cid" — EPIC
"Beowulf", for one — EPIC
"Beowulf," e.g. — EPOS
"Best actor" Oscar winner: 1976 — PETER FINCH
"Bestow on every _____ a limb" (J. Graham) — AIRTH
"Better _____ than never" — LATE
"Beware _____ of March!" — THE IDES
"Beware the _____" — IDES
"Beware!," in Brest — GARE
"Big Apple" dancer — ROCKETTE
"Big Apple" player — NEW YORK MET
"Big Blue" — IBM
"Big Island" city — HILO
"Big" creation theory — BANG
"Billy _____" — BUDD
"Bird thou never _____" — WERT
"Birds of Reason" poet Donald — DAVIE
"Bite the _____" — BULLET
"Black Beauty" author — SEWELL
"Black Gold" — OIL
"Bleak house" heroine — ADA
"Bleak House" lass — ADA
"Bless my _____!" — SOUL
"Blithe Spirit" author — COWARD
"Blondie" cartoonist Young — CHIC
"Blow, blow, _____": Shak. — THOU WINTER WIND
"Blue _____ Fly", Burl Ives song — TAIL
"Bluejays" stadium locale — TORONTO
"Bobbin" bird — ROBIN
"Body all _____": O. Hammerstein — ACHIN
"Body and _____" — SOUL
"Bombs bursting _____" — IN AIR
"Bon _____" — JOUR
"Bonae _____": L. — ARTES
"Boola" student — ELI
"Boot" land — ITALY
"Born again" candidate — SINNER
"Born in the _____": Springsteen — USA
"Born on a _____ ..." — MONDAY
"Borstal Boy" author — BEHAN
"Brat Farrar" author — TEY
"Bravo," Greek style — EUGE
"Breathless" star — GERE
"Brewster's _____": 1985 movie — MILLIONS
"Bride of Lammermoor" hero — EDGAR
"Bridget Loves _____" — BERNIE
"Brief _____": Tharp ballet — FLING
"Brief" approvals — OKS
"Brigadoon" composer — LOEWE
"Bright _____ button" — AS A
"Bring home the _____" — BACON
"Britannia rules _____" — THE WAVES
"Brother Rat" inst. — VMI
"Brown _____" — OCTOBER SALE
"Bubbles" author — SILLS
"Bubbly" — CHAMPAGNE
"Buffalo Bill" — CODY
"Build a better _____ ..." — MOUSETRAP
"Build it up with _____ steel ..." — IRON AND
"Bullitt" director — YATES
"Burnt Norton" poet — T S ELIOT
"Bus Stop" author — INGE
"Bus Stop" playwright — INGE
"Business as _____" — USUAL
"Busy _____" — AS A BEE
"Busy as _____" — A BEE
"But _____ begin": J. F. K. — LET US
"But _____ on forever": Tennyson — I GO
"But he's an _____ knave": Shak. — ARRANT
"But is it _____?" — ART
"But judge you as you _____": Shakespeare — ARE
"But only God can make _____" — A TREE
"But the end is not _____": Matt. 24 — YET
"But war's _____ ...": Cowper — A GAME
"Butterfield 8" author — OHARA
"By _____ bonny banks ..." — YON
"By all means!" — YOU BET
"By the _____ gods he swore" — NINE
"Bye" — TATA
"Bye-Bye Love" brothers — EVERLY
"C'est a _____" — LUI
"Cabaret" co-star — GREY
"Cabaret" director — FOSSE
"Cabaret" greeting — WELCOME
"Cabaret" lyrist — EBB
"Cactus Flower" star — GOLDIE HAWN
"Cagney _____ Lacey" — AND
"Cagney and Lacey" star — GLESS
"Cakes and _____": Maugham — ALE
"Call Me _____" — MADAM
"Call Me Madam" star — MERMAN
"Camelot" clan — KENNEDYS
"Camelot" mem. — KNT
"Camille" portrayer — GRETA
"Camino _____": T. Williams — REAL
"Camptown Races" composer — FOSTER
"Can do" servicemen — SEABEES
"Candy is dandy" poet — NASH
"Candy Striper" — AIDE
"Cantique de Noel" composer — ADAM
"Canvas" for Jack Frost — PANE
"Cara _____," 1954 song — MIA
"Card _____," Stravinsky ballet — PARTY
"Carmen" composer — BIZET
"Carmen" role — JOSE
"Carmina Burana" composer — ORFF
"Casablanca" heroine, et al. — ILSAS
"Casablanca" producer — HAL B WALLIS
"Casablanca" role — ILSA
"Casablanca" woman, et al. — ILSAS
"Casbah" actress — TOREN
"Casino _____," 007 spoof — ROYALE
"Cat on a Hot _____ Roof" — TIN
"Catcher in the _____" — RYE
"Catfish" was one — PRO
"Cats" author's monogram — TSE

"Cats" libretto author — ELIOT
"Caught like a rat _____" — IN A TRAP
"Cav" and _____, opera double bill — PAG
"Cavalleria Rusticana" mezzo — COLA
"Cave _____" — CANEM
"Celeste _____" (aria) — AIDA
"Certainly!" — TO BE SURE, YES
"Champagne Tony": 1964 British Open champ — LEMA
"Charley More _____ the Fair Thing" — SIGN
"Charley's _____" — AUNT
"Charlotte's _____": E.B. White — WEB
"Cheerful Little _____": golden oldie — EARFUL
"Cheers" e.g. — SITCOM
"Cheers" role — SAM
"Cheers" site — BAR ROOM
"Cheers" waitress — CARLA
"Cheery _____," Herrick poem — RIPE
"Cheyenne," for one — OATER
"Chicago piano" — POM POM
"Chicken of the sea" — TUNA
"Chicken", etc. — DARES
"Chickens" lady — MOTHER CAREY
"Child of the sun" — INCA
"Children of a _____ God" — LESSER
"Christ Stopped at _____": Carlo Levi — EBOLI
"Christina's World" painter — WYETH
"Cielo _____," Ponchielli aria — EMAR
"Cielo e _____," Ponchelli aria — MAR
"Citizen _____": 1941 film — KANE
"Citizen Kane" director — WELLES
"City of Light" — PARIS
"City of Victory" — CAIRO
"City Slickers" band leader — SPIKE JONES
"Clair de _____" — LUNE
"Claire's _____" — KNEE
"Clash by Night" dramatist — ODETS
"Classroom" for Zeno — STOA
"Cloister and the Hearth" author — READE
"Coal _____ Daughter" — MINERS
"Coal Miner's Daughter" Lynn — LORETTA
"Cocktails" for kiddies — SHIRLEY TEMPLES
"Coffee, Tea _____?" — OR ME
"Cogito, _____ sum": Descartes — ERGO
"Cold _____ Tree," Olive Burns novel — SASSY
"Collars" — ARRESTS
"Colonel _____ March" — BOGEY
"Colonial" workers — ANTS
"Come _____ these yellow sands": Shakespeare — UNTO
"Come in" — ENTER
"Come live with _____ ...": Donne — MEE
"Come Rain ..." composer — ARLEN
"Come to me, _____ to me ...": "Brigadoon" — BEND
"Comedy or Errors" role — ANGELO
"Comin' _____ the Rye" — THRO
"Coming of Age in _____": Margaret Mead — SAMOA
"Common Sense" author — PAINE
"Como _____?" — ESTA
"Comus" composer — ARNE
"Consumed the midnight _____" — oil
"Cookery is become _____": Burns — AN ART
"Core" subject, for short — MATH
"Cornish Wonder," English artist — OPIE
"Cosa _____" — NOSTRA
"Cosi fan _____" — TUTTE
"Cosmos" game — SOCCER
"Costly thy _____ as thy purse" — HABIT
"Could it be _____?": song — YOU
"Country" Slaughter — ENOS
"Cox and _____" — BOX
"Crazylegs" Hirsch — ELROY
"Crime and Punishment" heroine — SONIA
"Critique of Pure Reason" author — KANT
"Cry Me _____," Arthur Hamilton song — A RIVER
"Cry over _____ milk" — SPILT
"Cuckoo's Nest" builder — KEN KESEY
"Cyrano de Bergerac" playwright — ROSTAND
"Daily Planet" employee — LOIS LANE
"Dallas or Dyasty" — SOAP
"Dallas" is one — SOAP
"Dallas" name — EWING
"Dallas" subject — OIL
"Damn Yankees" composer — ADLER
"Damn Yankees" temptress — LOLA
"Damn Yankees" vamp — LOLA
"Dark Side of the _____" — MOON
"Dark Victory" actor — BRENT
"Darkness _____": Koestler novel — AT NOON
"Darling" director — JOHN SCHLESINGER
"Darling, Je Vous _____ Beaucoup" — AIME
"Das Kapital" author — MARX
"David Copperfield" character — EMLY
"Days _____ lives" — OF OUR
"Days of Our _____," soap opera — LIVES
"Days of Wine and _____" — ROSES
"De _____," Seneca essay — IRA
"Dead _____," Masefield novel — NED
"Dear _____" — BRUTUS
"Death be not _____ ...": Donne — PROUD
"Death Be Not Proud" poet — DONNE
"Death hath 10,000 several _____" — DOORS
"Death on the Nile" author — CHRISTIE
"Deck the Halls" refrain — FA LA LA
"Dedicated to the _____ Love" — ONE I
"Deep Purple" composer — DEROSE
"Demian" author — HESSE
"Den I wish _____ Dixie" — I WAS IN
"Der _____": Adenaur — ALTE
"Der Rosenkavalier" baron — OCHS
"Dernier _____" — CRI
"Desire _____ the Elms" — UNDER
"Desire Under the _____": O'Neill play — ELMS
"Deutschland uber _____" — ALLES
"Deutschland Uber _____" — ALLES
"Dial _____ Murder" — M FOR
"Diamond _____" — LIL
"Diana" singer — ANKA
"Dianetics" author Hubbard — L RON
"Diary of _____ housewife" — A MAD
"Die Lorelei" author — HEINE
"Die Lorelei" poet — HEINE
"Die Walkure" highlight — MAGIC FIRE MUSIC

"Dies _____" — IRAE
"Dies _____" — IRAE
"Diff'rent Strokes" actress — RAE
"Dirigo" is its motto — MAINE
"Dirty group of 1967 — DOZEN
"Disraeli" actor — ARLISS
"Divina Commedia" author — DANTE
"Divine Comedy" illustrator — DORE
"Divine Comedy" is one — EPIC
"Do _____ a Waltz?" — I HEAR
"Do _____ others ..." — UNTO
"Do _____ say": Selden on "Preaching" — AS I
"Do as I say, not _____" — AS I DO
"Do I _____ waltz?" — HEAR A
"Do You Believe in _____" — MAGIC
"Do You Know the Way _____ Jose?" — TO SAN
"Doctor Zhivago" heroine — LARA
"Doe _____, a female ..." — A DEER
"Doesn't know _____ about it" — BEANS
"Dog Day Afternoon" director — LUMET
"Dog Days" version of "a long time"? — A COLLIES AGE
"Dog Days" version of "bushed"? — BASSET TIRED
"Dog Days" version of "G.I."? — WHIPPET FACE
"Dog Days" version of "savage"? — TERRIER AT POODLE
"Doggone it!" — RATS
"Dolce far _____" — NIENTE
"Don Carlos" princess — EBOLI
"Don Giovanni" — OPERA
"Don't _____ on me." — TREAD
"Don't do that!" — STOP IT
"Don't look _____!" — AT ME
"Don't make _____!" — A SOUND
"Don't rain _____ Parade" — ON MY
"Don't rock _____!" — THE BOAT
"Don't throw bouquets _____" — AT ME
"Don't throw bouquets _____": "Oklahoma!" — AT ME
"Don't throw bouquets _____": Hammerstein — AT ME
"Don't you _____ sweet Alice?" — REMEMBER
"Don't!" — STOP
"Doubt truth to be _____": Hamlet — A LIAR
"Downstairs" personages — MAIDS
"Downtown" singer, a la the Irish? — PATULA CLARK
"Dragnet" force: Abbr. — LAPD
"Drake" poet — NOYES
"Dream Children ..." author — CHARLES LAMB
"Dreamgirls" dramatist — EYEN
"Driving Miss _____" — DAISY
"Drums Along the Mohawk" author — EDMONDS
"Duck Soup" actor — HARPO
"Dum spiro, _____" — SPERO
"Dynasty" actress — EVANS
"E _____ dell'anima," Verdi aria — IL SOL
"East Lynne" heroine — ISABEL
"East of _____": Steinbeck novel — EDEN
"East of Eden" character — ARON
"East of Eden" heroine — ABRA
"East of Eden" protagonist — CAL
"East of Eden" temptress — ABRA
"Easy _____ it!" — DOES
"Eat your cookie," _____ — SHE SNAPPED
"Ecce _____," Titian painting — HOMO
"Ecce homo" man — PILATE
"Echoi" composer — FOSS
"Edie was _____" — A LADY
"Educating _____": 1983 film — RITA
"Egmont" dramatist — GOETHE
"Eh?" — WHAT
"Either/Or" questioner — KIERKEGAARD
"El Caudillo" of Spain — FRANCO
"El Libertador" — BOLIVAR
"El Ropo" — STOGY
"Elegy" poet Thomas — GRAY
"Elephant Boy" actor — SABU
"Elephant Boy" co-director — KORDA
"Elephant Boy" star — SABU
"Ellie _____," post-Civil War hit — RHEE
"Elmer _____" — GANTRY
"Elmer Gantry" star — LANCASTER
"Emerald Port _____": 1983 TV serial — NAS
"Emergency" author: 1964 — RIVE
"Encore" — AGAIN
"End as _____": Willingham novel — A MAN
"Enigma Variations" composer — ELGAR
"Ernani" composer — VERDI
"Eroica" key — E FLAT
"Essay: _____ sally of the mind" (Johnson) — A LOOSE
"Esto perpetua" is its motto — IDAHO
"Et tu, _____!" — BRUTE
"Eugene _____," 1832 novel — ARAM
"Eugene Onegin" role — OLGA
"Everyone is _____ ...": Mark Twain — A MOON
"Everything's Coming _____": "Gypsy" song — UP ROSES
"Evita" role — PERON
"Evvvre-body _____": Durante — WANTS A GET IN DE ACT
"Evvvre-body _____": Durante — WANTS A GET IN DE ACT
"Exaggeration is truth _____": Gibran — THAT HAS LOST
"Excalibur" part — HILT
"Exiled" Red — PETE
"Exodus" author — URIS
"Exodus" character — ARI
"Exodus" name — ARI
"Exodus" novelist — URIS
"Exodus" role — ARI
"Eye in the sky" — SAMOS
"Eyes have they, but they _____" — SEE NOT
"F troop" fort — COURAGE
"Faerie Queene" poet — SPENSER
"Faith, as cold _____ be ...": Shak. — AS CAN
"Falcon Crest" family — CHANNING
"Family _____" — TIES
"Family Ties" role — ELYSE
"Fancy that" — IMAGINE
"Fat farm" — SPA
"Father Knows Best" family — ANDERSON
"Father of the _____" — BRIDE
"Fawlty Towers" star — CLEESE
"Fear of Flying" author — JONG
"Fedora" highlight — ARIA
"Feed _____, starve a fever" — A COLD
"Feliz _____ nuevo" — ANO
"Femme _____" — FATALE
"Festina _____" ("Make haste slowly") — LENTE
"Fickle and restless as _____": Heine — A FAWN

"Fiddler on the Roof" matchmaker — YENTE
"Fiddler" query — DO YOU LOVE ME
"Fighting _____" — IRISH
"Fill many a _____ of purest ray serene ...": — GEM
"Filthy" money — LUCRE
"Find _____, pick it up" — A PIN
"Finian's Rainbow" character — LEPRECHAUN
"Finian's Rainbow" role — LEP-RECHAUN
"Finnegans _____": Joyce — WAKE
"Fire's going out!" _____ — HE BELLOWED
"Fish Magic" painter — KLEE
"Five Foot Two, _____ Blue" — EYES OF
"Fixes," as a fight — RIGS
"Flamingo _____" — ROAD
"Flash Gordon" star — CRABBE
"Fleur-de- _____": Var. — LYS
"Flintstone's" child — PEBBLES
"Flow gently, sweet _____" — AFTON
"Flying Down to _____": 1933 film — RIO
"Flying" fish — SEA ROBIN
"Fog" poet — CARL SAND-BURG
"Folks down here _____ life of ease ..." — LIVE A
"Follow me _____!": Kipling — OME
"Folsom Prison Blues" composer — CASH
"For _____ a jolly ..." — HES
"For _____ and bells ...": Lowell — A CAP
"For _____ be Queen o' the May" — IM TO
"For _____ jolly good fellow ..." — HES A
"For _____ me as light and life": Burns — DEAR TO
"For _____ the Bell Tolls" — WHOM
"For art may _____" — ERR
"For Auld lang _____ ..." — SYNE
"For beauty lives with _____": Shak. — KINDNESS
"For Brutus _____ honourable man" — IS AN
"For Me and My _____" — GAL
"For Pete's _____!" — SAKE
"For want of _____ the shoe ..." — A NAIL
"For want of a nail _____ was lost" — THE SHOE
"For Whom the Bell Tolls" heroine — PILAR
"Forever _____ day" — AND A
"Forever _____" — AMBER
"Forever and Ever, _____": Travis hit — AMEN
"Forty _____" — CARATS
"Four Apostles" painter — DURER
"Fourscore and _____ years ago ..." — SEVEN
"Frae morn to _____ ...": Burns — EEN
"Frankenstein" — KARLOFF
"Free Wheeling" auth. — ONASH
"Friendly" pronoun — THEE
"From _____ 's coral strand ..." — INDIA
"From _____ Eternity" — HERE TO
"From _____ shining ..." — SEA TO
"From _____ to riches" — RAGS
"From pastures deep _____" (E.B. White) — IN FERN
"From the _____ all that hate us" — HAND OF
"From the gold _____ Heaven" (Rossetti) — BAR OF
"From the Terrace" author — OHARA
"Front porch" — FLAB
"Full _____ Jacket" — METAL
"Funny Girl" choreographer — HANEY
"Funny Girl" composer — STYNE
"Funny Girl" girl — BRICE
"Funny sheets" — COMICS
"Für _____": Beethoven bagatelle — ELISE
"Gallia _____ omnis divis ..." — EST
"Gang aft _____": Burns — AGLEY
"Gare Saint-Lazare" painter — MONET
"Gaslight" star — BOYER
"Gather ye _____ ...": Herrick — ROSEBUDS
"Gee whiz!" — GOSH
"Genesis" locale — EDEN
"Genesis" name — ABEL
"Gentlemen Prefer Blondes" author — LOOS
"George Herbert Walker _____" — BUSH
"George Washington _____ Here" — SLEPT
"George White's Scandals," e.g. — REVUE
"Georgy _____": L. Redgrave film — GIRL
"Get _____ the Church ..." — ME TO
"Get thee _____ nunnery" — TO A
"Ghosts" creator — IBSEN
"Ghosts" writer — IBSEN
"Giant" actor Sal _____ — MINEO
"Giant" creator — EDNA FERBER
"Giant" star — ROCK HUDSON
"Gigi" or "Gandhi" — OSCAR WINNER
"Gil _____" (Le Sage) — BLAS
"Giles Goat-Boy" creator — BARTH
"Gin a body _____ body": Burns — MEET A
"Giselle" composer Adolphe — ASTER
"Giselle" composer Adolphe _____ — ADAM
"Give 'em enough _____ ..." — ROPE
"Give _____: don't pollute" — A HOOT
"Give a _____ horse he can ride ..." — MAN A
"Give My _____ to Broadway" — REGARDS
"Gloomy Dean" — INGE
"Gloria _____" — PATRI
"Gloria in Excelsis _____" — DEO
"Go fly _____!" — A KITE
"Goblin Market" poet — ROS-SETTI
"God's Little _____" — ACRE
"Godfather" crime group — MAFIA
"Gold Bug" man — POE
"Golden Boy" playwright — ODETS
"Golden Girls" actress — GETTY
"Golden Treasury" entry — ODE
"Goldfish" painter — MATISSE
"Gone _____ Finnigan": Gillilan — AGIN
"Gone with the Wind," e.g. — HISTORICAL NOVEL
"Good _____!" (Charlie Brown's cry) — GRIEF
"Good _____": 1927 musical — NEWS
"Good Earth " role — OLAN
"Good Earth" -ling — OLAN
"Good Earth" heroine — OLAN
"Good enough!" — VERY WELL
"Good Night _____" — IRENE
"Goodbye, Mr. Chips" star — DONAT
"Goodnight _____" — IRENE

"Gorillas in the _____" — MIST
"Gotcha!" — AHA
"Grace under pressure" — POISE
"Graf _____" — SPEE
"Grand _____" — HOTEL
"Grand Old Man of Football" — STAGG
"Grand Ole _____" — OPRY
"Grand" actor John _____ — NEVILLE
"Grand" role — EDDA
"Great Catherine" playwright — SHAW
"Great!" — SWELL
"Great" components — LAKES
"Green _____" of TV — ACRES
"Green _____": TV series — ACRES
"Green Acres" handyman, et al. — EBS
"Green Gables" girl — ANNE
"Green Mansions" girl — RIMA
"Green Mansions" hero — ABEL
"Green Mansions" heroine — RIMA
"Green Pastures" role — AARON
"Greetings" org. — SSS
"Growing" place — GREEN HOUSE
"Guernica" painter — PICASSO
"Gulliver's Travels" creatures — YAHOOS
"Gunsmoke" Marshal Dillon — MATT
"Guys and Dolls" imprecation — LUCK BE A LADY
"Guys and Dolls" song — SUE ME
"Gymnopédies" composer — SATIE
"Gyp sheet" — CHEATING PAD
"H.M. Pulham, _____": Marquand — ESQ
"H.M. Pulham, _____": Marquand — ESQ
"H.M.S. Pinafore" lass — HEBE
"Half Magic" author — EAGER
"Halt, salts!" — AVAST
"Hammer and songs" instrument? — XYLOPHONE
"Hammerklavier" is one — SONATA
"Handy" Indian goddess — KALI
"Hansel and Gretel" prop — OVEN
"Happy Birthday _____" — TO YOU
"Happy Days Are Here Again" composer — AGER
"Hard _____!" — ALEE
"Hard Times" author — DICKENS
"Harper Valley _____" — PTA
"Has anybody here _____ Kelly?" — SEEN
"Have _____ day!" — A NICE
"Have a candy bar," _____ — HE SNICKERED
"Have Gun, Will Travel" role — PALADIN
"Have you _____ wool?" — ANY
"Have You Ever _____ Lonely?" — BEEN
"Hawkeye Pierce" portrayer — ALDA
"Haystack at Giverny" painter — MONET
"Haystacks" painter — MONET
"He _____ me to lie down ..." — MAKETH
"He hath _____ net for my feet" — SPREAD
"He hath spread _____ ..." — A NET
"He is ... _____ for the defenseless": Ingersoll — A SHIELD
"He was born in _____ ...": M. Arnold — A SHIP
"He was not born _____": Shak. — TO SHAME
"He wasted both toil _____": Cicero — AND OIL
"He will not _____ stopping here ...": Frost — SEE ME
"He's _____ Picker": Berlin — A RAG
"He's feeling his _____" — OATS
"Hear ye!" — OYEZ
"Heartburn" author Ephron — NORA
"Heidi" location — ALPS
"Hello Dolly" name — LEVI
"Hello" girl — DOLLY
"Help Me Make It _____ the Night" — THRU
"Henry _____ Little Secret": 1944 film — ALDRICHS
"Her eyes _____ Twilight fair": Wordsworth — AS STARS OF
"Here, _____ to their laws, we lie" — OBEDIENT
"Hernani" writer — HUGO
"Hey _____!" — THERE
"Hey there" — PST
"Hickety, pickety, my black _____" — HEN
"High _____ Windy Hill " — ON A
"High _____": 1952 film — NOON
"High _____": Anderson — TOR
"High _____": M. Anderson play — TOR
"High _____," 1959 song — HOPES
"High Noon" actress Jurado — KATE
"High Society" co-author — PARKER
"High" time — NOON
"Hinky _____ Parlay Voo" — DINKY
"His Eye _____ the Sparrow" — IS ON
"His wife could _____ lean" — EAT NO
"Hit the silk" — JUMP
"Hitchy _____": old-time revue — KOO
"Hitchy _____," ragtime hit — KOO
"Hold that tiger" — COLLEGE CHEER
"Holiday _____," 1942 film — INN
"Holiday" playwright — BARRY
"Holy Mountain" in Greece — ATHOS
"Holy" city? — TOLEDO
"Home _____" — ALONE
"Home, _____ Home" — SWEET
"Home, Sweet Home" author — PAYNE
"Home, Sweet Home" lyricist — PAYNE
"Home, Sweet Home" start — MID
"Homestead" artist — BENTON
"Honest _____" — ABE
"Honest _____" — ABE
"Honor Thy Father" author — TALESE
"Hope springs _____ ...": Pope — ETERNAL
"Horse power" for Cinderella's coach — MICE
"Hostess" Perle — MESTA
"How _____ the lady?": Shak. — DOTH
"How _____ to know" — WAS I
"How are the mighty _____": I Samuel — FALLEN
"How do I love _____?": — THEE
"How sweet _____" — IT IS
"How's that again?" — WHAT
"Hud" star — NEAL
"Hurry up" from HQ — ASAP
"I _____ a lass ...": Wither — LOVED
"I _____ a Teenage Werewolf" — WAS
"I _____ Camera" — AM A

"I _____ charmed life": Macbeth — BEAR A
"I _____ dance ..." — WONT
"I _____ Dancer": Nureyev film — AM A
"I _____ dream dear ..." — HAD A
"I _____ dream": M.L. King Jr. — HAD A
"I _____ fool!": Dickens — HATE A
"I _____ Have Eyes for You" — ONLY
"I _____ kick from champagne ..." — GET NO
"I _____ kick out of ... .." — GET A
"I _____ letter to my love" — SENT A
"I _____ man with seven wives" — MET A
"I _____ man" — MET A
"I _____ of Jeannie ..." — DREAM
"I _____ Parade" — LOVE A
"I _____ Rhapsody" — HEAR A
"I _____ Rhythm" — GOT
"I _____ the line" — TOED
"I _____ the songs" — WRITE
"I _____": Tony Martin song — GET IDEAS
"I am _____ a man": Shak. — TO GET
"I am _____": Louis XIV — THE STATE
"I am a lone _____ creetur ...": Dickens — LORN
"I am seeking _____": Diogenes — A MAN
"I Am Woman" singer Helen — REDDY
"I beg _____ pardon now": R. Wilbur — DEATHS
"I begin to smell _____": Cervantes — A RAT
"I Came, _____ ..." — I SAW
"I can't believe _____ the whole thing" — I ATE
"I cannot _____ lie" — TELL A
"I cannot tell _____" — A LIE
"I cast to earth _____" (Tennyson) — A SEED
"I could _____ horse!" — EAT A
"I didn't hear you" — WHAT
"I didn't know you _____" — CARED
"I do" alternative — YES
"I don't care a _____" — RAP
"I don't know's" base — THIRD
"I earn that I _____": Shak. — EAT
"I Enjoy Being _____" — A GIRL
"I Got You _____" — BABE
"I have _____ ...": M.L. King Jr. — A DREAM
"I have _____ the world ...": Byron — NOT LOVED
"I let _____ go out ..." — A SONG
"I let him in," _____ — SHE ADMITTED
"I like _____": 1952 motto — IKE
"I love _____ truly ..." — YOU
"I Love _____" — LUCY
"I Love Lucy" star — DESI
"I loved _____ ...": Wither — A LASS
"I loved you _____": Hamlet — EVER
"I Married _____" — DORA
"I mean it!" — SO THERE
"I met _____ with seven wives" — A MAN
"I never _____ man ...": Rogers — MET A
"I never _____ purple cow ..." — SAW A
"I never saw a _____": Dickinson — MOOR
"I Pagliacci" troupe-owner — CANIO
"I Promessi _____," Manzoni novel — SPOSI
"I Remember _____" — MAMA
"I Remember Mama" role — NELS
"I slept like _____" — A LOG
"I smell _____!" — A RAT
"I Wandered Lonely _____ Cloud" — AS A
"I Want _____ Just ..." — A GIRL
"I want a _____ just ..." — GIRL
"I will _____ and go now ...": Yeats — ARISE
"I will fear no _____ ..." — EVIL
"I Won't _____ Day Without You": Williams — LAST A
"I work in a lab," _____ — SHE RETORTED
"I" problem — EGOMANIA
"I'd hate to break up _____" — A SET
"I'd rather see than _____": Burgess — BE ONE
"I'd walk _____ ..." — A MILE
"I'll _____ World": 1945 comedy — TELL THE
"I'll learn him or _____": Twain — KILL HIM
"I'll say!" — OF COURSE
"I'll Take _____," 1965 film — SWEDEN
"I'm _____ wash that man ..." — GONNA
"I'm alive," _____ — HE BREATHED
"I'm all _____!" — EARS
"I'm dying," _____ — SHE CROAKED
"I'm eating _____" — MY HEART OUT
"I'm only _____ teetotaler ...": Shaw — A BEER
"I've _____ a secret" — GOT
"I've _____ every little star ..." — TOLD
"I've _____ Gal in Kalamazoo" — GOT A
"I've _____ to London ..." — BEEN
"I've Got _____ in Kalamazoo" — A GAL
"I've got _____" — AN IN
"I've Got a _____" — SECRET
"I've said _____ love" — ADIEU TO
"Iacta _____ est" — ALEA
"Ich _____," Prince of Wales motto — DIEN
"Ich bin _____ Berliner": J.F.K. — EIN
"Ida, _____ as Apple Cider" — SWEET
"If _____ a Hammer" — I HAD
"If _____ a Rich Man" — I WERE
"If _____ I should leave you ..." — EVER
"If _____ King" — I WERE
"If _____ My Way": 1913 song — I HAD
"If _____ You" — I HAD
"If I _____ King" — WERE
"If I _____ Million": 1932 movie — HAD A
"If I _____," Beatles song — FELL
"If You _____, But You Did," 1951 song — HADNT
"If you can't _____ heat ..." — STAND THE
"If You Knew _____" — SUSIE
"Ignorance _____" — IS BLISS
"Il _____" — DUCE
"Iliad" city — TROY
"Iliad" location — TROY
"Iliad" site — TROY
"Iliad," e.g. — EPIC
"Iliad," for one — EPIC
"In _____ we trust" — GOD
"In _____" — ESSE
"In _____" (having difficulty) — A SPOT
"In a cavern, _____" — IN A CANYON
"In God We Trust" e.g — MOTTO
"In God We Trust," for one — MOTTO
"In him _____ darkness": St. John — IS NO
"In hoc _____ vinces" — SIGNO

"In Like _____," 1967 Coburn film — FLINT
"In the _____ days ..." — OLDEN
"In the _____ of the Night" — STILL
"In the _____ of" (surrounded) — MIDST
"In the Boom Boom Room" playwright — RAGE
"In the wilderness, build me _____ ..." — A NEST
"In them hath _____ a tabernacle ...": Psalm 19:4 — TO LET
"In" — CHIC, TRENDY
"Inferno" poet — DANTE
"Inside Straight Club" site — ALGONQUIN
"Invisible Man" Claude — RAINS
"Iolanthe" player — PIER
"Ipanema" singer — ASTRUD
"Is _____ dagger ... ?": Shak. — THIS A
"Is it _____? Is it a plane?" — A BIRD
"Is it a hit _____ error?" — OR AN
"Is life _____?": Gilbert — A BOON
"Is there beauty _____?": Dostoyevsky — IN SODO
"Israel" poet's monogram — EAP
"It _____ ancient Mariner" — IS AN
"It _____ Fair" — ISNT
"It _____ necessarily so ..." — AINT
"It _____ Very Good Year" — WAS A
"It Ain't _____ Rain No Mo" — GONNA
"It dyes the _____": A. Meynell — WIDE AIR
"It had to be _____" — YOU
"It Had To Be _____" — YOU
"It Happened One Night" director — CAPRA
"It is a _____ told by an idiot ... .." — TALE
"It Seems Like Old Times" composer — STEPT
"It suits me to _____" — A TEE
"It was _____ of orders grey ...": WS — THE FRIAR
"It" girl of the 20's — BOW
"It's _____ ... world" — A MAD
"It's _____ country" — A FREE
"It's _____ to tell a lie" — A SIN
"It's _____ up" (too close to call) — A TOSS
"It's _____! — A BOY
"It's _____!" — A DEAL
"It's a sin to tell _____" — A LIE
"It's a sin to tell _____" — A LIE
"It's still the same _____ story ..." — OLD
"Jackie must have but _____ day ..." — A PENNY A
"Jacques _____ is Alive and Well ..." — BREL
"Jacta est _____!" — ALEA
"Jailhouse _____," Presley hit — ROCK
"Jalousie" composer: 1927 — GADE
"Jane _____" (Bronte) — EYRE
"Jane Eyre" author — BRONTE
"Jaws" director — STEVEN SPIELBERG
"Jaws" fish — SHARK
"Jelly Roll" Morton specialty — STOMP
"Jelly Roll" of jazz — MORTON
"Jeopardy!" and "Wheel of Fortune" — GAME SHOWS
"Jeopardy" offerings — ANSWERS
"Jerusalem Delivered" poet — TASSO
"Jerusalem the Golden" hymnologist — NEALE
"Jetsons" dog — ASTRO
"JFK" director — STONE
"Jog" or "Don't Jog" — DOCTORS ORDERS
"John Brown's Body" poet — BENET
"Johnny _____," Wyman movie — BELINDA
"Jolly _____," Hals painting — TRIO
"Joltin Joe" — DIMAG
"Jonathan Livingston Seagull" author — ADAMS
"Judith" composer — ARNE
"Julia" Oscar winner: 1977 — VANESSA REDGRAVE
"Jumbles" craft — SIEVE
"Junk" carrier — POSTMAN
"Just _____ doch-an'-dorris": Lauder — A WEE
"Just _____ in the dark" — A KISS
"Just _____ thought ..." — AS I
"Just _____!" — SAY NO
"Just When _____ You Most" — I NEEDED
"Kane and Abel" author — ARCHER
"Kate and _____" — ALLIE
"Keep the golden _____ between" — MEAN
"Kenilworth" heroine — AMY
"Key _____": Bogart film — LARGO
"Keystone" character — KOP
"Kidnapped" author's monogram — RLS
"Kind Hearts and _____" — CORONETS
"King _____ Road," 1965 song — OF THE
"King _____," J. Goodman film — RALPH
"King Lear" role — EDMUND, REGAN
"King of Swing" — BENNY
"King Olaf" composer — ELGAR
"King" Cole — NAT
"Kiss Me _____" — KATE
"Kiss Me Kate" composer — COLE PORTER
"Kiss of the Spider Woman" actress Braga — SONIA
"Kissing" plant — MISTLETOE
"Klute" star — FONDA
"Kon _____" — TIKI
"Krapp's _____ Tape": Beckett — LAST
"Krazy _____" — KAT
"L' _____ c'est moi" — ETAT
"L' _____ Espagnole," by Ravel — HEURE
"L'Ariesienne _____": Bizet — SUITE
"L'elisir d'amore" heroine — ADINA
"L.A. Law" actress — DEY
"L.A. Law's" Susan and family — DEYS
"La _____ aux Folles" — CAGE
"La _____," 1950 film — RONDE
"La Boheme" heroine — MIMI
"La Boheme" highlight — DUET
"La Boheme" role — MIMI
"La Douce" — IRMA
"La Douce" — IRMA
"La Plume de Ma _____" — TANTE
"La Sonnambula" heroine — AMINA
"La Strada" star Giulietta — MARSINI
"La Tosca" dramatist — SARDOU
"La Traviata" tune — ARIA
"La Tulipe _____": Dumas — NOIRE
"La Vie de Jesus" author — RENAN
"Lacta _____ est": the die is cast — ALEA
"Lacta alea _____" — EST
"Lady of the Lake" outlaw __ DHU
"Lady" of song — EADIE
"Laissez- _____" — FAIRE
"Lakme," e.g. — OPERA

"Lamp _____ My Feet" — UNTO
"Land of 10,000 Lakes" — MINNESOTA
"Land of the Dragon" — BHUTAN
"Landlord of New York" — ASTOR
"Las Vegas Nights" song: 1941 — DOLORES
"Last but not _____" — LEAST
"Last of the Mohicans" author — COOPER
"Laugh in" Johnson — ARTE
"Laugh in" star — DICK MARTIN
"Launching the Boat" painter — HOMER
"Lawrence of Arabia" director — LEAN
"Le _____ de la Rose," Fokine ballet — SPECTRE
"Le _____ Goriot": Balzac — PERE
"Le _____ Soleil" — ROI
"Le Coq _____": Rimsky-Korsakov opera — DOR
"Le Roi _____": Hugo play — SAMUSE
"Le Roi d'Ys" composer — LALO
"Leaning Tower" city — PISA
"Leave _____ Beaver" — IT TO
"Leave _____ to heaven": Shak. — HER
"Leave all _____ to the gods" — ELSE
"Leonore" poet — POE
"Les _____" — MAIDS
"Les _____": musical — GIRLS
"Les Bergeries" author — ANET
"Les Miserables" author — HUGO
"Les Miserables" domestic number — TROIS
"Les Mousquetaires" — TROIS
"Less _____ Zero," Bret Ellis novel — THAN
"Let _____ eat cake" — THEM
"Let _____": Beatles song — IT BE
"Let independence _____ boast" — BE OUR
"Let it _____" — SNOW
"Let no man put _____" — ASUNDER
"Let the _____ be burning" — LOWER LIGHTS
"Let's _____ little as we can": Shak. — MEET AS
"Let's Make _____" — A DEAL
"Let's Make a _____" — DEAL
"Li'l Abner" role — DAISY MAE
"Life _____ jest ...": Gay — IS A
"Life _____, life is ..." — IS REAL
"Life is Just _____ of Cherries" — A BOWL
"Life with _____" — FATHER
"Life with Father" name — DAY
"Light Horse" Harry — LEE
"Light October brew" — ALE
"Light of _____!": Herbert — MY EYE
"Like _____ from the blue" — A BOLT
"Like _____ in a china shop" — A BULL
"Like _____ of bricks" — A TON
"Like _____ without a tail ...": Shak. — A RAT
"Like Niobe, _____ tears": Shak. — ALL
"Lil Abner" cartoonist — CAPP
"Lili" film composer — KAPER
"Lily Maid of Astolat" — ELAINE
"Lions and tigers and bears, _____!" — OH MY
"Liquor is quicker" man — NASH
"Little _____ Echo" — SIR
"Little _____": Comic strip — IODINE
"Little Minister" author — BARRIE
"Little Shop of Horrors" store-keeper — FLORIST
"Little Women" sequel? — THE OLD WIVES TALE
"Little" Stowe girl — EVA
"Live free or _____" — DIE
"Lizzie Borden took _____": Anon. — AN AX
"Lohengrin" heroine — ELSA
"Lohengrin" lady — ELSA
"Lohengrin," for one — OPERA
"Lonely Boy" singer — ANKA
"Look _____ hands!" — MA NO
"Look here! — HIST
"Look Homeward, Angel" hero — GANT
"Lord Jim" actor — OTOOLE
"Lord, _____ I?": Matt. — IS IT
"Lord, is _____?": Matt. 26:22 — IT I
"Lorna _____" — DOONE
"Lorna _____" — DOONE
"Louise" or "Lohengrin" — OPERA
"Louise" or "Martha" — OPERA
"Love _____ to be purchased ..." — IS NOT
"Love _____": Jerome K. Jerome — IS LIKE THE MEASLES
"Love _____": Prov. 10:12 — COVERTH ALL SINS
"Love _____": Shak. — ALL TRUST A FEW
"Love _____": Song of Solomon — IS STRONG AS DEATH
"Love _____," 1951 film — HAS MANY FACES
"Love _____," 1952 film — IS BETTER THAN NEVER
"Love in _____ Climate": N. Mitford — A COLD
"Love Story" author Segal — ERICH
"Love Story" star — ONEAL
"Love your _____ ...": Tennyson — ENEMY
"Lower Manhattan" painter — MARIN
"Luck and Pluck" author — ALGER
"Lucky Jim" author — AMIS
"Lucky" folk — IRISH
"Lulu" and "Norma" — OPERAS
"Luncheon on the Grass" artist — MANET
"M _____ ..." — IS FOR THE MANY THINGS
"M*A*S*H" character — RADAR
"M*A*S*H" director Robert — ALTMAN
"M*A*S*H" land — KOREA
"M*A*S*H" star, et al. — ALDAS
"Macbeth does murder _____" — SLEEP
"Mack the _____" — KNIFE
"Mack the Knife" vocalist — DARIN
"Mad Dogs and Englishmen" composer — NOEL COWARD
"Mad Mad World" comic — JONATHAN WINTERS
"Madding crowd" chronicler — THOMAS HARDY
"Magic's" team — LAKERS
"Major _____," TV sitcom — DAD
"Major" constellation — URSA
"Make _____ Happy," 1960 song — SOME ONE
"Make My Day" Eastwood — CLINT
"Make us _____ of all eternity": Shak. — HEIRS
"Malcolm X" director — LEE
"Man _____ but little here below ..." — WANTS
"Man _____ Mancha" — OF LA
"Man _____ reasoning animal": Seneca — IS A
"Man Bites Dog" e.g. — NEWS
"Man is but _____": Pascal — A REED
"Man of _____," Flaherty film — ARAN
"Man of the red earth" — ADAM

"Man of the Year": 1947 — GEORGE C MARSHALL
"Man of the Year": 1958 — CHARLES DE GAULLE
"Man of the Year": 1964 — LYNDON JOHNSON
"Man-of-the-hour" — SANTA
"Mandy" singer — MANILOW
"Manhattan" lyricist — HART
"March King" of yore — SOUSA
"March of the _____" — TOYS
"Marching as _____" — TO WAR
"Marching" coins — DIMES
"Mares _____ ..." — EAT OATS
"Maria _____," Dorsey song — ELENA
"Marie" and "Dinah" — SONGS
"Marriage is _____": Cervantes — A NOOSE
"Marseillaise," e.g. — ANTHEM
"Marvelous _____" of the old Mets — MARV
"Mary _____ little lamb" — HAD A
"Mary _____" of film — DEARE
"Mary Magdalene" painter — RENI
"Masterpiece" on wheels — SHAY
"Matelot" author — LOTI
"Matter of Fact" columnist — ALSOP
"May the _____ be with you" — FORCE
"McGraw's boy" — MEL OTT
"McMillan and Wife" star — ROCK HUDSON
"McSorley's Bar" artist — SLOAN
"Mean machines" — HOT RODS
"Meek as _____" — A LAMB
"Men are April when they _____": W.S. — WOO
"Men die _____ idea does not": Lerner — BUT AN
"Mens sana in corpore _____" — SANO
"Merchant of Venice" role — PORTIA
"Merrily, merrily shall _____ now ...": Shak. — I LIVE
"Merry Mount" composer: 1894-1961 — HANSON
"Messe de Requiem" composer — FAURE
"Messiah" composer — HANDEL
"Methought I heard _____" (Macbeth) — A VOICE
"Middlemarch" author — ELIOT
"Midnight Cowboy" character — RATSO
"Midnight Cowboy" role — RATSO
"Mikado" role — KOKO
"Mike Hammer" star — STACY KEACH
"Mila 18" author — URIS
"Milton's the prince _____" (Byron) — OF POETS
"Miniver Cheevy, _____ late ..." — BORN TOO
"Miracle on 34th Street" employer — MACYS
"Miracle team" of 1969 — METS
"Miss _____ Regrets" — OTIS
"Miss Thompson," on stage — RAIN
"Moby Dick" — WHALE TALE
"Mommie _____" — DEAREST
"Mondo _____," 1963 documentary — CANE
"Money _____ everything" — ISNT
"Money _____ object" — IS NO
"Moon River" composer — HENRY MANCINI
"Moonlight", for one — SONATA
"Moonstruck" star — CHER
"Moonstruck" star, et al. — CHERS
"More matter with _____ art": Shak. — LESS
"Morning's at _____": Browning — SEVEN
"Most Happy _____" — FELLA
"Mother _____": Kipling — O MINE
"Motown" player — DETROIT LION
"Mourning becomes _____" — ELECTRA
"Mourning Becomes Electra" character — ORIN
"Mourning Becomes Electra" role — ORIN
"Mr. _____ Goes to Town" — DEEDS
"Mr. Midshipman _____" — EASY
"Much _____ About Nothing" — ADO
"Mugs" — PUSSES
"Mule Train" singer — LAINE
"Mum's the _____": Cervantes — WORD
"Murder _____," Lipsky novel — ONE
"Murder, _____ Said," 1962 film — SHE
"Murder, She _____" — WROTE
"Music _____ charms ..." — HATH
"My _____ and only" — ONE
"My _____ Flicka": 1943 film — FRIEND
"My _____ mouth" — HEARTS IN MY
"My _____ Sal" — GAL
"My _____": Twiggy musical — ONE AND ONLY
"My Antonia" author — WILLA CATHER
"My Antonia" character — MAREK
"My country _____ ..." — TIS
"My cup _____ over" — RUNNETH
"My Fair Lady" scene — ASCOT
"My Fair Lady" source — SHAW
"My Fair Lady" star — COOTE
"My Fair Lady" team — LERNER AND LOEWE
"My Friend Flicka" author Mary O'Hara _____ — ALSOP
"My Gal _____" — SAL
"My Life in Court" author — NIZER
"My Love is like _____ ..." — A RED
"My Name is _____ Lev": Potok — ASHER
"My Name Is _____": Saroyan — ARAM
"My Name is Asher _____" — LEV
"My Rosary" composer — NEVIN
"My Three _____" — SONS
"My Way" composer — ANKA
"My Wife's a Winsome _____ Thing": Burns — WEE
"My Wild _____" — IRISH ROSE
"Myth of Hercules" painter — RENI
"Name That _____" — TUNE
"Nana" actress — STEN
"Nana" novelist — ZOLA
"Nana" star: 1934 — STEN
"Nancy" rich kid — ROLLO
"Nashville" singer Blakley — RONEE
"Nearer, My God, to _____" — THEE
"Neat as _____" — A PIN
"Need _____ cry?": Burns — A BODY
"Nervous _____ cat" — AS A
"Nessun dorma," for one — ARIA
"Network" director — LUMET
"Night Music" playwright — ODETS
"Nightline" newsman — KOPPEL
"Nightmare" street — ELM

"Nightmare" street of films — ELM
"No _____!" — SIREE
"No _____": Sartre drama — EXIT
"No Exit" author — SARTRE
"No ifs, _____, or buts" — ANDS
"No man _____ island": Donne — IS AN
"No man is _____ his valet" — A HERO TO
"No man is a hero _____ valet" — TO HIS
"No problem!" — EASY
"No Siree!" participant — ROBERT SHERWOOD
"No Way" — NIX, NEVER
"No, No _____" — NANETTE
"Nolo contendere, el al." — PLEAS
"Nor iron bars _____" — A CAGE
"Norma _____" — RAE
"Norma _____": 1979 film — RAE
"Norma _____," Glaspell novel — ASHE
"Norma" opening — ACT I
"Norma" or "Martha" — OPERA
"Not on _____ life" — YOUR
"Not with _____ ...": T.S. Eliot — A BANG
"Nothing in Common" actor Bill, et al. — MACYS
"Nova" netwk. — PBS
"November's sky is chill and _____" — DREAR
"Novum Organum" author — BACON
"Now _____ me down to sleep ..." — I LAY
"Now I _____ ..." — LAY ME
"Now is the _____" — HOUR
"Now, _____": Bette Davis film — VOYAGER
"Now, knock when I _____ ...": Shak. — BID YOU
"O _____ Ben Jonson!" — RARE
"O _____" — SUSANNA
"O rare, Ben _____!" — JONSON
"O short-liv'd pride! _____?": Shak. — NOT FAIR
"O Sole _____" — MIO
"O sole _____" — MIO
"Oberon's" composer — WEBER
"Odi et _____": Horace — AMO
"Oedipus _____" — REX
"Of _____ and Men" — MICE
"Of _____ and the River" — TIME
"Of _____ I Sing" — THEE
"Of Mice and Men" role — LENNIE
"Of Thee _____" — I SING
"Of Thee I Sing" character — WINTERGREEN
"Off _____, on ...": Gillilan — AGIN
"Oh _____ good" — LADY BE
"Oh to _____ England ...": Browning — BE IN
"Oh! _____ danced ..." — HOW WE
"Oh, _____" (Forrest Tucker film) — SUSANNA
"Oh, _____, I long to hear you " — SHENANDOAH
"Oh, Give _____ home where ..." — ME A
"Oh, I am _____" — A COOK
"Oh, My _____" — PAPA
"Oh, Oh!" — OOPS
"Oh, that hurts" — OUCH
"Oh, What _____ Was Mary" — A PAL
"Okay!" — ALL RIGHT
"Oklahoma!" aunt — ELLER
"Oklahoma!" role — JUD
"Oklahoma!" star in 1955 — MACRAE
"Ol' Man _____": Louis Armstrong song — MOSE
"Old _____": Disney dog — YELLER
"Old Blue Eyes" — SINATRA
"Old Dog Tray" composer — FOSTER
"Old Dominion" state — VIRGINIA
"Old Glory," e.g. — BANNER
"Old Hat" — DATED
"Old Lady who lived in _____" — A SHOE
"Old MacDonald" refrain — EIEIO
"Old Rough and Ready" president — TAYLOR
"Oldtown Folks" author — STOWE
"Olympia" impressionist — MANET
"On _____ Pond": 1981 film — GOLDEN
"On a day _____ we pass the time.." — LIKE TODAY
"On Golden _____" — POND
"On the Beach" author — SHUTE
"On Your _____" — TOES
"Once _____ ..." — UPON
"Once _____ a time ..." — UPON
"Once _____ time ..." — UPON A
"Once in a _____" — BLUE MOON
"Once upon a _____" — MATTRESS
"One day _____ time" — AT A
"One Day at _____" — A TIME
"One leak will sink _____": Bunyan — A SHIP
"One-hoss _____" — SHAY
"Op. _____" (footnote) — CIT
"Operation Overlord" cmdr. — DDE
"Or set upon _____ bough ...": Yeats — A GOLDEN
"Ora pro _____" — NOBIS
"Oro y _____" (motto of MT) — PLATA
"Orphee" and "Le Repos" — COROTS
"Our Man _____," 1966 film — FLINT
"Out for the Christmas Trees" painter — GRANDMA MOSES
"Out of Africa" locale — KENYA
"Out on _____" — A LIMB
"Over _____" — THERE
"Over _____": W.W.I song — THERE
"Over Hill and _____" — DALE
"Over Hill and _____" — DALE
"Over the Rainbow" composer — ARLEN
"Over the Rainbow" songwriter — ARLEN
"Overboard" star — HAWN
"Oz" actor Bert — LAHR
"Oz" dog — TOTO
"Pacific" bird — DOVE
"Paddlin' _____ Home" — MADELIN
"Pagliacci" role — CANIO
"Pal Joey" author — OHARA
"Pal Joey" team — RODGERS AND HART
"Pale Horse, Pale _____" — RIDER
"Papa Bear" of football — HALAS
"Paper Moon" name — ONEAL
"Paradise Lost" author — MILTON
"Paradise Lost" character — SATAN
"Paradise Lost" playwright — ODETS
"Passage to India" heroine — ADELA
"Pathetique" or "Appassionata" — SONATA
"Patton," to Scott — ROLE
"Pay _____ mind" — IT NO
"Peace in _____ time" — OUR
"Peanuts" expletive — RATS
"Peanuts," e.g. — STRIP
"Peck's _____ Boy" — BAD
"Peer Gynt" _____ — SUITE

"Peer Gynt" author — IBSEN
"Peer Gynt" composer — GRIEG
"Penelope" composer — FAURE
"Penrod" penman — TARKINGTON
"People _____ Funny" — ARE
"People Will Say We're _____" — IN LOVE
"Perfect" number — TEN
"Peter _____" — PAN
"Peter Grimes," for one — OPERA
"Peter Pan" captain — HOOK
"Peter Pan" character — TINKERBELL
"Peter Pan" creator — BARRIE
"Peter Pan" pirate — SMEE
"Peter Pan" playwright — BARRIE
"Peyton Place" star — MALONE
"Pickwick Papers" author — DICKENS
"Picnic" playwright — INGE
"Picnic" won him a Pulitzer — INGE
"Pictures _____ Exhibition" — AT AN
"Pike's Peak or _____" — BUST
"Pilgrim at Tinker Creek" author — ANNIE DILLARD
"Pinafore" — SHIP
"Pinafore" insignia — HMS
"Pink Panther" Peter — SELLERS
"Pins and Needles" composer — HAROLD ROME
"Pinta" sister ship — NINA
"Pippin" director — FOSSE
"Pirates of Penzance" heroine — MABEL
"Platoon" director — STONE
"Play _____ it Lays": 1972 film — IT AS
"Play it again, _____" — SAM
"Playboy of the Western World" playwright — SYNGE
"Plaza _____" — SUITE
"Pleasure's _____" (Byron) — A SIN
"Pluck _____ rose ...": Shak. — A RED
"Poker Flats", author — HARTE
"Pomp and Circumstance" composer — ELGAR
"Pooh" creator — MILNE
"Poppycock!" — NONSENSE
"Porgy and Bess," e.g. — OPERA
"Portnoy's Complaint" penman — ROTH
"Portrait of _____" — A LADY
"Portrait of _____" — A LADY
"Preacher" of baseball — ROE
"Pretty _____ picture" — AS A
"Pretty maids all in _____" — A ROW
"Pretty Poison" star — TUESDAY WELD
"Profits than an _____ king" — IDLE
"Prometheus Unbound" poet — SHELLEY
"Prosit!" or "Cheers!" — TOAST
"Psycho-Cybernetics" author — MALTZ
"Push comes to _____": Tharp ballet — SHOVE
"Push" in Potsdam — STOSSE
"Puttin' on the _____," 1946 song — RITZ
"Quality Street" playwright — BARRIE
"Que _____ ...": Doris Day song — SERA
"Queen of the Jungle" and namesakes — SHEENAS
"Queenie" author — KORDA
"Quick _____ the Flit": 30's slogan — HENRY
"Quien _____?" — SABE
"Quiet!" — HUSH
"Quiet!" noises — SHS
"Quincy" actor Robert — ITO
"Quincy" co-star — ITO
"Quo _____?" — VADIS
"Quo Vadis?" emperor — NERO
"R.U.R." author — CAPEK
"R.U.R." protagonist — ROBOT
"Raging Bull" player — DENIRO
"Rainbow's End" author Steven P. _____ — ERIE
"Ramayama," e.g. — EPIC
"Rand" title strongman — ATLAS
"Raving, _____ money-mad": B.R. Newton — ROTTING
"Ready _____, here I come!" — OR NOT
"Red Badge" author — CRANE
"Red Roses for _____ Lady" — A BLUE
"Red Star over China" author — SNOW
"Regretful" miss of song — OTIS
"Remember _____ wife": Luke 17:32 — LOTS
"Remember the _____" — ALAMO
"Remington _____" — STEELE
"Republic" author — PLATO
"Requiem for _____" — A NUN
"Return of the _____" — JEDI
"Rhapsody _____" — IN BLUE
"Riders of the Purple Sage" author Zane — GREY
"Right away", to an RN — STAT
"Right you _____!" — ARE
"Righto!" — AYE
"Rigoletto" setting — MANTUA
"Ring" character — WOTAN
"Rio _____" — RITA
"Ripeness _____": King Lear — IS ALL
"Rob Peter _____ Paul" — TO PAY
"Roberta" composer — KERN
"Robin _____," old Irish song — ADAIR
"Robinson Crusoe" author — DEFOE
"Robinson Crusoe" creator — DEFOE
"Rock _____" — OF AGES
"Rock of _____" — AGES
"Rocked in the _____": Willard — CRADLE OF THE DEEP
"Rocket Man" singer — JOHN
"Roger, _____" — WILCO
"Romancero gitano" poet — LORCA
"Romancing the _____," 1984 film — STONE
"Rome of Hungary" — EGER
"Rooms _____" — TO LET
"Roots" co-star — AMOS
"Roots" role — KINTE
"Rose _____ rose" — IS A
"Rose of _____" — TRALEE
"Rosebud" in "Citizen Kane" — SLED
"Rosshalde" author — HESSE
"Rouse _____ his fair" (Scott) — THE LION
"Roxanna" author — DEFOE
"Rub-a- _____" — DUB DUB
"Rub-a-dub-dub" boat — TUB
"Rug" — TOUPEE
"Rule Britannia" composer — ARNE
"Ruler of the Queen's _____" — NAVEE
"Sail _____ Union ...": Longfellow — ON O
"Sail on, O _____!" — UNION
"Saint of the Gutters" — MOTHER TERESA
"Salem's _____" — LOT
"Samson et Dalila" composer Saint _____" — SAENS
"San Francisco" star — GABLE
"Sanford and _____" — SON
"Santa Claus is watching You" singer — STEVENS
"Santa Claus" star — MOORE
"Saratoga _____" — TRUNK
"Saratoga" was her last movie — HARLOW

"Satchmo" — LOUIS ARMSTRONG
"Saturday Night _____" — LIVE
"Saturday Night _____" (Travolta) — FEVER
"Saw wood" — SNORE
"Say good night, _____": G. Burns — GRACIE
"Say hey" Willy — MAYS
"Scenes from a Mall" star — ALLEN
"Schoolboy" of baseball — ROWE
"Scots, Wha _____ ..." (Robert Burns) — HAE
"Sea of Love" actress — BARKIN
"Second City" player — CHICAGO CUB
"Second hand _____" — ROSE
"See you later" — SO LONG
"Semper Fidelis" composer — SOUSA
"September _____" — MORN
"September _____": Neil Diamond song — MORN
"Serpico" author Peter — MAAS
"Sesame Street" grouch — OSCAR
"Sesame Street" name — ERNIE
"Sesame Street" resident — ERNIE
"Set me as _____ upon thine heart" — A SEAL
"Seven days _____" — A WEEK
"Seven Year Itch" actor — EWELL
"Sex, _____ and Videotape," 1989 film — LIES
"Sextet" source — LUCIA
"Shalom" — PEACE
"Shane" actor — LADD
"She _____ many children ..." — HAD SO
"She _____ Yellow Ribbon," 1949 film — WORE A
"She learn'd _____ at others' woe" (Gray) — TO MELT
"She painted it": Abbr. — PINX
"She was a _____": Wordsworth — PHANTOM OF DELIGHT
"She's wedded to the _____'s son": Scott — EARLIE
"Ship of _____" — FOOLS
"Ships of the desert" — CAMELS
"Short and stout" container — TEAPOT
"Show Boat" composer — KERN
"Show Me _____ Go Home" — THE WAY TO
"Showboat" author Ferber — EDNA
"Shrink" — ANALYST
"Shucks!" — DRAT
"Sic transit gloria _____" — MUNDI
"Silas _____" — MARNER
"Silas Marner" author — ELIOT
"Silent" Coolidge — CAL
"Silver lining" location — CLOUD
"Simon _____" ... — SAYS
"Sixteen Tons" singer — LAINE
"Slaughter on _____ Avenue" — TENTH
"Sleep like _____" — A TOP
"Sleeping Murder," e.g. — CHRISTIES MYSTERY
"Sleepy Time _____" — GAL
"Slippery" tree — ELM
"Slow boat" destination — CHINA
"Smell _____" — A RAT
"Smoke damage" event — FIRE SALE
"Smokey," for one — BEAR
"Snug as a bug in _____" — IN A RUG
"So _____": amen — BE IT
"So Big" author — FERBER
"Soft Watches" painter — DALI
"Sold for _____ of pottage" — A MESS
"Sold Out" notice — SRO
"Some _____ meat ...": Burns — HAE
"Some _____ Running" — CAME
"Some Like _____" — IT HOT
"Somebody Loves Me" singer Blossom — SEELEY
"Somewhat" suffix — ISH
"Somewhere _____ of Suez" — EAST
"Somewhere _____ the Rainbow" — OVER
"Song _____ Dance" — AND
"Songs and Sonnets" poet — DONNE
"Sons and Lovers" hero — MOREL
"South Pacific" highlight — SOME ENCHANTED EVENING
"South Pacific" nonpareil — DAME
"South Pacific" sine qua non — DAME
"Spandau" author — SPEER
"Spenser: For Hire" star — ROBERT URICH
"Spirits from the _____ deep" — VASTY
"Spitting" likeness — IMAGE
"Splitsville," once — RENO
"Spoils" winner — VICTOR
"Spoon River" poet's monogram — ELM
"Stanley & Livingstone" co-star — CEDRIC HARDWICKE
"Star _____" — TREK
"Star Trek" actor George — TAKEI
"Star Wars" captain — SOLO
"Star Wars" director — LUCAS
"Star Wars" hero — HAN SOLO
"Star Wars" princess — LEIA
"Star Wars" producer — LUCAS
"Star Wars" role — SOLO
"Star Wars" villain — VADER
"Stardust" composer — HOAGY CARMICHAEL
"Status stripe" designer — GUCCI
"Staying _____" — ALIVE
"Steel City" — PITTSBURGH
"Step _____!" — ON IT
"Steppenwolf" author — HESSE
"Stick close to your _____ ...": Gilbert — DESKS
"Sting like _____": Ali — A BEE
"Stompin" locale — SAVOY
"Stop, Pierre!" — ARRET
"Storm approaching!," — HE THUNDERED
"Street _____," Elmer Rice play — SCENE
"Street Scene" playwright — RICE
"Strike Up the Band" song: 1930 — SOON
"Strong as _____" — AN OX
"Stuart Little" — MOUSE TALE
"Stubborn Hope" poet — BRUTUS
"Stuffed Shirts" author — LUCE
"Sum, _____, fui ..." — ESSE
"Sunny" composer — KERN
"Superman" actor — REEVE
"Superman" Christopher — REEVE
"Sure!" — OKEY DOKE
"Surprise!" — AHA
"Sustineo _____," U.S.A.F. motto — ALAS
"Swan Lake" bend — PLIE
"Swan Lake" role — ODILE
"Swan Lake," for one — BALLET
"Swanee" composer — GEORGE GERSHWIN
"Swanee" lyricist — CAESAR
"Swann's _____": Proust — WAY
"Sweeney Todd" composer — SONDHEIM
"Sweet _____ Brown" — GEORGIA

"Sweet _____ O'Grady" — ROSIE
"Sweet _____! run softly ...": Spenser — THAMES
"Sweet _____" — ADELINE
"Sweet _____" — JENNIE LEE
"Sweet are the _____ of adversity" — USES
"Sweet Swan of _____!": Jonson — AVON
"Sweet" age — SIXTEEN
"Sweet" girl of song — GEORGIA BROWN
"Sweet" time — SIXTEEN
"Swifty," the agent — LAZAR
"Swinging _____," Haggard hit — DOORS
"Symphonie Espagnole" composer — LALO
"Ta-ta, Toledo" — ADIOS
"Tabula _____" — RASA
"Take _____ Leave It," old radio show — IT OR
"Take _____ your leader" — ME TO
"Take _____!" — THAT
"Take _____" (receptionist's request) — A SEAT
"Take _____, She's Mine" — HER
"Take Her, _____ Mine," 1963 film — SHES
"Take Me _____" 1959 song — ALONG
"Take Me _____": Gleason musical — ALONG
"Tamerlane" dramatist: 1701 — ROWE
"Tancredi" composer — ROSSINI
"Tara" for example — ESTATE
"Taras Bulba" author — GOGOL
"Tarry _____" — AWHILE
"Tarzan of the _____" — APES
"Tarzan" Barker — LES
"Tarzan" producer Lesser — SOL
"Te _____" — DEUM
"Tea for _____" — TWO
"Teach" to his classmates? — BLACKBEARD
"Teach", in college — PROF
"Tears" poet — REESE
"Tedious as _____ horse": King Henry IV — A TIRED
"Tell _____ Sweeney!" — IT TO
"Tell _____ the Marines!" — IT TO
"Tell me where is fancy _____ ..." — BRED
"Tempest" sprite — ARIEL
"Ten feet _____" — TALL
"Ten thousand saw _____ a glance": Wordsworth — I AT
"Tenant Farmer" painter — WYETH
"Tennis, _____?" — ANYONE
"Terry and the Pirates" villainess — DRAGON
"Thanks _____!" — A LOT
"Thanks _____" — A LOT
"Thar' _____ blows" — SHE
"That _____ is, so was he made": Bridges — A SHE
"That _____": Marlo Thomas role — GIRL
"That banner in the _____" — SKY
"That makes sense" — I SEE
"That neither is most _____" (Swinburne) — TO BLAME
"That rots itself _____ ...": Shak. — IN EASE
"That was no _____ ..." — LADY
"That which we call _____ ..." — A ROSE
"That's _____" — AMORE
"The _____ -King," Goethe ballad — ERL
"The _____ American" — UGLY
"The _____ and I" — EGG
"The _____ and the Dead" — NAKED
"The _____ Ape": D. Morris book — NAKED
"The _____ Archipelago": Solzhenitsyn — GULAG
"The _____ Around Us" — SEA
"The _____ Boys" — SUNSHINE
"The _____ but a morning star": Thoreau — SUN IS
"The _____ Came": 1939 film — RAINS
"The _____ Coast," Theroux novel — MOSQUITO
"The _____ Cometh" — ICEMAN
"The _____ connected to ..." — HIPBONES
"The _____ declare ...": Psalms — HEAVENS
"The _____ Dogs," Burns poem — TWA
"The _____ Duke": Wellington — IRON
"The _____ Eaters": Van Gogh — POTATO
"The _____ Emperor" — LAST
"The _____ Fair," Burns poem — HOLY
"The _____ Falcon" — MALTESE
"The _____ Fields": 1984 shocker — KILLING
"The _____ Game" — GIN
"The _____ Game," 1977 play — GIN
"The _____ Gang": 1969 movie — OVER THE HILL
"The _____ George Apley": Marquand novel — LATE
"The _____ Got Away": 1958 film — ONE THAT
"The _____ Green," E. Williams play — CORN IS
"The _____ Harp": Capote — GRASS
"The _____ Hill Mob" — LAVENDER
"The _____ Honeymoon"! old nonsense song — ABADABA
"The _____ Hunter" — DEER
"The _____ in Red" — LADY
"The _____ in the Crown" — JEWEL
"The _____ in the Rue Morgue" — MURDERS
"The _____ in Winter" — LION
"The _____ In," famous Clara Bow hit — FLEETS
"The _____ Incident" — OXBOW
"The _____ is an ugly lump": Kipling — CAMELS HUMP
"The _____ is cast": Caesar — DIE
"The _____ is in the pudding" — PROOF
"The _____ Kid" — CISCO
"The _____ lama": Nash — ONE L
"The _____ Legends": 1837 — INGOLDSBY
"The _____ Look Tonight," Fields/Kern hit — WAY YOU
"The _____ love ..." — ONE I
"The _____ Love Belongs ..." — ONE I
"The _____ Love" — ART OF
"The _____ Love" — MAN I, ONE I
"The _____ Love," Lupino film — MAN I
"The _____ Man" — THIN
"The _____ My Fingers," Arnold hit — TIPS OF
"The _____ of Good Women": Chaucer — LEGEND
"The _____ of Katie Elder": Wayne film — SONS
"The _____ of Kilimanjaro" — SNOWS
"The _____ of Miss Jean Brodie": 1969 film — PRIME
"The _____ of Night" — EDGE
"The _____ of Our Teeth" — SKIN
"The _____ of Pompeii" — LAST DAYS

"The _____ of Sleepy Hollow" — LEGEND
"The _____ of Spring": Stravinsky — RITE
"The _____ of St. Agnes" (Keats) — EVE
"The _____ of Summer" — BOYS
"The _____ of the crowd" — ROAR
"The _____ of the Guard": G. & S. — YEOMEN
"The _____ of the Kingdom" — KEYS
"The _____ of the Rings": Tolkien — LORD
"The _____ of the Worlds": H.G. Wells — WAR
"The _____ of Wrath" — GRAPES
"The _____ Old Moon" 1927 song — SAME
"The _____ or the Tiger" — LADY
"The _____ Park" — DEER
"The _____ Quartet": Paul Scott — RAJ
"The _____ Queene" — FAERIE
"The _____ Reason" (Paine) — AGE OF
"The _____ Red Line," Jones book — THIN
"The _____ Rose of Texas" — YELLOW
"The _____ Sanction" — LOO
"The _____ Sanction," 1975 film — EIGER
"The _____ Spain" — RAIN IN
"The _____ Spur," 1953 film — NAKED
"The _____ St. Agnes" — EVE OF
"The _____ the Golden West," 1938 film — GIRL OF
"The _____ the limit" — SKYS
"The _____ the Screw": Henry James — TURN OF
"The _____ their courses ..." — STARS IN
"The _____ to Bountiful" — TRIP
"The _____ Truth," Dunne-Grant film — AWFUL
"The _____" (radio oldie) — LONE RANGER
"The _____" by Dostoyevski — IDIOT
"The _____", Muni-Rainer movie — GOOD EARTH
"The _____": 1969 George Sanders pix — CANDYMAN
"The _____": 1979 Hepburn movie — CORN IS GREEN
"The _____": 1984 Uris book — HAJ
"The _____": Brando film — MEN
"The _____": Brando film — MEN
"The _____": Dostoyevski novel — IDIOT
"The _____": Dostoyevski novel — IDIOT
"The _____": Hamlet's last — REST IS SILENCE
"The _____": Harlow film of 1931 — IRONMAN
"The _____": Harlow film of 1931 — IRONMAN
"The _____": L. C. Douglas — ROBE
"The _____": Peck film — OMEN
"The _____": Straus operetta — CHOCOLATE SOLDIER
"The _____," 1851 tune — AR TRAVELER
"The _____," 1976 Polanski film — TENANT
"The _____," Hardy's poetic drama — DYNASTS
"The _____," Tom Cruise film — FIRM
"The 39 Steps" actor — DONAT
"The 400" — ELITE
"The Addams Family" star — ASTIN
"The Adding Machine" playwright — RICE
"The agony of de feet" — CORNS
"The Army of _____ law" — UNALTERABLE
"The Art of Love" poet — OVID
"The Babe" — RUTH
"The Bad _____": 1956 film — SEED
"The bad news" — BILL
"The Ballad of Reading _____" — GAOL
"The Ballad of the _____ Cafe": McCullers — SAD
"The Barber of Fleet Street" — SWEENEY TODD
"The Barefoot _____" — CONTESSA
"The Bartered Bride" composer — SMETANA
"The Bells of St. _____" — MARYS
"The best _____ schemes of ...": Burns — LAID
"The Beverly Hillbillies" family — CLAMPETT
"The Big Heat" director — LANG
"The Bigelow Papers Poet" — LOWELL
"The Blue Danube," for one — WALTZ
"The Bohemian Girl" composer — BALFE
"The Bold _____" — ONES
"The Boot" — ITALY
"The Breeze _____," 1940 song — AND I
"The Bride Came _____," Cagney film — COD
"The Bridge of San _____ Rey" — LUIS"
"The bright day _____," — IS DONE
"The Broken Jug" playwright — KLEIST
"The Burning Bush" author — UNDSET
"The Caine Mutiny" novelist — WOUK
"The Cat in the Hat" man — SEUSS
"The Catcher in the _____" — RYE
"The clink" — STIR
"The Cloister and the Hearth" author — READE
"The Cocktail Party" author — ELIOT
"The College Widow" author — ADE
"The Compleat _____": Walton — ANGLER
"The Complete Sherlock Holmes" — DOYLE
"The Conning Tower" columnists: Inits. — FPA
"The Conning Tower" monogram — FPA
"The Continent," to Brits — EUR
"The Cosby Show" family — HUXTABLE
"The Country Girl" dramatist — ODETS
"The Country Girl" star — KELLY
"The Crock of Gold" author — JAMES
"The Culture of Narcissism" author — LASCH
"The Divine Comedy" author — DANTE
"The Duino Elegies" poet — RILKE
"The Dunciad" poet — POPE
"The Dynamic _____" — DUO
"The Egg _____" — AND I
"The evil that men _____": Shak. — DO LIVES
"The eye of Greece," to Milton — ATHENS
"The Eyes are not _____": Eliot — HERE

"The Eyes of _____" — TEXAS
"The Facts of Life" Charlotte — RAE
"The Faerie Queene" damsel — UNA
"The Faerie Queene" heroine — UNA
"The fat _____ the fire": Heywood proverb — IS IN
"The First _____" — NOEL
"The Flowering Peach" playwright — ODETS
"The flowers that bloom in the spring _____" — TRA LA
"The Forsyte _____" — SAGA
"The Fountainhead" actress — NEAL
"The Fountainhead" writer — RAND
"The Friends of Eddie _____" — COYLE
"The Georgia Peach" — COBB
"The Ghost Writer" author — ROTH
"The Girl of the Golden West" — OPERA
"The Glass Key" star — LADD
"The Gloomy Dean" — INGE
"The Godfather" group — MAFIA
"The Godfather" star — BRANDO
"The Gods Must Be _____," 1981 film — CRAZY
"The Gold Bug" author — E A POE
"The Golden _____" — HORDE
"The Golden _____": Apuleius — ASS
"The Golden Bowl" author — HENRY JAMES
"The Good Earth" actress Luise — RAINER
"The Grapes of Wrath" character — OKIE
"The Grapes of Wrath" family — JOADS
"The Grass Harp" writer — TRUMAN CAPOTE
"The Great _____ Pepper" — WALDO
"The Great Gatsby" writer — FITZGERALD
"The Greatest" — ALI
"The Green _____," J. Wayne film — BERETS
"The guests _____ ...": Coleridge — ARE MET
"The Hairy _____" — APE
"The Haj" author — URIS
"The Hard Blue Sky" author — SHIRLEY ANN GRAU
"The Hardy Boys" pal — CHET
"The Heart is _____ Hunter" — A LONELY
"The Herne's _____," Yeats play — EGG
"The Highwayman" poet — NOYES
"The homage of _____": Byron — A TEAR
"The House Without a Key": detective — CHAN
"The Hunt For Red _____" — OCTOBER
"The Hunting of the _____": Carroll — SNARK
"The Informer" author O'Flaherty — LIAM
"The Irish are _____ people" (S. Johnson) — A FAIR
"The Jazz Singer" was one: 1927 — TALKIE
"The jig _____!" — IS UP
"The joke is _____" — ON ME
"The Joker" and others to Nicholson — ROLES
"The Jolly Toper" artist — HALS
"The Jungle" author — UPTON SINCLAIR
"The King _____" — AND I
"The King and I" role — ANNA
"The king can _____ wrong" — DO NO
"The King was in the _____ house" — COUNTING
"The Kiss" sculptor — RODIN
"The labor of _____ ...": Milton — AN AGE
"The Lady _____": 1979 film — IN RED
"The Lady and the Tramp" puppy — SCAMP
"The Lady or the _____?" — TIGER
"The Lady With _____" — A LAMP
"The Last _____" — HURRAH
"The Last Days of Pompeii" heroine — IONE
"The Last Frontier" — ALASKA
"The Last Word" — NEWEST
"The law is a _____": Dickens — ASS
"The liner, _____ a lady" — SHES
"The Liner, She's _____" A LADY
"The Lion of God" — ALI
"The Lone Eagle" — LINDY
"The Lone Ranger" Moore — CLAYTON
"The Love For Three _____" Prokofiev — ORANGES
"The Love for Three Oranges" — OPERA
"The Loved One" author — WAUGH
"The Magic Flute", e.g. — OPERA
"The Magic Mountain" author — MANN
"The Major" of radio's "Amateur Hour" — BOWES
"The Man With the _____": movie — GOLDEN ARM
"The Man With the Golden Arm" author — ALGREN
"The Man" of baseball — STAN
"The March King" — SOUSA
"The Marriage of Figaro" for one — OPERA
"The Merry _____ of Windsor": — WIVES
"The Merry Widow" composer — FRANZ LEHAR
"The Merry Widow" composer — LEHAR
"The Merry Widow" count — DANILO
"The Mikado" executioner — KOKO
"The Mikado" role — YUM YUM
"The Mill on the _____" — FLOSS
"The mind is like _____": Wilbur — A BAT
"The Moon _____" — AND I
"The Moor of Venice" — OTHELLO
"The Morning Watch" author: 1951 — AGEE
"The mother of all living" — EVE
"The mouse _____ the clock" — RAN UP
"The Mouse That _____" — ROARED
"The Murders in the _____ Morgue": Poe — RUE
"The Music Man" town — GARY
"The Myth of Sisyphus" author — CAMUS
"The Name of the Rose" author — ECO
"The Name of the Rose" author — ECO
"The Nazarene" author — ASCH
"The Necklace" author, with "de" — MAUPASSANT
"The Nerd" playwright — SHUE
"The Old Devils" author — AMIS
"The Old Wives' Tale" author — PEELE
"The Old Wives' Tale" dramatist — PEELE
"The Other Side of the Rainbow" author — TORME
"The Paper Chase" domestic? — JOHN HOUSEMAN

"The Pearl Fishers" tenor — NADIR
"The Perfect Fool" composer — HOLST
"The Plague" author — CAMUS
"The poet makes himself _____": Rimbaud — A SEER
"The Poisoned Stream" author: 1969 — HABE
"The Portrait of _____" — A LADY
"The Purloined Letter" penman — POE
"The Purple Fog" — TORME
"The Quare Fellow" dramatist — BEHAN
"The Queen of the _____": Rice — DAMNED
"The Rail-Splitter" — ABE LINCOLN
"The Rape of the Lock" author — POPE
"The Raven" poet — POE
"The Razor's _____", Maugham title — EDGE
"The Red and the Black" protagonist — SOREL
"The red planet" — MARS
"The Red" — ERIC
"The Rehearsal" painter — DEGAS
"The Revolt of Mamie _____" — STOVER
"The Rockford Files" star — JAMES GARNER
"The Rolling _____" — STONES
"The Rome of Hungary" — EGER
"The Rosary" composer — NEVIN
"The Rose _____": T. Williams opus — TATTOO
"The Rose of _____" — TRALEE
"The School for Wives" role — AGNES
"The Sea Wolf" author — JACK LONDON
"The Seven Little _____" — FOYS
"The Seven Year _____" — ITCH
"The Shape of Things _____": H.G. Wells — TO COME
"The Sheik of _____," 1921 song — ARABY
"The Shining _____" — HOUR
"The Shooting of Dan McGrew" — ROBERT SERVICE
"The signs of _____" (Matt) — THE TIMES
"The Song of the Earth" composer — MAHLER
"The Spy" author — COOPER
"The stag _____ ...": Scott — AT EVE
"The Stone _____" — AGE
"The Sultan of Sulu" playwright — ADE
"The Sun _____ Rises": Hemingway — ALSO
"The Sun Also _____" — RISES
"The Sweetheart of Sigma _____" — CHI
"The Sweetheart of Sigma _____" — CHI
"The Taming of the _____" — SHREW
"The Tempest" role — ARIEL
"The Tender _____" — TRAP
"The Terrible" — IVAN
"The Things _____ Last Summer" — WE DID
"The Things _____": Higginson — I MISS
"The Thinker" sculptor — RODIN
"The third day comes _____ ...": Shak. — A FROST
"The Third Man" director — REED
"The Thirty-_____ Steps" — NINE
"The Time Machine" race — ELOI
"The Tortoise and the Hare" — FABLE
"The Treasure of the Sierra _____" — MADRE
"The Turning Point" actress — SHIRLEY MACLAINE
"The Two Towers" author — TOLKIEN
"The two-l _____ ...": Ogden Nash — LLAMA
"The ultimate aphrodisiac" — POWER
"The Velvet Fog" — TORME
"The Village Blacksmith," for one — POEM
"The Waltons" grandpa — GEER
"The Wand of Youth" composer — ELGAR
"The Waste Land" author — ELIOT
"The Waste Land" author — ELIOT
"The Way of All _____": Butler — FLESH
"The Way We _____" — WERE
"The Wild Duck" playwright — IBSEN
"The Wind in the Willows" character — TOAD
"The Wizard of Oz" actor — LAHR
"The Wizard of Oz" notable — LAHR
"The wolf _____ the door!" — IS AT
"The Woman _____": Gene Wilder film — IN RED
"The word is _____ unto my feet" — A LAMP
"The World According to _____" — GARP
"The World of Words" author — PARTRIDGE
"The Wreck of the Mary _____" — DEARE
"The Yellow Rose of _____" — TEXAS
"Them" author — OATES
"Them" creatures — ANTS
"Then hey for _____ ...": Burns — A LASS
"There _____ a tavern in the town" — IS A
"There _____ crooked man ..." — WAS A
"There _____ time like the present" — IS NO
"There came _____ over all the land ...": Acts — A DEARTH
"There is _____ in love": I John 4:18 — NO FEAR
"There is _____ like an old ..." — NO FOOL
"There is many _____ 'twixt ..." — A SLIP
"There is no _____ but ignorance": Marlowe — SIN
"There is Nothing Like _____" — A DAME
"There ought to be _____" — A LAW
"There ought to be _____" — A LAW
"There was _____ danced ...": Shak. — A STAR
"There's _____ like home" — NO PLACE
"There's _____ like show ..." — NO BUSINESS
"There's many _____ twixt ..." — A SLIP
"There's no _____ like show ..." — BUSINESS
"There's no music in _____ ...": Ruskin — A REST
"There's not _____ of mine ...": Shak. — A NOTE
"Thereby hangs _____" — A TALE
"Thereby hangs _____" — A TALE
"Thereby hangs a _____ ...": — TALE
"They _____ serve who ..." — ALSO
"They _____ to Codura": 1969 movie — CAME
"They stumble that run _____" — FAST
"They went _____ way" — THATA

"They'd _____ every one" — EATEN
"They'll Do It Every Time" cartoonist — HATLO
"They're Biting" painter — KLEE
"Thief of Bagdad" thief — AHMED
"Thief of Baghdad" star — SABU
"Thin Man" star — ASTA
"Thine _____," Herbert song — ALONE
"Things are seldom what they _____" — SEEM
"Think of it" — IMAGINE
"Thirst-day" stop? — OASIS
"This _____ All": 1942 movie — ABOVE
"This _____ sudden!" — IS SO
"This _____ up" — END
"This Happy _____": 1944 film — BREED
"This Is Love" singer — ANKA
"This is the _____ primeval": Longfellow — FOREST
"This is the law and the _____" — PROPHETS
"This Nearly Was _____" — MINE
"This one's _____!" — ON ME
"This other _____ ...": Richard II — EDEN
"Thoroughly Modern _____": Andrews film — MILLIE
"Thou _____ not ..." — SHALT
"Thou would'st still be _____": Moore — ADORED
"Thousand Days" queen — ANNE
"Three _____ in the Fountain" — COINS
"Three Lives" author — STEIN
"Three Men _____ Horse" — ON A
"Three on _____," 1932 Bogart-Davis movie — A MATCH
"Three Sisters" character — MASHA
"Thus _____ Zarathustra": Nietzsche — SPAKE
"Thy _____ love my Shepherd is": Psalm — GOD OF
"Time _____ the essence" — IS OF
"Time _____ time" — AFTER
"Time _____!" — IS UP
"Time and _____ ..." — TIDE
"Time flies," e.g. — ADAGE
"Time is a great _____". — LEGALIZER
"Tin _____," 1987 film — MEN
"Tinker to _____ to Chance" — EVERS
"Tiny Alice" author — ALBEE
"Tiny Alice" playwright — ALBEE
"Tis _____ to be wise" — FOLLY
"To _____ and a bone ..." — A RAG
"To _____ and to Hold" — HAVE
"To _____ His Dulcinea," 1965 song — EACH
"To _____ His Own" — EACH
"To _____ human ..." — ERR IS
"To _____ in Dixie ..." — LIVE AND DIE
"To _____, With Love": Poitier film — SIR
"To a rag and _____ ..." Kipling — A BONE
"To be _____ ..." — OR NOT
"To be _____ to be" — OR NOT
"To fall _____ habit ...": Unamuno — INTO A
"To fetch _____ of water" — A PAIL
"To get her poor dog _____" — A BONE
"To Have and Have _____" — NOT
"To have and to _____ ..." — HOLD
"To Live and Die _____," 1985 film — IN LA
"To Sir, _____ Love" — WITH
"To sit upon _____": "King Henry VI" — A HILL
"To whom _____ today?": Anon. 1990 BC — DO I SPEAK
"Tobacco _____" — ROAD
"Today _____ man" — I AM A
"Today I _____ man" — AM A
"Tom Brown's Schoolday's" punisher — CAMER
"Tonight Show" host — LENO
"Tonight" host 1954-57 — ALLEN
"Tony _____," Sinatra film — ROME
"Too Many Cooks" sleuth — NERO WOLFE
"Tootsie" actress Teri — GARR
"Topaz" author — URIS
"Tosca" tune — ARIA
"Touch _____ the Cat" — NOT
"Tough Guy" actor Ray — ALDO
"Town Crier" performer — WOOLCOTT
"Toy Soldiers" star: 1991 — ASTIN
"Treasure Island" author's inits. — RLS
"Treasure Island" character — JOHN SILVER, PEW
"Tree _____ Window": Frost — AT MY
"Trees" poet — KILMER
"Tres _____" — BIEN
"Trinity" author — URIS
"Tristan and _____": Wagner opera — ISOLDE
"Tristram Shandy" author — STERNE
"Tru" Tony winner — MORSE
"True _____" — GRIT
"Trust _____," 1934 song — IN ME
"Tubby the _____" — TUBA
"Turandot" highlight — ARIA
"Turandot," for one — OPERA
"Turkish Bath" artist — INGRES
"Twelfth Night" clown — FESTE
"Twelfth Night" heroine — VIOLA
"Twenty _____ maidens we" (G&S) — LOVESICK
"Twenty Questions" words — IS IT
"Twice _____ tales": — TOLD
"Twilight Zone" author Serling — ROD
"Two Gentleman of _____" — VERONA
"Two Gentlemen" city — VERONA
"Two Years Before the _____" — MAST
"Two Years Before the Mast" author — DANA
"Typee" sequel — OMOO
"Typee" successor — OMOO
"U and _____": N. Mitford topic — NON U
"Ugly _____" (very homely) — AS SIN
"Uh huh" — I SEE
"Uh-huh!" — YUP
"'umble" Dickens character — HEEP
"Un bel di," for one — ARIA
"Un Femme de _____ Ans": Balzac — TRENTE
"Una _____ poco fa" — VOCE
"Unaccustomed _____ am" — AS I
"Uncle _____" — REMUS
"Uncle Miltie" — BERLE
"Uncle Tom's Cabin" author — STOWE
"Uncle Vanya" role — ELENA
"Unto us _____ is given" (Isaiah) — A SON
"Up _____ Now" (Eugene McCarthy autobiog.) — TIL
"Up _____," Al Smith's autobiography — TO NOW
"Up the lazy _____" — RIVER
"Up to _____," Al Smith's biography — NOW
"Upon the stroke _____ ...": "Richard III" — OF TEN
"Upstairs, Downstairs" role — PARLOR MAID

"Utopia" author — MORE
"Valley of the Dolls" author — SUSANN
"Valse _____": Sibelius — TRISTE
"Vaya con _____" — DIOS
"Venerable" theologian — BEDE
"Venus and _____": Shakespearean poem — ADONIS
"Very Good _____": Kern — EDDIE
"Vic and _____" — SADE
"Villa" composer — LEHAR
"Vissi d' _____", Puccini aria — ARTE
"Vissi d' _____," Puccini aria — ARTE
"Viva!" relative — OLE
"Vive _____!" — LE ROI
"Vive le _____!" — ROI
"Voltaire" star: 1933 — ARLISS
"Vulcan's chimney" — ETNA
"Wait 'Til the Sun Shines, _____" — NELLIE
"Wait till the sun shines, _____ ..." — NELLIE
"Waiting for Lefty" author — ODETS
"Waiting for the Robert _____" — E LEE
"Walking _____" (ecstatic) — ON AIR
"Waltzing _____" — MATILDA
"Wanted", poster word — ALIAS
"War and _____" — PEACE
"Wars of the _____" — ROSES
"Washington Post March" — SOUSA
"Wasn't that a _____ dish ..." — DAINTY
"Water Lilies" artist — MONET
"Water Mill" composer Teiji _____ — ITO
"Water Music" composer — HANDEL
"Watership Down" characters — RABBITS
"Watership Down" colony — WARREN
"We _____ amused!" — ARE NOT
"We _____ the World " — ARE
"We are not _____" — AMUSED
"We hold _____ truths" — THESE
"We yield our _____ thy soft mercy": Shak. — LIVES TO
"We're off _____ the Wizard" — TO SEE
"Wearing white for Easter _____" — TIME
"Welcome _____": Altman film — TO LA
"Well, _____ be!" — ILL
"Well-boiled icicles" man — SPOONER
"Werther" or "Lulu" — OPERA
"West _____ Story" — SIDE
"West Side Story" girl — ANITA
"West Side Story" heroine — MARIA
"What _____ can I say?" — ELSE
"What _____ God wrought" — HATH
"What _____ is new? — ELSE
"What _____ these mortals be" — FOOLS
"What _____ ye?" — AILS
"What _____!": Bette Davis line — A DUMP
"What _____": 1939 film — A LIFE
"What a pity!" — ALAS
"What do you have to _____ for yourself?" — SAY
"What Kind of Fool _____?" — AM I
"What was _____?" — THAT
"What's _____ for me?" — IN IT
"What's in _____?": Juliet — A NAME
"What's in a _____?" — NAME
"What, _____?" — NEVER
"Whatever _____ right": Pope — IS IS
"Whatever Lola wants Lola _____" — GETS
"When I _____ my lips": Shak. — OPE
"When I was _____ ...": W.S. Gilbert — A LAD
"When I was _____": "H.M.S. Pinafore" — A LAD
"When it's Springtime in the _____" — ROCKIES
"When the _____ breaks ..." — BOUGH
"When the sheep _____ the fauld ..." — ARE IN
"When yellow leaves, _____, or few ...": Shak. — OR NONE
"When you _____ a Tulip" — WORE
"When you wish upon _____" — A STAR
"Where _____ a will ..." — THERES
"Where _____ at": scene of action — ITS
"Where _____ meant than meets ..." (Milton) — MORE IS
"Where _____ now, the glory ... ?": Wordsworth — IS IT
"Where _____": action center — ITS AT
"Where Babies Come From" — STORK STORY
"Where have you _____?" — BEEN
"Where is _____ Heart?" Valentine query — YOUR
"Where men go at _____ day": Wharton — SET OF
"Where the _____ Are" — BOYS
"Where the Boys _____" — ARE
"While memory holds _____ ...": Shak. — A SEAT
"White as a _____" — SHEET
"Whither were you _____?" — AGOING
"Who _____ turn to?" — CAN I
"Who am _____ argue?" — I TO
"Who touches _____ ...": Whittier — A HAIR
"Who's afraid of Virginia _____?" — WOOLF
"Whom shall _____ ...": Isa. 6:8 — I SEND
"Whoopee!" of yore — EVOE
"Whose heart-strings are _____": Poe — A LUTE
"Whose Life _____ Anyway" — IS IT
"Whose woods these _____ think I know": Frost — ARE I
"Why meet we on the bridge of _____ ...?" — TIME
"Why meet we on the bridge of _____ ...?": — TIME
"Why, thou _____ God ...": Shak. — OWEST
"Will be," in a Doris Day hit — SERA
"Willard" creatures — RATS
"Win by _____" — A NOSE
"Winner _____" 1975 film — TAKE ALL
"Winnie _____ Pu": Lenard — ILLE
"Winnie the _____" — POOH
"Wiping something off _____": Kipling — A SLATE
"Wish _____ luck, amigo ..." — ME GOOD
"Wish you _____ here" — WERE
"Wish You Were Here" Composer — ROME
"Wishing hour" on New Year's Eve — MIDNITE
"With the blue ribbons _____" — ON IT
"With this ring I _____ wed" — THEE
"Wizard of Oz" dog — TOTO
"Woe _____!" — IS ME

"Woman of the _____": 1942 film — YEAR
"Woman of the Year": 1936 — WALLIS SIMPSON
"Wonderful Town" role — EILEEN
"Wool of bat, and tongue _____ ...": Shak. — OF DOG
"Workers of the world, _____!" — UNITE
"Worm of the Nile" — ASP
"Wouldn't _____ Loverly?" — IT BE
"Wreck of the Mary _____" — DEARE
"Wuthering Heights" locale — MOOR
"Yankee Doodle", man — COHAN
"Ye _____ Antique Shoppe" — OLDE
"Ye _____ Beauty Shoppe" — OLDE
"Ye _____ Gift Shoppe" — OLDE
"Ye _____ Shoppe" — OLDE
"Ye _____ Tea Shoppe" — OLDE
"Yeomen of the Guard" role — ELSIE
"Yes _____" (Davis) — I CAN
"Yes _____," Davis book — I CAN
"Yes _____," Sammy Davis's autobiography — I CAN
"Yes _____? Make up your mind!" — OR NO
"Yes, _____": humorous song — WE HAVE NO BANANAS
"Yes, sirree!" — INDEED
"Yesterday, December 7, 1941 _____ ...": F.D.R. — A DATE
"Yet gold _____ not ...": Spenser — ALL IS
"Yond Cassius _____ lean ..." — HAS A
"Yonder peasant, who _____?" — IS HE
"Yote _____" (Avila avowal) — AMO
"You _____ here" — ARE
"You _____ Love," 1927 song — ARE
"You _____ mouthful" — SAID A
"You _____ My Sunshine" — ARE
"You _____ right" — ARE SO
"You _____ seen nothin' yet" — AINT
"You _____ There" — ARE
"You bet!" — SURE
"You betcha" — YEH
"You can _____ horse ..." — LEAD A
"You can bet _____" — ON IT
"You can't fool _____ the people ..." (Lincoln) — ALL OF
"You Can't Get a Man with _____" — A GUN
"You can't pray _____": Huck Finn — A LIE
"You Can't Take It With You" director — CAPRA
"You mongrel," _____ — SHE MUTTERED
"You're _____"(You're great) — A DOLL
"You're right" — I SEE
"You're the _____ care for" — ONE I
"Young Man with _____": 1950 film — A HORN
"Younger _____ springtime ..." — THAN
"Your _____ Heart": Hank Williams hit — CHEATIN
"Your _____ or mine"? — PLACE
"Your Cheatin' Heart" composer — HANK WILLIAMS
"Zounds!" — EGAD

Quotations Beginning with Answer Blanks

"_____ Lang Syne" — AULD
"_____ ramblin' wreck ..." — IM A
"_____ 17", Holden's Oscar-winner — STALAG
"_____ a big bird" — EAST IS
"_____ a bird ... !" — ITS
"_____ a boy!" — ITS
"_____ a Camera" — I AM
"_____ a chance" — HASNT
"_____ a compass needle": R. Lowell — LEAN AS
"_____ a creature was ..." — NOT A
"_____ a customer" — ONE TO
"_____ a deal!" — ITS, LETS MAKE
"_____ a dingdong daddy ..." — IM A
"_____ a dream dear ..." — I HAD
"_____ a dream!" — I HAVE
"_____ a girl!" — ITS
"_____ a girl, just like ..." — I WANT
"_____ a Grecian Urn": Keats — ODE ON
"_____ a horse with wings!": Shak. — O FOR
"_____ a Hot Tin Roof" — CAT ON
"_____ a house": "The Tempest" — SO FAIR
"_____ a jolly good fellow" — HES
"_____ a kick out of you" — I GET
"_____ a little kinder": Guest — LET ME BE
"_____ a long way to ..." — ITS
"_____ a man who wasn't there" — I MET
"_____ a man with seven wives ..." — I MET
"_____ a Parade — I LOVE
"_____ a Rhapsody" — I HEARD
"_____ a Rose": 1925 song — ONLY
"_____ a Rose": Friml — ONLY
"_____ a small hotel ..." — THERES
"_____ a Song Go Out of My Heart" — I LET
"_____ a Time" — ONE DAY AT
"_____ a Wonderful Life" — ITS
"_____ Abby" — DEAR
"_____ Abner" — LIL
"_____ Adams — ALICE
"_____ afraid of life." Wm. James — BE NOT
"_____ Africa," 1985 Oscar winner — OUT OF
"_____ Afternoon": 1975 Pacino film — DOG DAY
"_____ against Thebes": Aeschylus — SEVEN
"_____ Age," book by Comfort — A GOOD
"_____ ahead, fall ..." — SPRING
"_____ Alaska": 1960 John Wayne film — NORTH TO
"_____ alive" — SAKES
"_____ Alive," Bee Gees hit — STAYIN
"_____ all in the game" — ITS
"_____ all over again" (Y. Berra) — DEJA VU
"_____ Alone" from "The Desert Song" — ONE
"_____ Along, Little Dogies" — GIT
"_____ Along," 1959 song — TAKE ME
"_____ also serve ..." — THEY
"_____ am, there ye may be ..." — WHERE I
"_____ amies," de Gaulle speech opener — MES
"_____ among wits": S. Johnson — A LORD
"_____ an ancient Mariner" (Coleridge) — IT IS

"_____ and a Woman": 1956 film — A MAN
"_____ and Abner" — LUM
"_____ and Ale," Maugham novel — CAKES
"_____ and anon" — EVER
"_____ and Away" — UP UP
"_____ and be merry" — EAT DRINK
"_____ and Bill" — MIN
"_____ and every ..." — EACH
"_____ and gap-tooth'd man ...": Tennyson — A GRAY
"_____ and I": 1947 Claudette Colbert movie — THE EGG
"_____ and I": G.W. Curtis — PRUE
"_____ and Ivory": Jackson-McCartney song — EBONY
"_____ and Ivory," 1982 hit song — EBONY
"_____ and Jew": 1987 Pulitzer winner — ARAB
"_____ and Lacey" — CAGNEY
"_____ and little fishes!" — YE GODS
"_____ and Lovers" — SONS
"_____ and Mabel," Gable film — CAIN
"_____ and Old Lace" — ARSENIC
"_____ and Peace" — WAR
"_____ and Prejudice" — PRIDE
"_____ and Sevens": O.Henry — SIXES
"_____ and Soul" — BODY
"_____ and the King of Siam" — ANNA
"_____ and the Man" — ARMS
"_____ and The Pendulum" — THE PIT
"_____ and the Swan" — LEDA
"_____ and the Wolf" — PETER
"_____ and tied" — ROPED
"_____ and to Hold" — TO HAVE
"_____ and Tyler Too!" — TIPPECANOE
"_____ and Whispers" — CRIES
"_____ and yet so far" — SO NEAR
"_____ angel" — IM NO
"_____ Angel," 1959 song — TEEN
"_____ any drop to drink" — NOR
"_____ are the times" ... — THESE
"_____ as a day in June?" — SO RARE
"_____ as a pin" — NEAT
"_____ as a Stranger": 1955 movie — NOT
"_____ as Apple Cider" — IDA SWEET
"_____ as I know" — AS FAR
"_____ as pie" — EASY
"_____ as we speak" — EVEN
"_____ ashes ending ..." — DAY OF WRATH
"_____ at a Time" of TV — ONE DAY
"_____ at Eight" — DINNER
"_____ at the voice of the bird": Eccl. — RISE UP
"_____ Attraction" — FATAL
"_____ au vin" — COQ
"_____ Aweigh" — ANCHORS
"_____ bad boy!" Lou Costello — IM A
"_____ Bad Boy" — PECKS
"_____ bad man": Spenser — A BOLD
"_____ bagatelle" — A MERE
"_____ Bailey" — BEETLE
"_____ Ballads" W.S.Gilbert — BAB
"_____ Barque," Nin work — SOLAR
"_____ be in England ...": R. Browning — OH TO
"_____ be married within ...": Dryden — I AM TO
"_____ be seeing you ..." — ILL
"_____ Beautiful Sea," — 1914 Song — BY THE
"_____ bed ..." — EARLY TO
"_____ been working on the railroad" — IVE
"_____ Before Dying" — A KISS
"_____ believe": Mark 9:24 — LORD I
"_____ Ben Johnson!" — O RARE
"_____ bien" — TRES
"_____ bin ein Berliner" — ICH
"_____ blanche": cold steel — ARMES
"_____ Blas" — GIL
"_____ Blu, Dip into di Blu" — NEL
"_____ Blue?": 1929 song — AM I
"_____ Blue?": musical query — AM I
"_____ Boat," Belafonte hit — BANANA
"_____ body meet a ..." — IF A
"_____ Body?": Sayers — WHOSE
"_____ bonnie banks ..." — BY YON
"_____ Boot" — DAS
"_____ Boot": 1981 film — DAS
"_____ Born" — A STAR IS
"_____ boy to do a man's work" — SEND A
"_____ boy!" — ATTA
"_____ Boys": sequel to "Little Women" — JOS
"_____ Boys," "Little Women" sequel — JOS
"_____ bragh" — ERIN GO
"_____ Brown's body" — JOHN
"_____ Brown," Jennifer Jones film — CLUNY
"_____ Bulba" — TARAS
"_____ but the brave ..." — NONE
"_____ But the Lonely Heart": 1944 film — NONE
"_____ Butterfly" — MADAM
"_____ Buttermilk Sky" — OLE
"_____ by any other name" ... — A ROSE
"_____ by land ..." — ONE IF
"_____ by the papers ..." — I SEE
"_____ c'est moi" — LETAP
"_____ Came Running": Jones — SOME
"_____ camera" — I AM A
"_____ can tell the truth ...": S. Butler — ANY FOOL
"_____ Can Wait" — HEAVEN
"_____ Can Whistle," Sondheim musical — ANYONE
"_____ Can" — YES I
"_____ Candy," T.Williams book — HARD
"_____ Cane," Jacopetti film — MONDO
"_____ Cantabile" — ANDANTE
"_____ cara," Bellini aria — ATEO
"_____ Cardboard Lover," 1942 film — HER
"_____ Care,": 1905 song — I DONT
"_____ Censare." Handel opera — GIULIO
"_____ Central Park": 1945 musical — UP IN
"_____ Chan," T.N. Page story — MARSE
"_____ Charley?": Bolger film — WHERES
"_____ Cheatin' Heart," 1952 song — YOUR
"_____ Chicago," 1938 movie — IN OLD
"_____ child is fair of face" — MONDAYS
"_____ Choice" — SOPHIES
"_____ class fightin' man": Kipling — A FIRST
"_____ Clear Day ..." — ON A
"_____ Clock Jump" — ONE O
"_____ clock scholar" — A TEN O
"_____ Clown" — BE A
"_____ cockhorse" — RIDE A
"_____ Coll", 1961 gangster film — MAD DOG

"_____ Comes to Shove": Tharp ballet — PUSH
"_____ company ..." — TWOS
"_____ conventional dither ..." — I AM IN A
"_____ Copy," TV program — HARD
"_____ corny as Kansas ..." — IM AS
"_____ count the ways ..." — LET ME
"_____ Cowhand," Mercer song — IM AN OLD
"_____ Crazy" — GIRL
"_____ Creatures Great and Small" — ALL
"_____ Crest" — FALCON
"_____ culpa!" — MEA
"_____ d'arte," Puccini aria — VISSI
"_____ d'Or," 1909 opera — LE COQ
"_____ d'Yvetot," Ibert opera — LE ROI
"_____ Dalloway," Woolf novel — MRS
"_____ Dance" — ANITRAS
"_____ Dance," Grieg comp osition — ANITRAS
"_____ Dancing Mood" — IM IN A
"_____ Date With an Angel" — GOT A
"_____ daughter"," 1970 movie — RYANS
"_____ day at a time" — ONE
"_____ Day's Night": first Beatles film — A HARD
"_____ Day's Night," Beatles film — A HARD
"_____ days"; youth — SALAD
"_____ de lune," Debussy opus — CLAIR
"_____ De-Lovely," Porter song — ITS
"_____ Death": Grieg — ASES
"_____ deer, a female ..." — DOE A
"_____ Dei" (prayer) — AGNUS
"_____ Delight": Sherwood play — IDIOTS
"_____ Delovely" — ITS
"_____ di Lammermoor": Donizetti — LUCIA
"_____ Diamond" — LEGS
"_____ Die," Gide work — IF IT
"_____ diem" — CARPE
"_____ Dieu!" — MON
"_____ diva": "Norma" aria — CAST A
"_____ diva," Bellini aria — CAST A
"_____ divided against ..." — A HOUSE
"_____ do all that may ..." (Macbeth) — I DARE
"_____ Do It": Cole Porter tune — LETS
"_____ Do This Sum" — I CANT
"_____ do we eat — WHEN
"_____ does it — EASY
"_____ Dogs and Englishmen ..." — MAD
"_____ Doll," Ellington-Strayhorn song — SATIN
"_____ Dolly" — HELLO
"_____ Dracula": 1943 movie — SON OF
"_____ Dream," in an opera — ELSAS
"_____ Dream," Wagner aria — ELSAS
"_____ Dreamer ..." — IM A
"_____ each life ..." — INTO
"_____ ears" — IM ALL
"_____ Earth" — PLANET
"_____ Easy," Sinatra favorite — NICE N
"_____ Eat Cake," 1933 musical — LET EM
"_____ ed Euridice" — ORFEO
"_____ Enterprise" — USS
"_____ entertain you" — LET ME
"_____ Entertainment" — THATS
"_____ est percipi" — ESSE
"_____ et labora" — ORA
"_____ Ever See a Dream Walking?" — DID YOU
"_____ evil" — SEE NO
"_____ evil" — SEE NO
"_____ Explain," Billie Holiday song — DONT
"_____ Eyed Jacks," 1961 film — ONE
"_____ Fables" — AESOPS
"_____ Fair" — ALLS
"_____ Family" (radio oldie) — PEPPER YOUNGS
"_____ Fan Tutti" — COSI
"_____ Faust": Busoni opera — DOKTOR
"_____ favor, Señor" — POR
"_____ Fideles" — ADESTE
"_____ Fire": Springsteen title — IM ON
"_____ first you don't succeed ..." — IF AT
"_____ flowing with milk and honey" — A LAND
"_____ Foolish Things ..." 1935 song — THESE
"_____ for a tooth" — A TOOTH
"_____ for Adano" — A BELL
"_____ for all ..." — ONE
"_____ for All Seasons" — A MAN
"_____ for Life" Kirk Douglas movie — LUST
"_____ For Me to Say" — ITS NOT
"_____ for Me" Lawford film — YOU
"_____ for naebody": Burns — I CARE
"_____ for tennis?" — ANY-ONE
"_____ for the million ..." — MISS
"_____ for the Misbegotten" — A MOON
"_____ for the money ..." — ONE
"_____ for the Seesaw": 1952 film — TWO
"_____ for the show" — TWO
"_____ for Your Money": Guinness flick — A RUN
"_____ for your thoughts — A PENNY
"_____ forgive those ..." — AS WE
"_____ forgiven" — ALL IS
"_____ free" — BORN
"_____ Freischutz" — DER
"_____ From the Vienna Woods": Strauss — TALES
"_____ Front Door" Pat Boone's single — AT MY
"_____ Fu": David Carradine series — KUNG
"_____ Funny That Way" — SHES
"_____ Gantry": Lewis novel — ELMER
"_____ Gay" — historic plane — ENOLA
"_____ Get it for You Wholesale" — I CAN
"_____ Get Next To You," 1970 song — I CANT
"_____ Get Started With You," — I CANT
"_____ Giovanni" — DON
"_____ Girl Just Like ...": 1911 song — I WANT A
"_____ girl" — ATTA, ITS A, THAT
"_____ girl": Marlo Thomas show — THAT
"_____ girl's best friend ..." — DIAMONDS ARE A
"_____ Girls" — LES
"_____ Girls": Kelly film — LES
"_____ give up the ship" — DONT
"_____ go again ..." — THERE I
"_____ go bragh" — ERIN
"_____ Goes": Cole Porter musical — ANYTHING

"_____ going out the door": Plutarch — I MET IT
"_____ Going-on" — WHATS
"_____ Good Day!" — HAVE A
"_____ Got a Crush on You" — IVE
"_____ Got A Secret" — IVE
"_____ Got Sixpence" — IVE
"_____ got that thing" — YOUVE
"_____ got the world on a string ... — IVE
"_____ Got to Be Me" — IVE
"_____ Got You Under My Skin" — IVE
"_____ gratia artis" — ARS
"_____ gratias" — DEO
"_____ Green Tomatoes" — FRIED
"_____ grief!" — GOOD
"_____ gris" (be tipsy, in Tours) — ETRE
"_____ Grit" — TRUE
"_____ groweth fast" — ILL
"_____ Grows in Brooklyn" — A TREE
"_____ Gun, Will Travel" — HAVE
"_____ gyre and gimble ..." — DID
"_____ had it!" — IVE
"_____ Hall": 1972 film — ANNIE
"_____ Hall": Allen flick — ANNIE
"_____ hand you cannot see": Tickell — I SEE A
"_____ Handle," 1938 Gable film — TOO HOT TO
"_____ hands I love ..." — PALE
"_____ Harold" — CHILDE
"_____ Harry," Eastwood film — DIRTY
"_____ has only nine lives": Twain — A CAT
"_____ have all the flowers gone? " — WHERE
"_____ Have I travel'd ...": Keats — MUCH
"_____ Have to do Is Dream" — ALL I
"_____ Hear a Waltz?" — DO I
"_____ Heart of Mine" — THIS
"_____ heart!" — HAVE A
"_____ Heidenieben": Strauss — EIN
"_____ Him in Paris": 1937 movie — I MET
"_____ History": Toynbee — A STUDY OF
"_____ Holiday" Hepburn movie — ROMAN
"_____ Home" McCartney song — EAT AT
"_____ homo" — ECCE
"_____ Hope" — RYANS
"_____ horse ...": Rev. 6:8 — A PALE
"_____ horse!" — GET A
"_____ House" — FULL
"_____ Houston" — MATT
"_____ I Did for Love," 1975 song — WHAT
"_____ I lay me ..." — NOW
"_____ I saw Elba" — ERE
"_____ I saw Elba" — ERE
"_____ I say, not ..." — DO AS
"_____ I sing" — OF THEE
"_____ I were a moron" — I WISH
"_____ I'm Adam" — MADAM
"_____ I," 1924 Gershwin song — SO AM
"_____ ideas" — I GET
"_____ if by land ..." — ONE
"_____ II," DeLillo novel — MAO
"_____ Ike" — I LIKE
"_____ in a while ..." — ONCE
"_____ in England now ...": Browning — OH TO BE
"_____ in fiery floods ...": Shak. — TO BATHE
"_____ In Heaven" — RAGE
"_____ in Her Ear" — A FLEA
"_____ in Love With Amy" — ONCE
"_____ in Love?": 1952 song — AM I
"_____ in my haste ..." — I SAID
"_____ in Paris" — APRIL
"_____ in St. Louis" — MEET ME
"_____ in the affairs of men": Shak. — A TIDE
"_____ in the dark — A LEAP
"_____ in the Dark," 1964 film — A SHOT
"_____ in the Dark," 1988 film — A CRY
"_____ in the Family" — ALL
"_____ in the hand ..." — A BIRD
"_____ in the Hat": Seuss — THE CAT
"_____ in the house? — A DOCTOR
"_____ in the saddle" — TALL
"_____ in the sky" — PIE
"_____ in the Sun — DUEL
"_____ in the Sun" — A PLACE
"_____ in the Sun": Peck film — A DUEL
"_____ in the Sun": Waugh — ISLAND
"_____ in the Sunset" — RED SAILS
"_____ in the woods" — BABES
"_____ in thee tonight" — ARE MET
"_____ in Time," Astaire's autobiogtraphy — STEPS
"_____ instant — IN AN
"_____ Irish Rose" — ABIES
"_____ iron" — PUMP
"_____ is ... a refuge from home life": Shaw — A HOTEL
"_____ is a rotten egg" — LAST ONE IN
"_____ is an Island" — NO MAN
"_____ is believing" — SEEING
"_____ is born" — A SON
"_____ is Born" — A STAR
"_____ is fair of face" — MONDAYS CHILD
"_____ is golden" — SILENCE
"_____ is good, and yet not" — SO SO
"_____ is humble". Cowper — WISDOM
"_____ is I set it down": Hamlet — MEET IT
"_____ is in Heaven" — AS IT
"_____ is it!" — THIS
"_____ is more": Browning — LESS
"_____ Is Not a Home": Adler — A HOUSE
"_____ is Silvia?" — WHO
"_____ is the forest primeval ..." — THIS
"_____ is the Night": Fitzgerald — TENDER
"_____ Is Your Life" — THIS
"_____ Island With You," 1948 film — ON AN
"_____ isn't so" — SAY IT
"_____ it a lovely day ..." — ISNT
"_____ It Again," 1926 song — SAY
"_____ It Be.": Beatles hit — LET
"_____ it down": Hamlet — I SET
"_____ it my way" — I DID
"_____ It Romantic?" — ISNT
"_____ it up" — WHOOP
"_____ It Up," Little Richard hit — RIP
"_____ it's at": scene of action — WHERE
"_____ It," 1940 song — SAY
"_____ Italian": Strauss — AUS
"_____ Iwo Jima": 1949 film — SANDS OF
"_____ Jim" — LORD
"_____ Jo" Griffith-Joyner — FLO
"_____ Joey" — PAL
"_____ jolly good ..." — HES A
"_____ Joy" — ODE TO
"_____ just my Bill" — HES
"_____ Kapital" — DAS
"_____ Karenina" — ANNA

"_____ Keys to Baldplate" — SEVEN
"_____ Kick Out of You" — I GET A
"_____ kingdom come ..." — THY
"_____ kleine Nachtmusik" — EINE
"_____ knees": 30's superlative — BEES
"_____ know" (Presley hit) — I GOTTA
"_____ knows no law" — NECESSITY
"_____ Kroger": Mann story — TONIO
"_____ la poupée," Offenbach song — AIR DE
"_____ la vista" — HASTA
"_____ Lady": Margaret Thatcher — IRON
"_____ Laugh-In" — ROWAN AND MARTINS
"_____ Lay Dying": Faulkner — AS I
"_____ Lazy River" — UP A
"_____ Leilani," Crosby hit — SWEET
"_____ Life Is It Anyway?": Dreyfuss movie — WHOSE
"_____ Like It" — AS YOU
"_____ Little, Love a little," Presley film — LIVE A
"_____ live and breathe" — AS I
"_____ longa, vita brevis" — ARS
"_____ Love Song" — PAGAN
"_____ Love You" — PS I
"_____ Love," 1982 film — MAKING
"_____ Lover," by Harry Crews — SCAR
"_____ Lucy" — I LOVE
"_____ Lynne," 1861 novel — EAST
"_____ Macabre" — DANSE
"_____ Make Believe" — ONLY
"_____ Male War Bride," 1949 film — I WAS A
"_____ Man Answers," Darin hit — IF A
"_____ man put asunder" — LET NO
"_____ Maria" — AVE
"_____ Marner" — SILAS
"_____ Mater," ancient hymn — STABAT
"_____ may look on a king": Heywood — A CAT
"_____ me your ears": Julius Caesar — LEND
"_____ me!" — WOE IS
"_____ meant to be lived": A.E. Roosevelt — LIFE WAS
"_____ Men": Cole Porter song — I HATE
"_____ Metropole," 1937 film — CAFE
"_____ Mia": 1954 hit — CARA
"_____ mio dulce ardor," Gluck aria — ODEL
"_____ Mir Bist Du Schön" — BEI
"_____ Misbehavin'" — AINT
"_____ Misérables" — LES
"_____ moi le déluge" — APRES
"_____ Murderer", N. Marsh mystery — ENTER A
"_____ my lady's chamber" — AND IN
"_____ My Souvenirs" — AMONG
"_____ my sunshine ..." — YOU ARE
"_____ My Way" — GOING
"_____ my word!" — UPON
"_____ my yellow basket" — I LOST
"_____ Named Sue" — A BOY
"_____ neater, sweeter maiden ...": Kipling — IVE A
"_____ Nell," Gershwin musical — OUR
"_____ no kick ..." — I GET
"_____ Not Alone": Muni movie — WE ARE
"_____ not, Duncan": Shak. — HEAR IT
"_____ o' My Heart" — PEG
"_____ o'clock scholar" — A TEN
"_____ o'clock scholar" — A TEN
"_____ of bricks" — A TON
"_____ of dreadful note": Macbeth — A DEED
"_____ of Endearment" — TERMS
"_____ of fat things ...": Isa. 25:6 — A FEAST
"_____ of Fire," 1981 film — CHARIOTS
"_____ of Fortune" — WHEEL
"_____ of Honey," Alpert hit — A TASTE
"_____ of Montezuma" — HALLS
"_____ of One's Own": Woolf — A ROOM
"_____ of robins ..." — A NEST
"_____ of robins" — A NEST
"_____ of snow-white horses ..." — A TEAM
"_____ of such a thing ...": Shak. — IN AWE
"_____ of thee" — TIS
"_____ of Two Cities" — A TALE
"_____ of Venus," 1940's musical — ONE TOUCH
"_____ Old Cow Hand" — IM AN
"_____ Old Gang of Mine" — THAT
"_____ old saw being apt here": Browning — SATANS
"_____ Old Smoky" — ON TOP OF
"_____ old-fashioned romance" — ITS AN
"_____ on parle ..." — ICI
"_____ on thin ice" — TREADS
"_____ Only Just Begun," P. Williams song — WEVE
"_____ or at sevens" — SIXES
"_____ or not ..." — TO BE
"_____ or sea ..." — ON LAND
"_____ Out": 1947 J. Mason film — ODD MAN
"_____ Pacific" — SOUTH
"_____ Packin' Mama," 1943 song — PISTOL
"_____ pale horse" (Bible) — BEHOLD A
"_____ parade" — I LOVE A
"_____ Paul" Kruger of Boer fame — OOM
"_____ peace" — REST IN
"_____ Peaks" — TWIN
"_____ penny, two a penny ..." — ONE A
"_____ people go ...": Exodus 5:1 — LET MY
"_____ people play" — GAMES
"_____ Performance": Tudor ballet — GALA
"_____ Perpetua": Idaho motto — ESTO
"_____ Perpetua," motto of Idaho — ESTO
"_____ pin and pick it up" — SEE A
"_____ Pinafore" — HMS
"_____ Pirate King ..." Gilbert & Sullivan — I AM A
"_____ plata" — OROY
"_____ Poems" — CHICAGO
"_____ Poetica" Horace — ARS
"_____ Poppa?": 1970 Segal film — WHERES
"_____ port in a storm" — ANY
"_____ Pretty" — I FEEL
"_____ pro nobis" — ORA
"_____ Promise": Maurois — TERRE
"_____ Pure": Martha aria — AH SO
"_____ Rabbit" — BRER
"_____ Rae" — NORMA
"_____ Ramsey": Richard Boone TV show — HEC
"_____ Rappaport": Herb Gardner play — IM NOT
"_____ Rebel," 1962 tune — HES A

"_____ Remember," 1960 song — TRY TO
"_____ Remember?" musical query — DID I
"_____ Restaurant" — ALICES
"_____ Restaurant" (Guthrie) — ALICES
"_____ Rex" — OEDIPUS
"_____ Rheingold" — DAS
"_____ Rhythm" — I GOT
"_____ rich. Rich is better" — BEEN
"_____ Richard's Almanac" — POOR
"_____ Rider," Eastwood film — PALE
"_____ Rides Again": 1939 film — DESTRY
"_____ Rigby" — ELEANOR
"_____ right with ...: Browning — ALLS
"_____ right with the world" — ALLS
"_____ road" — ONE FOR THE
"_____ robins in her hair" — A NEST OF
"_____ rod" — AARONS
"_____ Rookh," T. Moore work — LALLA
"_____ rose" — IS A
"_____ Rosenkavalier" — DER
"_____ sae weary ... ; Burns — AND I
"_____ said it" — YOU
"_____ sana ..." — MENS
"_____ Sanctorum" — ACTA
"_____ Sanctum" — INNER
"_____ santé!" — A VOTRE
"_____ saw a purple cow" — I NEVER
"_____ saw Elba" — ERE I
"_____ say more?" — NEED I
"_____ say, not ..." — DO AS I
"_____ says" — SIMON
"_____ Scared Stupid," 1991 film — ERNEST
"_____ sea to shining ..." — FROM
"_____ Seeing You," 1938 song — ILL BE
"_____ self-consuming fires" — WASTES IN
"_____ semper tyrannis" — SIC
"_____ Sensational," 1956 song — YOURE
"_____ sesame" — OPEN
"_____ Shall Have Music" — SHE
"_____ shall live your epitaph to make" — OR I
"_____ she blows!" — THAR
"_____ She Sweet?" — AINT
"_____ She's Mine" — TAKE HER
"_____ Shelter," Rolling Stones hit — GIMME
"_____ should have a good memory" — A LIAR
"_____ silly question ..." — ASK A
"_____ Silver" — HI HO
"_____ Since Eve" — EVER
"_____ sing like the birdies ..." — LETS ALL
"_____ Skies," Berlin prediction — BLUE
"_____ Sleep," Odets play — I CANT
"_____ Sloane" (TV show) — A MAN CALLED
"_____ Smile Be Your Umbrella" — LET A
"_____ Something to Me" — YOU DO
"_____ Song Go Out of My Heart" — I LET A
"_____ Song in My Heart" — WITH A
"_____ Song" — SAMS
"_____ Soul": Four Aces song — HEART AND
"_____ sow ..." — AS YE
"_____ Spee" — GRAF
"_____ Spiro, Spero" (S.C. motto) — DUM
"_____ Star State" — LONE
"_____ still a moment": Poe — HEART BE
"_____ stock and barrel" — LOCK
"_____ Stoops to Conquer" — SHE
"_____ Stop Me" (Bennett Cerf book) — TRY AND
"_____ strange place, this Limbo!": Coleridge — TIS A
"_____ Street Blues" — BEALE
"_____ Street": Douglas/Sheen film — WALL
"_____ Suspicion": Crawford film — ABOVE
"_____ Suspicion," 1943 film — ABOVE
"_____ sweet chariot ..." — SWING LOW
"_____ sweet song ..." — AN OLD
"_____ Sweetheart" — YOURE A
"_____ Swell": Rodgers and Hart tune — THOU
"_____ Sylphides" — LES
"_____ Sympathy" — TEA AND
"_____ take arms against ...: Shak. — OR TO
"_____ tale's best for winter": W.S. — A SAD
"_____ Talk," 1959 film — PILLOW
"_____ Talking": Rivers-Merryman — ENTER
"_____ tete": "Alouette" refrain — ETAL
"_____ than none"? — ALPHA LOAF IS BETA
"_____ than thou" — HOLIER
"_____ that kills": Housman — AN AIR
"_____ that kings/Have lipp'd ...": Shak. — A HAND
"_____ that rocks the cradle ..." — THE HAND
"_____ that will live in infamy": FDR — A DATE
"_____ that's the way it is" — AND
"_____ the ante" — UPS
"_____ the Antilles" — THE PEARL OF
"_____ the Apes" — PLANET OF
"_____ the Beloved Country" — CRY
"_____ the best of times" — IT WAS
"_____ the Cat" — FELIX
"_____ the Clowns," Sondheim song — SEND IN
"_____ the Conqueror": '88 Oscar film — PELLE
"_____ the curtains": Cowper — LET FALL
"_____ the fields we go" — OER
"_____ the Future," 1985 movie — BACK TO
"_____ the Great," E. Dumm cartoon — ALEC
"_____ the hills" — OLD AS
"_____ the Horrible" — HAGAR
"_____ the Jackal" — THE DAY OF
"_____ the King's Men" — ALL
"_____ the land of the free ..." — OER
"_____ the law excuses no man" — IGNORANCE OF
"_____ the light fantastic" — TRIP
"_____ the Likes of You" — I LIKE
"_____ the Lonely": Orbison song — ONLY
"_____ the money ..." — ONE FOR
"_____ the mood for love" — IM IN
"_____ the Moon," 1953 song — I SEE
"_____ the music" — FACE, STOP
"_____ the night before Christmas ..." — TWAS

"_____ the North": 1973 film — EMPERER OF
"_____ the ocean" — DEEP AS
"_____ the ocean" — GEM OF
"_____ the other — ONE OR
"_____ the Pecos": Mitchum movie — WEST OF
"_____ the ramparts ..." — OER
"_____ the ramparts ..." — OER
"_____ the Rear" (old song) — STEP TO
"_____ the Riveter" — ROSIE
"_____ the Rose": Young novel — SO RED
"_____ the season ..." — TIS
"_____ the season to be ..." — TIS
"_____ the Sheriff," 1974 tune — I SHOT
"_____ the show" — TWO FOR
"_____ the Single Girl" — SEX AND
"_____ the sparrow" — IS ON
"_____ the thought!" — PERISH
"_____ the Top": Porter — YOURE
"_____ the usual suspects"(Casablanca) — ROUND UP
"_____ the valley of death ..." — INTO
"_____ the Woods" — INTO
"_____ the worst too young!": Kipling — WE KNEW
"_____ the wrong way" — RUB
"_____ Theme": 1966 — LARAS
"_____ There" — OVER
"_____ There": 1954 song — HEY
"_____ there, you" — HEY
"_____ thing under the sun.": Eccl. 1:9 — NO NEW
"_____ Things Bright and Beautiful" — ALL
"_____ This House" — BLESS
"_____ This Must Be Belgium" — IF ITS TUESDAY
"_____ tho it be a cross ..." — EEN
"_____ thou now O soul": Whitman — DAREST
"_____ Three Lives" — I LED
"_____ three ships ..." — I SAW
"_____ Till Somebody Loves You" — YOURE NOBODY
"_____ Timberlane": Lewis novel — CASS
"_____ Time Next Year" — SAME
"_____ Time": Lupino film — IN OUR
"_____ Time," Roethke poem — IN A DARK
"_____ Times": Dickens novel — HARD
"_____ to be born ...": Eccles. — A TIME
"_____ to Be You," 1924 song — IT HAD
"_____ to bed" — AND SO
"_____ to bury Caesar ...": Shak. — I COME
"_____ to Handle," 1938 film — TOO HOT
"_____ to Live" (O'Hara) — A RAGE
"_____ to Live," 1958 film — I WANT
"_____ to my remains ...": Dryden — BE KIND
"_____ to the land of the dead": Auden — A LANE
"_____ to the public weal": Shak. — A FOE
"_____ to the System": Caine film — A SHOCK
"_____ to Watch Over Me" — SOMEONE
"_____ Tod": Grieg — ASES
"_____ Told Tales" — TWICE
"_____ Town": Wilder play — OUR
"_____ Town," 1938 Tracy film — BOYS
"_____ transit gloria mundi" — SIC
"_____ Tread on Me" — DONT
"_____ tricks?" — HOWS
"_____ Triplex," famous R.L.S. essay — AES
"_____ truly" — YRS
"_____ Tu," 1932 song — ERES
"_____ tu," baritone aria — ERI
"_____ tu," Verdi aria — ERI
"_____ Unis" — ETATS
"_____ unto my feet" — A LAMP
"_____ Up Doc?": 1972 film — WHATS
"_____ up!" — HANDS, WISE
"_____ up": excited — KEYED
"_____ up, wear it out" (New England maxim) — USE IT
"_____ Upon a Honeymoon": '42 Rogers film — ONCE
"_____ upon a Mattress" — ONCE
"_____ upon a time ..." — ONCE
"_____ us a child is born" — UNTO
"_____ us a son ..." — UNTO
"_____ usted Espanol?" — HABLA
"_____ vadis?" — QUO
"_____ Vice" — MIAMI
"_____ vincit amor" — OMNIA
"_____ virumque cano ...": Virgil — ARMA
"_____ walks in beauty ...": Byron — SHE
"_____ Waltz": Delibes — NAIL A
"_____ want for Christmas ..." — ALL I
"_____ Want to Set the World on Fire" — I DONT
"_____ War" — MAN O
"_____ Wars" — STAR
"_____ Was a Lady" — EADIE
"_____ Was a Lady": S. Foster — NELLY
"_____ was going to St. Ives" — AS I
"_____ was here": WW II graffiti — KILROY
"_____ was in the beginning ..." — AS IT
"_____ was one-and-twenty": Housman — WHEN I
"_____ was saying ..." — AS I
"_____ Way," Cahn-van Heusen song — ALL THE
"_____ we dance?" — SHALL
"_____ we devils?" — ARENT
"_____ we forget": Kipling — LEST
"_____ We Got Fun?": 1921 song — AINT
"_____ we have no bananas" — YES
"_____ Wedding": Garcia Lorca drama — BLOOD
"_____ Wednesday": T.S. Eliot — ASH
"_____ Well that Ends Well" — ALLS
"_____ went to Haiti!" — KATIE
"_____ were king ..." — IF I
"_____ Were the Days" — THOSE
"_____ what your country ..." J.F.K. — ASK NOT
"_____ when she is riggish": Shak. — BLESS HER
"_____ whiz" — GEE
"_____ whom I love ...": Meredith — SHE
"_____ Widow" — MERRY
"_____ Windermere's Fan" — LADY
"_____ Window" — REAR
"_____ Window": 1954 film — REAR
"_____ wise father ..." — IT IS A
"_____ with a view" — A ROOM
"_____ with Father" — LIFE
"_____ With Flowers" — SAY IT
"_____ With Judy": Taylor 1948 movie — A DATE

"_____ with Love" — TO SIR
"_____ With Love," Poitier film — TO SIR
"_____ with My Wife You Don't" — NOT
"_____ without a cause" — REBEL
"_____ Without Sunshine": Whitten novel — A DAY
"_____ woman's advice ...": T. Moore — ASK A
"_____ Women" — DESIGNING
"_____ Wonderland" — ALICE IN
"_____ wood" (superstitious words) — KNOCK ON
"_____ Work ...": G. Will book — MEN AT
"_____ World Turns" — AS THE
"_____ worry!" — NOT TO
"_____ Yankee Doodle Dandy" — IM A
"_____ yellow ribbon 'round ..." — TIE A
"_____ You Ain't Ma Baby?" — OR IS
"_____ You Glad You're You" — ARENT
"_____ You Like to Take a Walk?" — WOULD
"_____ you listening?" — ARE
"_____ You Sinner" — SING
"_____ you the superman": Nietzsche — I TEACH
"_____ you there?" — ARE
"_____ You Were Here" — WISH
"_____ Young Dream": Moore — LOVES
"_____ your fathers thus ...?": — DID NOT
"_____ your life" — NOT ON
"_____ Your Love Tonight": Elvis tune — I NEED
"_____ your pardon" — I BEG
"_____ Zauberflöte" — DIE
"_____" Tweed — BOSS
"_____' clock scholar ..." — A TEN O
"_____' ot sand an' ginger ..." Kipling — ESALL
"_____, a bone, ...": Kipling — A RAG
"_____, a deer ..." — DOE
"_____, Brute!" — ET TU
"_____, drink and be merry" — EAT
"_____, Father": Brit. TV comedy — BLESS ME
"_____, happy day": Tennyson — GO NOT
"_____, Just You" — SWEET SUE
"_____, my home is over Jordan" — DEEP RIVER
"_____, Nanette" — NO NO
"_____, one hope ..." J.R. Lowell — ONE LOVE
"_____, Rob Morris": Burns — AULD
"_____, Sam" — PLAY IT
"_____, Sharlie?": Pearl's Baron — VUS YOU DERE
"_____, shine ...": Isa. 60:1 — ARISE
"_____, slight man!": Julius Caesar — AWAY
"_____, the herald angels ..." — HARK
"_____, tho I walk through the valley ..." — YEA
"_____, We Have No Bananas" — YES
"_____, you noblest English" — ON ON
"_____, Zwei, Drei, ..." — EINS
"_____-feather'd sleep": Milton — DEWY
"_____-in-Boots" — PUSS
"_____-Tough," Reynolds film — SEMI
"_____-vous francais?" — PARLEZ

NOTES

NOTES

NOTES

NOTES

NOTES

NOTES